Maths for Business

Maths for Business

Selected chapters from:

College Mathematics for Business, Economics, Life Sciences, and Social Sciences
Fourteenth Edition, Global Edition
Raymond A. Barnett, Michael R. Ziegler, Karl E. Byleen and Christopher J. Stocker

Harlow, England • London • New York • Boston • San Francisco • Toronto • Sydney • Dubai • Singapore • Hong Kong
Tokyo • Seoul • Taipei • New Dehli • Cape Town • São Paulo • Mexico City • Madrid • Amsterdam • Munich • Paris • Milan

Pearson
KAO Two
KAO Park
Harlow
Essex CM17 9NA

And associated companies throughout the world

Visit us on the World Wide Web at:
www.pearson.com/uk

Compiled from:

College Mathematics for Business, Economics, Life Sciences, and Social Sciences
Fourteenth Edition, Global Edition
Raymond A. Barnett, Michael R. Ziegler, Karl E. Byleen and Christopher J. Stocker
ISBN 978-1-292-27049-4

ISBN 978-1-78764-408-3

Printed and bound in Great Britain by Ashford Colour Press, Gosport, Hampshire.

CONTENTS

Part 1

A Library of Elementary Functions

1 Linear Equations and Graphs

Introduction

How far will a glacier advance or retreat in the next ten years? The key to answering such a question, and to making other climate-related predictions, is mathematical modeling. In Chapter 1, we study one of the simplest mathematical models, a linear equation. We introduce a technique called linear regression to construct mathematical models from numerical data. We use mathematical models to predict average annual temperature and average annual precipitation (see Problems 23 and 24 in Section 1.3), the atmospheric concentration of carbon dioxide, the consumption of fossil fuels, and many other quantities in business, economics, life sciences, and social sciences.

1.1 Linear Equations and Inequalities

- Linear Equations
- Linear Inequalities
- Applications

The equation

$$3 - 2(x + 3) = \frac{x}{3} - 5$$

and the inequality

$$\frac{x}{2} + 2(3x - 1) \geq 5$$

are both first degree in one variable. In general, a **first-degree**, or **linear**, **equation** in one variable is any equation that can be written in the form

$$\textbf{Standard form:} \quad ax + b = 0 \qquad a \neq 0 \tag{1}$$

If the equality symbol, $=$, in (1) is replaced by $<$, $>$, $\leq$, or $\geq$, the resulting expression is called a **first-degree**, or **linear**, **inequality**.

A **solution** of an equation (or inequality) involving a single variable is a number that, when substituted for the variable, makes the equation (or inequality) true. The set of all solutions is called the **solution set**. To **solve an equation** (or inequality) means to find its solution set.

Knowing what is meant by the solution set is one thing; finding it is another. We start by recalling the idea of equivalent equations and equivalent inequalities. If we perform an operation on an equation (or inequality) that produces another equation (or inequality) with the same solution set, then the two equations (or inequalities) are said to be **equivalent**. The basic idea in solving equations or inequalities is to perform operations that produce simpler equivalent equations or inequalities and to continue the process until we obtain an equation or inequality with an obvious solution.

Linear Equations

Linear equations are generally solved using the following equality properties.

THEOREM 1 Equality Properties

An equivalent equation will result if

1. The same quantity is added to or subtracted from each side of a given equation.
2. Each side of a given equation is multiplied by or divided by the same nonzero quantity.

EXAMPLE 1 **Solving a Linear Equation** Solve and check:

$$8x - 3(x - 4) = 3(x - 4) + 6$$

SOLUTION

$$\begin{aligned} 8x - 3(x - 4) &= 3(x - 4) + 6 && \text{Use the distributive property.} \\ 8x - 3x + 12 &= 3x - 12 + 6 && \text{Combine like terms.} \\ 5x + 12 &= 3x - 6 && \text{Subtract } 3x \text{ from both sides.} \\ 2x + 12 &= -6 && \text{Subtract 12 from both sides.} \\ 2x &= -18 && \text{Divide both sides by 2.} \\ x &= -9 \end{aligned}$$

CHECK

$$\begin{aligned} 8x - 3(x - 4) &= 3(x - 4) + 6 \\ 8(-9) - 3[(-9) - 4] &\stackrel{?}{=} 3[(-9) - 4] + 6 \\ -72 - 3(-13) &\stackrel{?}{=} 3(-13) + 6 \\ -33 &\stackrel{\checkmark}{=} -33 \end{aligned}$$

Matched Problem 1 Solve and check: $3x - 2(2x - 5) = 2(x + 3) - 8$

Explore and Discuss 1

According to equality property 2, multiplying both sides of an equation by a nonzero number always produces an equivalent equation. What is the smallest positive number that you could use to multiply both sides of the following equation to produce an equivalent equation without fractions?

$$\frac{x + 1}{3} - \frac{x}{4} = \frac{1}{2}$$

EXAMPLE 2 **Solving a Linear Equation** Solve and check: $\frac{x + 2}{2} - \frac{x}{3} = 5$

SOLUTION What operations can we perform on

$$\frac{x + 2}{2} - \frac{x}{3} = 5$$

to eliminate the denominators? If we can find a number that is exactly divisible by each denominator, we can use the multiplication property of equality to clear the denominators. The LCD (least common denominator) of the fractions, 6, is exactly what we are looking for! Actually, any common denominator will do, but the LCD results in a simpler equivalent equation. So we multiply both sides of the equation by 6:

Reminder

Dashed boxes are used throughout the book to denote steps that are usually performed mentally.

$$6\left(\frac{x + 2}{2} - \frac{x}{3}\right) = 6 \cdot 5$$

$$\overset{3}{\cancel{6}} \cdot \frac{(x + 2)}{\underset{1}{\cancel{2}}} - \overset{2}{\cancel{6}} \cdot \frac{x}{\underset{1}{\cancel{3}}} = 30$$

$$\begin{aligned} 3(x + 2) - 2x &= 30 && \text{Use the distributive property.} \\ 3x + 6 - 2x &= 30 && \text{Combine like terms.} \\ x + 6 &= 30 && \text{Subtract 6 from both sides.} \\ x &= 24 \end{aligned}$$

CHECK

$$\begin{aligned} \frac{x + 2}{2} - \frac{x}{3} &= 5 \\ \frac{24 + 2}{2} - \frac{24}{3} &\stackrel{?}{=} 5 \\ 13 - 8 &\stackrel{?}{=} 5 \\ 5 &\stackrel{\checkmark}{=} 5 \end{aligned}$$

Matched Problem 2 Solve and check: $\frac{x + 1}{3} - \frac{x}{4} = \frac{1}{2}$

In many applications of algebra, formulas or equations must be changed to alternative equivalent forms. The following example is typical.

EXAMPLE 3 **Solving a Formula for a Particular Variable** If you deposit a principal P in an account that earns simple interest at an annual rate r, then the amount A in the account after t years is given by $A = P + Prt$. Solve for

(A) r in terms of A, P, and t

(B) P in terms of A, r, and t

SOLUTION (A)

$$A = P + Prt \quad \text{Reverse equation.}$$
$$P + Prt = A \quad \text{Subtract } P \text{ from both sides.}$$
$$Prt = A - P \quad \text{Divide both members by } Pt.$$
$$r = \frac{A - P}{Pt}$$

(B)

$$A = P + Prt \quad \text{Reverse equation.}$$
$$P + Prt = A \quad \text{Factor out } P \text{ (note the use of the distributive property).}$$
$$P(1 + rt) = A \quad \text{Divide by } (1 + rt).$$
$$P = \frac{A}{1 + rt}$$

Matched Problem 3 If a cardboard box has length L, width W, and height H, then its surface area is given by the formula $S = 2LW + 2LH + 2WH$. Solve the formula for

(A) L in terms of S, W, and H (B) H in terms of S, L, and W

Linear Inequalities

Before we start solving linear inequalities, let us recall what we mean by $<$ (less than) and $>$ (greater than). If a and b are real numbers, we write

$$a < b \quad a \text{ is less than } b$$

if there exists a positive number p such that $a + p = b$. Certainly, we would expect that if a positive number was added to any real number, the sum would be larger than the original. That is essentially what the definition states. If $a < b$, we may also write

$$b > a \quad b \text{ is greater than } a.$$

EXAMPLE 4 **Inequalities** Replace each question mark with either $<$ or $>$.

(A) 3 ? 5 (B) −6 ? −2 (C) 0 ? −10

SOLUTION

(A) $3 < 5$ because $3 + 2 = 5$.

(B) $-6 < -2$ because $-6 + 4 = -2$.

(C) $0 > -10$ because $-10 < 0$ (because $-10 + 10 = 0$).

Matched Problem 4 Replace each question mark with either $<$ or $>$.

(A) 2 ? 8 (B) −20 ? 0 (C) −3 ? −30

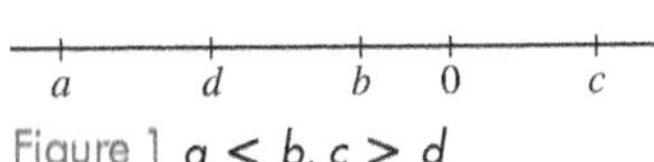

Figure 1 $a < b$, $c > d$

The inequality symbols have a very clear geometric interpretation on the real number line. If $a < b$, then a is to the left of b on the number line; if $c > d$, then c is to the right of d on the number line (Fig. 1). Check this geometric property with the inequalities in Example 4.

Explore and Discuss 2

Replace ? with $<$ or $>$ in each of the following:

(A) $-1 ? 3$ and $2(-1) ? 2(3)$

(B) $-1 ? 3$ and $-2(-1) ? -2(3)$

(C) $12 ? -8$ and $\frac{12}{4} ? \frac{-8}{4}$

(D) $12 ? -8$ and $\frac{12}{-4} ? \frac{-8}{-4}$

Based on these examples, describe the effect of multiplying both sides of an inequality by a number.

The procedures used to solve linear inequalities in one variable are almost the same as those used to solve linear equations in one variable, but with one important exception, as noted in item 3 of Theorem 2.

THEOREM 2 Inequality Properties

An equivalent inequality will result, and the **sense or direction will remain the same**, if each side of the original inequality

1. has the same real number added to or subtracted from it.
2. is multiplied or divided by the same *positive* number.

An equivalent inequality will result, and the **sense or direction will reverse**, if each side of the original inequality

3. is multiplied or divided by the same *negative* number.

Note: Multiplication by 0 and division by 0 are not permitted.

Therefore, we can perform essentially the same operations on inequalities that we perform on equations, with the exception that **the sense of the inequality reverses if we multiply or divide both sides by a negative number**. Otherwise, the sense of the inequality does not change. For example, if we start with the true statement

$$-3 > -7$$

and multiply both sides by 2, we obtain

$$-6 > -14$$

and the sense of the inequality stays the same. But if we multiply both sides of $-3 > -7$ by -2, the left side becomes 6 and the right side becomes 14, so we must write

$$6 < 14$$

to have a true statement. The sense of the inequality reverses.

If $a < b$, the **double inequality** $a < x < b$ means that $\boldsymbol{a < x}$ **and** $\boldsymbol{x < b}$; that is, x is between a and b. **Interval notation** is also used to describe sets defined by inequalities, as shown in Table 1.

The numbers a and b in Table 1 are called the **endpoints** of the interval. An interval is **closed** if it contains all its endpoints and **open** if it does not contain any of its endpoints. The intervals $[a, b]$, $(-\infty, a]$, and $[b, \infty)$ are closed, and the intervals (a, b), $(-\infty, a)$, and (b, ∞) are open. Note that the symbol ∞ (read infinity) is not a number. When we write $[b, \infty)$, we are simply referring to the interval that starts at b and continues indefinitely to the right. We never refer to ∞ as an endpoint, and we never write $[b, \infty]$. The interval $(-\infty, \infty)$ is the entire real number line.

Table 1 **Interval Notation**

Interval Notation	Inequality Notation	Line Graph
$[a, b]$	$a \le x \le b$	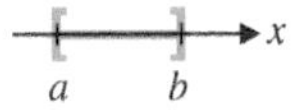
$[a, b)$	$a \le x < b$	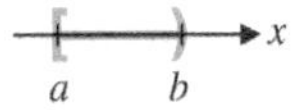
$(a, b]$	$a < x \le b$	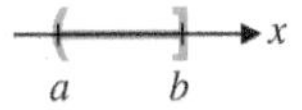
(a, b)	$a < x < b$	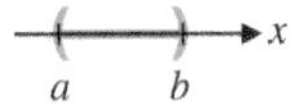
$(-\infty, a]$	$x \le a$	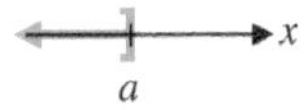
$(-\infty, a)$	$x < a$	
$[b, \infty)$	$x \ge b$	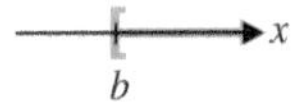
(b, ∞)	$x > b$	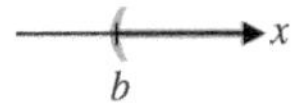

Note that an endpoint of a line graph in Table 1 has a square bracket through it if the endpoint is included in the interval; a parenthesis through an endpoint indicates that it is not included.

CONCEPTUAL INSIGHT

The notation $(2, 7)$ has two common mathematical interpretations: the ordered pair with first coordinate 2 and second coordinate 7, and the open interval consisting of all real numbers between 2 and 7. The choice of interpretation is usually determined by the context in which the notation is used. The notation $(2, -7)$ could be interpreted as an ordered pair but not as an interval. In interval notation, the left endpoint is always written first. So, $(-7, 2)$ is correct interval notation, but $(2, -7)$ is not.

EXAMPLE 5 **Interval and Inequality Notation, and Line Graphs**

(A) Write $[-2, 3)$ as a double inequality and graph.

(B) Write $x \ge -5$ in interval notation and graph.

SOLUTION

(A) $[-2, 3)$ is equivalent to $-2 \le x < 3$.

(B) $x \ge -5$ is equivalent to $[-5, \infty)$.

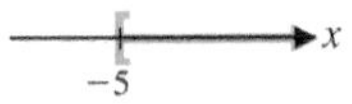

Matched Problem 5

(A) Write $(-7, 4]$ as a double inequality and graph.

(B) Write $x < 3$ in interval notation and graph.

Explore and Discuss 3

The solution to Example 5B shows the graph of the inequality $x \ge -5$. What is the graph of $x < -5$? What is the corresponding interval? Describe the relationship between these sets.

EXAMPLE 6 **Solving a Linear Inequality** Solve and graph:

$$2(2x + 3) < 6(x - 2) + 10$$

SOLUTION

$$2(2x + 3) < 6(x - 2) + 10 \quad \text{Remove parentheses.}$$
$$4x + 6 < 6x - 12 + 10 \quad \text{Combine like terms.}$$
$$4x + 6 < 6x - 2 \quad \text{Subtract } 6x \text{ from both sides.}$$
$$-2x + 6 < -2 \quad \text{Subtract 6 from both sides.}$$
$$-2x < -8 \quad \text{Divide both sides by } -2 \text{ and reverse the sense of the inequality.}$$
$$x > 4 \quad \text{or} \quad (4, \infty)$$

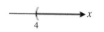

Notice that in the graph of $x > 4$, we use a parenthesis through 4, since the point 4 is not included in the graph.

Matched Problem 6 Solve and graph: $3(x - 1) \le 5(x + 2) - 5$

EXAMPLE 7 **Solving a Double Inequality** Solve and graph: $-3 < 2x + 3 \le 9$

SOLUTION We are looking for all numbers x such that $2x + 3$ is between -3 and 9, including 9 but not -3. We proceed as before except that we try to isolate x in the middle:

$$-3 < 2x + 3 \le 9$$
$$-3 - 3 < 2x + 3 - 3 \le 9 - 3$$
$$-6 < 2x \le 6$$
$$\frac{-6}{2} < \frac{2x}{2} \le \frac{6}{2}$$
$$-3 < x \le 3 \quad \text{or} \quad (-3, 3]$$

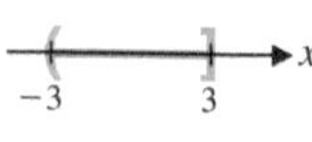

Matched Problem 7 Solve and graph: $-8 \le 3x - 5 < 7$

Note that a linear equation usually has exactly one solution, while a linear inequality usually has infinitely many solutions.

Applications

To realize the full potential of algebra, we must be able to translate real-world problems into mathematics. In short, we must be able to do word problems.

Here are some suggestions that will help you get started:

PROCEDURE For Solving Word Problems

1. Read the problem carefully and introduce a variable to represent an unknown quantity in the problem. Often the question asked in a problem will indicate the unknown quantity that should be represented by a variable.
2. Identify other quantities in the problem (known or unknown), and whenever possible, express unknown quantities in terms of the variable you introduced in Step 1.
3. Write a verbal statement using the conditions stated in the problem and then write an equivalent mathematical statement (equation or inequality).
4. Solve the equation or inequality and answer the questions posed in the problem.
5. Check the solution(s) in the original problem.

EXAMPLE 8 **Purchase Price** Alex purchases a big screen TV, pays 7% state sales tax, and is charged \$65 for delivery. If Alex's total cost is \$1,668.93, what was the purchase price of the TV?

SOLUTION

Step 1 **Introduce a variable for the unknown quantity.** After reading the problem, we decide to let x represent the purchase price of the TV.

Step 2 **Identify quantities in the problem.**

Delivery charge: \$65

Sales tax: $0.07x$

Total cost: \$1,668.93

Step 3 **Write a verbal statement and an equation.**

$$\text{Price} + \text{Delivery Charge} + \text{Sales Tax} = \text{Total Cost}$$
$$x + 65 + 0.07x = 1{,}668.93$$

Step 4 **Solve the equation and answer the question.**

$$x + 65 + 0.07x = 1{,}668.93 \quad \text{Combine like terms.}$$
$$1.07x + 65 = 1{,}668.93 \quad \text{Subtract 65 from both sides.}$$
$$1.07x = 1{,}603.93 \quad \text{Divide both sides by 1.07.}$$
$$x = 1{,}499$$

The price of the TV is \$1,499.

Step 5 **Check the answer in the original problem.**

$$\text{Price} = \$1{,}499.00$$
$$\text{Delivery charge} = \$\ \ 65.00$$
$$\text{Tax} = 0.07 \cdot 1{,}499 = \$\ 104.93$$
$$\text{Total} = \$1{,}668.93$$

Matched Problem 8 Mary paid 8.5% sales tax and a \$190 title and license fee when she bought a new car for a total of \$28,400. What is the purchase price of the car?

Any manufacturing company has **costs**, C, which include **fixed costs** such as plant overhead, product design, setup, and promotion; and **variable costs** that depend on the number of items produced. The **revenue**, R, is the amount of money received from the sale of its product. The company **breaks even** if the revenue is equal to the costs, that is, if $R = C$. Example 9 provides an introduction to cost, revenue, and break-even analysis.

EXAMPLE 9 **Break-Even Analysis** A manufacturing company makes bike computers. Fixed costs are \$48,000, and variable costs are \$12.40 per computer. If the computers are sold at a price of \$17.40 each, how many bike computers must be manufactured and sold in order for the company to break even?

SOLUTION

Step 1 Let x = number of bike computers manufactured and sold.

Step 2 C = Fixed costs + Variable costs

$= \$48{,}000 + \$12.40x$

$R = \$17.40x$

Step 3 The company breaks even if $R = C$; that is, if

$$\$17.40x = \$48,000 + \$12.40x$$

Step 4 $17.4x = 48,000 + 12.4x$ Subtract $12.4x$ from both sides.

$5x = 48,000$ Divide both sides by 5.

$x = 9,600$

The company must make and sell 9,600 bike computers to break even.

Step 5 Check:

Costs	Revenue
$48,000 + 12.4(9,600)$	$17.4(9,600)$
$= \$167,040$	$= \$167,040$

Matched Problem 9 How many bike computers would a company have to make and sell to break even if the fixed costs are \$36,000, variable costs are \$10.40 per computer, and the computers are sold to retailers for \$15.20 each?

EXAMPLE 10 **Consumer Price Index** The Consumer Price Index (CPI) is a measure of the average change in prices over time from a designated reference period, which equals 100. The index is based on prices of basic consumer goods and services. Table 2 lists the CPI for several years from 1960 to 2016. What net annual salary in 2016 would have the same purchasing power as a net annual salary of \$13,000 in 1960? Compute the answer to the nearest dollar. (*Source:* U.S. Bureau of Labor Statistics)

Table 2 CPI (1982–1984 = 100)

Year	Index
1960	29.6
1973	44.4
1986	109.6
1999	156.9
2016	241.7

SOLUTION

Step 1 Let $x =$ the purchasing power of an annual salary in 2016.

Step 2 Annual salary in 1960 $= \$13,000$

CPI in 1960 $= 29.6$

CPI in 2016 $= 241.7$

Step 3 The ratio of a salary in 2016 to a salary in 1960 is the same as the ratio of the CPI in 2016 to the CPI in 1960.

$$\frac{x}{13,000} = \frac{241.7}{29.6} \quad \text{Multiply both sides by 13,000.}$$

Step 4
$$x = 13,000 \cdot \frac{241.7}{29.6}$$
$$= \$106,152 \text{ per year}$$

Step 5 To check the answer, we confirm that the salary ratio agrees with the CPI ratio:

Salary Ratio	CPI Ratio
$\frac{106,152}{13,000} = 8.166$	$\frac{241.7}{29.6} = 8.166$

Matched Problem 10 What net annual salary in 1973 would have had the same purchasing power as a net annual salary of \$100,000 in 2016? Compute the answer to the nearest dollar.

Exercises 1.1

A *In Problems 1–6, solve for x.*

1. $5x + 3 = x + 23$
2. $7x - 6 = 5x - 24$
3. $9(4 - x) = 2(x + 7)$
4. $3(x + 6) = 5 - 2(x + 1)$
5. $\frac{x + 1}{4} = \frac{x}{2} + 5$
6. $\frac{2x + 1}{3} - \frac{5x}{2} = 4$

In Problems 7–12, write the interval as an inequality or double inequality.

7. $[4, 13)$
8. $(-3, 5]$
9. $(-2, 7)$
10. $[-6, -1]$
11. $(-\infty, 4]$
12. $[9, \infty)$

In Problems 13–18, write the solution set using interval notation.

13. $-8 < x \le 2$
14. $-1 \le x < 5$
15. $2x < 18$
16. $3x \ge 12$
17. $15 \le -3x < 21$
18. $-8 < -4x \le 12$

B *In Problems 19–32, find the solution set.*

19. $\frac{x}{4} + \frac{1}{2} = \frac{1}{8}$
20. $\frac{m}{3} - 4 = \frac{2}{3}$
21. $\frac{y}{-5} > \frac{3}{2}$
22. $\frac{x}{-4} < \frac{5}{6}$
23. $2u + 4 = 5u + 1 - 7u$
24. $-3y + 9 + y = 13 - 8y$
25. $10x + 25(x - 3) = 275$
26. $-3(4 - x) = 5 - (x + 1)$
27. $3 - y \le 4(y - 3)$
28. $x - 2 \ge 2(x - 5)$
29. $\frac{x}{5} - \frac{x}{6} = \frac{6}{5}$
30. $\frac{y}{4} - \frac{y}{3} = \frac{1}{2}$
31. $\frac{m}{5} - 3 < \frac{3}{5} - \frac{m}{2}$
32. $\frac{u}{2} - \frac{2}{3} < \frac{u}{3} + 2$

In Problems 33–36, solve and graph.

33. $2 \le 3x - 7 < 14$
34. $-4 \le 5x + 6 < 21$
35. $-4 \le \frac{9}{5}C + 32 \le 68$
36. $-1 \le \frac{2}{3}t + 5 \le 11$

In Problems 37–42, solve for the indicated variable.

37. $3x - 4y = 12$; for y
38. $y = -\frac{2}{3}x + 8$; for x
39. $Ax + By = C$; for y $(B \ne 0)$
40. $y = mx + b$; for m
41. $F = \frac{9}{5}C + 32$; for C
42. $C = \frac{5}{9}(F - 32)$; for F

C *In Problems 43 and 44, solve and graph.*

43. $-3 \le 4 - 7x < 18$
44. $-10 \le 8 - 3u \le -6$
45. If both a and b are positive numbers and b/a is greater than 1, then is $a - b$ positive or negative?
46. If both a and b are negative numbers and b/a is greater than 1, then is $a - b$ positive or negative?

Applications

47. **Ticket sales.** A rock concert brought in \$432,500 on the sale of 9,500 tickets. If the tickets sold for \$35 and \$55 each, how many of each type of ticket were sold?
48. **Parking meter coins.** An all-day parking meter takes only dimes and quarters. If it contains 100 coins with a total value of \$14.50, how many of each type of coin are in the meter?
49. **IRA.** You have \$500,000 in an IRA (Individual Retirement Account) at the time you retire. You have the option of investing this money in two funds: Fund A pays 5.2% annually and Fund B pays 7.7% annually. How should you divide your money between Fund A and Fund B to produce an annual interest income of \$34,000?
50. **IRA.** Refer to Problem 49. How should you divide your money between Fund A and Fund B to produce an annual interest income of \$30,000?
51. **Car prices.** If the price change of cars parallels the change in the CPI (see Table 2 in Example 10), what would a car sell for (to the nearest dollar) in 2016 if a comparable model sold for \$10,000 in 1999?
52. **Home values.** If the price change in houses parallels the CPI (see Table 2 in Example 10), what would a house valued at \$200,000 in 2016 be valued at (to the nearest dollar) in 1960?
53. **Retail and wholesale prices.** Retail prices in a department store are obtained by marking up the wholesale price by 40%. That is, the retail price is obtained by adding 40% of the wholesale price to the wholesale price.
    (A) What is the retail price of a suit if the wholesale price is \$300?
    (B) What is the wholesale price of a pair of jeans if the retail price is \$77?
54. **Retail and sale prices.** Sale prices in a department store are obtained by marking down the retail price by 15%. That is, the sale price is obtained by subtracting 15% of the retail price from the retail price.
    (A) What is the sale price of a hat that has a retail price of \$60?
    (B) What is the retail price of a dress that has a sale price of \$136?

55. Equipment rental. A golf course charges \$52 for a round of golf using a set of their clubs, and \$44 if you have your own clubs. If you buy a set of clubs for \$270, how many rounds must you play to recover the cost of the clubs?

56. Equipment rental. The local supermarket rents carpet cleaners for \$20 a day. These cleaners use shampoo in a special cartridge that sells for \$16 and is available only from the supermarket. A home carpet cleaner can be purchased for \$300. Shampoo for the home cleaner is readily available for \$9 a bottle. Past experience has shown that it takes two shampoo cartridges to clean the 10-foot-by-12-foot carpet in your living room with the rented cleaner. Cleaning the same area with the home cleaner will consume three bottles of shampoo. If you buy the home cleaner, how many times must you clean the living-room carpet to make buying cheaper than renting?

57. Sales commissions. One employee of a computer store is paid a base salary of \$2,000 a month plus an 8% commission on all sales over \$7,000 during the month. How much must the employee sell in one month to earn a total of \$4,000 for the month?

58. Sales commissions. A second employee of the computer store in Problem 57 is paid a base salary of \$3,000 a month plus a 5% commission on all sales during the month.

(A) How much must this employee sell in one month to earn a total of \$4,000 for the month?

(B) Determine the sales level at which both employees receive the same monthly income.

(C) If employees can select either of these payment methods, how would you advise an employee to make this selection?

59. Break-even analysis. A publisher for a promising new novel figures fixed costs (overhead, advances, promotion, copy editing, typesetting) at \$55,000, and variable costs (printing, paper, binding, shipping) at \$1.60 for each book produced. If the book is sold to distributors for \$11 each, how many must be produced and sold for the publisher to break even?

60. Break-even analysis. The publisher of a new book figures fixed costs at \$92,000 and variable costs at \$2.10 for each book produced. If the book is sold to distributors for \$15 each, how many must be sold for the publisher to break even?

61. Break-even analysis. The publisher in Problem 59 finds that rising prices for paper increase the variable costs to \$2.10 per book.

(A) Discuss possible strategies the company might use to deal with this increase in costs.

(B) If the company continues to sell the books for \$11, how many books must they sell now to make a profit?

(C) If the company wants to start making a profit at the same production level as before the cost increase, how much should they sell the book for now?

62. Break-even analysis. The publisher in Problem 60 finds that rising prices for paper increase the variable costs to \$2.70 per book.

(A) Discuss possible strategies the company might use to deal with this increase in costs.

(B) If the company continues to sell the books for \$15, how many books must they sell now to make a profit?

(C) If the company wants to start making a profit at the same production level as before the cost increase, how much should they sell the book for now?

63. Wildlife management. A naturalist estimated the total number of rainbow trout in a certain lake using the capture–mark–recapture technique. He netted, marked, and released 200 rainbow trout. A week later, allowing for thorough mixing, he again netted 200 trout, and found 8 marked ones among them. Assuming that the proportion of marked fish in the second sample was the same as the proportion of all marked fish in the total population, estimate the number of rainbow trout in the lake.

64. Temperature conversion. If the temperature for a 24-hour period at an Antarctic station ranged between $-49°F$ and $14°F$ (that is, $-49 \le F \le 14$), what was the range in degrees Celsius? [*Note:* $F = \frac{9}{5}C + 32$.]

65. Psychology. The IQ (intelligence quotient) is found by dividing the mental age (MA), as indicated on standard tests, by the chronological age (CA) and multiplying by 100. For example, if a child has a mental age of 12 and a chronological age of 8, the calculated IQ is 150. If a 9-year-old girl has an IQ of 140, compute her mental age.

66. Psychology. Refer to Problem 65. If the IQ of a group of 12-year-old children varies between 80 and 140, what is the range of their mental ages?

Answers to Matched Problems

1. $x = 4$

2. $x = 2$

3. (A) $L = \dfrac{S - 2WH}{2W + 2H}$ (B) $H = \dfrac{S - 2LW}{2L + 2W}$

4. (A) $<$ (B) $<$ (C) $>$

5. (A) $-7 < x \le 4$; (B) $(-\infty, 3)$

6. $x \ge -4$ or $[-4, \infty)$

7. $-1 \le x < 4$ or $[-1, 4)$

8. \$26,000

9. 7,500 bike computers

10. \$18,370

1.2 Graphs and Lines

- Cartesian Coordinate System
- Graphs of $Ax + By = C$
- Slope of a Line
- Equations of Lines: Special Forms
- Applications

In this section, we will consider one of the most basic geometric figures—a line. When we use the term *line* in this book, we mean *straight line*. We will learn how to recognize and graph a line and how to use information concerning a line to find its equation. Examining the graph of any equation often results in additional insight into the nature of the equation's solutions.

Cartesian Coordinate System

Recall that to form a **Cartesian** or **rectangular coordinate system**, we select two real number lines—one horizontal and one vertical—and let them cross through their origins as indicated in Figure 1. Up and to the right are the usual choices for the positive directions. These two number lines are called the **horizontal axis** and the **vertical axis**, or, together, the **coordinate axes**. The horizontal axis is usually referred to as the ***x* axis** and the vertical axis as the ***y* axis**, and each is labeled accordingly. The coordinate axes divide the plane into four parts called **quadrants**, which are numbered counterclockwise from I to IV (see Fig. 1).

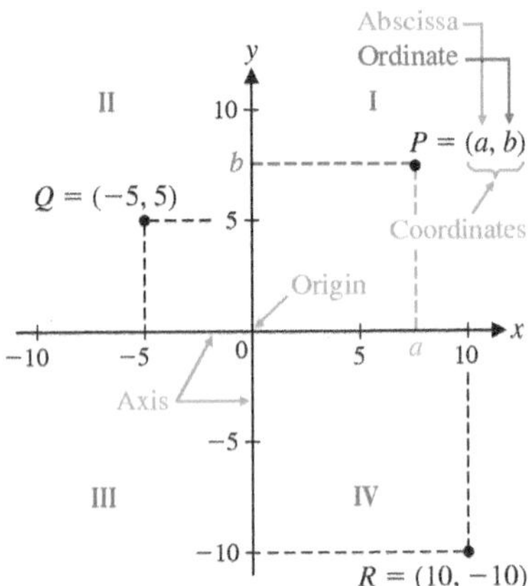

Figure 1 The Cartesian (rectangular) coordinate system

Now we want to assign *coordinates* to each point in the plane. Given an arbitrary point P in the plane, pass horizontal and vertical lines through the point (Fig. 1). The vertical line will intersect the horizontal axis at a point with coordinate a, and the horizontal line will intersect the vertical axis at a point with coordinate b. These two numbers, written as the **ordered pair** (a, b), form the **coordinates** of the point P. The first coordinate, a, is called the **abscissa** of P; the second coordinate, b, is called the **ordinate** of P. The abscissa of Q in Figure 1 is -5, and the ordinate of Q is 5. The coordinates of a point can also be referenced in terms of the axis labels. The ***x* coordinate** of R in Figure 1 is 10, and the ***y* coordinate** of R is -10. The point with coordinates $(0, 0)$ is called the **origin**.

The procedure we have just described assigns to each point P in the plane a unique pair of real numbers (a, b). Conversely, if we are given an ordered pair of real numbers (a, b), then, reversing this procedure, we can determine a unique point P in the plane. Thus,

There is a one-to-one correspondence between the points in a plane and the elements in the set of all ordered pairs of real numbers.

This is often referred to as the **fundamental theorem of analytic geometry**.

Graphs of $Ax + By = C$

In Section 1.1, we called an equation of the form $ax + b = 0$ $(a \neq 0)$ a linear equation in one variable. Now we want to consider linear equations in two variables:

DEFINITION Linear Equations in Two Variables

A **linear equation in two variables** is an equation that can be written in the **standard form**

$$Ax + By = C$$

where A, B, and C are constants (A and B not both 0), and x and y are variables.

A **solution** of an equation in two variables is an ordered pair of real numbers that satisfies the equation. For example, $(4, 3)$ is a solution of $3x - 2y = 6$. The **solution set** of an equation in two variables is the set of all solutions of the equation. The **graph** of an equation is the graph of its solution set.

Explore and Discuss 1

(A) As noted earlier, $(4, 3)$ is a solution of the equation

$$3x - 2y = 6$$

Find three more solutions of this equation. Plot these solutions in a Cartesian coordinate system. What familiar geometric shape could be used to describe the solution set of this equation?

(B) Repeat part (A) for the equation $x = 2$.

(C) Repeat part (A) for the equation $y = -3$.

In Explore and Discuss 1, you may have recognized that the graph of each equation is a (straight) line. Theorem 1 confirms this fact.

THEOREM 1 Graph of a Linear Equation in Two Variables

The graph of any equation of the form

$$Ax + By = C \qquad (A \text{ and } B \text{ not both } 0) \qquad (1)$$

is a line, and any line in a Cartesian coordinate system is the graph of an equation of this form.

If $A \neq 0$ and $B \neq 0$, then equation (1) can be written as

$$y = -\frac{A}{B}x + \frac{C}{B} = mx + b, m \neq 0$$

If $A = 0$ and $B \neq 0$, then equation (1) can be written as

$$y = \frac{C}{B}$$

and its graph is a **horizontal line**. If $A \neq 0$ and $B = 0$, then equation (1) can be written as

$$x = \frac{C}{A}$$

and its graph is a **vertical line**. To graph equation (1), or any of its special cases, plot any two points in the solution set and use a straightedge to draw the line through these two points. The points where the line crosses the axes are often the easiest to find. The ***y* intercept** is the y coordinate of the point where the graph crosses the y axis, and the ***x* intercept** is the x coordinate of the point where the graph crosses the x axis. To find the y intercept, let $x = 0$ and solve for y. To find the x intercept, let $y = 0$ and solve for x. It is a good idea to find a third point as a check point.

Reminder

If the x intercept is a and the y intercept is b, then the graph of the line passes through the points $(a, 0)$ and $(0, b)$. It is common practice to refer to both the numbers a and b and the points $(a, 0)$ and $(0, b)$ as the x and y intercepts of the line.

EXAMPLE 1 **Using Intercepts to Graph a Line** Graph: $3x - 4y = 12$

SOLUTION Find and plot the y intercept, the x intercept, and a check point (Fig. 2).

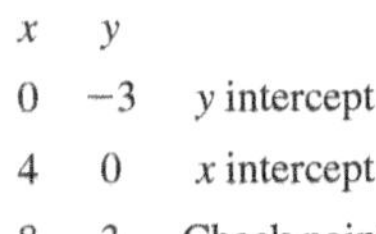

x	y	
0	−3	y intercept
4	0	x intercept
8	3	Check point

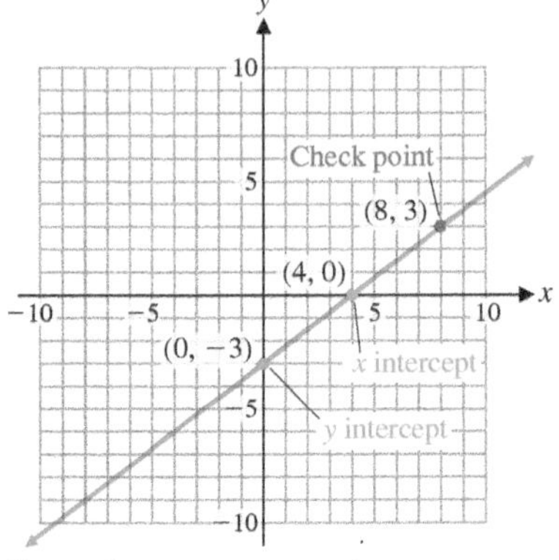

Figure 2

Matched Problem 1 Graph: $4x - 3y = 12$

The icon in the margin is used throughout this book to identify optional graphing calculator activities that are intended to give you additional insight into the concepts under discussion. You may have to consult the manual for your calculator for the details necessary to carry out these activities.

EXAMPLE 2 **Using a Graphing Calculator** Graph $3x - 4y = 12$ on a graphing calculator and find the intercepts.

SOLUTION First, we solve $3x - 4y = 12$ for y.

$$3x - 4y = 12 \qquad \text{Add } -3x \text{ to both sides.}$$

$$-4y = -3x + 12 \qquad \text{Divide both sides by } -4.$$

$$y = \frac{-3x + 12}{-4} \qquad \text{Simplify.}$$

$$y = \frac{3}{4}x - 3 \qquad (2)$$

Now we enter the right side of equation (2) in a calculator (Fig. 3A), enter values for the window variables (Fig. 3B), and graph the line (Fig. 3C). (The numerals to the left and right of the screen in Figure 3C are Xmin and Xmax, respectively. Similarly, the numerals below and above the screen are Ymin and Ymax.)

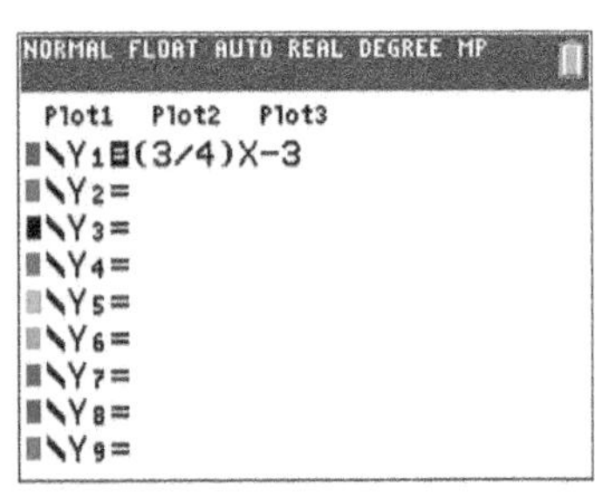

(A)

```
NORMAL FLOAT AUTO REAL DEGREE MP
WINDOW
 Xmin=-10
 Xmax=10
 Xscl=1
 Ymin=-5
 Ymax=5
 Yscl=1
 Xres=1
 ΔX=0.07575757575757
 TraceStep=0.151515151515...
```

(B)

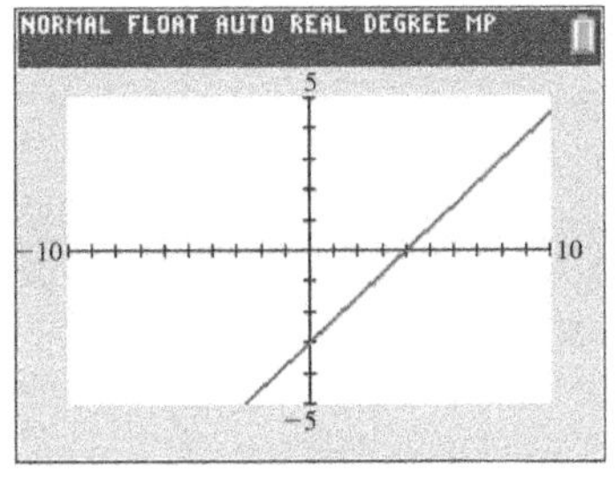

(C)

Figure 3 Graphing a line on a graphing calculator

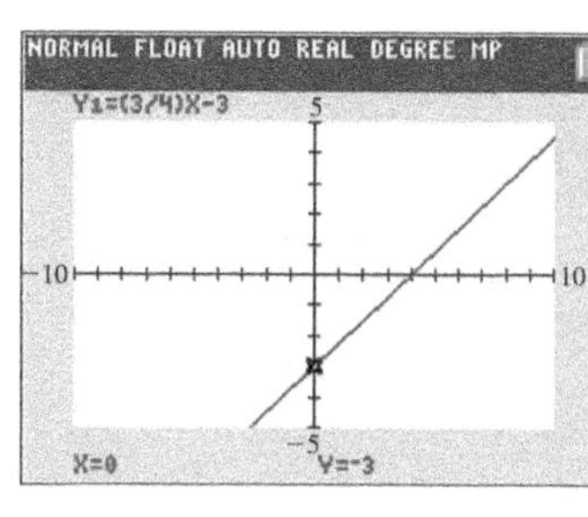

(A)

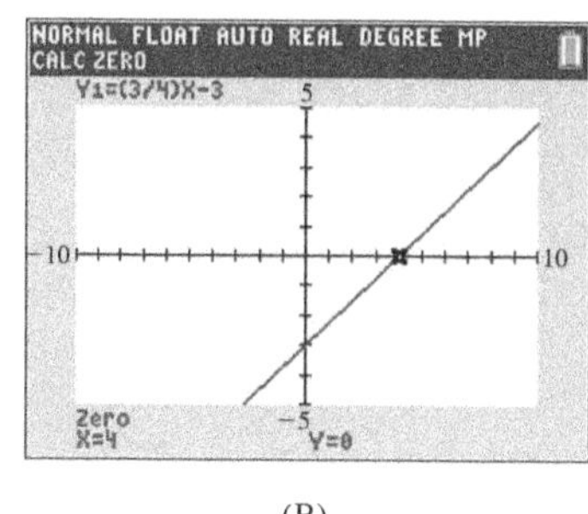

(B)

Figure 4 Using TRACE and ZERO on a graphing calculator

Next we use two calculator commands to find the intercepts: TRACE (Fig. 4A) and ZERO (Fig. 4B). The y intercept is -3 (Fig. 4A), and the x intercept is 4 (Fig. 4B).

Matched Problem 2 Graph $4x - 3y = 12$ on a graphing calculator and find the intercepts.

EXAMPLE 3 **Horizontal and Vertical Lines**

(A) Graph $x = -4$ and $y = 6$ simultaneously in the same rectangular coordinate system.

(B) Write the equations of the vertical and horizontal lines that pass through the point $(7, -5)$.

SOLUTION

(A) The line $x = -4$ consists of all points with x coordinate -4. To graph it, draw the vertical line through $(-4, 0)$. The line $y = 6$ consists of all points with y coordinate 6. To graph it, draw the horizontal line through $(0, 6)$. See Figure 5.

(B) Horizontal line through $(7, -5)$: $y = -5$
Vertical line through $(7, -5)$: $x = 7$

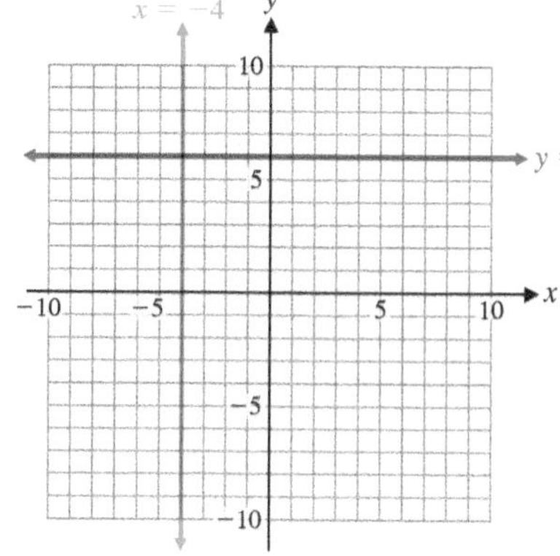

Figure 5

Matched Problem 3

(A) Graph $x = 5$ and $y = -3$ simultaneously in the same rectangular coordinate system.

(B) Write the equations of the vertical and horizontal lines that pass through the point $(-8, 2)$.

Slope of a Line

If we take two points, (x_1, y_1) and (x_2, y_2), on a line, then the ratio of the change in y to the change in x is called the **slope** of the line. In a sense, slope provides a measure of the "steepness" of a line relative to the x axis. The change in x is often called the **run**, and the change in y is the **rise**.

DEFINITION Slope of a Line

If a line passes through two distinct points, (x_1, y_1) and (x_2, y_2) (see Fig. 6), then its slope is given by the formula

$$m = \frac{y_2 - y_1}{x_2 - x_1} \qquad x_1 \neq x_2$$

$$= \frac{\text{vertical change (rise)}}{\text{horizontal change (run)}}$$

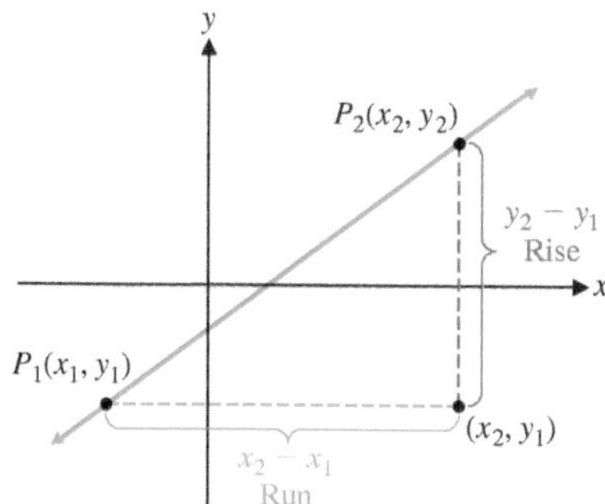

Figure 6

For a horizontal line, y does not change; its slope is 0. For a vertical line, x does not change; $x_1 = x_2$ so its slope is not defined. In general, the slope of a line may be positive, negative, 0, or not defined. Each case is illustrated geometrically in Table 1.

Table 1 Geometric Interpretation of Slope

Line	Rising as x moves from left to right	Falling as x moves from left to right	Horizontal	Vertical
Slope	Positive	Negative	0	Not defined
Example				

CONCEPTUAL INSIGHT

One property of real numbers discussed in Appendix A, Section A.1, is

$$\frac{-a}{-b} = -\frac{-a}{b} = -\frac{a}{-b} = \frac{a}{b}, \quad b \neq 0$$

This property implies that the slope of the line through A and B is equal to the slope of the line through B and A. For example, if $A = (4, 3)$ and $B = (1, 2)$, then

$B = (1, 2) \qquad A = (4, 3)$

$A = (4, 3) \qquad B = (1, 2)$

$$m = \frac{2 - 3}{1 - 4} = \frac{-1}{-3} = \frac{1}{3} = \frac{3 - 2}{4 - 1}$$

A property of similar triangles (see the back of the book) ensures that the slope of a line is the same for any pair of distinct points on the line (Fig. 7).

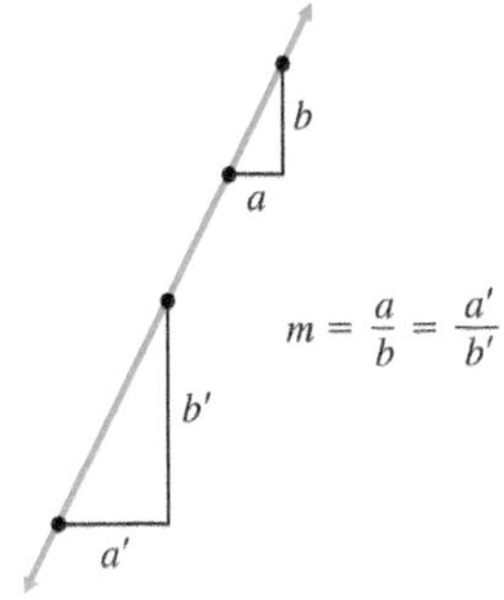

Figure 7

EXAMPLE 4 **Finding Slopes** Sketch a line through each pair of points, and find the slope of each line.

(A) $(-3, -2), (3, 4)$
(B) $(-1, 3), (2, -3)$
(C) $(-2, -3), (3, -3)$
(D) $(-2, 4), (-2, -2)$

SOLUTION

(A)

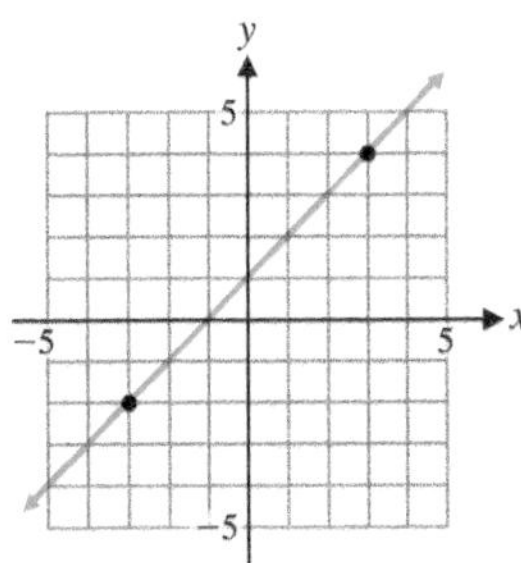

$$m = \frac{4 - (-2)}{3 - (-3)} = \frac{6}{6} = 1$$

(B)

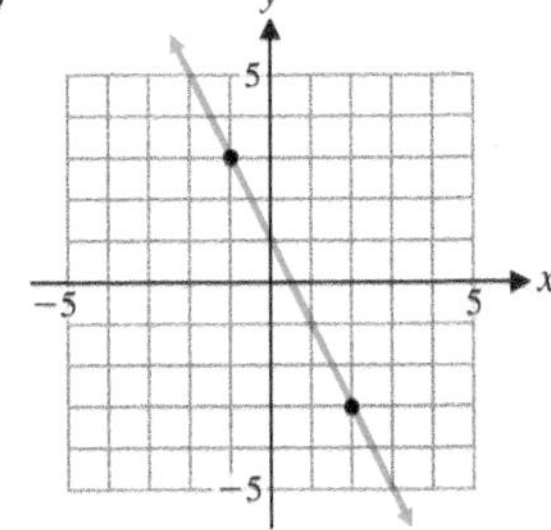

$$m = \frac{-3 - 3}{2 - (-1)} = \frac{-6}{3} = -2$$

(C)

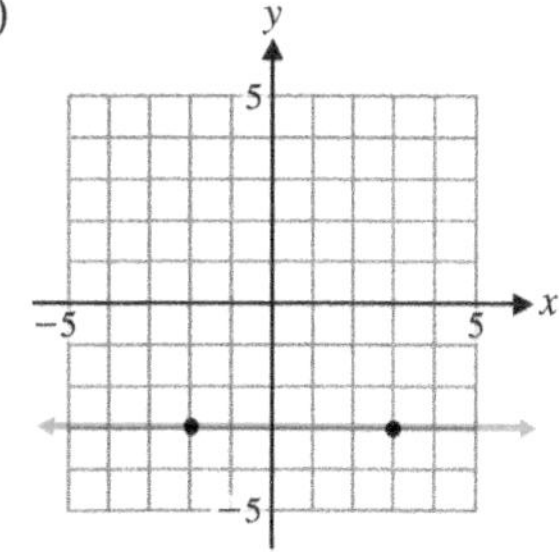

$$m = \frac{-3 - (-3)}{3 - (-2)} = \frac{0}{5} = 0$$

(D)

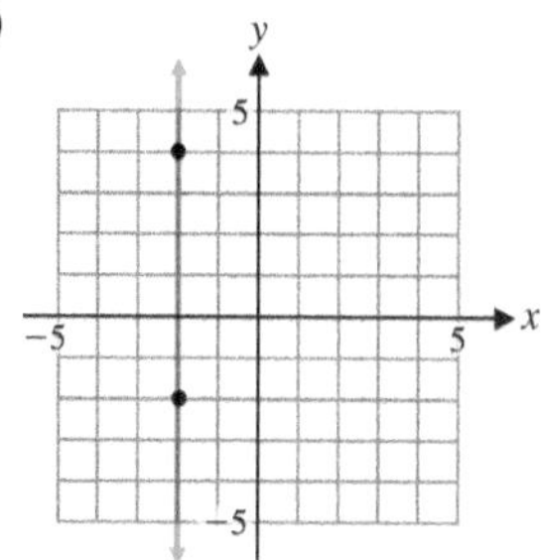

$$m = \frac{-2 - 4}{-2 - (-2)} = \frac{-6}{0}$$

Slope is not defined.

Matched Problem 4 Find the slope of the line through each pair of points.

(A) $(-2, 4), (3, 4)$ (B) $(-2, 4), (0, -4)$

(C) $(-1, 5), (-1, -2)$ (D) $(-1, -2), (2, 1)$

Equations of Lines: Special Forms

Let us start by investigating why $y = mx + b$ is called the *slope-intercept form* for a line.

Explore and Discuss 2

(A) Graph $y = x + b$ for $b = -5, -3, 0, 3$, and 5 simultaneously in the same coordinate system. Verbally describe the geometric significance of b.

(B) Graph $y = mx - 1$ for $m = -2, -1, 0, 1$, and 2 simultaneously in the same coordinate system. Verbally describe the geometric significance of m.

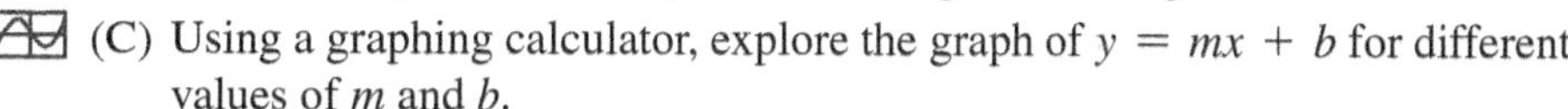

(C) Using a graphing calculator, explore the graph of $y = mx + b$ for different values of m and b.

As you may have deduced from Explore and Discuss 2, constants m and b in $y = mx + b$ have the following geometric interpretations.

If we let $x = 0$, then $y = b$. So the graph of $y = mx + b$ crosses the y axis at $(0, b)$. The constant b is the *y intercept*. For example, the y intercept of the graph of $y = -4x - 1$ is -1.

To determine the geometric significance of m, we proceed as follows: If $y = mx + b$, then by setting $x = 0$ and $x = 1$, we conclude that $(0, b)$ and $(1, m + b)$ lie on its graph (Fig. 8). The slope of this line is given by:

$$\text{Slope} = \frac{y_2 - y_1}{x_2 - x_1} = \frac{(m + b) - b}{1 - 0} = m$$

So m is the slope of the line given by $y = mx + b$.

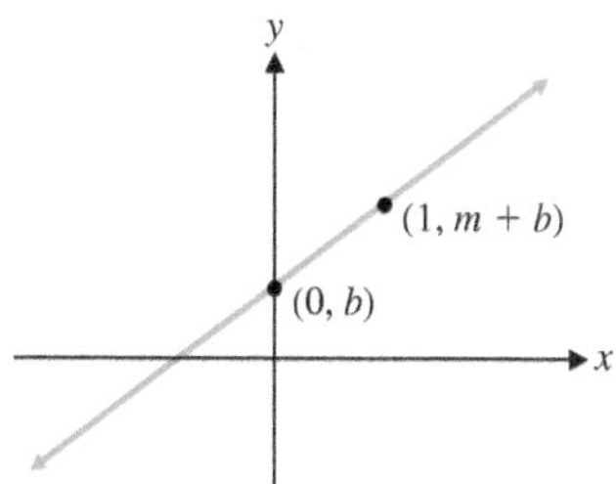

Figure 8

DEFINITION Slope-Intercept Form

The equation

$$y = mx + b \qquad m = \text{slope}, b = y \text{ intercept} \tag{3}$$

is called the **slope-intercept form** of an equation of a line.

EXAMPLE 5 **Using the Slope-Intercept Form**

(A) Find the slope and y intercept, and graph $y = -\frac{2}{3}x - 3$.

(B) Write the equation of the line with slope $\frac{2}{3}$ and y intercept -2.

SOLUTION

(A) Slope $= m = -\frac{2}{3}$; y intercept $= b = -3$.

To graph the line, first plot the y intercept $(0, -3)$. Then, since the slope is $-\frac{2}{3}$, locate a second point on the line by moving 3 units in the x direction (run) and -2 units in the y direction (rise). Draw the line through these two points (see Fig. 9).

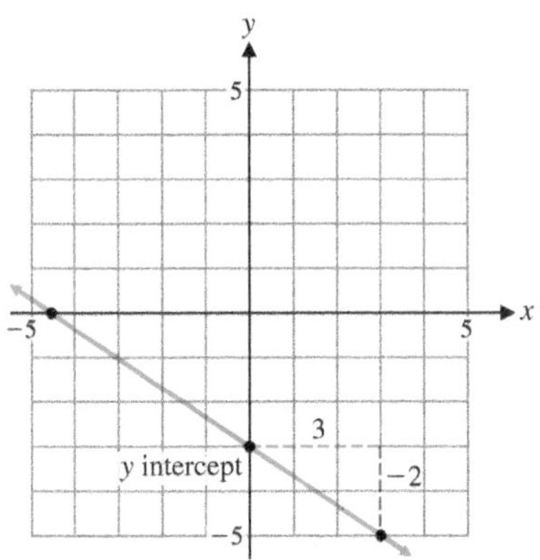

Figure 9

(B) $m = \frac{2}{3}$ and $b = -2$; so, $y = \frac{2}{3}x - 2$

Matched Problem 5 Write the equation of the line with slope $\frac{1}{2}$ and y intercept -1. Graph.

Suppose that a line has slope m and passes through a fixed point (x_1, y_1). If the point (x, y) is any other point on the line (Fig. 10), then

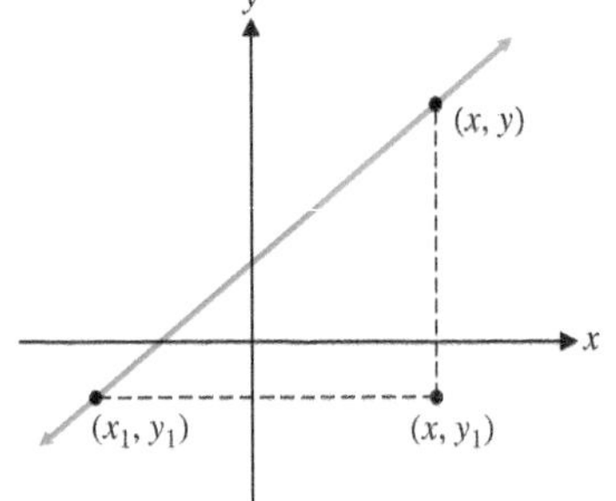

Figure 10

$$\frac{y - y_1}{x - x_1} = m$$

That is,

$$y - y_1 = m(x - x_1) \tag{4}$$

We now observe that (x_1, y_1) also satisfies equation (4) and conclude that equation (4) is an equation of a line with slope m that passes through (x_1, y_1).

DEFINITION Point-Slope Form

An equation of a line with slope m that passes through (x_1, y_1) is

$$y - y_1 = m(x - x_1) \tag{4}$$

which is called the **point-slope form** of an equation of a line.

The point-slope form is extremely useful, since it enables us to find an equation for a line if we know its slope and the coordinates of a point on the line or if we know the coordinates of two points on the line.

EXAMPLE 6 **Using the Point-Slope Form**

(A) Find an equation for the line that has slope $\frac{1}{2}$ and passes through $(-4, 3)$. Write the final answer in the form $Ax + By = C$.

(B) Find an equation for the line that passes through the points $(-3, 2)$ and $(-4, 5)$. Write the resulting equation in the form $y = mx + b$.

SOLUTION

(A) Use $y - y_1 = m(x - x_1)$. Let $m = \frac{1}{2}$ and $(x_1, y_1) = (-4, 3)$. Then

$$y - 3 = \tfrac{1}{2}[x - (-4)]$$

$$y - 3 = \tfrac{1}{2}(x + 4) \qquad \text{Multiply both sides by 2.}$$

$$2y - 6 = x + 4$$

$$-x + 2y = 10 \quad \text{or} \quad x - 2y = -10$$

(B) First, find the slope of the line by using the slope formula:

$$m = \frac{y_2 - y_1}{x_2 - x_1} = \frac{5 - 2}{-4 - (-3)} = \frac{3}{-1} = -3$$

Now use $y - y_1 = m(x - x_1)$ with $m = -3$ and $(x_1, y_1) = (-3, 2)$:

$$y - 2 = -3[x - (-3)]$$

$$y - 2 = -3(x + 3)$$

$$y - 2 = -3x - 9$$

$$y = -3x - 7$$

Matched Problem 6

(A) Find an equation for the line that has slope $\frac{2}{3}$ and passes through $(6, -2)$. Write the resulting equation in the form $Ax + By = C, A > 0$.

(B) Find an equation for the line that passes through $(2, -3)$ and $(4, 3)$. Write the resulting equation in the form $y = mx + b$.

The various forms of the equation of a line that we have discussed are summarized in Table 2 for quick reference.

Table 2 **Equations of a Line**

Standard form	$Ax + By = C$	A and B not both 0
Slope-intercept form	$y = mx + b$	Slope: m; y intercept: b
Point-slope form	$y - y_1 = m(x - x_1)$	Slope: m; point: (x_1, y_1)
Horizontal line	$y = b$	Slope: 0
Vertical line	$x = a$	Slope: undefined

Applications

We will now see how equations of lines occur in certain applications.

EXAMPLE 7 **Cost Equation** The management of a company that manufactures skateboards has fixed costs (costs at 0 output) of \$300 per day and total costs of \$4,300 per day at an output of 100 skateboards per day. Assume that cost C is linearly related to output x.

(A) Find the slope of the line joining the points associated with outputs of 0 and 100, that is, the line passing through $(0, 300)$ and $(100, 4{,}300)$.

(B) Find an equation of the line relating output to cost. Write the final answer in the form $C = mx + b$.

(C) Graph the cost equation from part (B) for $0 \le x \le 200$.

SOLUTION

(A) $$m = \frac{y_2 - y_1}{x_2 - x_1} = \frac{4{,}300 - 300}{100 - 0} = \frac{4{,}000}{100} = 40$$

(B) We must find an equation of the line that passes through $(0, 300)$ with slope 40. We use the slope-intercept form:

$$C = mx + b$$
$$C = 40x + 300$$

(C) To graph $C = 40x + 300$ for $0 \le x \le 200$, we first calculate $C(200)$:

$$C(200) = 40(200) + 300 = 8{,}300$$

Plot the points $(200, 8{,}300)$ and $(0, 300)$ and draw the line segment joining them (see Fig. 11).

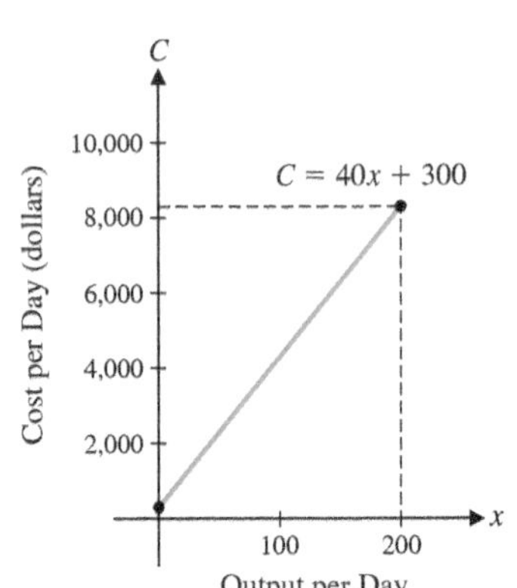

Figure 11

In Example 7, the *fixed cost* of \$300 per day covers plant cost, insurance, and so on. This cost is incurred whether or not there is any production. The *variable cost* is $40x$, which depends on the day's output. Since increasing production from x to $x + 1$ will increase the cost by \$40 (from $40x + 300$ to $40x + 340$), the slope 40 can be interpreted as the **rate of change** of the cost function with respect to production x.

Matched Problem 7 Answer parts (A) and (B) in Example 7 for fixed costs of \$250 per day and total costs of \$3,450 per day at an output of 80 skateboards per day.

In a free competitive market, the price of a product is determined by the relationship between supply and demand. If there is a surplus—that is, the supply is greater than the demand—the price tends to come down. If there is a shortage—that is, the demand is greater than the supply—the price tends to go up. The price tends to move toward an equilibrium price at which the supply and demand are equal. Example 8 introduces the basic concepts.

EXAMPLE 8 **Supply and Demand** At a price of \$9.00 per box of oranges, the supply is 320,000 boxes and the demand is 200,000 boxes. At a price of \$8.50 per box, the supply is 270,000 boxes and the demand is 300,000 boxes.

(A) Find a price–supply equation of the form $p = mx + b$, where p is the price in dollars and x is the corresponding supply in thousands of boxes.

(B) Find a price–demand equation of the form $p = mx + b$, where p is the price in dollars and x is the corresponding demand in thousands of boxes.

(C) Graph the price–supply and price–demand equations in the same coordinate system and find their point of intersection.

SOLUTION

(A) To find a price–supply equation of the form $p = mx + b$, we must find two points of the form (x, p) that are on the supply line. From the given supply data, $(320, 9)$ and $(270, 8.5)$ are two such points. First, find the slope of the line:

$$m = \frac{9 - 8.5}{320 - 270} = \frac{0.5}{50} = 0.01$$

Now use the point-slope form to find the equation of the line:

$$p - p_1 = m(x - x_1) \qquad (x_1, p_1) = (320, 9)$$

$$p - 9 = 0.01(x - 320)$$

$$p - 9 = 0.01x - 3.2$$

$$p = 0.01x + 5.8 \qquad \text{Price–supply equation}$$

(B) From the given demand data, $(200, 9)$ and $(300, 8.5)$ are two points on the demand line.

$$m = \frac{8.5 - 9}{300 - 200} = \frac{-0.5}{100} = -0.005$$

$$p - p_1 = m(x - x_1) \qquad \text{Substitute } x_1 = 200,\ p_1 = 9.$$

$$p - 9 = -0.005(x - 200)$$

$$p - 9 = -0.005x + 1$$

$$p = -0.005x + 10 \qquad \text{Price–demand equation}$$

(C) From part (A), we plot the points $(320, 9)$ and $(270, 8.5)$ and then draw the line through them. We do the same with the points $(200, 9)$ and $(300, 8.5)$ from part (B) (Fig. 12). (Note that we restricted the axes to intervals that contain these data points.) To find the intersection point of the two lines, we equate the right-hand sides of the price–supply and price–demand equations and solve for x:

Price–supply Price–demand

$$0.01x + 5.8 = -0.005x + 10$$

$$0.015x = 4.2$$

$$x = 280$$

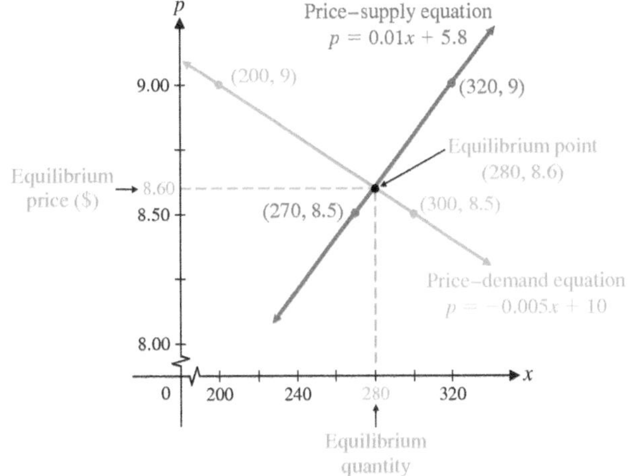

Figure 12 Graphs of price–supply and price–demand equations

Now use the price–supply equation to find p when $x = 280$:

$$p = 0.01x + 5.8$$

$$p = 0.01(280) + 5.8 = 8.6$$

As a check, we use the price–demand equation to find p when $x = 280$:

$$p = -0.005x + 10$$

$$p = -0.005(280) + 10 = 8.6$$

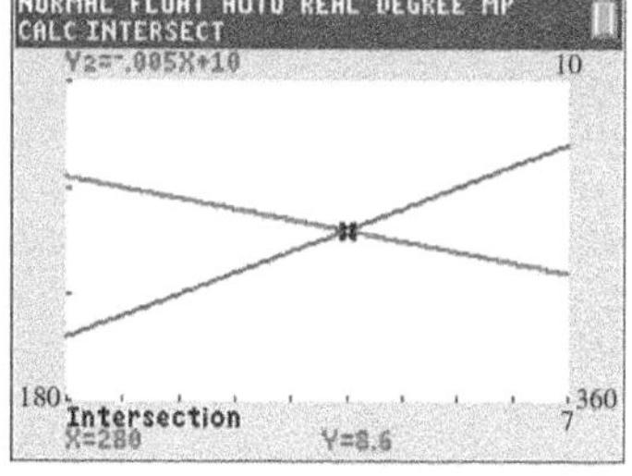

Figure 13 Finding an intersection point

The lines intersect at $(280, 8.6)$. The intersection point of the price–supply and price–demand equations is called the **equilibrium point**, and its coordinates are the **equilibrium quantity** (280) and the **equilibrium price** ($8.60). These terms are illustrated in Figure 12. The intersection point can also be found by using the INTERSECT command on a graphing calculator (Fig. 13). To summarize, the price of a box of oranges tends toward the equilibrium price of $8.60, at which the supply and demand are both equal to 280,000 boxes.

Matched Problem 8 At a price of $12.59 per box of grapefruit, the supply is 595,000 boxes and the demand is 650,000 boxes. At a price of $13.19 per box, the supply is 695,000 boxes and the demand is 590,000 boxes. Assume that the relationship between price and supply is linear and that the relationship between price and demand is linear.

(A) Find a price–supply equation of the form $p = mx + b$.

(B) Find a price–demand equation of the form $p = mx + b$.

(C) Find the equilibrium point.

Exercises 1.2

A *Problems 1–4 refer to graphs (A)–(D).*

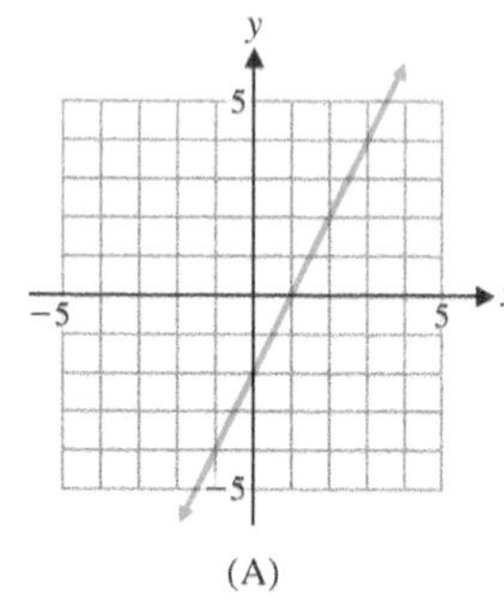
(A)

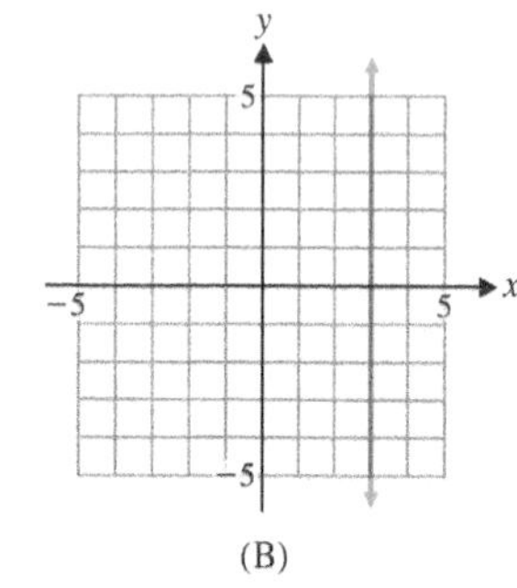
(B)

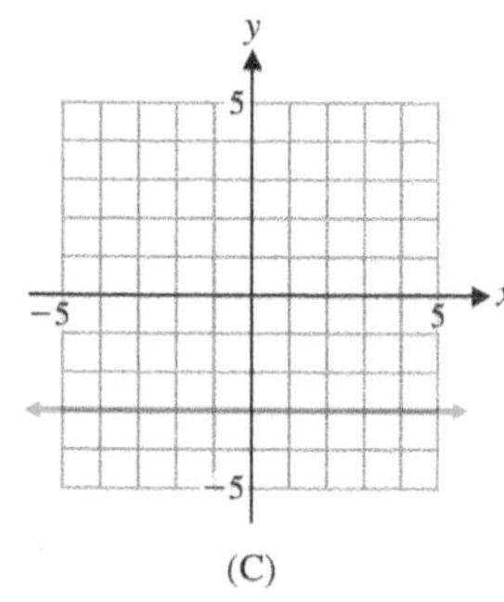
(C)

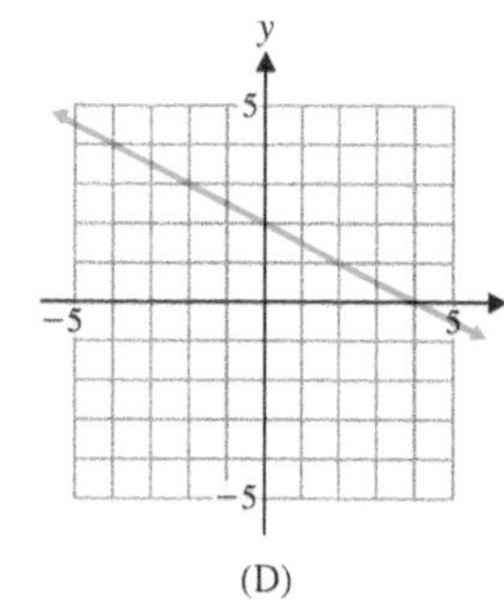
(D)

1. Identify the graph(s) of lines with a negative slope.

2. Identify the graph(s) of lines with a positive slope.

3. Identify the graph(s) of any lines with slope zero.

4. Identify the graph(s) of any lines with undefined slope.

In Problems 5–8, sketch a graph of each equation in a rectangular coordinate system.

5. $y = 2x - 3$

6. $y = \frac{x}{2} + 1$

7. $2x + 3y = 12$

8. $8x - 3y = 24$

In Problems 9–14, find the slope and y intercept of the graph of each equation.

9. $y = 5x - 7$

10. $y = 3x + 2$

11. $y = -\frac{5}{2}x - 9$

12. $y = -\frac{10}{3}x + 4$

13. $y = \frac{x}{4} + \frac{2}{3}$

14. $y = \frac{x}{5} - \frac{1}{2}$

In Problems 15–20, find the slope and x intercept of the graph of each equation.

15. $y = 2x + 10$

16. $y = -4x + 12$

17. $8x - y = 40$

18. $3x + y = 6$

19. $-6x + 7y = 42$

20. $9x + 2y = 4$

In Problems 21–24, write an equation of the line with the indicated slope and y intercept.

21. Slope = 2
y intercept = 1

22. Slope = 1
y intercept = 5

23. Slope = $-\frac{1}{3}$
y intercept = 6

24. Slope = $\frac{6}{7}$
y intercept = $-\frac{9}{2}$

B *In Problems 25–28, use the graph of each line to find the x intercept, y intercept, and slope. Write the slope-intercept form of the equation of the line.*

25.

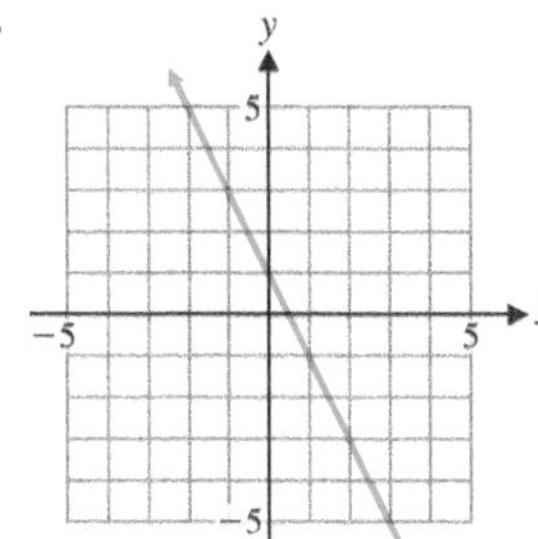

26.

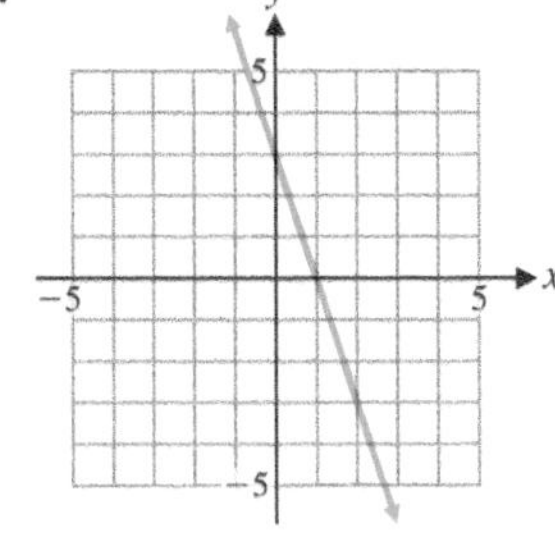

27.

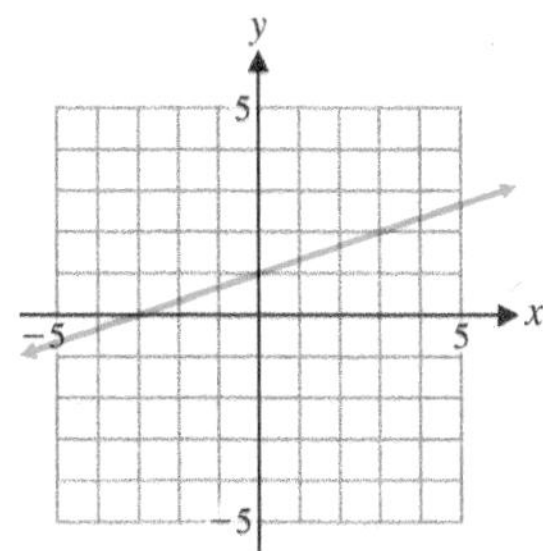

28.

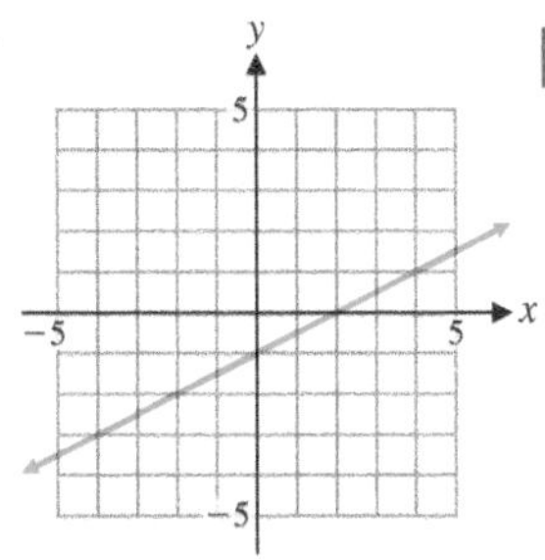

In Problems 29–34, sketch a graph of each equation or pair of equations in a rectangular coordinate system.

29. $y = -\frac{2}{3}x - 2$

30. $y = -\frac{3}{2}x + 1$

31. $3x - 2y = 10$

32. $5x - 6y = 15$

33. $x = 3; y = -2$

34. $x = -3; y = 2$

In Problems 35–40, find the slope of the graph of each equation.

35. $4x + y = 3$

36. $5x - y = -2$

37. $3x + 5y = 15$

38. $2x - 3y = 18$

39. $-4x + 2y = 9$

40. $-x + 8y = 4$

41. Given $Ax + By = 12$, graph each of the following three cases in the same coordinate system.

(A) $A = 2$ and $B = 0$

(B) $A = 0$ and $B = 3$

(C) $A = 3$ and $B = 4$

42. Given $Ax + By = 24$, graph each of the following three cases in the same coordinate system.

(A) $A = 6$ and $B = 0$

(B) $A = 0$ and $B = 8$

(C) $A = 2$ and $B = 3$

43. Graph $y = 25x + 200, x \geq 0$.

44. Graph $y = 40x + 160, x \geq 0$.

45. (A) Graph $y = 1.2x - 4.2$ in a rectangular coordinate system.

(B) Find the x and y intercepts algebraically to one decimal place.

(C) Graph $y = 1.2x - 4.2$ in a graphing calculator.

(D) Find the x and y intercepts to one decimal place using TRACE and the ZERO command.

46. (A) Graph $y = -0.8x + 5.2$ in a rectangular coordinate system.

(B) Find the x and y intercepts algebraically to one decimal place.

(C) Graph $y = -0.8x + 5.2$ in a graphing calculator.

(D) Find the x and y intercepts to one decimal place using TRACE and the ZERO command.

In Problems 47–50, write the equations of the vertical and horizontal lines through each point.

47. $(4, -3)$

48. $(-5, 6)$

49. $(-1.5, -3.5)$

50. $(2.6, 3.8)$

C *In Problems 51–58, write the slope-intercept form of the equation of the line with the indicated slope that goes through the given point.*

51. $m = 5; (3, 0)$

52. $m = 4; (0, 6)$

53. $m = -2; (-1, 9)$

54. $m = -10; (2, -5)$

55. $m = \frac{1}{3}; (-4, -8)$

56. $m = \frac{2}{7}; (7, 1)$

57. $m = -3.2; (5.8, 12.3)$

58. $m = 0.9; (2.3, 6.7)$

In Problems 59–66,

(A) *Find the slope of the line that passes through the given points.*

(B) *Find the standard form of the equation of the line.*

(C) *Find the slope-intercept form of the equation of the line.*

59. $(2, 5)$ and $(5, 7)$

60. $(1, 2)$ and $(3, 5)$

61. $(-2, -1)$ and $(2, -6)$

62. $(2, 3)$ and $(-3, 7)$

63. $(5, 3)$ and $(5, -3)$

64. $(1, 4)$ and $(0, 4)$

65. $(-2, 5)$ and $(3, 5)$

66. $(2, 0)$ and $(2, -3)$

67. Discuss the relationship among the graphs of the lines with equation $y = mx + 2$, where m is any real number.

68. Discuss the relationship among the graphs of the lines with equation $y = -0.5x + b$, where b is any real number.

Applications

69. **Cost analysis.** A donut shop has a fixed cost of \$124 per day and a variable cost of \$0.12 per donut. Find the total daily cost of producing x donuts. How many donuts can be produced for a total daily cost of \$250?

70. Cost analysis. A small company manufactures picnic tables. The weekly fixed cost is \$1,200 and the variable cost is \$45 per table. Find the total weekly cost of producing x picnic tables. How many picnic tables can be produced for a total weekly cost of \$4,800?

71. Cost analysis. A plant can manufacture 80 golf clubs per day for a total daily cost of \$7,647 and 100 golf clubs per day for a total daily cost of \$9,147.

(A) Assuming that daily cost and production are linearly related, find the total daily cost of producing x golf clubs.

(B) Graph the total daily cost for $0 \le x \le 200$.

(C) Interpret the slope and y intercept of this cost equation.

72. Cost analysis. A plant can manufacture 50 tennis rackets per day for a total daily cost of \$3,855 and 60 tennis rackets per day for a total daily cost of \$4,245.

(A) Assuming that daily cost and production are linearly related, find the total daily cost of producing x tennis rackets.

(B) Graph the total daily cost for $0 \le x \le 100$.

(C) Interpret the slope and y intercept of this cost equation.

73. Business—Markup policy. A drugstore sells a drug costing \$85 for \$112 and a drug costing \$175 for \$238.

(A) If the markup policy of the drugstore is assumed to be linear, write an equation that expresses retail price R in terms of cost C (wholesale price).

(B) What does a store pay (to the nearest dollar) for a drug that retails for \$185?

74. Business—Markup policy. A clothing store sells a shirt costing \$20 for \$33 and a jacket costing \$60 for \$93.

(A) If the markup policy of the store is assumed to be linear, write an equation that expresses retail price R in terms of cost C (wholesale price).

(B) What does a store pay for a suit that retails for \$240?

75. Business—Depreciation. A farmer buys a new tractor for \$157,000 and assumes that it will have a trade-in value of \$82,000 after 10 years. The farmer uses a constant rate of depreciation (commonly called **straight-line depreciation**—one of several methods permitted by the IRS) to determine the annual value of the tractor.

(A) Find a linear model for the depreciated value V of the tractor t years after it was purchased.

(B) What is the depreciated value of the tractor after 6 years?

(C) When will the depreciated value fall below \$70,000?

(D) Graph V for $0 \le t \le 20$ and illustrate the answers from parts (B) and (C) on the graph.

76. Business—Depreciation. A charter fishing company buys a new boat for \$224,000 and assumes that it will have a trade-in value of \$115,200 after 16 years.

(A) Find a linear model for the depreciated value V of the boat t years after it was purchased.

(B) What is the depreciated value of the boat after 10 years?

(C) When will the depreciated value fall below \$100,000?

(D) Graph V for $0 \le t \le 30$ and illustrate the answers from (B) and (C) on the graph.

77. Boiling point. The temperature at which water starts to boil is called its **boiling point** and is linearly related to the altitude. Water boils at 212°F at sea level and at 193.6°F at an altitude of 10,000 feet. (*Source:* biggreenegg.com)

(A) Find a relationship of the form $T = mx + b$ where T is degrees Fahrenheit and x is altitude in thousands of feet.

(B) Find the boiling point at an altitude of 3,500 feet.

(C) Find the altitude if the boiling point is 200°F.

(D) Graph T and illustrate the answers to (B) and (C) on the graph.

78. Boiling point. The temperature at which water starts to boil is also linearly related to barometric pressure. Water boils at 212°F at a pressure of 29.9 inHg (inches of mercury) and at 191°F at a pressure of 28.4 inHg. (*Source:* biggreenegg.com)

(A) Find a relationship of the form $T = mx + b$, where T is degrees Fahrenheit and x is pressure in inches of mercury.

(B) Find the boiling point at a pressure of 31 inHg.

(C) Find the pressure if the boiling point is 199°F.

(D) Graph T and illustrate the answers to (B) and (C) on the graph.

79. Flight conditions. In stable air, the air temperature drops about 3.6°F for each 1,000-foot rise in altitude. (*Source:* Federal Aviation Administration)

(A) If the temperature at sea level is 70°F, write a linear equation that expresses temperature T in terms of altitude A in thousands of feet.

(B) At what altitude is the temperature 34°F?

80. Flight navigation. The airspeed indicator on some aircraft is affected by the changes in atmospheric pressure at different altitudes. A pilot can estimate the true airspeed by observing the indicated airspeed and adding to it about 1.6% for every 1,000 feet of altitude. (*Source:* Megginson Technologies Ltd.)

(A) A pilot maintains a constant reading of 200 miles per hour on the airspeed indicator as the aircraft climbs from sea level to an altitude of 10,000 feet. Write a linear equation that expresses true airspeed T (in miles per hour) in terms of altitude A (in thousands of feet).

(B) What would be the true airspeed of the aircraft at 6,500 feet?

81. Demographics. The average number of persons per household in the United States has been shrinking steadily for as long as statistics have been kept and is approximately linear with respect to time. In 1980 there were about 2.76 persons per household, and in 2015 about 2.54. (*Source:* U.S. Census Bureau)

(A) If N represents the average number of persons per household and t represents the number of years since 1980, write a linear equation that expresses N in terms of t.

(B) Use this equation to estimate household size in the year 2030.

82. Demographics. The **median** household income divides the households into two groups: the half whose income is less than or equal to the median, and the half whose income is greater than the median. The median household income in the United States grew from about \$30,000 in 1990 to about \$55,775 in 2015. (*Source:* U.S. Census Bureau)

(A) If I represents the median household income and t represents the number of years since 1990, write a linear equation that expresses I in terms of t.

(B) Use this equation to estimate median household income in the year 2030.

83. Cigarette smoking. The percentage of female cigarette smokers in the United States declined from 21.0% in 2000 to 13.6% in 2015. (*Source:* Centers for Disease Control)

(A) Find a linear equation relating percentage of female smokers (f) to years since 2000 (t).

(B) Use this equation to predict the year in which the percentage of female smokers falls below 7%.

84. Cigarette smoking. The percentage of male cigarette smokers in the United States declined from 25.7% in 2000 to 16.7% in 2015. (*Source:* Centers for Disease Control)

(A) Find a linear equation relating percentage of male smokers (m) to years since 2000 (t).

(B) Use this equation to predict the year in which the percentage of male smokers falls below 7%.

85. Supply and demand. At a price of \$9.00 per bushel, the supply of soybeans is 3,600 million bushels and the demand is 4,000 million bushels. At a price of \$9.50 per bushel, the supply is 4,100 million bushels and the demand is 3,500 million bushels.

(A) Find a price–supply equation of the form $p = mx + b$.

(B) Find a price–demand equation of the form $p = mx + b$.

(C) Find the equilibrium point.

(D) Graph the price–supply equation, price–demand equation, and equilibrium point in the same coordinate system.

86. Supply and demand. At a price of \$3.20 per bushel, the supply of corn is 9,800 million bushels and the demand is 9,200 million bushels. At a price of \$2.95 per bushel, the supply is 9,300 million bushels and the demand is 9,700 million bushels.

(A) Find a price–supply equation of the form $p = mx + b$.

(B) Find a price–demand equation of the form $p = mx + b$.

(C) Find the equilibrium point.

(D) Graph the price–supply equation, price–demand equation, and equilibrium point in the same coordinate system.

87. Physics. Hooke's law states that the relationship between the stretch s of a spring and the weight w causing the stretch is linear. For a particular spring, a 5-pound weight causes a stretch of 2 inches, while with no weight, the stretch of the spring is 0.

(A) Find a linear equation that expresses s in terms of w.

(B) What is the stretch for a weight of 20 pounds?

(C) What weight will cause a stretch of 3.6 inches?

88. Physics. The distance d between a fixed spring and the floor is a linear function of the weight w attached to the bottom of the spring. The bottom of the spring is 18 inches from the floor when the weight is 3 pounds, and 10 inches from the floor when the weight is 5 pounds.

(A) Find a linear equation that expresses d in terms of w.

(B) Find the distance from the bottom of the spring to the floor if no weight is attached.

(C) Find the smallest weight that will make the bottom of the spring touch the floor. (Ignore the height of the weight.)

Answers to Matched Problems

1.

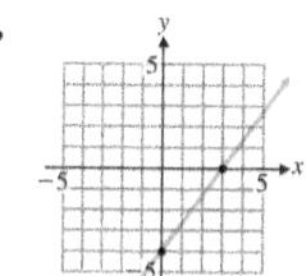

2. y intercept $= -4$, x intercept $= 3$

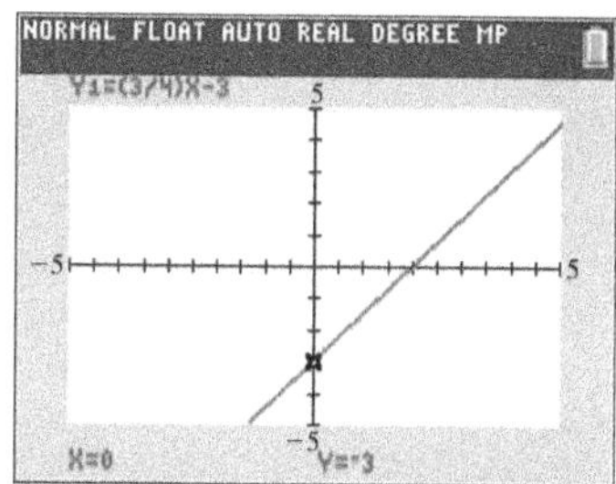

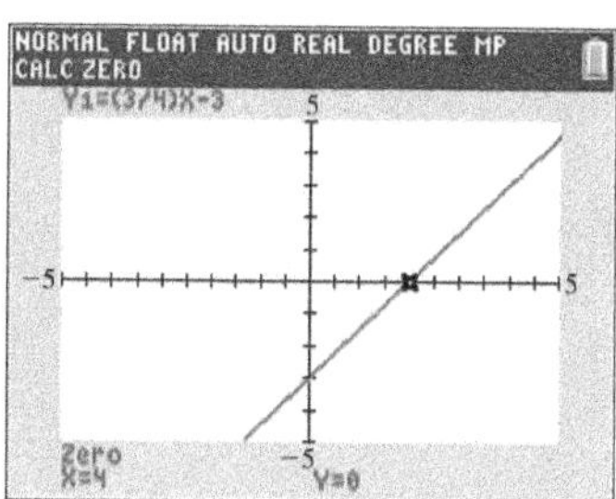

3. (A)

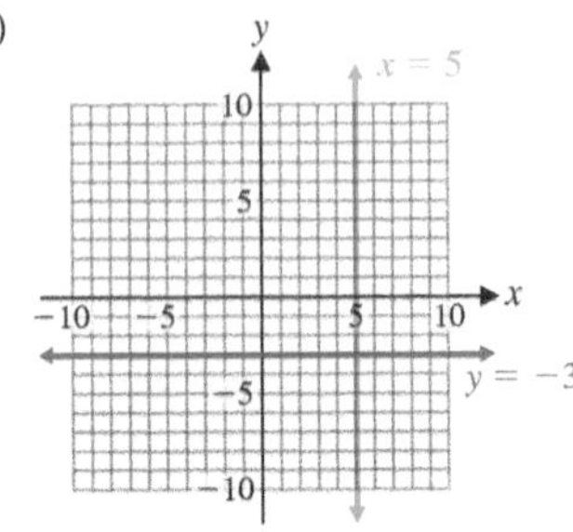

(B) Horizontal line: $y = 2$; vertical line: $x = -8$

4. (A) 0 (B) -4
(C) Not defined (D) 1

5. $y = \frac{1}{2}x - 1$

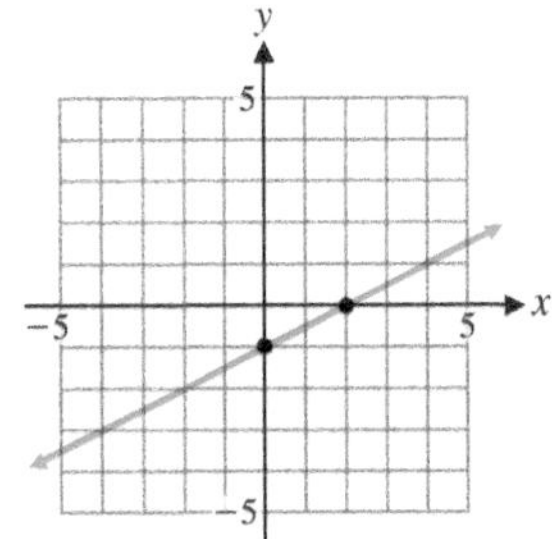

6. (A) $2x - 3y = 18$ (B) $y = 3x - 9$

7. (A) $m = 40$ (B) $C = 40x + 250$

8. (A) $p = 0.006x + 9.02$ (B) $p = -0.01x + 19.09$
(C) $(629, 12.80)$

1.3 Linear Regression

- Slope as a Rate of Change
- Linear Regression

Mathematical modeling is the process of using mathematics to solve real-world problems. This process can be broken down into three steps (Fig. 1):

Step 1 *Construct* the **mathematical model** (that is, a mathematics problem that, when solved, will provide information about the real-world problem).

Step 2 *Solve* the mathematical model.

Step 3 *Interpret* the solution to the mathematical model in terms of the original real-world problem.

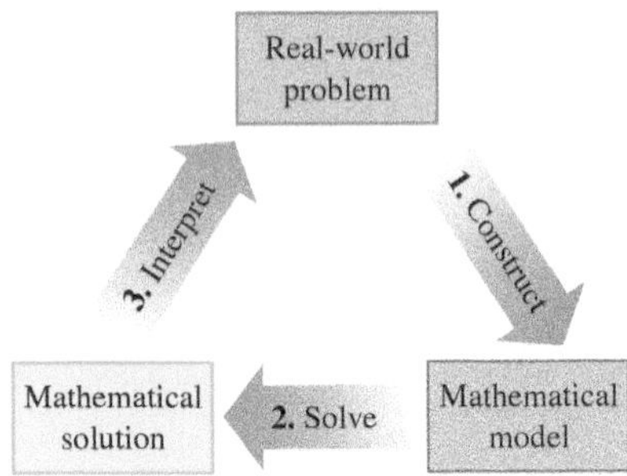

Figure 1

In more complex problems, this cycle may have to be repeated several times to obtain the required information about the real-world problem. In this section, we will discuss one of the simplest mathematical models, a linear equation. With the aid of a graphing calculator or computer, we also will learn how to analyze a linear model based on real-world data.

Slope as a Rate of Change

If x and y are related by the equation $y = mx + b$, where m and b are constants with $m \neq 0$, then x and y are **linearly related**. If (x_1, y_1) and (x_2, y_2) are two distinct points on this line, then the slope of the line is

$$m = \frac{y_2 - y_1}{x_2 - x_1} = \frac{\text{Change in } y}{\text{Change in } x} \tag{1}$$

In applications, ratio (1) is called the **rate of change** of y with respect to x. Since the slope of a line is unique, **the rate of change of two linearly related variables is constant**. Here are some examples of familiar rates of change: miles per hour, revolutions per minute, price per pound, passengers per plane, and so on. If the relationship between x and y is not linear, ratio (1) is called the **average rate of change** of y with respect to x.

EXAMPLE 1 **Estimating Body Surface Area** Appropriate doses of medicine for both animals and humans are often based on body surface area (BSA). Since weight is much easier to determine than BSA, veterinarians use the weight of an animal to estimate BSA. The following linear equation expresses BSA for canines in terms of weight:

$$a = 16.12w + 375.6$$

where a is BSA in square inches and w is weight in pounds. (*Source:* Veterinary Oncology Consultants, PTY LTD)

(A) Interpret the slope of the BSA equation.

(B) What is the effect of a one-pound increase in weight?

SOLUTION

(A) The rate-of-change of BSA with respect to weight is 16.12 square inches per pound.

(B) Since slope is the ratio of rise to run, increasing w by 1 pound (run) increases a by 16.12 square inches (rise).

Matched Problem 1 The equation $a = 28.55w + 118.7$ expresses BSA for felines in terms of weight, where a is BSA in square inches and w is weight in pounds.

(A) Interpret the slope of the BSA equation.

(B) What is the effect of a one-pound increase in weight?

Explore and Discuss 1

As illustrated in Example 1A, the slope m of a line with equation $y = mx + b$ has two interpretations:

1. m is the rate of change of y with respect to x.
2. Increasing x by one unit will change y by m units.

How are these two interpretations related?

Parachutes are used to deliver cargo to areas that cannot be reached by other means. The **rate of descent** of the cargo is the rate of change of altitude with respect to time. The absolute value of the rate of descent is called the **speed** of the cargo. At low altitudes, the altitude of the cargo and the time in the air are linearly related. The appropriate rate of descent varies widely with the item. Bulk food (rice, flour, beans, etc.) and clothing can tolerate nearly any rate of descent under 40 ft/sec. Machinery and electronics (pumps, generators, radios, etc.) should generally be dropped at 15 ft/sec or less. Butler Tactical Parachute Systems in Roanoke, Virginia, manufactures a variety of canopies for dropping cargo. The following example uses information taken from the company's brochures.

EXAMPLE 2 **Finding the Rate of Descent** A 100-pound cargo of delicate electronic equipment is dropped from an altitude of 2,880 feet and lands 200 seconds later. (*Source:* Butler Tactical Parachute Systems)

(A) Find a linear model relating altitude a (in feet) and time in the air t (in seconds).

(B) How fast is the cargo moving when it lands?

SOLUTION

(A) If $a = mt + b$ is the linear equation relating altitude a and time in air t, then the graph of this equation must pass through the following points:

$$(t_1, a_1) = (0, 2{,}880) \qquad \text{Cargo is dropped from plane.}$$

$$(t_2, a_2) = (200, 0) \qquad \text{Cargo lands.}$$

The slope of this line is

$$m = \frac{a_2 - a_1}{t_2 - t_1} = \frac{0 - 2{,}880}{200 - 0} = -14.4$$

and the equation of this line is

$$a - 0 = -14.4(t - 200)$$

$$a = -14.4t + 2{,}880$$

(B) The rate of descent is the slope $m = -14.4$, so the speed of the cargo at landing is $|-14.4| = 14.4$ ft/sec.

Matched Problem 2 A 400-pound load of grain is dropped from an altitude of 2,880 feet and lands 80 seconds later.

(A) Find a linear model relating altitude a (in feet) and time in the air t (in seconds).

(B) How fast is the cargo moving when it lands?

Linear Regression

In real-world applications, we often encounter numerical data in the form of a table. **Regression analysis** is a process for finding a function that provides a useful model for a set of data points. Graphs of equations are often called **curves**, and regression analysis is also referred to as **curve fitting**. In the next example, we use a linear model obtained by using **linear regression** on a graphing calculator.

EXAMPLE 3 **Diamond Prices** Prices for round-shaped diamonds taken from an online trader are given in Table 1.

(A) A linear model for the data in Table 1 is given by

$$p = 6{,}140c - 480 \tag{2}$$

where p is the price of a diamond weighing c carats. (We will discuss the source of models like this later in this section.) Plot the points in Table 1 on a Cartesian coordinate system, producing a *scatter plot*, and graph the model on the same axes.

(B) Interpret the slope of the model in (2).

(C) Use the model to estimate the cost of a 0.85-carat diamond and the cost of a 1.2-carat diamond. Round answers to the nearest dollar.

(D) Use the model to estimate the weight of a diamond (to two decimal places) that sells for $4,000.

Table 1 Round-Shaped Diamond Prices

Weight (carats)	Price
0.5	$2,790
0.6	$3,191
0.7	$3,694
0.8	$4,154
0.9	$5,018
1.0	$5,898

Source: www.tradeshop.com

SOLUTION

(A) A **scatter plot** is simply a graph of the points in Table 1 (Fig. 2A). To add the graph of the model to the scatter plot, we find any two points that satisfy equation (2) [we choose $(0.4, 1{,}976)$ and $(1.1, 6{,}274)$]. Plotting these points and drawing a line through them gives us Figure 2B.

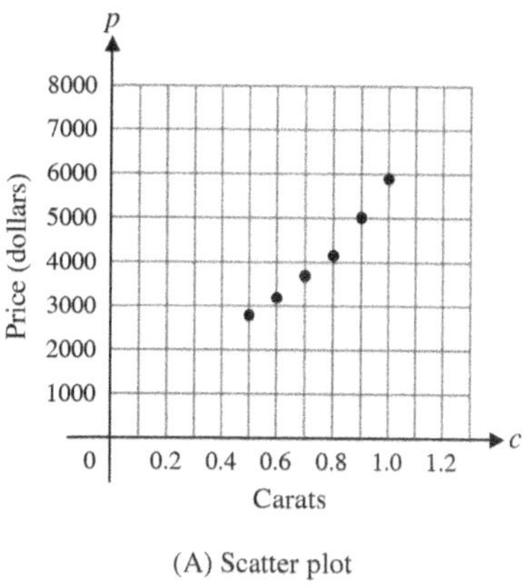

(A) Scatter plot

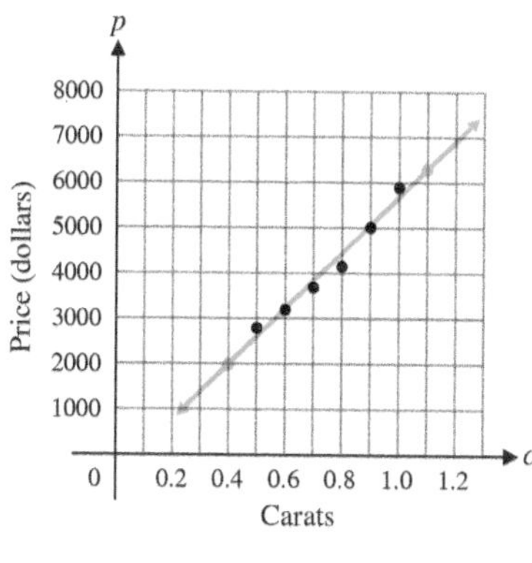

(B) Linear model

Figure 2

(B) The rate of change of the price of a diamond with respect to its weight is 6,140. Increasing the weight by one carat will increase the price by about $6,140.

(C) The graph of the model (Fig. 2B) does not pass through any of the points in the scatter plot, but it comes close to all of them. [Verify this by evaluating equation (2) at $c = 0.5, 0.6, \ldots, 1$.] So we can use equation (2) to approximate points not in Table 1.

$$c = 0.85 \qquad\qquad c = 1.2$$

$$p \approx 6{,}140(0.85) - 480 \qquad p \approx 6{,}140(1.2) - 480$$

$$= \$4{,}739 \qquad\qquad = \$6{,}888$$

A 0.85-carat diamond will cost about $4,739, and a 1.2-carat diamond will cost about $6,888.

(D) To find the weight of a $4,000 diamond, we solve the following equation for c:

$$6{,}140c - 480 = 4{,}000 \qquad \text{Add 480 to both sides.}$$

$$6{,}140c = 4{,}480 \qquad \text{Divide both sides by 6,140.}$$

$$c = \frac{4{,}480}{6{,}140} \approx 0.73 \qquad \text{Rounded to two decimal places.}$$

A $4,000 diamond will weigh about 0.73 carat.

Table 2 Emerald-Shaped Diamond Prices

Weight (carats)	Price
0.5	$1,677
0.6	$2,353
0.7	$2,718
0.8	$3,218
0.9	$3,982
1.0	$4,510

Source: www.tradeshop.com

Matched Problem 3 Prices for emerald-shaped diamonds from an online trader are given in Table 2. Repeat Example 3 for this data with the linear model

$$p = 5{,}600c - 1{,}100$$

where p is the price of an emerald-shaped diamond weighing c carats.

The model we used in Example 3 was obtained using a technique called **linear regression**, and the model is called the **regression line**. This technique produces a line that is the **best fit** for a given data set. (The line of best fit is the line that minimizes the sum of the squares of the vertical distances from the data points to the line.) Although you can find a linear regression line by hand, we prefer to leave the calculations to a graphing calculator or a computer. Don't be concerned if you don't have either of these electronic devices. We will supply the regression model in most of the applications we discuss, as we did in Example 3.

Explore and Discuss 2

As stated previously, we used linear regression to produce the model in Example 3. If you have a graphing calculator that supports linear regression, then you can find this model. The linear regression process varies greatly from one calculator to another. Consult the user's manual for the details of linear regression. The screens in Figure 3 are related to the construction of the model in Example 3 on a Texas Instruments TI-84 Plus CE.

(A) Produce similar screens on your graphing calculator.

(B) Do the same for Matched Problem 3.

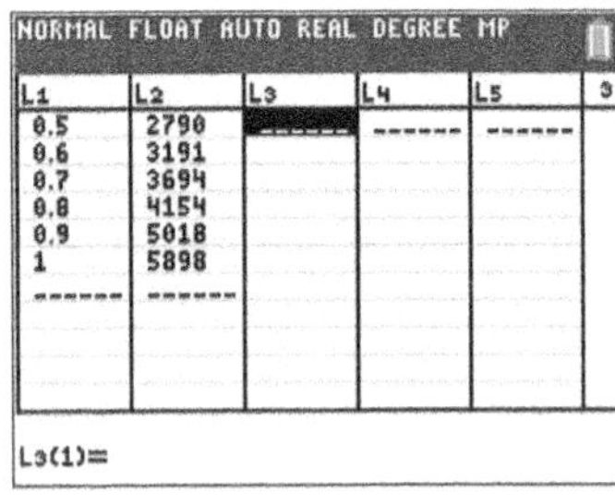

(A) Entering the data

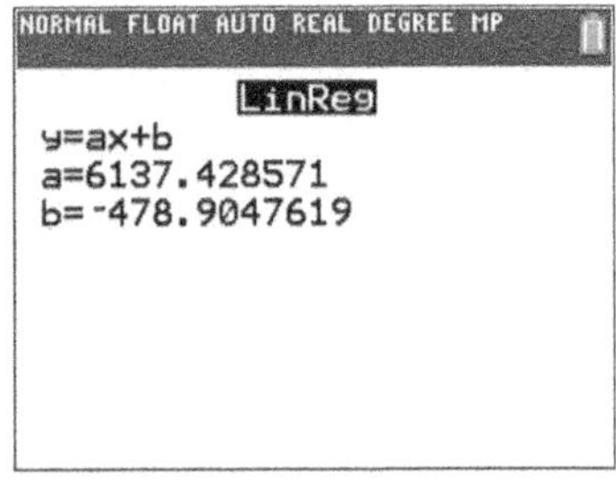

(B) Finding the model

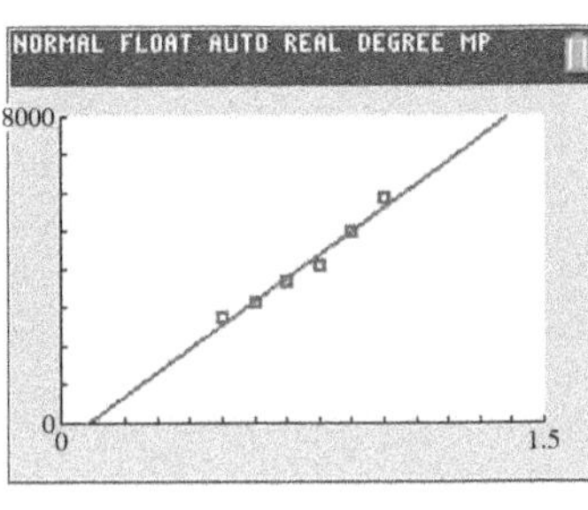

(C) Graphing the data and the model

Figure 3 Linear regression on a graphing calculator

In Example 3, we used the regression model to approximate points that were not given in Table 1 but would fit between points in the table. This process is called **interpolation**. In the next example, we use a regression model to approximate points outside the given data set. This process is called **extrapolation**, and the approximations are often referred to as **predictions**.

EXAMPLE 4 **Atmospheric Concentration of Carbon Dioxide** Table 3 contains information about the concentration of carbon dioxide (CO_2) in the atmosphere. The linear regression model for the data is

$$C = 360 + 2.04t$$

where C is the concentration (in parts per million) of carbon dioxide and t is the time in years with $t = 0$ corresponding to the year 1995.

(A) Interpret the slope of the regression line as a rate of change.

(B) Use the regression model to predict the concentration of CO_2 in the atmosphere in 2025.

Table 3 Atmospheric Concentration of CO_2 (parts per million)

1995	2000	2005	2010	2015
361	370	380	390	402

Source: National Oceanic and Atmospheric Administration

SOLUTION

(A) The slope $m = 2.04$ is the rate of change of concentration of CO_2 with respect to time. Since the slope is positive, the concentration of CO_2 is increasing at a rate of 2.04 parts per million per year.

(B) If $t = 30$, then

$$C = 360 + 2.04(30) \approx 421$$

So the model predicts that the atmospheric concentration of CO_2 will be approximately 421 parts per million in 2025.

Matched Problem 4 Using the model of Example 4, estimate the concentration of carbon dioxide in the atmosphere in the year 1990.

Forest managers estimate growth, volume, yield, and forest potential. One common measure is the diameter of a tree at breast height (Dbh), which is defined as the diameter of the tree at a point 4.5 feet above the ground on the uphill side of the tree. Example 5 uses Dbh to estimate the height of balsam fir trees.

EXAMPLE 5 **Forestry** A linear regression model for the height of balsam fir trees is

$$h = 3.8d + 18.73$$

where d is Dbh in inches and h is the height in feet.

(A) Interpret the slope of this model.

(B) What is the effect of a 1-inch increase in Dbh?

(C) Estimate the height of a balsam fir with a Dbh of 8 inches. Round your answer to the nearest foot.

(D) Estimate the Dbh of a balsam fir that is 30 feet tall. Round your answer to the nearest inch.

SOLUTION

(A) The rate of change of height with respect to breast height diameter is 3.8 feet per inch.

(B) Height increases by 3.8 feet.

(C) We must find h when $d = 8$:

$$h = 3.8d + 18.73 \qquad \text{Substitute } d = 8.$$

$$h = 3.8(8) + 18.73 \qquad \text{Evaluate.}$$

$$h = 49.13 \approx 49 \text{ ft}$$

(D) We must find d when $h = 30$:

$$h = 3.8d + 18.73 \qquad \text{Substitute } h = 30.$$

$$30 = 3.8d + 18.73 \qquad \text{Subtract 18.73 from both sides.}$$

$$11.27 = 3.8d \qquad \text{Divide both sides by 3.8.}$$

$$d = \frac{11.27}{3.8} \approx 3 \text{ in.}$$

The data used to produce the regression model in Example 5 are from the Jack Haggerty Forest at Lakehead University in Canada (Table 4). We used the popular

Table 4 **Height and Diameter of the Balsam Fir**

Dbh (in.)	Height (ft)	Dbh (in.)	Height (ft)	Dbh (in.)	Height (ft)	Dbh (in.)	Height (ft)
6.5	51.8	6.4	44.0	3.1	19.7	4.6	26.6
8.6	50.9	4.4	46.9	7.1	55.8	4.8	33.1
5.7	49.2	6.5	52.2	6.3	32.8	3.1	28.5
4.9	46.3	4.1	46.9	2.4	26.2	3.2	29.2
6.4	44.3	8.8	51.2	2.5	29.5	5.0	34.1
4.1	46.9	5.0	36.7	6.9	45.9	3.0	28.2
1.7	13.1	4.9	34.1	2.4	32.8	4.8	33.8
1.8	19.0	3.8	32.2	4.3	39.4	4.4	35.4
3.2	20.0	5.5	49.2	7.3	36.7	11.3	55.4
5.1	46.6	6.3	39.4	10.9	51.5	3.7	32.2

Source: Jack Haggerty Forest, Lakehead University, Canada

spreadsheet Excel to produce a scatter plot of the data in Table 4 and to find the regression model (Fig. 4).

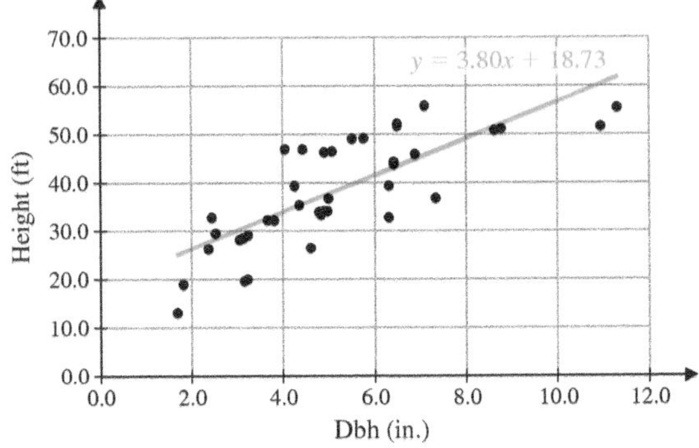

Figure 4 Linear regression with a spreadsheet

Matched Problem 5 Figure 5 shows the scatter plot for white spruce trees in the Jack Haggerty Forest at Lakehead University in Canada. A regression model produced by a spreadsheet (Fig. 5), after rounding, is

$$h = 1.8d + 34$$

where d is Dbh in inches and h is the height in feet.

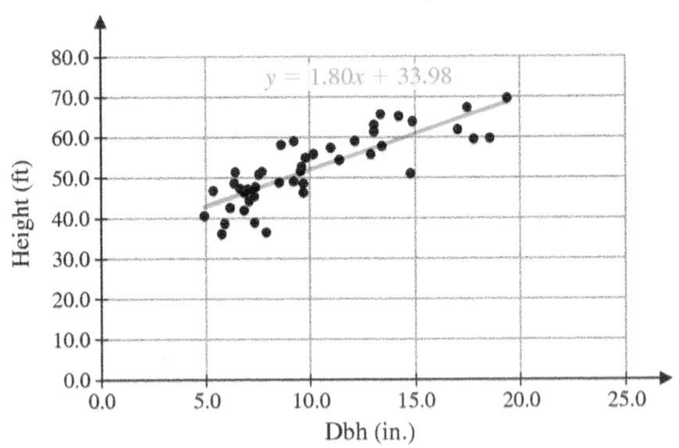

Figure 5 Linear regression for white spruce trees

(A) Interpret the slope of this model.

(B) What is the effect of a 1-inch increase in Dbh?

(C) Estimate the height of a white spruce with a Dbh of 10 inches. Round your answer to the nearest foot.

(D) Estimate the Dbh of a white spruce that is 65 feet tall. Round your answer to the nearest inch.

Exercises 1.3

Applications

1. **Ideal weight.** Dr. J. D. Robinson published the following estimate of the ideal body weight of a woman:

$$49 \text{ kg} + 1.7 \text{ kg for each inch over 5 ft}$$

(A) Find a linear model for Robinson's estimate of the ideal weight of a woman using w for ideal body weight (in kilograms) and h for height over 5 ft (in inches).

(B) Interpret the slope of the model.

(C) If a woman is 5′4″ tall, what does the model predict her weight to be?

(D) If a woman weighs 60 kg, what does the model predict her height to be?

2. **Ideal weight.** Dr. J. D. Robinson also published the following estimate of the ideal body weight of a man:

$$52 \text{ kg} + 1.9 \text{ kg for each inch over 5 ft}$$

(A) Find a linear model for Robinson's estimate of the ideal weight of a man using w for ideal body weight (in kilograms) and h for height over 5 ft (in inches).

(B) Interpret the slope of the model.

(C) If a man is 5′8″ tall, what does the model predict his weight to be?

(D) If a man weighs 70 kg, what does the model predict his height to be?

3. **Underwater pressure.** At sea level, the weight of the atmosphere exerts a pressure of 14.7 pounds per square inch, commonly referred to as 1 **atmosphere of pressure**. As an object descends in water, pressure P and depth d are linearly related. In salt water, the pressure at a depth of 33 ft is 2 atms, or 29.4 pounds per square inch.

(A) Find a linear model that relates pressure P (in pounds per square inch) to depth d (in feet).

(B) Interpret the slope of the model.

(C) Find the pressure at a depth of 50 ft.

(D) Find the depth at which the pressure is 4 atms.

4. **Underwater pressure.** Refer to Problem 3. In fresh water, the pressure at a depth of 34 ft is 2 atms, or 29.4 pounds per square inch.

(A) Find a linear model that relates pressure P (in pounds per square inch) to depth d (in feet).

(B) Interpret the slope of the model.

(C) Find the pressure at a depth of 50 ft.

(D) Find the depth at which the pressure is 4 atms.

5. **Rate of descent—Parachutes.** At low altitudes, the altitude of a parachutist and time in the air are linearly related. A jump at 2,880 ft using the U.S. Army's T-10 parachute system lasts 120 secs.

(A) Find a linear model relating altitude a (in feet) and time in the air t (in seconds).

(B) Find the rate of descent for a T-10 system.

(C) Find the speed of the parachutist at landing.

6. **Rate of descent—Parachutes.** The U.S Army is considering a new parachute, the Advanced Tactical Parachute System (ATPS). A jump at 2,880 ft using the ATPS system lasts 180 secs.

(A) Find a linear model relating altitude a (in feet) and time in the air t (in seconds).

(B) Find the rate of descent for an ATPS system parachute.

(C) Find the speed of the parachutist at landing.

7. **Speed of sound.** The speed of sound through air is linearly related to the temperature of the air. If sound travels at 331 m/sec at 0°C and at 343 m/sec at 20°C, construct a linear model relating the speed of sound (s) and the air temperature (t). Interpret the slope of this model. (*Source:* Engineering Toolbox)

8. **Speed of sound.** The speed of sound through sea water is linearly related to the temperature of the water. If sound travels at 1,403 m/sec at 0°C and at 1,481 m/sec at 20°C, construct a linear model relating the speed of sound (s) and the air temperature (t). Interpret the slope of this model. (*Source:* Engineering Toolbox)

9. **Energy production.** Table 5 lists U.S. fossil fuel production as a percentage of total energy production for selected years. A linear regression model for this data is

$$y = -0.19x + 83.75$$

where x represents years since 1985 and y represents the corresponding percentage of total energy production.

Table 5 U.S. Fossil Fuel Production

Year	Production (%)
1985	85
1990	83
1995	81
2000	80
2005	79
2010	78
2015	80

Source: Energy Information Administration

(A) Draw a scatter plot of the data and a graph of the model on the same axes.

(B) Interpret the slope of the model.

(C) Use the model to predict fossil fuel production in 2025.

(D) Use the model to estimate the first year for which fossil fuel production is less than 70% of total energy production.

10. **Energy consumption.** Table 6 lists U.S. fossil fuel consumption as a percentage of total energy consumption for selected years. A linear regression model for this data is

$$y = -0.14x + 86.18$$

where x represents years since 1985 and y represents the corresponding percentage of fossil fuel consumption.

Table 6 U.S. Fossil Fuel Consumption

Year	Consumption (%)
1985	86
1990	85
1995	85
2000	84
2005	85
2010	83
2015	81

Source: Energy Information Administration

(A) Draw a scatter plot of the data and a graph of the model on the same axes.

(B) Interpret the slope of the model.

(C) Use the model to predict fossil fuel consumption in 2025.

(D) Use the model to estimate the first year for which fossil fuel consumption is less than 80% of total energy consumption.

11. **Cigarette smoking.** The data in Table 7 shows that the percentage of female cigarette smokers in the United States declined from 22.1% in 1997 to 13.6% in 2015.

Table 7 **Percentage of Smoking Prevalence among U.S. Adults**

Year	Males (%)	Females (%)
1997	27.6	22.1
2000	25.7	21.0
2003	24.1	19.2
2006	23.9	18.0
2010	21.5	17.3
2015	16.7	13.6

Source: Centers for Disease Control

(A) Applying linear regression to the data for females in Table 7 produces the model

$$f = -0.45t + 22.20$$

where f is percentage of female smokers and t is time in years since 1997. Draw a scatter plot of the female smoker data and a graph of the regression model on the same axes.

(B) Estimate the first year in which the percentage of female smokers is less than 10%.

12. **Cigarette smoking.** The data in Table 7 shows that the percentage of male cigarette smokers in the United States declined from 27.6% in 1997 to 16.7% in 2015.

(A) Applying linear regression to the data for males in Table 7 produces the model

$$m = -0.56t + 27.82$$

where m is percentage of male smokers and t is time in years since 1997. Draw a scatter plot of the male smoker data and a graph of the regression model.

(B) Estimate the first year in which the percentage of male smokers is less than 10%.

13. **Licensed drivers.** Table 8 contains the state population and the number of licensed drivers in the state (both in millions) for the states with population under 1 million in 2014. The regression model for this data is

$$y = 0.75x$$

where x is the state population (in millions) and y is the number of licensed drivers (in millions) in the state.

(A) Draw a scatter plot of the data and a graph of the model on the same axes.

Table 8 **Licensed Drivers in 2014**

State	Population	Licensed Drivers
Alaska	0.74	0.53
Delaware	0.94	0.73
Montana	1.00	0.77
North Dakota	0.74	0.53
South Dakota	0.85	0.61
Vermont	0.63	0.55
Wyoming	0.58	0.42

Source: Bureau of Transportation Statistics

(B) If the population of Hawaii in 2014 was about 1.4 million, use the model to estimate the number of licensed drivers in Hawaii in 2014 to the nearest thousand.

(C) If the number of licensed drivers in Maine in 2014 was about 1,019,000, use the model to estimate the population of Maine in 2014 to the nearest thousand.

14. **Licensed drivers.** Table 9 contains the state population and the number of licensed drivers in the state (both in millions) for the most populous states in 2014. The regression model for this data is

$$y = 0.62x + 0.29$$

where x is the state population (in millions) and y is the number of licensed drivers (in millions) in the state.

Table 9 **Licensed Drivers in 2014**

State	Population	Licensed Drivers
California	39	25
Florida	20	14
Illinois	13	8
New York	20	11
Ohio	12	8
Pennsylvania	13	9
Texas	27	16

Source: Bureau of Transportation Statistics

(A) Draw a scatter plot of the data and a graph of the model on the same axes.

(B) If the population of Michigan in 2014 was about 9.9 million, use the model to estimate the number of licensed drivers in Michigan in 2014 to the nearest thousand.

(C) If the number of licensed drivers in Georgia in 2014 was about 6.7 million, use the model to estimate the population of Georgia in 2014 to the nearest thousand.

15. **Net sales.** A linear regression model for the net sales data in Table 10 is

$$S = 15.85t + 250.1$$

where S is net sales and t is time since 2000 in years.

Table 10 **Walmart Stores, Inc.**

Billions of U.S. Dollars	2008	2009	2010	2011	2012	2015
Net sales	374	401	405	419	444	488
Operating income	21.9	22.8	24.0	25.5	26.6	27.3

Source: Walmart Stores, Inc.

(A) Draw a scatter plot of the data and a graph of the model on the same axes.

(B) Predict Walmart's net sales for 2026.

16. Operating income. A linear regression model for the operating income data in Table 10 is

$$I = 0.82t + 15.84$$

where I is operating income and t is time since 2000 in years.

(A) Draw a scatter plot of the data and a graph of the model on the same axes.

(B) Predict Walmart's annual operating income for 2026.

17. Freezing temperature. Ethylene glycol and propylene glycol are liquids used in antifreeze and deicing solutions. Ethylene glycol is listed as a hazardous chemical by the Environmental Protection Agency, while propylene glycol is generally regarded as safe. Table 11 lists the freezing temperature for various concentrations (as a percentage of total weight) of each chemical in a solution used to deice airplanes. A linear regression model for the ethylene glycol data in Table 11 is

$$E = -0.55T + 31$$

where E is the percentage of ethylene glycol in the deicing solution and T is the temperature at which the solution freezes.

Table 11 **Freezing Temperatures**

Freezing Temperature (°F)	Ethylene Glycol (% Wt.)	Propylene Glycol (% Wt.)
−50	56	58
−40	53	55
−30	49	52
−20	45	48
−10	40	43
0	33	36
10	25	29
20	16	19

Source: T. Labuza, University of Minnesota

(A) Draw a scatter plot of the data and a graph of the model on the same axes.

(B) Use the model to estimate the freezing temperature to the nearest degree of a solution that is 30% ethylene glycol.

(C) Use the model to estimate the percentage of ethylene glycol in a solution that freezes at 15°F.

18. Freezing temperature. A linear regression model for the propylene glycol data in Table 11 is

$$P = -0.54T + 34$$

where P is the percentage of propylene glycol in the deicing solution and T is the temperature at which the solution freezes.

(A) Draw a scatter plot of the data and a graph of the model on the same axes.

(B) Use the model to estimate the freezing temperature to the nearest degree of a solution that is 30% propylene glycol.

(C) Use the model to estimate the percentage of propylene glycol in a solution that freezes at 15°F.

19. Forestry. The figure contains a scatter plot of 100 data points for black spruce trees and the linear regression model for this data.

(A) Interpret the slope of the model.

(B) What is the effect of a 1-in. increase in Dbh?

(C) Estimate the height of a black spruce with a Dbh of 15 in. Round your answer to the nearest foot.

(D) Estimate the Dbh of a black spruce that is 25 ft tall. Round your answer to the nearest inch.

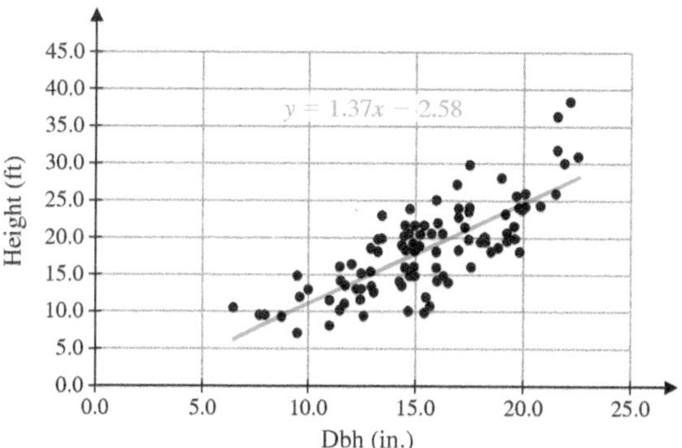

black spruce
Source: Lakehead University

20. Forestry. The figure contains a scatter plot of 100 data points for black walnut trees and the linear regression model for this data.

(A) Interpret the slope of the model.

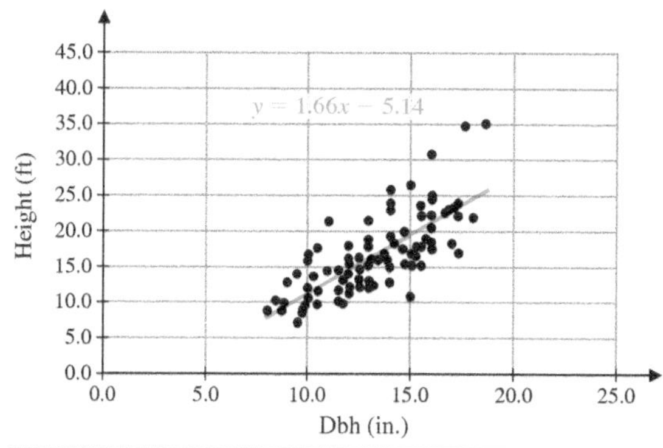

black walnut
Source: Kagen Research

(B) What is the effect of a 1-in. increase in Dbh?

(C) Estimate the height of a black walnut with a Dbh of 12 in. Round your answer to the nearest foot.

(D) Estimate the Dbh of a black walnut that is 25 ft tall. Round your answer to the nearest inch.

21. Undergraduate enrollment. Table 12 lists fall undergraduate enrollment by gender in U.S. degree-granting institutions. The figure contains a scatter plot and regression line for each data set, where x represents years since 1980 and y represents enrollment (in millions).

(A) Interpret the slope of each model.

(B) Use the regression models to predict the male and female undergraduate enrollments in 2025.

(C) Use the regression models to estimate the first year in which female undergraduate enrollment will exceed male undergraduate enrollment by at least 3 million.

Table 12 Fall Undergraduate Enrollment (in millions)

Year	Male	Female
1980	5.00	5.47
1990	5.38	6.58
2000	5.78	7.38
2010	7.84	10.25
2014	7.59	9.71

Source: National Center for Education Statistics

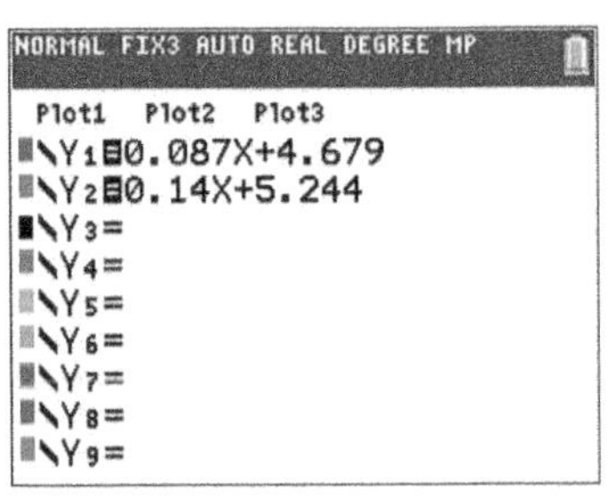

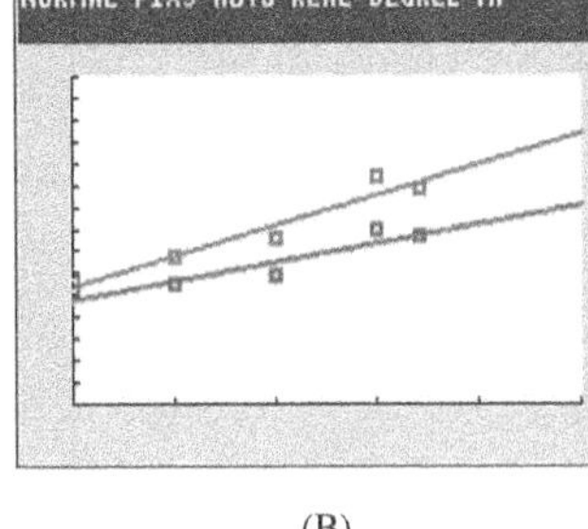

(A) (B)

Figure for 21

22. Graduate enrollment. Table 13 lists fall graduate enrollment by gender in U.S. degree-granting institutions. The figure contains a scatter plot and regression line for each data set, where x represents years since 1980 and y represents enrollment (in millions).

(A) Interpret the slope of each model.

(B) Use the regression models to predict the male and female graduate enrollments in 2025.

(C) Use the regression models to estimate the first year in which female graduate enrollment will exceed male graduate enrollment by at least 1 million.

Table 13 Fall Graduate Enrollment (in millions)

Year	Male	Female
1980	0.87	0.75
1990	0.90	0.96
2000	0.94	1.21
2010	1.21	1.73
2014	1.21	1.70

Source: National Center for Education Statistics

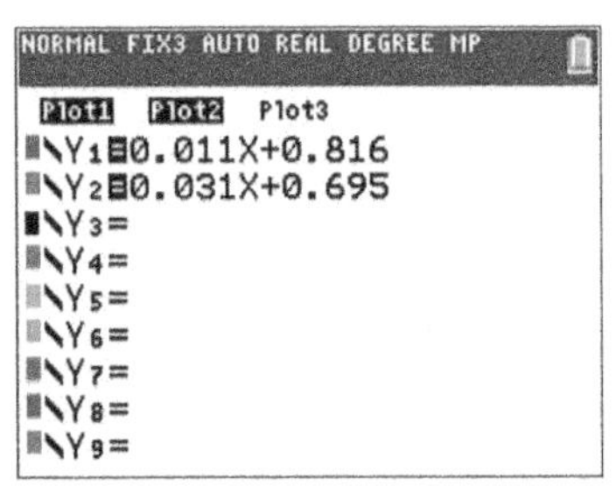

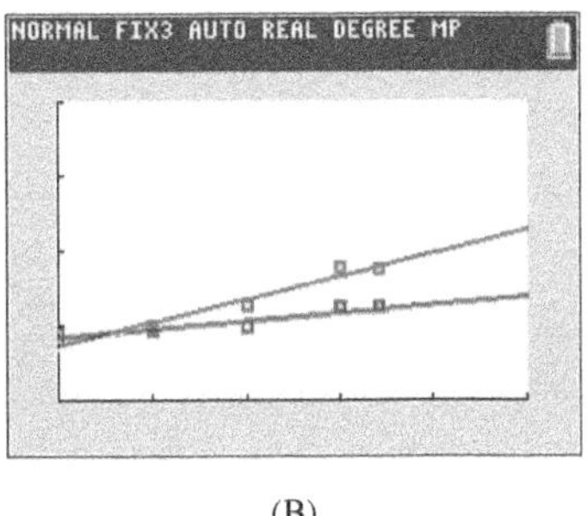

(A) (B)

Figure for 22

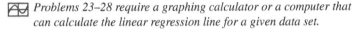

Problems 23–28 require a graphing calculator or a computer that can calculate the linear regression line for a given data set.

23. Climate. Find a linear regression model for the data on average annual temperature in Table 14, where x is years since 1960 and y is temperature (in °F). (Round regression coefficients to three decimal places). Use the model to estimate the average annual temperature in the contiguous United States in 2025.

Table 14 Climate Data for the Contiguous United States

Year	Average Annual Temperature (°F)	Average Annual Precipitation (in)
1965	51.69	29.80
1975	51.50	33.03
1985	51.30	29.97
1995	52.65	32.69
2005	53.64	30.08
2015	54.40	34.59

Source: National Oceanic and Atmospheric Administration

24. Climate. Find a linear regression model for the data on average annual precipitation in Table 14, where x is years since 1960 and y is precipitation (in inches). (Round regression coefficients to three decimal places). Use the model to estimate the average annual precipitation in the contiguous United States in 2025.

25. Olympic Games. Find a linear regression model for the men's 100-meter freestyle data given in Table 15, where x is years since 1990 and y is winning time (in seconds). Do the same for the women's 100-meter freestyle data. (Round regression coefficients to three decimal places.) Do these models indicate that the women will eventually catch up with the men?

Table 15 Winning Times in Olympic Swimming Events

	100-Meter Freestyle		200-Meter Backstroke	
	Men	Women	Men	Women
1992	49.02	54.65	1:58.47	2:07.06
1996	48.74	54.50	1.58.54	2:07.83
2000	48.30	53.83	1:56.76	2:08.16
2004	48.17	53.84	1:54.76	2:09.16
2008	47.21	53.12	1:53.94	2:05.24
2012	47.52	53.00	1:53.41	2:04.06
2016	47.58	52.70	1:53:62	2:05.99

Source: www.infoplease.com

26. **Olympic Games.** Find a linear regression model for the men's 200-meter backstroke data given in Table 15, where x is years since 1990 and y is winning time (in seconds). Do the same for the women's 200-meter backstroke data. (Round regression coefficients to three decimal places.) Do these models indicate that the women will eventually catch up with the men?

27. **Supply and demand.** Table 16 contains price–supply data and price–demand data for corn. Find a linear regression model for the price–supply data where x is supply (in billions of bushels) and y is price (in dollars). Do the same for the price–demand data. (Round regression coefficients to two decimal places.) Find the equilibrium price for corn.

Table 16 Supply and Demand for U.S. Corn

Price ($/bu)	Supply (billion bu)	Price ($/bu)	Demand (billion bu)
2.15	6.29	2.07	9.78
2.29	7.27	2.15	9.35
2.36	7.53	2.22	8.47
2.48	7.93	2.34	8.12
2.47	8.12	2.39	7.76
2.55	8.24	2.47	6.98

Source: www.usda.gov/nass/pubs/histdata.htm

28. **Supply and demand.** Table 17 contains price–supply data and price–demand data for soybeans. Find a linear regression model for the price–supply data where x is supply (in billions of bushels) and y is price (in dollars). Do the same for the price–demand data. (Round regression coefficients to two decimal places.) Find the equilibrium price for soybeans.

Table 17 Supply and Demand for U.S. Soybeans

Price ($/bu)	Supply (billion bu)	Price ($/bu)	Demand (billion bu)
5.15	1.55	4.93	2.60
5.79	1.86	5.48	2.40
5.88	1.94	5.71	2.18
6.07	2.08	6.07	2.05
6.15	2.15	6.40	1.95
6.25	2.27	6.66	1.85

Source: www.usda.gov/nass/pubs/histdata.htm

Answers to Matched Problems

1. (A) The rate of change of BSA with respect to weight is 28.55 square inches per pound.

(B) Increasing w by 1 pound increases a by 28.55 square inches.

2. (A) $a = -36t + 2{,}880$

(B) 36 ft/sec

3. (A)

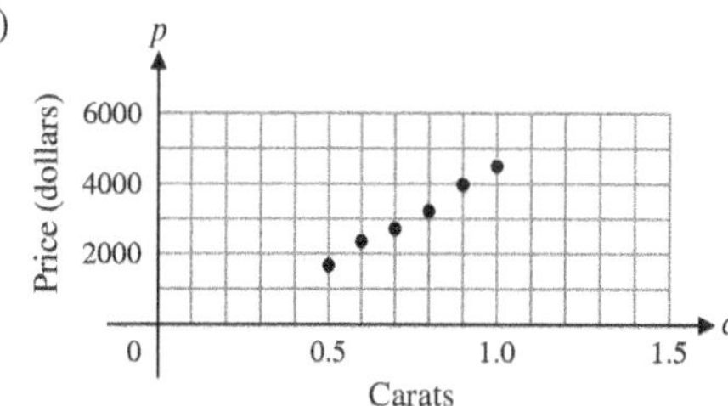

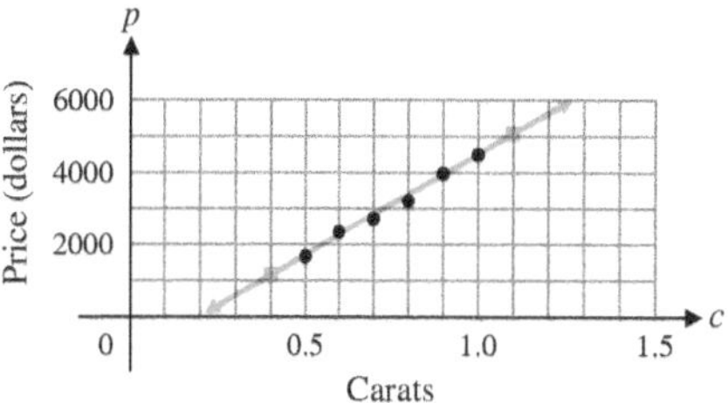

(B) The rate of change of the price of a diamond with respect to its weight is $5,600. Increasing the weight by one carat will increase the price by about $5,600.

(C) $3,660; $5,620

(D) 0.91 carat

4. Approximately 350 parts per million.

5. (A) The slope is 1.8, so the rate of change of height with respect to breast height diameter is 1.8 feet per inch.

(B) Height increases by 1.8 feet.

(C) 52 ft

(D) 17 in.

2 Functions and Graphs

Introduction

Many marine species are dependent on light from the sun. They will be found near the surface of the ocean, because light intensity decreases dramatically with depth. We use the function concept, one of the most important ideas in mathematics, to express the precise relationship between light intensity and ocean depth (see Problems 63 and 64 in Section 2.5).

The study of mathematics beyond the elementary level requires a firm understanding of a basic list of elementary functions (see *A Library of Elementary Functions* at the back of the book). In Chapter 2, we introduce the elementary functions and study their properties, graphs, and many applications.

2.1 Functions

- Equations in Two Variables
- Definition of a Function
- Functions Specified by Equations
- Function Notation
- Applications

We introduce the general notion of a *function* as a correspondence between two sets. Then we restrict attention to functions for which the two sets are both sets of real numbers. The most useful are those functions that are specified by equations in two variables. We discuss the terminology and notation associated with functions, graphs of functions, and applications.

Equations in Two Variables

The graph of an equation of the form $Ax + By = C$, where A and B are not both zero, is a line. Because a line is determined by any two of its points, such an equation is easy to graph: Just plot *any* two points in its solution set and sketch the unique line through them (Fig. 1).

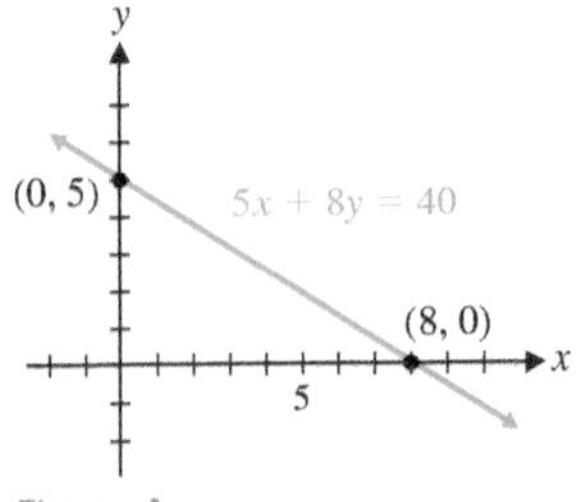

Figure 1

More complicated equations in two variables, such as $y = 9 - x^2$ or $x^2 = y^4$, are more difficult to graph. To **sketch the graph** of an equation, we plot enough points from its solution set in a rectangular coordinate system so that the total graph is apparent, and then we connect these points with a smooth curve. This process is called **point-by-point plotting**.

EXAMPLE 1 **Point-by-Point Plotting** Sketch the graph of each equation.

(A) $y = 9 - x^2$ (B) $x^2 = y^4$

SOLUTION

(A) Make up a table of solutions—that is, ordered pairs of real numbers that satisfy the given equation. For easy mental calculation, choose integer values for x.

x	−4	−3	−2	−1	0	1	2	3	4
y	−7	0	5	8	9	8	5	0	−7

After plotting these solutions, if there are any portions of the graph that are unclear, plot additional points until the shape of the graph is apparent. Then join all the plotted points with a smooth curve (Fig. 2). Arrowheads are used to indicate that the graph continues beyond the portion shown here with no significant changes in shape.

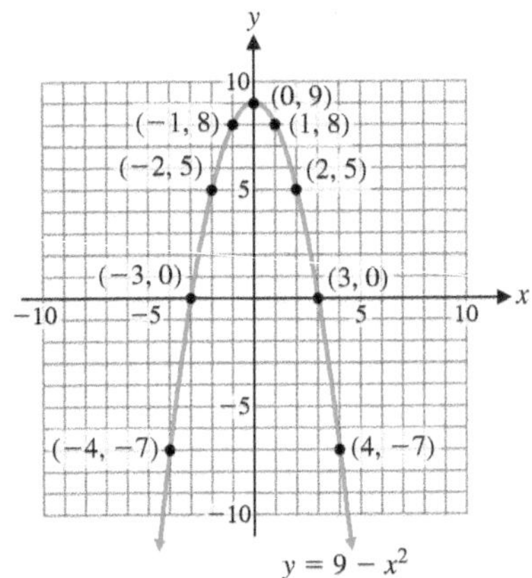

Figure 2 $y = 9 - x^2$

(B) Again we make a table of solutions—here it may be easier to choose integer values for y and calculate values for x. Note, for example, that if $y = 2$, then $x = \pm 4$; that is, the ordered pairs $(4, 2)$ and $(-4, 2)$ are both in the solution set.

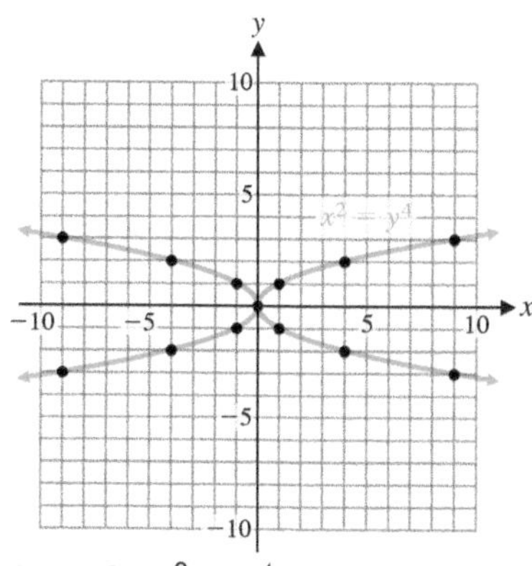

Figure 3 $x^2 = y^4$

x	± 9	± 4	± 1	0	± 1	± 4	± 9
y	-3	-2	-1	0	1	2	3

We plot these points and join them with a smooth curve (Fig. 3).

Matched Problem 1 Sketch the graph of each equation.

(A) $y = x^2 - 4$

(B) $y^2 = \dfrac{100}{x^2 + 1}$

Explore and Discuss 1

To graph the equation $y = -x^3 + 3x$, we use point-by-point plotting to obtain the graph in Figure 4.

x	y
-1	-2
0	0
1	2

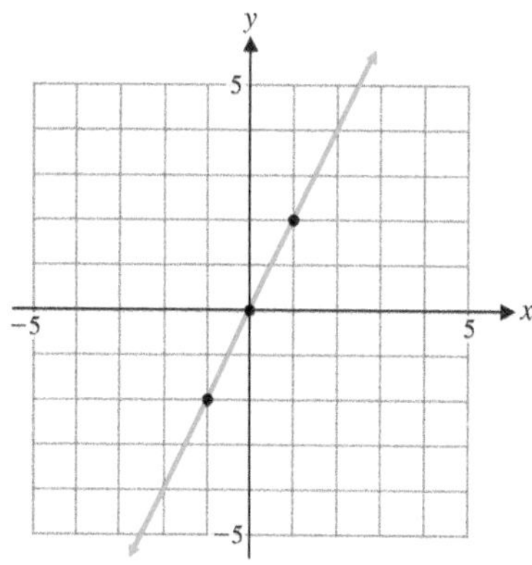

Figure 4

(A) Do you think this is the correct graph of the equation? Why or why not?

(B) Add points on the graph for $x = -2, -1.5, -0.5, 0.5, 1.5$, and 2.

(C) Now, what do you think the graph looks like? Sketch your version of the graph, adding more points as necessary.

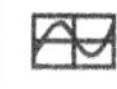

(D) Graph this equation on a graphing calculator and compare it with your graph from part (C).

The icon in the margin is used throughout this book to identify optional graphing calculator activities that are intended to give you additional insight into the concepts under discussion. You may have to consult the manual for your graphing calculator for the details necessary to carry out these activities. For example, to graph the equation in Explore and Discuss 1 on most graphing calculators, you must enter the equation (Fig. 5A) and the window variables (Fig. 5B).

As Explore and Discuss 1 illustrates, the shape of a graph may not be apparent from your first choice of points. Using point-by-point plotting, it may be difficult to find points in the solution set of the equation, and it may be difficult to determine when you have found enough points to understand the shape of the graph. We will supplement the technique of point-by-point plotting with a detailed analysis of several basic equations, giving you the ability to sketch graphs with accuracy and confidence.

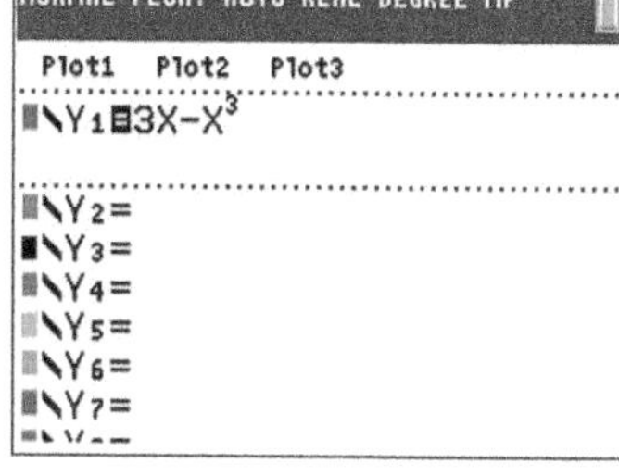

(A)

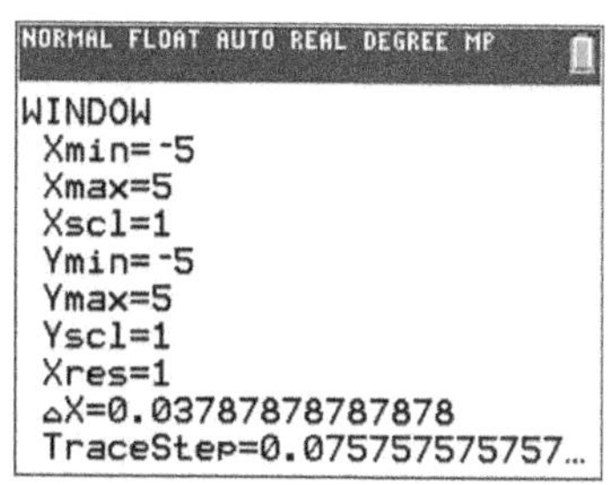

(B)

Figure 5

Definition of a Function

Central to the concept of function is correspondence. You are familiar with correspondences in daily life. For example,

To each person, there corresponds an annual income.
To each item in a supermarket, there corresponds a price.
To each student, there corresponds a grade-point average.
To each day, there corresponds a maximum temperature.
For the manufacture of x items, there corresponds a cost.
For the sale of x items, there corresponds a revenue.
To each square, there corresponds an area.
To each number, there corresponds its cube.

One of the most important aspects of any science is the establishment of correspondences among various types of phenomena. Once a correspondence is known, predictions can be made. A cost analyst would like to predict costs for various levels of output in a manufacturing process, a medical researcher would like to know the correspondence between heart disease and obesity, a psychologist would like to predict the level of performance after a subject has repeated a task a given number of times, and so on.

What do all of these examples have in common? Each describes the matching of elements from one set with the elements in a second set.

Consider Tables 1–3. Tables 1 and 2 specify functions, but Table 3 does not. Why not? The definition of the term *function* will explain.

Table 1

Domain	Range
Number	*Cube*
−2 →	−8
−1 →	−1
0 →	0
1 →	1
2 →	8

Table 2

Domain	Range
Number	*Square*
−2 →	4
−1 →	1
0 →	0
1 →	1
2 →	4

Table 3

Domain	Range
Number	*Square root*
0 →	0
1 →	1, −1
4 →	2, −2
9 →	3, −3

DEFINITION Function

A **function** is a correspondence between two sets of elements such that to each element in the first set, there corresponds one and only one element in the second set.

The first set is called the **domain**, and the set of corresponding elements in the second set is called the **range**.

Tables 1 and 2 specify functions since to each domain value, there corresponds exactly one range value (for example, the cube of -2 is -8 and no other number). On the other hand, Table 3 does not specify a function since to at least one domain value, there corresponds more than one range value (for example, to the domain value 9, there corresponds -3 and 3, both square roots of 9).

Explore and Discuss 2

Consider the set of students enrolled in a college and the set of faculty members at that college. Suppose we define a correspondence between the two sets by saying that a student corresponds to a faculty member if the student is currently enrolled in a course taught by that faculty member. Is this correspondence a function? Discuss.

Functions Specified by Equations

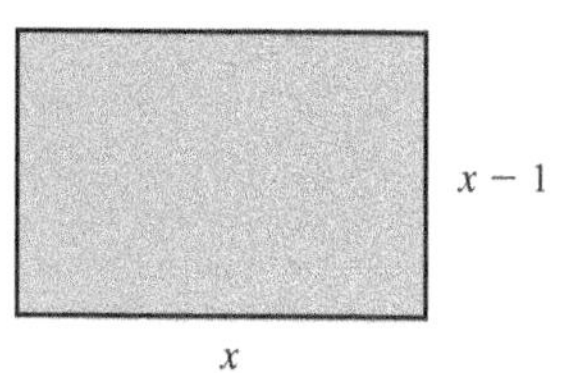

Figure 6

Most of the functions in this book will have domains and ranges that are (infinite) sets of real numbers. The **graph** of such a function is the set of all points (x, y) in the Cartesian plane such that x is an element of the domain and y is the corresponding element in the range. The correspondence between domain and range elements is often specified by an equation in two variables. Consider, for example, the equation for the area of a rectangle with width 1 inch less than its length (Fig. 6). If x is the length, then the area y is given by

$$y = x(x - 1) \qquad x \geq 1$$

For each **input** x (length), we obtain an **output** y (area). For example,

If $x = 5$, then $y = 5(5 - 1) = 5 \cdot 4 = 20$.

If $x = 1$, then $y = 1(1 - 1) = 1 \cdot 0 = 0$.

If $x = \sqrt{5}$, then $y = \sqrt{5}(\sqrt{5} - 1) = 5 - \sqrt{5}$
≈ 2.7639.

The input values are domain values, and the output values are range values. The equation assigns each domain value x a range value y. The variable x is called an *independent variable* (since values can be "independently" assigned to x from the domain), and y is called a *dependent variable* (since the value of y "depends" on the value assigned to x). In general, any variable used as a placeholder for domain values is called an **independent variable**; any variable that is used as a placeholder for range values is called a **dependent variable**.

When does an equation specify a function?

DEFINITION Functions Specified by Equations

If in an equation in two variables, we get exactly one output (value for the dependent variable) for each input (value for the independent variable), then the equation specifies a function. The graph of such a function is just the graph of the specifying equation.

If we get more than one output for a given input, the equation does not specify a function.

EXAMPLE 2 **Functions and Equations** Determine which of the following equations specify functions with independent variable x.

(A) $4y - 3x = 8$, x a real number (B) $y^2 - x^2 = 9$, x a real number

SOLUTION

(A) Solving for the dependent variable y, we have

$$4y - 3x = 8$$
$$4y = 8 + 3x \qquad (1)$$
$$y = 2 + \frac{3}{4}x$$

Since each input value x corresponds to exactly one output value $\left(y = 2 + \frac{3}{4}x\right)$, we see that equation (1) specifies a function.

(B) Solving for the dependent variable y, we have

$$y^2 - x^2 = 9$$
$$y^2 = 9 + x^2 \qquad (2)$$
$$y = \pm\sqrt{9 + x^2}$$

Since $9 + x^2$ is always a positive real number for any real number x, and since each positive real number has two square roots, then to each input value x there corresponds two output values ($y = -\sqrt{9 + x^2}$ and $y = \sqrt{9 + x^2}$). For example, if $x = 4$, then equation (2) is satisfied for $y = 5$ and for $y = -5$. So equation (2) does not specify a function.

Reminder

Each positive real number u has two square roots: $\sqrt{u}$, the principal square root, and $-\sqrt{u}$, the negative of the principal square root (see Appendix A, Section A.6).

Matched Problem 2 Determine which of the following equations specify functions with independent variable x.

(A) $y^2 - x^4 = 9$, x a real number (B) $3y - 2x = 3$, x a real number

Since the graph of an equation is the graph of all the ordered pairs that satisfy the equation, it is very easy to determine whether an equation specifies a function by examining its graph. The graphs of the two equations we considered in Example 2 are shown in Figure 7.

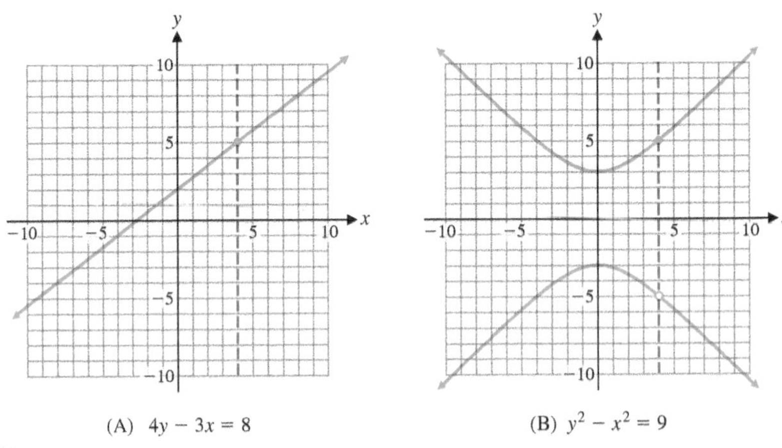

Figure 7

In Figure 7A, notice that any vertical line will intersect the graph of the equation $4y - 3x = 8$ in exactly one point. This shows that to each x value, there corresponds exactly one y value, confirming our conclusion that this equation specifies a function. On the other hand, Figure 7B shows that there exist vertical lines that intersect the graph of $y^2 - x^2 = 9$ in two points. This indicates that there exist x values to which there correspond two different y values and verifies our conclusion that this equation does not specify a function. These observations are generalized in Theorem 1.

THEOREM 1 Vertical-Line Test for a Function

An equation specifies a function if each vertical line in the coordinate system passes through, at most, one point on the graph of the equation.

If any vertical line passes through two or more points on the graph of an equation, then the equation does not specify a function.

The function graphed in Figure 7A is an example of a *linear function.* The vertical-line test implies that equations of the form $y = mx + b$, where $m \neq 0$, specify functions; they are called **linear functions**. Similarly, equations of the form $y = b$ specify functions; they are called **constant functions**, and their graphs are horizontal lines. The vertical-line test implies that equations of the form $x = a$ do not specify functions; note that the graph of $x = a$ is a vertical line.

In Example 2, the domains were explicitly stated along with the given equations. In many cases, this will not be done. Unless stated to the contrary, we shall adhere to the following convention regarding domains and ranges for functions specified by equations:

If a function is specified by an equation and the domain is not indicated, then we assume that the domain is the set of all real-number replacements of the independent variable (inputs) that produce real values for the dependent variable (outputs). The range is the set of all outputs corresponding to input values.

EXAMPLE 3 **Finding a Domain** Find the domain of the function specified by the equation $y = \sqrt{4 - x}$, assuming that x is the independent variable.

SOLUTION For y to be real, $4 - x$ must be greater than or equal to 0; that is,

$$4 - x \geq 0$$

$$-x \geq -4$$

$$x \leq 4 \qquad \text{Sense of inequality reverses when both sides are divided by } -1.$$

Domain: $x \leq 4$ (inequality notation) or $(-\infty, 4]$ (interval notation)

Matched Problem 3 Find the domain of the function specified by the equation $y = \sqrt{x - 2}$, assuming x is the independent variable.

Function Notation

We have seen that a function involves two sets, a domain and a range, and a correspondence that assigns to each element in the domain exactly one element in the range. Just as we use letters as names for numbers, now we will use letters as names for functions. For example, f and g may be used to name the functions specified by the equations $y = 2x + 1$ and $y = x^2 + 2x - 3$:

$$f\colon \quad y = 2x + 1$$

$$g\colon \quad y = x^2 + 2x - 3 \tag{3}$$

If x represents an element in the domain of a function f, then we frequently use the symbol

$$f(x)$$

in place of y to designate the number in the range of the function f to which x is paired (Fig. 8). This symbol does *not* represent the product of f and x. The symbol $f(x)$ is read as "f of x," "f at x," or "the value of f at x." Whenever we write $y = f(x)$, we assume that the variable x is an independent variable and that both y and $f(x)$ are dependent variables.

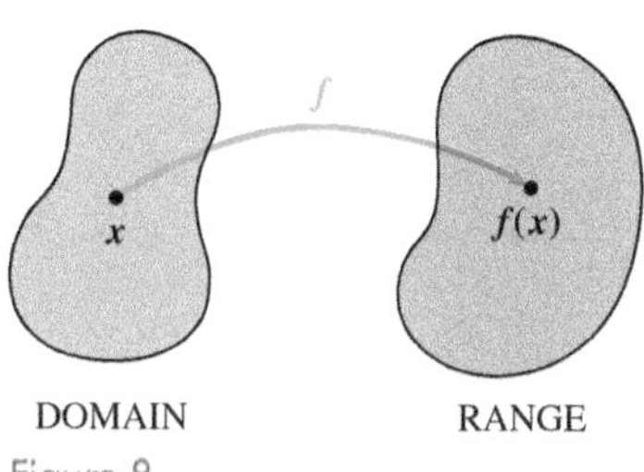

Figure 8

Using function notation, we can now write functions f and g in equation (3) as

$$f(x) = 2x + 1 \qquad \text{and} \qquad g(x) = x^2 + 2x - 3$$

Let us find $f(3)$ and $g(-5)$. To find $f(3)$, we replace x with 3 wherever x occurs in $f(x) = 2x + 1$ and evaluate the right side:

$$f(x) = 2x + 1$$
$$f(3) = 2 \cdot 3 + 1$$
$$= 6 + 1 = 7 \qquad \text{For input 3, the output is 7.}$$

Therefore,

$$f(3) = 7 \qquad \text{The function } f \text{ assigns the range value 7 to the domain value 3.}$$

To find $g(-5)$, we replace each x by -5 in $g(x) = x^2 + 2x - 3$ and evaluate the right side:

$$g(x) = x^2 + 2x - 3$$
$$g(-5) = (-5)^2 + 2(-5) - 3$$
$$= 25 - 10 - 3 = 12 \qquad \text{For input } -5\text{, the output is 12.}$$

Therefore,

$$g(-5) = 12 \qquad \text{The function } g \text{ assigns the range value 12 to the domain value } -5.$$

It is very important to understand and remember the definition of $f(x)$:

For any element x in the domain of the function f, the symbol $f(x)$ represents the element in the range of f corresponding to x in the domain of f. If x is an input value, then $f(x)$ is the corresponding output value. If x is an element that is not in the domain of f, then f *is not defined at* x and $f(x)$ *does not exist.*

EXAMPLE 4 **Function Evaluation** For $f(x) = 12/(x - 2)$, $g(x) = 1 - x^2$, and $h(x) = \sqrt{x - 1}$, evaluate:

(A) $f(6)$ (B) $g(-2)$ (C) $h(-2)$ (D) $f(0) + g(1) - h(10)$

SOLUTION

(A) $f(6) = \dfrac{12}{6 - 2} = \dfrac{12}{4} = 3$

(B) $g(-2) = 1 - (-2)^2 = 1 - 4 = -3$

(C) $h(-2) = \sqrt{-2 - 1} = \sqrt{-3}$

But $\sqrt{-3}$ is not a real number. Since we have agreed to restrict the domain of a function to values of x that produce real values for the function, -2 is not in the domain of h, and $h(-2)$ does not exist.

(D) $f(0) + g(1) - h(10) = \dfrac{12}{0 - 2} + (1 - 1^2) - \sqrt{10 - 1}$

$$= \frac{12}{-2} + 0 - \sqrt{9}$$
$$= -6 - 3 = -9$$

Reminder

Dashed boxes are used throughout the book to represent steps that are usually performed mentally.

Matched Problem 4 Use the functions in Example 4 to find

(A) $f(-2)$ (B) $g(-1)$ (C) $h(-8)$ (D) $\dfrac{f(3)}{h(5)}$

EXAMPLE 5 **Finding Domains** Find the domains of functions f, g, and h:

$$f(x) = \frac{12}{x - 2} \qquad g(x) = 1 - x^2 \qquad h(x) = \sqrt{x - 1}$$

SOLUTION *Domain of f:* $12/(x - 2)$ represents a real number for all replacements of x by real numbers except for $x = 2$ (division by 0 is not defined). Thus, $f(2)$ does not exist, and the domain of f is the set of all real numbers except 2. We often indicate this by writing

$$f(x) = \frac{12}{x - 2} \qquad x \neq 2$$

Domain of g: The domain is R, the set of all real numbers, since $1 - x^2$ represents a real number for all replacements of x by real numbers.

Domain of h: The domain is the set of all real numbers x such that $\sqrt{x - 1}$ is a real number; so

$$x - 1 \geq 0$$

$$x \geq 1 \quad \text{or, in interval notation,} \quad [1, \infty)$$

Matched Problem 5 Find the domains of functions F, G, and H:

$$F(x) = x^2 - 3x + 1 \qquad G(x) = \frac{5}{x + 3} \qquad H(x) = \sqrt{2 - x}$$

In addition to evaluating functions at specific numbers, it is important to be able to evaluate functions at expressions that involve one or more variables. For example, the **difference quotient**

$$\frac{f(x + h) - f(x)}{h} \qquad x \text{ and } x + h \text{ in the domain of } f,\ h \neq 0$$

is studied extensively in calculus.

CONCEPTUAL INSIGHT

In algebra, you learned to use parentheses for grouping variables. For example,

$$2(x + h) = 2x + 2h$$

Now we are using parentheses in the function symbol $f(x)$. For example, if $f(x) = x^2$, then

$$f(x + h) = (x + h)^2 = x^2 + 2xh + h^2$$

Note that $f(x) + f(h) = x^2 + h^2 \neq f(x + h)$. That is, the function name f does not distribute across the grouped variables $(x + h)$, as the "2" does in $2(x + h)$ (see Appendix A, Section A.2).

EXAMPLE 6 **Using Function Notation** For $f(x) = x^2 - 2x + 7$, find

(A) $f(a)$

(B) $f(a + h)$

(C) $f(a + h) - f(a)$

(D) $\dfrac{f(a + h) - f(a)}{h}, \quad h \neq 0$

SOLUTION

(A) $f(a) = a^2 - 2a + 7$

(B) $f(a + h) = (a + h)^2 - 2(a + h) + 7 = a^2 + 2ah + h^2 - 2a - 2h + 7$

(C) $f(a + h) - f(a) = (a^2 + 2ah + h^2 - 2a - 2h + 7) - (a^2 - 2a + 7)$

$= 2ah + h^2 - 2h$

(D) $\dfrac{f(a+h) - f(a)}{h} = \dfrac{2ah + h^2 - 2h}{h} = \dfrac{h(2a + h - 2)}{h}$ Because $h \neq 0$, $\dfrac{h}{h} = 1$.

$= 2a + h - 2$

Matched Problem 6 Repeat Example 6 for $f(x) = x^2 - 4x + 9$.

Applications

If we reduce the price of a product, will we generate more revenue? If we increase production, will our profits rise? **Profit–loss analysis** is a method for answering such questions in order to make sound business decisions.

Here are the basic concepts of profit–loss analysis: A manufacturing company has **costs**, C, which include **fixed costs** such as plant overhead, product design, setup, and promotion and **variable costs** that depend on the number of items produced. The **revenue**, R, is the amount of money received from the sale of its product. The company takes a **loss** if $R < C$, **breaks even** if $R = C$, and has a **profit** if $R > C$. The **profit** P is equal to revenue minus cost; that is, $P = R - C$. (So the company takes a loss if $P < 0$, breaks even if $P = 0$, and has a profit if $P > 0$.) To predict its revenue, a company uses a **price–demand** function, $p(x)$, determined using historical data or sampling techniques, that specifies the relationship between the demand x and the price p. A point (x, p) is on the graph of the price–demand function if x items can be sold at a price of $\$p$ per item. (Normally, a reduction in the price p will increase the demand x, so the graph of the price–demand function is expected to go downhill as you move from left to right.) The revenue R is equal to the number of items sold multiplied by the price per item; that is, $R = xp$.

Cost, revenue, and profit can be written as functions $C(x)$, $R(x)$, and $P(x)$ of the independent variable x, the number of items manufactured and sold. The functions $C(x)$, $R(x)$, $P(x)$, and $p(x)$ often have the following forms, where a, b, m, and n are positive constants determined from the context of a particular problem:

Cost function

$C(x) = a + bx$ $C =$ fixed costs + variable costs

Price–demand function

$p(x) = m - nx$ x is the number of items that can be sold at $\$p$ per item

Revenue function

$R(x) = xp$ $R =$ number of items sold × price per item

$= x(m - nx)$

Profit function

$P(x) = R(x) - C(x)$

$= x(m - nx) - (a + bx)$

CAUTION Do not confuse the price–demand function $p(x)$ with the profit function $P(x)$. Price is always denoted by the lowercase p. Profit is always denoted by the uppercase P. Note that the revenue and profit functions, $R(x)$ and $P(x)$, depend on the price–demand function $p(x)$, but $C(x)$ does not. ▲

Example 7 and Matched Problem 7 provide an introduction to profit–loss analysis.

EXAMPLE 7

Price–Demand and Revenue A manufacturer of a popular digital camera wholesales the camera to retail outlets throughout the United Kingdom. Using statistical methods, the financial department in the company produced the price–demand data in Table 4, where p is the wholesale price per camera at which x million cameras are sold. Notice that as the price goes down, the number sold goes up.

Table 4 **Price–Demand**

x (millions)	$p(\$)$
2	87
5	68
8	53
12	37

Using special analytical techniques (regression analysis), an analyst obtained the following price–demand function to model the Table 4 data:

$$p(x) = 94.8 - 5x \qquad 1 \le x \le 15 \tag{4}$$

Table 5 **Revenue**

x (millions)	$R(x)$ (million \$)
1	90
3	
6	
9	
12	
15	

(A) Plot the data in Table 4. Then sketch a graph of the price–demand function in the same coordinate system.

(B) What is the company's revenue function for this camera, and what is its domain?

(C) Complete Table 5, computing revenues to the nearest million dollars.

(D) Plot the data in Table 5. Then sketch a graph of the revenue function using these points.

(E) Graph the revenue function on a graphing calculator.

SOLUTION

(A) The four data points are plotted in Figure 9. Note that $p(1) = 89.8$ and $p(15) = 19.8$. So the graph of the price–demand function is the line through (1, 89.8) and (15, 19.8) (see Fig. 9).

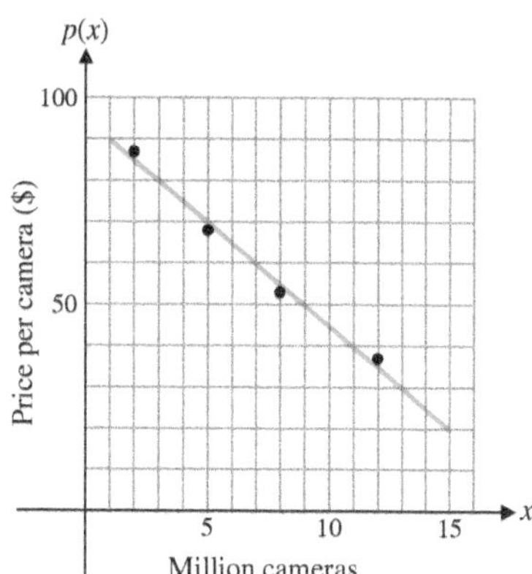

Figure 9 **Price–demand**

In Figure 9, notice that the model approximates the actual data in Table 4, and it is assumed that it gives realistic and useful results for all other values of x between 1 million and 15 million.

(B) $R(x) = xp(x) = x(94.8 - 5x)$ million dollars

Domain: $1 \le x \le 15$

[Same domain as the price–demand function, equation (4).]

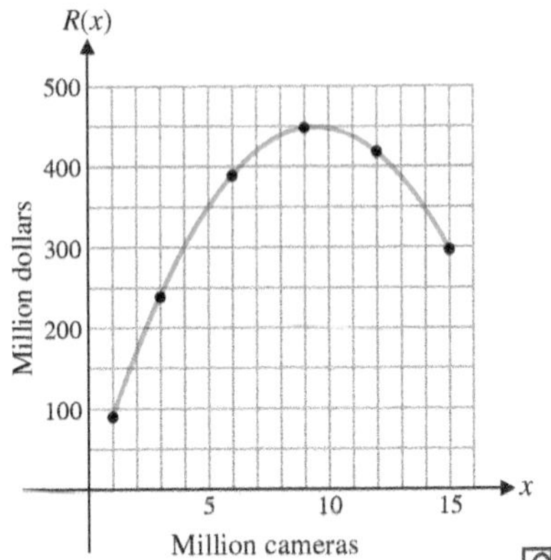

Figure 10

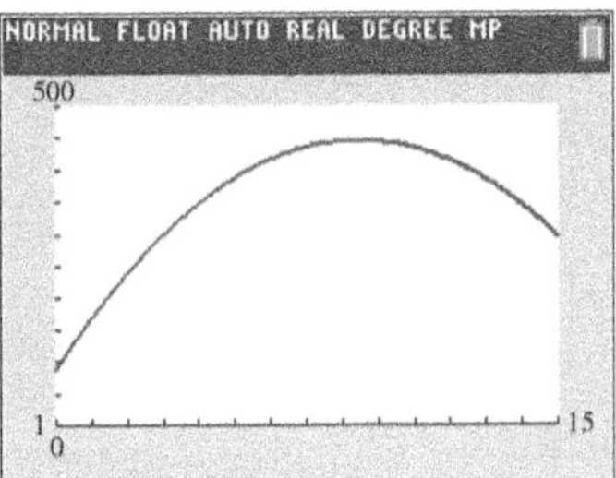

Figure 11

(C)

Table 5 **Revenue**

x (millions)	$R(x)$ (million $)
1	90
3	239
6	389
9	448
12	418
15	297

(D) The six points from Table 5 are plotted in Figure 10. The graph of the revenue function is the smooth curve drawn through those six points.

(E) Figure 11 shows the graph of $R(x) = x(94.8 - 5x)$ on a graphing calculator.

Matched Problem 7 The financial department in Example 7, using statistical techniques, produced the data in Table 6, where $C(x)$ is the cost in millions of dollars for manufacturing and selling x million cameras.

Table 6 **Cost Data**

x (millions)	$C(x)$ (million $)
1	175
5	260
8	305
12	395

Using special analytical techniques (regression analysis), an analyst produced the following cost function to model the Table 6 data:

$$C(x) = 156 + 19.7x \qquad 1 \le x \le 15 \tag{5}$$

(A) Plot the data in Table 6. Then sketch a graph of equation (5) in the same coordinate system.

(B) Using the revenue function from Example 7(B), what is the company's profit function for this camera, and what is its domain?

(C) Complete Table 7, computing profits to the nearest million dollars.

Table 7 **Profit**

x (millions)	$P(x)$ (million $)
1	−86
3	
6	
9	
12	
15	

(D) Plot the data in Table 7. Then sketch a graph of the profit function using these points.

(E) Graph the profit function on a graphing calculator.

Exercises 2.1

A *In Problems 1–8, use point-by-point plotting to sketch the graph of each equation.*

1. $y = x + 1$

2. $x = y + 1$

3. $x = y^2$

4. $y = x^2$

5. $y = x^3$

6. $x = y^3$

7. $xy = -6$

8. $xy = 12$

Indicate whether each table in Problems 9–14 specifies a function.

9.

Domain		Range
3	→	0
5	→	1
7	→	2

10.

Domain		Range
−1	→	5
−2	→	7
−3	→	9

11. **Domain** **Range**

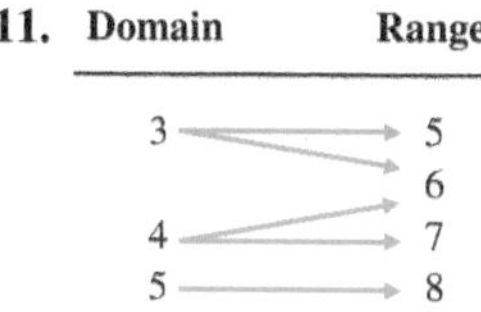

12.

Domain		Range
8	→	0
9	→	1
	↘	2
10	→	3

13. **Domain** **Range**

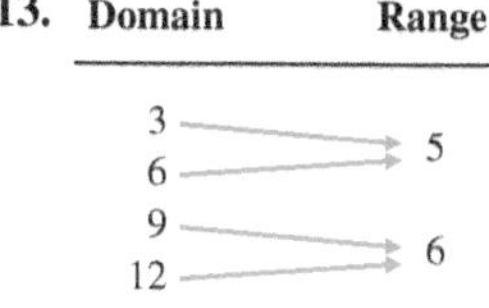

14. **Domain** **Range**

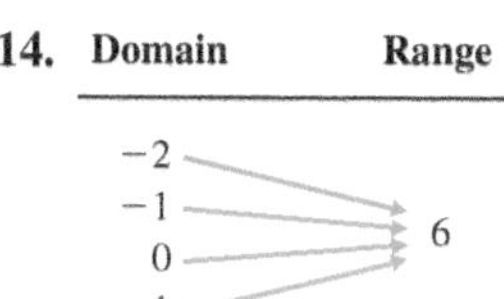

Indicate whether each graph in Problems 15–20 specifies a function.

15.

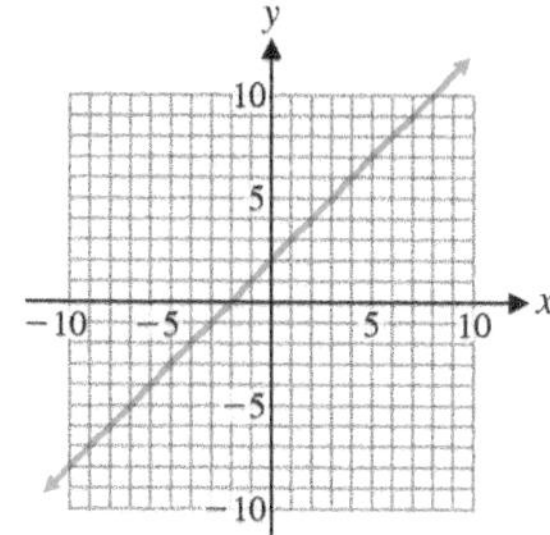

16.

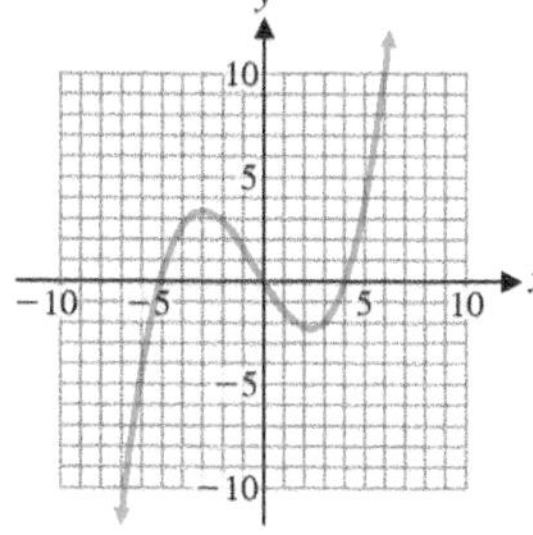

17.

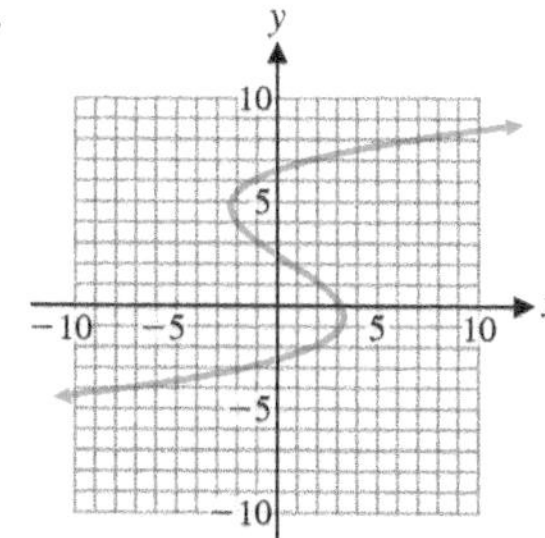

18.

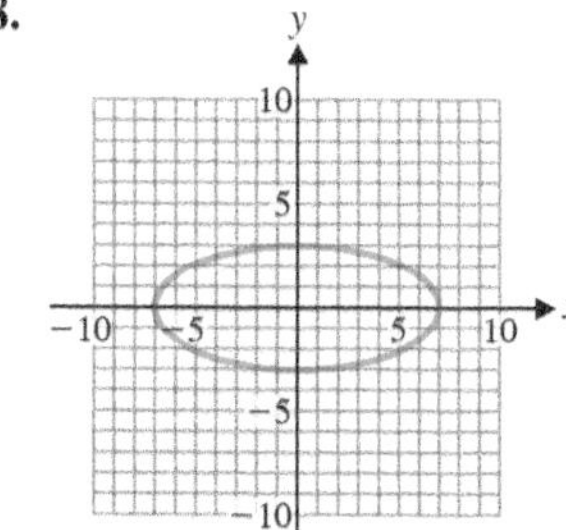

19.

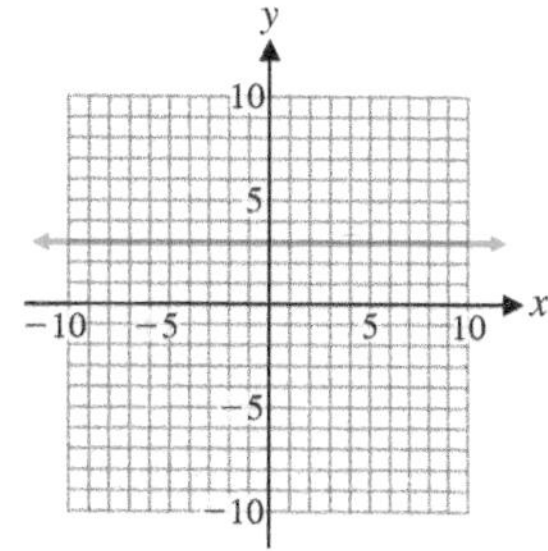

20.

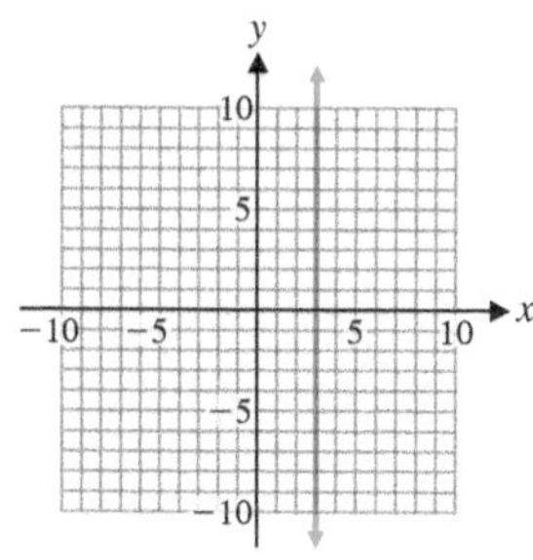

In Problems 21–28, each equation specifies a function with independent variable x. Determine whether the function is linear, constant, or neither.

21. $y = -3x + \frac{1}{8}$

22. $y = 4x + \frac{1}{x}$

23. $7x + 5y = 3$

24. $2x - 4y - 6 = 0$

25. $y - 5x = 4 - 3x^2$

26. $x + xy + 1 = 0$

27. $y - x^2 + 2 = 10 - x^2$

28. $\frac{y - x}{2} + \frac{3 + 2x}{4} = 1$

In Problems 29–36, use point-by-point plotting to sketch the graph of each function.

29. $f(x) = 1 - x$

30. $f(x) = \frac{x}{2} - 3$

31. $f(x) = x^2 - 1$

32. $f(x) = 3 - x^2$

33. $f(x) = 4 - x^3$

34. $f(x) = x^3 - 2$

35. $f(x) = \frac{8}{x}$

36. $f(x) = \frac{-6}{x}$

In Problems 37 and 38, the three points in the table are on the graph of the indicated function f. Do these three points provide sufficient information for you to sketch the graph of $y = f(x)$? Add more points to the table until you are satisfied that your sketch is a good representation of the graph of $y = f(x)$ for $-5 \le x \le 5$.

37.

x	−1	0	1
$f(x)$	−1	0	1

$f(x) = \frac{2x}{x^2 + 1}$

38.

x	0	1	2
$f(x)$	0	1	2

$f(x) = \frac{3x^2}{x^2 + 2}$

In Problems 39–46, use the following graph of a function f to determine x or y to the nearest integer, as indicated. Some problems may have more than one answer.

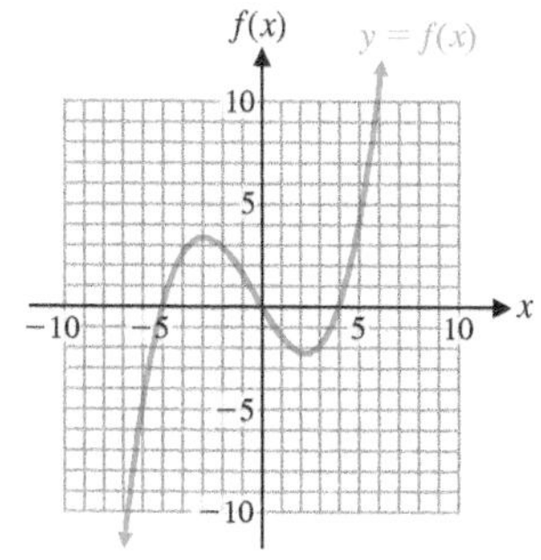

39. $y = f(-5)$

40. $y = f(4)$

41. $y = f(3)$

42. $y = f(-2)$

43. $f(x) = 0, x < 0$

44. $f(x) = -2$

45. $f(x) = -5$

46. $f(x) = 0$

B *In Problems 47–52, find the domain of each function.*

47. $F(x) = 2x^3 - x^2 + 3$

48. $H(x) = 7 - 2x^2 - x^4$

49. $f(x) = \dfrac{x - 2}{x + 4}$

50. $g(x) = \dfrac{x + 5}{x - 6}$

51. $g(x) = \sqrt{7 - x}$

52. $F(x) = \dfrac{8}{\sqrt{9 + x}}$

In Problems 53–60, does the equation specify a function with independent variable x? If so, find the domain of the function. If not, find a value of x to which there corresponds more than one value of y.

53. $2x + 5y = 10$

54. $6x - 7y = 21$

55. $y(x + y) = 4$

56. $x(x + y) = 4$

57. $x^{-3} + y^3 = 27$

58. $x^2 + y^2 = 9$

59. $x^3 - y^2 = 0$

60. $\sqrt{x} - y^3 = 0$

In Problems 61–74, find and simplify the expression if $f(x) = x^2 - 4$.

61. $f(5x)$

62. $f(-3x)$

63. $f(x + 3)$

64. $f(x - 1)$

65. $f(x^2)$

66. $f(x^3)$

67. $f(\sqrt{x})$

68. $f(\sqrt[4]{x})$

69. $f(2) + f(h)$

70. $f(-3) + f(h)$

71. $f(2 + h)$

72. $f(-3 + h)$

73. $f(2 + h) - f(2)$

74. $f(-3 + h) - f(-3)$

C *In Problems 75–80, find and simplify each of the following, assuming* $h \neq 0$ *in (C).*

(A) $f(x + h)$

(B) $f(x + h) - f(x)$

(C) $\dfrac{f(x + h) - f(x)}{h}$

75. $f(x) = 4x - 3$

76. $f(x) = -3x + 9$

77. $f(x) = 4x^2 - 7x + 6$

78. $f(x) = 3x^2 + 5x - 8$

79. $f(x) = x(20 - x)$

80. $f(x) = x(x + 50)$

Problems 81–84 refer to the area A and perimeter P of a rectangle with length l and width w (see the figure).

A = lw
P = 2l + 2w
w
l

81. The area of a rectangle is 25 sq in. Express the perimeter $P(w)$ as a function of the width w, and state the domain of this function.

82. The area of a rectangle is 216 sq ft. Express the perimeter $P(l)$ as a function of the length l, and state the domain of this function.

83. The perimeter of a rectangle is 100 m. Express the area $A(l)$ as a function of the length l, and state the domain of this function.

84. The perimeter of a rectangle is 160 m. Express the area $A(w)$ as a function of the width w, and state the domain of this function.

Applications

85. Price–demand. A company manufactures memory chips for microcomputers. Its marketing research department, using statistical techniques, collected the data shown in Table 8, where p is the wholesale price per chip at which x million chips can be sold. Using special analytical techniques (regression analysis), an analyst produced the following price–demand function to model the data:

$$p(x) = 75 - 3x \qquad 1 \le x \le 20$$

Table 8 **Price–Demand**

x (millions)	p($)
1	72
4	63
9	48
14	33
20	15

(A) Plot the data points in Table 8, and sketch a graph of the price–demand function in the same coordinate system.

(B) What would be the estimated price per chip for a demand of 7 million chips? For a demand of 11 million chips?

86. Price–demand. A company manufactures notebook computers. Its marketing research department, using statistical techniques, collected the data shown in Table 9, where p is the wholesale price per computer at which x thousand computers can be sold. Using special analytical techniques (regression analysis), an analyst produced the following price–demand function to model the data:

$$p(x) = 2{,}000 - 60x \qquad 1 \le x \le 25$$

Table 9 **Price–Demand**

x (thousands)	p($)
1	1,940
8	1,520
16	1,040
21	740
25	500

(A) Plot the data points in Table 9, and sketch a graph of the price–demand function in the same coordinate system.

(B) What would be the estimated price per computer for a demand of 11,000 computers? For a demand of 18,000 computers?

87. Revenue.

(A) Using the price–demand function

$$p(x) = 75 - 3x \qquad 1 \le x \le 20$$

from Problem 85, write the company's revenue function and indicate its domain.

(B) Complete Table 10, computing revenues to the nearest million dollars.

Table 10 **Revenue**

x (millions)	$R(x)$ (million $)
1	72
4	
8	
12	
16	
20	

(C) Plot the points from part (B) and sketch a graph of the revenue function using these points. Choose millions for the units on the horizontal and vertical axes.

88. Revenue.

(A) Using the price–demand function

$$p(x) = 2{,}000 - 60x \qquad 1 \le x \le 25$$

from Problem 86, write the company's revenue function and indicate its domain.

(B) Complete Table 11, computing revenues to the nearest thousand dollars.

Table 11 **Revenue**

x (thousands)	$R(x)$ (thousand $)
1	1,940
5	
10	
15	
20	
25	

(C) Plot the points from part (B) and sketch a graph of the revenue function using these points. Choose thousands for the units on the horizontal and vertical axes.

89. Profit. The financial department for the company in Problems 85 and 87 established the following cost function for producing and selling x million memory chips:

$$C(x) = 125 + 16x \text{ million dollars}$$

(A) Write a profit function for producing and selling x million memory chips and indicate its domain.

(B) Complete Table 12, computing profits to the nearest million dollars.

Table 12 **Profit**

x (millions)	$P(x)$ (million $)
1	−69
4	
8	
12	
16	
20	

(C) Plot the points in part (B) and sketch a graph of the profit function using these points.

90. Profit. The financial department for the company in Problems 86 and 88 established the following cost function for producing and selling x thousand notebook computers:

$$C(x) = 4{,}000 + 500x \text{ thousand dollars}$$

(A) Write a profit function for producing and selling x thousand notebook computers and indicate its domain.

(B) Complete Table 13, computing profits to the nearest thousand dollars.

Table 13 **Profit**

x (thousands)	$P(x)$ (thousand $)
1	−2,560
5	
10	
15	
20	
25	

(C) Plot the points in part (B) and sketch a graph of the profit function using these points.

91. Muscle contraction. In a study of the speed of muscle contraction in frogs under various loads, British biophysicist A. W. Hill determined that the weight w (in grams) placed on the muscle and the speed of contraction v (in centimeters per second) are approximately related by an equation of the form

$$(w + a)(v + b) = c$$

where a, b, and c are constants. Suppose that for a certain muscle, $a = 15$, $b = 1$, and $c = 90$. Express v as a function of w. Find the speed of contraction if a weight of 16 g is placed on the muscle.

92. Politics. The percentage s of seats in the House of Commons won by Conservatives and the percentage v of votes cast for Conservatives (when expressed as decimal fractions) are related by the equation

$$8v - 5s = 1 \qquad 0 < s < 1, \quad 0.125 < v < 0.75$$

(A) Express v as a function of s and find the percentage of votes required for the Conservatives to win 51% of the seats.

(B) Express s as a function of v and find the percentage of seats won if the Conservatives receive 51% of the votes.

Answers to Matched Problems

1. (A)

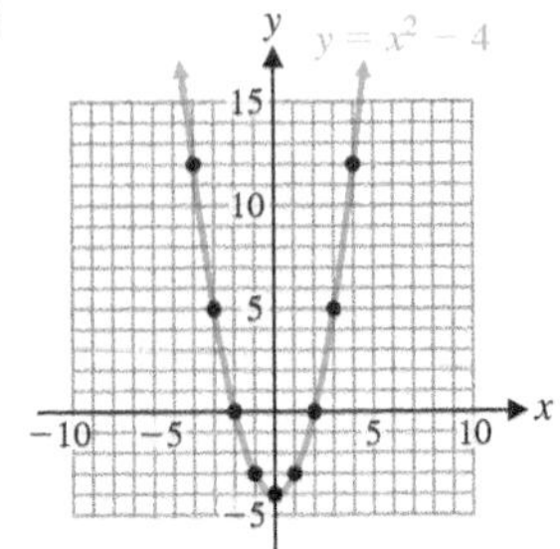

(B)

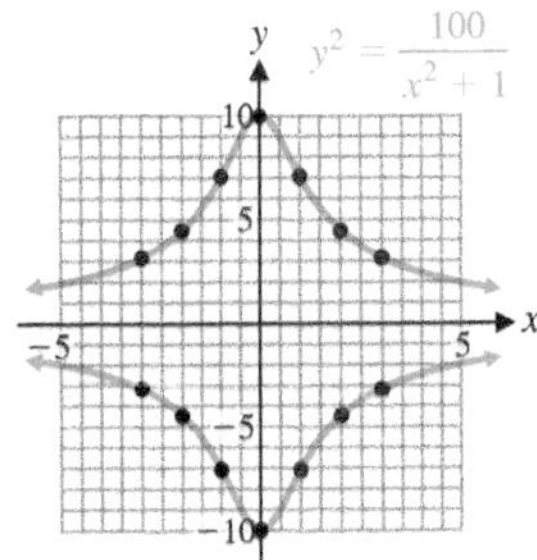

2. (A) Does not specify a function
   (B) Specifies a function
3. $x \geq 2$ (inequality notation) or $[2, \infty)$ (interval notation)
4. (A) -3 (B) 0
   (C) Does not exist (D) 6
5. Domain of F: R; domain of G: all real numbers except -3; domain of H: $x \leq 2$ (inequality notation) or $(-\infty, 2]$ (interval notation)
6. (A) $a^2 - 4a + 9$
   (B) $a^2 + 2ah + h^2 - 4a - 4h + 9$
   (C) $2ah + h^2 - 4h$
   (D) $2a + h - 4$
7. (A)

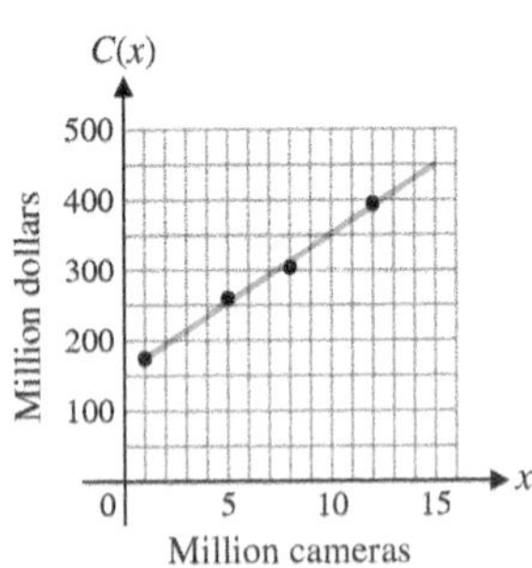

(B) $P(x) = R(x) - C(x)$
$= x(94.8 - 5x) - (156 + 19.7x)$;
domain: $1 \leq x \leq 15$

(C) Table 7 **Profit**

x (millions)	$P(x)$ (million \$)
1	−86
3	24
6	115
9	115
12	25
15	−155

(D) [graph of $P(x)$: Million dollars vs. Million cameras]

(E)

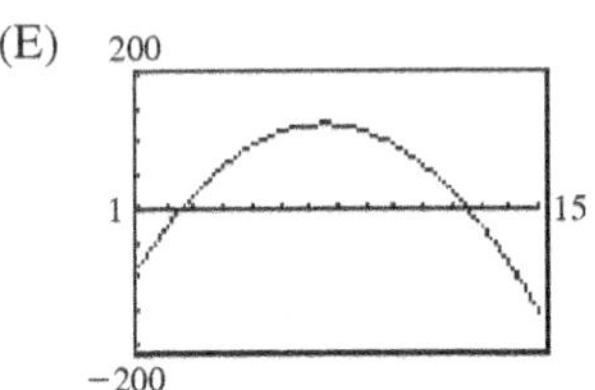

2.2 Elementary Functions: Graphs and Transformations

- A Beginning Library of Elementary Functions
- Vertical and Horizontal Shifts
- Reflections, Stretches, and Shrinks
- Piecewise-Defined Functions

Each of the functions

$$g(x) = x^2 - 4 \qquad h(x) = (x - 4)^2 \qquad k(x) = -4x^2$$

can be expressed in terms of the function $f(x) = x^2$:

$$g(x) = f(x) - 4 \qquad h(x) = f(x - 4) \qquad k(x) = -4f(x)$$

In this section, we will see that the graphs of functions g, h, and k are closely related to the graph of function f. Insight gained by understanding these relationships will help us analyze and interpret the graphs of many different functions.

A Beginning Library of Elementary Functions

As you progress through this book, you will repeatedly encounter a small number of elementary functions. We will identify these functions, study their basic properties, and include them in a library of elementary functions (see the references at the back of the book). This library will become an important addition to your mathematical toolbox and can be used in any course or activity where mathematics is applied.

We begin by placing six basic functions in our library.

DEFINITION Basic Elementary Functions

$f(x) = x$	Identity function
$h(x) = x^2$	Square function
$m(x) = x^3$	Cube function
$n(x) = \sqrt{x}$	Square root function
$p(x) = \sqrt[3]{x}$	Cube root function
$g(x) = \lvert x \rvert$	Absolute value function

These elementary functions can be evaluated by hand for certain values of x and with a calculator for all values of x for which they are defined.

EXAMPLE 1 **Evaluating Basic Elementary Functions** Evaluate each basic elementary function at

(A) $x = 64$ (B) $x = -12.75$

Round any approximate values to four decimal places.

SOLUTION

(A) $f(64) = 64$

$h(64) = 64^2 = 4{,}096$ Use a calculator.

$m(64) = 64^3 = 262{,}144$ Use a calculator.

$n(64) = \sqrt{64} = 8$

$p(64) = \sqrt[3]{64} = 4$

$g(64) = |64| = 64$

(B) $f(-12.75) = -12.75$

$h(-12.75) = (-12.75)^2 = 162.5625$ Use a calculator.

$m(-12.75) = (-12.75)^3 \approx -2{,}072.6719$ Use a calculator.

$n(-12.75) = \sqrt{-12.75}$ Not a real number.

$p(-12.75) = \sqrt[3]{-12.75} \approx -2.3362$ Use a calculator.

$g(-12.75) = |-12.75| = 12.75$

Matched Problem 1 Evaluate each basic elementary function at

(A) $x = 729$ (B) $x = -5.25$

Round any approximate values to four decimal places.

Remark Most computers and graphing calculators use ABS(x) to represent the absolute value function. The following representation can also be useful:

$$|x| = \sqrt{x^2}$$

Figure 1 shows the graph, range, and domain of each of the basic elementary functions.

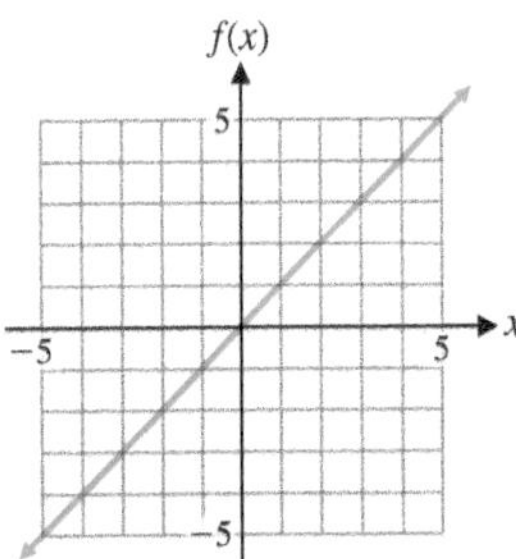

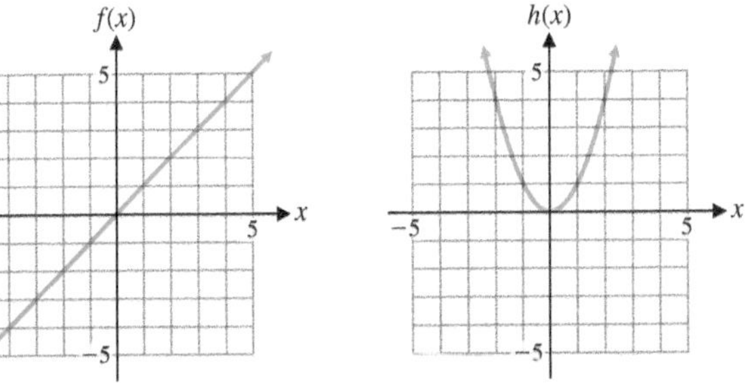

(A) **Identity function**
$f(x) = x$
Domain: R
Range: R

(B) **Square function**
$h(x) = x^2$
Domain: R
Range: $[0, \infty)$

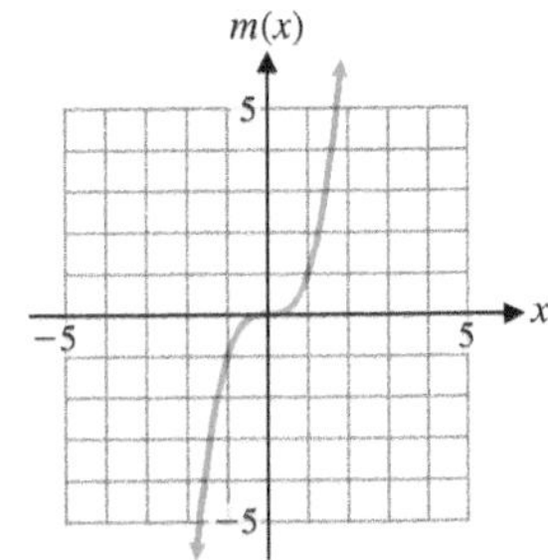

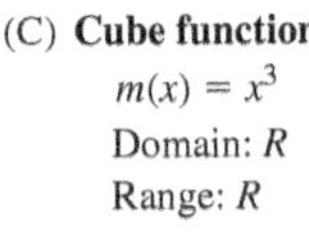

(C) **Cube function**
$m(x) = x^3$
Domain: R
Range: R

Reminder

Letters used to designate these functions may vary from context to context; R is the set of all real numbers.

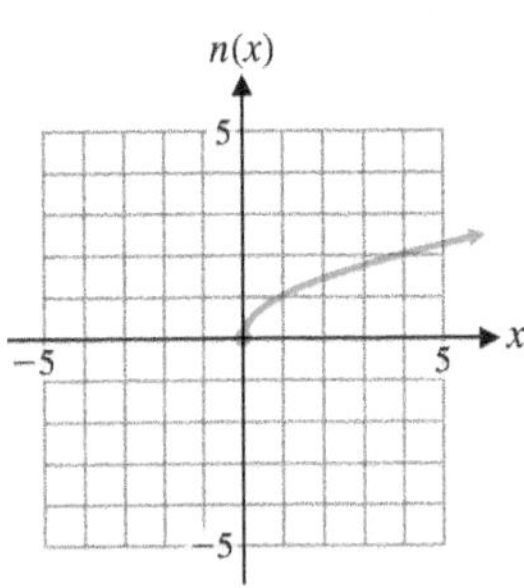

(D) **Square root function**
$n(x) = \sqrt{x}$
Domain: $[0, \infty)$
Range: $[0, \infty)$

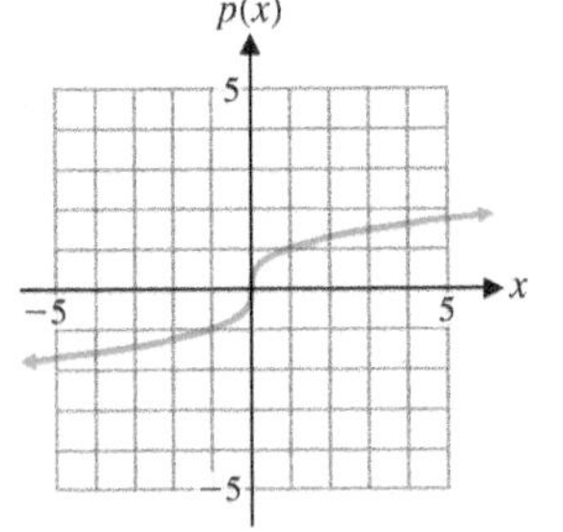

(E) **Cube root function**
$p(x) = \sqrt[3]{x}$
Domain: R
Range: R

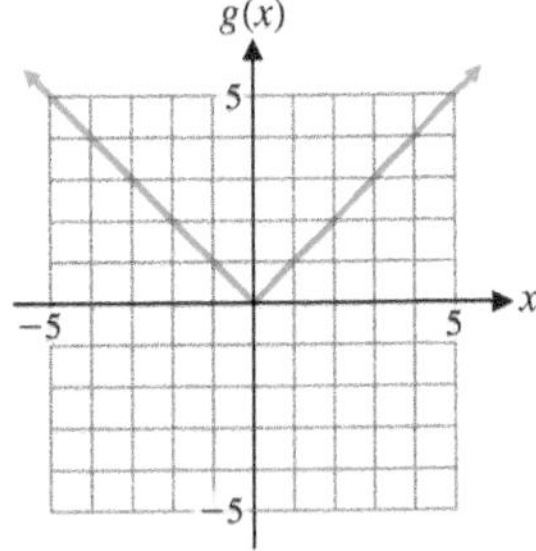

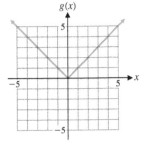

(F) **Absolute value function**
$g(x) = |x|$
Domain: R
Range: $[0, \infty)$

Figure 1 Some basic functions and their graphs

CONCEPTUAL INSIGHT

Absolute Value In beginning algebra, absolute value is often interpreted as distance from the origin on a real number line (see Appendix A, Section A.1).

distance $= 6 = -(-6)$ distance $= 5$

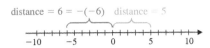

−10 −5 0 5 10

If $x < 0$, then $-x$ is the *positive* distance from the origin to x, and if $x > 0$, then x is the positive distance from the origin to x. Thus,

$$|x| = \begin{cases} -x & \text{if } x < 0 \\ x & \text{if } x \geq 0 \end{cases}$$

Vertical and Horizontal Shifts

If a new function is formed by performing an operation on a given function, then the graph of the new function is called a **transformation** of the graph of the original function. For example, graphs of $y = f(x) + k$ and $y = f(x + h)$ are transformations of the graph of $y = f(x)$.

Explore and Discuss 1

Let $f(x) = x^2$.

(A) Graph $y = f(x) + k$ for $k = -4, 0$, and 2 simultaneously in the same coordinate system. Describe the relationship between the graph of $y = f(x)$ and the graph of $y = f(x) + k$ for any real number k.

(B) Graph $y = f(x + h)$ for $h = -4, 0$, and 2 simultaneously in the same coordinate system. Describe the relationship between the graph of $y = f(x)$ and the graph of $y = f(x + h)$ for any real number h.

EXAMPLE 2

Vertical and Horizontal Shifts

(A) How are the graphs of $y = |x| + 4$ and $y = |x| - 5$ related to the graph of $y = |x|$? Confirm your answer by graphing all three functions simultaneously in the same coordinate system.

(B) How are the graphs of $y = |x + 4|$ and $y = |x - 5|$ related to the graph of $y = |x|$? Confirm your answer by graphing all three functions simultaneously in the same coordinate system.

SOLUTION

(A) The graph of $y = |x| + 4$ is the same as the graph of $y = |x|$ shifted upward 4 units, and the graph of $y = |x| - 5$ is the same as the graph of $y = |x|$ shifted downward 5 units. Figure 2 confirms these conclusions. [It appears that the graph of $y = f(x) + k$ is the graph of $y = f(x)$ shifted up if k is positive and down if k is negative.]

(B) The graph of $y = |x + 4|$ is the same as the graph of $y = |x|$ shifted to the left 4 units, and the graph of $y = |x - 5|$ is the same as the graph of $y = |x|$ shifted to the right 5 units. Figure 3 confirms these conclusions. [It appears that the graph of $y = f(x + h)$ is the graph of $y = f(x)$ shifted right if h is negative and left if h is positive—the opposite of what you might expect.]

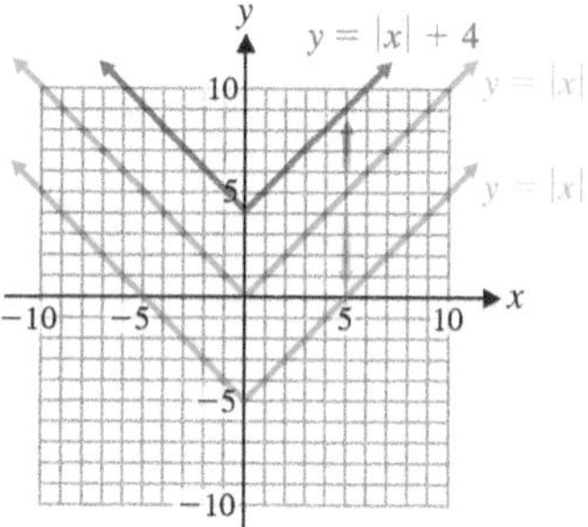

Figure 2 Vertical shifts

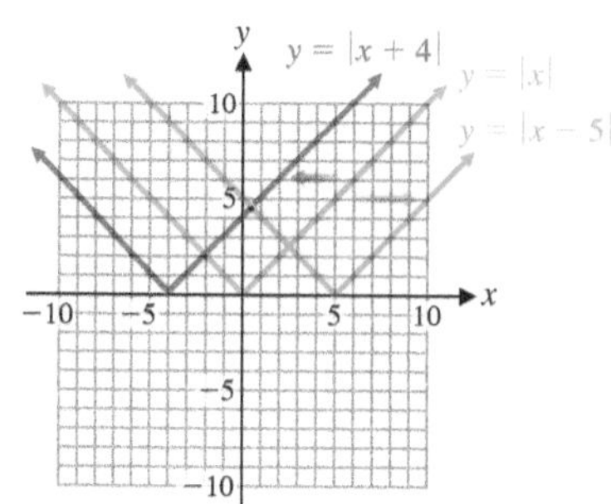

Figure 3 Horizontal shifts

Matched Problem 2

(A) How are the graphs of $y = \sqrt{x} + 5$ and $y = \sqrt{x} - 4$ related to the graph of $y = \sqrt{x}$? Confirm your answer by graphing all three functions simultaneously in the same coordinate system.

(B) How are the graphs of $y = \sqrt{x + 5}$ and $y = \sqrt{x - 4}$ related to the graph of $y = \sqrt{x}$? Confirm your answer by graphing all three functions simultaneously in the same coordinate system.

Comparing the graphs of $y = f(x) + k$ with the graph of $y = f(x)$, we see that the graph of $y = f(x) + k$ can be obtained from the graph of $y = f(x)$ by **vertically translating** (shifting) the graph of the latter upward k units if k is positive and downward $|k|$ units if k is negative. Comparing the graphs of $y = f(x + h)$ with the graph of $y = f(x)$, we see that the graph of $y = f(x + h)$ can be obtained from the graph of $y = f(x)$ by **horizontally translating** (shifting) the graph of the latter h units to the left if h is positive and $|h|$ units to the right if h is negative.

EXAMPLE 3 **Vertical and Horizontal Translations (Shifts)** The graphs in Figure 4 are either horizontal or vertical shifts of the graph of $f(x) = x^2$. Write appropriate equations for functions H, G, M, and N in terms of f.

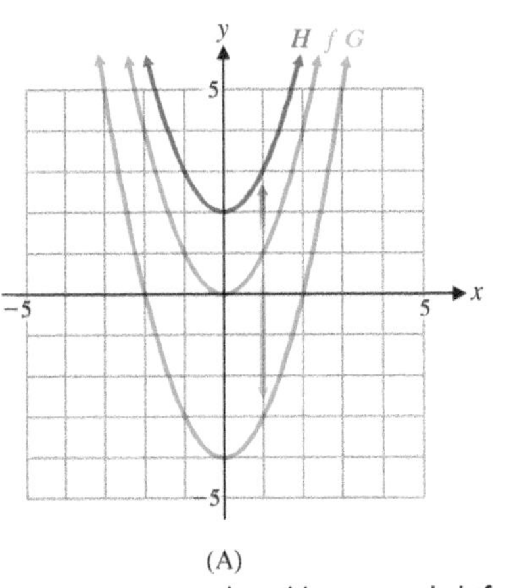

(A) (B)

Figure 4 Vertical and horizontal shifts

SOLUTION Functions H and G are vertical shifts given by

$$H(x) = x^2 + 2 \qquad G(x) = x^2 - 4$$

Functions M and N are horizontal shifts given by

$$M(x) = (x + 2)^2 \qquad N(x) = (x - 3)^2$$

Matched Problem 3 The graphs in Figure 5 are either horizontal or vertical shifts of the graph of $f(x) = \sqrt[3]{x}$. Write appropriate equations for functions H, G, M, and N in terms of f.

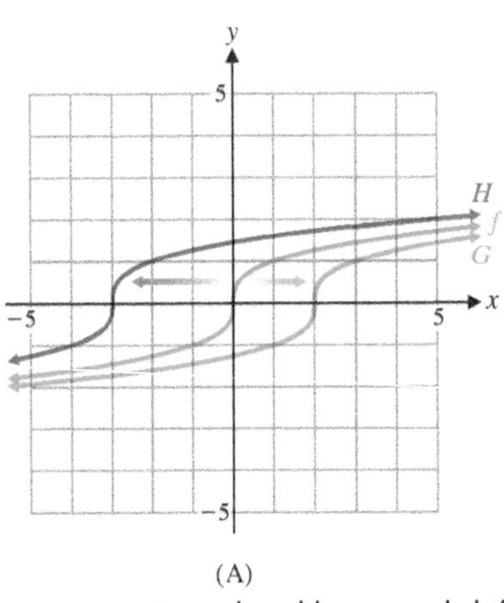

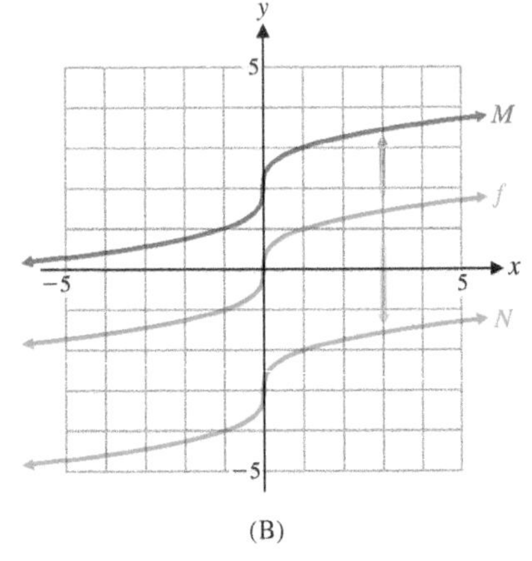

(A) (B)

Figure 5 Vertical and horizontal shifts

Reflections, Stretches, and Shrinks

We now investigate how the graph of $y = Af(x)$ is related to the graph of $y = f(x)$ for different real numbers A.

Explore and Discuss 2

(A) Graph $y = Ax^2$ for $A = 1, 4$, and $\frac{1}{4}$ simultaneously in the same coordinate system.

(B) Graph $y = Ax^2$ for $A = -1, -4$, and $-\frac{1}{4}$ simultaneously in the same coordinate system.

(C) Describe the relationship between the graph of $h(x) = x^2$ and the graph of $G(x) = Ax^2$ for any real number A.

Comparing $y = Af(x)$ to $y = f(x)$, we see that the graph of $y = Af(x)$ can be obtained from the graph of $y = f(x)$ by multiplying each ordinate value of the latter by A. The result is a **vertical stretch** of the graph of $y = f(x)$ if $A > 1$, a **vertical shrink** of the graph of $y = f(x)$ if $0 < A < 1$, and a **reflection in the x axis** if $A = -1$. If A is a negative number other than -1, then the result is a combination of a reflection in the x axis and either a vertical stretch or a vertical shrink.

EXAMPLE 4 **Reflections, Stretches, and Shrinks**

(A) How are the graphs of $y = 2|x|$ and $y = 0.5|x|$ related to the graph of $y = |x|$? Confirm your answer by graphing all three functions simultaneously in the same coordinate system.

(B) How is the graph of $y = -2|x|$ related to the graph of $y = |x|$? Confirm your answer by graphing both functions simultaneously in the same coordinate system.

SOLUTION

(A) The graph of $y = 2|x|$ is a vertical stretch of the graph of $y = |x|$ by a factor of 2, and the graph of $y = 0.5|x|$ is a vertical shrink of the graph of $y = |x|$ by a factor of 0.5. Figure 6 confirms this conclusion.

(B) The graph of $y = -2|x|$ is a reflection in the x axis and a vertical stretch of the graph of $y = |x|$. Figure 7 confirms this conclusion.

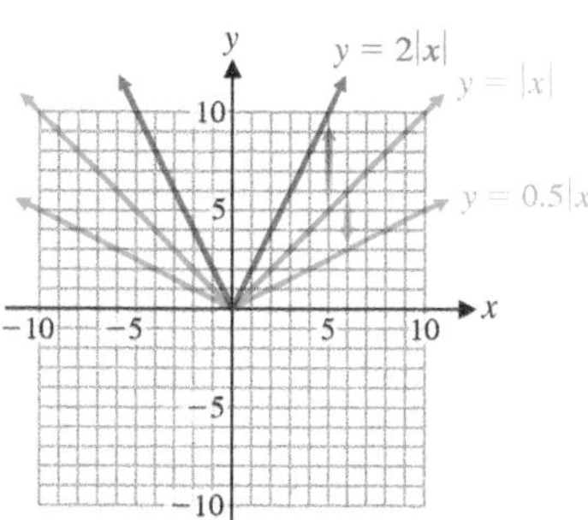

Figure 6 Vertical stretch and shrink

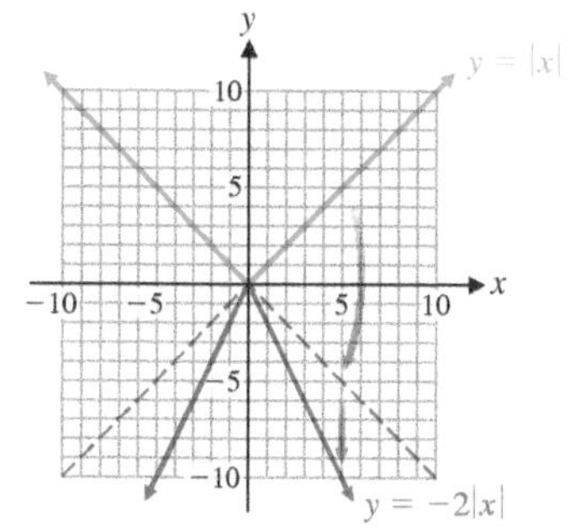

Figure 7 Reflection and vertical stretch

Matched Problem 4

(A) How are the graphs of $y = 2x$ and $y = 0.5x$ related to the graph of $y = x$? Confirm your answer by graphing all three functions simultaneously in the same coordinate system.

(B) How is the graph of $y = -0.5x$ related to the graph of $y = x$? Confirm your answer by graphing both functions in the same coordinate system.

The various transformations considered above are summarized in the following box for easy reference:

SUMMARY Graph Transformations

Vertical Translation:

$$y = f(x) + k \quad \begin{cases} k > 0 & \text{Shift graph of } y = f(x) \text{ up } k \text{ units.} \\ k < 0 & \text{Shift graph of } y = f(x) \text{ down } |k| \text{ units.} \end{cases}$$

Horizontal Translation:

$$y = f(x + h) \quad \begin{cases} h > 0 & \text{Shift graph of } y = f(x) \text{ left } h \text{ units.} \\ h < 0 & \text{Shift graph of } y = f(x) \text{ right } |h| \text{ units.} \end{cases}$$

Reflection:

$$y = -f(x) \quad \text{Reflect the graph of } y = f(x) \text{ in the } x \text{ axis.}$$

Vertical Stretch and Shrink:

$$y = Af(x) \quad \begin{cases} A > 1 & \text{Stretch graph of } y = f(x) \text{ vertically by multiplying each ordinate value by } A. \\ 0 < A < 1 & \text{Shrink graph of } y = f(x) \text{ vertically by multiplying each ordinate value by } A. \end{cases}$$

Explore and Discuss 3

Explain why applying any of the graph transformations in the summary box to a linear function produces another linear function.

EXAMPLE 5 **Combining Graph Transformations** Discuss the relationship between the graphs of $y = -|x - 3| + 1$ and $y = |x|$. Confirm your answer by graphing both functions simultaneously in the same coordinate system.

SOLUTION The graph of $y = -|x - 3| + 1$ is a reflection of the graph of $y = |x|$ in the x axis, followed by a horizontal translation of 3 units to the right and a vertical translation of 1 unit upward. Figure 8 confirms this description.

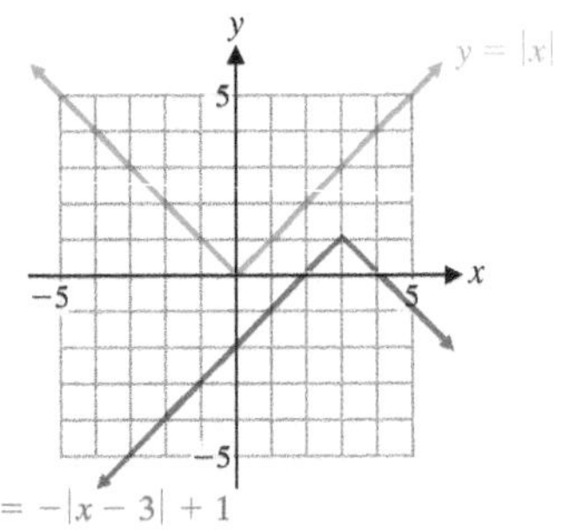

Figure 8 Combined transformations

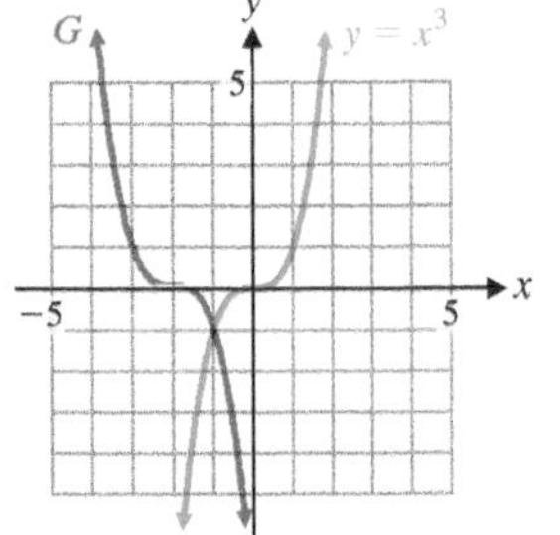

Figure 9 Combined transformations

Matched Problem 5 The graph of $y = G(x)$ in Figure 9 involves a reflection and a translation of the graph of $y = x^3$. Describe how the graph of function G is related to the graph of $y = x^3$ and find an equation of the function G.

Piecewise-Defined Functions

Earlier we noted that the absolute value of a real number x can be defined as

$$|x| = \begin{cases} -x & \text{if } x < 0 \\ x & \text{if } x \geq 0 \end{cases}$$

Notice that this function is defined by different rules for different parts of its domain. Functions whose definitions involve more than one rule are called **piecewise-defined functions**. Graphing one of these functions involves graphing each rule over the appropriate portion of the domain (Fig. 10). In Figure 10C, notice that an open dot is used to show that the point $(0, -2)$ is not part of the graph and a solid dot is used to show that (0, 2) is part of the graph.

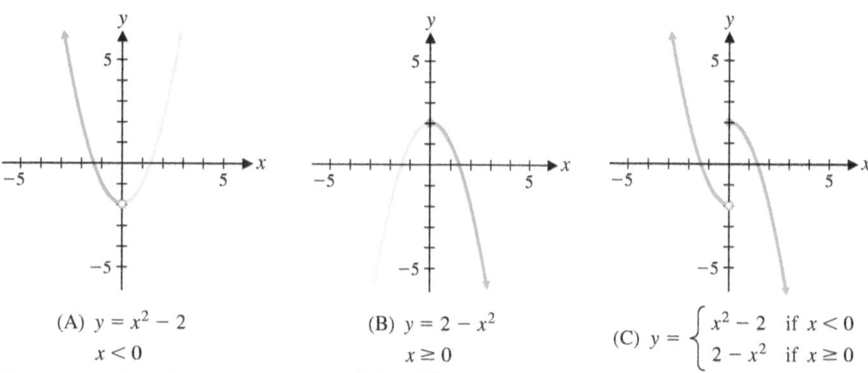

Figure 10 Graphing a piecewise-defined function

EXAMPLE 6 **Graphing Piecewise-Defined Functions** Graph the piecewise-defined function

$$g(x) = \begin{cases} x + 1 & \text{if } 0 \leq x < 2 \\ 0.5x & \text{if } x \geq 2 \end{cases}$$

SOLUTION If $0 \leq x < 2$, then the first rule applies and the graph of g lies on the line $y = x + 1$ (a vertical shift of the identity function $y = x$). If $x = 0$, then (0, 1) lies on $y = x + 1$; we plot (0, 1) with a solid dot (Fig. 11) because $g(0) = 1$. If $x = 2$, then (2, 3) lies on $y = x + 1$; we plot (2, 3) with an open dot because $g(2) \neq 3$. The line segment from (0, 1) to (2, 3) is the graph of g for $0 \leq x < 2$. If $x \geq 2$, then the second rule applies and the graph of g lies on the line $y = 0.5x$ (a vertical shrink of the identity function $y = x$). If $x = 2$, then (2, 1) lies on the line $y = 0.5x$; we plot (2, 1) with a solid dot because $g(2) = 1$. The portion of $y = 0.5x$ that starts at (2, 1) and extends to the right is the graph of g for $x \geq 2$.

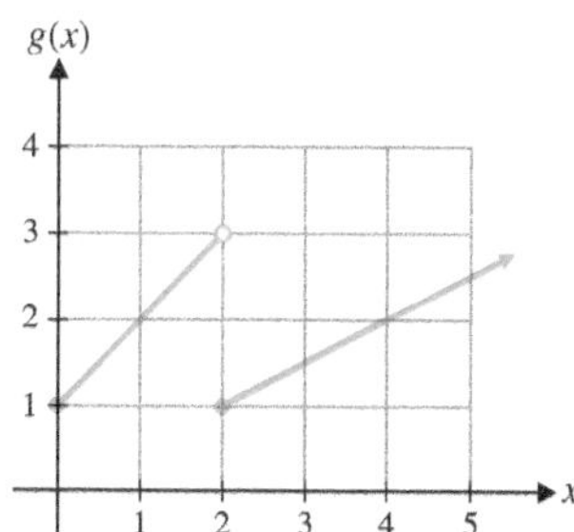

Figure 11

Matched Problem 6 Graph the piecewise-defined function

$$h(x) = \begin{cases} -2x + 4 & \text{if } 0 \leq x \leq 2 \\ x - 1 & \text{if } x > 2 \end{cases}$$

As the next example illustrates, piecewise-defined functions occur naturally in many applications.

EXAMPLE 7 **Natural Gas Rates** Easton Utilities uses the rates shown in Table 1 to compute the monthly cost of natural gas for each customer. Write a piecewise definition for the cost of consuming x CCF (cubic hundred feet) of natural gas and graph the function.

Table 1 Charges per Month

\$0.7866 per CCF for the first 5 CCF
\$0.4601 per CCF for the next 35 CCF
\$0.2508 per CCF for all over 40 CCF

SOLUTION If $C(x)$ is the cost, in dollars, of using x CCF of natural gas in one month, then the first line of Table 1 implies that

$$C(x) = 0.7866x \quad \text{if } 0 \le x \le 5$$

Note that $C(5) = 3.933$ is the cost of 5 CCF. If $5 < x \le 40$, then $x - 5$ represents the amount of gas that cost \$0.4601 per CCF, $0.4601(x - 5)$ represents the cost of this gas, and the total cost is

$$C(x) = 3.933 + 0.4601(x - 5)$$

If $x > 40$, then

$$C(x) = 20.0365 + 0.2508(x - 40)$$

where $20.0365 = C(40)$, the cost of the first 40 CCF. Combining all these equations, we have the following piecewise definition for $C(x)$:

$$C(x) = \begin{cases} 0.7866x & \text{if } 0 \le x \le 5 \\ 3.933 + 0.4601(x - 5) & \text{if } 5 < x \le 40 \\ 20.0365 + 0.2508(x - 40) & \text{if } x > 40 \end{cases}$$

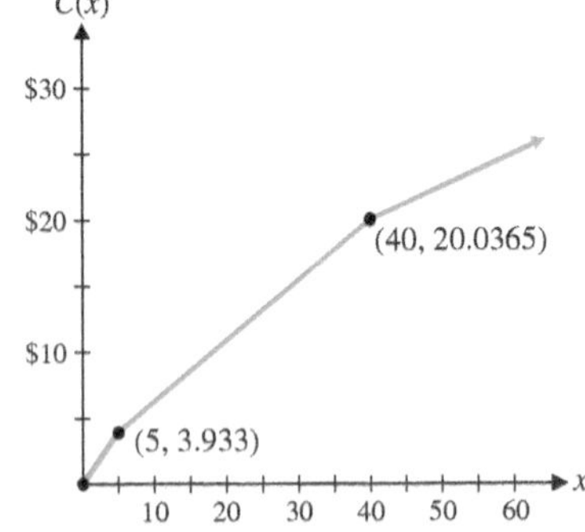

Figure 12 Cost of purchasing x CCF of natural gas

To graph C, first note that each rule in the definition of C represents a transformation of the identity function $f(x) = x$. Graphing each transformation over the indicated interval produces the graph of C shown in Figure 12.

Matched Problem 7 Trussville Utilities uses the rates shown in Table 2 to compute the monthly cost of natural gas for residential customers. Write a piecewise definition for the cost of consuming x CCF of natural gas and graph the function.

Table 2 Charges per Month

\$0.7675 per CCF for the first 50 CCF
\$0.6400 per CCF for the next 150 CCF
\$0.6130 per CCF for all over 200 CCF

Exercises 2.2

A *In Problems 1–10, find the domain and range of each function.*

1. $f(x) = x^2 - 4$
2. $f(x) = 1 + \sqrt{x}$
3. $f(x) = 7 - 2x$
4. $f(x) = x^2 + 12$
5. $f(x) = 8 - \sqrt{x}$
6. $f(x) = 5x + 3$
7. $f(x) = 27 + \sqrt[3]{x}$
8. $f(x) = 20 - 18|x|$
9. $f(x) = 6|x| + 9$
10. $f(x) = -8 + \sqrt[3]{x}$

In Problems 11–26, graph each of the functions using the graphs of functions f and g below.

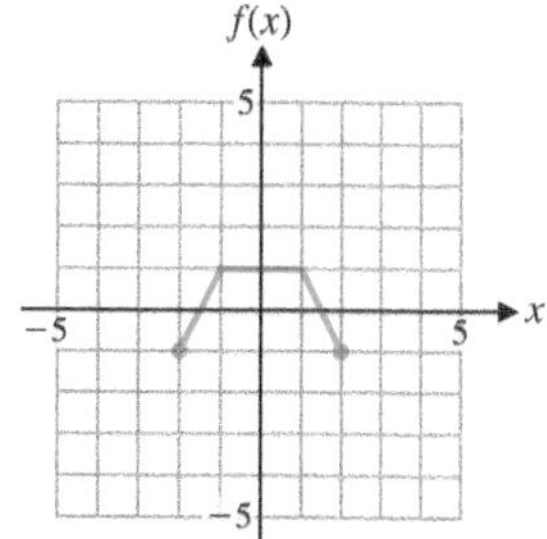
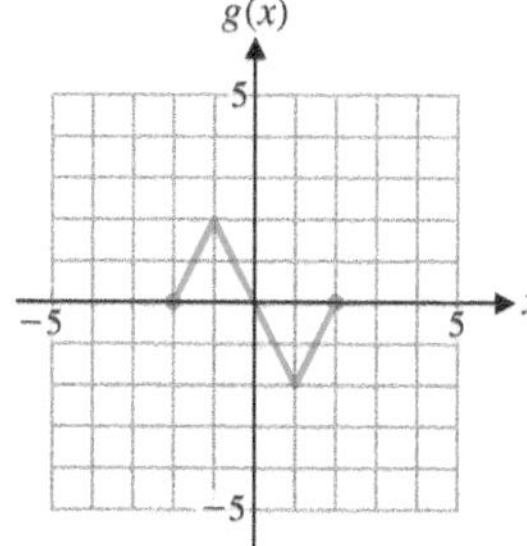

11. $y = f(x) + 2$ **12.** $y = g(x) - 1$

13. $y = f(x + 2)$ **14.** $y = g(x - 1)$

15. $y = g(x - 3)$ **16.** $y = f(x + 3)$

17. $y = g(x) - 3$ **18.** $y = f(x) + 3$

19. $y = -f(x)$ **20.** $y = -g(x)$

21. $y = 0.5g(x)$ **22.** $y = 2f(x)$

23. $y = 2f(x) + 1$ **24.** $y = -0.5g(x) + 3$

25. $y = 2(f(x) + 1)$ **26.** $y = -(0.5g(x) + 3)$

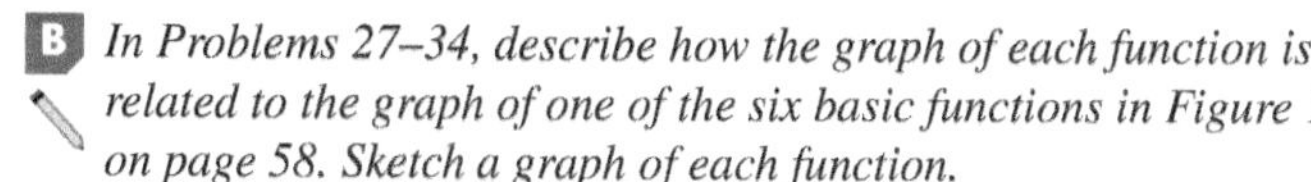

B *In Problems 27–34, describe how the graph of each function is related to the graph of one of the six basic functions in Figure 1 on page 58. Sketch a graph of each function.*

27. $g(x) = -|x + 3|$ **28.** $h(x) = -|x - 5|$

29. $f(x) = (x - 4)^2 - 3$ **30.** $m(x) = (x + 3)^2 + 4$

31. $f(x) = 7 - \sqrt{x}$ **32.** $g(x) = -6 + \sqrt[3]{x}$

33. $h(x) = -3|x|$ **34.** $m(x) = -0.4x^2$

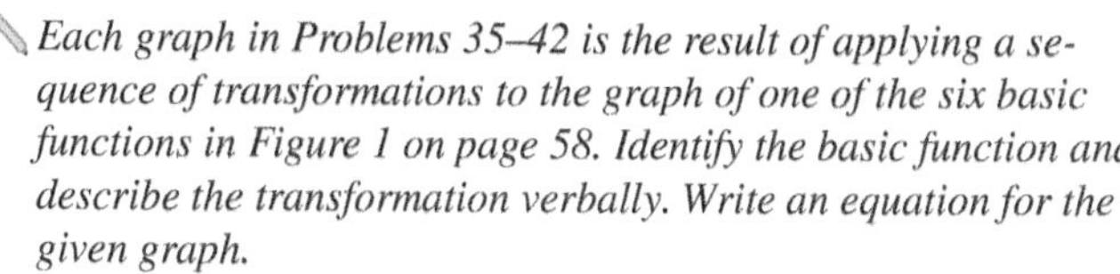

Each graph in Problems 35–42 is the result of applying a sequence of transformations to the graph of one of the six basic functions in Figure 1 on page 58. Identify the basic function and describe the transformation verbally. Write an equation for the given graph.

35.

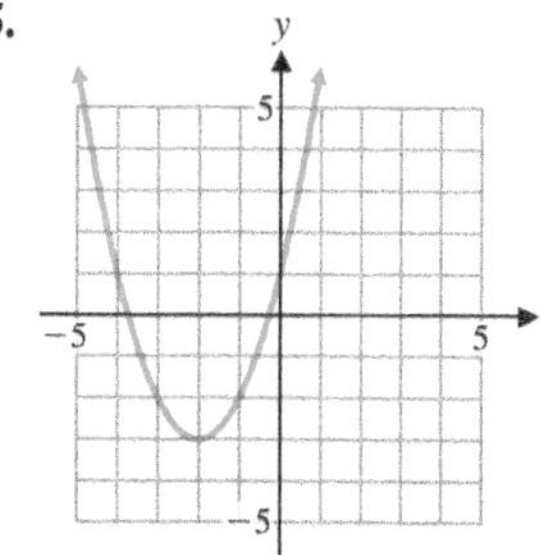

36.

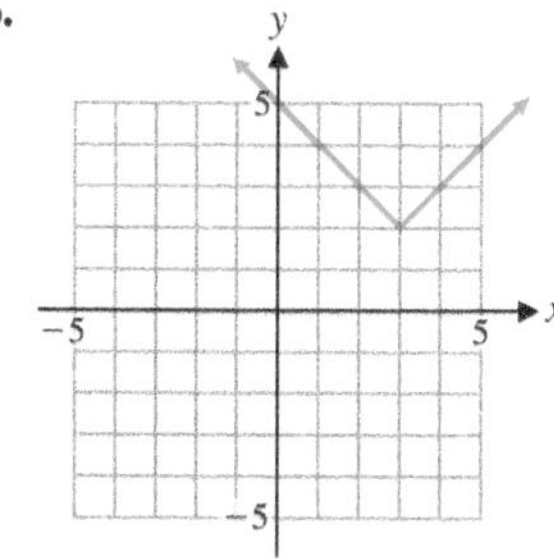

37.

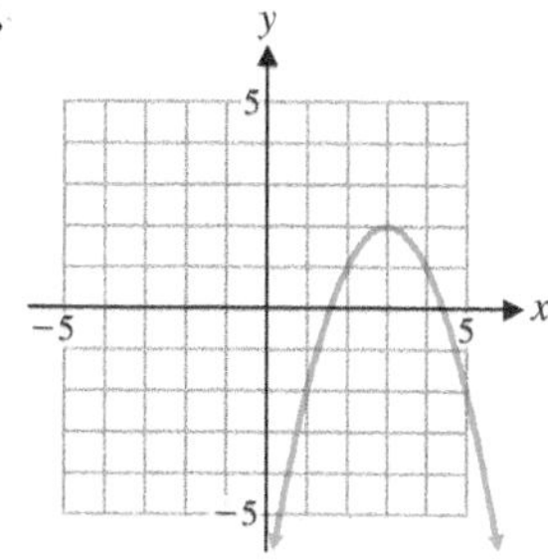

38.

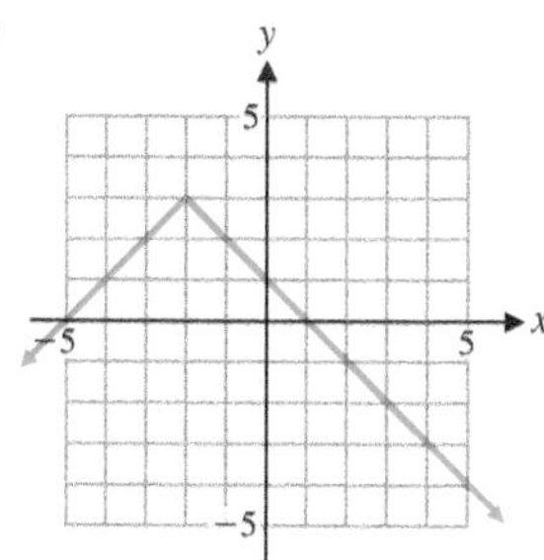

39.

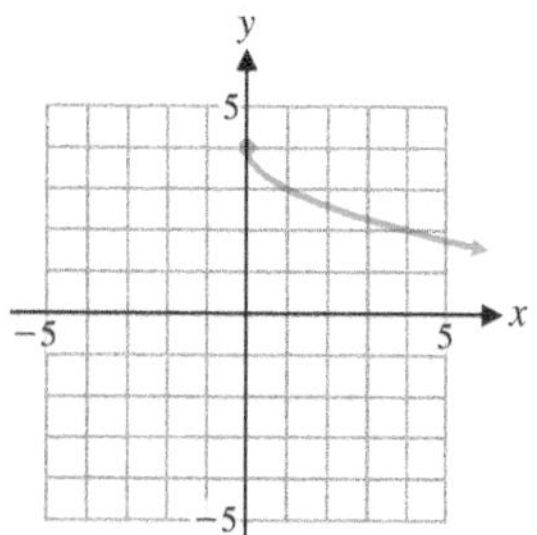

40.

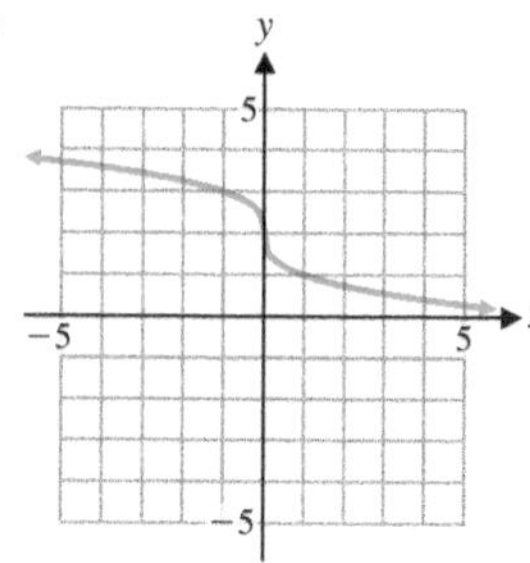

41.

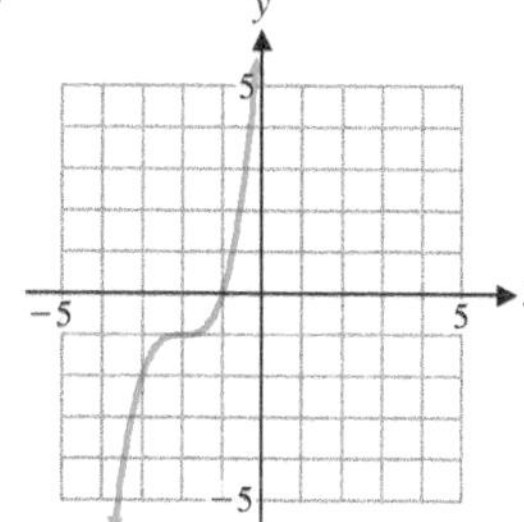

42.

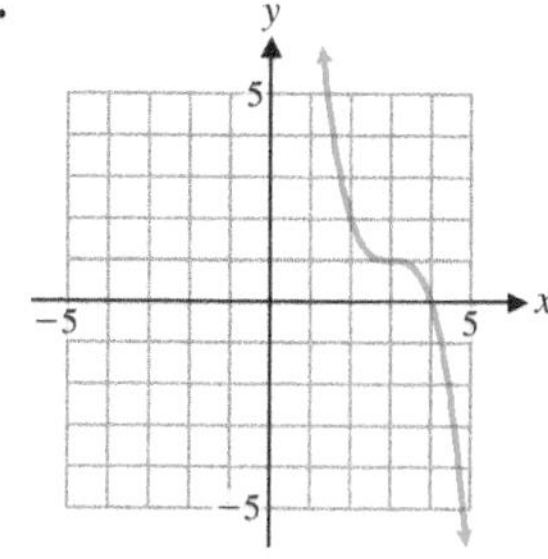

In Problems 43–48, the graph of the function g is formed by applying the indicated sequence of transformations to the given function f. Find an equation for the function g and graph g using $-5 \le x \le 5$ *and* $-5 \le y \le 5$.

43. The graph of $f(x) = \sqrt{x}$ is shifted 3 units to the left and 2 units up.

44. The graph of $f(x) = \sqrt[3]{x}$ is shifted 2 units to the right and 3 units down.

45. The graph of $f(x) = |x|$ is reflected in the x axis and shifted to the left 3 units.

46. The graph of $f(x) = |x|$ is reflected in the x axis and shifted to the right 1 unit.

47. The graph of $f(x) = x^3$ is reflected in the x axis and shifted 2 units to the right and down 1 unit.

48. The graph of $f(x) = x^2$ is reflected in the x axis and shifted to the left 2 units and up 4 units.

Graph each function in Problems 49–54.

49. $f(x) = \begin{cases} 2 - 2x & \text{if } x < 2 \\ x - 2 & \text{if } x \ge 2 \end{cases}$

50. $g(x) = \begin{cases} x + 1 & \text{if } x < -1 \\ 2 + 2x & \text{if } x \ge -1 \end{cases}$

51. $h(x) = \begin{cases} 5 + 0.5x & \text{if } 0 \le x \le 10 \\ -10 + 2x & \text{if } x > 10 \end{cases}$

52. $h(x) = \begin{cases} 10 + 2x & \text{if } 0 \le x \le 20 \\ 40 + 0.5x & \text{if } x > 20 \end{cases}$

53. $h(x) = \begin{cases} 2x & \text{if } 0 \le x \le 20 \\ x + 20 & \text{if } 20 < x \le 40 \\ 0.5x + 40 & \text{if } x > 40 \end{cases}$

54. $h(x) = \begin{cases} 4x + 20 & \text{if } 0 \le x \le 20 \\ 2x + 60 & \text{if } 20 < x \le 100 \\ -x + 360 & \text{if } x > 100 \end{cases}$

C *Each of the graphs in Problems 55–60 involves a reflection in the x axis and/or a vertical stretch or shrink of one of the basic functions in Figure 1 on page 58. Identify the basic function, and describe the transformation verbally. Write an equation for the given graph.*

55.

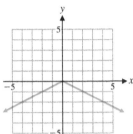

56.

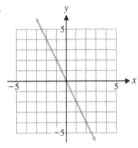

57.

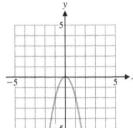

58.

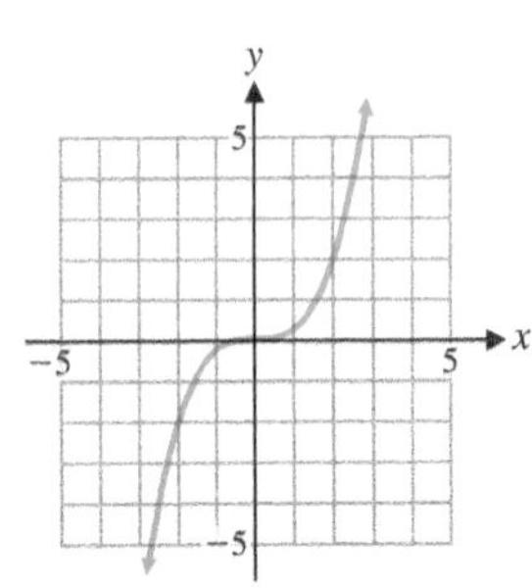

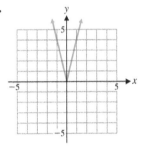

59.

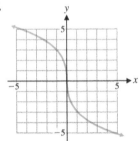

60.

Changing the order in a sequence of transformations may change the final result. Investigate each pair of transformations in Problems 61–66 to determine if reversing their order can produce a different result. Support your conclusions with specific examples and/or mathematical arguments. (The graph of $y = f(-x)$ is the reflection of $y = f(x)$ in the y axis.)

61. Vertical shift; horizontal shift

62. Vertical shift; reflection in y axis

63. Vertical shift; reflection in x axis

64. Horizontal shift; vertical stretch

65. Horizontal shift; reflection in y axis

66. Horizontal shift; horizontal shrink

Applications

67. Price–demand. A retail chain sells bicycle helmets. The retail price $p(x)$ (in dollars) and the weekly demand x for a particular model are related by

$$p(x) = 115 - 4\sqrt{x} \qquad 9 \le x \le 289$$

(A) Describe how the graph of function p can be obtained from the graph of one of the basic functions in Figure 1 on page 58.

(B) Sketch a graph of function p using part (A) as an aid.

68. Price–supply. The manufacturer of the bicycle helmets in Problem 67 is willing to supply x helmets at a price of $p(x)$ as given by the equation

$$p(x) = 4\sqrt{x} \qquad 9 \le x \le 289$$

(A) Describe how the graph of function p can be obtained from the graph of one of the basic functions in Figure 1 on page 58.

(B) Sketch a graph of function p using part (A) as an aid.

69. Hospital costs. Using statistical methods, the financial department of a hospital arrived at the cost equation

$$C(x) = 0.00048(x - 500)^3 + 60{,}000 \qquad 100 \le x \le 1{,}000$$

where $C(x)$ is the cost in dollars for handling x cases per month.

(A) Describe how the graph of function C can be obtained from the graph of one of the basic functions in Figure 1 on page 58.

(B) Sketch a graph of function C using part (A) and a graphing calculator as aids.

70. Price–demand. A company manufactures and sells in-line skates. Its financial department has established the price–demand function

$$p(x) = 190 - 0.013(x - 10)^2 \qquad 10 \le x \le 100$$

where $p(x)$ is the price at which x thousand pairs of in-line skates can be sold.

(A) Describe how the graph of function p can be obtained from the graph of one of the basic functions in Figure 1 on page 58.

(B) Sketch a graph of function p using part (A) and a graphing calculator as aids.

71. Electricity rates. Table 3 shows the electricity rates charged by Origin Energy for the state of Victoria in Australia. The daily supply charge is a fixed daily charge, independent of the kWh (kilowatt-hours) used during the day.

(A) Write a piecewise definition of the daily charge $V(x)$ for a customer who uses x kWh in a day.

(B) Graph $V(x)$.

Table 3 Victoria

Daily supply charge \$1.34
First 11 kWh at \$0.32 per kWh
Over 11 kWh at \$0.35 per kWh

72. **Electricity rates.** Table 4 shows the electricity rates charged by Origin Energy for the regions in South Australia.

(A) Write a piecewise definition of the daily charge $S(x)$ for a customer who uses x kWh in a day.

(B) Graph $S(x)$.

Table 4 South Australia

Daily supply charge, \$0.90
First 11 kWh at \$0.40 per kWh
Over 11 kWh at \$0.43 per kWh

73. **Real estate property tax.** Table 5 shows real estate property tax rates in Peru.

(A) Write a piecewise definition for $T(x)$, the amount of tax units due on a real estate's value of x tax units (1 tax unit is approximately \$1,265).

(B) Graph $T(x)$.

(C) Find the amount of tax units due on a taxable value of 30 tax units. Of 90 tax units.

Table 5 Peru Real Estate Property Tax

Over	But not over	Amount of tax units due is
0 tax units	15 tax units	0.2% of the property value
15 tax units	60 tax units	0.03 tax units plus 0.6% of excess over 15 tax units
60 tax units		0.30 tax units plus 1.0% of excess over 60 tax units

74. **Real estate property tax.** Table 6 shows real estate property tax rates in Bolivia.

(A) Write a piecewise definition for $T(x)$, the tax due on a real estate's value of x bolivianos Bs.

(B) Graph $T(x)$.

(C) Find the tax due on a taxable value of 300,000 Bs. Of 500,000 Bs. Of 1,000,000 Bs.

Table 6 Bolivia Real Estate Property Tax

Over	But not over	Tax due is
Bs 0	Bs 200,000	0.35% of the property value
Bs 200,000	Bs 400,000	Bs 700 plus 0.50% of excess over Bs 200,000
Bs 400,000	Bs 600,000	Bs 1,700 plus 1.00% of excess over Bs 400,000
Bs 600,000		Bs 3,700 plus 1.50% of excess over Bs 600,000

75. **Human weight.** A good approximation of the normal weight of a person 60 inches or taller but not taller than 80 inches is given by $w(x) = 5.5x - 220$, where x is height in inches and $w(x)$ is weight in pounds.

(A) Describe how the graph of function w can be obtained from the graph of one of the basic functions in Figure 1, page 58.

(B) Sketch a graph of function w using part (A) as an aid.

76. **Herpetology.** The average weight of a particular species of snake is given by $w(x) = 463x^3$, $0.2 \le x \le 0.8$, where x is length in meters and $w(x)$ is weight in grams.

(A) Describe how the graph of function w can be obtained from the graph of one of the basic functions in Figure 1, page 58.

(B) Sketch a graph of function w using part (A) as an aid.

77. **Safety research.** Under ideal conditions, if a person driving a vehicle slams on the brakes and skids to a stop, the speed of the vehicle $v(x)$ (in miles per hour) is given approximately by $v(x) = C\sqrt{x}$, where x is the length of skid marks (in feet) and C is a constant that depends on the road conditions and the weight of the vehicle. For a particular vehicle, $v(x) = 7.08\sqrt{x}$ and $4 \le x \le 144$.

(A) Describe how the graph of function v can be obtained from the graph of one of the basic functions in Figure 1, page 58.

(B) Sketch a graph of function v using part (A) as an aid.

78. **Learning.** A production analyst has found that on average it takes a new person $T(x)$ minutes to perform a particular assembly operation after x performances of the operation, where $T(x) = 10 - \sqrt[3]{x}$, $0 \le x \le 125$.

(A) Describe how the graph of function T can be obtained from the graph of one of the basic functions in Figure 1, page 58.

(B) Sketch a graph of function T using part (A) as an aid.

Answers to Matched Problems

1. (A) $f(729) = 729$, $h(729) = 531{,}441$, $m(729) = 387{,}420{,}489$, $n(729) = 27$, $p(729) = 9$, $g(729) = 729$

(B) $f(-5.25) = -5.25$, $h(-5.25) = 27.5625$, $m(-5.25) = -144.7031$, $n(-5.25)$ is not a real number, $p(-5.25) = -1.7380$, $g(-5.25) = 5.25$

2. (A) The graph of $y = \sqrt{x} + 5$ is the same as the graph of $y = \sqrt{x}$ shifted upward 5 units, and the graph of $y = \sqrt{x} - 4$ is the same as the graph of $y = \sqrt{x}$ shifted downward 4 units. The figure confirms these conclusions.

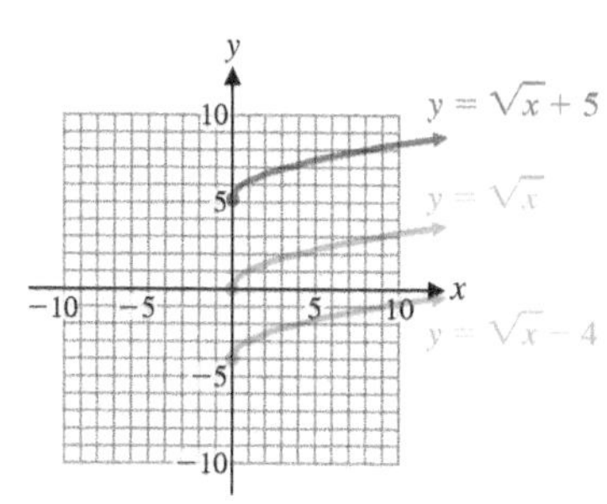

(B) The graph of $y = \sqrt{x + 5}$ is the same as the graph of $y = \sqrt{x}$ shifted to the left 5 units, and the graph of $y = \sqrt{x - 4}$ is the same as the graph of $y = \sqrt{x}$ shifted to the right 4 units. The figure confirms these conclusions.

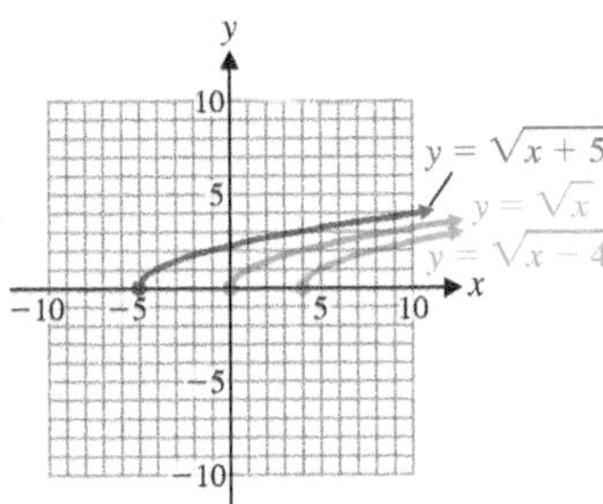

3. $H(x) = \sqrt[3]{x + 3}$, $G(x) = \sqrt[3]{x - 2}$, $M(x) = \sqrt[3]{x} + 2$, $N(x) = \sqrt[3]{x} - 3$

4. (A) The graph of $y = 2x$ is a vertical stretch of the graph of $y = x$, and the graph of $y = 0.5x$ is a vertical shrink of the graph of $y = x$. The figure confirms these conclusions.

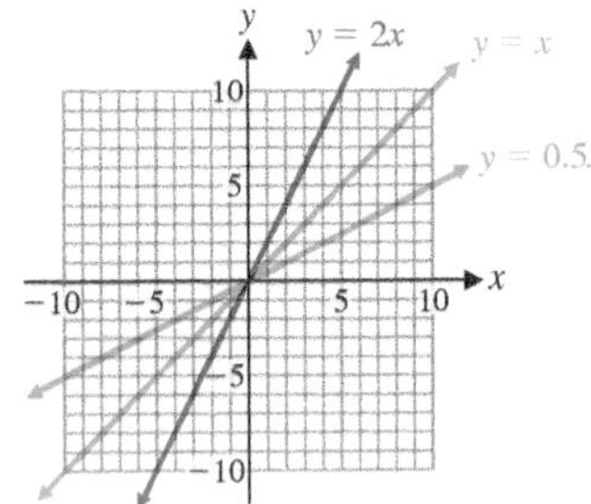

(B) The graph of $y = -0.5x$ is a vertical shrink and a reflection in the x axis of the graph of $y = x$. The figure confirms this conclusion.

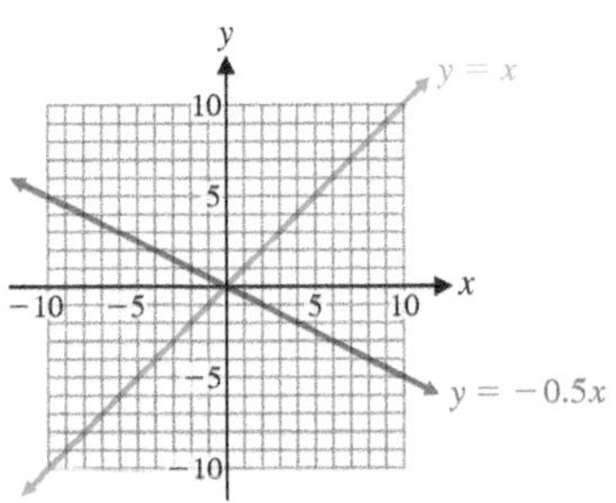

5. The graph of function G is a reflection in the x axis and a horizontal translation of 2 units to the left of the graph of $y = x^3$. An equation for G is $G(x) = -(x + 2)^3$.

6.

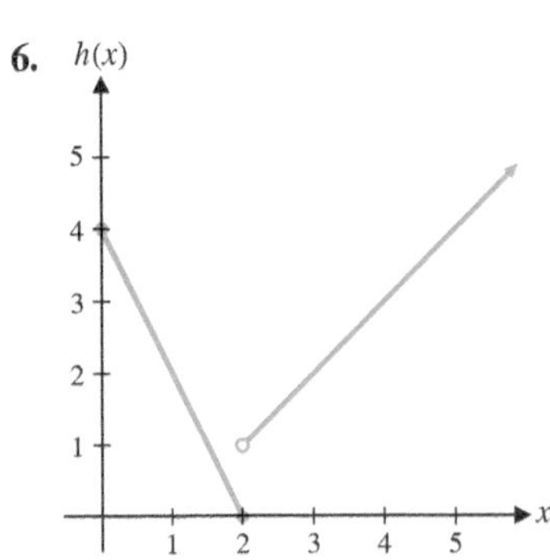

7. $C(x) = \begin{cases} 0.7675x & \text{if } 0 \le x \le 50 \\ 38.375 + 0.64(x - 50) & \text{if } 50 < x \le 200 \\ 134.375 + 0.613(x - 200) & \text{if } 200 < x \end{cases}$

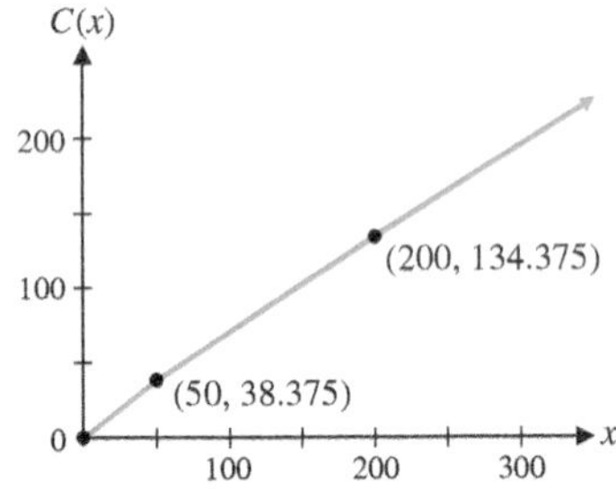

2.3 Quadratic Functions

- Quadratic Functions, Equations, and Inequalities
- Properties of Quadratic Functions and Their Graphs
- Applications

If the degree of a linear function is increased by one, we obtain a *second-degree function,* usually called a *quadratic function,* another basic function that we will need in our library of elementary functions. We will investigate relationships between quadratic functions and the solutions to quadratic equations and inequalities. Other important properties of quadratic functions will also be investigated, including maxima and minima. We will then be in a position to solve important practical problems such as finding production levels that will generate maximum revenue or maximum profit.

Quadratic Functions, Equations, and Inequalities

The graph of the square function $h(x) = x^2$ is shown in Figure 1. Notice that the graph is symmetric with respect to the y axis and that $(0, 0)$ is the lowest point on the graph. Let's explore the effect of applying graph transformations to the graph of h.

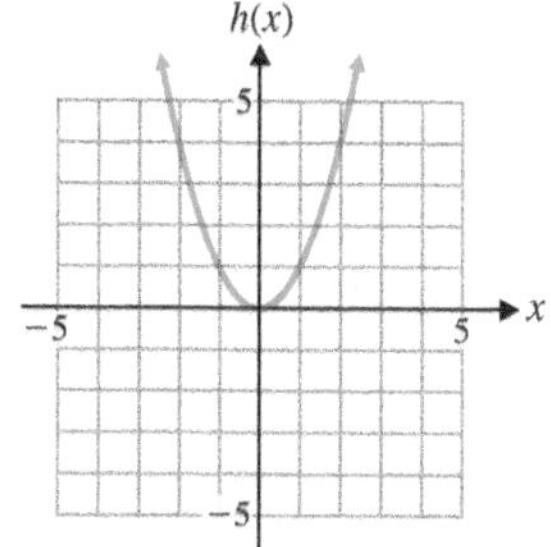

Figure 1 Square function $h(x) = x^2$

Explore and Discuss 1

Indicate how the graph of each function is related to the graph of the function $h(x) = x^2$. Find the highest or lowest point, whichever exists, on each graph.

(A) $f(x) = (x - 3)^2 - 7 = x^2 - 6x + 2$
(B) $g(x) = 0.5(x + 2)^2 + 3 = 0.5x^2 + 2x + 5$
(C) $m(x) = -(x - 4)^2 + 8 = -x^2 + 8x - 8$
(D) $n(x) = -3(x + 1)^2 - 1 = -3x^2 - 6x - 4$

The graphs of the functions in Explore and Discuss 1 are similar in shape to the graph of the square function in Figure 1. All are *parabolas.* The arc of a basketball shot is a parabola. Reflecting telescopes, solar furnaces, and automobile headlights are some of the many applications of parabolas. Each of the functions in Explore and Discuss 1 is a *quadratic function.*

DEFINITION Quadratic Functions

If a, b, and c are real numbers with $a \neq 0$, then the function

$$f(x) = ax^2 + bx + c \qquad \text{Standard form}$$

is a **quadratic function** and its graph is a **parabola**.

CONCEPTUAL INSIGHT

If x is any real number, then $ax^2 + bx + c$ is also a real number. According to the agreement on domain and range in Section 2.1, the domain of a quadratic function is R, the set of real numbers.

We will discuss methods for determining the range of a quadratic function later in this section. Typical graphs of quadratic functions are illustrated in Figure 2.

Reminder

The *union* of two sets A and B, denoted $A \cup B$, is the set of all elements that belong to A or B (or both). So the set of all real numbers x such that $x^2 - 4 \geq 0$ (see Fig. 2A) is $(-\infty, -2] \cup [2, \infty)$.

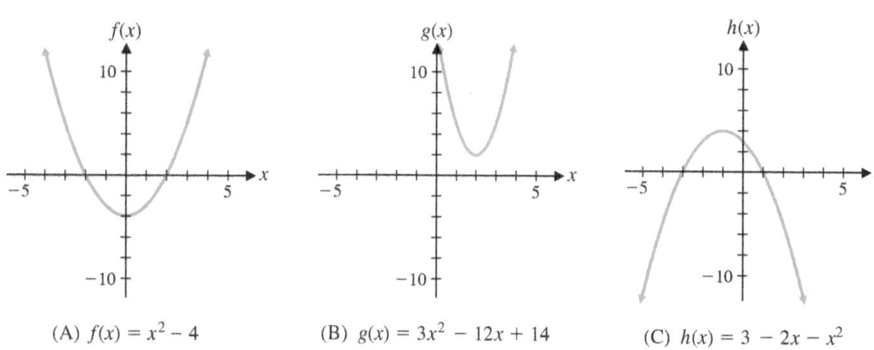

Figure 2 Graphs of quadratic functions

CONCEPTUAL INSIGHT

An x intercept of a function is also called a **zero** of the function. The x intercept of a linear function can be found by solving the linear equation $y = mx + b = 0$ for x, $m \neq 0$ (see Section 1.2). Similarly, the x intercepts of a quadratic function can be found by solving the quadratic equation $y = ax^2 + bx + c = 0$

for x, $a \neq 0$. Several methods for solving quadratic equations are discussed in Appendix B, Section B.7. The most popular of these is the **quadratic formula**.

If $ax^2 + bx + c = 0$, $a \neq 0$, then

$$x = \frac{-b \pm \sqrt{b^2 - 4ac}}{2a}, \text{ provided } b^2 - 4ac \geq 0$$

EXAMPLE 1 **Intercepts, Equations, and Inequalities**

(A) Sketch a graph of $f(x) = -x^2 + 5x + 3$ in a rectangular coordinate system.

(B) Find x and y intercepts algebraically to four decimal places.

(C) Graph $f(x) = -x^2 + 5x + 3$ in a standard viewing window.

(D) Find the x and y intercepts to four decimal places using TRACE and ZERO on your graphing calculator.

(E) Solve the quadratic inequality $-x^2 + 5x + 3 \geq 0$ graphically to four decimal places using the results of parts (A) and (B) or (C) and (D).

(F) Solve the equation $-x^2 + 5x + 3 = 4$ graphically to four decimal places using INTERSECT on your graphing calculator.

SOLUTION

(A) Hand-sketch a graph of f by drawing a smooth curve through the plotted points (Fig. 3).

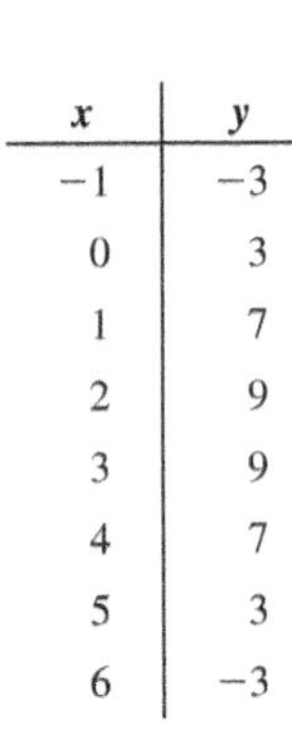

x	y
−1	−3
0	3
1	7
2	9
3	9
4	7
5	3
6	−3

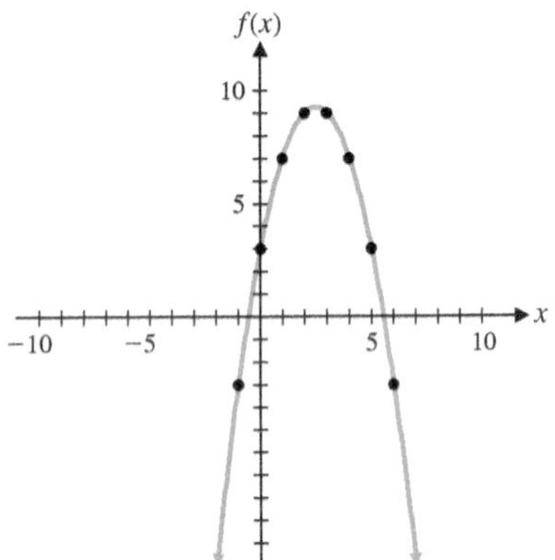

Figure 3

(B) Find intercepts algebraically:

y intercept: $f(0) = -(0)^2 + 5(0) + 3 = 3$

x intercepts: $f(x) = -x^2 + 5x + 3 = 0$ Use the quadratic formula.

$$x = \frac{-b \pm \sqrt{b^2 - 4ac}}{2a}$$ Substitute $a = -1$, $b = 5$, $c = 3$.

$$x = \frac{-(5) \pm \sqrt{5^2 - 4(-1)(3)}}{2(-1)}$$ Simplify.

$$= \frac{-5 \pm \sqrt{37}}{-2} = -0.5414 \quad \text{or} \quad 5.5414$$

(C) Use in a graphing calculator (Fig. 4).

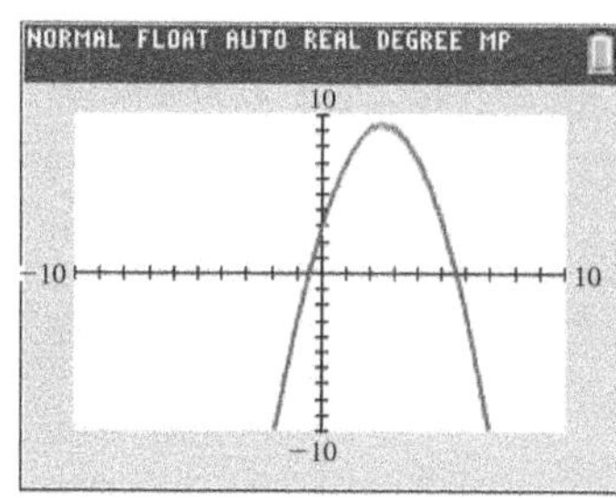

Figure 4

(D) Find intercepts using a graphing calculator (Fig. 5).

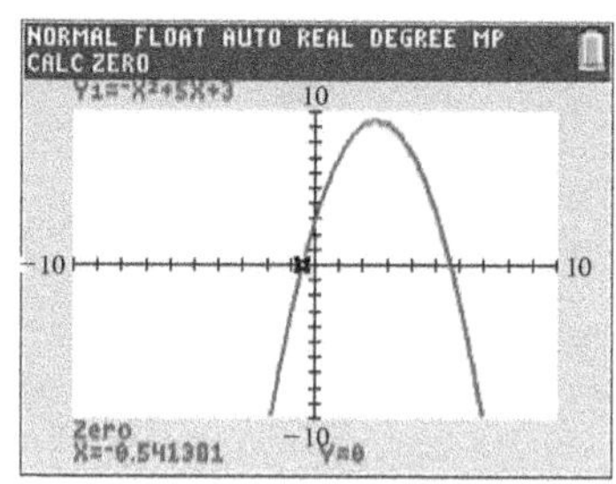

(A) x intercept: -0.5414

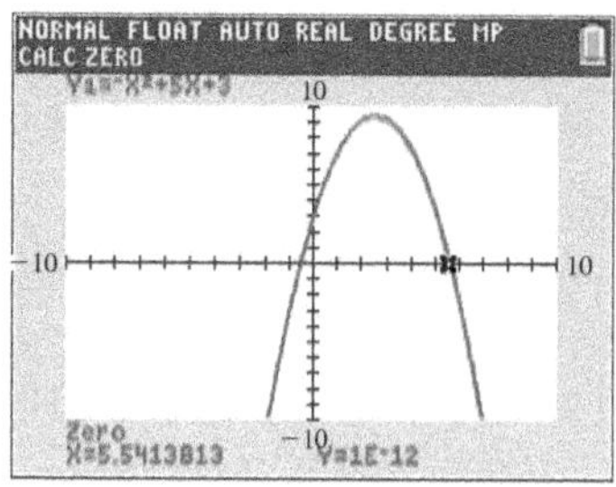

(B) x intercept: 5.5414

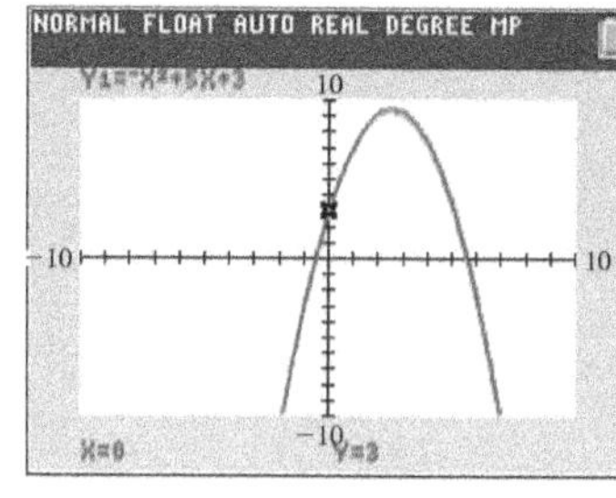

(C) y intercept: 3

Figure 5

(E) Solve $-x^2 + 5x + 3 \geq 0$ graphically: The quadratic inequality

$$-x^2 + 5x + 3 \geq 0$$

holds for those values of x for which the graph of $f(x) = -x^2 + 5x + 3$ in the figures in parts (A) and (C) is at or above the x axis. This happens for x between the two x intercepts [found in part (B) or (D)], including the two x intercepts. The solution set for the quadratic inequality is $-0.5414 \leq x \leq 5.5414$ or $[-0.5414, 5.5414]$.

(F) Solve the equation $-x^2 + 5x + 3 = 4$ using a graphing calculator (Fig. 6).

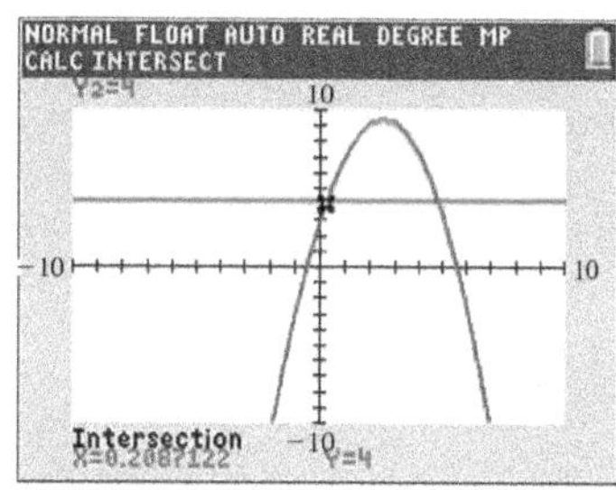

(A) $-x^2 + 5x + 3 = 4$ at $x = 0.2087$

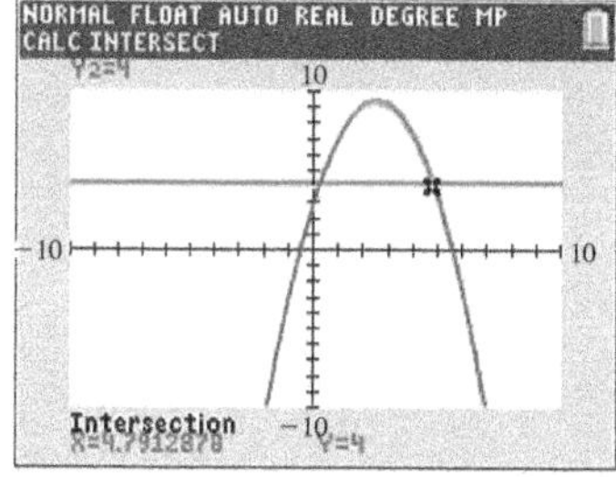

(B) $-x^2 + 5x + 3 = 4$ at $x = 4.7913$

Figure 6

Matched Problem 1

(A) Sketch a graph of $g(x) = 2x^2 - 5x - 5$ in a rectangular coordinate system.

(B) Find x and y intercepts algebraically to four decimal places.

(C) Graph $g(x) = 2x^2 - 5x - 5$ in a standard viewing window.

(D) Find the x and y intercepts to four decimal places using TRACE and the ZERO command on your graphing calculator.

(E) Solve $2x^2 - 5x - 5 \geq 0$ graphically to four decimal places using the results of parts (A) and (B) or (C) and (D).

(F) Solve the equation $2x^2 - 5x - 5 = -3$ graphically to four decimal places using INTERSECT on your graphing calculator.

Explore and Discuss 2

How many x intercepts can the graph of a quadratic function have? How many y intercepts? Explain your reasoning.

Properties of Quadratic Functions and Their Graphs

Many useful properties of the quadratic function can be uncovered by transforming

$$f(x) = ax^2 + bx + c \quad a \neq 0$$

into the **vertex form**

$$f(x) = a(x - h)^2 + k$$

The process of *completing the square* (see Appendix B.7) is central to the transformation. We illustrate the process through a specific example and then generalize the results.

Consider the quadratic function given by

$$f(x) = -2x^2 + 16x - 24 \tag{1}$$

We use completing the square to transform this function into vertex form:

$$\begin{aligned} f(x) &= -2x^2 + 16x - 24 && \text{Factor the coefficient of } x^2 \text{ out of the first two terms.} \\ &= -2(x^2 - 8x) - 24 \\ &= -2(x^2 - 8x + ?) - 24 && \text{Add 16 to complete the square inside the parentheses. Because of the } -2 \text{ outside the parentheses, we have actually added } -32\text{, so we must add 32 to the outside.} \\ &= -2(x^2 - 8x + 16) - 24 + 32 && \text{Factor, simplify} \\ &= -2(x - 4)^2 + 8 && \text{The transformation is complete and can be checked by multiplying out.} \end{aligned}$$

Therefore,

$$f(x) = -2(x - 4)^2 + 8 \tag{2}$$

If $x = 4$, then $-2(x - 4)^2 = 0$ and $f(4) = 8$. For any other value of x, the negative number $-2(x - 4)^2$ is added to 8, making it smaller. Therefore,

$$f(4) = 8$$

is the *maximum value* of $f(x)$ for all x. Furthermore, if we choose any two x values that are the same distance from 4, we will obtain the same function value. For example, $x = 3$ and $x = 5$ are each one unit from $x = 4$ and their function values are

$$f(3) = -2(3 - 4)^2 + 8 = 6$$
$$f(5) = -2(5 - 4)^2 + 8 = 6$$

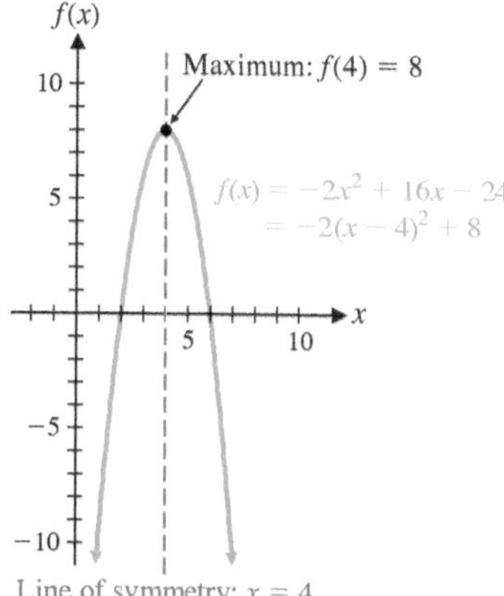

Figure 7 Graph of a quadratic function

Therefore, the vertical line $x = 4$ is a line of symmetry. That is, if the graph of equation (1) is drawn on a piece of paper and the paper is folded along the line $x = 4$, then the two sides of the parabola will match exactly. All these results are illustrated by graphing equations (1) and (2) and the line $x = 4$ simultaneously in the same coordinate system (Fig. 7).

From the preceding discussion, we see that as x moves from left to right, $f(x)$ is increasing on $(-\infty, 4]$, and decreasing on $[4, \infty)$, and that $f(x)$ can assume no value greater than 8. Thus,

$$\text{Range of } f: \quad y \leq 8 \quad \text{or} \quad (-\infty, 8]$$

In general, the graph of a quadratic function is a parabola with line of symmetry parallel to the vertical axis. The lowest or highest point on the parabola, whichever exists, is called the **vertex**. The maximum or minimum value of a quadratic function always occurs at the vertex of the parabola. The line of symmetry through the vertex is called the **axis** of the parabola. In the example above, $x = 4$ is the axis of the parabola and $(4, 8)$ is its vertex.

CONCEPTUAL INSIGHT

Applying the graph transformation properties discussed in Section 2.2 to the transformed equation,

$$\begin{aligned} f(x) &= -2x^2 + 16x - 24 \\ &= -2(x - 4)^2 + 8 \end{aligned}$$

we see that the graph of $f(x) = -2x^2 + 16x - 24$ is the graph of $g(x) = x^2$ vertically stretched by a factor of 2, reflected in the x axis, and shifted to the right 4 units and up 8 units, as shown in Figure 8.

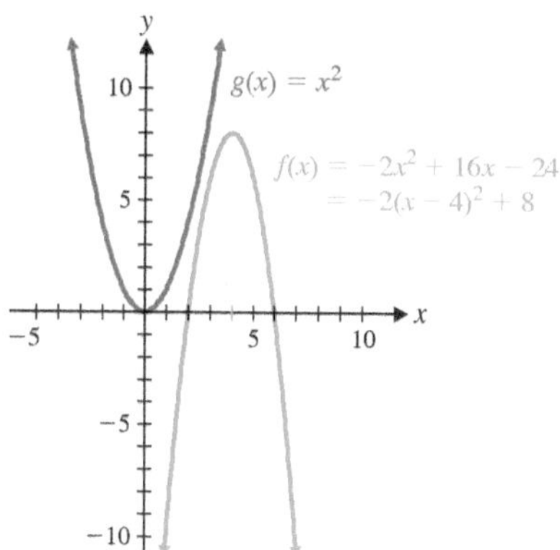

Figure 8 Graph of **f** is the graph of **g** transformed

Note the important results we have obtained from the vertex form of the quadratic function f:

- The vertex of the parabola
- The axis of the parabola
- The maximum value of $f(x)$
- The range of the function f
- The relationship between the graph of $g(x) = x^2$ and the graph of $f(x) = -2x^2 + 16x - 24$

The preceding discussion is generalized to all quadratic functions in the following summary:

SUMMARY Properties of a Quadratic Function and Its Graph

Given a quadratic function and the vertex form obtained by completing the square

$$f(x) = ax^2 + bx + c \qquad a \neq 0 \quad \text{Standard form}$$
$$= a(x - h)^2 + k \qquad \text{Vertex form}$$

we summarize general properties as follows:

1. The graph of f is a parabola that opens upward if $a > 0$, downward if $a < 0$ (Fig. 9).

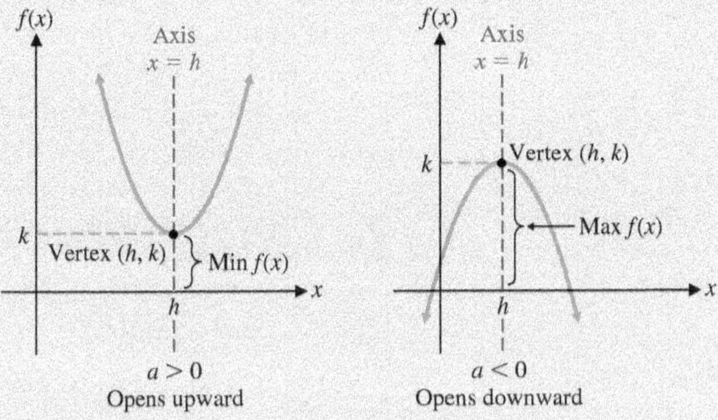

Figure 9

2. Vertex: (h, k) (parabola increases on one side of the vertex and decreases on the other)
3. Axis (of symmetry): $x = h$ (parallel to y axis)
4. $f(h) = k$ is the minimum if $a > 0$ and the maximum if $a < 0$
5. Domain: All real numbers. Range: $(-\infty, k]$ if $a < 0$ or $[k, \infty)$ if $a > 0$
6. The graph of f is the graph of $g(x) = ax^2$ translated horizontally h units and vertically k units.

EXAMPLE 2 **Analyzing a Quadratic Function** Given the quadratic function

$$f(x) = 0.5\,x^2 - 6x + 21$$

(A) Find the vertex form for f.

(B) Find the vertex and the maximum or minimum. State the range of f.

(C) Describe how the graph of function f can be obtained from the graph of $g(x) = x^2$ using transformations.

(D) Sketch a graph of function f in a rectangular coordinate system.

(E) Graph function f using a suitable viewing window.

(F) Find the vertex and the maximum or minimum using the appropriate graphing calculator command.

SOLUTION

(A) Complete the square to find the vertex form:

$$\begin{aligned} f(x) &= 0.5\,x^2 - 6x + 21 \\ &= 0.5(x^2 - 12x + ?) + 21 \\ &= 0.5(x^2 - 12x + 36) + 21 - 18 \\ &= 0.5(x - 6)^2 + 3 \end{aligned}$$

(B) From the vertex form, we see that $h = 6$ and $k = 3$. Thus, vertex: $(6, 3)$; minimum: $f(6) = 3$; range: $y \geq 3$ or $[3, \infty)$.

(C) The graph of $f(x) = 0.5(x - 6)^2 + 3$ is the same as the graph of $g(x) = x^2$ vertically shrunk by a factor of 0.5, and shifted to the right 6 units and up 3 units.

(D) Graph in a rectangular coordinate system (Fig. 10).

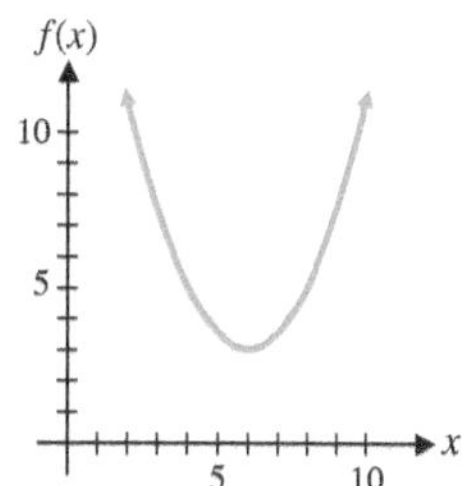

Figure 10

(E) Use a graphing calculator (Fig. 11).

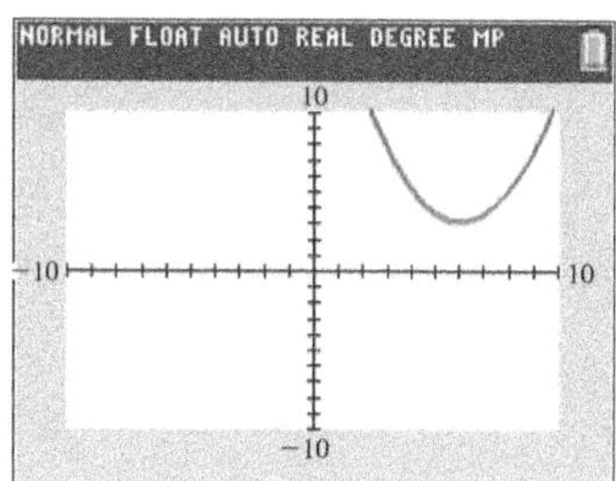

Figure 11

(F) Find the vertex and minimum using the minimum command (Fig. 12).

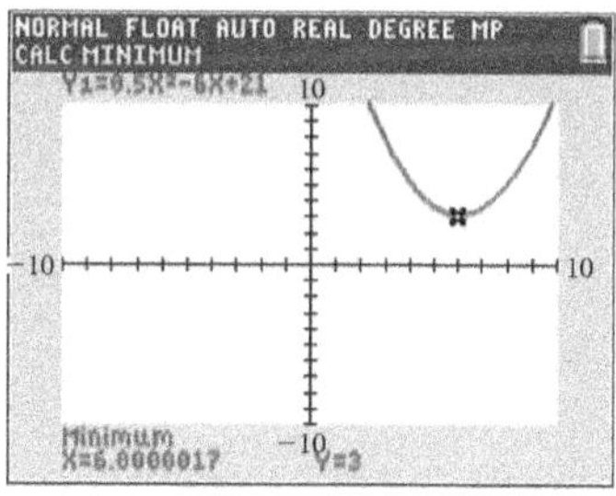

Figure 12

Vertex: $(6, 3)$; minimum: $f(6) = 3$

Matched Problem 2 Given the quadratic function $f(x) = -0.25x^2 - 2x + 2$

(A) Find the vertex form for f.

(B) Find the vertex and the maximum or minimum. State the range of f.

(C) Describe how the graph of function f can be obtained from the graph of $g(x) = x^2$ using transformations.

(D) Sketch a graph of function f in a rectangular coordinate system.

(E) Graph function f using a suitable viewing window.

(F) Find the vertex and the maximum or minimum using the appropriate graphing calculator command.

Applications

EXAMPLE 3 **Maximum Revenue** This is a continuation of Example 7 in Section 2.1. Recall that the financial department in the company that produces a digital camera arrived at the following price–demand function and the corresponding revenue function:

$$p(x) = 94.8 - 5x \qquad \text{Price–demand function}$$

$$R(x) = xp(x) = x(94.8 - 5x) \qquad \text{Revenue function}$$

where $p(x)$ is the wholesale price per camera at which x million cameras can be sold and $R(x)$ is the corresponding revenue (in millions of dollars). Both functions have domain $1 \le x \le 15$.

(A) Find the value of x to the nearest thousand cameras that will generate the maximum revenue. What is the maximum revenue to the nearest thousand dollars? Solve the problem algebraically by completing the square.

(B) What is the wholesale price per camera (to the nearest dollar) that generates the maximum revenue?

(C) Graph the revenue function using an appropriate viewing window.

(D) Find the value of x to the nearest thousand cameras that will generate the maximum revenue. What is the maximum revenue to the nearest thousand dollars? Solve the problem graphically using the maximum command.

SOLUTION

(A) Algebraic solution:

$$\begin{aligned} R(x) &= x(94.8 - 5x) \\ &= -5x^2 + 94.8x \\ &= -5(x^2 - 18.96x + ?) \\ &= -5(x^2 - 18.96x + 89.8704) + 449.352 \\ &= -5(x - 9.48)^2 + 449.352 \end{aligned}$$

The maximum revenue of 449.352 million dollars (\$449,352,000) occurs when $x = 9.480$ million cameras (9,480,000 cameras).

(B) Finding the wholesale price per camera: Use the price–demand function for an output of 9.480 million cameras:

$$\begin{aligned} p(x) &= 94.8 - 5x \\ p(9.480) &= 94.8 - 5(9.480) \\ &= \$47 \text{ per camera} \end{aligned}$$

(C) Use a graphing calculator (Fig. 13).

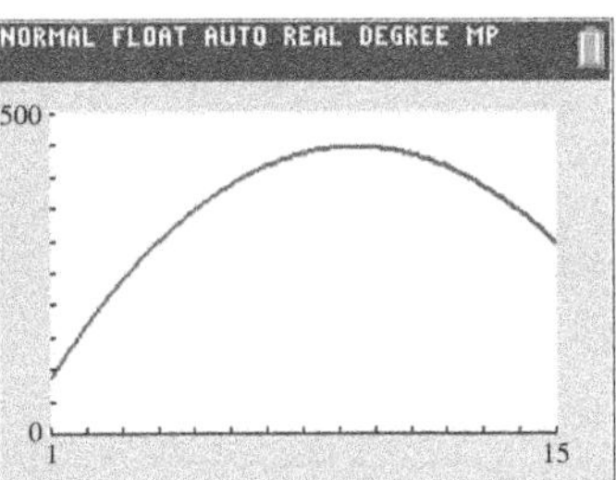

Figure 13

(D) Use the maximum command on a graphing calculator (Fig. 14).

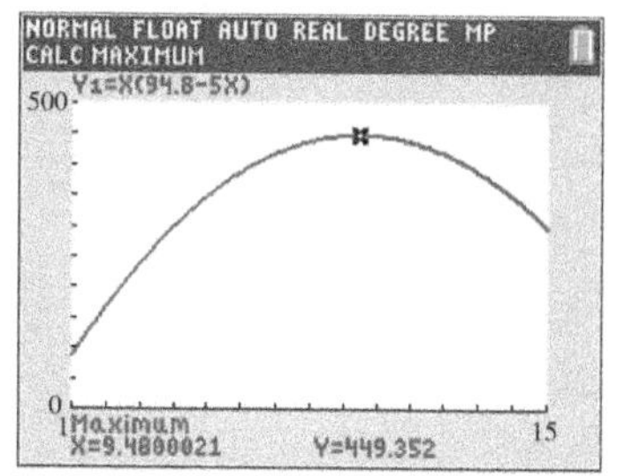

Figure 14

The manufacture and sale of 9.480 million cameras (9,480,000 cameras) will generate a maximum revenue of 449.352 million dollars ($449,352,000).

Matched Problem 3 The financial department in Example 3, using statistical and analytical techniques (see Matched Problem 7 in Section 2.1), arrived at the cost function

$$C(x) = 156 + 19.7x \quad \text{Cost function}$$

where $C(x)$ is the cost (in millions of dollars) for manufacturing and selling x million cameras.

(A) Using the revenue function from Example 3 and the preceding cost function, write an equation for the profit function.

(B) Find the value of x to the nearest thousand cameras that will generate the maximum profit. What is the maximum profit to the nearest thousand dollars? Solve the problem algebraically by completing the square.

(C) What is the wholesale price per camera (to the nearest dollar) that generates the maximum profit?

(D) Graph the profit function using an appropriate viewing window.

(E) Find the output to the nearest thousand cameras that will generate the maximum profit. What is the maximum profit to the nearest thousand dollars? Solve the problem graphically using the maximum command.

EXAMPLE 4 **Break-Even Analysis** Use the revenue function from Example 3 and the cost function from Matched Problem 3:

$$R(x) = x(94.8 - 5x) \quad \text{Revenue function}$$

$$C(x) = 156 + 19.7x \quad \text{Cost function}$$

Both have domain $1 \le x \le 15$.

(A) Sketch the graphs of both functions in the same coordinate system.

(B) **Break-even points** are the production levels at which $R(x) = C(x)$. Find the break-even points algebraically to the nearest thousand cameras.

(C) Plot both functions simultaneously in the same viewing window.

(D) Use INTERSECT to find the break-even points graphically to the nearest thousand cameras.

(E) Recall that a loss occurs if $R(x) < C(x)$ and a profit occurs if $R(x) > C(x)$. For what values of x (to the nearest thousand cameras) will a loss occur? A profit?

SOLUTION

(A) Sketch the functions (Fig. 15).

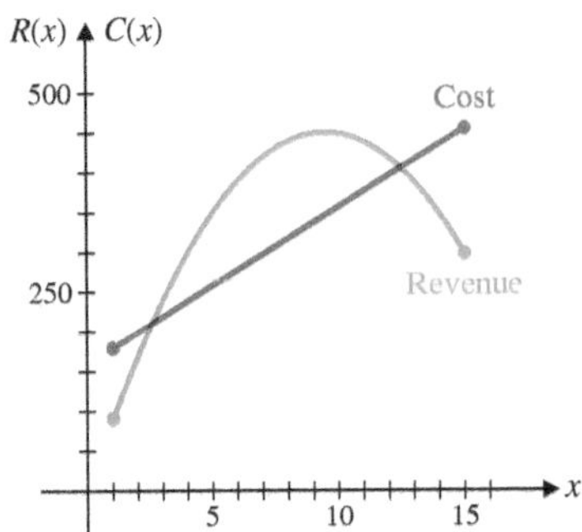

Figure 15

(B) Find x such that $R(x) = C(x)$:

$$x(94.8 - 5x) = 156 + 19.7x \quad \text{Simplify.}$$

$$-5x^2 + 75.1x - 156 = 0 \quad \text{Use the quadratic formula.}$$

$$x = \frac{-75.1 \pm \sqrt{75.1^2 - 4(-5)(-156)}}{2(-5)}$$

$$= \frac{-75.1 \pm \sqrt{2{,}520.01}}{-10}$$

$$x = 2.490 \quad \text{and} \quad 12.530$$

The company breaks even at $x = 2.490$ million cameras (2,490,000 cameras) and at $x = 12.530$ million cameras (12,530,000 cameras).

(C) Use a graphing calculator (Fig. 16).

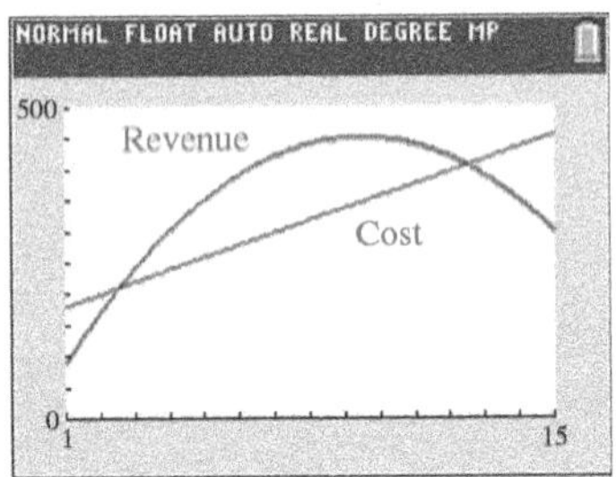

Figure 16

(D) Use INTERSECT on a graphing calculator (Fig. 17).

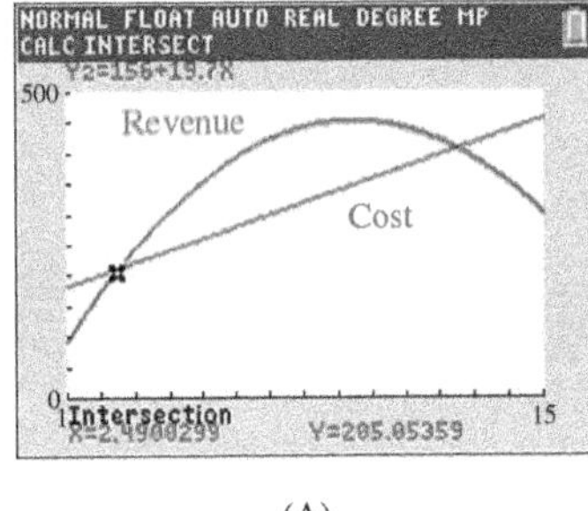

(A)

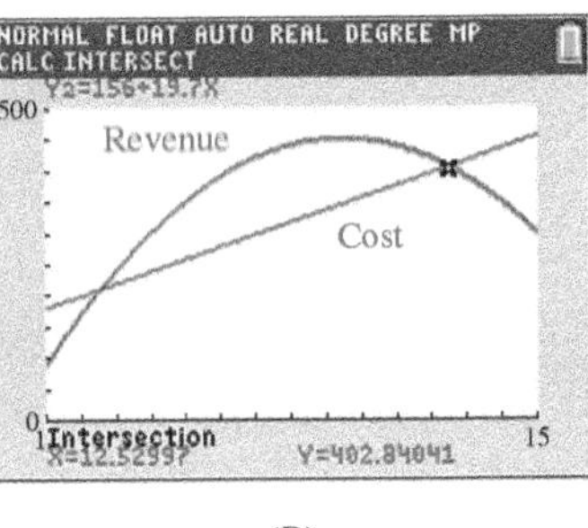

(B)

Figure 17

The company breaks even at $x = 2.490$ million cameras (2,490,000 cameras) and at $x = 12.530$ million cameras (12,530,000 cameras).

(E) Use the results from parts (A) and (B) or (C) and (D):

$$\text{Loss:} \quad 1 \le x < 2.490 \quad \text{or} \quad 12.530 < x \le 15$$

$$\text{Profit:} \quad 2.490 < x < 12.530$$

Matched Problem 4 Use the profit equation from Matched Problem 3:

$$\begin{aligned} P(x) &= R(x) - C(x) \\ &= -5x^2 + 75.1x - 156 \qquad \text{Profit function} \end{aligned}$$

$$\text{Domain:} \quad 1 \le x \le 15$$

(A) Sketch a graph of the profit function in a rectangular coordinate system.

(B) Break-even points occur when $P(x) = 0$. Find the break-even points algebraically to the nearest thousand cameras.

(C) Plot the profit function in an appropriate viewing window.

(D) Find the break-even points graphically to the nearest thousand cameras.

(E) A loss occurs if $P(x) < 0$, and a profit occurs if $P(x) > 0$. For what values of x (to the nearest thousand cameras) will a loss occur? A profit?

A visual inspection of the plot of a data set might indicate that a parabola would be a better model of the data than a straight line. In that case, rather than using linear regression to fit a linear model to the data, we would use **quadratic regression** on a graphing calculator to find the function of the form $y = ax^2 + bx + c$ that best fits the data.

EXAMPLE 5 **Outboard Motors** Table 1 gives performance data for a boat powered by an Evinrude outboard motor. Use quadratic regression to find the best model of the form $y = ax^2 + bx + c$ for fuel consumption y (in miles per gallon) as a function of speed x (in miles per hour). Estimate the fuel consumption (to one decimal place) at a speed of 12 miles per hour.

Table 1

rpm	mph	mpg
2,500	10.3	4.1
3,000	18.3	5.6
3,500	24.6	6.6
4,000	29.1	6.4
4,500	33.0	6.1
5,000	36.0	5.4
5,400	38.9	4.9

SOLUTION Enter the data in a graphing calculator (Fig. 18A) and find the quadratic regression equation (Fig. 18B). The data set and the regression equation are graphed in Figure 18C. Using trace, we see that the estimated fuel consumption at a speed of 12 mph is 4.5 mpg.

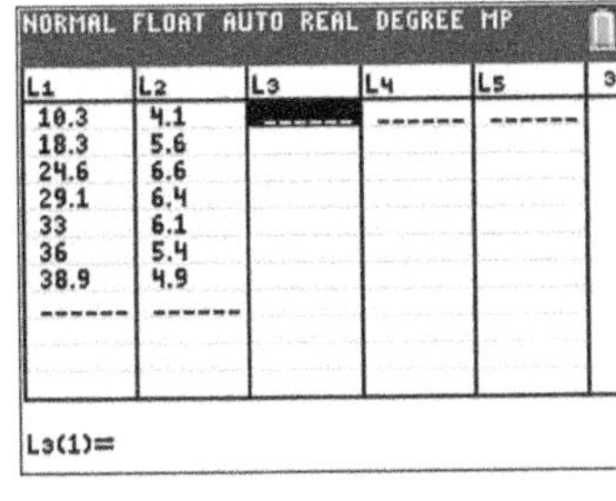

(A)

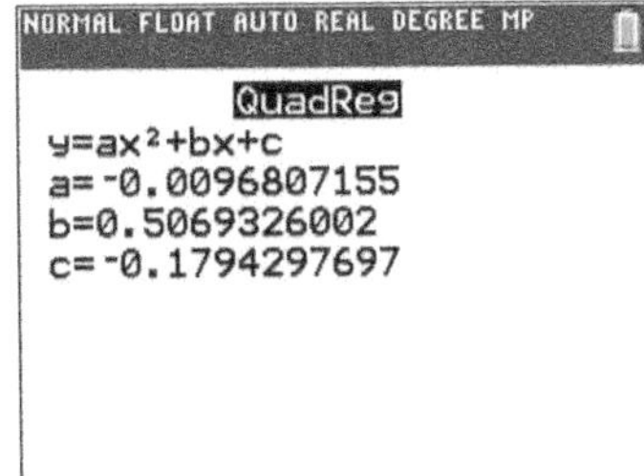

(B)

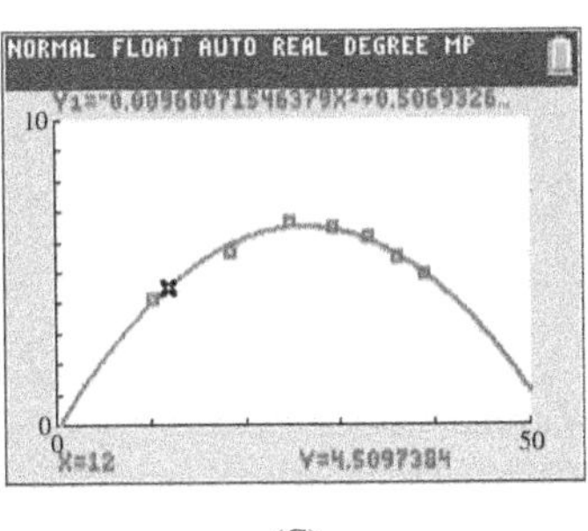

(C)

Figure 18

Matched Problem 5 Refer to Table 1. Use quadratic regression to find the best model of the form $y = ax^2 + bx + c$ for boat speed y (in miles per hour) as a function of engine speed x (in revolutions per minute). Estimate the boat speed (in miles per hour, to one decimal place) at an engine speed of 3,400 rpm.

Exercises 2.3

A *In Problems 1–8, find the vertex form of each quadratic function by completing the square.*

1. $f(x) = x^2 - 10x$

2. $f(x) = x^2 + 16x$

3. $f(x) = x^2 + 20x + 50$

4. $f(x) = x^2 - 12x - 8$

5. $f(x) = -2x^2 + 4x - 5$

6. $f(x) = 4x^2 - 24x + 26$

7. $f(x) = 2x^2 + 2x + 1$

8. $f(x) = -5x^2 + 15x - 11$

In Problems 9–12, write a brief verbal description of the relationship between the graph of the indicated function and the graph of $y = x^2$.

9. $f(x) = x^2 - 4x + 3$

10. $g(x) = x^2 - 2x - 5$

11. $m(x) = -x^2 + 10x - 16$

12. $n(x) = -x^2 + 8x - 9$

13. Match each equation with a graph of one of the functions f, g, m, or n in the figure.

(A) $y = -(x + 2)^2 + 1$ (B) $y = (x - 2)^2 - 1$

(C) $y = (x + 2)^2 - 1$ (D) $y = -(x - 2)^2 + 1$

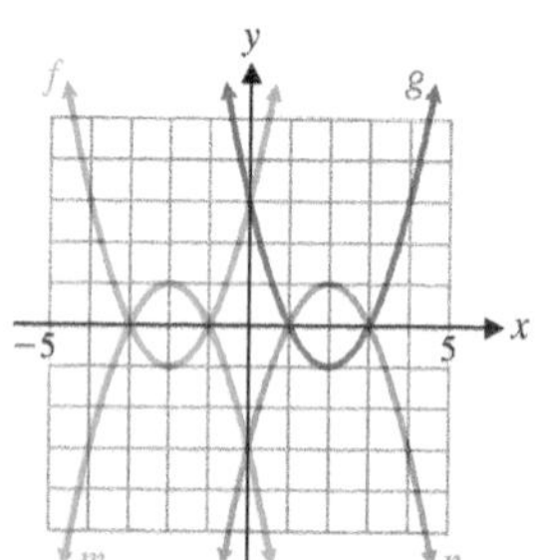

14. Match each equation with a graph of one of the functions f, g, m, or n in the figure.

(A) $y = (x - 3)^2 - 4$ (B) $y = -(x + 3)^2 + 4$

(C) $y = -(x - 3)^2 + 4$ (D) $y = (x + 3)^2 - 4$

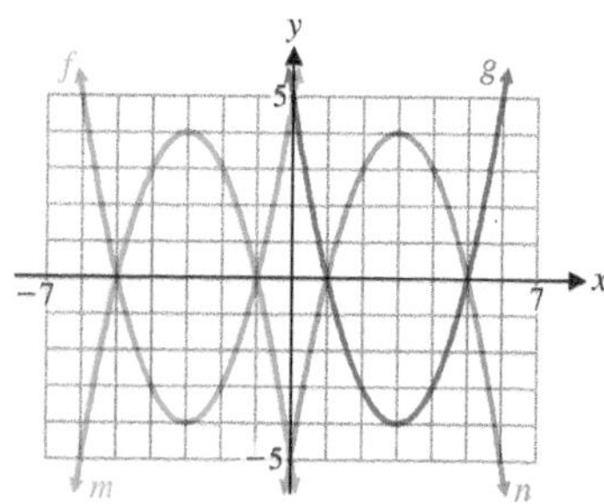

For the functions indicated in Problems 15–18, find each of the following to the nearest integer by referring to the graphs for Problems 13 and 14.

(A) *Intercepts* (B) *Vertex*

(C) *Maximum or minimum* (D) *Range*

15. Function n in the figure for Problem 13

16. Function m in the figure for Problem 14

17. Function f in the figure for Problem 13

18. Function g in the figure for Problem 14

In Problems 19–22, find each of the following:

(A) *Intercepts* (B) *Vertex*

(C) *Maximum or minimum* (D) *Range*

19. $f(x) = -(x - 3)^2 + 2$

20. $g(x) = -(x + 2)^2 + 3$

21. $m(x) = (x + 1)^2 - 2$

22. $n(x) = (x - 4)^2 - 3$

B *In Problems 23–26, write an equation for each graph in the form $y = a(x - h)^2 + k$, where a is either 1 or -1 and h and k are integers.*

23.

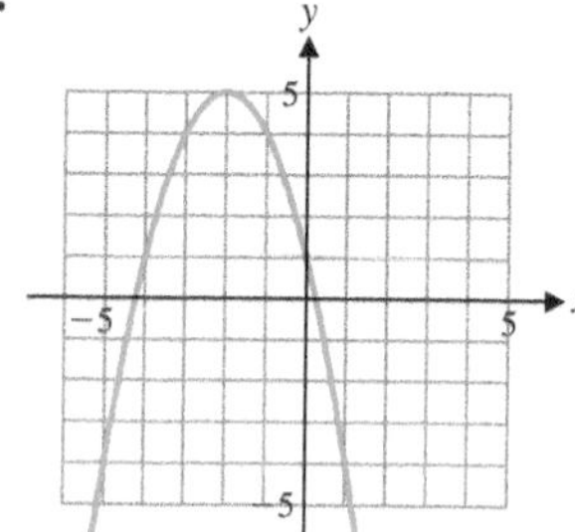

24.

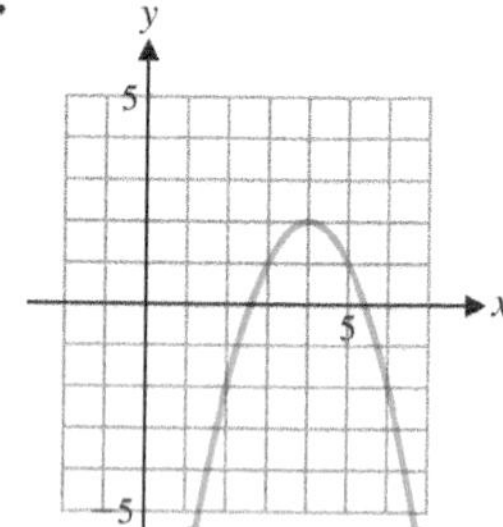

25.

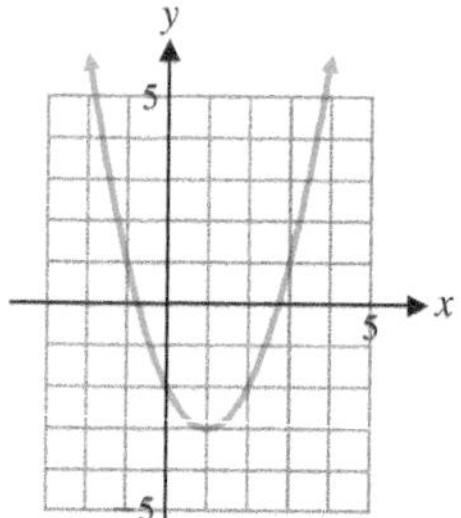

26.

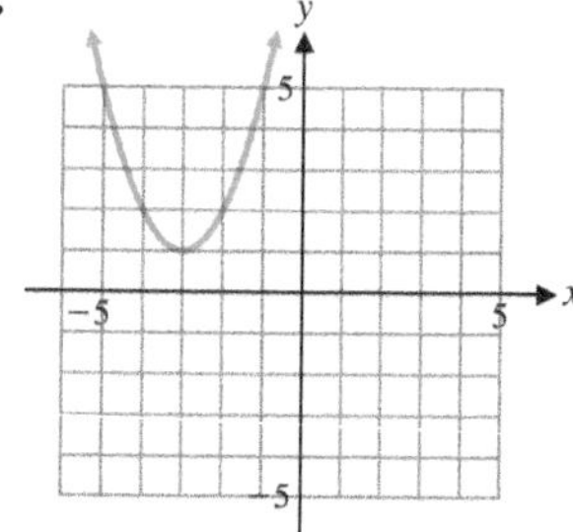

In Problems 27–32, find the vertex form for each quadratic function. Then find each of the following:

(A) *Intercepts* (B) *Vertex*

(C) *Maximum or minimum* (D) *Range*

27. $f(x) = x^2 - 8x + 12$

28. $g(x) = x^2 - 12x + 27$

29. $r(x) = -4x^2 + 16x - 15$

30. $s(x) = -4x^2 - 8x - 3$

31. $u(x) = 0.5x^2 - 2x + 5$

32. $v(x) = 0.5x^2 + 6x + 19$

33. Let $f(x) = 0.3x^2 - x - 8$. Solve each equation graphically to two decimal places.

(A) $f(x) = 4$ (B) $f(x) = -1$ (C) $f(x) = -9$

34. Let $g(x) = -0.6x^2 + 3x + 4$. Solve each equation graphically to two decimal places.
(A) $g(x) = -2$ (B) $g(x) = 5$ (C) $g(x) = 8$

35. Let $f(x) = 125x - 6x^2$. Find the maximum value of f to four decimal places graphically.

36. Let $f(x) = 100x - 7x^2 - 10$. Find the maximum value of f to four decimal places graphically.

C *In Problems 37–40, first write each function in vertex form; then find each of the following (to two decimal places):*

(A) *Intercepts* (B) *Vertex*

(C) *Maximum or minimum* (D) *Range*

37. $g(x) = 0.25x^2 - 1.5x - 7$

38. $m(x) = 0.20x^2 - 1.6x - 1$

39. $f(x) = -0.12x^2 + 0.96x + 1.2$

40. $n(x) = -0.25x^2 - 4.50x - 9.75$

In Problems 41–44, use interval notation to write the solution set of the inequality.

41. $(x - 3)(x + 5) > 0$

42. $(x + 6)(x - 3) < 0$

43. $x^2 + x - 6 \le 0$

44. $x^2 + 9x + 14 \ge 0$

Solve Problems 45–50 graphically to two decimal places using a graphing calculator.

45. $2 - 5x - x^2 = 0$

46. $7 + 3x - 2x^2 = 0$

47. $1.9x^2 - 1.5x - 5.6 < 0$

48. $3.4 + 2.9x - 1.1x^2 \ge 0$

49. $2.8 + 3.1x - 0.9x^2 \le 0$

50. $1.8x^2 - 3.1x - 4.9 > 0$

51. Given that f is a quadratic function with maximum $f(x) = f(-4) = -9$, find the axis, vertex, range, and x intercepts.

52. Given that f is a quadratic function with minimum $f(x) = f(3) = 7$, find the axis, vertex, range, and x intercepts.

In Problems 53–56,

(A) *Graph f and g in the same coordinate system.*

(B) *Solve $f(x) = g(x)$ algebraically to two decimal places.*

(C) *Solve $f(x) > g(x)$ using parts (A) and (B).*

(D) *Solve $f(x) < g(x)$ using parts (A) and (B).*

53. $f(x) = -0.4x(x - 10)$
$g(x) = 0.3x + 5$
$0 \le x \le 10$

54. $f(x) = -0.7x(x - 7)$
$g(x) = 0.5x + 3.5$
$0 \le x \le 7$

55. $f(x) = -0.9x^2 + 7.2x$
$g(x) = 1.2x + 5.5$
$0 \le x \le 8$

56. $f(x) = -0.7x^2 + 6.3x$
$g(x) = 1.1x + 4.8$
$0 \le x \le 9$

57. How can you tell from the graph of a quadratic function whether it has exactly one real zero?

58. How can you tell from the graph of a quadratic function whether it has no real zeros?

59. How can you tell from the standard form $y = ax^2 + bx + c$ whether a quadratic function has two real zeros?

60. How can you tell from the standard form $y = ax^2 + bx + c$ whether a quadratic function has exactly one real zero?

61. How can you tell from the vertex form $y = a(x - h)^2 + k$ whether a quadratic function has no real zeros?

62. How can you tell from the vertex form $y = a(x - h)^2 + k$ whether a quadratic function has two real zeros?

In Problems 63 and 64, assume that a, b, c, h, and k are constants with $a \ne 0$ such that

$$ax^2 + bx + c = a(x - h)^2 + k$$

for all real numbers x.

63. Show that $h = -\dfrac{b}{2a}$.

64. Show that $k = \dfrac{4ac - b^2}{4a}$.

Applications

65. **Tire mileage.** An automobile tire manufacturer collected the data in the table relating tire pressure x (in pounds per square inch) and mileage (in thousands of miles):

x	Mileage
28	45
30	52
32	55
34	51
36	47

A mathematical model for the data is given by

$$f(x) = -0.518x^2 + 33.3x - 481$$

(A) Complete the following table. Round values of $f(x)$ to one decimal place.

x	Mileage	$f(x)$
28	45	
30	52	
32	55	
34	51	
36	47	

(B) Sketch the graph of f and the mileage data in the same coordinate system.

(C) Use the modeling function $f(x)$ to estimate the mileage for a tire pressure of 31 lbs/sq in. and for 35 lbs/sq in. Round answers to two decimal places.

(D) Write a brief description of the relationship between tire pressure and mileage.

66. Automobile production. The table shows the retail market share of passenger cars (excluding minivehicles) from Toyota Motor Corporation as a percentage of the Japanese market.

Year	Market Share
1985	41.8%
1990	41.9%
1995	40.0%
2000	43.2%
2005	43.6%
2010	48.5%

A mathematical model for this data is given by

$$f(x) = 0.0237x^2 - 0.59x + 44.52$$

where $x = 0$ corresponds to 1980.

(A) Complete the following table. Round values of $f(x)$ to two decimal places.

x	Market Share	$f(x)$
5	41.8	
10	41.9	
15	40.0	
20	43.2	
25	43.6	
30	48.5	

(B) Sketch the graph of f and the market share data in the same coordinate system.

(C) Use values of the modeling function f to estimate Toyota's market share in 2020 and in 2023.

(D) Write a brief verbal description of Toyota's market share from 1985 to 2010.

**67. Tire mileage.** Using quadratic regression on a graphing calculator, show that the quadratic function that best fits the data on tire mileage in Problem 65 is

$$f(x) = -0.518x^2 + 33.3x - 481$$

**68. Automobile production.** Using quadratic regression on a graphing calculator, show that the quadratic function that best fits the data on market share in Problem 66 is

$$f(x) = 0.0237x^2 - 0.59x + 44.52$$

69. Revenue. The marketing research department for a company that manufactures and sells memory chips for microcomputers established the following price–demand and revenue functions:

$p(x) = 75 - 3x$ Price–demand function

$R(x) = xp(x) = x(75 - 3x)$ Revenue function

where $p(x)$ is the wholesale price in dollars at which x million chips can be sold, and $R(x)$ is in millions of dollars. Both functions have domain $1 \le x \le 20$.

(A) Sketch a graph of the revenue function in a rectangular coordinate system.

(B) Find the value of x that will produce the maximum revenue. What is the maximum revenue?

(C) What is the wholesale price per chip that produces the maximum revenue?

70. Revenue. The marketing research department for a company that manufactures and sells notebook computers established the following price–demand and revenue functions:

$p(x) = 2{,}000 - 60x$ Price–demand function

$R(x) = xp(x)$ Revenue function

$= x(2{,}000 - 60x)$

where $p(x)$ is the wholesale price in dollars at which x thousand computers can be sold, and $R(x)$ is in thousands of dollars. Both functions have domain $1 \le x \le 25$.

(A) Sketch a graph of the revenue function in a rectangular coordinate system.

(B) Find the value of x that will produce the maximum revenue. What is the maximum revenue to the nearest thousand dollars?

(C) What is the wholesale price per computer (to the nearest dollar) that produces the maximum revenue?

71. Break-even analysis. Use the revenue function from Problem 69 and the given cost function:

$R(x) = x(75 - 3x)$ Revenue function

$C(x) = 125 + 16x$ Cost function

where x is in millions of chips, and $R(x)$ and $C(x)$ are in millions of dollars. Both functions have domain $1 \le x \le 20$.

(A) Sketch a graph of both functions in the same rectangular coordinate system.

(B) Find the break-even points to the nearest thousand chips.

(C) For what values of x will a loss occur? A profit?

72. Break-even analysis. Use the revenue function from Problem 70, and the given cost function:

$R(x) = x(2{,}000 - 60x)$ Revenue function

$C(x) = 4{,}000 + 500x$ Cost function

where x is thousands of computers, and $C(x)$ and $R(x)$ are in thousands of dollars. Both functions have domain $1 \le x \le 25$.

(A) Sketch a graph of both functions in the same rectangular coordinate system.

(B) Find the break-even points.

(C) For what values of x will a loss occur? A profit?

73. Profit-loss analysis. Use the revenue and cost functions from Problem 71:

$R(x) = x(75 - 3x)$ Revenue function

$C(x) = 125 + 16x$ Cost function

where x is in millions of chips, and $R(x)$ and $C(x)$ are in millions of dollars. Both functions have domain $1 \le x \le 20$.

(A) Form a profit function P, and graph R, C, and P in the same rectangular coordinate system.

(B) Discuss the relationship between the intersection points of the graphs of R and C and the x intercepts of P.

(C) Find the x intercepts of P and the break-even points to the nearest thousand chips.

(D) Find the value of x (to the nearest thousand chips) that produces the maximum profit. Find the maximum profit (to the nearest thousand dollars), and compare with Problem 69B.

74. Profit-loss analysis. Use the revenue function from Problem 70 and the given cost function:

$$R(x) = x(2{,}000 - 60x) \quad \text{Revenue function}$$
$$C(x) = 4{,}000 + 500x \quad \text{Cost function}$$

where x is thousands of computers, and $R(x)$ and $C(x)$ are in thousands of dollars. Both functions have domain $1 \le x \le 25$.

(A) Form a profit function P, and graph R, C, and P in the same rectangular coordinate system.

(B) Discuss the relationship between the intersection points of the graphs of R and C and the x intercepts of P.

(C) Find the x intercepts of P and the break-even points.

(D) Find the value of x that produces the maximum profit. Find the maximum profit and compare with Problem 70B.

75. Medicine. The French physician Poiseuille was the first to discover that blood flows faster near the center of an artery than near the edge. Experimental evidence has shown that the rate of flow v (in centimeters per second) at a point x centimeters from the center of an artery (see the figure) is given by

$$v = f(x) = 1{,}000(0.04 - x^2) \quad 0 \le x \le 0.2$$

Find the distance from the center that the rate of flow is 20 centimeters per second. Round answer to two decimal places.

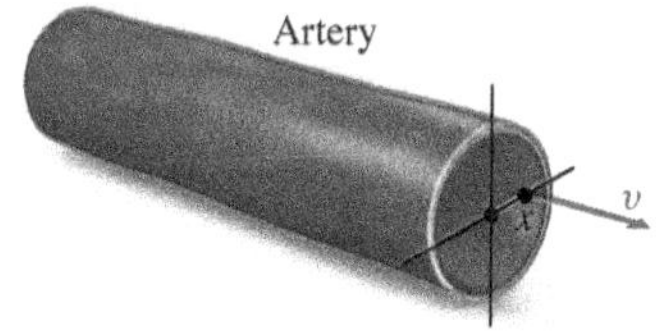

Figure for 75 and 76

76. Medicine. Refer to Problem 75. Find the distance from the center that the rate of flow is 30 centimeters per second. Round answer to two decimal places.

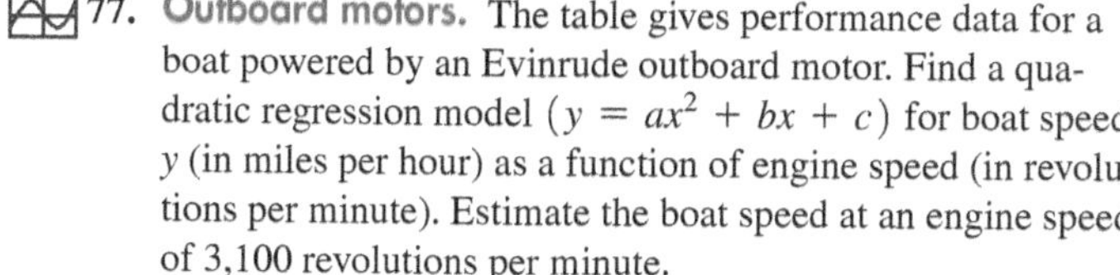

77. Outboard motors. The table gives performance data for a boat powered by an Evinrude outboard motor. Find a quadratic regression model $(y = ax^2 + bx + c)$ for boat speed y (in miles per hour) as a function of engine speed (in revolutions per minute). Estimate the boat speed at an engine speed of 3,100 revolutions per minute.

Table for 77 and 78

rpm	mph	mpg
1,500	4.5	8.2
2,000	5.7	6.9
2,500	7.8	4.8
3,000	9.6	4.1
3,500	13.4	3.7

78. Outboard motors. The table gives performance data for a boat powered by an Evinrude outboard motor. Find a quadratic regression model $(y = ax^2 + bx + c)$ for fuel consumption y (in miles per gallon) as a function of engine speed (in revolutions per minute). Estimate the fuel consumption at an engine speed of 2,300 revolutions per minute.

Answers to Matched Problems

1. (A)

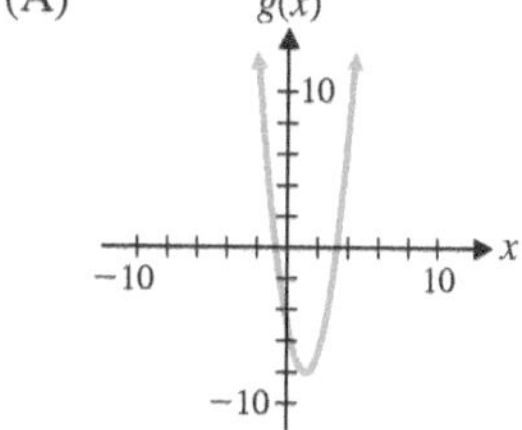

(B) x intercepts: $-0.7656, 3.2656$; y intercept: -5

(C)

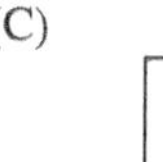

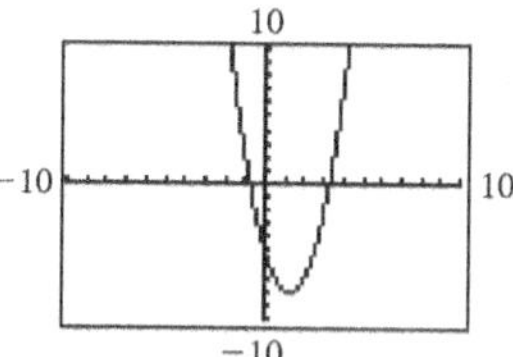

(D) x intercepts: $-0.7656, 3.2656$; y intercept: -5

(E) $x \le -0.7656$ or $x \ge 3.2656$; or $(-\infty, -0.7656]$ or $[3.2656, \infty)$

(F) $x = -0.3508, 2.8508$

2. (A) $f(x) = -0.25(x + 4)^2 + 6$.

(B) Vertex: $(-4, 6)$; maximum: $f(-4) = 6$; range: $y \le 6$ or $(-\infty, 6]$

(C) The graph of $f(x) = -0.25(x + 4)^2 + 6$ is the same as the graph of $g(x) = x^2$ vertically shrunk by a factor of 0.25, reflected in the x axis, and shifted 4 units to the left and 6 units up.

(D)

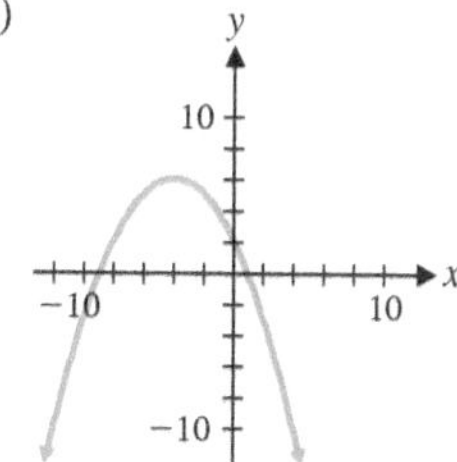

(E)

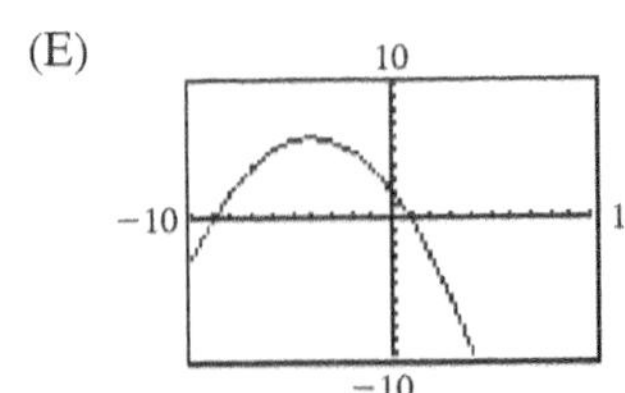

(F) Vertex: $(-4, 6)$; maximum: $f(-4) = 6$

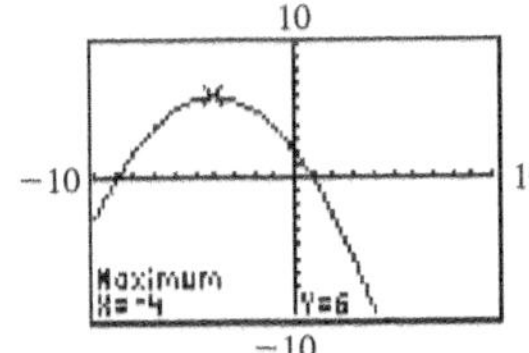

3. (A) $P(x) = R(x) - C(x) = -5x^2 + 75.1x - 156$

   (B) $P(x) = R(x) - C(x) = -5(x - 7.51)^2 + 126.0005$; the manufacture and sale of 7,510,000 cameras will produce a maximum profit of \$126,001,000.

   (C) $p(7.510) = \$57$

   (D)

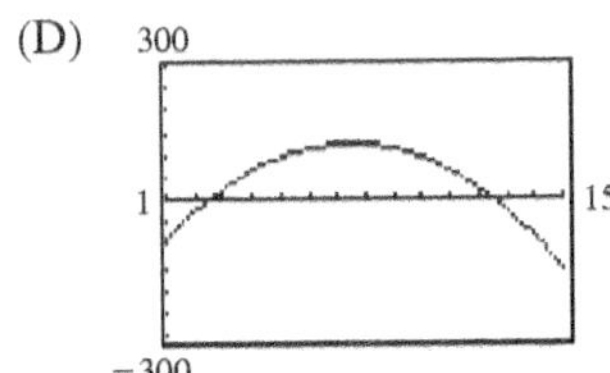

   (E)

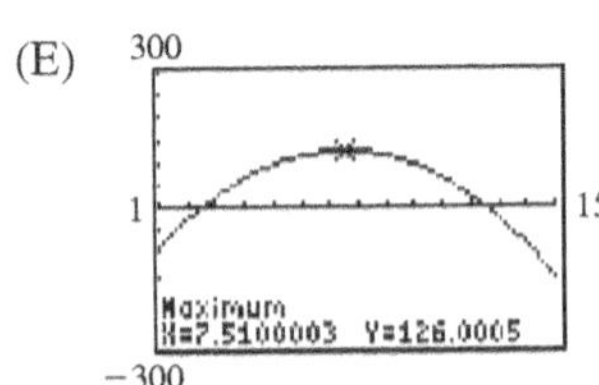

The manufacture and sale of 7,510,000 cameras will produce a maximum profit of \$126,001,000. (Notice that maximum profit does not occur at the same value of x where maximum revenue occurs.)

4. (A)

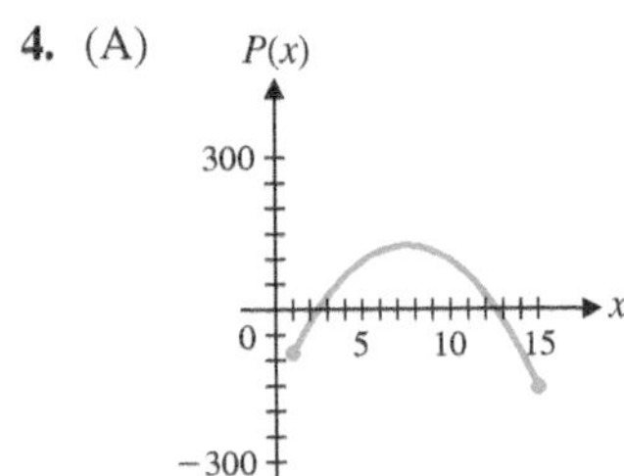

   (B) $x = 2.490$ million cameras (2,490,000 cameras) and $x = 12.530$ million cameras (12,530,000 cameras)

   (C)

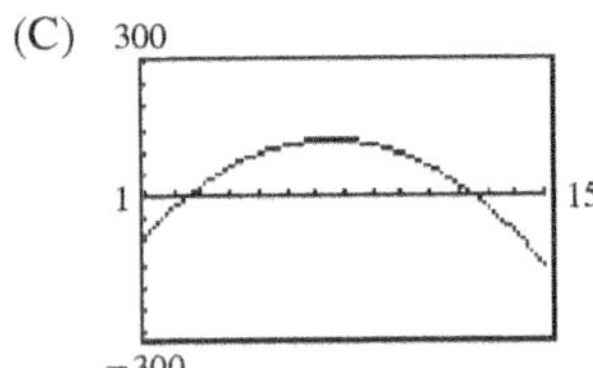

   (D) $x = 2.490$ million cameras (2,490,000 cameras) and $x = 12.530$ million cameras (12,530,000 cameras)

   (E) Loss: $1 \le x < 2.490$ or $12.530 < x \le 15$; profit: $2.490 < x < 12.530$

5.

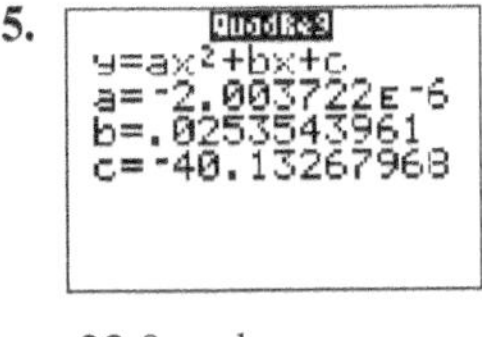

22.9 mph

2.4 Polynomial and Rational Functions

- Polynomial Functions
- Regression Polynomials
- Rational Functions
- Applications

Linear and quadratic functions are special cases of the more general class of *polynomial functions*. Polynomial functions are a special case of an even larger class of functions, the *rational functions*. We will describe the basic features of the graphs of polynomial and rational functions. We will use these functions to solve real-world problems where linear or quadratic models are inadequate, for example, to determine the relationship between length and weight of a species of fish, or to model the training of new employees.

Polynomial Functions

A linear function has the form $f(x) = mx + b$ (where $m \neq 0$) and is a polynomial function of degree 1. A quadratic function has the form $f(x) = ax^2 + bx + c$ (where $a \neq 0$) and is a polynomial function of degree 2. Here is the general definition of a polynomial function.

DEFINITION Polynomial Function

A **polynomial function** is a function that can be written in the form

$$f(x) = a_n x^n + a_{n-1}x^{n-1} + \cdots + a_1 x + a_0$$

for n a nonnegative integer, called the **degree** of the polynomial. The coefficients $a_0, a_1, \ldots, a_n$ are real numbers with $a_n \neq 0$. The **domain** of a polynomial function is the set of all real numbers.

Figure 1 shows graphs of representative polynomial functions of degrees 1 through 6. The figure, which also appears on the inside back cover, suggests some general properties of graphs of polynomial functions.

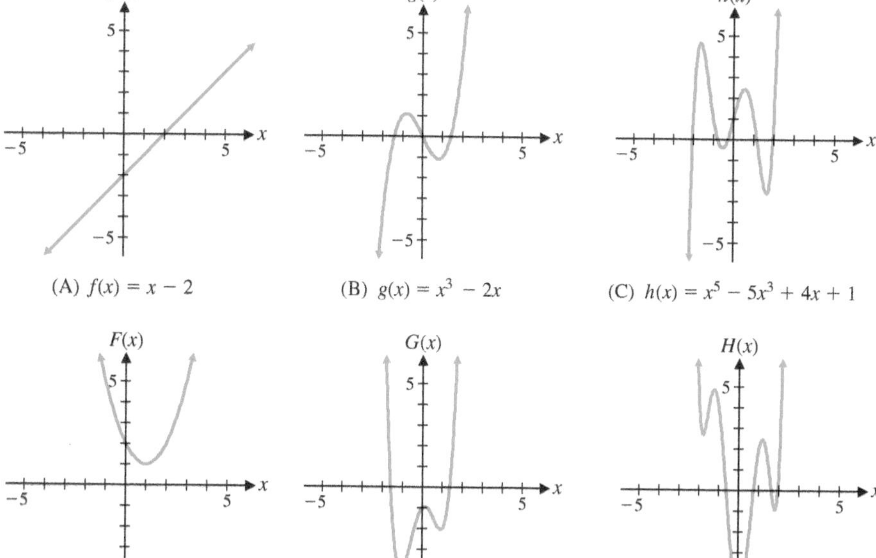

(A) $f(x) = x - 2$ (B) $g(x) = x^3 - 2x$ (C) $h(x) = x^5 - 5x^3 + 4x + 1$

(D) $F(x) = x^2 - 2x + 2$ (E) $G(x) = 2x^4 - 4x^2 + x - 1$ (F) $H(x) = x^6 - 7x^4 + 14x^2 - x - 5$

Figure 1 Graphs of polynomial functions

Notice that the odd-degree polynomial graphs start negative, end positive, and cross the x axis at least once. The even-degree polynomial graphs start positive, end positive, and may not cross the x axis at all. In all cases in Figure 1, the **leading coefficient**—that is, the coefficient of the highest-degree term—was chosen positive. If any leading coefficient had been chosen negative, then we would have a similar graph but reflected in the x axis.

A polynomial of degree n can have, at most, n linear factors. Therefore, the graph of a polynomial function of positive degree n can intersect the x axis at most n times. Note from Figure 1 that a polynomial of degree n may intersect the x axis fewer than n times. An x intercept of a function is also called a **zero** or **root** of the function.

Reminder

Only real numbers can be x intercepts. Functions may have complex zeros that are not real numbers, but such zeros, which are not x intercepts, will not be discussed in this book.

The graph of a polynomial function is **continuous**, with no holes or breaks. That is, the graph can be drawn without removing a pen from the paper. Also, the graph of a polynomial has no sharp corners. Figure 2 shows the graphs of two functions—one that is not continuous, and the other that is continuous but with a sharp corner. Neither function is a polynomial.

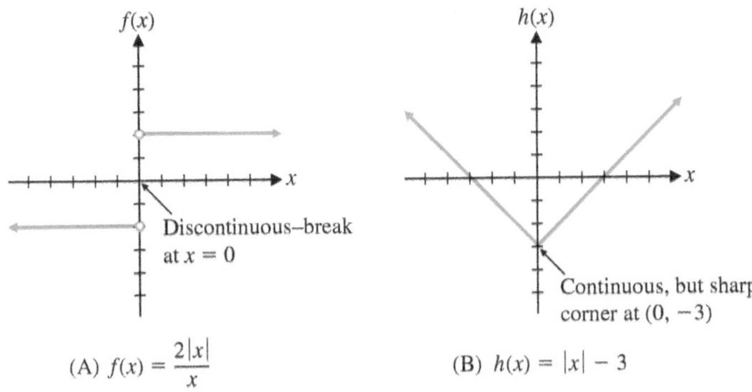

(A) $f(x) = \frac{2|x|}{x}$ (B) $h(x) = |x| - 3$

Figure 2 Discontinuous and sharp-corner functions

Regression Polynomials

In Section A.3, we see that regression techniques can be used to fit a straight line to a set of data. Linear functions are not the only ones that can be applied in this manner. Most graphing calculators have the ability to fit a variety of curves to a given set of data. We will discuss polynomial regression models in this section and other types of regression models in later sections.

EXAMPLE 1 **Estimating the Weight of a Fish** Using the length of a fish to estimate its weight is of interest to both scientists and sport anglers. The data in Table 1 give the average weights of lake trout for certain lengths. Use the data and regression techniques to find a polynomial model that can be used to estimate the weight of a lake trout for any length. Estimate (to the nearest ounce) the weights of lake trout of lengths 39, 40, 41, 42, and 43 inches, respectively.

Table 1 Lake Trout

Length (in.)	Weight (oz)	Length (in.)	Weight (oz)
x	y	x	y
10	5	30	152
14	12	34	226
18	26	38	326
22	56	44	536
26	96		

SOLUTION The graph of the data in Table 1 (Fig. 3A) indicates that a linear regression model would not be appropriate in this case. And, in fact, we would not expect a linear relationship between length and weight. Instead, it is more likely that the weight would be related to the cube of the length. We use a cubic regression polynomial to model the data (Fig. 3B). Figure 3C adds the graph of the polynomial model to the graph of the data. The graph in Figure 3C shows that this cubic polynomial

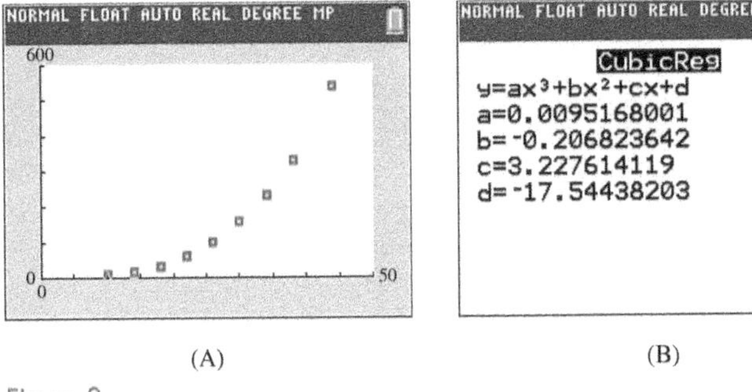

(A) (B)

Figure 3

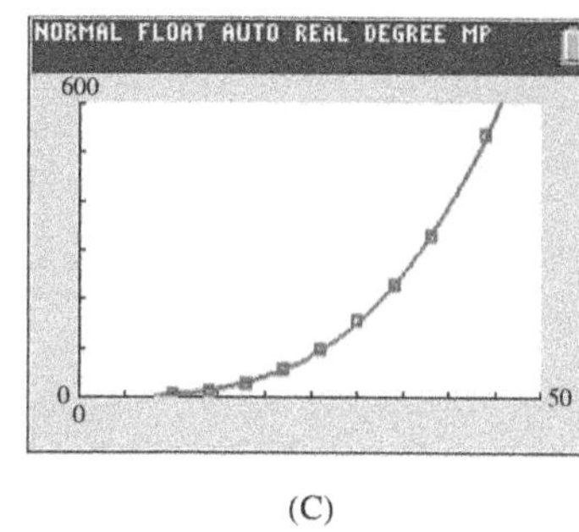

(C)

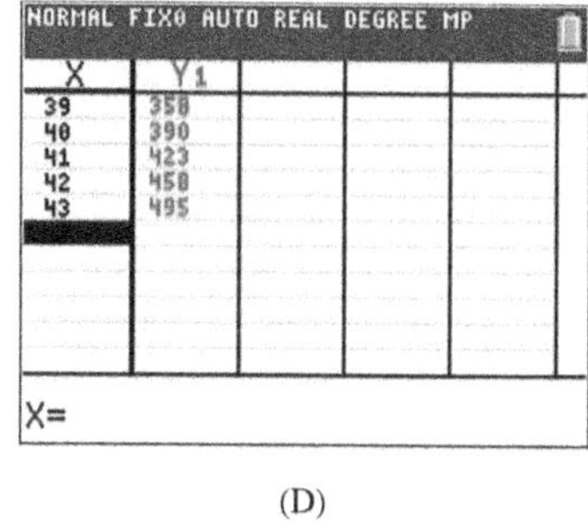

(D)

does provide a good fit for the data. (We will have more to say about the choice of functions and the accuracy of the fit provided by regression analysis later in the book.) Figure 3D shows the estimated weights for the lengths requested.

Matched Problem 1 The data in Table 2 give the average weights of pike for certain lengths. Use a cubic regression polynomial to model the data. Estimate (to the nearest ounce) the weights of pike of lengths 39, 40, 41, 42, and 43 inches, respectively.

Table 2 **Pike**

Length (in.)	Weight (oz)	Length (in.)	Weight (oz)
x	y	x	y
10	5	30	108
14	12	34	154
18	26	38	210
22	44	44	326
26	72	52	522

Rational Functions

Just as rational numbers are defined in terms of quotients of integers, *rational functions* are defined in terms of quotients of polynomials. The following equations specify rational functions:

$$f(x) = \frac{1}{x} \quad g(x) = \frac{x-2}{x^2 - x - 6} \quad h(x) = \frac{x^3 - 8}{x}$$

$$p(x) = 3x^2 - 5x \quad q(x) = 7 \quad r(x) = 0$$

DEFINITION Rational Function

A **rational function** is any function that can be written in the form

$$f(x) = \frac{n(x)}{d(x)} \qquad d(x) \neq 0$$

where $n(x)$ and $d(x)$ are polynomials. The **domain** is the set of all real numbers such that $d(x) \neq 0$.

Figure 4 shows the graphs of representative rational functions. Note, for example, that in Figure 4A the line $x = 2$ is a *vertical asymptote* for the function. The graph of f gets closer to this line as x gets closer to 2. The line $y = 1$ in Figure 4A is a *horizontal asymptote* for the function. The graph of f gets closer to this line as x increases or decreases without bound.

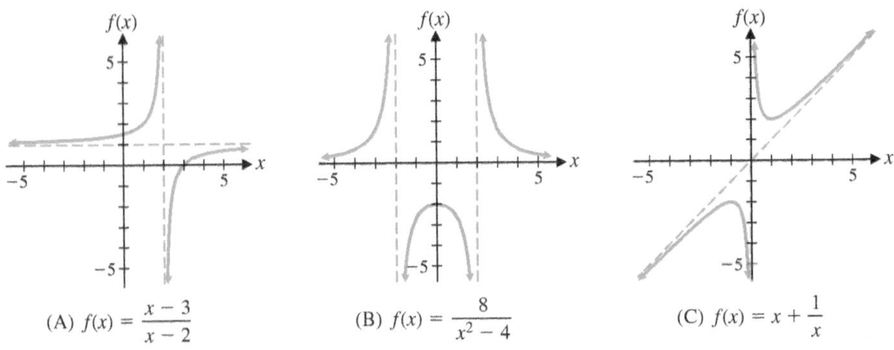

Figure 4 **Graphs of rational functions**

The number of vertical asymptotes of a rational function $f(x) = n(x)/d(x)$ is at most equal to the degree of $d(x)$. A rational function has at most one horizontal asymptote (note that the graph in Fig. 4C does not have a horizontal asymptote). Moreover, the graph of a rational function approaches the horizontal asymptote (when one exists) both as x increases and decreases without bound.

EXAMPLE 2 **Graphing Rational Functions** Given the rational function

$$f(x) = \frac{3x}{x^2 - 4}$$

(A) Find the domain.
(B) Find the x and y intercepts.
(C) Find the equations of all vertical asymptotes.
(D) If there is a horizontal asymptote, find its equation.
(E) Using the information from (A)–(D) and additional points as necessary, sketch a graph of f.

SOLUTION

(A) $x^2 - 4 = (x - 2)(x + 2)$, so the denominator is 0 if $x = -2$ or $x = 2$. Therefore the domain is the set of all real numbers except -2 and 2.

(B) *x intercepts:* $f(x) = 0$ only if $3x = 0$, or $x = 0$. So the only x intercept is 0.
y intercept:

$$f(0) = \frac{3 \cdot 0}{0^2 - 4} = \frac{0}{-4} = 0$$

So the y intercept is 0.

(C) Consider individually the values of x for which the denominator is 0, namely, 2 and -2, found in part (A).

(i) If $x = 2$, the numerator is 6, and the denominator is 0, so $f(2)$ is undefined. But for numbers just to the right of 2 (like 2.1, 2.01, 2.001), the numerator is close to 6, and the denominator is a positive number close to 0, so the fraction $f(x)$ is large and positive. For numbers just to the left of 2 (like 1.9, 1.99, 1.999), the numerator is close to 6, and the denominator is a negative number close to 0, so the fraction $f(x)$ is large (in absolute value) and negative. Therefore, the line $x = 2$ is a vertical asymptote, and $f(x)$ is positive to the right of the asymptote, and negative to the left.

(ii) If $x = -2$, the numerator is -6, and the denominator is 0, so $f(2)$ is undefined. But for numbers just to the right of -2 (like $-1.9, -1.99, -1.999$), the numerator is close to -6, and the denominator is a negative number close to 0, so the fraction $f(x)$ is large and positive. For numbers just to the left of -2 (like $-2.1, -2.01, -2.001$), the numerator is close to -6, and the denominator is a positive number close to 0, so the fraction $f(x)$ is large (in absolute value) and negative. Therefore, the line $x = -2$ is a vertical asymptote, and $f(x)$ is positive to the right of the asymptote and negative to the left.

(D) Rewrite $f(x)$ by dividing each term in the numerator and denominator by the highest power of x in $f(x)$.

$$f(x) = \frac{3x}{x^2 - 4} = \frac{\frac{3x}{x^2}}{\frac{x^2}{x^2} - \frac{4}{x^2}} = \frac{\frac{3}{x}}{1 - \frac{4}{x^2}}$$

As x increases or decreases without bound, the numerator tends to 0 and the denominator tends to 1; so, $f(x)$ tends to 0. The line $y = 0$ is a horizontal asymptote.

(E) Use the information from parts (A)–(D) and plot additional points as necessary to complete the graph, as shown in Figure 5.

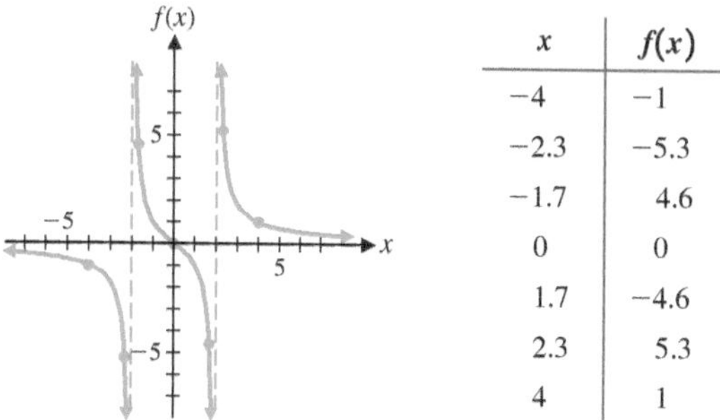

x	$f(x)$
−4	−1
−2.3	−5.3
−1.7	4.6
0	0
1.7	−4.6
2.3	5.3
4	1

Figure 5

Matched Problem 2 Given the rational function $g(x) = \dfrac{3x + 3}{x^2 - 9}$

(A) Find the domain.
(B) Find the x and y intercepts.
(C) Find the equations of all vertical asymptotes.
(D) If there is a horizontal asymptote, find its equation.
(E) Using the information from parts (A)–(D) and additional points as necessary, sketch a graph of g.

CONCEPTUAL INSIGHT

Consider the rational function

$$g(x) = \frac{3x^2 - 12x}{x^3 - 4x^2 - 4x + 16} = \frac{3x(x - 4)}{(x^2 - 4)(x - 4)}$$

The numerator and denominator of g have a common zero, $x = 4$. If $x \neq 4$, then we can cancel the factor $x - 4$ from the numerator and denominator, leaving the function $f(x)$ of Example 2. So the graph of g (Fig. 6) is identical to the graph of f (Fig. 5), except that the graph of g has an open dot at $(4, 1)$, indicating that 4 is not in the domain of g. In particular, f and g have the same asymptotes. Note that the line $x = 4$ is *not* a vertical asymptote of g, even though 4 is a zero of its denominator.

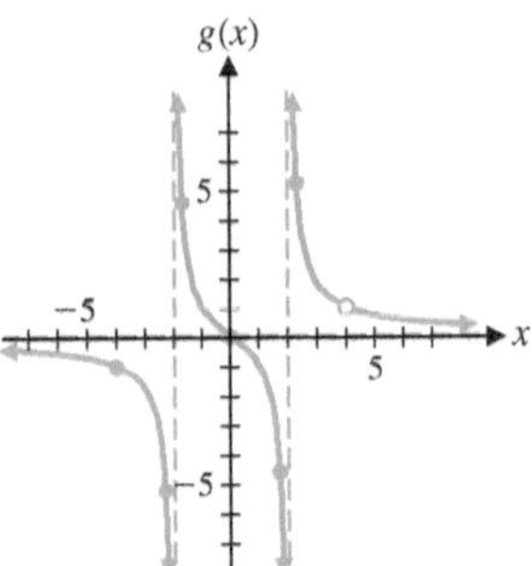

Figure 6

Graphing rational functions is aided by locating vertical and horizontal asymptotes first, if they exist. The following general procedure is suggested by Example 2 and the Conceptual Insight above.

PROCEDURE Vertical and Horizontal Asymptotes of Rational Functions

Consider the rational function

$$f(x) = \frac{n(x)}{d(x)}$$

where $n(x)$ and $d(x)$ are polynomials.

Vertical asymptotes:

Case 1. Suppose $n(x)$ and $d(x)$ have no real zero in common. If c is a real number such that $d(c) = 0$, then the line $x = c$ is a vertical asymptote of the graph of f.

Case 2. If $n(x)$ and $d(x)$ have one or more real zeros in common, cancel common linear factors, and apply Case 1 to the reduced function. (The reduced function has the same asymptotes as f.)

Horizontal asymptote:

Case 1. If degree $n(x) <$ degree $d(x)$, then $y = 0$ is the horizontal asymptote.

Case 2. If degree $n(x) =$ degree $d(x)$, then $y = a/b$ is the horizontal asymptote, where a is the leading coefficient of $n(x)$, and b is the leading coefficient of $d(x)$.

Case 3. If degree $n(x) >$ degree $d(x)$, there is no horizontal asymptote.

Example 2 illustrates Case 1 of the procedure for horizontal asymptotes. Cases 2 and 3 are illustrated in Example 3 and Matched Problem 3.

EXAMPLE 3 **Finding Asymptotes** Find the vertical and horizontal asymptotes of the rational function

$$f(x) = \frac{3x^2 + 3x - 6}{2x^2 - 2}$$

SOLUTION Vertical asymptotes We factor the numerator $n(x)$ and the denominator $d(x)$:

$$n(x) = 3(x^2 + x - 2) = 3(x - 1)(x + 2)$$
$$d(x) = 2(x^2 - 1) = 2(x - 1)(x + 1)$$

The reduced function is

$$\frac{3(x + 2)}{2(x + 1)}$$

which, by the procedure, has the vertical asymptote $x = -1$. Therefore, $x = -1$ is the only vertical asymptote of f.

Horizontal asymptote Both $n(x)$ and $d(x)$ have degree 2 (Case 2 of the procedure for horizontal asymptotes). The leading coefficient of the numerator $n(x)$ is 3, and the leading coefficient of the denominator $d(x)$ is 2. So $y = 3/2$ is the horizontal asymptote.

Matched Problem 3 Find the vertical and horizontal asymptotes of the rational function

$$f(x) = \frac{x^3 - 4x}{x^2 + 5x}$$

Explore and Discuss 1

A function f is **bounded** if the entire graph of f lies between two horizontal lines. The only polynomials that are bounded are the constant functions, but there are many rational functions that are bounded. Give an example of a bounded rational function, with domain the set of all real numbers, that is not a constant function.

Applications

Rational functions occur naturally in many types of applications.

EXAMPLE 4 Employee Training A company that manufactures computers has established that, on the average, a new employee can assemble $N(t)$ components per day after t days of on-the-job training, as given by

$$N(t) = \frac{50t}{t + 4} \qquad t \geq 0$$

Sketch a graph of N, $0 \leq t \leq 100$, including any vertical or horizontal asymptotes. What does $N(t)$ approach as t increases without bound?

SOLUTION Vertical asymptotes None for $t \geq 0$

Horizontal asymptote

$$N(t) = \frac{50t}{t + 4} = \frac{50}{1 + \frac{4}{t}}$$

$N(t)$ approaches 50 (the leading coefficient of $50t$ divided by the leading coefficient of $t + 4$) as t increases without bound. So $y = 50$ is a horizontal asymptote.

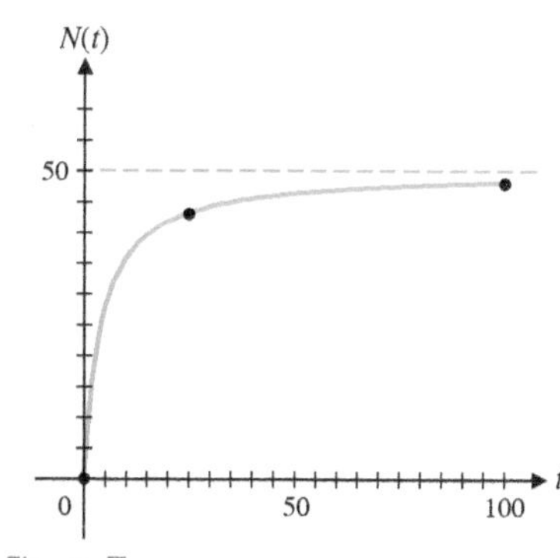

Figure 7

Sketch of graph Note that $N(0) = 0$, $N(25) \approx 43$, and $N(100) \approx 48$. We draw a smooth curve through (0, 0), (25, 43) and (100, 48) (Fig. 7).

$N(t)$ approaches 50 as t increases without bound. It appears that 50 components per day would be the upper limit that an employee would be expected to assemble.

Matched Problem 4 Repeat Example 4 for $N(t) = \dfrac{25t + 5}{t + 5} \quad t \geq 0$.

Exercises 2.4

A *In Problems 1–10, for each polynomial function find the following:*

(A) *Degree of the polynomial*

(B) *All x intercepts*

(C) *The y intercept*

1. $f(x) = 7x + 21$

2. $f(x) = x^2 - 5x + 6$

3. $f(x) = x^2 + 9x + 20$

4. $f(x) = 30 - 3x$

5. $f(x) = x^2 + 2x^6 + 3x^4 + 15$

6. $f(x) = 5x^4 + 3x^2 + x^{10} + 7x^8 + 9$

7. $f(x) = x^2(x + 6)^3$

8. $f(x) = (x - 8)^2(x + 4)^3$

9. $f(x) = (x^2 - 25)(x^3 + 8)^3$

10. $f(x) = (2x - 5)^2(x^2 - 9)^4$

Each graph in Problems 11–18 is the graph of a polynomial function. Answer the following questions for each graph:

(A) *What is the minimum degree of a polynomial function that could have the graph?*

(B) *Is the leading coefficient of the polynomial negative or positive?*

11.

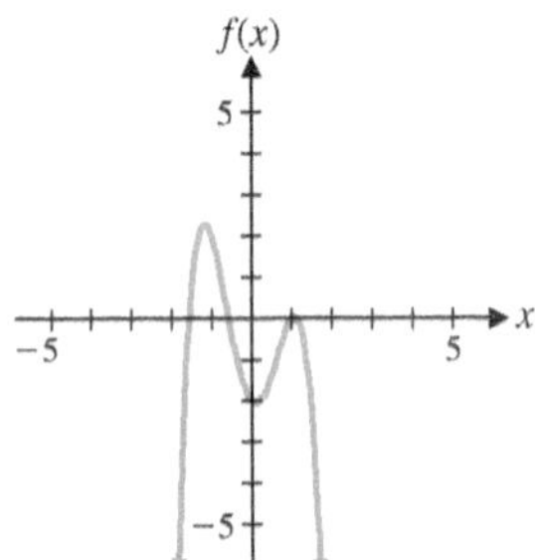

12.

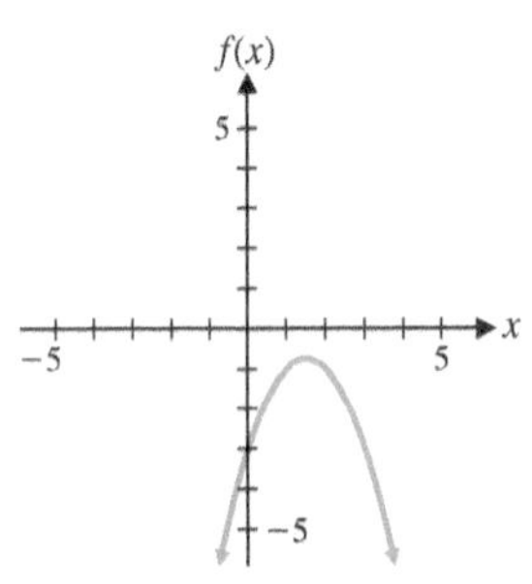

13.

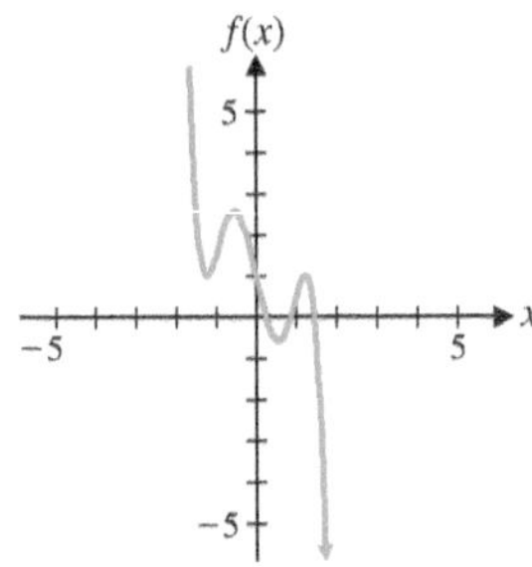

14.

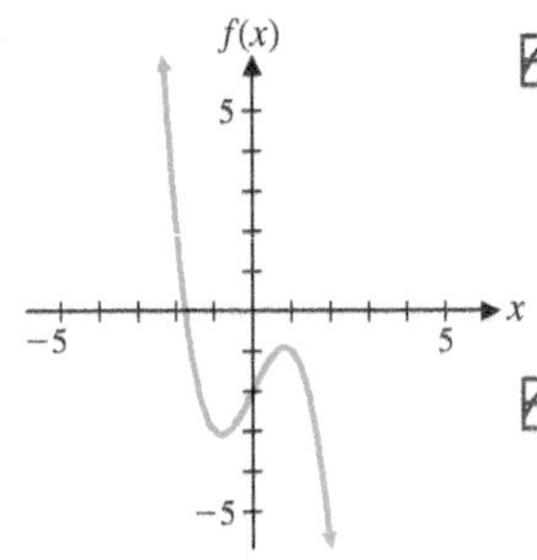

15.

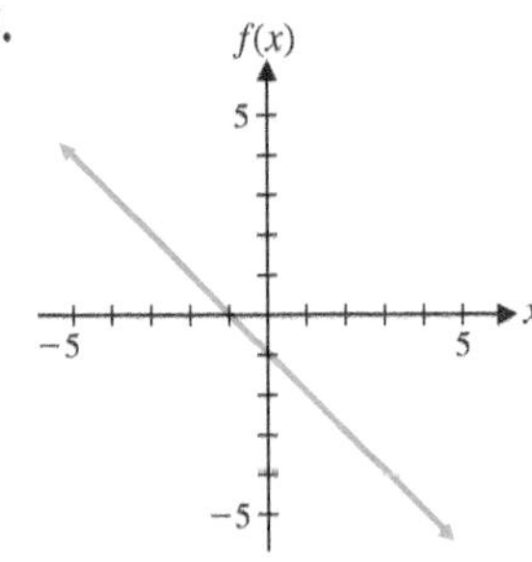

16.

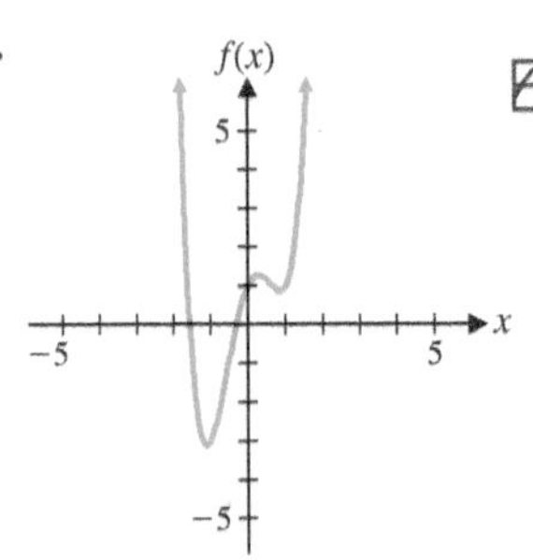

17.

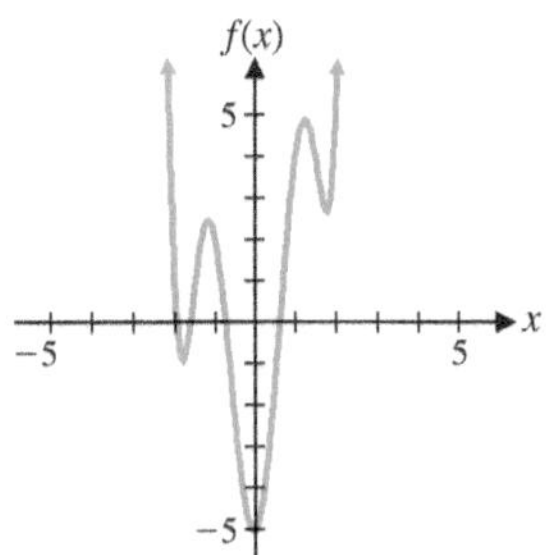

18.

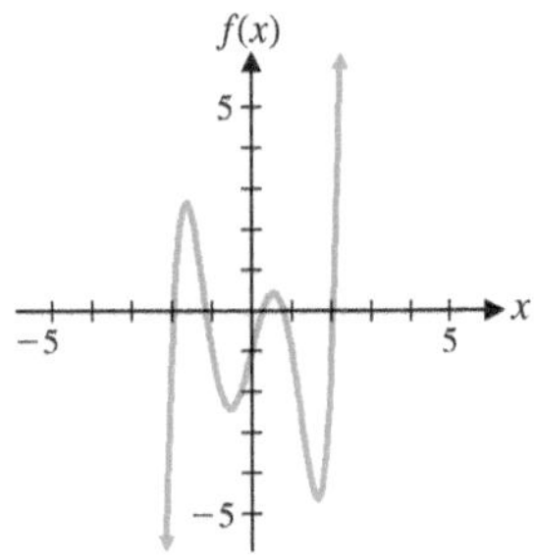

19. What is the maximum number of x intercepts that a polynomial of degree 10 can have?

20. What is the maximum number of x intercepts that a polynomial of degree 11 can have?

21. What is the minimum number of x intercepts that a polynomial of degree 9 can have? Explain.

22. What is the minimum number of x intercepts that a polynomial of degree 6 can have? Explain.

B *For each rational function in Problems 23–28,*

(A) *Find the intercepts for the graph.*

(B) *Determine the domain.*

(C) *Find any vertical or horizontal asymptotes for the graph.*

(D) *Sketch any asymptotes as dashed lines. Then sketch a graph of $y = f(x)$.*

23. $f(x) = \dfrac{x + 2}{x - 2}$

24. $f(x) = \dfrac{x - 3}{x + 3}$

25. $f(x) = \dfrac{3x}{x + 2}$

26. $f(x) = \dfrac{2x}{x - 3}$

27. $f(x) = \dfrac{4 - 2x}{x - 4}$

28. $f(x) = \dfrac{3 - 3x}{x - 2}$

29. Compare the graph of $y = 2x^4$ to the graph of $y = 2x^4 - 5x^2 + x + 2$ in the following two viewing windows:

(A) $-5 \le x \le 5, -5 \le y \le 5$

(B) $-5 \le x \le 5, -500 \le y \le 500$

30. Compare the graph of $y = x^3$ to the graph of $y = x^3 - 2x + 2$ in the following two viewing windows:

(A) $-5 \le x \le 5, -5 \le y \le 5$

(B) $-5 \le x \le 5, -500 \le y \le 500$

31. Compare the graph of $y = -x^5$ to the graph of $y = -x^5 + 4x^3 - 4x + 1$ in the following two viewing windows:

(A) $-5 \le x \le 5, -5 \le y \le 5$

(B) $-5 \le x \le 5, -500 \le y \le 500$

32. Compare the graph of $y = -x^5$ to the graph of $y = -x^5 + 5x^3 - 5x + 2$ in the following two viewing windows:

(A) $-5 \le x \le 5, -5 \le y \le 5$

(B) $-5 \le x \le 5, -500 \le y \le 500$

In Problems 33–40, find the equation of any horizontal asymptote.

33. $f(x) = \dfrac{4x^3 + x^2 - 10}{5x^3 + 7x^2 + 9}$

34. $f(x) = \dfrac{6x^4 - x^3 + 2}{4x^4 + 10x + 5}$

35. $f(x) = \dfrac{1 - 5x + x^2}{2 + 3x + 4x^2}$

36. $f(x) = \dfrac{8 - x^3}{1 + 2x^3}$

37. $f(x) = \dfrac{x^4 + 2x^2 + 1}{1 - x^5}$

38. $f(x) = \dfrac{3 + 5x}{x^2 + x + 3}$

39. $f(x) = \dfrac{x^2 + 6x + 1}{x - 5}$

40. $f(x) = \dfrac{x^2 + x^4 + 1}{x^3 + 2x - 4}$

In Problems 41–46, find the equations of any vertical asymptotes.

41. $f(x) = \dfrac{x^2 + 1}{(x^2 - 1)(x^2 - 9)}$

42. $f(x) = \dfrac{x^2 - 16}{(x^2 - 25)(x^2 - 36)}$

43. $f(x) = \dfrac{x^2 - x - 6}{x^2 - 3x - 10}$

44. $f(x) = \dfrac{x^2 - 8x + 7}{x^2 + 7x - 8}$

45. $f(x) = \dfrac{x^2 - 49x}{x^3 - 49x}$

46. $f(x) = \dfrac{x^2 + x - 2}{x^3 - 3x^2 + 2x}$

C *For each rational function in Problems 47–52,*

(A) *Find any intercepts for the graph.*

(B) *Find any vertical and horizontal asymptotes for the graph.*

(C) *Sketch any asymptotes as dashed lines. Then sketch a graph of f.*

(D) *Graph the function in a standard viewing window using a graphing calculator.*

47. $f(x) = \dfrac{2x^2}{x^2 - x - 6}$

48. $f(x) = \dfrac{3x^2}{x^2 + x - 6}$

49. $f(x) = \dfrac{6 - 2x^2}{x^2 - 9}$

50. $f(x) = \dfrac{3 - 3x^2}{x^2 - 4}$

51. $f(x) = \dfrac{-4x + 24}{x^2 + x - 6}$

52. $f(x) = \dfrac{5x - 10}{x^2 + x - 12}$

53. Write an equation for the lowest-degree polynomial function with the graph and intercepts shown in the figure.

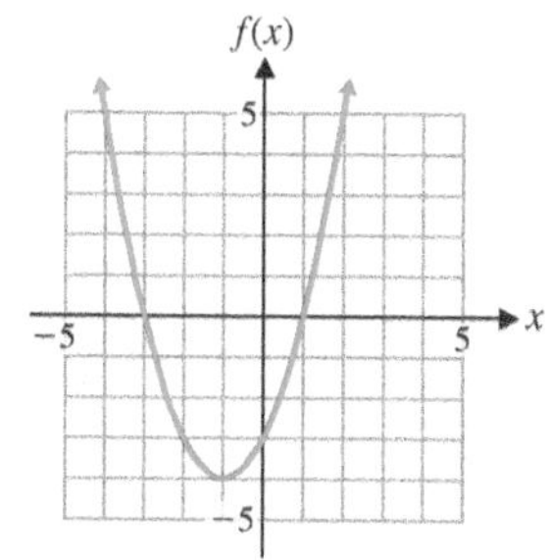

54. Write an equation for the lowest-degree polynomial function with the graph and intercepts shown in the figure.

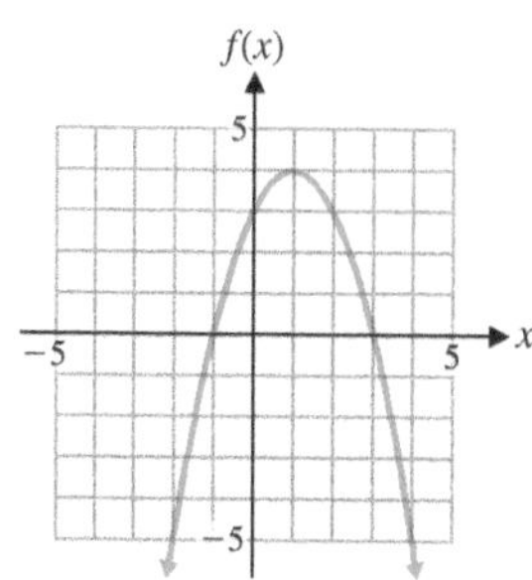

55. Write an equation for the lowest-degree polynomial function with the graph and intercepts shown in the figure.

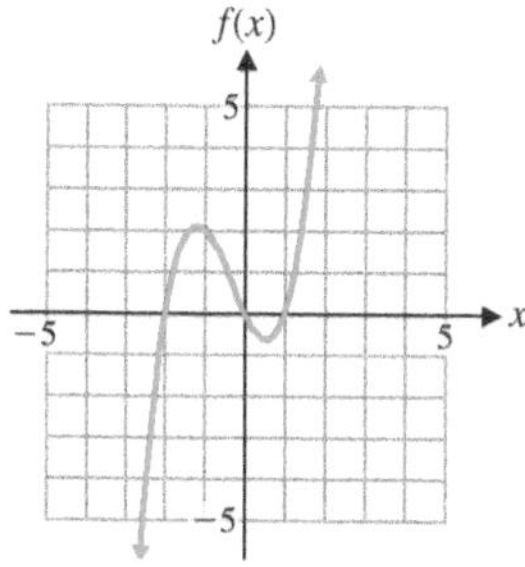

56. Write an equation for the lowest-degree polynomial function with the graph and intercepts shown in the figure.

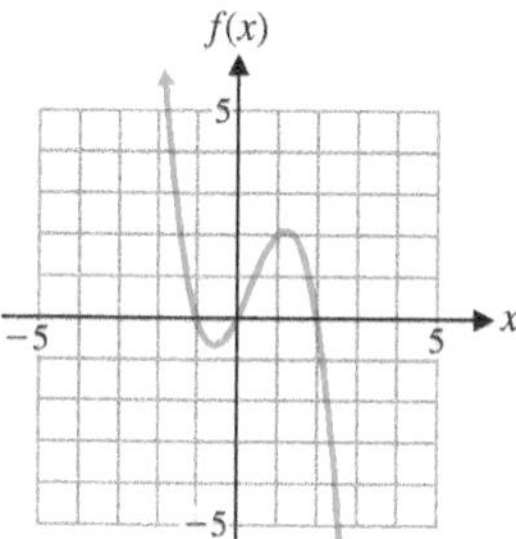

Applications

57. **Average cost.** A company manufacturing snowboards has fixed costs of \$200 per day and total costs of \$3,800 per day at a daily output of 20 boards.

(A) Assuming that the total cost per day, $C(x)$, is linearly related to the total output per day, x, write an equation for the cost function.

(B) The average cost per board for an output of x boards is given by $\overline{C}(x) = C(x)/x$. Find the average cost function.

(C) Sketch a graph of the average cost function, including any asymptotes, for $1 \le x \le 30$.

(D) What does the average cost per board tend to as production increases?

58. **Average cost.** A company manufacturing surfboards has fixed costs of \$300 per day and total costs of \$5,100 per day at a daily output of 20 boards.

(A) Assuming that the total cost per day, $C(x)$, is linearly related to the total output per day, x, write an equation for the cost function.

(B) The average cost per board for an output of x boards is given by $\overline{C}(x) = C(x)/x$. Find the average cost function.

(C) Sketch a graph of the average cost function, including any asymptotes, for $1 \leq x \leq 30$.

(D) What does the average cost per board tend to as production increases?

59. **Replacement time.** An office copier has an initial price of \$2,500. A service contract costs \$200 for the first year and increases \$50 per year thereafter. It can be shown that the total cost of the copier after n years is given by

$$C(n) = 2{,}500 + 175n + 25n^2$$

The average cost per year for n years is given by $\overline{C}(n) = C(n)/n$.

(A) Find the rational function $\overline{C}$.

(B) Sketch a graph of $\overline{C}$ for $2 \leq n \leq 20$.

(C) When is the average cost per year at a minimum, and what is the minimum average annual cost? [*Hint:* Refer to the sketch in part (B) and evaluate $\overline{C}(n)$ at appropriate integer values until a minimum value is found.] The time when the average cost is minimum is frequently referred to as the **replacement time** for the piece of equipment.

(D) Graph the average cost function $\overline{C}$ on a graphing calculator and use an appropriate command to find when the average annual cost is at a minimum.

60. **Minimum average cost.** Financial analysts in a company that manufactures DVD players arrived at the following daily cost equation for manufacturing x DVD players per day:

$$C(x) = x^2 + 2x + 2{,}000$$

The average cost per unit at a production level of x players per day is $\overline{C}(x) = C(x)/x$.

(A) Find the rational function $\overline{C}$.

(B) Sketch a graph of $\overline{C}$ for $5 \leq x \leq 150$.

(C) For what daily production level (to the nearest integer) is the average cost per unit at a minimum, and what is the minimum average cost per player (to the nearest cent)? [*Hint:* Refer to the sketch in part (B) and evaluate $\overline{C}(x)$ at appropriate integer values until a minimum value is found.]

(D) Graph the average cost function $\overline{C}$ on a graphing calculator and use an appropriate command to find the daily production level (to the nearest integer) at which the average cost per player is at a minimum. What is the minimum average cost to the nearest cent?

61. **Minimum average cost.** A consulting firm, using statistical methods, provided a veterinary clinic with the cost equation

$$C(x) = 0.00048(x - 500)^3 + 60{,}000$$
$$100 \leq x \leq 1{,}000$$

where $C(x)$ is the cost in dollars for handling x cases per month. The average cost per case is given by $\overline{C}(x) = C(x)/x$.

(A) Write the equation for the average cost function $\overline{C}$.

(B) Graph $\overline{C}$ on a graphing calculator.

(C) Use an appropriate command to find the monthly caseload for the minimum average cost per case. What is the minimum average cost per case?

62. **Minimum average cost.** The financial department of a hospital, using statistical methods, arrived at the cost equation

$$C(x) = 20x^3 - 360x^2 + 2{,}300x - 1{,}000$$
$$1 \leq x \leq 12$$

where $C(x)$ is the cost in thousands of dollars for handling x thousand cases per month. The average cost per case is given by $\overline{C}(x) = C(x)/x$.

(A) Write the equation for the average cost function $\overline{C}$.

(B) Graph $\overline{C}$ on a graphing calculator.

(C) Use an appropriate command to find the monthly caseload for the minimum average cost per case. What is the minimum average cost per case to the nearest dollar?

63. **Diet.** Table 3 shows the per capita consumption of ice cream in the United States for selected years since 1987.

(A) Let x represent the number of years since 1980 and find a cubic regression polynomial for the per capita consumption of ice cream.

(B) Use the polynomial model from part (A) to estimate (to the nearest tenth of a pound) the per capita consumption of ice cream in 2023.

Table 3 **Per Capita Consumption of Ice Cream**

Year	Ice Cream (pounds)
1987	18.0
1992	15.8
1997	15.7
2002	16.4
2007	14.9
2012	13.4
2014	12.8

Source: U.S. Department of Agriculture

64. **Diet.** Refer to Table 4.

(A) Let x represent the number of years since 2000 and find a cubic regression polynomial for the per capita consumption of eggs.

(B) Use the polynomial model from part (A) to estimate (to the nearest integer) the per capita consumption of eggs in 2023.

Table 4 Per Capita Consumption of Eggs

Year	Number of Eggs
2002	255
2004	257
2006	258
2008	247
2010	243
2012	254
2014	263

Source: U.S. Department of Agriculture

Table 5 Marriages and Divorces (per 1,000 population)

Date	Marriages	Divorces
1960	8.5	2.2
1970	10.6	3.5
1980	10.6	5.2
1990	9.8	4.7
2000	8.5	4.1
2010	6.8	3.6

Source: National Center for Health Statistics

65. Physiology. In a study on the speed of muscle contraction in frogs under various loads, researchers W. O. Fems and J. Marsh found that the speed of contraction decreases with increasing loads. In particular, they found that the relationship between speed of contraction v (in centimeters per second) and load x (in grams) is given approximately by

$$v(x) = \frac{26 + 0.06x}{x} \quad x \geq 5$$

(A) What does $v(x)$ approach as x increases?

(B) Sketch a graph of function v.

66. Learning theory. In 1917, L. L. Thurstone, a pioneer in quantitative learning theory, proposed the rational function

$$f(x) = \frac{a(x + c)}{(x + c) + b}$$

to model the number of successful acts per unit time that a person could accomplish after x practice sessions. Suppose that for a particular person enrolled in a typing class,

$$f(x) = \frac{55(x + 1)}{(x + 8)} \quad x \geq 0$$

where $f(x)$ is the number of words per minute the person is able to type after x weeks of lessons.

(A) What does $f(x)$ approach as x increases?

(B) Sketch a graph of function f, including any vertical or horizontal asymptotes.

67. Marriage. Table 5 shows the marriage and divorce rates per 1,000 population for selected years since 1960.

(A) Let x represent the number of years since 1960 and find a cubic regression polynomial for the marriage rate.

(B) Use the polynomial model from part (A) to estimate the marriage rate (to one decimal place) for 2025.

68. Divorce. Refer to Table 5.

(A) Let x represent the number of years since 1960 and find a cubic regression polynomial for the divorce rate.

(B) Use the polynomial model from part (A) to estimate the divorce rate (to one decimal place) for 2025.

Answers to Matched Problems

1.

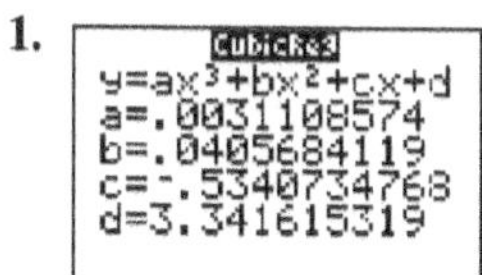

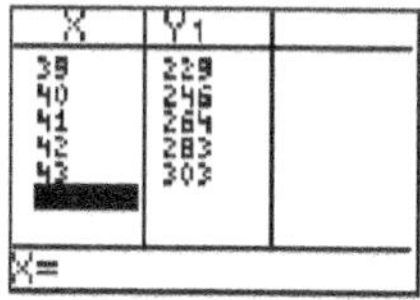

2. (A) Domain: all real numbers except -3 and 3

(B) x intercept: -1; y intercept: $-\frac{1}{3}$

(C) Vertical asymptotes: $x = -3$ and $x = 3$;

(D) Horizontal asymptote: $y = 0$

(E)

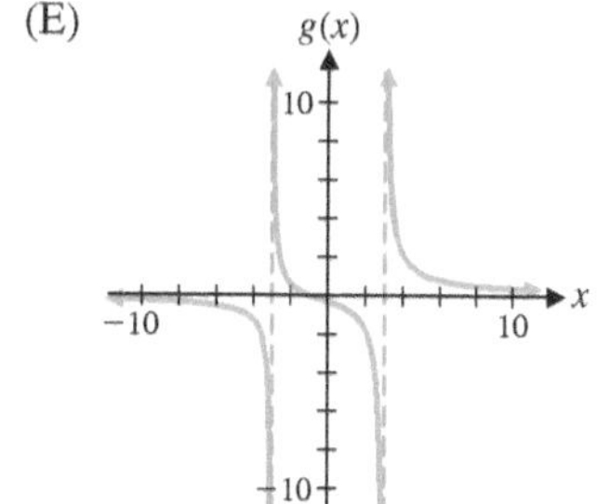

3. Vertical asymptote: $x = -5$
Horizontal asymptote: none

4. No vertical asymptotes for $t \geq 0$; $y = 25$ is a horizontal asymptote. $N(t)$ approaches 25 as t increases without bound. It appears that 25 components per day would be the upper limit that an employee would be expected to assemble.

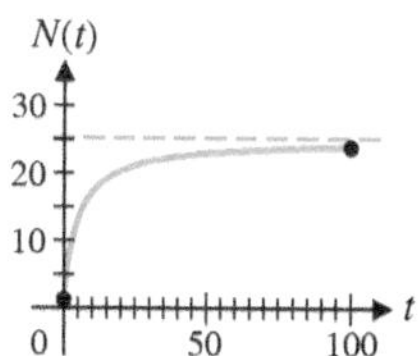

2.5 Exponential Functions

- Exponential Functions
- Base *e* Exponential Function
- Growth and Decay Applications
- Compound Interest

This section introduces an important class of functions called *exponential functions.* These functions are used extensively in modeling and solving a wide variety of real-world problems, including growth of money at compound interest, growth of populations, radioactive decay, and learning associated with the mastery of such devices as a new computer or an assembly process in a manufacturing plant.

Exponential Functions

We start by noting that

$$f(x) = 2^x \quad \text{and} \quad g(x) = x^2$$

are not the same function. Whether a variable appears as an exponent with a constant base or as a base with a constant exponent makes a big difference. The function g is a quadratic function, which we have already discussed. The function f is a new type of function called an *exponential function.* In general,

DEFINITION Exponential Function

The equation

$$f(x) = b^x \quad b > 0, b \neq 1$$

defines an **exponential function** for each different constant b, called the **base**. The **domain** of f is the set of all real numbers, and the **range** of f is the set of all positive real numbers.

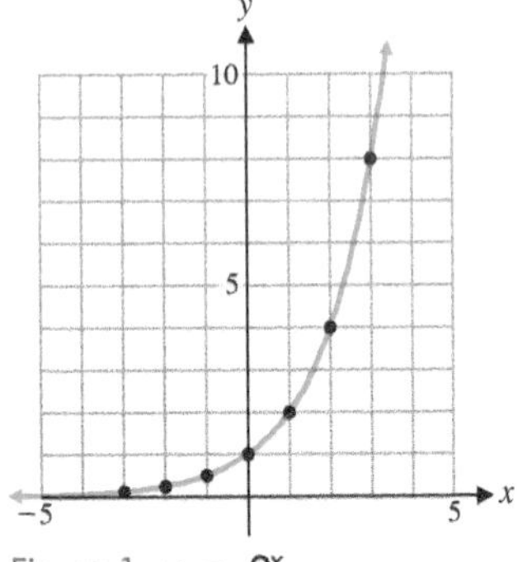

Figure 1 $y = 2^x$

We require the base b to be positive to avoid imaginary numbers such as $(-2)^{1/2} = \sqrt{-2} = i\sqrt{2}$. We exclude $b = 1$ as a base, since $f(x) = 1^x = 1$ is a constant function, which we have already considered.

When asked to hand-sketch graphs of equations such as $y = 2^x$ or $y = 2^{-x}$, many students do not hesitate. [*Note:* $2^{-x} = 1/2^x = (1/2)^x$.] They make tables by assigning integers to x, plot the resulting points, and then join these points with a smooth curve as in Figure 1. The only catch is that we have not defined 2^x for all real numbers. From Appendix B, Section B.6, we know what 2^5, 2^{-3}, $2^{2/3}$, $2^{-3/5}$, $2^{1.4}$, and $2^{-3.14}$ mean (that is, 2^p, where p is a rational number), but what does

$$2^{\sqrt{2}}$$

mean? The question is not easy to answer at this time. In fact, a precise definition of $2^{\sqrt{2}}$ must wait for more advanced courses, where it is shown that

$$2^x$$

names a positive real number for x any real number, and that the graph of $y = 2^x$ is as indicated in Figure 1.

It is useful to compare the graphs of $y = 2^x$ and $y = 2^{-x}$ by plotting both on the same set of coordinate axes, as shown in Figure 2A. The graph of

$$f(x) = b^x \quad b > 1 \text{ (Fig. 2B)}$$

looks very much like the graph of $y = 2^x$, and the graph of

$$f(x) = b^x \quad 0 < b < 1 \text{ (Fig. 2B)}$$

looks very much like the graph of $y = 2^{-x}$. Note that in both cases the x axis is a horizontal asymptote for the graphs.

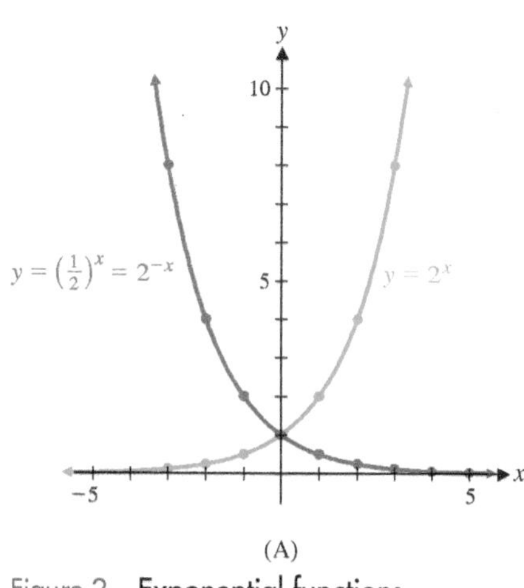

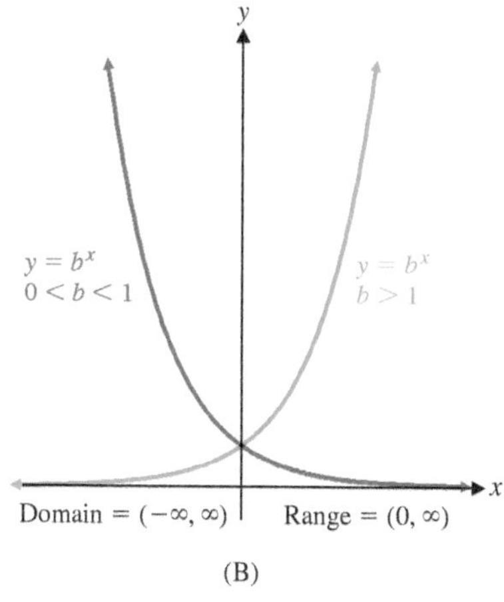

Figure 2 Exponential functions

The graphs in Figure 2 suggest the following general properties of exponential functions, which we state without proof:

THEOREM 1 Basic Properties of the Graph of $f(x) = b^x$, $b > 0$, $b \neq 1$

1. All graphs will pass through the point $(0, 1)$. *$b^0 = 1$ for any permissible base b.*
2. All graphs are continuous curves, with no holes or jumps.
3. The x axis is a horizontal asymptote.
4. If $b > 1$, then b^x increases as x increases.
5. If $0 < b < 1$, then b^x decreases as x increases.

CONCEPTUAL INSIGHT

Recall that the graph of a rational function has at most one horizontal asymptote and that it approaches the horizontal asymptote (if one exists) both as $x \to \infty$ *and* as $x \to -\infty$ (see Section 2.4). The graph of an exponential function, on the other hand, approaches its horizontal asymptote as $x \to \infty$ *or* as $x \to -\infty$, but not both. In particular, there is no rational function that has the same graph as an exponential function.

The use of a calculator with the key y^x, or its equivalent, makes the graphing of exponential functions almost routine. Example 1 illustrates the process.

EXAMPLE 1 **Graphing Exponential Functions** Sketch a graph of $y = (\frac{1}{2})4^x$, $-2 \le x \le 2$.

SOLUTION Use a calculator to create the table of values shown. Plot these points, and then join them with a smooth curve as in Figure 3.

x	y
−2	0.031
−1	0.125
0	0.50
1	2.00
2	8.00

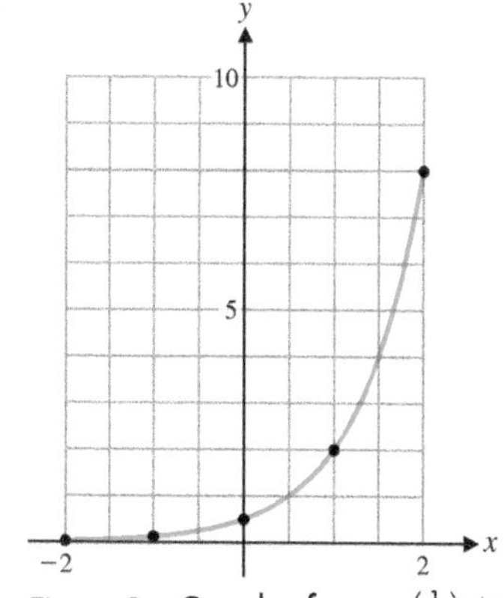

Figure 3 Graph of $y = (\frac{1}{2})4^x$

Matched Problem 1 Sketch a graph of $y = (\frac{1}{2})4^{-x}$, $-2 \le x \le 2$.

Exponential functions, whose domains include irrational numbers, obey the familiar laws of exponents discussed in Appendix B, Section B.6 for rational exponents. We summarize these exponent laws here and add two other important and useful properties.

THEOREM 2 Properties of Exponential Functions

For a and b positive, $a \neq 1, b \neq 1$, and x and y real,

1. Exponent laws:

$$a^x a^y = a^{x+y} \qquad \frac{a^x}{a^y} = a^{x-y} \qquad \frac{4^{2y}}{4^{5y}} = 4^{2y-5y} = 4^{-3y}$$

$$(a^x)^y = a^{xy} \qquad (ab)^x = a^x b^x \qquad \left(\frac{a}{b}\right)^x = \frac{a^x}{b^x}$$

2. $a^x = a^y$ if and only if $x = y$ — If $7^{5t+1} = 7^{3t-3}$, then $5t + 1 = 3t - 3$, and $t = -2$.

3. For $x \neq 0$,
$a^x = b^x$ if and only if $a = b$ — If $a^5 = 2^5$, then $a = 2$.

Reminder

$(-2)^2 = 2^2$, but this equation does not contradict property 3 of Theorem 2. In Theorem 2, both a and b must be positive.

Base e Exponential Function

Of all the possible bases b we can use for the exponential function $y = b^x$, which ones are the most useful? If you look at the keys on a calculator, you will probably see 10^x and e^x. It is clear why base 10 would be important, because our number system is a base 10 system. But what is e, and why is it included as a base? It turns out that base e is used more frequently than all other bases combined. The reason for this is that certain formulas and the results of certain processes found in calculus and more advanced mathematics take on their simplest form if this base is used. This is why you will see e used extensively in expressions and formulas that model real-world phenomena. In fact, its use is so prevalent that you will often hear people refer to $y = e^x$ as *the* exponential function.

The base e is an irrational number and, like π, it cannot be represented exactly by any finite decimal or fraction. However, e can be approximated as closely as we like by evaluating the expression

$$\left(1 + \frac{1}{x}\right)^x \tag{1}$$

for sufficiently large values of x. What happens to the value of expression (1) as x increases without bound? Think about this for a moment before proceeding. Maybe you guessed that the value approaches 1, because

$$1 + \frac{1}{x}$$

approaches 1, and 1 raised to any power is 1. Let us see if this reasoning is correct by actually calculating the value of the expression for larger and larger values of x. Table 1 summarizes the results.

Table 1

x	$\left(1 + \frac{1}{x}\right)^x$
1	2
10	2.593 74...
100	2.704 81...
1,000	2.716 92...
10,000	2.718 14...
100,000	2.718 26...
1,000,000	2.718 28...

Interestingly, the value of expression (1) is never close to 1 but seems to be approaching a number close to 2.7183. In fact, as x increases without bound, the value of expression (1) approaches an irrational number that we call e. The irrational number e to 12 decimal places is

$$e = 2.718\,281\,828\,459$$

Compare this value of e with the value of e^1 from a calculator.

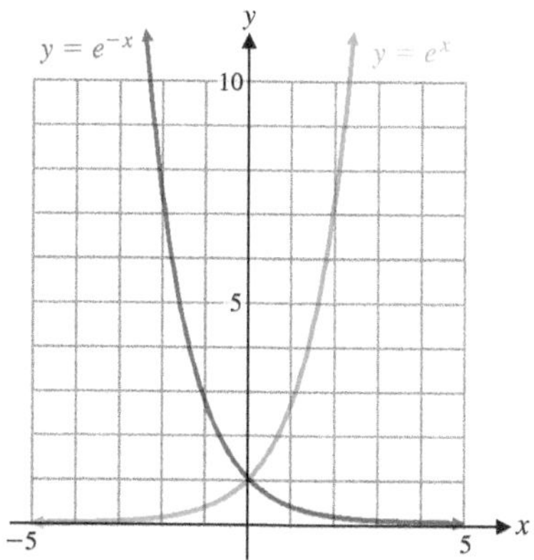

Figure 4

DEFINITION Exponential Functions with Base e and Base $1/e$

The exponential functions with base e and base $1/e$, respectively, are defined by

$$y = e^x \quad \text{and} \quad y = e^{-x}$$

Domain: $(-\infty, \infty)$

Range: $(0, \infty)$ (see Fig. 4)

Explore and Discuss 1

Graph the functions $f(x) = e^x$, $g(x) = 2^x$, and $h(x) = 3^x$ on the same set of coordinate axes. At which values of x do the graphs intersect? For positive values of x, which of the three graphs lies above the other two? Below the other two? How does your answer change for negative values of x?

Growth and Decay Applications

Functions of the form $y = ce^{kt}$, where c and k are constants and the independent variable t represents time, are often used to model population growth and radioactive decay. Note that if $t = 0$, then $y = c$. So the constant c represents the initial population (or initial amount). The constant k is called the **relative growth rate** and has the following interpretation: Suppose that $y = ce^{kt}$ models the population of a country, where y is the number of persons and t is time in years. If the relative growth rate is $k = 0.02$, then at any time t, the population is growing at a rate of $0.02y$ persons (that is, 2% of the population) per year.

We say that **population is growing continuously at relative growth rate k** to mean that the population y is given by the model $y = ce^{kt}$.

EXAMPLE 2 **Exponential Growth** Cholera, an intestinal disease, is caused by a cholera bacterium that multiplies exponentially. The number of bacteria grows continuously at relative growth rate 1.386, that is,

$$N = N_0 e^{1.386t}$$

where N is the number of bacteria present after t hours and N_0 is the number of bacteria present at the start $(t = 0)$. If we start with 25 bacteria, how many bacteria (to the nearest unit) will be present

(A) In 0.6 hour? (B) In 3.5 hours?

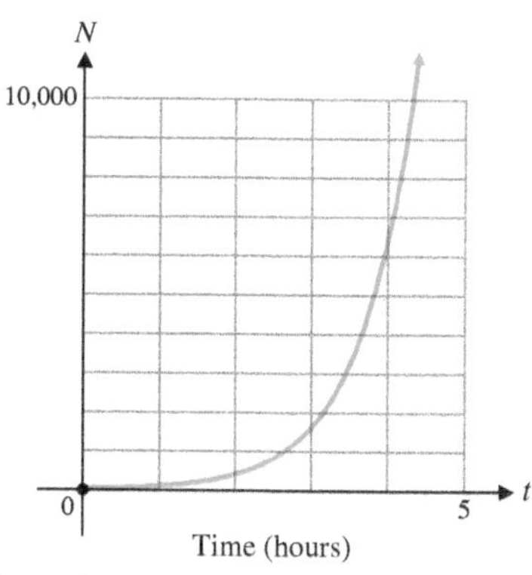

Figure 5

SOLUTION Substituting $N_0 = 25$ into the preceding equation, we obtain

$$N = 25e^{1.386t} \quad \text{The graph is shown in Figure 5.}$$

(A) Solve for N when $t = 0.6$:

$$N = 25e^{1.386(0.6)} \quad \text{Use a calculator.}$$
$$= 57 \text{ bacteria}$$

(B) Solve for N when $t = 3.5$:

$$N = 25e^{1.386(3.5)} \quad \text{Use a calculator.}$$
$$= 3{,}197 \text{ bacteria}$$

Matched Problem 2 Refer to the exponential growth model for cholera in Example 2. If we start with 55 bacteria, how many bacteria (to the nearest unit) will be present

(A) In 0.85 hour? (B) In 7.25 hours?

EXAMPLE 3 **Exponential Decay** Cosmic-ray bombardment of the atmosphere produces neutrons, which in turn react with nitrogen to produce radioactive carbon-14 (^{14}C). Radioactive ^{14}C enters all living tissues through carbon dioxide, which is first absorbed by plants. As long as a plant or animal is alive, ^{14}C is maintained in the living organism at a constant level. Once the organism dies, however, ^{14}C decays according to the equation

$$A = A_0e^{-0.000124t}$$

where A is the amount present after t years and A_0 is the amount present at time $t = 0$.

(A) If 500 milligrams of ^{14}C is present in a sample from a skull at the time of death, how many milligrams will be present in the sample in 15,000 years? Compute the answer to two decimal places.

(B) The **half-life** of ^{14}C is the time t at which the amount present is one-half the amount at time $t = 0$. Use Figure 6 to estimate the half-life of ^{14}C.

SOLUTION Substituting $A_0 = 500$ in the decay equation, we have

$$A = 500e^{-0.000124t} \quad \text{See the graph in Figure 6.}$$

(A) Solve for A when $t = 15{,}000$:

$$A = 500e^{-0.000124(15{,}000)} \quad \text{Use a calculator.}$$
$$= 77.84 \text{ milligrams}$$

Figure 6

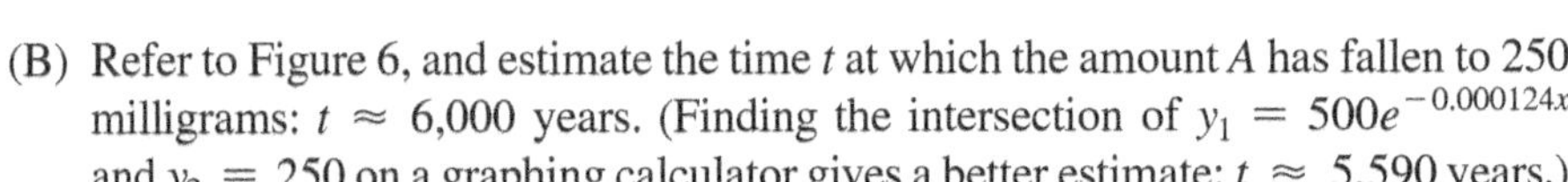

(B) Refer to Figure 6, and estimate the time t at which the amount A has fallen to 250 milligrams: $t \approx 6{,}000$ years. (Finding the intersection of $y_1 = 500e^{-0.000124x}$ and $y_2 = 250$ on a graphing calculator gives a better estimate: $t \approx 5{,}590$ years.)

Matched Problem 3 Refer to the exponential decay model in Example 3. How many milligrams of ^{14}C would have to be present at the beginning in order to have 25 milligrams present after 18,000 years? Compute the answer to the nearest milligram.

If you buy a new car, it is likely to depreciate in value by several thousand dollars during the first year you own it. You would expect the value of the car to decrease in each subsequent year, but not by as much as in the previous year. If you drive the car long enough, its resale value will get close to zero. An exponential decay function will often be a good model of depreciation; a linear or quadratic function would not be suitable (why?). We can use **exponential regression** on a graphing calculator to find the function of the form $y = ab^x$ that best fits a data set.

EXAMPLE 4 **Depreciation** Table 2 gives the market value of a hybrid sedan (in dollars) x years after its purchase. Find an exponential regression model of the form $y = ab^x$ for this data set. Estimate the purchase price of the hybrid. Estimate the value of the hybrid 10 years after its purchase. Round answers to the nearest dollar.

Table 2

x	Value ($)
1	12,575
2	9,455
3	8,115
4	6,845
5	5,225
6	4,485

SOLUTION Enter the data into a graphing calculator (Fig. 7A) and find the exponential regression equation (Fig. 7B). The estimated purchase price is $y_1(0) = \$14,910$. The data set and the regression equation are graphed in Figure 7C. Using trace, we see that the estimated value after 10 years is $1,959.

(A)

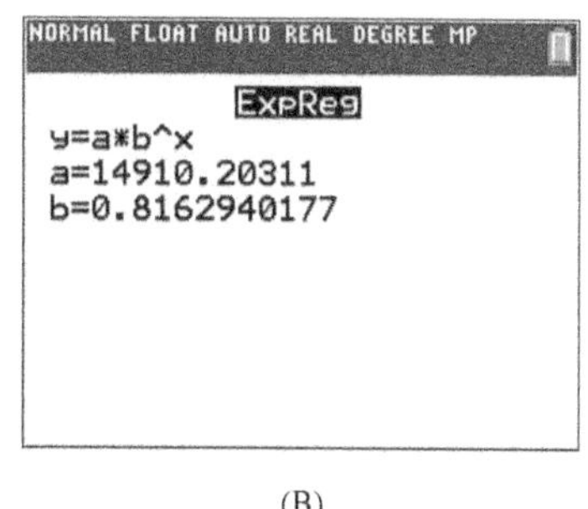

(B)

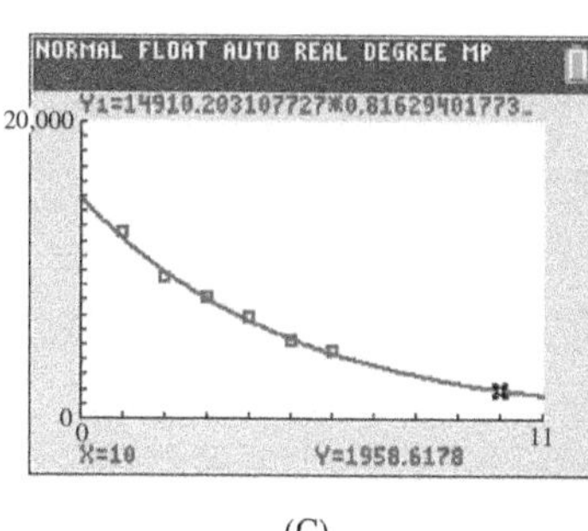

(C)

Figure 7

Matched Problem 4 Table 3 gives the market value of a midsize sedan (in dollars) x years after its purchase. Find an exponential regression model of the form $y = ab^x$ for this data set. Estimate the purchase price of the sedan. Estimate the value of the sedan 10 years after its purchase. Round answers to the nearest dollar.

Table 3

x	Value ($)
1	23,125
2	19,050
3	15,625
4	11,875
5	9,450
6	7,125

Compound Interest

The fee paid to use another's money is called **interest**. It is usually computed as a percent (called **interest rate**) of the principal over a given period of time. If, at the end of a payment period, the interest due is reinvested at the same rate, then the interest earned as well as the principal will earn interest during the next payment period. Interest paid on interest reinvested is called **compound interest** and may be calculated using the following compound interest formula:

If a **principal P (present value)** is invested at an annual **rate r** (expressed as a decimal) compounded m times a year, then the **amount A (future value)** in the account at the end of t years is given by

$$A = P\left(1 + \frac{r}{m}\right)^{mt} \quad \text{Compound interest formula}$$

For given r and m, the amount A is equal to the principal P multiplied by the exponential function b^t, where $b = (1 + r/m)^m$.

EXAMPLE 5 **Compound Growth** If $1,000 is invested in an account paying 10% compounded monthly, how much will be in the account at the end of 10 years? Compute the answer to the nearest cent.

SOLUTION We use the compound interest formula as follows:

$$A = P\left(1 + \frac{r}{m}\right)^{mt}$$

$$= 1{,}000\left(1 + \frac{0.10}{12}\right)^{(12)(10)} \quad \text{Use a calculator.}$$

$$= \$2{,}707.04$$

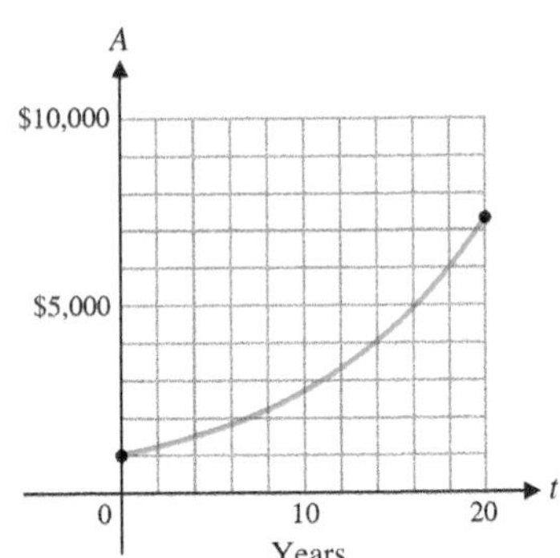

Figure 8

The graph of

$$A = 1{,}000\left(1 + \frac{0.10}{12}\right)^{12t}$$

for $0 \le t \le 20$ is shown in Figure 8.

Matched Problem 5 If you deposit $5,000 in an account paying 9% compounded daily, how much will you have in the account in 5 years? Compute the answer to the nearest cent.

Explore and Discuss 2

Suppose that $1,000 is deposited in a savings account at an annual rate of 5%. Guess the amount in the account at the end of 1 year if interest is compounded (1) quarterly, (2) monthly, (3) daily, (4) hourly. Use the compound interest formula to compute the amounts at the end of 1 year to the nearest cent. Discuss the accuracy of your initial guesses.

Explore and Discuss 2 suggests that if $1,000 were deposited in a savings account at an annual interest rate of 5%, then the amount at the end of 1 year would be less than $1,051.28, even if interest were compounded every minute or every second. The limiting value, approximately $1,051.271 096, is said to be the amount in the account if interest were compounded continuously.

If a principal, P, is invested at an annual rate, r, and compounded continuously, then the amount in the account at the end of t years is given by

$$A = Pe^{rt} \quad \text{Continuous compound interest formula}$$

where the constant $e \approx 2.718\,28$ is the base of the exponential function.

EXAMPLE 6 **Continuous Compound Interest** If \$1,000 is invested in an account paying 10% compounded continuously, how much will be in the account at the end of 10 years? Compute the answer to the nearest cent.

SOLUTION We use the continuous compound interest formula:

$$A = Pe^{rt} = 1000e^{0.10(10)} = 1000e = \$2{,}718.28$$

Compare with the answer to Example 5.

Matched Problem 6 If you deposit \$5,000 in an account paying 9% compounded continuously, how much will you have in the account in 5 years? Compute the answer to the nearest cent.

The formulas for compound interest and continuous compound interest are summarized below for convenient reference.

SUMMARY

Compound Interest: $A = P\left(1 + \frac{r}{m}\right)^{mt}$

Continuous Compound Interest: $A = Pe^{rt}$

where A = amount (future value) at the end of t years
P = principal (present value)
r = annual rate (expressed as a decimal)
m = number of compounding periods per year
t = time in years

Exercises 2.5

A **1.** Match each equation with the graph of f, g, h, or k in the figure.

(A) $y = 2^x$ (B) $y = (0.2)^x$

(C) $y = 4^x$ (D) $y = \left(\frac{1}{3}\right)^x$

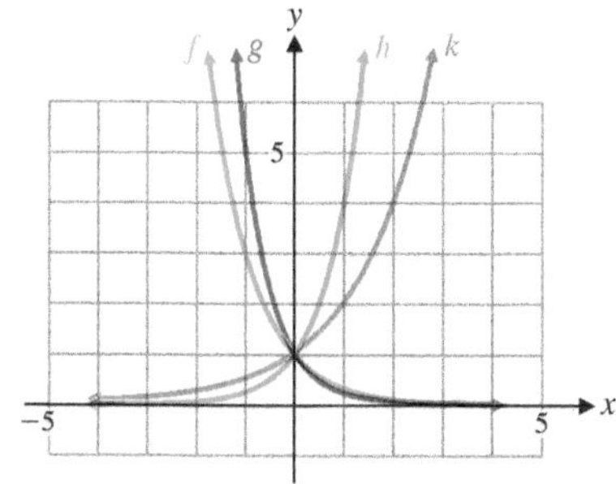

2. Match each equation with the graph of f, g, h, or k in the figure.

(A) $y = \left(\frac{1}{4}\right)^x$ (B) $y = (0.5)^x$

(C) $y = 5^x$ (D) $y = 3^x$

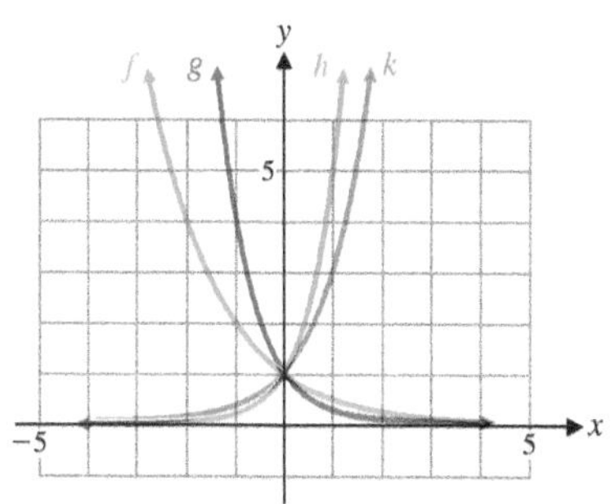

Graph each function in Problems 3–10 over the indicated interval.

3. $y = 5^x$; $[-2, 2]$

4. $y = 3^x$; $[-3, 3]$

5. $y = \left(\frac{1}{5}\right)^x = 5^{-x}$; $[-2, 2]$

6. $y = \left(\frac{1}{3}\right)^x = 3^{-x}$; $[-3, 3]$

7. $f(x) = -5^x$; $[-2, 2]$

8. $g(x) = -3^{-x}$; $[-3, 3]$

9. $y = -e^{-x}$; $[-3, 3]$

10. $y = -e^x$; $[-3, 3]$

B *In Problems 11–18, describe verbally the transformations that can be used to obtain the graph of g from the graph of f (see Section 2.2).*

11. $g(x) = -2^x$; $f(x) = 2^x$

12. $g(x) = 2^{x-2}$; $f(x) = 2^x$

13. $g(x) = 3^{x+1}$; $f(x) = 3^x$

14. $g(x) = -3^x$; $f(x) = 3^x$

15. $g(x) = e^x + 1$; $f(x) = e^x$

16. $g(x) = e^x - 2$; $f(x) = e^x$

17. $g(x) = 2e^{-(x+2)}$; $f(x) = e^{-x}$

18. $g(x) = 0.25e^{-(x-4)}$; $f(x) = e^{-x}$

19. Use the graph of f shown in the figure to sketch the graph of each of the following.

(A) $y = f(x) - 1$ (B) $y = f(x + 2)$

(C) $y = 3f(x) - 2$ (D) $y = 2 - f(x - 3)$

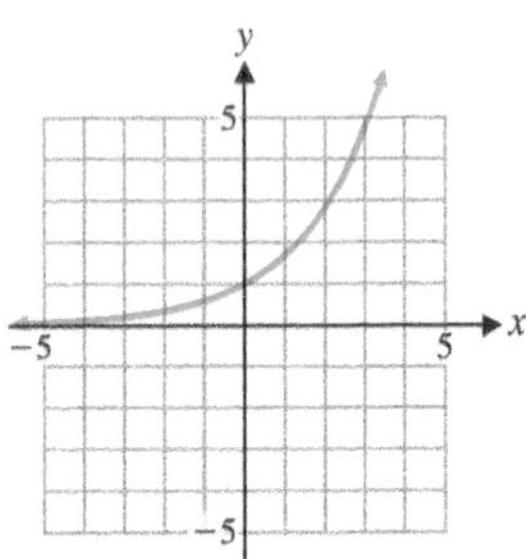

Figure for 19 and 20

20. Use the graph of f shown in the figure to sketch the graph of each of the following.

(A) $y = f(x) + 2$ (B) $y = f(x - 3)$

(C) $y = 2f(x) - 4$ (D) $y = 4 - f(x + 2)$

In Problems 21–26, graph each function over the indicated interval.

21. $f(t) = 2^{t/10}$; $[-30, 30]$ **22.** $G(t) = 3^{t/100}$; $[-200, 200]$

23. $y = -3 + e^{1+x}$; $[-4, 2]$ **24.** $N = 1 + e^{x-3}$; $[-2, 6]$

25. $y = e^{|x|}$; $[-3, 3]$ **26.** $y = e^{-|x|}$; $[-3, 3]$

27. Find all real numbers a such that $a^2 = a^{-2}$. Explain why this does not violate the second exponential function property in Theorem 2 on page 98.

28. Find real numbers a and b such that $a \neq b$ but $a^4 = b^4$. Explain why this does not violate the third exponential function property in Theorem 2 on page 98.

In Problems 29–38, solve each equation for x.

29. $2^{2x+5} = 2^{101}$ **30.** $3^{x+4} = 3^{2x-5}$

31. $9^{x^2} = 9^{4x+21}$ **32.** $5^{x^2-x} = 5^{42}$

33. $(3x + 9)^5 = 32x^5$ **34.** $(5x + 6)^7 = 111^7$

35. $(x + 5)^2 = (2x - 14)^2$ **36.** $(2x + 1)^2 = (3x - 1)^2$

37. $(5x + 18)^4 = (x + 6)^4$ **38.** $(8x - 11)^6 = (7x - 19)^6$

C *In Problems 39–46, solve each equation for x. (Remember: $e^x \neq 0$ and $e^{-x} \neq 0$ for all values of x).*

39. $xe^{-x} + 7e^{-x} = 0$ **40.** $10xe^x - 5e^x = 0$

41. $2x^2e^x - 8e^x = 0$ **42.** $3x^2e^{-x} - 48e^{-x} = 0$

43. $e^{4x} - e = 0$ **44.** $e^{4x} + e = 0$

45. $e^{3x-1} + e = 0$ **46.** $e^{3x-1} - e = 0$

Graph each function in Problems 47–50 over the indicated interval.

47. $h(x) = x(2^x)$; $[-5, 0]$ **48.** $m(x) = x(3^{-x})$; $[0, 3]$

49. $N = \dfrac{100}{1 + e^{-t}}$; $[0, 5]$ **50.** $N = \dfrac{300}{1 + 4e^{-t}}$; $[0, 5]$

Applications

In all problems involving days, a 365-day year is assumed.

51. Continuous compound interest. Find the value of an investment of \$100,000 in 9 years if it earns an annual rate of 2.85% compounded continuously.

52. Continuous compound interest. Find the value of an investment of \$24,000 in 7 years if it earns an annual rate of 4.35% compounded continuously.

53. Compound growth. Suppose that \$2,500 is invested at 7% compounded quarterly. How much money will be in the account in

(A) $\frac{3}{4}$ year? (B) 15 years?

Compute answers to the nearest cent.

54. Compound growth. Suppose that \$4,000 is invested at 6% compounded weekly. How much money will be in the account in

(A) $\frac{1}{2}$ year? (B) 10 years?

Compute answers to the nearest cent.

55. Finance. A person wishes to have \$15,000 cash for a new car 5 years from now. How much should be placed in an account now, if the account pays 6.75% compounded weekly? Compute the answer to the nearest dollar.

56. Finance. A couple just had a baby. How much should they invest now at 5.5% compounded daily in order to have \$40,000 for the child's education 17 years from now? Compute the answer to the nearest dollar.

57. Money growth. Commonwealth Bank of Australia offers term deposits with different interest payment options. The rates for 24-month term deposits are the following:

(A) 2.40% compounded four weekly

(B) 2.50% compounded six monthly

(C) 2.60% compounded annually

Compute the value of \$10,000 invested in each interest payment option at the end of 2 years.

58. Money growth. Bankwest, a division of Commonwealth Bank of Australia, offers online term deposits with different interest payment options. The rates for 60-month term deposits are the following:

(A) 2.62% compounded monthly

(B) 2.62% compounded quarterly

(C) 2.63% compounded semiannually

(D) 2.65% compounded annually

Compute the value of $10,000 invested in each interest payment option at the end of 5 years.

59. Advertising. A company is trying to introduce a new product to as many people as possible through television advertising in a large metropolitan area with 2 million possible viewers. A model for the number of people N (in millions) who are aware of the product after t days of advertising was found to be

$$N = 2(1 - e^{-0.037t})$$

Graph this function for $0 \le t \le 50$. What value does N approach as t increases without bound?

60. Learning curve. People assigned to assemble circuit boards for a computer manufacturing company undergo on-the-job training. From past experience, the learning curve for the average employee is given by

$$N = 40(1 - e^{-0.12t})$$

where N is the number of boards assembled per day after t days of training. Graph this function for $0 \le t \le 30$. What is the maximum number of boards an average employee can be expected to produce in 1 day?

61. Internet users. Table 4 shows the number of individuals worldwide who could access the internet from home for selected years since 2000.

(A) Let x represent the number of years since 2000 and find an exponential regression model ($y = ab^x$) for the number of internet users.

(B) Use the model to estimate the number of internet users in 2024.

Table 4 **Internet Users (billions)**

Year	Users
2000	0.41
2004	0.91
2008	1.58
2012	2.02
2016	3.42

Source: Internet Stats Live

62. Mobile data traffic. Table 5 shows estimates of mobile data traffic, in exabytes (10^{18} bytes) per month, for years from 2015 to 2020.

(A) Let x represent the number of years since 2015 and find an exponential regression model ($y = ab^x$) for mobile data traffic.

(B) Use the model to estimate the mobile data traffic in 2025.

Table 5 **Mobile Data Traffic (exabytes per month)**

Year	Traffic
2015	3.7
2016	6.2
2017	9.9
2018	14.9
2019	21.7
2020	30.6

Source: Cisco Systems Inc.

63. Marine biology. Marine life depends on the microscopic plant life that exists in the photic zone, a zone that goes to a depth where only 1% of surface light remains. In some waters with a great deal of sediment, the photic zone may go down only 15 to 20 feet. In some murky harbors, the intensity of light d feet below the surface is given approximately by

$$I = I_0 e^{-0.23d}$$

where I_0 is the intensity of light at the surface. What percentage of the surface light will reach a depth of

(A) 10 feet? (B) 20 feet?

64. Marine biology. Refer to Problem 63. Light intensity I relative to depth d (in feet) for one of the clearest bodies of water in the world, the Sargasso Sea, can be approximated by

$$I = I_0 e^{-0.00942d}$$

where I_0 is the intensity of light at the surface. What percentage of the surface light will reach a depth of

(A) 50 feet? (B) 100 feet?

65. Population growth. In 2015, the estimated population of South Sudan was 12 million with a relative growth rate of 4.02%.

(A) Write an equation that models the population growth in South Sudan, letting 2015 be year 0.

(B) Based on the model, what is the expected population of South Sudan in 2025?

66. Population growth. In 2015, the estimated population of Brazil was 204 million with a relative growth rate of 0.77%.

(A) Write an equation that models the population growth in Brazil, letting 2015 be year 0.

(B) Based on the model, what is the expected population of Brazil in 2030?

67. Population growth. In 2015, the estimated population of Japan was 127 million with a relative growth rate of −0.16%.

(A) Write an equation that models the population growth in Japan, letting 2015 be year 0.

(B) Based on the model, what is the expected population in Japan in 2030?

68. World population growth. From the dawn of humanity to 1830, world population grew to one billion people. In 100 more years (by 1930) it grew to two billion, and 3 billion more were added in only 60 years (by 1990). In 2016, the estimated world population was 7.4 billion with a relative growth rate of 1.13%.

(A) Write an equation that models the world population growth, letting 2016 be year 0.

(B) Based on the model, what is the expected world population (to the nearest hundred million) in 2025? In 2033?

Answers to Matched Problems

1.

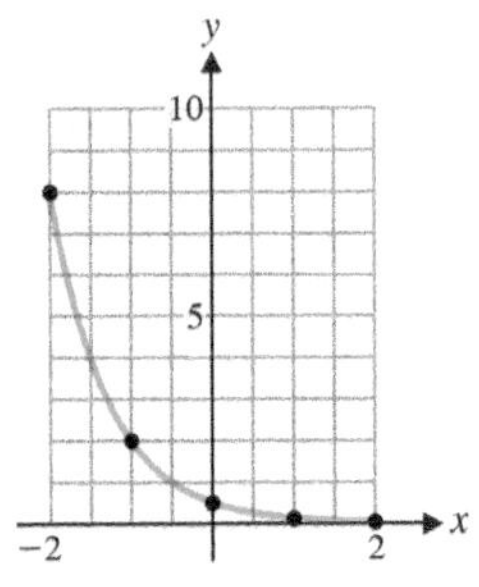

2. (A) 179 bacteria (B) 1,271,659 bacteria
3. 233 mg
4. Purchase price: \$30,363; value after 10 yr: \$2,864

5. \$7,841.13
6. \$7,841.56

2.6 Logarithmic Functions

- Inverse Functions
- Logarithmic Functions
- Properties of Logarithmic Functions
- Calculator Evaluation of Logarithms
- Applications

Find the exponential function keys 10^x and e^x on your calculator. Close to these keys you will find the LOG and LN keys. The latter two keys represent *logarithmic functions,* and each is closely related to its nearby exponential function. In fact, the exponential function and the corresponding logarithmic function are said to be *inverses* of each other. In this section we will develop the concept of inverse functions and use it to define a logarithmic function as the inverse of an exponential function. We will then investigate basic properties of logarithmic functions, use a calculator to evaluate them for particular values of x, and apply them to real-world problems.

Logarithmic functions are used in modeling and solving many types of problems. For example, the decibel scale is a logarithmic scale used to measure sound intensity, and the Richter scale is a logarithmic scale used to measure the force of an earthquake. An important business application has to do with finding the time it takes money to double if it is invested at a certain rate compounded a given number of times a year or compounded continuously. This requires the solution of an exponential equation, and logarithms play a central role in the process.

Inverse Functions

Look at the graphs of $f(x) = \frac{x}{2}$ and $g(x) = \frac{|x|}{2}$ in Figure 1:

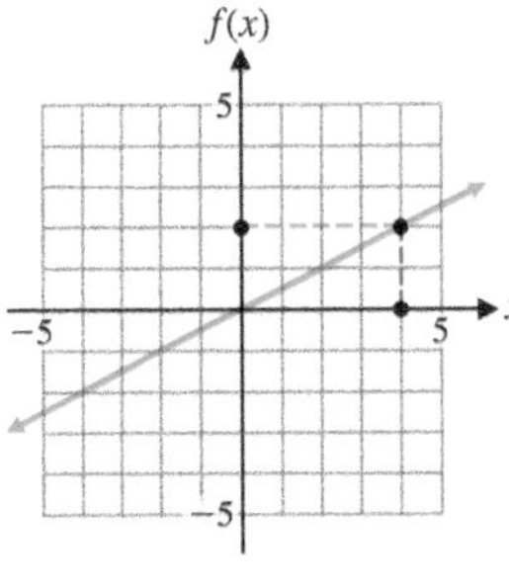

(A) $f(x) = \frac{x}{2}$

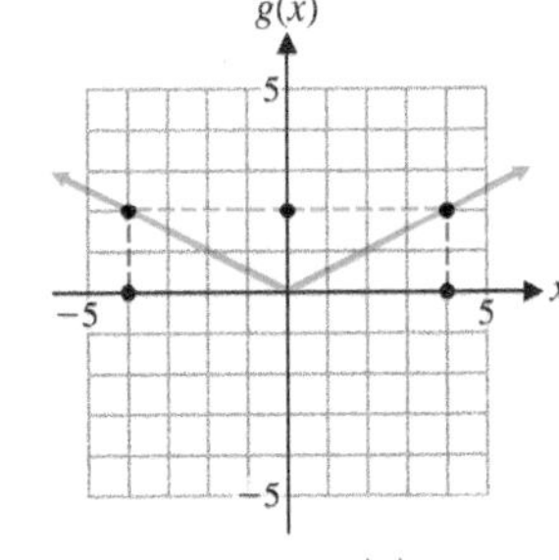

(B) $g(x) = \frac{|x|}{2}$

Figure 1

Because both f and g are functions, each domain value corresponds to exactly one range value. For which function does each range value correspond to exactly one domain value? This is the case only for function f. Note that for function f, the range value 2 corresponds to the domain value 4. For function g the range value 2 corresponds to both -4 and 4. Function f is said to be *one-to-one.*

DEFINITION One-to-One Functions

A function f is said to be **one-to-one** if each range value corresponds to exactly one domain value.

Reminder

We say that the function f is **increasing** on an interval (a, b) if $f(x_2) > f(x_1)$ whenever $a < x_1 < x_2 < b$ and f is **decreasing** on (a, b) if $f(x_2) < f(x_1)$ whenever $a < x_1 < x_2 < b$.

It can be shown that any continuous function that is either increasing or decreasing for all domain values is one-to-one. If a continuous function increases for some domain values and decreases for others, then it cannot be one-to-one. Figure 1 shows an example of each case.

Explore and Discuss 1

Graph $f(x) = 2^x$ and $g(x) = x^2$. For a range value of 4, what are the corresponding domain values for each function? Which of the two functions is one-to-one? Explain why.

Starting with a one-to-one function f, we can obtain a new function called the *inverse* of f.

DEFINITION Inverse of a Function

If f is a one-to-one function, then the **inverse** of f is the function formed by interchanging the independent and dependent variables for f. Thus, if (a, b) is a point on the graph of f, then (b, a) is a point on the graph of the inverse of f.

Note: If f is not one-to-one, then f **does not have an inverse.**

In this course, we are interested in the inverses of exponential functions, called *logarithmic functions.*

Logarithmic Functions

If we start with the exponential function f defined by

$$y = 2^x \tag{1}$$

and interchange the variables, we obtain the inverse of f:

$$x = 2^y \tag{2}$$

We call the inverse the **logarithmic function with base 2**, and write

$$y = \log_2 x \quad \text{if and only if} \quad x = 2^y$$

We can graph $y = \log_2 x$ by graphing $x = 2^y$ since they are equivalent. Any ordered pair of numbers on the graph of the exponential function will be on the graph of the logarithmic function if we interchange the order of the components. For example, $(3, 8)$ satisfies equation (1) and $(8, 3)$ satisfies equation (2). The graphs of $y = 2^x$ and $y = \log_2 x$ are shown in Figure 2. Note that if we fold the paper along the dashed line $y = x$ in Figure 2, the two graphs match exactly. The line $y = x$ is a line of symmetry for the two graphs.

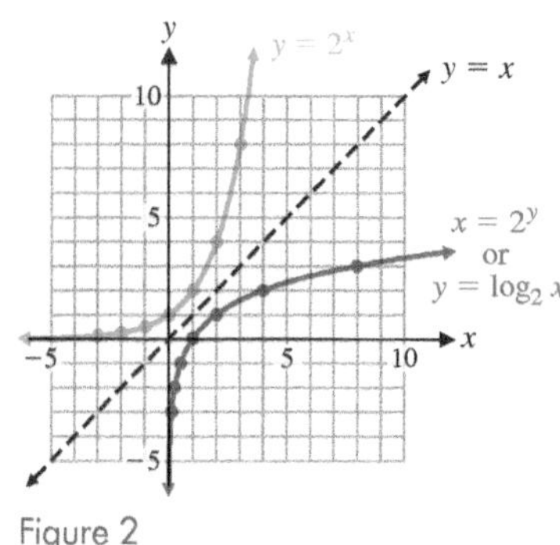

Figure 2

Exponential Function		Logarithmic Function	
x	$y = 2^x$	$x = 2^y$	y
-3	$\frac{1}{8}$	$\frac{1}{8}$	-3
-2	$\frac{1}{4}$	$\frac{1}{4}$	-2
-1	$\frac{1}{2}$	$\frac{1}{2}$	-1
0	1	1	0
1	2	2	1
2	4	4	2
3	8	8	3

Ordered pairs reversed

In general, since the graphs of all exponential functions of the form $f(x) = b^x$, $b \neq 1$, $b > 0$, are either increasing or decreasing, exponential functions have inverses.

DEFINITION Logarithmic Functions

The inverse of an exponential function is called a **logarithmic function**. For $b > 0$ and $b \neq 1$,

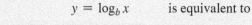

Logarithmic form		Exponential form
$y = \log_b x$	is equivalent to	$x = b^y$

The **log to the base b of x** is the exponent to which b must be raised to obtain x. [*Remember:* A logarithm is an exponent.] The **domain** of the logarithmic function is the set of all positive real numbers, which is also the range of the corresponding exponential function, and the **range** of the logarithmic function is the set of all real numbers, which is also the domain of the corresponding exponential function. Typical graphs of an exponential function and its inverse, a logarithmic function, are shown in Figure 3.

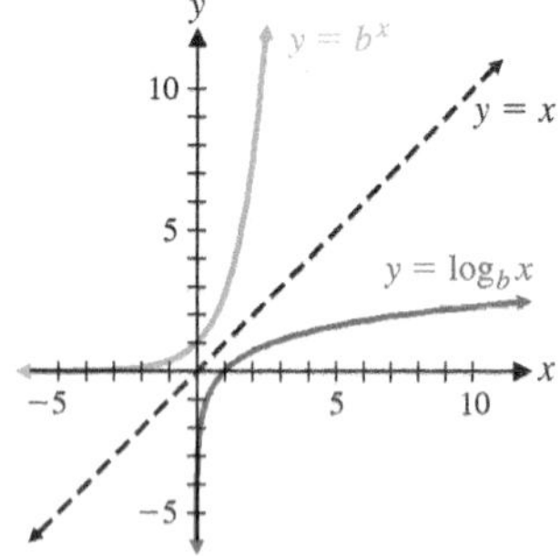

Figure 3

CONCEPTUAL INSIGHT

Because the domain of a logarithmic function consists of the positive real numbers, the entire graph of a logarithmic function lies to the right of the y axis. In contrast, the graphs of polynomial and exponential functions intersect every vertical line, and the graphs of rational functions intersect all but a finite number of vertical lines.

The following examples involve converting logarithmic forms to equivalent exponential forms, and vice versa.

EXAMPLE 1 **Logarithmic–Exponential Conversions** Change each logarithmic form to an equivalent exponential form:

(A) $\log_5 25 = 2$ (B) $\log_9 3 = \frac{1}{2}$ (C) $\log_2\left(\frac{1}{4}\right) = -2$

SOLUTION

(A) $\log_5 25 = 2$ is equivalent to $25 = 5^2$

(B) $\log_9 3 = \frac{1}{2}$ is equivalent to $3 = 9^{1/2}$

(C) $\log_2\left(\frac{1}{4}\right) = -2$ is equivalent to $\frac{1}{4} = 2^{-2}$

Matched Problem 1 Change each logarithmic form to an equivalent exponential form:

(A) $\log_3 9 = 2$ (B) $\log_4 2 = \frac{1}{2}$ (C) $\log_3\left(\frac{1}{9}\right) = -2$

EXAMPLE 2 **Exponential–Logarithmic Conversions** Change each exponential form to an equivalent logarithmic form:

(A) $64 = 4^3$ (B) $6 = \sqrt{36}$ (C) $\frac{1}{8} = 2^{-3}$

SOLUTION

(A) $64 = 4^3$ is equivalent to $\log_4 64 = 3$

(B) $6 = \sqrt{36}$ is equivalent to $\log_{36} 6 = \frac{1}{2}$

(C) $\frac{1}{8} = 2^{-3}$ is equivalent to $\log_2\left(\frac{1}{8}\right) = -3$

Matched Problem 2 Change each exponential form to an equivalent logarithmic form:

(A) $49 = 7^2$ (B) $3 = \sqrt{9}$ (C) $\frac{1}{3} = 3^{-1}$

To gain a deeper understanding of logarithmic functions and their relationship to exponential functions, we consider a few problems where we want to find x, b, or y in $y = \log_b x$, given the other two values. All values are chosen so that the problems can be solved exactly without a calculator.

EXAMPLE 3 **Solutions of the Equation $y = \log_b x$** Find y, b, or x, as indicated.

(A) Find y: $y = \log_4 16$ (B) Find x: $\log_2 x = -3$

(C) Find b: $\log_b 100 = 2$

SOLUTION

(A) $y = \log_4 16$ is equivalent to $16 = 4^y$. So,

$$y = 2$$

(B) $\log_2 x = -3$ is equivalent to $x = 2^{-3}$. So,

$$x = \frac{1}{2^3} = \frac{1}{8}$$

(C) $\log_b 100 = 2$ is equivalent to $100 = b^2$. So,

$$b = 10$$ Recall that b cannot be negative.

Matched Problem 3 Find y, b, or x, as indicated.

(A) Find y: $y = \log_9 27$ (B) Find x: $\log_3 x = -1$

(C) Find b: $\log_b 1{,}000 = 3$

Properties of Logarithmic Functions

The properties of exponential functions (Section 2.5) lead to properties of logarithmic functions. For example, consider the exponential property $b^x b^y = b^{x+y}$. Let $M = b^x$, $N = b^y$. Then

$$\log_b MN = \log_b(b^x b^y) = \log_b b^{x+y} = x + y = \log_b M + \log_b N$$

So $\log_b MN = \log_b M + \log_b N$, that is, the logarithm of a product is the sum of the logarithms. Similarly, the logarithm of a quotient is the difference of the logarithms. These properties are among the eight useful properties of logarithms that are listed in Theorem 1.

THEOREM 1 Properties of Logarithmic Functions

If b, M, and N are positive real numbers, $b \neq 1$, and p and x are real numbers, then

1. $\log_b 1 = 0$
2. $\log_b b = 1$
3. $\log_b b^x = x$
4. $b^{\log_b x} = x, \quad x > 0$
5. $\log_b MN = \log_b M + \log_b N$
6. $\log_b \frac{M}{N} = \log_b M - \log_b N$
7. $\log_b M^p = p \log_b M$
8. $\log_b M = \log_b N$ if and only if $M = N$

EXAMPLE 4 **Using Logarithmic Properties** Use logarithmic properties to write in simpler form:

(A) $\log_b \frac{wx}{yz}$ (B) $\log_b (wx)^{3/5}$ (C) $e^{x \log_e b}$ (D) $\frac{\log_e x}{\log_e b}$

SOLUTION

(A)
$$\log_b \frac{wx}{yz} = \log_b wx - \log_b yz$$
$$= \log_b w + \log_b x - (\log_b y + \log_b z)$$
$$= \log_b w + \log_b x - \log_b y - \log_b z$$

(B) $\log_b (wx)^{3/5} = \frac{3}{5} \log_b wx = \frac{3}{5}(\log_b w + \log_b x)$

(C) $e^{x \log_e b} = e^{\log_e b^x} = b^x$

(D) $\frac{\log_e x}{\log_e b} = \frac{\log_e (b^{\log_b x})}{\log_e b} = \frac{(\log_b x)(\log_e b)}{\log_e b} = \log_b x$

Matched Problem 4 Write in simpler form, as in Example 4.

(A) $\log_b \frac{R}{ST}$ (B) $\log_b \left(\frac{R}{S}\right)^{2/3}$ (C) $2^{u \log_2 b}$ (D) $\frac{\log_2 x}{\log_2 b}$

The following examples and problems will give you additional practice in using basic logarithmic properties.

EXAMPLE 5 **Solving Logarithmic Equations** Find x so that

$$\tfrac{3}{2}\log_b 4 - \tfrac{2}{3}\log_b 8 + \log_b 2 = \log_b x$$

SOLUTION

$$\tfrac{3}{2}\log_b 4 - \tfrac{2}{3}\log_b 8 + \log_b 2 = \log_b x \quad \text{Use property 7.}$$
$$\log_b 4^{3/2} - \log_b 8^{2/3} + \log_b 2 = \log_b x \quad \text{Simplify.}$$
$$\log_b 8 - \log_b 4 + \log_b 2 = \log_b x \quad \text{Use properties 5 and 6.}$$
$$\log_b \frac{8 \cdot 2}{4} = \log_b x \quad \text{Simplify.}$$
$$\log_b 4 = \log_b x \quad \text{Use property 8.}$$
$$x = 4$$

Matched Problem 5 Find x so that $3 \log_b 2 + \frac{1}{2}\log_b 25 - \log_b 20 = \log_b x$.

EXAMPLE 6 **Solving Logarithmic Equations** Solve: $\log_{10} x + \log_{10}(x + 1) = \log_{10} 6$.

SOLUTION

$$\log_{10} x + \log_{10}(x + 1) = \log_{10} 6 \quad \text{Use property 5.}$$
$$\log_{10}[x(x + 1)] = \log_{10} 6 \quad \text{Use property 8.}$$
$$x(x + 1) = 6 \quad \text{Expand.}$$
$$x^2 + x - 6 = 0 \quad \text{Solve by factoring.}$$
$$(x + 3)(x - 2) = 0$$
$$x = -3, 2$$

We must exclude $x = -3$, since the domain of the function $\log_{10} x$ is $(0, \infty)$; so $x = 2$ is the only solution.

Matched Problem 6 Solve: $\log_3 x + \log_3(x - 3) = \log_3 10$.

Calculator Evaluation of Logarithms

Of all possible logarithmic bases, e and 10 are used almost exclusively. Before we can use logarithms in certain practical problems, we need to be able to approximate the logarithm of any positive number either to base 10 or to base e. And conversely, if we are given the logarithm of a number to base 10 or base e, we need to be able to approximate the number. Historically, tables were used for this purpose, but now calculators make computations faster and far more accurate.

Common logarithms are logarithms with base 10. **Natural logarithms** are logarithms with base e. Most calculators have a key labeled "log" (or "LOG") and a key labeled "ln" (or "LN"). The former represents a common (base 10) logarithm and the latter a natural (base e) logarithm. In fact, "log" and "ln" are both used extensively in mathematical literature, and whenever you see either used in this book without a base indicated, they will be interpreted as follows:

Common logarithm: $\log x$ **means** $\log_{10} x$
Natural logarithm: $\ln x$ **means** $\log_e x$

Finding the common or natural logarithm using a calculator is very easy. On some calculators, you simply enter a number from the domain of the function and press LOG or LN. On other calculators, you press either LOG or LN, enter a number from the domain, and then press ENTER. Check the user's manual for your calculator.

EXAMPLE 7 **Calculator Evaluation of Logarithms** Use a calculator to evaluate each to six decimal places:

(A) $\log 3{,}184$ (B) $\ln 0.000\,349$ (C) $\log(-3.24)$

SOLUTION

(A) $\log 3{,}184 = 3.502\,973$

(B) $\ln 0.000\,349 = -7.960\,439$

(C) $\log(-3.24) =$ Error -3.24 is not in the domain of the log function.

Matched Problem 7 Use a calculator to evaluate each to six decimal places:

(A) $\log 0.013\,529$ (B) $\ln 28.693\,28$ (C) $\ln(-0.438)$

Given the logarithm of a number, how do you find the number? We make direct use of the logarithmic-exponential relationships, which follow from the definition of logarithmic function given at the beginning of this section.

$$\log x = y \quad \text{is equivalent to} \quad x = 10^y$$
$$\ln x = y \quad \text{is equivalent to} \quad x = e^y$$

EXAMPLE 8 **Solving $\log_b x = y$ for x** Find x to four decimal places, given the indicated logarithm:

(A) $\log x = -2.315$ (B) $\ln x = 2.386$

SOLUTION

(A) $\log x = -2.315$ Change to equivalent exponential form.

$x = 10^{-2.315}$ Evaluate with a calculator.

$= 0.0048$

(B) $\ln x = 2.386$ Change to equivalent exponential form.

$x = e^{2.386}$ Evaluate with a calculator.

$= 10.8699$

Matched Problem 8 Find x to four decimal places, given the indicated logarithm:

(A) $\ln x = -5.062$ (B) $\log x = 2.0821$

We can use logarithms to solve exponential equations.

EXAMPLE 9 **Solving Exponential Equations** Solve for x to four decimal places:

(A) $10^x = 2$ (B) $e^x = 3$ (C) $3^x = 4$

SOLUTION

(A) $10^x = 2$ Take common logarithms of both sides.

$\log 10^x = \log 2$ Use property 3.

$x = \log 2$ Use a calculator.

$= 0.3010$ To four decimal places

$e^x = 3$ Take natural logarithms of both sides.

(B) $\ln e^x = \ln 3$ Use property 3.

$x = \ln 3$ Use a calculator.

$= 1.0986$ To four decimal places

(C) $3^x = 4$ Take either natural or common logarithms of both sides. (We choose common logarithms.)

$\log 3^x = \log 4$ Use property 7.

$x \log 3 = \log 4$ Solve for x.

$x = \dfrac{\log 4}{\log 3}$ Use a calculator.

$= 1.2619$ To four decimal places

Matched Problem 9 Solve for x to four decimal places:

(A) $10^x = 7$ (B) $e^x = 6$ (C) $4^x = 5$

Exponential equations can also be solved graphically by graphing both sides of an equation and finding the points of intersection. Figure 4 illustrates this approach for the equations in Example 9.

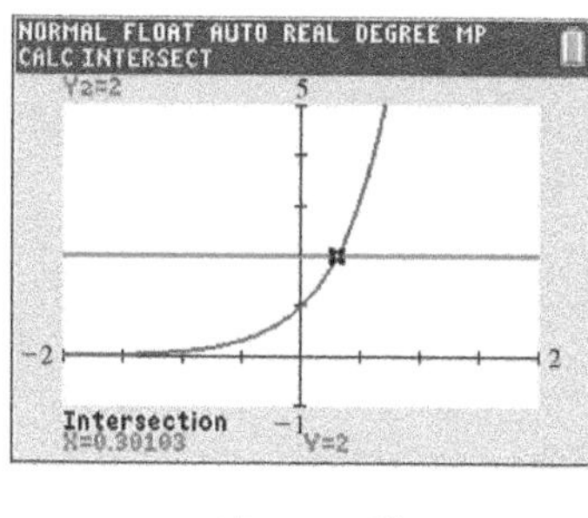

(A) $y_1 = 10^x$
$y_2 = 2$

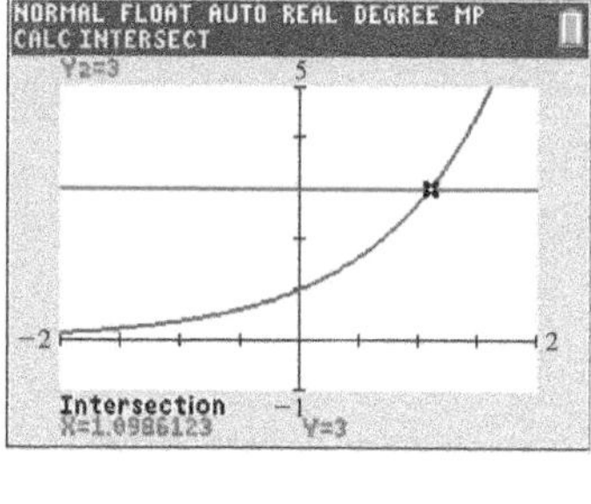

(B) $y_1 = e^x$
$y_2 = 3$

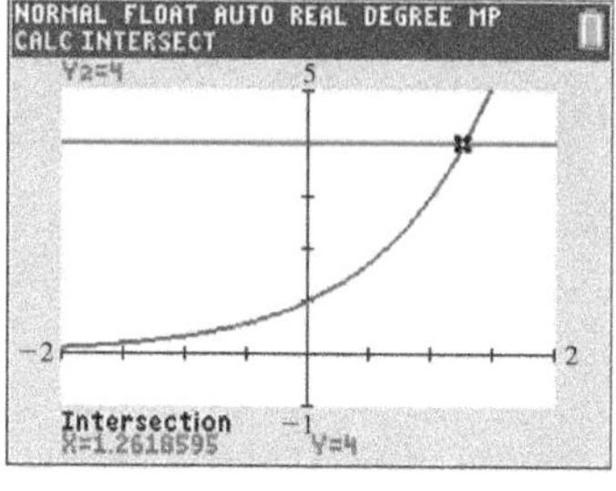

(C) $y_1 = 3^x$
$y_2 = 4$

Figure 4 Graphical solution of exponential equations

Explore and Discuss 2

Discuss how you could find $y = \log_5 38.25$ using either natural or common logarithms on a calculator. [*Hint:* Start by rewriting the equation in exponential form.]

Remark In the usual notation for natural logarithms, the simplifications of Example 4, parts (C) and (D) on page 110, become

$$e^{x \ln b} = b^x \qquad \text{and} \qquad \frac{\ln x}{\ln b} = \log_b x$$

With these formulas, we can change an exponential function with base b, or a logarithmic function with base b, to expressions involving exponential or logarithmic functions, respectively, to the base e. Such **change-of-base formulas** are useful in calculus.

Applications

A convenient and easily understood way of comparing different investments is to use their **doubling times**—the length of time it takes the value of an investment to double. Logarithm properties, as you will see in Example 10, provide us with just the right tool for solving some doubling-time problems.

EXAMPLE 10 **Doubling Time for an Investment** How long (to the next whole year) will it take money to double if it is invested at 20% compounded annually?

SOLUTION We use the compound interest formula discussed in Section 2.5:

$$A = P\left(1 + \frac{r}{m}\right)^{mt} \qquad \text{Compound interest}$$

The problem is to find t, given $r = 0.20$, $m = 1$, and $A = 2P$; that is,

$$2P = P(1 + 0.2)^t$$

$$2 = 1.2^t$$

Solve for t by taking the natural or common logarithm of both sides (we choose the natural logarithm).

$$1.2^t = 2$$

$$\ln 1.2^t = \ln 2$$

$$t \ln 1.2 = \ln 2 \quad \text{Use property 7.}$$

$$t = \frac{\ln 2}{\ln 1.2} \quad \text{Use a calculator.}$$

$$\approx 3.8 \text{ years} \quad [\textit{Note: } (\ln 2)/(\ln 1.2) \neq \ln 2 - \ln 1.2]$$

$$\approx 4 \text{ years} \quad \text{To the next whole year}$$

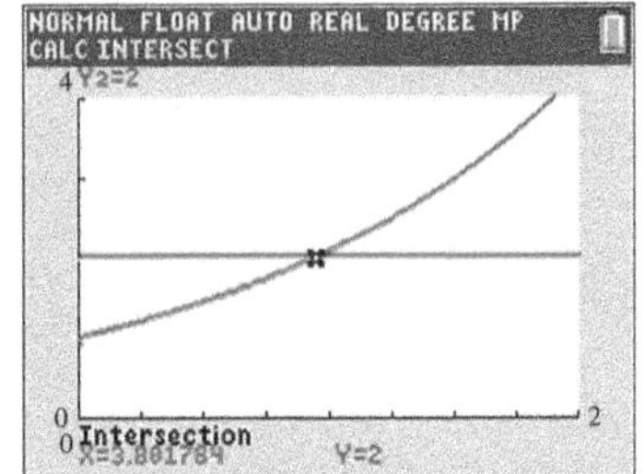

Figure 5 $y_1 = 1.2^x$, $y_2 = 2$

When interest is paid at the end of 3 years, the money will not be doubled; when paid at the end of 4 years, the money will be slightly more than doubled.

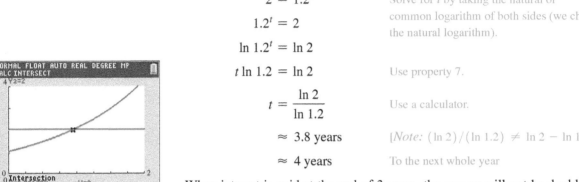

Example 10 can also be solved graphically by graphing both sides of the equation $2 = 1.2^t$, and finding the intersection point (Fig. 5).

Matched Problem 10 How long (to the next whole year) will it take money to triple if it is invested at 13% compounded annually?

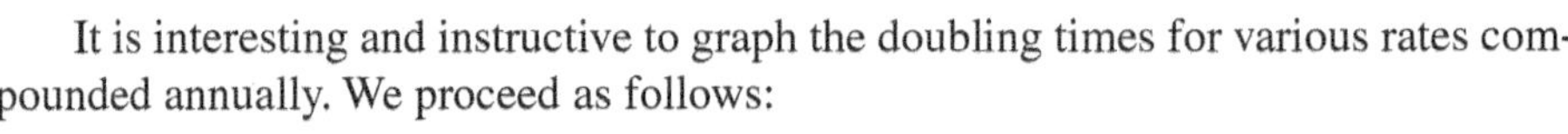

It is interesting and instructive to graph the doubling times for various rates compounded annually. We proceed as follows:

$$A = P(1 + r)^t$$

$$2P = P(1 + r)^t$$

$$2 = (1 + r)^t$$

$$(1 + r)^t = 2$$

$$\ln (1 + r)^t = \ln 2$$

$$t \ln (1 + r) = \ln 2$$

$$t = \frac{\ln 2}{\ln(1 + r)}$$

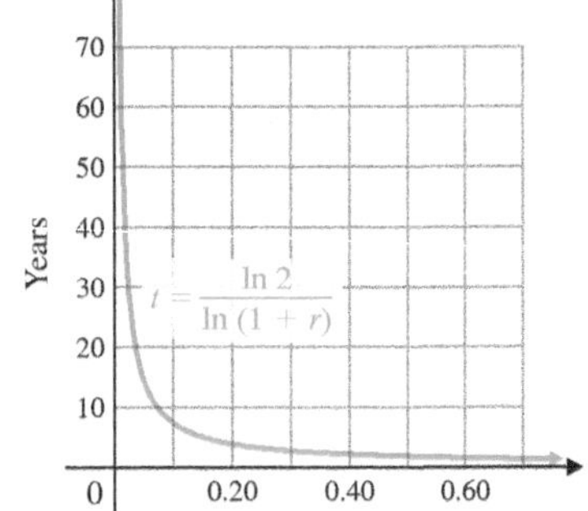

Figure 6

Figure 6 shows the graph of this equation (doubling time in years) for interest rates compounded annually from 1 to 70% (expressed as decimals). Note the dramatic change in doubling time as rates change from 1 to 20% (from 0.01 to 0.20).

Among increasing functions, the logarithmic functions (with bases $b > 1$) increase much more slowly for large values of x than either exponential or polynomial functions. When a visual inspection of the plot of a data set indicates a slowly increasing function, a logarithmic function often provides a good model. We use **logarithmic regression** on a graphing calculator to find the function of the form $y = a + b \ln x$ that best fits the data.

EXAMPLE 11 **Home Ownership Rates** The U.S. Census Bureau published the data in Table 1 on home ownership rates. Let x represent time in years with $x = 0$ representing 1900. Use logarithmic regression to find the best model of the form $y = a + b \ln x$ for the home ownership rate y as a function of time x. Use the model to predict the home ownership rate in the United States in 2025 (to the nearest tenth of a percent).

Table 1 Home Ownership Rates

Year	Rate (%)
1950	55.0
1960	61.9
1970	62.9
1980	64.4
1990	64.2
2000	67.4
2010	66.9

SOLUTION Enter the data in a graphing calculator (Fig. 7A) and find the logarithmic regression equation (Fig. 7B). The data set and the regression equation are graphed in Figure 7C. Using trace, we predict that the home ownership rate in 2025 would be 69.8%.

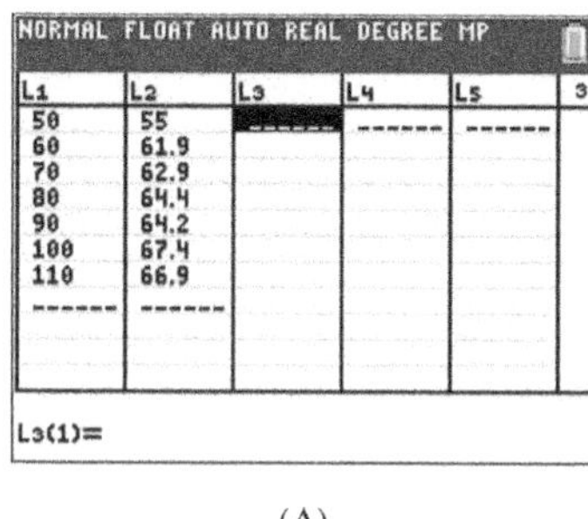

(A)

NORMAL FLOAT AUTO REAL DEGREE MP

LnReg
y=a+blnx
a=4.113162084
b=13.59644935

(B)

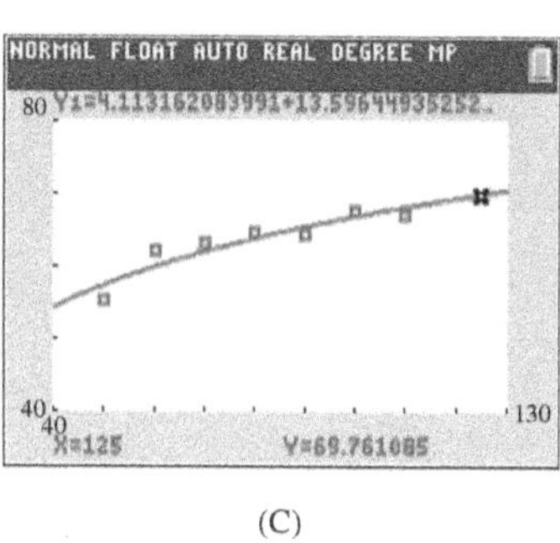

(C)

Figure 7

Matched Problem 11 Refer to Example 11. Use the model to predict the home ownership rate in the United States in 2030 (to the nearest tenth of a percent).

CAUTION Note that in Example 11 we let $x = 0$ represent 1900. If we let $x = 0$ represent 1940, for example, we would obtain a different logarithmic regression equation. We would *not* let $x = 0$ represent 1950 (the first year in Table 1) or any later year, because logarithmic functions are undefined at 0. ▲

Exercises 2.6

A *For Problems 1–6, rewrite in equivalent exponential form.*

1. $\log_3 27 = 3$

2. $\log_2 32 = 5$

3. $\log_{10} 1 = 0$

4. $\log_e 1 = 0$

5. $\log_4 8 = \frac{3}{2}$

6. $\log_8 16 = \frac{4}{3}$

For Problems 7–12, rewrite in equivalent logarithmic form.

7. $49 = 7^2$

8. $36 = 6^2$

9. $8 = 4^{3/2}$

10. $8 = 16^{3/4}$

11. $A = b^u$

12. $M = b^x$

In Problems 13–22, evaluate the expression without using a calculator.

13. $\log_{10} 1{,}000{,}000$

14. $\log_{10} \frac{1}{1{,}000}$

15. $\log_{10} \frac{1}{100{,}000}$

16. $\log_{10} 10{,}000$

17. $\log_2 128$

18. $\log_3 \frac{1}{243}$

19. $\ln e^{-3}$

20. $e^{\ln(-1)}$

21. $e^{\ln(-3)}$

22. $\ln e^{-1}$

For Problems 23–28, write in simpler form, as in Example 4.

23. $\log_b \frac{P}{Q}$

24. $\log_b FG$

25. $\log_b L^5$

26. $\log_b w^{26}$

27. $3^{p \log_3 q}$

28. $\frac{\log_3 P}{\log_3 R}$

B *For Problems 29–38, find x, y, or b without using a calculator.*

29. $\log_{10} x = -1$

30. $\log_{10} x = 1$

31. $\log_b 64 = 3$

32. $\log_b \frac{1}{25} = 2$

33. $\log_2 \frac{1}{8} = y$

34. $\log_{49} 7 = y$

35. $\log_b 81 = -4$

36. $\log_b 10{,}000 = 2$

37. $\log_4 x = \frac{3}{2}$

38. $\log_{27} x = \frac{4}{3}$

In Problems 39–46, discuss the validity of each statement. If the statement is always true, explain why. If not, give a counterexample.

39. Every polynomial function is one-to-one.

40. Every polynomial function of odd degree is one-to-one.

41. If g is the inverse of a function f, then g is one-to-one.

42. The graph of a one-to-one function intersects each vertical line exactly once.

43. The inverse of $f(x) = 2x$ is $g(x) = x/2$.

44. The inverse of $f(x) = x^2$ is $g(x) = \sqrt{x}$.

45. If f is one-to-one, then the domain of f is equal to the range of f.

46. If g is the inverse of a function f, then f is the inverse of g.

C *Find x in Problems 47–54.*

47. $\log_b x = \frac{2}{3}\log_b 8 + \frac{1}{2}\log_b 9 - \log_b 6$

48. $\log_b x = \frac{2}{3}\log_b 27 + 2\log_b 2 - \log_b 3$

49. $\log_b x = \frac{3}{2}\log_b 4 - \frac{2}{3}\log_b 8 + 2\log_b 2$

50. $\log_b x = \frac{1}{2}\log_b 36 + \frac{1}{3}\log_b 125 - \frac{1}{2}\log_b 100$

51. $\log_b x + \log_b (x - 4) = \log_b 21$

52. $\log_b(x + 2) + \log_b x = \log_b 24$

53. $\log_{10}(x - 1) - \log_{10}(x + 1) = 1$

54. $\log_{10}(x + 6) - \log_{10}(x - 3) = 1$

Graph Problems 55 and 56 by converting to exponential form first.

55. $y = \log_2 (x - 2)$

56. $y = \log_3 (x + 2)$

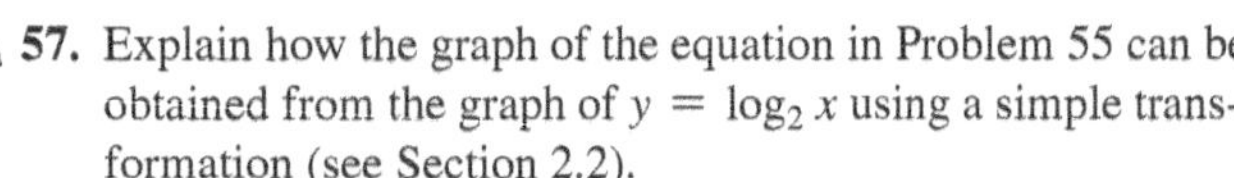

57. Explain how the graph of the equation in Problem 55 can be obtained from the graph of $y = \log_2 x$ using a simple transformation (see Section 2.2).

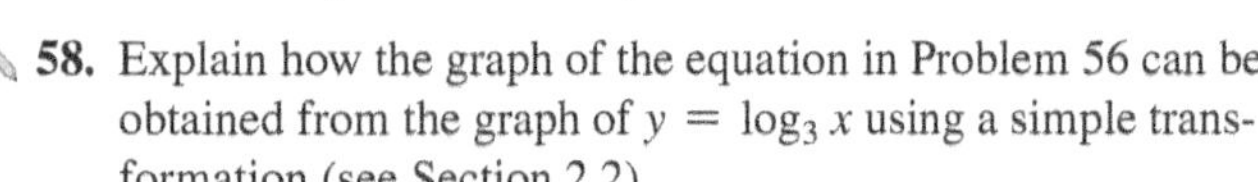

58. Explain how the graph of the equation in Problem 56 can be obtained from the graph of $y = \log_3 x$ using a simple transformation (see Section 2.2).

59. What are the domain and range of the function defined by $y = 1 + \ln(x + 1)$?

60. What are the domain and range of the function defined by $y = \log(x - 1) - 1$?

For Problems 61 and 62, evaluate to five decimal places using a calculator.

61. (A) $\log 3{,}527.2$ (B) $\log 0.006\,913\,2$
(C) $\ln 277.63$ (D) $\ln 0.040\,883$

62. (A) $\log 72.604$ (B) $\log 0.033\,041$
(C) $\ln 40{,}257$ (D) $\ln 0.005\,926\,3$

For Problems 63 and 64, find x to four decimal places.

63. (A) $\log x = 1.1285$ (B) $\log x = -2.0497$
(C) $\ln x = 2.7763$ (D) $\ln x = -1.8879$

64. (A) $\log x = 2.0832$ (B) $\log x = -1.1577$
(C) $\ln x = 3.1336$ (D) $\ln x = -4.3281$

For Problems 65–70, solve each equation to four decimal places.

65. $10^x = 12$

66. $10^x = 153$

67. $e^x = 5.432$

68. $e^x = 0.3059$

69. $1.005^{12t} = 3$

70. $1.234^{5t} = 6$

Graph Problems 71–78 using a calculator and point-by-point plotting. Indicate increasing and decreasing intervals.

71. $y = \ln x$

72. $y = -\ln x$

73. $y = |\ln x|$

74. $y = \ln|x|$

75. $y = 3\ln(x + 4)$

76. $y = 3\ln x + 4$

77. $y = 4\ln x - 3$

78. $y = 4\ln(x - 3)$

79. Explain why the logarithm of 1 for any permissible base is 0.

80. Explain why 1 is not a suitable logarithmic base.

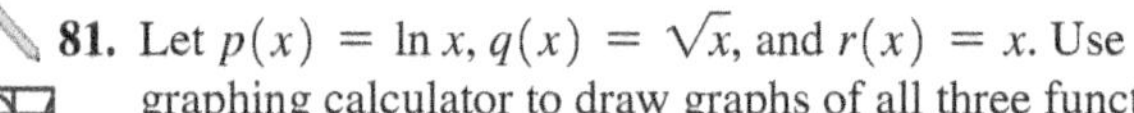

81. Let $p(x) = \ln x$, $q(x) = \sqrt{x}$, and $r(x) = x$. Use a graphing calculator to draw graphs of all three functions in the same viewing window for $1 \le x \le 16$. Discuss what it means for one function to be larger than another on an interval, and then order the three functions from largest to smallest for $1 < x \le 16$.

82. Let $p(x) = \log x$, $q(x) = \sqrt[3]{x}$, and $r(x) = x$. Use a graphing calculator to draw graphs of all three functions in the same viewing window for $1 \le x \le 16$. Discuss what it means for one function to be smaller than another on an interval, and then order the three functions from smallest to largest for $1 < x \le 16$.

Applications

83. Doubling time. In its first 10 years the Gabelli Growth Fund produced an average annual return of 21.36%. Assume that money invested in this fund continues to earn 21.36% compounded annually. How long (to the nearest year) will it take money invested in this fund to double?

84. Doubling time. In its first 10 years the Janus Flexible Income Fund produced an average annual return of 9.58%. Assume that money invested in this fund continues to earn 9.58% compounded annually. How long (to the nearest year) will it take money invested in this fund to double?

85. Investing. How many years (to two decimal places) will it take \$1,000 to grow to \$1,800 if it is invested at 6% compounded quarterly? Compounded daily?

86. Investing. How many years (to two decimal places) will it take \$5,000 to grow to \$7,500 if it is invested at 8% compounded semiannually? Compounded monthly?

87. Continuous compound interest. How many years (to two decimal places) will it take an investment of \$35,000 to grow to \$50,000 if it is invested at 4.75% compounded continuously?

88. Continuous compound interest. How many years (to two decimal places) will it take an investment of \$17,000 to grow to \$41,000 if it is invested at 2.95% compounded continuously?

89. Supply and demand. A cordless screwdriver is sold through a national chain of discount stores. A marketing company established price–demand and price–supply tables (Tables 2 and 3), where x is the number of screwdrivers people are willing to buy and the store is willing to sell each month at a price of p dollars per screwdriver.

(A) Find a logarithmic regression model $(y = a + b \ln x)$ for the data in Table 2. Estimate the demand (to the nearest unit) at a price level of \$50.

Table 2 **Price–Demand**

x	$p = D(x)$ (\$)
1,000	91
2,000	73
3,000	64
4,000	56
5,000	53

(B) Find a logarithmic regression model $(y = a + b \ln x)$ for the data in Table 3. Estimate the supply (to the nearest unit) at a price level of \$50.

Table 3 **Price–Supply**

x	$p = S(x)$ (\$)
1,000	9
2,000	26
3,000	34
4,000	38
5,000	41

(C) Does a price level of \$50 represent a stable condition, or is the price likely to increase or decrease? Explain.

90. Equilibrium point. Use the models constructed in Problem 89 to find the equilibrium point. Write the equilibrium price to the nearest cent and the equilibrium quantity to the nearest unit.

91. Sound intensity: decibels. Because of the extraordinary range of sensitivity of the human ear (a range of over 1,000 million millions to 1), it is helpful to use a logarithmic scale, rather than an absolute scale, to measure sound intensity over this range. The unit of measure is called the *decibel,* after the inventor of the telephone, Alexander Graham Bell. If we let N be the number of decibels, I the power of the sound in question (in watts per square centimeter), and I_0 the power of sound just below the threshold of hearing (approximately 10^{-16} watt per square centimeter), then

$$I = I_0 10^{N/10}$$

Show that this formula can be written in the form

$$N = 10 \log \frac{I}{I_0}$$

92. Sound intensity: decibels. Use the formula in Problem 91 (with $I_0 = 10^{-16}\ \text{W/cm}^2$) to find the decibel ratings of the following sounds:

(A) Whisper: $10^{-13}\ \text{W/cm}^2$

(B) Normal conversation: $3.16 \times 10^{-10}\ \text{W/cm}^2$

(C) Heavy traffic: $10^{-8}\ \text{W/cm}^2$

(D) Jet plane with afterburner: $10^{-1}\ \text{W/cm}^2$

93. Agriculture. Table 4 shows the yield (in bushels per acre) and the total production (in millions of bushels) for corn in the United States for selected years since 1950. Let x represent years since 1900. Find a logarithmic regression model $(y = a + b \ln x)$ for the yield. Estimate (to the nearest bushel per acre) the yield in 2024.

Table 4 **United States Corn Production**

Year	x	Yield (bushels per acre)	Total Production (million bushels)
1950	50	38	2,782
1960	60	56	3,479
1970	70	81	4,802
1980	80	98	6,867
1990	90	116	7,802
2000	100	140	10,192
2010	110	153	12,447

94. Agriculture. Refer to Table 4. Find a logarithmic regression model $(y = a + b \ln x)$ for the total production. Estimate (to the nearest million) the production in 2024.

95. World population. If the world population is now 7.4 billion people and if it continues to grow at an annual rate of 1.1% compounded continuously, how long (to the nearest year) would it take before there is only 1 square yard of land per person? (The Earth contains approximately 1.68×10^{14} square yards of land.)

96. Archaeology: carbon-14 dating. The radioactive carbon-14 $\left({}^{14}\text{C}\right)$ in an organism at the time of its death decays according to the equation

$$A = A_0 e^{-0.000124t}$$

where t is time in years and A_0 is the amount of ^{14}C present at time $t = 0$. (See Example 3 in Section 2.5.) Estimate the age of a skull uncovered in an archaeological site if 10% of the original amount of ^{14}C is still present. [*Hint:* Find t such that $A = 0.1A_0$.]

Answers to Matched Problems

1. (A) $9 = 3^2$ (B) $2 = 4^{1/2}$ (C) $\frac{1}{9} = 3^{-2}$
2. (A) $\log_7 49 = 2$ (B) $\log_9 3 = \frac{1}{2}$ (C) $\log_3\left(\frac{1}{3}\right) = -1$
3. (A) $y = \frac{3}{2}$ (B) $x = \frac{1}{3}$ (C) $b = 10$
4. (A) $\log_b R - \log_b S - \log_b T$ (B) $\frac{2}{3}(\log_b R - \log_b S)$ (C) b^u (D) $\log_b x$
5. $x = 2$
6. $x = 5$
7. (A) $-1.868\,734$ (B) 3.356 663 (C) Not defined
8. (A) 0.0063 (B) 120.8092
9. (A) 0.8451 (B) 1.7918 (C) 1.1610
10. 9 yr
11. 70.3%

Chapter 2 Summary and Review

Important Terms, Symbols, and Concepts

2.1 Functions

EXAMPLES

- **Point-by-point plotting** may be used to **sketch the graph** of an equation in two variables: Plot enough points from its solution set in a rectangular coordinate system so that the total graph is apparent and then connect these points with a smooth curve. — Ex. 1, p. 42
- A **function** is a correspondence between two sets of elements such that to each element in the first set there corresponds one and only one element in the second set. The first set is called the **domain** and the set of corresponding elements in the second set is called the **range**.
- If x is a placeholder for the elements in the domain of a function, then x is called the **independent variable** or the **input**. If y is a placeholder for the elements in the range, then y is called the **dependent variable** or the **output**.
- If in an equation in two variables we get exactly one output for each input, then the equation specifies a function. The graph of such a function is just the graph of the specifying equation. If we get more than one output for a given input, then the equation does not specify a function. — Ex. 2, p. 45
- The **vertical-line test** can be used to determine whether or not an equation in two variables specifies a function (Theorem 1, p. 28).
- The functions specified by equations of the form $y = mx + b$, where $m \neq 0$, are called **linear functions**. Functions specified by equations of the form $y = b$ are called **constant functions**.
- If a function is specified by an equation and the domain is not indicated, we agree to assume that the domain is the set of all inputs that produce outputs that are real numbers. — Ex. 3, p. 47; Ex. 5, p. 49
- The symbol $f(x)$ represents the element in the range of f that corresponds to the element x of the domain. — Ex. 4, p. 48; Ex. 6, p. 49
- **Break-even** and **profit–loss** analysis use a cost function C and a revenue function R to determine when a company will have a loss $(R < C)$, will break even $(R = C)$, or will have a profit $(R > C)$. Typical **cost, revenue, profit,** and **price–demand functions** are given on page 50. — Ex. 7, p. 51

2.2 Elementary Functions: Graphs and Transformations

- The graphs of **six basic elementary functions** (the identity function, the square and cube functions, the square root and cube root functions, and the absolute value function) are shown on page 58. — Ex. 1, p. 57
- Performing an operation on a function produces a **transformation** of the graph of the function. The basic graph transformations, **vertical and horizontal translations** (shifts), **reflection in the x axis**, and **vertical stretches and shrinks**, are summarized on page 62. — Ex. 2, p. 59; Ex. 3, p. 60; Ex. 4, p. 61; Ex. 5, p. 62; Ex. 6, p. 63; Ex. 7, p. 64
- A **piecewise-defined function** is a function whose definition involves more than one rule.

2.3 Quadratic Functions

- If a, b, and c are real numbers with $a \neq 0$, then the function — Ex. 1, p. 70

$$f(x) = ax^2 + bx + c \qquad \text{Standard form}$$

is a **quadratic function** in **standard form** and its graph is a **parabola**.

- The quadratic formula

$$x = \frac{-b \pm \sqrt{b^2 - 4ac}}{2a} \qquad b^2 - 4ac \geq 0$$

can be used to find the x intercepts of a quadratic function.

- Completing the square in the standard form of a quadratic function produces the **vertex form**

$$f(x) = a(x - h)^2 + k \qquad \text{Vertex form}$$

- From the vertex form of a quadratic function, we can read off the vertex, axis of symmetry, maximum or minimum, and range, and can easily sketch the graph (page 74). Ex. 2, p. 74 Ex. 3, p. 76
- If a revenue function $R(x)$ and a cost function $C(x)$ intersect at a point (x_0, y_0), then both this point and its x coordinate x_0 are referred to as **break-even points**. Ex. 4, p. 77
- **Quadratic regression** on a graphing calculator produces the function of the form $y = ax^2 + bx + c$ that best fits a data set. Ex. 5, p. 79

2.4 Polynomial and Rational Functions

- A **polynomial function** is a function that can be written in the form

$$f(x) = a_nx^n + a_{n-1}x^{n-1} + \cdots + a_1x + a_0$$

for n a nonnegative integer called the **degree** of the polynomial. The coefficients $a_0, a_1, \ldots, a_n$ are real numbers with **leading coefficient** $a_n \neq 0$. The **domain** of a polynomial function is the set of all real numbers. Graphs of representative polynomial functions are shown on page 85 and at the back of the book.

- The graph of a polynomial function of degree n can intersect the x axis at most n times. An x intercept is also called a **zero** or **root**.
- The graph of a polynomial function has no sharp corners and is **continuous**; that is; it has no holes or breaks.
- **Polynomial regression** produces a polynomial of specified degree that best fits a data set. Ex. 1, p. 86
- A **rational function** is any function that can be written in the form

$$f(x) = \frac{n(x)}{d(x)} \qquad d(x) \neq 0$$

where $n(x)$ and $d(x)$ are polynomials. The **domain** is the set of all real numbers such that $d(x) \neq 0$. Graphs of representative rational functions are shown on page 88 and at the back of the book.

- Unlike polynomial functions, a rational function can have vertical asymptotes [but not more than the degree of the denominator $d(x)$] and at most one horizontal asymptote. Ex. 2, p. 88
- A procedure for finding the vertical and horizontal asymptotes of a rational function is given on page 90. Ex. 3, p. 90 Ex. 4, p. 91

2.5 Exponential Functions

- An **exponential function** is a function of the form

$$f(x) = b^x$$

where $b \neq 1$ is a positive constant called the **base**. The **domain** of f is the set of all real numbers, and the **range** is the set of positive real numbers.

- The graph of an exponential function is continuous, passes through $(0, 1)$, and has the x axis as a horizontal asymptote. If $b > 1$, then b^x increases as x increases; if $0 < b < 1$, then b^x decreases as x increases (Theorem 1, p. 79). Ex. 1, p. 97
- Exponential functions obey the familiar laws of exponents and satisfy additional properties (Theorem 2, p. 80).
- The base that is used most frequently in mathematics is the irrational number $e \approx 2.7183$.

2.5 Exponential Functions (*Continued*)

- Exponential functions can be used to model population growth and radioactive decay. Ex. 2, p. 99
- **Exponential regression** on a graphing calculator produces the function of the form $y = ab^x$ that best fits a data set. Ex. 3, p. 100 Ex. 4, p. 101
- Exponential functions are used in computations of **compound interest** and **continuous compound interest**: Ex. 5, p. 102 Ex. 6, p. 103

$$A = P\left(1 + \frac{r}{m}\right)^{mt} \qquad \text{Compound interest}$$

$$A = Pe^{rt} \qquad \text{Continuous compound interest}$$

(see summary on page 103).

2.6 Logarithmic Functions

- A function is said to be **one-to-one** if each range value corresponds to exactly one domain value.
- The **inverse** of a one-to-one function f is the function formed by interchanging the independent and dependent variables of f. That is, (a,b) is a point on the graph of f if and only if (b,a) is a point on the graph of the inverse of f. A function that is not one-to-one does not have an inverse.
- The inverse of the exponential function with base b is called the **logarithmic function with base** $\boldsymbol{b}$, denoted $y = \log_b x$. The **domain** of $\log_b x$ is the set of all positive real numbers (which is the range of b^x), and the range of $\log_b x$ is the set of all real numbers (which is the domain of b^x).
- Because $\log_b x$ is the inverse of the function b^x, Ex. 1, p. 108 Ex. 2, p. 109 Ex. 3, p. 109

Logarithmic form		Exponential form
$y = \log_b x$	is equivalent to	$x = b^y$

- Properties of logarithmic functions can be obtained from corresponding properties of exponential functions (Theorem 1, p. 110). Ex. 4, p. 110 Ex. 5, p. 110 Ex. 6, p. 111
- Logarithms to the base 10 are called **common logarithms**, often denoted simply by $\log x$. Logarithms to the base e are called **natural logarithms**, often denoted by $\ln x$. Ex. 7, p. 111 Ex. 8, p. 112
- Logarithms can be used to find an investment's **doubling time**—the length of time it takes for the value of an investment to double. Ex. 9, p. 112 Ex. 10, p. 113
- **Logarithmic regression** on a graphing calculator produces the function of the form $y = a + b\ln x$ that best fits a data set. Ex. 11, p. 114

Review Exercises

Work through all the problems in this chapter review and check your answers in the back of the book. Answers to all review problems are there along with section numbers in italics to indicate where each type of problem is discussed. Where weaknesses show up, review appropriate sections in the text.

A *In Problems 1–3, use point-by-point plotting to sketch the graph of each equation.*

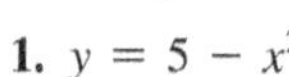

1. $y = 5 - x^2$
2. $x^2 = y^2$
3. $y^2 = 4x^2$
4. Indicate whether each graph specifies a function:

(A)

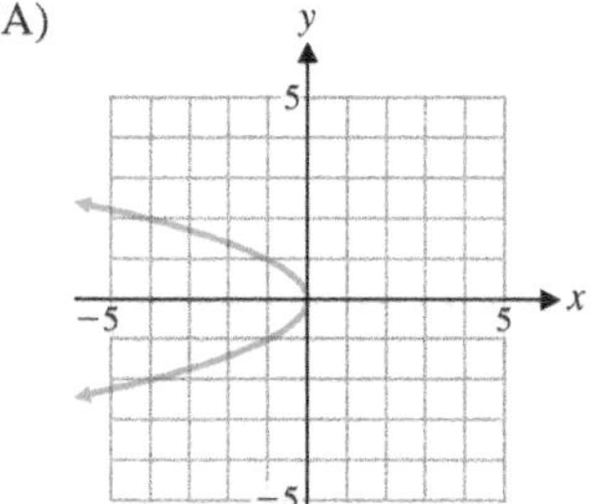

(B)

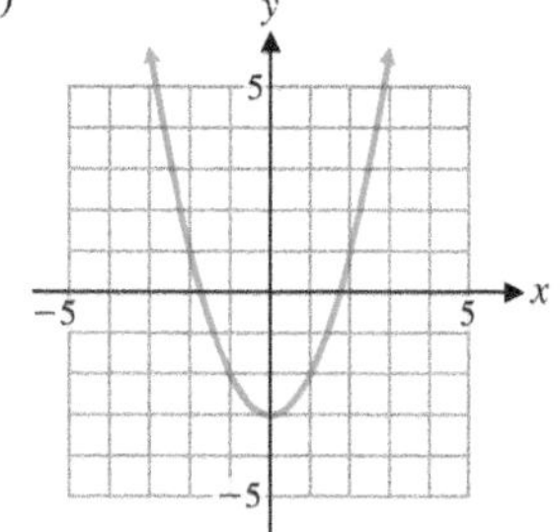

(C)

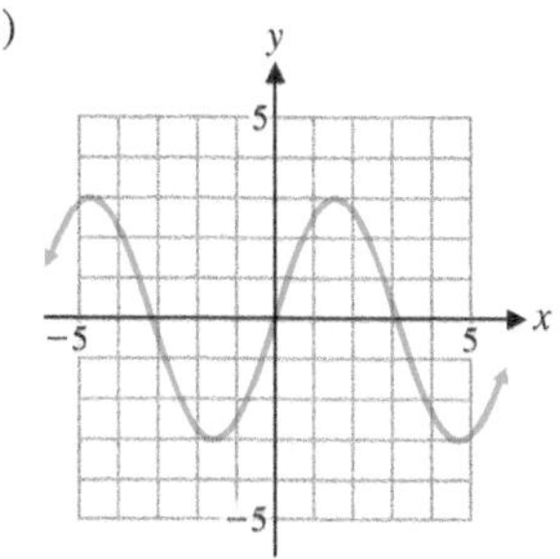

(D)

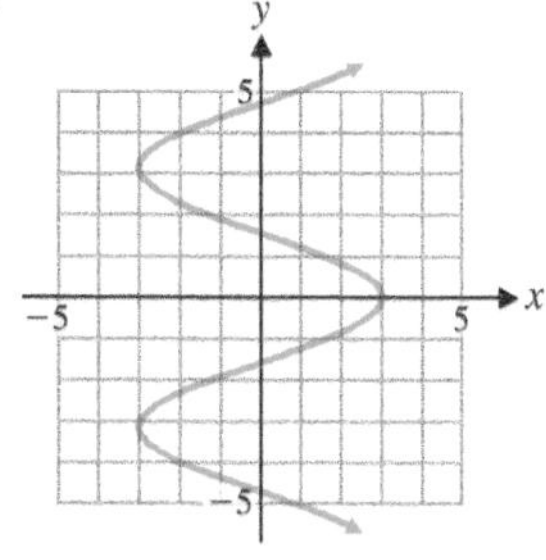

5. For $f(x) = 2x - 1$ and $g(x) = 2x^2 + 3x$, find:

(A) $f(-1) + g(-2)$ (B) $f(-2) \cdot g(0)$

(C) $\frac{g(-1)}{f(2)}$ (D) $\frac{f(2)}{g(-1)}$

6. Write in logarithmic form using base e: $u = e^v$.

7. Write in exponential form using base e: $\ln m = k$.

8. Write in logarithmic form using base e: $k = e^x$.

9. Write in logarithmic form using base 10: $m = 10^z$.

Solve Problems 10–12 for x exactly without using a calculator.

10. $\log_4 x = 3$ **11.** $\log_x 49 = 2$

12. $\log_3 27 = x$

Solve Problems 13–16 for x to three decimal places.

13. $10^x = 130.6$ **14.** $e^x = 200$

15. $\log x = 2.15$ **16.** $\ln x = -1.147$

17. Use the graph of function f in the figure to determine (to the nearest integer) x or y as indicated.

(A) $y = f(0)$ (B) $4 = f(x)$

(C) $y = f(3)$ (D) $3 = f(x)$

(E) $y = f(-6)$ (F) $-1 = f(x)$

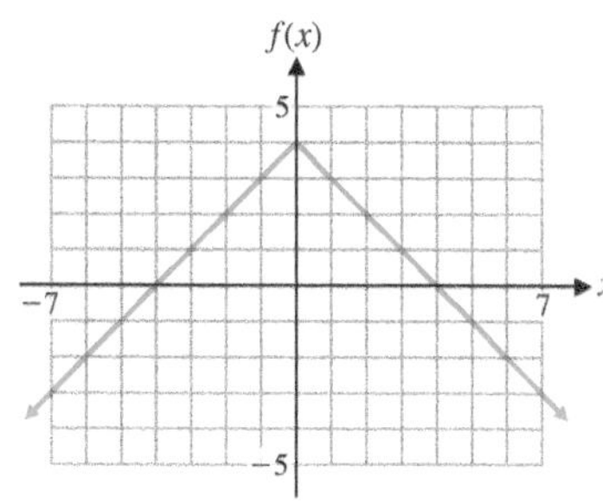

B **18.** Sketch a graph of each of the functions in parts (A)–(D) using the graph of function f in the figure below.

(A) $y = -f(x)$ (B) $y = f(x) + 4$

(C) $y = f(x - 2)$ (D) $y = -f(x + 3) - 3$

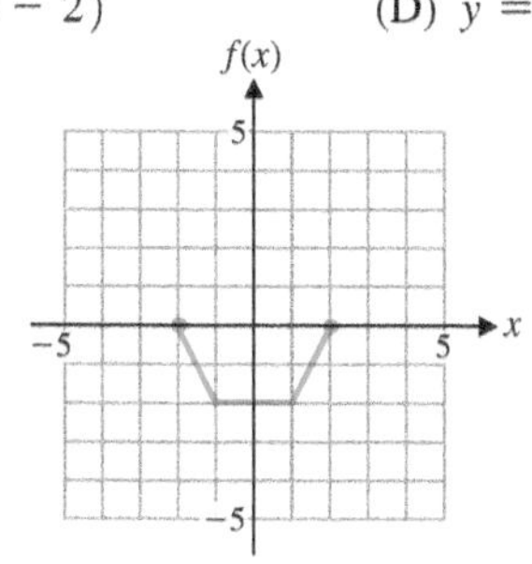

19. Complete the square and find the standard form for the quadratic function

$$f(x) = -x^2 + 4x$$

Then write a brief verbal description of the relationship between the graph of f and the graph of $y = x^2$.

20. Match each equation with a graph of one of the functions f, g, m, or n in the figure.

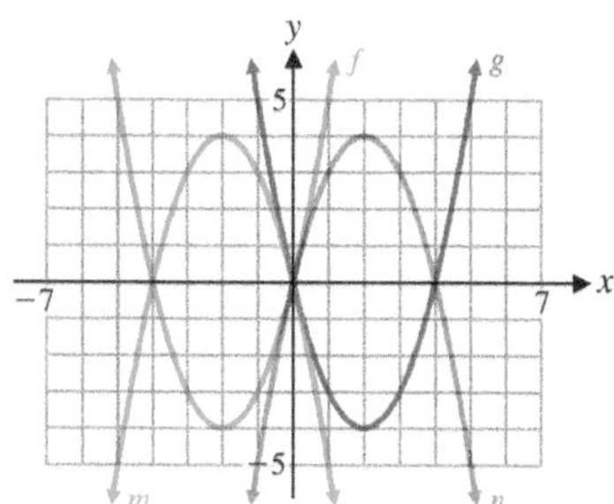

(A) $y = (x - 2)^2 - 4$ (B) $y = -(x + 2)^2 + 4$

(C) $y = -(x - 2)^2 + 4$ (D) $y = (x + 2)^2 - 4$

21. Referring to the graph of function f in the figure for Problem 20 and using known properties of quadratic functions, find each of the following to the nearest integer:

(A) Intercepts (B) Vertex

(C) Maximum or minimum (D) Range

In Problems 22–25, each equation specifies a function. Determine whether the function is linear, quadratic, constant, or none of these.

22. $y = 4 - x + 3x^2$ **23.** $y = \frac{1 + 5x}{6}$

24. $y = \frac{7 - 4x}{2x}$ **25.** $y = 8x + 2(10 - 4x)$

Solve Problems 26–33 for x exactly without using a calculator.

26. $\log(x + 5) = \log(2x - 3)$ **27.** $2\ln(x - 1) = \ln(x^2 - 5)$

28. $9^{x-1} = 3^{1+x}$ **29.** $e^{2x} = e^{x^2-3}$

30. $12x^2e^x = 4xe^x$ **31.** $\log_{1/3} 9 = x$

32. $\log_x 8 = -3$ **33.** $\log_9 x = \frac{3}{2}$

Solve Problems 34–41 for x to four decimal places.

34. $x = 3(e^{1.49})$ **35.** $x = 230(10^{-0.161})$

36. $\log x = -2.0144$ **37.** $\ln x = 0.3618$

38. $35 = 7(3^x)$ **39.** $0.001 = e^{0.03x}$

40. $8{,}000 = 4{,}000(1.08^x)$ **41.** $5^{2x-3} = 7.08$

42. Find the domain of each function:

(A) $f(x) = \frac{2x - 5}{x^2 - x - 6}$ (B) $g(x) = \frac{3x}{\sqrt{5 - x}}$

43. Find the vertex form for $f(x) = 4x^2 + 4x - 3$ and then find the intercepts, the vertex, the maximum or minimum, and the range.

44. Let $f(x) = e^x - 2$ and $g(x) = \ln(x + 1)$. Find all points of intersection for the graphs of f and g. Round answers to two decimal places.

In Problems 45 and 46, use point-by-point plotting to sketch the graph of each function.

45. $f(x) = \dfrac{50}{x^2 + 1}$ **46.** $f(x) = \dfrac{-66}{2 + x^2}$

If $f(x) = 5x + 1$, *find and simplify each of the following in Problems 47–50.*

47. $f(f(0))$ **48.** $f(f(-1))$

49. $f(2x - 1)$ **50.** $f(4 - x)$

51. Let $f(x) = 3 - 2x$. Find

(A) $f(2)$ (B) $f(2 + h)$

(C) $f(2 + h) - f(2)$ (D) $\dfrac{f(2 + h) - f(2)}{h}, h \neq 0$

52. Let $f(x) = 4 - 3x$. Find

(A) $f(3)$ (B) $f(3 + h)$

(C) $f(3 + h) - f(3)$ (D) $\dfrac{f(3 + h) - f(3)}{h}, h \neq 0$

53. Explain how the graph of $m(x) = -|x - 6|$ is related to the graph of $y = |x|$.

54. Explain how the graph of $g(x) = 0.6x^3 + 5$ is related to the graph of $y = x^3$.

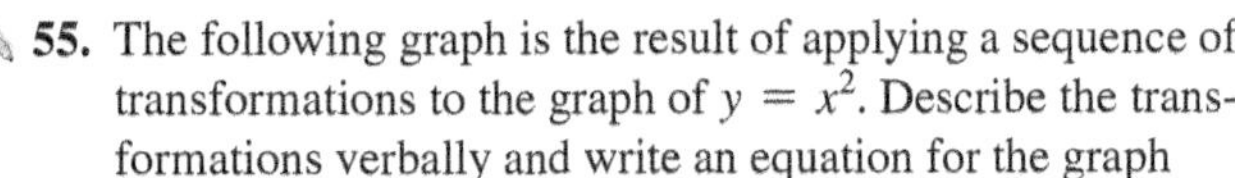

55. The following graph is the result of applying a sequence of transformations to the graph of $y = x^2$. Describe the transformations verbally and write an equation for the graph

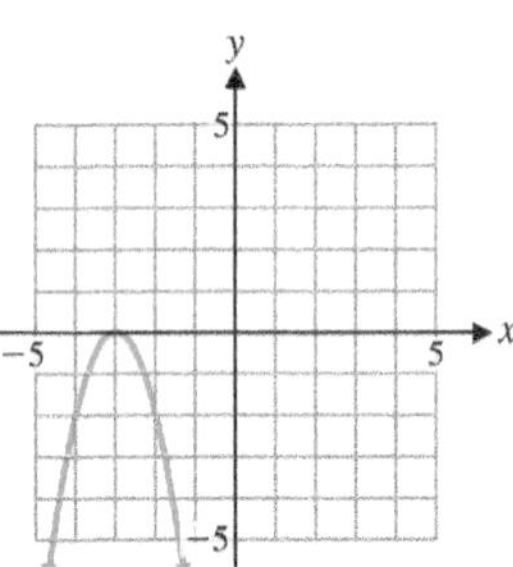

56. The graph of a function f is formed by vertically stretching the graph of $y = \sqrt{x}$ by a factor of 2, and shifting it to the left 3 units and down 1 unit. Find an equation for function f and graph it for $-5 \leq x \leq 5$ and $-5 \leq y \leq 5$.

In Problems 57–59, find the equation of any horizontal asymptote.

57. $f(x) = \dfrac{5x + 4}{x^2 - 3x + 1}$ **58.** $f(x) = \dfrac{3x^2 + 2x - 1}{4x^2 - 5x + 3}$

59. $f(x) = \dfrac{x^2 + 4}{100x + 1}$

In Problems 60 and 61, find the equations of any vertical asymptotes.

60. $f(x) = \dfrac{x^2 + 100}{x^2 - 100}$ **61.** $f(x) = \dfrac{x^2 + 3x}{x^2 + 2x}$

In Problems 62–67, discuss the validity of each statement. If the statement is always true, explain why. If not, give a counterexample.

62. Every polynomial function is a rational function.

63. Every rational function is a polynomial function.

64. The graph of every rational function has at least one vertical asymptote.

65. The graph of every exponential function has a horizontal asymptote.

66. The graph of every logarithmic function has a vertical asymptote.

67. There exists a rational function that has both a vertical and horizontal asymptote.

68. Sketch the graph of f for $x \geq 0$.

$$f(x) = \begin{cases} 9 + 0.3x & \text{if } 0 \leq x \leq 20 \\ 5 + 0.2x & \text{if } x > 20 \end{cases}$$

69. Sketch the graph of g for $x \geq 0$.

$$f(x) = \begin{cases} 0.5x + 5 & \text{if } 0 \leq x \leq 10 \\ 1.2x - 2 & \text{if } 10 < x \leq 30 \\ 2x - 26 & \text{if } x > 30 \end{cases}$$

70. Write an equation for the graph shown in the form $y = a(x - h)^2 + k$, where a is either -1 or $+1$ and h and k are integers.

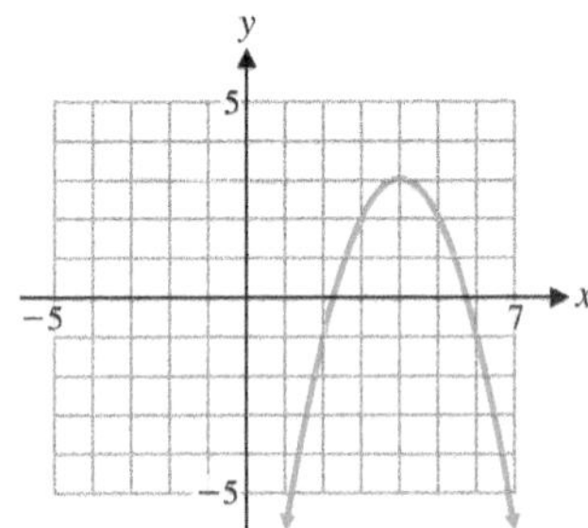

71. Given $f(x) = -0.4x^2 + 3.2x + 1.2$, find the following algebraically (to one decimal place) without referring to a graph:

(A) Intercepts (B) Vertex

(C) Maximum or minimum (D) Range

72. Graph $f(x) = -0.4x^2 + 3.2x + 1.2$ in a graphing calculator and find the following (to one decimal place) using TRACE and appropriate commands:

(A) Intercepts (B) Vertex

(C) Maximum or minimum (D) Range

73. Noting that $\pi = 3.141\,592\,654\ldots$ and $\sqrt{2} = 1.414\,213\,562\ldots$ explain why the calculator results shown here are obvious. Discuss similar connections between the natural logarithmic function and the exponential function with base e.

```
NORMAL FLOAT AUTO REAL DEGREE MP
log(10^π)
                    3.141592654
10^log(√2)
                    1.414213562
```

Solve Problems 74–77 exactly without using a calculator.

74. $\log x - \log 8 = \log 4 - \log(x + 4)$

75. $\ln(x + 4) - \ln(2x - 1) = \ln x$

76. $\ln(x + 6) - \ln 2x = 2 \ln 2$

77. $\log 3x^2 = 2 + \log 9x$

78. Write $\ln y = -7t + \ln b$ in an exponential form free of logarithms. Then solve for y in terms of the remaining variables.

79. Explain why 1 cannot be used as a logarithmic base.

80. The following graph is the result of applying a sequence of transformations to the graph of $y = \sqrt[3]{x}$. Describe the transformations verbally, and write an equation for the graph.

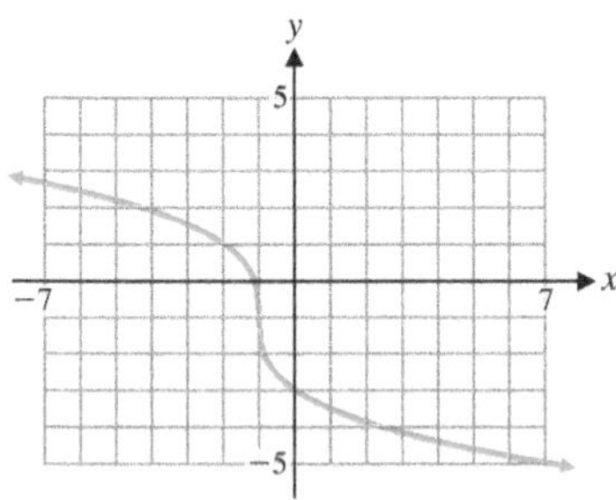

81. Given $G(x) = 0.4x^2 + 1.6x - 6.5$, find the following algebraically (to three decimal places) without the use of a graph:

(A) Intercepts (B) Vertex

(C) Maximum or minimum (D) Range

82. Graph $G(x) = 0.3x^2 + 1.2x - 6.9$ in a standard viewing window. Then find each of the following (to one decimal place) using appropriate commands.

(A) Intercepts (B) Vertex

(C) Maximum or minimum (D) Range

Applications

In all problems involving days, a 365-day year is assumed.

83. Electricity rates. The table shows the electricity rates charged by Easton Utilities in the summer months.

(A) Write a piecewise definition of the monthly charge $S(x)$ (in dollars) for a customer who uses x kWh in a summer month.

(B) Graph $S(x)$.

Energy Charge (June–September)
\$3.00 for the first 20 kWh or less
5.70¢ per kWh for the next 180 kWh
3.46¢ per kWh for the next 800 kWh
2.17¢ per kWh for all over 1,000 kWh

84. Money growth. Provident Bank of Cincinnati, Ohio, offered a certificate of deposit that paid 1.25% compounded quarterly. If a \$5,000 CD earns this rate for 5 years, how much will it be worth?

85. Money growth. Capital One Bank of Glen Allen, Virginia, offered a certificate of deposit that paid 1.05% compounded daily. If a \$5,000 CD earns this rate for 5 years, how much will it be worth?

86. Money growth. How long will it take for money invested at 6.59% compounded monthly to triple?

87. Money growth. How long will it take for money invested at 7.39% compounded continuously to double?

88. Break-even analysis. The research department in a company that manufactures AM/FM clock radios established the following price-demand, cost, and revenue functions:

$$p(x) = 50 - 1.25x \quad \text{Price–demand function}$$
$$C(x) = 160 + 10x \quad \text{Cost function}$$
$$R(x) = xp(x) = x(50 - 1.25x) \quad \text{Revenue function}$$

where x is in thousands of units, and $C(x)$ and $R(x)$ are in thousands of dollars. All three functions have domain $1 \le x \le 40$.

(A) Graph the cost function and the revenue function simutaneously in the same coordinate system.

(B) Determine algebraically when $R = C$. Then, with the aid of part (A), determine when $R < C$ and $R > C$ to the nearest unit.

(C) Determine algebraically the maximum revenue (to the nearest thousand dollars) and the output (to the nearest unit) that produces the maximum revenue. What is the wholesale price of the radio (to the nearest dollar) at this output?

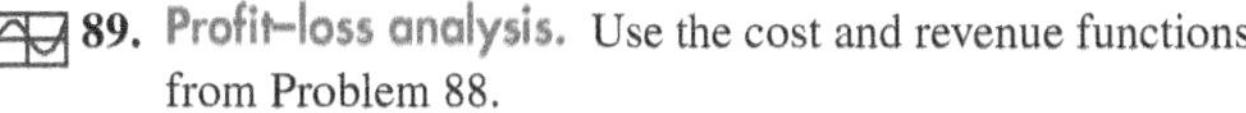

89. Profit–loss analysis. Use the cost and revenue functions from Problem 88.

(A) Write a profit function and graph it in a graphing calculator.

(B) Determine graphically when $P = 0$, $P < 0$, and $P > 0$ to the nearest unit.

(C) Determine graphically the maximum profit (to the nearest thousand dollars) and the output (to the nearest unit) that produces the maximum profit. What is the wholesale price of the radio (to the nearest dollar) at this output? [Compare with Problem 88C.]

90. Construction. A construction company has 840 feet of chain-link fence that is used to enclose storage areas for equipment and materials at construction sites. The supervisor wants to set up two identical rectangular storage areas sharing a common fence (see the figure).

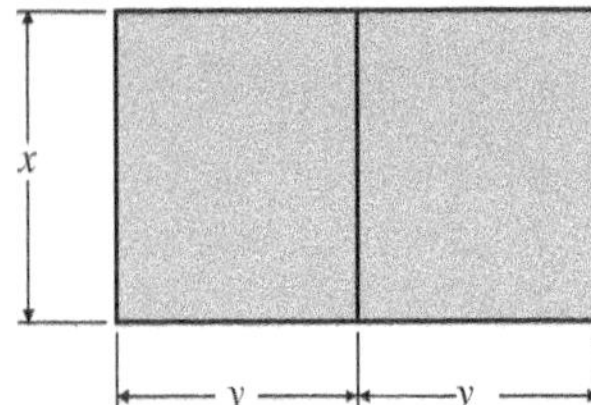

Assuming that all fencing is used,

(A) Express the total area $A(x)$ enclosed by both pens as a function of x.

(B) From physical considerations, what is the domain of the function A?

(C) Graph function A in a rectangular coordinate system.

(D) Use the graph to discuss the number and approximate locations of values of x that would produce storage areas with a combined area of 25,000 square feet.

(E) Approximate graphically (to the nearest foot) the values of x that would produce storage areas with a combined area of 25,000 square feet.

(F) Determine algebraically the dimensions of the storage areas that have the maximum total combined area. What is the maximum area?

91. Equilibrium point. A company is planning to introduce a 10-piece set of nonstick cookware. A marketing company established price–demand and price–supply tables for selected prices (Tables 1 and 2), where x is the number of cookware sets people are willing to buy and the company is willing to sell each month at a price of p dollars per set.

(A) Find a quadratic regression model for the data in Table 1. Estimate the demand at a price level of \$180.

(B) Find a linear regression model for the data in Table 2. Estimate the supply at a price level of \$180.

(C) Does a price level of \$180 represent a stable condition, or is the price likely to increase or decrease? Explain.

Table 1 **Price–Demand**

x	$p = D(x)(\$)$
985	330
2,145	225
2,950	170
4,225	105
5,100	50

Table 2 **Price–Supply**

x	$p = S(x)(\$)$
985	30
2,145	75
2,950	110
4,225	155
5,100	190

(D) Use the models in parts (A) and (B) to find the equilibrium point. Write the equilibrium price to the nearest cent and the equilibrium quantity to the nearest unit.

92. Crime statistics. According to data published by the FBI, the crime index in the United States has shown a downward trend since the early 1990s (Table 3).

(A) Find a cubic regression model for the crime index if $x = 0$ represents 1987.

(B) Use the cubic regression model to predict the crime index in 2025.

Table 3 **Crime Index**

Year	Crimes per 100,000 Inhabitants
1987	5,550
1992	5,660
1997	4,930
2002	4,125
2007	3,749
2010	3,350
2013	3,099

93. Medicine. One leukemic cell injected into a healthy mouse will divide into 2 cells in about $\frac{1}{2}$ day. At the end of the day these 2 cells will divide into 4. This doubling continues until 1 billion cells are formed; then the animal dies with leukemic cells in every part of the body.

(A) Write an equation that will give the number N of leukemic cells at the end of t days.

(B) When, to the nearest day, will the mouse die?

94. Marine biology. The intensity of light entering water is reduced according to the exponential equation

$$I = I_0 e^{-kd}$$

where I is the intensity d feet below the surface, I_0 is the intensity at the surface, and k is the coefficient of extinction. Measurements in the Sargasso Sea have indicated that half of the surface light reaches a depth of 73.6 feet. Find k (to five decimal places), and find the depth (to the nearest foot) at which 1% of the surface light remains.

95. Agriculture. The number of dairy cows on farms in the United States is shown in Table 4 for selected years since 1950. Let 1940 be year 0.

Table 4 Dairy Cows on Farms in the United States

Year	Dairy Cows (thousands)
1950	23,853
1960	19,527
1970	12,091
1980	10,758
1990	10,015
2000	9,190
2010	9,117

(A) Find a logarithmic regression model $(y = a + b \ln x)$ for the data. Estimate (to the nearest thousand) the number of dairy cows in 2023.

(B) Explain why it is not a good idea to let 1950 be year 0.

96. Population growth. The population of some countries has a relative growth rate of 3% (or more) per year. At this rate, how many years (to the nearest tenth of a year) will it take a population to double?

97. Medicare. The annual expenditures for Medicare (in billions of dollars) by the U.S. government for selected years since 1980 are shown in Table 5. Let x represent years since 1980.

(A) Find an exponential regression model $(y = ab^x)$ for the data. Estimate (to the nearest billion) the annual expenditures in 2025.

(B) When will the annual expenditures exceed two trillion dollars?

Table 5 Medicare Expenditures

Year	Billion $
1980	37
1985	72
1990	111
1995	181
2000	197
2005	299
2010	452
2015	546

Part 2

Finite Mathematics

3 Mathematics of Finance

Introduction

How do I choose the right loan for college? Would it be better to take the dealer's financing or the rebate for my new car? How much should my parents offer for the new home they want to buy? To make wise decisions in such matters, you need a basic understanding of the mathematics of finance.

In Chapter 3 we study the mathematics of simple and compound interest, ordinary annuities, auto loans, and home mortage loans (see Problems 47–48 in Section 3.4). You will need a calculator with logarithmic and exponential keys. A graphing calculator would be even better: It can help you visualize the rate at which an investment grows or the rate at which principal on a loan is amortized.

You may wish to review arithmetic and geometric sequences, discussed in Appendix C.2, before beginning this chapter.

Finally, to avoid repeating the following reminder many times, we emphasize it here: Throughout the chapter, interest rates are to be converted to decimal form before they are used in a formula.

3.1 Simple Interest

- The Simple Interest Formula
- Simple Interest and Investments

The Simple Interest Formula

Simple interest is used on short-term notes—often of duration less than 1 year. The concept of simple interest, however, forms the basis of much of the rest of the material developed in this chapter, for which time periods may be much longer than a year.

If you deposit a sum of money P in a savings account or if you borrow a sum of money P from a lender, then P is referred to as the **principal**. When money is borrowed—whether it is a savings institution borrowing from you when you deposit money in your account, or you borrowing from a lender—a fee is charged for the money borrowed. This fee is rent paid for the use of another's money, just as rent is paid for the use of another's house. The fee is called **interest**. It is usually computed as a percentage (called the **interest rate**) of the principal over a given period of time. The interest rate, unless otherwise stated, is an annual rate. **Simple interest** is given by the following formula:

Reminder

To write a percentage as a decimal, divide by 100 and delete the % sign. To write a decimal as a percentage, multiply by 100 and add the % sign. So 12% and 0.12 are equivalent expressions.

DEFINITION Simple Interest

$$I = Prt \qquad (1)$$

where I = interest
P = principal
r = annual simple interest rate (written as a decimal)
t = time in years

For example, the interest on a loan of \$100 at 12% for 9 months would be

$$\begin{aligned} I &= Prt && \text{Convert 12\% to a decimal (0.12)} \\ &= (100)(0.12)(0.75) && \text{and 9 months to years } (\tfrac{9}{12} = 0.75). \\ &= \$9 \end{aligned}$$

At the end of 9 months, the borrower would repay the principal (\$100) plus the interest (\$9), or a total of \$109.

In general, if a principal P is borrowed at a rate r, then after t years, the borrower will owe the lender an amount A that will include the principal P plus the interest I. Since P is the amount that is borrowed now and A is the amount that must be paid back in the future, P is often referred to as the **present value** and A as the **future value**. The formula relating A and P follows:

THEOREM 1 Simple Interest

$$\begin{aligned} A &= P + Prt \\ &= P(1 + rt) \qquad (2) \end{aligned}$$

where A = amount, or future value
P = principal, or present value
r = annual simple interest rate (written as a decimal)
t = time in years

Given any three of the four variables A, P, r, and t in (2), we can solve for the fourth. The following examples illustrate several types of common problems that can be solved by using formula (2).

EXAMPLE 1 **Total Amount Due on a Loan** Find the total amount due on a loan of \$800 at 9% simple interest at the end of 4 months.

SOLUTION To find the amount A (future value) due in 4 months, we use formula (2) with $P = 800$, $r = 0.09$, and $t = \frac{4}{12} = \frac{1}{3}$ year. Thus,

$$\begin{aligned} A &= P(1 + rt) \\ &= 800\left[1 + 0.09\left(\tfrac{1}{3}\right)\right] \\ &= 800(1.03) \\ &= \$824 \end{aligned}$$

Matched Problem 1 Find the total amount due on a loan of \$500 at 12% simple interest at the end of 30 months.

Explore and Discuss 1

(A) Your sister has loaned you \$1,000 with the understanding that you will repay the principal plus 4% simple interest when you can. How much would you owe her if you repaid the loan after 1 year? After 2 years? After 5 years? After 10 years?

(B) How is the interest after 10 years related to the interest after 1 year? After 2 years? After 5 years?

(C) Explain why your answers are consistent with the fact that for simple interest, the graph of future value as a function of time is a straight line (Fig. 1).

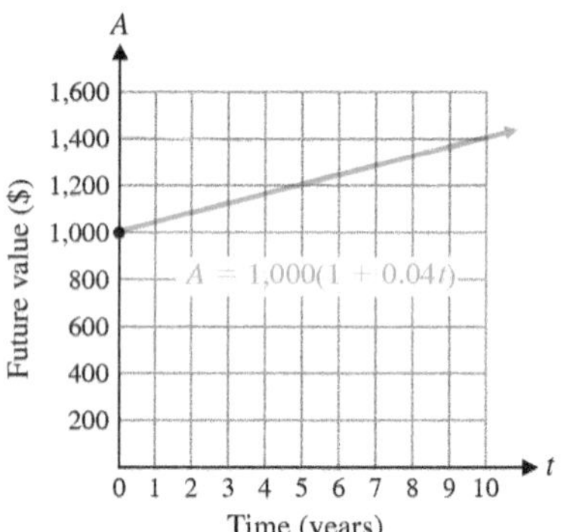

Figure 1

EXAMPLE 2 **Present Value of an Investment** If you want to earn an annual rate of 10% on your investments, how much (to the nearest cent) should you pay for a note that will be worth \$5,000 in 9 months?

SOLUTION We again use formula (2), but now we are interested in finding the principal P (present value), given $A = \$5{,}000$, $r = 0.1$, and $t = \frac{9}{12} = 0.75$ year. Thus,

$$\begin{aligned} A &= P(1 + rt) && \text{Replace } A, r, \text{ and } t \text{ with the given values, and solve for } P. \\ 5{,}000 &= P[1 + 0.1(0.75)] \\ 5{,}000 &= (1.075)P \\ P &= \$4{,}651.16 \end{aligned}$$

Matched Problem 2 Repeat Example 2 with a time period of 6 months.

CONCEPTUAL INSIGHT

If we consider future value A as a function of time t with the present value P and the annual rate r being fixed, then $A = P + Prt$ is a linear function of t with y intercept P and slope Pr. For example, if $P = 1{,}000$ and $r = 0.04$ (Fig. 1), then

$$A = 1{,}000(1 + 0.04t) = 1{,}000 + 40t$$

is a linear function with y intercept 1,000 and slope 40.

Simple Interest and Investments

Because simple interest is used on short-term notes, the time period is often given in days rather than months or years. How should a time period given in days be converted to years? In this section, we will divide by 360, assuming a 360-day year called a *banker's year*. In other sections, we will assume a 365-day year. The choice will always be clearly stated. This assumption does not affect calculations in which the time period is not given in days. If the time period is given in months or quarters, for example, we would divide by 12 or 4, respectively, to convert the time period to years.

EXAMPLE 3 **Interest Rate Earned on a Note** T-bills (Treasury bills) are one of the instruments that the U.S. Treasury Department uses to finance the public debt. If you buy a 180-day T-bill with a maturity value of \$10,000 for \$9,893.78, what annual simple interest rate will you earn? (Express answer as a percentage, correct to three decimal places.)

SOLUTION Again we use formula (2), but this time we are interested in finding r, given $P = \$9{,}893.78$, $A = \$10{,}000$, and $t = 180/360 = 0.5$ year.

$$\begin{aligned} A &= P(1 + rt) \\ 10{,}000 &= 9{,}893.78(1 + 0.5r) \\ 10{,}000 &= 9{,}893.78 + 4{,}946.89r \\ 106.22 &= 4{,}946.89r \\ r &= \frac{106.22}{4{,}946.89} \approx 0.02147 \quad \text{or} \quad 2.147\% \end{aligned}$$

Replace P, A, and t with the given values, and solve for r.

Matched Problem 3 Repeat Example 3, assuming that you pay \$9,828.74 for the T-bill.

EXAMPLE 4 **Interest Rate Earned on an Investment** Suppose that after buying a new car you decide to sell your old car to a friend. You accept a 270-day note for \$3,500 at 10% simple interest as payment. (Both principal and interest are paid at the end of 270 days.) Sixty days later you find that you need the money and sell the note to a third party for \$3,550. What annual interest rate will the third party receive for the investment? Express the answer as a percentage, correct to three decimal places.

SOLUTION

Step 1 Find the amount that will be paid at the end of 270 days to the holder of the note.

$$\begin{aligned} A &= P(1 + rt) \\ &= \$3{,}500\left[1 + (0.1)\left(\tfrac{270}{360}\right)\right] \\ &= \$3{,}762.50 \end{aligned}$$

Step 2 For the third party, we are to find the annual rate of interest r required to make \$3,550 grow to \$3,762.50 in 210 days $(270 - 60)$; that is, we are to find r (which is to be converted to $100r\%$), given $A = \$3{,}762.50$, $P = \$3{,}550$, and $t = \frac{210}{360}$.

$$A = P + Prt \qquad \text{Solve for } r.$$

$$r = \frac{A - P}{Pt}$$

$$r = \frac{3{,}762.50 - 3{,}550}{(3{,}550)\left(\frac{210}{360}\right)} \approx 0.10262 \quad \text{or} \quad 10.262\%$$

Matched Problem 4 Repeat Example 4 assuming that 90 days after it was initially signed, the note was sold to a third party for \$3,500.

Some online discount brokerage firms offer flat rates for trading stock, but many still charge commissions based on the transaction amount (principal). Table 1 shows the commission schedule for one of these firms.

Table 1 Commission Schedule

Principal	Commission
\$0–\$2,499	\$29 + 1.6% of principal
\$2,500–\$9,999	\$49 + 0.8% of principal
\$10,000+	\$99 + 0.3% of principal

EXAMPLE 5 **Interest on an Investment** An investor purchases 50 shares of a stock at \$47.52 per share. After 200 days, the investor sells the stock for \$52.19 per share. Using Table 1, find the annual rate of interest earned by this investment. Express the answer as a percentage, correct to three decimal places.

SOLUTION The principal referred to in Table 1 is the value of the stock. The total cost for the investor is the cost of the stock plus the commission:

$$47.52(50) = \$2{,}376 \qquad \text{Principal}$$

$$29 + 0.016(2{,}376) = \$67.02 \qquad \text{Commission, using line 1 of Table 1}$$

$$2{,}376 + 67.02 = \$2{,}443.02 \qquad \text{Total investment}$$

When the stock is sold, the commission is subtracted from the proceeds of the sale and the remainder is returned to the investor:

$$52.19(50) = \$2{,}609.50 \qquad \text{Principal}$$

$$49 + 0.008(2{,}609.50) = \$69.88 \qquad \text{Commission, using line 2 of Table 1}$$

$$2{,}609.50 - 69.88 = \$2{,}539.62 \qquad \text{Total return}$$

Now using formula (2) with $A = 2{,}539.62$, $P = 2{,}443.02$, and $t = \frac{200}{360} = \frac{5}{9}$, we have

$$A = P(1 + rt)$$

$$2{,}539.62 = 2{,}443.02\left(1 + \frac{5}{9}r\right)$$

$$= 2{,}443.02 + 1{,}357.23r$$

$$96.60 = 1{,}357.23r$$

$$r = \frac{96.60}{1{,}357.23} \approx 0.07117 \quad \text{or} \quad 7.117\%$$

Matched Problem 5 Repeat Example 5 if 500 shares of stock were purchased for \$17.64 per share and sold 270 days later for \$22.36 per share.

CONCEPTUAL INSIGHT

The commission schedule in Table 1 specifies a piecewise-defined function C with independent variable p, the principal (see Section 1.2).

$$C = \begin{cases} 29 + 0.016p & \text{if } 0 \le p < 2{,}500 \\ 49 + 0.008p & \text{if } 2{,}500 \le p < 10{,}000 \\ 99 + 0.003p & \text{if } 10{,}000 \le p \end{cases}$$

Two credit card accounts may differ in a number of ways, including annual interest rates, credit limits, minimum payments, annual fees, billing cycles, and even the methods for calculating interest. A common method for calculating the interest owed on a credit card is the **average daily balance method.** In this method, a balance is calculated at the end of each day, incorporating any purchases, credits, or payments that were made that day. Interest is calculated at the end of the billing cycle on the average of those daily balances. The average daily balance method is considered in Example 6.

EXAMPLE 6 **Credit Card Accounts** A credit card has an annual interest rate of 21.99%, and interest is calculated by the average daily balance method. In a 30-day billing cycle, purchases of \$56.75, \$184.36, and \$49.19 were made on days 12, 19, and 24, respectively, and a payment of \$100.00 was credited to the account on day 10. If the unpaid balance at the start of the billing cycle was \$842.67, how much interest will be charged at the end of the billing cycle? What will the unpaid balance be at the start of the next billing cycle?

SOLUTION First calculate the unpaid balance on each day of the billing cycle:

$$\begin{aligned} &\text{Days } 1\text{–}9: && \$842.67 \\ &\text{Days } 10\text{–}11: && \$842.67 - \$100.00 = \$742.67 \\ &\text{Days } 12\text{–}18: && \$742.67 + \$56.75 = \$799.42 \\ &\text{Days } 19\text{–}23: && \$799.42 + \$184.36 = \$983.78 \\ &\text{Days } 24\text{–}30: && \$983.78 + \$49.19 = \$1{,}032.97 \end{aligned}$$

So the unpaid balance was \$842.67 for the first 9 days of the billing cycle, \$742.67 for the next 2 days, \$799.42 for the next 7 days, and so on. To calculate the average daily balance, we find the sum of the 30 daily balances, and then divide by 30:

$$\begin{aligned} \text{Sum: } & 9(\$842.67) + 2(\$742.67) + 7(\$799.42) + 5(\$983.78) \\ & + 7(\$1032.97) = \$26{,}815.00 \end{aligned}$$

$$\text{Average daily balance: } \$26{,}815.00/30 = \$893.83$$

To calculate the interest, use the formula $I = Prt$ with $P = \$893.83$, $r = 0.2199$, and $t = 30/360$:

$$I = Prt = \$893.83(0.2199)(30/360) = \$16.38$$

Therefore, the interest charged at the end of the billing cycle is \$16.38, and the unpaid balance at the start of the next cycle is \$1,032.97 + \$16.38 = \$1,049.35.

Matched Problem 6 A credit card has an annual interest rate of 16.99%, and interest is calculated by the average daily balance method. In a 30-day billing cycle, purchases of \$345.86 and \$246.71 were made on days 9 and 16, respectively, and a payment of \$500.00 was credited to the account on day 15. If the unpaid balance at the start of the billing cycle was \$1,792.19, how much interest will be charged at the end of the billing cycle? What will the unpaid balance be at the start of the next billing cycle?

Exercises 3.1

W Skills Warm-up Exercises

In Problems 1–4, if necessary, review Section B.1.

1. If your state sales tax rate is 5.65%, how much tax will you pay on a bicycle that sells for \$449.99?
2. If your state sales tax rate is 8.25%, what is the total cost of a motor scooter that sells for \$1,349.95?
3. A baseball team had a 103–58 win–loss record. Find its winning percentage to the nearest percentage point.
4. A basketball team played 21 games with a winning percentage of 81%. How many games did it lose?

In Problems 5–8, give the slope and y intercept of each line. (If necessary, review Section 1.2.)

5. $y = 12{,}000 + 120x$
6. $y = 15{,}000 + 300x$
7. $y = 2{,}000(1 + 0.025x)$
8. $y = 5{,}000(1 + 0.035x)$

A *In Problems 9–16, convert the given interest rate to decimal form if it is given as a percentage, and to a percentage if it is given in decimal form.*

9. 6.2%
10. 0.085
11. 0.137
12. 4.35%
13. 0.25%
14. 0.0019
15. 0.0084
16. 0.765%

In Problems 17–24, convert the given time period to years, in reduced fraction form, assuming a 360-day year [this assumption does not affect the number of quarters (4), months (12), or weeks (52) in a year].

17. 180 days
18. 9 months
19. 4 months
20. 90 days
21. 5 quarters
22. 6 weeks
23. 24 weeks
24. 7 quarters

In Problems 25–32, use formula (1) for simple interest to find each of the indicated quantities.

25. $P = \$300$; $r = 7\%$; $t = 2$ years; $I = ?$
26. $P = \$950$; $r = 9\%$; $t = 1$ year; $I = ?$
27. $I = \$36$; $r = 4\%$; $t = 6$ months; $P = ?$
28. $I = \$15$; $r = 8\%$; $t = 3$ quarters; $P = ?$
29. $I = \$48$; $P = \$600$; $t = 240$ days; $r = ?$
30. $I = \$28$; $P = \$700$; $t = 13$ weeks; $r = ?$
31. $I = \$60$; $P = \$2{,}400$; $r = 5\%$; $t = ?$
32. $I = \$84$; $P = \$7{,}200$; $r = 3.5\%$; $t = ?$

B *In Problems 33–40, use formula (2) for the amount to find each of the indicated quantities.*

33. $P = \$4{,}500$; $r = 10\%$; $t = 1$ quarter; $A = ?$
34. $P = \$8{,}000$; $r = 6.5\%$; $t = 90$ days; $A = ?$
35. $A = \$910$; $r = 16\%$; $t = 13$ weeks; $P = ?$
36. $A = \$6{,}608$; $r = 24\%$; $t = 3$ quarters; $P = ?$
37. $A = \$24{,}780$; $P = \$21{,}000$; $t = 8$ months; $r = ?$
38. $A = \$22{,}135$; $P = \$19{,}000$; $t = 39$ weeks; $r = ?$
39. $A = \$736$; $P = \$640$; $r = 15\%$; $t = ?$
40. $A = \$610$; $P = \$600$; $r = 5\%$; $t = ?$

C *In Problems 41–46, solve each formula for the indicated variable.*

41. $I = Prt$; for r
42. $I = Prt$; for P
43. $A = P + Prt$; for P
44. $A = P + Prt$; for r
45. $A = P(1 + rt)$; for t
46. $I = Prt$; for t

47. Discuss the similarities and differences in the graphs of future value A as a function of time t if \$1,000 is invested at simple interest at rates of 4%, 8%, and 12%, respectively (see the figure).

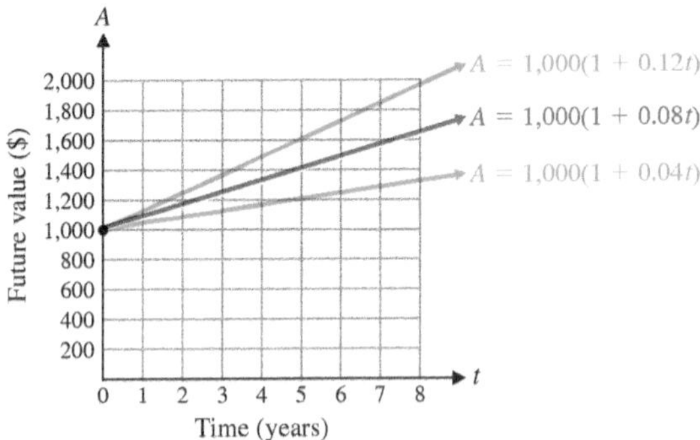

48. Discuss the similarities and differences in the graphs of future value A as a function of time t for loans of \$400, \$800, and \$1,200, respectively, each at 7.5% simple interest (see the figure).

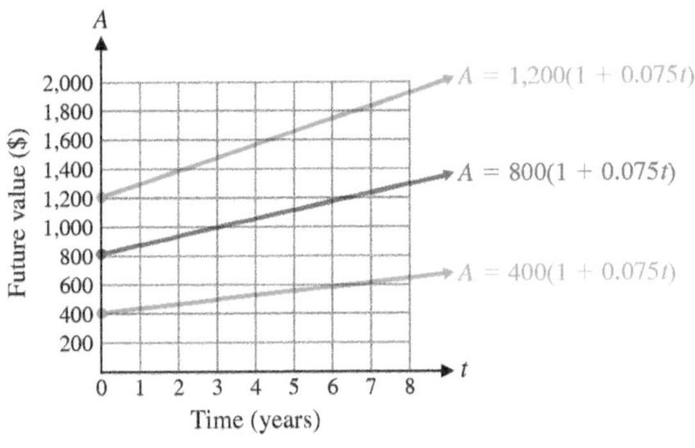

Applications*

In all problems involving days, a 360-day year is assumed. When annual rates are requested as an answer, express the rate as a percentage, correct to three decimal places, unless directed otherwise. Round dollar amounts to the nearest cent.

49. If $3,000 is loaned for 4 months at a 4.5% annual rate, how much interest is earned?

50. If $5,000 is loaned for 9 months at a 6.2% annual rate, how much interest is earned?

51. How much interest will you have to pay for a 60-day loan of $500, if a 36% annual rate is charged?

52. If a 50% annual rate is charged, how much interest will be owed on a loan of $1,000 for 30 days?

53. A loan of $7,260 was repaid at the end of 8 months. What size repayment check (principal and interest) was written, if an 8% annual rate of interest was charged?

54. A loan of $10,000 was repaid at the end of 6 months. What amount (principal and interest) was repaid, if a 6.5% annual rate of interest was charged?

55. A loan of $4,000 was repaid at the end of 10 months with a check for $4,270. What annual rate of interest was charged?

56. A check for $3,097.50 was used to retire a 5-month $3,000 loan. What annual rate of interest was charged?

57. If you paid $30 to a loan company for the use of $1,000 for 60 days, what annual rate of interest did they charge?

58. If you paid $120 to a loan company for the use of $2,000 for 90 days, what annual rate of interest did they charge?

59. A radio commercial for a loan company states: "You only pay 29¢ a day for each $500 borrowed." If you borrow $1,500 for 120 days, what amount will you repay, and what annual interest rate is the company charging?

60. George finds a company that charges 59¢ per day for each $1,000 borrowed. If he borrows $3,000 for 60 days, what amount will he repay, and what annual interest rate will he pay the company?

61. What annual interest rate is earned by a 13-week T-bill with a maturity value of $1,000 that sells for $989.37?

62. What annual interest rate is earned by a 33-day T-bill with a maturity value of $1,000 that sells for $996.16?

63. What is the purchase price of a 50-day T-bill with a maturity value of $1,000 that earns an annual interest rate of 5.53%?

64. What is the purchase price of a 26-week T-bill with a maturity value of $1,000 that earns an annual interest rate of 4.903%?

*The authors wish to thank Professor Roy Luke of Pierce College and Professor Dennis Pence of Western Michigan University for their many useful suggestions of applications for this chapter.

In Problems 65 and 66, assume that the minimum payment on a credit card is the greater of $20 or 2% of the unpaid balance.

65. Find the minimum payment on an unpaid balance of $1,215.45.

66. Find the minimum payment on an unpaid balance of $936.24.

In Problems 67 and 68, assume that the minimum payment on a credit card is the greater of $27 or 3% of the unpaid balance.

67. Find the minimum payment on an unpaid balance of $815.69.

68. Find the minimum payment on an unpaid balance of $927.38.

69. For services rendered, an attorney accepts a 90-day note for $5,500 at 8% simple interest from a client. (Both interest and principal are repaid at the end of 90 days.) Wishing to use her money sooner, the attorney sells the note to a third party for $5,560 after 30 days. What annual interest rate will the third party receive for the investment?

70. To complete the sale of a house, the seller accepts a 180-day note for $10,000 at 7% simple interest. (Both interest and principal are repaid at the end of 180 days.) Wishing to use the money sooner for the purchase of another house, the seller sells the note to a third party for $10,124 after 60 days. What annual interest rate will the third party receive for the investment?

Use the commission schedule from Company A shown in Table 2 to find the annual rate of interest earned by each investment in Problems 71 and 72.

Table 2 Company A

Principal	Commission
Under $3,000	$25 + 1.8% of principal
$3,000–$10,000	$37 + 1.4% of principal
Over $10,000	$107 + 0.7% of principal

71. An investor purchases 200 shares at $14.20 a share, holds the stock for 39 weeks, and then sells the stock for $15.75 a share.

72. An investor purchases 450 shares at $21.40 a share, holds the stock for 26 weeks, and then sells the stock for $24.60 a share.

Use the commission schedule from Company B shown in Table 3 to find the annual rate of interest earned by each investment in Problems 73 and 74.

Table 3 Company B

Principal	Commission
Under $3,000	$32 + 1.8% of principal
$3,000–$10,000	$56 + 1% of principal
Over $10,000	$106 + 0.5% of principal

73. An investor purchases 215 shares at $45.75 a share, holds the stock for 300 days, and then sells the stock for $51.90 a share.

74. An investor purchases 75 shares at $37.90 a share, holds the stock for 150 days, and then sells the stock for $41.20 a share.

Many tax preparation firms offer their clients a refund anticipation loan (RAL). For a fee, the firm will give a client his refund when the return is filed. The loan is repaid when the IRS refund is sent to the firm. The RAL fee is equivalent to the interest charge for a loan. The schedule in Table 4 is from a major RAL lender. Use this schedule to find the annual rate of interest for the RALs in Problems 75–78.

Table 4

RAL Amount	RAL Fee
\$0–\$500	\$29.00
\$501–\$1,000	\$39.00
\$1,001–\$1,500	\$49.00
\$1,501–\$2,000	\$69.00
\$2,001–\$5,000	\$89.00

75. A client receives a \$475 RAL, which is paid back in 20 days.

76. A client receives a \$1,100 RAL, which is paid back in 30 days.

77. A client receives a \$1,900 RAL, which is paid back in 15 days.

78. A client receives a \$3,000 RAL, which is paid back in 25 days.

In Problems 79–82, assume that the annual interest rate on a credit card is 25.74% and interest is calculated by the average daily balance method.

79. The unpaid balance at the start of a 28-day billing cycle was \$955.13. A \$5,000 purchase was made on the first day of the billing cycle and a \$50 payment was credited to the account on day 21. How much interest will be charged at the end of the billing cycle?

80. The unpaid balance at the start of a 28-day billing cycle was \$955.13. A \$50 payment was credited to the account on day 21 of the billing cycle and a \$5,000 purchase was made on the last day of the billing cycle. How much interest will be charged at the end of the billing cycle?

81. The unpaid balance at the start of a 28-day billing cycle was \$1,472.35. Purchases of \$154.15 and \$38.76 were made on days 5 and 12, respectively, and a payment of \$250 was credited to the account on day 18. Find the unpaid balance at the end of the billing cycle.

82. The unpaid balance at the start of a 28-day billing cycle was \$1,837.23. Purchases of \$126.54 and \$52.89 were made on days 21 and 27, respectively, and a payment of \$100 was credited to the account on day 20. Find the unpaid balance at the end of the billing cycle.

In Problems 83–86, assume that the annual interest rate on a credit card is 19.99% and interest is calculated by the average daily balance method.

83. The unpaid balance at the start of a 30-day billing cycle was \$654.71. No purchases were made during the billing cycle and a payment of \$654.71 was credited to the account on day 21. Find the unpaid balance at the end of the billing cycle.

84. The unpaid balance at the start of a 30-day billing cycle was \$1,583.44. No purchases were made during the billing cycle and a payment of \$1,583.44 was credited to the account on day 21. Find the unpaid balance at the end of the billing cycle.

85. The unpaid balance at the start of a 30-day billing cycle was \$725.38. A purchase of \$49.82 was made on day 15. No payment was made during the billing cycle and a late fee of \$37 was charged to the account on day 25. Find the unpaid balance at the end of the billing cycle.

86. The unpaid balance at the start of a 30-day billing cycle was \$475.17. A purchase of \$125.93 was made on day 3. No payment was made during the billing cycle and a late fee of \$37 was charged to the account on day 25. Find the unpaid balance at the end of the billing cycle.

A ***payday loan*** *or* ***short-term loan*** *is a loan that is repaid either on the next payday or over a short term. In Problems 87–90, assume a 365-day year to express the annual interest rate as a percentage, rounded to the nearest integer.*

87. In the UK, if you use a short-term loan from Wonga Group Limited to borrow £400 for a period of two weeks, you have to repay £444.80. Find the annual interest rate for this loan.

88. In South Africa, if you use a short-term loan from Wonga Group Limited to borrow R3,000 for a period of 12 days, you have to repay R3,530.04. Find the annual interest rate for this loan.

89. In Spain, if you use a short-term loan from Wonga Group Limited to borrow €250 for a period of 18 days, you have to repay €257.43. Find the annual interest rate for this loan.

90. In Spain, if you use a short-term loan from Wonga Group Limited to borrow €300 for a period of 25 days, you have to repay €329.70. Find the annual interest rate for this loan.

Answers to Matched Problems

1. \$650 **2.** \$4,761.90 **3.** 3.485%
4. 15.0% **5.** 31.439% **6.** \$26.94; \$1,911.70

3.2 Compound and Continuous Compound Interest

- Compound Interest
- Continuous Compound Interest
- Growth and Time
- Annual Percentage Yield

Compound Interest

If at the end of a payment period the interest due is reinvested at the same rate, then the interest as well as the original principal will earn interest during the next payment period. Interest paid on interest reinvested is called **compound interest**.

For example, suppose you deposit \$1,000 in a bank that pays 8% compounded quarterly. How much will the bank owe you at the end of a year? *Compounding quarterly* means that earned interest is paid to your account at the end of each 3-month period and that interest as well as the principal earns interest for the next quarter. Using the simple interest formula (2) from the preceding section, we compute the amount in the account at the end of the first quarter after interest has been paid:

$$\begin{aligned} A &= P(1 + rt) \\ &= 1{,}000[1 + 0.08(\tfrac{1}{4})] \\ &= 1{,}000(1.02) = \$1{,}020 \end{aligned}$$

Now, \$1,020 is your new principal for the second quarter. At the end of the second quarter, after interest is paid, the account will have

$$\begin{aligned} A &= \$1{,}020[1 + 0.08(\tfrac{1}{4})] \\ &= \$1{,}020(1.02) = \$1{,}040.40 \end{aligned}$$

Similarly, at the end of the third quarter, you will have

$$\begin{aligned} A &= \$1{,}040.40[1 + 0.08(\tfrac{1}{4})] \\ &= \$1{,}040.40(1.02) = \$1{,}061.21 \end{aligned}$$

Finally, at the end of the fourth quarter, the account will have

$$\begin{aligned} A &= \$1{,}061.21[1 + 0.08(\tfrac{1}{4})] \\ &= \$1{,}061.21(1.02) = \$1{,}082.43 \end{aligned}$$

How does this compounded amount compare with simple interest? The amount with simple interest would be

$$\begin{aligned} A &= P(1 + rt) \\ &= \$1{,}000[1 + 0.08(1)] \\ &= \$1{,}000(1.08) = \$1{,}080 \end{aligned}$$

We see that compounding quarterly yields \$2.43 more than simple interest would provide.

Let's look over the calculations for compound interest above to see if we can uncover a pattern that might lead to a general formula for computing compound interest:

$$\begin{aligned} A &= 1{,}000(1.02) && \text{End of first quarter} \\ A &= [1{,}000(1.02)](1.02) = 1{,}000(1.02)^2 && \text{End of second quarter} \\ A &= [1{,}000(1.02)^2](1.02) = 1{,}000(1.02)^3 && \text{End of third quarter} \\ A &= [1{,}000(1.02)^3](1.02) = 1{,}000(1.02)^4 && \text{End of fourth quarter} \end{aligned}$$

It appears that at the end of n quarters, we would have

$$A = 1{,}000(1.02)^n \qquad \text{End of } n\text{th quarter}$$

or

$$\begin{aligned} A &= 1{,}000[1 + 0.08(\tfrac{1}{4})]^n \\ &= 1{,}000[1 + \tfrac{0.08}{4}]^n \end{aligned}$$

where $\frac{0.08}{4} = 0.02$ is the interest rate per quarter. Since interest rates are generally quoted as *annual nominal rates*, the **rate per compounding period** is found by dividing the annual nominal rate by the number of compounding periods per year.

In general, if P is the principal earning interest compounded m times a year at an annual rate of r, then (by repeated use of the simple interest formula, using $i = r/m$, the rate per period) the amount A at the end of each period is

$$A = P(1 + i) \quad \text{End of first period}$$
$$A = [P(1 + i)](1 + i) = P(1 + i)^2 \quad \text{End of second period}$$
$$A = [P(1 + i)^2](1 + i) = P(1 + i)^3 \quad \text{End of third period}$$
$$\vdots$$
$$A = [P(1 + i)^{n-1}](1 + i) = P(1 + i)^n \quad \text{End of } n\text{th period}$$

We summarize this important result in Theorem 1:

THEOREM 1 Compound Interest

$$A = P(1 + i)^n \qquad (1)$$

where $i = r/m$ and A = amount (future value) at the end of n periods
P = principal (present value)
r = annual nominal rate*
m = number of compounding periods per year
i = rate per compounding period
n = total number of compounding periods

* This is often shortened to "annual rate" or just "rate."

CONCEPTUAL INSIGHT

Formula (1) of Theorem 1 is equivalent to the formula

$$A = P\left(1 + \frac{r}{m}\right)^{mt} \qquad (2)$$

where t is the time, in years, that the principal is invested. For a compound interest calculation, formula (2) may seem more natural to use than (1), if r (the annual interest rate) and t (time in years) are given. On the other hand, if i (the interest rate per period), and n (the number of compounding periods) are given, formula (1) may seem easier to use. It is not necessary to memorize both formulas, but it is important to understand how they are related.

EXAMPLE 1 **Comparing Interest for Various Compounding Periods** If \$1,000 is invested at 8% compounded

(A) annually, (B) semiannually,

(C) quarterly, (D) monthly,

what is the amount after 5 years? Write answers to the nearest cent.

SOLUTION

(A) Compounding annually means that there is one interest payment period per year. So, $n = 5$ and $i = r = 0.08$.

$$A = P(1 + i)^n$$
$$= 1{,}000(1 + 0.08)^5 \quad \text{Use a calculator.}$$
$$= 1{,}000(1.469\ 328)$$
$$= \$1{,}469.33 \quad \text{Interest earned} = A - p = \$469.33.$$

(B) Compounding semiannually means that there are two interest payment periods per year. The number of payment periods in 5 years is $n = 2(5) = 10$, and the interest rate per period is

$$i = \frac{r}{m} = \frac{0.08}{2} = 0.04$$

$$\begin{aligned} A &= P(1 + i)^n \\ &= 1{,}000(1 + 0.04)^{10} && \text{Use a calculator.} \\ &= 1{,}000(1.480\,244) \\ &= \$1{,}480.24 && \text{Interest earned} = A - P = \$480.24. \end{aligned}$$

(C) Compounding quarterly means that there are four interest payments per year. So, $n = 4(5) = 20$ and $i = \frac{0.08}{4} = 0.02$.

$$\begin{aligned} A &= P(1 + i)^n \\ &= 1{,}000(1 + 0.02)^{20} && \text{Use a calculator.} \\ &= 1{,}000(1.485\,947) \\ &= \$1{,}485.95 && \text{Interest earned} = A - P = \$485.95. \end{aligned}$$

Reminder

The bar over the 6 in $i = 0.006\,66\overline{6}$ indicates a repeating decimal expansion. Rounding i to a small number of decimal places, such as 0.007 or 0.0067, can result in round-off errors. To avoid this, use as many decimal places for i as your calculator is capable of displaying.

(D) Compounding monthly means that there are twelve interest payments per year. So, $n = 12(5) = 60$ and $i = \frac{0.08}{12} = 0.006\,66\overline{6}$ (see the Reminder).

$$\begin{aligned} A &= P(1 + i)^n \\ &= 1{,}000\left(1 + \frac{0.08}{12}\right)^{60} && \text{Use a calculator.} \\ &= 1{,}000(1.489\,846) \\ &= \$1{,}489.85 && \text{Interest earned} = A - P = \$489.85. \end{aligned}$$

Matched Problem 1 Repeat Example 1 with an annual interest rate of 6% over an 8-year period.

Continuous Compound Interest

In Example 1, we considered an investment of \$1,000 at an annual rate of 8%. We calculated the amount after 5 years for interest compounded annually, semiannually, quarterly, and monthly. What would happen to the amount if interest were compounded daily, or every minute, or every second?

Although the difference in amounts in Example 1 between compounding semiannually and annually is \$1,480.24 − \$1,469.33 = \$10.91, the difference between compounding monthly and quarterly is only \$1,489.85 − \$1,485.95 = \$3.90. This suggests that as the number m of compounding periods per year increases without bound, the amount will approach some limiting value. To see that this is indeed the case, we rewrite the amount A as follows:

$$\begin{aligned} A &= P(1 + i)^n && \text{Substitute } i = \frac{r}{m},\ n = mt. \\ &= P\left(1 + \frac{r}{m}\right)^{mt} && \text{Multiply the exponent by } \frac{r}{r}\ (=1). \\ &= P\left(1 + \frac{r}{m}\right)^{[m/r]rt} && \text{Let } x = \frac{m}{r}\text{; then } \frac{1}{x} = \frac{r}{m}. \\ &= P\left(1 + \frac{1}{x}\right)^{xrt} && \text{Use a law of exponents: } a^{xy} = (a^x)^y. \\ &= P\left[\left(1 + \frac{1}{x}\right)^x\right]^{rt} \end{aligned}$$

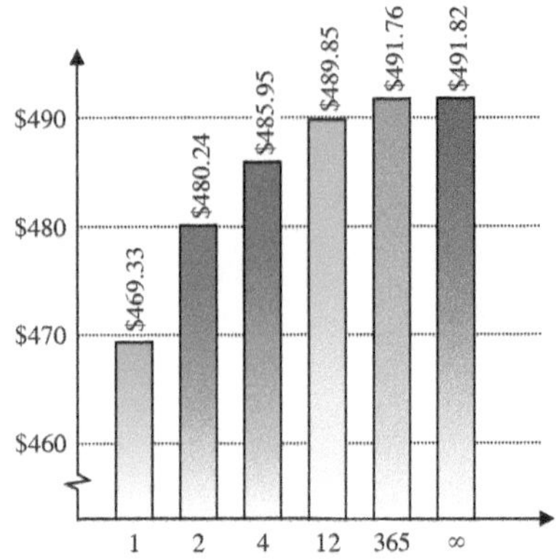

Figure 1 Interest on $1,000 for 5 years at 8% with various compounding periods

As the number m of compounding periods increases without bound, so does x. So the expression in square brackets gets close to the irrational number $e \approx 2.7183$ (see Table 1 in Section 1.5), and the amount approaches the limiting value

$$A = Pe^{rt} = 1{,}000e^{0.08(5)} \approx \$1{,}491.8247$$

In other words, no matter how often interest is compounded, the amount in the account after 5 years will never equal or exceed $1,491.83. Therefore, the interest $I(=A-P)$ will never equal or exceed $491.83 (Fig. 1).

CONCEPTUAL INSIGHT

One column in Figure 1 is labeled with the symbol ∞, read as "infinity." This symbol does not represent a real number. We use ∞ to denote the process of allowing m, the number of compounding periods per year, to get larger and larger with no upper limit on its size.

The formula we have obtained, $A = Pe^{rt}$, is known as the **continuous compound interest formula**. It is used when interest is **compounded continuously**, that is, when the number of compounding periods per year increases without bound.

THEOREM 2 Continuous Compound Interest Formula

If a principal P is invested at an annual rate r (expressed as a decimal) compounded continuously, then the amount A in the account at the end of t years is given by

$$A = Pe^{rt} \tag{3}$$

EXAMPLE 2 **Compounding Daily and Continuously** What amount will an account have after 2 years if $5,000 is invested at an annual rate of 8%

(A) compounded daily? (B) compounded continuously?

Compute answers to the nearest cent.

SOLUTION

(A) Use the compound interest formula

$$A = P\left(1 + \frac{r}{m}\right)^{mt}$$

with $P = 5{,}000$, $r = 0.08$, $m = 365$, and $t = 2$:

$$A = 5{,}000\left(1 + \frac{0.08}{365}\right)^{(365)(2)} \quad \text{Use a calculator.}$$

$$= \$5{,}867.45$$

(B) Use the continuous compound interest formula

$$A = Pe^{rt}$$

with $P = 5{,}000$, $r = 0.08$, and $t = 2$:

$$A = 5{,}000e^{(0.08)(2)} \quad \text{Use a calculator.}$$

$$= \$5{,}867.55$$

CAUTION In Example 2B, do not use the approximation 2.7183 for e; it is not accurate enough to compute the correct amount to the nearest cent. Instead, use your calculator's built-in e. Avoid any rounding off until the end of the calculation, when you round the amount to the nearest cent.

Matched Problem 2 What amount will an account have after 1.5 years if \$8,000 is invested at an annual rate of 9%

(A) compounded weekly? (B) compounded continuously?

Compute answers to the nearest cent.

CONCEPTUAL INSIGHT

The continuous compound interest formula $A = Pe^{rt}$ is identical, except for the names of the variables, to the equation $y = ce^{kt}$ that we used to model population growth in Section 1.5. Like the growth of an investment that earns continuous compound interest, we usually consider the population growth of a country to be continuous: Births and deaths occur all the time, not just at the end of a month or quarter.

Growth and Time

How much should you invest now to have a given amount at a future date? What annual rate of return have your investments earned? How long will it take your investment to double in value? The formulas for compound interest and continuous compound interest can be used to answer such questions. If the values of all but one of the variables in the formula are known, then we can solve for the remaining variable.

EXAMPLE 3 **Finding Present Value** How much should you invest now at 10% to have \$8,000 toward the purchase of a car in 5 years if interest is

(A) compounded quarterly? (B) compounded continuously?

SOLUTION

(A) We are given a future value $A = \$8{,}000$ for a compound interest investment, and we need to find the present value P given $i = \frac{0.10}{4} = 0.025$ and $n = 4(5) = 20$.

$$
\begin{aligned}
A &= P(1 + i)^n \\
8{,}000 &= P(1 + 0.025)^{20} \\
P &= \frac{8{,}000}{(1 + 0.025)^{20}} \qquad \text{Use a calculator.} \\
&= \frac{8{,}000}{1.638\,616} \\
&= \$4{,}882.17
\end{aligned}
$$

Your initial investment of \$4,882.17 will grow to \$8,000 in 5 years.

(B) We are given $A = \$8{,}000$ for an investment at continuous compound interest, and we need to find the present value P given $r = 0.10$ and $t = 5$.

$$
\begin{aligned}
A &= Pe^{rt} \\
8{,}000 &= Pe^{0.10(5)} \\
P &= \frac{8{,}000}{e^{0.10(5)}} \qquad \text{Use a calculator.} \\
P &= \$4{,}852.25
\end{aligned}
$$

Your initial investment of \$4,852.25 will grow to \$8,000 in 5 years.

Matched Problem 3 How much should new parents invest at 8% to have \$80,000 toward their child's college education in 17 years if interest is

(A) compounded semiannually? (B) compounded continuously?

A graphing calculator is a useful tool for studying compound interest. In Figure 2, we use a spreadsheet to illustrate the growth of the investment in Example 3A both numerically and graphically. Similar results can be obtained from most graphing calculators.

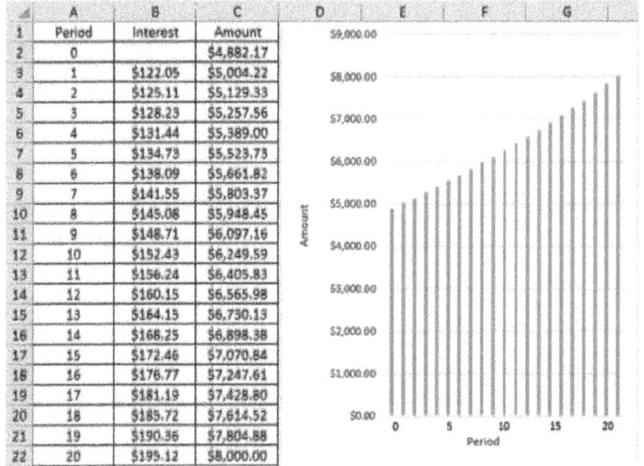

Period	Interest	Amount
0		$4,882.17
1	$122.05	$5,004.22
2	$125.11	$5,129.33
3	$128.23	$5,257.56
4	$131.44	$5,389.00
5	$134.73	$5,523.73
6	$138.09	$5,661.82
7	$141.55	$5,803.37
8	$145.08	$5,948.45
9	$148.71	$6,097.16
10	$152.43	$6,249.59
11	$156.24	$6,405.83
12	$160.15	$6,565.98
13	$164.15	$6,730.13
14	$168.25	$6,898.38
15	$172.46	$7,070.84
16	$176.77	$7,247.61
17	$181.19	$7,428.80
18	$185.72	$7,614.52
19	$190.36	$7,804.88
20	$195.12	$8,000.00

Figure 2 Growth of $4,882.17 at 10% compounded quarterly for 5 years

Solving the compound interest formula or the continuous compound interest formula for r enables us to determine the rate of growth of an investment.

EXAMPLE 4 **Computing Growth Rate** Figure 3 shows that a $10,000 investment in a growth-oriented mutual fund over a 10-year period would have grown to $126,000. What annual nominal rate would produce the same growth if interest was:

(A) compounded annually? (B) compounded continuously?

Express answers as percentages, rounded to three decimal places.

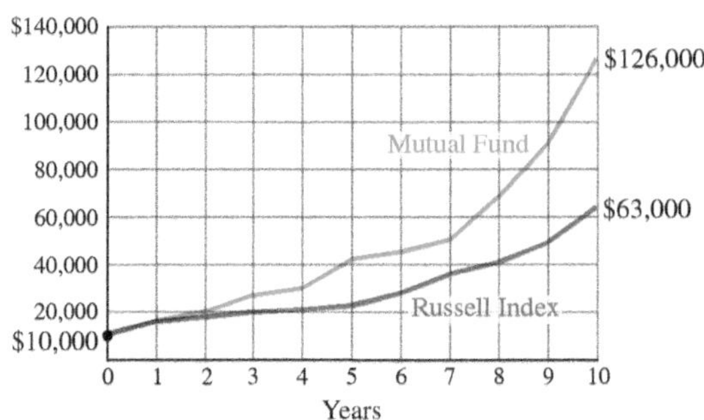

Figure 3 Growth of a $10,000 investment

SOLUTION

(A)
$$126{,}000 = 10{,}000(1 + r)^{10}$$
$$12.6 = (1 + r)^{10}$$
$$\sqrt[10]{12.6} = 1 + r$$
$$r = \sqrt[10]{12.6} - 1 = 0.28836 \quad \text{or} \quad 28.836\%$$

(B)
$$126{,}000 = 10{,}000e^{r(10)}$$
$$12.6 = e^{10r} \quad \text{Take ln of both sides.}$$
$$\ln 12.6 = 10r$$
$$r = \frac{\ln 12.6}{10} = 0.25337 \quad \text{or} \quad 25.337\%$$

Matched Problem 4 The Russell Index tracks the average performance of various groups of stocks. Figure 3 shows that, on average, a \$10,000 investment in midcap growth funds over a 10-year period would have grown to \$63,000. What annual nominal rate would produce the same growth if interest were

(A) compounded annually? (B) compounded continuously?

Express answers as percentages, rounded to three decimal places.

CONCEPTUAL INSIGHT

We can solve $A = P(1 + i)^n$ for n using a property of logarithms:

$$\log_b M^p = p \log_b M$$

Theoretically, any base can be used for the logarithm, but most calculators only evaluate logarithms with base 10 (denoted log) or base e (denoted ln).

Finally, if we solve the compound interest formula for n (or the continuous compound interest formula for t), we can determine the **growth time** of an investment—the time it takes a given principal to grow to a particular value (the shorter the time, the greater the return on the investment).

Example 5 illustrates three methods for solving for growth time.

EXAMPLE 5 **Computing Growth Time** How long will it take \$10,000 to grow to \$12,000 if it is invested at 9% compounded monthly?

SOLUTION

Method 1. Use logarithms and a calculator:

$$A = P(1 + i)^n$$
$$12{,}000 = 10{,}000\left(1 + \frac{0.09}{12}\right)^n$$
$$1.2 = 1.0075^n$$

Now, solve for n by taking logarithms of both sides:

$$\ln 1.2 = \ln 1.0075^n \quad \text{We choose the natural logarithm (base } e\text{)}$$
$$\ln 1.2 = n \ln 1.0075 \quad \text{and use the property } \ln M^p = p \ln M.$$
$$n = \frac{\ln 1.2}{\ln 1.0075}$$
$$\approx 24.40 \approx 25 \text{ months} \quad \text{or} \quad 2 \text{ years and } 1 \text{ month}$$

Note: 24.40 is rounded up to 25 to guarantee reaching \$12,000 since interest is paid at the end of each month.

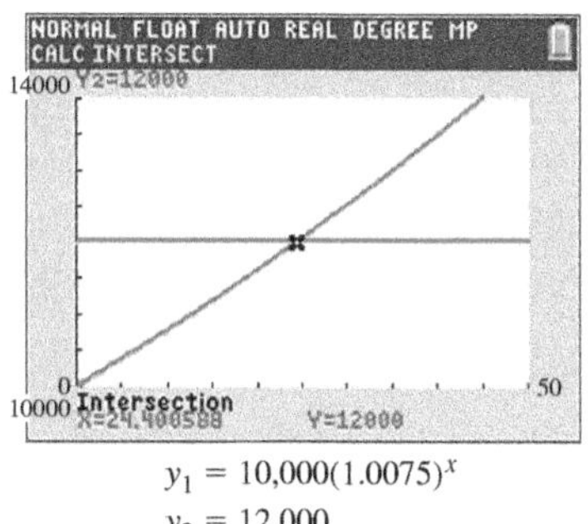

$y_1 = 10{,}000(1.0075)^x$
$y_2 = 12{,}000$

Figure 4

Method 2. Use a graphing calculator: To solve this problem using graphical approximation techniques, we graph both sides of the equation $12{,}000 = 10{,}000(1.0075)^n$ and find that the graphs intersect at $x = n = 24.40$ months (Fig. 4). So the growth time is 25 months.

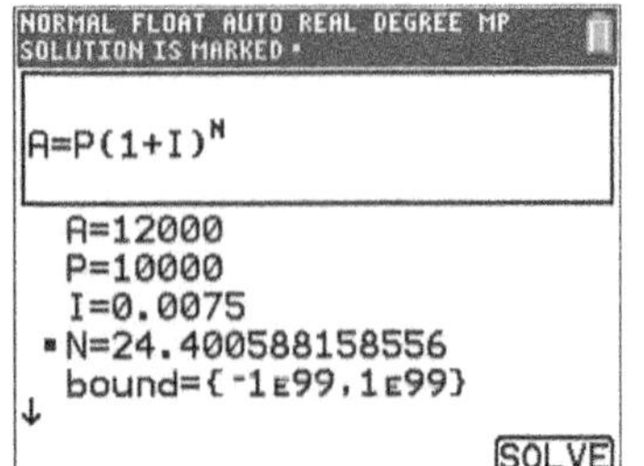

Figure 5 TI-84 Plus CE equation solver

Method 3. Most graphing calculators have an approximation process that is referred to as an **equation solver**. Figure 5 shows the equation solver on a TI-84 Plus CE. After entering values for three of the four variables, the solver will approximate the value of the remaining variable. Once again, we see that the growth time is 25 months (Fig. 5).

Matched Problem 5 How long will it take \$10,000 to grow to \$25,000 if it is invested at 8% compounded quarterly?

Annual Percentage Yield

Table 1 lists the rate and compounding period for certificates of deposit (CDs) offered by four banks. How can we tell which of these CDs has the best return?

Table 1 Certificates of Deposit (CDs)

Bank	Rate	Compounded
Advanta	4.93%	monthly
DeepGreen	4.95%	daily
Charter One	4.97%	quarterly
Liberty	4.94%	continuously

Explore and Discuss 1

Determine the value after 1 year of a \$1,000 CD purchased from each of the banks in Table 1. Which CD offers the greatest return? Which offers the least return?

If a principal P is invested at an annual rate r compounded m times a year, then the amount after 1 year is

$$A = P\left(1 + \frac{r}{m}\right)^m$$

The simple interest rate that will produce the same amount A in 1 year is called the **annual percentage yield** (APY). To find the APY, we proceed as follows:

$$\begin{pmatrix}\text{amount at}\\ \text{simple interest}\\ \text{after 1 year}\end{pmatrix} = \begin{pmatrix}\text{amount at}\\ \text{compound interest}\\ \text{after 1 year}\end{pmatrix}$$

$$P(1 + \text{APY}) = P\left(1 + \frac{r}{m}\right)^m \qquad \text{Divide both sides by } P.$$

$$1 + \text{APY} = \left(1 + \frac{r}{m}\right)^m \qquad \text{Isolate APY on the left side.}$$

$$\text{APY} = \left(1 + \frac{r}{m}\right)^m - 1$$

If interest is compounded continuously, then the amount after 1 year is $A = Pe^r$. So to find the annual percentage yield, we solve the equation

$$P(1 + \text{APY}) = Pe^r$$

for APY, obtaining $\text{APY} = e^r - 1$. We summarize our results in Theorem 3.

THEOREM 3 Annual Percentage Yield

If a principal is invested at the annual (nominal) rate r compounded m times a year, then the annual percentage yield is

$$\text{APY} = \left(1 + \frac{r}{m}\right)^m - 1$$

If a principal is invested at the annual (nominal) rate r compounded continuously, then the annual percentage yield is

$$\text{APY} = e^r - 1$$

The annual percentage yield is also referred to as the **effective rate** or **true interest rate**.

Compound rates with different compounding periods cannot be compared directly (see Explore and Discuss 1). But since the annual percentage yield is a simple interest rate, the annual percentage yields for two different compound rates can be compared.

EXAMPLE 6 **Using APY to Compare Investments** Find the APYs (expressed as a percentage, correct to three decimal places) for each of the banks in Table 1 and compare these CDs.

SOLUTION

$$\text{Advanta: APY} = \left(1 + \frac{0.0493}{12}\right)^{12} - 1 = 0.05043 \quad \text{or} \quad 5.043\%$$

$$\text{DeepGreen: APY} = \left(1 + \frac{0.0495}{365}\right)^{365} - 1 = 0.05074 \quad \text{or} \quad 5.074\%$$

$$\text{Charter One: APY} = \left(1 + \frac{0.0497}{4}\right)^{4} - 1 = 0.05063 \quad \text{or} \quad 5.063\%$$

$$\text{Liberty: APY} = e^{0.0494} - 1 = 0.05064 \quad \text{or} \quad 5.064\%$$

Comparing these APYs, we conclude that the DeepGreen CD will have the largest return and the Advanta CD will have the smallest.

Matched Problem 6 Southern Pacific Bank offered a 1-year CD that paid 4.8% compounded daily and Washington Savings Bank offered one that paid 4.85% compounded quarterly. Find the APY (expressed as a percentage, correct to three decimal places) for each CD. Which has the higher return?

EXAMPLE 7 **Computing the Annual Nominal Rate Given the APY** A savings and loan wants to offer a CD with a monthly compounding rate that has an APY of 7.5%. What annual nominal rate compounded monthly should it use?

Check with a graphing calculator.

SOLUTION

$$\text{APY} = \left(1 + \frac{r}{m}\right)^m - 1$$

$$0.075 = \left(1 + \frac{r}{12}\right)^{12} - 1$$

$$1.075 = \left(1 + \frac{r}{12}\right)^{12}$$

$$\sqrt[12]{1.075} = 1 + \frac{r}{12}$$

$$\sqrt[12]{1.075} - 1 = \frac{r}{12}$$

$$r = 12(\sqrt[12]{1.075} - 1) \qquad \text{Use a calculator.}$$

$$= 0.072\,539 \quad \text{or} \quad 7.254\%$$

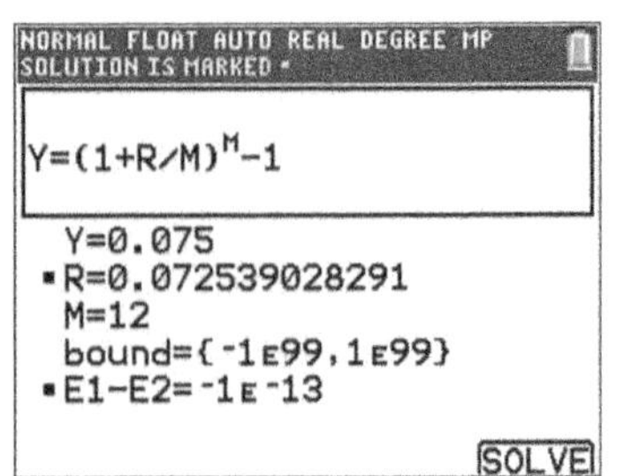

Figure 6 TI-84 Plus CE equation solver

So an annual nominal rate of 7.254% compounded monthly is equivalent to an APY of 7.5%.

CHECK We use an equation solver on a graphing calculator to check this result (Fig. 6).

Matched Problem 7 What is the annual nominal rate compounded quarterly for a bond that has an APY of 5.8%?

Each compound interest problem involves two interest rates. Referring to Example 5, $r = 0.09$ or 9% is the annual nominal compounding rate, and $i = r/12 = 0.0075$ or 0.75% is the interest rate per month. Do not confuse these two rates by using r in place of i in the compound interest formula. If interest is compounded annually, then $i = r/1 = r$. In all other cases, r and i are not the same. ▲

Explore and Discuss 2

(A) Which would be the better way to invest $1,000: at 9% simple interest for 10 years, or at 7% compounded monthly for 10 years?

(B) Explain why the graph of future value as a function of time is a straight line for simple interest, but for compound interest the graph curves upward (see Fig. 7).

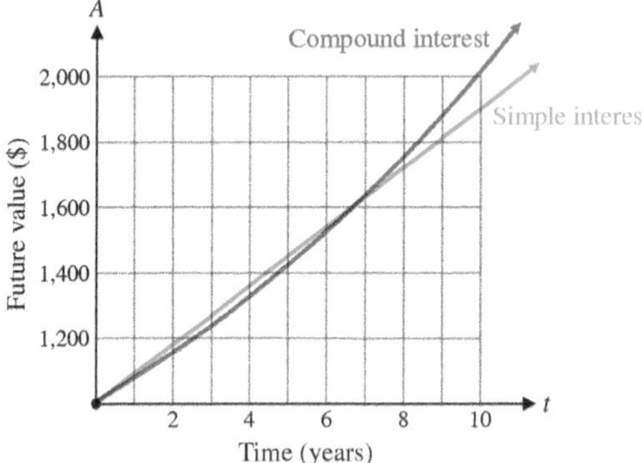

Figure 7

CONCEPTUAL INSIGHT

The two curves in Figure 7 intersect at $t = 0$ and again near $t = 7$. The t coordinate of each intersection point is a solution of the equation

$$1{,}000(1 + 0.09t) = 1{,}000(1 + 0.07/12)^{12t}$$

Don't try to use algebra to solve this equation. It can't be done. But the solutions are easily approximated on a graphing calculator (Fig. 8).

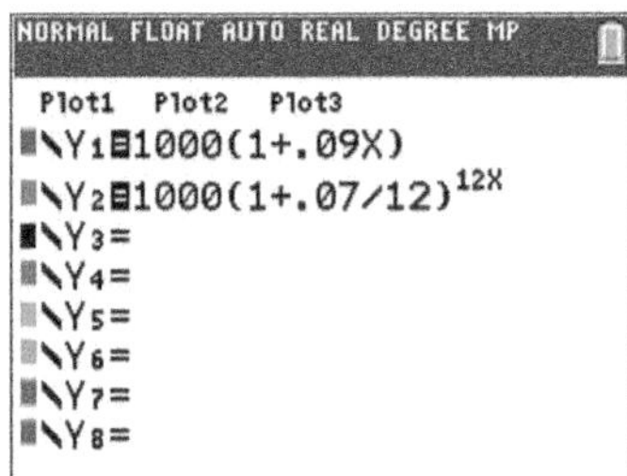

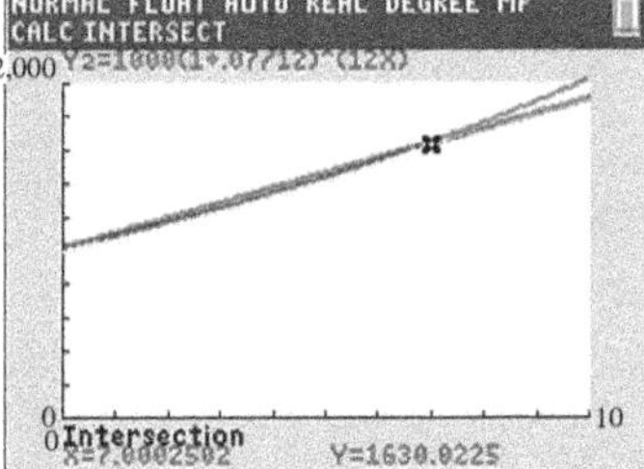

Figure 8

Exercises 3.2

Find all dollar amounts to the nearest cent. When an interest rate is requested as an answer, express the rate as a percentage correct to two decimal places, unless directed otherwise. In all problems involving days, use a 365-day year.

W **Skills Warm-up Exercises**

In Problems 1–8, solve the equation for the unknown quantity. (If necessary, review sections B.7, 1.5, and 1.6.)

1. $1{,}641.6 = \mathrm{P}(1.2)^3$

2. $2{,}652.25 = \mathrm{P}(1.03)^2$

3. $12x^3 = 58{,}956$

4. $100x^4 = 15{,}006.25$

5. $6.75 = 3(1 + i)^2$

6. $13.72 = 5(1 + i)^3$

7. $14{,}641 = 10{,}000(1.1)^n$

8. $2{,}488.32 = 1{,}000(1.2)^n$

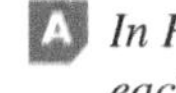

A *In Problems 9–12, use compound interest formula (1) to find each of the indicated values.*

9. $P = \$5{,}000;\ i = 0.005;\ n = 36;\ A = ?$

10. $P = \$2{,}800;\ i = 0.003;\ n = 24;\ A = ?$

11. $A = \$8{,}000;\ i = 0.02;\ n = 32;\ P = ?$

12. $A = \$15{,}000;\ i = 0.01;\ n = 28;\ P = ?$

In Problems 13–20, use the continuous compound interest formula (3) to find each of the indicated values.

13. $P = \$2{,}450;\ r = 8.12\%;\ t = 3$ years; $A = ?$

14. $P = \$995;\ r = 22\%;\ t = 2$ years; $A = ?$

15. $A = \$3{,}450;\ r = 7.65\%;\ t = 9$ years; $P = ?$

16. $A = \$19{,}000;\ r = 7.69\%;\ t = 5$ years; $P = ?$

17. $A = \$88{,}000;\ P = \$71{,}153;\ r = 8.5\%;\ t = ?$

18. $A = \$32{,}982;\ P = \$27{,}200;\ r = 5.93\%;\ t = ?$

19. $A = \$15{,}875;\ P = \$12{,}100;\ t = 48$ months; $r = ?$

20. $A = \$23{,}600;\ P = \$19{,}150;\ t = 60$ months; $r = ?$

In Problems 21–28, use the given annual interest rate r and the compounding period to find i, the interest rate per compounding period.

21. 6.6% compounded quarterly

22. 3.84% compounded monthly

23. 10.2% compounded monthly

24. 2.94% compounded semiannually

25. 7.3% compounded daily

26. 5.44% compounded quarterly

27. 4.86% compounded semiannually

28. 10.95% compounded daily

In Problems 29–36, use the given interest rate i per compounding period to find r, the annual rate.

29. 1.73% per half-year

30. 2.34% per quarter

31. 0.53% per month

32. 0.012% per day

33. 2.19% per quarter

34. 3.69% per half-year

35. 0.006% per day

36. 0.47% per month

B **37.** If \$100 is invested at 6% compounded

(A) annually (B) quarterly (C) monthly

what is the amount after 4 years? How much interest is earned?

38. If \$2,000 is invested at 7% compounded

(A) annually (B) quarterly (C) monthly

what is the amount after 5 years? How much interest is earned?

39. If \$5,000 is invested at 5% compounded monthly, what is the amount after

(A) 2 years? (B) 4 years?

40. If \$20,000 is invested at 4% compounded monthly, what is the amount after

(A) 5 years? (B) 8 years?

41. If \$8,000 is invested at 7% compounded continuously, what is the amount after 6 years?

42. If \$30,000 is invested at 9.75% compounded continuously, what is the amount after 10 years?

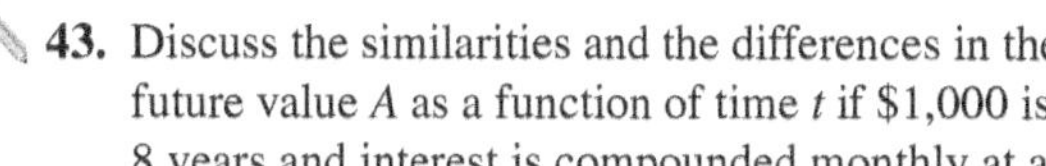

43. Discuss the similarities and the differences in the graphs of future value A as a function of time t if \$1,000 is invested for 8 years and interest is compounded monthly at annual rates of 4%, 8%, and 12%, respectively (see the figure).

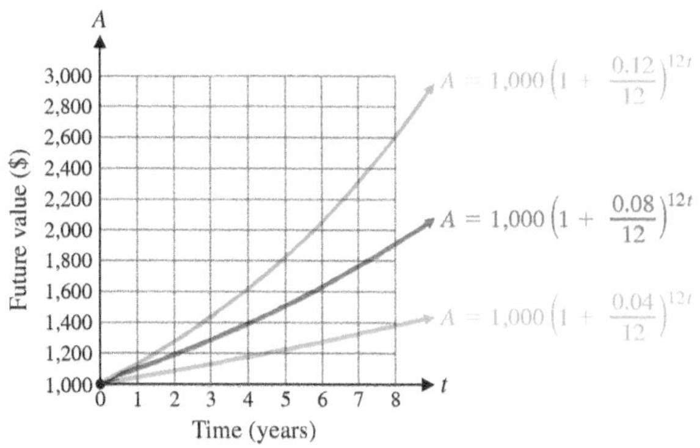

44. Discuss the similarities and differences in the graphs of future value A as a function of time t for loans of \$4,000, \$8,000, and \$12,000, respectively, each at 7.5% compounded monthly for 8 years (see the figure).

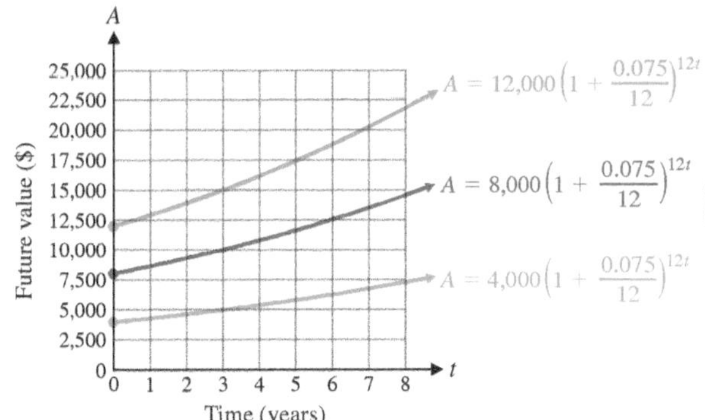

45. If \$1,000 is invested in an account that earns 9.75% compounded annually for 6 years, find the interest earned during each year and the amount in the account at the end of each year. Organize your results in a table.

46. If \$2,000 is invested in an account that earns 8.25% compounded annually for 5 years, find the interest earned during each year and the amount in the account at the end of each year. Organize your results in a table.

47. If an investment company pays 6% compounded semiannually, how much should you deposit now to have \$10,000
(A) 5 years from now? (B) 10 years from now?

48. If an investment company pays 8% compounded quarterly, how much should you deposit now to have \$6,000
(A) 3 years from now? (B) 6 years from now?

49. If an investment earns 9% compounded continuously, how much should you deposit now to have \$25,000
(A) 36 months from now? (B) 9 years from now?

50. If an investment earns 12% compounded continuously, how much should you deposit now to have \$4,800
(A) 48 months from now? (B) 7 years from now?

51. What is the annual percentage yield (APY) for money invested at an annual rate of
(A) 3.9% compounded monthly?
(B) 2.3% compounded quarterly?

52. What is the annual percentage yield (APY) for money invested at an annual rate of
(A) 4.32% compounded monthly?
(B) 4.31% compounded daily?

53. What is the annual percentage yield (APY) for money invested at an annual rate of
(A) 5.15% compounded continuously?
(B) 5.20% compounded semiannually?

54. What is the annual percentage yield (APY) for money invested at an annual rate of
(A) 3.05% compounded quarterly?
(B) 2.95% compounded continuously?

55. How long will it take \$4,000 to grow to \$9,000 if it is invested at 7% compounded monthly?

56. How long will it take \$7,000 to grow to \$9,800 if it is invested at 5.6% compounded quarterly?

57. How long will it take \$7,000 to grow to \$9,800 if it is invested at 5.6% compounded continuously?

58. How long will it take \$42,000 to grow to \$60,276 if it is invested at 4.25% compounded continuously?

C *In Problems 59 and 60, use compound interest formula (1) to find n to the nearest larger integer value.*

59. $A = 2P; i = 0.06; n = ?$

60. $A = 3P; i = 0.07; n = ?$

61. How long will it take money to double if it is invested at
(A) 10% compounded quarterly?
(B) 12% compounded quarterly?

62. How long will it take money to double if it is invested at
(A) 8% compounded semiannually?
(B) 7% compounded semiannually?

63. How long will it take money to double if it is invested at
(A) 3% compounded continuously?
(B) 6% compounded continuously?

64. How long will it take money to triple if it is invested at
(A) 3% compounded continuously?
(B) 6% compounded continuously?

Applications

65. A newborn child receives a \$20,000 gift toward college from her grandparents. How much will the \$20,000 be worth in 17 years if it is invested at 7% compounded quarterly?

66. A person with \$14,000 is trying to decide whether to purchase a car now, or to invest the money at 6.5% compounded semiannually and then buy a more expensive car. How much will be available for the purchase of a car at the end of 3 years?

67. What will a \$210,000 house cost 10 years from now if the inflation rate over that period averages 3% compounded annually?

68. If the inflation rate averages 4% per year compounded annually for the next 5 years, what will a car that costs \$17,000 now cost 5 years from now?

69. Rental costs for office space have been going up at 4.8% per year compounded annually for the past 5 years. If office space rent is now \$25 per square foot per month, what were the rental rates 5 years ago?

70. In a suburb, housing costs have been increasing at 5.2% per year compounded annually for the past 8 years. A house worth \$260,000 now would have had what value 8 years ago?

71. (A) If an investment of \$100 were made in 1776, and if it earned 3% compounded quarterly, how much would it be worth in 2026?

(B) Discuss the effect of compounding interest monthly, daily, and continuously (rather than quarterly) on the \$100 investment.

(C) Use a graphing calculator to graph the growth of the investment of part (A).

72. (A) Starting with formula (1), derive each of the following formulas:

$$P = \frac{A}{(1+i)^n}, \quad i = \left(\frac{A}{P}\right)^{1/n} - 1, \quad n = \frac{\ln A - \ln P}{\ln(1+i)}$$

(B) Explain why it is unnecessary to memorize the formulas above for P, i, and n if you know formula (1).

73. A promissory note will pay \$50,000 at maturity 6 years from now. If you pay \$28,000 for the note now, what rate compounded continuously would you earn?

74. If you deposit \$10,000 in a savings account now, what rate compounded continuously would be required for you to withdraw \$12,500 at the end of 4 years?

75. You have saved \$7,000 toward the purchase of a car costing \$9,000. How long will the \$7,000 have to be invested at 9% compounded monthly to grow to \$9,000? (Round up to the next-higher month if not exact.)

76. A married couple has \$15,000 toward the purchase of a house. For the house that the couple wants to buy, a down payment of \$20,000 is required. How long will the money have to be invested at 7% compounded quarterly to grow to \$20,000? (Round up to the next-higher quarter if not exact.)

77. An Individual Retirement Account (IRA) has \$20,000 in it, and the owner decides not to add any more money to the account other than interest earned at 6% compounded daily. How much will be in the account 35 years from now when the owner reaches retirement age?

78. If \$1 had been placed in a bank account in the year 1066 and forgotten until now, how much would be in the account at the end of 2026 if the money earned 2% interest compounded annually? 2% simple interest? (Now you can see the power of compounding and why inactive accounts are closed after a relatively short period of time.)

79. How long will it take money to double if it is invested at 7% compounded daily? 8.2% compounded continuously?

80. How long will it take money to triple if it is invested at 5% compounded daily? 6% compounded continuously?

81. In a conversation with a friend, you note that you have two real estate investments, one that has doubled in value in the past 9 years and another that has doubled in value in the past 12 years. Your friend says that the first investment has been growing at approximately 8% compounded annually and the second at 6% compounded annually. How did your friend make these estimates? The **rule of 72** states that the annual compound rate of growth r of an investment that doubles in n years can be approximated by $r = 72/n$. Construct a table comparing the exact rate of growth and the approximate rate provided by the rule of 72 for doubling times of $n = 6, 7, \ldots, 12$ years. Round both rates to one decimal place.

82. Refer to Problem 81. Show that the exact annual compound rate of growth of an investment that doubles in n years is given by $r = 100(2^{1/n} - 1)$. Graph this equation and the rule of 72 on a graphing calculator for $5 \le n \le 20$.

Solve Problems 83–86 using graphical approximation techniques on a graphing calculator.

83. How long does it take for a \$2,400 investment at 13% compounded quarterly to be worth more than a \$3,000 investment at 6% compounded quarterly?

84. How long does it take for a \$4,800 investment at 8% compounded monthly to be worth more than a \$5,000 investment at 5% compounded monthly?

85. One investment pays 10% simple interest and another pays 7% compounded annually. Which investment would you choose? Why?

86. One investment pays 9% simple interest and another pays 6% compounded monthly. Which investment would you choose? Why?

87. What is the annual nominal rate compounded daily for a bond that has an annual percentage yield of 3.39%?

88. What is the annual nominal rate compounded monthly for a bond that has an annual percentage yield of 2.95%?

89. What annual nominal rate compounded monthly has the same annual percentage yield as 7% compounded continuously?

90. What annual nominal rate compounded continuously has the same annual percentage yield as 6% compounded monthly?

Problems 91–94 refer to zero coupon bonds. A ***zero coupon bond*** *is a bond that is sold now at a discount and will pay its* ***face value*** *at some time in the future when it matures—no interest payments are made.*

91. A zero coupon bond with a face value of \$30,000 matures in 15 years. What should the bond be sold for now if its rate of return is to be 4.348% compounded annually?

92. A zero coupon bond with a face value of \$20,000 matures in 10 years. What should the bond be sold for now if its rate of return is to be 4.194% compounded annually?

93. If you pay \$4,126 for a 20-year zero coupon bond with a face value of \$10,000, what is your annual compound rate of return?

94. If you pay \$32,000 for a 5-year zero coupon bond with a face value of \$40,000, what is your annual compound rate of return?

The buying and selling commission schedule shown in the table is from an online discount brokerage firm. Taking into consideration the buying and selling commissions in this schedule, find the annual compound rate of interest earned by each investment in Problems 95–98.

Transaction Size	Commission Rate
\$0–\$1,500	\$29 + 2.5% of principal
\$1,501–\$6,000	\$57 + 0.6% of principal
\$6,001–\$22,000	\$75 + 0.30% of principal
\$22,001–\$50,000	\$97 + 0.20% of principal
\$50,001–\$500,000	\$147 + 0.10% of principal
\$500,001+	\$247 + 0.08% of principal

95. An investor purchases 100 shares of stock at \$65 per share, holds the stock for 5 years, and then sells the stock for \$125 a share.

96. An investor purchases 300 shares of stock at \$95 per share, holds the stock for 3 years, and then sells the stock for \$156 a share.

97. An investor purchases 200 shares of stock at \$28 per share, holds the stock for 4 years, and then sells the stock for \$55 a share.

98. An investor purchases 400 shares of stock at \$48 per share, holds the stock for 6 years, and then sells the stock for \$147 a share.

Answers to Matched Problems

1. (A) \$1,593.85 (B) \$1,604.71
   (C) \$1,610.32 (D) \$1,614.14
2. (A) \$9,155.23 (B) \$9,156.29
3. (A) \$21,084.17 (B) \$20,532.86
4. (A) 20.208% (B) 18.405%
5. 47 quarters, or 11 years and 3 quarters
6. Southern Pacific Bank: 4.917%
   Washington Savings Bank: 4.939%
   Washington Savings Bank has the higher return.
7. 5.678%

3.3 Future Value of an Annuity; Sinking Funds

- Future Value of an Annuity
- Sinking Funds
- Approximating Interest Rates

Future Value of an Annuity

An **annuity** is any sequence of equal periodic payments. If payments are made at the end of each time interval, then the annuity is called an **ordinary annuity**. We consider only ordinary annuities in this book. The amount, or **future value**, of an annuity is the sum of all payments plus all interest earned.

Suppose you decide to deposit \$100 every 6 months into an account that pays 6% compounded semiannually. If you make six deposits, one at the end of each interest payment period, over 3 years, how much money will be in the account after the last deposit is made? To solve this problem, let's look at it in terms of a time line. Using the compound amount formula $A = P(1 + i)^n$, we can find the value of each deposit after it has earned compound interest up through the sixth deposit, as shown in Figure 1.

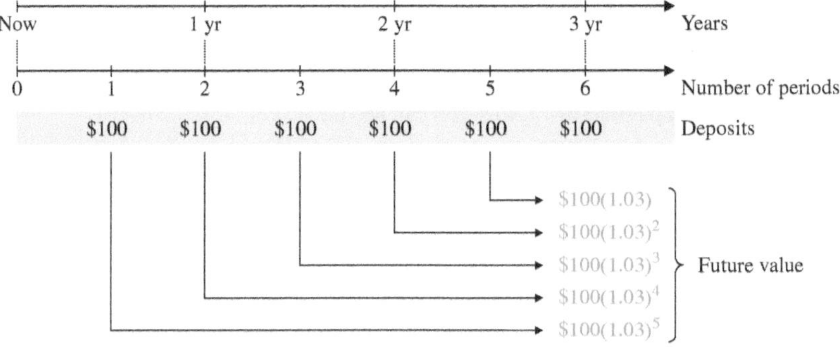

Figure 1

We could, of course, evaluate each of the future values in Figure 1 using a calculator and then add the results to find the amount in the account at the time of the sixth deposit—a tedious project at best. Instead, we take another approach, which leads directly to a formula that will produce the same result in a few steps (even when the number of deposits is very large). We start by writing the total amount in the account after the sixth deposit in the form

$$S = 100 + 100(1.03) + 100(1.03)^2 + 100(1.03)^3 + 100(1.03)^4 + 100(1.03)^5 \quad (1)$$

We would like a simple way to sum these terms. Let us multiply each side of (1) by 1.03 to obtain

$$1.03S = 100(1.03) + 100(1.03)^2 + 100(1.03)^3 + 100(1.03)^4 + 100(1.03)^5 + 100(1.03)^6 \quad (2)$$

Subtracting equation (1) from equation (2), left side from left side and right side from right side, we obtain

$$1.03S - S = 100(1.03)^6 - 100 \qquad \text{Factor each side.}$$

$$0.03S = 100[(1.03)^6 - 1] \qquad \text{Divide by 0.03.}$$

$$S = 100\frac{(1 + 0.03)^6 - 1}{0.03} \qquad \text{We write } S \text{ in this form to observe a general pattern.} \quad (3)$$

In general, if R is the periodic deposit, i the rate per period, and n the number of periods, then the future value is given by

$$S = R + R(1 + i) + R(1 + i)^2 + \cdots + R(1 + i)^{n-1} \qquad \text{Note how this compares to (1).} \quad (4)$$

and proceeding as in the above example, we obtain the general formula for the future value of an ordinary annuity:

$$S = R\frac{(1 + i)^n - 1}{i} \qquad \text{Note how this compares to (3).} \quad (5)$$

Returning to the example above, we use a calculator to complete the problem:

$$S = 100\frac{(1.03)^6 - 1}{0.03} \qquad \text{For improved accuracy, keep all values in the calculator until the end; round to the required number of decimal places.}$$

$$= \$646.84$$

CONCEPTUAL INSIGHT

In general, an expression of the form

$$a + ar + ar^2 + \cdots + ar^{n-1}$$

is called a finite geometric series (each term is obtained from the preceding term by multiplying by r). The sum of the terms of a finite geometric series is (see Section C.2)

$$a + ar + ar^2 + \cdots + ar^{n-1} = a\frac{r^n - 1}{r - 1}$$

If $a = R$ and $r = 1 + i$, then equation (4) is the sum of the terms of a finite geometric series and, using the preceding formula, we have

$$S = R + R(1 + i) + R(1 + i)^2 + \cdots + R(1 + i)^{n-1}$$

$$= R\frac{(1 + i)^n - 1}{1 + i - 1} \qquad a = R, r = 1 + i$$

$$= R\frac{(1 + i)^n - 1}{i} \quad (5)$$

So formula (5) is a direct consequence of the sum formula for a finite geometric series.

It is common to use FV (future value) for S and PMT (payment) for R in formula (5). Making these changes, we have the formula in Theorem 1.

THEOREM 1 Future Value of an Ordinary Annuity

$$FV = PMT\frac{(1+i)^n - 1}{i} \tag{6}$$

where
FV = future value (amount)
PMT = periodic payment
i = rate per period
n = number of payments (periods)

Note: Payments are made at the end of each period.

EXAMPLE 1 **Future Value of an Ordinary Annuity** What is the value of an annuity at the end of 20 years if \$2,000 is deposited each year into an account earning 8.5% compounded annually? How much of this value is interest?

SOLUTION To find the value of the annuity, use formula (6) with $PMT = \$2{,}000$, $i = r = 0.085$, and $n = 20$.

$$FV = PMT\frac{(1+i)^n - 1}{i}$$

$$= 2{,}000\frac{(1.085)^{20} - 1}{0.085} = \$96{,}754.03 \qquad \text{Use a calculator.}$$

To find the amount of interest earned, subtract the total amount deposited in the annuity (20 payments of \$2,000) from the total value of the annuity after the 20th payment.

$$\text{Deposits} = 20(2{,}000) = \$40{,}000$$

$$\text{Interest} = \text{value} - \text{deposits} = 96{,}754.03 - 40{,}000 = \$56{,}754.03$$

Figure 2, which was generated using a spreadsheet, illustrates the growth of this account over 20 years.

	A	B	C	D
1	Period	Payment	Interest	Balance
2	1	\$2,000.00	\$0.00	\$2,000.00
3	2	\$2,000.00	\$170.00	\$4,170.00
4	3	\$2,000.00	\$354.45	\$6,524.45
5	4	\$2,000.00	\$554.58	\$9,079.03
6	5	\$2,000.00	\$771.72	\$11,850.75
7	6	\$2,000.00	\$1,007.31	\$14,858.06
8	7	\$2,000.00	\$1,262.94	\$18,120.99
9	8	\$2,000.00	\$1,540.28	\$21,661.28
10	9	\$2,000.00	\$1,841.21	\$25,502.49
11	10	\$2,000.00	\$2,167.71	\$29,670.20
12	11	\$2,000.00	\$2,521.97	\$34,192.17
13	12	\$2,000.00	\$2,906.33	\$39,098.50
14	13	\$2,000.00	\$3,323.37	\$44,421.87
15	14	\$2,000.00	\$3,775.86	\$50,197.73
16	15	\$2,000.00	\$4,266.81	\$56,464.54
17	16	\$2,000.00	\$4,799.49	\$63,264.02
18	17	\$2,000.00	\$5,377.44	\$70,641.47
19	18	\$2,000.00	\$6,004.52	\$78,645.99
20	19	\$2,000.00	\$6,684.91	\$87,330.90
21	20	\$2,000.00	\$7,423.13	\$96,754.03
22	Totals	\$40,000.00	\$56,754.03	

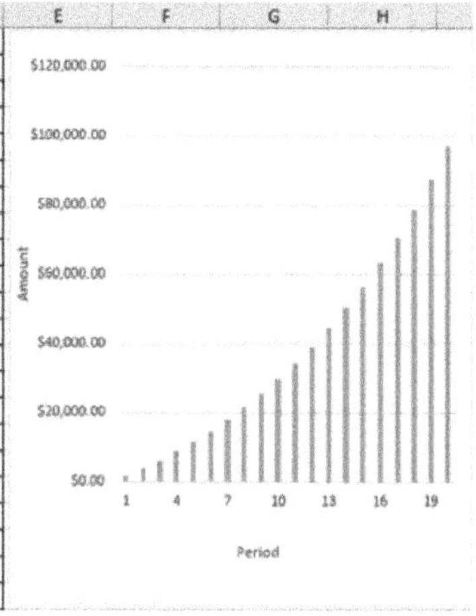

Figure 2 Ordinary annuity at 8.5% compounded annually for 20 years

Matched Problem 1 What is the value of an annuity at the end of 10 years if \$1,000 is deposited every 6 months into an account earning 8% compounded semiannually? How much of this value is interest?

The table in Figure 2 is called a **balance sheet**. Let's take a closer look at the construction of this table. The first line is a special case because the payment is made at the end of the period and no interest is earned. Each subsequent line of the table is computed as follows:

payment	+ interest	+ old balance	= new balance	
2,000	+ 0.085(2,000)	+ 2,000	= 4,170	Period 2
2,000	+ 0.085(4,170)	+ 4,170	= 6,524.45	Period 3

And so on. The amounts at the bottom of each column in the balance sheet agree with the results we obtained by using formula (6), as you would expect. Although balance sheets are appropriate for certain situations, we will concentrate on applications of formula (6). There are many important problems that can be solved only by using this formula.

Explore and Discuss 1

(A) Discuss the similarities and differences in the graphs of future value FV as a function of time t for ordinary annuities in which \$100 is deposited each month for 8 years and interest is compounded monthly at annual rates of 4%, 8%, and 12%, respectively (Fig. 3).

(B) Discuss the connections between the graph of the equation $y = 100t$, where t is time in months, and the graphs of part (A).

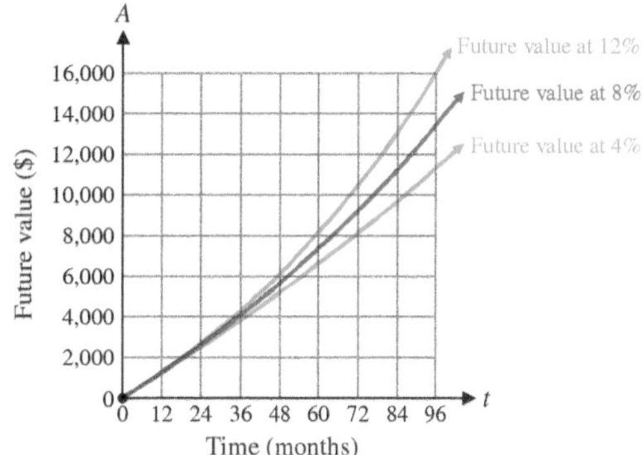

Figure 3

Sinking Funds

The formula for the future value of an ordinary annuity has another important application. Suppose the parents of a newborn child decide that on each of the child's birthdays up to the 17th year, they will deposit \$$PMT$ in an account that pays 6% compounded annually. The money is to be used for college expenses. What should the annual deposit (\$$PMT$) be in order for the amount in the account to be \$80,000 after the 17th deposit?

We are given FV, i, and n in formula (6), and we must find PMT:

$$FV = PMT\frac{(1+i)^n - 1}{i}$$

$$80{,}000 = PMT\frac{(1.06)^{17} - 1}{0.06} \qquad \text{Solve for } PMT.$$

$$PMT = 80{,}000\frac{0.06}{(1.06)^{17} - 1} \qquad \text{Use a calculator.}$$

$$= \$2{,}835.58 \text{ per year}$$

An annuity of 17 annual deposits of \$2,835.58 at 6% compounded annually will amount to \$80,000 in 17 years.

This is an example of a *sinking fund problem.* In general, any account that is established for accumulating funds to meet future obligations or debts is called a **sinking fund**. If the payments are to be made in the form of an ordinary annuity, then we have only to solve formula (6) for the **sinking fund payment** *PMT*:

$$PMT = FV\frac{i}{(1+i)^n - 1} \qquad (7)$$

It is important to understand that formula (7), which is convenient to use, is simply a variation of formula (6). You can always find the sinking fund payment by first substituting the appropriate values into formula (6) and then solving for *PMT*, as we did in the college fund example discussed above. Or you can substitute directly into formula (7), as we do in the next example. Use whichever method is easier for you.

EXAMPLE 2 **Computing the Payment for a Sinking Fund** A company estimates that it will have to replace a piece of equipment at a cost of \$800,000 in 5 years. To have this money available in 5 years, a sinking fund is established by making equal monthly payments into an account paying 6.6% compounded monthly.

(A) How much should each payment be?

(B) How much interest is earned during the last year?

SOLUTION

(A) To find *PMT*, we can use either formula (6) or (7). We choose formula (7) with $FV = \$800{,}000$, $i = \frac{0.066}{12} = 0.0055$, and $n = 12 \cdot 5 = 60$:

$$\begin{aligned} PMT &= FV\frac{i}{(1+i)^n - 1} \\ &= 800{,}000\frac{0.0055}{(1.0055)^{60} - 1} \\ &= \$11{,}290.42 \text{ per month} \end{aligned}$$

(B) To find the interest earned during the fifth year, we first use formula (6) with $PMT = \$11{,}290.42$, $i = 0.0055$, and $n = 12 \cdot 4 = 48$ to find the amount in the account after 4 years:

$$\begin{aligned} FV &= PMT\frac{(1+i)^n - 1}{i} \\ &= 11{,}290.42\frac{(1.0055)^{48} - 1}{0.0055} \\ &= \$618{,}277.04 && \text{Amount after 4 years} \end{aligned}$$

During the 5th year, the amount in the account grew from \$618,277.04 to \$800,000. A portion of this growth was due to the 12 monthly payments of \$11,290.42. The remainder of the growth was interest. Thus,

$$\begin{aligned} 800{,}000 - 618{,}277.04 &= 181{,}722.96 && \text{Growth in the 5th year} \\ 12 \cdot 11{,}290.42 &= 135{,}485.04 && \text{Payments during the 5th year} \\ 181{,}722.96 - 135{,}485.04 &= \$46{,}237.92 && \text{Interest during the 5th year} \end{aligned}$$

Matched Problem 2 A bond issue is approved for building a marina in a city. The city is required to make regular payments every 3 months into a sinking fund paying 5.4% compounded quarterly. At the end of 10 years, the bond obligation will be retired with a cost of \$5,000,000.

(A) What should each payment be?

(B) How much interest is earned during the 10th year?

EXAMPLE 3 **Growth in an IRA** Jane deposits \$2,000 annually into a Roth IRA that earns 6.85% compounded annually. (The interest earned by a Roth IRA is tax free.) Due to a change in employment, these deposits stop after 10 years, but the account continues to earn interest until Jane retires 25 years after the last deposit was made. How much is in the account when Jane retires?

SOLUTION First, we use the future value formula with $PMT = \$2{,}000$, $i = 0.0685$, and $n = 10$ to find the amount in the account after 10 years:

$$\begin{aligned} FV &= PMT\frac{(1+i)^n - 1}{i} \\ &= 2{,}000\frac{(1.0685)^{10} - 1}{0.0685} \\ &= \$27{,}437.89 \end{aligned}$$

Now we use the compound interest formula from Section 3.2 with $P = \$27{,}437.89$, $i = 0.0685$, and $n = 25$ to find the amount in the account when Jane retires:

$$\begin{aligned} A &= P(1+i)^n \\ &= 27{,}437.89(1.0685)^{25} \\ &= \$143{,}785.10 \end{aligned}$$

Matched Problem 3 Refer to Example 3. Mary starts a Roth IRA earning the same rate of interest at the time Jane stops making payments into her IRA. How much must Mary deposit each year for the next 25 years in order to have the same amount at retirement as Jane?

Explore and Discuss 2

Refer to Example 3 and Matched Problem 3. What was the total amount Jane deposited in order to have \$143,785.10 at retirement? What was the total amount Mary deposited in order to have the same amount at retirement? Do you think it is advisable to start saving for retirement as early as possible?

Approximating Interest Rates

Algebra can be used to solve the future value formula (6) for PMT or n but not for i. However, graphical techniques or equation solvers can be used to approximate i to as many decimal places as desired.

EXAMPLE 4 **Approximating an Interest Rate** A person makes monthly deposits of \$100 into an ordinary annuity. After 30 years, the annuity is worth \$160,000. What annual rate compounded monthly has this annuity earned during this 30-year period? Express the answer as a percentage, correct to two decimal places.

SOLUTION Substituting $FV = \$160{,}000$, $PMT = \$100$, and $n = 30(12) = 360$ in (6) produces the following equation:

$$160{,}000 = 100\frac{(1+i)^{360}-1}{i}$$

We can approximate the solution to this equation by using graphical techniques (Figs. 4A, 4B) or an equation solver (Fig. 4C). From Figure 4B or 4C, we see that $i = 0.006\,956\,7$ and $12(i) = 0.083\,480\,4$. So the annual rate (to two decimal places) is $r = 8.35\%$.

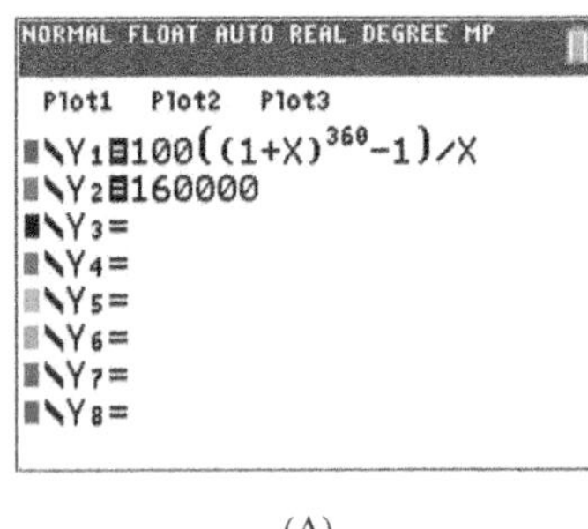

(A)

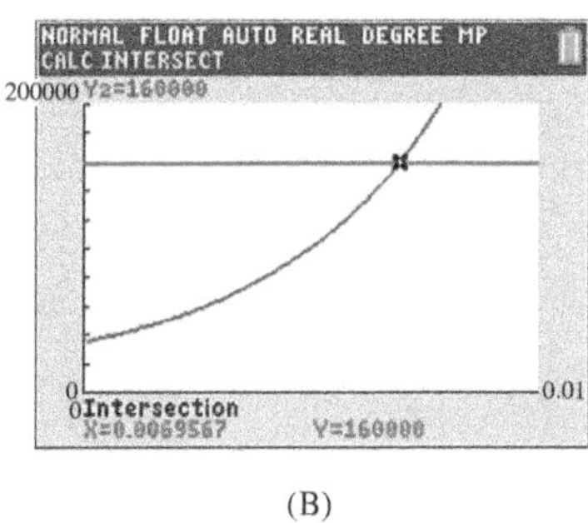

(B)

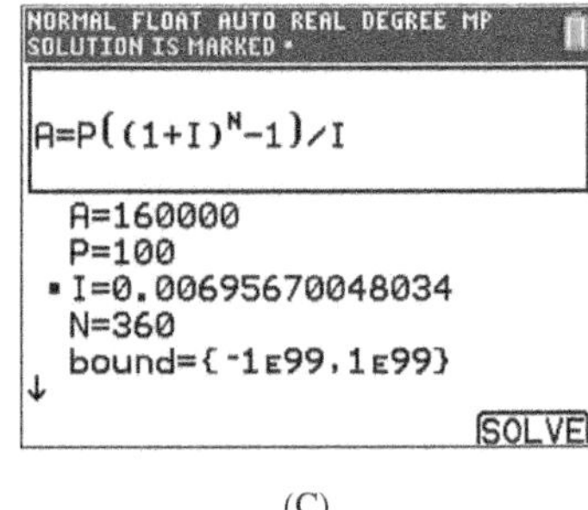

(C)

Figure 4

Matched Problem 4 A person makes annual deposits of \$1,000 into an ordinary annuity. After 20 years, the annuity is worth \$55,000. What annual compound rate has this annuity earned during this 20-year period? Express the answer as a percentage, correct to two decimal places.

Exercises 3.3

W Skills Warm-up Exercises

In Problems 1–8, find the sum of the finite geometric series $a + ar + ar^2 + \cdots + ar^{n-1}$. *(If necessary, review Section C.2.)*

1. $1 + 2 + 4 + 8 + \cdots + 2^9$
2. $1 + 5 + 25 + 125 + \cdots + 5^8$
3. $a = 30, r = 1, n = 100$
4. $a = 25, r = -1, n = 81$
5. $a = 10, r = 3, n = 15$
6. $a = 5, r = 7, n = 8$

A *In Problems 7–14, find i (the rate per period) and n (the number of periods) for each annuity.*

7. Quarterly deposits of \$500 are made for 20 years into an annuity that pays 8% compounded quarterly.
8. Monthly deposits of \$350 are made for 6 years into an annuity that pays 6% compounded monthly.
9. Semiannual deposits of \$900 are made for 12 years into an annuity that pays 7.5% compounded semiannually.
10. Annual deposits of \$2,500 are made for 15 years into an annuity that pays 6.25% compounded annually.
11. Monthly deposits of \$345 are made for 7 years into an annuity that pays 7.8% compounded monthly.
12. Semiannual deposits of \$1,900 are made for 7 years into an annuity that pays 8.5% compounded semiannually.
13. Annual deposits of \$1,750 are made for 15 years into an annuity that pays 6.25% compounded annually.
14. Quarterly deposits of \$1,200 are made for 18 years into an annuity that pays 7.6% compounded quarterly.

B *In Problems 15–22, use the future value formula (6) to find each of the indicated values.*

15. $n = 20$; $i = 0.03$; $PMT = \$500$; $FV = ?$
16. $n = 25$; $i = 0.04$; $PMT = \$100$; $FV = ?$
17. $FV = \$5{,}000$; $n = 15$; $i = 0.01$; $PMT = ?$
18. $FV = \$3{,}500$; $n = 16$; $i = 0.07$; $PMT = ?$
19. $FV = \$4{,}000$; $i = 0.02$; $PMT = 200$; $n = ?$
20. $FV = \$7{,}500$; $i = 0.06$; $PMT = 300$; $n = ?$
21. $FV = \$7{,}600$; $PMT = \$500$; $n = 10$; $i = ?$ (Round answer to two decimal places.)
22. $FV = \$4{,}100$; $PMT = \$100$; $n = 20$; $i = ?$ (Round answer to two decimal places.)

C

23. Explain what is meant by an ordinary annuity.
24. Explain why no interest is credited to an ordinary annuity at the end of the first period.

25. Solve the future value formula (6) for n.

26. Solve the future value formula (6) for i if $n = 2$.

Applications

27. Guaranty Income Life offered an annuity that pays 6.65% compounded monthly. If $500 is deposited into this annuity every month, how much is in the account after 10 years? How much of this is interest?

28. Nationwide Bank in the UK offered an annuity that pays 6.95% compounded monthly. If $800 is deposited into this annuity every month, how much is in the account after 12 years? How much of this is interest?

29. In order to accumulate enough money for a down payment on a house, a couple deposits $300 per month into an account paying 6% compounded monthly. If payments are made at the end of each period, how much money will be in the account in 5 years?

30. A self-employed person has a Keogh retirement plan. (This type of plan is free of taxes until money is withdrawn.) If deposits of $7,500 are made each year into an account paying 8% compounded annually, how much will be in the account after 20 years?

31. A bank in Netherlands offered an annuity that pays 6.15% compounded monthly. What equal monthly deposit should be made into this annuity in order to have $125,000 in 25 years?

32. A bank in Belgium offered an annuity that pays 5.95% compounded monthly. What equal monthly deposit should be made into this annuity in order to have $250,000 in 20 years?

33. A company estimates that it will need $100,000 in 8 years to replace a computer. If it establishes a sinking fund by making fixed monthly payments into an account paying 7.5% compounded monthly, how much should each payment be?

34. Parents have set up a sinking fund in order to have $120,000 in 15 years for their children's college education. How much should be paid semiannually into an account paying 6.8% compounded semiannually?

35. If $1,000 is deposited at the end of each year for 5 years into an ordinary annuity earning 8.32% compounded annually, construct a balance sheet showing the interest earned during each year and the balance at the end of each year.

36. If $2,000 is deposited at the end of each quarter for 2 years into an ordinary annuity earning 7.9% compounded quarterly, construct a balance sheet showing the interest earned during each quarter and the balance at the end of each quarter.

37. Beginning in January, a person plans to deposit $100 at the end of each month into an account earning 6% compounded monthly. Each year taxes must be paid on the interest earned during that year. Find the interest earned during each year for the first 3 years.

38. If $500 is deposited each quarter into an account paying 8% compounded quarterly for 3 years, find the interest earned during each of the 3 years.

39. Bob makes his first $1,000 deposit into an IRA earning 6.4% compounded annually on his 24th birthday and his last $1,000 deposit on his 35th birthday (12 equal deposits in all). With no additional deposits, the money in the IRA continues to earn 6.4% interest compounded annually until Bob retires on his 65th birthday. How much is in the IRA when Bob retires?

40. Refer to Problem 39. John procrastinates and does not make his first $1,000 deposit into an IRA until he is 36, but then he continues to deposit $1,000 each year until he is 65 (30 deposits in all). If John's IRA also earns 6.4% compounded annually, how much is in his IRA when he makes his last deposit on his 65th birthday?

41. Refer to Problems 39 and 40. How much would John have to deposit each year in order to have the same amount at retirement as Bob has?

42. Refer to Problems 39 and 40. Suppose that Bob decides to continue to make $1,000 deposits into his IRA every year until his 65th birthday. If John still waits until he is 36 to start his IRA, how much must he deposit each year in order to have the same amount at age 65 as Bob has?

43. Bank Australia offered an Online Saver account with an APY of 1.663%.

    (A) If interest is compounded monthly, what is the equivalent annual nominal rate?

    (B) If you wish to have $40,000 in this account after 6 years, what equal deposit should you make each month?

44. RaboDirect, a division of Rabobank Australia Limited, offered a High Interest Savings Account with an APY of 3.093%.

    (A) If interest is compounded monthly, what is the equivalent annual nominal rate?

    (B) If a company wishes to have $250,000 in this account after 5 years, what equal deposit should be made each month?

45. You can afford monthly deposits of $200 into an account that pays 5.7% compounded monthly. How long will it be until you have $7,000? (Round to the next-higher month if not exact.)

46. A company establishes a sinking fund for upgrading office equipment with monthly payments of $2,000 into an account paying 6.6% compounded monthly. How long will it be before the account has $100,000? (Round up to the next-higher month if not exact.)

In Problems 47–50, use graphical approximation techniques or an equation solver to approximate the desired interest rate. Express each answer as a percentage, correct to two decimal places.

47. A person makes annual payments of $1,000 into an ordinary annuity. At the end of 5 years, the amount in the annuity is $5,840. What annual nominal compounding rate has this annuity earned?

48. A person invests $2,000 annually in an IRA. At the end of 6 years, the amount in the fund is $14,000. What annual nominal compounding rate has this fund earned?

49. An employee opens a credit union account and deposits \$120 at the end of each month. After one year, the account contains \$1,444.96. What annual nominal rate compounded monthly has the account earned?

50. An employee opens a credit union account and deposits \$90 at the end of each month. After two years, the account contains \$2,177.48. What annual nominal rate compounded monthly has the account earned?

In Problems 51 and 52, use graphical approximation techniques to answer the questions.

51. When would an ordinary annuity consisting of quarterly payments of \$500 at 6% compounded quarterly be worth more than a principal of \$5,000 invested at 4% simple interest?

52. When would an ordinary annuity consisting of monthly payments of \$200 at 5% compounded monthly be worth more than a principal of \$10,000 invested at 7.5% compounded monthly?

Answers to Matched Problems

1. Value: \$29,778.08; interest: \$9,778.08
2. (A) \$95,094.67 (B) \$248,628.88
3. \$2,322.73
4. 9.64%

3.4 Present Value of an Annuity; Amortization

- Present Value of an Annuity
- Amortization
- Amortization Schedules
- General Problem-Solving Strategy

Present Value of an Annuity

How much should you deposit in an account paying 6% compounded semiannually in order to be able to withdraw \$1,000 every 6 months for the next 3 years? (After the last payment is made, no money is to be left in the account.)

Actually, we are interested in finding the present value of each \$1,000 that is paid out during the 3 years. We can do this by solving for P in the compound interest formula:

$$A = P(1 + i)^n$$

$$P = \frac{A}{(1 + i)^n} = A(1 + i)^{-n}$$

The rate per period is $i = \frac{0.06}{2} = 0.03$. The present value P of the first payment is $1{,}000(1.03)^{-1}$, the present value of the second payment is $1{,}000(1.03)^{-2}$, and so on. Figure 1 shows this in terms of a time line.

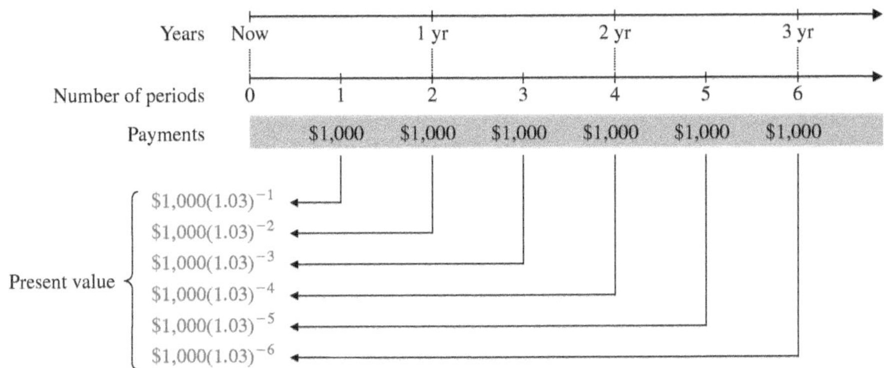

Figure 1

We could evaluate each of the present values in Figure 1 using a calculator and add the results to find the total present values of all the payments (which will be the amount needed now to buy the annuity). Since this is a tedious process, particularly when the number of payments is large, we will use the same device we used in the preceding section to produce a formula that will accomplish the same result in a couple of steps. We start by writing the sum of the present values in the form

$$P = 1{,}000(1.03)^{-1} + 1{,}000(1.03)^{-2} + \cdots + 1{,}000(1.03)^{-6} \quad (1)$$

Multiplying both sides of equation (1) by 1.03, we obtain

$$1.03P = 1{,}000 + 1{,}000(1.03)^{-1} + \cdots + 1{,}000(1.03)^{-5} \quad (2)$$

Now subtract equation (1) from equation (2):

$$1.03P - P = 1{,}000 - 1{,}000(1.03)^{-6}$$ Factor each side.

$$0.03P = 1{,}000[1 - (1 + 0.03)^{-6}]$$ Divide by 0.03.

$$P = 1{,}000\frac{1 - (1 + 0.03)^{-6}}{0.03} \quad (3)$$ We write P in this form to observe a general pattern.

In general, if R is the periodic payment, i the rate per period, and n the number of periods, then the present value of all payments is given by

$$P = R(1 + i)^{-1} + R(1 + i)^{-2} + \cdots + R(1 + i)^{-n}$$ Note how this compares to (1).

Proceeding as in the above example, we obtain the general formula for the present value of an ordinary annuity:

$$P = R\frac{1 - (1 + i)^{-n}}{i} \quad (4)$$ Note how this compares to (3).

Returning to the preceding example, we use a calculator to complete the problem:

$$P = 1{,}000\frac{1 - (1.03)^{-6}}{0.03}$$
$$= \$5{,}417.19$$

CONCEPTUAL INSIGHT

Formulas (3) and (4) can also be established by using the sum formula for a finite geometric series (see Section C.2):

$$a + ar + ar^2 + \cdots + ar^{n-1} = a\frac{r^n - 1}{r - 1}$$

It is common to use PV (present value) for P and PMT (payment) for R in formula (4). Making these changes, we have the following:

THEOREM 1 Present Value of an Ordinary Annuity

$$PV = PMT\frac{1 - (1 + i)^{-n}}{i} \quad (5)$$

where
PV = present value of all payments
PMT = periodic payment
i = rate per period
n = number of periods

Note: Payments are made at the end of each period.

EXAMPLE 1 **Present Value of an Annuity** What is the present value of an annuity that pays \$200 per month for 5 years if money is worth 6% compounded monthly?

SOLUTION To solve this problem, use formula (5) with $PMT = \$200$, $i = \frac{0.06}{12} = 0.005$, and $n = 12(5) = 60$:

$$\begin{aligned} PV &= PMT\frac{1 - (1 + i)^{-n}}{i} \\ &= 200\frac{1 - (1.005)^{-60}}{0.005} \qquad \text{Use a calculator.} \\ &= \$10{,}345.11 \end{aligned}$$

Matched Problem 1 How much should you deposit in an account paying 8% compounded quarterly in order to receive quarterly payments of \$1,000 for the next 4 years?

EXAMPLE 2 **Retirement Planning** Lincoln Benefit Life offered an ordinary annuity that earned 6.5% compounded annually. A person plans to make equal annual deposits into this account for 25 years and then make 20 equal annual withdrawals of \$25,000, reducing the balance in the account to zero. How much must be deposited annually to accumulate sufficient funds to provide for these payments? How much total interest is earned during this entire 45-year process?

SOLUTION This problem involves both future and present values. Figure 2 illustrates the flow of money into and out of the annuity.

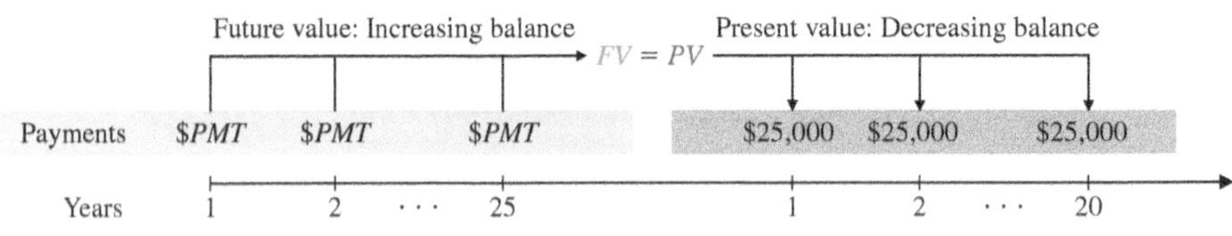

Figure 2

Since we are given the required withdrawals, we begin by finding the present value necessary to provide for these withdrawals. Using formula (5) with $PMT = \$25{,}000$, $i = 0.065$, and $n = 20$, we have

$$\begin{aligned} PV &= PMT\frac{1 - (1 + i)^{-n}}{i} \\ &= 25{,}000\frac{1 - (1.065)^{-20}}{0.065} \qquad \text{Use a calculator.} \\ &= \$275{,}462.68 \end{aligned}$$

Now we find the deposits that will produce a future value of \$275,462.68 in 25 years. Using formula (7) from Section 3.3 with $FV = \$275{,}462.68$, $i = 0.065$, and $n = 25$, we have

$$\begin{aligned} PMT &= FV\frac{i}{(1 + i)^{n} - 1} \\ &= 275{,}462.68\frac{0.065}{(1.065)^{25} - 1} \qquad \text{Use a calculator.} \\ &= \$4{,}677.76 \end{aligned}$$

Thus, depositing \$4,677.76 annually for 25 years will provide for 20 annual withdrawals of \$25,000. The interest earned during the entire 45-year process is

$$\begin{aligned} \text{interest} &= (\text{total withdrawals}) - (\text{total deposits}) \\ &= 20(25{,}000) - 25(\$4{,}677.76) \\ &= \$383{,}056 \end{aligned}$$

Matched Problem 2 Refer to Example 2. If \$2,000 is deposited annually for the first 25 years, how much can be withdrawn annually for the next 20 years?

Amortization

The present value formula for an ordinary annuity, formula (5), has another important use. Suppose that you borrow \$5,000 from a bank to buy a car and agree to repay the loan in 36 equal monthly payments, including all interest due. If the bank charges 1% per month on the unpaid balance (12% per year compounded monthly), how much should each payment be to retire the total debt, including interest, in 36 months?

Actually, the bank has bought an annuity from you. The question is: If the bank pays you \$5,000 (present value) for an annuity paying them \$*PMT* per month for 36 months at 12% interest compounded monthly, what are the monthly payments (*PMT*)? (Note that the value of the annuity at the end of 36 months is zero.) To find *PMT*, we have only to use formula (5) with $PV = \$5{,}000$, $i = 0.01$, and $n = 36$:

$$PV = PMT\frac{1 - (1 + i)^{-n}}{i}$$

$$5{,}000 = PMT\frac{1 - (1.01)^{-36}}{0.01} \qquad \text{Solve for } PMT \text{ and use a calculator.}$$

$$PMT = \$166.07 \text{ per month}$$

At \$166.07 per month, the car will be yours after 36 months. That is, you have *amortized* the debt in 36 equal monthly payments. (*Mort* means "death"; you have "killed" the loan in 36 months.) In general, **amortizing a debt** means that the debt is retired in a given length of time by equal periodic payments that include compound interest. We are interested in computing the equal periodic payments. Solving the present value formula (5) for *PMT* in terms of the other variables, we obtain the following **amortization formula**:

$$PMT = PV\frac{i}{1 - (1 + i)^{-n}} \tag{6}$$

Formula (6) is simply a variation of formula (5), and either formula can be used to find the periodic payment *PMT*.

EXAMPLE 3 **Monthly Payment and Total Interest on an Amortized Debt** Assume that you buy a TV for \$800 and agree to pay for it in 18 equal monthly payments at $1\frac{1}{2}\%$ interest per month on the unpaid balance.

(A) How much are your payments? (B) How much interest will you pay?

SOLUTION

(A) Use formula (5) or (6) with $PV = \$800$, $i = 0.015$, $n = 18$, and solve for *PMT*:

$$\begin{aligned} PMT &= PV\frac{i}{1 - (1 + i)^{-n}} \\ &= 800\frac{0.015}{1 - (1.015)^{-18}} \qquad \text{Use a calculator.} \\ &= \$51.04 \text{ per month} \end{aligned}$$

(B) Total interest paid = (amount of all payments) − (initial loan)

$$= 18(\$51.04) - \$800$$

$$= \$118.72$$

Matched Problem 3 If you sell your car to someone for $2,400 and agree to finance it at 1% per month on the unpaid balance, how much should you receive each month to amortize the loan in 24 months? How much interest will you receive?

Explore and Discuss 1

To purchase a home, a family plans to sign a mortgage of $70,000 at 8% on the unpaid balance. Discuss the advantages and disadvantages of a 20-year mortgage as opposed to a 30-year mortgage. Include a comparison of monthly payments and total interest paid.

Amortization Schedules

What happens if you are amortizing a debt with equal periodic payments and later decide to pay off the remainder of the debt in one lump-sum payment? This occurs each time a home with an outstanding mortgage is sold. In order to understand what happens in this situation, we must take a closer look at the amortization process. We begin with an example that allows us to examine the effect each payment has on the debt.

EXAMPLE 4 **Constructing an Amortization Schedule** If you borrow $500 that you agree to repay in six equal monthly payments at 1% interest per month on the unpaid balance, how much of each monthly payment is used for interest and how much is used to reduce the unpaid balance?

SOLUTION First, we compute the required monthly payment using formula (5) or (6). We choose formula (6) with $PV = \$500$, $i = 0.01$, and $n = 6$:

$$PMT = PV\frac{i}{1 - (1 + i)^{-n}}$$

$$= 500\frac{0.01}{1 - (1.01)^{-6}} \quad \text{Use a calculator.}$$

$$= \$86.27 \text{ per month}$$

At the end of the first month, the interest due is

$$\$500(0.01) = \$5.00$$

The amortization payment is divided into two parts, payment of the interest due and reduction of the unpaid balance (repayment of principal):

Monthly payment		Interest due		Unpaid balance reduction
$86.27	=	$5.00	+	$81.27

The unpaid balance for the next month is

Previous unpaid balance		Unpaid balance reduction		New unpaid balance
$500.00	−	$81.27	=	$418.73

At the end of the second month, the interest due on the unpaid balance of \$418.73 is

$$\$418.73(0.01) = \$4.19$$

Thus, at the end of the second month, the monthly payment of \$86.27 covers interest and unpaid balance reduction as follows:

$$\$86.27 = \$4.19 + \$82.08$$

and the unpaid balance for the third month is

$$\$418.73 - \$82.08 = \$336.65$$

This process continues until all payments have been made and the unpaid balance is reduced to zero. The calculations for each month are listed in Table 1, often referred to as an **amortization schedule.**

Table 1 Amortization Schedule

Payment Number	Payment	Interest	Unpaid Balance Reduction	Unpaid Balance
0				\$500.00
1	\$86.27	\$5.00	\$81.27	418.73
2	86.27	4.19	82.08	336.65
3	86.27	3.37	82.90	253.75
4	86.27	2.54	83.73	170.02
5	86.27	1.70	84.57	85.45
6	86.30	0.85	85.45	0.00
Totals	\$517.65	\$17.65	\$500.00	

Matched Problem 4 Construct the amortization schedule for a \$1,000 debt that is to be amortized in six equal monthly payments at 1.25% interest per month on the unpaid balance.

CONCEPTUAL INSIGHT

In Table 1, notice that the last payment had to be increased by \$0.03 in order to reduce the unpaid balance to zero. This small discrepancy is due to rounding the monthly payment and the entries in the interest column to two decimal places.

Suppose that a family is making monthly payments on a home mortgage loan. If the family decides to borrow money to make home improvements, they might take out a *home equity loan*. The amount of the loan will depend on the *equity* in their home, defined as the current net market value (the amount that would be received if the home were sold, after subtracting all costs involved in selling the house) minus the unpaid loan balance:

$$\textbf{Equity} = (\textbf{current net market value}) - (\textbf{unpaid loan balance}).$$

Similarly, if a family decides to sell the home they own and buy a more expensive home, the equity in their current home will be an important factor in determining the new home price that they can afford.

EXAMPLE 5 **Equity in a Home** A family purchased a home 10 years ago for \$80,000. The home was financed by paying 20% down and signing a 30-year mortgage at 9% on the unpaid balance. The net market value of the house is now \$120,000, and the family wishes to sell the house. How much equity (to the nearest dollar) does the family have in the house now after making 120 monthly payments?

SOLUTION How can we find the unpaid loan balance after 10 years or 120 monthly payments? One way to proceed would be to construct an amortization schedule, but this would require a table with 120 lines. Fortunately, there is an easier way. The unpaid balance after 120 payments is the amount of the loan that can be paid off with the remaining 240 monthly payments (20 remaining years on the loan). Since the lending institution views a loan as an annuity that they bought from the family, **the unpaid balance of a loan with *n* remaining payments is the present value of that annuity and can be computed by using formula (5)**. Since formula (5) requires knowledge of the monthly payment, we compute *PMT* first using formula (6).

Step 1 Find the monthly payment:

$$PMT = PV\frac{i}{1-(1+i)^{-n}} \qquad PV = (0.80)(\$80{,}000) = \$64{,}000,\quad i = \tfrac{0.09}{12} = 0.0075$$

$$= 64{,}000\frac{0.0075}{1-(1.0075)^{-360}} \qquad n = 12(30) = 360$$

$$= \$514.96 \text{ per month} \qquad \text{Use a calculator.}$$

Step 2 Find the present value of a \$514.96 per month, 20-year annuity:

$$PV = PMT\frac{1-(1+i)^{-n}}{i} \qquad PMT = \$514.96,\quad n = 12(20) = 240$$

$$= 514.96\frac{1-(1.0075)^{-240}}{0.0075} \qquad i = \tfrac{0.09}{12} = 0.0075 \quad \text{Use a calculator.}$$

$$= \$57{,}235 \qquad \text{Unpaid loan balance}$$

Step 3 Find the equity:

$$\begin{aligned}\text{equity} &= (\text{current net market value}) - (\text{unpaid loan balance})\\ &= \$120{,}000 - \$57{,}235\\ &= \$62{,}765\end{aligned}$$

So the equity in the home is \$62,765. In other words, if the family sells the house for \$120,000 net, the family will walk away with \$62,765 after paying off the unpaid loan balance of \$57,235.

Matched Problem 5 A couple purchased a home 20 years ago for \$65,000. The home was financed by paying 20% down and signing a 30-year mortgage at 8% on the unpaid balance. The net market value of the house is now \$130,000, and the couple wishes to sell the house. How much equity (to the nearest dollar) does the couple have in the house now after making 240 monthly payments?

The unpaid loan balance in Example 5 may seem a surprisingly large amount to owe after having made payments for 10 years, but long-term amortizations start out with very small reductions in the unpaid balance. For example, the interest due at the end of the very first period of the loan in Example 5 was

$$\$64{,}000(0.0075) = \$480.00$$

The first monthly payment was divided as follows:

$$\underset{\text{Monthly payment}}{\$514.96} - \underset{\text{Interest due}}{\$480.00} = \underset{\text{Unpaid balance reduction}}{\$34.96}$$

Only \$34.96 was applied to the unpaid balance.

Explore and Discuss 2

(A) A family has an \$85,000, 30-year mortgage at 9.6% compounded monthly. Show that the monthly payments are \$720.94.

(B) Explain why the equation

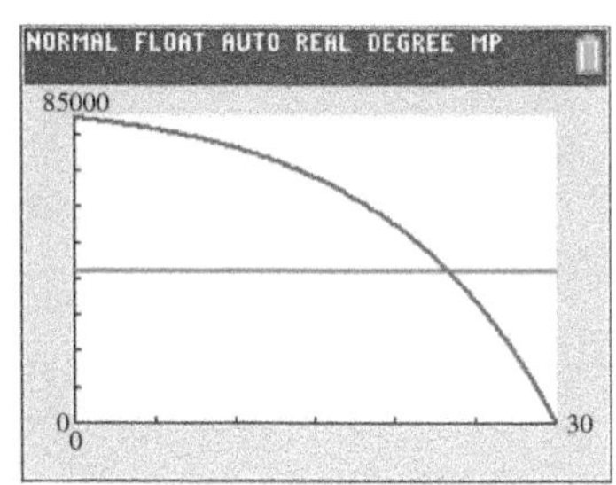

Figure 3

$$y = 720.94\frac{1 - (1.008)^{-12(30-x)}}{0.008}$$

gives the unpaid balance of the loan after x years.

(C) Find the unpaid balance after 5 years, after 10 years, and after 15 years.

(D) When does the unpaid balance drop below half of the original \$85,000?

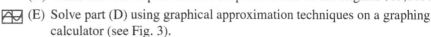

(E) Solve part (D) using graphical approximation techniques on a graphing calculator (see Fig. 3).

EXAMPLE 6 **Automobile Financing** You have negotiated a price of \$25,200 for a new Bison pickup truck. Now you must choose between 0% financing for 48 months or a \$3,000 rebate. If you choose the rebate, you can obtain a credit union loan for the balance at 4.5% compounded monthly for 48 months. Which option should you choose?

SOLUTION If you choose 0% financing, your monthly payment will be

$$PMT_1 = \frac{25{,}200}{48} = \$525$$

If you choose the \$3,000 rebate, and borrow \$22,200 at 4.5% compounded monthly for 48 months, the monthly payment is

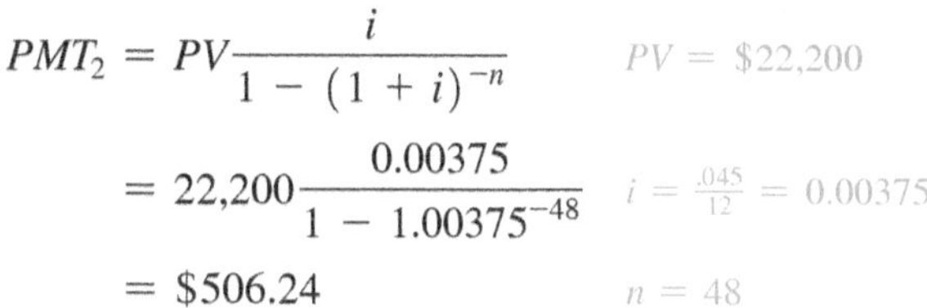

$$PMT_2 = PV\frac{i}{1 - (1 + i)^{-n}} \qquad PV = \$22{,}200$$

$$= 22{,}200\frac{0.00375}{1 - 1.00375^{-48}} \qquad i = \frac{.045}{12} = 0.00375$$

$$= \$506.24 \qquad n = 48$$

You should choose the \$3,000 rebate. You will save $525 - 506.24 = \$18.76$ monthly or $48(18.76) = \$900.48$ over the life of the loan.

Matched Problem 6 Which option should you choose if your credit union raises its loan rate to 7.5% compounded monthly and all other data remain the same?

EXAMPLE 7 **Credit Cards** The annual interest rate on a credit card is 18.99%. How long will it take to pay off an unpaid balance of \$847.29 if no new purchases are made and the minimum payment of \$20.00 is made each month?

SOLUTION It is necessary to make some simplifying assumptions because the lengths of the billing cycles, the days on which payments are credited, and the method for calculating interest are not specified. So we assume that there are 12 equal billing cycles per year, and that the \$20 payments are credited at the end of each cycle. With these assumptions, it is reasonable to use the present value formula with $PV = \$847.29$, $PMT = \$20.00$, and $i = 0.1899/12$ in order to solve for n, the number of payments:

$$PV = PMT\frac{1 - (1 + i)^{-n}}{i} \qquad \text{Multiply by } i \text{ and divide by } PMT.$$

$$i(PV/PMT) = 1 - (1 + i)^{-n} \qquad \text{Solve for } (1 + i)^{-n}.$$

$$(1 + i)^{-n} = 1 - i(PV/PMT) \qquad \text{Take the ln of both sides.}$$

$$-n \ln(1 + i) = \ln(1 - i(PV/PMT)) \qquad \text{Solve for } n.$$

$$n = -\frac{\ln(1 - i(PV/PMT))}{\ln(1 + i)} \qquad \text{Substitute } i = 0.1899/12,$$

$$n \approx 70.69 \qquad PV = \$847.29, \text{ and } PMT = \$20.$$

We conclude that the unpaid balance will be paid off in 71 months.

Matched Problem 7 The annual interest rate on a credit card is 24.99%. How long will it take to pay off an unpaid balance of \$1,485.73 if no new purchases are made and a \$50.00 payment is made each month?

General Problem-Solving Strategy

After working the problems in Exercises 3.4, it is important to work the problems in the Review Exercises. This will give you valuable experience in distinguishing among the various types of problems we have considered in this chapter. It is impossible to completely categorize all the problems you will encounter, but you may find the following guidelines helpful in determining which of the four basic formulas is involved in a particular problem. Be aware that some problems may involve more than one of these formulas and others may not involve any of them.

SUMMARY Strategy for Solving Mathematics of Finance Problems

Step 1 Determine whether the problem involves a single payment or a sequence of equal periodic payments. Simple and compound interest problems involve a single present value and a single future value. Ordinary annuities may be concerned with a present value or a future value but always involve a sequence of equal periodic payments.

Step 2 If a single payment is involved, determine whether simple or compound interest is used. Often simple interest is used for durations of a year or less and compound interest for longer periods.

Step 3 If a sequence of periodic payments is involved, determine whether the payments are being made into an account that is increasing in value—a future value problem—or the payments are being made out of an account that is decreasing in value—a present value problem. Remember that amortization problems always involve the present value of an ordinary annuity.

Steps 1–3 will help you choose the correct formula for a problem, as indicated in Figure 4. Then you must determine the values of the quantities in the formula that are given in the problem and those that must be computed, and solve the problem.

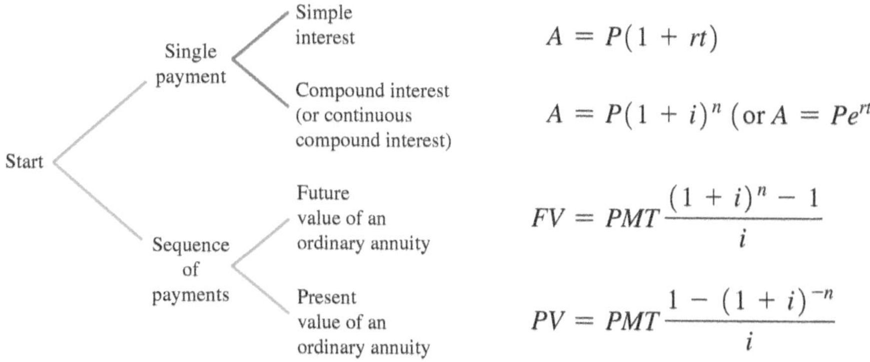

Figure 4 Selecting the correct formula for a problem

Exercises 3.4

W **Skills Warm-up Exercises**

In Problems 1–6, find the sum of the finite geometric series $a + ar + ar^2 + \cdots + ar^{n-1}$. Write the answer as a quotient of integers. (If necessary, review Section C.2).

1. $1 + \frac{1}{2} + \frac{1}{4} + \frac{1}{8} + \cdots + \frac{1}{2^8}$

2. $1 + \frac{1}{5} + \frac{1}{25} + \frac{1}{125} + \cdots + \frac{1}{5^7}$

3. $30 + 3 + \frac{3}{10} + \frac{3}{100} + \cdots + \frac{3}{1{,}000{,}000}$

4. $10{,}000 + 1{,}000 + 100 + 10 + \cdots + \frac{1}{10{,}000}$

5. $1 - \frac{1}{3} + \frac{1}{9} - \frac{1}{27} + \cdots + \frac{1}{3^6}$

6. $1 - \frac{1}{10} + \frac{1}{100} - \frac{1}{1{,}000} + \frac{1}{10{,}000} - \frac{1}{100{,}000}$

A *In Problems 7–14, find i (the rate per period) and n (the number of periods) for each loan at the given annual rate.*

7. Monthly payments of \$87.65 are made for 7 years to repay a loan at 5.4% compounded monthly.

8. Semiannual payments of \$3,200 are made for 12 years to repay a loan at 9.9% compounded semiannually.

9. Quarterly payments of \$975 are made for 10 years to repay a loan at 9.9% compounded quarterly.

10. Annual payments of \$1,045 are made for 5 years to repay a loan at 4.75% compounded annually.

11. Semiannual payments of \$1,250 are made for 25 years to repay a loan at 6.75% compounded semiannually.

12. Quarterly payments of \$610 are made for 6 years to repay loan at 8.24% compounded quarterly.

13. Annual payments of \$5,195 are made for 9 years to repay a loan at 5.48% compounded annually.

14. Monthly payments of \$433 are made for 3 years to repay a loan at 10.8% compounded monthly.

B *In Problems 15–22, use formula (5) or (6) to solve each problem.*

15. $n = 30$; $i = 0.04$; $PMT = \$200$; $PV = ?$

16. $n = 24$; $i = 0.015$; $PMT = \$250$; $PV = ?$

17. $PV = \$40{,}000$; $n = 96$; $i = 0.0075$; $PMT = ?$

18. $PV = \$25{,}000$; $n = 48$; $i = 0.0095$; $PMT = ?$

19. $PV = \$5{,}000$; $i = 0.01$; $PMT = \$200$; $n = ?$

20. $PV = \$12{,}000$; $i = 0.0125$; $PMT = \$750$; $n = ?$

21. $PV = \$9{,}000$; $PMT = \$600$; $n = 20$; $i = ?$ (Round answer to three decimal places.)

22. $PV = \$12{,}000$; $PMT = \$400$; $n = 40$; $i = ?$ (Round answer to three decimal places.)

C

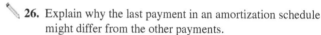

23. Explain what is meant by the present value of an ordinary annuity.

24. Solve the present value formula (5) for n.

25. Explain how an ordinary annuity is involved when you take out an auto loan from a bank.

26. Explain why the last payment in an amortization schedule might differ from the other payments.

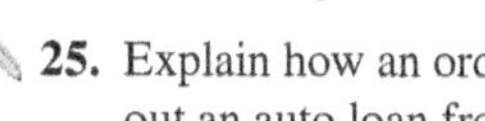

Applications

27. A bank offers a 9-year ordinary annuity with a guaranteed rate of 3.70% compounded annually. How much should you pay for one of these annuities if you want to receive payments of \$8,000 annually over the 9-year period?

28. A bank offers a 5-year ordinary annuity with a guaranteed rate of 3.30% compounded annually. How much should you pay for one of these annuities if you want to receive payments of \$5,000 annually over the 5-year period?

29. E-Loan, an online lending service, offers a 36-month auto loan at 7.56% compounded monthly to applicants with good credit ratings. If you have a good credit rating and can afford monthly payments of $350, how much can you borrow from E-Loan? What is the total interest you will pay for this loan?

30. E-Loan offers a 36-month auto loan at 9.84% compounded monthly to applicants with fair credit ratings. If you have a fair credit rating and can afford monthly payments of $350, how much can you borrow from E-Loan? What is the total interest you will pay for this loan?

31. If you buy a computer directly from the manufacturer for $2,500 and agree to repay it in 48 equal installments at 1.25% interest per month on the unpaid balance, how much are your monthly payments? How much total interest will be paid?

32. If you buy a computer directly from the manufacturer for $3,500 and agree to repay it in 60 equal installments at 1.75% interest per month on the unpaid balance, how much are your monthly payments? How much total interest will be paid?

In Problems 33–36, assume that no new purchases are made with the credit card.

33. The annual interest rate on a credit card is 16.99%. If a payment of $100.00 is made each month, how long will it take to pay off an unpaid balance of $2,487.56?

34. The annual interest rate on a credit card is 24.99%. If a payment of $100.00 is made each month, how long will it take to pay off an unpaid balance of $2,487.56?

35. The annual interest rate on a credit card is 14.99%. If the minimum payment of $20 is made each month, how long will it take to pay off an unpaid balance of $937.14?

36. The annual interest rate on a credit card is 22.99%. If the minimum payment of $25 is made each month, how long will it take to pay off an unpaid balance of $860.22?

Problems 37 and 38 refer to the following ads.

37. The ad for a Bison sedan claims that a monthly payment of $299 constitutes 0% financing. Explain why that is false. Find the annual interest rate compounded monthly that is actually being charged for financing $17,485 with 72 monthly payments of $299.

2020 BISON SEDAN
Zero down – 0% financing
$299 per month*
Buy for $17,485.

* Bison sedan, 0% down, 0% for 72 months

2020 BISON SUV
Zero down – 0% financing
$399 per month*
Buy for $23,997.

* Bison SUV, 0% down, 0% for 72 months

38. The ad for a Bison SUV claims that a monthly payment of $399 constitutes 0% financing. Explain why that is false. Find the annual interest rate compounded monthly that is actually being charged for financing $23,997 with 72 monthly payments of $399.

39. You want to purchase an automobile for $27,300. The dealer offers you 0% financing for 60 months or a $5,000 rebate. You can obtain 6.3% financing for 60 months at the local bank. Which option should you choose? Explain.

40. You want to purchase an automobile for $28,500. The dealer offers you 0% financing for 60 months or a $6,000 rebate. You can obtain 6.2% financing for 60 months at the local bank. Which option should you choose? Explain.

41. A sailboat costs $35,000. You pay 20% down and amortize the rest with equal monthly payments over a 12-year period. If you must pay 8.75% compounded monthly, what is your monthly payment? How much interest will you pay?

42. A recreational vehicle costs $80,000. You pay 10% down and amortize the rest with equal monthly payments over a 7-year period. If you pay 9.25% compounded monthly, what is your monthly payment? How much interest will you pay?

43. Construct the amortization schedule for a $5,000 debt that is to be amortized in eight equal quarterly payments at 2.8% interest per quarter on the unpaid balance.

44. Construct the amortization schedule for a $10,000 debt that is to be amortized in six equal quarterly payments at 2.6% interest per quarter on the unpaid balance.

45. A woman borrows $6,000 at 9% compounded monthly, which is to be amortized over 3 years in equal monthly payments. For tax purposes, she needs to know the amount of interest paid during each year of the loan. Find the interest paid during the first year, the second year, and the third year of the loan. [*Hint:* Find the unpaid balance after 12 payments and after 24 payments.]

46. A man establishes an annuity for retirement by depositing $50,000 into an account that pays 7.2% compounded monthly. Equal monthly withdrawals will be made each month for 5 years, at which time the account will have a zero balance. Each year taxes must be paid on the interest earned by the account during that year. How much interest was earned during the first year? [*Hint:* The amount in the account at the end of the first year is the present value of a 4-year annuity.]

47. Some friends tell you that they paid £2,400 down on a new car and are to pay £299 per month for 48 months. If interest is 3.9% compounded monthly, what was the selling price of the car? How much interest will they pay in 48 months?

48. A couple is thinking about buying a new car costing £20,000. The couple must pay 15% down, and the rest is to be amortized over 48 months in equal monthly payments. If money costs 2.9% compounded monthly, what will the monthly payment be? How much total interest will be paid over 48 months?

49. A student receives a federally backed student loan of $6,000 at 3.5% interest compounded monthly. After finishing college in 2 years, the student must amortize the loan in the next 4 years by making equal monthly payments. What will the payments be and what total interest will the student pay? [*Hint:* This is a two-part problem. First, find the amount of the debt at the end of the first 2 years; then amortize this amount over the next 4 years.]

50. A person establishes a sinking fund for retirement by contributing $7,500 per year at the end of each year for 20 years. For the next 20 years, equal yearly payments are withdrawn, at the end of which time the account will have a zero balance. If

money is worth 9% compounded annually, what yearly payments will the person receive for the last 20 years?

51. A family has a $150,000, 30-year mortgage at 6.1% compounded monthly. Find the monthly payment. Also find the unpaid balance after

(A) 10 years (B) 20 years

(C) 25 years

52. A family has a $210,000, 20-year mortgage at 6.75% compounded monthly. Find the monthly payment. Also find the unpaid balance after

(A) 5 years (B) 10 years

(C) 15 years

53. A family has a $129,000, 20-year mortgage at 7.2% compounded monthly.

(A) Find the monthly payment and the total interest paid.

(B) Suppose the family decides to add an extra $102.41 to its mortgage payment each month starting with the very first payment. How long will it take the family to pay off the mortgage? How much interest will be saved?

54. At the time they retire, a couple has $200,000 in an account that pays 8.4% compounded monthly.

(A) If the couple decides to withdraw equal monthly payments for 10 years, at the end of which time the account will have a zero balance, how much should the couple withdraw each month?

(B) If the couple decides to withdraw $3,000 a month until the balance in the account is zero, how many withdrawals can the couple make?

55. An ordinary annuity that earns 7.5% compounded monthly has a current balance of $500,000. The owner of the account is about to retire and has to decide how much to withdraw from the account each month. Find the number of withdrawals under each of the following options:

(A) $5,000 monthly (B) $4,000 monthly

(C) $3,000 monthly

56. Refer to Problem 55. If the account owner decides to withdraw $3,000 monthly, how much is in the account after 10 years? After 20 years? After 30 years?

57. An ordinary annuity pays 7.44% compounded monthly.

(A) A person deposits $100 monthly for 30 years and then makes equal monthly withdrawals for the next 15 years, reducing the balance to zero. What are the monthly withdrawals? How much interest is earned during the entire 45-year process?

(B) If the person wants to make withdrawals of $2,000 per month for the last 15 years, how much must be deposited monthly for the first 30 years?

58. An ordinary annuity pays 6.48% compounded monthly.

(A) A person wants to make equal monthly deposits into the account for 15 years in order to then make equal monthly withdrawals of $1,500 for the next 20 years, reducing the balance to zero. How much should be deposited each month for the first 15 years? What is the total interest earned during this 35-year process?

(B) If the person makes monthly deposits of $1,000 for the first 15 years, how much can be withdrawn monthly for the next 20 years?

59. A couple wishes to borrow money using the equity in their home for collateral. A loan company will loan the couple up to 70% of their equity. The couple purchased the home 12 years ago for $179,000. The home was financed by paying 20% down and signing a 30-year mortgage at 8.4% on the unpaid balance. Equal monthly payments were made to amortize the loan over the 30-year period. The net market value of the house is now $215,000. After making the 144th payment, the couple applied to the loan company for the maximum loan. How much (to the nearest dollar) will the couple receive?

60. A person purchased a house 10 years ago for $160,000. The house was financed by paying 20% down and signing a 30-year mortgage at 7.75% on the unpaid balance. Equal monthly payments were made to amortize the loan over a 30-year period. The owner now (after the 120th payment) wishes to refinance the house due to a need for additional cash. If the loan company agrees to a new 30-year mortgage of 80% of the new appraised value of the house, which is $225,000, how much cash (to the nearest dollar) will the owner receive after repaying the balance of the original mortgage?

61. A person purchased a $145,000 home 10 years ago by paying 20% down and signing a 30-year mortgage at 7.9% compounded monthly. Interest rates have dropped and the owner wants to refinance the unpaid balance by signing a new 20-year mortgage at 5.5% compounded monthly. How much interest will refinancing save?

62. A person purchased a $200,000 home 20 years ago by paying 20% down and signing a 30-year mortgage at 13.2% compounded monthly. Interest rates have dropped and the owner wants to refinance the unpaid balance by signing a new 10-year mortgage at 8.2% compounded monthly. How much interest will refinancing save?

63. Discuss the similarities and differences in the graphs of unpaid balance as a function of time for 30-year mortgages of $50,000, $75,000, and $100,000, respectively, each at 9% compounded monthly (see the figure). Include computations of the monthly payment and total interest paid in each case.

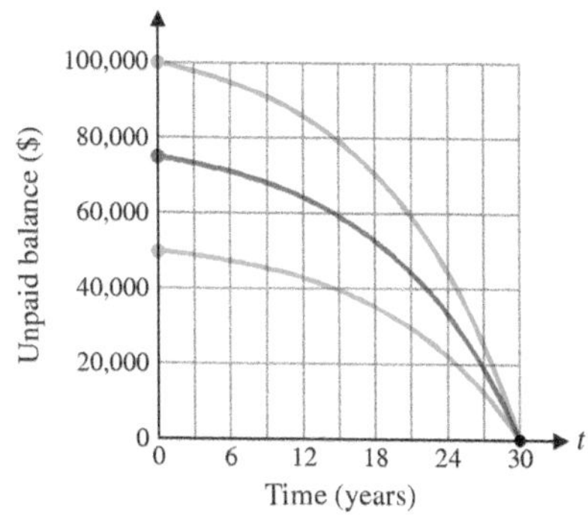

Figure for 63

64. Discuss the similarities and differences in the graphs of unpaid balance as a function of time for 30-year mortgages of $60,000 at rates of 7%, 10%, and 13%, respectively (see the figure). Include computations of the monthly payment and total interest paid in each case.

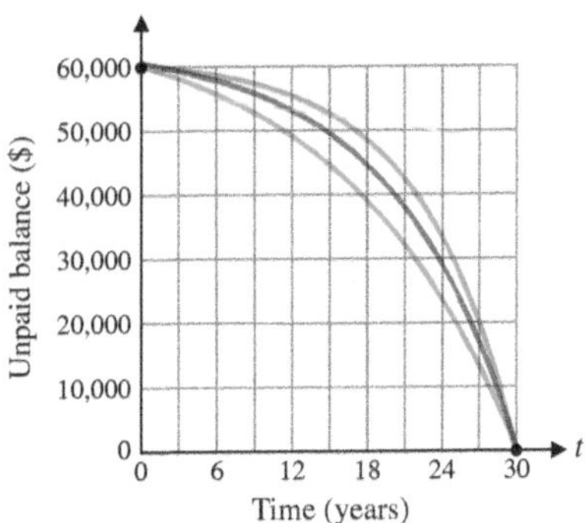

In Problems 65–68, use graphical approximation techniques or an equation solver to approximate the desired interest rate. Express each answer as a percentage, correct to two decimal places.

65. A discount electronics store offers to let you pay for a $1,000 stereo in 12 equal $90 installments. The store claims that since you repay $1,080 in 1 year, the $80 finance charge represents an 8% annual rate. This would be true if you repaid the loan in a single payment at the end of the year. But since you start repayment after 1 month, this is an amortized loan, and 8% is not the correct rate. What is the annual nominal compounding rate for this loan?

66. A $2,000 computer can be financed by paying $100 per month for 2 years. What is the annual nominal compounding rate for this loan?

67. The owner of a small business has received two offers of purchase. The first prospective buyer offers to pay the owner $100,000 in cash now. The second offers to pay the owner $10,000 now and monthly payments of $1,200 for 10 years. In effect, the second buyer is asking the owner for a $90,000 loan. If the owner accepts the second offer, what annual nominal compounding rate will the owner receive for financing this purchase?

68. At the time they retire, a couple has $200,000 invested in an annuity. The couple can take the entire amount in a single payment, or receive monthly payments of $2,000 for 15 years. If the couple elects to receive the monthly payments, what annual nominal compounding rate will the couple earn on the money invested in the annuity?

Answers to Matched Problems

1. $13,577.71 **2.** $10,688.87

3. $PMT = \$112.98/\text{mo}$; total interest = $311.52

4.

Payment Number	Payment	Interest	Unpaid Balance Reduction	Unpaid Balance
0				$1,000.00
1	$174.03	$12.50	$161.53	838.47
2	174.03	10.48	163.55	674.92
3	174.03	8.44	165.59	509.33
4	174.03	6.37	167.66	341.67
5	174.03	4.27	169.76	171.91
6	174.06	2.15	171.91	0.00
Totals	$1,044.21	$44.21	$1,000.00	

5. $98,551 **6.** Choose the 0% financing. **7.** 47 months

Chapter 3 Summary and Review

Important Terms, Symbols, and Concepts

3.1 Simple Interest

EXAMPLES

- **Interest** is the fee paid for the use of a sum of money P, called the **principal. Simple interest** is given by

$$I = Prt$$

where I = interest
P = principal
r = annual simple interest rate (written as a decimal)
t = time in years

- If a principal P **(present value)** is borrowed, then the **amount** A **(future value)** is the total of the principal and the interest:

$$A = P + Prt$$
$$= P(1 + rt)$$

- The **average daily balance method** is a common method for calculating the interest owed on a credit card. The formula $I = Prt$ is used, but a daily balance is calculated for each day of the billing cycle, and P is the average of those daily balances.

Ex. 1, p. 130
Ex. 2, p. 130
Ex. 3, p. 131
Ex. 4, p. 131
Ex. 5, p. 132
Ex. 6, p. 133

3.2 Compound and Continuous Compound Interest

- **Compound interest** is interest paid on the principal plus reinvested interest. The future and present values are related by Ex. 1, p. 138

$$A = P(1 + i)^n$$

where $i = r/m$ and
A = amount or future value
P = principal or present value
r = annual nominal rate (or just rate)
m = number of compounding periods per year
i = rate per compounding period
n = total number of compounding periods

- If a principal P is invested at an annual rate r earning **continuous compound interest**, then the amount A after t years is given by Ex. 2, p. 140 Ex. 3, p. 141 Ex. 4, p. 142

$$A = Pe^{rt}$$

- The **growth time** of an investment is the time it takes for a given principal to grow to a particular amount. Three methods for finding the growth time are as follows: Ex. 5, p. 143
  1. Use logarithms and a calculator.
  2. Use graphical approximation on a graphing calculator.
  3. Use an **equation solver** on a graphing calculator or a computer.
- The **annual percentage yield** (APY; also called the **effective rate** or **true interest rate**) is the simple interest rate that would earn the same amount as a given annual rate for which interest is compounded.
- If a principal is invested at the annual rate r compounded m times a year, then the annual percentage yield is given by Ex. 6, p. 145

$$\text{APY} = \left(1 + \frac{r}{m}\right)^m - 1$$

- If a principal is invested at the annual rate r compounded continuously, then the annual percentage yield is given by Ex. 7, p. 145

$$\text{APY} = e^r - 1$$

- A **zero coupon bond** is a bond that is sold now at a discount and will pay its **face value** at some time in the future when it matures.

3.3 Future Value of an Annuity; Sinking Funds

- An **annuity** is any sequence of equal periodic payments. If payments are made at the end of each time interval, then the annuity is called an **ordinary annuity**. The amount, or **future value**, of an annuity is the sum of all payments plus all interest earned and is given by Ex. 1, p. 152 Ex. 3, p. 155 Ex. 4, p. 155

$$FV = PMT\frac{(1 + i)^n - 1}{i}$$

where FV = future value (amount)
PMT = periodic payment
i = rate per period
n = number of payments (periods)

- A **balance sheet** is a table that shows the interest and balance for each payment of an annuity.
- An account that is established to accumulate funds to meet future obligations or debts is called a **sinking fund**. The **sinking fund payment** can be found by solving the future value formula for PMT: Ex. 2, p. 154

$$PMT = FV\frac{i}{(1 + i)^n - 1}$$

3.4 Present Value of an Annuity; Amortization

- If equal payments are made from an account until the amount in the account is 0, the payment and the **present value** are related by the following formula: Ex. 1, p. 160 Ex. 2, p. 160

$$PV = PMT\frac{1 - (1 + i)^{-n}}{i}$$

where PV = present value of all payments
PMT = periodic payment
i = rate per period
n = number of periods

- **Amortizing** a debt means that the debt is retired in a given length of time by equal periodic payments that include compound interest. Solving the present value formula for the payment gives us the **amortization formula**: Ex. 3, p. 161 Ex. 6, p. 165 Ex. 7, p. 165

$$PMT = PV\frac{i}{1 - (1 + i)^{-n}}$$

- An **amortization schedule** is a table that shows the interest due and the balance reduction for each payment of a loan. Ex. 4, p. 162
- The **equity** in a property is the difference between the current net market value and the unpaid loan balance. The unpaid balance of a loan with n **remaining payments** is given by the present value formula. Ex. 5, p. 163
- A strategy for solving problems in the mathematics of finance is presented on page 166.

Review Exercises

Work through all the problems in this chapter review and check your answers in the back of the book. Answers to all review problems are there along with section numbers in italics to indicate where each type of problem is discussed. Where weaknesses show up, review appropriate sections in the text.

In Problems 1–4, find the indicated quantity, given $A = P(1 + rt)$.

1. $A = ?$; $P = \$200$; $r = 9\%$; $t = 8$ months

2. $A = \$900$; $P = ?$; $r = 14\%$; $t = 3$ month

3. $A = \$312$; $P = \$250$; $r = 7\%$; $t = ?$

4. $A = \$3,120$; $P = \$3,000$; $r = ?$; $t = 8$ months

In Problems 5 and 6, find the indicated quantity, given $A = P(1 + i)^n$.

5. $A = ?$; $P = \$1,400$; $i = 0.004$; $n = 30$

6. $A = \$6,000$; $P = ?$; $i = 0.006$; $n = 62$

In Problems 7 and 8, find the indicated quantity, given $A = Pe^{rt}$.

7. $A = ?$; $P = \$5,400$; $r = 5.8\%$; $t = 2$ years

8. $A = 45,000$; $P = ?$; $r = 9.4\%$; $t = 72$ months

B *In Problems 9 and 10, find the indicated quantity, given*

$$FV = PMT\frac{(1 + i)^n - 1}{i}$$

9. $FV = \$10,000$; $PMT = ?$; $i = 0.016$; $n = 54$

10. $FV = ?$; $PMT = \$1,200$; $i = 0.004$; $n = 72$

In Problems 11 and 12, find the indicated quantity, given

$$PV = PMT\frac{1 - (1 + i)^{-n}}{i}$$

11. $FV = ?$; $PMT = \$3,500$; $i = 0.03$; $n = 14$

12. $FV = \$9,000$; $PMT = ?$; $i = 0.0065$; $n = 16$

C **13.** Solve the equation $2,500 = 1,000(1.06)^n$ for n to the nearest integer using:

(A) Logarithms

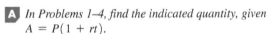

(B) Graphical approximation techniques or an equation solver on a graphing calculator

14. Solve the equation

$$5{,}000 = 100\frac{(1.01)^n - 1}{0.01}$$

for n to the nearest integer using:

(A) Logarithms

(B) Graphical approximation techniques or an equation solver on a graphing calculator.

Applications

Find all dollar amounts correct to the nearest cent. When an interest rate is requested as an answer, express the rate as a percentage, correct to two decimal places.

15. You need to borrow $4,000 for 9 months. The local bank is willing to supply the money at 9% simple interest. Calculate the amount of interest that will be paid on the loan for the stated period and the total amount required at the end of the period.

16. Grandparents deposited $6,000 into a grandchild's account toward a college education. How much money (to the nearest dollar) will be in the account 17 years from now if the account earns 7% compounded monthly?

17. How much should you pay for a corporate bond paying 6.6% compounded monthly in order to have $25,000 in 10 years?

18. An investment account pays 5.4% compounded annually. Construct a balance sheet showing the interest earned during each year and the balance at the end of each year for 4 years if

(A) A single deposit of $400 is made at the beginning of the first year.

(B) Four deposits of $100 are made at the end of each year.

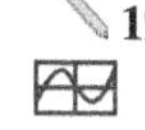

19. One investment pays 13% simple interest and another 9% compounded annually. Which investment would you choose? Why?

20. A $10,000 retirement account is left to earn interest at 7% compounded daily. How much money will be in the account 40 years from now when the owner reaches 65? (Use a 365-day year and round answer to the nearest dollar.)

21. A couple wishes to have $40,000 in 6 years for the down payment on a house. At what rate of interest compounded continuously must $25,000 be invested now to accomplish this goal?

22. Which is the better investment and why: 9% compounded quarterly or 9.25% compounded annually?

23. What is the value of an ordinary annuity at the end of 8 years if $200 per month is deposited into an account earning 7.2% compounded monthly? How much of this value is interest?

24. A payday lender charges $60 for a loan of $500 for 15 days. Find the annual interest rate. (Use a 360-day year.)

25. The annual interest rate on a credit card is 25.74% and interest is calculated by the average daily balance method. The unpaid balance at the start of a 30-day billing cycle was $1,672.18. A purchase of $265.12 was made on day 8 and a payment of $250 was credited to the account on day 20. Find the unpaid balance at the end of the billing cycle. (Use a 360-day year.)

26. What will a $23,000 car cost (to the nearest dollar) 5 years from now if the inflation rate over that period averages 5% compounded annually?

27. What would the $23,000 car in Problem 25 have cost (to the nearest dollar) 5 years ago if the inflation rate over that period had averaged 5% compounded annually?

28. A loan of $2,500 was repaid at the end of 10 months with a check for $2,812.50. What annual rate of interest was charged?

29. You want to purchase an automobile for $21,600. The dealer offers you 0% financing for 48 months or a $3,000 rebate. You can obtain 4.8% financing for 48 months at the local bank. Which option should you choose? Explain.

30. Find the annual percentage yield on a bond earning 6.25% if interest is compounded

(A) monthly.

(B) continuously.

31. You have $5,000 toward the purchase of a boat that will cost $6,000. How long will it take the $5,000 to grow to $6,000 if it is invested at 9% compounded quarterly? (Round up to the next-higher quarter if not exact.)

32. How long will it take money to double if it is invested at 6% compounded monthly? 9% compounded monthly? (Round up to the next-higher month if not exact.)

33. Starting on his 21st birthday, and continuing on every birthday up to and including his 65th, John deposits $2,000 a year into an IRA. How much (to the nearest dollar) will be in the account on John's 65th birthday, if the account earns:

(A) 7% compounded annually?

(B) 11% compounded annually?

34. If you just sold a stock for $17,388.17 (net) that cost you $12,903.28 (net) 3 years ago, what annual compound rate of return did you make on your investment?

35. The table shows the fees for refund anticipation loans (RALs) offered by an online tax preparation firm. Find the annual rate of interest for each of the following loans. Assume a 360-day year.

(A) A $400 RAL paid back in 15 days

(B) A $1,800 RAL paid back in 21 days

RAL Amount	RAL Fee
$10–$500	$29.00
$501–$1,000	$39.00
$1,001–$1,500	$49.00
$1,501–$2,000	$69.00
$2,001–$5,000	$82.00

36. Lincoln Benefit Life offered an annuity that pays 5.5% compounded monthly. What equal monthly deposit should be made into this annuity in order to have $50,000 in 5 years?

37. A person wants to establish an annuity for retirement purposes. He wants to make quarterly deposits for 20 years so that he can then make quarterly withdrawals of $5,000 for 10 years. The annuity earns 7.32% interest compounded quarterly.

    (A) How much will have to be in the account at the time he retires?

    (B) How much should be deposited each quarter for 20 years in order to accumulate the required amount?

    (C) What is the total amount of interest earned during the 30-year period?

38. If you borrow $4,000 from an online lending firm for the purchase of a computer and agree to repay it in 48 equal installments at 0.9% interest per month on the unpaid balance, how much are your monthly payments? How much total interest will be paid?

39. A company decides to establish a sinking fund to replace a piece of equipment in 6 years at an estimated cost of $50,000. To accomplish this, they decide to make fixed monthly payments into an account that pays 6.12% compounded monthly. How much should each payment be?

40. How long will it take money to double if it is invested at 7.5% compounded daily? 7.5% compounded annually?

41. A student receives a student loan for $8,000 at 5.5% interest compounded monthly to help her finish the last 1.5 years of college. Starting 1 year after finishing college, the student must amortize the loan in the next 5 years by making equal monthly payments. What will the payments be and what total interest will the student pay?

42. If you invest $5,650 in an account paying 8.65% compounded continuously, how much money will be in the account at the end of 10 years?

43. A company makes a payment of $1,200 each month into a sinking fund that earns 6% compounded monthly. Use graphical approximation techniques on a graphing calculator to determine when the fund will be worth $100,000.

44. A couple has a $50,000, 20-year mortgage at 9% compounded monthly. Use graphical approximation techniques on a graphing calculator to determine when the unpaid balance will drop below $10,000.

45. A loan company advertises in the paper that you will pay only 8¢ a day for each $100 borrowed. What annual rate of interest are they charging? (Use a 360-day year.)

46. Construct the amortization schedule for a $1,000 debt that is to be amortized in four equal quarterly payments at 2.5% interest per quarter on the unpaid balance.

47. You can afford monthly deposits of only $300 into an account that pays 7.98% compounded monthly. How long will it be until you will have $9,000 to purchase a used car? (Round to the next-higher month if not exact.)

48. A company establishes a sinking fund for plant retooling in 6 years at an estimated cost of $850,000. How much should be invested semiannually into an account paying 8.76% compounded semiannually? How much interest will the account earn in the 6 years?

49. What is the annual nominal rate compounded monthly for a CD that has an annual percentage yield of 2.50%?

50. If you buy a 13-week T-bill with a maturity value of $5,000 for $4,922.15 from the U.S. Treasury Department, what annual interest rate will you earn?

51. In order to save enough money for the down payment on a condominium, a young couple deposits $200 each month into an account that pays 7.02% interest compounded monthly. If the couple needs $10,000 for a down payment, how many deposits will the couple have to make?

52. A business borrows $80,000 at 9.42% interest compounded monthly for 8 years.

    (A) What is the monthly payment?

    (B) What is the unpaid balance at the end of the first year?

    (C) How much interest was paid during the first year?

53. You unexpectedly inherit $10,000 just after you have made the 72nd monthly payment on a 30-year mortgage of $60,000 at 8.2% compounded monthly. Discuss the relative merits of using the inheritance to reduce the principal of the loan or to buy a certificate of deposit paying 7% compounded monthly.

54. Your parents are considering a $75,000, 30-year mortgage to purchase a new home. The bank at which they have done business for many years offers a rate of 7.54% compounded monthly. A competitor is offering 6.87% compounded monthly. Would it be worthwhile for your parents to switch banks? Explain.

55. How much should a $5,000 face value zero coupon bond, maturing in 5 years, be sold for now, if its rate of return is to be 5.6% compounded annually?

56. If you pay $5,695 for a $10,000 face value zero coupon bond that matures in 10 years, what is your annual compound rate of return?

57. If an investor wants to earn an annual interest rate of 6.4% on a 26-week T-bill with a maturity value of $5,000, how much should the investor pay for the T-bill?

58. Two years ago you borrowed $10,000 at 12% interest compounded monthly, which was to be amortized over 5 years. Now you have acquired some additional funds and decide that you want to pay off this loan. What is the unpaid balance after making equal monthly payments for 2 years?

59. What annual nominal rate compounded monthly has the same annual percentage yield as 7.28% compounded quarterly?

60. (A) A man deposits $2,000 in an IRA on his 21st birthday and on each subsequent birthday up to, and including, his 29th (nine deposits in all). The account earns 8% compounded annually. If he leaves the money in the

account without making any more deposits, how much will he have on his 65th birthday, assuming the account continues to earn the same rate of interest?

(B) How much would be in the account (to the nearest dollar) on his 65th birthday if he had started the deposits on his 30th birthday and continued making deposits on each birthday until (and including) his 65th birthday?

61. A promissory note will pay \$27,000 at maturity 10 years from now. How much money should you be willing to pay now if money is worth 5.5% compounded continuously?

62. In a new housing development, the houses are selling for \$100,000 and require a 20% down payment. The buyer is given a choice of 30-year or 15-year financing, both at 7.68% compounded monthly.

(A) What is the monthly payment for the 30-year choice? For the 15-year choice?

(B) What is the unpaid balance after 10 years for the 30-year choice? For the 15-year choice?

63. A loan company will loan up to 60% of the equity in a home. A family purchased their home 8 years ago for \$83,000. The home was financed by paying 20% down and signing a 30-year mortgage at 8.4% for the balance. Equal monthly payments were made to amortize the loan over the 30-year period. The market value of the house is now \$95,000. After making the 96th payment, the family applied to the loan company for the maximum loan. How much (to the nearest dollar) will the family receive?

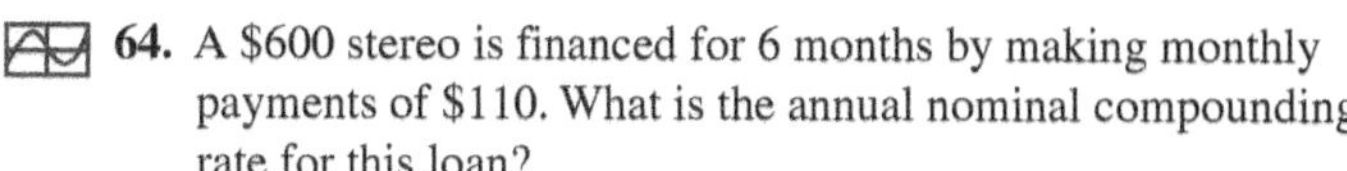

64. A \$600 stereo is financed for 6 months by making monthly payments of \$110. What is the annual nominal compounding rate for this loan?

65. A person deposits \$2,000 each year for 25 years into an IRA. When she retires immediately after making the 25th deposit, the IRA is worth \$220,000.

(A) Find the interest rate earned by the IRA over the 25-year period leading up to retirement.

(B) Assume that the IRA continues to earn the interest rate found in part (A). How long can the retiree withdraw \$30,000 per year? How long can she withdraw \$24,000 per year?

4 Systems of Linear Equations; Matrices

Introduction

Traffic congestion in urban areas is a major problem. Traffic control by on-ramp metering, traffic signals, and message signs is one approach to reducing congestion. Traffic control by vehicle-to-vehicle communication shows promise for the future. The mathematical prerequisite for solving problems in traffic flow is the ability to solve systems of linear equations (see Problems 97 and 98 in Section 4.3).

In Chapter 4 we discuss methods for solving systems of two linear equations by hand calculation. We also introduce matrix methods, including Gauss–Jordan elimination, that can be used to solve systems with many equations on a calculator or computer. We consider a number of important applications, including resource allocation, production scheduling, and economic planning.

4.1 Review: Systems of Linear Equations in Two Variables

- Systems of Linear Equations in Two Variables
- Graphing
- Substitution
- Elimination by Addition
- Applications

Systems of Linear Equations in Two Variables

To establish basic concepts, let's consider the following simple example: If 2 adult tickets and 1 child ticket cost \$32, and if 1 adult ticket and 3 child tickets cost \$36, what is the price of each?

$$\begin{aligned} \text{Let: } & x = \text{price of adult ticket} \\ & y = \text{price of child ticket} \\ \text{Then: } & 2x + y = 32 \\ & x + 3y = 36 \end{aligned}$$

Now we have a system of two linear equations in two variables. It is easy to find ordered pairs (x, y) that satisfy one or the other of these equations. For example, the ordered pair $(16, 0)$ satisfies the first equation but not the second, and the ordered pair $(24, 4)$ satisfies the second but not the first. To solve this system, we must find all ordered pairs of real numbers that satisfy both equations at the same time. In general, we have the following definition:

DEFINITION Systems of Two Linear Equations in Two Variables

Given the **linear system**

$$\begin{aligned} ax + by &= h \\ cx + dy &= k \end{aligned}$$

where a, b, c, d, h, and k are real constants, a pair of numbers $x = x_0$ and $y = y_0$ [also written as an ordered pair (x_0, y_0)] is a **solution** of this system if each equation is satisfied by the pair. The set of all such ordered pairs is called the **solution set** for the system. To **solve** a system is to find its solution set.

We will consider three methods of solving such systems: *graphing, substitution,* and *elimination by addition*. Each method has its advantages, depending on the situation.

Graphing

Recall that the graph of a line is a graph of all the ordered pairs that satisfy the equation of the line. To solve the ticket problem by graphing, we graph both equations in the same coordinate system. The coordinates of any points that the graphs have in common must be solutions to the system since they satisfy both equations.

EXAMPLE 1 **Solving a System by Graphing** Solve the ticket problem by graphing:

$$\begin{aligned} 2x + y &= 32 \\ x + 3y &= 36 \end{aligned}$$

SOLUTION An easy way to find two distinct points on the first line is to find the x and y intercepts. Substitute $y = 0$ to find the x intercept ($2x = 32$, so $x = 16$), and substitute $x = 0$ to find the y intercept ($y = 32$). Then draw the line through

Reminder

Recall that we may graph a line by finding its intercepts (Section A.2). For the equation $2x + y = 32$:

$$\text{If } x = 0, \text{ then } y = 32.$$

$$\text{If } y = 0, \text{ then } x = 16.$$

This gives the points (0, 32) and (16, 0), which uniquely define the line.

(16, 0) and (0, 32). After graphing both lines in the same coordinate system (Fig. 1), estimate the coordinates of the intersection point:

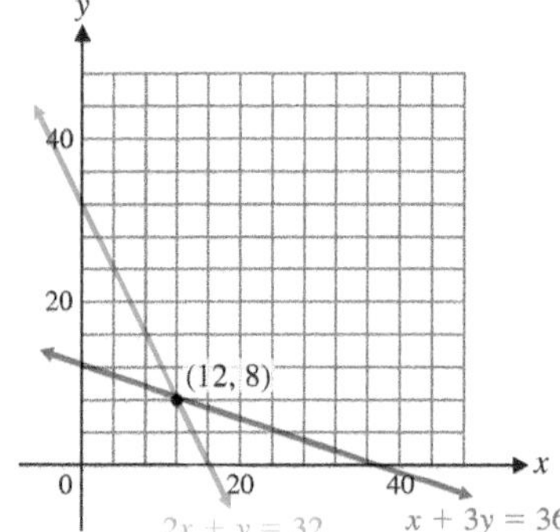

Figure 1

$x = \$12$ Adult ticket

$y = \$8$ Child ticket

$$2x + y = 32 \qquad x + 3y = 36$$

CHECK $2(12) + 8 \stackrel{?}{=} 32 \qquad 12 + 3(8) \stackrel{?}{=} 36$

$$32 \stackrel{\checkmark}{=} 32 \qquad 36 \stackrel{\checkmark}{=} 36$$

Check that (12, 8) satisfies each of the original equations.

Matched Problem 1 Solve by graphing and check:

$$2x - y = -3$$
$$x + 2y = -4$$

It is clear that Example 1 has exactly one solution since the lines have exactly one point in common. In general, lines in a rectangular coordinate system are related to each other in one of the three ways illustrated in the next example.

EXAMPLE 2 **Solving a System by Graphing** Solve each of the following systems by graphing:

(A) $x - 2y = 2$
$x + y = 5$

(B) $x + 2y = -4$
$2x + 4y = 8$

(C) $2x + 4y = 8$
$x + 2y = 4$

SOLUTION

(A)

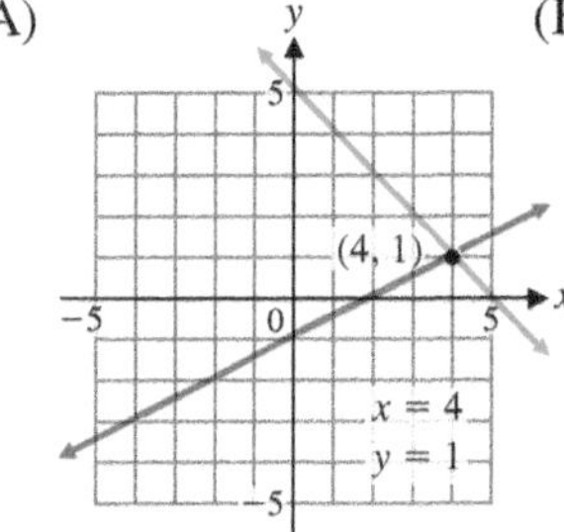

Intersection at one point only—exactly one solution

(B)

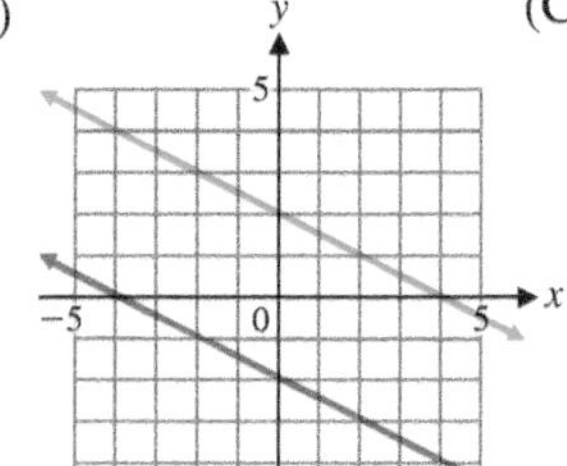

Lines are parallel (each has slope $-\frac{1}{2}$)—no solutions

(C)

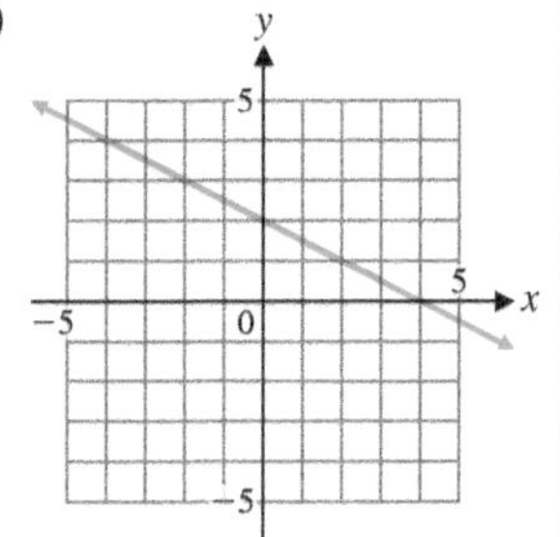

Lines coincide—infinite number of solutions

Matched Problem 2 Solve each of the following systems by graphing:

(A) $x + y = 4$
$2x - y = 2$

(B) $6x - 3y = 9$
$2x - y = 3$

(C) $2x - y = 4$
$6x - 3y = -18$

We introduce some terms that describe the different types of solutions to systems of equations.

DEFINITION Systems of Linear Equations: Basic Terms

A system of linear equations is **consistent** if it has one or more solutions and **inconsistent** if no solutions exist. Furthermore, a consistent system is said to be **independent** if it has exactly one solution (often referred to as the **unique solution**) and **dependent** if it has more than one solution. Two systems of equations are **equivalent** if they have the same solution set.

Referring to the three systems in Example 2, the system in part (A) is consistent and independent with the unique solution $x = 4, y = 1$. The system in part (B) is inconsistent. And the system in part (C) is consistent and dependent with an infinite number of solutions (all points on the two coinciding lines).

⚠ CAUTION Given a system of equations, do not confuse the *number of variables* with the *number of solutions*. The systems of Example 2 involve two variables, x and y. A solution to such a system is a *pair* of numbers, one for x and one for y. So the system in Example 2A has two variables, but exactly one solution, namely, $x = 4, y = 1$. ▲

Explore and Discuss 1

Can a consistent and dependent system have exactly two solutions? Exactly three solutions? Explain.

By graphing a system of two linear equations in two variables, we gain useful information about the solution set of the system. In general, any two lines in a coordinate plane must intersect in exactly one point, be parallel, or coincide (have identical graphs). So the systems in Example 2 illustrate the only three possible types of solutions for systems of two linear equations in two variables. These ideas are summarized in Theorem 1.

THEOREM 1 Possible Solutions to a Linear System

The linear system

$$\begin{aligned} ax + by &= h \\ cx + dy &= k \end{aligned}$$

must have

(A) Exactly one solution — Consistent and independent

or

(B) No solution — Inconsistent

or

(C) Infinitely many solutions — Consistent and dependent

There are no other possibilities.

In the past, one drawback to solving systems by graphing was the inaccuracy of hand-drawn graphs. Graphing calculators have changed that. Graphical solutions on a graphing calculator provide an accurate approximation of the solution to a system of linear equations in two variables. Example 3 demonstrates this.

EXAMPLE 3 **Solving a System Using a Graphing Calculator** Solve to two decimal places using graphical approximation techniques on a graphing calculator:

$$5x + 2y = 15$$
$$2x - 3y = 16$$

SOLUTION First, solve each equation for y:

$$5x + 2y = 15 \qquad\qquad 2x - 3y = 16$$
$$2y = -5x + 15 \qquad\qquad -3y = -2x + 16$$
$$y = -2.5x + 7.5 \qquad\qquad y = \frac{2}{3}x - \frac{16}{3}$$

Next, enter each equation in the graphing calculator (Fig. 2A), graph in an appropriate viewing window, and approximate the intersection point (Fig. 2B).

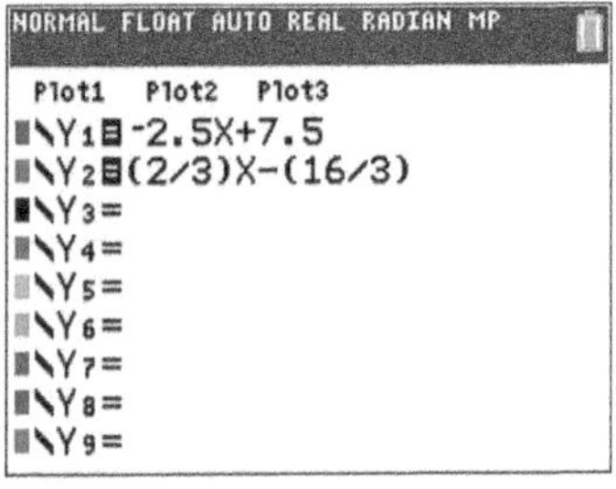

(A) Equation definitions

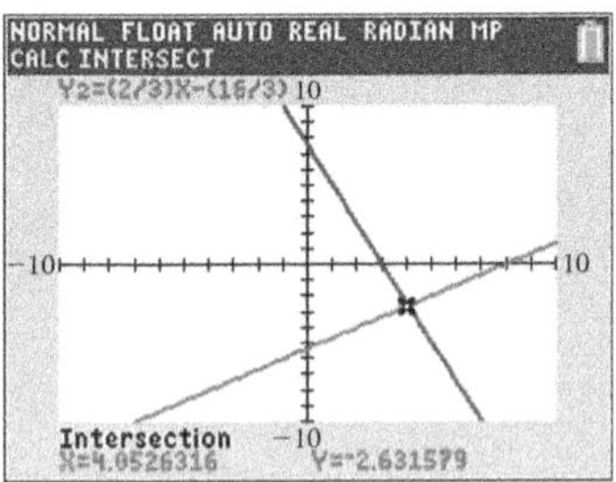

(B) Intersection points

Figure 2

Rounding the values in Figure 2B to two decimal places, we see that the solution is $x = 4.05$ and $y = -2.63$, or $(4.05, -2.63)$.

CHECK

$$5x + 2y = 15 \qquad\qquad 2x - 3y = 16$$
$$5(4.05) + 2(-2.63) \stackrel{?}{=} 15 \qquad\qquad 2(4.05) - 3(-2.63) \stackrel{?}{=} 16$$
$$14.99 \stackrel{\checkmark}{\approx} 15 \qquad\qquad 15.99 \stackrel{\checkmark}{\approx} 16$$

The checks are sufficiently close but, due to rounding, not exact.

Matched Problem 3 Solve to two decimal places using graphical approximation techniques on a graphing calculator:

$$2x - 5y = -25$$
$$4x + 3y = 5$$

Graphical methods help us to visualize a system and its solutions, reveal relationships that might otherwise be hidden, and, with the assistance of a graphing calculator, provide accurate approximations to solutions.

Substitution

Now we review an algebraic method that is easy to use and provides exact solutions to a system of two equations in two variables, provided that solutions exist. In this method, first we choose one of two equations in a system and solve for one variable in terms of the other. (We make a choice that avoids fractions, if possible.) Then we **substitute** the result into the other equation and solve the resulting linear equation in one variable. Finally, we substitute this result back into the results of the first step to find the second variable.

EXAMPLE 4 **Solving a System by Substitution** Solve by substitution:

$$\begin{aligned} 5x + y &= 4 \\ 2x - 3y &= 5 \end{aligned}$$

SOLUTION Solve either equation for one variable in terms of the other; then substitute into the remaining equation. In this problem, we avoid fractions by choosing the first equation and solving for y in terms of x:

$$\begin{aligned} 5x + y &= 4 && \text{Solve the first equation for } y \text{ in terms of } x. \\ y &= 4 - 5x && \text{Substitute into the second equation.} \end{aligned}$$

$$\begin{aligned} 2x - 3y &= 5 && \text{Second equation} \\ 2x - 3(4 - 5x) &= 5 && \text{Solve for } x. \\ 2x - 12 + 15x &= 5 \\ 17x &= 17 \\ x &= 1 \end{aligned}$$

Now, replace x with 1 in $y = 4 - 5x$ to find y:

$$\begin{aligned} y &= 4 - 5x \\ y &= 4 - 5(1) \\ y &= -1 \end{aligned}$$

The solution is $x = 1, y = -1$ or $(1, -1)$.

CHECK

$$\begin{aligned} 5x + y &= 4 \\ 5(1) + (-1) &\stackrel{?}{=} 4 \\ 4 &\stackrel{\checkmark}{=} 4 \end{aligned} \qquad \begin{aligned} 2x - 3y &= 5 \\ 2(1) - 3(-1) &\stackrel{?}{=} 5 \\ 5 &\stackrel{\checkmark}{=} 5 \end{aligned}$$

Matched Problem 4 Solve by substitution:

$$\begin{aligned} 3x + 2y &= -2 \\ 2x - y &= -6 \end{aligned}$$

Explore and Discuss 2

Return to Example 2 and solve each system by substitution. Based on your results, describe how you can recognize a dependent system or an inconsistent system when using substitution.

Elimination by Addition

The methods of graphing and substitution both work well for systems involving two variables. However, neither is easily extended to larger systems. Now we turn to **elimination by addition**. This is probably the most important method of solution. It readily generalizes to larger systems and forms the basis for computer-based solution methods.

To solve an equation such as $2x - 5 = 3$, we perform operations on the equation until we reach an equivalent equation whose solution is obvious (see Appendix B, Section B.7).

$$\begin{aligned} 2x - 5 &= 3 && \text{Add 5 to both sides.} \\ 2x &= 8 && \text{Divide both sides by 2.} \\ x &= 4 \end{aligned}$$

Theorem 2 indicates that we can solve systems of linear equations in a similar manner.

THEOREM 2 Operations That Produce Equivalent Systems

A system of linear equations is transformed into an equivalent system if

(A) Two equations are interchanged.
(B) An equation is multiplied by a nonzero constant.
(C) A constant multiple of one equation is added to another equation.

Any one of the three operations in Theorem 2 can be used to produce an equivalent system, but the operations in parts (B) and (C) will be of most use to us now. Part (A) becomes useful when we apply the theorem to larger systems. The use of Theorem 2 is best illustrated by examples.

EXAMPLE 5 **Solving a System Using Elimination by Addition** Solve the following system using elimination by addition:

$$\begin{aligned} 3x - 2y &= 8 \\ 2x + 5y &= -1 \end{aligned}$$

SOLUTION We use Theorem 2 to eliminate one of the variables, obtaining a system with an obvious solution:

$$\begin{aligned} 3x - 2y &= 8 \\ 2x + 5y &= -1 \end{aligned}$$

Multiply the top equation by 5 and the bottom equation by 2 (Theorem 2B).

$$\begin{aligned} 5(3x - 2y) &= 5(8) \\ 2(2x + 5y) &= 2(-1) \end{aligned}$$

$$\begin{aligned} 15x - 10y &= 40 \\ 4x + 10y &= -2 \\ \hline 19x \qquad &= 38 \end{aligned}$$

Add the top equation to the bottom equation (Theorem 2C), eliminating the y terms.

Divide both sides by 19, which is the same as multiplying the equation by $\frac{1}{19}$ (Theorem 2B).

$$x = 2$$

This equation paired with either of the two original equations produces a system equivalent to the original system.

Knowing that $x = 2$, we substitute this number back into either of the two original equations (we choose the second) to solve for y:

$$\begin{aligned} 2(2) + 5y &= -1 \\ 5y &= -5 \\ y &= -1 \end{aligned}$$

The solution is $x = 2$, $y = -1$ or $(2, -1)$.

CHECK

$$\begin{aligned} 3x - 2y &= 8 \\ 3(2) - 2(-1) &\stackrel{?}{=} 8 \\ 8 &\stackrel{\checkmark}{=} 8 \end{aligned} \qquad \begin{aligned} 2x + 5y &= -1 \\ 2(2) + 5(-1) &\stackrel{?}{=} -1 \\ -1 &\stackrel{\checkmark}{=} -1 \end{aligned}$$

Matched Problem 5 Solve the following system using elimination by addition:

$$\begin{aligned} 5x - 2y &= 12 \\ 2x + 3y &= 1 \end{aligned}$$

Let's see what happens in the elimination process when a system has either no solution or infinitely many solutions. Consider the following system:

$$\begin{aligned} 2x + 6y &= -3 \\ x + 3y &= 2 \end{aligned}$$

Multiplying the second equation by -2 and adding, we obtain

$$\begin{aligned} 2x + 6y &= -3 \\ -2x - 6y &= -4 \\ \hline 0 &= -7 \quad \text{Not possible} \end{aligned}$$

We have obtained a contradiction. The assumption that the original system has solutions must be false. So the system has no solutions, and its solution set is the empty set. The graphs of the equations are parallel lines, and the system is inconsistent.

Now consider the system

$$\begin{aligned} x - \tfrac{1}{2}y &= 4 \\ -2x + y &= -8 \end{aligned}$$

If we multiply the top equation by 2 and add the result to the bottom equation, we obtain

$$\begin{aligned} 2x - y &= 8 \\ -2x + y &= -8 \\ \hline 0 &= 0 \end{aligned}$$

Obtaining $0 = 0$ implies that the equations are equivalent; that is, their graphs coincide and the system is dependent. If we let $x = k$, where k is any real number, and solve either equation for y, we obtain $y = 2k - 8$. So $(k, 2k - 8)$ is a solution to this system for any real number k. The variable k is called a **parameter** and replacing k with a real number produces a **particular solution** to the system. For example, some particular solutions to this system are

$k = -1$	$k = 2$	$k = 5$	$k = 9.4$
$(-1, -10)$	$(2, -4)$	$(5, 2)$	$(9.4, 10.8)$

Applications

Many real-world problems are solved readily by constructing a mathematical model consisting of two linear equations in two variables and applying the solution methods that we have discussed. We shall examine two applications in detail.

EXAMPLE 6 **Diet** Jasmine wants to use milk and orange juice to increase the amount of calcium and vitamin A in her daily diet. An ounce of milk contains 37 milligrams of calcium and 57 micrograms* of vitamin A. An ounce of orange juice contains 5 milligrams of calcium and 65 micrograms of vitamin A. How many ounces of milk and orange juice should Jasmine drink each day to provide exactly 500 milligrams of calcium and 1,200 micrograms of vitamin A?

SOLUTION The first step in solving an application problem is to introduce the proper variables. Often, the question asked in the problem will guide you in this decision. Reading the last sentence in Example 6, we see that we must determine a certain number of ounces of milk and orange juice. So we introduce variables to represent these unknown quantities:

$$\begin{aligned} x &= \text{number of ounces of milk} \\ y &= \text{number of ounces of orange juice} \end{aligned}$$

* A microgram (μg) is one millionth (10^{-6}) of a gram.

Next, we summarize the given information using a table. It is convenient to organize the table so that the quantities represented by the variables correspond to columns in the table (rather than to rows) as shown.

	Milk	Orange Juice	Total Needed
Calcium	37 mg/oz	5 mg/oz	500 mg
Vitamin A	57 μg/oz	65 μg/oz	1,200 μg

Now we use the information in the table to form equations involving x and y:

$$\begin{pmatrix}\text{calcium in } x \text{ oz}\\ \text{of milk}\end{pmatrix} + \begin{pmatrix}\text{calcium in } y \text{ oz}\\ \text{of orange juice}\end{pmatrix} = \begin{pmatrix}\text{total calcium}\\ \text{needed (mg)}\end{pmatrix}$$

$$37x \quad + \quad 5y \quad = \quad 500$$

$$\begin{pmatrix}\text{vitamin A in } x \text{ oz}\\ \text{of milk}\end{pmatrix} + \begin{pmatrix}\text{vitamin A in } y \text{ oz}\\ \text{of orange juice}\end{pmatrix} = \begin{pmatrix}\text{total vitamin A}\\ \text{needed } (\mu\text{g})\end{pmatrix}$$

$$57x \quad + \quad 65y \quad = \quad 1{,}200$$

So we have the following model to solve:

$$\begin{aligned} 37x + 5y &= 500 \\ 57x + 65y &= 1{,}200 \end{aligned}$$

We can multiply the first equation by -13 and use elimination by addition:

$$\begin{aligned} -481x - 65y &= -6{,}500 \\ 57x + 65y &= 1{,}200 \\ \hline -424x \qquad &= -5{,}300 \\ x &= 12.5 \end{aligned} \qquad \begin{aligned} 37(12.5) + 5y &= 500 \\ 5y &= 37.5 \\ y &= 7.5 \end{aligned}$$

Drinking 12.5 ounces of milk and 7.5 ounces of orange juice each day will provide Jasmine with the required amounts of calcium and vitamin A.

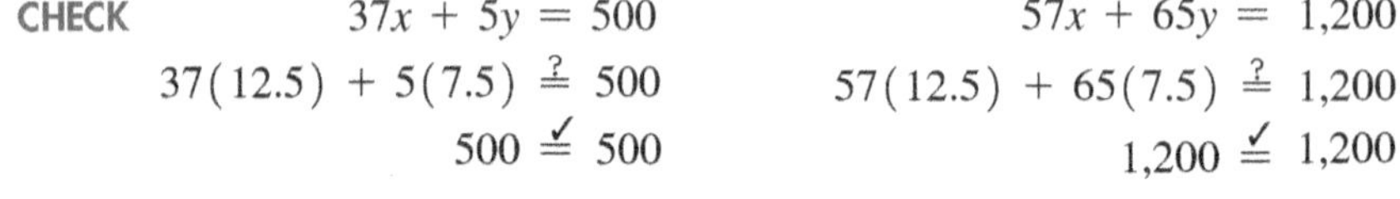

CHECK

$$\begin{aligned} 37x + 5y &= 500 \\ 37(12.5) + 5(7.5) &\stackrel{?}{=} 500 \\ 500 &\stackrel{\checkmark}{=} 500 \end{aligned} \qquad \begin{aligned} 57x + 65y &= 1{,}200 \\ 57(12.5) + 65(7.5) &\stackrel{?}{=} 1{,}200 \\ 1{,}200 &\stackrel{\checkmark}{=} 1{,}200 \end{aligned}$$

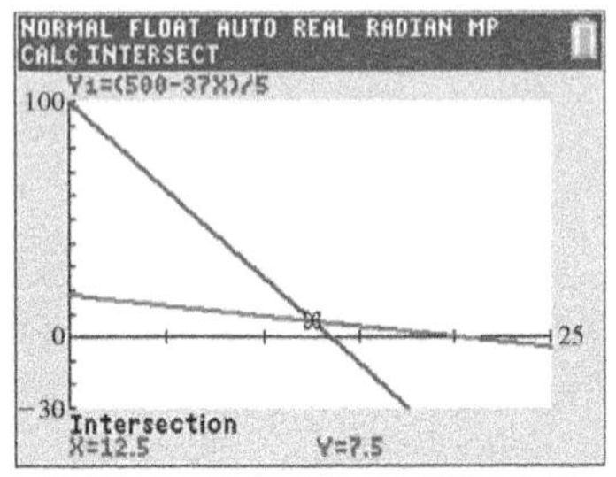

Figure 3

$y_1 = (500 - 37x)/5$

$y_2 = (1{,}200 - 57x)/65$

Figure 3 illustrates a solution to Example 6 using graphical approximation techniques.

Matched Problem 6 Dennis wants to use cottage cheese and yogurt to increase the amount of protein and calcium in his daily diet. An ounce of cottage cheese contains 3 grams of protein and 15 milligrams of calcium. An ounce of yogurt contains 1 gram of protein and 41 milligrams of calcium. How many ounces of cottage cheese and yogurt should Dennis eat each day to provide exactly 62 grams of protein and 760 milligrams of calcium?

In a free market economy, the price of a product is determined by the relationship between supply and demand. Suppliers are more willing to supply a product at higher prices. So when the price is high, the supply is high. If the relationship between price and supply is linear, then the graph of the price–supply equation is a line with positive slope. On the other hand, consumers of a product are generally less willing to buy a product at higher prices. So when the price is high, demand is low. If the relationship between price and demand is linear, the graph of the price–demand equation is a line with negative slope. In a free competitive market, the price of a product tends to move toward an **equilibrium price**, in which the supply and demand are equal; that common value of the supply and demand is the **equilibrium quantity**. To find the equilibrium price, we solve the system consisting of the price–supply and price–demand equations.

EXAMPLE 7 **Supply and Demand** At a price of \$1.88 per pound, the supply for cherries in a large city is 16,000 pounds, and the demand is 10,600 pounds. When the price drops to \$1.46 per pound, the supply decreases to 10,000 pounds, and the demand increases to 12,700 pounds. Assume that the price–supply and price–demand equations are linear.

(A) Find the price–supply equation.

(B) Find the price–demand equation.

(C) Find the supply and demand at a price of \$2.09 per pound.

(D) Find the supply and demand at a price of \$1.32 per pound.

(E) Use the substitution method to find the equilibrium price and equilibrium demand.

SOLUTION

(A) Let p be the price per pound, and let x be the quantity in thousands of pounds. Then (16, 1.88) and (10, 1.46) are solutions of the price–supply equation. Use the point–slope form for the equation of a line, $y - y_1 = m(x - x_1)$, to obtain the price–supply equation:

$$p - 1.88 = \frac{1.46 - 1.88}{10 - 16}(x - 16) \quad \text{Simplify.}$$

$$p - 1.88 = 0.07(x - 16) \quad \text{Solve for } p.$$

$$p = 0.07x + 0.76 \quad \text{Price–supply equation}$$

(B) Again, let p be the price per pound, and let x be the quantity in thousands of pounds. Then (10.6, 1.88) and (12.7, 1.46) are solutions of the price–demand equation.

$$p - 1.88 = \frac{1.46 - 1.88}{12.7 - 10.6}(x - 10.6) \quad \text{Simplify.}$$

$$p - 1.88 = -0.2(x - 10.6) \quad \text{Solve for } p.$$

$$p = -0.2x + 4 \quad \text{Price–demand equation}$$

(C) Substitute $p = 2.09$ into the price–supply equation, and also into the price–demand equation, and solve for x:

Price–supply equation	Price–demand equation
$p = 0.07x + 0.76$	$p = -0.2x + 4$
$2.09 = 0.07x + 0.76$	$2.09 = -0.2x + 4$
$x = 19$	$x = 9.55$

At a price of \$2.09 per pound, the supply is 19,000 pounds of cherries and the demand is 9,550 pounds. (The supply is greater than the demand, so the price will tend to come down.)

(D) Substitute $p = 1.32$ in each equation and solve for x:

Price–supply equation	Price–demand equation
$p = 0.07x + 0.76$	$p = -0.2x + 4$
$1.32 = 0.07x + 0.76$	$1.32 = -0.2x + 4$
$x = 8$	$x = 13.4$

At a price of \$1.32 per pound, the supply is 8,000 pounds of cherries, and the demand is 13,400 pounds. (The demand is greater than the supply, so the price will tend to go up.)

(E) We solve the linear system

$$p = 0.07x + 0.76 \qquad \text{Price–supply equation}$$

$$p = -0.2x + 4 \qquad \text{Price–demand equation}$$

using substitution (substitute $p = -0.2x + 4$ in the first equation):

$$-0.2x + 4 = 0.07x + 0.76$$

$$-0.27x = -3.24 \qquad \text{Equilibrium quantity}$$

$$x = 12 \text{ thousand pounds}$$

Now substitute $x = 12$ into the price–demand equation:

$$p = -0.2(12) + 4$$

$$p = \$1.60 \text{ per pound} \qquad \text{Equilibrium price}$$

The results are interpreted graphically in Figure 4 (it is customary to refer to the graphs of price–supply and price–demand equations as "curves" even when they are lines). Note that if the price is above the equilibrium price of \$1.60 per pound, the supply will exceed the demand and the price will come down. If the price is below the equilibrium price of \$1.60 per pound, the demand will exceed the supply and the price will go up. So the price will stabilize at \$1.60 per pound. At this equilibrium price, suppliers will supply 12,000 pounds of cherries and consumers will purchase 12,000 pounds.

Figure 4

Matched Problem 7 Find the equilibrium quantity and equilibrium price, and graph the following price–supply and price–demand equations:

$$p = 0.08q + 0.66 \qquad \text{Price–supply equation}$$

$$p = -0.1q + 3 \qquad \text{Price–demand equation}$$

Exercises 4.1

Skills Warm-up Exercises

W *In Problems 1–6, find the x and y coordinates of the intersection of the given lines. (If necessary, review Section A.2).*

1. $y = 5x + 7$ and the y axis
2. $y = 5x + 7$ and the x axis
3. $3x + 4y = 72$ and the x axis
4. $3x + 4y = 72$ and the y axis
5. $6x - 5y = 120$ and $x = 5$
6. $6x - 5y = 120$ and $y = 9$

In Problems 7 and 8, find an equation in point–slope form, $y - y_1 = m(x - x_1)$, of the line through the given points.

7. (2, 7) and (4, −5).
8. (5, 39) and (−7, 3).

A *Match each system in Problems 9–12 with one of the following graphs, and use the graph to solve the system.*

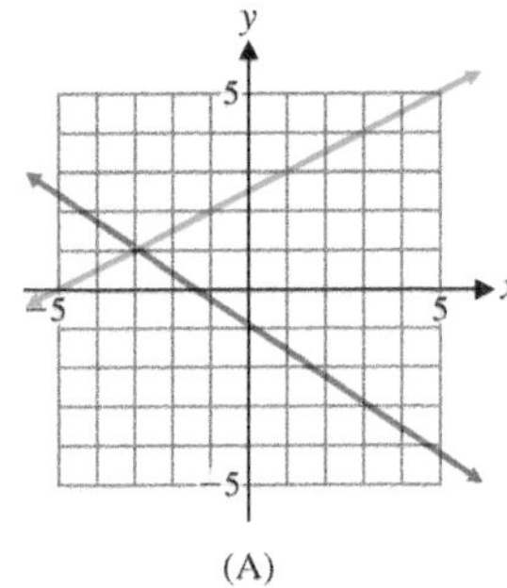

(A)

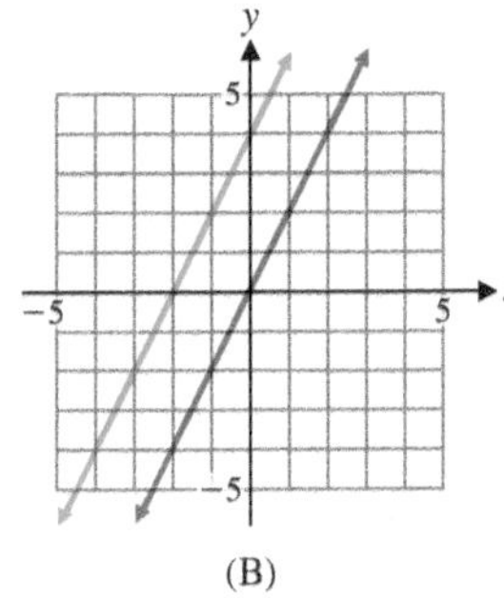

(B)

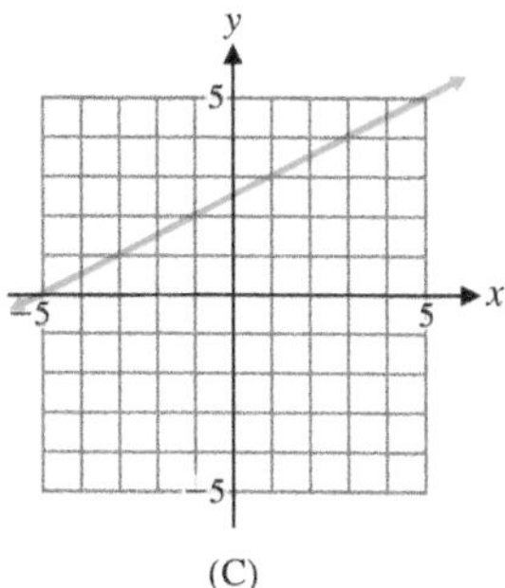

(C)

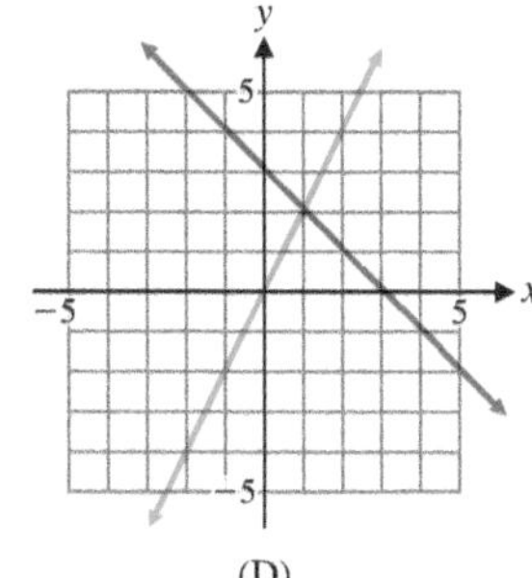

(D)

9. $-4x + 2y = 8$, $2x - y = 0$

10. $x + y = 3$, $2x - y = 0$

11. $-x + 2y = 5$, $2x + 3y = -3$

12. $2x - 4y = -10$, $-x + 2y = 5$

Solve Problems 13–16 by graphing.

13. $3x - y = 2$, $x + 2y = 10$

14. $8x - 3y = 27$, $5x + 3y = 12$

15. $m + 2n = 4$, $2m + 4n = -8$

16. $3u + 5v = 15$, $6u + 10v = -30$

Solve Problems 17–20 using substitution.

17. $y = 2x - 3$, $x + 2y = 14$

18. $y = x - 4$, $x + 3y = 12$

19. $2x + y = 6$, $x - y = -3$

20. $3x - y = 7$, $2x + 3y = 1$

Solve Problems 21–24 using elimination by addition.

21. $3u - 2v = 12$, $7u + 2v = 8$

22. $2x - 3y = -8$, $5x + 3y = 1$

23. $2m - n = 10$, $m - 2n = -4$

24. $2x + 3y = 1$, $3x - y = 7$

B *Solve Problems 25–34 using substitution or elimination by addition.*

25. $6x - 2y = 4$, $5x + 3y = 8$

26. $3x + 9y = 6$, $4x - 3y = 8$

27. $4x - 2y = 10$, $-6x + 3y = 15$

28. $-5x + 15y = 10$, $5x - 15y = 10$

29. $4x - 2y = 10$, $-6x + 3y = -15$

30. $-5x + 15y = 10$, $5x - 15y = -10$

31. $3m + 5n = 7$, $2m + 10n = 12$

32. $8m - 9n = 12$, $3m - 15n = 51$

33. $x + y = 1$, $0.3x + 0.5y = 0.7$

34. $x + 2y = 3$, $0.2x + 0.5y = 0.4$

In Problems 35–42, solve the system. Note that each solution can be found mentally, without the use of a calculator or pencil-and-paper calculation; try to visualize the graphs of both lines.

35. $x + 0y = 7$, $0x + y = 3$

36. $x + 0y = -4$, $0x + y = 9$

37. $6x + 0y = 7$, $0x + 9y = -8$

38. $6x + 0y = 7$, $0x + 4y = 9$

39. $x + y = 0$, $x - y = 0$

40. $-2x + y = 0$, $5x - y = 0$

41. $x - 2y = 4$, $0x + y = 5$

42. $x + 6y = -1$, $0x + y = -4$

43. In a free competitive market, if the supply of a good is greater than the demand, will the price tend to go up or come down?

44. In a free competitive market, if the demand for a good is greater than the supply, will the price tend to go up or come down?

Problems 45–48 are concerned with the linear system

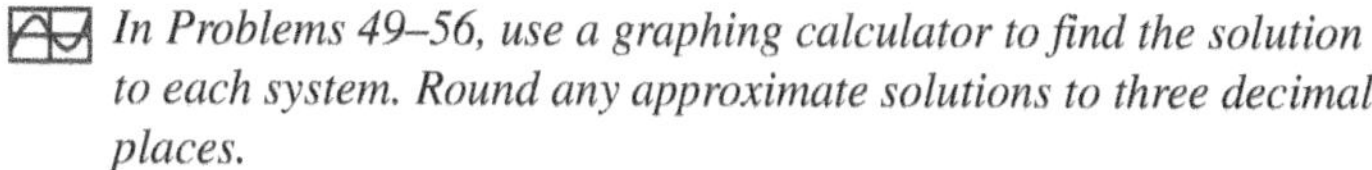

$$y = mx + b$$
$$y = nx + c$$

where m, b, n, and c are nonzero constants.

45. If the system has a unique solution, discuss the relationships among the four constants.

46. If the system has no solution, discuss the relationships among the four constants.

47. If the system has an infinite number of solutions, discuss the relationships among the four constants.

48. If $m = 0$, how many solutions does the system have?

In Problems 49–56, use a graphing calculator to find the solution to each system. Round any approximate solutions to three decimal places.

49. $y = 9x - 10$, $y = -7x + 8$

50. $y = 3x - 18$, $y = -17x + 51$

51. $y = 0.2x + 0.7$, $y = 0.2x - 0.1$

52. $y = -1.7x + 2.3$, $y = -1.7x - 1.3$

53. $3x - 2y = 15$, $4x + 3y = 13$

54. $3x - 7y = -20$, $2x + 5y = 8$

55. $-2.4x + 3.5y = 0.1$, $-1.7x + 2.6y = -0.2$

56. $4.2x + 5.4y = -12.9$, $6.4x + 3.7y = -4.5$

C *In Problems 57–62, graph the equations in the same coordinate system. Find the coordinates of any points where two or more lines intersect. Is there a point that is a solution to all three equations?*

57. $x - 2y = -6$, $2x + y = 8$, $x + 2y = -2$

58. $x + y = 3$, $x + 3y = 15$, $3x - y = 5$

59. $x + y = 1$, $x - 2y = -8$, $3x + y = -3$

60. $x - y = 6$, $x - 2y = 8$, $x + 4y = -4$

61. $4x - 3y = -24$, $2x + 3y = 12$, $8x - 6y = 24$

62. $2x + 3y = 18$, $2x - 6y = -6$, $4x + 6y = -24$

63. The coefficients of the three systems given below are similar. One might guess that the solution sets to the three systems would be nearly identical. Develop evidence for or against this guess by considering graphs of the systems and solutions obtained using substitution or elimination by addition.

(A) $5x + 4y = 4$
$11x + 9y = 4$

(B) $5x + 4y = 4$
$11x + 8y = 4$

(C) $5x + 4y = 4$
$10x + 8y = 4$

64. Repeat Problem 63 for the following systems:

(A) $6x - 5y = 10$
$-13x + 11y = -20$

(B) $6x - 5y = 10$
$-13x + 10y = -20$

(C) $6x - 5y = 10$
$-12x + 10y = -20$

Applications

65. Supply and demand for T-shirts. Suppose that the supply and demand equations for printed T-shirts for a particular week are

$p = 0.7q + 3$ Price–supply equation
$p = -1.7q + 15$ Price–demand equation

where p is the price in dollars and q is the quantity in hundreds.

(A) Find the supply and demand (to the nearest unit) if T-shirts are \$4 each. Discuss the stability of the T-shirt market at this price level.

(B) Find the supply and demand (to the nearest unit) if T-shirts are \$9 each. Discuss the stability of the T-shirt market at this price level.

(C) Find the equilibrium price and quantity.

(D) Graph the two equations in the same coordinate system and identify the equilibrium point, supply curve, and demand curve.

66. Supply and demand for caps. Suppose that the supply and demand for printed caps for a particular week are

$p = 0.4q + 3.2$ Price–supply equation
$p = -1.9q + 17$ Price–demand equation

where p is the price in dollars and q is the quantity in hundreds.

(A) Find the supply and demand (to the nearest unit) if caps are \$4 each. Discuss the stability of that specific cap market at this price level.

(B) Find the supply and demand (to the nearest unit) if caps are \$9 each. Discuss the stability of the cap market at this price level.

(C) Find the equilibrium price and quantity.

(D) Graph the two equations in the same coordinate system and identify the equilibrium point, supply curve, and demand curve.

67. Supply and demand for soybeans. At \$4.80 per bushel, the annual supply for soybeans in the Midwest is 1.9 billion bushels, and the annual demand is 2.0 billion bushels. When the price increases to \$5.10 per bushel, the annual supply increases to 2.1 billion bushels, and the annual demand decreases to 1.8 billion bushels. Assume that the price–supply and price–demand equations are linear. (*Source:* U.S. Census Bureau)

(A) Find the price–supply equation.

(B) Find the price–demand equation.

(C) Find the equilibrium price and quantity.

(D) Graph the two equations in the same coordinate system and identify the equilibrium point, supply curve, and demand curve.

68. Supply and demand for corn. At \$2.13 per bushel, the annual supply for corn in the Midwest is 8.9 billion bushels and the annual demand is 6.5 billion bushels. When the price falls to \$1.50 per bushel, the annual supply decreases to 8.2 billion bushels and the annual demand increases to 7.4 billion bushels. Assume that the price–supply and price–demand equations are linear. (*Source:* U.S. Census Bureau)

(A) Find the price–supply equation.

(B) Find the price–demand equation.

(C) Find the equilibrium price and quantity.

(D) Graph the two equations in the same coordinate system and identify the equilibrium point, supply curve, and demand curve.

69. Break-even analysis. A small plant manufactures riding lawn mowers. The plant has fixed costs (leases, insurance, etc.) of \$48,000 per day and variable costs (labor, materials, etc.) of \$1,400 per unit produced. The mowers are sold for \$1,800 each. So the cost and revenue equations are

$y = 48{,}000 + 1{,}400x$ Cost equation
$y = 1{,}800x$ Revenue equation

where x is the total number of mowers produced and sold each day. The daily costs and revenue are in dollars.

(A) How many units must be manufactured and sold each day for the company to break even?

(B) Graph both equations in the same coordinate system and show the break-even point. Interpret the regions between the lines to the left and to the right of the break-even point.

70. Break-even analysis. Repeat Problem 69 with the cost and revenue equations

$y = 65{,}000 + 1{,}100x$ Cost equation
$y = 1{,}600x$ Revenue equation

71. Break-even analysis. A company markets exercise DVDs that sell for \$19.95, including shipping and handling. The monthly fixed costs (advertising, rent, etc.) are \$24,000 and the variable costs (materials, shipping, etc) are \$7.45 per DVD.

(A) Find the cost equation and the revenue equation.

(B) How many DVDs must be sold each month for the company to break even?

(C) Graph the cost and revenue equations in the same coordinate system and show the break-even point. Interpret the regions between the lines to the left and to the right of the break-even point.

72. Break-even analysis. Repeat Problem 71 if the monthly fixed costs increase to $27,200, the variable costs increase to $9.15, and the company raises the selling price of the DVDs to $21.95.

73. Delivery charges. Global Parcel, an international package delivery service, charges a base price for overnight delivery of packages weighing 1 kg or less and a surcharge for each additional kg (or fraction thereof). A customer is billed €13.68 for shipping a 3-kg package and €24.60 for a 10-kg package. Find the base price and the surcharge for each additional kg.

74. Delivery charges. Refer to Problem 73. Parcel Express, a competing overnight delivery service, informs the customer in Problem 73 that they would ship the 3-kg package for €14.75 and the 10-kg package for €23.78.

(A) If Parcel Express computes its cost in the same manner as Global Parcel, find the base price and the surcharge for Parcel Express.

(B) Devise a simple rule that the customer can use to choose the cheaper of the two services for each package shipped. Justify your answer.

75. Coffee blends. A coffee company uses Colombian and Brazilian coffee beans to produce two blends, robust and mild. A pound of the robust blend requires 12 ounces of Colombian beans and 4 ounces of Brazilian beans. A pound of the mild blend requires 6 ounces of Colombian beans and 10 ounces of Brazilian beans. Coffee is shipped in 132-pound burlap bags. The company has 50 bags of Colombian beans and 40 bags of Brazilian beans on hand. How many pounds of each blend should the company produce in order to use all the available beans?

76. Coffee blends. Refer to Problem 75.

(A) If the company decides to discontinue production of the robust blend and produce only the mild blend, how many pounds of the mild blend can the company produce? How many beans of each type will the company use? Are there any beans that are not used?

(B) Repeat part (A) if the company decides to discontinue production of the mild blend and produce only the robust blend.

77. Animal diet. Animals in an experiment are to be kept under a strict diet. Each animal should receive 20 grams of protein and 6 grams of fat. The laboratory technician is able to purchase two food mixes: Mix A has 10% protein and 6% fat; mix B has 20% protein and 2% fat. How many grams of each mix should be used to obtain the right diet for one animal?

78. Fertilizer. A fruit grower uses two types of fertilizer in an orange grove, brand A and brand B. Each bag of brand A contains 8 pounds of nitrogen and 4 pounds of phosphoric acid. Each bag of brand B contains 7 pounds of nitrogen and 6 pounds of phosphoric acid. Tests indicate that the grove needs 720 pounds of nitrogen and 500 pounds of phosphoric acid. How many bags of each brand should be used to provide the required amounts of nitrogen and phosphoric acid?

79. Electronics. A supplier for the electronics industry manufactures keyboards and screens for graphing calculators at plants in Mexico and Taiwan. The hourly production rates at each plant are given in the table. How many hours should each plant be operated to exactly fill an order for 4,000 keyboards and 4,000 screens?

Plant	Keyboards	Screens
Mexico	40	32
Taiwan	20	32

80. Sausage. A company produces Italian sausages and bratwursts at plants in Green Bay and Sheboygan. The hourly production rates at each plant are given in the table. How many hours should each plant operate to exactly fill an order for 62,250 Italian sausages and 76,500 bratwursts?

Plant	Italian Sausage	Bratwurst
Green Bay	800	800
Sheboygan	500	1,000

81. Physics. An object dropped off the top of a tall building falls vertically with constant acceleration. If s is the distance of the object above the ground (in feet) t seconds after its release, then s and t are related by an equation of the form $s = a + bt^2$, where a and b are constants. Suppose the object is 180 feet above the ground 1 second after its release and 132 feet above the ground 2 seconds after its release.

(A) Find the constants a and b.

(B) How tall is the building?

(C) How long does the object fall?

82. Physics. Repeat Problem 81 if the object is 240 feet above the ground after 1 second and 192 feet above the ground after 2 seconds.

83. Earthquakes. An earthquake emits a primary wave and a secondary wave. Near the surface of the Earth the primary wave travels at 5 miles per second and the secondary wave at 3 miles per second. From the time lag between the two waves arriving at a given receiving station, it is possible to estimate the distance to the quake. Suppose a station measured a time difference of 16 seconds between the arrival of the two waves. How long did each wave travel, and how far was the earthquake from the station?

84. Sound waves. A ship using sound-sensing devices above and below water recorded a surface explosion 6 seconds sooner by its underwater device than its above-water device. Sound travels in air at 1,100 feet per second and in seawater at 5,000 feet per second. How long did it take each sound wave to reach the ship? How far was the explosion from the ship?

85. Psychology. People approach certain situations with "mixed emotions." For example, public speaking often brings forth the positive response of recognition and the negative response of failure. Which dominates? J. S. Brown, in an experiment on approach and avoidance, trained rats by feeding them from a goal box. The rats received mild electric shocks from the same goal box. This established an approach–avoidance conflict relative to the goal box. Using an appropriate apparatus, Brown arrived at the following relationships:

$$p = -\tfrac{1}{5}d + 70 \qquad \text{Approach equation}$$

$$p = -\tfrac{4}{3}d + 230 \qquad \text{Avoidance equation}$$

where $30 \le d \le 172.5$. The approach equation gives the pull (in grams) toward the food goal box when the rat is placed d centimeters away from it. The avoidance equation gives the pull (in grams) away from the shock goal box when the rat is placed d centimeters from it.

(A) Graph the approach equation and the avoidance equation in the same coordinate system.

(B) Find the value of d for the point of intersection of these two equations.

(C) What do you think the rat would do when placed the distance d from the box found in part (B)?

(*Source: Journal of Comparative and Physiological Psychology*, 41:450–465.)

Answers to Matched Problems

1. $x = -2, y = -1$

$$\begin{aligned} 2x - y &= -3 \\ 2(-2) - (-1) &\overset{?}{=} -3 \\ -3 &\overset{\checkmark}{=} -3 \\ x + 2y &= -4 \\ (-2) + 2(-1) &\overset{?}{=} -4 \\ -4 &\overset{\checkmark}{=} -4 \end{aligned}$$

$2x - y = -3$ $\quad$ $x + 2y = -4$ $\quad$ $(-2, -1)$

2. (A) $x = 2, y = 2$
   (B) Infinitely many solutions
   (C) No solution
3. $x = -1.92, y = 4.23$
4. $x = -2, y = 2$
5. $x = 2, y = -1$
6. 16.5 oz of cottage cheese, 12.5 oz of yogurt
7. Equilibrium quantity = 13 thousand pounds; equilibrium price = \$1.70 per pound

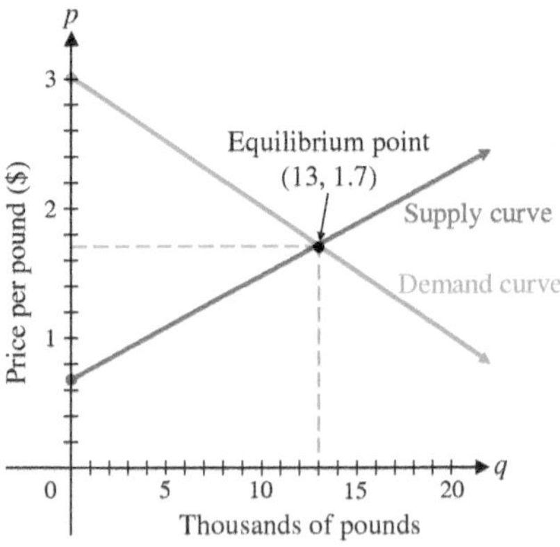

4.2 Systems of Linear Equations and Augmented Matrices

- Matrices
- Solving Linear Systems Using Augmented Matrices
- Summary

Most linear systems of any consequence involve large numbers of equations and variables. It is impractical to try to solve such systems by hand. In the past, these complex systems could be solved only on large computers. Now there are a wide array of approaches to solving linear systems, ranging from graphing calculators to software and spreadsheets. In the rest of this chapter, we develop several *matrix methods* for solving systems with the understanding that these methods are generally used with a graphing calculator. It is important to keep in mind that we are not presenting these techniques as efficient methods for solving linear systems by hand. Instead, we emphasize formulation of mathematical models and interpretation of the results—two activities that graphing calculators cannot perform for you.

Matrices

In solving systems of equations using elimination by addition, the coefficients of the variables and the constant terms played a central role. The process can be made more efficient for generalization and computer work by the introduction of a mathematical form called a *matrix*. A **matrix** is a rectangular array of numbers written within brackets. Two examples are

$$A = \begin{bmatrix} 1 & -4 & 5 \\ 7 & 0 & -2 \end{bmatrix} \qquad B = \begin{bmatrix} -4 & 5 & 12 \\ 0 & 1 & 8 \\ -3 & 10 & 9 \\ -6 & 0 & -1 \end{bmatrix} \tag{1}$$

Each number in a matrix is called an **element** of the matrix. Matrix A has 6 elements arranged in 2 rows and 3 columns. Matrix B has 12 elements arranged in 4 rows and 3 columns. If a matrix has m rows and n columns, it is called an $\boldsymbol{m \times n}$ **matrix** (read "m by n matrix"). The expression $m \times n$ is called the **size** of the matrix, and the numbers m and n are called the **dimensions** of the matrix. It is important to note that the number of rows is always given first. Referring to equations (1), A is a 2×3 matrix and B is a 4×3 matrix. A matrix with n rows and n columns is called a **square matrix of order** $\boldsymbol{n}$. A matrix with only 1 column is called a **column matrix**, and a matrix with only 1 row is called a **row matrix**.

$$\underset{\text{Square matrix of order 3}}{\overset{3 \times 3}{\begin{bmatrix} 0.5 & 0.2 & 1.0 \\ 0.0 & 0.3 & 0.5 \\ 0.7 & 0.0 & 0.2 \end{bmatrix}}} \qquad \underset{\text{Column matrix}}{\overset{4 \times 1}{\begin{bmatrix} 3 \\ -2 \\ 1 \\ 0 \end{bmatrix}}} \qquad \underset{\text{Row matrix}}{\overset{1 \times 4}{\begin{bmatrix} 2 & \frac{1}{2} & 0 & -\frac{2}{3} \end{bmatrix}}}$$

The **position** of an element in a matrix is given by the row and column containing the element. This is usually denoted using **double subscript notation** a_{ij}, where i is the row and j is the column containing the element a_{ij}, as illustrated below:

$$A = \begin{bmatrix} 1 & -4 & 5 \\ 7 & 0 & -2 \end{bmatrix} \qquad \begin{matrix} a_{11} = 1, & a_{12} = -4, & a_{13} = 5 \\ a_{21} = 7, & a_{22} = 0, & a_{23} = -2 \end{matrix}$$

Note that a_{12} is read "a sub one two" (*not* "a sub twelve"). The elements $a_{11} = 1$ and $a_{22} = 0$ make up the *principal diagonal* of A. In general, the **principal diagonal** of a matrix A consists of the elements $a_{11}, a_{22}, a_{33}, \dots$.

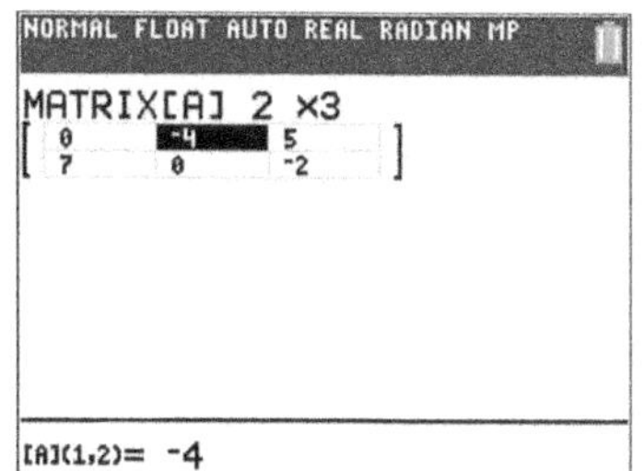

Figure 1 Matrix notation on a graphing calculator

Remark—Most graphing calculators are capable of storing and manipulating matrices. Figure 1 shows matrix A displayed in the editing screen of a graphing calculator. The size of the matrix is given at the top of the screen. The position and value of the currently selected element is given at the bottom. Note that a comma is used in the notation for the position. This is common practice on many graphing calculators but not in mathematical literature. In a spreadsheet, matrices are referred to by their location (upper left corner to lower right corner), using either row and column numbers (Fig. 2A) or row numbers and column letters (Fig. 2B).

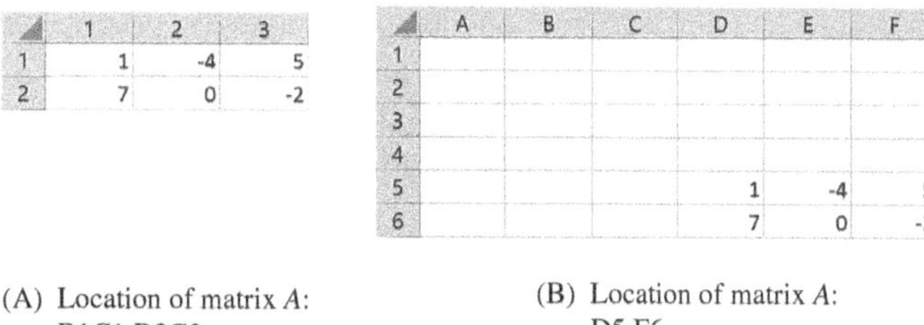

	1	2	3
1	1	-4	5
2	7	0	-2

	A	B	C	D	E	F
1						
2						
3						
4						
5				1	-4	5
6				7	0	-2

(A) Location of matrix A: R1C1:R2C3

(B) Location of matrix A: D5:F6

Figure 2 Matrix notation in a spreadsheet

Matrices serve as a shorthand for solving systems of linear equations. Associated with the system

$$\begin{aligned} 2x - 3y &= 5 \\ x + 2y &= -3 \end{aligned} \tag{2}$$

are its **coefficient matrix, constant matrix**, and **augmented matrix**:

Coefficient matrix	Constant matrix	Augmented matrix
$\begin{bmatrix} 2 & -3 \\ 1 & 2 \end{bmatrix}$	$\begin{bmatrix} 5 \\ -3 \end{bmatrix}$	$\left[\begin{array}{cc\|c} 2 & -3 & 5 \\ 1 & 2 & -3 \end{array}\right]$

Note that the augmented matrix is just the coefficient matrix, augmented by the constant matrix. The vertical bar is included only as a visual aid to separate the coefficients from the constant terms. The augmented matrix contains all of the essential information about the linear system—everything but the names of the variables.

For ease of generalization to the larger systems in later sections, we will change the notation for the variables in system (2) to a subscript form. That is, in place of x and y, we use x_1 and x_2, respectively, and system (2) is rewritten as

$$\begin{aligned} 2x_1 - 3x_2 &= 5 \\ x_1 + 2x_2 &= -3 \end{aligned}$$

In general, associated with each linear system of the form

$$\begin{aligned} a_{11}x_1 + a_{12}x_2 &= k_1 \\ a_{21}x_1 + a_{22}x_2 &= k_2 \end{aligned} \tag{3}$$

where x_1 and x_2 are variables, is the *augmented matrix* of the system:

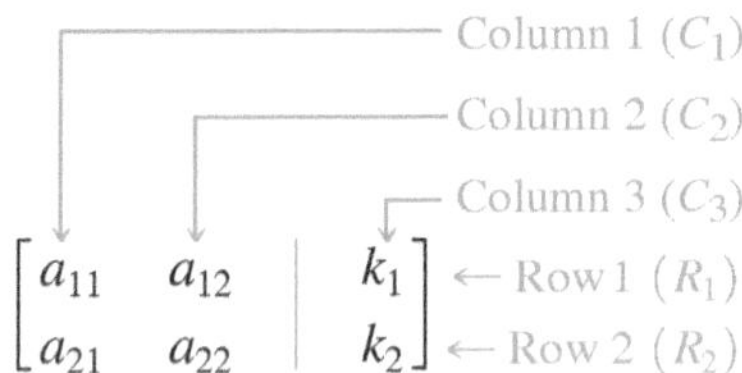

This matrix contains the essential parts of system (3). Our objective is to learn how to manipulate augmented matrices in order to solve system (3), if a solution exists. The manipulative process is closely related to the elimination process discussed in Section 4.1.

Recall that two linear systems are said to be equivalent if they have the same solution set. In Theorem 2, Section 4.1, we used the operations listed below to transform linear systems into equivalent systems:

(A) Two equations are interchanged.
(B) An equation is multiplied by a nonzero constant.
(C) A constant multiple of one equation is added to another equation.

Paralleling the earlier discussion, we say that two augmented matrices are **row equivalent**, denoted by the symbol ~ placed between the two matrices, if they are augmented matrices of equivalent systems of equations. How do we transform augmented matrices into row-equivalent matrices? We use Theorem 1, which is a direct consequence of the operations listed in Section 4.1.

THEOREM 1 Operations That Produce Row-Equivalent Matrices

An augmented matrix is transformed into a row-equivalent matrix by performing any of the following **row operations**:

(A) Two rows are interchanged $(R_i \leftrightarrow R_j)$.
(B) A row is multiplied by a nonzero constant $(kR_i \rightarrow R_i)$.
(C) A constant multiple of one row is added to another row $(kR_j + R_i \rightarrow R_i)$.

Note: The arrow $\rightarrow$ means "replaces."

Solving Linear Systems Using Augmented Matrices

We illustrate the use of Theorem 1 by several examples.

EXAMPLE 1 **Solving a System Using Augmented Matrix Methods** Solve using augmented matrix methods:

$$\begin{aligned} 3x_1 + 4x_2 &= 1 \\ x_1 - 2x_2 &= 7 \end{aligned} \tag{4}$$

SOLUTION We start by writing the augmented matrix corresponding to system (4):

$$\left[\begin{array}{cc|c} 3 & 4 & 1 \\ 1 & -2 & 7 \end{array}\right] \tag{5}$$

Our objective is to use row operations from Theorem 1 to try to transform matrix (5) into the form

$$\left[\begin{array}{cc|c} 1 & 0 & m \\ 0 & 1 & n \end{array}\right] \tag{6}$$

where m and n are real numbers. Then the solution to system (4) will be obvious, since matrix (6) will be the augmented matrix of the following system (a row in an augmented matrix always corresponds to an equation in a linear system):

$$\begin{aligned} x_1 &= m \qquad & x_1 + 0x_2 &= m \\ x_2 &= n \qquad & 0x_1 + x_2 &= n \end{aligned}$$

Now we use row operations to transform matrix (5) into form (6).

Step 1 To get a 1 in the upper left corner, we interchange R_1 and R_2 (Theorem 1A):

$$\left[\begin{array}{cc|c} 3 & 4 & 1 \\ 1 & -2 & 7 \end{array}\right] \begin{array}{c} R_1 \leftrightarrow R_2 \\ \sim \end{array} \left[\begin{array}{cc|c} 1 & -2 & 7 \\ 3 & 4 & 1 \end{array}\right]$$

Step 2 To get a 0 in the lower left corner, we multiply R_1 by (-3) and add to R_2 (Theorem 1C)—this changes R_2 but not R_1. Some people find it useful to write $(-3R_1)$ outside the matrix to help reduce errors in arithmetic, as shown:

$$\left[\begin{array}{cc|c} 1 & -2 & 1 \\ 3 & 4 & 7 \end{array}\right] \begin{array}{c} \\ (-3)R_1 \mathbin{\tilde{+}} R_2 \rightarrow R_2 \end{array} \left[\begin{array}{cc|c} 1 & -2 & 7 \\ 0 & 10 & -20 \end{array}\right]$$
$$\begin{array}{ccc} -3 & 6 & -21 \end{array}$$

Step 3 To get a 1 in the second row, second column, we multiply R_2 by $\frac{1}{10}$ (Theorem 1B):

$$\left[\begin{array}{cc|c} 1 & -2 & 7 \\ 0 & 10 & -20 \end{array}\right] \tfrac{1}{10}R_2 \underset{\sim}{\rightarrow} R_2 \left[\begin{array}{cc|c} 1 & -2 & 7 \\ 0 & 1 & -2 \end{array}\right]$$

Step 4 To get a 0 in the first row, second column, we multiply R_2 by 2 and add the result to R_1 (Theorem 1C)—this changes R_1 but not R_2:

$$\begin{array}{ccc} 0 & 2 & -4 \end{array}$$
$$\left[\begin{array}{cc|c} 1 & -2 & 7 \\ 0 & 1 & -2 \end{array}\right] \begin{array}{c} 2R_2 + R1 \rightarrow R1 \\ \sim \end{array} \left[\begin{array}{cc|c} 1 & 0 & 3 \\ 0 & 1 & -2 \end{array}\right]$$

We have accomplished our objective! The last matrix is the augmented matrix for the system

$$\begin{aligned} x_1 &= 3 \qquad & x_1 + 0x_2 &= 3 \\ x_2 &= -2 \qquad & 0x_1 + x_2 &= -2 \end{aligned} \tag{7}$$

Since system (7) is equivalent to system (4), our starting system, we have solved system (4); that is, $x_1 = 3$ and $x_2 = -2$.

CHECK

$$3x_1 + 4x_2 = 1 \qquad x_1 - 2x_2 = 7$$
$$3(3) + 4(-2) \stackrel{?}{=} 1 \qquad 3 - 2(-2) \stackrel{?}{=} 7$$
$$1 \stackrel{\checkmark}{=} 1 \qquad 7 \stackrel{\checkmark}{=} 7$$

The preceding process may be written more compactly as follows:

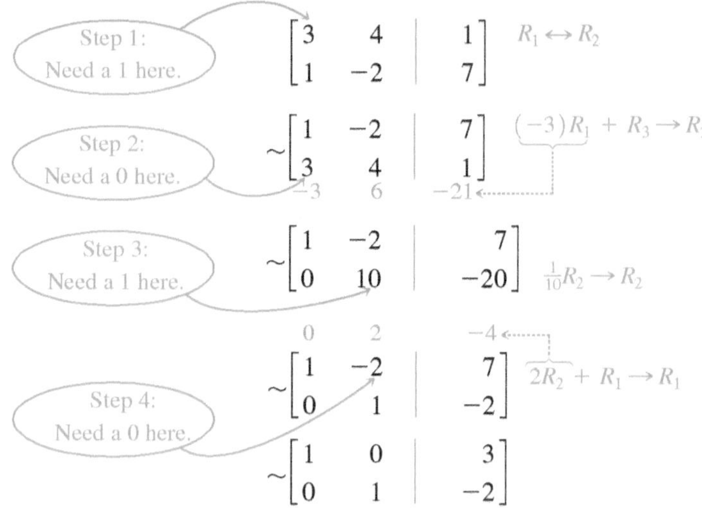

$$\begin{bmatrix} 3 & 4 & | & 1 \\ 1 & -2 & | & 7 \end{bmatrix} \quad R_1 \leftrightarrow R_2$$

$$\sim \begin{bmatrix} 1 & -2 & | & 7 \\ 3 & 4 & | & 1 \end{bmatrix} \quad (-3)R_1 + R_2 \to R_2$$

$$\sim \begin{bmatrix} 1 & -2 & | & 7 \\ 0 & 10 & | & -20 \end{bmatrix} \quad \tfrac{1}{10}R_2 \to R_2$$

$$\sim \begin{bmatrix} 1 & -2 & | & 7 \\ 0 & 1 & | & -2 \end{bmatrix} \quad 2R_2 + R_1 \to R_1$$

$$\sim \begin{bmatrix} 1 & 0 & | & 3 \\ 0 & 1 & | & -2 \end{bmatrix}$$

Therefore, $x_1 = 3$ and $x_2 = -2$.

Matched Problem 1 Solve using augmented matrix methods:

$$2x_1 - x_2 = -7$$
$$x_1 + 2x_2 = 4$$

Many graphing calculators can perform row operations. Figure 3 shows the results of performing the row operations used in the solution of Example 1. Consult your manual for the details of performing row operations on your graphing calculator.

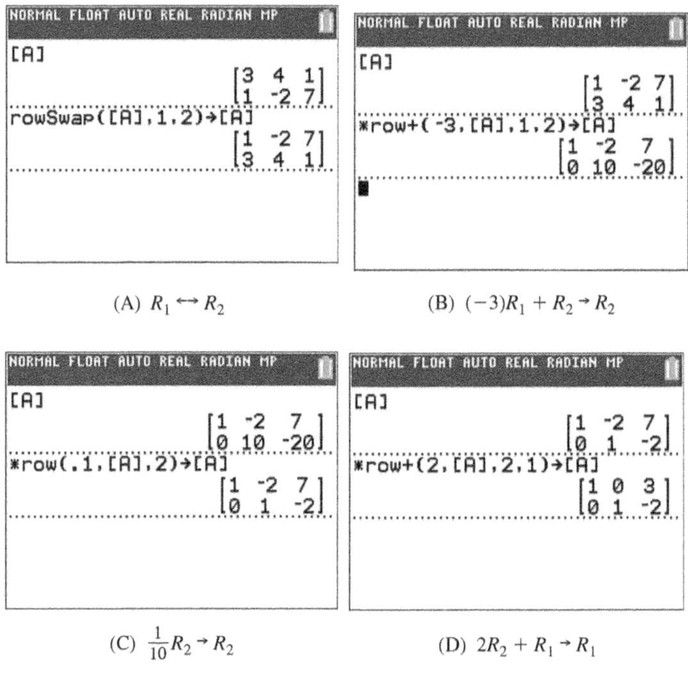

Figure 3 Row operations on a graphing calculator

Explore and Discuss 1

The summary following the solution of Example 1 shows five augmented matrices. Write the linear system that each matrix represents, solve each system graphically, and discuss the relationships among these solutions.

EXAMPLE 2 **Solving a System Using Augmented Matrix Methods** Solve using augmented matrix methods:

$$2x_1 - 3x_2 = 6$$
$$3x_1 + 4x_2 = \frac{1}{2}$$

SOLUTION

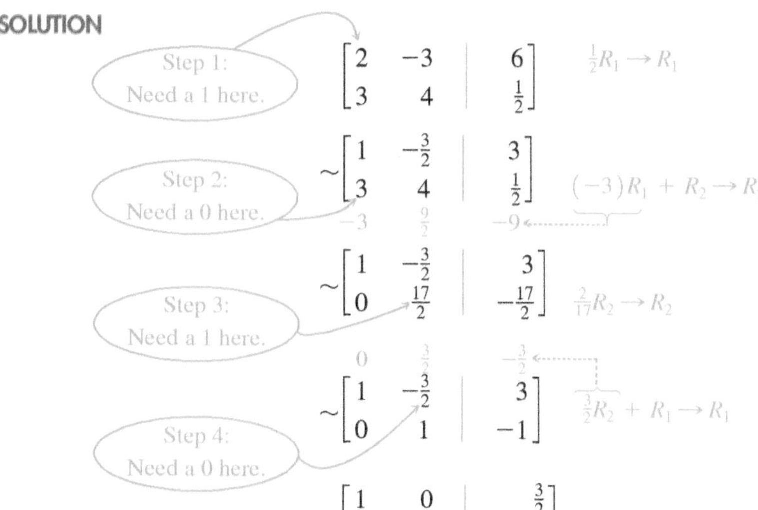

$$\begin{bmatrix} 2 & -3 & | & 6 \\ 3 & 4 & | & \frac{1}{2} \end{bmatrix} \quad \tfrac{1}{2}R_1 \to R_1$$

$$\sim \begin{bmatrix} 1 & -\frac{3}{2} & | & 3 \\ 3 & 4 & | & \frac{1}{2} \end{bmatrix} \quad (-3)R_1 + R_2 \to R_2$$

$$\quad -3 \quad \tfrac{9}{2} \qquad -9$$

$$\sim \begin{bmatrix} 1 & -\frac{3}{2} & | & 3 \\ 0 & \frac{17}{2} & | & -\frac{17}{2} \end{bmatrix} \quad \tfrac{2}{17}R_2 \to R_2$$

$$\quad 0 \quad \tfrac{3}{2} \qquad -\tfrac{3}{2}$$

$$\sim \begin{bmatrix} 1 & -\frac{3}{2} & | & 3 \\ 0 & 1 & | & -1 \end{bmatrix} \quad \tfrac{3}{2}R_2 + R_1 \to R_1$$

$$\sim \begin{bmatrix} 1 & 0 & | & \frac{3}{2} \\ 0 & 1 & | & -1 \end{bmatrix}$$

So, $x_1 = \frac{3}{2}$ and $x_2 = -1$. The check is left for you.

Matched Problem 2 Solve using augmented matrix methods:

$$5x_1 - 2x_2 = 11$$
$$2x_1 + 3x_2 = \frac{5}{2}$$

EXAMPLE 3 **Solving a System Using Augmented Matrix Methods** Solve using augmented matrix methods:

$$\begin{aligned} 2x_1 - x_2 &= 4 \\ -6x_1 + 3x_2 &= -12 \end{aligned} \tag{8}$$

SOLUTION

$$\begin{bmatrix} 2 & -1 & | & 4 \\ -6 & 3 & | & -12 \end{bmatrix} \quad \begin{matrix} \tfrac{1}{2}R_1 \to R_1 \text{ (to get a 1 in the upper left corner)} \\ \tfrac{1}{3}R_2 \to R_2 \text{ (this simplifies } R_2\text{)} \end{matrix}$$

$$\sim \begin{bmatrix} 1 & -\frac{1}{2} & | & 2 \\ -2 & 1 & | & -4 \end{bmatrix} \quad 2R_1 + R_2 \to R_2 \text{ (to get a 0 in the lower left corner)}$$

$$\quad 2 \quad -1 \qquad 4$$

$$\sim \begin{bmatrix} 1 & -\frac{1}{2} & | & 2 \\ 0 & 0 & | & 0 \end{bmatrix}$$

The last matrix corresponds to the system

$$\begin{aligned} x_1 - \frac{1}{2}x_2 &= 2 \qquad & x_1 - \frac{1}{2}x_2 &= 2 \\ 0 &= 0 \qquad & 0x_1 + 0x_2 &= 0 \end{aligned} \tag{9}$$

This system is equivalent to the original system. Geometrically, the graphs of the two original equations coincide, and there are infinitely many solutions. In general, if we end up with a row of zeros in an augmented matrix for a two-equation, two-variable system, the system is dependent, and there are infinitely many solutions.

We represent the infinitely many solutions using the same method that was used in Section 4.1, that is, by introducing a parameter. We start by solving $x_1 - \frac{1}{2}x_2 = 2$, the first equation in system (9), for either variable in terms of the other. We choose to solve for x_1 in terms of x_2 because it is easier:

$$x_1 = \frac{1}{2}x_2 + 2 \tag{10}$$

Now we introduce a parameter t (we can use other letters, such as k, s, p, q, and so on, to represent a parameter also). If we let $x_2 = t$, then for any real number t,

$$\begin{aligned} x_1 &= \frac{1}{2}t + 2 \\ x_2 &= t \end{aligned} \tag{11}$$

represents a solution of system (8). Using ordered-pair notation, we write: For any real number t,

$$\left(\frac{1}{2}t + 2, t\right) \tag{12}$$

is a solution of system (8). More formally, we write

$$\text{solution set} = \left\{\left(\frac{1}{2}t + 2, t\right) \middle| t \in R\right\} \tag{13}$$

Typically we use the less formal notations (11) or (12) to represent the solution set for problems of this type.

CHECK The following is a check that system (11) provides a solution to system (8) for any real number t:

$$\begin{aligned} 2x_1 - x_2 &= 4 \\ 2\left(\frac{1}{2}t + 2\right) - t &\stackrel{?}{=} 4 \\ t + 4 - t &\stackrel{?}{=} 4 \\ 4 &\stackrel{\checkmark}{=} 4 \end{aligned} \qquad \begin{aligned} -6x_1 + 3x_2 &= -12 \\ -6\left(\frac{1}{2}t + 2\right) + 3t &\stackrel{?}{=} -12 \\ -3t - 12 + 3t &\stackrel{?}{=} -12 \\ -12 &\stackrel{\checkmark}{=} -12 \end{aligned}$$

Matched Problem 3 Solve using augmented matrix methods:

$$\begin{aligned} -2x_1 + 6x_2 &= 6 \\ 3x_1 - 9x_2 &= -9 \end{aligned}$$

Explore and Discuss 2

The solution of Example 3 involved three augmented matrices. Write the linear system that each matrix represents, solve each system graphically, and discuss the relationships among these solutions.

EXAMPLE 4 **Solving a System Using Augmented Matrix Methods** Solve using augmented matrix methods:

$$\begin{aligned} 2x_1 + 6x_2 &= -3 \\ x_1 + 3x_2 &= 2 \end{aligned}$$

SOLUTION

$$\left[\begin{array}{cc|c} 2 & 6 & -3 \\ 1 & 3 & 2 \end{array}\right] \quad R_1 \leftrightarrow R_2$$

$$\sim \left[\begin{array}{cc|c} 1 & 3 & 2 \\ 2 & 6 & -3 \end{array}\right] \quad (-2)R_1 + R_2 \rightarrow R_2$$

$$\begin{array}{ccc} -2 & -6 & -4 \end{array}$$

$$\sim \left[\begin{array}{cc|c} 1 & 3 & 2 \\ 0 & 0 & -7 \end{array}\right] \quad R_2 \text{ implies the contradiction } 0 = -7.$$

This is the augmented matrix of the system

$$\begin{aligned} x_1 + 3x_2 &= 2 & \quad x_1 + 3x_2 &= 2 \\ 0 &= -7 & \quad 0x_1 + 0x_2 &= -7 \end{aligned}$$

The second equation is not satisfied by any ordered pair of real numbers. As we saw in Section 4.1, the original system is inconsistent and has no solution. If in a row of an augmented matrix, we obtain all zeros to the left of the vertical bar and a nonzero number to the right, the system is inconsistent and there are no solutions.

Matched Problem 4 Solve using augmented matrix methods:

$$\begin{aligned} 2x_1 - x_2 &= 3 \\ 4x_1 - 2x_2 &= -1 \end{aligned}$$

Summary

Examples 2, 3, and 4 illustrate the three possible solution types for a system of two linear equations in two variables, as discussed in Theorem 1, Section 4.1. Examining the final matrix form in each of these solutions leads to the following summary.

SUMMARY Possible Final Matrix Forms for a System of Two Linear Equations in Two Variables

Form 1: Exactly one solution (consistent and independent)	Form 2: Infinitely many solutions (consistent and dependent)	Form 3: No solution (inconsistent)
$\left[\begin{array}{cc\|c} 1 & 0 & m \\ 0 & 1 & n \end{array}\right]$	$\left[\begin{array}{cc\|c} 1 & m & n \\ 0 & 0 & 0 \end{array}\right]$	$\left[\begin{array}{cc\|c} 1 & m & n \\ 0 & 0 & p \end{array}\right]$

m, n, p are real numbers; $p \neq 0$

The process of solving systems of equations described in this section is referred to as **Gauss–Jordan elimination**. We formalize this method in the next section so that it will apply to systems of any size, including systems where the number of equations and the number of variables are not the same.

Exercises 4.2

W **Skills Warm-up Exercises**

Problems 1–14 refer to the following matrices: (If necessary, review the terminology at the beginning of Section 4.2.)

$$A = \begin{bmatrix} 2 & -4 & 0 \\ 6 & 1 & -5 \end{bmatrix}$$

$$B = \begin{bmatrix} -1 & 9 & 0 \\ -4 & 8 & 7 \\ 2 & 4 & 0 \end{bmatrix}$$

$$C = \begin{bmatrix} 2 & -3 & 0 \end{bmatrix}$$

$$D = \begin{bmatrix} -5 \\ 8 \end{bmatrix}$$

1. How many elements are there in A? In C?
2. How many elements are there in B? In D?
3. What is the size of B? Of D?
4. What is the size of A? Of C?
5. Which of the matrices is a column matrix?
6. Which of the matrices is a row matrix?
7. Which of the matrices is a square matrix?
8. Which of the matrices does not contain the element 0?

A

9. List the elements on the principal diagonal of A.
10. List the elements on the principal diagonal of B.
11. For matrix B, list the elements b_{21}, b_{12}, b_{33}.
12. For matrix A, list the elements a_{21}, a_{12}.
13. For matrix C, find $c_{11} + c_{12} + c_{13}$.
14. For matrix D, find $d_{11} + d_{21}$.

In Problems 15–18, write the coefficient matrix and the augmented matrix of the given system of linear equations.

15. $3x_1 + 5x_2 = 8$
$2x_1 - 4x_2 = -7$

16. $5x_1 + 7x_2 = 11$
$-4x_1 + 9x_2 = 16$

17. $x_1 + 4x_2 = 15$
$6x_1 = 18$

18. $5x_1 - x_2 = 10$
$3x_2 = 21$

In Problems 19–22, write the system of linear equations that is represented by the given augmented matrix. Assume that the variables are x_1 and x_2.

19. $\left[\begin{array}{cc|c} 2 & 5 & 7 \\ 1 & 4 & 9 \end{array}\right]$

20. $\left[\begin{array}{cc|c} 0 & 3 & 15 \\ -8 & 2 & 25 \end{array}\right]$

21. $\left[\begin{array}{cc|c} 4 & 0 & -10 \\ 0 & 8 & 40 \end{array}\right]$

22. $\left[\begin{array}{cc|c} 1 & -3 & 5 \\ 0 & 1 & 7 \end{array}\right]$

Perform the row operations indicated in Problems 23–34 on the following matrix:

$$\left[\begin{array}{cc|c} 2 & -4 & 6 \\ 1 & -3 & 5 \end{array}\right]$$

23. $R_1 \leftrightarrow R_2$

24. $R_2 \leftrightarrow R_1$

25. $2R_2 \rightarrow R_2$

26. $-2R_2 \rightarrow R_2$

27. $R_1 + R_2 \rightarrow R_1$

28. $R_1 + R_2 \rightarrow R_2$

29. $-\frac{1}{2}R_1 \rightarrow R_1$

30. $\frac{1}{2}R_1 \rightarrow R_1$

31. $(-1)R_2 + R_1 \rightarrow R_1$

32. $(-2)R_2 + R_1 \rightarrow R_1$

33. $(-3)R_2 + R_1 \rightarrow R_1$

34. $(-\frac{1}{2})R_1 + R_2 \rightarrow R_2$

Each of the matrices in Problems 35–42 is the result of performing a single row operation on the matrix A shown below. Identify the row operation.

$$A = \left[\begin{array}{cc|c} -1 & 2 & -3 \\ 6 & -3 & 12 \end{array}\right]$$

35. $\left[\begin{array}{cc|c} -1 & 2 & -3 \\ 2 & -1 & 4 \end{array}\right]$

36. $\left[\begin{array}{cc|c} -6 & 12 & -18 \\ 6 & -3 & 12 \end{array}\right]$

37. $\left[\begin{array}{cc|c} -1 & 2 & -3 \\ 0 & 9 & -6 \end{array}\right]$

38. $\left[\begin{array}{cc|c} 3 & 0 & 5 \\ 6 & -3 & 12 \end{array}\right]$

39. $\left[\begin{array}{cc|c} 1 & 1 & 1 \\ 6 & -3 & 12 \end{array}\right]$

40. $\left[\begin{array}{cc|c} -1 & 2 & -3 \\ 2 & 5 & 0 \end{array}\right]$

41. $\left[\begin{array}{cc|c} 6 & -3 & 12 \\ -1 & 2 & -3 \end{array}\right]$

42. $\left[\begin{array}{cc|c} -1 & 2 & -3 \\ 0 & 9 & -6 \end{array}\right]$

Solve Problems 43–46 using augmented matrix methods. Graph each solution set. Discuss the differences between the graph of an equation in the system and the graph of the system's solution set.

43. $3x_1 - 2x_2 = 6$
$4x_1 - 3x_2 = 6$

44. $x_1 - 2x_2 = 5$
$-2x_1 + 4x_2 = -10$

45. $3x_1 - 2x_2 = -3$
$-6x_1 + 4x_2 = 6$

46. $x_1 - 2x_2 = 1$
$-2x_1 + 5x_2 = 2$

Solve Problems 47 and 48 using augmented matrix methods. Write the linear system represented by each augmented matrix in your solution, and solve each of these systems graphically. Discuss the relationships among the solutions of these systems.

47. $x_1 + x_2 = 5$
$x_1 - x_2 = 1$

48. $x_1 - x_2 = 2$
$x_1 + x_2 = 6$

Each of the matrices in Problems 49–54 is the final matrix form for a system of two linear equations in the variables x_1 and x_2. Write the solution of the system.

49. $\left[\begin{array}{cc|c} 1 & 0 & -4 \\ 0 & 1 & 6 \end{array}\right]$

50. $\left[\begin{array}{cc|c} 1 & 0 & -4 \\ 0 & 1 & 7 \end{array}\right]$

51. $\left[\begin{array}{cc|c} 1 & 3 & 2 \\ 0 & 0 & 4 \end{array}\right]$

52. $\left[\begin{array}{cc|c} 1 & -2 & 7 \\ 0 & 0 & -9 \end{array}\right]$

53. $\left[\begin{array}{cc|c} 1 & -2 & 15 \\ 0 & 0 & 0 \end{array}\right]$

54. $\left[\begin{array}{cc|c} 1 & 7 & -9 \\ 0 & 0 & 0 \end{array}\right]$

B *Solve Problems 55–74 using augmented matrix methods.*

55. $\begin{aligned} x_1 - 2x_2 &= 1 \\ 2x_1 - x_2 &= 5 \end{aligned}$

56. $\begin{aligned} x_1 + 3x_2 &= 1 \\ 3x_1 - 2x_2 &= 14 \end{aligned}$

57. $\begin{aligned} x_1 - 3x_2 &= 9 \\ -2x_1 + x_2 &= -8 \end{aligned}$

58. $\begin{aligned} x_1 - 3x_2 &= -5 \\ -3x_1 - x_2 &= 5 \end{aligned}$

59. $\begin{aligned} 3x_1 - x_2 &= 2 \\ x_1 + 2x_2 &= 10 \end{aligned}$

60. $\begin{aligned} 2x_1 + x_2 &= 0 \\ x_1 - 2x_2 &= -5 \end{aligned}$

61. $\begin{aligned} x_1 + 2x_2 &= 4 \\ 2x_1 + 4x_2 &= -8 \end{aligned}$

62. $\begin{aligned} 2x_1 - 3x_2 &= -2 \\ -4x_1 + 6x_2 &= 7 \end{aligned}$

63. $\begin{aligned} 2x_1 + x_2 &= 6 \\ x_1 - x_2 &= -3 \end{aligned}$

64. $\begin{aligned} 3x_1 - x_2 &= -5 \\ x_1 + 3x_2 &= 5 \end{aligned}$

65. $\begin{aligned} 3x_1 - 6x_2 &= -9 \\ -2x_1 + 4x_2 &= 6 \end{aligned}$

66. $\begin{aligned} 2x_1 - 4x_2 &= -2 \\ -3x_1 + 6x_2 &= 3 \end{aligned}$

67. $\begin{aligned} 4x_1 - 2x_2 &= 2 \\ -6x_1 + 3x_2 &= -3 \end{aligned}$

68. $\begin{aligned} -6x_1 + 2x_2 &= 4 \\ 3x_1 - x_2 &= -2 \end{aligned}$

69. $\begin{aligned} 2x_1 + x_2 &= 1 \\ 4x_1 - x_2 &= -7 \end{aligned}$

70. $\begin{aligned} 2x_1 - x_2 &= -8 \\ 2x_1 + x_2 &= 8 \end{aligned}$

71. $\begin{aligned} 4x_1 - 6x_2 &= 8 \\ -6x_1 + 9x_2 &= -10 \end{aligned}$

72. $\begin{aligned} 2x_1 - 4x_2 &= -4 \\ -3x_1 + 6x_2 &= 4 \end{aligned}$

73. $\begin{aligned} -6x_1 + 8x_2 &= -18 \\ 9x_1 - 12x_2 &= 27 \end{aligned}$

74. $\begin{aligned} -2x_1 + 4x_2 &= 4 \\ 3x_1 - 6x_2 &= -6 \end{aligned}$

C *Solve Problems 75–80 using augmented matrix methods.*

75. $\begin{aligned} 3x_1 - x_2 &= 7 \\ 2x_1 + 3x_2 &= 1 \end{aligned}$

76. $\begin{aligned} 2x_1 - 3x_2 &= -8 \\ 5x_1 + 3x_2 &= 1 \end{aligned}$

77. $\begin{aligned} 3x_1 + 2x_2 &= 4 \\ 2x_1 - x_2 &= 5 \end{aligned}$

78. $\begin{aligned} 5x_1 + 2x_2 &= 23 \\ 7x_1 - 6x_2 &= -3 \end{aligned}$

79. $\begin{aligned} 0.2x_1 - 0.5x_2 &= 0.07 \\ 0.8x_1 - 0.3x_2 &= 0.79 \end{aligned}$

80. $\begin{aligned} 0.3x_1 - 0.6x_2 &= 0.18 \\ 0.5x_1 - 0.2x_2 &= 0.54 \end{aligned}$

Solve Problems 81–84 using augmented matrix methods. Use a graphing calculator to perform the row operations.

81. $\begin{aligned} 0.8x_1 + 2.88x_2 &= 4 \\ 1.25x_1 + 4.34x_2 &= 5 \end{aligned}$

82. $\begin{aligned} 2.7x_1 - 15.12x_2 &= 27 \\ 3.25x_1 - 18.52x_2 &= 33 \end{aligned}$

83. $\begin{aligned} 4.8x_1 - 40.32x_2 &= 295.2 \\ -3.75x_1 + 28.7x_2 &= -211.2 \end{aligned}$

84. $\begin{aligned} 5.7x_1 - 8.55x_2 &= -35.91 \\ 4.5x_1 + 5.73x_2 &= 76.17 \end{aligned}$

Answers to Matched Problems

1. $x_1 = -2, x_2 = 3$
2. $x_1 = 2, x_2 = -\frac{1}{2}$
3. The system is dependent. For t any real number, a solution is $x_1 = 3t - 3, x_2 = t$.
4. Inconsistent—no solution

4.3 Gauss–Jordan Elimination

- Reduced Matrices
- Solving Systems by Gauss–Jordan Elimination
- Application

Now that you have had some experience with row operations on simple augmented matrices, we consider systems involving more than two variables. We will not require a system to have the same number of equations as variables. Just as for systems of two linear equations in two variables, any linear system, regardless of the number of equations or number of variables, has either

1. Exactly one solution (consistent and independent), or
2. Infinitely many solutions (consistent and dependent), or
3. No solution (inconsistent).

Reduced Matrices

In the preceding section we used row operations to transform the augmented matrix for a system of two equations in two variables,

$$\left[\begin{array}{cc|c} a_{11} & a_{12} & k_1 \\ a_{21} & a_{22} & k_2 \end{array}\right] \qquad \begin{aligned} a_{11}x_1 + a_{12}x_2 &= k_1 \\ a_{21}x_1 + a_{22}x_2 &= k_2 \end{aligned}$$

into one of the following simplified forms:

$$\overset{\text{Form 1}}{\left[\begin{array}{cc|c} 1 & 0 & m \\ 0 & 1 & n \end{array}\right]} \quad \overset{\text{Form 2}}{\left[\begin{array}{cc|c} 1 & m & n \\ 0 & 0 & 0 \end{array}\right]} \quad \overset{\text{Form 3}}{\left[\begin{array}{cc|c} 1 & m & n \\ 0 & 0 & p \end{array}\right]} \qquad (1)$$

where m, n, and p are real numbers, $p \neq 0$. Each of these reduced forms represents a system that has a different type of solution set, and no two of these forms are row equivalent.

For large linear systems, it is not practical to list all such simplified forms; there are too many of them. Instead, we give a general definition of a simplified form called a **reduced matrix**, which can be applied to all matrices and systems, regardless of size.

DEFINITION Reduced Form

A matrix is said to be in **reduced row echelon form**, or, more simply, in **reduced form**, if

1. Each row consisting entirely of zeros is below any row having at least one nonzero element.
2. The leftmost nonzero element in each row is 1.
3. All other elements in the column containing the leftmost 1 of a given row are zeros.
4. The leftmost 1 in any row is to the right of the leftmost 1 in the row above.

The following matrices are in reduced form. Check each one carefully to convince yourself that the conditions in the definition are met.

Note that a row of a reduced matrix may have a leftmost 1 in the last column.

$$\left[\begin{array}{cc|c} 1 & 0 & 2 \\ 0 & 1 & -3 \end{array}\right] \quad \left[\begin{array}{ccc|c} 1 & 0 & 0 & 2 \\ 0 & 1 & 0 & -1 \\ 0 & 0 & 1 & 3 \end{array}\right] \quad \left[\begin{array}{cc|c} 1 & 0 & 3 \\ 0 & 1 & -1 \\ 0 & 0 & 0 \end{array}\right]$$

$$\left[\begin{array}{cccc|c} 1 & 4 & 0 & 0 & -3 \\ 0 & 0 & 1 & 0 & 2 \\ 0 & 0 & 0 & 1 & 6 \end{array}\right] \quad \left[\begin{array}{ccc|c} 1 & 0 & 4 & 0 \\ 0 & 1 & 3 & 0 \\ 0 & 0 & 0 & 1 \end{array}\right]$$

EXAMPLE 1 **Reduced Forms** The following matrices are not in reduced form. Indicate which condition in the definition is violated for each matrix. State the row operation(s) required to transform the matrix into reduced form, and find the reduced form.

(A) $\left[\begin{array}{cc|c} 0 & 1 & -2 \\ 1 & 0 & 3 \end{array}\right]$ (B) $\left[\begin{array}{ccc|c} 1 & 2 & -2 & 3 \\ 0 & 0 & 1 & -1 \end{array}\right]$

(C) $\left[\begin{array}{cc|c} 1 & 0 & -3 \\ 0 & 0 & 0 \\ 0 & 1 & -2 \end{array}\right]$ (D) $\left[\begin{array}{ccc|c} 1 & 0 & 0 & -1 \\ 0 & 2 & 0 & 3 \\ 0 & 0 & 1 & -5 \end{array}\right]$

SOLUTION

(A) Condition 4 is violated: The leftmost 1 in row 2 is not to the right of the leftmost 1 in row 1. Perform the row operation $R_1 \leftrightarrow R_2$ to obtain

$$\left[\begin{array}{cc|c} 1 & 0 & 3 \\ 0 & 1 & -2 \end{array}\right]$$

(B) Condition 3 is violated: The column containing the leftmost 1 in row 2 has a nonzero element above the 1. Perform the row operation $2R_2 + R_1 \to R_1$ to obtain

$$\left[\begin{array}{ccc|c} 1 & 2 & 0 & 1 \\ 0 & 0 & 1 & -1 \end{array}\right]$$

(C) Condition 1 is violated: The second row contains all zeros and is not below any row having at least one nonzero element. Perform the row operation $R_2 \leftrightarrow R_3$ to obtain

$$\left[\begin{array}{cc|c} 1 & 0 & -3 \\ 0 & 1 & -2 \\ 0 & 0 & 0 \end{array}\right]$$

(D) Condition 2 is violated: The leftmost nonzero element in row 2 is not a 1. Perform the row operation $\frac{1}{2}R_2 \to R_2$ to obtain

$$\left[\begin{array}{ccc|c} 1 & 0 & 0 & -1 \\ 0 & 1 & 0 & \frac{3}{2} \\ 0 & 0 & 1 & -5 \end{array}\right]$$

Matched Problem 1 The matrices below are not in reduced form. Indicate which condition in the definition is violated for each matrix. State the row operation(s) required to transform the matrix into reduced form, and find the reduced form.

(A) $\left[\begin{array}{cc|c} 1 & 0 & 2 \\ 0 & 3 & -6 \end{array}\right]$

(B) $\left[\begin{array}{ccc|c} 1 & 5 & 4 & 3 \\ 0 & 1 & 2 & -1 \\ 0 & 0 & 0 & 0 \end{array}\right]$

(C) $\left[\begin{array}{ccc|c} 0 & 1 & 0 & -3 \\ 1 & 0 & 0 & 0 \\ 0 & 0 & 1 & 2 \end{array}\right]$

(D) $\left[\begin{array}{ccc|c} 1 & 2 & 0 & 3 \\ 0 & 0 & 0 & 0 \\ 0 & 0 & 1 & 4 \end{array}\right]$

Solving Systems by Gauss–Jordan Elimination

We are now ready to outline the Gauss–Jordan method for solving systems of linear equations. The method systematically transforms an augmented matrix into a reduced form. The system corresponding to a reduced augmented matrix is called a **reduced system**. As we shall see, reduced systems are easy to solve.

The Gauss–Jordan elimination method is named after the German mathematician Carl Friedrich Gauss (1777–1885) and the German geodesist Wilhelm Jordan (1842–1899). Gauss, one of the greatest mathematicians of all time, used a method of solving systems of equations in his astronomical work that was later generalized by Jordan to solve problems in large-scale surveying.

EXAMPLE 2 **Solving a System Using Gauss–Jordan Elimination** Solve by Gauss–Jordan elimination:

$$\begin{aligned} 2x_1 - 2x_2 + x_3 &= 3 \\ 3x_1 + x_2 - x_3 &= 7 \\ x_1 - 3x_2 + 2x_3 &= 0 \end{aligned}$$

SOLUTION Write the augmented matrix and follow the steps indicated at the right.

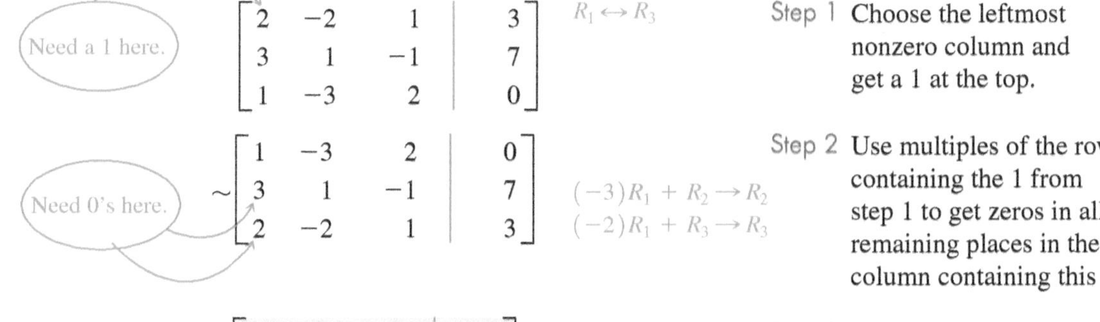

$$\begin{bmatrix} 2 & -2 & 1 & | & 3 \\ 3 & 1 & -1 & | & 7 \\ 1 & -3 & 2 & | & 0 \end{bmatrix} \quad R_1 \leftrightarrow R_3$$

Step 1 Choose the leftmost nonzero column and get a 1 at the top.

$$\sim \begin{bmatrix} 1 & -3 & 2 & | & 0 \\ 3 & 1 & -1 & | & 7 \\ 2 & -2 & 1 & | & 3 \end{bmatrix} \quad \begin{matrix} (-3)R_1 + R_2 \rightarrow R_2 \\ (-2)R_1 + R_3 \rightarrow R_3 \end{matrix}$$

Step 2 Use multiples of the row containing the 1 from step 1 to get zeros in all remaining places in the column containing this 1.

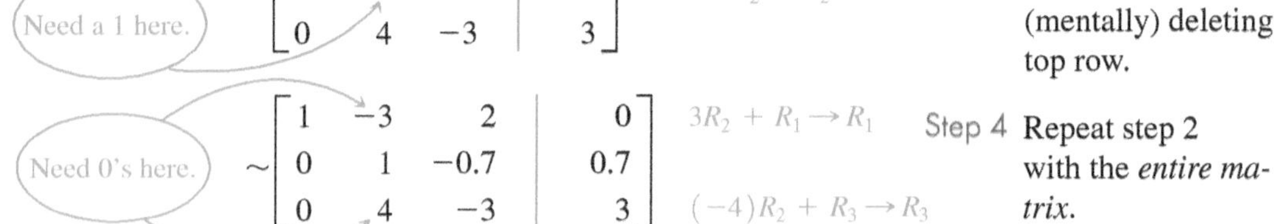

$$\sim \begin{bmatrix} 1 & -3 & 2 & | & 0 \\ 0 & 10 & -7 & | & 7 \\ 0 & 4 & -3 & | & 3 \end{bmatrix} \quad 0.1R_2 \rightarrow R_2$$

Step 3 Repeat step 1 with the *submatrix* formed by (mentally) deleting the top row.

$$\sim \begin{bmatrix} 1 & -3 & 2 & | & 0 \\ 0 & 1 & -0.7 & | & 0.7 \\ 0 & 4 & -3 & | & 3 \end{bmatrix} \quad \begin{matrix} 3R_2 + R_1 \rightarrow R_1 \\ (-4)R_2 + R_3 \rightarrow R_3 \end{matrix}$$

Step 4 Repeat step 2 with the *entire matrix*.

$$\sim \begin{bmatrix} 1 & 0 & -0.1 & | & 2.1 \\ 0 & 1 & -0.7 & | & 0.7 \\ 0 & 0 & -0.2 & | & 0.2 \end{bmatrix} \quad (-5)R_3 \rightarrow R_3$$

Step 3 Repeat step 1 with the *submatrix* formed by (mentally) deleting the top rows.

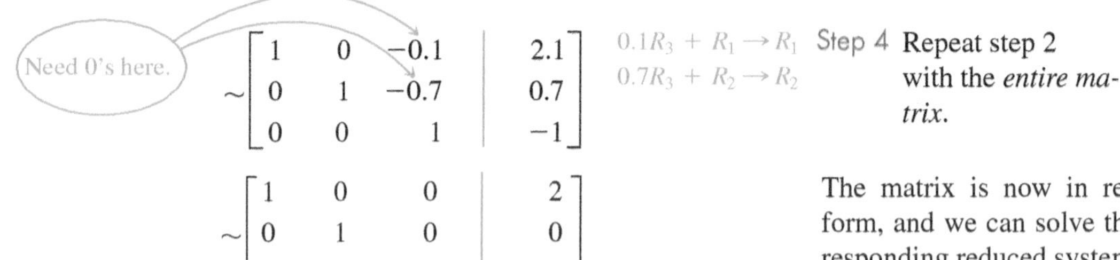

$$\sim \begin{bmatrix} 1 & 0 & -0.1 & | & 2.1 \\ 0 & 1 & -0.7 & | & 0.7 \\ 0 & 0 & 1 & | & -1 \end{bmatrix} \quad \begin{matrix} 0.1R_3 + R_1 \rightarrow R_1 \\ 0.7R_3 + R_2 \rightarrow R_2 \end{matrix}$$

Step 4 Repeat step 2 with the *entire matrix*.

$$\sim \begin{bmatrix} 1 & 0 & 0 & | & 2 \\ 0 & 1 & 0 & | & 0 \\ 0 & 0 & 1 & | & -1 \end{bmatrix}$$

The matrix is now in reduced form, and we can solve the corresponding reduced system.

$$\begin{aligned} x_1 \qquad\qquad &= 2 \\ x_2 \qquad &= 0 \\ x_3 &= -1 \end{aligned}$$

The solution to this system is $x_1 = 2, x_2 = 0, x_3 = -1$. You should check this solution in the original system.

Matched Problem 2 Solve by Gauss–Jordan elimination:

$$\begin{aligned} 3x_1 + x_2 - 2x_3 &= 2 \\ x_1 - 2x_2 + x_3 &= 3 \\ 2x_1 - x_2 - 3x_3 &= 3 \end{aligned}$$

PROCEDURE Gauss–Jordan Elimination

Step 1 Choose the leftmost nonzero column and use appropriate row operations to get a 1 at the top.

Step 2 Use multiples of the row containing the 1 from step 1 to get zeros in all remaining places in the column containing this 1.

Step 3 Repeat step 1 with the **submatrix** formed by (mentally) deleting the row used in step 2 and all rows above this row.

Step 4 Repeat step 2 with the **entire matrix,** including the rows deleted mentally. Continue this process until the entire matrix is in reduced form.

Note: If at any point in this process we obtain a row with all zeros to the left of the vertical line and a nonzero number to the right, we can stop before we find the reduced form since we will have a contradiction: $0 = n, n \neq 0$. We can then conclude that the system has no solution.

Remarks

1. Even though each matrix has a unique reduced form, the sequence of steps presented here for transforming a matrix into a reduced form is not unique. For example, it is possible to use row operations in such a way that computations involving fractions are minimized. But we emphasize again that we are not interested in the most efficient hand methods for transforming small matrices into reduced forms. Our main interest is in giving you a little experience with a method that is suitable for solving large-scale systems on a graphing calculator or computer.
2. Most graphing calculators have the ability to find reduced forms. Figure 1 illustrates the solution of Example 2 on a TI-84 Plus CE graphing calculator using the rref command (rref is an acronym for reduced row echelon form). Notice that in row 2 and column 4 of the reduced form the graphing calculator has displayed the very small number –3.5E – 13, instead of the exact value 0. This is a common occurrence on a graphing calculator and causes no problems. Just replace any very small numbers displayed in scientific notation with 0.

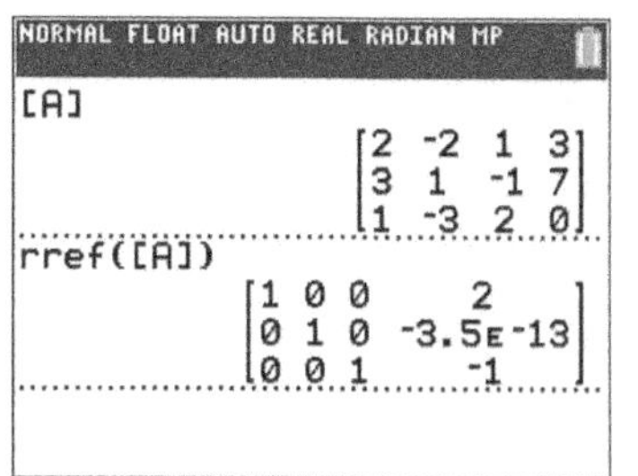

Figure 1 Gauss–Jordan elimination on a graphing calculator

EXAMPLE 3 **Solving a System Using Gauss–Jordan Elimination** Solve by Gauss–Jordan elimination:

$$\begin{aligned} 2x_1 - 4x_2 + x_3 &= -4 \\ 4x_1 - 8x_2 + 7x_3 &= 2 \\ -2x_1 + 4x_2 - 3x_3 &= 5 \end{aligned}$$

SOLUTION

$$\left[\begin{array}{rrr|r} 2 & -4 & 1 & -4 \\ 4 & -8 & 7 & 2 \\ -2 & 4 & -3 & 5 \end{array}\right] \quad 0.5R_1 \to R_1$$

$$\sim \left[\begin{array}{rrr|r} 1 & -2 & 0.5 & -2 \\ 4 & -8 & 7 & 2 \\ -2 & 4 & -3 & 5 \end{array}\right] \quad \begin{array}{l} (-4)R_1 + R_2 \to R_2 \\ 2R_1 + R_3 \to R_3 \end{array}$$

$$\sim \left[\begin{array}{rrr|r} 1 & -2 & 0.5 & -2 \\ 0 & 0 & 5 & 10 \\ 0 & 0 & -2 & 1 \end{array}\right] \quad 0.2R_2 \to R_2$$

Note that column 3 is the leftmost nonzero column in this submatrix.

$$\sim \left[\begin{array}{rrr|r} 1 & -2 & 0.5 & -2 \\ 0 & 0 & 1 & 2 \\ 0 & 0 & -2 & 1 \end{array}\right] \quad \begin{array}{l} (-0.5)R_2 + R_1 \to R_1 \\ \\ 2R_2 + R_3 \to R_3 \end{array}$$

$$\sim \left[\begin{array}{rrr|r} 1 & -2 & 0 & -3 \\ 0 & 0 & 1 & 2 \\ 0 & 0 & 0 & 5 \end{array}\right]$$

We stop the Gauss–Jordan elimination, even though the matrix is not in reduced form, since the last row produces a contradiction.

The system has no solution.

Matched Problem 3 Solve by Gauss–Jordan elimination:

$$\begin{aligned} 2x_1 - 4x_2 - x_3 &= -8 \\ 4x_1 - 8x_2 + 3x_3 &= 4 \\ -2x_1 + 4x_2 + x_3 &= 11 \end{aligned}$$

CAUTION Figure 2 shows the solution to Example 3 on a graphing calculator with a built-in reduced-form routine. Notice that the graphing calculator does not stop when a contradiction first occurs but continues on to find the reduced form. Nevertheless, the last row in the reduced form still produces a contradiction. Do not confuse this type of reduced form with one that represents a consistent system (see Fig. 1).

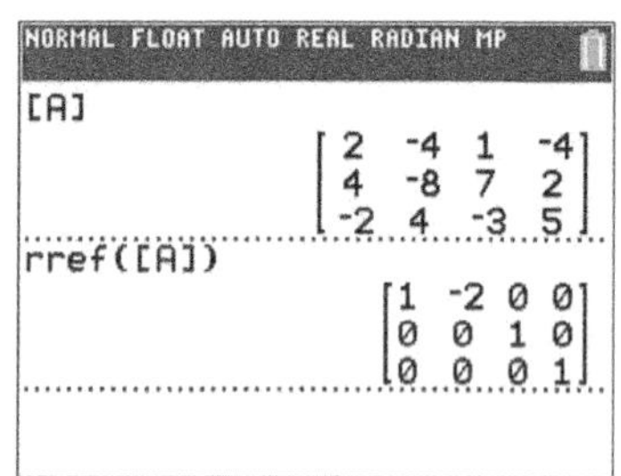

Figure 2 Recognizing contradictions on a graphing calculator

EXAMPLE 4 **Solving a System Using Gauss–Jordan Elimination** Solve by Gauss–Jordan elimination:

$$\begin{aligned} 3x_1 + 6x_2 - 9x_3 &= 15 \\ 2x_1 + 4x_2 - 6x_3 &= 10 \\ -2x_1 - 3x_2 + 4x_3 &= -6 \end{aligned}$$

SOLUTION

$$\left[\begin{array}{rrr|r} 3 & 6 & -9 & 15 \\ 2 & 4 & -6 & 10 \\ -2 & -3 & 4 & -6 \end{array}\right] \qquad \tfrac{1}{3}R_1 \to R_1$$

$$\sim \left[\begin{array}{rrr|r} 1 & 2 & -3 & 5 \\ 2 & 4 & -6 & 10 \\ -2 & -3 & 4 & -6 \end{array}\right] \qquad \begin{array}{l} (-2)R_1 + R_2 \to R_2 \\ 2R_1 + R_3 \to R_3 \end{array}$$

$$\sim \left[\begin{array}{rrr|r} 1 & 2 & -3 & 5 \\ 0 & 0 & 0 & 0 \\ 0 & 1 & -2 & 4 \end{array}\right] \qquad R_2 \leftrightarrow R_3$$

Note that we must interchange rows 2 and 3 to obtain a nonzero entry at the top of the second column of this submatrix.

$$\sim \left[\begin{array}{rrr|r} 1 & 2 & -3 & 5 \\ 0 & 1 & -2 & 4 \\ 0 & 0 & 0 & 0 \end{array}\right] \qquad (-2)R_2 + R_1 \to R_1$$

$$\sim \left[\begin{array}{rrr|r} 1 & 0 & 1 & -3 \\ 0 & 1 & -2 & 4 \\ 0 & 0 & 0 & 0 \end{array}\right]$$

The matrix is now in reduced form. Write the corresponding reduced system and solve.

⚠ CAUTION All-zero rows do not necessarily indicate that there are infinitely many solutions. These rows show that some of the information given by the equations was redundant. ▲

$$\begin{aligned} x_1 + x_3 &= -3 \\ x_2 - 2x_3 &= 4 \end{aligned}$$

We discard the equation corresponding to the third (all zero) row in the reduced form, since it is satisfied by all values of x_1, x_2, and x_3.

Note that the leftmost variable in each equation appears in one and only one equation. We solve for the leftmost variables x_1 and x_2 in terms of the remaining variable, x_3:

$$\begin{aligned} x_1 &= -x_3 - 3 \\ x_2 &= 2x_3 + 4 \end{aligned}$$

If we let $x_3 = t$, then for any real number t,

$$\begin{aligned} x_1 &= -t - 3 \\ x_2 &= 2t + 4 \\ x_3 &= t \end{aligned}$$

You should check that $(-t - 3, 2t + 4, t)$ is a solution of the original system for any real number t. Some particular solutions are

$t = 0$	$t = -2$	$t = 3.5$
$(-3, 4, 0)$	$(-1, 0, -2)$	$(-6.5, 11, 3.5)$

More generally,

If the number of leftmost 1's in a reduced augmented coefficient matrix is less than the number of variables in the system and there are no contradictions, then the system is dependent and has infinitely many solutions.

Describing the solution set to such a dependent system is not difficult. In a reduced system without contradictions, the **leftmost variables** correspond to the leftmost 1's in the corresponding reduced augmented matrix. The definition of reduced form for an augmented matrix ensures that each leftmost variable in the corresponding reduced system appears in one and only one equation of the system. Solving for each leftmost variable in terms of the remaining variables and writing a general solution to the system is usually easy. Example 5 illustrates a slightly more involved case.

Matched Problem 4 Solve by Gauss–Jordan elimination:

$$\begin{aligned} 2x_1 - 2x_2 - 4x_3 &= -2 \\ 3x_1 - 3x_2 - 6x_3 &= -3 \\ -2x_1 + 3x_2 + x_3 &= 7 \end{aligned}$$

Explore and Discuss 1

Explain why the definition of reduced form ensures that each leftmost variable in a reduced system appears in one and only one equation and no equation contains more than one leftmost variable. Discuss methods for determining whether a consistent system is independent or dependent by examining the reduced form.

EXAMPLE 5 **Solving a System Using Gauss–Jordan Elimination** Solve by Gauss–Jordan elimination:

$$\begin{aligned} x_1 + 2x_2 + 4x_3 + x_4 - x_5 &= 1 \\ 2x_1 + 4x_2 + 8x_3 + 3x_4 - 4x_5 &= 2 \\ x_1 + 3x_2 + 7x_3 \qquad\quad + 3x_5 &= -2 \end{aligned}$$

SOLUTION

$$\left[\begin{array}{ccccc|c} 1 & 2 & 4 & 1 & -1 & 1 \\ 2 & 4 & 8 & 3 & -4 & 2 \\ 1 & 3 & 7 & 0 & 3 & -2 \end{array}\right] \quad \begin{array}{l} (-2)R_1 + R_2 \to R_2 \\ (-1)R_1 + R_3 \to R_3 \end{array}$$

$$\sim \left[\begin{array}{ccccc|c} 1 & 2 & 4 & 1 & -1 & 1 \\ 0 & 0 & 0 & 1 & -2 & 0 \\ 0 & 1 & 3 & -1 & 4 & -3 \end{array}\right] \quad R_2 \leftrightarrow R_3$$

$$\sim \left[\begin{array}{ccccc|c} 1 & 2 & 4 & 1 & -1 & 1 \\ 0 & 1 & 3 & -1 & 4 & -3 \\ 0 & 0 & 0 & 1 & -2 & 0 \end{array}\right] \quad (-2)R_2 + R_1 \to R_1$$

$$\sim \left[\begin{array}{ccccc|c} 1 & 0 & -2 & 3 & -9 & 7 \\ 0 & 1 & 3 & -1 & 4 & -3 \\ 0 & 0 & 0 & 1 & -2 & 0 \end{array}\right] \quad \begin{array}{l} (-3)R_3 + R_1 \to R_1 \\ R_3 + R_2 \to R_2 \end{array}$$

$$\sim \left[\begin{array}{ccccc|c} 1 & 0 & -2 & 0 & -3 & 7 \\ 0 & 1 & 3 & 0 & 2 & -3 \\ 0 & 0 & 0 & 1 & -2 & 0 \end{array}\right] \quad \text{Matrix is in reduced form.}$$

$$\begin{aligned} x_1 - 2x_3 - 3x_5 &= 7 \\ x_2 + 3x_3 + 2x_5 &= -3 \\ x_4 - 2x_5 &= 0 \end{aligned}$$

Solve for the leftmost variables x_1, x_2, and x_4 in terms of the remaining variables x_3 and x_5:

$$\begin{aligned} x_1 &= 2x_3 + 3x_5 + 7 \\ x_2 &= -3x_3 - 2x_5 - 3 \\ x_4 &= 2x_5 \end{aligned}$$

If we let $x_3 = s$ and $x_5 = t$, then for any real numbers s and t,

$$\begin{aligned} x_1 &= 2s + 3t + 7 \\ x_2 &= -3s - 2t - 3 \\ x_3 &= s \\ x_4 &= 2t \\ x_5 &= t \end{aligned}$$

is a solution. The check is left for you.

Matched Problem 5 Solve by Gauss–Jordan elimination:

$$\begin{aligned} x_1 - x_2 + 2x_3 \qquad - 2x_5 &= 3 \\ -2x_1 + 2x_2 - 4x_3 - x_4 + x_5 &= -5 \\ 3x_1 - 3x_2 + 7x_3 + x_4 - 4x_5 &= 6 \end{aligned}$$

Application

Dependent systems of linear equations provide an excellent opportunity to discuss mathematical modeling in more detail. The process of using mathematics to solve real-world problems can be broken down into three steps (Fig. 3):

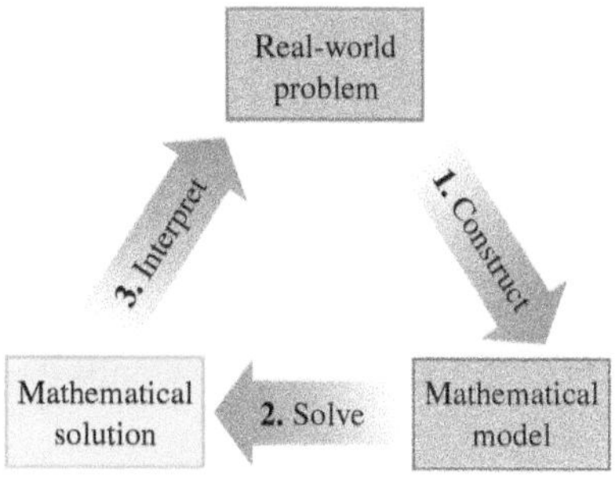

Figure 3

Step 1 *Construct* a mathematical model whose solution will provide information about the real-world problem.

Step 2 *Solve* the mathematical model.

Step 3 *Interpret* the solution to the mathematical model in terms of the original real-world problem.

In more complex problems, this cycle may have to be repeated several times to obtain the required information about the real-world problem.

EXAMPLE 6 **Purchasing** A company that rents small moving trucks wants to purchase 25 trucks with a combined capacity of 28,000 cubic feet. Three different types of trucks are available: a 10-foot truck with a capacity of 350 cubic feet, a 14-foot truck with a capacity of 700 cubic feet, and a 24-foot truck with a capacity of 1,400 cubic feet. How many of each type of truck should the company purchase?

SOLUTION The question in this example indicates that the relevant variables are the number of each type of truck:

$$\begin{aligned} x_1 &= \text{number of 10-foot trucks} \\ x_2 &= \text{number of 14-foot trucks} \\ x_3 &= \text{number of 24-foot trucks} \end{aligned}$$

Next we form the mathematical model:

$$\begin{aligned} x_1 + x_2 + x_3 &= 25 && \text{Total number of trucks} \\ 350x_1 + 700x_2 + 1{,}400x_3 &= 28{,}000 && \text{Total capacity} \end{aligned} \qquad (2)$$

Now we form the augmented matrix of the system and solve by Gauss–Jordan elimination:

$$\left[\begin{array}{ccc|c} 1 & 1 & 1 & 25 \\ 350 & 700 & 1{,}400 & 28{,}000 \end{array}\right] \quad \tfrac{1}{350}R_2 \to R_2$$

$$\sim \left[\begin{array}{ccc|c} 1 & 1 & 1 & 25 \\ 1 & 2 & 4 & 80 \end{array}\right] \quad -R_1 + R_2 \to R_2$$

$$\sim \left[\begin{array}{ccc|c} 1 & 1 & 1 & 25 \\ 0 & 1 & 3 & 55 \end{array}\right] \quad -R_2 + R_1 \to R_1$$

$$\sim \left[\begin{array}{ccc|c} 1 & 0 & -2 & -30 \\ 0 & 1 & 3 & 55 \end{array}\right] \quad \text{Matrix is in reduced form.}$$

$$\begin{aligned} x_1 - 2x_3 &= -30 \quad \text{or} \quad x_1 = 2x_3 - 30 \\ x_2 + 3x_3 &= 55 \quad \text{or} \quad x_2 = -3x_3 + 55 \end{aligned}$$

Let $x_3 = t$. Then for t any real number,

$$\begin{aligned} x_1 &= 2t - 30 \\ x_2 &= -3t + 55 \\ x_3 &= t \end{aligned} \qquad (3)$$

is a solution to mathematical model (2).

Now we must interpret this solution in terms of the original problem. Since the variables x_1, x_2, and x_3 represent numbers of trucks, they must be nonnegative real numbers. And since we can't purchase a fractional number of trucks, each must be a nonnegative whole number. Since $t = x_3$, it follows that t must also be a nonnegative whole number. The first and second equations in model (3) place additional restrictions on the values that t can assume:

$$x_1 = 2t - 30 \geq 0 \quad \text{implies that} \quad t \geq 15$$

$$x_2 = -3t + 55 \geq 0 \quad \text{implies that} \quad t \leq \frac{55}{3} = 18\tfrac{1}{3}$$

So the only possible values of t that will produce meaningful solutions to the original problem are 15, 16, 17, and 18. That is, the only combinations of 25 trucks that will result in a combined capacity of 28,000 cubic feet are $x_1 = 2t - 30$ 10-foot trucks, $x_2 = -3t + 55$ 14-foot trucks, and $x_3 = t$ 24-foot trucks, where $t = 15, 16, 17$, or 18. A table is a convenient way to display these solutions:

	10-Foot Truck	14-Foot Truck	24-Foot Truck
t	x_1	x_2	x_3
15	0	10	15
16	2	7	16
17	4	4	17
18	6	1	18

Matched Problem 6 A company that rents small moving trucks wants to purchase 16 trucks with a combined capacity of 19,200 cubic feet. Three different types of trucks are available: a cargo van with a capacity of 300 cubic feet, a 15-foot truck with a capacity of 900 cubic feet, and a 24-foot truck with a capacity of 1,500 cubic feet. How many of each type of truck should the company purchase?

Explore and Discuss 2

Refer to Example 6. The rental company charges \$19.95 per day for a 10-foot truck, \$29.95 per day for a 14-foot truck, and \$39.95 per day for a 24-foot truck. Which of the four possible choices in the table would produce the largest daily income from truck rentals?

Exercises 4.3

Skills Warm-up Exercises

W *In Problems 1–4, write the augmented matrix of the system of linear equations. (If necessary, review the terminology of Section 4.2.)*

1. $\begin{aligned} x_1 + 2x_2 + 3x_3 &= 12 \\ x_1 + 7x_2 - 5x_3 &= 15 \end{aligned}$

2. $\begin{aligned} 4x_1 + x_2 &= 8 \\ 3x_1 - 5x_2 &= 6 \\ x_1 + 9x_2 &= 4 \end{aligned}$

3. $\begin{aligned} x_1 \quad\quad + 6x_3 &= 2 \\ x_2 - x_3 &= 5 \\ x_1 + 3x_2 \quad\quad &= 7 \end{aligned}$

4. $\begin{aligned} 3x_1 + 4x_2 \quad\quad &= 10 \\ x_1 \quad\quad + 5x_3 &= 15 \\ -x_2 + x_3 &= 20 \end{aligned}$

In Problems 5–8, write the system of linear equations that is represented by the augmented matrix. Assume that the variables are $x_1, x_2, \ldots$.

5. $\left[\begin{array}{rr|r} 1 & -3 & 4 \\ 3 & 2 & 5 \\ -1 & 6 & 3 \end{array}\right]$

6. $\left[\begin{array}{rrr|r} -1 & 8 & -3 & 0 \\ 9 & -2 & 0 & 8 \end{array}\right]$

7. $\left[\begin{array}{cccc|c} 5 & -2 & 0 & 8 & 4 \end{array}\right]$

8. $\left[\begin{array}{ccc|c} 1 & 0 & -1 & 1 \\ -1 & 1 & 0 & 3 \\ 0 & 2 & 1 & -5 \end{array}\right]$

A *In Problems 9–18, if a matrix is in reduced form, say so. If not, explain why and indicate a row operation that completes the next step of Gauss–Jordan elimination.*

9. $\left[\begin{array}{cc|c} 1 & 0 & 3 \\ 0 & 1 & -2 \end{array}\right]$

10. $\left[\begin{array}{cc|c} 0 & 1 & 3 \\ 1 & 0 & -2 \end{array}\right]$

11. $\left[\begin{array}{cc|c} 0 & 1 & 5 \\ 1 & 0 & -1 \end{array}\right]$

12. $\left[\begin{array}{cc|c} 1 & 0 & 5 \\ 0 & 1 & -1 \end{array}\right]$

13. $\left[\begin{array}{ccc|c} 4 & 12 & -8 & 16 \\ 0 & 3 & -6 & 0 \\ 0 & 7 & -2 & 6 \end{array}\right]$

14. $\left[\begin{array}{ccc|c} 5 & 10 & -5 & -15 \\ 0 & 2 & -2 & 7 \\ 0 & 5 & -1 & 0 \end{array}\right]$

15. $\left[\begin{array}{ccc|c} 1 & 5 & -7 & 2 \\ 0 & 1 & -6 & 0 \\ 0 & 7 & -2 & 6 \end{array}\right]$

16. $\left[\begin{array}{ccc|c} 1 & 10 & -5 & -15 \\ 0 & 0 & -2 & 6 \\ 0 & 0 & 0 & 0 \end{array}\right]$

17. $\left[\begin{array}{ccc|c} 1 & 2 & 2 & 9 \\ 0 & 0 & -2 & 8 \\ 0 & 0 & 0 & 0 \end{array}\right]$

18. $\left[\begin{array}{ccc|c} 1 & 0 & -5 & -15 \\ 0 & 1 & -2 & 7 \\ 0 & 5 & -1 & 0 \end{array}\right]$

In Problems 19–28, write the solution of the linear system corresponding to each reduced augmented matrix.

19. $\left[\begin{array}{ccc|c} 1 & 0 & 0 & -2 \\ 0 & 1 & 0 & 3 \\ 0 & 0 & 1 & 0 \end{array}\right]$

20. $\left[\begin{array}{cccc|c} 1 & 0 & 0 & 0 & -2 \\ 0 & 1 & 0 & 0 & 0 \\ 0 & 0 & 1 & 0 & 1 \\ 0 & 0 & 0 & 1 & 3 \end{array}\right]$

21. $\left[\begin{array}{ccc|c} 1 & 0 & -2 & 3 \\ 0 & 1 & 1 & -5 \\ 0 & 0 & 0 & 0 \end{array}\right]$

22. $\left[\begin{array}{ccc|c} 1 & -2 & 0 & -3 \\ 0 & 0 & 1 & 5 \\ 0 & 0 & 0 & 0 \end{array}\right]$

23. $\left[\begin{array}{cc|c} 1 & 0 & 0 \\ 0 & 1 & 0 \\ 0 & 0 & 1 \end{array}\right]$

24. $\left[\begin{array}{cc|c} 1 & 0 & 7 \\ 0 & 1 & -8 \\ 0 & 0 & 0 \end{array}\right]$

25. $\left[\begin{array}{ccc|c} 1 & 0 & -3 & 5 \\ 0 & 1 & 2 & -7 \end{array}\right]$

26. $\left[\begin{array}{ccc|c} 1 & 0 & 1 & -4 \\ 0 & 1 & -1 & 6 \end{array}\right]$

27. $\left[\begin{array}{cccc|c} 1 & -2 & 0 & -3 & -5 \\ 0 & 0 & 1 & 3 & 2 \end{array}\right]$

28. $\left[\begin{array}{cccc|c} 1 & 0 & -2 & 3 & 4 \\ 0 & 1 & -1 & 2 & -1 \end{array}\right]$

29. In which of Problems 19, 21, 23, 25, and 27 is the number of leftmost ones equal to the number of variables?

30. In which of Problems 20, 22, 24, 26, and 28 is the number of leftmost ones equal to the number of variables?

31. In which of Problems 19, 21, 23, 25, and 27 is the number of leftmost ones less than the number of variables?

32. In which of Problems 20, 22, 24, 26, and 28 is the number of leftmost ones less than the number of variables?

In Problems 33–38, discuss the validity of each statement about linear systems. If the statement is always true, explain why. If not, give a counterexample.

33. If the number of leftmost ones is equal to the number of variables, then the system has exactly one solution.

34. If the number of leftmost ones is less than the number of variables, then the system has infinitely many solutions.

35. If the number of leftmost ones is equal to the number of variables and the system is consistent, then the system has exactly one solution.

36. If the number of leftmost ones is less than the number of variables and the system is consistent, then the system has infinitely many solutions.

37. If there is an all-zero row, then the system has infinitely many solutions.

38. If there are no all-zero rows, then the system has exactly one solution.

B *Use row operations to change each matrix in Problems 39–46 to reduced form.*

39. $\left[\begin{array}{cc|c} 1 & 2 & -1 \\ 0 & 1 & 3 \end{array}\right]$

40. $\left[\begin{array}{cc|c} 1 & 3 & 1 \\ 0 & 2 & -4 \end{array}\right]$

41. $\left[\begin{array}{ccc|c} 1 & 1 & 1 & 16 \\ 2 & 3 & 4 & 25 \end{array}\right]$

42. $\left[\begin{array}{ccc|c} 1 & 1 & 1 & 8 \\ 3 & 5 & 7 & 30 \end{array}\right]$

43. $\left[\begin{array}{ccc|c} 1 & 0 & -3 & 1 \\ 0 & 1 & 2 & 0 \\ 0 & 0 & 3 & -6 \end{array}\right]$

44. $\left[\begin{array}{ccc|c} 1 & 0 & 4 & 0 \\ 0 & 1 & -3 & -1 \\ 0 & 0 & -2 & 2 \end{array}\right]$

45. $\left[\begin{array}{ccc|c} 1 & 2 & -2 & -1 \\ 0 & 3 & -6 & -3 \\ 0 & -1 & 2 & 1 \end{array}\right]$

46. $\left[\begin{array}{ccc|c} 1 & -2 & 3 & -5 \\ 0 & 4 & -8 & -4 \\ 0 & -1 & 2 & 1 \end{array}\right]$

Solve Problems 47–62 using Gauss–Jordan elimination.

47. $\begin{aligned} 2x_1 + 4x_2 - 10x_3 &= -2 \\ 3x_1 + 9x_2 - 21x_3 &= 0 \\ x_1 + 5x_2 - 12x_3 &= 1 \end{aligned}$

48. $\begin{aligned} 3x_1 + 5x_2 - x_3 &= -7 \\ x_1 + x_2 + x_3 &= -1 \\ 2x_1 + 11x_3 &= 7 \end{aligned}$

49. $\begin{aligned} 3x_1 + 8x_2 - x_3 &= -18 \\ 2x_1 + x_2 + 5x_3 &= 8 \\ 2x_1 + 4x_2 + 2x_3 &= -4 \end{aligned}$

50. $\begin{aligned} 2x_1 + 6x_2 + 15x_3 &= -12 \\ 4x_1 + 7x_2 + 13x_3 &= -10 \\ 3x_1 + 6x_2 + 12x_3 &= -9 \end{aligned}$

51. $\begin{aligned} 2x_1 - x_2 - 3x_3 &= 8 \\ x_1 - 2x_2 &= 7 \end{aligned}$

52. $\begin{aligned} 2x_1 + 4x_2 - 6x_3 &= 10 \\ 3x_1 + 3x_2 - 3x_3 &= 6 \end{aligned}$

53. $\begin{aligned} 2x_1 - x_2 &= 0 \\ 3x_1 + 2x_2 &= 7 \\ x_1 - x_2 &= -1 \end{aligned}$

54. $\begin{aligned} 2x_1 - x_2 &= 0 \\ 3x_1 + 2x_2 &= 7 \\ x_1 - x_2 &= -2 \end{aligned}$

55. $\begin{aligned} 3x_1 - 4x_2 - x_3 &= 1 \\ 2x_1 - 3x_2 + x_3 &= 1 \\ x_1 - 2x_2 + 3x_3 &= 2 \end{aligned}$

56. $\begin{aligned} 3x_1 + 7x_2 - x_3 &= 11 \\ x_1 + 2x_2 - x_3 &= 3 \\ 2x_1 + 4x_2 - 2x_3 &= 10 \end{aligned}$

57. $$\begin{aligned} 3x_1 - 2x_2 + x_3 &= -7 \\ 2x_1 + x_2 - 4x_3 &= 0 \\ x_1 + x_2 - 3x_3 &= 1 \end{aligned}$$

58. $$\begin{aligned} 2x_1 + 3x_2 + 5x_3 &= 21 \\ x_1 - x_2 - 5x_3 &= -2 \\ 2x_1 + x_2 - x_3 &= 11 \end{aligned}$$

59. $$\begin{aligned} 2x_1 + 4x_2 - 2x_3 &= 2 \\ -3x_1 - 6x_2 + 3x_3 &= -3 \end{aligned}$$

60. $$\begin{aligned} 4x_1 - 16x_2 + 8x_3 &= -20 \\ -5x_1 + 20x_2 - 10x_3 &= 25 \end{aligned}$$

61. $$\begin{aligned} 4x_1 - x_2 + 2x_3 &= 3 \\ -4x_1 + x_2 - 3x_3 &= -10 \\ 8x_1 - 2x_2 + 9x_3 &= -1 \end{aligned}$$

62. $$\begin{aligned} 4x_1 - 2x_2 + 2x_3 &= 5 \\ -6x_1 + 3x_2 - 3x_3 &= -2 \\ 10x_1 - 5x_2 + 9x_3 &= 4 \end{aligned}$$

63. Consider a consistent system of three linear equations in three variables. Discuss the nature of the system and its solution set if the reduced form of the augmented coefficient matrix has

(A) One leftmost 1 (B) Two leftmost 1's

(C) Three leftmost 1's (D) Four leftmost 1's

64. Consider a system of three linear equations in three variables. Give examples of two reduced forms that are not row-equivalent if the system is

(A) Consistent and dependent

(B) Inconsistent

C *Solve Problems 65–70 using Gauss–Jordan elimination.*

65. $$\begin{aligned} x_1 + 2x_2 - 4x_3 - x_4 &= 7 \\ 2x_1 + 5x_2 - 9x_3 - 4x_4 &= 16 \\ x_1 + 5x_2 - 7x_3 - 7x_4 &= 13 \end{aligned}$$

66. $$\begin{aligned} 2x_1 + 4x_2 + 5x_3 + 4x_4 &= 8 \\ x_1 + 2x_2 + 2x_3 + x_4 &= 3 \end{aligned}$$

67. $$\begin{aligned} x_1 - x_2 + 3x_3 - 2x_4 &= 1 \\ -2x_1 + 4x_2 - 3x_3 + x_4 &= 0.5 \\ 3x_1 - x_2 + 10x_3 - 4x_4 &= 2.9 \\ 4x_1 - 3x_2 + 8x_3 - 2x_4 &= 0.6 \end{aligned}$$

68. $$\begin{aligned} x_1 + x_2 + 4x_3 + x_4 &= 1.3 \\ -x_1 + x_2 - x_3 &= 1.1 \\ 2x_1 + x_3 + 3x_4 &= -4.4 \\ 2x_1 + 5x_2 + 11x_3 + 3x_4 &= 5.6 \end{aligned}$$

69. $$\begin{aligned} x_1 - 2x_2 + x_3 + x_4 + 2x_5 &= 2 \\ -2x_1 + 4x_2 + 2x_3 + 2x_4 - 2x_5 &= 0 \\ 3x_1 - 6x_2 + x_3 + x_4 + 5x_5 &= 4 \\ -x_1 + 2x_2 + 3x_3 + x_4 + x_5 &= 3 \end{aligned}$$

70. $$\begin{aligned} x_1 - 3x_2 + x_3 + x_4 + 2x_5 &= 2 \\ -x_1 + 5x_2 + 2x_3 + 2x_4 - 2x_5 &= 0 \\ 2x_1 - 6x_2 + 2x_3 + 2x_4 + 4x_5 &= 4 \\ -x_1 + 3x_2 - x_3 + x_5 &= -3 \end{aligned}$$

71. Find a, b, and c so that the graph of the quadratic equation $y = ax^2 + bx + c$ passes through the points $(-2, 9)$, $(1, -9)$, and $(4, 9)$.

72. Find a, b, and c so that the graph of the quadratic equation $y = ax^2 + bx + c$ passes through the points $(-1, -5)$, $(2, 7)$, and $(5, 1)$.

Applications

Construct a mathematical model for each of the following problems. (The answers in the back of the book include both the mathematical model and the interpretation of its solution.) Use Gauss–Jordan elimination to solve the model and then interpret the solution.

73. **Boat production.** A small manufacturing plant makes three types of inflatable boats: one-person, two-person, and four-person models. Each boat requires the services of three departments, as listed in the table. The cutting, assembly, and packaging departments have available a maximum of 380, 330, and 120 labor-hours per week, respectively.

Department	One-Person Boat	Two-Person Boat	Four-Person Boat
Cutting	0.5 hr	1.0 hr	1.5 hr
Assembly	0.6 hr	0.9 hr	1.2 hr
Packaging	0.2 hr	0.3 hr	0.5 hr

(A) How many boats of each type must be produced each week for the plant to operate at full capacity?

(B) How is the production schedule in part (A) affected if the packaging department is no longer used?

(C) How is the production schedule in part (A) affected if the four-person boat is no longer produced?

74. **Production scheduling.** Repeat Problem 73 assuming that the cutting, assembly, and packaging departments have available a maximum of 350, 330, and 115 labor-hours per week, respectively.

75. **Tank car leases.** A chemical manufacturer wants to lease a fleet of 24 railroad tank cars with a combined carrying capacity of 520,000 gallons. Tank cars with three different carrying capacities are available: 8,000 gallons, 16,000 gallons, and 24,000 gallons. How many of each type of tank car should be leased?

76. **Airplane leases.** A corporation wants to lease a fleet of 12 airplanes with a combined carrying capacity of 220 passengers. The three available types of planes carry 10, 15, and 20 passengers, respectively. How many of each type of plane should be leased?

77. **Tank car leases.** Refer to Problem 75. The cost of leasing an 8,000-gallon tank car is \$450 per month, a 16,000-gallon tank car is \$650 per month, and a 24,000-gallon tank car is \$1,150 per month. Which of the solutions to Problem 75 would minimize the monthly leasing cost?

78. **Airplane leases.** Refer to Problem 76. The cost of leasing a 10-passenger airplane is \$8,000 per month, a 15-passenger airplane is \$14,000 per month, and a 20-passenger airplane is \$16,000 per month. Which of the solutions to Problem 76 would minimize the monthly leasing cost?

79. **Income tax.** A corporation has a taxable income of \$7,650,000. At this income level, the federal income tax rate is 50%, the state tax rate is 20%, and the local tax rate is 10%. If each tax rate is applied to the total taxable income, the resulting tax liability for the corporation would be 80% of taxable income. However, it is customary to deduct taxes paid to one agency before computing taxes for the other agencies. Assume that the federal taxes are based on the income that remains after the state and local taxes are deducted, and that state and local taxes are computed in a similar manner. What is the tax liability of the corporation (as a percentage of taxable income) if these deductions are taken into consideration?

80. **Income tax.** Repeat Problem 79 if local taxes are not allowed as a deduction for federal and state taxes.

81. **Taxable income.** As a result of several mergers and acquisitions, stock in four companies has been distributed among the companies. Each row of the following table gives the percentage of stock in the four companies that a particular company owns and the annual net income of each company (in millions of dollars):

	Percentage of Stock Owned in Company				Annual Net Income
Company	A	B	C	D	Million \$
A	71	8	3	7	3.2
B	12	81	11	13	2.6
C	11	9	72	8	3.8
D	6	2	14	72	4.4

So company *A* holds 71% of its own stock, 8% of the stock in company *B*, 3% of the stock in company *C*, etc. For the purpose of assessing a state tax on corporate income, the taxable income of each company is defined to be its share of its own annual net income plus its share of the taxable income of each of the other companies, as determined by the percentages in the table. What is the taxable income of each company (to the nearest thousand dollars)?

82. **Taxable income.** Repeat Problem 81 if tax law is changed so that the taxable income of a company is defined to be all of its own annual net income plus its share of the taxable income of each of the other companies.

83. **Nutrition.** A dietitian in a hospital is to arrange a special diet composed of three basic foods. The diet is to include exactly 340 units of calcium, 180 units of iron, and 220 units of vitamin A. The number of units per ounce of each special ingredient for each of the foods is indicated in the table.

	Units per Ounce		
	Food A	Food B	Food C
Calcium	30	10	20
Iron	10	10	20
Vitamin A	10	30	20

(A) How many ounces of each food must be used to meet the diet requirements?

(B) How is the diet in part (A) affected if food *C* is not used?

(C) How is the diet in part (A) affected if the vitamin A requirement is dropped?

84. **Nutrition.** Repeat Problem 83 if the diet is to include exactly 400 units of calcium, 160 units of iron, and 240 units of vitamin A.

85. **Plant food.** A farmer can buy four types of plant food. Each barrel of mix *A* contains 30 pounds of phosphoric acid, 50 pounds of nitrogen, and 30 pounds of potash; each barrel of mix *B* contains 30 pounds of phosphoric acid, 75 pounds of nitrogen, and 20 pounds of potash; each barrel of mix *C* contains 30 pounds of phosphoric acid, 25 pounds of nitrogen, and 20 pounds of potash; and each barrel of mix *D* contains 60 pounds of phosphoric acid, 25 pounds of nitrogen, and 50 pounds of potash. Soil tests indicate that a particular field needs 900 pounds of phosphoric acid, 750 pounds of nitrogen, and 700 pounds of potash. How many barrels of each type of food should the farmer mix together to supply the necessary nutrients for the field?

86. **Animal feed.** In a laboratory experiment, rats are to be fed 5 packets of food containing a total of 80 units of vitamin E. There are four different brands of food packets that can be used. A packet of brand *A* contains 5 units of vitamin E, a packet of brand *B* contains 10 units of vitamin E, a packet of brand *C* contains 15 units of vitamin E, and a packet of brand *D* contains 20 units of vitamin E. How many packets of each brand should be mixed and fed to the rats?

87. **Plant food.** Refer to Problem 85. The costs of the four mixes are Mix *A*, \$46; Mix *B*, \$72; Mix *C*, \$57; and Mix *D*, \$63. Which of the solutions to Problem 85 would minimize the cost of the plant food?

88. **Animal feed.** Refer to Problem 86. The costs of the four brands are Brand *A*, \$1.50; Brand *B*, \$3.00; Brand *C*, \$3.75; and Brand *D*, \$2.25. Which of the solutions to Problem 86 would minimize the cost of the rat food?

89. **Population growth.** The population of Spain was approximately 34 million in 1970, 39 million in 1990, and 46 million in 2010. Construct a model for this data by finding a quadratic equation whose graph passes through the points (0,34), (20,39), and (40,46). Use this model to estimate the population in 2030.

90. **Population growth.** The population of Turkey was approximately 35 million in 1970, 56 million in 1990, and 73 million in 2010. Construct a model for this data by finding a quadratic equation whose graph passes through the points (0,35), (20,56), and (40,73). Use this model to estimate the population in 2030.

91. **Female life expectancy.** The life expectancy for females born during 1980–1985 was approximately 77.6 years. This grew to 78 years during 1985–1990 and to 78.6 years during 1990–1995. Construct a model for this data by finding a quadratic equation whose graph passes through the points (0, 77.6), (5, 78), and (10, 78.6). Use this model to estimate the life expectancy for females born between 1995 and 2000 and for those born between 2000 and 2005.

92. **Male life expectancy.** The life expectancy for males born during 1980–1985 was approximately 70.7 years. This grew to 71.1 years during 1985–1990 and to 71.8 years during 1990–1995. Construct a model for this data by finding a

quadratic equation whose graph passes through the points (0, 70.7), (5, 71.1), and (10, 71.8). Use this model to estimate the life expectancy for males born between 1995 and 2000 and for those born between 2000 and 2005.

93. Female life expectancy. Refer to Problem 91. Subsequent data indicated that life expectancy grew to 79.1 years for females born during 1995–2000 and to 79.7 years for females born during 2000–2005. Add the points (15, 79.1) and (20, 79.7) to the data set in Problem 91. Use a graphing calculator to find a quadratic regression model for all five data points. Graph the data and the model in the same viewing window.

94. Male life expectancy. Refer to Problem 92. Subsequent data indicated that life expectancy grew to 73.2 years for males born during 1995–2000 and to 74.3 years for males born during 2000–2005. Add the points (15, 73.2) and (20, 74.3) to the data set in Problem 92. Use a graphing calculator to find a quadratic regression model for all five data points. Graph the data and the model in the same viewing window.

95. Sociology. Two sociologists have grant money to study school busing in a particular city. They wish to conduct an opinion survey using 600 telephone contacts and 400 house contacts. Survey company *A* has personnel to do 30 telephone and 10 house contacts per hour; survey company *B* can handle 20 telephone and 20 house contacts per hour. How many hours should be scheduled for each firm to produce exactly the number of contacts needed?

96. Sociology. Repeat Problem 95 if 650 telephone contacts and 350 house contacts are needed.

97. Traffic flow. The rush-hour traffic flow for a network of four one-way streets in a city is shown in the figure. The numbers next to each street indicate the number of vehicles per hour that enter and leave the network on that street. The variables x_1, x_2, x_3, and x_4 represent the flow of traffic between the four intersections in the network.

(A) For a smooth traffic flow, the number of vehicles entering each intersection should always equal the number leaving. For example, since 1,200 vehicles enter the intersection of Old Street and Baker Street each hour and $x_1 + x_4$ vehicles leave this intersection, we see that $x_1 + x_4 = 1{,}200$. Find the equations determined by the traffic flow at each of the other three intersections.

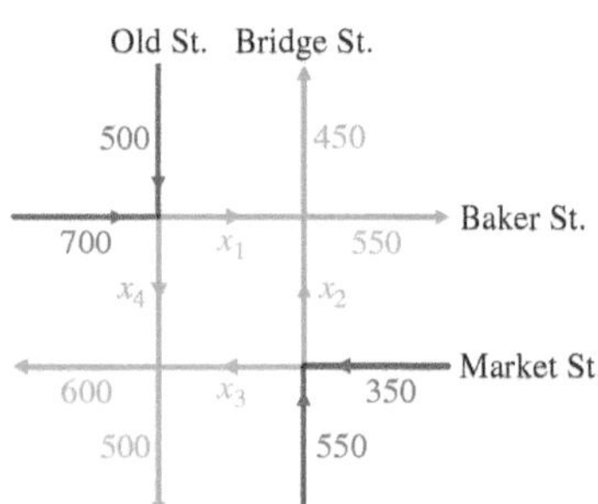

(B) Find the solution to the system in part (A).

(C) What is the maximum number of vehicles that can travel from Baker Street to Market Street on Old Street? What is the minimum number?

(D) If traffic lights are adjusted so that 600 vehicles per hour travel from Baker Street to Market Street on Old Street, determine the flow around the rest of the network.

98. Traffic flow. Refer to Problem 97. Closing Bridge Street north of Baker Street for construction changes the traffic flow for the network as indicated in the figure. Repeat parts (A)–(D) of Problem 97 for this traffic flow.

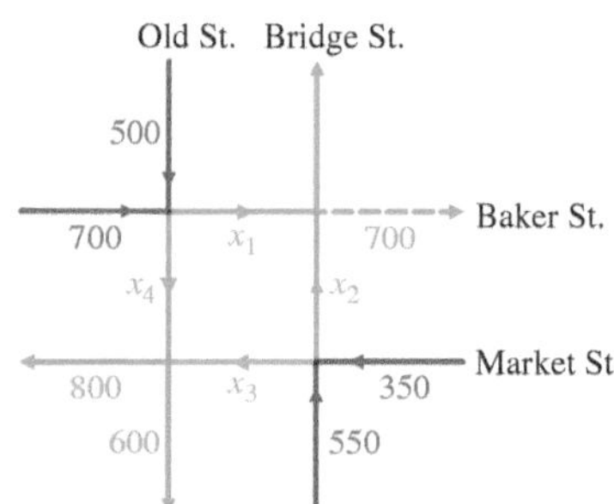

Answers to Matched Problems

1. (A) Condition 2 is violated: The 3 in row 2 and column 2 should be a 1. Perform the operation $\frac{1}{3}R_2 \rightarrow R_2$ to obtain

$$\left[\begin{array}{cc|c} 1 & 0 & 2 \\ 0 & 1 & -2 \end{array}\right]$$

(B) Condition 3 is violated: The 5 in row 1 and column 2 should be a 0. Perform the operation $(-5)R_2 + R_1 \rightarrow R_1$ to obtain

$$\left[\begin{array}{ccc|c} 1 & 0 & -6 & 8 \\ 0 & 1 & 2 & -1 \\ 0 & 0 & 0 & 0 \end{array}\right]$$

(C) Condition 4 is violated. The leftmost 1 in the second row is not to the right of the leftmost 1 in the first row. Perform the operation $R_1 \leftrightarrow R_2$ to obtain

$$\left[\begin{array}{ccc|c} 1 & 0 & 0 & 0 \\ 0 & 1 & 0 & -3 \\ 0 & 0 & 1 & 2 \end{array}\right]$$

(D) Condition 1 is violated: The all-zero second row should be at the bottom. Perform the operation $R_2 \leftrightarrow R_3$ to obtain

$$\left[\begin{array}{ccc|c} 1 & 2 & 0 & 3 \\ 0 & 0 & 1 & 4 \\ 0 & 0 & 0 & 0 \end{array}\right]$$

2. $x_1 = 1, x_2 = -1, x_3 = 0$

3. Inconsistent; no solution

4. $x_1 = 5t + 4, x_2 = 3t + 5, x_3 = t$, t any real number

5. $x_1 = s + 7, x_2 = s, x_3 = t - 2, x_4 = -3t - 1, x_5 = t$, s and t any real numbers

6. $t - 8$ cargo vans, $-2t + 24$ 15-foot trucks, and t 24-foot trucks, where $t = 8, 9, 10, 11$, or 12

4.4 Matrices: Basic Operations

- Addition and Subtraction
- Product of a Number k and a Matrix M
- Matrix Product

In the two preceding sections we introduced the important idea of matrices. In this and following sections, we develop this concept further. Matrices are both an ancient and a current mathematical concept. References to matrices and systems of equations can be found in Chinese manuscripts dating back to about 200 B.C. More recently, computers have made matrices a useful tool for a wide variety of applications. Most graphing calculators and computers are capable of performing calculations with matrices.

As we will see, matrix addition and multiplication are similar to real number addition and multiplication in many respects, but there are some important differences. A brief review of Appendix B, Section B.1, where real number operations are discussed, will help you understand the similarities and the differences.

Addition and Subtraction

Before we can discuss arithmetic operations for matrices, we have to define equality for matrices. Two matrices are **equal** if they have the same size and their corresponding elements are equal. For example,

$$\underset{2 \times 3}{\begin{bmatrix} a & b & c \\ d & e & f \end{bmatrix}} = \underset{2 \times 3}{\begin{bmatrix} u & v & w \\ x & y & z \end{bmatrix}} \quad \text{if and only if} \quad \begin{matrix} a = u & b = v & c = w \\ d = x & e = y & f = z \end{matrix}$$

The **sum of two matrices of the same size** is the matrix with elements that are the sum of the corresponding elements of the two given matrices. Addition is not defined for matrices of different sizes.

EXAMPLE 1 Matrix Addition

(A) $\begin{bmatrix} a & b \\ c & d \end{bmatrix} + \begin{bmatrix} w & x \\ y & z \end{bmatrix} = \begin{bmatrix} (a+w) & (b+x) \\ (c+y) & (d+z) \end{bmatrix}$

(B) $\begin{bmatrix} 2 & -3 & 0 \\ 1 & 2 & -5 \end{bmatrix} + \begin{bmatrix} 3 & 1 & 2 \\ -3 & 2 & 5 \end{bmatrix} = \begin{bmatrix} 5 & -2 & 2 \\ -2 & 4 & 0 \end{bmatrix}$

(C) $\begin{bmatrix} 5 & 0 & -2 \\ 1 & -3 & 8 \end{bmatrix} + \begin{bmatrix} -1 & 7 \\ 0 & 6 \\ -2 & 8 \end{bmatrix}$ Not defined

Matched Problem 1 Add: $\begin{bmatrix} 3 & 2 \\ -1 & -1 \\ 0 & 3 \end{bmatrix} + \begin{bmatrix} -2 & 3 \\ 1 & -1 \\ 2 & -2 \end{bmatrix}$

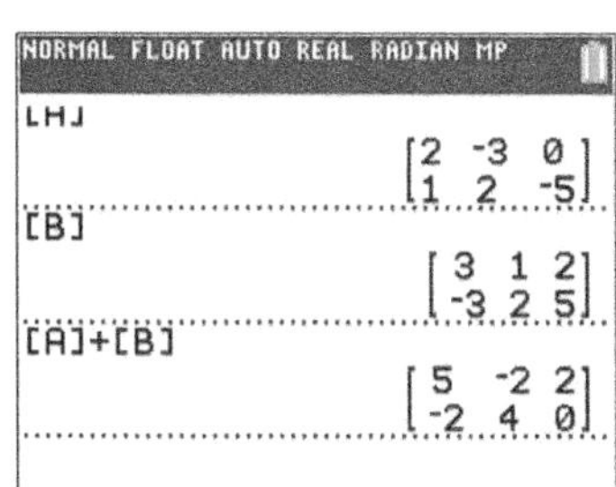

Figure 1 Addition on a graphing calculator

Graphing calculators can be used to solve problems involving matrix operations. Figure 1 illustrates the solution to Example 1B on a TI-84 Plus CE.

Because we add two matrices by adding their corresponding elements, it follows from the properties of real numbers that matrices of the same size are commutative and associative relative to addition. That is, if A, B, and C are matrices of the same size, then

Commutative: $A + B = B + A$

Associative: $(A + B) + C = A + (B + C)$

A matrix with elements that are all zeros is called a **zero matrix**. For example,

$$[0 \quad 0 \quad 0] \quad \begin{bmatrix} 0 & 0 \\ 0 & 0 \end{bmatrix} \quad \begin{bmatrix} 0 \\ 0 \\ 0 \\ 0 \end{bmatrix} \quad \begin{bmatrix} 0 & 0 & 0 & 0 \\ 0 & 0 & 0 & 0 \\ 0 & 0 & 0 & 0 \end{bmatrix}$$

are zero matrices of different sizes. [*Note:* The simpler notation "0" is often used to denote the zero matrix of an arbitrary size.] The **negative of a matrix *M***, denoted by $-M$, is a matrix with elements that are the negatives of the elements in M. Thus, if

$$M = \begin{bmatrix} a & b \\ c & d \end{bmatrix} \quad \text{then} \quad -M = \begin{bmatrix} -a & -b \\ -c & -d \end{bmatrix}$$

Note that $M + (-M) = 0$ (a zero matrix).

If A and B are matrices of the same size, we define **subtraction** as follows:

$$A - B = A + (-B)$$

So to subtract matrix B from matrix A, we simply add the negative of B to A.

EXAMPLE 2 **Matrix Subtraction**

$$\begin{bmatrix} 3 & -2 \\ 5 & 0 \end{bmatrix} - \begin{bmatrix} -2 & 2 \\ 3 & 4 \end{bmatrix} = \begin{bmatrix} 3 & -2 \\ 5 & 0 \end{bmatrix} + \begin{bmatrix} 2 & -2 \\ -3 & -4 \end{bmatrix} = \begin{bmatrix} 5 & -4 \\ 2 & -4 \end{bmatrix}$$

Matched Problem 2 Subtract: $[2 \quad -3 \quad 5] - [3 \quad -2 \quad 1]$

EXAMPLE 3 **Matrix Equations** Find a, b, c, and d so that

$$\begin{bmatrix} a & b \\ c & d \end{bmatrix} - \begin{bmatrix} 2 & -1 \\ -5 & 6 \end{bmatrix} = \begin{bmatrix} 4 & 3 \\ -2 & 4 \end{bmatrix}$$

SOLUTION

$$\begin{bmatrix} a & b \\ c & d \end{bmatrix} - \begin{bmatrix} 2 & -1 \\ -5 & 6 \end{bmatrix} = \begin{bmatrix} 4 & 3 \\ -2 & 4 \end{bmatrix}$$ Subtract the matrices on the left side.

$$\begin{bmatrix} a - 2 & b - (-1) \\ c - (-5) & d - 6 \end{bmatrix} = \begin{bmatrix} 4 & 3 \\ -2 & 4 \end{bmatrix}$$ Remove parentheses.

$$\begin{bmatrix} a - 2 & b + 1 \\ c + 5 & d - 6 \end{bmatrix} = \begin{bmatrix} 4 & 3 \\ -2 & 4 \end{bmatrix}$$ Use the definition of *equality* to change this matrix equation into four real number equations.

$$a - 2 = 4 \qquad b + 1 = 3 \qquad c + 5 = -2 \qquad d - 6 = 4$$

$$a = 6 \qquad b = 2 \qquad c = -7 \qquad d = 10$$

Matched Problem 3 Find a, b, c, and d so that

$$\begin{bmatrix} a & b \\ c & d \end{bmatrix} - \begin{bmatrix} -4 & 2 \\ 1 & -3 \end{bmatrix} = \begin{bmatrix} -2 & 5 \\ 8 & 2 \end{bmatrix}$$

Product of a Number k and a Matrix M

The **product of a number k and a matrix M**, denoted by kM, is a matrix formed by multiplying each element of M by k.

EXAMPLE 4 **Multiplication of a Matrix by a Number**

$$-2\begin{bmatrix} 3 & -1 & 0 \\ -2 & 1 & 3 \\ 0 & -1 & -2 \end{bmatrix} = \begin{bmatrix} -6 & 2 & 0 \\ 4 & -2 & -6 \\ 0 & 2 & 4 \end{bmatrix}$$

Matched Problem 4 Find: $10\begin{bmatrix} 1.3 \\ 0.2 \\ 3.5 \end{bmatrix}$

The next example illustrates the use of matrix operations in an applied setting.

EXAMPLE 5 **Sales Commissions** Ms. Smith and Mr. Jones are salespeople in a new-car agency that sells only two models. August was the last month for this year's models, and next year's models were introduced in September. Gross dollar sales for each month are given in the following matrices:

$$\begin{matrix} & \text{August sales} \\ & \begin{matrix} \text{Compact} & \text{Luxury} \end{matrix} \\ \begin{matrix} \text{Ms. Smith} \\ \text{Mr. Jones} \end{matrix} & \begin{bmatrix} \$54{,}000 & \$88{,}000 \\ \$126{,}000 & 0 \end{bmatrix} = A \end{matrix} \qquad \begin{matrix} \text{September sales} \\ \begin{matrix} \text{Compact} & \text{Luxury} \end{matrix} \\ \begin{bmatrix} \$228{,}000 & \$368{,}000 \\ \$304{,}000 & \$322{,}000 \end{bmatrix} = B \end{matrix}$$

For example, Ms. Smith had $54,000 in compact sales in August, and Mr. Jones had $322,000 in luxury car sales in September.

(A) What were the combined dollar sales in August and September for each salesperson and each model?

(B) What was the increase in dollar sales from August to September?

(C) If both salespeople receive 5% commissions on gross dollar sales, compute the commission for each person for each model sold in September.

SOLUTION

$$\text{(A)}\ A + B = \begin{matrix} \begin{matrix} \text{Compact} & \text{Luxury} \end{matrix} \\ \begin{bmatrix} \$282{,}000 & \$456{,}000 \\ \$430{,}000 & \$322{,}000 \end{bmatrix} \end{matrix} \begin{matrix} \text{Ms. Smith} \\ \text{Mr. Jones} \end{matrix}$$

$$\text{(B)}\ B - A = \begin{matrix} \begin{matrix} \text{Compact} & \text{Luxury} \end{matrix} \\ \begin{bmatrix} \$174{,}000 & \$280{,}000 \\ \$178{,}000 & \$322{,}000 \end{bmatrix} \end{matrix} \begin{matrix} \text{Ms. Smith} \\ \text{Mr. Jones} \end{matrix}$$

$$\text{(C)}\ 0.05B = \begin{bmatrix} (0.05)(\$228{,}000) & (0.05)(\$368{,}000) \\ (0.05)(\$304{,}000) & (0.05)(\$322{,}000) \end{bmatrix}$$

$$= \begin{bmatrix} \$11{,}400 & \$18{,}400 \\ \$15{,}200 & \$16{,}100 \end{bmatrix} \begin{matrix} \text{Ms. Smith} \\ \text{Mr. Jones} \end{matrix}$$

Matched Problem 5 Repeat Example 5 with

$$A = \begin{bmatrix} \$45{,}000 & \$77{,}000 \\ \$106{,}000 & \$22{,}000 \end{bmatrix} \quad \text{and} \quad B = \begin{bmatrix} \$190{,}000 & \$345{,}000 \\ \$266{,}000 & \$276{,}000 \end{bmatrix}$$

Figure 2 illustrates a solution for Example 5 on a spreadsheet.

	A	B	C	D	E	F	G	H	I
1		August Sales			September Sales			September Commissions	
2		Compact	Luxury		Compact	Luxury		Compact	Luxury
3	Smith	$ 54,000	$ 88,000		$228,000	$368,000		$ 11,400	$ 18,400
4	Jones	$126,000	$ 0		$304,000	$322,000		$ 15,200	$ 16,100
5									
6		Combined Sales			Sales Increase				
7	Smith	$282,000	$456,000		$174,000	$280,000			
8	Jones	$430,000	$322,000		$178,000	$322,000			

Figure 2

Matrix Product

Matrix multiplication was introduced by the English mathematician Arthur Cayley (1821–1895) in studies of systems of linear equations and linear transformations. Although this multiplication may seem strange at first, it is extremely useful in many practical problems.

We start by defining the product of two special matrices, a row matrix and a column matrix.

DEFINITION Product of a Row Matrix and a Column Matrix

The **product** of a $1 \times n$ row matrix and an $n \times 1$ column matrix is a 1×1 matrix given by

$$\underset{1 \times n}{[a_1\ a_2\ \dots\ a_n]} \underset{n \times 1}{\begin{bmatrix} b_1 \\ b_2 \\ \vdots \\ b_n \end{bmatrix}} = [a_1b_1 + a_2b_2 + \cdots + a_nb_n]$$

Note that the number of elements in the row matrix and in the column matrix must be the same for the product to be defined.

EXAMPLE 6 **Product of a Row Matrix and a Column Matrix**

$$[2\quad -3\quad 0]\begin{bmatrix} -5 \\ 2 \\ -2 \end{bmatrix} = [(2)(-5) + (-3)(2) + (0)(-2)]$$

$$= [-10 - 6 + 0] = [-16]$$

Matched Problem 6 $[-1\quad 0\quad 3\quad 2]\begin{bmatrix} 2 \\ 3 \\ 4 \\ -1 \end{bmatrix} = ?$

Refer to Example 6. The distinction between the real number -16 and the 1×1 matrix $[-16]$ is a technical one, and it is common to see 1×1 matrices written as real numbers without brackets. In the work that follows, we will frequently refer to 1×1 matrices as real numbers and omit the brackets whenever it is convenient to do so.

EXAMPLE 7 **Labor Costs** A factory produces a slalom water ski that requires 3 labor-hours in the assembly department and 1 labor-hour in the finishing department. Assembly personnel receive \$9 per hour and finishing personnel receive \$6 per hour. Total labor cost per ski is given by the product:

$$\begin{bmatrix} 3 & 1 \end{bmatrix} \begin{bmatrix} 9 \\ 6 \end{bmatrix} = [(3)(9) + (1)(6)] = [27 + 6] = [33] \quad \text{or} \quad \$33 \text{ per ski}$$

Matched Problem 7 If the factory in Example 7 also produces a trick water ski that requires 5 labor-hours in the assembly department and 1.5 labor-hours in the finishing department, write a product between appropriate row and column matrices that will give the total labor cost for this ski. Compute the cost.

We now use the product of a $1 \times n$ row matrix and an $n \times 1$ column matrix to extend the definition of matrix product to more general matrices.

DEFINITION Matrix Product

If A is an $m \times p$ matrix and B is a $p \times n$ matrix, then the **matrix product** of A and B, denoted AB, is an $m \times n$ matrix whose element in the ith row and jth column is the real number obtained from the product of the ith row of A and the jth column of B. If the number of columns in A does not equal the number of rows in B, the matrix product AB is **not defined**.

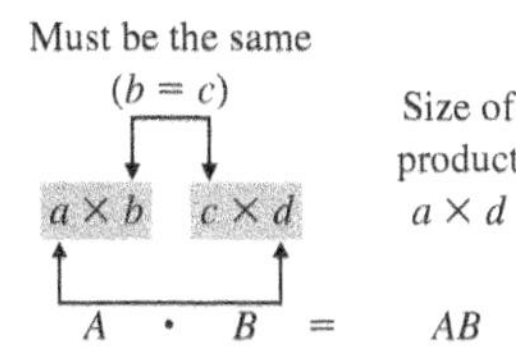

Figure 3

It is important to check sizes before starting the multiplication process. If A is an $a \times b$ matrix and B is a $c \times d$ matrix, then if $b = c$, the product AB will exist and will be an $a \times d$ matrix (see Fig. 3). If $b \neq c$, the product AB does not exist. The definition is not as complicated as it might first seem. An example should help clarify the process.

For

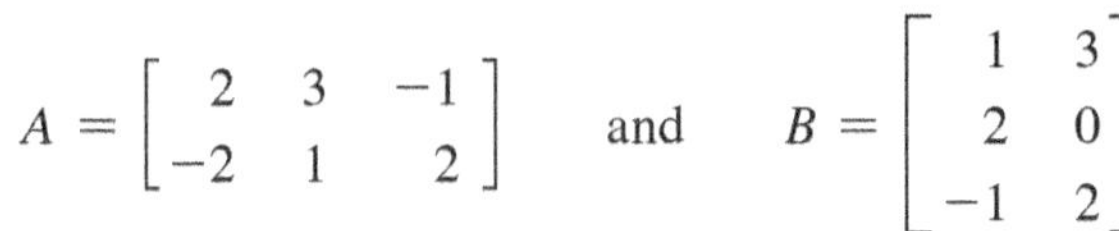

$$A = \begin{bmatrix} 2 & 3 & -1 \\ -2 & 1 & 2 \end{bmatrix} \quad \text{and} \quad B = \begin{bmatrix} 1 & 3 \\ 2 & 0 \\ -1 & 2 \end{bmatrix}$$

A is 2×3 and B is 3×2, so AB is 2×2. To find the first row of AB, we take the product of the first row of A with every column of B and write each result as a real number, not as a 1×1 matrix. The second row of AB is computed in the same manner. The four products of row and column matrices used to produce the four elements in AB are shown in the following dashed box. These products are usually calculated mentally or with the aid of a calculator, and need not be written out. The shaded portions highlight the steps involved in computing the element in the first row and second column of AB.

$$\overset{2 \times 3}{\begin{bmatrix} 2 & 3 & -1 \\ -2 & 1 & 2 \end{bmatrix}} \overset{3 \times 2}{\begin{bmatrix} 1 & 3 \\ 2 & 0 \\ -1 & 2 \end{bmatrix}} = \begin{bmatrix} \begin{bmatrix} 2 & 3 & -1 \end{bmatrix} \begin{bmatrix} 1 \\ 2 \\ -1 \end{bmatrix} & \begin{bmatrix} 2 & 3 & -1 \end{bmatrix} \begin{bmatrix} 3 \\ 0 \\ 2 \end{bmatrix} \\ \begin{bmatrix} -2 & 1 & 2 \end{bmatrix} \begin{bmatrix} 1 \\ 2 \\ -1 \end{bmatrix} & \begin{bmatrix} -2 & 1 & 2 \end{bmatrix} \begin{bmatrix} 3 \\ 0 \\ 2 \end{bmatrix} \end{bmatrix}$$

$$= \begin{bmatrix} (2)(1) + (3)(2) + (-1)(-1) & (2)(3) + (3)(0) + (-1)(2) \\ (-2)(1) + (1)(2) + (2)(-1) & (-2)(3) + (1)(0) + (2)(2) \end{bmatrix} = \overset{2 \times 2}{\begin{bmatrix} 9 & 4 \\ -2 & -2 \end{bmatrix}}$$

EXAMPLE 8 **Matrix Multiplication** Find the indicated matrix product, if it exists, where:

$$A = \begin{bmatrix} 2 & 1 \\ 1 & 0 \\ -1 & 2 \end{bmatrix} \quad B = \begin{bmatrix} 1 & -1 & 0 & 1 \\ 2 & 1 & 2 & 0 \end{bmatrix} \quad C = \begin{bmatrix} 2 & 6 \\ -1 & -3 \end{bmatrix}$$

$$D = \begin{bmatrix} 1 & 2 \\ 3 & 6 \end{bmatrix} \quad E = \begin{bmatrix} 2 & -3 & 0 \end{bmatrix} \quad F = \begin{bmatrix} -5 \\ 2 \\ -2 \end{bmatrix}$$

(A) $$AB = \overset{3 \times 2}{\begin{bmatrix} 2 & 1 \\ 1 & 0 \\ -1 & 2 \end{bmatrix}} \overset{2 \times 4}{\begin{bmatrix} 1 & -1 & 0 & 1 \\ 2 & 1 & 2 & 0 \end{bmatrix}}$$

$$= \begin{bmatrix} (2)(1)+(1)(2) & (2)(-1)+(1)(1) & (2)(0)+(1)(2) & (2)(1)+(1)(0) \\ (1)(1)+(0)(2) & (1)(-1)+(0)(1) & (1)(0)+(0)(2) & (1)(1)+(0)(0) \\ (-1)(1)+(2)(2) & (-1)(-1)+(2)(1) & (-1)(0)+(2)(2) & (-1)(1)+(2)(0) \end{bmatrix}$$

$$= \overset{3 \times 4}{\begin{bmatrix} 4 & -1 & 2 & 2 \\ 1 & -1 & 0 & 1 \\ 3 & 3 & 4 & -1 \end{bmatrix}}$$

(B) $$BA = \overset{2 \times 4}{\begin{bmatrix} 1 & -1 & 0 & 1 \\ 2 & 1 & 2 & 0 \end{bmatrix}} \overset{3 \times 2}{\begin{bmatrix} 2 & 1 \\ 1 & 0 \\ -1 & 2 \end{bmatrix}} \quad \text{Not defined}$$

(C) $$CD = \begin{bmatrix} 2 & 6 \\ -1 & -3 \end{bmatrix} \begin{bmatrix} 1 & 2 \\ 3 & 6 \end{bmatrix} = \begin{bmatrix} (2)(1)+(6)(3) & (2)(2)+(6)(6) \\ (-1)(1)+(-3)(3) & (-1)(2)+(-3)(6) \end{bmatrix}$$

$$= \begin{bmatrix} 20 & 40 \\ -10 & -20 \end{bmatrix}$$

(D) $$DC = \begin{bmatrix} 1 & 2 \\ 3 & 6 \end{bmatrix} \begin{bmatrix} 2 & 6 \\ -1 & -3 \end{bmatrix} = \begin{bmatrix} (1)(2)+(2)(-1) & (1)(6)+(2)(-3) \\ (3)(2)+(6)(-1) & (3)(6)+(6)(-3) \end{bmatrix}$$

$$= \begin{bmatrix} 0 & 0 \\ 0 & 0 \end{bmatrix}$$

(E) $$EF = \begin{bmatrix} 2 & -3 & 0 \end{bmatrix} \begin{bmatrix} -5 \\ 2 \\ -2 \end{bmatrix} = \begin{bmatrix} (2)(-5)+(-3)(2)+(0)(-2) \end{bmatrix} = \begin{bmatrix} -16 \end{bmatrix}$$

$$\text{(F) } FE = \begin{bmatrix} -5 \\ 2 \\ -2 \end{bmatrix} [2 \quad -3 \quad 0] = \begin{bmatrix} (-5)(2) & (-5)(-3) & (-5)(0) \\ (2)(2) & (2)(-3) & (2)(0) \\ (-2)(2) & (-2)(-3) & (-2)(0) \end{bmatrix}$$

$$= \begin{bmatrix} -10 & 15 & 0 \\ 4 & -6 & 0 \\ -4 & 6 & 0 \end{bmatrix}$$

$$\text{(G) } A^{2*} = AA = \underset{3 \times 2}{\begin{bmatrix} 2 & 1 \\ 1 & 0 \\ -1 & 2 \end{bmatrix}} \underset{3 \times 2}{\begin{bmatrix} 2 & 1 \\ 1 & 0 \\ -1 & 2 \end{bmatrix}} \quad \text{Not defined}$$

$$\text{(H) } C^2 = CC = \begin{bmatrix} 2 & 6 \\ -1 & -3 \end{bmatrix} \begin{bmatrix} 2 & 6 \\ -1 & -3 \end{bmatrix}$$

$$= \begin{bmatrix} (2)(2)+(6)(-1) & (2)(6)+(6)(-3) \\ (-1)(2)+(-3)(-1) & (-1)(6)+(-3)(-3) \end{bmatrix}$$

$$= \begin{bmatrix} -2 & -6 \\ 1 & 3 \end{bmatrix}$$

Matched Problem 8 Find each product, if it is defined:

(A) $\begin{bmatrix} -1 & 0 & 3 & -2 \\ 1 & 2 & 2 & 0 \end{bmatrix} \begin{bmatrix} -1 & 1 \\ 2 & 3 \\ 1 & 0 \end{bmatrix}$ (B) $\begin{bmatrix} -1 & 1 \\ 2 & 3 \\ 1 & 0 \end{bmatrix} \begin{bmatrix} -1 & 0 & 3 & -2 \\ 1 & 2 & 2 & 0 \end{bmatrix}$

(C) $\begin{bmatrix} 1 & 2 \\ -1 & -2 \end{bmatrix} \begin{bmatrix} -2 & 4 \\ 1 & -2 \end{bmatrix}$ (D) $\begin{bmatrix} -2 & 4 \\ 1 & -2 \end{bmatrix} \begin{bmatrix} 1 & 2 \\ -1 & -2 \end{bmatrix}$

(E) $[3 \quad -2 \quad 1] \begin{bmatrix} 4 \\ 2 \\ 3 \end{bmatrix}$ (F) $\begin{bmatrix} 4 \\ 2 \\ 3 \end{bmatrix} [3 \quad -2 \quad 1]$

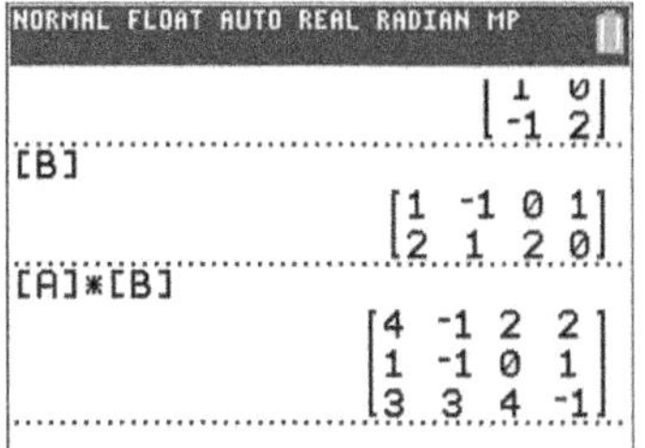

Figure 4 Multiplication on a graphing calculator

Figure 4 illustrates a graphing calculator solution to Example 8A. What would you expect to happen if you tried to solve Example 8B on a graphing calculator?

CONCEPTUAL INSIGHT

In the arithmetic of real numbers, it does not matter in which order we multiply. For example, $5 \times 7 = 7 \times 5$. In matrix multiplication, however, it does make a difference. That is, AB does not always equal BA, even if both multiplications are defined and both products are the same size (see Examples 8C and 8D).

Matrix multiplication is not commutative.

The zero property of real numbers states that if the product of two real numbers is 0, then one of the numbers must be 0 (see Appendix B, Section B.1). This property is very important when solving equations. For example,

(Continued)

*Following standard algebraic notation, we write $A^2 = AA$, $A^3 = AAA$, and so on.

$$x^2 - 4x + 3 = 0$$

$$(x - 1)(x - 3) = 0$$

$$x - 1 = 0 \quad \text{or} \quad x - 3 = 0$$

$$x = 1 \qquad\qquad x = 3$$

For matrices, it is possible to find nonzero matrices A and B such that AB is a zero matrix (see Example 8D).

The zero property does not hold for matrix multiplication.

Explore and Discuss 1

In addition to the commutative and zero properties, there are other significant differences between real number multiplication and matrix multiplication.

(A) In real number multiplication, the only real number whose square is 0 is the real number 0 ($0^2 = 0$). Find at least one 2×2 matrix A with all elements nonzero such that $A^2 = 0$, where 0 is the 2×2 zero matrix.

(B) In real number multiplication, the only nonzero real number that is equal to its square is the real number 1 ($1^2 = 1$). Find at least one 2×2 matrix B with all elements nonzero such that $B^2 = B$.

EXAMPLE 9 **Matrix Multiplication** Find a, b, c, and d so that

$$\begin{bmatrix} 2 & -1 \\ 5 & 3 \end{bmatrix}\begin{bmatrix} a & b \\ c & d \end{bmatrix} = \begin{bmatrix} -6 & 17 \\ 7 & 4 \end{bmatrix}$$

SOLUTION The product of the matrices on the left side of the equation is

$$\begin{bmatrix} 2 & -1 \\ 5 & 3 \end{bmatrix}\begin{bmatrix} a & b \\ c & d \end{bmatrix} = \begin{bmatrix} 2a - c & 2b - d \\ 5a + 3c & 5b + 3d \end{bmatrix}$$

Therefore,

$$2a - c = -6 \qquad 2b - d = 17$$

$$5a + 3c = 7 \qquad 5b + 3d = 4$$

This gives a system of two equations in the variables a and c, and a second system of two equations in the variables b and d. Each system can be solved by substitution, or elimination by addition, or Gauss–Jordan elimination (the details are omitted). The solution of the first system is $a = -1$, $c = 4$, and the solution of the second system is $b = 5$, $d = -7$.

Matched Problem 9 Find a, b, c, and d so that

$$\begin{bmatrix} 6 & -5 \\ 0 & 3 \end{bmatrix}\begin{bmatrix} a & b \\ c & d \end{bmatrix} = \begin{bmatrix} -16 & 64 \\ 24 & -6 \end{bmatrix}$$

Now we consider an application of matrix multiplication.

EXAMPLE 10 **Labor Costs** We can combine the time requirements for slalom and trick water skis discussed in Example 7 and Matched Problem 7 into one matrix:

$$\begin{array}{l} \\ \\ \text{Trick ski} \\ \text{Slalom ski} \end{array} \begin{array}{c} \text{Labor-hours per ski} \\ \begin{array}{cc} \text{Assembly department} & \text{Finishing department} \end{array} \\ \begin{bmatrix} 5\text{ hr} & 1.5\text{ hr} \\ 3\text{ hr} & 1\ \ \text{hr} \end{bmatrix} = L \end{array}$$

Now suppose that the company has two manufacturing plants, one in California and the other in Maryland, and that their hourly rates for each department are given in the following matrix:

$$\begin{array}{l} \\ \\ \text{Assembly department} \\ \text{Finishing department} \end{array} \begin{array}{c} \text{Hourly wages} \\ \begin{array}{cc} \text{California} & \text{Maryland} \end{array} \\ \begin{bmatrix} \$12 & \$13 \\ \$7 & \$8 \end{bmatrix} = H \end{array}$$

Since H and L are both 2×2 matrices, we can take the product of H and L in either order and the result will be a 2×2 matrix:

$$HL = \begin{bmatrix} 12 & 13 \\ 7 & 8 \end{bmatrix} \begin{bmatrix} 5 & 1.5 \\ 3 & 1 \end{bmatrix} = \begin{bmatrix} 99 & 31 \\ 59 & 18.5 \end{bmatrix}$$

$$LH = \begin{bmatrix} 5 & 1.5 \\ 3 & 1 \end{bmatrix} \begin{bmatrix} 12 & 13 \\ 7 & 8 \end{bmatrix} = \begin{bmatrix} 70.5 & 77 \\ 43 & 47 \end{bmatrix}$$

How can we interpret the elements in these products? Let's begin with the product HL. The element 99 in the first row and first column of HL is the product of the first row matrix of H and the first column matrix of L:

$$\begin{array}{cc} \text{CA} & \text{MD} \end{array} \atop [12 \quad 13] \begin{bmatrix} 5 \\ 3 \end{bmatrix} \begin{array}{l} \text{Trick} \\ \text{Slalom} \end{array} = 12(5) + 13(3) = 60 + 39 = 99$$

Notice that \$60 is the labor cost for assembling a trick ski at the California plant and \$39 is the labor cost for assembling a slalom ski at the Maryland plant. Although both numbers represent labor costs, it makes no sense to add them together. They do not pertain to the same type of ski or to the same plant. So even though the product HL happens to be defined mathematically, it has no useful interpretation in this problem.

Now let's consider the product LH. The element 70.5 in the first row and first column of LH is given by the following product:

$$\begin{array}{cc} \text{Assembly} & \text{Finishing} \end{array} \atop [5 \qquad 1.5] \begin{bmatrix} 12 \\ 7 \end{bmatrix} \begin{array}{l} \text{Assembly} \\ \text{Finishing} \end{array} = 5(12) + 1.5(7) = 60 + 10.5 = 70.5$$

This time, \$60 is the labor cost for assembling a trick ski at the California plant and \$10.50 is the labor cost for finishing a trick ski at the California plant. So the sum is the total labor cost for producing a trick ski at the California plant. The other elements in LH also represent total labor costs, as indicated by the row and column labels shown below:

$$\begin{array}{c} \text{Labor costs per ski} \\ \begin{array}{cc} \text{CA} & \text{MD} \end{array} \\ LH = \begin{bmatrix} \$70.50 & \$77 \\ \$43 & \$47 \end{bmatrix} \end{array} \begin{array}{l} \\ \\ \text{Trick} \\ \text{Slalom} \end{array}$$

Figure 5 shows a solution to Example 9 on a spreadsheet.

	A	B	C	D	E	F	G
1		Labor-hours per ski				Hourly wages	
2		Assembly	Finishing			California	Maryland
3	Trick ski	5	1.5		Assembly	\$ 12.00	\$ 13.00
4	Slalom ski	3	1		Finishing	\$ 7.00	\$ 8.00
5							
6		Labor costs per ski					
7		California	Maryland				
8	Trick ski	\$ 75.50	\$ 77.00				
9	Slalom ski	\$ 43.00	\$ 47.00				

Figure 5 Matrix multiplication in a spreadsheet: The command MMULT(B3:C4, F3:G4) produces the matrix in B8:C9

Matched Problem 10 Refer to Example 10. The company wants to know how many hours to schedule in each department in order to produce 2,000 trick skis and 1,000 slalom skis. These production requirements can be represented by either of the following matrices:

$$\begin{matrix} & \text{Trick skis} & \text{Slalom skis} \\ P = & [2{,}000 & 1{,}000] \end{matrix} \qquad Q = \begin{bmatrix} 2{,}000 \\ 1{,}000 \end{bmatrix} \begin{matrix} \text{Trick skis} \\ \text{Slalom skis} \end{matrix}$$

Using the labor-hour matrix L from Example 10, find PL or LQ, whichever has a meaningful interpretation for this problem, and label the rows and columns accordingly.

CONCEPTUAL INSIGHT

Example 10 and Matched Problem 10 illustrate an important point about matrix multiplication. Even if you are using a graphing calculator to perform the calculations in a matrix product, it is still necessary for you to know the definition of matrix multiplication so that you can interpret the results correctly.

Exercises 4.4

Skills Warm-up Exercises

W *In Problems 1–14, perform the indicated operation, if possible. (If necessary, review the definitions at the beginning of Section 4.4.)*

1. $[1 \quad 5] + [3 \quad 10]$

2. $\begin{bmatrix} 3 \\ 2 \end{bmatrix} - \begin{bmatrix} 7 \\ -4 \end{bmatrix}$

3. $\begin{bmatrix} 2 & 0 \\ -3 & 6 \end{bmatrix} - \begin{bmatrix} 0 & -4 \\ -1 & 0 \end{bmatrix}$

4. $\begin{bmatrix} -9 & 2 \\ 8 & 0 \end{bmatrix} + \begin{bmatrix} 9 & 0 \\ 0 & 8 \end{bmatrix}$

5. $\begin{bmatrix} 3 \\ 6 \end{bmatrix} + \begin{bmatrix} -1 & 9 \end{bmatrix}$

6. $4\begin{bmatrix} 2 & -6 & 1 \\ 8 & 5 & -3 \end{bmatrix}$

7. $7\begin{bmatrix} 3 & -5 & 9 & 4 \end{bmatrix}$

8. $[10 \quad 12] + \begin{bmatrix} 4 \\ 3 \end{bmatrix}$

A **9.** $\begin{bmatrix} 3 & 4 \\ -1 & -2 \end{bmatrix}\begin{bmatrix} -1 \\ 2 \end{bmatrix}$

10. $\begin{bmatrix} -1 & 1 \\ 2 & -3 \end{bmatrix}\begin{bmatrix} 4 \\ -2 \end{bmatrix}$

11. $\begin{bmatrix} 2 & -3 \\ 1 & 2 \end{bmatrix}\begin{bmatrix} 1 & -1 \\ 0 & -2 \end{bmatrix}$

12. $\begin{bmatrix} -5 & 4 \\ 3 & -2 \end{bmatrix}\begin{bmatrix} -6 & 7 \\ -8 & 9 \end{bmatrix}$

13. $\begin{bmatrix} 1 & -1 \\ 0 & -2 \end{bmatrix}\begin{bmatrix} 2 & -3 \\ 1 & 2 \end{bmatrix}$

14. $\begin{bmatrix} -6 & 7 \\ -8 & 9 \end{bmatrix}\begin{bmatrix} -5 & 4 \\ 3 & -2 \end{bmatrix}$

In Problems 15–22, find the matrix product. Note that each product can be found mentally, without the use of a calculator or pencil-and-paper calculations.

15. $\begin{bmatrix} 5 & 0 \\ 0 & 5 \end{bmatrix}\begin{bmatrix} 1 & 2 \\ 3 & 4 \end{bmatrix}$

16. $\begin{bmatrix} 3 & 0 \\ 0 & 3 \end{bmatrix}\begin{bmatrix} 1 & 3 \\ 5 & 7 \end{bmatrix}$

17. $\begin{bmatrix} 1 & 2 \\ 3 & 4 \end{bmatrix}\begin{bmatrix} 5 & 0 \\ 0 & 5 \end{bmatrix}$

18. $\begin{bmatrix} 1 & 3 \\ 5 & 7 \end{bmatrix}\begin{bmatrix} 3 & 0 \\ 0 & 3 \end{bmatrix}$

19. $\begin{bmatrix} 0 & 1 \\ 0 & 0 \end{bmatrix}\begin{bmatrix} 3 & 5 \\ 7 & 9 \end{bmatrix}$

20. $\begin{bmatrix} 0 & 0 \\ 1 & 0 \end{bmatrix}\begin{bmatrix} 2 & 4 \\ 6 & 8 \end{bmatrix}$

21. $\begin{bmatrix} 3 & 5 \\ 7 & 9 \end{bmatrix}\begin{bmatrix} 0 & 1 \\ 0 & 0 \end{bmatrix}$

22. $\begin{bmatrix} 2 & 4 \\ 6 & 8 \end{bmatrix}\begin{bmatrix} 0 & 0 \\ 1 & 0 \end{bmatrix}$

B *Find the products in Problems 23–30.*

23. $[3 \quad -2]\begin{bmatrix} -5 \\ 4 \end{bmatrix}$

24. $[-3 \quad 5]\begin{bmatrix} 2 \\ -4 \end{bmatrix}$

25. $\begin{bmatrix} -5 \\ 4 \end{bmatrix}[3 \quad -2]$

26. $\begin{bmatrix} 2 \\ -4 \end{bmatrix}[-3 \quad 5]$

27. $[-1 \quad 0 \quad 1]\begin{bmatrix} 2 \\ 1 \\ 3 \end{bmatrix}$

28. $[1 \quad -2 \quad 3]\begin{bmatrix} 6 \\ -5 \\ 0 \end{bmatrix}$

29. $\begin{bmatrix} 2 \\ 1 \\ 3 \end{bmatrix}[-1 \quad 0 \quad 1]$

30. $\begin{bmatrix} 6 \\ -5 \\ 0 \end{bmatrix}[1 \quad -2 \quad 3]$

Problems 31–48 refer to the following matrices:

$$A = \begin{bmatrix} 2 & -1 & 3 \\ 0 & 4 & -2 \end{bmatrix} \quad B = \begin{bmatrix} -3 & 1 \\ 2 & 5 \end{bmatrix}$$

$$C = \begin{bmatrix} -1 & 0 & 2 \\ 4 & -3 & 1 \\ -2 & 3 & 5 \end{bmatrix} \quad D = \begin{bmatrix} 3 & -2 \\ 0 & -1 \\ 1 & 2 \end{bmatrix}$$

Perform the indicated operations, if possible.

31. AC

32. CA

33. CD

34. DC

35. B^2

36. C^2

37. $B + AD$

38. $C + DA$

39. $(0.1)DB$

40. $(0.2)CD$

41. $(3)BA + (4)AC$

42. $(2)DB + (5)CD$

43. $(-2)BA + (6)CD$

44. $(-1)AC + (3)DB$

45. ACD

46. CDA

47. DBA

48. BAD

49. If a and b are nonzero real numbers,

$$A = \begin{bmatrix} a & a \\ b & b \end{bmatrix}, \quad \text{and} \quad B = \begin{bmatrix} a & a \\ -a & -a \end{bmatrix}$$

find AB and BA.

50. If a and b are nonzero real numbers,

$$A = \begin{bmatrix} a & b \\ -a & -b \end{bmatrix}, \quad \text{and} \quad B = \begin{bmatrix} a & a \\ a & a \end{bmatrix}$$

find AB and BA.

51. If a and b are nonzero real numbers and

$$A = \begin{bmatrix} ab & b^2 \\ -a^2 & -ab \end{bmatrix}$$

find A^2.

52. If a and b are nonzero real numbers and

$$A = \begin{bmatrix} ab & b - ab^2 \\ a & 1 - ab \end{bmatrix}$$

find A^2.

In Problems 53 and 54, use a graphing calculator to calculate $B, B^2, B^3, \ldots$ and $AB, AB^2, AB^3, \ldots$. Describe any patterns you observe in each sequence of matrices.

53. $A = [0.3 \quad 0.7]$ and $B = \begin{bmatrix} 0.4 & 0.6 \\ 0.2 & 0.8 \end{bmatrix}$

54. $A = [0.8 \quad 0.2]$ and $B = \begin{bmatrix} 0.6 & 0.4 \\ 0.1 & 0.9 \end{bmatrix}$

C **55.** Find a, b, c, and d so that

$$\begin{bmatrix} a & b \\ c & d \end{bmatrix} + \begin{bmatrix} 2 & -3 \\ 0 & 1 \end{bmatrix} = \begin{bmatrix} 1 & -2 \\ 3 & -4 \end{bmatrix}$$

56. Find w, x, y, and z so that

$$\begin{bmatrix} 7 & -8 \\ 0 & 9 \end{bmatrix} + \begin{bmatrix} w & x \\ y & z \end{bmatrix} = \begin{bmatrix} 4 & -5 \\ 6 & 0 \end{bmatrix}$$

57. Find a, b, c, and d so that

$$\begin{bmatrix} 1 & -2 \\ 2 & -3 \end{bmatrix}\begin{bmatrix} a & b \\ c & d \end{bmatrix} = \begin{bmatrix} 1 & 0 \\ 3 & 2 \end{bmatrix}$$

58. Find a, b, c, and d so that

$$\begin{bmatrix} 1 & 3 \\ 1 & 4 \end{bmatrix}\begin{bmatrix} a & b \\ c & d \end{bmatrix} = \begin{bmatrix} 6 & -5 \\ 7 & -7 \end{bmatrix}$$

In Problems 59–62, determine whether the statement is true or false.

59. There exist two 1×1 matrices A and B such that $AB \neq BA$.

60. There exist two 2×2 matrices A and B such that $AB \neq BA$.

61. There exist two nonzero 2×2 matrices A and B such that AB is the 2×2 zero matrix.

62. There exist two nonzero 1×1 matrices A and B such that AB is the 1×1 zero matrix.

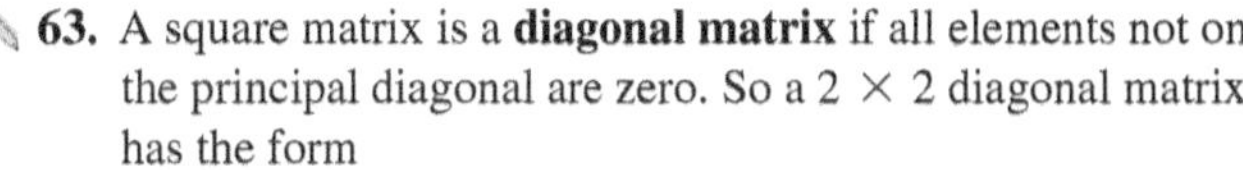

63. A square matrix is a **diagonal matrix** if all elements not on the principal diagonal are zero. So a 2×2 diagonal matrix has the form

$$A = \begin{bmatrix} a & 0 \\ 0 & d \end{bmatrix}$$

where a and d are real numbers. Discuss the validity of each of the following statements. If the statement is always true, explain why. If not, give examples.

(A) If A and B are 2×2 diagonal matrices, then $A + B$ is a 2×2 diagonal matrix.

(B) If A and B are 2×2 diagonal matrices, then AB is a 2×2 diagonal matrix.

(C) If A and B are 2×2 diagonal matrices, then $AB = BA$.

64. A square matrix is an **upper triangular matrix** if all elements below the principal diagonal are zero. So a 2×2 upper triangular matrix has the form

$$A = \begin{bmatrix} a & b \\ 0 & d \end{bmatrix}$$

where a, b, and d are real numbers. Discuss the validity of each of the following statements. If the statement is always true, explain why. If not, give examples.

(A) If A and B are 2×2 upper triangular matrices, then $A + B$ is a 2×2 upper triangular matrix.

(B) If A and B are 2×2 upper triangular matrices, then AB is a 2×2 upper triangular matrix.

(C) If A and B are 2×2 upper triangular matrices, then $AB = BA$.

Applications

65. Cost analysis. A company with two different plants manufactures guitars and banjos. Its production costs for each instrument are given in the following matrices:

$$\begin{array}{c} \text{Plant X} \\ \begin{array}{r} \\ \text{Materials} \\ \text{Labor} \end{array} \begin{array}{c} \text{Guitar} \quad \text{Banjo} \\ \begin{bmatrix} \$47 & \$39 \\ \$90 & \$125 \end{bmatrix} \end{array} = A \end{array} \qquad \begin{array}{c} \text{Plant Y} \\ \begin{array}{c} \text{Guitar} \quad \text{Banjo} \\ \begin{bmatrix} \$56 & \$42 \\ \$84 & \$115 \end{bmatrix} \end{array} = B \end{array}$$

Find $\frac{1}{2}(A + B)$, the average cost of production for the two plants.

66. Cost analysis. If both labor and materials at plant X in Problem 65 are increased by 20%, find $\frac{1}{2}(1.2A + B)$, the new average cost of production for the two plants.

67. Markup. An import car dealer sells three models of a car. The retail prices and the current dealer invoice prices (costs) for the basic models and options indicated are given in the following two matrices (where "Air" means air-conditioning):

Retail price

	Basic Car	Air	AM/FM radio	Cruise control
Model A	\$35,075	\$2,560	\$1,070	\$640
Model B	\$39,045	\$1,840	\$770	\$460
Model C	\$45,535	\$3,400	\$1,415	\$850

$= M$

Dealer invoice price

	Basic Car	Air	AM/FM radio	Cruise control
Model A	\$30,996	\$2,050	\$850	\$510
Model B	\$34,857	\$1,585	\$660	\$395
Model C	\$41,667	\$2,890	\$1,200	\$725

$= N$

We define the markup matrix to be $M - N$ (**markup** is the difference between the retail price and the dealer invoice price). Suppose that the value of the dollar has had a sharp decline and the dealer invoice price is to have an across-the-board 15% increase next year. To stay competitive with domestic cars, the dealer increases the retail prices 10%. Calculate a markup matrix for next year's models and the options indicated. (Compute results to the nearest dollar.)

68. Markup. Referring to Problem 67, what is the markup matrix resulting from a 20% increase in dealer invoice prices and an increase in retail prices of 15%? (Compute results to the nearest dollar.)

69. Labor costs. A company with manufacturing plants located in Italy (IT) and Poland (PL) has labor-hour and wage requirements for the manufacture of three types of shelving units as given in the following two matrices:

Labor-hours per shelving unit

$M =$

Cutting department	Assembly department	Packaging department	
0.7 hr	0.8 hr	0.3 hr	Small shelving unit
1.1 hr	1.3 hr	0.4 hr	Medium shelving unit
1.6 hr	1.7 hr	0.5 hr	Large shelving unit

Hourly wages

$N =$

IT	PL	
€12.45	€9.95	Cutting department
€9.55	€7.35	Assembly department
€7.75	€5.65	Packaging department

(A) Find the labor costs for a medium shelving unit manufactured at the Italian plant.

(B) Find the labor costs for a small shelving unit manufactured at the Polish plant.

(C) Discuss possible interpretations of the elements in the matrix products MN and NM.

(D) If either of the products MN or NM has a meaningful interpretation, find the product and label its rows and columns.

70. Inventory value. A personal computer retail company sells five different computer models through three stores. The inventory of each model on hand in each store is summarized in matrix M. Wholesale (W) and retail (R) values of each model computer are summarized in matrix N.

Model

$M =$

A	B	C	D	E	
4	2	3	7	1	Store 1
2	3	5	0	6	Store 2
10	4	3	4	3	Store 3

$N =$

W	R	Model
\$700	\$840	A
\$1,400	\$1,800	B
\$1,800	\$2,400	C
\$2,700	\$3,300	D
\$3,500	\$4,900	E

(A) What is the retail value of the inventory at store 2?

(B) What is the wholesale value of the inventory at store 3?

(C) If either product MN or NM has a meaningful interpretation, find the product and label its rows and columns. What do the entries represent?

(D) Discuss methods of matrix multiplication that can be used to find the total inventory of each model on hand at all three stores. State the matrices that can be used and perform the necessary operations.

71. Cereal. A nutritionist for a cereal company blends two cereals in three different mixes. The amounts of protein, carbohydrate, and fat (in grams per ounce) in each cereal are given by matrix M. The amounts of each cereal used in the three mixes are given by matrix N.

$$\begin{array}{l} \qquad\quad \text{Cereal A} \qquad \text{Cereal B} \\ M = \begin{bmatrix} 4\text{ g/oz} & 2\text{ g/oz} \\ 20\text{ g/oz} & 16\text{ g/oz} \\ 3\text{ g/oz} & 1\text{ g/oz} \end{bmatrix} \begin{matrix} \text{Protein} \\ \text{Carbohydrate} \\ \text{Fat} \end{matrix} \end{array}$$

$$\begin{array}{l} \qquad\ \text{Mix X} \quad \text{Mix Y} \quad \text{Mix Z} \\ N = \begin{bmatrix} 15\text{ oz} & 10\text{ oz} & 5\text{ oz} \\ 5\text{ oz} & 10\text{ oz} & 15\text{ oz} \end{bmatrix} \begin{matrix} \text{Cereal A} \\ \text{Cereal B} \end{matrix} \end{array}$$

(A) Find the amount of protein in mix X.

(B) Find the amount of fat in mix Z.

(C) Discuss possible interpretations of the elements in the matrix products MN and NM.

(D) If either of the products MN or NM has a meaningful interpretation, find the product and label its rows and columns.

72. Heredity. Gregor Mendel (1822–1884) made discoveries that revolutionized the science of genetics. In one experiment, he crossed dihybrid yellow round peas (yellow and round are dominant characteristics; the peas also contained genes for the recessive characteristics green and wrinkled) and obtained peas of the types indicated in the matrix:

$$\begin{array}{l} \qquad\qquad\ \ \text{Round} \quad \text{Wrinkled} \\ \begin{matrix} \text{Yellow} \\ \text{Green} \end{matrix} \begin{bmatrix} 315 & 101 \\ 108 & 32 \end{bmatrix} = M \end{array}$$

Suppose he carried out a second experiment of the same type and obtained peas of the types indicated in this matrix:

$$\begin{array}{l} \qquad\qquad\ \ \text{Round} \quad \text{Wrinkled} \\ \begin{matrix} \text{Yellow} \\ \text{Green} \end{matrix} \begin{bmatrix} 370 & 128 \\ 110 & 36 \end{bmatrix} = N \end{array}$$

If the results of the two experiments are combined, discuss matrix multiplication methods that can be used to find the following quantities. State the matrices that can be used and perform the necessary operations.

(A) The total number of peas in each category

(B) The total number of peas in all four categories

(C) The percentage of peas in each category

73. Politics. In a local London election, a public relations firm promoted its candidate in three ways: telephone calls, house calls, and letters. The cost per contact is given in matrix M, and the number of contacts of each type made in two adjacent boroughs is given in matrix N.

$$\begin{array}{l} \qquad\ \text{Cost per contact} \\ M = \begin{bmatrix} £0.90 \\ £3.45 \\ £1.15 \end{bmatrix} \begin{matrix} \text{Telephone call} \\ \text{House call} \\ \text{Letter} \end{matrix} \end{array}$$

$$\begin{array}{l} \qquad\ \begin{matrix} \text{Telephone} \\ \text{call} \end{matrix} \quad \begin{matrix} \text{House} \\ \text{call} \end{matrix} \quad \text{Letter} \\ N = \begin{bmatrix} 1{,}300 & 800 & 6{,}000 \\ 2{,}100 & 1200 & 7{,}000 \end{bmatrix} \begin{matrix} \text{Greenwich} \\ \text{Bromley} \end{matrix} \end{array}$$

(A) Find the total amount spent in Greenwich.

(B) Find the total amount spent in Bromley.

(C) If either product MN or NM has a meaningful interpretation, find the product and label its rows and columns. What do the entries represent?

(D) Discuss methods of matrix multiplication that can be used to find the total number of telephone calls, house calls, and letters. State the matrices that can be used and perform the necessary operations.

74. Test averages. A teacher has given four tests to a class of five students and stored the results in the following matrix:

$$\begin{array}{l} \qquad\qquad\qquad\quad \text{Tests} \\ \qquad\qquad\ \ 1 \quad\ 2 \quad\ 3 \quad\ 4 \\ \begin{matrix} \text{Ann} \\ \text{Bob} \\ \text{Carol} \\ \text{Dan} \\ \text{Eric} \end{matrix} \begin{bmatrix} 78 & 84 & 81 & 86 \\ 91 & 65 & 84 & 92 \\ 95 & 90 & 92 & 91 \\ 75 & 82 & 87 & 91 \\ 83 & 88 & 81 & 76 \end{bmatrix} = M \end{array}$$

Discuss methods of matrix multiplication that the teacher can use to obtain the information indicated below. In each case, state the matrices to be used and then perform the necessary operations.

(A) The average on all four tests for each student, assuming that all four tests are given equal weight

(B) The average on all four tests for each student, assuming that the first three tests are given equal weight and the fourth is given twice this weight

(C) The class average on each of the four tests

Answers to Matched Problems

1. $\begin{bmatrix} 1 & 5 \\ 0 & -2 \\ 2 & 1 \end{bmatrix}$ **2.** $[-1 \quad -1 \quad 4]$ **3.** $\begin{matrix} a = -6 \\ b = 7 \\ c = 9 \\ d = -1 \end{matrix}$ **4.** $\begin{bmatrix} 13 \\ 2 \\ 35 \end{bmatrix}$

5. (A) $\begin{bmatrix} \$235{,}000 & \$422{,}000 \\ \$372{,}000 & \$298{,}000 \end{bmatrix}$

(B) $\begin{bmatrix} \$145{,}000 & \$268{,}000 \\ \$160{,}000 & \$254{,}000 \end{bmatrix}$

(C) $\begin{bmatrix} \$9{,}500 & \$17{,}250 \\ \$13{,}300 & \$13{,}800 \end{bmatrix}$

6. [8] **7.** $[5 \quad 1.5]\begin{bmatrix} 9 \\ 6 \end{bmatrix} = [54]$, or \$54

8. (A) Not defined

(B) $\begin{bmatrix} 2 & 2 & -1 & 2 \\ 1 & 6 & 12 & -4 \\ -1 & 0 & 3 & -2 \end{bmatrix}$ (C) $\begin{bmatrix} 0 & 0 \\ 0 & 0 \end{bmatrix}$

(D) $\begin{bmatrix} -6 & -12 \\ 3 & 6 \end{bmatrix}$ (E) [11]

(F) $\begin{bmatrix} 12 & -8 & 4 \\ 6 & -4 & 2 \\ 9 & -6 & 3 \end{bmatrix}$

9. $a = 4, c = 8, b = 9, d = -2$

10. $PL = \begin{array}{l} \ \ \text{Assembly} \quad \text{Finishing} \\ [13{,}000 \qquad 4{,}000] \end{array}$ Labor-hours

4.5 Inverse of a Square Matrix

- Identity Matrix for Multiplication
- Inverse of a Square Matrix
- Application: Cryptography

Identity Matrix for Multiplication

Does the set of all matrices of a given size have an identity element for multiplication? That is, if M is an arbitrary $m \times n$ matrix, does there exist an identity element I such that $IM = MI = M$? The answer, in general, is no. However, the set of all **square matrices of order n** (matrices with n rows and n columns) does have an identity element.

DEFINITION Identity Matrix

The **identity element for multiplication** for the set of all square matrices of order n is the square matrix of order n, denoted by I, with 1's along the principal diagonal (from the upper left corner to the lower right) and 0's elsewhere.

For example,

$$\begin{bmatrix} 1 & 0 \\ 0 & 1 \end{bmatrix} \quad \text{and} \quad \begin{bmatrix} 1 & 0 & 0 \\ 0 & 1 & 0 \\ 0 & 0 & 1 \end{bmatrix}$$

are the identity matrices for all square matrices of order 2 and 3, respectively.

Most graphing calculators have a built-in command for generating the identity matrix of a given order (see Fig. 1).

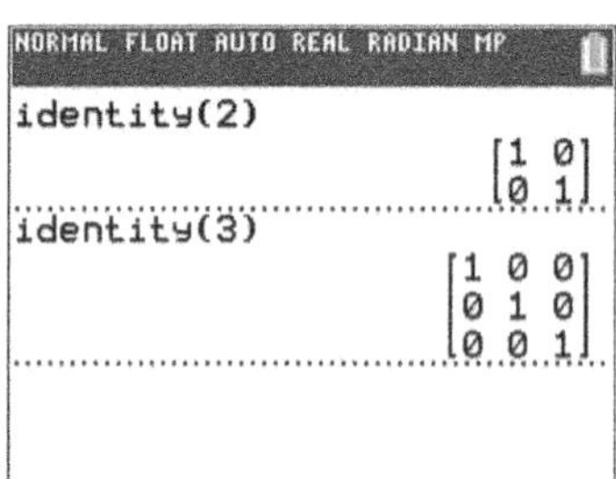

Figure 1 Identity matrices

EXAMPLE 1 Identity Matrix Multiplication

(A) $\begin{bmatrix} 1 & 0 & 0 \\ 0 & 1 & 0 \\ 0 & 0 & 1 \end{bmatrix}\begin{bmatrix} 3 & -2 & 5 \\ 0 & 2 & -3 \\ -1 & 4 & -2 \end{bmatrix} = \begin{bmatrix} 3 & -2 & 5 \\ 0 & 2 & -3 \\ -1 & 4 & -2 \end{bmatrix}$

(B) $\begin{bmatrix} 3 & -2 & 5 \\ 0 & 2 & -3 \\ -1 & 4 & -2 \end{bmatrix}\begin{bmatrix} 1 & 0 & 0 \\ 0 & 1 & 0 \\ 0 & 0 & 1 \end{bmatrix} = \begin{bmatrix} 3 & -2 & 5 \\ 0 & 2 & -3 \\ -1 & 4 & -2 \end{bmatrix}$

(C) $\begin{bmatrix} 1 & 0 \\ 0 & 1 \end{bmatrix}\begin{bmatrix} 2 & -1 & 3 \\ -2 & 0 & 4 \end{bmatrix} = \begin{bmatrix} 2 & -1 & 3 \\ -2 & 0 & 4 \end{bmatrix}$

(D) $\begin{bmatrix} 2 & -1 & 3 \\ -2 & 0 & 4 \end{bmatrix}\begin{bmatrix} 1 & 0 & 0 \\ 0 & 1 & 0 \\ 0 & 0 & 1 \end{bmatrix} = \begin{bmatrix} 2 & -1 & 3 \\ -2 & 0 & 4 \end{bmatrix}$

Matched Problem 1 Multiply:

(A) $\begin{bmatrix} 1 & 0 \\ 0 & 1 \end{bmatrix}\begin{bmatrix} 2 & -3 \\ 5 & 7 \end{bmatrix}$ and $\begin{bmatrix} 2 & -3 \\ 5 & 7 \end{bmatrix}\begin{bmatrix} 1 & 0 \\ 0 & 1 \end{bmatrix}$

(B) $\begin{bmatrix} 1 & 0 & 0 \\ 0 & 1 & 0 \\ 0 & 0 & 1 \end{bmatrix}\begin{bmatrix} 4 & 2 \\ 3 & -5 \\ 6 & 8 \end{bmatrix}$ and $\begin{bmatrix} 4 & 2 \\ 3 & -5 \\ 6 & 8 \end{bmatrix}\begin{bmatrix} 1 & 0 \\ 0 & 1 \end{bmatrix}$

In general, we can show that if M is a square matrix of order n and I is the identity matrix of order n, then

$$IM = MI = M$$

If M is an $m \times n$ matrix that is not square $(m \neq n)$, it is still possible to multiply M on the left and on the right by an identity matrix, but not with the same size identity matrix (see Example 1C and D). To avoid the complications involved with associating two different identity matrices with each nonsquare matrix, we restrict our attention in this section to square matrices.

Explore and Discuss 1

The only real number solutions to the equation $x^2 = 1$ are $x = 1$ and $x = -1$.

(A) Show that $A = \begin{bmatrix} 0 & 1 \\ 1 & 0 \end{bmatrix}$ satisfies $A^2 = I$, where I is the 2×2 identity.

(B) Show that $B = \begin{bmatrix} 0 & -1 \\ -1 & 0 \end{bmatrix}$ satisfies $B^2 = I$.

(C) Find a 2×2 matrix with all elements nonzero whose square is the 2×2 identity matrix.

Inverse of a Square Matrix

If r is an arbitary real number, then its **additive inverse** is the solution x to the equation $r + x = 0$. So the additive inverse of 3 is -3, and the additive inverse of -7 is 7. Similarly, if M is an arbitary $m \times n$ matrix, then M has an additive inverse $-M$, whose elements are just the additive inverses of the elements of M.

The situation is more complicated for *multiplicative* inverses. The **multiplicative inverse** of an arbitrary real number r is the solution x to the equation $r \cdot x = 1$. So the multiplicative inverse of 3 is $\frac{1}{3}$, and the multiplicative inverse of $\frac{-15}{4}$ is $\frac{-4}{15}$. Every real number has a multiplicative inverse except for 0. Because the equation $0 \cdot x = 1$ has no real solution, 0 does not have a multiplicative inverse.

Can we extend the multiplicative inverse concept to matrices? That is, given a matrix M, can we find another matrix N such that $MN = NM = I$, the matrix identity for multiplication? To begin, we consider the size of these matrices. Let M be an $n \times m$ matrix and N a $p \times q$ matrix. If both MN and NM are defined, then $m = p$ and $q = n$ (Fig. 2). If $MN = NM$, then $n = p$ and $q = m$ (Fig. 3). Thus, we have $m = p = n = q$. In other words, M and N must be square matrices of the same order. Later we will see that not all square matrices have inverses.

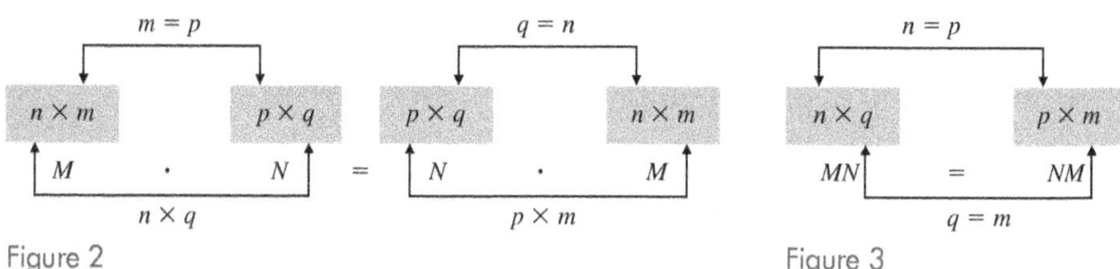

Figure 2

Figure 3

DEFINITION Inverse of a Square Matrix

Let M be a square matrix of order n and I be the identity matrix of order n. If there exists a matrix M^{-1} (read "M inverse") such that

$$M^{-1}M = MM^{-1} = I$$

then M^{-1} is called the **multiplicative inverse of M** or, more simply, the **inverse of M**. If no such matrix exists, then M is said to be a **singular matrix**.

Let us use the definition above to find M^{-1} for

$$M = \begin{bmatrix} 2 & 3 \\ 1 & 2 \end{bmatrix}$$

We are looking for

$$M^{-1} = \begin{bmatrix} a & c \\ b & d \end{bmatrix}$$

such that

$$MM^{-1} = M^{-1}M = I$$

So we write

$$\overset{M}{\begin{bmatrix} 2 & 3 \\ 1 & 2 \end{bmatrix}} \overset{M^{-1}}{\begin{bmatrix} a & c \\ b & d \end{bmatrix}} = \overset{I}{\begin{bmatrix} 1 & 0 \\ 0 & 1 \end{bmatrix}}$$

and try to find a, b, c, and d so that the product of M and M^{-1} is the identity matrix I. Multiplying M and M^{-1} on the left side, we obtain

$$\begin{bmatrix} (2a + 3b) & (2c + 3d) \\ (a + 2b) & (c + 2d) \end{bmatrix} = \begin{bmatrix} 1 & 0 \\ 0 & 1 \end{bmatrix}$$

which is true only if

$$\begin{aligned} 2a + 3b &= 1 \\ a + 2b &= 0 \end{aligned} \qquad\qquad \begin{aligned} 2c + 3d &= 0 \\ c + 2d &= 1 \end{aligned}$$

Use Gauss–Jordan elimination to solve each system.

$$\left[\begin{array}{cc|c} 2 & 3 & 1 \\ 1 & 2 & 0 \end{array}\right] \quad R_1 \leftrightarrow R_2 \qquad \left[\begin{array}{cc|c} 2 & 3 & 0 \\ 1 & 2 & 1 \end{array}\right] \quad R_1 \leftrightarrow R_2$$

$$\left[\begin{array}{cc|c} 1 & 2 & 0 \\ 2 & 3 & 1 \end{array}\right] \quad (-2)R_1 + R_2 \rightarrow R_2 \qquad \left[\begin{array}{cc|c} 1 & 2 & 1 \\ 2 & 3 & 0 \end{array}\right] \quad (-2)R_1 + R_2 \rightarrow R_2$$

$$\left[\begin{array}{cc|c} 1 & 2 & 0 \\ 0 & -1 & 1 \end{array}\right] \quad (-1)R_2 \rightarrow R_2 \qquad \left[\begin{array}{cc|c} 1 & 2 & 1 \\ 0 & -1 & -2 \end{array}\right] \quad (-1)R_2 \rightarrow R_2$$

$$\left[\begin{array}{cc|c} 1 & 2 & 0 \\ 0 & 1 & -1 \end{array}\right] \quad (-2)R_2 + R_1 \rightarrow R_1 \qquad \left[\begin{array}{cc|c} 1 & 2 & 1 \\ 0 & 1 & 2 \end{array}\right] \quad (-2)R_2 + R_1 \rightarrow R_1$$

$$\left[\begin{array}{cc|c} 1 & 0 & 2 \\ 0 & 1 & -1 \end{array}\right] \qquad \left[\begin{array}{cc|c} 1 & 0 & -3 \\ 0 & 1 & 2 \end{array}\right]$$

$a = 2, b = -1 \qquad c = -3, d = 2$

$$M^{-1} = \begin{bmatrix} a & c \\ b & d \end{bmatrix} = \begin{bmatrix} 2 & -3 \\ -1 & 2 \end{bmatrix}$$

CHECK

$$\overset{M}{\begin{bmatrix} 2 & 3 \\ 1 & 2 \end{bmatrix}} \overset{M^{-1}}{\begin{bmatrix} 2 & -3 \\ -1 & 2 \end{bmatrix}} = \overset{I}{\begin{bmatrix} 1 & 0 \\ 0 & 1 \end{bmatrix}} = \overset{M^{-1}}{\begin{bmatrix} 2 & -3 \\ -1 & 2 \end{bmatrix}} \overset{M}{\begin{bmatrix} 2 & 3 \\ 1 & 2 \end{bmatrix}}$$

Unlike nonzero real numbers, inverses do not always exist for square matrices. For example, if

$$N = \begin{bmatrix} 2 & 1 \\ 4 & 2 \end{bmatrix}$$

then, using the previous process, we are led to the systems

$$\begin{aligned} 2a + b &= 1 \\ 4a + 2b &= 0 \end{aligned} \qquad \begin{aligned} 2c + d &= 0 \\ 4c + 2d &= 1 \end{aligned}$$

Use Gauss–Jordan elimination to solve each system.

$$\left[\begin{array}{cc|c} 2 & 1 & 1 \\ 4 & 2 & 0 \end{array}\right] \quad (-2)R_1 + R_2 \to R_2 \qquad \left[\begin{array}{cc|c} 2 & 1 & 0 \\ 4 & 2 & 1 \end{array}\right] \quad (-2)R_1 + R_2 \to R_2$$

$$\left[\begin{array}{cc|c} 2 & 1 & 0 \\ 0 & 0 & -2 \end{array}\right] \qquad \left[\begin{array}{cc|c} 2 & 1 & 0 \\ 0 & 0 & 1 \end{array}\right]$$

The last row of each augmented matrix contains a contradiction. So each system is inconsistent and has no solution. We conclude that N^{-1} does not exist and N is a singular matrix.

Being able to find inverses, when they exist, leads to direct and simple solutions to many practical problems. In the next section, we show how inverses can be used to solve systems of linear equations.

The method outlined previously for finding M^{-1}, if it exists, gets very involved for matrices of order larger than 2. Now that we know what we are looking for, we can use augmented matrices (see Sections 4.2 and 4.3) to make the process more efficient.

EXAMPLE 2 **Finding the Inverse of a Matrix** Find the inverse, if it exists, of the matrix

$$M = \begin{bmatrix} 1 & -1 & 1 \\ 0 & 2 & -1 \\ 2 & 3 & 0 \end{bmatrix}$$

SOLUTION We start as before and write

$$\overset{M}{\begin{bmatrix} 1 & -1 & 1 \\ 0 & 2 & -1 \\ 2 & 3 & 0 \end{bmatrix}} \overset{M^{-1}}{\begin{bmatrix} a & d & g \\ b & e & h \\ c & f & i \end{bmatrix}} = \overset{I}{\begin{bmatrix} 1 & 0 & 0 \\ 0 & 1 & 0 \\ 0 & 0 & 1 \end{bmatrix}}$$

which is true only if

$$\begin{aligned} a - \ \ b + c &= 1 \\ 2b - c &= 0 \\ 2a + 3b \qquad &= 0 \end{aligned} \qquad \begin{aligned} d - \ \ e + f &= 0 \\ 2e - f &= 1 \\ 2d + 3e \qquad &= 0 \end{aligned} \qquad \begin{aligned} g - \ \ h + i &= 0 \\ 2h - i &= 0 \\ 2g + 3h \qquad &= 1 \end{aligned}$$

Now we write augmented matrices for each of the three systems:

$$\overset{\text{First}}{\left[\begin{array}{ccc|c} 1 & -1 & 1 & 1 \\ 0 & 2 & -1 & 0 \\ 2 & 3 & 0 & 0 \end{array}\right]} \quad \overset{\text{Second}}{\left[\begin{array}{ccc|c} 1 & -1 & 1 & 0 \\ 0 & 2 & -1 & 1 \\ 2 & 3 & 0 & 0 \end{array}\right]} \quad \overset{\text{Third}}{\left[\begin{array}{ccc|c} 1 & -1 & 1 & 0 \\ 0 & 2 & -1 & 0 \\ 2 & 3 & 0 & 1 \end{array}\right]}$$

Since each matrix to the left of the vertical bar is the same, exactly the same row operations can be used on each augmented matrix to transform it into a reduced form. We can speed up the process substantially by combining all three augmented matrices into the single augmented matrix form below:

$$\left[\begin{array}{ccc|ccc} 1 & -1 & 1 & 1 & 0 & 0 \\ 0 & 2 & -1 & 0 & 1 & 0 \\ 2 & 3 & 0 & 0 & 0 & 1 \end{array}\right] = [M \mid I] \tag{1}$$

We now try to perform row operations on matrix (1) until we obtain a row-equivalent matrix of the form

$$\overset{I \qquad\qquad\quad B}{\left[\begin{array}{ccc|ccc} 1 & 0 & 0 & a & d & g \\ 0 & 1 & 0 & b & e & h \\ 0 & 0 & 1 & c & f & i \end{array}\right]} = [I \mid B] \tag{2}$$

If this can be done, the new matrix B to the right of the vertical bar will be M^{-1}. Now let's try to transform matrix (1) into a form like matrix (2). We follow the same sequence of steps as we did in the solution of linear systems by Gauss–Jordan elimination (see Section 4.3).

$$\overset{M \qquad\qquad\qquad I}{\left[\begin{array}{ccc|ccc} 1 & -1 & 1 & 1 & 0 & 0 \\ 0 & 2 & -1 & 0 & 1 & 0 \\ 2 & 3 & 0 & 0 & 0 & 1 \end{array}\right]} \qquad (-2)R_1 + R_3 \rightarrow R_3$$

$$\sim \left[\begin{array}{ccc|ccc} 1 & -1 & 1 & 1 & 0 & 0 \\ 0 & 2 & -1 & 0 & 1 & 0 \\ 0 & 5 & -2 & -2 & 0 & 1 \end{array}\right] \qquad \tfrac{1}{2}R_2 \rightarrow R_2$$

$$\sim \left[\begin{array}{ccc|ccc} 1 & -1 & 1 & 1 & 0 & 0 \\ 0 & 1 & -\frac{1}{2} & 0 & \frac{1}{2} & 0 \\ 0 & 5 & -2 & -2 & 0 & 1 \end{array}\right] \qquad \begin{array}{l} R_2 + R_1 \rightarrow R_1 \\ (-5)R_2 + R_3 \rightarrow R_3 \end{array}$$

$$\sim\left[\begin{array}{ccc|ccc} 1 & 0 & \frac{1}{2} & 1 & \frac{1}{2} & 0 \\ 0 & 1 & -\frac{1}{2} & 0 & \frac{1}{2} & 0 \\ 0 & 0 & \frac{1}{2} & -2 & -\frac{5}{2} & 1 \end{array}\right] \quad 2R_3 \to R_3$$

$$\sim\left[\begin{array}{ccc|ccc} 1 & 0 & \frac{1}{2} & 1 & \frac{1}{2} & 0 \\ 0 & 1 & -\frac{1}{2} & 0 & \frac{1}{2} & 0 \\ 0 & 0 & 1 & -4 & -5 & 2 \end{array}\right] \quad \begin{array}{l} (-\frac{1}{2})R_3 + R_1 \to R_1 \\ \frac{1}{2}R_3 + R_2 \to R_2 \end{array}$$

$$\sim\left[\begin{array}{ccc|ccc} 1 & 0 & 0 & 3 & 3 & -1 \\ 0 & 1 & 0 & -2 & -2 & 1 \\ 0 & 0 & 1 & -4 & -5 & 2 \end{array}\right] = [I \mid B]$$

Converting back to systems of equations equivalent to our three original systems, we have

$$\begin{array}{lll} a = 3 & d = 3 & g = -1 \\ b = -2 & e = -2 & h = 1 \\ c = -4 & f = -5 & i = 2 \end{array}$$

And these are just the elements of M^{-1} that we are looking for!

$$M^{-1} = \begin{bmatrix} 3 & 3 & -1 \\ -2 & -2 & 1 \\ -4 & -5 & 2 \end{bmatrix}$$

Note that this is the matrix to the right of the vertical line in the last augmented matrix. That is, $M^{-1} = B$.

Since the definition of matrix inverse requires that

$$M^{-1}M = I \qquad \text{and} \qquad MM^{-1} = I \tag{3}$$

it appears that we must compute both $M^{-1}M$ and MM^{-1} to check our work. However, it can be shown that if one of the equations in (3) is satisfied, the other is also satisfied. So to check our answer it is sufficient to compute either $M^{-1}M$ or MM^{-1}; we do not need to do both.

CHECK

$$M^{-1}M = \begin{bmatrix} 3 & 3 & -1 \\ -2 & -2 & 1 \\ -4 & -5 & 2 \end{bmatrix}\begin{bmatrix} 1 & -1 & 1 \\ 0 & 2 & -1 \\ 2 & 3 & 0 \end{bmatrix} = \begin{bmatrix} 1 & 0 & 0 \\ 0 & 1 & 0 \\ 0 & 0 & 1 \end{bmatrix} = I$$

Matched Problem 2 Let $M = \begin{bmatrix} 3 & -1 & 1 \\ -1 & 1 & 0 \\ 1 & 0 & 1 \end{bmatrix}$.

(A) Form the augmented matrix $[M \mid I]$.

(B) Use row operations to transform $[M \mid I]$ into $[I \mid B]$.

(C) Verify by multiplication that $B = M^{-1}$ (that is, show that $BM = I$).

The procedure shown in Example 2 can be used to find the inverse of any square matrix, if the inverse exists, and will also indicate when the inverse does not exist. These ideas are summarized in Theorem 1.

THEOREM 1 Inverse of a Square Matrix *M*

If $[M \mid I]$ is transformed by row operations into $[I \mid B]$, then the resulting matrix B is M^{-1}. However, if we obtain all 0's in one or more rows to the left of the vertical line, then M^{-1} does not exist.

Explore and Discuss 2

(A) Suppose that the square matrix M has a row of all zeros. Explain why M has no inverse.

(B) Suppose that the square matrix M has a column of all zeros. Explain why M has no inverse.

EXAMPLE 3 **Finding a Matrix Inverse** Find M^{-1}, given $M = \begin{bmatrix} 4 & -1 \\ -6 & 2 \end{bmatrix}$.

SOLUTION

$$\left[\begin{array}{rr|rr} 4 & -1 & 1 & 0 \\ -6 & 2 & 0 & 1 \end{array}\right] \quad \tfrac{1}{4}R_1 \rightarrow R_1$$

$$\sim \left[\begin{array}{rr|rr} 1 & -\frac{1}{4} & \frac{1}{4} & 0 \\ -6 & 2 & 0 & 1 \end{array}\right] \quad 6R_1 + R_2 \rightarrow R_2$$

$$\sim \left[\begin{array}{rr|rr} 1 & -\frac{1}{4} & \frac{1}{4} & 0 \\ 0 & \frac{1}{2} & \frac{3}{2} & 1 \end{array}\right] \quad 2R_2 \rightarrow R_2$$

$$\sim \left[\begin{array}{rr|rr} 1 & -\frac{1}{4} & \frac{1}{4} & 0 \\ 0 & 1 & 3 & 2 \end{array}\right] \quad \tfrac{1}{4}R_2 + R_1 \rightarrow R_1$$

$$\sim \left[\begin{array}{rr|rr} 1 & 0 & 1 & \frac{1}{2} \\ 0 & 1 & 3 & 2 \end{array}\right]$$

Therefore,

$$M^{-1} = \begin{bmatrix} 1 & \frac{1}{2} \\ 3 & 2 \end{bmatrix}$$

Check by showing that $M^{-1}M = I$.

Matched Problem 3 Find M^{-1}, given $M = \begin{bmatrix} 2 & -6 \\ 1 & -2 \end{bmatrix}$.

Most graphing calculators and spreadsheets can compute matrix inverses, as illustrated in Figure 4 for the solution to Example 3.

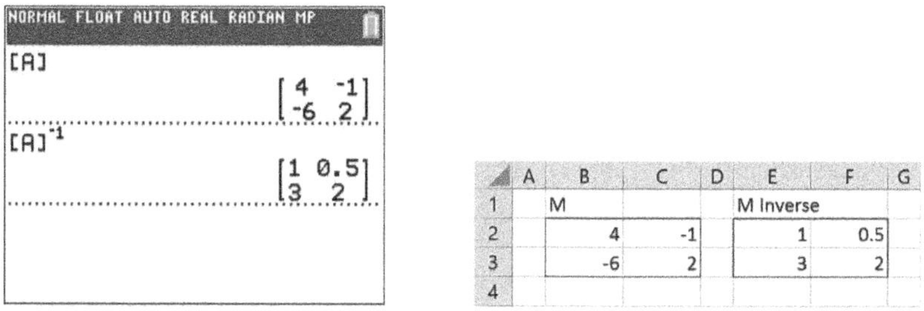

(A) The command $[A]^{-1}$ produces the inverse on this graphing calculator

	A	B	C	D	E	F	G
1		M			M Inverse		
2		4	-1		1	0.5	
3		-6	2		3	2	
4							

(B) The command MINVERSE (B2:C3) produces the inverse in this spreadsheet

Figure 4 Finding a matrix inverse

Explore and Discuss 3

The inverse of

$$A = \begin{bmatrix} a & b \\ c & d \end{bmatrix}$$

is

$$A^{-1} = \begin{bmatrix} \dfrac{d}{ad - bc} & \dfrac{-b}{ad - bc} \\ \dfrac{-c}{ad - bc} & \dfrac{a}{ad - bc} \end{bmatrix} = \frac{1}{D}\begin{bmatrix} d & -b \\ -c & a \end{bmatrix} \qquad D = ad - bc$$

provided that $D \neq 0$.

(A) Use matrix multiplication to verify this formula. What can you conclude about A^{-1} if $D = 0$?

(B) Use this formula to find the inverse of matrix M in Example 3.

EXAMPLE 4 **Finding a Matrix Inverse** Find M^{-1}, given $M = \begin{bmatrix} 2 & -4 \\ -3 & 6 \end{bmatrix}$.

SOLUTION

$$\left[\begin{array}{cc|cc} 2 & -4 & 1 & 0 \\ -3 & 6 & 0 & 1 \end{array}\right] \quad \tfrac{1}{2}R_1 \to R_1$$

$$\sim \left[\begin{array}{cc|cc} 1 & -2 & \frac{1}{2} & 0 \\ -3 & 6 & 0 & 1 \end{array}\right] \quad 3R_1 + R_2 \to R_2$$

$$\sim \left[\begin{array}{cc|cc} 1 & -2 & \frac{1}{2} & 0 \\ 0 & 0 & \frac{3}{2} & 1 \end{array}\right]$$

We have all 0's in the second row to the left of the vertical bar; therefore, the inverse does not exist.

Matched Problem 4 Find N^{-1}, given $N = \begin{bmatrix} 3 & 1 \\ 6 & 2 \end{bmatrix}$.

Square matrices that do not have inverses are called singular matrices. Graphing calculators and spreadsheets recognize singular matrices and generally respond with some type of error message, as illustrated in Figure 5 for the solution to Example 4.

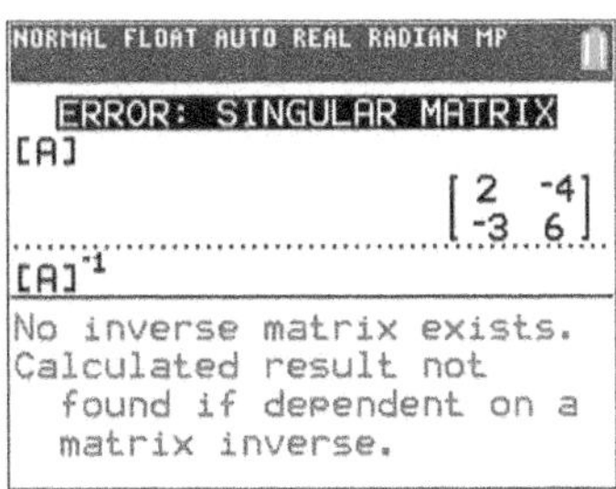

(A) A graphing calculator displays a clear error message

	A	B	C	D	E	F	G
1		M			M Inverse		
2		2	-4		#NUM!	#NUM!	
3		-3	6		#NUM!	#NUM!	
4							

(B) A spreadsheet displays a more cryptic error message

Figure 5

Application: Cryptography

Matrix inverses can provide a simple and effective procedure for encoding and decoding messages. To begin, assign the numbers 1–26 to the letters in the alphabet, as shown below. Also assign the number 0 to a blank to provide for space between words. (A more sophisticated code could include both capital and lowercase letters and punctuation symbols.)

Blank	A	B	C	D	E	F	G	H	I	J	K	L	M	N	O	P	Q	R	S	T	U	V	W	X	Y	Z
0	1	2	3	4	5	6	7	8	9	10	11	12	13	14	15	16	17	18	19	20	21	22	23	24	25	26

The message "SECRET CODE" corresponds to the sequence

19 5 3 18 5 20 0 3 15 4 5

Any matrix whose elements are positive integers and whose inverse exists can be used as an **encoding matrix**. For example, to use the 2×2 matrix

$$A = \begin{bmatrix} 4 & 3 \\ 1 & 1 \end{bmatrix}$$

to encode the preceding message, first we divide the numbers in the sequence into groups of 2 and use these groups as the columns of a matrix B with 2 rows:

$$B = \begin{bmatrix} 19 & 3 & 5 & 0 & 15 & 5 \\ 5 & 18 & 20 & 3 & 4 & 0 \end{bmatrix}$$

Proceed down the columns, not across the rows.

Notice that we added an extra blank at the end of the message to make the columns come out even. Then we multiply this matrix on the left by A:

$$AB = \begin{bmatrix} 4 & 3 \\ 1 & 1 \end{bmatrix}\begin{bmatrix} 19 & 3 & 5 & 0 & 15 & 5 \\ 5 & 18 & 20 & 3 & 4 & 0 \end{bmatrix}$$

$$= \begin{bmatrix} 91 & 66 & 80 & 9 & 72 & 20 \\ 24 & 21 & 25 & 3 & 19 & 5 \end{bmatrix}$$

The coded message is

91 24 66 21 80 25 9 3 72 19 20 5

This message can be decoded simply by putting it back into matrix form and multiplying on the left by the **decoding matrix** A^{-1}. Since A^{-1} is easily determined if A is known, the encoding matrix A is the only key needed to decode messages that are encoded in this manner.

EXAMPLE 5 **Cryptography** The message

46 84 85 28 47 46 4 5 10 30 48 72 29 57 38 38 57 95

was encoded with the matrix A shown next. Decode this message.

$$A = \begin{bmatrix} 1 & 1 & 1 \\ 2 & 1 & 2 \\ 2 & 3 & 1 \end{bmatrix}$$

SOLUTION Since the encoding matrix A is 3×3, we begin by entering the coded message in the columns of a matrix C with three rows:

$$C = \begin{bmatrix} 46 & 28 & 4 & 30 & 29 & 38 \\ 84 & 47 & 5 & 48 & 57 & 57 \\ 85 & 46 & 10 & 72 & 38 & 95 \end{bmatrix}$$

If B is the matrix containing the uncoded message, then B and C are related by $C = AB$. To recover B, we find A^{-1} (details omitted) and multiply both sides of the equation $C = AB$ by A^{-1}:

$$B = A^{-1}C$$

$$= \begin{bmatrix} -5 & 2 & 1 \\ 2 & -1 & 0 \\ 4 & -1 & -1 \end{bmatrix}\begin{bmatrix} 46 & 28 & 4 & 30 & 29 & 38 \\ 84 & 47 & 5 & 48 & 57 & 57 \\ 85 & 46 & 10 & 72 & 38 & 95 \end{bmatrix}$$

$$= \begin{bmatrix} 23 & 0 & 0 & 18 & 7 & 19 \\ 8 & 9 & 3 & 12 & 1 & 19 \\ 15 & 19 & 1 & 0 & 21 & 0 \end{bmatrix}$$

Writing the numbers in the columns of this matrix in sequence and using the correspondence between numbers and letters noted earlier produces the decoded message:

23	8	15	0	9	19	0	3	1	18	12	0	7	1	21	19	19	0
W	H	O		I	S		C	A	R	L		G	A	U	S	S	

The answer to this question can be found earlier in this chapter.

Matched Problem 5 The message below was also encoded with the matrix A in Example 5. Decode this message:

46 84 85 28 47 46 32 41 78 25 42 53 25 37 63 43 71 83 19 37 25

Exercises 4.5

Skills Warm-up Exercises

W

In Problems 1–4, find the additive inverse and the multiplicative inverse, if defined, of each real number. (If necessary, review Section B.1).

1. (A) 4 (B) -3 (C) 0
2. (A) -7 (B) 2 (C) -1
3. (A) $\frac{2}{3}$ (B) $\frac{-1}{7}$ (C) 1.6
4. (A) $\frac{6}{7}$ (B) $\frac{23}{45}$ (C) -0.8

A

In Problems 5–8, does the given matrix have a multiplicative inverse? Explain your answer.

5. $\begin{bmatrix} 2 & 5 \end{bmatrix}$ 6. $\begin{bmatrix} 4 \\ 8 \end{bmatrix}$ 7. $\begin{bmatrix} 0 & 0 \\ 0 & 0 \end{bmatrix}$ 8. $\begin{bmatrix} 1 & 0 \\ 0 & 1 \end{bmatrix}$

In Problems 9–18, find the matrix products. Note that each product can be found mentally, without the use of a calculator or pencil-and-paper calculations.

9. (A) $\begin{bmatrix} 1 & 0 \\ 0 & 0 \end{bmatrix}\begin{bmatrix} 2 & -3 \\ 4 & 5 \end{bmatrix}$ (B) $\begin{bmatrix} 2 & -3 \\ 4 & 5 \end{bmatrix}\begin{bmatrix} 1 & 0 \\ 0 & 0 \end{bmatrix}$

10. (A) $\begin{bmatrix} 1 & 0 \\ 0 & 0 \end{bmatrix}\begin{bmatrix} -1 & 6 \\ 5 & 2 \end{bmatrix}$ (B) $\begin{bmatrix} -1 & 6 \\ 5 & 2 \end{bmatrix}\begin{bmatrix} 1 & 0 \\ 0 & 0 \end{bmatrix}$

11. (A) $\begin{bmatrix} 0 & 0 \\ 0 & 1 \end{bmatrix}\begin{bmatrix} 2 & -3 \\ 4 & 5 \end{bmatrix}$ (B) $\begin{bmatrix} 2 & -3 \\ 4 & 5 \end{bmatrix}\begin{bmatrix} 0 & 0 \\ 0 & 1 \end{bmatrix}$

12. (A) $\begin{bmatrix} 0 & 0 \\ 0 & 1 \end{bmatrix}\begin{bmatrix} 6 & -7 \\ -8 & 9 \end{bmatrix}$ (B) $\begin{bmatrix} 6 & -7 \\ -8 & 9 \end{bmatrix}\begin{bmatrix} 0 & 0 \\ 0 & 1 \end{bmatrix}$

13. (A) $\begin{bmatrix} 1 & 0 \\ 0 & 1 \end{bmatrix}\begin{bmatrix} 2 & -3 \\ 4 & 5 \end{bmatrix}$ (B) $\begin{bmatrix} 2 & -3 \\ 4 & 5 \end{bmatrix}\begin{bmatrix} 1 & 0 \\ 0 & 1 \end{bmatrix}$

14. (A) $\begin{bmatrix} 1 & 0 \\ 0 & 1 \end{bmatrix}\begin{bmatrix} -1 & 6 \\ 5 & 2 \end{bmatrix}$ (B) $\begin{bmatrix} -1 & 6 \\ 5 & 2 \end{bmatrix}\begin{bmatrix} 1 & 0 \\ 0 & 1 \end{bmatrix}$

15. $\begin{bmatrix} 1 & 0 & 0 \\ 0 & 1 & 0 \\ 0 & 0 & 1 \end{bmatrix}\begin{bmatrix} -2 & 1 & 3 \\ 2 & 4 & -2 \\ 5 & 1 & 0 \end{bmatrix}$

16. $\begin{bmatrix} 1 & 0 & 0 \\ 0 & 1 & 0 \\ 0 & 0 & 1 \end{bmatrix}\begin{bmatrix} 1 & -2 & 3 \\ -4 & 5 & -6 \\ 7 & -8 & 9 \end{bmatrix}$

17. $\begin{bmatrix} -2 & 1 & 3 \\ 2 & 4 & -2 \\ 5 & 1 & 0 \end{bmatrix}\begin{bmatrix} 1 & 0 & 0 \\ 0 & 1 & 0 \\ 0 & 0 & 1 \end{bmatrix}$

18. $\begin{bmatrix} 1 & -2 & 3 \\ -4 & 5 & -6 \\ 7 & -8 & 9 \end{bmatrix}\begin{bmatrix} 1 & 0 & 0 \\ 0 & 1 & 0 \\ 0 & 0 & 1 \end{bmatrix}$

In Problems 19–28, examine the product of the two matrices to determine if each is the inverse of the other.

19. $\begin{bmatrix} 3 & -4 \\ -2 & 3 \end{bmatrix}$; $\begin{bmatrix} 3 & 4 \\ 2 & 3 \end{bmatrix}$

20. $\begin{bmatrix} -2 & -1 \\ -4 & 2 \end{bmatrix}$; $\begin{bmatrix} 1 & -1 \\ 2 & -2 \end{bmatrix}$

21. $\begin{bmatrix} 2 & 2 \\ -1 & -1 \end{bmatrix}$; $\begin{bmatrix} 1 & 1 \\ -1 & -1 \end{bmatrix}$

22. $\begin{bmatrix} 5 & -7 \\ -2 & 3 \end{bmatrix}$; $\begin{bmatrix} 3 & 7 \\ 2 & 5 \end{bmatrix}$

23. $\begin{bmatrix} -5 & 2 \\ -8 & 3 \end{bmatrix}$; $\begin{bmatrix} 3 & -2 \\ 8 & -5 \end{bmatrix}$

24. $\begin{bmatrix} 7 & 4 \\ -5 & -3 \end{bmatrix}$; $\begin{bmatrix} 3 & 4 \\ -5 & -7 \end{bmatrix}$

25. $\begin{bmatrix} 1 & -3 & -5 \\ -2 & 3 & 5 \\ -1 & 1 & 2 \end{bmatrix}$; $\begin{bmatrix} -1 & -1 & 0 \\ 1 & 3 & -5 \\ -1 & -2 & 3 \end{bmatrix}$

26. $\begin{bmatrix} 1 & 0 & 1 \\ -3 & 1 & -2 \\ 0 & 0 & 1 \end{bmatrix}$; $\begin{bmatrix} 1 & 0 & -1 \\ 3 & 1 & -1 \\ 0 & 0 & 1 \end{bmatrix}$

27. $\begin{bmatrix} 3 & -1 & 1 \\ 2 & 5 & -4 \\ 0 & 2 & 1 \end{bmatrix}$; $\begin{bmatrix} 1 & -2 & 0 \\ 3 & 4 & 0 \\ -2 & 1 & 0 \end{bmatrix}$

28. $\begin{bmatrix} 1 & 0 & -1 \\ 3 & 1 & -1 \\ 0 & 0 & 0 \end{bmatrix}$; $\begin{bmatrix} 1 & 0 & -1 \\ -3 & 1 & -2 \\ 0 & 0 & 1 \end{bmatrix}$

Without performing any row operations, explain why each of the matrices in Problems 29–38 does not have an inverse.

29. $\begin{bmatrix} 1 & 2 & 0 \\ -3 & 2 & -1 \end{bmatrix}$

30. $\begin{bmatrix} -2 & 3 & -1 \\ 4 & 0 & 1 \end{bmatrix}$

31. $\begin{bmatrix} 1 & -2 \\ 3 & 0 \\ 2 & -1 \end{bmatrix}$

32. $\begin{bmatrix} 0 & -1 \\ 2 & -2 \\ 1 & -3 \end{bmatrix}$

33. $\begin{bmatrix} 0 & 1 \\ 0 & -2 \end{bmatrix}$

34. $\begin{bmatrix} 0 & -1 \\ 0 & 2 \end{bmatrix}$

35. $\begin{bmatrix} 1 & -2 \\ 0 & 0 \end{bmatrix}$

36. $\begin{bmatrix} -1 & 2 \\ 0 & 0 \end{bmatrix}$

37. $\begin{bmatrix} 1 & -3 \\ -3 & 9 \end{bmatrix}$

38. $\begin{bmatrix} -1 & 2 \\ 1 & -2 \end{bmatrix}$

B *Given M in Problems 39–48, find M^{-1} and show that $M^{-1}M = I$.*

39. $\begin{bmatrix} -1 & 0 \\ -3 & 1 \end{bmatrix}$

40. $\begin{bmatrix} 1 & -5 \\ 0 & -1 \end{bmatrix}$

41. $\begin{bmatrix} 1 & 2 \\ 1 & 3 \end{bmatrix}$

42. $\begin{bmatrix} 2 & 1 \\ 5 & 3 \end{bmatrix}$

43. $\begin{bmatrix} 1 & 2 \\ 4 & 9 \end{bmatrix}$

44. $\begin{bmatrix} 2 & 1 \\ 1 & 1 \end{bmatrix}$

45. $\begin{bmatrix} 1 & -3 & 0 \\ 0 & 1 & 1 \\ 2 & -1 & 4 \end{bmatrix}$

46. $\begin{bmatrix} 2 & 3 & 0 \\ 1 & 2 & 3 \\ 0 & -1 & -5 \end{bmatrix}$

47. $\begin{bmatrix} 1 & 1 & 0 \\ 2 & 3 & -1 \\ 1 & 0 & 2 \end{bmatrix}$

48. $\begin{bmatrix} 1 & 1 & 1 \\ 2 & 1 & 0 \\ 4 & 3 & 1 \end{bmatrix}$

Find the inverse of each matrix in Problems 49–56, if it exists.

49. $\begin{bmatrix} 4 & 3 \\ -3 & -2 \end{bmatrix}$

50. $\begin{bmatrix} -4 & 3 \\ -5 & 4 \end{bmatrix}$

51. $\begin{bmatrix} 2 & 6 \\ 3 & 9 \end{bmatrix}$

52. $\begin{bmatrix} 2 & -4 \\ -3 & 6 \end{bmatrix}$

53. $\begin{bmatrix} 2 & 1 \\ 4 & 3 \end{bmatrix}$

54. $\begin{bmatrix} -5 & 3 \\ 2 & -2 \end{bmatrix}$

55. $\begin{bmatrix} 3 & -1 \\ -5 & 35 \end{bmatrix}$

56. $\begin{bmatrix} 5 & -10 \\ -2 & 24 \end{bmatrix}$

In Problems 57–60, find the inverse. Note that each inverse can be found mentally, without the use of a calculator or pencil-and-paper calculations.

57. $\begin{bmatrix} 3 & 0 \\ 0 & 3 \end{bmatrix}$

58. $\begin{bmatrix} 5 & 0 \\ 0 & 5 \end{bmatrix}$

59. $\begin{bmatrix} 2 & 0 \\ 0 & \frac{1}{2} \end{bmatrix}$

60. $\begin{bmatrix} 3 & 0 \\ 0 & -\frac{1}{4} \end{bmatrix}$

C *Find the inverse of each matrix in Problems 61–68, if it exists.*

61. $\begin{bmatrix} -5 & -2 & -2 \\ 2 & 1 & 0 \\ 1 & 0 & 1 \end{bmatrix}$

62. $\begin{bmatrix} 2 & -2 & 4 \\ 1 & 1 & 1 \\ 1 & 0 & 1 \end{bmatrix}$

63. $\begin{bmatrix} 2 & 1 & 1 \\ 1 & 1 & 0 \\ -1 & -1 & 0 \end{bmatrix}$

64. $\begin{bmatrix} 1 & -1 & 0 \\ 2 & -1 & 1 \\ 0 & 1 & 1 \end{bmatrix}$

65. $\begin{bmatrix} -1 & -2 & 2 \\ 4 & 3 & 0 \\ 4 & 0 & 4 \end{bmatrix}$

66. $\begin{bmatrix} 4 & 2 & 2 \\ 4 & 2 & 0 \\ 5 & 0 & 5 \end{bmatrix}$

67. $\begin{bmatrix} 2 & -1 & -2 \\ -4 & 2 & 8 \\ 6 & -2 & -1 \end{bmatrix}$

68. $\begin{bmatrix} -1 & -1 & 4 \\ 3 & 3 & -22 \\ -2 & -1 & 19 \end{bmatrix}$

69. Show that $(A^{-1})^{-1} = A$ for: $A = \begin{bmatrix} 4 & 3 \\ 3 & 2 \end{bmatrix}$

70. Show that $(AB)^{-1} = B^{-1}A^{-1}$ for

$$A = \begin{bmatrix} 4 & 3 \\ 3 & 2 \end{bmatrix} \quad \text{and} \quad B = \begin{bmatrix} 2 & 5 \\ 3 & 7 \end{bmatrix}$$

71. Discuss the existence of M^{-1} for 2×2 diagonal matrices of the form

$$M = \begin{bmatrix} a & 0 \\ 0 & d \end{bmatrix}$$

Generalize your conclusions to $n \times n$ diagonal matrices.

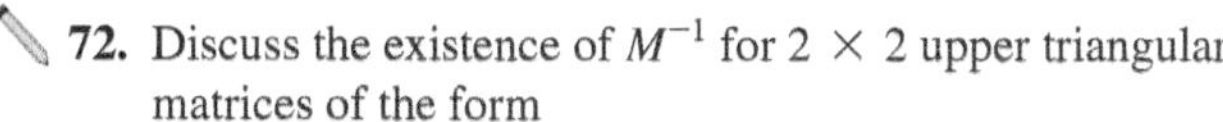

72. Discuss the existence of M^{-1} for 2×2 upper triangular matrices of the form

$$M = \begin{bmatrix} a & b \\ 0 & d \end{bmatrix}$$

Generalize your conclusions to $n \times n$ upper triangular matrices.

In Problems 73–75, find A^{-1} and A^2.

73. $\begin{bmatrix} -1 & 3 \\ 0 & 1 \end{bmatrix}$ **74.** $\begin{bmatrix} -5 & 4 \\ -6 & 5 \end{bmatrix}$ **75.** $\begin{bmatrix} 5 & -3 \\ 8 & -5 \end{bmatrix}$

76. Based on your observations in Problems 73–75, if $A = A^{-1}$ for a square matrix A, what is A^2? Give a mathematical argument to support your conclusion.

Applications

Problems 77–80 refer to the encoding matrix

$$A = \begin{bmatrix} 1 & 2 \\ 1 & 3 \end{bmatrix}$$

77. Cryptography. Encode the message "WINGARDIUM LEVIOSA" using matrix A.

78. Cryptography. Encode the message "FINITE INCANTATEM" using matrix A.

79. Cryptography. The following message was encoded with matrix A. Decode this message:

52 70 17 21 5 5 29 43 4 4 52 70 25
35 29 33 15 18 5 5

80. Cryptography. The following message was encoded with matrix A. Decode this message:

36 44 5 5 38 56 55 75 18 23 56 75
22 33 37 55 27 40 53 79 59 81

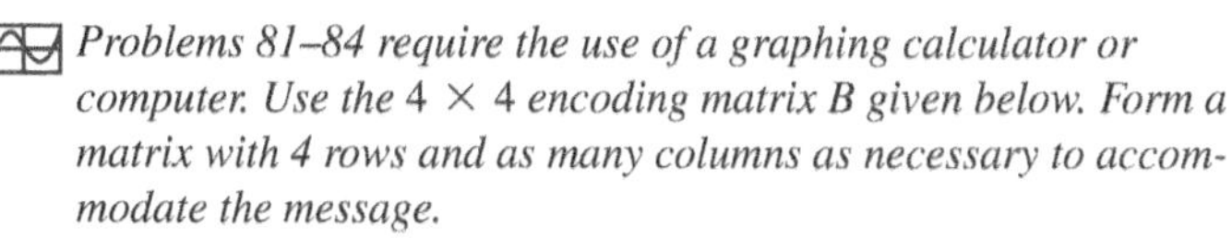

Problems 81–84 require the use of a graphing calculator or computer. Use the 4×4 encoding matrix B given below. Form a matrix with 4 rows and as many columns as necessary to accommodate the message.

$$B = \begin{bmatrix} 2 & 2 & 1 & 3 \\ 1 & 2 & 2 & 1 \\ 1 & 1 & 0 & 1 \\ 2 & 3 & 2 & 3 \end{bmatrix}$$

81. Cryptography. Encode the message "DEPART ISTANBUL ORIENT EXPRESS" using matrix B.

82. Cryptography. Encode the message "SAIL FROM LISBON IN MORNING" using matrix B.

83. Cryptography. The following message was encoded with matrix B. Decode this message:

85 74 27 109 31 27 13 40 139 73 58 154
61 70 18 93 69 59 23 87 18 13 9 22

84. Cryptography. The following message was encoded with matrix B. Decode this message:

75 61 28 94 35 22 13 40 49 21 16 52
42 45 19 64 38 55 10 65 69 75 24 102
67 49 19 82 10 5 5 10

Problems 85–88 require the use of a graphing calculator or a computer. Use the 5×5 encoding matrix C given below. Form a matrix with 5 rows and as many columns as necessary to accommodate the message.

$$C = \begin{bmatrix} 1 & 0 & 1 & 0 & 1 \\ 0 & 1 & 1 & 0 & 3 \\ 2 & 1 & 1 & 1 & 1 \\ 0 & 0 & 1 & 0 & 2 \\ 1 & 1 & 1 & 2 & 1 \end{bmatrix}$$

85. Cryptography. Encode the message "THE EAGLE HAS LANDED" using matrix C.

86. Cryptography. Encode the message "ONE IF BY LAND AND TWO IF BY SEA" using matrix C.

87. Cryptography. The following message was encoded with matrix C. Decode this message:

37 72 58 45 56 30 67 50 46 60 27 77
41 45 39 28 24 52 14 37 32 58 70 36
76 22 38 70 12 67

88. Cryptography. The following message was encoded with matrix C. Decode this message:

25 75 55 35 50 43 83 54 60 53 25 13
59 9 53 15 35 40 15 45 33 60 60 36
51 15 7 37 0 22

Answers to Matched Problems

1. (A) $\begin{bmatrix} 2 & -3 \\ 5 & 7 \end{bmatrix}$ (B) $\begin{bmatrix} 4 & 2 \\ 3 & -5 \\ 6 & 8 \end{bmatrix}$

2. (A) $\left[\begin{array}{rrr|rrr} 3 & -1 & 1 & 1 & 0 & 0 \\ -1 & 1 & 0 & 0 & 1 & 0 \\ 1 & 0 & 1 & 0 & 0 & 1 \end{array}\right]$

(B) $\left[\begin{array}{rrr|rrr} 1 & 0 & 0 & 1 & 1 & -1 \\ 0 & 1 & 0 & 1 & 2 & -1 \\ 0 & 0 & 1 & -1 & -1 & 2 \end{array}\right]$

(C) $\begin{bmatrix} 1 & 1 & -1 \\ 1 & 2 & -1 \\ -1 & -1 & 2 \end{bmatrix}\begin{bmatrix} 3 & -1 & 1 \\ -1 & 1 & 0 \\ 1 & 0 & 1 \end{bmatrix} = \begin{bmatrix} 1 & 0 & 0 \\ 0 & 1 & 0 \\ 0 & 0 & 1 \end{bmatrix}$

3. $\begin{bmatrix} -1 & 3 \\ -\frac{1}{2} & 1 \end{bmatrix}$

4. Does not exist

5. WHO IS WILHELM JORDAN

4.6 Matrix Equations and Systems of Linear Equations

- Matrix Equations
- Matrix Equations and Systems of Linear Equations
- Application

The identity matrix and inverse matrix discussed in the preceding section can be put to immediate use in the solution of certain simple matrix equations. Being able to solve a matrix equation gives us another important method of solving systems of equations, provided that the system is independent and has the same number of variables as equations. If the system is dependent or if it has either fewer or more variables than equations, we must return to the Gauss–Jordan method of elimination.

Matrix Equations

Solving simple matrix equations is similar to solving real number equations but with two important differences:

1. there is *no* operation of division for matrices, and
2. matrix multiplication is *not* commutative.

Compare the real number equation $4x = 9$ and the matrix equation $AX = B$. The real number equation can be solved by dividing both sides of the equation by 4. However, that approach cannot be used for $AX = B$, because there is no operation of division for matrices. Instead, we note that $4x = 9$ can be solved by multiplying both sides of the equation by $\frac{1}{4}$, the multiplicative inverse of 4. So we solve $AX = B$ by multiplying both sides of the equation, *on the left*, by A^{-1}, the inverse of A. Because matrix multiplication is not commutative, multiplying both sides of an equation on the left by A^{-1} is different from multiplying both sides of an equation on the right by A^{-1}. In the case of $AX = B$, it is multiplication on the left that is required. The details are presented in Example 1.

In solving matrix equations, we will be guided by the properties of matrices summarized in Theorem 1.

THEOREM 1 Basic Properties of Matrices

Assuming that all products and sums are defined for the indicated matrices A, B, C, I, and 0, then

Addition Properties

Associative:	$(A + B) + C = A + (B + C)$
Commutative:	$A + B = B + A$
Additive identity:	$A + 0 = 0 + A = A$
Additive inverse:	$A + (-A) = (-A) + A = 0$

Multiplication Properties

Associative property:	$A(BC) = (AB)C$
Multiplicative identity:	$AI = IA = A$
Multiplicative inverse:	If A is a square matrix and A^{-1} exists, then $AA^{-1} = A^{-1}A = I$.

Combined Properties

Left distributive:	$A(B + C) = AB + AC$
Right distributive:	$(B + C)A = BA + CA$

Equality

Addition:	If $A = B$, then $A + C = B + C$.
Left multiplication:	If $A = B$, then $CA = CB$.
Right multiplication:	If $A = B$, then $AC = BC$.

EXAMPLE 1 **Solving a Matrix Equation** Given an $n \times n$ matrix A and $n \times 1$ column matrices B and X, solve $AX = B$ for X. Assume that all necessary inverses exist.

SOLUTION We are interested in finding a column matrix X that satisfies the matrix equation $AX = B$. To solve this equation, we multiply both sides on the left by A^{-1} to isolate X on the left side.

$$\begin{aligned} AX &= B && \text{Use the left multiplication property.} \\ A^{-1}(AX) &= A^{-1}B && \text{Use the associative property.} \\ (A^{-1}A)X &= A^{-1}B && A^{-1}A = I \\ IX &= A^{-1}B && IX = X \\ X &= A^{-1}B \end{aligned}$$

Matched Problem 1 Given an $n \times n$ matrix A and $n \times 1$ column matrices B, C, and X, solve $AX + C = B$ for X. Assume that all necessary inverses exist.

CAUTION Do not mix the left multiplication property and the right multiplication property. If $AX = B$, then

$$A^{-1}(AX) \neq BA^{-1}$$

Matrix Equations and Systems of Linear Equations

Now we show how independent systems of linear equations with the same number of variables as equations can be solved. First, convert the system into a matrix equation of the form $AX = B$, and then use $X = A^{-1}B$ as obtained in Example 1.

EXAMPLE 2 **Using Inverses to Solve Systems of Equations** Use matrix inverse methods to solve the system:

$$\begin{aligned} x_1 - x_2 + x_3 &= 1 \\ 2x_2 - x_3 &= 1 \\ 2x_1 + 3x_2 \quad &= 1 \end{aligned} \tag{1}$$

SOLUTION The inverse of the coefficient matrix

$$A = \begin{bmatrix} 1 & -1 & 1 \\ 0 & 2 & -1 \\ 2 & 3 & 0 \end{bmatrix}$$

provides an efficient method for solving this system. To see how, we convert system (1) into a matrix equation:

$$\overset{A}{\begin{bmatrix} 1 & -1 & 1 \\ 0 & 2 & -1 \\ 2 & 3 & 0 \end{bmatrix}} \overset{X}{\begin{bmatrix} x_1 \\ x_2 \\ x_3 \end{bmatrix}} = \overset{B}{\begin{bmatrix} 1 \\ 1 \\ 1 \end{bmatrix}} \tag{2}$$

Check that matrix equation (2) is equivalent to system (1) by finding the product of the left side and then equating corresponding elements on the left with those on the right.

We are interested in finding a column matrix X that satisfies the matrix equation $AX = B$. In Example 1 we found that if A^{-1} exists, then

$$X = A^{-1}B$$

The inverse of A was found in Example 2, Section 4.5, to be

$$A^{-1} = \begin{bmatrix} 3 & 3 & -1 \\ -2 & -2 & 1 \\ -4 & -5 & 2 \end{bmatrix}$$

Therefore,

$$\overset{X}{\begin{bmatrix} x_1 \\ x_2 \\ x_3 \end{bmatrix}} = \overset{A^{-1}}{\begin{bmatrix} 3 & 3 & -1 \\ -2 & -2 & 1 \\ -4 & -5 & 2 \end{bmatrix}} \overset{B}{\begin{bmatrix} 1 \\ 1 \\ 1 \end{bmatrix}} = \begin{bmatrix} 5 \\ -3 \\ -7 \end{bmatrix}$$

and we can conclude that $x_1 = 5, x_2 = -3$, and $x_3 = -7$. Check this result in system (1).

Matched Problem 2 Use matrix inverse methods to solve the system:

$$\begin{aligned} 3x_1 - x_2 + x_3 &= 1 \\ -x_1 + x_2 &= 3 \\ x_1 + x_3 &= 2 \end{aligned}$$

[*Note:* The inverse of the coefficient matrix was found in Matched Problem 2, Section 4.5.]

At first glance, using matrix inverse methods seems to require the same amount of effort as using Gauss–Jordan elimination. In either case, row operations must be applied to an augmented matrix involving the coefficients of the system. The advantage of the inverse matrix method becomes readily apparent when solving a number of systems with a common coefficient matrix and different constant terms.

EXAMPLE 3 **Using Inverses to Solve Systems of Equations** Use matrix inverse methods to solve each of the following systems:

(A)
$$\begin{aligned} x_1 - x_2 + x_3 &= 3 \\ 2x_2 - x_3 &= 1 \\ 2x_1 + 3x_2 &= 4 \end{aligned}$$

(B)
$$\begin{aligned} x_1 - x_2 + x_3 &= -5 \\ 2x_2 - x_3 &= 2 \\ 2x_1 + 3x_2 &= -3 \end{aligned}$$

SOLUTION Notice that both systems have the same coefficient matrix A as system (1) in Example 2. Only the constant terms have changed. We can use A^{-1} to solve these systems just as we did in Example 2.

(A)

$$\overset{X}{\begin{bmatrix} x_1 \\ x_2 \\ x_3 \end{bmatrix}} = \overset{A^{-1}}{\begin{bmatrix} 3 & 3 & -1 \\ -2 & -2 & 1 \\ -4 & -5 & 2 \end{bmatrix}} \overset{B}{\begin{bmatrix} 3 \\ 1 \\ 4 \end{bmatrix}} = \begin{bmatrix} 8 \\ -4 \\ -9 \end{bmatrix}$$

$x_1 = 8, x_2 = -4$, and $x_3 = -9$.

(B)

$$\overset{X}{\begin{bmatrix} x_1 \\ x_2 \\ x_3 \end{bmatrix}} = \overset{A^{-1}}{\begin{bmatrix} 3 & 3 & -1 \\ -2 & -2 & 1 \\ -4 & -5 & 2 \end{bmatrix}} \overset{B}{\begin{bmatrix} -5 \\ 2 \\ -3 \end{bmatrix}} = \begin{bmatrix} -6 \\ 3 \\ 4 \end{bmatrix}$$

$x_1 = -6, x_2 = 3$, and $x_3 = 4$.

Matched Problem 3 Use matrix inverse methods to solve each of the following systems (see Matched Problem 2):

(A)
$$\begin{aligned} 3x_1 - x_2 + x_3 &= 3 \\ -x_1 + x_2 \qquad &= -3 \\ x_1 + \qquad x_3 &= 2 \end{aligned}$$

(B)
$$\begin{aligned} 3x_1 - x_2 + x_3 &= -5 \\ -x_1 + x_2 \qquad &= 1 \\ x_1 \qquad + x_3 &= -4 \end{aligned}$$

As Examples 2 and 3 illustrate, inverse methods are very convenient for hand calculations because once the inverse is found, it can be used to solve any new system formed by changing only the constant terms. Since most graphing calculators and computers can compute the inverse of a matrix, this method also adapts readily to graphing calculator and spreadsheet solutions (Fig. 1). However, if your graphing calculator (or spreadsheet) also has a built-in procedure for finding the reduced form of an augmented matrix, it is just as convenient to use Gauss–Jordan elimination. Furthermore, Gauss–Jordan elimination can be used in all cases and, as noted below, matrix inverse methods cannot always be used.

	A	B	C	D	E	F	G	H	I	J	K
1			A			B	X		B	X	
2		1	-1	1		3	8		-5	-6	
3		0	2	-1		1	-4		2	3	
4		2	3	0		4	-9		-3	4	
5											

Figure 1 Using inverse methods on a spreadsheet: The values in G2:G4 are produced by the command MMULT (MINVERSE(B2:D4),F2:F4)

SUMMARY Using Inverse Methods to Solve Systems of Equations

If the number of equations in a system equals the number of variables and the coefficient matrix has an inverse, then the system will always have a unique solution that can be found by using the inverse of the coefficient matrix to solve the corresponding matrix equation.

Matrix equation	Solution
$AX = B$	$X = A^{-1}B$

CONCEPTUAL INSIGHT

There are two cases where inverse methods will not work:

Case 1. The coefficient matrix is singular.

Case 2. The number of variables is not the same as the number of equations.

In either case, use Gauss–Jordan elimination.

Application

The following application illustrates the usefulness of the inverse matrix method for solving systems of equations.

EXAMPLE 4 **Investment Analysis** An investment advisor currently has two types of investments available for clients: a conservative investment A that pays 5% per year and a higher risk investment B that pays 10% per year. Clients may divide their investments between the two to achieve any total return desired between 5% and 10%. However, the higher the desired return, the higher the risk. How should each client invest to achieve the indicated return?

	Client			
	1	2	3	k
Total investment	\$20,000	\$50,000	\$10,000	k_1
Annual return desired	\$ 1,200	\$ 3,750	\$ 900	k_2
	(6%)	(7.5%)	(9%)	

SOLUTION The answer to this problem involves six quantities, two for each client. Utilizing inverse matrices provides an efficient way to find these quantities. We will solve the problem for an arbitrary client k with unspecified amounts k_1 for the total investment and k_2 for the annual return. (Do not confuse k_1 and k_2 with variables. Their values are known—they just differ for each client.)

Let x_1 = amount invested in A by a given client

x_2 = amount invested in B by a given client

Then we have the following mathematical model:

$$x_1 + x_2 = k_1 \quad \text{Total invested}$$
$$0.05x_1 + 0.1x_2 = k_2 \quad \text{Total annual return desired}$$

Write as a matrix equation:

$$\overset{A}{\begin{bmatrix} 1 & 1 \\ 0.05 & 0.1 \end{bmatrix}} \overset{X}{\begin{bmatrix} x_1 \\ x_2 \end{bmatrix}} = \overset{B}{\begin{bmatrix} k_1 \\ k_2 \end{bmatrix}}$$

If A^{-1} exists, then

$$X = A^{-1}B$$

We now find A^{-1} by starting with the augmented matrix $[A \mid I]$ and proceeding as discussed in Section 4.5:

$$\left[\begin{array}{cc|cc} 1 & 1 & 1 & 0 \\ 0.05 & 0.1 & 0 & 1 \end{array}\right] \quad 20R_2 \to R_2$$

$$\sim \left[\begin{array}{cc|cc} 1 & 1 & 1 & 0 \\ 1 & 2 & 0 & 20 \end{array}\right] \quad (-1)R_1 + R_2 \to R_2$$

$$\sim \left[\begin{array}{cc|cc} 1 & 1 & 1 & 0 \\ 0 & 1 & -1 & 20 \end{array}\right] \quad (-1)R_2 + R_1 \to R_1$$

$$\sim \left[\begin{array}{cc|cc} 1 & 0 & 2 & -20 \\ 0 & 1 & -1 & 20 \end{array}\right]$$

Therefore,

$$A^{-1} = \begin{bmatrix} 2 & -20 \\ -1 & 20 \end{bmatrix} \qquad \text{Check: } \overset{A^{-1}}{\begin{bmatrix} 2 & -20 \\ -1 & 20 \end{bmatrix}} \overset{A}{\begin{bmatrix} 1 & 1 \\ 0.1 & 0.2 \end{bmatrix}} = \overset{I}{\begin{bmatrix} 1 & 0 \\ 0 & 1 \end{bmatrix}}$$

and

$$\overset{X}{\begin{bmatrix} x_1 \\ x_2 \end{bmatrix}} = \overset{A^{-1}}{\begin{bmatrix} 2 & -20 \\ -1 & 20 \end{bmatrix}} \overset{B}{\begin{bmatrix} k_1 \\ k_2 \end{bmatrix}}$$

To solve each client's investment problem, we replace k_1 and k_2 with appropriate values from the table and multiply by A^{-1}:

Client 1

$$\begin{bmatrix} x_1 \\ x_2 \end{bmatrix} = \begin{bmatrix} 2 & -20 \\ -1 & 20 \end{bmatrix} \begin{bmatrix} 20{,}000 \\ 1{,}200 \end{bmatrix} = \begin{bmatrix} 16{,}000 \\ 4{,}000 \end{bmatrix}$$

Solution: $x_1 = \$16{,}000$ in investment A, $x_2 = \$4{,}000$ in investment B

Client 2

$$\begin{bmatrix} x_1 \\ x_2 \end{bmatrix} = \begin{bmatrix} 2 & -20 \\ -1 & 20 \end{bmatrix} \begin{bmatrix} 50{,}000 \\ 3{,}750 \end{bmatrix} = \begin{bmatrix} 25{,}000 \\ 25{,}000 \end{bmatrix}$$

Solution: $x_1 = \$25{,}000$ in investment A, $x_2 = \$25{,}000$ in investment B

Client 3

$$\begin{bmatrix} x_1 \\ x_2 \end{bmatrix} = \begin{bmatrix} 2 & -20 \\ -1 & 20 \end{bmatrix} \begin{bmatrix} 10{,}000 \\ 900 \end{bmatrix} = \begin{bmatrix} 2{,}000 \\ 8{,}000 \end{bmatrix}$$

Solution: $x_1 = \$2{,}000$ in investment A, $x_2 = \$8{,}000$ in investment B

Matched Problem 4 Repeat Example 4 with investment A paying 4% and investment B paying 12%.

Figure 2 illustrates a solution to Example 4 on a spreadsheet.

	A	B	C	D	E	F	G	H
1			Clients					
2		1	2	3		A		
3	Total Investment	$ 20,000	$ 50,000	$ 10,000		1	1	
4	Annual Return	$ 1,200	$ 3,750	$ 900		0.05	0.1	
5	Amount Invested in A	$ 16,000	$ 25,000	$ 2,000				
6	Amount Invested in B	$ 4,000	$ 25,000	$ 8,000				
7								

Figure 2

Explore and Discuss 1

Refer to the mathematical model in Example 4:

$$\overset{A}{\begin{bmatrix} 1 & 1 \\ 0.05 & 0.1 \end{bmatrix}} \overset{X}{\begin{bmatrix} x_1 \\ x_2 \end{bmatrix}} = \overset{B}{\begin{bmatrix} k_1 \\ k_2 \end{bmatrix}} \quad (3)$$

(A) Does matrix equation (3) always have a solution for any constant matrix B?

(B) Do all these solutions make sense for the original problem? If not, give examples.

(C) If the total investment is $k_1 = \$10{,}000$, describe all possible annual returns k_2.

Exercises 4.6

Skills Warm-up Exercises

W *In Problems 1–8, solve each equation for x, where x represents a real number. (If necessary, review Section A.1).*

1. $5x = -3$

2. $4x = 9$

3. $4x = 8x + 7$

4. $6x = -3x + 14$

5. $6x + 8 = -2x + 17$

6. $-4x + 3 = 5x + 12$

7. $10 - 3x = 7x + 9$

8. $2x + 7x + 1 = 8x + 3 - x$

A *Write Problems 9–12 as systems of linear equations without matrices.*

9. $\begin{bmatrix} 3 & 1 \\ 2 & -1 \end{bmatrix} \begin{bmatrix} x_1 \\ x_2 \end{bmatrix} = \begin{bmatrix} 5 \\ -4 \end{bmatrix}$

10. $\begin{bmatrix} -3 & 2 \\ 6 & -7 \end{bmatrix} \begin{bmatrix} x_1 \\ x_2 \end{bmatrix} = \begin{bmatrix} 1 \\ -8 \end{bmatrix}$

11. $\begin{bmatrix} -3 & 1 & 0 \\ 2 & 0 & 1 \\ -1 & 3 & -2 \end{bmatrix} \begin{bmatrix} x_1 \\ x_2 \\ x_3 \end{bmatrix} = \begin{bmatrix} 3 \\ -4 \\ 2 \end{bmatrix}$

12. $\begin{bmatrix} 2 & -1 & 0 \\ -2 & 3 & -1 \\ 4 & 0 & 3 \end{bmatrix}\begin{bmatrix} x_1 \\ x_2 \\ x_3 \end{bmatrix} = \begin{bmatrix} 6 \\ -4 \\ 7 \end{bmatrix}$

Write each system in Problems 13–16 as a matrix equation of the form $AX = B$.

13. $\begin{aligned} 3x_1 - 4x_2 &= 1 \\ 2x_1 + x_2 &= 5 \end{aligned}$

14. $\begin{aligned} 2x_1 + x_2 &= 8 \\ -5x_1 + 3x_2 &= -4 \end{aligned}$

15. $\begin{aligned} x_1 - 3x_2 + 2x_3 &= -3 \\ -2x_1 + 3x_2 \quad\quad &= 1 \\ x_1 + x_2 + 4x_3 &= -2 \end{aligned}$

16. $\begin{aligned} 4x_1 - 3x_2 + 2x_3 &= -1 \\ -3x_1 + 5x_2 \quad\quad &= 7 \\ 2x_1 \quad\quad - 6x_3 &= -8 \end{aligned}$

Find x_1 and x_2 in Problems 17–20.

17. $\begin{bmatrix} x_1 \\ x_2 \end{bmatrix} = \begin{bmatrix} 3 & -2 \\ 1 & 4 \end{bmatrix}\begin{bmatrix} -2 \\ 1 \end{bmatrix}$

18. $\begin{bmatrix} x_1 \\ x_2 \end{bmatrix} = \begin{bmatrix} -2 & 1 \\ -1 & 2 \end{bmatrix}\begin{bmatrix} 3 \\ -2 \end{bmatrix}$

19. $\begin{bmatrix} x_1 \\ x_2 \end{bmatrix} = \begin{bmatrix} -4 & 3 \\ 5 & -6 \end{bmatrix}\begin{bmatrix} 2 \\ -7 \end{bmatrix}$

20. $\begin{bmatrix} x_1 \\ x_2 \end{bmatrix} = \begin{bmatrix} 3 & -1 \\ 0 & 2 \end{bmatrix}\begin{bmatrix} -2 \\ 1 \end{bmatrix}$

In Problems 21–24, find x_1 and x_2.

21. $\begin{bmatrix} 1 & -1 \\ 1 & -2 \end{bmatrix}\begin{bmatrix} x_1 \\ x_2 \end{bmatrix} = \begin{bmatrix} 5 \\ 7 \end{bmatrix}$

22. $\begin{bmatrix} 1 & 3 \\ 1 & 4 \end{bmatrix}\begin{bmatrix} x_1 \\ x_2 \end{bmatrix} = \begin{bmatrix} 9 \\ 6 \end{bmatrix}$

23. $\begin{bmatrix} 1 & 1 \\ 2 & -3 \end{bmatrix}\begin{bmatrix} x_1 \\ x_2 \end{bmatrix} = \begin{bmatrix} 15 \\ 10 \end{bmatrix}$

24. $\begin{bmatrix} 1 & 1 \\ 3 & -2 \end{bmatrix}\begin{bmatrix} x_1 \\ x_2 \end{bmatrix} = \begin{bmatrix} 10 \\ 20 \end{bmatrix}$

In Problems 25–30, solve for x_1 and x_2.

25. $\begin{bmatrix} 1 & 3 \\ 1 & 1 \end{bmatrix}\begin{bmatrix} x_1 \\ x_2 \end{bmatrix} + \begin{bmatrix} 5 \\ 2 \end{bmatrix} = \begin{bmatrix} 14 \\ 7 \end{bmatrix}$

26. $\begin{bmatrix} 2 & 1 \\ 1 & 3 \end{bmatrix}\begin{bmatrix} x_1 \\ x_2 \end{bmatrix} + \begin{bmatrix} 3 \\ 5 \end{bmatrix} = \begin{bmatrix} 10 \\ 16 \end{bmatrix}$

27. $\begin{bmatrix} 2 & 6 \\ -4 & -12 \end{bmatrix}\begin{bmatrix} x_1 \\ x_2 \end{bmatrix} + \begin{bmatrix} 5 \\ 2 \end{bmatrix} = \begin{bmatrix} 14 \\ 7 \end{bmatrix}$

28. $\begin{bmatrix} 2 & 1 \\ -6 & -3 \end{bmatrix}\begin{bmatrix} x_1 \\ x_2 \end{bmatrix} + \begin{bmatrix} 3 \\ 5 \end{bmatrix} = \begin{bmatrix} 10 \\ 16 \end{bmatrix}$

29. $\begin{bmatrix} 4 & 2 \\ 3 & 1 \end{bmatrix}\begin{bmatrix} x_1 \\ x_2 \end{bmatrix} - \begin{bmatrix} 4 \\ 3 \end{bmatrix} = \begin{bmatrix} 14 \\ 8 \end{bmatrix}$

30. $\begin{bmatrix} 3 & 2 \\ 2 & 1 \end{bmatrix}\begin{bmatrix} x_1 \\ x_2 \end{bmatrix} - \begin{bmatrix} 4 \\ 1 \end{bmatrix} = \begin{bmatrix} 4 \\ 3 \end{bmatrix}$

B *In Problems 31–38, write each system as a matrix equation and solve using inverses. [Note: The inverses were found in Problems 41–48, Exercises 4.5.]*

31. $\begin{aligned} x_1 + 2x_2 &= k_1 \\ x_1 + 3x_2 &= k_2 \end{aligned}$

(A) $k_1 = 1, k_2 = 3$

(B) $k_1 = 3, k_2 = 5$

(C) $k_1 = -2, k_2 = 1$

32. $\begin{aligned} 2x_1 + x_2 &= k_1 \\ 5x_1 + 3x_2 &= k_2 \end{aligned}$

(A) $k_1 = 2, k_2 = 13$

(B) $k_1 = 2, k_2 = 4$

(C) $k_1 = 1, k_2 = -3$

33. $\begin{aligned} x_1 + 2x_2 &= k_1 \\ 4x_1 + 9x_2 &= k_2 \end{aligned}$

(A) $k_1 = 1, k_2 = 2$

(B) $k_1 = -3, k_2 = 4$

(C) $k_1 = 2, k_2 = -1$

34. $\begin{aligned} 2x_1 + x_2 &= k_1 \\ x_1 + x_2 &= k_2 \end{aligned}$

(A) $k_1 = -1, k_2 = -2$

(B) $k_1 = 2, k_2 = 3$

(C) $k_1 = 2, k_2 = 0$

35. $\begin{aligned} x_1 - 3x_2 \quad\quad &= k_1 \\ x_2 + x_3 &= k_2 \\ 2x_1 - x_2 + 4x_3 &= k_3 \end{aligned}$

(A) $k_1 = 1, k_2 = 0, k_3 = 2$

(B) $k_1 = -1, k_2 = 1, k_3 = 0$

(C) $k_1 = 2, k_2 = -2, k_3 = 1$

36. $\begin{aligned} 2x_1 + 3x_2 \quad\quad &= k_1 \\ x_1 + 2x_2 + 3x_3 &= k_2 \\ -x_2 - 5x_3 &= k_3 \end{aligned}$

(A) $k_1 = 0, k_2 = 2, k_3 = 1$

(B) $k_1 = -2, k_2 = 0, k_3 = 1$

(C) $k_1 = 3, k_2 = 1, k_3 = 0$

37. $\begin{aligned} x_1 + x_2 \quad\quad &= k_1 \\ 2x_1 + 3x_2 - x_3 &= k_2 \\ x_1 \quad\quad + 2x_3 &= k_3 \end{aligned}$

(A) $k_1 = 2, k_2 = 0, k_3 = 4$

(B) $k_1 = 0, k_2 = 4, k_3 = -2$

(C) $k_1 = 4, k_2 = 2, k_3 = 0$

38. $\begin{aligned} x_1 + x_2 + x_3 &= k_1 \\ 2x_1 + x_2 \quad\quad &= k_2 \\ 4x_1 + 3x_2 + x_3 &= k_3 \end{aligned}$

(A) $k_1 = 0, k_2 = 3, k_3 = 6$

(B) $k_1 = -3, k_2 = 0, k_3 = 6$

(C) $k_1 = 3, k_2 = 6, k_3 = 0$

In Problems 39–44, the matrix equation is not solved correctly. Explain the mistake and find the correct solution. Assume that the indicated inverses exist.

39. $AX = B, X = \frac{B}{A}$

40. $XA = B, X = \frac{B}{A}$

41. $XA = B, X = A^{-1}B$

42. $AX = B, X = BA^{-1}$

43. $AX = BA, X = A^{-1}BA, X = B$

44. $XA = AB, X = ABA^{-1}, X = B$

In Problems 45–50, explain why the system cannot be solved by matrix inverse methods. Discuss methods that could be used and then solve the system.

45. $\begin{aligned} -3x_1 + 9x_2 &= -6 \\ 6x_1 - 18x_2 &= 9 \end{aligned}$

46. $\begin{aligned} -3x_1 + 9x_2 &= -6 \\ 6x_1 - 18x_2 &= 12 \end{aligned}$

47. $x_1 - 3x_2 - 2x_3 = -1$
$-2x_1 + 6x_2 + 4x_3 = 3$

48. $x_1 - 3x_2 - 2x_3 = -1$
$-2x_1 + 7x_2 + 3x_3 = 3$

49. $x_1 - 2x_2 + 3x_3 = 1$
$2x_1 - 3x_2 - 2x_3 = 3$
$x_1 - x_2 - 5x_3 = 2$

50. $x_1 - 2x_2 + 3x_3 = 1$
$2x_1 - 3x_2 - 2x_3 = 3$
$x_1 - x_2 - 5x_3 = 4$

C *For $n \times n$ matrices A and B, and $n \times 1$ column matrices C, D, and X, solve each matrix equation in Problems 51–56 for X. Assume that all necessary inverses exist.*

51. $AX - BX = C$

52. $AX + BX = C$

53. $AX + X = C$

54. $AX - X = C$

55. $AX - C = D - BX$

56. $AX + C = BX + D$

In Problems 57 and 58, solve for x_1 and x_2.

57. $\begin{bmatrix} 5 & 10 \\ 4 & 7 \end{bmatrix}\begin{bmatrix} x_1 \\ x_2 \end{bmatrix} - \begin{bmatrix} 2 & -1 \\ 3 & 3 \end{bmatrix}\begin{bmatrix} x_1 \\ x_2 \end{bmatrix} = \begin{bmatrix} 97 \\ 35 \end{bmatrix}$

58. $\begin{bmatrix} 5 & 1 \\ 2 & 2 \end{bmatrix}\begin{bmatrix} x_1 \\ x_2 \end{bmatrix} + \begin{bmatrix} -3 & 2 \\ 1 & 3 \end{bmatrix}\begin{bmatrix} x_1 \\ x_2 \end{bmatrix} = \begin{bmatrix} 20 \\ 31 \end{bmatrix}$

In Problems 59–62, write each system as a matrix equation and solve using the inverse coefficient matrix. Use a graphing calculator or computer to perform the necessary calculations.

59. $x_1 + 5x_2 + 6x_3 = 76$
$2x_1 + 3x_2 + 8x_3 = 92$
$11x_1 + 9x_2 + 4x_3 = 181$

60. $8x_1 + 7x_2 + 6x_3 = 25$
$2x_1 + 3x_2 + 4x_3 = 37$
$x_1 + x_3 = 49$

61. $2x_1 + x_2 + 5x_3 + 5x_4 = 37$
$3x_1 - 4x_2 + 3x_3 + 2x_4 = 0$
$7x_1 + 3x_2 + 8x_3 + 4x_4 = 45$
$5x_1 + 9x_2 + 6x_3 + 7x_4 = 94$

62. $x_1 + 4x_2 - x_3 + 4x_4 = 11$
$3x_1 + x_2 + 4x_3 + x_4 = 27$
$2x_1 + 7x_2 + x_3 - 8x_4 = 31$
$6x_1 + 4x_3 - 5x_4 = 47$

Applications

Construct a mathematical model for each of the following problems. (The answers in the back of the book include both the mathematical model and the interpretation of its solution.) Use matrix inverse methods to solve the model and then interpret the solution.

63. Concert tickets. A concert hall has 10,000 seats and two categories of ticket prices, $25 and $35. Assume that all seats in each category can be sold.

	Concert		
	1	2	3
Tickets sold	10,000	10,000	10,000
Return required	$275,000	$300,000	$325,000

(A) How many tickets of each category should be sold to bring in each of the returns indicated in the table?

(B) Is it possible to bring in a return of $200,000? Of $400,000? Explain.

(C) Describe all the possible returns.

64. Parking receipts. Parking fees at a zoo are $5.00 for local residents and $7.50 for all others. At the end of each day, the total number of vehicles parked that day and the gross receipts for the day are recorded, but the number of vehicles in each category is not. The following table contains the relevant information for a recent 4-day period:

	Day			
	1	2	3	4
Vehicles parked	1,200	1,550	1,740	1,400
Gross receipts	$7,125	$9,825	$11,100	$8,650

(A) How many vehicles in each category used the zoo's parking facilities each day?

(B) If 1,200 vehicles are parked in one day, is it possible to take in gross receipts of $5,000? Of $10,000? Explain.

(C) Describe all possible gross receipts on a day when 1,200 vehicles are parked.

65. Production scheduling. A supplier manufactures car and truck frames at two different plants. The production rates (in frames per hour) for each plant are given in the table:

Plant	Car Frames	Truck Frames
A	10	5
B	8	8

How many hours should each plant be scheduled to operate to exactly fill each of the orders in the following table?

	Orders		
	1	2	3
Car frames	3,000	2,800	2,600
Truck frames	1,600	2,000	2,200

66. Production scheduling. Labor and material costs for manufacturing two guitar models are given in the table:

Guitar Model	Labor Cost	Material Cost
A	$30	$20
B	$40	$30

(A) If a total of $3,000 a week is allowed for labor and material, how many of each model should be produced each week to use exactly each of the allocations of the $3,000 indicated in the following table?

	Weekly Allocation		
	1	2	3
Labor	$1,800	$1,750	$1,720
Material	$1,200	$1,250	$1,280

(B) Is it possible to use an allocation of $1,600 for labor and $1,400 for material? Of $2,000 for labor and $1,000 for material? Explain.

67. Incentive plan. A small company provides an incentive plan for its top executives. Each executive receives as a bonus a percentage of the portion of the annual profit that remains after the bonuses for the other executives have been deducted (see the table). If the company has an annual profit of $2 million, find the bonus for each executive. Round each bonus to the nearest hundred dollars.

Officer	Bonus
President	3%
Executive vice president	2.5%
Associate vice president	2%
Assistant vice president	1.5%

68. Incentive plan. Repeat Problem 67 if the company decides to include a 0.7% bonus for the sales manager in the incentive plan.

69. Diets. A biologist has available two commercial food mixes containing the percentage of protein and fat given in the table.

Mix	Protein(%)	Fat(%)
A	20	4
B	14	3

(A) How many ounces of each mix should be used to prepare each of the diets listed in the following table?

	Diet		
	1	2	3
Protein	80 oz	90 oz	100 oz
Fat	17 oz	18 oz	21 oz

(B) Is it possible to prepare a diet consisting of 100 ounces of protein and 22 ounces of fat? Of 80 ounces of protein and 15 ounces of fat? Explain.

70. Education. A state university system is planning to hire new faculty at the rank of lecturer or instructor for several of its two-year community colleges. The number of sections taught and the annual salary (in thousands of dollars) for each rank are given in the table.

	Rank	
	Lecturer	Instructor
Sections taught	3	4
Annual salary (thousand $)	20	25

The number of sections taught by new faculty and the amount budgeted for salaries (in thousands of dollars) at each of the colleges are given in the following table. How many faculty of each rank should be hired at each college to exactly meet the demand for sections and completely exhaust the salary budget?

	Community College		
	1	2	3
Demand for sections	30	33	35
Salary budget (thousand $)	200	210	220

Answers to Matched Problems

1.
$$\begin{aligned} AX + C &= B \\ (AX + C) - C &= B - C \\ AX + (C - C) &= B - C \\ AX + 0 &= B - C \\ AX &= B - C \\ A^{-1}(AX) &= A^{-1}(B - C) \\ (A^{-1}A)X &= A^{-1}(B - C) \\ IX &= A^{-1}(B - C) \\ X &= A^{-1}(B - C) \end{aligned}$$

2. $x_1 = 2, x_2 = 5, x_3 = 0$

3. (A) $x_1 = -2, x_2 = -5, x_3 = 4$
   (B) $x_1 = 0, x_2 = 1, x_3 = -4$

4. $A^{-1} = \begin{bmatrix} 1.5 & -12.5 \\ -0.5 & 12.5 \end{bmatrix}$; client 1: $15,000 in *A* and $5,000 in *B*; client 2: $28,125 in *A* and $21,875 in *B*; client 3: $3,750 in *A* and $6,250 in *B*

4.7 Leontief Input–Output Analysis

- Two-Industry Model
- Three-Industry Model

An important application of matrices and their inverses is **input–output analysis.** Wassily Leontief (1905–1999), the primary force behind this subject, was awarded the Nobel Prize in economics in 1973 because of the significant impact his work had on economic planning for industrialized countries. Among other things, he conducted a comprehensive study of how 500 sectors of the U.S. economy interacted with each other. Of course, large-scale computers played a crucial role in this analysis.

Our investigation will be more modest. In fact, we start with an economy comprised of only two industries. From these humble beginnings, ideas and definitions will evolve that can be readily generalized for more realistic economies. Input–output analysis attempts to establish equilibrium conditions under which industries in an economy have just enough output to satisfy each other's demands in addition to final (outside) demands.

Two-Industry Model

We start with an economy comprised of only two industries, electric company E and water company W. Output for both companies is measured in dollars. The electric company uses both electricity and water (inputs) in the production of electricity (output), and the water company uses both electricity and water (inputs) in the production of water (output). Suppose that the production of each dollar's worth of electricity requires \$0.30 worth of electricity and \$0.10 worth of water, and the production of each dollar's worth of water requires \$0.20 worth of electricity and \$0.40 worth of water. If the final demand (the demand from all other users of electricity and water) is

$$d_1 = \$12 \text{ million for electricity}$$

$$d_2 = \$8 \text{ million for water}$$

how much electricity and water should be produced to meet this final demand?

To begin, suppose that the electric company produces \$12 million worth of electricity and the water company produces \$8 million worth of water. Then the production processes of the companies would require

Electricity required to produce electricity — Electricity required to produce water

$$0.3(12) + 0.2(8) = \$5.2 \text{ million of electricity}$$

and

Water required to produce electricity — Water required to produce water

$$0.1(12) + 0.4(8) = \$4.4 \text{ million of water}$$

leaving only \$6.8 million of electricity and \$3.6 million of water to satisfy the final demand. To meet the internal demands of both companies and to end up with enough electricity for the final outside demand, both companies must produce more than just the final demand. In fact, they must produce exactly enough to meet their own internal demands plus the final demand. To determine the total output that each company must produce, we set up a system of equations.

If

$$x_1 = \text{total output from electric company}$$

$$x_2 = \text{total output from water company}$$

then, reasoning as before, the internal demands are

$$0.3x_1 + 0.2x_2 \quad \text{Internal demand for electricity}$$

$$0.1x_1 + 0.4x_2 \quad \text{Internal demand for water}$$

Combining the internal demand with the final demand produces the following system of equations:

Total output — Internal demand — Final demand

$$\begin{aligned} x_1 &= 0.3x_1 + 0.2x_2 + d_1 \\ x_2 &= 0.1x_1 + 0.4x_2 + d_2 \end{aligned} \qquad (1)$$

or, in matrix form,

$$\begin{bmatrix} x_1 \\ x_2 \end{bmatrix} = \begin{bmatrix} 0.3 & 0.2 \\ 0.1 & 0.4 \end{bmatrix} \begin{bmatrix} x_1 \\ x_2 \end{bmatrix} + \begin{bmatrix} d_1 \\ d_2 \end{bmatrix}$$

or

$$X = MX + D \qquad (2)$$

where

$$D = \begin{bmatrix} d_1 \\ d_2 \end{bmatrix} \quad \text{Final demand matrix}$$

$$X = \begin{bmatrix} x_1 \\ x_2 \end{bmatrix} \quad \text{Output matrix}$$

$$M = \begin{matrix} & \begin{matrix} E & W \end{matrix} \\ \begin{matrix} E \\ W \end{matrix} & \begin{bmatrix} 0.3 & 0.2 \\ 0.1 & 0.4 \end{bmatrix} \end{matrix} \quad \text{Technology matrix}$$

The **technology matrix** is the heart of input–output analysis. The elements in the technology matrix are determined as follows (read from left to right and then up):

$$\begin{matrix} & & \text{Output} & \\ & & E & W \\ & & \uparrow & \uparrow \\ \text{Input} & \begin{matrix} E \rightarrow \\ \\ W \rightarrow \end{matrix} & \left[\begin{matrix} \begin{pmatrix} \text{input from } E \\ \text{to produce \$1} \\ \text{of electricity} \end{pmatrix} \\ \begin{pmatrix} \text{input from } W \\ \text{to produce \$1} \\ \text{of electricity} \end{pmatrix} \end{matrix} \right. & \left. \begin{matrix} \begin{pmatrix} \text{input from } E \\ \text{to produce \$1} \\ \text{of water} \end{pmatrix} \\ \begin{pmatrix} \text{input from } W \\ \text{to produce \$1} \\ \text{of water} \end{pmatrix} \end{matrix} \right] = M \end{matrix}$$

CONCEPTUAL INSIGHT

Labeling the rows and columns of the technology matrix with the first letter of each industry is an important part of the process. The same order must be used for columns as for rows, and that same order must be used for the entries of D (the final demand matrix) and the entries of X (the output matrix). In this book we normally label the rows and columns in alphabetical order.

Now we solve equation (2) for X. We proceed as in Section 4.6:

$$\begin{aligned} X &= MX + D \\ X - MX &= D \\ IX - MX &= D \qquad I = \begin{bmatrix} 1 & 0 \\ 0 & 1 \end{bmatrix} \\ (I - M)X &= D \\ X &= (I - M)^{-1}D \qquad \text{Assuming } I - M \text{ has an inverse} \end{aligned} \tag{3}$$

Omitting the details of the calculations, we find

$$I - M = \begin{bmatrix} 0.7 & -0.2 \\ -0.1 & 0.6 \end{bmatrix} \quad \text{and} \quad (I - M)^{-1} = \begin{bmatrix} 1.5 & 0.5 \\ 0.25 & 1.75 \end{bmatrix}$$

Then we have

$$\begin{bmatrix} x_1 \\ x_2 \end{bmatrix} = \begin{bmatrix} 1.5 & 0.5 \\ 0.25 & 1.75 \end{bmatrix} \begin{bmatrix} d_1 \\ d_2 \end{bmatrix} = \begin{bmatrix} 1.5 & 0.5 \\ 0.25 & 1.75 \end{bmatrix} \begin{bmatrix} 12 \\ 8 \end{bmatrix} = \begin{bmatrix} 22 \\ 17 \end{bmatrix} \tag{4}$$

Therefore, the electric company must produce an output of \$22 million and the water company must produce an output of \$17 million so that each company can meet both internal and final demands.

CHECK We use equation (2) to check our work:

$$X = MX + D$$

$$\begin{bmatrix} 22 \\ 17 \end{bmatrix} \stackrel{?}{=} \begin{bmatrix} 0.3 & 0.2 \\ 0.1 & 0.4 \end{bmatrix} \begin{bmatrix} 22 \\ 17 \end{bmatrix} + \begin{bmatrix} 12 \\ 8 \end{bmatrix}$$

$$\begin{bmatrix} 22 \\ 17 \end{bmatrix} \stackrel{?}{=} \begin{bmatrix} 10 \\ 9 \end{bmatrix} + \begin{bmatrix} 12 \\ 8 \end{bmatrix}$$

$$\begin{bmatrix} 22 \\ 17 \end{bmatrix} \stackrel{\checkmark}{=} \begin{bmatrix} 22 \\ 17 \end{bmatrix}$$

To solve this input–output problem on a graphing calculator, simply store matrices M, D, and I in memory; then use equation (3) to find X and equation (2) to check your results. Figure 1 illustrates this process on a graphing calculator.

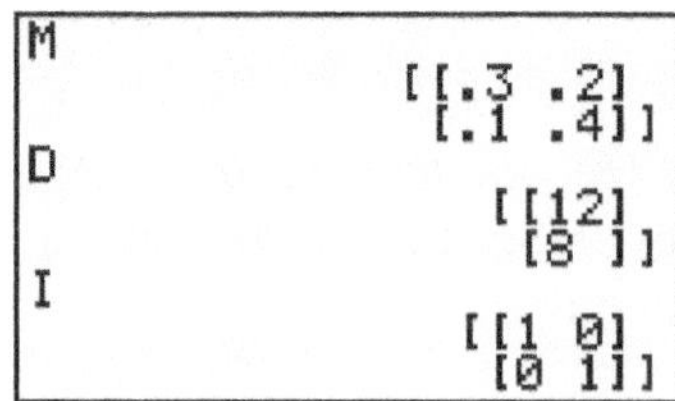

(A) Store M, D, and I in the graphing calculator's memory

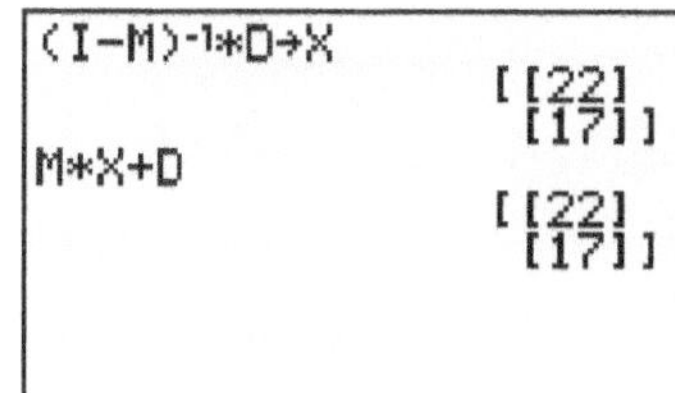

(B) Compute X and check in equation (2)

Figure 1

Actually, equation (4) solves the original problem for arbitrary final demands d_1 and d_2. This is very useful, since equation (4) gives a quick solution not only for the final demands stated in the original problem but also for various other projected final demands. If we had solved system (1) by Gauss–Jordan elimination, then we would have to start over for each new set of final demands.

Suppose that in the original problem the projected final demands 5 years from now are $d_1 = 24$ and $d_2 = 16$. To determine each company's output for this projection, we simply substitute these values into equation (4) and multiply:

$$\begin{bmatrix} x_1 \\ x_2 \end{bmatrix} = \begin{bmatrix} 1.5 & 0.5 \\ 0.25 & 1.75 \end{bmatrix} \begin{bmatrix} 24 \\ 16 \end{bmatrix} = \begin{bmatrix} 44 \\ 34 \end{bmatrix}$$

We summarize these results for convenient reference.

SUMMARY Solution to a Two-Industry Input–Output Problem

Given two industries, C_1 and C_2, with

Technology matrix, Output matrix, Final demand matrix

$$M = \begin{matrix} C_1 \\ C_2 \end{matrix} \overset{\begin{matrix} C_1 & C_2 \end{matrix}}{\begin{bmatrix} a_{11} & a_{12} \\ a_{21} & a_{22} \end{bmatrix}} \quad X = \begin{bmatrix} x_1 \\ x_2 \end{bmatrix} \quad D = \begin{bmatrix} d_1 \\ d_2 \end{bmatrix}$$

where a_{ij} is the input required from C_i to produce a dollar's worth of output for C_j, the solution to the input–output matrix equation

Total output, Internal demand, Final demand

$$X = MX + D$$

is

$$X = (I - M)^{-1}D \qquad (3)$$

assuming that $I - M$ has an inverse.

Three-Industry Model

Equations (2) and (3) in the solution to a two-industry input–output problem are the same for a three-industry economy, a four-industry economy, or an economy with n industries (where n is any natural number). The steps we took going from equation (2) to equation (3) hold for arbitrary matrices as long as the matrices have the correct sizes and $(I - M)^{-1}$ exists.

Explore and Discuss 1

If equations (2) and (3) are valid for an economy with n industries, discuss the size of all the matrices in each equation.

The next example illustrates the application of equations (2) and (3) to a three-industry economy.

EXAMPLE 1 **Input–Output Analysis** An economy is based on three sectors, agriculture (A), energy (E), and manufacturing (M). Production of a dollar's worth of agriculture requires an input of \$0.20 from the agriculture sector and \$0.40 from the energy sector. Production of a dollar's worth of energy requires an input of \$0.20 from the energy sector and \$0.40 from the manufacturing sector. Production of a dollar's worth of manufacturing requires an input of \$0.10 from the agriculture sector, \$0.10 from the energy sector, and \$0.30 from the manufacturing sector. Find the output from each sector that is needed to satisfy a final demand of \$20 billion for agriculture, \$10 billion for energy, and \$30 billion for manufacturing.

SOLUTION Since this is a three-industry problem, the technology matrix will be a 3×3 matrix, and the output and final demand matrices will be 3×1 column matrices.

To begin, we form a blank 3×3 technology matrix and label the rows and columns in alphabetical order.

Technology matrix

$$\text{Input}\quad \begin{array}{c} \\ A \\ E \\ M \end{array} \overset{\text{Output}}{\begin{array}{c} A\ E\ M \\ \left[\begin{array}{ccc} & & \\ & & \\ & & \end{array}\right] \end{array}} = M$$

Now we analyze the production information given in the problem, beginning with agriculture.

"Production of a dollar's worth of agriculture requires an input of \$0.20 from the agriculture sector and \$0.40 from the energy sector."

We organize this information in a table and then insert it in the technology matrix. Since manufacturing is not mentioned in the agriculture production information, the input from manufacturing is \$0.

Agriculture

Input Output

$$\begin{array}{l} A \xrightarrow{0.2} A \\ E \xrightarrow{0.4} A \\ M \xrightarrow{0} A \end{array} \qquad \begin{array}{c} \\ A \\ E \\ M \end{array} \begin{array}{c} A \quad\ E \quad\ M \\ \left[\begin{array}{ccc} 0.2 & & \\ 0.4 & & \\ 0 & & \end{array}\right] \end{array}$$

"Production of a dollar's worth of energy requires an input of \$0.20 from the energy sector and \$0.40 from the manufacturing sector."

Energy

Input Output

$$\begin{array}{l} A \xrightarrow[0.2]{0} E \\ E \xrightarrow[0.4]{} E \\ M \longrightarrow E \end{array} \qquad \begin{array}{c} \\ A \\ E \\ M \end{array} \begin{array}{c} \begin{array}{ccc} A & E & M \end{array} \\ \begin{bmatrix} 0.2 & 0 & \\ 0.4 & 0.2 & \\ 0 & 0.4 & \end{bmatrix} \end{array}$$

"Production of a dollar's worth of manufacturing requires an input of \$0.10 from the agriculture sector, \$0.10 from the energy sector, and \$0.30 from the manufacturing sector."

Manufacturing

Input Output

$$\begin{array}{l} A \xrightarrow{0.1} M \\ E \xrightarrow{0.1} M \\ M \xrightarrow{0.3} M \end{array} \qquad \begin{array}{c} \\ A \\ E \\ M \end{array} \begin{array}{c} \begin{array}{ccc} A & E & M \end{array} \\ \begin{bmatrix} 0.2 & 0 & 0.1 \\ 0.4 & 0.2 & 0.1 \\ 0 & 0.4 & 0.3 \end{bmatrix} \end{array}$$

Therefore,

Technology matrix / Final demand matrix / Output matrix

$$M = \begin{array}{c} A \\ E \\ M \end{array} \begin{array}{c} \begin{array}{ccc} A & E & M \end{array} \\ \begin{bmatrix} 0.2 & 0 & 0.1 \\ 0.4 & 0.2 & 0.1 \\ 0 & 0.4 & 0.3 \end{bmatrix} \end{array} \qquad D = \begin{bmatrix} 20 \\ 10 \\ 30 \end{bmatrix} \qquad X = \begin{bmatrix} x_1 \\ x_2 \\ x_3 \end{bmatrix}$$

where M, X, and D satisfy the input–output equation $X = MX + D$. Since the solution to this equation is $X = (I - M)^{-1}D$, we must first find $I - M$ and then $(I - M)^{-1}$. Omitting the details of the calculations, we have

$$I - M = \begin{bmatrix} 0.8 & 0 & -0.1 \\ -0.4 & 0.8 & -0.1 \\ 0 & -0.4 & 0.7 \end{bmatrix}$$

and

$$(I - M)^{-1} = \begin{bmatrix} 1.3 & 0.1 & 0.2 \\ 0.7 & 1.4 & 0.3 \\ 0.4 & 0.8 & 1.6 \end{bmatrix}$$

So the output matrix X is given by

$$\overset{X}{\begin{bmatrix} x_1 \\ x_2 \\ x_3 \end{bmatrix}} = \overset{(I - M)^{-1}}{\begin{bmatrix} 1.3 & 0.1 & 0.2 \\ 0.7 & 1.4 & 0.3 \\ 0.4 & 0.8 & 1.6 \end{bmatrix}} \overset{D}{\begin{bmatrix} 20 \\ 10 \\ 30 \end{bmatrix}} = \begin{bmatrix} 33 \\ 37 \\ 64 \end{bmatrix}$$

An output of \$33 billion for agriculture, \$37 billion for energy, and \$64 billion for manufacturing will meet the given final demands. You should check this result in equation (2).

Figure 2 illustrates a spreadsheet solution for Example 1.

	A	B	C	D	E	F	G	H	I	J	K	L	M
1		Technology Matrix M								Final		Output	
2		A	E	M			I-M			Demand			
3	A	0.2	0	0.1		0.8	0	-0.1		20		33	
4	E	0.4	0.2	0.1		-0.4	0.8	-0.1		10		37	
5	M	0	0.4	0.3		0	-0.4	0.7		30		64	
6													

Figure 2 The command MMULT(MINVERSE(F3:H5), J3:J5) produces the output in L3:L5

Matched Problem 1 An economy is based on three sectors, coal, oil, and transportation. Production of a dollar's worth of coal requires an input of \$0.20 from the coal sector and \$0.40 from the transportation sector. Production of a dollar's worth of oil requires an input of \$0.10 from the oil sector and \$0.20 from the transportation sector. Production of a dollar's worth of transportation requires an input of \$0.40 from the coal sector, \$0.20 from the oil sector, and \$0.20 from the transportation sector.

(A) Find the technology matrix M.

(B) Find $(I - M)^{-1}$.

(C) Find the output from each sector that is needed to satisfy a final demand of \$30 billion for coal, \$10 billion for oil, and \$20 billion for transportation.

Exercises 4.7

Skills Warm-up Exercises

W *In Problems 1–8, solve each equation for x, where x represents a real number. (If necessary, review Section A.1.)*

1. $x = 3x + 6$

2. $x = 4x - 5$

3. $x = 0.9x + 10$

4. $x = 0.6x + 84$

5. $x = 0.2x + 3.2$

6. $x = 0.3x + 4.2$

7. $x = 0.68x + 2.56$

8. $x = 0.89x + 10.23$

A *Problems 9–14 pertain to the following input–output model: Assume that an economy is based on two industrial sectors, agriculture (A) and energy (E). The technology matrix M and final demand matrices (in billions of dollars) are*

$$\begin{array}{c} \\ A \\ E \end{array}\begin{array}{c} \begin{array}{cc} A & E \end{array} \\ \begin{bmatrix} 0.4 & 0.2 \\ 0.2 & 0.1 \end{bmatrix} \end{array} = M$$

$$D_1 = \begin{bmatrix} 6 \\ 4 \end{bmatrix} \quad D_2 = \begin{bmatrix} 8 \\ 5 \end{bmatrix} \quad D_3 = \begin{bmatrix} 12 \\ 9 \end{bmatrix}$$

9. How much input from A and E are required to produce a dollar's worth of output for A?

10. How much input from A and E are required to produce a dollar's worth of output for E?

11. Find $I - M$ and $(I - M)^{-1}$.

12. Find the output for each sector that is needed to satisfy the final demand D_1.

13. Repeat Problem 12 for D_2.

14. Repeat Problem 12 for D_3.

B *Problems 15–20 pertain to the following input–output model: Assume that an economy is based on three industrial sectors: agriculture (A), building (B), and energy (E). The technology matrix M and final demand matrices (in billions of dollars) are*

$$\begin{array}{c} \\ A \\ B \\ E \end{array}\begin{array}{c} \begin{array}{ccc} A & B & E \end{array} \\ \begin{bmatrix} 0.2 & 0.3 & 0.2 \\ 0.1 & 0.2 & 0.1 \\ 0.1 & 0.3 & 0.1 \end{bmatrix} \end{array} = M$$

$$D_1 = \begin{bmatrix} 10 \\ 15 \\ 20 \end{bmatrix} \quad D_2 = \begin{bmatrix} 15 \\ 10 \\ 5 \end{bmatrix}$$

15. How much input from A, B, and E are required to produce a dollar's worth of output for B?

16. How much of each of E's output dollars is required as input for each of the three sectors?

17. Find $I - M$.

18. Find $(I - M)^{-1}$.
Show that $(I - M)^{-1}(I - M) = I$.

19. Use $(I - M)^{-1}$ in Problem 18 to find the output for each sector that is needed to satisfy the final demand D_1.

20. Repeat Problem 19 for D_2.

In Problems 21–26, find $(I - M)^{-1}$ and X.

21. $M = \begin{bmatrix} 0.1 & 0.2 \\ 0.9 & 0.8 \end{bmatrix}$; $D = \begin{bmatrix} 15 \\ 45 \end{bmatrix}$

22. $M = \begin{bmatrix} 0.4 & 0.2 \\ 0.6 & 0.8 \end{bmatrix}$; $D = \begin{bmatrix} 30 \\ 50 \end{bmatrix}$

23. $M = \begin{bmatrix} 0.2 & 0.4 \\ 0.4 & 0.3 \end{bmatrix}; \quad D = \begin{bmatrix} 25 \\ 35 \end{bmatrix}$

24. $M = \begin{bmatrix} 0.4 & 0.1 \\ 0.2 & 0.3 \end{bmatrix}; \quad D = \begin{bmatrix} 15 \\ 20 \end{bmatrix}$

C 25. $M = \begin{bmatrix} 0.3 & 0.1 & 0.3 \\ 0.2 & 0.1 & 0.2 \\ 0.1 & 0.1 & 0.1 \end{bmatrix}; \quad D = \begin{bmatrix} 20 \\ 5 \\ 10 \end{bmatrix}$

26. $M = \begin{bmatrix} 0.3 & 0.2 & 0.3 \\ 0.1 & 0.1 & 0.1 \\ 0.1 & 0.2 & 0.1 \end{bmatrix}; \quad D = \begin{bmatrix} 10 \\ 25 \\ 15 \end{bmatrix}$

27. The technology matrix for an economy based on agriculture (A) and manufacturing (M) is

$$M = \begin{matrix} & A & M \\ A & 0.3 & 0.25 \\ M & 0.1 & 0.25 \end{matrix}$$

(A) Find the output for each sector that is needed to satisfy a final demand of \$40 million for agriculture and \$40 million for manufacturing.

(B) Discuss the effect on the final demand if the agriculture output in part (A) is increased by \$20 million and manufacturing output remains unchanged.

28. The technology matrix for an economy based on energy (E) and transportation (T) is

$$M = \begin{matrix} & E & T \\ E & 0.25 & 0.25 \\ T & 0.4 & 0.2 \end{matrix}$$

(A) Find the output for each sector that is needed to satisfy a final demand of \$50 million for energy and \$50 million for transportation.

(B) Discuss the effect on the final demand if the transportation output in part (A) is increased by \$40 million and the energy output remains unchanged.

29. Refer to Problem 27. Fill in the elements in the following technology matrix.

$$T = \begin{matrix} & M & A \\ M & & \\ A & & \end{matrix}$$

Use this matrix to solve Problem 27. Discuss any differences in your calculations and in your answers.

30. Refer to Problem 28. Fill in the elements in the following technology matrix.

$$T = \begin{matrix} & T & E \\ T & & \\ E & & \end{matrix}$$

Use this matrix to solve Problem 28. Discuss any differences in your calculations and in your answers.

31. The technology matrix for an economy based on energy (E) and mining (M) is

$$M = \begin{matrix} & E & M \\ E & 0.2 & 0.3 \\ M & 0.4 & 0.3 \end{matrix}$$

The management of these two sectors would like to set the total output level so that the final demand is always 40% of the total output. Discuss methods that could be used to accomplish this objective.

32. The technology matrix for an economy based on automobiles (A) and construction (C) is

$$M = \begin{matrix} & A & C \\ A & 0.1 & 0.4 \\ C & 0.1 & 0.1 \end{matrix}$$

The management of these two sectors would like to set the total output level so that the final demand is always 70% of the total output. Discuss methods that could be used to accomplish this objective.

33. All the technology matrices in the text have elements between 0 and 1. Why is this the case? Would you ever expect to find an element in a technology matrix that is negative? That is equal to 0? That is equal to 1? That is greater than 1?

34. The sum of the elements in a column of any of the technology matrices in the text is less than 1. Why is this the case? Would you ever expect to find a column with a sum equal to 1? Greater than 1? How would you describe an economic system where the sum of the elements in every column of the technology matrix is 1?

Applications

35. **Coal, steel.** An economy is based on two industrial sectors, coal and steel. Production of a dollar's worth of coal requires an input of \$0.10 from the coal sector and \$0.20 from the steel sector. Production of a dollar's worth of steel requires an input of \$0.20 from the coal sector and \$0.40 from the steel sector. Find the output for each sector that is needed to satisfy a final demand of \$20 billion for coal and \$10 billion for steel.

36. **Transportation, manufacturing.** An economy is based on two sectors, transportation and manufacturing. Production of a dollar's worth of transportation requires an input of \$0.10 from each sector and production of a dollar's worth of manufacturing requires an input of \$0.40 from each sector. Find the output for each sector that is needed to satisfy a final demand of \$5 billion for transportation and \$20 billion for manufacturing.

37. **Agriculture, tourism.** The economy of a small island nation is based on two sectors, agriculture and tourism. Production of a dollar's worth of agriculture requires an input of \$0.20 from agriculture and \$0.20 from tourism. Production of a dollar's worth of tourism requires an input of \$0.50 from agriculture and \$0.25 from tourism. Find the output from each sector that is needed to satisfy a final demand of \$50 million for agriculture and \$90 million for tourism.

38. **Agriculture, oil.** The economy of a country is based on two sectors, agriculture and oil. Production of a dollar's worth of agriculture requires an input of \$0.40 from agriculture and \$0.35 from oil. Production of a dollar's worth of oil requires

an input of \$0.20 from agriculture and \$0.05 from oil. Find the output from each sector that is needed to satisfy a final demand of \$40 million for agriculture and \$250 million for oil.

39. **Agriculture, manufacturing, energy.** An economy is based on three sectors, agriculture, manufacturing, and energy. Production of a dollar's worth of agriculture requires inputs of \$0.20 from agriculture, \$0.20 from manufacturing, and \$0.20 from energy. Production of a dollar's worth of manufacturing requires inputs of \$0.40 from agriculture, \$0.10 from manufacturing, and \$0.10 from energy. Production of a dollar's worth of energy requires inputs of \$0.30 from agriculture, \$0.10 from manufacturing, and \$0.10 from energy. Find the output for each sector that is needed to satisfy a final demand of \$10 billion for agriculture, \$15 billion for manufacturing, and \$20 billion for energy.

40. **Electricity, natural gas, oil.** A large energy company produces electricity, natural gas, and oil. The production of a dollar's worth of electricity requires inputs of \$0.30 from electricity, \$0.10 from natural gas, and \$0.20 from oil. Production of a dollar's worth of natural gas requires inputs of \$0.30 from electricity, \$0.10 from natural gas, and \$0.20 from oil. Production of a dollar's worth of oil requires inputs of \$0.10 from each sector. Find the output for each sector that is needed to satisfy a final demand of \$25 billion for electricity, \$15 billion for natural gas, and \$20 billion for oil.

41. **Four sectors.** An economy is based on four sectors, agriculture (A), energy (E), labor (L), and manufacturing (M). The table gives the input requirements for a dollar's worth of output for each sector, along with the projected final demand (in billions of dollars) for a 3-year period. Find the output for each sector that is needed to satisfy each of these final demands. Round answers to the nearest billion dollars.

		Output				Final Demand		
		A	E	L	M	1	2	3
Input	A	0.05	0.17	0.23	0.09	23	32	55
	E	0.07	0.12	0.15	0.19	41	48	62
	L	0.25	0.08	0.03	0.32	18	21	25
	M	0.11	0.19	0.28	0.16	31	33	35

42. Repeat Problem 41 with the following table:

		Output				Final Demand		
		A	E	L	M	1	2	3
Input	A	0.07	0.09	0.27	0.12	18	22	37
	E	0.14	0.07	0.21	0.24	26	31	42
	L	0.17	0.06	0.02	0.21	12	19	28
	M	0.15	0.13	0.31	0.19	41	45	49

Answers to Matched Problems

1. (A) $\begin{bmatrix} 0.2 & 0 & 0.4 \\ 0 & 0.1 & 0.2 \\ 0.4 & 0.2 & 0.2 \end{bmatrix}$ (B) $\begin{bmatrix} 1.7 & 0.2 & 0.9 \\ 0.2 & 1.2 & 0.4 \\ 0.9 & 0.4 & 1.8 \end{bmatrix}$

(C) \$71 billion for coal, \$26 billion for oil, and \$67 billion for transportation

Chapter 4 Summary and Review

Important Terms, Symbols, and Concepts

4.1 Review: Systems of Linear Equations in Two Variables

EXAMPLES

- The **solution** of a system is an ordered pair of real numbers that satisfies each equation in the system. Solution by **graphing** is one method that can be used to find a solution. Ex. 1, p. 177; Ex. 2, p. 178
- A linear system is **consistent** and **independent** if it has a unique solution, **consistent** and **dependent** if it has more than one solution, and **inconsistent** if it has no solution. A linear system that is consistent and dependent actually has an infinite number of solutions.
- A **graphing calculator** provides accurate solutions to a linear system. Ex. 3, p. 180
- The **substitution** method can also be used to solve linear systems. Ex. 4, p. 181
- The **method of elimination by addition** is easily extended to larger systems. Ex. 5, p. 182

4.2 Systems of Linear Equations and Augmented Matrices

- A **matrix** is a rectangular array of real numbers. **Row operations** performed on an **augmented matrix** produce equivalent systems (Theorem 1, page 192). Ex. 1, p. 193; Ex. 2, p. 195
- There are only three possible final forms for the augmented matrix for a linear system of two equations in two variables (p. 197). Ex. 3, p. 195; Ex. 4, p. 197

4.3 Gauss–Jordan Elimination

- There are many possibilities for the final **reduced form** of the augmented matrix of a larger system of linear equations. Reduced form is defined on page 200.
- The **Gauss–Jordan elimination procedure** is described on pages 202 and 203.

Ex. 1, p. 200
Ex. 2, p. 201
Ex. 3, p. 203
Ex. 4, p. 204
Ex. 5, p. 205

4.4 Matrices: Basic Operations

- Two matrices are **equal** if they are the same size and their corresponding elements are equal. The **sum** of two matrices of the same size is the matrix with elements that are the sum of the corresponding elements of the two given matrices. Ex. 1, p. 213
- The **negative of a matrix** is the matrix with elements that are the negatives of the given matrix. If A and B are matrices of the same size, then B can be subtracted from A by adding the negative of B to A. Ex. 2, p. 214
- Matrix equations involving addition and subtraction are solved much like real number equations. Ex. 3, p. 214
- The product of a real number k and a matrix M is the matrix formed by multiplying each element of M by k. Ex. 4, p. 215
- The product of a row matrix and a column matrix is defined on page 216. Ex. 6, p. 216
- The matrix product of an $m \times p$ matrix with a $p \times n$ is defined on page 217. Ex. 8, p. 218

4.5 Inverse of a Square Matrix

- The **identity matrix** for multiplication is defined on page 226.
- The **inverse** of a square matrix is defined on page 228.

Ex. 1, p. 226
Ex. 2, p. 229
Ex. 3, p. 232
Ex. 4, p. 233

4.6 Matrix Equations and Systems of Linear Equations

- Basic properties of matrices are summarized in Theorem 1 on page 238.
- **Matrix inverse methods** for solving systems of equations are described in the Summary on page 241.

Ex. 1, p. 239
Ex. 2, p. 239
Ex. 3, p. 240

4.7 Leontief Input–Output Analysis

- Leontief **input–output** analysis is summarized on page 249. Ex. 1, p. 250

Review Exercises

Work through all the problems in this chapter review and check your answers in the back of the book. Answers to all problems are there along with section numbers in italics to indicate where each type of problem is discussed. Where weaknesses show up, review appropriate sections in the text.

1. Solve the following system by graphing:

$$\begin{aligned} 2x - y &= 4 \\ x - 2y &= -4 \end{aligned}$$

2. Solve the system in Problem 1 by substitution.

3. If a matrix is in reduced form, say so. If not, explain why and state the row operation(s) necessary to transform the matrix into reduced form.

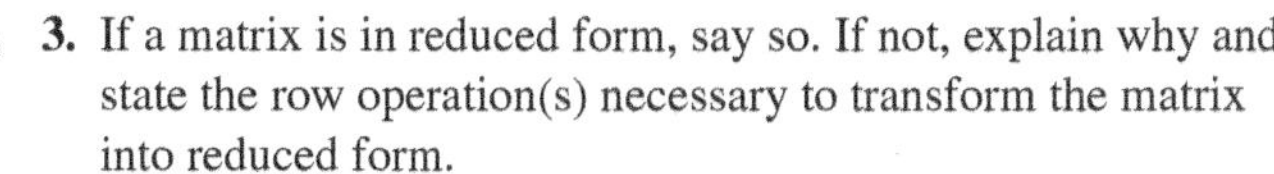

(A) $\left[\begin{array}{cc|c} 0 & 1 & 2 \\ 1 & 0 & 3 \end{array}\right]$ (B) $\left[\begin{array}{cc|c} 1 & 0 & 2 \\ 0 & 3 & 3 \end{array}\right]$

(C) $\left[\begin{array}{ccc|c} 1 & 0 & 1 & 2 \\ 0 & 1 & 1 & 3 \end{array}\right]$ (D) $\left[\begin{array}{ccc|c} 1 & 1 & 0 & 2 \\ 0 & 1 & 1 & 3 \end{array}\right]$

4. Given matrices A and B,

$$A = \begin{bmatrix} 5 & 3 & -1 & 0 & 2 \\ -4 & 8 & 1 & 3 & 0 \end{bmatrix} \qquad B = \begin{bmatrix} -3 & 2 \\ 0 & 4 \\ -1 & 7 \end{bmatrix}$$

(A) What is the size of A? Of B?

(B) Find a_{24}, a_{15}, b_{31}, and b_{22}.

(C) Is AB defined? Is BA defined?

5. Find x_1 and x_2:

(A) $\begin{bmatrix} 1 & -2 \\ 1 & -3 \end{bmatrix}\begin{bmatrix} x_1 \\ x_2 \end{bmatrix} = \begin{bmatrix} 4 \\ 2 \end{bmatrix}$

(B) $\begin{bmatrix} 5 & 3 \\ 1 & 1 \end{bmatrix}\begin{bmatrix} x_1 \\ x_2 \end{bmatrix} + \begin{bmatrix} 25 \\ 14 \end{bmatrix} = \begin{bmatrix} 18 \\ 22 \end{bmatrix}$

In Problems 6–14, perform the operations that are defined, given the following matrices:

$$A = \begin{bmatrix} 1 & 2 \\ 3 & 1 \end{bmatrix} \quad B = \begin{bmatrix} 2 & 1 \\ 1 & 1 \end{bmatrix} \quad C = [2 \quad 3] \quad D = \begin{bmatrix} 1 \\ 2 \end{bmatrix}$$

6. $A + 2B$ **7.** $3B + D$

8. $2A + B$ **9.** BD

10. BC **11.** AD

12. DC **13.** CA

14. $C + A$

15. Find the inverse of the matrix A given below by appropriate row operations on $[A \mid I]$. Show that $A^{-1}A = I$.

$$A = \begin{bmatrix} 4 & 3 \\ 3 & 2 \end{bmatrix}$$

16. Solve the following system using elimination by addition:

$$\begin{aligned} 3m_1 + 4m_2 &= 3 \\ 2m_1 + 3m_2 &= 3 \end{aligned}$$

17. Solve the system in Problem 16 by performing appropriate row operations on the augmented matrix of the system.

18. Solve the system in Problem 16 by writing the system as a matrix equation and using the inverse of the coefficient matrix (see Problem 15). Also, solve the system if the constants 3 and 5 are replaced by 7 and 10, respectively. By 4 and 2, respectively.

In Problems 19–24, perform the operations that are defined, given the following matrices:

$$A = \begin{bmatrix} 2 & -2 \\ 1 & 0 \\ 3 & 2 \end{bmatrix} \quad B = \begin{bmatrix} -1 \\ 2 \\ 3 \end{bmatrix} \quad C = [2 \quad 1 \quad 3]$$

$$D = \begin{bmatrix} 3 & -2 & 1 \\ -1 & 1 & 2 \end{bmatrix} \quad E = \begin{bmatrix} 3 & -4 \\ -1 & 0 \end{bmatrix}$$

19. $A + B$ **20.** $E + DA$

21. $DA - 3E$ **22.** BC

23. CB **24.** $AD - BC$

25. Find the inverse of the matrix A given below by appropriate row operations on $[A \mid I]$. Show that $A^{-1}A = I$.

$$A = \begin{bmatrix} 1 & 2 & 3 \\ 2 & 3 & 4 \\ 1 & 2 & 1 \end{bmatrix}$$

26. Solve by Gauss–Jordan elimination:

(A)
$$\begin{aligned} x_1 + 2x_2 + 3x_3 &= 1 \\ 2x_1 + 3x_2 + 4x_3 &= 3 \\ x_1 + 2x_2 + x_3 &= 3 \end{aligned}$$

(B)
$$\begin{aligned} x_1 + 2x_2 - x_3 &= 2 \\ 2x_1 + 3x_2 + x_3 &= -3 \\ 3x_1 + 5x_2 \quad &= -1 \end{aligned}$$

(C)
$$\begin{aligned} x_1 + x_2 + x_3 &= 8 \\ 3x_1 + 2x_2 + 4x_3 &= 21 \end{aligned}$$

27. Solve the system in Problem 26A by writing the system as a matrix equation and using the inverse of the coefficient matrix (see Problem 25). Also, solve the system if the constants 1, 3, and 3 are replaced by 0, 0, and −2, respectively. By −3, −4, and 1, respectively.

28. Discuss the relationship between the number of solutions of the following system and the constant k.

$$\begin{aligned} 2x_1 - 6x_2 &= 4 \\ -x_1 + kx_2 &= -2 \end{aligned}$$

29. An economy is based on two sectors, agriculture and energy. Given the technology matrix M and the final demand matrix D (in billions of dollars), find $(I - M)^{-1}$ and the output matrix X:

$$M = \begin{matrix} & \begin{matrix} A & E \end{matrix} \\ \begin{matrix} A \\ E \end{matrix} & \begin{bmatrix} 0.2 & 0.15 \\ 0.4 & 0.3 \end{bmatrix} \end{matrix} \quad D = \begin{matrix} A \\ E \end{matrix} \begin{bmatrix} 30 \\ 20 \end{bmatrix}$$

30. Use the matrix M in Problem 29 to fill in the elements in the following technology matrix.

$$T = \begin{matrix} & \begin{matrix} E & A \end{matrix} \\ \begin{matrix} E \\ A \end{matrix} & \begin{bmatrix} & \\ & \end{bmatrix} \end{matrix}$$

Use this matrix to solve Problem 29. Discuss any differences in your calculations and in your answers.

31. An economy is based on two sectors, coal and steel. Given the technology matrix M and the final demand matrix D (in billions of dollars), find $(I - M)^{-1}$ and the output matrix X:

$$M = \begin{matrix} & \begin{matrix} C & S \end{matrix} \\ \begin{matrix} C \\ S \end{matrix} & \begin{bmatrix} 0.45 & 0.65 \\ 0.55 & 0.35 \end{bmatrix} \end{matrix} \quad D = \begin{matrix} C \\ S \end{matrix} \begin{bmatrix} 40 \\ 10 \end{bmatrix}$$

32. Use graphical approximation techniques on a graphing calculator to find the solution of the following system to two decimal places:

$$\begin{aligned} x - 5y &= -5 \\ 2x + 3y &= 12 \end{aligned}$$

33. Find the inverse of the matrix A given below. Show that $A^{-1}A = I$.

$$A = \begin{bmatrix} 4 & 5 & 6 \\ 4 & 5 & -4 \\ 1 & 1 & 1 \end{bmatrix}$$

34. Solve the system

$$\begin{aligned} 0.04x_1 + 0.05x_2 + 0.06x_3 &= 360 \\ 0.04x_1 + 0.05x_2 - 0.04x_3 &= 120 \\ x_1 + x_2 + x_3 &= 7{,}000 \end{aligned}$$

by writing it as a matrix equation and using the inverse of the coefficient matrix. (Before starting, multiply the first two equations by 100 to eliminate decimals. Also, see Problem 33.)

35. Solve Problem 34 by Gauss–Jordan elimination.

36. Given the technology matrix M and the final demand matrix D (in billions of dollars), find $(I - M)^{-1}$ and the output matrix X:

$$M = \begin{bmatrix} 0.2 & 0 & 0.4 \\ 0.1 & 0.3 & 0.1 \\ 0 & 0.4 & 0.2 \end{bmatrix} \quad D = \begin{bmatrix} 40 \\ 20 \\ 30 \end{bmatrix}$$

37. Discuss the number of solutions for a system of n equations in n variables if the coefficient matrix
    (A) Has an inverse.
    (B) Does not have an inverse.

38. Discuss the number of solutions for the system corresponding to the reduced form shown below if
    (A) $m \neq 0$
    (B) $m = 0$ and $n \neq 0$
    (C) $m = 0$ and $n = 0$

$$\left[\begin{array}{ccc|c} 1 & 0 & -2 & 5 \\ 0 & 1 & 3 & 3 \\ 0 & 0 & m & n \end{array}\right]$$

39. One solution to the input–output equation $X = MX + D$ is given by $X = (I - M)^{-1}D$. Discuss the validity of each step in the following solutions of this equation. (Assume that all necessary inverses exist.) Are both solutions correct?

(A)
$$\begin{aligned} X &= MX + D \\ X - MX &= D \\ X(I - M) &= D \\ X &= D(I - M)^{-1} \end{aligned}$$

(B)
$$\begin{aligned} X &= MX + D \\ -D &= MX - X \\ -D &= (M - I)X \\ X &= (M - I)^{-1}(-D) \end{aligned}$$

Applications

40. **Break-even analysis.** A computer design company is preparing to market a new computer. The company's fixed costs for research, development, and tooling are $253,000 and the variable costs are $35.50 per unit. The company is planning to sell each unit at a market price of $199.99.
    (A) Find the cost and revenue equations.
    (B) Find the break-even point.
    (C) Graph both equations in the same coordinate system and show the break-even point. Use the graph to determine the production levels that will result in a profit and in a loss.

41. **Resource allocation.** An international mining company has two mines in Port Hedland and Jack Hills. The composition of the ore from each field is given in the table. How many tons of ore from each mine should be used to obtain exactly 6 tons of nickel and 8 tons of copper?

Mine	Nickel (%)	Copper (%)
Port Hedland	2	4
Jack Hills	3	2

42. **Resource allocation.**
    (A) Set up Problem 41 as a matrix equation and solve using the inverse of the coefficient matrix.
    (B) Solve Problem 41 as in part (A) if 7.5 tons of nickel and 7 tons of copper are needed.

43. **Business leases.** A grain company wants to lease a fleet of 20 covered hopper railcars with a combined capacity of 108,000 cubic feet. Hoppers with three different carrying capacities are available: 3,000 cubic feet, 4,500 cubic feet, and 6,000 cubic feet.
    (A) How many of each type of hopper should they lease?
    (B) The monthly rates for leasing these hoppers are $180 for 3,000 cubic feet, $225 for 4,500 cubic feet, and $325 for 6,000 cubic feet. Which of the solutions in part (A) would minimize the monthly leasing costs?

44. **Material costs.** A manufacturer wishes to make two different bronze alloys in a metal foundry. The quantities of copper, tin, and zinc needed are indicated in matrix M. The costs for these materials (in dollars per pound) from two suppliers are summarized in matrix N. The company must choose one supplier or the other.

$$M = \begin{array}{c} \text{Copper} \quad \text{Tin} \quad \text{Zinc} \\ \begin{bmatrix} 4{,}800\text{ lb} & 600\text{ lb} & 300\text{ lb} \\ 6{,}000\text{ lb} & 1{,}400\text{ lb} & 700\text{ lb} \end{bmatrix} \end{array} \begin{array}{l} \text{Alloy 1} \\ \text{Alloy 2} \end{array}$$

$$N = \begin{array}{c} \text{Supplier A} \quad \text{Supplier B} \\ \begin{bmatrix} \$0.75 & \$0.70 \\ \$6.50 & \$6.70 \\ \$0.40 & \$0.50 \end{bmatrix} \end{array} \begin{array}{l} \text{Copper} \\ \text{Tin} \\ \text{Zinc} \end{array}$$

    (A) Discuss possible interpretations of the elements in the matrix products MN and NM.
    (B) If either product MN or NM has a meaningful interpretation, find the product and label its rows and columns.
    (C) Discuss methods of matrix multiplication that can be used to determine the supplier that will provide the necessary materials at the lowest cost.

45. **Labor costs.** A company with manufacturing plants in Tokyo and Osaka has labor-hour and wage requirements for the manufacture of two inexpensive calculators as given in matrices M and N below:

Labor-hours per calculator

$$M = \begin{array}{c} \begin{array}{ccc} \text{Fabricating department} & \text{Assembly department} & \text{Packaging department} \end{array} \\ \begin{bmatrix} 0.15\text{ hr} & 0.10\text{ hr} & 0.05\text{ hr} \\ 0.25\text{ hr} & 0.20\text{ hr} & 0.05\text{ hr} \end{bmatrix} \end{array} \begin{array}{l} \text{Model A} \\ \text{Model B} \end{array}$$

Hourly wages

$$N = \begin{array}{c} \begin{array}{cc} \text{Tokyo plant} & \text{Osaka plant} \end{array} \\ \begin{bmatrix} \$12 & \$10 \\ \$15 & \$12 \\ \$\ 7 & \$\ 6 \end{bmatrix} \end{array} \begin{array}{l} \text{Fabricating department} \\ \text{Assembly department} \\ \text{Packaging department} \end{array}$$

    (A) Find the labor cost for producing one model B calculator at the Tokyo plant.
    (B) Discuss possible interpretations of the elements in the matrix products MN and NM.

(C) If either product MN or NM has a meaningful interpretation, find the product and label its rows and columns.

46. **Investment analysis.** A person has $5,000 to invest, part at 5% and the rest at 10%. How much should be invested at each rate to yield $400 per year? Solve using augmented matrix methods.

47. **Investment analysis.** Solve Problem 46 by using a matrix equation and the inverse of the coefficient matrix.

48. **Investment analysis.** In Problem 46, is it possible to have an annual yield of $200? Of $600? Describe all possible annual yields.

49. **Ticket prices.** An outdoor amphitheater has 25,000 seats. Ticket prices are $8, $12, and $20, and the number of tickets priced at $8 must equal the number priced at $20. How many tickets of each type should be sold (assuming that all seats can be sold) to bring in each of the returns indicated in the table? Solve using the inverse of the coefficient matrix.

	Concert		
	1	2	3
Tickets sold	25,000	25,000	25,000
Return required	$320,000	$330,000	$340,000

50. **Ticket prices.** Discuss the effect on the solutions to Problem 49 if it is no longer required to have an equal number of $8 tickets and $20 tickets.

51. **Input–output analysis.** Consider a hypothetical economy that depends on two basic products, wheat and oil. Production of 1 metric ton of wheat requires an input of 0.25 metric tons of wheat and 0.33 metric tons of oil. Production of 1 metric ton of oil requires 0.08 metric tons of wheat and 0.11 metric tons of oil.

(A) Find the output of each item that is needed to satisfy a final demand of 500 metric tons of wheat and 1000 metric tons of oil.

(B) Find the output of each item that is needed to satisfy a final demand of 800 metric tons of wheat and 2000 metric tons of oil.

52. **Cryptography.** The following message was encoded with the matrix B shown below. Decode the message.

7 25 30 19 6 24 20 8 28 5 14 14
9 23 28 15 6 21 13 1 14 21 26 29

$$B = \begin{bmatrix} 1 & 1 & 0 \\ 1 & 0 & 1 \\ 1 & 1 & 1 \end{bmatrix}$$

53. **Traffic flow.** The rush-hour traffic flow (in vehicles per hour) for a network of four one-way streets is shown in the figure.

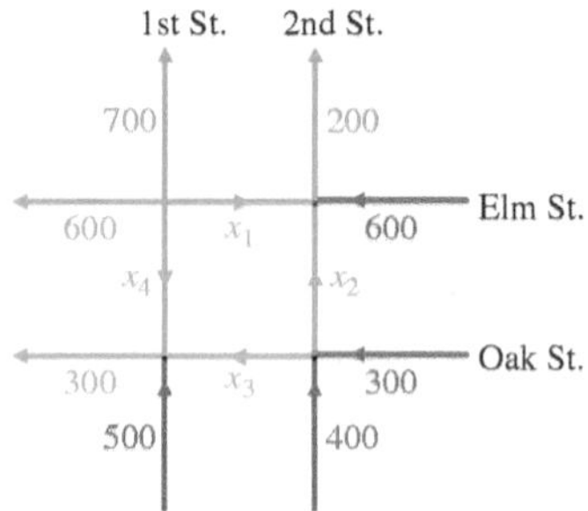

(A) Write the system of equations determined by the flow of traffic through the four intersections.

(B) Find the solution of the system in part (A).

(C) What is the maximum number of vehicles per hour that can travel from Oak Street to Elm Street on 1st Street? What is the minimum number?

(D) If traffic lights are adjusted so that 500 vehicles per hour travel from Oak Street to Elm Street on 1st Street, determine the flow around the rest of the network.

5 Linear Inequalities and Linear Programming

Introduction

Real-world problems often involve limitations on materials, time, and money. To express such constraints mathematically, we formulate systems of inequalities. In Chapter 5 we discuss systems of inequalities in two variables and introduce a relatively new mathematical tool called linear programming. Linear programming can be used to determine how two different alloys of bronze should be combined to produce window frames (see Problems 59 and 60 in Section 5.1).

5.1 Linear Inequalities in Two Variables

- Graphing Linear Inequalities in Two Variables
- Application

Graphing Linear Inequalities in Two Variables

We know how to graph first-degree equations such as

$$y = 2x - 3 \quad \text{and} \quad 2x - 3y = 5$$

but how do we graph first-degree inequalities such as the following?

$$y \leq 2x - 3 \quad \text{and} \quad 2x - 3y > 5$$

We will find that graphing these inequalities is similar to graphing the equations, but first we must discuss some important subsets of a plane in a rectangular coordinate system.

A line divides the plane into two regions called **half-planes**. A vertical line divides it into **left** and **right half-planes**; a nonvertical line divides it into **upper** and **lower half-planes**. In either case, the dividing line is called the **boundary line** of each half-plane, as indicated in Figure 1.

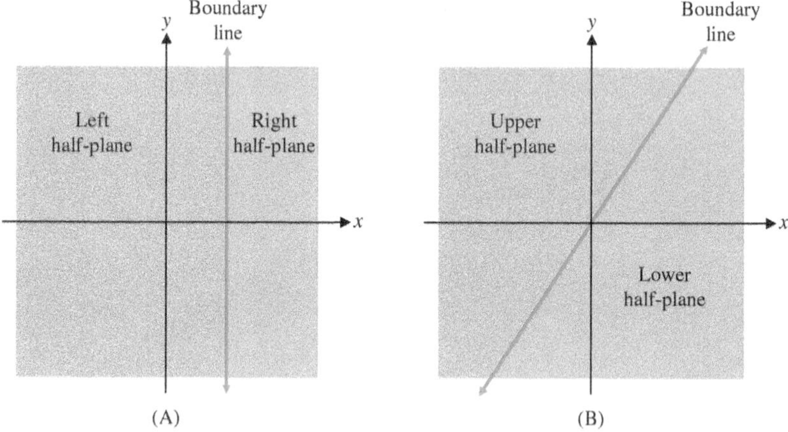

Figure 1

To find the half-planes determined by a linear equation such as $y - x = -2$, we rewrite the equation as $y = x - 2$. For any given value of x, there is exactly one value for y such that (x, y) lies on the line. For example, for $x = 4$, we have $y = 4 - 2 = 2$. For the same x and smaller values of y, the point (x, y) will lie below the line since $y < x - 2$. So the lower half-plane corresponds to the solution of the inequality $y < x - 2$. Similarly, the upper half-plane corresponds to $y > x - 2$, as shown in Figure 2.

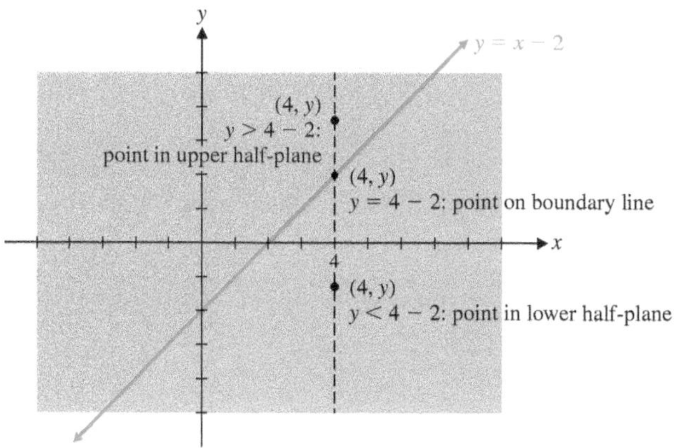

Figure 2

The four inequalities formed from $y = x - 2$, replacing the $=$ sign by $>$, $\geq$, $<$, and $\leq$, respectively, are

$$y > x - 2 \qquad y \geq x - 2 \qquad y < x - 2 \qquad y \leq x - 2$$

The graph of each is a half-plane, excluding the boundary line for $<$ and $>$ and including the boundary line for $\leq$ and $\geq$. In Figure 3, the half-planes are indicated with small arrows on the graph of $y = x - 2$ and then graphed as shaded regions. Excluded boundary lines are shown as dashed lines, and included boundary lines are shown as solid lines.

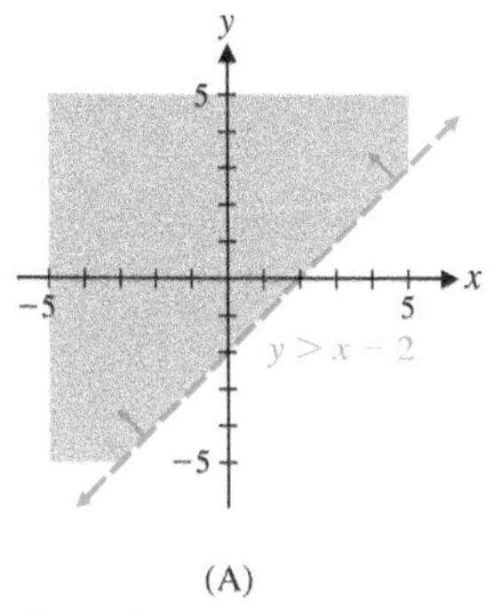

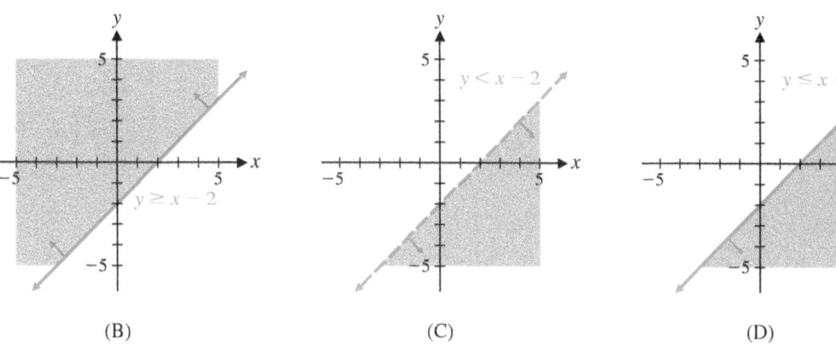

Figure 3

Figure 4 shows the graphs of Figures 3B and 3D on a graphing calculator. Note that it is impossible to show a dotted boundary line when using shading on a calculator.

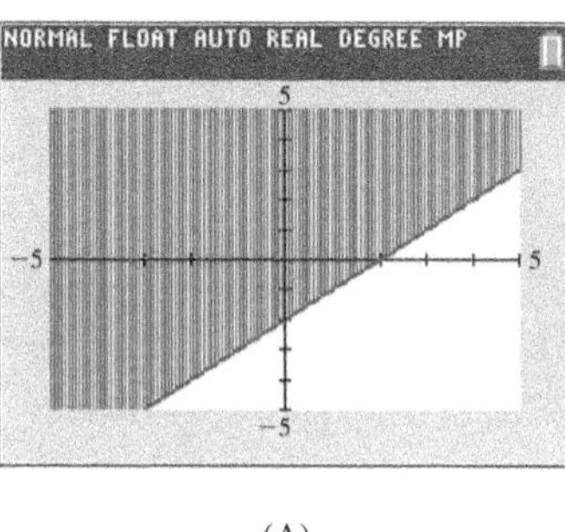

(A)

(B)

Figure 4

The preceding discussion suggests the following theorem, which is stated without proof:

THEOREM 1 Graphs of Linear Inequalities

The graph of the linear inequality

$$Ax + By < C \qquad \text{or} \qquad Ax + By > C$$

with $B \neq 0$, is either the upper half-plane or the lower half-plane (but not both) determined by the line $Ax + By = C$.

If $B = 0$ and $A \neq 0$, the graph of

$$Ax < C \qquad \text{or} \qquad Ax > C$$

is either the left half-plane or the right half-plane (but not both) determined by the line $Ax = C$.

As a consequence of this theorem, we state a simple and fast mechanical procedure for graphing linear inequalities.

PROCEDURE Graphing Linear Inequalities

Step 1 First graph $Ax + By = C$ as a dashed line if equality is not included in the original statement, or as a solid line if equality is included.

Step 2 Choose a test point anywhere in the plane not on the line [the origin $(0, 0)$ usually requires the least computation], and substitute the coordinates into the inequality.

Step 3 Does the test point satisfy the original inequality? If so, shade the half-plane that contains the test point. If not, shade the opposite half-plane.

EXAMPLE 1 **Graphing a Linear Inequality** Graph $2x - 3y \le 6$.

Reminder

Recall that the line $2x - 3y = 6$ can be graphed by finding any two points on the line. The x and y intercepts are usually a good choice (see Fig. 5).

x	y
0	−2
3	0

SOLUTION

Step 1 Graph $2x - 3y = 6$ as a solid line, since equality is included in the original statement (Fig. 5).

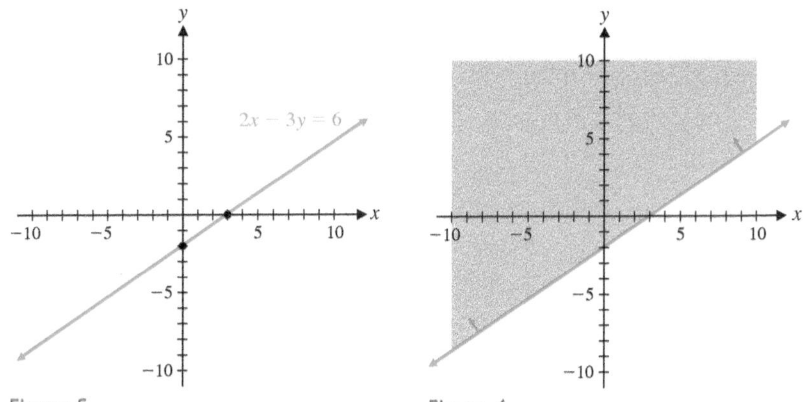

Figure 5 Figure 6

Step 2 Pick a convenient test point above or below the line. The origin $(0, 0)$ requires the least computation, so substituting $(0, 0)$ into the inequality, we get

$$2x - 3y \le 6$$
$$2(0) - 3(0) = 0 \le 6$$

This is a true statement; therefore, the point $(0, 0)$ is in the solution set.

Step 3 The line $2x - 3y = 6$ and the half-plane containing the origin form the graph of $2x - 3y \le 6$, as shown in Figure 6.

Matched Problem 1 Graph $6x - 3y > 18$.

Explore and Discuss 1

In Step 2 of Example 1, $(0, 0)$ was used as a test point in graphing a linear inequality. Describe those linear inequalities for which $(0, 0)$ is not a valid test point. In that case, how would you choose a test point to make calculation easy?

EXAMPLE 2 **Graphing Inequalities** Graph

(A) $y > -3$ (B) $2x \le 5$ (C) $x \le 3y$

SOLUTION

(A) Step 1 Graph the horizontal line $y = -3$ as a dashed line, since equality is not included in the original statement (Fig. 7).

Step 2 Substituting $x = 0$ and $y = 0$ in the inequality produces a true statement, so the point $(0, 0)$ is in the solution set.

Step 3 The graph of the solution set is the upper half-plane, excluding the boundary line (Fig. 8).

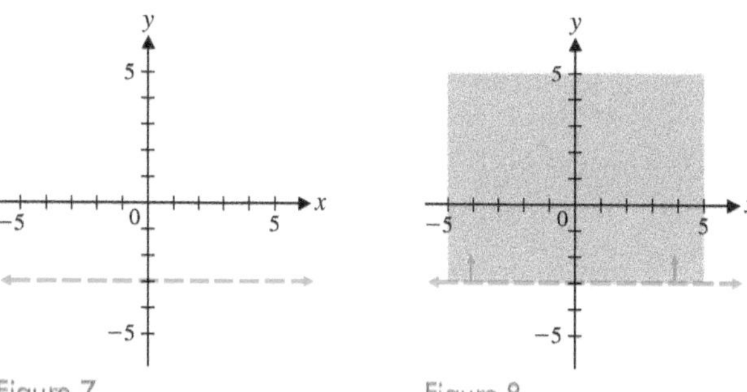

Figure 7 Figure 8

(B) Step 1 Graph the vertical line $2x = 5$ as a solid line, since equality is included in the original statement (Fig. 9).

Step 2 Substituting $x = 0$ and $y = 0$ in the inequality produces a true statement, so the point $(0, 0)$ is in the solution set.

Step 3 The graph of the solution set is the left half-plane, including the boundary line (Fig. 10).

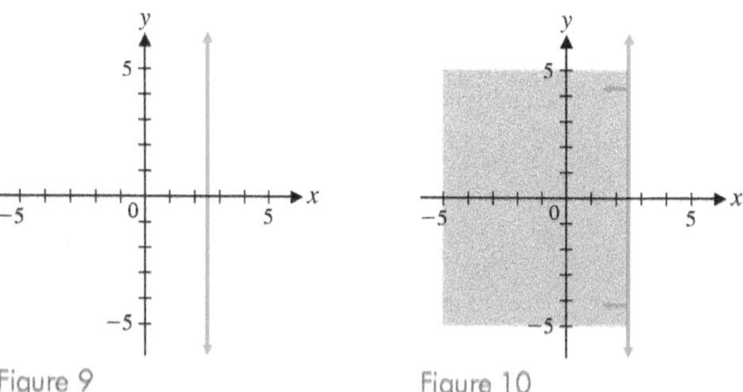

Figure 9 Figure 10

(C) Step 1 Graph the line $x = 3y$ as a solid line, since equality is included in the original statement (Fig. 11).

Step 2 Since the line passes through the origin, we must use a different test point. We choose $(0, 2)$ for a test point and conclude that this point is in the solution set.

Step 3 The graph of the solution set is the upper half-plane, including the boundary line (Fig. 12).

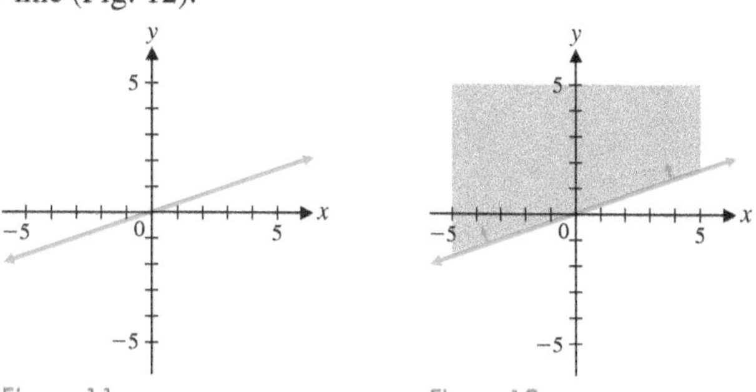

Figure 11 Figure 12

Matched Problem 2 Graph

(A) $y < 4$ (B) $4x \geq -9$ (C) $3x \geq 2y$

EXAMPLE 3 **Interpreting a Graph** Find the linear inequality whose graph is given in Figure 13. Write the boundary line equation in the form $Ax + By = C$, where A, B, and C are integers, before stating the inequality.

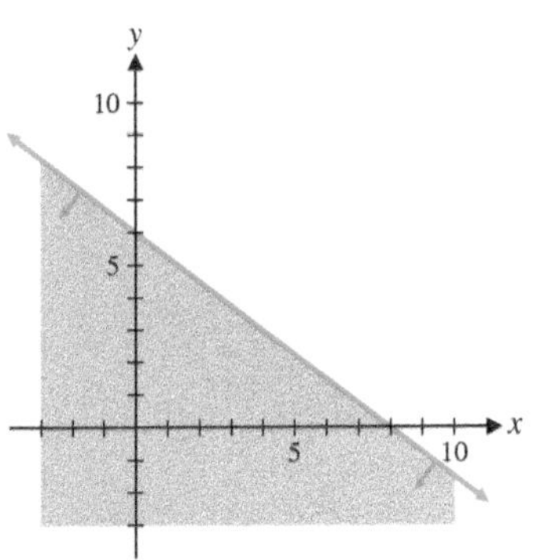
Figure 13

SOLUTION The boundary line (Fig. 13) passes through the points $(0, 6)$ and $(8, 0)$. We use the slope-intercept form to find the equation of this line:

$$\text{Slope: } m = \frac{0 - 6}{8 - 0} = -\frac{6}{8} = -\frac{3}{4}$$

$$y \text{ intercept: } b = 6$$

$$\text{Boundary line equation: } y = -\frac{3}{4}x + 6 \qquad \text{Multiply both sides by 4.}$$

$$4y = -3x + 24 \qquad \text{Add } 3x \text{ to both sides.}$$

$$3x + 4y = 24 \qquad \text{Form: } Ax + By = C$$

Since $(0, 0)$ is in the shaded region in Figure 13 and the boundary line is solid, the graph in Figure 13 is the graph of $3x + 4y \le 24$.

Matched Problem 3 Find the linear inequality whose graph is given in Figure 14. Write the boundary line equation in the form $Ax + By = C$, where A, B, and C are integers, before stating the inequality.

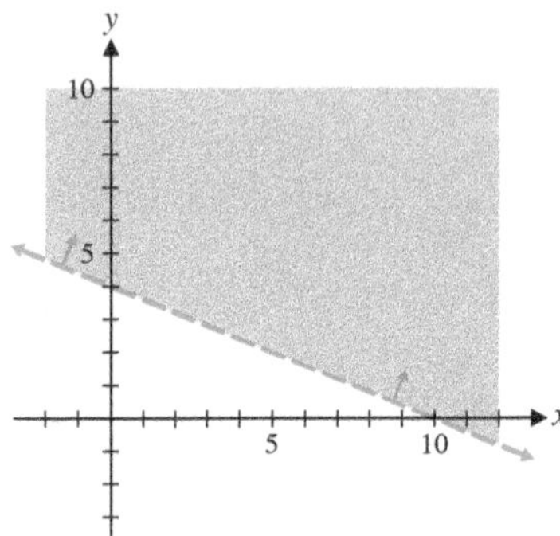
Figure 14

Application

EXAMPLE 4 **Sales** A concert promoter wants to book a rock group for a stadium concert. A ticket for admission to the stadium playing field will cost \$125, and a ticket for a seat in the stands will cost \$175. The group wants to be guaranteed total ticket sales of at least \$700,000. How many tickets of each type must be sold to satisfy the group's guarantee? Express the answer as a linear inequality and draw its graph.

SOLUTION

Let x = Number of tickets sold for the playing field

y = Number of tickets sold for seats in the stands

We use these variables to translate the following statement from the problem into a mathematical statement:

The group wants to be guaranteed total ticket sales of at least \$700,000.

$$\begin{pmatrix}\text{Sales for the}\\ \text{playing field}\end{pmatrix} + \begin{pmatrix}\text{Sales for seats}\\ \text{in the stands}\end{pmatrix} \begin{pmatrix}\text{At}\\ \text{least}\end{pmatrix} \begin{pmatrix}\text{Total sales}\\ \text{guaranteed}\end{pmatrix}$$

$$125x + 175y \ge 700{,}000$$

Dividing both sides of this inequality by 25, x, and y must satisfy

$$5x + 7y \ge 28{,}000$$

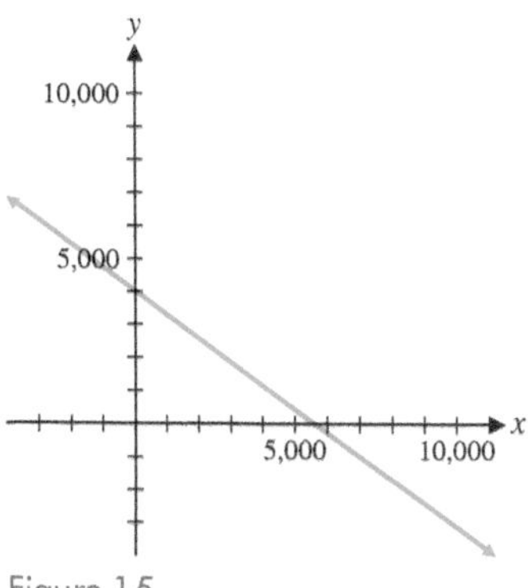

Figure 15

We use the three-step procedure to graph this inequality.

Step 1 Graph $5x + 7y = 28{,}000$ as a solid line (Fig. 15).

Step 2 Substituting $x = 0$ and $y = 0$ in the inequality produces a false statement, so the point $(0, 0)$ is not in the solution set.

Step 3 The graph of the inequality is the upper half-plane including the boundary line (Fig. 16), but does this graph really represent ticket sales?

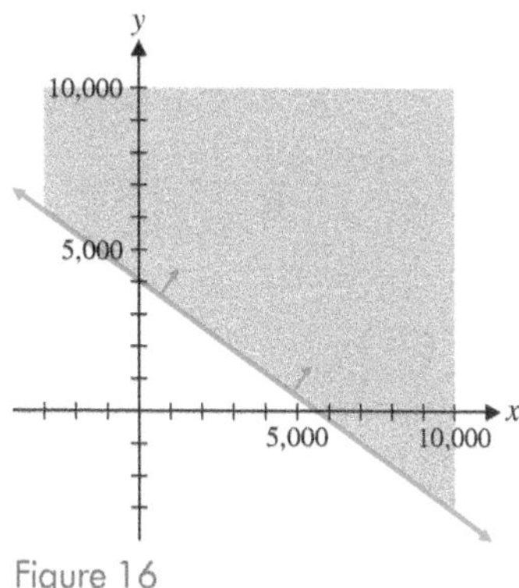

Figure 16

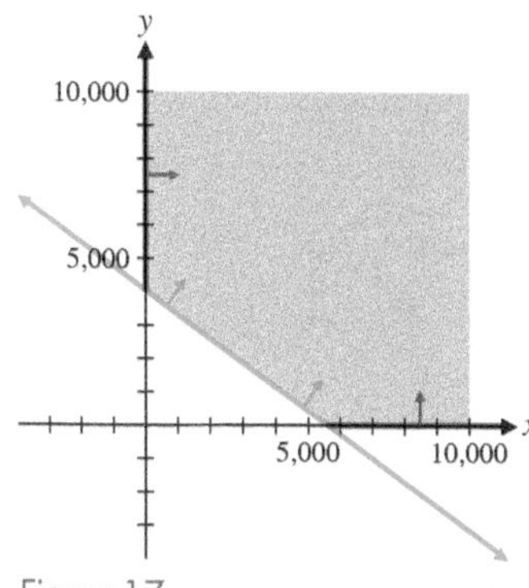

Figure 17

The shaded region in Figure 16 contains points in the second quadrant (where $x < 0$) and the fourth quadrant (where $y < 0$). It is not possible to sell a negative number of tickets, so we must restrict both x and y to the first quadrant. With this restriction, the solution becomes

$$5x + 7y \geq 28{,}000$$
$$x \geq 0, \ y \geq 0$$

and the graph is shown in Figure 17. There is yet another restriction on x and y. It is not possible to sell a fractional number of tickets, so both x and y must be integers. So the solutions of the original problem correspond to those points of the shaded region in Figure 17 that have integer coordinates. This restriction is not indicated in Figure 17, because the points with integer coordinates are too close together (about 9,000 such points per inch) to be visually distinguishable from other points.

Matched Problem 4 A food vendor at a rock concert sells sandwiches for \$4 and fish and chips for \$5. How many of these must be sold to produce sales of at least \$1,000? Express the answer as a linear inequality and draw its graph.

Exercises 5.1

Skills Warm-up Exercises

W *For Problems 1–8, if necessary, review Section A.2.*

1. Is the point $(3, 5)$ on the line $y = 2x + 1$?

2. Is the point $(7, 9)$ on the line $y = 3x - 11$?

3. Is the point $(3, 5)$ in the solution set of $y \leq 2x + 1$?

4. Is the point $(7, 9)$ in the solution set of $y \leq 3x - 11$?

5. Is the point $(10, 12)$ on the line $13x - 11y = 2$?

6. Is the point $(21, 25)$ on the line $30x - 27y = 1$?

7. Is the point $(10, 12)$ in the solution set of $13x - 11y \geq 2$?

8. Is the point $(21, 25)$ in the solution set of $30x - 27y \leq 1$?

A *Graph each inequality in Problems 9–18.*

9. $y \leq x - 1$

10. $y > x + 1$

11. $3x - 2y > 6$

12. $2x - 5y \leq 10$

13. $x \geq -4$

14. $y < 5$

15. $5x + 7y \geq 35$

16. $4x + 8y \geq 32$

17. $5x \leq -2y$

18. $6x \geq 4y$

In Problems 19–22,

(A) *graph the set of points that satisfy the inequality.*

(B) *graph the set of points that do not satisfy the inequality.*

19. $3x + 5y < 30$

20. $3x + 4y > 24$

21. $5x - 2y \geq 20$

22. $3x - 5y \leq 30$

In Problems 23–32, define the variable and translate the sentence into an inequality.

23. There are fewer than 10 applicants.

24. She consumes no more than 900 calories per day.

25. He practices no less than 2.5 hours per day.

26. The average attendance is less than 15,000.

27. The success rate of the project is under 20%.

28. The discount is at least 5%.

29. The annual fee is over $45,000.

30. The population is greater than 500,000.

31. The enrollment is at most 30.

32. Mileage exceeds 35 miles per gallon.

B *In Exercises 33–38, state the linear inequality whose graph is given in the figure. Write the boundary-line equation in the form $Ax + By = C$, where A, B, and C are integers, before stating the inequality.*

33.

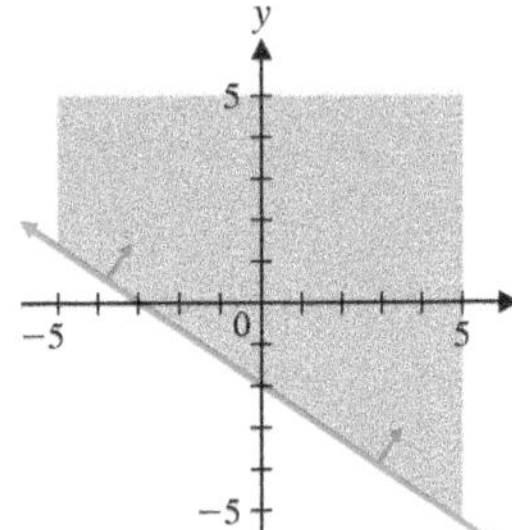

34.

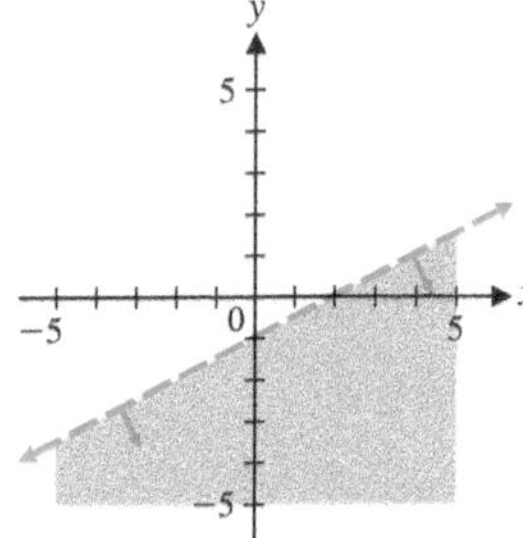

35.

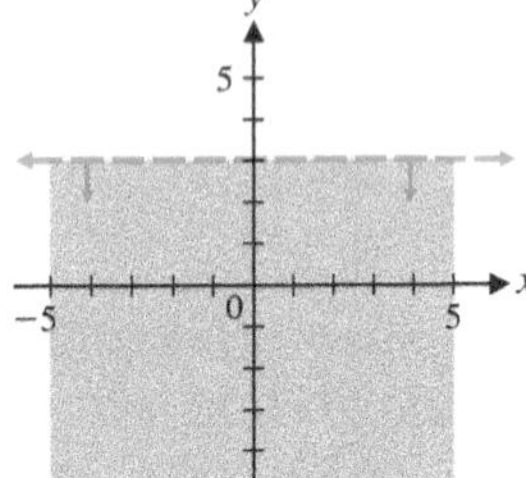

36.

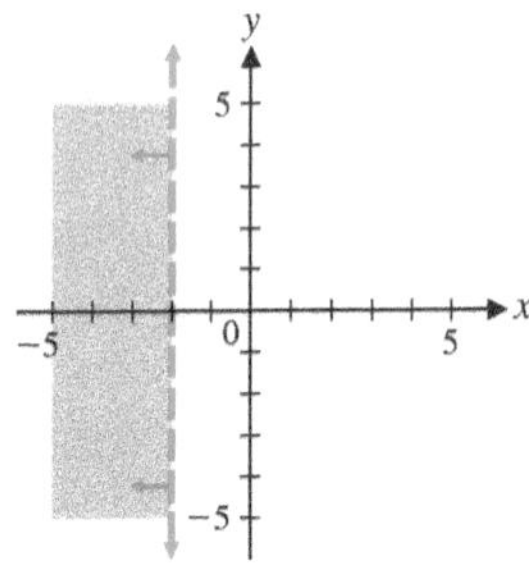

37.

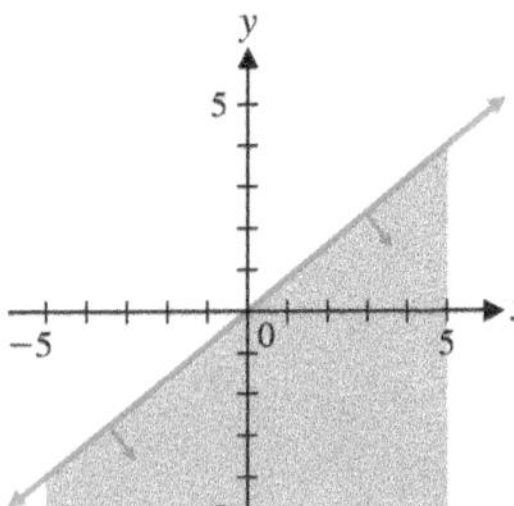

38.

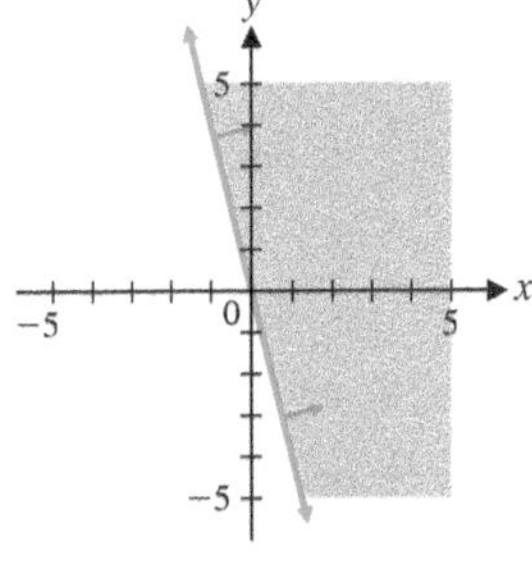

In Problems 39–44, define two variables and translate the sentence into an inequality.

39. Enrollment in finite mathematics plus enrollment in calculus is less than 300.

40. New-car sales and used-car sales combined are at most $500,000.

41. Revenue is at least $20,000 under the cost.

42. The Conservative candidate beat the Labor candidate by at least seven percentage points.

43. The number of grams of protein in rice is more than double the number of grams of protein in potato.

44. The plane is at least 500 miles closer to Cape Town than to Johannesburg.

C *In Problems 45–54, graph each inequality subject to the non-negative restrictions.*

45. $15x + 50y \le 4{,}500,\ x \ge 0,\ y \ge 0$

46. $24x + 30y > 7{,}200,\ x \ge 0,\ y \ge 0$

47. $60x - 35y > 0,\ x \ge 0,\ y \ge 0$

48. $16x - 12y \ge 4{,}800,\ x \ge 0,\ y \ge 0$

49. $-18x + 30y \ge 2{,}700,\ x \ge 0,\ y \ge 0$

50. $-14x + 22y < 1{,}540,\ x \ge 0,\ y \ge 0$

51. $12x - 8y < 4{,}800,\ x \ge 0,\ y \ge 0$

52. $-35x + 75y \le 0,\ x \ge 0,\ y \ge 0$

53. $25x + 75y < -600,\ x \ge 0,\ y \ge 0$

54. $75x + 25y > -600,\ x \ge 0,\ y \ge 0$

Applications

In Problems 55–66, express your answer as a linear inequality with appropriate nonnegative restrictions and draw its graph.

55. Seed costs. Seed costs for a farmer are $90 per acre for corn and $70 per acre for soybeans. How many acres of each crop should the farmer plant if he wants to spend no more than $11,000 on seed?

56. Labor costs. Labor costs for a farmer are $120 per acre for corn and $100 per acre for soybeans. How many acres of each crop should the farmer plant if he wants to spend no more than $15,000 on labor?

57. Fertilizer. A farmer wants to use two brands of fertilizer for his corn crop. Brand *A* contains 26% nitrogen, 3% phosphate, and 3% potash. Brand *B* contains 16% nitrogen, 8% phosphate, and 8% potash.

(*Source:* Spectrum Analytic, Inc.)

(A) How many pounds of each brand of fertilizer should he add to each acre if he wants to add at least 120 pounds of nitrogen to each acre?

(B) How many pounds of each brand of fertilizer should he add to each acre if he wants to add at most 28 pounds of phosphate to each acre?

58. **Fertilizer.** A farmer wants to use two brands of fertilizer for his soybean crop. Brand A contains 18% nitrogen, 24% phosphate, and 12% potash. Brand B contains 5% nitrogen, 10% phosphate, and 15% potash.

(*Source:* Spectrum Analytic, Inc.)

(A) How many pounds of each brand of fertilizer should he add to each acre if he wants to add at least 50 pounds of phosphate to each acre?

(B) How many pounds of each brand of fertilizer should he add to each acre if he wants to add at most 60 pounds of potash to each acre?

59. **Alloy.** A producer uses two alloys of bronze to produce window frames: commercial bronze that is 90% copper and 10% zinc and architectural bronze that is 57% copper, 40% zinc, and 3% lead. How many kilograms of each alloy should the producer use to produce a frame that is at least 75% copper?

60. **Alloy.** Refer to Exercise 59. How many kilograms of each alloy should the producer use to produce a frame that is at least 30% zinc?

61. **Customized vehicles.** A company uses sedans and minivans to produce custom vehicles for transporting hotel guests to and from airports. Plant A can produce 10 sedans and 8 minivans per week, and Plant B can produce 8 sedans and 6 minivans per week. How many weeks should each plant operate in order to produce at least 400 sedans?

62. **Customized vehicles.** Refer to Exercise 61. How many weeks should each plant operate in order to produce at least 480 minivans?

63. **Political advertising.** A candidate has budgeted $10,000 to spend on radio and television advertising. A radio ad costs $200 per 30-second spot, and a television ad costs $800 per 30-second spot. How many radio and television spots can the candidate purchase without exceeding the budget?

64. **Political advertising.** Refer to Problem 63. The candidate decides to replace the television ads with newspaper ads that cost $500 per ad. How many radio spots and newspaper ads can the candidate purchase without exceeding the budget?

65. **Mattresses.** A company produces foam mattresses in two sizes: regular and king. It takes 5 minutes to cut the foam for a regular mattress and 6 minutes for a king mattress. If the cutting department has 50 labor-hours available each day, how many regular and king mattresses can be cut in one day?

66. **Mattresses.** Refer to Problem 65. It takes 15 minutes to cover a regular mattress and 20 minutes to cover a king mattress. If the covering department has 160 labor-hours available each day, how many regular and king mattresses can be covered in one day?

Answers to Matched Problems

1.

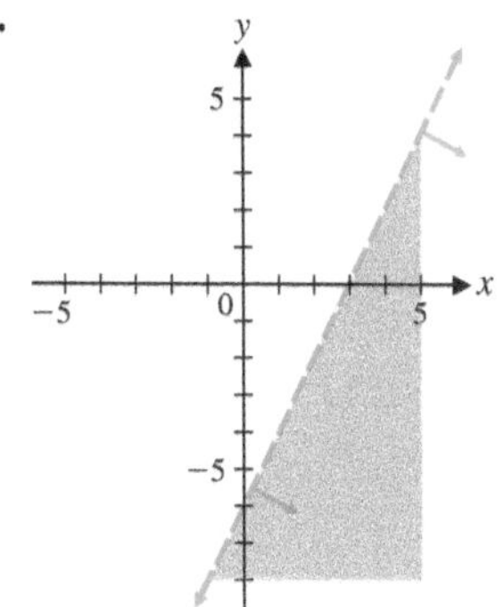

2. (A)

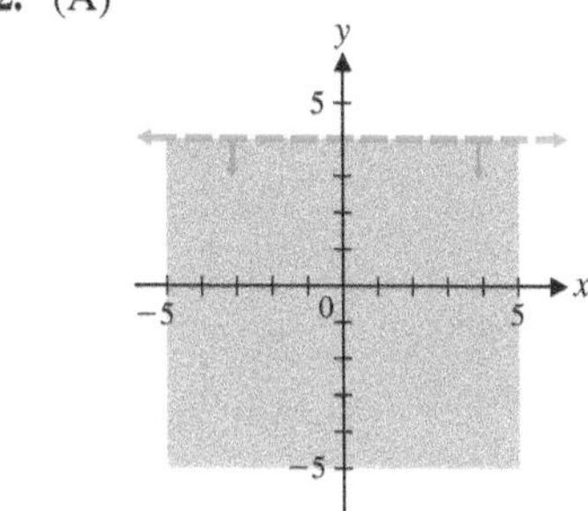

(B) (C)

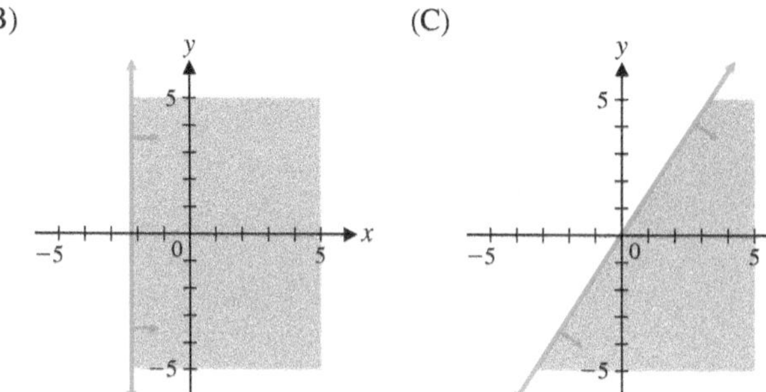

3. $2x + 5y > 20$

4. Let x = Number of hot dogs sold

y = Number of hamburgers sold

$4x + 5y \geq 1{,}000 \qquad x \geq 0, y \geq 0$

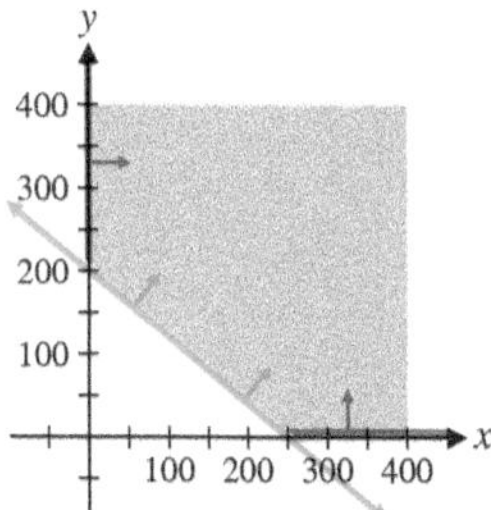

5.2 Systems of Linear Inequalities in Two Variables

- Solving Systems of Linear Inequalities Graphically
- Applications

Solving Systems of Linear Inequalities Graphically

We now consider systems of linear inequalities such as

$$\begin{aligned} x + y &\geq 6 \\ 2x - y &\geq 0 \end{aligned} \quad \text{and} \quad \begin{aligned} 2x + y &\leq 22 \\ x + y &\leq 13 \\ 2x + 5y &\leq 50 \\ x &\geq 0 \\ y &\geq 0 \end{aligned}$$

We wish to **solve** such systems **graphically**—that is, to find the graph of all ordered pairs of real numbers (x, y) that simultaneously satisfy all the inequalities in the system. The graph is called the **solution region** for the system (the solution region is also known as the **feasible region**). To find the solution region, we graph each inequality in the system and then take the intersection of all the graphs. To simplify the discussion that follows, *we consider only systems of linear inequalities where equality is included in each statement in the system.*

EXAMPLE 1 **Solving a System of Linear Inequalities Graphically** Solve the following system of linear inequalities graphically:

$$\begin{aligned} x + y &\geq 6 \\ 2x - y &\geq 0 \end{aligned}$$

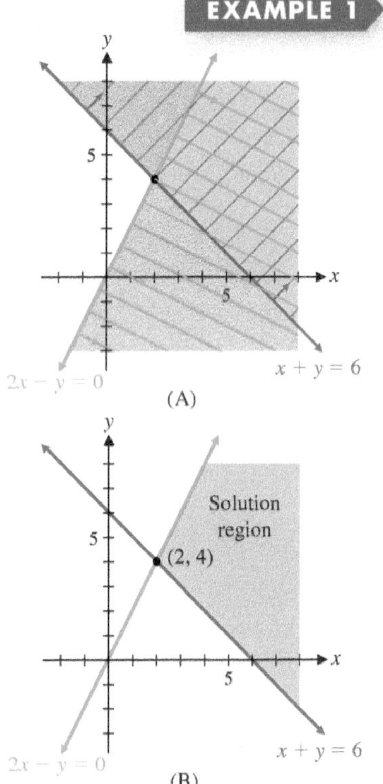

Figure 1

SOLUTION Graph the line $x + y = 6$ and shade the region that satisfies the linear inequality $x + y \geq 6$. This region is shaded with red lines in Figure 1A. Next, graph the line $2x - y = 0$ and shade the region that satisfies the inequality $2x - y \geq 0$. This region is shaded with blue lines in Figure 1A. The solution region for the system of inequalities is the intersection of these two regions. This is the region shaded in both red and blue (cross-hatched) in Figure 1A and redrawn in Figure 1B with only the solution region shaded. The coordinates of any point in the shaded region of Figure 1B specify a solution to the system. For example, the points $(2, 4)$, $(6, 3)$, and $(7.43, 8.56)$ are three of infinitely many solutions, as can be easily checked. The intersection point $(2, 4)$ is obtained by solving the equations $x + y = 6$ and $2x - y = 0$ simultaneously using any of the techniques discussed in Chapter 4.

Matched Problem 1 Solve the following system of linear inequalities graphically:

$$\begin{aligned} 3x + y &\leq 21 \\ x - 2y &\leq 0 \end{aligned}$$

CONCEPTUAL INSIGHT

To check that you have shaded a solution region correctly, choose a test point in the region and check that it satisfies each inequality in the system. For example, choosing the point $(5, 4)$ in the shaded region in Figure 1B, we have

$$\begin{aligned} x + y &\geq 6 \\ 5 + 4 &\overset{?}{\geq} 6 \\ 9 &\overset{\checkmark}{\geq} 6 \end{aligned} \qquad \begin{aligned} 2x - y &\geq 0 \\ 10 - 4 &\overset{?}{\geq} 0 \\ 6 &\overset{\checkmark}{\geq} 0 \end{aligned}$$

The points of intersection of the lines that form the boundary of a solution region will play a fundamental role in the solution of linear programming problems, which are discussed in the next section.

DEFINITION Corner Point

A **corner point** of a solution region is a point in the solution region that is the intersection of two boundary lines.

For example, the point $(2, 4)$ is the only corner point of the solution region in Example 1 (Fig. 1B).

EXAMPLE 2 **Solving a System of Linear Inequalities Graphically** Solve the following system of linear inequalities graphically and find the corner points:

$$\begin{aligned} 2x + y &\le 22 \\ x + y &\le 13 \\ 2x + 5y &\le 50 \\ x &\ge 0 \\ y &\ge 0 \end{aligned}$$

SOLUTION The inequalities $x \ge 0$ and $y \ge 0$ indicate that the solution region will lie in the first quadrant. So we can restrict our attention to that portion of the plane. First, we graph the lines

$$\begin{aligned} 2x + y &= 22 \\ x + y &= 13 \\ 2x + 5y &= 50 \end{aligned}$$

Find the x and y intercepts of each line; then sketch the line through these points.

Next, choosing $(0, 0)$ as a test point, we see that the graph of each of the first three inequalities in the system consists of its corresponding line and the half-plane lying below the line, as indicated by the small arrows in Figure 2. The solution region of the system consists of the points in the first quadrant that simultaneously lie on or below all three of these lines (see the shaded region in Fig. 2).

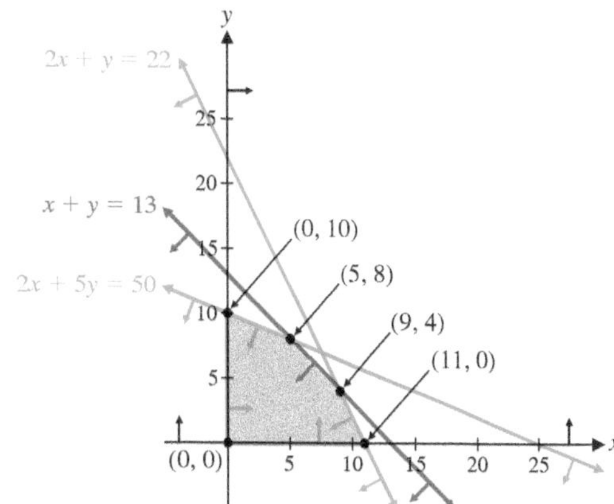

Figure 2

The corner points $(0, 0)$, $(0, 10)$, and $(11, 0)$ can be determined from the graph. The other two corner points are determined as follows:

Solve the system	Solve the system
$2x + 5y = 50$	$2x + y = 22$
$x + y = 13$	$x + y = 13$
to obtain $(5, 8)$.	to obtain $(9, 4)$.

Note that the lines $2x + 5y = 50$ and $2x + y = 22$ also intersect, but the intersection point is not part of the solution region and so is not a corner point.

Matched Problem 2 Solve the following system of linear inequalities graphically and find the corner points:

$$\begin{aligned} 5x + y &\geq 20 \\ x + y &\geq 12 \\ x + 3y &\geq 18 \\ x &\geq 0 \\ y &\geq 0 \end{aligned}$$

If we compare the solution regions of Examples 1 and 2, we see that there is a fundamental difference between these two regions. We can draw a circle around the solution region in Example 2; however, it is impossible to include all the points in the solution region in Example 1 in any circle, no matter how large we draw it. This leads to the following definition:

DEFINITION Bounded and Unbounded Solution Regions

A solution region of a system of linear inequalities is **bounded** if it can be enclosed within a circle. If it cannot be enclosed within a circle, it is **unbounded**.

The solution region for Example 2 is bounded, and the solution region for Example 1 is unbounded. This definition will be important in the next section.

Explore and Discuss 1

Determine whether the solution region of each system of linear inequalities is bounded or unbounded.

(A) $y \leq 1$, $x \geq 0$, $y \geq 0$

(B) $x \leq 100$, $y \leq 200$, $x \geq 0$, $y \geq 0$

(C) $x \leq y$, $y \leq x$, $x \geq 0$, $y \geq 0$

Applications

EXAMPLE 3 **Nutrition** A patient on a brown rice and skim milk diet is required to have at least 800 calories and at least 32 grams of protein per day. Each serving of brown rice contains 200 calories and 5 grams of protein. Each serving of skim milk contains 80 calories and 8 grams of protein. How many servings of each food should be eaten per day to meet the minimum daily requirements?

SOLUTION To answer the question, we need to solve for x and y, where

x = number of daily servings of brown rice

y = number of daily servings of skim milk

We arrange the information given in the problem in a table, with columns corresponding to x and y.

	Brown Rice	Skim Milk	Minimum Daily Requirement
Calories	200 cal/svg	80 cal/svg	800 cal
Protein	5 g/svg	8 g/svg	32 g

The number of calories in x servings of brown rice is $200x$, and the number of calories in y servings of skim milk is $80y$. So, to meet the minimum daily requirement for calories, $200x + 80y$ must be greater than or equal to 800. This gives the first of the inequalities below. The second inequality expresses the condition that the minimum daily requirement for protein is met. The last two inequalities express the fact that the number of servings of each food cannot be a negative number.

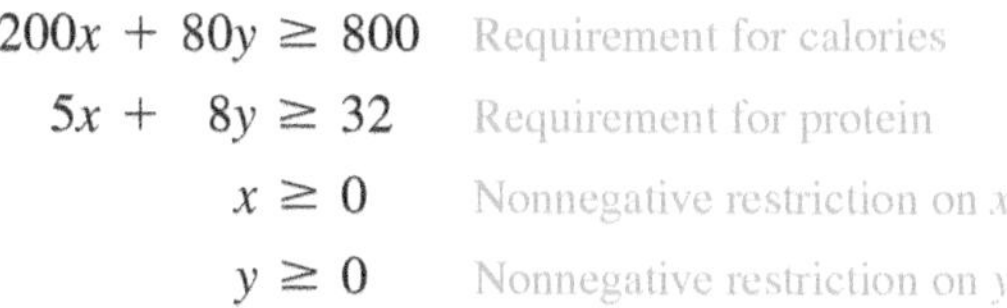

$$
\begin{aligned}
200x + 80y &\ge 800 && \text{Requirement for calories}\\
5x + 8y &\ge 32 && \text{Requirement for protein}\\
x &\ge 0 && \text{Nonnegative restriction on } x\\
y &\ge 0 && \text{Nonnegative restriction on } y
\end{aligned}
$$

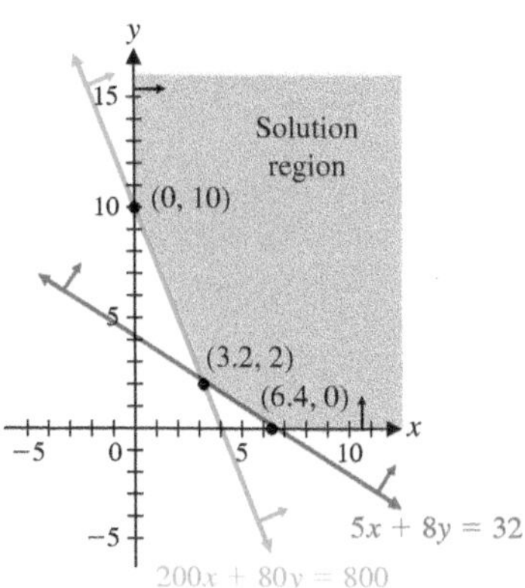

Figure 3

We graph this system of inequalities, and shade the solution region (Figure 3). Each point in the shaded area, including the straight-line boundaries, will meet the minimum daily requirements for calories and protein; any point outside the shaded area will not. For example, 4 servings of brown rice and 2 servings of skim milk will meet the minimum daily requirements, but 3 servings of brown rice and 2 servings of skim milk will not. Note that the solution region is unbounded.

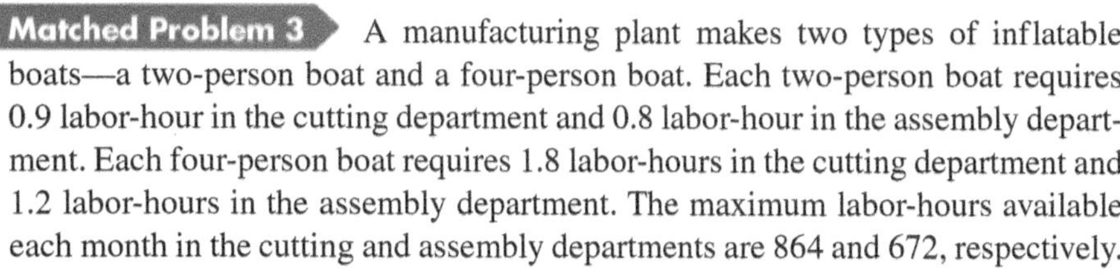

Matched Problem 3 A manufacturing plant makes two types of inflatable boats—a two-person boat and a four-person boat. Each two-person boat requires 0.9 labor-hour in the cutting department and 0.8 labor-hour in the assembly department. Each four-person boat requires 1.8 labor-hours in the cutting department and 1.2 labor-hours in the assembly department. The maximum labor-hours available each month in the cutting and assembly departments are 864 and 672, respectively.

(A) Summarize this information in a table.

(B) If x two-person boats and y four-person boats are manufactured each month, write a system of linear inequalities that reflects the conditions indicated. Graph the feasible region.

Exercises 5.2

Skills Warm-up Exercises

W *For Problems 1–8, if necessary, review Section A.2. Problems 1–4 refer to the following system of linear inequalities:*

$$
\begin{aligned}
4x + y &\le 20\\
3x + 5y &\le 37\\
x &\ge 0\\
y &\ge 0
\end{aligned}
$$

1. Is the point $(3, 5)$ in the solution region?

2. Is the point $(4, 5)$ in the solution region?

3. Is the point $(3, 6)$ in the solution region?

4. Is the point $(2, 6)$ in the solution region?

Problems 5–8 refer to the following system of linear inequalities:

$$
\begin{aligned}
5x + y &\le 32\\
7x + 4y &\ge 45\\
x &\ge 0\\
y &\ge 0
\end{aligned}
$$

5. Is the point $(4, 3)$ in the solution region?

6. Is the point $(5, 3)$ in the solution region?

7. Is the point $(6, 2)$ in the solution region?

8. Is the point $(5, 2)$ in the solution region?

A *In Problems 9–12, match the solution region of each system of linear inequalities with one of the four regions shown in the figure.*

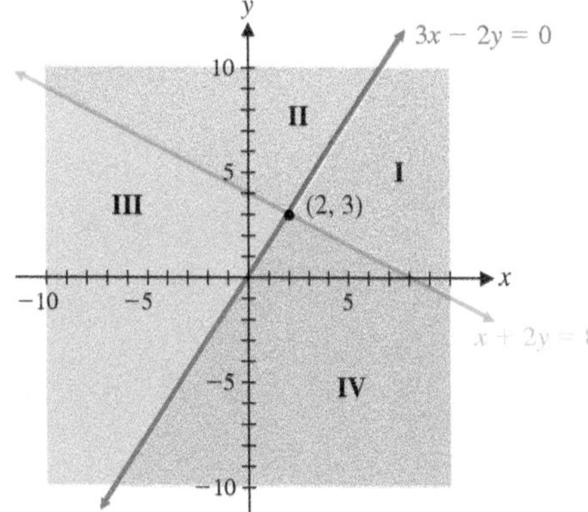

9. $x + 2y \le 8$
$3x - 2y \ge 0$

10. $x + 2y \ge 8$
$3x - 2y \le 0$

11. $x + 2y \ge 8$
$3x - 2y \ge 0$

12. $x + 2y \le 8$
$3x - 2y \le 0$

In Problems 13–16, solve each system of linear inequalities graphically.

13. $3x + y \geq 6$
$x \leq 4$

14. $3x + 4y \leq 12$
$y \geq -3$

15. $x - 2y \leq 12$
$2x + y \geq 4$

16. $2x + 5y \leq 20$
$x - 5y \geq -5$

B *In Problems 17–20, match the solution region of each system of linear inequalities with one of the four regions shown in the figure. Identify the corner points of each solution region.*

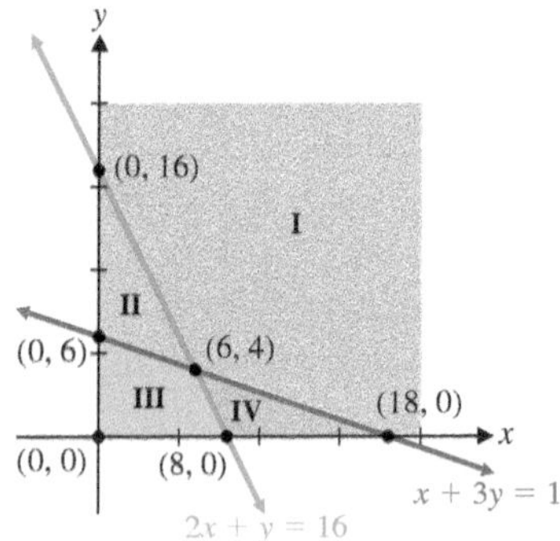

17. $x + 3y \leq 18$
$2x + y \geq 16$
$x \geq 0$
$y \geq 0$

18. $x + 3y \leq 18$
$2x + y \leq 16$
$x \geq 0$
$y \geq 0$

19. $x + 3y \geq 18$
$2x + y \geq 16$
$x \geq 0$
$y \geq 0$

20. $x + 3y \geq 18$
$2x + y \leq 16$
$x \geq 0$
$y \geq 0$

In Problems 21–28, is the solution region bounded or unbounded?

21. $5x - 4y \leq 10$
$x \geq 0$
$y \geq 0$

22. $x + 2y \geq 4$
$x \geq 0$
$y \geq 0$

23. $5x - 2y \geq 10$
$x \geq 0$
$y \geq 0$

24. $4x - 3y \leq 12$
$x \geq 0$
$y \geq 0$

25. $-x + y \leq 4$
$x \leq 10$
$x \geq 0$
$y \geq 0$

26. $x - y \leq 3$
$x \leq 9$
$x \geq 0$
$y \geq 0$

27. $2x + 5y \geq 12$
$x + 4y \leq 12$
$x \geq 0$
$y \geq 0$

28. $-x + 2y \leq 2$
$2x - y \leq 2$
$x \geq 0$
$y \geq 0$

Solve the systems in Problems 29–38 graphically and indicate whether each solution region is bounded or unbounded. Find the coordinates of each corner point.

29. $2x + 3y \leq 12$
$x \geq 0$
$y \geq 0$

30. $3x + 4y \leq 24$
$x \geq 0$
$y \geq 0$

31. $3x + 4y \geq 24$
$x + y \geq 7$
$x \geq 0$
$y \geq 0$

32. $6x + 3y \leq 24$
$3x + 6y \leq 30$
$x \geq 0$
$y \geq 0$

33. $4x + y \leq 8$
$x + 4y \leq 17$
$x \geq 0$
$y \geq 0$

34. $4x + 3y \geq 24$
$3x + 4y \geq 8$
$x \geq 0$
$y \geq 0$

35. $3x + 8y \geq 24$
$x + y \geq 5$
$3x + 2y \geq 12$
$x \geq 0$
$y \geq 0$

36. $3x + y \leq 21$
$x + y \leq 9$
$x + 3y \leq 21$
$x \geq 0$
$y \geq 0$

37. $5x + 4y \geq 48$
$x + 2y \geq 12$
$x + y \geq 11$
$x \geq 0$
$y \geq 0$

38. $3x + y \geq 24$
$x + y \geq 16$
$x + 3y \geq 30$
$x \geq 0$
$y \geq 0$

C *Solve the systems in Problems 39–48 graphically and indicate whether each solution region is bounded or unbounded. Find the coordinates of each corner point.*

39. $2x - y \leq 1$
$x + 2y \leq 13$
$y \geq 15$

40. $x + y \leq 11$
$x + 5y \geq 15$
$2x + y \geq 12$

41. $x + 2y \leq 18$
$2x + y \leq 21$
$x + y \geq 10$

42. $2x + 3y \geq 24$
$x + 3y \leq 15$
$y \geq 4$

43. $x - y \geq 1$
$2x - y \geq 3$
$0 \leq y \leq 6$

44. $2x + 3y \geq 12$
$-x + 3y \leq 3$
$0 \leq y \leq 5$

45. $x - y \geq 0$
$x + y \leq 5$
$x + 2y \leq 6$
$y \geq 1$

46. $x + y \leq 10$
$5x + 3y \geq 15$
$-2x + 3y \leq 15$
$2x - 5y \leq 6$

47. $16x + 13y \leq 120$
$3x + 4y \geq 25$
$-4x + 3y \leq 11$

48. $2x + 2y \leq 21$
$-10x + 5y \leq 24$
$3x + 5y \geq 37$

Problems 49 and 50 introduce an algebraic process for finding the corner points of a solution region without drawing a graph. We will discuss this process later in the chapter.

49. Consider the following system of inequalities and corresponding boundary lines:

$$\begin{aligned} 3x + 4y &\le 36 \qquad & 3x + 4y &= 36 \\ 3x + 2y &\le 30 \qquad & 3x + 2y &= 30 \\ x &\ge 0 \qquad & x &= 0 \\ y &\ge 0 \qquad & y &= 0 \end{aligned}$$

(A) Use algebraic methods to find the intersection points (if any exist) for each possible pair of boundary lines. (There are six different possible pairs.)

(B) Test each intersection point in all four inequalities to determine which are corner points.

50. Repeat Problem 49 for

$$\begin{aligned} 2x + y &\le 16 \qquad & 2x + y &= 16 \\ 2x + 3y &\le 36 \qquad & 2x + 3y &= 36 \\ x &\ge 0 \qquad & x &= 0 \\ y &\ge 0 \qquad & y &= 0 \end{aligned}$$

Applications

51. Water skis. A manufacturing company makes two types of water skis, a trick ski and a slalom ski. The trick ski requires 6 labor-hours for fabricating and 1 labor-hour for finishing. The slalom ski requires 4 labor-hours for fabricating and 1 labor-hour for finishing. The maximum labor-hours available per day for fabricating and finishing are 108 and 24, respectively. If x is the number of trick skis and y is the number of slalom skis produced per day, write a system of linear inequalities that indicates appropriate restraints on x and y. Find the set of feasible solutions graphically for the number of each type of ski that can be produced.

52. Furniture. A furniture manufacturing company manufactures dining-room tables and chairs. A table requires 8 labor-hours for assembling and 2 labor-hours for finishing. A chair requires 2 labor-hours for assembling and 1 labor-hour for finishing. The maximum labor-hours available per day for assembly and finishing are 400 and 120, respectively. If x is the number of tables and y is the number of chairs produced per day, write a system of linear inequalities that indicates appropriate restraints on x and y. Find the set of feasible solutions graphically for the number of tables and chairs that can be produced.

53. Water skis. Refer to Problem 51. The company makes a profit of \$50 on each trick ski and a profit of \$60 on each slalom ski.

(A) If the company makes 10 trick skis and 10 slalom skis per day, the daily profit will be \$1,100. Are there other production schedules that will result in a daily profit of \$1,100? How are these schedules related to the graph of the line $50x + 60y = 1{,}100$?

(B) Find a production schedule that will produce a daily profit greater than \$1,100 and repeat part (A) for this schedule.

(C) Discuss methods for using lines like those in parts (A) and (B) to find the largest possible daily profit.

54. Furniture. Refer to Problem 52. The company makes a profit of \$50 on each table and a profit of \$15 on each chair.

(A) If the company makes 20 tables and 20 chairs per day, the daily profit will be \$1,300. Are there other production schedules that will result in a daily profit of \$1,300? How are these schedules related to the graph of the line $50x + 15y = 1{,}300$?

(B) Find a production schedule that will produce a daily profit greater than \$1,300 and repeat part (A) for this schedule.

(C) Discuss methods for using lines like those in parts (A) and (B) to find the largest possible daily profit.

55. Plant food. A farmer can buy two types of plant food, mix A and mix B. Each cubic yard of mix A contains 20 pounds of phosphoric acid, 30 pounds of nitrogen, and 5 pounds of potash. Each cubic yard of mix B contains 10 pounds of phosphoric acid, 30 pounds of nitrogen, and 10 pounds of potash. The minimum monthly requirements are 460 pounds of phosphoric acid, 960 pounds of nitrogen, and 220 pounds of potash. If x is the number of cubic yards of mix A used and y is the number of cubic yards of mix B used, write a system of linear inequalities that indicates appropriate restraints on x and y. Find the set of feasible solutions graphically for the amounts of mix A and mix B that can be used.

56. Nutrition. A dietitian in a hospital is to arrange a special diet using two foods. Each ounce of food M contains 30 units of calcium, 10 units of iron, and 10 units of vitamin A. Each ounce of food N contains 10 units of calcium, 10 units of iron, and 30 units of vitamin A. The minimum requirements in the diet are 360 units of calcium, 160 units of iron, and 240 units of vitamin A. If x is the number of ounces of food M used and y is the number of ounces of food N used, write a system of linear inequalities that reflects the conditions indicated. Find the set of feasible solutions graphically for the amount of each kind of food that can be used.

57. Psychology. A psychologist uses two types of boxes when studying mice and rats. Each mouse spends 10 minutes per day in box A and 20 minutes per day in box B. Each rat spends 20 minutes per day in box A and 10 minutes per day in box B. The total maximum time available per day is 800 minutes for box A and 640 minutes for box B. If x is the number of mice used and y the number of rats used, write a system of linear inequalities that indicates appropriate restrictions on x and y. Find the set of feasible solutions graphically.

Answers to Matched Problems

1.

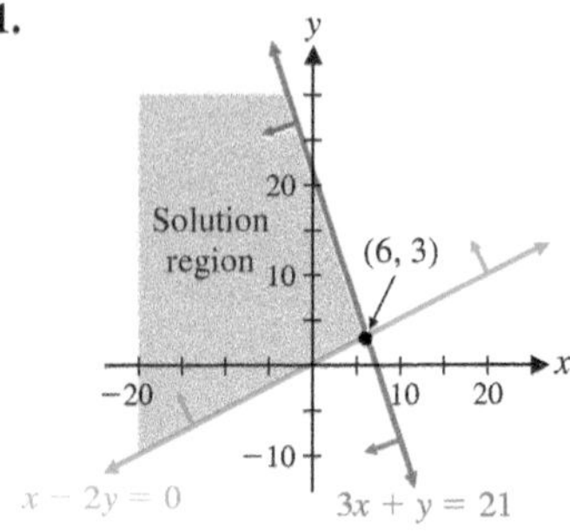

2.

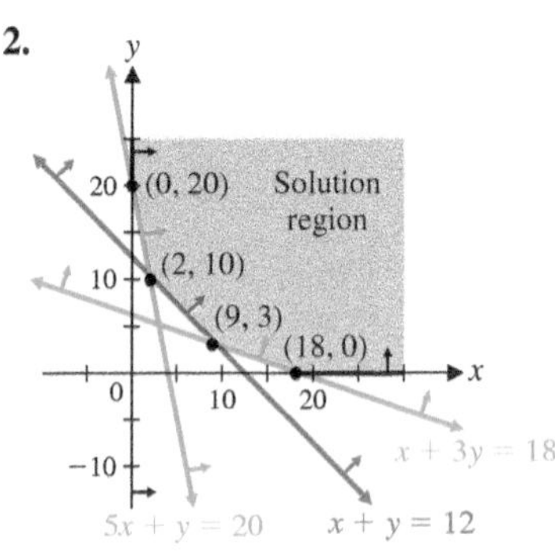

3. (A)

	Labor-Hours Required		Maximum Labor-Hours Available per Month
	Two-Person Boat	Four-Person Boat	
Cutting Department	0.9	1.8	864
Assembly Department	0.8	1.2	672

(B) $0.9x + 1.8y \le 864$

$0.8x + 1.2y \le 672$

$x \ge 0$

$y \ge 0$

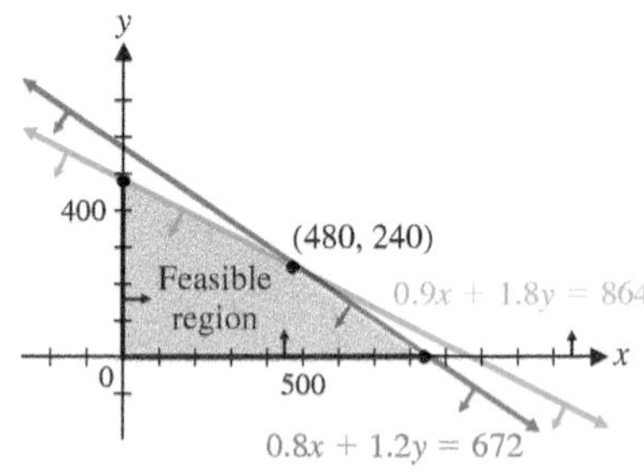

5.3 Linear Programming in Two Dimensions: A Geometric Approach

- A Linear Programming Problem
- General Description of Linear Programming
- Geometric Method for Solving Linear Programming Problems
- Applications

Several problems discussed in the preceding section are related to a more general type of problem called a *linear programming problem.* **Linear programming** is a mathematical process that has been developed to help management in decision making. We introduce this topic by considering an example in detail, using an intuitive geometric approach. Insight gained from this approach will prove invaluable when later we consider an algebraic approach that is less intuitive but necessary to solve most real-world problems.

A Linear Programming Problem

We begin our discussion with a concrete example. The solution method will suggest two important theorems and a simple general geometric procedure for solving linear programming problems in two variables.

EXAMPLE 1 **Production Scheduling** A manufacturer of lightweight mountain tents makes a standard model and an expedition model. Each standard tent requires 1 labor-hour from the cutting department and 3 labor-hours from the assembly department. Each expedition tent requires 2 labor-hours from the cutting department and 4 labor-hours from the assembly department. The maximum labor-hours available per day in the cutting and assembly departments are 32 and 84, respectively. If the company makes a profit of \$50 on each standard tent and \$80 on each expedition tent, how many tents of each type should be manufactured each day to maximize the total daily profit (assuming that all tents can be sold)?

SOLUTION This is an example of a linear programming problem. We begin by analyzing the question posed in this example.

According to the question, the *objective* of management is to maximize profit. Since the profits for standard and expedition tents differ, management must decide how many of each type of tent to manufacture. So it is reasonable to introduce the following **decision variables**:

$$\text{Let } x = \text{number of standard tents produced per day}$$
$$y = \text{number of expedition tents produced per day}$$

Now we summarize the manufacturing requirements, objectives, and restrictions in Table 1, with the decision variables related to the columns in the table.

Table 1

	Labor-Hours per Tent		Maximum Labor-Hours Available per Day
	Standard Model	Expedition Model	
Cutting department	1	2	32
Assembly department	3	4	84
Profit per tent	\$50	\$80	

Using the last line of Table 1, we form the **objective function**, in this case the profit P, in terms of the decision variables (we assume that all tents manufactured are sold):

$$P = 50x + 80y \quad \text{Objective function}$$

The **objective** is to find values of the decision variables that produce the **optimal value** (in this case, maximum value) of the objective function.

The form of the objective function indicates that the profit can be made as large as we like, simply by producing enough tents. But any manufacturing company has limits imposed by available resources, plant capacity, demand, and so on. These limits are referred to as **problem constraints**. Using the information in Table 1, we can determine two problem constraints.

$$\begin{pmatrix}\text{daily cutting}\\ \text{time for } x\\ \text{standard tents}\end{pmatrix} + \begin{pmatrix}\text{daily cutting}\\ \text{time for } y\\ \text{expedition tents}\end{pmatrix} \le \begin{pmatrix}\text{maximum labor-}\\ \text{hours available}\\ \text{per day}\end{pmatrix} \quad \begin{matrix}\text{Cutting}\\ \text{department}\\ \text{constraint}\end{matrix}$$
$$1x \quad + \quad 2y \quad \le \quad 32$$

$$\begin{pmatrix}\text{daily assembly}\\ \text{time for } x\\ \text{standard tents}\end{pmatrix} + \begin{pmatrix}\text{daily assembly}\\ \text{time for } y\\ \text{expedition tents}\end{pmatrix} \le \begin{pmatrix}\text{maximum labor-}\\ \text{hours available}\\ \text{per day}\end{pmatrix} \quad \begin{matrix}\text{Assembly}\\ \text{department}\\ \text{constraint}\end{matrix}$$
$$3x \quad + \quad 4y \quad \le \quad 84$$

It is not possible to manufacture a negative number of tents; thus, we have the **nonnegative constraints**

$$x \ge 0 \text{ and } y \ge 0$$

which we usually write in the form

$$x, y \ge 0 \quad \text{Nonnegative constraints}$$

We now have a **mathematical model** for the problem under consideration:

$$\begin{aligned}
\text{Maximize} \quad & P = 50x + 80y && \text{Objective function}\\
\text{subject to} \quad & \left.\begin{aligned} x + 2y &\le 32\\ 3x + 4y &\le 84 \end{aligned}\right\} && \text{Problem constraints}\\
& x, y \ge 0 && \text{Nonnegative constraints}
\end{aligned}$$

Solving the set of linear inequality constraints **graphically**, we obtain the feasible region for production schedules (Fig. 1).

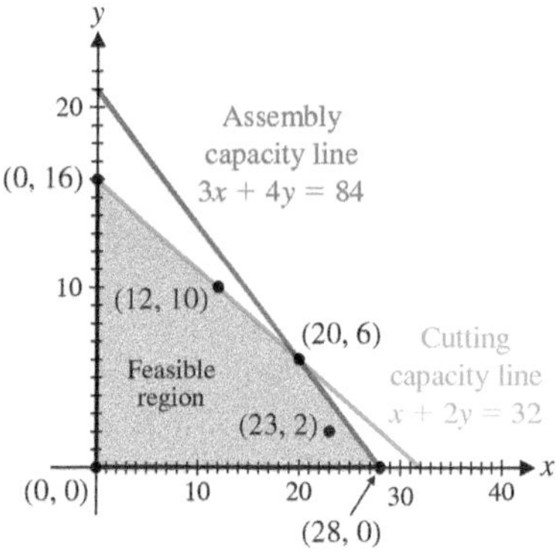

Figure 1

By choosing a production schedule (x, y) from the feasible region, a profit can be determined using the objective function

$$P = 50x + 80y$$

For example, if $x = 12$ and $y = 10$, the profit for the day would be

$$\begin{aligned} P &= 50(12) + 80(10) \\ &= \$1{,}400 \end{aligned}$$

Or if $x = 23$ and $y = 2$, the profit for the day would be

$$\begin{aligned} P &= 50(23) + 80(2) \\ &= \$1{,}310 \end{aligned}$$

Out of all possible production schedules (x, y) from the feasible region, which schedule(s) produces the *maximum* profit? This is a **maximization problem**. Since point-by-point checking is impossible (there are infinitely many points to check), we must find another way.

By assigning P in $P = 50x + 80y$ a particular value and plotting the resulting equation in the coordinate system shown in Figure 1, we obtain a **constant-profit line**. Every point in the feasible region on this line represents a production schedule that will produce the same profit. By doing this for a number of values for P, we obtain a family of constant-profit lines (Fig. 2) that are parallel to each other, since they all have the same slope. To see this, we write $P = 50x + 80y$ in the slope-intercept form

$$y = -\frac{5}{8}x + \frac{P}{80}$$

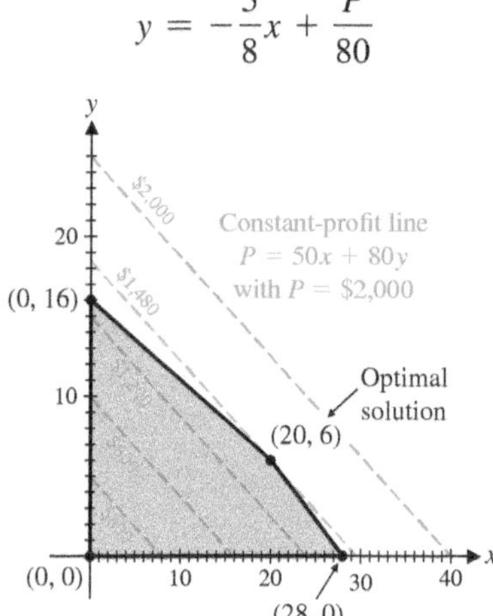

Figure 2 **Constant-profit lines**

and note that for any profit P, the constant-profit line has slope $-\frac{5}{8}$. We also observe that as the profit P increases, the y intercept ($P/80$) increases, and the line moves away from the origin.

Therefore, the maximum profit occurs at a point where a constant-profit line is the farthest from the origin but still in contact with the feasible region, in this example, at $(20, 6)$ (see Fig. 2). So profit is maximized if the manufacturer makes 20 standard tents and 6 expedition tents per day, and the maximum profit is

$$P = 50(20) + 80(6)$$
$$= \$1{,}480$$

The point $(20, 6)$ is called an **optimal solution** to the problem because it maximizes the objective (profit) function and is in the feasible region. In general, it appears that a maximum profit occurs at one of the corner points. We also note that the minimum profit $(P = 0)$ occurs at the corner point $(0, 0)$.

Matched Problem 1 A manufacturing plant makes two types of inflatable boats—a two-person boat and a four-person boat. Each two-person boat requires 0.9 labor-hour from the cutting department and 0.8 labor-hour from the assembly department. Each four-person boat requires 1.8 labor-hours from the cutting department and 1.2 labor-hours from the assembly department. The maximum labor-hours available per month in the cutting department and the assembly department are 864 and 672, respectively. The company makes a profit of \$25 on each two-person boat and \$40 on each four-person boat.

(A) Identify the decision variables.

(B) Summarize the relevant material in a table similar to Table 1 in Example 1.

(C) Write the objective function P.

(D) Write the problem constraints and nonnegative constraints.

(E) Graph the feasible region. Include graphs of the objective function for $P = \$5{,}000$, $P = \$10{,}000$, $P = \$15{,}000$, and $P = \$21{,}600$.

(F) From the graph and constant-profit lines, determine how many boats should be manufactured each month to maximize the profit. What is the maximum profit?

Before proceeding further, let's summarize the steps we used to form the model in Example 1.

PROCEDURE Constructing a Model for an Applied Linear Programming Problem

Step 1 Introduce decision variables.

Step 2 Summarize relevant material in table form, relating columns to the decision variables, if possible (see Table 1).

Step 3 Determine the objective and write a linear objective function.

Step 4 Write problem constraints using linear equations and/or inequalities.

Step 5 Write nonnegative constraints.

Explore and Discuss 1

Refer to the feasible region S shown in Figure 3.

(A) Let $P = x + y$. Graph the constant-profit lines through the points $(5, 5)$ and $(10, 10)$. Place a straightedge along the line with the smaller profit and slide it in the direction of increasing profit, without changing its slope. What is the maximum value of P? Where does this maximum value occur?

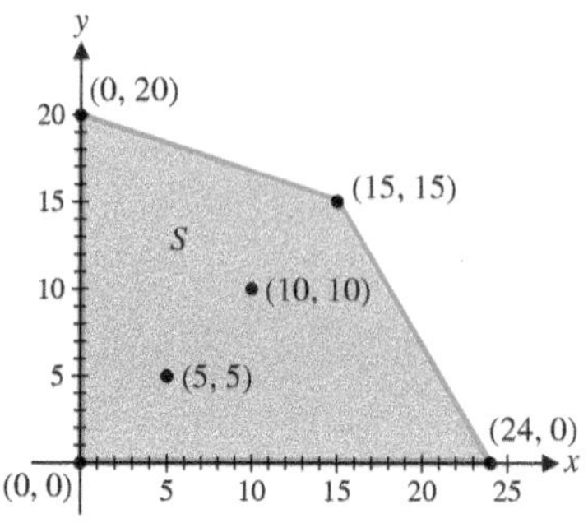

Figure 3

(B) Repeat part (A) for $P = x + 10y$.

(C) Repeat part (A) for $P = 10x + y$.

General Description of Linear Programming

In Example 1 and Matched Problem 1, the optimal solution occurs at a corner point of the feasible region. Is this always the case? The answer is a qualified yes, as we will see in Theorem 1. First, we give a few general definitions.

A **linear programming problem** is one that is concerned with finding the **optimal value** (maximum or minimum value) of a linear **objective function** z of the form

$$z = ax + by, \text{ where } a \text{ and } b \text{ do not both } = 0$$

and the **decision variables** x and y are subject to **problem constraints** in the form of $\leq$ or $\geq$ linear inequalities and equations. In addition, the decision variables must satisfy the **nonnegative constraints** $x \geq 0, y \geq 0$. The set of points satisfying both the problem constraints and the nonnegative constraints is called the **feasible region** for the problem. Any point in the feasible region that produces the optimal value of the objective function over the feasible region is called an **optimal solution**.

THEOREM 1 Fundamental Theorem of Linear Programming

If the optimal value of the objective function in a linear programming problem exists, then that value must occur at one or more of the corner points of the feasible region.

Theorem 1 provides a simple procedure for solving a linear programming problem, *provided that the problem has an optimal solution—not all do*. In order to use Theorem 1, we must know that the problem under consideration has an optimal solution. Theorem 2 provides some conditions that will ensure that a linear programming problem has an optimal solution.

THEOREM 2 Existence of Optimal Solutions

(A) If the feasible region for a linear programming problem is bounded, then both the maximum value and the minimum value of the objective function always exist.

(B) If the feasible region is unbounded and the coefficients of the objective function are positive, then the minimum value of the objective function exists but the maximum value does not.

(C) If the feasible region is empty (that is, there are no points that satisfy all the constraints), then both the maximum value and the minimum value of the objective function do not exist.

Geometric Method for Solving Linear Programming Problems

The preceding discussion leads to the following procedure for the geometric solution of linear programming problems with two decision variables:

PROCEDURE Geometric Method for Solving a Linear Programming Problem with Two Decision Variables

Step 1 Graph the feasible region. Then, if an optimal solution exists according to Theorem 2, find the coordinates of each corner point.

Step 2 Construct a **corner point table** listing the value of the objective function at each corner point.

Step 3 Determine the optimal solution(s) from the table in Step 2.

Step 4 For an applied problem, interpret the optimal solution(s) in terms of the original problem.

Before we consider more applications, let's use this procedure to solve some linear programming problems where the model has already been determined.

EXAMPLE 2 **Solving a Linear Programming Problem**

(A) Minimize and maximize $z = 3x + y$

subject to

$$\begin{aligned} 2x + y &\le 20 \\ 10x + y &\ge 36 \\ 2x + 5y &\ge 36 \\ x, y &\ge 0 \end{aligned}$$

(B) Minimize and maximize $z = 10x + 20y$

subject to

$$\begin{aligned} 6x + 2y &\ge 36 \\ 2x + 4y &\ge 32 \\ y &\le 20 \\ x, y &\ge 0 \end{aligned}$$

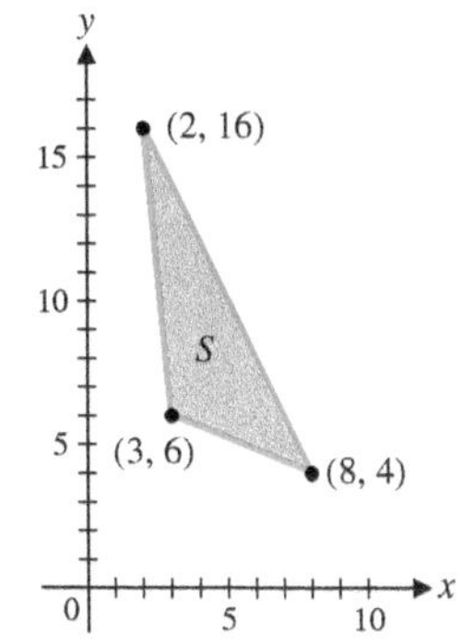

Figure 4

SOLUTION

(A) Step 1 Graph the feasible region S (Fig. 4). Then, after checking Theorem 2 to determine whether an optimal solution exists, find the coordinates of each corner point. Since S is bounded, z will have both a maximum and a minimum value on S (Theorem 2A) and these will both occur at corner points (Theorem 1).

Step 2 Evaluate the objective function at each corner point, as shown in the table.

Corner Point	
(x, y)	$z = 3x + y$
$(3, 6)$	15
$(2, 16)$	22
$(8, 4)$	28

Step 3 Determine the optimal solutions from Step 2. Examining the values in the table, we see that the minimum value of z is 15 at $(3, 6)$ and the maximum value of z is 28 at $(8, 4)$.

(B) Step 1 Graph the feasible region S (Fig. 5). Then, after checking Theorem 2 to determine whether an optimal solution exists, find the coordinates of each corner point. Since S is unbounded and the coefficients of the

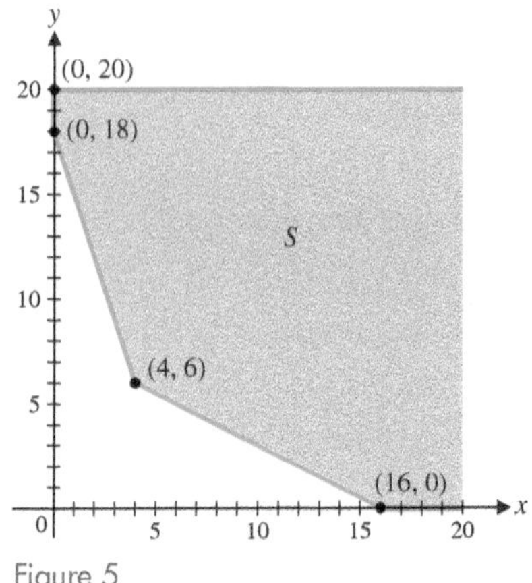

Figure 5

objective function are positive, z has a minimum value on S but no maximum value (Theorem 2B).

Step 2 Evaluate the objective function at each corner point, as shown in the table.

Corner Point	
(x, y)	$z = 10x + 20y$
$(0, 20)$	400
$(0, 18)$	360
$(4, 6)$	160
$(16, 0)$	160

Step 3 Determine the optimal solution from Step 2. The minimum value of z is 160 at $(4, 6)$ and at $(16, 0)$.

The solution to Example 2B is a **multiple optimal solution**. In general, if two corner points are both optimal solutions to a linear programming problem, then any point on the line segment joining them is also an optimal solution. This is the only way that optimal solutions can occur at noncorner points.

Matched Problem 2

(A) Maximize and minimize $z = 4x + 2y$ subject to the constraints given in Example 2A.

(B) Maximize and minimize $z = 20x + 5y$ subject to the constraints given in Example 2B.

CONCEPTUAL INSIGHT

Determining that an optimal solution exists is a critical step in the solution of a linear programming problem. If you skip this step, you may examine a corner point table like the one in the solution of Example 2B and erroneously conclude that the maximum value of the objective function is 400.

Explore and Discuss 2

In Example 2B we saw that there was no optimal solution for the problem of maximizing the objective function z over the feasible region S. We want to add an additional constraint to modify the feasible region so that an optimal solution for the maximization problem does exist. Which of the following constraints will accomplish this objective?

(A) $x \le 20$ (B) $y \ge 4$ (C) $x \le y$ (D) $y \le x$

For an illustration of Theorem 2C, consider the following:

$$\begin{aligned} \text{Maximize} \quad & P = 2x + 3y \\ \text{subject to} \quad & x + y \ge 8 \\ & x + 2y \le 8 \\ & 2x + y \le 10 \\ & x, y \ge 0 \end{aligned}$$

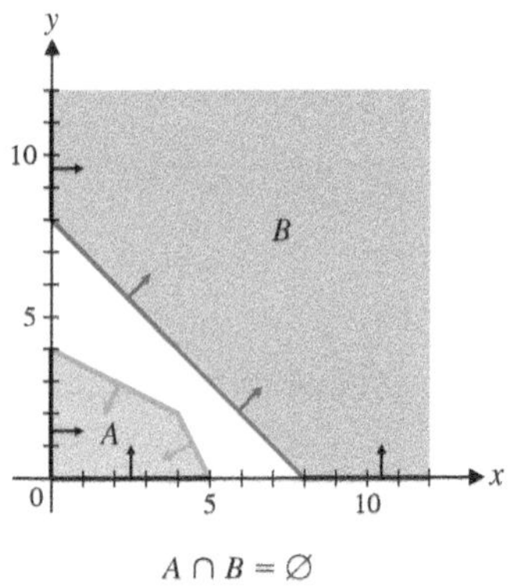

Figure 6

The intersection of the graphs of the constraint inequalities is the empty set (Fig. 6); so the *feasible region is empty*. If this happens, the problem should be reexamined to see if it has been formulated properly. If it has, the management may have to reconsider items such as labor-hours, overtime, budget, and supplies allocated to the project in order to obtain a nonempty feasible region and a solution to the original problem.

Applications

EXAMPLE 3 **Medication** A hospital patient is required to have at least 84 units of drug A and 120 units of drug B each day (assume that an overdose of either drug is harmless). Each gram of substance M contains 10 units of drug A and 8 units of drug B, and each gram of substance N contains 2 units of drug A and 4 units of drug B. Now, suppose that both M and N contain an undesirable drug D: 3 units per gram in M and 1 unit per gram in N. How many grams of each of substances M and N should be mixed to meet the minimum daily requirements and simultaneously minimize the intake of drug D? How many units of the undesirable drug D will be in this mixture?

SOLUTION First we construct the mathematical model.

Step 1 Introduce decision variables. According to the questions asked, we must decide how many grams of substances M and N should be mixed to form the daily dose of medication. These two quantities are the decision variables:

$$x = \text{number of grams of substance } M \text{ used}$$

$$y = \text{number of grams of substance } N \text{ used}$$

Step 2 Summarize relevant material in a table, relating the columns to substances M and N.

	Amount of Drug per Gram		Minimum Daily Requirement
	Substance M	Substance N	
Drug A	10 units/gram	2 units/gram	84 units
Drug B	8 units/gram	4 units/gram	120 units
Drug D	3 units/gram	1 unit/gram	

Step 3 Determine the objective and the objective function. The objective is to minimize the amount of drug D in the daily dose of medication. Using the decision variables and the information in the table, we form the linear objective function

$$C = 3x + y$$

Step 4 Write the problem constraints. The constraints in this problem involve minimum requirements, so the inequalities will take a different form:

$$10x + 2y \ge 84 \quad \text{Drug } A \text{ constraint}$$

$$8x + 4y \ge 120 \quad \text{Drug } B \text{ constraint}$$

Step 5 Add the nonnegative constraints and summarize the model.

$$\begin{aligned} \text{Minimize} \quad & C = 3x + y && \text{Objective function} \\ \text{subject to} \quad & 10x + 2y \ge 84 && \text{Drug } A \text{ constraint} \\ & 8x + 4y \ge 120 && \text{Drug } B \text{ constraint} \\ & x, y \ge 0 && \text{Nonnegative constraints} \end{aligned}$$

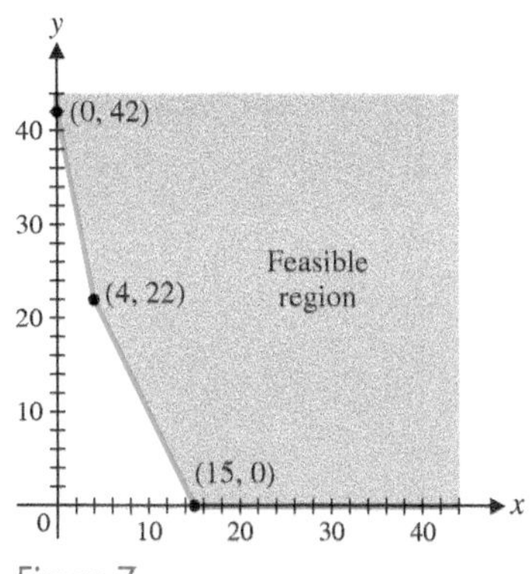

Figure 7

Corner Point	
(x, y)	$C = 3x + y$
$(0, 42)$	42
$(4, 22)$	34
$(15, 0)$	45

Now we use the geometric method to solve the problem.

Step 1 Graph the feasible region (Fig. 7). Then, after checking Theorem 2 to determine whether an optimal solution exists, find the coordinates of each corner point. Since the feasible region is unbounded and the coefficients of the objective function are positive, this minimization problem has a solution.

Step 2 Evaluate the objective function at each corner point, as shown in the table.

Step 3 Determine the optimal solution from Step 2. The optimal solution is $C = 34$ at the corner point $(4, 22)$.

Step 4 Interpret the optimal solution in terms of the original problem. If we use 4 grams of substance M and 22 grams of substance N, we will supply the minimum daily requirements for drugs A and B and minimize the intake of the undesirable drug D at 34 units. (Any other combination of M and N from the feasible region will result in a larger amount of the undesirable drug D.)

Matched Problem 3 A chicken farmer can buy a special food mix A at 20¢ per pound and a special food mix B at 40¢ per pound. Each pound of mix A contains 3,000 units of nutrient N_1 and 1,000 units of nutrient N_2; each pound of mix B contains 4,000 units of nutrient N_1 and 4,000 units of nutrient N_2. If the minimum daily requirements for the chickens collectively are 36,000 units of nutrient N_1 and 20,000 units of nutrient N_2, how many pounds of each food mix should be used each day to minimize daily food costs while meeting (or exceeding) the minimum daily nutrient requirements? What is the minimum daily cost? Construct a mathematical model and solve using the geometric method.

CONCEPTUAL INSIGHT

Refer to Example 3. If we change the minimum requirement for drug B from 120 to 125, the optimal solution changes to 3.6 grams of substance M and 24.1 grams of substance N, correct to one decimal place.

Now refer to Example 1. If we change the maximum labor-hours available per day in the assembly department from 84 to 79, the solution changes to 15 standard tents and 8.5 expedition tents.

We can measure 3.6 grams of substance M and 24.1 grams of substance N, but how can we make 8.5 tents? Should we make 8 tents? Or 9 tents? If the solutions to a problem must be integers and the optimal solution found graphically involves decimals, then rounding the decimal value to the nearest integer does not always produce the *optimal integer solution* (see Problem 44, Exercises 5.3). Finding optimal integer solutions to a linear programming problem is called *integer programming* and requires special techniques that are beyond the scope of this book. As mentioned earlier, if we encounter a solution like 8.5 tents per day, we will interpret this as an *average* value over many days of production.

Exercises 5.3

W **Skills Warm-up Exercises**

In Problems 1–8, if necessary, review Theorem 1. In Problems 1–4, the feasible region is the set of points on and inside the rectangle with vertices $(0, 0)$, $(12, 0)$, $(0, 5)$, and $(12, 5)$. Find the maximum and minimum values of the objective function Q over the feasible region.

1. $Q = 7x + 14y$ **2.** $Q = 3x + 15y$

3. $Q = 10x - 12y$ **4.** $Q = -9x + 20y$

In Problems 5–8, the feasible region is the set of points on and inside the triangle with vertices $(0, 0)$, $(8, 0)$, and $(0, 10)$. Find the maximum and minimum values of the objective function Q over the feasible region.

5. $Q = -4x - 3y$ **6.** $Q = 3x + 2y$

7. $Q = -6x + 4y$ **8.** $Q = 10x - 8y$

A *In Problems 9–12, graph the constant-profit lines through $(3, 3)$ and $(6, 6)$. Use a straightedge to identify the corner point where the maximum profit occurs (see Explore and Discuss 1). Confirm your answer by constructing a corner-point table.*

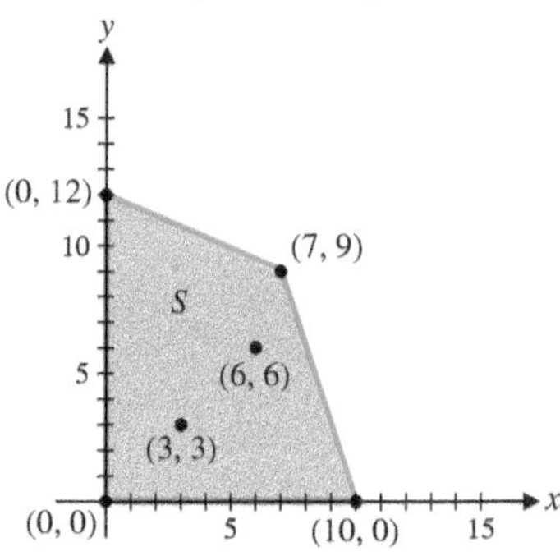

9. $P = x + y$ **10.** $P = 4x + y$

11. $P = 3x + 7y$ **12.** $P = 9x + 3y$

In Problems 13–16, graph the constant-cost lines through (9, 9) and (12, 12). Use a straightedge to identify the corner point where the minimum cost occurs. Confirm your answer by constructing a corner-point table.

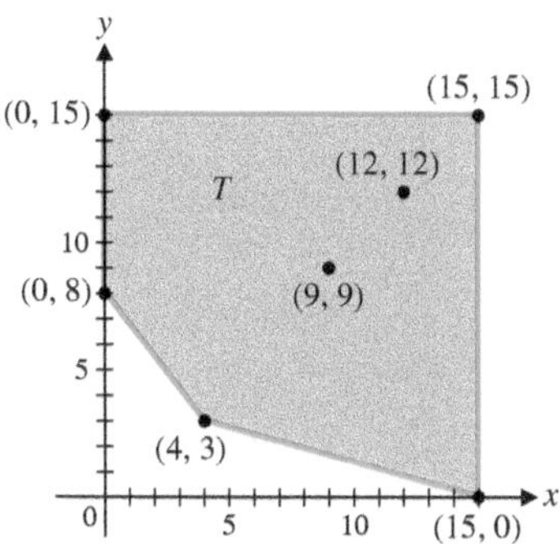

13. $C = 7x + 4y$

14. $C = 7x + 9y$

15. $C = 3x + 8y$

16. $C = 2x + 11y$

B *Solve the linear programming problems stated in Problems 17–38.*

17. Maximize $P = 18x + 13y$
subject to $3x + 2y \le 12$
$x, y \ge 0$

18. Maximize $P = 30x + 12y$
subject to $3x + y \le 18$
$x, y \ge 0$

19. Minimize $C = 5x + 7y$
subject to $x + 2y \ge 10$
$x, y \ge 0$

20. Minimize $C = 15x + 25y$
subject to $4x + 7y \ge 28$
$x, y \ge 0$

21. Maximize $P = 20x + 10y$
subject to $5x + 3y \le 42$
$3x + y \le 24$
$x, y \ge 0$

22. Maximize $P = 3x + 2y$
subject to $6x + 3y \le 24$
$3x + 6y \le 30$
$x, y \ge 0$

23. Minimize and maximize
$z = 5x + 2y$
subject to $x + y \ge 5$
$x + 2y \ge 6$
$x, y \ge 0$

24. Minimize and maximize
$z = 8x + 7y$
subject to $4x + 3y \ge 24$
$3x + 4y \ge 8$
$x, y \ge 0$

25. Minimize and maximize
$z = 50x + 40y$
subject to $3x + 8y \ge 24$
$x + y \ge 5$
$3x + 2y \ge 12$
$x, y \ge 0$

26. Maximize $P = 20x + 10y$
subject to $3x + y \le 21$
$x + y \le 9$
$x + 3y \le 21$
$x, y \ge 0$

27. Maximize $P = 25x + 15y$
subject to $x - y \le -4$
$x + y \le 8$
$x - y \le 4$
$x, y \ge 0$

28. Minimize and maximize
$z = 400x + 100y$
subject to $3x + y \ge 24$
$x + y \ge 16$
$x + 3y \ge 30$
$x, y \ge 0$

29. Minimize and maximize
$P = 30x + 10y$
subject to $2x + 2y \ge 4$
$6x + 4y \le 36$
$2x + y \le 10$
$x, y \ge 0$

30. Minimize and maximize
$P = 2x + y$
subject to $x + y \ge 2$
$6x + 4y \le 36$
$4x + 2y \le 20$
$x, y \ge 0$

31. Minimize and maximize
$P = 3x + 5y$
subject to $x + 2y \le 6$
$x + y \le 4$
$2x + 3y \ge 12$
$x, y \ge 0$

32. Minimize and maximize
$P = -x + 3y$
subject to $2x - y \ge 4$
$-x + 2y \le 4$
$y \le 6$
$x, y \ge 0$

33. Minimize and maximize

$$P = 6x + 3y$$

subject to
$$\begin{aligned} 4x + y &\ge 80 \\ x + 5y &\ge 115 \\ 3x + 2y &\le 150 \\ x, y &\ge 0 \end{aligned}$$

34. Minimize and maximize

$$P = 12x + 14y$$

subject to
$$\begin{aligned} -2x + y &\ge 6 \\ x + y &\le 15 \\ 3x - y &\ge 0 \\ x, y &\ge 0 \end{aligned}$$

35. Maximize $P = 25x + 20y$

subject to
$$\begin{aligned} 0.8x + 0.1y &\le 160 \\ 2.8x + 0.4y &\le 560 \\ 0.04x + 0.02y &\le 20 \\ x, y &\ge 0 \end{aligned}$$

36. Minimize $C = 30x + 10y$

subject to
$$\begin{aligned} 1.8x + 0.9y &\ge 270 \\ 0.3x + 0.2y &\ge 54 \\ 0.01x + 0.03y &\ge 3.9 \\ x, y &\ge 0 \end{aligned}$$

37. Maximize $P = 525x + 478y$

subject to
$$\begin{aligned} 275x + 322y &\le 3{,}381 \\ 350x + 340y &\le 3{,}762 \\ 425x + 306y &\le 4{,}114 \\ x, y &\ge 0 \end{aligned}$$

38. Maximize $P = 300x + 460y$

subject to
$$\begin{aligned} 245x + 452y &\le 4{,}181 \\ 290x + 379y &\le 3{,}888 \\ 390x + 299y &\le 4{,}407 \\ x, y &\ge 0 \end{aligned}$$

C *In Problems 39 and 40, explain why Theorem 2 cannot be used to conclude that a maximum or minimum value exists. Graph the feasible regions and use graphs of the objective function $z = x - y$ for various values of z to discuss the existence of a maximum value and a minimum value.*

39. Minimize and maximize

$$z = x - y$$

subject to
$$\begin{aligned} x - 2y &\le 0 \\ 2x - y &\le 6 \\ x, y &\ge 0 \end{aligned}$$

40. Minimize and maximize

$$z = x - y$$

subject to
$$\begin{aligned} x - 2y &\ge -6 \\ 2x - y &\ge 0 \\ x, y &\ge 0 \end{aligned}$$

Problems 41–48 refer to the bounded feasible region with corner points $O = (0, 0)$, $A = (0, 5)$, $B = (4, 3)$, and $C = (5, 0)$ that is determined by the system of inequalities

$$\begin{aligned} x + 2y &\le 10 \\ 3x + y &\le 15 \\ x, y &\ge 0 \end{aligned}$$

41. If $P = ax + 10y$, find all numbers a such that the maximum value of P occurs only at B.

42. If $P = ax + 10y$, find all numbers a such that the maximum value of P occurs only at A.

43. If $P = ax + 10y$, find all numbers a such that the maximum value of P occurs only at C.

44. If $P = ax + 10y$, find all numbers a such that the maximum value of P occurs at both A and B.

45. If $P = ax + 10y$, find all numbers a such that the maximum value of P occurs at both B and C.

46. If $P = ax + 10y$, find all numbers a such that the minimum value of P occurs only at C.

47. If $P = ax + 10y$, find all numbers a such that the minimum value of P occurs at both O and C.

48. If $P = ax + 10y$, explain why the minimum value of P cannot occur at B.

Applications

In Problems 49–64, construct a mathematical model in the form of a linear programming problem. (The answers in the back of the book for these application problems include the model.) Then solve by the geometric method.

49. Water skis. A manufacturing company makes two types of water skis—a trick ski and a slalom ski. The relevant manufacturing data are given in the table below.

	Labor-Hours per Ski		Maximum Labor-Hours
Department	Trick Ski	Slalom Ski	Available per Day
Fabricating	6	4	108
Finishing	1	1	24

(A) If the profit on a trick ski is \$40 and the profit on a slalom ski is \$30, how many of each type of ski should be manufactured each day to realize a maximum profit? What is the maximum profit?

(B) Discuss the effect on the production schedule and the maximum profit if the profit on a slalom ski decreases to \$25.

(C) Discuss the effect on the production schedule and the maximum profit if the profit on a slalom ski increases to \$45.

50. Furniture. A furniture manufacturing company manufactures dining-room tables and chairs. The relevant manufacturing data are given in the table below.

Department	Labor-Hours per Unit		Maximum Labor-Hours Available per Day
	Table	Chair	
Assembly	8	2	400
Finishing	2	1	120
Profit per unit	$90	$25	

(A) How many tables and chairs should be manufactured each day to realize a maximum profit? What is the maximum profit?

(B) Discuss the effect on the production schedule and the maximum profit if the marketing department of the company decides that the number of chairs produced should be at least four times the number of tables produced.

51. **Production scheduling.** A furniture company has two plants that produce the lumber used in manufacturing tables and chairs. In 1 day of operation, plant A can produce the lumber required to manufacture 20 tables and 60 chairs, and plant B can produce the lumber required to manufacture 25 tables and 50 chairs. The company needs enough lumber to manufacture at least 200 tables and 500 chairs.

(A) If it costs $1,000 to operate plant A for 1 day and $900 to operate plant B for 1 day, how many days should each plant be operated to produce a sufficient amount of lumber at a minimum cost? What is the minimum cost?

(B) Discuss the effect on the operating schedule and the minimum cost if the daily cost of operating plant A is reduced to $600 and all other data in part (A) remain the same.

(C) Discuss the effect on the operating schedule and the minimum cost if the daily cost of operating plant B is reduced to $800 and all other data in part (A) remain the same.

52. **Mobiles.** A mobile firm manufactures two types of mobiles: a dial pad model and a touch screen model. The production of a dial pad mobile requires a capital expenditure of $100 and 8 hours of labor. The production of a touch screen mobile requires a capital expenditure of $50 and 24 hours of labor. The firm has a capital of $5,000 and 5,000 labor hours available for the production of dial pad and touch screen mobiles.

(A) What is the maximum number of mobiles the company is capable of manufacturing?

(B) If each dial pad mobile contributes a profit of $75 and each touch screen mobile contributes a profit of $25, how much profit will the company make by producing the maximum number of mobiles determined in part (A)? Is this the maximum profit? If not, what is the maximum profit?

53. **Transportation.** The officers of a high school senior class are planning to rent buses and vans for a class trip. Each bus can transport 40 students, requires 3 chaperones, and costs $1,200 to rent. Each van can transport 8 students, requires 1 chaperone, and costs $100 to rent. Since there are 400 students in the senior class that may be eligible to go on the trip, the officers must plan to accommodate at least 400 students. Since only 36 parents have volunteered to serve as chaperones, the officers must plan to use at most 36 chaperones. How many vehicles of each type should the officers rent in order to minimize the transportation costs? What are the minimal transportation costs?

54. **Transportation.** Refer to Problem 53. If each van can transport 7 people and there are 35 available chaperones, show that the optimal solution found graphically involves decimals. Find all feasible solutions with integer coordinates and identify the one that minimizes the transportation costs. Can this optimal integer solution be obtained by rounding the optimal decimal solution? Explain.

55. **Investment.** An investor has $60,000 to invest in a CD and a mutual fund. The CD yields 5% and the mutual fund yields an average of 9%. The mutual fund requires a minimum investment of $10,000, and the investor requires that at least twice as much should be invested in CDs as in the mutual fund. How much should be invested in CDs and how much in the mutual fund to maximize the return? What is the maximum return?

56. **Investment.** An investor has $24,000 to invest in bonds of AAA and B qualities. The AAA bonds yield an average of 6%, and the B bonds yield 10%. The investor requires that at least three times as much money should be invested in AAA bonds as in B bonds. How much should be invested in each type of bond to maximize the return? What is the maximum return?

57. **Pollution control.** Because of new federal regulations on pollution, a chemical plant introduced a new, more expensive process to supplement or replace an older process used in the production of a particular chemical. The older process emitted 20 grams of sulfur dioxide and 40 grams of particulate matter into the atmosphere for each gallon of chemical produced. The new process emits 5 grams of sulfur dioxide and 20 grams of particulate matter for each gallon produced. The company makes a profit of 60¢ per gallon and 20¢ per gallon on the old and new processes, respectively.

(A) If the government allows the plant to emit no more than 16,000 grams of sulfur dioxide and 30,000 grams of particulate matter daily, how many gallons of the chemical should be produced by each process to maximize daily profit? What is the maximum daily profit?

(B) Discuss the effect on the production schedule and the maximum profit if the government decides to restrict emissions of sulfur dioxide to 11,500 grams daily and all other data remain unchanged.

(C) Discuss the effect on the production schedule and the maximum profit if the government decides to restrict emissions of sulfur dioxide to 7,200 grams daily and all other data remain unchanged.

58. **Capital expansion.** A fast-food chain plans to expand by opening several new restaurants. The chain operates two types of restaurants, drive-through and full-service. A drive-through restaurant costs $100,000 to construct, requires 5 employees, and has an expected annual revenue of $200,000. A full-service restaurant costs $150,000 to construct, requires 15 employees, and has an expected annual revenue of $500,000. The chain has $2,400,000 in capital available for expansion. Labor contracts require that they hire no more than 210 employees, and licensing restrictions require that they open no more than 20 new restaurants. How many

restaurants of each type should the chain open in order to maximize the expected revenue? What is the maximum expected revenue? How much of their capital will they use and how many employees will they hire?

59. **Fertilizer.** A fruit grower can use two types of fertilizer in his orange grove, brand *A* and brand *B*. The amounts (in pounds) of nitrogen, phosphoric acid, and chloride in a bag of each brand are given in the table. Tests indicate that the grove needs at least 1,000 pounds of phosphoric acid and at most 400 pounds of chloride.

	Pounds per Bag	
	Brand *A*	Brand *B*
Nitrogen	8	3
Phosphoric acid	4	4
Chloride	2	1

(A) If the grower wants to maximize the amount of nitrogen added to the grove, how many bags of each mix should be used? How much nitrogen will be added?

(B) If the grower wants to minimize the amount of nitrogen added to the grove, how many bags of each mix should be used? How much nitrogen will be added?

60. **Nutrition.** A dietitian is to arrange a special diet composed of two foods, *M* and *N*. Each ounce of food *M* contains 30 units of calcium, 10 units of iron, 10 units of vitamin A, and 8 units of cholesterol. Each ounce of food *N* contains 10 units of calcium, 10 units of iron, 30 units of vitamin A, and 4 units of cholesterol. If the minimum daily requirements are 360 units of calcium, 160 units of iron, and 240 units of vitamin A, how many ounces of each food should be used to meet the minimum requirements and at the same time minimize the cholesterol intake? What is the minimum cholesterol intake?

61. **Plant food.** A farmer can buy two types of plant food, mix *A* and mix *B*. Each cubic yard of mix *A* contains 20 pounds of phosphoric acid, 30 pounds of nitrogen, and 5 pounds of potash. Each cubic yard of mix *B* contains 10 pounds of phosphoric acid, 30 pounds of nitrogen, and 10 pounds of potash. The minimum monthly requirements are 460 pounds of phosphoric acid, 960 pounds of nitrogen, and 220 pounds of potash. If mix *A* costs $30 per cubic yard and mix *B* costs $35 per cubic yard, how many cubic yards of each mix should the farmer blend to meet the minimum monthly requirements at a minimal cost? What is this cost?

62. **Animal food.** A laboratory technician in a medical research center is asked to formulate a diet from two commercially packaged foods, food *A* and food *B*, for a group of animals. Each ounce of food *A* contains 8 units of fat, 16 units of carbohydrate, and 2 units of protein. Each ounce of food *B* contains 4 units of fat, 32 units of carbohydrate, and 8 units of protein. The minimum daily requirements are 176 units of fat, 1,024 units of carbohydrate, and 384 units of protein. If food *A* costs 5¢ per ounce and food *B* costs 5¢ per ounce, how many ounces of each food should be used to meet the minimum daily requirements at the least cost? What is the cost for this amount of food?

63. **Psychology.** A psychologist uses two types of boxes with mice and rats. The amount of time (in minutes) that each mouse and each rat spends in each box per day is given in the table. What is the maximum number of mice and rats that can be used in this experiment? How many mice and how many rats produce this maximum?

	Time		Maximum Time
	Mice	Rats	Available per Day
Box *A*	10 min	20 min	800 min
Box *B*	20 min	10 min	640 min

64. **Music.** A music academy conducts a training course in vocal and guitar for both amateurs and professionals. Allocation of classes and cost of conducting the classes are given in the table. How many classes of vocal and guitar should be arranged to minimize the cost and meet the class-hour requirements? What is the minimum weekly cost of conducting classes?

	Class-Hours		Minimum Class-Hours to Be
	Vocal	Guitar	Attended
Amateurs	2	3	15
Professionals	1	2	8
Costs per class	$7	$12	

Answers to Matched Problems

1. (A) $x =$ number of two-person boats produced each month
$y =$ number of four-person boats produced each month

(B)

	Labor-Hours Required		Maximum Labor-Hours Available
	Two-Person Boat	Four-Person Boat	per Month
Cutting department	0.9	1.8	864
Assembly department	0.8	1.2	672
Profit per boat	$25	$40	

(C) $P = 25x + 40y$

(D) $0.9x + 1.8y \le 864$
$0.8x + 1.2y \le 672$
$x, y \ge 0$

(E)

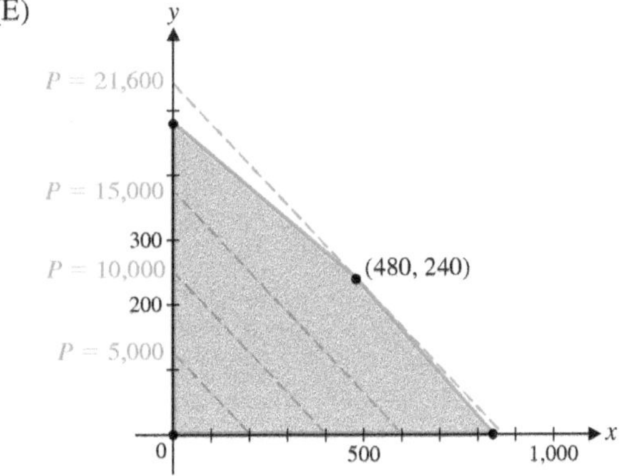

(F) 480 two-person boats, 240 four-person boats; Max $P = \$21{,}600$ per month

2. (A) Min $z = 24$ at $(3, 6)$; Max $z = 40$ at $(2, 16)$ and $(8, 4)$ (multiple optimal solution)
(B) Min $z = 90$ at $(0, 18)$; no maximum value

3. Min $C = 0.2x + 0.4y$
subject to $3{,}000x + 4{,}000y \geq 36{,}000$
$1{,}000x + 4{,}000y \geq 20{,}000$
$x, y \geq 0$
8 lb of mix A, 3 lb of mix B; Min $C = \$2.80$ per day

Chapter 5 Summary and Review

Important Terms, Symbols, and Concepts

5.1 Linear Inequalities in Two Variables

EXAMPLES

- A line divides the plane into two regions called **half-planes**. A vertical line divides the plane into **left** and **right half-planes**; a nonvertical line divides it into **upper** and **lower half-planes**. In either case, the dividing line is called the **boundary line** of each half-plane. Ex. 1, p. 262; Ex. 2, p. 262
- The **graph of a linear inequality** is the half-plane obtained by following the procedure on page 262. Ex. 3, p. 264
- The variables in an applied problem are often required to be nonnegative. Ex. 4, p. 264

5.2 System of Linear Inequalities in Two Variables

- The **solution region** (also called the **feasible region**) of a system of linear inequalities is the graph of all ordered pairs that simultaneously satisfy all the inequalities in the system. Ex. 1, p. 268
- A **corner point** of a solution region is a point in the region that is the intersection of two boundary lines. Ex. 2, p. 269
- A solution region is **bounded** if it can be enclosed in a circle and **unbounded** if it cannot. Ex. 3, p. 270

5.3 Linear Programming in Two Dimensions: A Geometric Approach

- The problem of finding the optimal (maximum or minimum) value of a linear objective function on a feasible region is called a **linear programming problem**. Ex. 1, p. 274
- The optimal value (if it exists) of the objective function in a linear programming problem must occur at one (or more) of the corner points of the feasible region (Theorem 1, page 278). Existence criteria are described in Theorem 2, page 278, and a solution procedure is listed on page 279. Ex. 2, p. 279; Ex. 3, p. 281

Review Exercises

Work through all the problems in this chapter review and check answers in the back of the book. Answers to all review problems are there, and following each answer is a number in italics indicating the section in which that type of problem is discussed. Where weaknesses show up, review appropriate sections in the text.

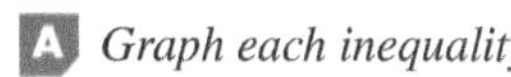
A *Graph each inequality.*

1. $2y < 4x + 3$
2. $4y - 8x \leq 20$

Graph the systems in Problems 3–6 and indicate whether each solution region is bounded or unbounded. Find the coordinates of each corner point.

3. $5x + 9y \leq 90$
$x, y \geq 0$

4. $15x + 16y \geq 1{,}200$
$x, y \geq 0$

5. $3x + y \leq 7$
$2x + 8y \leq 26$
$x, y \geq 0$

6. $3x + y \geq 9$
$2x + 4y \geq 16$
$x, y \geq 0$

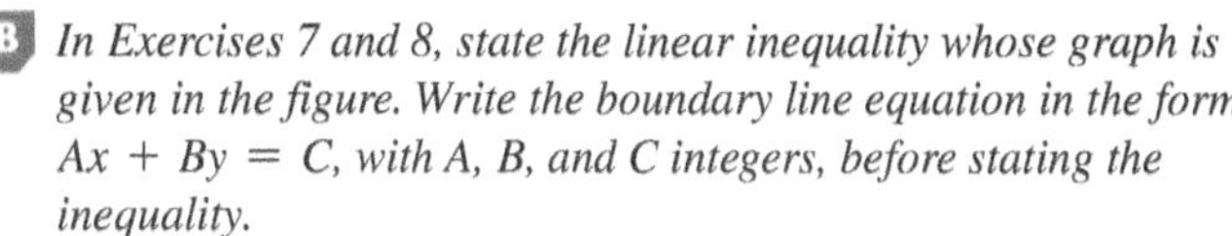
B *In Exercises 7 and 8, state the linear inequality whose graph is given in the figure. Write the boundary line equation in the form $Ax + By = C$, with A, B, and C integers, before stating the inequality.*

7.

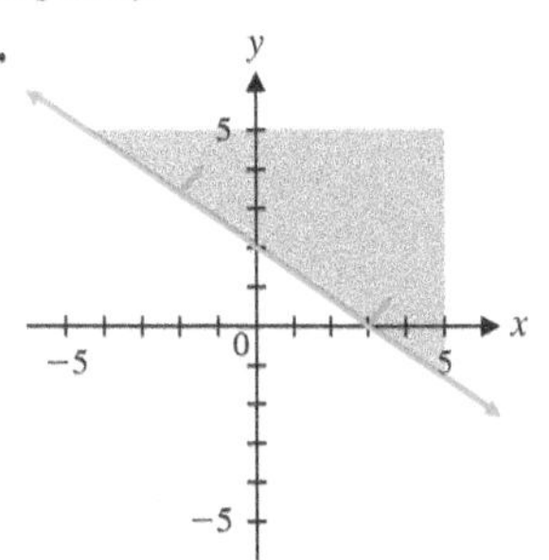

8.

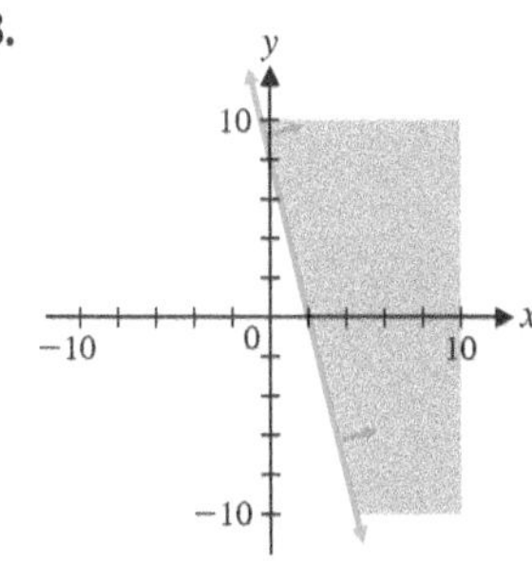

Solve the linear programming problems in Problems 9–13.

9. Maximize $P = 3x + 2y$
subject to $x + 3y \leq 6$
$x + 2y \leq 9$
$x, y \geq 0$

10. Maximize $P = 2x + 5y$

subject to
$$\begin{aligned} 2x + y &\geq 12 \\ x + 2y &\leq 18 \\ x, y &\geq 0 \end{aligned}$$

C 11. Maximize $P = 3x + 4y$

subject to
$$\begin{aligned} x + 2y &\leq 12 \\ x + y &\leq 7 \\ 2x + y &\leq 10 \\ x, y &\geq 0 \end{aligned}$$

12. Minimize $C = 8x + 3y$

subject to
$$\begin{aligned} x + y &\geq 10 \\ 2x + y &\geq 15 \\ x &\geq 3 \\ x, y &\geq 0 \end{aligned}$$

13. Maximize $P = 4x + 3y$

subject to
$$\begin{aligned} 2x + y &\geq 12 \\ x + y &\geq 8 \\ x &\leq 12 \\ y &\leq 12 \\ x, y &\geq 0 \end{aligned}$$

Applications

14. **Electronics.** A company uses two machines to solder circuit boards, an oven and a wave soldering machine. A circuit board for a calculator needs 4 minutes in the oven and 2 minutes on the wave machine, while a circuit board for a toaster requires 3 minutes in the oven and 1 minute on the wave machine. (*Source*: Universal Electronics)

(A) How many circuit boards for calculators and toasters can be produced if the oven is available for 5 hours? Express your answer as a linear inequality with appropriate nonnegative restrictions and draw its graph.

(B) How many circuit boards for calculators and toasters can be produced if the wave machine is available for 2 hours? Express your answer as a linear inequality with appropriate nonnegative restrictions and draw its graph.

In Problems 15 and 16, construct a mathematical model in the form of a linear programming problem. (The answers in the back of the book for these application problems include the model.) Then solve the problem by the indicated method.

15. **Sail manufacture.** South Shore Sail Loft manufactures regular and competition sails. Each regular sail takes 2 hours to cut and 4 hours to sew. Each competition sail takes 3 hours to cut and 10 hours to sew. There are 150 hours available in the cutting department and 380 hours available in the sewing department.

(A) If the Loft makes a profit of \$100 on each regular sail and \$200 on each competition sail, how many sails of each type should the company manufacture to maximize its profit? What is the maximum profit?

(B) An increase in the demand for competition sails causes the profit on a competition sail to rise to \$260. Discuss the effect of this change on the number of sails manufactured and on the maximum profit.

(C) A decrease in the demand for competition sails causes the profit on a competition sail to drop to \$140. Discuss the effect of this change on the number of sails manufactured and on the maximum profit.

16. **Animal food.** A special diet for laboratory animals is to contain at least 850 units of vitamins, 800 units of minerals, and 1,150 calories. There are two feed mixes available, mix *A* and mix *B*. A gram of mix *A* contains 2 units of vitamins, 2 units of minerals, and 4 calories. A gram of mix *B* contains 5 units of vitamins, 4 units of minerals, and 5 calories.

(A) If mix *A* costs \$0.04 per gram and mix *B* costs \$0.09 per gram, how many grams of each mix should be used to satisfy the requirements of the diet at minimal cost? What is the minimum cost?

(B) If the price of mix *B* decreases to \$0.06 per gram, discuss the effect of this change on the solution in part (A).

(C) If the price of mix *B* increases to \$0.12 per gram, discuss the effect of this change on the solution in part (A).

Part 3

Calculus

6 Limits and the Derivative

Introduction

How do algebra and calculus differ? The two words *static* and *dynamic* probably come as close as any to expressing the difference between the two disciplines. In algebra, we solve equations for a particular value of a variable—a static notion. In calculus, we are interested in how a change in one variable affects another variable—a dynamic notion.

Isaac Newton (1642–1727) of England and Gottfried Wilhelm von Leibniz (1646–1716) of Germany developed calculus independently to solve problems concerning motion. Today calculus is used not just in the physical sciences, but also in business, economics, life sciences, and social sciences—any discipline that seeks to understand dynamic phenomena.

In Chapter 6 we introduce the *derivative*, one of the two key concepts of calculus. Both key concepts depend on the notion of *limit*, which is explained in Sections 6.1 and 6.2. We consider many applications of limits and derivatives. See, for example, Problem 91 in Section 6.5 on the connection between advertising expenditures and power boat sales.

6.1 Introduction to Limits

- Functions and Graphs: Brief Review
- Limits: A Graphical Approach
- Limits: An Algebraic Approach
- Limits of Difference Quotients

Basic to the study of calculus is the concept of a *limit.* This concept helps us to describe, in a precise way, the behavior of $f(x)$ when x is close, but not equal, to a particular value c. In this section, we develop an intuitive and informal approach to evaluating limits.

Functions and Graphs: Brief Review

The graph of the function $y = f(x) = x + 2$ is the graph of the set of all ordered pairs $(x, f(x))$. For example, if $x = 2$, then $f(2) = 4$ and $(2, f(2)) = (2, 4)$ is a point on the graph of f. Figure 1 shows $(-1, f(-1))$, $(1, f(1))$, and $(2, f(2))$ plotted on the graph of f. Notice that the domain values -1, 1, and 2 are associated with the x axis and the range values $f(-1) = 1, f(1) = 3$, and $f(2) = 4$ are associated with the y axis.

Given x, it is sometimes useful to read $f(x)$ directly from the graph of f. Example 1 reviews this process.

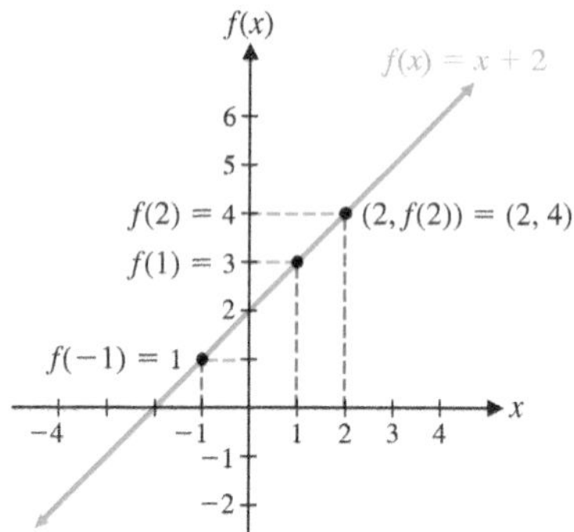

Figure 1

EXAMPLE 1 **Finding Values of a Function from Its Graph** Complete the following table, using the given graph of the function g.

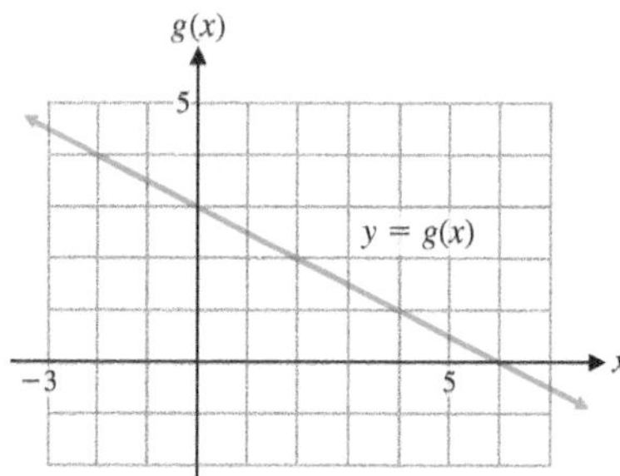

x	$g(x)$
−2	
1	
3	
4	

SOLUTION To determine $g(x)$, proceed vertically from the x value on the x axis to the graph of g and then horizontally to the corresponding y value $g(x)$ on the y axis (as indicated by the dashed lines).

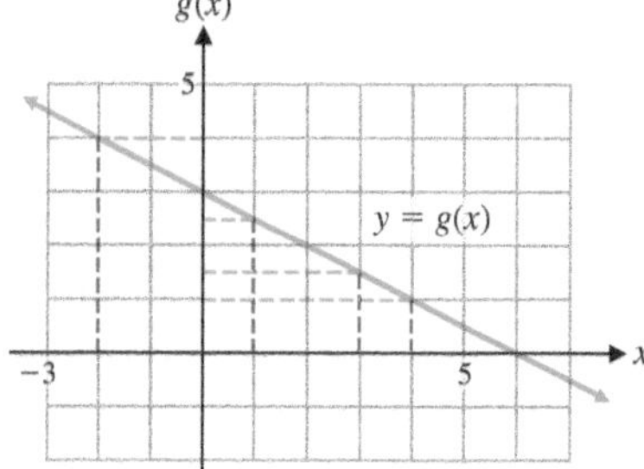

x	$g(x)$
−2	4.0
1	2.5
3	1.5
4	1.0

Matched Problem 1 Complete the following table, using the given graph of the function h.

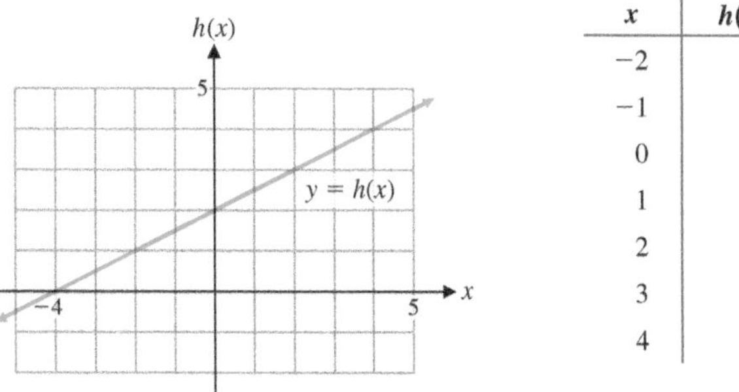

x	$h(x)$
−2	
−1	
0	
1	
2	
3	
4	

Limits: A Graphical Approach

We introduce the important concept of a *limit* through an example, which leads to an intuitive definition of the concept.

EXAMPLE 2 **Analyzing a Limit** Let $f(x) = x + 2$. Discuss the behavior of the values of $f(x)$ when x is close to 2.

SOLUTION We begin by drawing a graph of f that includes the domain value $x = 2$ (Fig. 2).

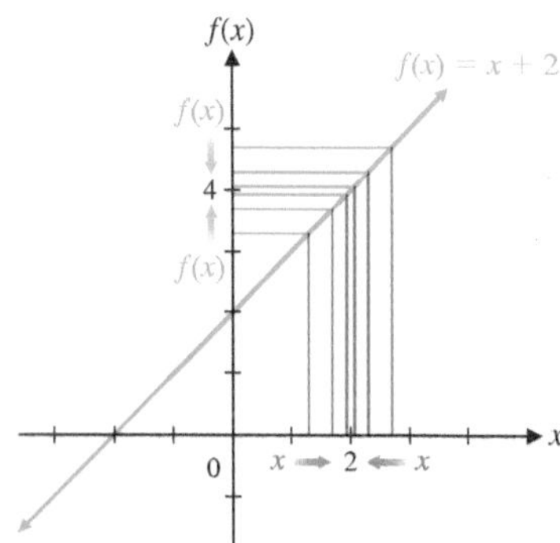

Figure 2

In Figure 2, we are using a static drawing to describe a dynamic process. This requires careful interpretation. The thin vertical lines in Figure 2 represent values of x that are close to 2. The corresponding horizontal lines identify the value of $f(x)$ associated with each value of x. [Example 1 dealt with the relationship between x and $f(x)$ on a graph.] The graph in Figure 2 indicates that as the values of x get closer and closer to 2 on either side of 2, the corresponding values of $f(x)$ get closer and closer to 4. Symbolically, we write

$$\lim_{x \to 2} f(x) = 4$$

This equation is read as "The limit of $f(x)$ as x approaches 2 is 4." Note that $f(2) = 4$. That is, the value of the function at 2 and the limit of the function as x approaches 2 are the same. This relationship can be expressed as

$$\lim_{x \to 2} f(x) = f(2) = 4$$

Graphically, this means that there is no hole or break in the graph of f at $x = 2$.

Matched Problem 2 Let $f(x) = x + 1$. Discuss the behavior of the values of $f(x)$ when x is close to 1.

We now present an informal definition of the important concept of a limit. A precise definition is not needed for our discussion, but one is given in a footnote.*

DEFINITION Limit

We write

$$\lim_{x \to c} f(x) = L \quad \text{or} \quad f(x) \to L \text{ as } x \to c$$

if the functional value $f(x)$ is close to the single real number L whenever x is close, but not equal, to c (on either side of c).

Note: The existence of a limit at c has nothing to do with the value of the function at c. In fact, c may not even be in the domain of f. However, the function must be defined on both sides of c.

Reminder:

The absolute value of a positive or negative number is positive. The absolute value of 0 is 0.

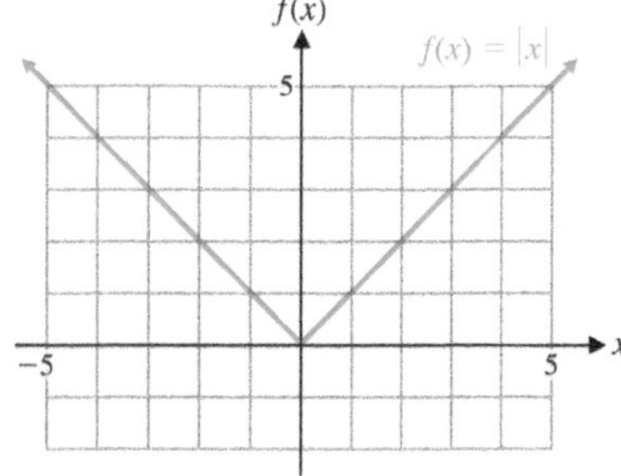

Figure 3

The next example involves the **absolute value function**:

$$f(x) = |x| = \begin{cases} -x & \text{if } x < 0 \\ x & \text{if } x \geq 0 \end{cases} \qquad \begin{array}{l} f(-2) = |-2| = -(-2) = 2 \\ f(3) = |3| = 3 \end{array}$$

The graph of f is shown in Figure 3.

EXAMPLE 3 **Analyzing a Limit** Let $h(x) = |x|/x$. Explore the behavior of $h(x)$ for x near, but not equal, to 0. Find $\lim_{x \to 0} h(x)$ if it exists.

SOLUTION The function h is defined for all real numbers except 0 [$h(0) = |0|/0$ is undefined]. For example,

$$h(-2) = \frac{|-2|}{-2} = \frac{2}{-2} = -1$$

Note that if x is any negative number, then $h(x) = -1$ (if $x < 0$, then the numerator $|x|$ is positive but the denominator x is negative, so $h(x) = |x|/x = -1$). If x is any positive number, then $h(x) = 1$ (if $x > 0$, then the numerator $|x|$ is equal to the denominator x, so $h(x) = |x|/x = 1$). Figure 4 illustrates the behavior of $h(x)$ for x near 0. Note that the absence of a solid dot on the vertical axis indicates that h is not defined when $x = 0$.

When x is near 0 (on either side of 0), is $h(x)$ near one specific number? The answer is "No," because $h(x)$ is -1 for $x < 0$ and 1 for $x > 0$. Consequently, we say that

$$\lim_{x \to 0} \frac{|x|}{x} \text{ does not exist}$$

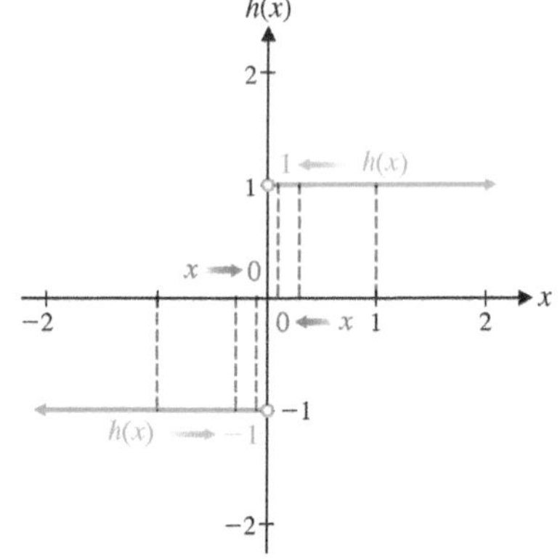

Figure 4

Neither $h(x)$ nor the limit of $h(x)$ exists at $x = 0$. However, the limit from the left and the limit from the right both exist at 0, but they are not equal.

Matched Problem 3 Graph

$$h(x) = \frac{x - 2}{|x - 2|}$$

and find $\lim_{x \to 2} h(x)$ if it exists.

In Example 3, we see that the values of the function $h(x)$ approach two different numbers, depending on the direction of approach, and it is natural to refer to these values as "the limit from the left" and "the limit from the right." These experiences suggest that the notion of **one-sided limits** will be very useful in discussing basic limit concepts.

*To make the informal definition of *limit* precise, we must make the word *close* more precise. This is done as follows: We write $\lim_{x \to c} f(x) = L$ if, for each $e > 0$, there exists a $d > 0$ such that $|f(x) - L| < e$ whenever $0 < |x - c| < d$. This definition is used to establish particular limits and to prove many useful properties of limits that will be helpful in finding particular limits.

DEFINITION One-Sided Limits

We write

$$\lim_{x\to c^-} f(x) = K \qquad x \to c^- \text{ is read "}x\text{ approaches }c\text{ from the left" and means } x \to c \text{ and } x < c.$$

and call K the **limit from the left** or the **left-hand limit** if $f(x)$ is close to K whenever x is close to, but to the left of, c on the real number line. We write

$$\lim_{x\to c^+} f(x) = L \qquad x \to c^+ \text{ is read "}x\text{ approaches }c\text{ from the right" and means } x \to c \text{ and } x > c.$$

and call L the **limit from the right** or the **right-hand limit** if $f(x)$ is close to L whenever x is close to, but to the right of, c on the real number line.

If no direction is specified in a limit statement, we will always assume that the limit is **two-sided** or **unrestricted**. Theorem 1 states an important relationship between one-sided limits and unrestricted limits.

THEOREM 1 On the Existence of a Limit

For a (two-sided) limit to exist, the limit from the left and the limit from the right must exist and be equal. That is,

$$\lim_{x\to c} f(x) = L \text{ if and only if } \lim_{x\to c^-} f(x) = \lim_{x\to c^+} f(x) = L$$

In Example 3,

$$\lim_{x\to 0^-} \frac{|x|}{x} = -1 \qquad \text{and} \qquad \lim_{x\to 0^+} \frac{|x|}{x} = 1$$

Since the left- and right-hand limits are *not* the same,

$$\lim_{x\to 0} \frac{|x|}{x} \text{ does not exist}$$

EXAMPLE 4 **Analyzing Limits Graphically** Given the graph of the function f in Figure 5, discuss the behavior of $f(x)$ for x near (A) -1, (B) 1, and (C) 2.

SOLUTION

(A) Since we have only a graph to work with, we use vertical and horizontal lines to relate the values of x and the corresponding values of $f(x)$. For any x near -1 on either side of -1, we see that the corresponding value of $f(x)$, determined by a horizontal line, is close to 1. We then have $f(-1) = \lim_{x\to -1} f(x)$.

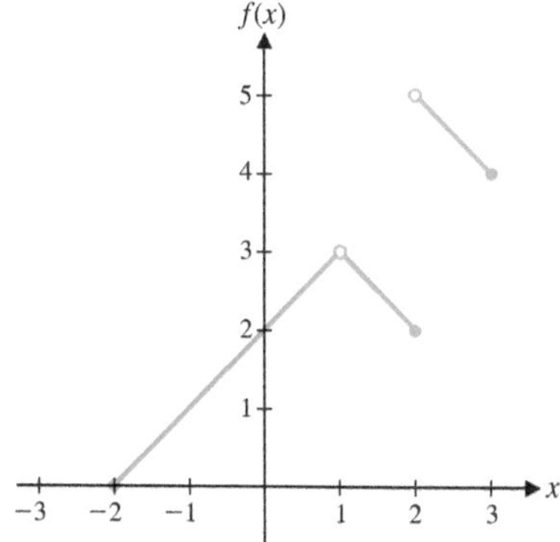

Figure 5

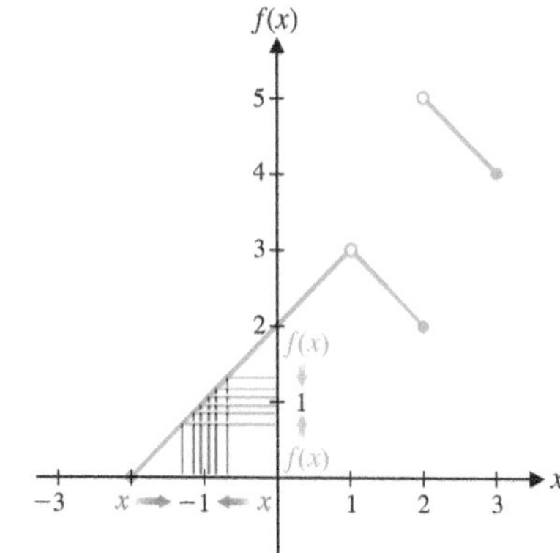

$$\lim_{x\to -1^-} f(x) = 1$$
$$\lim_{x\to -1^+} f(x) = 1$$
$$\lim_{x\to -1} f(x) = 1$$
$$f(-1) = 1$$

(B) Again, for any x near, but not equal to, 1, the vertical and horizontal lines indicate that the corresponding value of $f(x)$ is close to 3. The open dot at (1, 3), together with the absence of a solid dot anywhere on the vertical line through $x = 1$, indicates that $f(1)$ is not defined.

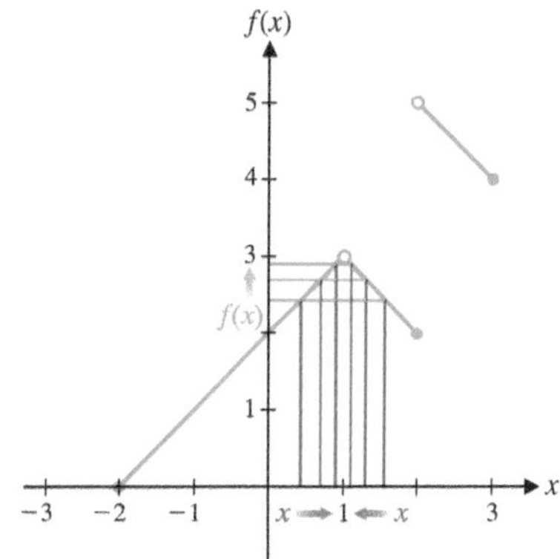

$$\lim_{x\to 1^-} f(x) = 3$$
$$\lim_{x\to 1^+} f(x) = 3$$
$$\lim_{x\to 1} f(x) = 3$$
$f(1)$ not defined

(C) The abrupt break in the graph at $x = 2$ indicates that the behavior of the graph near $x = 2$ is more complicated than in the two preceding cases. If x is close to 2 on the left side of 2, the corresponding horizontal line intersects the y axis at a point close to 2. If x is close to 2 on the right side of 2, the corresponding horizontal line intersects the y axis at a point close to 5. This is a case where the one-sided limits are different.

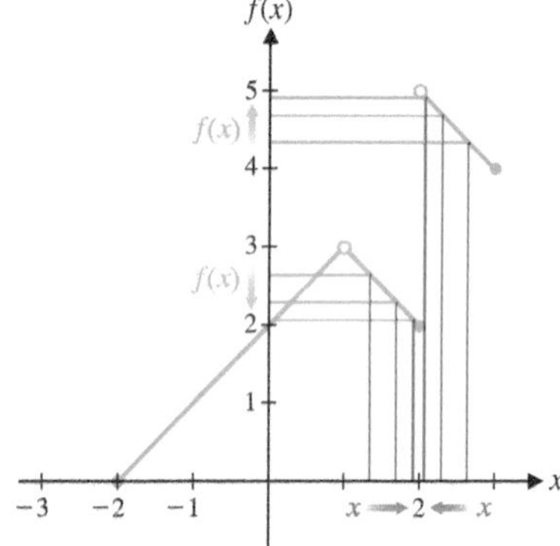

$$\lim_{x\to 2^-} f(x) = 2$$
$$\lim_{x\to 2^+} f(x) = 5$$
$\lim_{x\to 2} f(x)$ does not exist
$$f(2) = 2$$

Matched Problem 4 Given the graph of the function f shown in Figure 6, discuss the following, as we did in Example 4:

(A) Behavior of $f(x)$ for x near 0

(B) Behavior of $f(x)$ for x near 1

(C) Behavior of $f(x)$ for x near 3

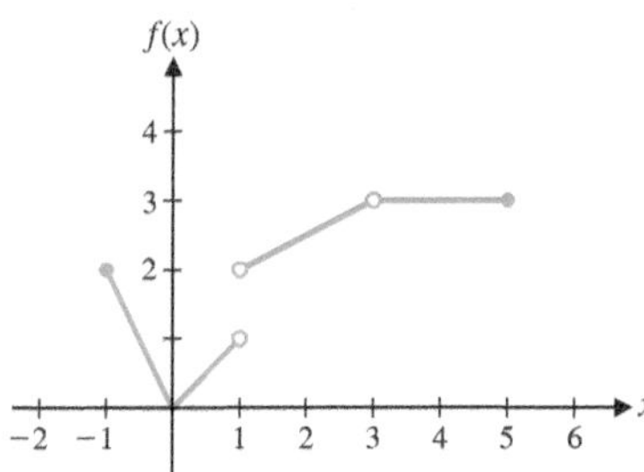

Figure 6

CONCEPTUAL INSIGHT

In Example 4B, note that $\lim_{x \to 1} f(x)$ exists even though f is not defined at $x = 1$ and the graph has a hole at $x = 1$. In general, the value of a function at $x = c$ has no effect on the limit of the function as x approaches c.

Limits: An Algebraic Approach

Graphs are very useful tools for investigating limits, especially if something unusual happens at the point in question. However, many of the limits encountered in calculus are routine and can be evaluated quickly with a little algebraic simplification, some intuition, and basic properties of limits. The following list of properties of limits forms the basis for this approach:

THEOREM 2 Properties of Limits

Let f and g be two functions, and assume that

$$\lim_{x \to c} f(x) = L \qquad \lim_{x \to c} g(x) = M$$

where L and M are real numbers (both limits exist). Then

1. $\lim_{x \to c} k = k$ for any constant k
2. $\lim_{x \to c} x = c$
3. $\lim_{x \to c} [f(x) + g(x)] = \lim_{x \to c} f(x) + \lim_{x \to c} g(x) = L + M$
4. $\lim_{x \to c} [f(x) - g(x)] = \lim_{x \to c} f(x) - \lim_{x \to c} g(x) = L - M$
5. $\lim_{x \to c} kf(x) = k \lim_{x \to c} f(x) = kL$ for any constant k
6. $\lim_{x \to c} [f(x) \cdot g(x)] = [\lim_{x \to c} f(x)][\lim_{x \to c} g(x)] = LM$
7. $\lim_{x \to c} \dfrac{f(x)}{g(x)} = \dfrac{\lim_{x \to c} f(x)}{\lim_{x \to c} g(x)} = \dfrac{L}{M}$ if $M \neq 0$
8. $\lim_{x \to c} \sqrt[n]{f(x)} = \sqrt[n]{\lim_{x \to c} f(x)} = \sqrt[n]{L}$ if $L > 0$ or n is odd

Each property in Theorem 2 is also valid if $x \to c$ is replaced everywhere by $x \to c^-$ or replaced everywhere by $x \to c^+$.

Explore and Discuss 1

The properties listed in Theorem 2 can be paraphrased in brief verbal statements. For example, property 3 simply states that *the limit of a sum is equal to the sum of the limits.* Write brief verbal statements for the remaining properties in Theorem 2.

EXAMPLE 5 **Using Limit Properties** Find $\lim_{x \to 3} (x^2 - 4x)$.

SOLUTION Using Property 4,

$$\lim_{x \to 3} (x^2 - 4x) = \lim_{x \to 3} x^2 - \lim_{x \to 3} 4x \qquad \text{Use properties 5 and 6}$$

$$= \left(\lim_{x \to 3} x\right) \cdot \left(\lim_{x \to 3} x\right) - 4 \lim_{x \to 3} x \qquad \text{Use exponents}$$

$$= \left(\lim_{x \to 3} x\right)^2 - 4 \lim_{x \to 3} x \qquad \text{Use Property 2}$$

$$= 3^2 - 4 \cdot 3 = -3$$

So, omitting the steps in the dashed boxes,

$$\lim_{x\to 3}(x^2 - 4x) = 3^2 - 4\cdot 3 = -3$$

Matched Problem 5 Find $\lim_{x\to -2}(x^2 + 5x)$.

If $f(x) = x^2 - 4$ and c is any real number, then, just as in Example 5

$$\lim_{x\to c} f(x) = \lim_{x\to c}(x^2 - 4x) = c^2 - 4c = f(c)$$

So the limit can be found easily by evaluating the function f at c.

This simple method for finding limits is very useful, because there are many functions that satisfy the property

$$\lim_{x\to c} f(x) = f(c) \tag{1}$$

Any polynomial function

$$f(x) = a_n x^n + a_{n-1}x^{n-1} + \cdots + a_0$$

satisfies (1) for any real number c. Also, any rational function

$$r(x) = \frac{n(x)}{d(x)}$$

where $n(x)$ and $d(x)$ are polynomials, satisfies (1) provided c is a real number for which $d(c) \neq 0$.

THEOREM 3 Limits of Polynomial and Rational Functions

1. $\lim_{x\to c} f(x) = f(c)$ for f any polynomial function.
2. $\lim_{x\to c} r(x) = r(c)$ for r any rational function with a nonzero denominator at $x = c$.

If Theorem 3 is applicable, the limit is easy to find: *Simply evaluate the function at c.*

EXAMPLE 6 **Evaluating Limits** Find each limit.

(A) $\lim_{x\to 2}(x^3 - 5x - 1)$ (B) $\lim_{x\to -1}\sqrt{2x^2 + 3}$ (C) $\lim_{x\to 4}\frac{2x}{3x + 1}$

SOLUTION

(A) Use Theorem 3 to get $\lim_{x\to 2}(x^3 - 5x - 1) = 2^3 - 5\cdot 2 - 1 = -3$

(B) Using Property 8, $\lim_{x\to -1}\sqrt{2x^2 + 3} = \sqrt{\lim_{x\to -1}(2x^2 + 3)}$ Use Theorem 3

$$= \sqrt{2(-1)^2 + 3}$$

$$= \sqrt{5}$$

(C) Use Theorem 3 to get $\lim_{x\to 4}\frac{2x}{3x + 1} = \frac{2\cdot 4}{3\cdot 4 + 1}$

$$= \frac{8}{13}$$

Matched Problem 6 Find each limit.

(A) $\lim_{x\to -1}(x^4 - 2x + 3)$ (B) $\lim_{x\to 2}\sqrt{3x^2 - 6}$ (C) $\lim_{x\to -2}\frac{x^2}{x^2 + 1}$

EXAMPLE 7 **Evaluating Limits** Let

$$f(x) = \begin{cases} x^2 + 1 & \text{if } x < 2 \\ x - 1 & \text{if } x > 2 \end{cases}$$

Find:

(A) $\lim_{x \to 2^-} f(x)$ (B) $\lim_{x \to 2^+} f(x)$ (C) $\lim_{x \to 2} f(x)$ (D) $f(2)$

SOLUTION

(A) $\lim_{x \to 2^-} f(x) = \lim_{x \to 2^-} (x^2 + 1)$ If $x < 2$, $f(x) = x^2 + 1$.

$= 2^2 + 1 = 5$

(B) $\lim_{x \to 2^+} f(x) = \lim_{x \to 2^+} (x - 1)$ If $x > 2$, $f(x) = x - 1$.

$= 2 - 1 = 1$

(C) Since the one-sided limits are not equal, $\lim_{x \to 2} f(x)$ does not exist.

(D) Because the definition of f does not assign a value to f for $x = 2$, only for $x < 2$ and $x > 2$, $f(2)$ does not exist.

Matched Problem 7 Let

$$f(x) = \begin{cases} 2x + 3 & \text{if } x < 5 \\ -x + 12 & \text{if } x > 5 \end{cases}$$

Find:

(A) $\lim_{x \to 5^-} f(x)$ (B) $\lim_{x \to 5^+} f(x)$ (C) $\lim_{x \to 5} f(x)$ (D) $f(5)$

It is important to note that there are restrictions on some of the limit properties. In particular, if $\lim_{x \to c} f(x) = 0$ and $\lim_{x \to c} g(x) = 0$, then finding $\lim_{x \to c} \frac{f(x)}{g(x)}$ may present some difficulties, since limit property 7 (the limit of a quotient) does not apply when $\lim_{x \to c} g(x) = 0$. The next example illustrates some techniques that can be useful in this situation.

EXAMPLE 8 **Evaluating Limits** Find each limit.

(A) $\lim_{x \to 2} \frac{x^2 - 4}{x - 2}$ (B) $\lim_{x \to -1} \frac{x|x + 1|}{x + 1}$

SOLUTION

(A) Note that $\lim_{x \to 2} x^2 - 4 = 2^2 - 4 = 0$ and $\lim_{x \to 2} x - 2 = 2 - 2 = 0$. Algebraic simplification is often useful in such a case when the numerator and denominator both have limit 0.

$$\lim_{x \to 2} \frac{x^2 - 4}{x - 2} = \lim_{x \to 2} \frac{(x - 2)(x + 2)}{x - 2} \quad \text{Cancel } \frac{x - 2}{x - 2}$$

$$= \lim_{x \to 2} (x + 2) = 4$$

(B) One-sided limits are helpful for limits involving the absolute value function.

$$\lim_{x \to -1^+} \frac{x|x + 1|}{x + 1} = \lim_{x \to -1^+} (x) = -1 \quad \text{If } x > -1, \text{ then } \frac{|x + 1|}{x + 1} = 1.$$

$$\lim_{x \to -1^-} \frac{x|x + 1|}{x + 1} = \lim_{x \to -1^-} (-x) = 1 \quad \text{If } x < -1, \text{ then } \frac{|x + 1|}{x + 1} = -1.$$

Since the limit from the left and the limit from the right are not the same, we conclude that

$$\lim_{x \to -1} \frac{x|x + 1|}{x + 1} \quad \text{does not exist}$$

Matched Problem 8 Find each limit.

(A) $\lim_{x \to -3} \frac{x^2 + 4x + 3}{x + 3}$ (B) $\lim_{x \to 4} \frac{x^2 - 16}{|x - 4|}$

CONCEPTUAL INSIGHT

In the solution to Example 8A we used the following algebraic identity:

$$\frac{x^2 - 4}{x - 2} = \frac{(x - 2)(x + 2)}{x - 2} = x + 2, \quad x \neq 2$$

The restriction $x \neq 2$ is necessary here because the first two expressions are not defined at $x = 2$. Why didn't we include this restriction in the solution? When x approaches 2 in a limit problem, it is assumed that x is close, but not equal, to 2. It is important that you understand that both of the following statements are valid:

$$\lim_{x \to 2} \frac{x^2 - 4}{x - 2} = \lim_{x \to 2} (x + 2) \quad \text{and} \quad \frac{x^2 - 4}{x - 2} = x + 2, \quad x \neq 2$$

Limits like those in Example 8 occur so frequently in calculus that they are given a special name.

DEFINITION Indeterminate Form

If $\lim_{x \to c} f(x) = 0$ and $\lim_{x \to c} g(x) = 0$, then $\lim_{x \to c} \frac{f(x)}{g(x)}$ is said to be **indeterminate**, or, more specifically, a **0/0 indeterminate form**.

The term *indeterminate* is used because the limit of an indeterminate form may or may not exist (see Examples 8A and 8B).

CAUTION The expression $0/0$ does not represent a real number and should never be used as the value of a limit. If a limit is a $0/0$ indeterminate form, further investigation is always required to determine whether the limit exists and to find its value if it does exist. ▲

If the denominator of a quotient approaches 0 and the numerator approaches a nonzero number, then the limit of the quotient is not an indeterminate form. In fact, in this case the limit of the quotient does not exist.

THEOREM 4 Limit of a Quotient

If $\lim_{x \to c} f(x) = L, L \neq 0$, and $\lim_{x \to c} g(x) = 0$,

then

$$\lim_{x \to c} \frac{f(x)}{g(x)} \quad \text{does not exist}$$

EXAMPLE 9 **Indeterminate Forms** Is the limit expression a $0/0$ indeterminate form? Find the limit or explain why the limit does not exist.

(A) $\lim_{x \to 1} \frac{x - 1}{x^2 + 1}$ (B) $\lim_{x \to 1} \frac{x - 1}{x^2 - 1}$ (C) $\lim_{x \to 1} \frac{x + 1}{x^2 - 1}$

SOLUTION

(A) $\lim_{x\to1}(x-1)=0$ but $\lim_{x\to1}(x^2+1)=2$. So no, the limit expression is not a $0/0$ indeterminate form. By property 7 of Theorem 2,

$$\lim_{x\to1}\frac{x-1}{x^2+1}=\frac{0}{2}=0$$

(B) $\lim_{x\to1}(x-1)=0$ and $\lim_{x\to1}(x^2-1)=0$. So yes, the limit expression is a $0/0$ indeterminate form. We factor x^2-1 to simplify the limit expression and find the limit:

$$\lim_{x\to1}\frac{x-1}{x^2-1}=\lim_{x\to1}\frac{x-1}{(x-1)(x+1)}=\lim_{x\to1}\frac{1}{x+1}=\frac{1}{2}$$

(C) $\lim_{x\to1}(x+1)=2$ and $\lim_{x\to1}(x^2-1)=0$. So no, the limit expression is not a $0/0$ indeterminate form. By Theorem 4,

$$\lim_{x\to1}\frac{x+1}{x^2-1}\quad\text{does not exist}$$

Matched Problem 9 Is the limit expression a $0/0$ indeterminate form? Find the limit or explain why the limit does not exist.

(A) $\lim_{x\to3}\frac{x+1}{x+3}$ (B) $\lim_{x\to3}\frac{x-3}{x^2+9}$ (C) $\lim_{x\to3}\frac{x^2-9}{x-3}$

Limits of Difference Quotients

Let the function f be defined in an open interval containing the number a. One of the most important limits in calculus is the limit of the **difference quotient**,

$$\lim_{h\to0}\frac{f(a+h)-f(a)}{h}\tag{2}$$

If

$$\lim_{h\to0}[f(a+h)-f(a)]=0$$

as it often does, then limit (2) is an indeterminate form.

EXAMPLE 10 **Limit of a Difference Quotient** Find the following limit for $f(x)=4x-5$:

$$\lim_{h\to0}\frac{f(3+h)-f(3)}{h}$$

SOLUTION

$$\begin{aligned}\lim_{h\to0}\frac{f(3+h)-f(3)}{h}&=\lim_{h\to0}\frac{[4(\mathbf{3+h})-5]-[4(\mathbf{3})-5]}{h}\\&=\lim_{h\to0}\frac{12+4h-5-12+5}{h}\\&=\lim_{h\to0}\frac{4h}{h}=\lim_{h\to0}4=4\end{aligned}$$

Since this is a $0/0$ indeterminate form and property 7 in Theorem 2 does not apply, we proceed with algebraic simplification.

Matched Problem 10 Find the following limit for $f(x)=7-2x$:

$$\lim_{h\to0}\frac{f(4+h)-f(4)}{h}.$$

Explore and Discuss 2

If $f(x) = \frac{1}{x}$, explain why $\lim_{h \to 0} \frac{f(3+h) - f(3)}{h} = -\frac{1}{9}$.

Exercises 6.1

Skills Warm-up Exercises

W *In Problems 1–8, factor each polynomial into the product of first-degree factors with integer coefficients. (If necessary, review Section A.3.)*

1. $x^2 - 81$ **2.** $x^2 - 64$

3. $x^2 - 4x - 21$ **4.** $x^2 + 5x - 36$

5. $x^3 - 7x^2 + 12x$ **6.** $x^3 + 15x^2 + 50x$

7. $6x^2 - x - 1$ **8.** $12x^2 - 5x - 2$

In Problems 9–16, use the graph of the function f shown to estimate the indicated limits and function values.

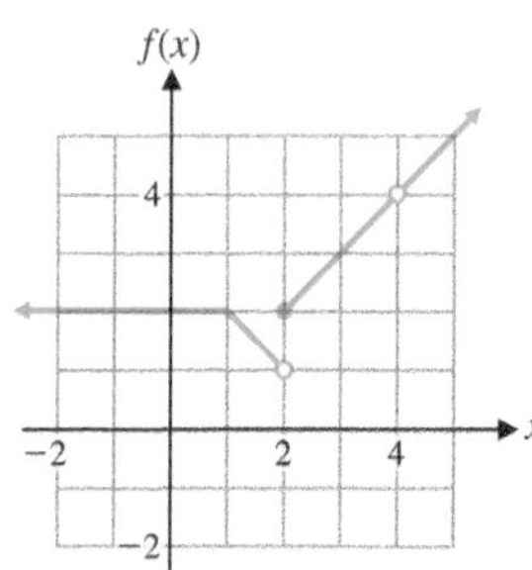

Figure for 9–16

A **9.** $f(-0.5)$ **10.** $f(0.5)$

11. $f(1.75)$ **12.** $f(2.25)$

13. (A) $\lim_{x \to 0^-} f(x)$ (B) $\lim_{x \to 0^+} f(x)$ (C) $\lim_{x \to 0} f(x)$ (D) $f(0)$

14. (A) $\lim_{x \to 1^-} f(x)$ (B) $\lim_{x \to 1^+} f(x)$ (C) $\lim_{x \to 1} f(x)$ (D) $f(1)$

15. (A) $\lim_{x \to 2^-} f(x)$ (B) $\lim_{x \to 2^+} f(x)$ (C) $\lim_{x \to 2} f(x)$ (D) $f(2)$

16. (A) $\lim_{x \to 4^-} f(x)$ (B) $\lim_{x \to 4^+} f(x)$ (C) $\lim_{x \to 4} f(x)$ (D) $f(4)$

In Problems 17–24, use the graph of the function g shown to estimate the indicated limits and function values.

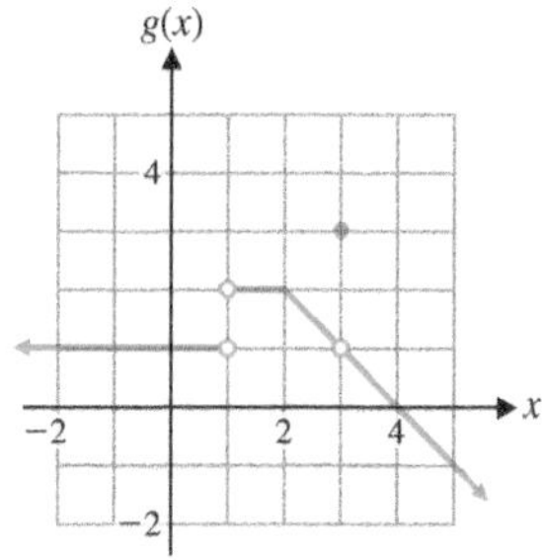

Figure for 17–24

17. $g(1.9)$ **18.** $g(2.1)$

19. $g(3.5)$ **20.** $g(2.5)$

21. (A) $\lim_{x \to 1^-} g(x)$ (B) $\lim_{x \to 1^+} g(x)$ (C) $\lim_{x \to 1} g(x)$ (D) $g(1)$

22. (A) $\lim_{x \to 2^-} g(x)$ (B) $\lim_{x \to 2^+} g(x)$ (C) $\lim_{x \to 2} g(x)$ (D) $g(2)$

23. (A) $\lim_{x \to 3^-} g(x)$ (B) $\lim_{x \to 3^+} g(x)$ (C) $\lim_{x \to 3} g(x)$ (D) $g(3)$

24. (A) $\lim_{x \to 4^-} g(x)$ (B) $\lim_{x \to 4^+} g(x)$ (C) $\lim_{x \to 4} g(x)$ (D) $g(4)$

In Problems 25–28, use the graph of the function f shown to estimate the indicated limits and function values.

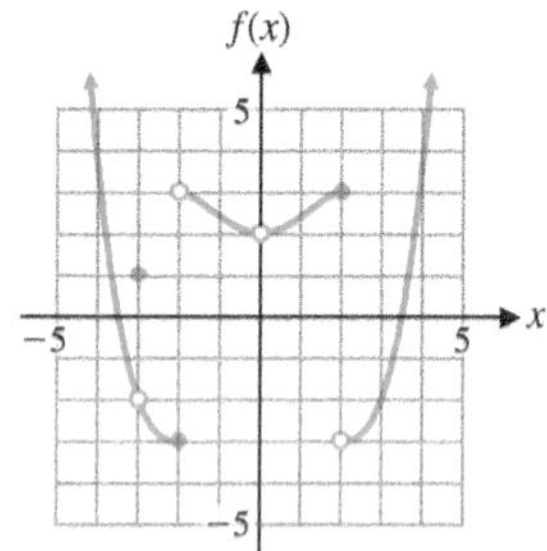

Figure for 25–28

25. (A) $\lim_{x \to -3^+} f(x)$ (B) $\lim_{x \to -3^-} f(x)$ (C) $\lim_{x \to -3} f(x)$ (D) $f(-3)$

26. (A) $\lim_{x \to -2^+} f(x)$ (B) $\lim_{x \to -2^-} f(x)$ (C) $\lim_{x \to -2} f(x)$ (D) $f(-2)$

27. (A) $\lim_{x \to 0^+} f(x)$ (B) $\lim_{x \to 0^-} f(x)$ (C) $\lim_{x \to 0} f(x)$ (D) $f(0)$

28. (A) $\lim_{x \to 2^+} f(x)$ (B) $\lim_{x \to 2^-} f(x)$ (C) $\lim_{x \to 2} f(x)$ (D) $f(2)$

B *In Problems 29–38, find each limit if it exists.*

29. $\lim_{x \to 3} 4x$ **30.** $\lim_{x \to -6} 5x$

31. $\lim_{x \to -4} (x + 5)$ **32.** $\lim_{x \to 5} (x - 3)$

33. $\lim_{x \to 2} x(x - 4)$ **34.** $\lim_{x \to -3} x(x + 5)$

35. $\lim_{x \to -3} \frac{x}{x + 5}$ **36.** $\lim_{x \to 4} \frac{x - 2}{x}$

37. $\lim_{x \to 1} \sqrt{5x + 4}$ **38.** $\lim_{x \to -2} \sqrt{17 - 4x}$

Given that $\lim_{x\to 1} f(x) = -5$ and $\lim_{x\to 1} g(x) = 4$, find the indicated limits in Problems 39–46.

39. $\lim_{x\to 1} (-3)f(x)$

40. $\lim_{x\to 1} 2g(x)$

41. $\lim_{x\to 1} [2f(x) + g(x)]$

42. $\lim_{x\to 1} [3g(x) - 4f(x)]$

43. $\lim_{x\to 1} \dfrac{2 - f(x)}{x + g(x)}$

44. $\lim_{x\to 1} \dfrac{3 - f(x)}{1 - 4g(x)}$

45. $\lim_{x\to 1} \sqrt{g(x) - f(x)}$

46. $\lim_{x\to 1} \sqrt[3]{5g(x) + 7x}$

In Problems 47–50, sketch a possible graph of a function that satisfies the given conditions.

47. $f(0) = 1;\ \lim_{x\to 0^-} f(x) = 3;\ \lim_{x\to 0^+} f(x) = 1$

48. $f(1) = -2;\ \lim_{x\to 1^-} f(x) = 2;\ \lim_{x\to 1^+} f(x) = -2$

49. $f(-2) = 2;\ \lim_{x\to -2^-} f(x) = 1;\ \lim_{x\to -2^+} f(x) = 1$

50. $f(0) = -1;\ \lim_{x\to 0^-} f(x) = 2;\ \lim_{x\to 0^+} f(x) = 2$

In Problems 51–66, find each indicated quantity if it exists.

51. Let $f(x) = \begin{cases} 1 - x^2 & \text{if } x \le 0 \\ 1 + x^2 & \text{if } x > 0 \end{cases}$. Find

(A) $\lim_{x\to 0^+} f(x)$ (B) $\lim_{x\to 0^-} f(x)$

(C) $\lim_{x\to 0} f(x)$ (D) $f(0)$

52. Let $f(x) = \begin{cases} 2 + x & \text{if } x \le 0 \\ 2 - x & \text{if } x > 0 \end{cases}$. Find

(A) $\lim_{x\to 0^+} f(x)$ (B) $\lim_{x\to 0^-} f(x)$

(C) $\lim_{x\to 0} f(x)$ (D) $f(0)$

53. Let $f(x) = \begin{cases} x^2 & \text{if } x < 1 \\ 2x & \text{if } x > 1 \end{cases}$. Find

(A) $\lim_{x\to 1^+} f(x)$ (B) $\lim_{x\to 1^-} f(x)$

(C) $\lim_{x\to 1} f(x)$ (D) $f(1)$

54. Let $f(x) = \begin{cases} x + 3 & \text{if } x < -2 \\ \sqrt{x + 2} & \text{if } x > -2 \end{cases}$. Find

(A) $\lim_{x\to -2^+} f(x)$ (B) $\lim_{x\to -2^-} f(x)$

(C) $\lim_{x\to -2} f(x)$ (D) $f(-2)$

55. Let $f(x) = \begin{cases} \dfrac{x^2 - 9}{x + 3} & \text{if } x < 0 \\ \dfrac{x^2 - 9}{x - 3} & \text{if } x > 0 \end{cases}$. Find

(A) $\lim_{x\to -3} f(x)$ (B) $\lim_{x\to 0} f(x)$

(C) $\lim_{x\to 3} f(x)$

56. Let $f(x) = \begin{cases} \dfrac{x}{x + 3} & \text{if } x < 0 \\ \dfrac{x}{x - 3} & \text{if } x > 0 \end{cases}$. Find

(A) $\lim_{x\to -3} f(x)$ (B) $\lim_{x\to 0} f(x)$

(C) $\lim_{x\to 3} f(x)$

57. Let $f(x) = \dfrac{|x - 1|}{x - 1}$. Find

(A) $\lim_{x\to 1^+} f(x)$ (B) $\lim_{x\to 1^-} f(x)$

(C) $\lim_{x\to 1} f(x)$ (D) $f(1)$

58. Let $f(x) = \dfrac{x - 3}{|x - 3|}$. Find

(A) $\lim_{x\to 3^+} f(x)$ (B) $\lim_{x\to 3^-} f(x)$

(C) $\lim_{x\to 3} f(x)$ (D) $f(3)$

59. Let $f(x) = \dfrac{x - 2}{x^2 - 2x}$. Find

(A) $\lim_{x\to 0} f(x)$ (B) $\lim_{x\to 2} f(x)$

(C) $\lim_{x\to 4} f(x)$

60. Let $f(x) = \dfrac{x + 3}{x^2 + 3x}$. Find

(A) $\lim_{x\to -3} f(x)$ (B) $\lim_{x\to 0} f(x)$

(C) $\lim_{x\to 3} f(x)$

61. Let $f(x) = \dfrac{x^2 - x - 6}{x + 2}$. Find

(A) $\lim_{x\to -2} f(x)$ (B) $\lim_{x\to 0} f(x)$

(C) $\lim_{x\to 3} f(x)$

62. Let $f(x) = \dfrac{x^2 + x - 6}{x + 3}$. Find

(A) $\lim_{x\to -3} f(x)$ (B) $\lim_{x\to 0} f(x)$

(C) $\lim_{x\to 2} f(x)$

63. Let $f(x) = \dfrac{(x + 2)^2}{x^2 - 4}$. Find

(A) $\lim_{x\to -2} f(x)$ (B) $\lim_{x\to 0} f(x)$

(C) $\lim_{x\to 2} f(x)$

64. Let $f(x) = \dfrac{x^2 - 1}{(x + 1)^2}$. Find

(A) $\lim_{x\to -1} f(x)$ (B) $\lim_{x\to 0} f(x)$

(C) $\lim_{x\to 1} f(x)$

65. Let $f(x) = \dfrac{2x^2 - 3x - 2}{x^2 + x - 6}$. Find

(A) $\lim_{x\to 2} f(x)$ (B) $\lim_{x\to 0} f(x)$

(C) $\lim_{x\to 1} f(x)$

66. Let $f(x) = \dfrac{3x^2 + 2x - 1}{x^2 + 3x + 2}$. Find

(A) $\lim_{x\to -3} f(x)$ (B) $\lim_{x\to -1} f(x)$

(C) $\lim_{x\to 2} f(x)$

In Problems 67–72, discuss the validity of each statement. If the statement is always true, explain why. If not, give a counterexample.

67. If $\lim_{x\to 1} f(x) = 0$ and $\lim_{x\to 1} g(x) = 0$, then $\lim_{x\to 1} \dfrac{f(x)}{g(x)} = 0$.

68. If $\lim_{x\to 1} f(x) = 1$ and $\lim_{x\to 1} g(x) = 1$, then $\lim_{x\to 1} \dfrac{f(x)}{g(x)} = 1$.

69. If f is a function such that $\lim_{x\to 0} f(x)$ exists, then $f(0)$ exists.

70. If f is a function such that $f(0)$ exists, then $\lim_{x\to 0} f(x)$ exists.

71. If f is a polynomial, then, as x approaches 0, the right-hand limit exists and is equal to the left-hand limit.

72. If f is a rational function, then, as x approaches 0, the right-hand limit exists and is equal to the left-hand limit.

C *In Problems 73–80, is the limit expression a 0/0 indeterminate form? Find the limit or explain why the limit does not exist.*

73. $\lim_{x\to 4} \dfrac{(x+2)(x-4)}{(x-1)(x-4)}$

74. $\lim_{x\to -3} \dfrac{x-2}{x+3}$

75. $\lim_{x\to 1} \dfrac{x-5}{x-1}$

76. $\lim_{x\to 6} \dfrac{(x+9)(x-6)}{(x-6)(x-3)}$

77. $\lim_{x\to 7} \dfrac{x^2-49}{x^2-4x-21}$

78. $\lim_{x\to 5} \dfrac{x^2-7x+10}{x^2-4x-5}$

79. $\lim_{x\to -1} \dfrac{x^2+3x+2}{x^2-3x+2}$

80. $\lim_{x\to -4} \dfrac{x^2-6x+9}{x^2+6x+9}$

Compute the following limit for each function in Problems 81–88.

$$\lim_{h\to 0} \frac{f(2+h)-f(2)}{h}$$

81. $f(x) = 3x + 1$

82. $f(x) = 4x - 5$

83. $f(x) = x^2 + 1$

84. $f(x) = x^2 - 6x$

85. $f(x) = -7x + 9$

86. $f(x) = -4x + 13$

87. $f(x) = |x + 1|$

88. $f(x) = -3|x|$

89. Let f be defined by

$$f(x) = \begin{cases} 1 + mx & \text{if } x \le 1 \\ 4 - mx & \text{if } x > 1 \end{cases}$$

where m is a constant.

(A) Graph f for $m = 1$, and find

$$\lim_{x\to 1^-} f(x) \quad \text{and} \quad \lim_{x\to 1^+} f(x)$$

(B) Graph f for $m = 2$, and find

$$\lim_{x\to 1^-} f(x) \quad \text{and} \quad \lim_{x\to 1^+} f(x)$$

(C) Find m so that

$$\lim_{x\to 1^-} f(x) = \lim_{x\to 1^+} f(x)$$

and graph f for this value of m.

(D) Write a brief verbal description of each graph. How does the graph in part (C) differ from the graphs in parts (A) and (B)?

90. Let f be defined by

$$f(x) = \begin{cases} -3m + 0.5x & \text{if } x \le 2 \\ 3m - x & \text{if } x > 2 \end{cases}$$

where m is a constant.

(A) Graph f for $m = 0$, and find

$$\lim_{x\to 2^-} f(x) \quad \text{and} \quad \lim_{x\to 2^+} f(x)$$

(B) Graph f for $m = 1$, and find

$$\lim_{x\to 2^-} f(x) \quad \text{and} \quad \lim_{x\to 2^+} f(x)$$

(C) Find m so that

$$\lim_{x\to 2^-} f(x) = \lim_{x\to 2^+} f(x)$$

and graph f for this value of m.

(D) Write a brief verbal description of each graph. How does the graph in part (C) differ from the graphs in parts (A) and (B)?

Applications

91. Car Sharing. A car sharing service offers a membership plan with a \$50 per month fee that includes 10 hours of driving each month and charges \$9 for each additional hour.

(A) Write a piecewise definition of the cost $F(x)$ for a month in which a member uses a car for x hours.

(B) Graph $F(x)$ for $0 < x \le 15$

(C) Find $\lim_{x\to 10^-} F(x)$, $\lim_{x\to 10^+} F(x)$, and $\lim_{x\to 10} F(x)$, whichever exist.

92. Car Sharing. A car sharing service offers a membership plan with no monthly fee. Members who use a car for at most 10 hours are charged \$15 per hour. Members who use a car for more than 10 hours are charged \$10 per hour.

(A) Write a piecewise definition of the cost $G(x)$ for a month in which a member uses a car for x hours.

(B) Graph $G(x)$ for $0 < x \le 20$

(C) Find $\lim_{x\to 10^-} G(x)$, $\lim_{x\to 10^+} G(x)$, and $\lim_{x\to 10} G(x)$, whichever exist.

93. Car Sharing. Refer to Problems 91 and 92. Write a brief verbal comparison of the two services described for customers who use a car for 10 hours or less in a month.

94. Car Sharing. Refer to Problems 91 and 92. Write a brief verbal comparison of the two services described for customers who use a car for more than 10 hours in a month.

A company sells custom embroidered apparel and promotional products. Table 1 shows the volume discounts offered by the company, where x is the volume of a purchase in dollars. Problems 95 and 96 deal with two different interpretations of this discount method.

Table 1 **Volume Discount (Excluding Tax)**

Volume (\$x)	Discount Amount
$\$300 \le x < \$1{,}000$	3%
$\$1{,}000 \le x < \$3{,}000$	5%
$\$3{,}000 \le x < \$5{,}000$	7%
$\$5{,}000 \le x$	10%

95. Volume discount. Assume that the volume discounts in Table 1 apply to the entire purchase. That is, if the volume x satisfies $\$300 \le x < \$1{,}000$, then the entire purchase is discounted 3%. If the volume x satisfies $\$1{,}000 \le x < \$3{,}000$, the entire purchase is discounted 5%, and so on.

(A) If x is the volume of a purchase before the discount is applied, then write a piecewise definition for the discounted price $D(x)$ of this purchase.

(B) Use one-sided limits to investigate the limit of $D(x)$ as x approaches \$1,000. As x approaches \$3,000.

96. Volume discount. Assume that the volume discounts in Table 1 apply only to that portion of the volume in each interval. That is, the discounted price for a \$4,000 purchase would be computed as follows:

$$300 + 0.97(700) + 0.95(2{,}000) + 0.93(1{,}000) = 3{,}809$$

(A) If x is the volume of a purchase before the discount is applied, then write a piecewise definition for the discounted price $P(x)$ of this purchase.

(B) Use one-sided limits to investigate the limit of $P(x)$ as x approaches \$1,000. As x approaches \$3,000.

(C) Compare this discount method with the one in Problem 95. Does one always produce a lower price than the other? Discuss.

97. Pollution A state charges polluters an annual fee of \$20 per ton for each ton of pollutant emitted into the atmosphere, up to a maximum of 4,000 tons. No fees are charged for emissions beyond the 4,000-ton limit. Write a piecewise definition of the fees $F(x)$ charged for the emission of x tons of pollutant in a year. What is the limit of $F(x)$ as x approaches 4,000 tons? As x approaches 8,000 tons?

98. Pollution Refer to Problem 97. The average fee per ton of pollution is given by $A(x) = F(x)/x$. Write a piecewise definition of $A(x)$. What is the limit of $A(x)$ as x approaches 4,000 tons? As x approaches 8,000 tons?

99. Voter turnout. Statisticians often use piecewise-defined functions to predict outcomes of elections. For the following functions f and g, find the limit of each function as x approaches 5 and as x approaches 10.

$$f(x) = \begin{cases} 0 & \text{if } x \le 5 \\ 0.8 - 0.08x & \text{if } 5 < x < 10 \\ 0 & \text{if } 10 \le x \end{cases}$$

$$g(x) = \begin{cases} 0 & \text{if } x \le 5 \\ 0.8x - 0.04x^2 - 3 & \text{if } 5 < x < 10 \\ 1 & \text{if } 10 \le x \end{cases}$$

Answers to Matched Problems

1.

x	−2	−1	0	1	2	3	4
$h(x)$	1.0	1.5	2.0	2.5	3.0	3.5	4.0

2. $\lim_{x\to1} f(x) = 2$

3. 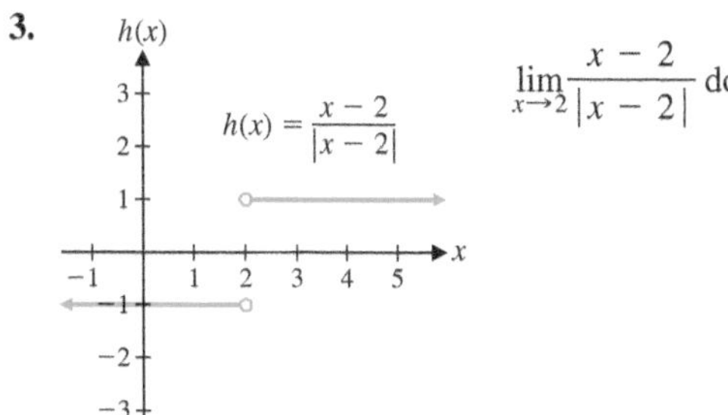

$\lim_{x\to2} \frac{x-2}{|x-2|}$ does not exist

4. (A) $\lim_{x\to0^-} f(x) = 0$
$\lim_{x\to0^+} f(x) = 0$
$\lim_{x\to0} f(x) = 0$
$f(0) = 0$

(B) $\lim_{x\to1^-} f(x) = 1$
$\lim_{x\to1^+} f(x) = 2$
$\lim_{x\to1} f(x)$ does not exist
$f(1)$ not defined

(C) $\lim_{x\to3^-} f(x) = 3$
$\lim_{x\to3^+} f(x) = 3$
$\lim_{x\to3} f(x) = 3$ $f(3)$ not defined

5. −6

6. (A) 6
(B) $\sqrt{6}$
(C) $\frac{4}{5}$

7. (A) 13
(B) 7
(C) Does not exist
(D) Not defined

8. (A) −2
(B) Does not exist

9. (A) No; $\frac{2}{3}$
(B) No; 0
(C) Yes; 6

10. −2

6.2 Infinite Limits and Limits at Infinity

- Infinite Limits
- Locating Vertical Asymptotes
- Limits at Infinity
- Finding Horizontal Asymptotes

In this section, we consider two new types of limits: infinite limits and limits at infinity. Infinite limits and vertical asymptotes are used to describe the behavior of functions that are unbounded near $x = a$. Limits at infinity and horizontal asymptotes are used to describe the behavior of functions as x assumes arbitrarily large positive values or arbitrarily large negative values. Although we will include graphs to illustrate basic concepts, we postpone a discussion of graphing techniques until Chapter 8.

Infinite Limits

The graph of $f(x) = \dfrac{1}{x-1}$ (Fig. 1) indicates that

$$\lim_{x \to 1^+} \frac{1}{x-1}$$

does not exist. There does not exist a real number L that the values of $f(x)$ approach as x approaches 1 from the right. Instead, as x approaches 1 from the right, the values of $f(x)$ are positive and become larger and larger; that is, $f(x)$ increases without bound (Table 1). We express this behavior symbolically as

$$\lim_{x \to 1^+} \frac{1}{x-1} = \infty \quad \text{or} \quad f(x) = \frac{1}{x-1} \to \infty \quad \text{as} \quad x \to 1^+ \tag{1}$$

Since ∞ is a not a real number, *the limit in (1) does not exist*. We are using the symbol ∞ to describe the manner in which the limit fails to exist, and we call this situation an **infinite limit**. We use ∞ to describe positive growth without bound, we use $-\infty$ to describe negative growth without bound, and we use $\pm\infty$ to mean "∞ or $-\infty$". If x approaches 1 from the left, the values of $f(x)$ are negative and become larger and larger in absolute value; that is, $f(x)$ decreases through negative values without bound (Table 2). We express this behavior symbolically as

$$\lim_{x \to 1^-} \frac{1}{x-1} = -\infty \quad \text{or} \quad f(x) = \frac{1}{x-1} \to -\infty \quad \text{as} \quad x \to 1^- \tag{2}$$

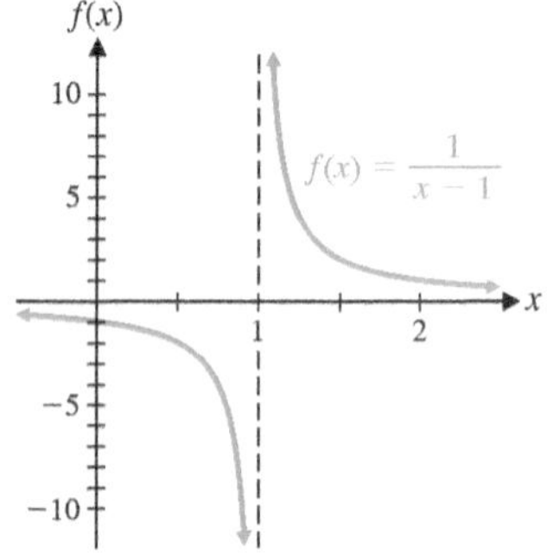

Figure 1

Table 1

x	$f(x) = \dfrac{1}{x-1}$
1.1	10
1.01	100
1.001	1,000
1.0001	10,000
1.00001	100,000
1.000001	1,000,000

Table 2

x	$f(x) = \dfrac{1}{x-1}$
0.9	−10
0.99	−100
0.999	−1,000
0.9999	−10,000
0.99999	−100,000
0.999999	−1,000,000

The one-sided limits in (1) and (2) describe the behavior of the graph as $x \to 1$ (Fig. 1). Does the two-sided limit of $f(x)$ as $x \to 1$ exist? No, because neither of the one-sided limits exists. Also, there is no reasonable way to use the symbol ∞ to describe the behavior of $f(x)$ as $x \to 1$ on both sides of 1. We say that

$$\lim_{x \to 1} \frac{1}{x-1} \text{ does not exist.}$$

Explore and Discuss 1

Let $g(x) = \dfrac{1}{(x-1)^2}$.

Construct tables for $g(x)$ as $x \to 1^+$ and as $x \to 1^-$. Use these tables and infinite limits to discuss the behavior of $g(x)$ near $x = 1$.

We used the dashed vertical line $x = 1$ in Figure 1 to illustrate the infinite limits as x approaches 1 from the right and from the left. We call this line a *vertical asymptote*.

DEFINITION Infinite Limits and Vertical Asymptotes

The vertical line $x = a$ is a **vertical asymptote** for the graph of $y = f(x)$ if

$$f(x) \to \infty \quad \text{or} \quad f(x) \to -\infty \quad \text{as} \quad x \to a^+ \quad \text{or} \quad x \to a^-$$

[That is, if $f(x)$ either increases or decreases without bound as x approaches a from the right or from the left].

Locating Vertical Asymptotes

How do we locate vertical asymptotes? If f is a polynomial function, then $\lim_{x \to a} f(x)$ is equal to the real number $f(a)$ [Theorem 3, Section 6.1]. So *a polynomial function has no vertical asymptotes*. Similarly (again by Theorem 3, Section 6.1), *a vertical asymptote of a rational function can occur only at a zero of its denominator*. Theorem 1 provides a simple procedure for locating the vertical asymptotes of a rational function.

THEOREM 1 Locating Vertical Asymptotes of Rational Functions

If $f(x) = n(x)/d(x)$ is a rational function, $d(c) = 0$ and $n(c) \neq 0$, then the line $x = c$ is a vertical asymptote of the graph of f.

If $f(x) = n(x)/d(x)$ and both $n(c) = 0$ and $d(c) = 0$, then the limit of $f(x)$ as x approaches c involves an indeterminate form and Theorem 1 does not apply:

$$\lim_{x \to c} f(x) = \lim_{x \to c} \frac{n(x)}{d(x)} \qquad \frac{0}{0} \text{ indeterminate form}$$

Algebraic simplification is often useful in this situation.

EXAMPLE 1 **Locating Vertical Asymptotes** Let $f(x) = \dfrac{x^2 + x - 2}{x^2 - 1}$.

Reminder:

We no longer write "does not exist" for limits of ∞ or $-\infty$.

Describe the behavior of f at each zero of the denominator. Use ∞ and $-\infty$ when appropriate. Identify all vertical asymptotes.

SOLUTION Let $n(x) = x^2 + x - 2$ and $d(x) = x^2 - 1$. Factoring the denominator, we see that

$$d(x) = x^2 - 1 = (x - 1)(x + 1)$$

has two zeros: $x = -1$ and $x = 1$.

First, we consider $x = -1$. Since $d(-1) = 0$ and $n(-1) = -2 \neq 0$, Theorem 1 tells us that the line $x = -1$ is a vertical asymptote. So at least one of the one-sided limits at $x = -1$ must be either ∞ or $-\infty$. Examining tables of values of f for x near -1 or a graph on a graphing calculator will show which is the case. From Tables 3 and 4, we see that

$$\lim_{x \to -1^-} \frac{x^2 + x - 2}{x^2 - 1} = -\infty \quad \text{and} \quad \lim_{x \to -1^+} \frac{x^2 + x - 2}{x^2 - 1} = \infty$$

Table 3

x	$f(x) = \dfrac{x^2 + x - 2}{x^2 - 1}$
-1.1	-9
-1.01	-99
-1.001	-999
-1.0001	$-9{,}999$
-1.00001	$-99{,}999$

Table 4

x	$f(x) = \dfrac{x^2 + x - 2}{x^2 - 1}$
-0.9	11
-0.99	101
-0.999	1,001
-0.9999	10,001
-0.99999	100,001

Now we consider the other zero of $d(x)$, $x = 1$. This time $n(1) = 0$ and Theorem 1 does not apply. We use algebraic simplification to investigate the behavior of the function at $x = 1$:

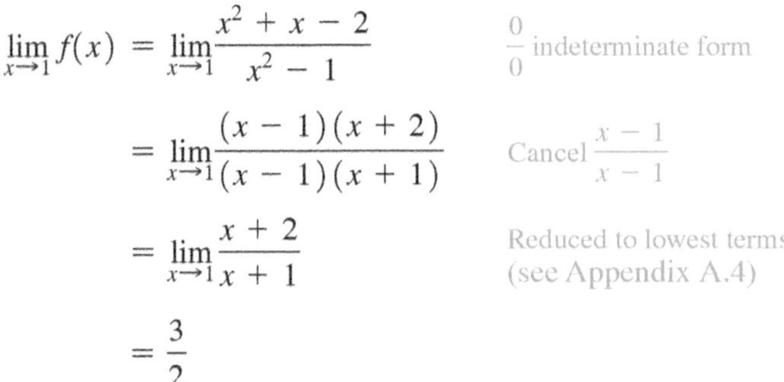

$$\lim_{x\to 1} f(x) = \lim_{x\to 1}\frac{x^2 + x - 2}{x^2 - 1} \qquad \frac{0}{0} \text{ indeterminate form}$$

$$= \lim_{x\to 1}\frac{(x-1)(x+2)}{(x-1)(x+1)} \qquad \text{Cancel } \frac{x-1}{x-1}$$

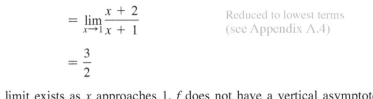

$$= \lim_{x\to 1}\frac{x+2}{x+1} \qquad \text{Reduced to lowest terms (see Appendix A.4)}$$

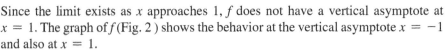

$$= \frac{3}{2}$$

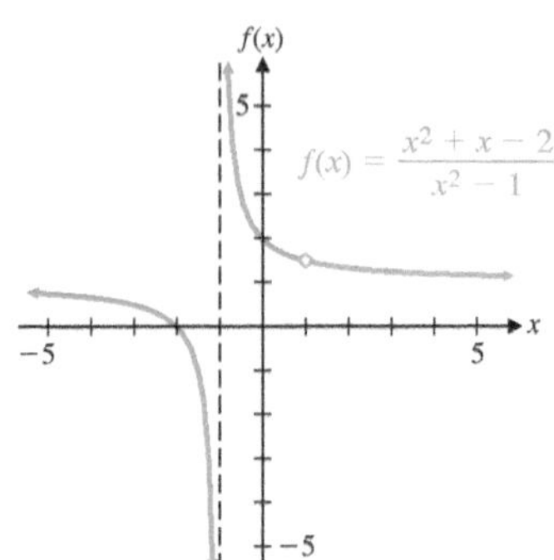

Figure 2

Since the limit exists as x approaches 1, f does not have a vertical asymptote at $x = 1$. The graph of f (Fig. 2) shows the behavior at the vertical asymptote $x = -1$ and also at $x = 1$.

Matched Problem 1 Let $f(x) = \frac{x - 3}{x^2 - 4x + 3}$.

Describe the behavior of f at each zero of the denominator. Use ∞ and $-\infty$ when appropriate. Identify all vertical asymptotes.

EXAMPLE 2 **Locating Vertical Asymptotes** Let $f(x) = \frac{x^2 + 20}{5(x-2)^2}$.

Describe the behavior of f at each zero of the denominator. Use ∞ and $-\infty$ when appropriate. Identify all vertical asymptotes.

SOLUTION Let $n(x) = x^2 + 20$ and $d(x) = 5(x-2)^2$. The only zero of $d(x)$ is $x = 2$. Since $n(2) = 24 \neq 0$, f has a vertical asymptote at $x = 2$ (Theorem 1). Tables 5 and 6 show that $f(x) \to \infty$ as $x \to 2$ from either side, and we have

$$\lim_{x\to 2^+}\frac{x^2 + 20}{5(x-2)^2} = \infty \quad \text{and} \quad \lim_{x\to 2^-}\frac{x^2 + 20}{5(x-2)^2} = \infty$$

Table 5

x	$f(x) = \frac{x^2 + 20}{5(x-2)^2}$
2.1	488.2
2.01	48,080.02
2.001	4,800,800.2

Table 6

x	$f(x) = \frac{x^2 + 20}{5(x-2)^2}$
1.9	472.2
1.99	47,920.02
1.999	4,799,200.2

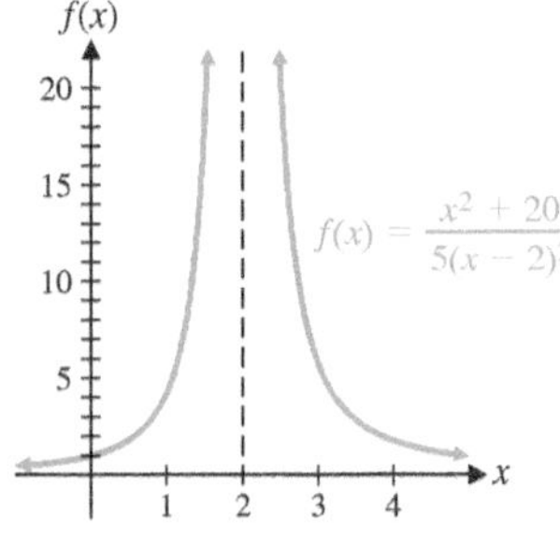

Figure 3

The denominator d has no other zeros, so f does not have any other vertical asymptotes. The graph of f (Fig. 3) shows the behavior at the vertical asymptote $x = 2$. Because the left- and right-hand limits are both infinite, we write

$$\lim_{x\to 2}\frac{x^2 + 20}{5(x-2)^2} = \infty$$

Matched Problem 2 Let $f(x) = \frac{x - 1}{(x+3)^2}$.

Describe the behavior of f at each zero of the denominator. Use ∞ and $-\infty$ when appropriate. Identify all vertical asymptotes.

CONCEPTUAL INSIGHT

When is it correct to say that a limit does not exist, and when is it correct to use ∞ or $-\infty$? It depends on the situation. Table 7 lists the infinite limits that we discussed in Examples 1 and 2.

Table 7

Right-Hand Limit	Left-Hand Limit	Two-Sided Limit
$\lim_{x\to -1^+} \frac{x^2+x-2}{x^2-1} = \infty$	$\lim_{x\to -1^-} \frac{x^2+x-2}{x^2-1} = -\infty$	$\lim_{x\to -1} \frac{x^2+x-2}{x^2-1}$ does not exist
$\lim_{x\to 2^+} \frac{x^2+20}{5(x-2)^2} = \infty$	$\lim_{x\to 2^-} \frac{x^2+20}{5(x-2)^2} = \infty$	$\lim_{x\to 2} \frac{x^2+20}{5(x-2)^2} = \infty$

The instructions in Examples 1 and 2 said that we should use infinite limits to describe the behavior at vertical asymptotes. If we had been asked to *evaluate* the limits, with no mention of ∞ or asymptotes, then the correct answer would be that **all of these limits do not exist**. Remember, ∞ is a symbol used to describe the behavior of functions at vertical asymptotes.

Limits at Infinity

The symbol ∞ can also be used to indicate that an independent variable is increasing or decreasing without bound. We write $x \to \infty$ to indicate that x is increasing without bound through positive values and $x \to -\infty$ to indicate that x is decreasing without bound through negative values. We begin by considering power functions of the form x^p and $1/x^p$ where p is a positive real number.

If p is a positive real number, then x^p increases as x increases. There is no upper bound on the values of x^p. We indicate this behavior by writing

$$\lim_{x\to\infty} x^p = \infty \quad \text{or} \quad x^p \to \infty \quad \text{as} \quad x \to \infty$$

Since the reciprocals of very large numbers are very small numbers, it follows that $1/x^p$ approaches 0 as x increases without bound. We indicate this behavior by writing

$$\lim_{x\to\infty} \frac{1}{x^p} = 0 \quad \text{or} \quad \frac{1}{x^p} \to 0 \quad \text{as} \quad x \to \infty$$

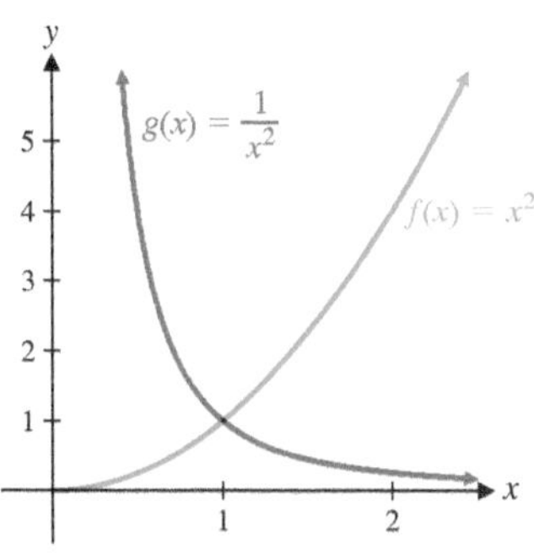

Figure 4

Figure 4 illustrates the preceding behavior for $f(x) = x^2$ and $g(x) = 1/x^2$, and we write

$$\lim_{x\to\infty} f(x) = \infty \quad \text{and} \quad \lim_{x\to\infty} g(x) = 0$$

Limits of power functions as x decreases without bound behave in a similar manner, with two important differences. First, if x is negative, then x^p is not defined for all values of p. For example, $x^{1/2} = \sqrt{x}$ is not defined for negative values of x. Second, if x^p is defined, then it may approach ∞ or $-\infty$, depending on the value of p. For example,

$$\lim_{x\to-\infty} x^2 = \infty \quad \text{but} \quad \lim_{x\to-\infty} x^3 = -\infty$$

For the function g in Figure 4, the line $y = 0$ (the x axis) is called a *horizontal asymptote*. In general, a line $y = b$ is a **horizontal asymptote** of the graph of $y = f(x)$ if $f(x)$ approaches b as either x increases without bound or x decreases without bound. Symbolically, $y = b$ is a horizontal asymptote if either

$$\lim_{x\to-\infty} f(x) = b \quad \text{or} \quad \lim_{x\to\infty} f(x) = b$$

In the first case, the graph of f will be close to the horizontal line $y = b$ for large (in absolute value) negative x. In the second case, the graph will be close to the horizontal

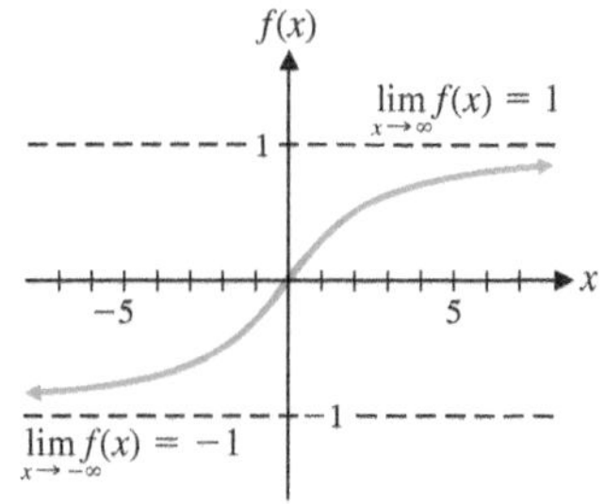

Figure 5

line $y = b$ for large positive x. Figure 5 shows the graph of a function with two horizontal asymptotes: $y = 1$ and $y = -1$.

Theorem 2 summarizes the various possibilities for limits of power functions as x increases or decreases without bound.

THEOREM 2 Limits of Power Functions at Infinity

If p is a positive real number and k is any real number except 0, then

1. $\lim_{x\to-\infty} \frac{k}{x^p} = 0$ **2.** $\lim_{x\to\infty} \frac{k}{x^p} = 0$

3. $\lim_{x\to-\infty} kx^p = \infty$ or $-\infty$ **4.** $\lim_{x\to\infty} kx^p = \infty$ or $-\infty$

provided that x^p is a real number for negative values of x. The limits in 3 and 4 will be either $-\infty$ or ∞, depending on k and p.

How can we use Theorem 2 to evaluate limits at infinity? It turns out that the limit properties listed in Theorem 2, Section 6.1, are also valid if we replace the statement $x \to c$ with $x \to \infty$ or $x \to -\infty$.

EXAMPLE 3 **Limit of a Polynomial Function at Infinity** Let $p(x) = 2x^3 - x^2 - 7x + 3$. Find the limit of $p(x)$ as x approaches ∞ and as x approaches $-\infty$.

SOLUTION Since limits of power functions of the form $1/x^p$ approach 0 as x approaches ∞ or $-\infty$, it is convenient to work with these reciprocal forms whenever possible. If we factor out the term involving the highest power of x, then we can write $p(x)$ as

$$p(x) = 2x^3\left(1 - \frac{1}{2x} - \frac{7}{2x^2} + \frac{3}{2x^3}\right)$$

Using Theorem 2 above and Theorem 2 in Section 6.1, we write

$$\lim_{x\to\infty}\left(1 - \frac{1}{2x} - \frac{7}{2x^2} + \frac{3}{2x^3}\right) = 1 - 0 - 0 + 0 = 1$$

For large values of x,

$$\left(1 - \frac{1}{2x} - \frac{7}{2x^2} + \frac{3}{2x^3}\right) \approx 1$$

and

$$p(x) = 2x^3\left(1 - \frac{1}{2x} - \frac{7}{2x^2} + \frac{3}{2x^3}\right) \approx 2x^3$$

Since $2x^3 \to \infty$ as $x \to \infty$, it follows that

$$\lim_{x\to\infty} p(x) = \lim_{x\to\infty} 2x^3 = \infty$$

Similarly, $2x^3 \to -\infty$ as $x \to -\infty$ implies that

$$\lim_{x\to-\infty} p(x) = \lim_{x\to-\infty} 2x^3 = -\infty$$

So the behavior of $p(x)$ for large values is the same as the behavior of the highest-degree term, $2x^3$.

Matched Problem 3 Let $p(x) = -4x^4 + 2x^3 + 3x$. Find the limit of $p(x)$ as x approaches ∞ and as x approaches $-\infty$.

The term with highest degree in a polynomial is called the **leading term**. In the solution to Example 3, the limits at infinity of $p(x) = 2x^3 - x^2 - 7x + 3$ were the same as the limits of the leading term $2x^3$. Theorem 3 states that this is true for any polynomial of degree greater than or equal to 1.

THEOREM 3 Limits of Polynomial Functions at Infinity

If

$$p(x) = a_n x^n + a_{n-1}x^{n-1} + \cdots + a_1 x + a_0,\ a_n \neq 0,\ n \geq 1$$

then

$$\lim_{x\to\infty} p(x) = \lim_{x\to\infty} a_n x^n = \infty \text{ or } -\infty$$

and

$$\lim_{x\to-\infty} p(x) = \lim_{x\to-\infty} a_n x^n = \infty \text{ or } -\infty$$

Each limit will be either $-\infty$ or ∞, depending on a_n and n.

A polynomial of degree 0 is a constant function $p(x) = a_0$, and its limit as x approaches ∞ or $-\infty$ is the number a_0. For any polynomial of degree 1 or greater, Theorem 3 states that the limit as x approaches ∞ or $-\infty$ cannot be equal to a number. This means that **polynomials of degree 1 or greater never have horizontal asymptotes.**

A pair of limit expressions of the form

$$\lim_{x\to\infty} f(x) = A, \quad \lim_{x\to-\infty} f(x) = B$$

where A and B are ∞, $-\infty$, or real numbers, describes the **end behavior** of the function f. The first of the two limit expressions describes the **right end behavior** and the second describes the **left end behavior**. By Theorem 3, the end behavior of any nonconstant polynomial function is described by a pair of infinite limits.

EXAMPLE 4 **End Behavior of a Polynomial** Give a pair of limit expressions that describe the end behavior of each polynomial.

(A) $p(x) = 3x^3 - 500x^2$ (B) $p(x) = 3x^3 - 500x^4$

SOLUTION

(A) By Theorem 3,

$$\lim_{x\to\infty} (3x^3 - 500x^2) = \lim_{x\to\infty} 3x^3 = \infty \qquad \text{Right end behavior}$$

and

$$\lim_{x\to-\infty} (3x^3 - 500x^2) = \lim_{x\to-\infty} 3x^3 = -\infty \qquad \text{Left end behavior}$$

(B) By Theorem 3,

$$\lim_{x\to\infty} (3x^3 - 500x^4) = \lim_{x\to\infty} (-500x^4) = -\infty \qquad \text{Right end behavior}$$

and

$$\lim_{x\to-\infty} (3x^3 - 500x^4) = \lim_{x\to-\infty} (-500x^4) = -\infty \qquad \text{Left end behavior}$$

Matched Problem 4 Give a pair of limit expressions that describe the end behavior of each polynomial.

(A) $p(x) = 300x^2 - 4x^5$ (B) $p(x) = 300x^6 - 4x^5$

EXAMPLE 5 **Sales Analysis** The total number of downloads D (in millions) of a new app t months after it is released is given by

$$D(t) = \frac{3t^2}{2t^2 + 100}.$$

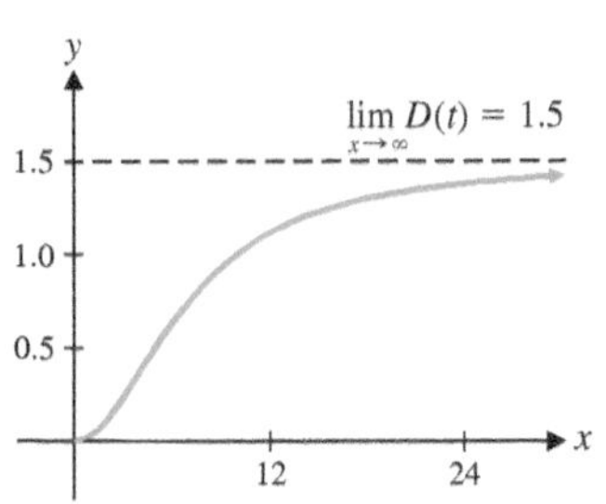

Figure 6

Find and interpret $\lim_{t\to\infty} D(t)$. Use Figure 6 to confirm your answer.

SOLUTION Factoring the highest-degree term out of the numerator and the highest-degree term out of the denominator, we write

$$D(t) = \frac{3t^2}{2t^2} \cdot \frac{1}{1 + \frac{100}{2t^2}}$$

$$\lim_{t\to\infty} D(t) = \lim_{t\to\infty} \frac{3t^2}{2t^2} \cdot \lim_{t\to\infty} \frac{1}{1 + \frac{100}{2t^2}} = \frac{3}{2} \cdot \frac{1}{1 + 0} = \frac{3}{2}.$$

Over time, the total number of downloads will approach 1.5 million. Figure 6 shows that as $t \to \infty$, $D(t) \to 1.5$.

Matched Problem 5 If the total number of downloads D (in millions) of a new app t months after it is released is given by $D(t) = \frac{4t^2}{5t^2 + 70}$, find and interpret $\lim_{t\to\infty} D(t)$.

Finding Horizontal Asymptotes

Since a rational function is the ratio of two polynomials, it is not surprising that reciprocals of powers of x can be used to analyze limits of rational functions at infinity. For example, consider the rational function

$$f(x) = \frac{3x^2 - 5x + 9}{2x^2 + 7}$$

Factoring the highest-degree term out of the numerator and the highest-degree term out of the denominator, we write

$$f(x) = \frac{3x^2}{2x^2} \cdot \frac{1 - \frac{5}{3x} + \frac{3}{x^2}}{1 + \frac{7}{2x^2}}$$

$$\lim_{x\to\infty} f(x) = \lim_{x\to\infty} \frac{3x^2}{2x^2} \cdot \lim_{x\to\infty} \frac{1 - \frac{5}{3x} + \frac{3}{x^2}}{1 + \frac{7}{2x^2}} = \frac{3}{2} \cdot \frac{1 - 0 + 0}{1 + 0} = \frac{3}{2}$$

The behavior of this rational function as x approaches infinity is determined by the ratio of the highest-degree term in the numerator ($3x^2$) to the highest-degree term in the denominator ($2x^2$). Theorem 2 can be used to generalize this result to any rational function. Theorem 4 lists the three possible outcomes.

THEOREM 4 Limits of Rational Functions at Infinity and Horizontal Asymptotes of Rational Functions

(A) If $f(x) = \dfrac{a_m x^m + a_{m-1}x^{m-1} + \cdots + a_1 x + a_0}{b_n x^n + b_{n-1}x^{n-1} + \cdots + b_1 x + b_0}$, $a_m \neq 0, b_n \neq 0$

then $\lim_{x\to\infty} f(x) = \lim_{x\to\infty} \dfrac{a_m x^m}{b_n x^n}$ and $\lim_{x\to-\infty} f(x) = \lim_{x\to-\infty} \dfrac{a_m x^m}{b_n x^n}$

(B) There are three possible cases for these limits:

1. If $m < n$, then $\lim_{x\to\infty} f(x) = \lim_{x\to-\infty} f(x) = 0$, and the line $y = 0$ (the x axis) is a horizontal asymptote of $f(x)$.
2. If $m = n$, then $\lim_{x\to\infty} f(x) = \lim_{x\to-\infty} f(x) = \dfrac{a_m}{b_n}$, and the line $y = \dfrac{a_m}{b_n}$ is a horizontal asymptote of $f(x)$.
3. If $m > n$, then each limit will be ∞ or $-\infty$, depending on m, n, a_m, and b_n, and $f(x)$ does not have a horizontal asymptote.

Notice that in cases 1 and 2 of Theorem 4, the limit is the same if x approaches ∞ or $-\infty$. So, **a rational function can have at most one horizontal asymptote** (see Fig. 7).

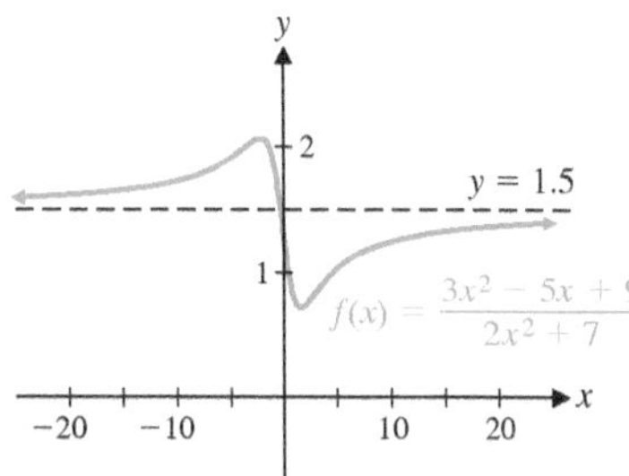

Figure 7

CONCEPTUAL INSIGHT

The graph of f in Figure 7 dispels the misconception that the graph of a function cannot cross a horizontal asymptote. Horizontal asymptotes give us information about the graph of a function only as $x \to \infty$ and $x \to -\infty$, not at any specific value of x.

EXAMPLE 6 **Finding Horizontal Asymptotes** Find all horizontal asymptotes, if any, of each function.

(A) $f(x) = \dfrac{5x^3 - 2x^2 + 1}{4x^3 + 2x - 7}$

(B) $f(x) = \dfrac{3x^4 - x^2 + 1}{8x^6 - 10}$

(C) $f(x) = \dfrac{2x^5 - x^3 - 1}{6x^3 + 2x^2 - 7}$

SOLUTION We will make use of part A of Theorem 4.

(A) $\lim_{x\to\infty} f(x) = \lim_{x\to\infty} \frac{5x^3 - 2x^2 + 1}{4x^3 + 2x - 7} = \lim_{x\to\infty} \frac{5x^3}{4x^3} = \frac{5}{4}$

The line $y = 5/4$ is a horizontal asymptote of $f(x)$. We may also use Theorem 4, part B2.

(B) $\lim_{x\to\infty} f(x) = \lim_{x\to\infty} \frac{3x^4 - x^2 + 1}{8x^6 - 10} = \lim_{x\to\infty} \frac{3x^4}{8x^6} = \lim_{x\to\infty} \frac{3}{8x^2} = 0$

The line $y = 0$ (the x axis) is a horizontal asymptote of $f(x)$. We may also use Theorem 4, part B1.

(C) $\lim_{x\to\infty} f(x) = \lim_{x\to\infty} \frac{2x^5 - x^3 - 1}{6x^3 + 2x^2 - 7} = \lim_{x\to\infty} \frac{2x^5}{6x^3} = \lim_{x\to\infty} \frac{x^2}{3} = \infty$

The function $f(x)$ has no horizontal asymptotes. This agrees with Theorem 4, part B3.

Matched Problem 6 Find all horizontal asymptotes, if any, of each function.

(A) $f(x) = \frac{4x^3 - 5x + 8}{2x^4 - 7}$ (B) $f(x) = \frac{5x^6 + 3x}{2x^5 - x - 5}$

(C) $f(x) = \frac{2x^3 - x + 7}{4x^3 + 3x^2 - 100}$

An accurate sketch of the graph of a rational function requires knowledge of both vertical and horizontal asymptotes. As we mentioned earlier, we are postponing a detailed discussion of graphing techniques until Section 8.4.

EXAMPLE 7 Find all vertical and horizontal asymptotes of the function

$$f(x) = \frac{2x^2 - 5}{x^2 + 5x + 4}$$

SOLUTION Let $n(x) = 2x^2 - 5$ and $d(x) = x^2 + 5x + 4 = (x + 1)(x + 4)$. The denominator $d(x) = 0$ at $x = -1$ and $x = -4$. Since the numerator $n(x)$ is not zero at these values of x [$n(-1) = -3$ and $n(-4) = 27$], by Theorem 1 there are two vertical asymptotes of f: the line $x = -1$ and the line $x = -4$. Since

$$\lim_{x\to\infty} f(x) = \lim_{x\to\infty} \frac{2x^2 - 5}{x^2 + 5x + 4} = \lim_{x\to\infty} \frac{2x^2}{x^2} = 2$$

the horizontal asymptote is the line $y = 2$ (Theorem 3).

Matched Problem 7 Find all vertical and horizontal asymptotes of the function $f(x) = \frac{x^2 - 9}{x^2 - 4}$.

Exercises 6.2

Skills Warm-up Exercises

W *In Problems 1–8, find an equation of the form $Ax + By = C$ for the given line.*

1. The horizontal line through $(0, 4)$
2. The vertical line through $(5, 0)$
3. The vertical line through $(-6, 3)$
4. The horizontal line through $(7, 1)$
5. The line through $(-2, 9)$ that has slope 2
6. The line through $(4, -5)$ that has slope -6
7. The line through $(9, 0)$ and $(0, 7)$
8. The line through $(-1, 20)$ and $(1, 30)$

A *Problems 9–16 refer to the following graph of $y = f(x)$.*

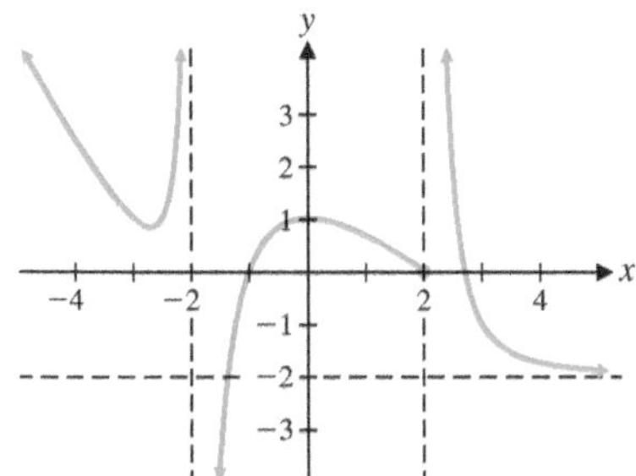

Figure for 9–16

9. $\lim_{x\to\infty} f(x) = ?$
10. $\lim_{x\to-\infty} f(x) = ?$
11. $\lim_{x\to-2^+} f(x) = ?$
12. $\lim_{x\to-2^-} f(x) = ?$
13. $\lim_{x\to-2} f(x) = ?$
14. $\lim_{x\to2^+} f(x) = ?$
15. $\lim_{x\to2^-} f(x) = ?$
16. $\lim_{x\to2} f(x) = ?$

In Problems 17–24, find each limit. Use $-\infty$ and ∞ when appropriate.

17. $f(x) = \dfrac{x}{x-5}$

(A) $\lim_{x\to5^-} f(x)$ (B) $\lim_{x\to5^+} f(x)$ (C) $\lim_{x\to5} f(x)$

18. $f(x) = \dfrac{x^2}{x+3}$

(A) $\lim_{x\to-3^-} f(x)$ (B) $\lim_{x\to-3^+} f(x)$ (C) $\lim_{x\to-3} f(x)$

19. $f(x) = \dfrac{4-5x}{(x-6)^2}$

(A) $\lim_{x\to6^-} f(x)$ (B) $\lim_{x\to6^+} f(x)$ (C) $\lim_{x\to6} f(x)$

20. $f(x) = \dfrac{2x+2}{(x+2)^2}$

(A) $\lim_{x\to-2^-} f(x)$ (B) $\lim_{x\to-2^+} f(x)$ (C) $\lim_{x\to-2} f(x)$

21. $f(x) = \dfrac{x^2+x-2}{x-1}$

(A) $\lim_{x\to1^-} f(x)$ (B) $\lim_{x\to1^+} f(x)$ (C) $\lim_{x\to1} f(x)$

22. $f(x) = \dfrac{x^2+x+2}{x-1}$

(A) $\lim_{x\to1^-} f(x)$ (B) $\lim_{x\to1^+} f(x)$ (C) $\lim_{x\to1} f(x)$

23. $f(x) = \dfrac{x^2-3x+2}{x+2}$

(A) $\lim_{x\to-2^-} f(x)$ (B) $\lim_{x\to-2^+} f(x)$ (C) $\lim_{x\to-2} f(x)$

24. $f(x) = \dfrac{x^2+x-2}{x+2}$

(A) $\lim_{x\to-2^-} f(x)$ (B) $\lim_{x\to-2^+} f(x)$ (C) $\lim_{x\to-2} f(x)$

In Problems 25–32, find (A) the leading term of the polynomial, (B) the limit as x approaches ∞, and (C) the limit as x approaches $-\infty$.

25. $p(x) = 15 + 3x^2 - 5x^3$
26. $p(x) = 10 - x^6 + 7x^3$
27. $p(x) = 9x^2 - 6x^4 + 7x$
28. $p(x) = -x^5 + 2x^3 + 9x$
29. $p(x) = x^2 + 7x + 12$
30. $p(x) = 5x + x^3 - 8x^2$
31. $p(x) = x^4 + 2x^5 - 11x$
32. $p(x) = 2 - 3x^4 - 5x^6$

B *In Problems 33–40, find each function value and limit. Use $-\infty$ or ∞ where appropriate.*

33. $f(x) = \dfrac{4x+7}{5x-9}$

(A) $f(10)$ (B) $f(100)$ (C) $\lim_{x\to\infty} f(x)$

34. $f(x) = \dfrac{2-3x^3}{7+4x^3}$

(A) $f(5)$ (B) $f(10)$ (C) $\lim_{x\to\infty} f(x)$

35. $f(x) = \dfrac{5x^2+11}{7x-2}$

(A) $f(20)$ (B) $f(50)$ (C) $\lim_{x\to\infty} f(x)$

36. $f(x) = \dfrac{5x+11}{7x^3-2}$

(A) $f(-8)$ (B) $f(-16)$ (C) $\lim_{x\to-\infty} f(x)$

37. $f(x) = \dfrac{7x^4-14x^2}{6x^5+3}$

(A) $f(-6)$ (B) $f(-12)$ (C) $\lim_{x\to-\infty} f(x)$

38. $f(x) = \dfrac{4x^7-8x}{6x^4+9x^2}$

(A) $f(-3)$ (B) $f(-6)$ (C) $\lim_{x\to-\infty} f(x)$

39. $f(x) = \dfrac{10-7x^3}{4+x^3}$

(A) $f(-10)$ (B) $f(-20)$ (C) $\lim_{x\to-\infty} f(x)$

40. $f(x) = \dfrac{3+x}{5+4x}$

(A) $f(-50)$ (B) $f(-100)$ (C) $\lim_{x\to-\infty} f(x)$

In Problems 41–50, use $-\infty$ or ∞ where appropriate to describe the behavior at each zero of the denominator and identify all vertical asymptotes.

41. $f(x) = \dfrac{3x}{x-2}$
42. $f(x) = \dfrac{2x}{x-5}$

43. $f(x) = \frac{x+1}{x^2-1}$

44. $f(x) = \frac{x-3}{x^2+9}$

45. $f(x) = \frac{x-3}{x^2+1}$

46. $f(x) = \frac{x-5}{x^2-16}$

47. $f(x) = \frac{x^2-4x-21}{x^2-3x-10}$

48. $f(x) = \frac{x^2-1}{x^3+3x^2+2x}$

49. $f(x) = \frac{x^2-4}{x^3+x^2-2x}$

50. $f(x) = \frac{x^2+2x-15}{x^2+2x-8}$

In Problems 51–64, find all horizontal and vertical asymptotes.

51. $f(x) = \frac{2x}{x+2}$

52. $f(x) = \frac{3x+2}{x-4}$

53. $f(x) = \frac{x^2+1}{x^2-1}$

54. $f(x) = \frac{9-x^2}{9+x^2}$

55. $f(x) = \frac{x^3}{x^2+6}$

56. $f(x) = \frac{x}{x^2-4}$

57. $f(x) = \frac{x}{x^2+4}$

58. $f(x) = \frac{x^2+9}{x}$

59. $f(x) = \frac{x^2}{x-3}$

60. $f(x) = \frac{x+5}{x^2}$

61. $f(x) = \frac{2x^2+3x-2}{x^2-x-2}$

62. $f(x) = \frac{2x^2+7x+12}{2x^2+5x-12}$

63. $f(x) = \frac{3x^2-x-2}{x^2-5x+4}$

64. $f(x) = \frac{x^2-x-12}{2x^2+5x-12}$

C *In Problems 65–68, give a limit expression that describes the right end behavior of the function.*

65. $f(x) = \frac{x+3}{x^2-5}$

66. $f(x) = \frac{3+4x+x^2}{5-x}$

67. $f(x) = \frac{x^2-5}{x+3}$

68. $f(x) = \frac{3x^2+1}{6x^2+5x}$

In Problems 69–72, give a limit expression that describes the left end behavior of the function.

69. $f(x) = \frac{5-2x^2}{1+8x^2}$

70. $f(x) = \frac{2x+3}{x^2-1}$

71. $f(x) = \frac{x^2+3}{4-5x}$

72. $f(x) = \frac{6-x^4}{1+2x}$

In Problems 73–78, discuss the validity of each statement. If the statement is always true, explain why. If not, give a counterexample.

73. A rational function has at least one vertical asymptote.

74. A rational function has at most one vertical asymptote.

75. A rational function has at least one horizontal asymptote.

76. A rational function has at most one horizontal asymptote.

77. A polynomial function of degree ≥ 1 has neither horizontal nor vertical asymptotes.

78. The graph of a rational function cannot cross a horizontal asymptote.

79. Theorem 3 states that

$$\lim_{x\to\infty} (a_n x^n + a_{n-1}x^{n-1} + \cdots + a_0) = \pm\infty.$$

What conditions must n and a_n satisfy for the limit to be ∞? For the limit to be $-\infty$?

80. Theorem 3 also states that

$$\lim_{x\to-\infty} (a_n x^n + a_{n-1}x^{n-1} + \cdots + a_0) = \pm\infty.$$

What conditions must n and a_n satisfy for the limit to be ∞? For the limit to be $-\infty$?

Applications

81. **Average cost.** A small company manufacturing chairs has fixed costs of $300 per day and total costs of $1,500 per day for a daily output of 30 chairs.

(A) Assuming that the total cost per day $C(x)$ is linearly related to the total output per day x, write an equation for the cost function.

(B) The average cost per chair for an output of x chairs is given by $\overline{C}(x) = C(x)/x$. Find the average cost function.

(C) Sketch a graph of the average cost function, including any asymptotes, for $1 \leq x \leq 40$.

(D) What does the average cost per chair tend to as production increases?

82. **Average cost.** A small company manufacturing tables has fixed costs of $400 per day and total costs of $2,500 per day for a daily output of 30 tables.

(A) Assuming that the total cost per day $C(x)$ is linearly related to the total output per day x, write an equation for the cost function.

(B) The average cost per table for an output of x tables is given by $\overline{C}(x) = C(x)/x$. Find the average cost function.

(C) Sketch a graph of the average cost function, including any asymptotes, for $1 \leq x \leq 40$.

(D) What does the average cost per table tend to as production increases?

83. **Operating System Updates.** A newly released smartphone operating system gives users an update notice every time they download a new app. The percentage P of users that have installed the new update after t days is given by

$$P(t) = \frac{100t^2}{t^2+100}.$$

(A) What percentage of users have installed the new update after 5 days? After 10 days? After 20 days?

(B) What happens to $P(t)$ as $t \to \infty$?

84. Operating System Updates. A newly released smartphone operating system gives users an immediate notice to update but no further reminders. The percent P of users that have installed the new update after t days is given by $P(t) = \frac{99t^2}{t^2 + 50}$.

(A) What percentage of users have installed the new update after 5 days? After 10 days? After 20 days?

(B) What happens to $P(t)$ as $t \to \infty$?

85. Drug concentration. A drug is administered to a patient through an IV drip. The drug concentration (in milligrams/milliliter) in the bloodstream t hours after the drip was started by $C(t) = \frac{5t^2(t + 50)}{t^3 + 100}$. Find and interpret $\lim_{t\to\infty} C(t)$.

86. Drug concentration. A drug is administered to a patient through an injection. The drug concentration (in milligrams/milliliter) in the bloodstream t hours after the injection is given by $C(t) = \frac{5t(t + 50)}{t^3 + 100}$. Find and interpret $\lim_{t\to\infty} C(t)$.

87. Pollution. In Silicon Valley, a number of computer-related manufacturing firms were contaminating underground water supplies with toxic chemicals stored in leaking underground containers. A water quality control agency ordered the companies to take immediate corrective action and contribute to a monetary pool for the testing and cleanup of the underground contamination. Suppose that the monetary pool (in millions of dollars) for the testing and cleanup is given by

$$P(x) = \frac{2x}{1 - x} \qquad 0 \le x < 1$$

where x is the percentage (expressed as a decimal) of the total contaminant removed.

(A) How much must be in the pool to remove 90% of the contaminant?

(B) How much must be in the pool to remove 95% of the contaminant?

(C) Find $\lim_{x\to 1^-} P(x)$ and discuss the implications of this limit.

88. Employee training. A company producing computer components has established that, on average, a new employee can assemble $N(t)$ components per day after t days of on-the-job training, as given by

$$N(t) = \frac{100t}{t + 9} \qquad t \ge 0$$

(A) How many components per day can a new employee assemble after 6 days of on-the-job training?

(B) How many days of on-the-job training will a new employee need to reach the level of 70 components per day?

(C) Find $\lim_{t\to\infty} N(t)$ and discuss the implications of this limit.

89. Biochemistry. In 1913, biochemists Leonor Michaelis and Maude Menten proposed the rational function model (see figure)

$$v(s) = \frac{V_{max}\, s}{K_M + s}$$

for the velocity of the enzymatic reaction v, where s is the substrate concentration. The constants V_{max} and K_M are determined from experimental data.

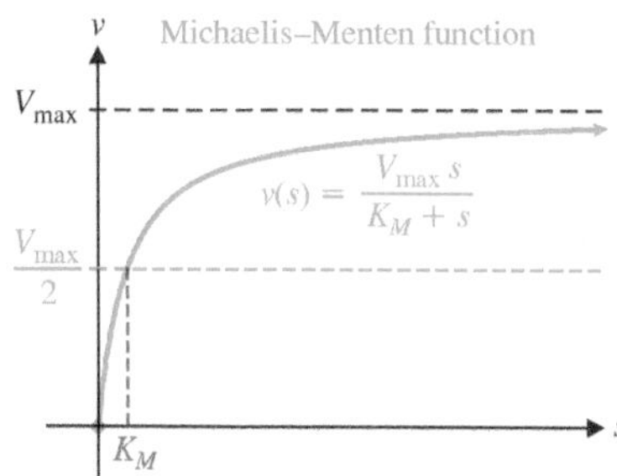

(A) Show that $\lim_{s\to\infty} v(s) = V_{max}$.

(B) Show that $v(K_M) = \frac{V_{max}}{2}$.

(C) Table 8 (*Source:* Michaelis and Menten (1913) *Biochem. Z.* 49, 333–369) lists data for the substrate saccharose treated with an enzyme.

Table 8

s	v
5.2	0.866
10.4	1.466
20.8	2.114
41.6	2.666
83.3	3.236
167	3.636
333	3.636

Plot the points in Table 8 on graph paper and estimate V_{max} to the nearest integer. To estimate K_M, add the horizontal line $v = \frac{V_{max}}{2}$ to your graph, connect successive points on the graph with straight-line segments, and estimate the value of s (to the nearest multiple of 10) that satisfies $v(s) = \frac{V_{max}}{2}$.

(D) Use the constants V_{max} and K_M from part (C) to form a Michaelis–Menten function for the data in Table 8.

(E) Use the function from part (D) to estimate the velocity of the enzyme reaction when the saccharose is 15 and to estimate the saccharose when the velocity is 3.

90. Biochemistry. Table 9 (*Source:* Institute of Chemistry, Macedonia) lists data for the substrate sucrose treated with the enzyme invertase. We want to model these data with a Michaelis–Menten function.

Table 9

s	v
2.92	18.2
5.84	26.5
8.76	31.1
11.7	33
14.6	34.9
17.5	37.2
23.4	37.1

(A) Plot the points in Table 9 on graph paper and estimate V_{max} to the nearest integer. To estimate K_M, add the horizontal line $v = \frac{V_{max}}{2}$ to your graph, connect successive points on the graph with straight-line segments, and estimate the value of s (to the nearest integer) that satisfies $v(s) = \frac{V_{max}}{2}$.

(B) Use the constants V_{max} and K_M from part (A) to form a Michaelis–Menten function for the data in Table 9.

(C) Use the function from part (B) to estimate the velocity of the enzyme reaction when the sucrose is 9 and to estimate the sucrose when the velocity is 32.

91. **Physics.** The coefficient of thermal expansion (CTE) is a measure of the expansion of an object subjected to extreme temperatures. To model this coefficient, we use a Michaelis–Menten function of the form

$$C(T) = \frac{C_{max}T}{M + T} \qquad \text{(Problem 89)}$$

where C = CTE, T is temperature in K (degrees Kelvin), and C_{max} and M are constants. Table 10 (*Source:* National Physical Laboratory) lists the coefficients of thermal expansion for nickel and for copper at various temperatures.

Table 10 **Coefficients of Thermal Expansion**

T (K)	Nickel	Copper
100	6.6	10.3
200	11.3	15.2
293	13.4	16.5
500	15.3	18.3
800	16.8	20.3
1,100	17.8	23.7

(A) Plot the points in columns 1 and 2 of Table 10 on graph paper and estimate C_{max} to the nearest integer. To estimate M, add the horizontal line CTE $= \frac{C_{max}}{2}$ to your graph, connect successive points on the graph with straight-line segments, and estimate the value of T (to the nearest multiple of fifty) that satisfies $C(T) = \frac{C_{max}}{2}$.

(B) Use the constants $\frac{C_{max}}{2}$ and M from part (A) to form a Michaelis–Menten function for the CTE of nickel.

(C) Use the function from part (B) to estimate the CTE of nickel at 600 K and to estimate the temperature when the CTE of nickel is 12.

92. **Physics.** Repeat Problem 91 for the CTE of copper (column 3 of Table 10).

Answers to Matched Problems

1. Vertical asymptote: $x = 1$; $\lim_{x\to 1^+} f(x) = \infty$, $\lim_{x\to 1^-} f(x) = -\infty$ $\lim_{x\to 3} f(x) = 1/2$ so f does not have a vertical asymptote at $x = 3$
2. Vertical asymptote: $x = -3$; $\lim_{x\to -3^+} f(x) = \lim_{x\to -3^-} f(x) = -\infty$
3. $\lim_{x\to\infty} p(x) = \lim_{x\to -\infty} p(x) = -\infty$
4. (A) $\lim_{x\to\infty} p(x) = -\infty$, $\lim_{x\to -\infty} p(x) = \infty$
   (B) $\lim_{x\to\infty} p(x) = \infty$, $\lim_{x\to -\infty} p(x) = \infty$
5. $\lim_{t\to\infty} D(t) = 0.8$; Over time, the total number of downloads will approach 0.8 million.
6. (A) $y = 0$ (B) No horizontal asymptotes
   (C) $y = 1/2$
7. Vertical asymptotes: $x = -2, x = 2$; horizontal asymptote: $y = 1$

6.3 Continuity

- Continuity
- Continuity Properties
- Solving Inequalities Using Continuity Properties

Theorem 3 in Section 6.1 states that if f is a polynomial function or a rational function with a nonzero denominator at $x = c$, then

$$\lim_{x\to c} f(x) = f(c) \qquad (1)$$

Functions that satisfy equation (1) are said to be *continuous* at $x = c$. A firm understanding of continuous functions is essential for sketching and analyzing graphs. We will also see that continuity properties provide a simple and efficient method for solving inequalities—a tool that we will use extensively in later sections.

Continuity

Compare the graphs shown in Figure 1. Notice that two of the graphs are broken; that is, they cannot be drawn without lifting a pen off the paper. Informally, a function is *continuous over an interval* if its graph over the interval can be drawn without removing a pen from the paper. A function whose graph is broken (disconnected) at $x = c$ is said to be *discontinuous* at $x = c$. Function f (Fig. 1A) is continuous for all x. Function g (Fig. 1B) is discontinuous at $x = 2$ but is continuous over any interval that does not include 2. Function h (Fig. 1C) is discontinuous at $x = 0$ but is continuous over any interval that does not include 0.

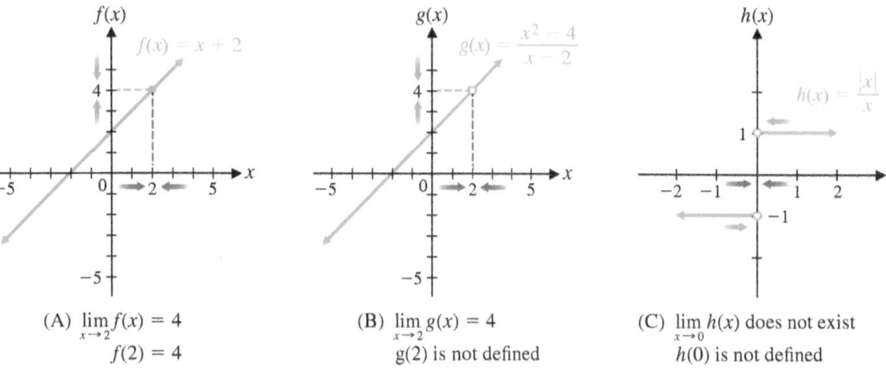

(A) $\lim_{x \to 2} f(x) = 4$, $f(2) = 4$
(B) $\lim_{x \to 2} g(x) = 4$, $g(2)$ is not defined
(C) $\lim_{x \to 0} h(x)$ does not exist, $h(0)$ is not defined

Figure 1

Most graphs of natural phenomena are continuous, whereas many graphs in business and economics applications have discontinuities. Figure 2A illustrates temperature variation over a 24-hour period—a continuous phenomenon. Figure 2B illustrates warehouse inventory over a 1-week period—a discontinuous phenomenon.

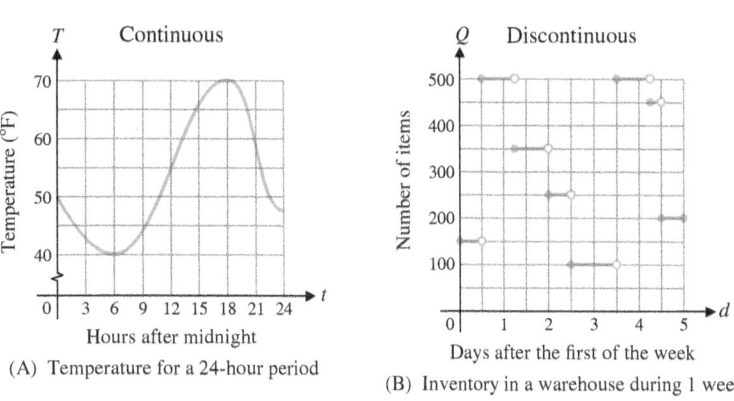

(A) Temperature for a 24-hour period
(B) Inventory in a warehouse during 1 week

Figure 2

Explore and Discuss 1

(A) Write a brief verbal description of the temperature variation illustrated in Figure 2A, including estimates of the high and low temperatures during the period shown and the times at which they occurred.

(B) Write a brief verbal description of the changes in inventory illustrated in Figure 2B, including estimates of the changes in inventory and the times at which those changes occurred.

The preceding discussion leads to the following formal definition of continuity:

Reminder:

We use (a, b) to represent all points between $x = a$ and $x = b$, not including a and b. See Table 1 in Section 1.1 for a review of interval notation.

DEFINITION Continuity

A function f is **continuous at the point $x = c$ if**

1. $\lim_{x \to c} f(x)$ exists **2.** $f(c)$ exists **3.** $\lim_{x \to c} f(x) = f(c)$

A function is **continuous on the open interval (a, b)** if it is continuous at each point on the interval.

If one or more of the three conditions in the definition fails, then the function is **discontinuous** at $x = c$.

EXAMPLE 1

Continuity of a Function Defined by a Graph Use the definition of continuity to discuss the continuity of the function whose graph is shown in Figure 3.

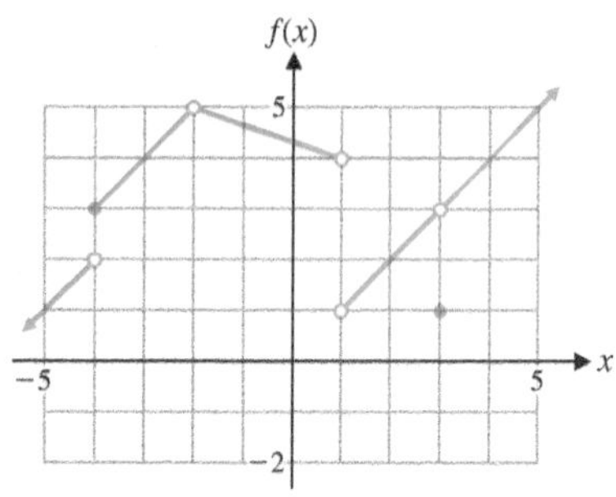

Figure 3

SOLUTION We begin by identifying the points of discontinuity. Examining the graph, we see breaks or holes at $x = -4, -2, 1$, and 3. Now we must determine which conditions in the definition of continuity are not satisfied at each of these points. In each case, we find the value of the function and the limit of the function at the point in question.

Discontinuity at $x = -4$:

$$\lim_{x \to -4^-} f(x) = 2$$
$$\lim_{x \to -4^+} f(x) = 3$$
$$\lim_{x \to -4} f(x) \text{ does not exist}$$
$$f(-4) = 3$$

Since the one-sided limits are different, the limit does not exist (Section 6.1).

So, f is not continuous at $x = -4$ because condition 1 is not satisfied.

Discontinuity at $x = -2$:

$$\lim_{x \to -2^-} f(x) = 5$$
$$\lim_{x \to -2^+} f(x) = 5$$
$$\lim_{x \to -2} f(x) = 5$$
$$f(-2) \text{ does not exist}$$

The hole at $(-2, 5)$ indicates that 5 is not the value of f at -2. Since there is no solid dot elsewhere on the vertical line $x = -2$, $f(-2)$ is not defined.

So even though the limit as x approaches -2 exists, f is not continuous at $x = -2$ because condition 2 is not satisfied.

Discontinuity at $x = 1$:

$$\lim_{x \to 1^-} f(x) = 4$$
$$\lim_{x \to 1^+} f(x) = 1$$
$$\lim_{x \to 1} f(x) \text{ does not exist}$$
$$f(1) \text{ does not exist}$$

This time, f is not continuous at $x = 1$ because neither of conditions 1 and 2 is satisfied.

Discontinuity at $x = 3$:

$$\lim_{x \to 3^-} f(x) = 3$$
$$\lim_{x \to 3^+} f(x) = 3$$
$$\lim_{x \to 3} f(x) = 3$$
$$f(3) = 1$$

The solid dot at (3, 1) indicates that $f(3) = 1$.

Conditions 1 and 2 are satisfied, but f is not continuous at $x = 3$ because condition 3 is not satisfied.

Having identified and discussed all points of discontinuity, we can now conclude that f is continuous except at $x = -4, -2, 1$, and 3.

CONCEPTUAL INSIGHT

Rather than list the points where a function is discontinuous, sometimes it is useful to state the intervals on which the function is continuous. Using the set operation **union,** denoted by $\cup$, we can express the set of points where the function in Example 1 is continuous as follows:

$$(-\infty, -4) \cup (-4, -2) \cup (-2, 1) \cup (1, 3) \cup (3, \infty)$$

Matched Problem 1 Use the definition of continuity to discuss the continuity of the function whose graph is shown in Figure 4.

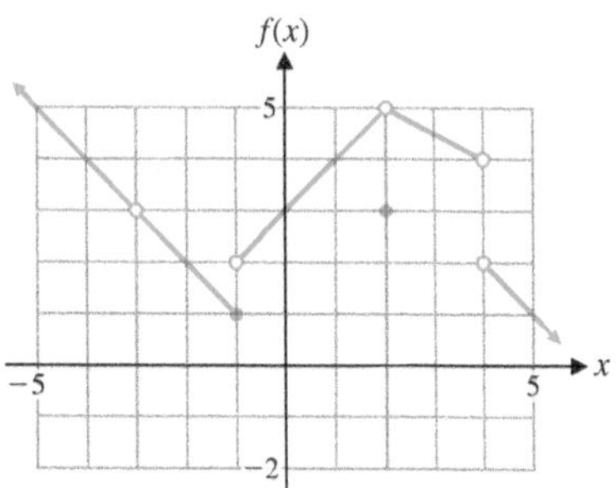

Figure 4

For functions defined by equations, it is important to be able to locate points of discontinuity by examining the equation.

EXAMPLE 2 **Continuity of Functions Defined by Equations** Using the definition of continuity, discuss the continuity of each function at the indicated point(s).

(A) $f(x) = x + 2$ at $x = 2$

(B) $g(x) = \dfrac{x^2 - 4}{x - 2}$ at $x = 2$

(C) $h(x) = \dfrac{|x|}{x}$ at $x = 0$ and at $x = 1$

SOLUTION

(A) f is continuous at $x = 2$, since

$$\lim_{x \to 2} f(x) = 4 = f(2) \qquad \text{See Figure 1A.}$$

(B) g is not continuous at $x = 2$, since $g(2) = 0/0$ is not defined. See Figure 1B.

(C) h is not continuous at $x = 0$, since $h(0) = |0|/0$ is not defined; also, $\lim_{x \to 0} h(x)$ does not exist.

h is continuous at $x = 1$, since

$$\lim_{x \to 1} \frac{|x|}{x} = 1 = h(1) \qquad \text{See Figure 1C.}$$

Matched Problem 2 Using the definition of continuity, discuss the continuity of each function at the indicated point(s).

(A) $f(x) = x + 1$ at $x = 1$

(B) $g(x) = \dfrac{x^2 - 1}{x - 1}$ at $x = 1$

(C) $h(x) = \dfrac{x - 2}{|x - 2|}$ at $x = 2$ and at $x = 0$

We can also talk about one-sided continuity, just as we talked about one-sided limits. For example, a function is said to be **continuous on the right** at $x = c$ if $\lim_{x \to c^+} f(x) = f(c)$ and **continuous on the left** at $x = c$ if $\lim_{x \to c^-} f(x) = f(c)$. A function is **continuous on the closed interval [a, b]** if it is continuous on the open interval (a, b) and is continuous both on the right at a and on the left at b.

Figure 5A illustrates a function that is continuous on the closed interval $[-1, 1]$. Figure 5B illustrates a function that is continuous on the half-closed interval $[0, \infty)$.

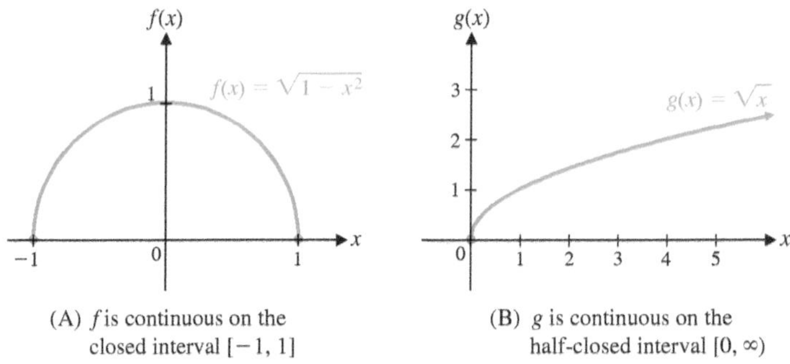

Figure 5 Continuity on closed and half-closed intervals

Continuity Properties

Functions have some useful **general continuity properties**:

PROPERTIES General Continuity properties

If two functions are continuous on the same interval, then their sum, difference, product, and quotient are continuous on the same interval except for values of x that make a denominator 0.

These properties, along with Theorem 1, enable us to determine intervals of continuity for some important classes of functions without having to look at their graphs or use the three conditions in the definition.

THEOREM 1 Continuity Properties of Some Specific Functions

(A) A constant function $f(x) = k$, where k is a constant, is continuous for all x.

$f(x) = 7$ is continuous for all x.

(B) For n a positive integer, $f(x) = x^n$ is continuous for all x.

$f(x) = x^5$ is continuous for all x.

(C) A polynomial function is continuous for all x.
$2x^3 - 3x^2 + x - 5$ is continuous for all x.

(D) A rational function is continuous for all x except those values that make a denominator 0.
$\frac{x^2 + 1}{x - 1}$ is continuous for all x except $x = 1$, a value that makes the denominator 0.

(E) For n an odd positive integer greater than 1, $\sqrt[n]{f(x)}$ is continuous wherever $f(x)$ is continuous.
$\sqrt[3]{x^2}$ is continuous for all x.

(F) For n an even positive integer, $\sqrt[n]{f(x)}$ is continuous wherever $f(x)$ is continuous and nonnegative.
$\sqrt[4]{x}$ is continuous on the interval $[0, \infty)$.

Parts (C) and (D) of Theorem 1 are the same as Theorem 3 in Section 6.1. They are repeated here to emphasize their importance.

EXAMPLE 3 **Using Continuity Properties** Using Theorem 1 and the general properties of continuity, determine where each function is continuous.

(A) $f(x) = x^2 - 2x + 1$ (B) $f(x) = \frac{x}{(x + 2)(x - 3)}$

(C) $f(x) = \sqrt[3]{x^2 - 4}$ (D) $f(x) = \sqrt{x - 2}$

SOLUTION

(A) Since f is a polynomial function, f is continuous for all x.

(B) Since f is a rational function, f is continuous for all x except -2 and 3 (values that make the denominator 0).

(C) The polynomial function $x^2 - 4$ is continuous for all x. Since $n = 3$ is odd, f is continuous for all x.

(D) The polynomial function $x - 2$ is continuous for all x and nonnegative for $x \geq 2$. Since $n = 2$ is even, f is continuous for $x \geq 2$, or on the interval $[2, \infty)$.

Matched Problem 3 Using Theorem 1 and the general properties of continuity, determine where each function is continuous.

(A) $f(x) = x^4 + 2x^2 + 1$ (B) $f(x) = \frac{x^2}{(x + 1)(x - 4)}$

(C) $f(x) = \sqrt{x - 4}$ (D) $f(x) = \sqrt[3]{x^3 + 1}$

Solving Inequalities Using Continuity Properties

One of the basic tools for analyzing graphs in calculus is a special line graph called a *sign chart*. We will make extensive use of this type of chart in later sections. In the discussion that follows, we use continuity properties to develop a simple and efficient procedure for constructing sign charts.

Suppose that a function f is continuous over the interval (1, 8) and $f(x) \neq 0$ for any x in (1, 8). Suppose also that $f(2) = 5$, a positive number. Is it possible for $f(x)$ to be negative for any x in the interval (1, 8)? The answer is "no." If $f(7)$ were -3, for example, as shown in Figure 6, then how would it be possible to join the points (2, 5) and (7, -3) with the graph of a continuous function without crossing the x axis between 1 and 8 at least once? [Crossing the x axis would violate our assumption

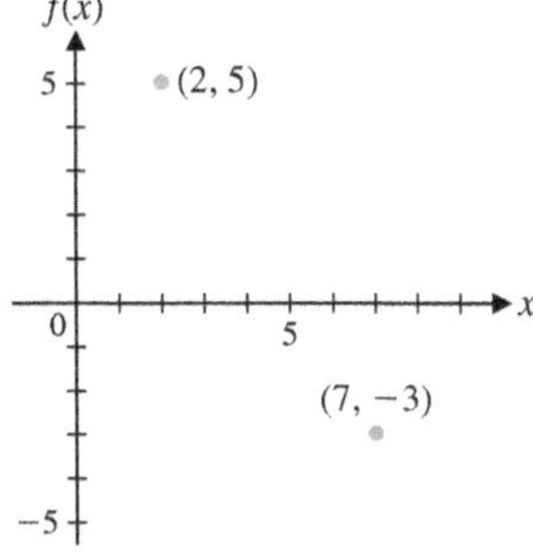

Figure 6

that $f(x) \neq 0$ for any x in $(1, 8)$.] We conclude that $f(x)$ must be positive for all x in $(1, 8)$. If $f(2)$ were negative, then, using the same type of reasoning, $f(x)$ would have to be negative over the entire interval $(1, 8)$.

In general, **if f is continuous and $f(x) \neq 0$ on the interval (a, b), then $f(x)$ cannot change sign on (a, b).** This is the essence of Theorem 2.

THEOREM 2 Sign Properties on an Interval (a, b)

If f is continuous on (a, b) and $f(x) \neq 0$ for all x in (a, b), then either $f(x) > 0$ for all x in (a, b) or $f(x) < 0$ for all x in (a, b).

Theorem 2 provides the basis for an effective method of solving many types of inequalities. Example 4 illustrates the process.

EXAMPLE 4 **Solving an Inequality** Solve $\frac{x+1}{x-2} > 0$.

SOLUTION We start by using the left side of the inequality to form the function f.

$$f(x) = \frac{x+1}{x-2}$$

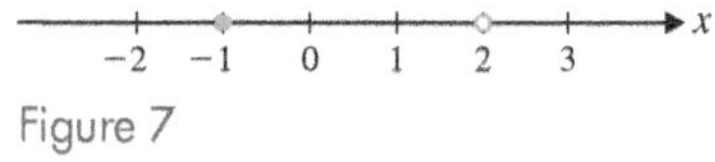

Figure 7

Test Numbers

x	$f(x)$
-2	$\frac{1}{4}$ (+)
0	$-\frac{1}{2}$ (−)
3	4 (+)

The denominator is equal to 0 if $x = 2$, and the numerator is equal to 0 if $x = -1$. So the rational function f is discontinuous at $x = 2$, and $f(x) = 0$ for $x = -1$ (a fraction is 0 when the numerator is 0 and the denominator is not 0). We plot $x = 2$ and $x = -1$, which we call *partition numbers*, on a real number line (Fig. 7). (Note that the dot at 2 is open because the function is not defined at $x = 2$.) The partition numbers 2 and -1 determine three open intervals: $(-\infty, -1)$, $(-1, 2)$, and $(2, \infty)$. The function f is continuous and nonzero on each of these intervals. From Theorem 2, we know that $f(x)$ does not change sign on any of these intervals. We can find the sign of $f(x)$ on each of the intervals by selecting a **test number** in each interval and evaluating $f(x)$ at that number. Since any number in each subinterval will do, we choose test numbers that are easy to evaluate: -2, 0, and 3. The table in the margin shows the results.

The sign of $f(x)$ at each test number is the same as the sign of $f(x)$ over the interval containing that test number. Using this information, we construct a **sign chart** for $f(x)$ as shown in Figure 8.

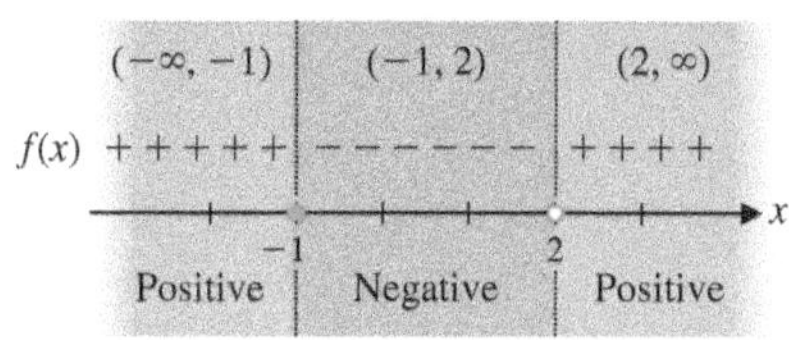

Figure 8

From the sign chart, we can easily write the solution of the given nonlinear inequality:

$f(x) > 0$	for	$x < -1$ or $x > 2$	Inequality notation
		$(-\infty, -1) \cup (2, \infty)$	Interval notation

Matched Problem 4 Solve $\frac{x^2 - 1}{x - 3} < 0$.

Most of the inequalities we encounter will involve strict inequalities ($>$ or $<$). If it is necessary to solve inequalities of the form $\geq$ or $\leq$, we simply include the endpoint x of any interval if f is defined at x and $f(x)$ satisfies the given inequality. For example, from the sign chart in Figure 8, the solution of the inequality

$$\frac{x+1}{x-2} \geq 0 \quad \text{is} \quad \begin{matrix} x \leq -1 \quad \text{or} \quad x > 2 & \text{Inequality notation} \\ (-\infty, -1] \cup (2, \infty) & \text{Interval notation} \end{matrix}$$

Example 4 illustrates a general procedure for constructing sign charts.

DEFINITION

A real number x is a **partition number** for a function f if f is discontinuous at x or $f(x) = 0$.

Suppose that p_1 and p_2 are consecutive partition numbers for f; that is, there are no partition numbers in the open interval (p_1, p_2). Then f is continuous on (p_1, p_2) [since there are no points of discontinuity in that interval], so f does not change sign on (p_1, p_2) [since $f(x) \neq 0$ for x in that interval]. In other words, **partition numbers determine open intervals on which f does not change sign**. By using a test number from each interval, we can construct a sign chart for f on the real number line. It is then easy to solve the inequality $f(x) < 0$ or the inequality $f(x) > 0$.

We summarize the procedure for constructing sign charts in the following box.

PROCEDURE Constructing Sign Charts

Given a function f,

Step 1 Find all partition numbers of f:

(A) Find all numbers x such that f is discontinuous at x. (Rational functions are discontinuous at values of x that make a denominator 0.)

(B) Find all numbers x such that $f(x) = 0$. (For a rational function, this occurs where the numerator is 0 and the denominator is not 0.)

Step 2 Plot the numbers found in step 1 on a real number line, dividing the number line into intervals.

Step 3 Select a test number in each open interval determined in step 2 and evaluate $f(x)$ at each test number to determine whether $f(x)$ is positive $(+)$ or negative $(-)$ in each interval.

Step 4 Construct a sign chart, using the real number line in step 2. This will show the sign of $f(x)$ on each open interval.

There is an alternative to step 3 in the procedure for constructing sign charts that may save time if the function $f(x)$ is written in factored form. The key is to determine the sign of each factor in the numerator and denominator of $f(x)$. We will illustrate with Example 4. The partition numbers -1 and 2 divide the x axis into three open intervals. If $x > 2$, then both the numerator and denominator are positive, so $f(x) > 0$. If $-1 < x < 2$, then the numerator is positive but the denominator is negative, so $f(x) < 0$. If $x < -1$, then both the numerator and denominator are negative, so $f(x) > 0$. Of course both approaches, the test number approach and the sign of factors approach, give the same sign chart.

EXAMPLE 5 **Positive Profit** A bakery estimates its annual profits from the production and sale of x loaves of bread per year to be $P(x)$ dollars, where $P(x) = 6x - 0.001x^2 - 5000$. For which values of x does the bakery make a profit selling bread?

SOLUTION We follow the procedure for constructing a sign chart for $P(x)$. Since $P(x)$ is a polynomial, $P(x)$ is continuous everywhere. To find where $P(x) = 0$, we first factor $P(x)$.

$$P(x) = 6x - 0.001x^2 - 5000 = -0.001(x - 1000)(x - 5000)$$

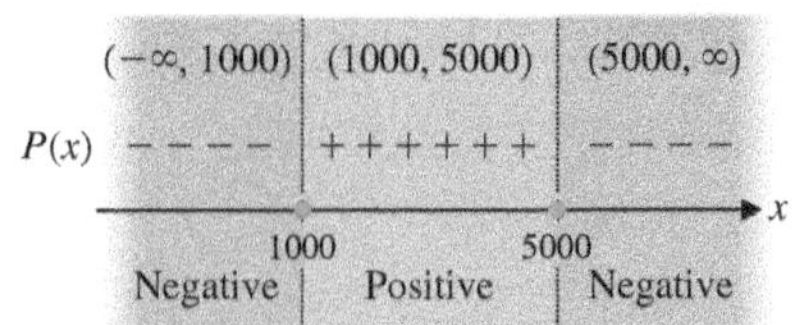

Figure 9

Test Numbers

x	$P(x)$
0	−5000 (−)
2000	3000 (+)
10000	−45000 (−)

Since $x - 1000 = 0$ when $x = 1000$ and $x - 5000 = 0$ when $x = 5000$, these are our two partition numbers.

We next plot $x = 1000$ and $x = 5000$ on the real number line and test the points $x = 0$, $x = 2000$, and $x = 10000$ to get the sign chart in Figure 9.

The annual profit from the sale of bread is positive if $1000 < x < 5000$. The bakery should make more than 1000 loaves but less than 5000 loaves of bread each year.

Matched Problem 5 The bakery estimates its annual profits from raisin bread to be $P(x) = -0.001x^2 + 7x - 6000$. For which values of x does the bakery make a profit selling raisin bread?

Exercises 6.3

Skills Warm-up Exercises

W *In Problems 1–8, use interval notation to specify the given interval.*

1. The set of all real numbers from −3 to 5, including −3 and 5

2. The set of all real numbers from −8 to −4, excluding −8 but including −4

3. $\{x \mid -10 < x < 100\}$

4. $\{x \mid 0.1 \le x \le 0.3\}$

5. $\{x \mid x^2 > 25\}$

6. $\{x \mid x^2 \ge 16\}$

7. $\{x \mid x \le -3 \text{ or } x > 4\}$

8. $\{x \mid x < 6 \text{ or } x \ge 9\}$

A *In Problems 9–14, sketch a possible graph of a function that satisfies the given conditions at $x = 1$ and discuss the continuity of f at $x = 1$.*

9. $f(1) = 2$ and $\lim_{x \to 1} f(x) = 2$

10. $f(1) = -2$ and $\lim_{x \to 1} f(x) = 2$

11. $f(1) = 2$ and $\lim_{x \to 1} f(x) = -2$

12. $f(1) = -2$ and $\lim_{x \to 1} f(x) = -2$

13. $f(1) = -2$, $\lim_{x \to 1^-} f(x) = 2$, and $\lim_{x \to 1^+} f(x) = -2$

14. $f(1) = 2$, $\lim_{x \to 1^-} f(x) = 2$, and $\lim_{x \to 1^+} f(x) = -2$

Problems 15–22 refer to the function f shown in the figure. Use the graph to estimate the indicated function values and limits.

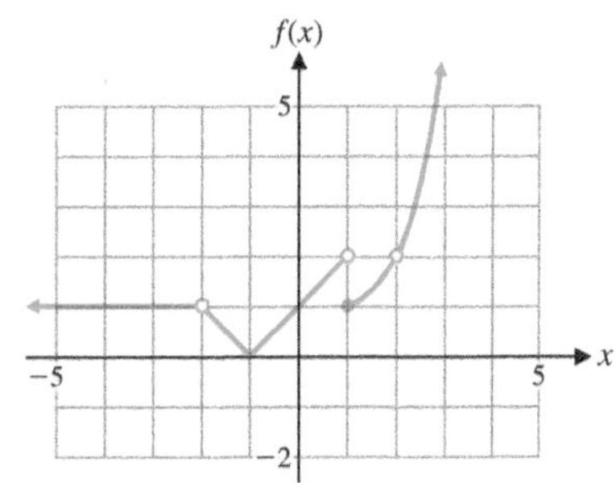

Figure for 15–22

15. $f(0.9)$

16. $f(-2.1)$

17. $f(1.1)$

18. $f(-1.9)$

19. (A) $\lim_{x \to 1^-} f(x)$ (B) $\lim_{x \to 1^+} f(x)$
(C) $\lim_{x \to 1} f(x)$ (D) $f(1)$
(E) Is f continuous at $x = 1$? Explain.

20. (A) $\lim_{x \to 2^-} f(x)$ (B) $\lim_{x \to 2^+} f(x)$
(C) $\lim_{x \to 2} f(x)$ (D) $f(2)$
(E) Is f continuous at $x = 2$? Explain.

21. (A) $\lim_{x \to -2^-} f(x)$ (B) $\lim_{x \to -2^+} f(x)$
(C) $\lim_{x \to -2} f(x)$ (D) $f(-2)$
(E) Is f continuous at $x = -2$? Explain.

22. (A) $\lim_{x \to -1^-} f(x)$ (B) $\lim_{x \to -1^+} f(x)$
(C) $\lim_{x \to -1} f(x)$ (D) $f(-1)$
(E) Is f continuous at $x = -1$? Explain.

Problems 23–30 refer to the function g shown in the figure. Use the graph to estimate the indicated function values and limits.

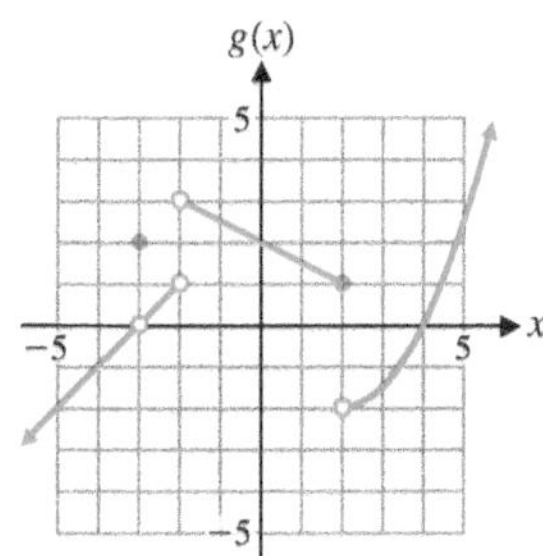

Figure for 23–30

23. $g(-3.1)$

24. $g(-2.1)$

25. $g(-2.9)$

26. $g(-1.9)$

27. (A) $\lim_{x \to -4^-} g(x)$ (B) $\lim_{x \to -4^+} g(x)$
(C) $\lim_{x \to -4} g(x)$ (D) $g(-4)$
(E) Is g continuous at $x = -4$? Explain.

28. (A) $\lim_{x \to 0^-} g(x)$ (B) $\lim_{x \to 0^+} g(x)$
(C) $\lim_{x \to 0} g(x)$ (D) $g(0)$
(E) Is g continuous at $x = 0$? Explain.

29. (A) $\lim_{x \to 1^-} g(x)$ (B) $\lim_{x \to 1^+} g(x)$
(C) $\lim_{x \to 1} g(x)$ (D) $g(1)$
(E) Is g continuous at $x = 1$? Explain.

30. (A) $\lim_{x \to 4^-} g(x)$ (B) $\lim_{x \to 4^+} g(x)$
(C) $\lim_{x \to 4} g(x)$ (D) $g(4)$
(E) Is g continuous at $x = 4$? Explain.

Use Theorem 1 to determine where each function in Problems 31–40 is continuous.

31. $f(x) = 3x - 4$
32. $h(x) = 4 - 2x$
33. $g(x) = \dfrac{3x}{x + 2}$
34. $k(x) = \dfrac{7x}{x - 8}$
35. $m(x) = \dfrac{x + 1}{x^2 + 3x - 4}$
36. $n(x) = \dfrac{x - 2}{x^2 - 2x - 3}$
37. $F(x) = \dfrac{2x}{x^2 + 9}$
38. $G(x) = \dfrac{1 - x^2}{x^2 + 1}$
39. $M(x) = \dfrac{x - 1}{4x^2 - 9}$
40. $N(x) = \dfrac{x^2 + 4}{4 - 25x^2}$

B *In Problems 41–46, find all partition numbers of the function.*

41. $f(x) = \dfrac{3x + 8}{x - 4}$
42. $f(x) = \dfrac{2x + 7}{5x - 1}$
43. $f(x) = \dfrac{1 - x^2}{1 + x^2}$
44. $f(x) = \dfrac{x^2 + 4}{x^2 - 9}$
45. $f(x) = \dfrac{x^2 - x - 56}{x^2 - 4x}$
46. $f(x) = \dfrac{x^3 + x}{x^2 - x - 42}$

In Problems 47–54, use a sign chart to solve each inequality. Express answers in inequality and interval notation.

47. $x^2 - x - 12 < 0$
48. $x^2 - 2x - 8 < 0$
49. $x^2 + 21 > 10x$
50. $x^2 + 7x > -10$
51. $x^3 < 4x$
52. $x^4 - 36x^2 > 0$
53. $\dfrac{x^2 + 5x}{x - 3} > 0$
54. $\dfrac{x - 4}{x^2 + 2x} < 0$

55. Use the graph of f to determine where
(A) $f(x) > 0$ (B) $f(x) < 0$
Express answers in interval notation.

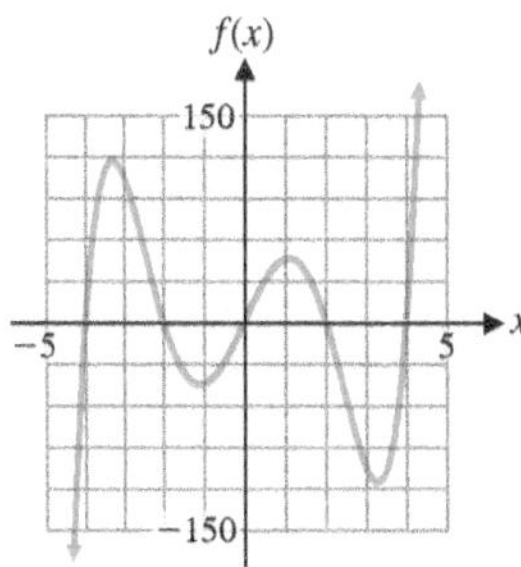

56. Use the graph of g to determine where
(A) $g(x) > 0$ (B) $g(x) < 0$
Express answers in interval notation.

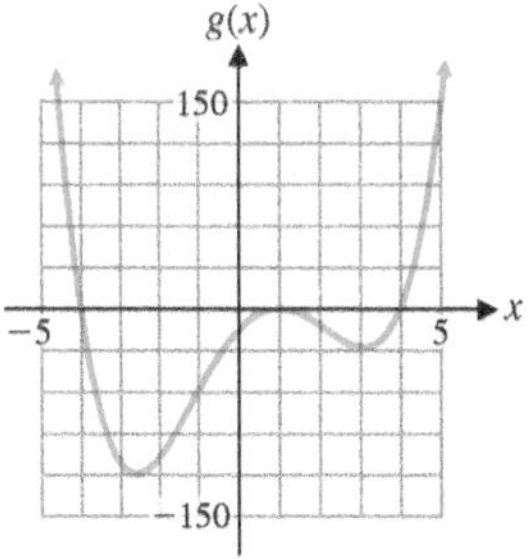

In Problems 57–60, use a graphing calculator to approximate the partition numbers of each function $f(x)$ to four decimal places. Then solve the following inequalities:

(A) $f(x) > 0$ (B) $f(x) < 0$

Express answers in interval notation.

57. $f(x) = x^4 - 6x^2 + 3x + 5$
58. $f(x) = x^4 - 4x^2 - 2x + 2$
59. $f(x) = \dfrac{3 + 6x - x^3}{x^2 - 1}$
60. $f(x) = \dfrac{x^3 - 5x + 1}{x^2 - 1}$

Use Theorem 1 to determine where each function in Problems 61–68 is continuous. Express the answer in interval notation.

61. $\sqrt{x - 6}$
62. $\sqrt{7 - x}$
63. $\sqrt[3]{5 - x}$
64. $\sqrt[3]{x - 8}$
65. $\sqrt{x^2 - 9}$
66. $\sqrt{4 - x^2}$
67. $\sqrt{x^2 + 1}$
68. $\sqrt[3]{x^4 + 5}$

In Problems 69–74, graph f, locate all points of discontinuity, and discuss the behavior of f at these points.

69. $f(x) = \begin{cases} 1 + x & \text{if } x < 1 \\ 5 - x & \text{if } x \geq 1 \end{cases}$

70. $f(x) = \begin{cases} x^2 & \text{if } x \leq 1 \\ 2x & \text{if } x > 1 \end{cases}$

71. $f(x) = \begin{cases} 1 + x & \text{if } x \le 2 \\ 5 - x & \text{if } x > 2 \end{cases}$

72. $f(x) = \begin{cases} x^2 & \text{if } x \le 2 \\ 2x & \text{if } x > 2 \end{cases}$

73. $f(x) = \begin{cases} -x & \text{if } x < 0 \\ 1 & \text{if } x = 0 \\ x & \text{if } x > 0 \end{cases}$

74. $f(x) = \begin{cases} 1 & \text{if } x < 0 \\ 0 & \text{if } x = 0 \\ 1 + x & \text{if } x > 0 \end{cases}$

C *Problems 75 and 76 refer to the **greatest integer function**, which is denoted by $[\![x]\!]$ and is defined as*

$$[\![x]\!] = \textit{greatest integer} \le x$$

For example,

$$[\![-3.6]\!] = \textit{greatest integer} \le -3.6 = -4$$
$$[\![2]\!] = \textit{greatest integer} \le 2 = 2$$
$$[\![2.5]\!] = \textit{greatest integer} \le 2.5 = 2$$

The graph of $f(x) = [\![x]\!]$ is shown. There, we can see that

$$[\![x]\!] = -2 \quad \textit{for} \quad -2 \le x < -1$$
$$[\![x]\!] = -1 \quad \textit{for} \quad -1 \le x < 0$$
$$[\![x]\!] = 0 \quad \textit{for} \quad 0 \le x < 1$$
$$[\![x]\!] = 1 \quad \textit{for} \quad 1 \le x < 2$$
$$[\![x]\!] = 2 \quad \textit{for} \quad 2 \le x < 3$$

and so on.

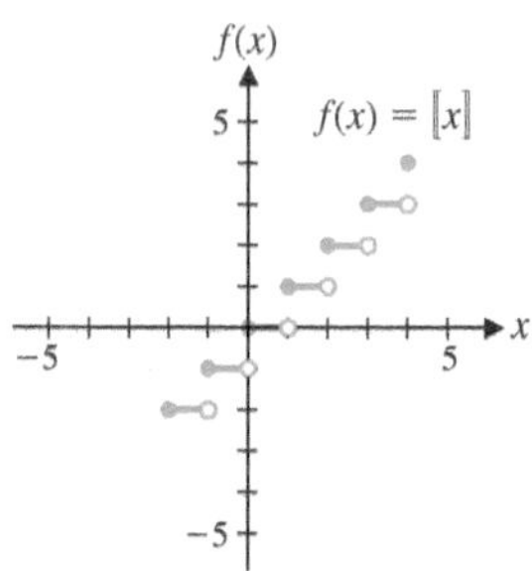

Figure for 75 and 76

75. (A) Is f continuous from the right at $x = 0$?

(B) Is f continuous from the left at $x = 0$?

(C) Is f continuous on the open interval $(0, 1)$?

(D) Is f continuous on the closed interval $[0, 1]$?

(E) Is f continuous on the half-closed interval $[0, 1)$?

76. (A) Is f continuous from the right at $x = 2$?

(B) Is f continuous from the left at $x = 2$?

(C) Is f continuous on the open interval $(1, 2)$?

(D) Is f continuous on the closed interval $[1, 2]$?

(E) Is f continuous on the half-closed interval $[1, 2)$?

In Problems 77–82, discuss the validity of each statement. If the statement is always true, explain why. If not, give a counterexample.

77. A polynomial function is continuous for all real numbers.

78. A rational function is continuous for all but finitely many real numbers.

79. If f is a function that is continuous at $x = 0$ and $x = 2$, then f is continuous at $x = 1$.

80. If f is a function that is continuous on the open interval $(0, 2)$, then f is continuous at $x = 1$.

81. If f is a function that has no partition numbers in the interval (a, b), then f is continuous on (a, b).

82. The greatest integer function (see Problem 75) is a rational function.

In Problems 83–86, sketch a possible graph of a function f that is continuous for all real numbers and satisfies the given conditions. Find the x intercepts of f.

83. $f(x) < 0$ on $(-\infty, -5)$ and $(2, \infty)$; $f(x) > 0$ on $(-5, 2)$

84. $f(x) > 0$ on $(-\infty, -4)$ and $(3, \infty)$; $f(x) < 0$ on $(-4, 3)$

85. $f(x) < 0$ on $(-\infty, -6)$ and $(-1, 4)$; $f(x) > 0$ on $(-6, -1)$ and $(4, \infty)$

86. $f(x) > 0$ on $(-\infty, -3)$ and $(2, 7)$; $f(x) < 0$ on $(-3, 2)$ and $(7, \infty)$

87. The function $f(x) = 2/(1 - x)$ satisfies $f(0) = 2$ and $f(2) = -2$. Is f equal to 0 anywhere on the interval $(-1, 3)$? Does this contradict Theorem 2? Explain.

88. The function $f(x) = 8/(x - 5)$ satisfies $f(1) = -2$ and $f(7) = 4$. Is f equal to 0 anywhere on the interval $(-2, 8)$? Does this contradict Theorem 2? Explain.

Applications

89. **Postal rates.** First-class postage in 2016 was \$0.47 for the first ounce (or any fraction thereof) and \$0.21 for each additional ounce (or fraction thereof) up to a maximum weight of 3.5 ounces.

(A) Write a piecewise definition of the first-class postage $P(x)$ for a letter weighing x ounces.

(B) Graph $P(x)$ for $0 < x \le 3.5$.

(C) Is $P(x)$ continuous at $x = 2.5$? At $x = 3$? Explain.

90. **Bike Rental.** A bike rental service charges \$15 for the first hour (or any fraction thereof) and \$10 for each additional hour (or fraction thereof) up to a maximum of 8 hours.

(A) Write a piecewise definition of the charge $R(x)$ for a rental lasting x hours.

(B) Graph $R(x)$ for $0 < x \le 8$.

(C) Is $R(x)$ continuous at $x = 3.5$? At $x = 4$? Explain.

91. Postal rates. Discuss the differences between the function $Q(x) = 0.47 + 0.21[\![x]\!]$ and the function $P(x)$ defined in Problem 89. (The symbol $[\![x]\!]$ is defined in problems 75 and 76.)

92. Bike Rental. Discuss the differences between the function $S(x) = 15 + 10[\![x]\!]$ and $R(x)$ defined in Problem 90. (The symbol $[\![x]\!]$ is defined in problems 75 and 76.)

93. Natural-gas rates. Table 1 shows the rates for natural gas charged by Origin Energy of the Australian Gas Networks for the Adelaide distribution zone. The daily supply charge is a fixed daily charge, independent of the amount of gas used per day.

Table 1 **Adelaide Distribution Zone**

Daily supply charge	71 cents
First 50 MJ	3.9 cents per MJ
Over 50 MJ	1.9 cents per MJ

(A) Write a piecewise definition of the daily charge $S(x)$ for a customer who uses x MJ (megajoules).

(B) Graph $S(x)$.

(C) Is $S(x)$ continuous at $x = 50$? Explain.

94. Natural-gas rates. Table 2 shows the rates for natural gas charged by Origin Energy of the Australian Gas Networks for the Brisbane distribution zone. The daily supply charge is a fixed daily charge, independent of the amount of gas used per day.

Table 2 **Brisbane Distribution Zone**

Daily supply charge	70 cents
First 8 MJ	5.5 cents per MJ
Next 19 MJ	3.9 cents per MJ
Over 27 MJ	2.8 cents per MJ

(A) Write a piecewise definition of the monthly charge $S(x)$ for a customer who uses x MJ.

(B) Graph $S(x)$.

(C) Is $S(x)$ continuous at $x = 8$? At $x = 27$? Explain.

95. Income. A personal-computer salesperson receives a base salary of \$1,000 per month and a commission of 5% of all sales over \$10,000 during the month. If the monthly sales are \$20,000 or more, then the salesperson is given an additional \$500 bonus. Let $E(s)$ represent the person's earnings per month as a function of the monthly sales s.

(A) Graph $E(s)$ for $0 \le s \le 30{,}000$.

(B) Find $\lim_{s \to 10{,}000} E(s)$ and $E(10{,}000)$.

(C) Find $\lim_{s \to 20{,}000} E(s)$ and $E(20{,}000)$.

(D) Is E continuous at $s = 10{,}000$? At $s = 20{,}000$?

96. Equipment rental. An office equipment rental and leasing company rents copiers for \$10 per day (and any fraction thereof) or for \$50 per 7-day week. Let $C(x)$ be the cost of renting a copier for x days.

(A) Graph $C(x)$ for $0 \le x \le 10$.

(B) Find $\lim_{x \to 4.5} C(x)$ and $C(4.5)$.

(C) Find $\lim_{x \to 8} C(x)$ and $C(8)$.

(D) Is C continuous at $x = 4.5$? At $x = 8$?

97. Animal supply. A medical laboratory raises its own rabbits. The number of rabbits $N(t)$ available at any time t depends on the number of births and deaths. When a birth or death occurs, the function N generally has a discontinuity, as shown in the figure.

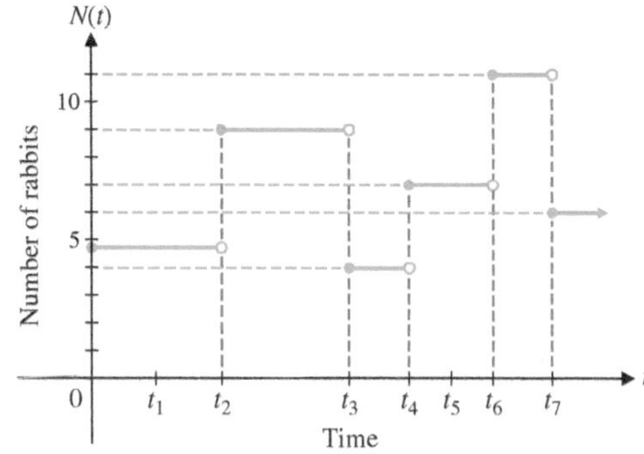

(A) Where is the function N discontinuous?

(B) $\lim_{t \to t_5} N(t) = ?$; $N(t_5) = ?$

(C) $\lim_{t \to t_3} N(t) = ?$; $N(t_3) = ?$

98. Learning. The graph shown represents the history of a person learning the material on limits and continuity in this book. At time t_2, the student's mind goes blank during a quiz. At time t_4, the instructor explains a concept particularly well, then suddenly a big jump in understanding takes place.

(A) Where is the function p discontinuous?

(B) $\lim_{t \to t_1} p(t) = ?$; $p(t_1) = ?$

(C) $\lim_{t \to t_2} p(t) = ?$; $p(t_2) = ?$

(D) $\lim_{t \to t_4} p(t) = ?$; $p(t_4) = ?$

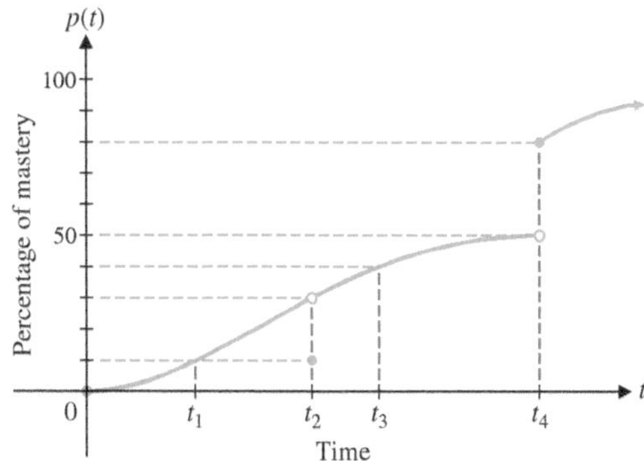

Answers to Matched Problems

1. f is not continuous at $x = -3, -1, 2$, and 4.
   $x = -3$: $\lim_{x \to -3} f(x) = 3$, but $f(-3)$ does not exist
   $x = -1$: $f(-1) = 1$, but $\lim_{x \to -1} f(x)$ does not exist
   $x = 2$: $\lim_{x \to 2} f(x) = 5$, but $f(2) = 3$
   $x = 4$: $\lim_{x \to 4} f(x)$ does not exist, and $f(4)$ does not exist

*A British thermal unit (Btu) is the amount of heat required to raise the temperature of 1 pound of water 1 degree Fahrenheit, and a therm is 100,000 Btu.

2. (A) f is continuous at $x = 1$, since $\lim_{x \to 1} f(x) = 2 = f(1)$.
   (B) g is not continuous at $x = 1$, since $g(1)$ is not defined.
   (C) h is not continuous at $x = 2$ for two reasons: $h(2)$ does not exist and $\lim_{x \to 2} h(x)$ does not exist.
   h is continuous at $x = 0$, since $\lim_{x \to 0} h(x) = -1 = h(0)$.
3. (A) Since f is a polynomial function, f is continuous for all x.
   (B) Since f is a rational function, f is continuous for all x except -1 and 4 (values that make the denominator 0).
   (C) The polynomial function $x - 4$ is continuous for all x and nonnegative for $x \geq 4$. Since $n = 2$ is even, f is continuous for $x \geq 4$, or on the interval $[4, \infty)$.
   (D) The polynomial function $x^3 + 1$ is continuous for all x. Since $n = 3$ is odd, f is continuous for all x.
4. $-\infty < x < -1$ or $1 < x < 3$; $(-\infty, -1) \cup (1, 3)$
5. $1000 < x < 6000$

6.4 The Derivative

- Rate of Change
- Slope of the Tangent Line
- The Derivative
- Nonexistence of the Derivative

We will now make use of the limit concepts developed in Sections 6.1, 6.2, and 6.3 to solve the two important problems illustrated in Figure 1. The solution of each of these apparently unrelated problems involves a common concept called the *derivative.*

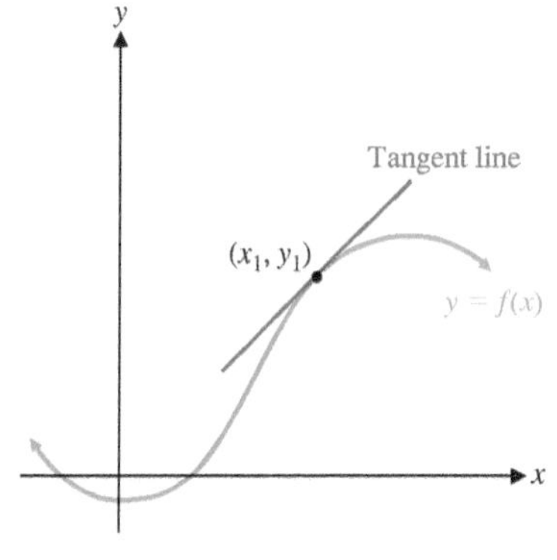

(A) Find the equation of the tangent line at (x_1, y_1) given $y = f(x)$

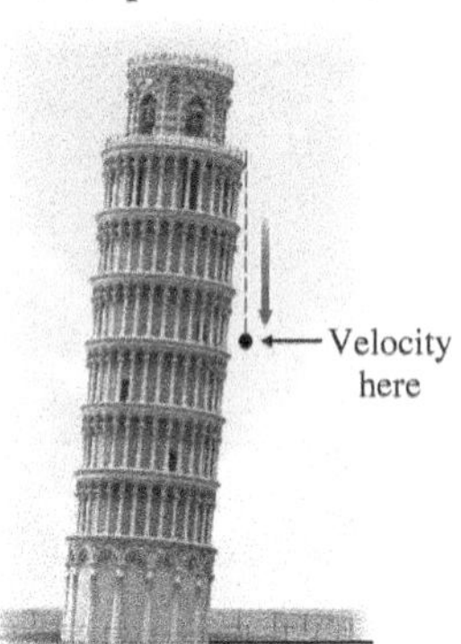

(B) Find the instantaneous velocity of a falling object

Figure 1 Two basic problems of calculus

Rate of Change

If you pass mile marker 120 on the interstate highway at 9 a.m. and mile marker 250 at 11 a.m., then the *average rate of change* of distance with respect to time, also known as *average velocity*, is

$$\frac{250 - 120}{11 - 9} = \frac{130}{2} = 65 \text{ miles per hour}$$

Of course your speedometer reading, that is, the *instantaneous rate of change*, or *instantaneous velocity*, might well have been 75 mph at some moment between 9 a.m. and 11 a.m.

We will define the concepts of average rate of change and instantaneous rate of change more generally, and will apply them in situations that are unrelated to velocity.

DEFINITION Average Rate of Change

For $y = f(x)$, the **average rate of change from $x = a$ to $x = a + h$** is

$$\frac{f(a + h) - f(a)}{(a + h) - a} = \frac{f(a + h) - f(a)}{h} \qquad h \neq 0 \qquad (1)$$

Note that the numerator and denominator in (1) are differences, so (1) is a **difference quotient** (see Section 2.1).

EXAMPLE 1 **Revenue Analysis** The revenue (in dollars) from the sale of x plastic planter boxes is given by

$$R(x) = 20x - 0.02x^2 \qquad 0 \le x \le 1{,}000$$

and is graphed in Figure 2.

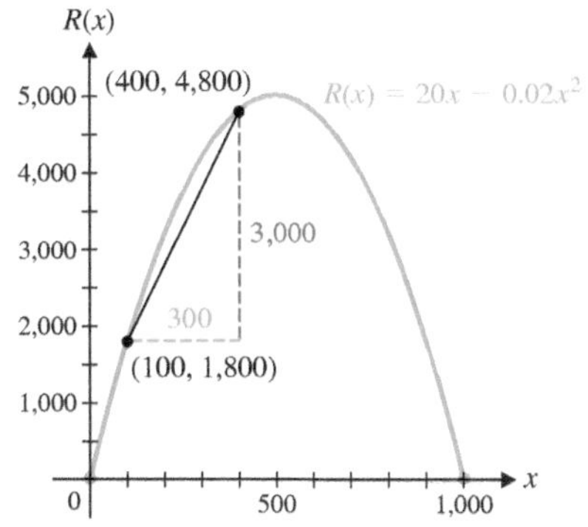

Figure 2

(A) What is the change in revenue if production is changed from 100 planters to 400 planters?

(B) What is the average rate of change in revenue for this change in production?

SOLUTION

(A) The change in revenue is given by

$$R(400) - R(100) = 20(400) - 0.02(400)^2 - [20(100) - 0.02(100)^2]$$
$$= 4{,}800 - 1{,}800 = \$3{,}000$$

Increasing production from 100 planters to 400 planters will increase revenue by \$3,000.

(B) To find the average rate of change in revenue, we divide the change in revenue by the change in production:

$$\frac{R(400) - R(100)}{400 - 100} = \frac{3{,}000}{300} = \$10$$

The average rate of change in revenue is \$10 per planter when production is increased from 100 to 400 planters.

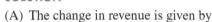

Matched Problem 1 Refer to the revenue function in Example 1.

(A) What is the change in revenue if production is changed from 600 planters to 800 planters?

(B) What is the average rate of change in revenue for this change in production?

EXAMPLE 2 **Velocity** A small steel ball dropped from a tower will fall a distance of y feet in x seconds, as given approximately by the formula

$$y = f(x) = 16x^2$$

Figure 3 shows the position of the ball on a coordinate line (positive direction down) at the end of 0, 1, 2, and 3 seconds.

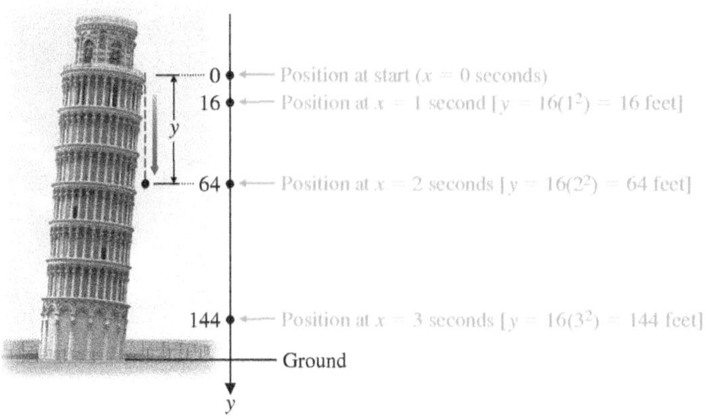

Figure 3

(A) Find the average velocity from $x = 2$ seconds to $x = 3$ seconds.

(B) Find and simplify the average velocity from $x = 2$ seconds to $x = 2 + h$ seconds, $h \neq 0$.

(C) Find the limit of the expression from part (B) as $h \to 0$ if that limit exists.

(D) Discuss possible interpretations of the limit from part (C).

SOLUTION

(A) Recall the formula $d = rt$, which can be written in the form

$$r = \frac{d}{t} = \frac{\text{Distance covered}}{\text{Elapsed time}} = \text{Average velocity}$$

For example, if a person drives from San Francisco to Los Angeles (a distance of about 420 miles) in 7 hours, then the average velocity is

$$r = \frac{d}{t} = \frac{420}{7} = 60 \text{ miles per hour}$$

Sometimes the person will be traveling faster and sometimes slower, but the average velocity is 60 miles per hour. In our present problem, the average velocity of the steel ball from $x = 2$ seconds to $x = 3$ seconds is

$$\begin{aligned}\text{Average velocity} &= \frac{\text{Distance covered}}{\text{Elapsed time}} \\ &= \frac{f(3) - f(2)}{3 - 2} \\ &= \frac{16(3)^2 - 16(2)^2}{1} = 80 \text{ feet per second}\end{aligned}$$

We see that if $y = f(x)$ is the position of the falling ball, then the average velocity is simply the average rate of change of $f(x)$ with respect to time x.

(B) Proceeding as in part (A), we have

$$\begin{aligned}\text{Average velocity} &= \frac{\text{Distance covered}}{\text{Elapsed time}} \\ &= \frac{f(2 + h) - f(2)}{h} && \text{Difference quotient} \\ &= \frac{16(2 + h)^2 - 16(2)^2}{h} && \text{Simplify this 0/0 indeterminate form.} \\ &= \frac{64 + 64h + 16h^2 - 64}{h} \\ &= \frac{h(64 + 16h)}{h} = 64 + 16h \qquad h \neq 0\end{aligned}$$

Notice that if $h = 1$, the average velocity is 80 feet per second, which is the result in part (A).

(C) The limit of the average velocity expression from part (B) as $h \to 0$ is

$$\begin{aligned}\lim_{h \to 0} \frac{f(2 + h) - f(2)}{h} &= \lim_{h \to 0} (64 + 16h) \\ &= 64 \text{ feet per second}\end{aligned}$$

(D) The average velocity over smaller and smaller time intervals approaches 64 feet per second. This limit can be interpreted as the velocity of the ball at the *instant* that the ball has been falling for exactly 2 seconds. Therefore, 64 feet per second is referred to as the **instantaneous velocity** at $x = 2$ seconds, and we have solved one of the basic problems of calculus (see Fig. 1B).

Matched Problem 2 For the falling steel ball in Example 2, find

(A) The average velocity from $x = 1$ second to $x = 2$ seconds

(B) The average velocity (in simplified form) from $x = 1$ second to $x = 1 + h$ seconds, $h \neq 0$

(C) The instantaneous velocity at $x = 1$ second

The ideas in Example 2 can be applied to the average rate of change of any function.

DEFINITION Instantaneous Rate of Change

For $y = f(x)$, the **instantaneous rate of change at $x = a$** is

$$\lim_{h \to 0} \frac{f(a + h) - f(a)}{h} \tag{2}$$

if the limit exists.

The adjective *instantaneous* is often omitted with the understanding that the phrase **rate of change** always refers to the instantaneous rate of change and not the average rate of change. Similarly, **velocity** always refers to the instantaneous rate of change of distance with respect to time.

Slope of the Tangent Line

So far, our interpretations of the difference quotient have been numerical in nature. Now we want to consider a geometric interpretation.

In geometry, a line that intersects a circle in two points is called a *secant line*, and a line that intersects a circle in exactly one point is called a *tangent line* (Fig. 4). If the point Q in Figure 4 is moved closer and closer to the point P, then the angle between the secant line through P and Q and the tangent line at P gets smaller and smaller. We will generalize the geometric concepts of secant line and tangent line of a circle and will use them to study graphs of functions.

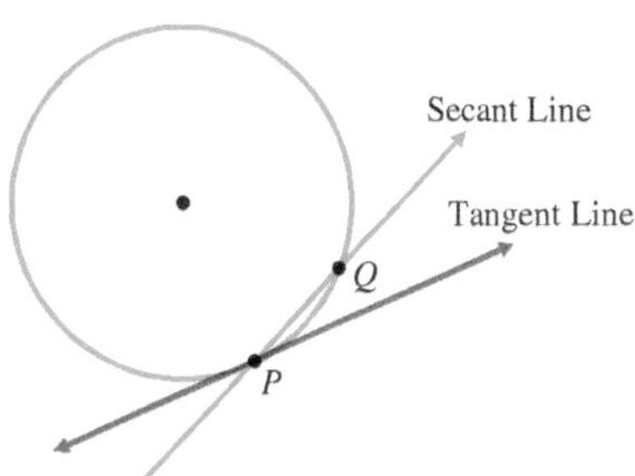

Figure 4 Secant line and tangent line of a circle

Reminder:

The slope of the line through the points (x_1, y_1) and (x_2, y_2) is the difference of the y coordinates divided by the difference of the x coordinates.

$$m = \frac{y_2 - y_1}{x_2 - x_1}$$

A line through two points on the graph of a function is called a **secant line**. If $(a, f(a))$ and $(a + h, f(a + h))$ are two points on the graph of $y = f(x)$, then we

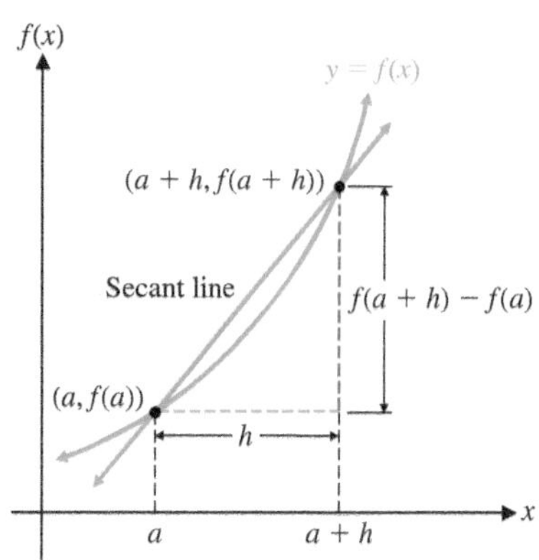

Figure 5 Secant line

can use the slope formula from Section 1.2 to find the slope of the secant line through these points (Fig. 5).

$$\textbf{Slope of secant line} = \frac{y_2 - y_1}{x_2 - x_1} = \frac{f(a + h) - f(a)}{(a + h) - a}$$

$$= \frac{f(a + h) - f(a)}{h} \qquad \text{Difference quotient}$$

The difference quotient can be interpreted as both the average rate of change and the slope of the secant line.

EXAMPLE 3 **Slope of a Secant Line** Given $f(x) = x^2$,

(A) Find the slope of the secant line for $a = 1$ and $h = 2$ and 1, respectively. Graph $y = f(x)$ and the two secant lines.

(B) Find and simplify the slope of the secant line for $a = 1$ and h any nonzero number.

(C) Find the limit of the expression in part (B).

(D) Discuss possible interpretations of the limit in part (C).

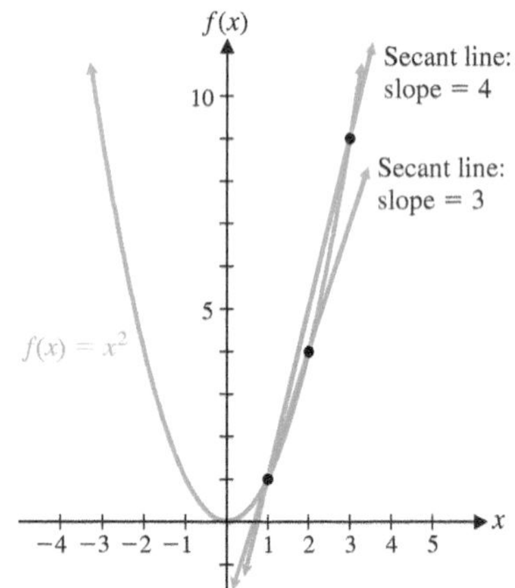

Figure 6 Secant lines

SOLUTION

(A) For $a = 1$ and $h = 2$, the secant line goes through $(1, f(1)) = (1, 1)$ and $(3, f(3)) = (3, 9)$, and its slope is

$$\frac{f(1 + 2) - f(1)}{2} = \frac{3^2 - 1^2}{2} = 4$$

For $a = 1$ and $h = 1$, the secant line goes through $(1, f(1)) = (1, 1)$ and $(2, f(2)) = (2, 4)$, and its slope is

$$\frac{f(1 + 1) - f(1)}{1} = \frac{2^2 - 1^2}{1} = 3$$

The graphs of $y = f(x)$ and the two secant lines are shown in Figure 6.

(B) For $a = 1$ and h any nonzero number, the secant line goes through $(1, f(1)) = (1, 1)$ and $(1 + h, f(1 + h)) = (1 + h, (1 + h)^2)$, and its slope is

$$\frac{f(1 + h) - f(1)}{h} = \frac{(1 + h)^2 - 1^2}{h} \qquad \text{Square the binomial.}$$

$$= \frac{1 + 2h + h^2 - 1}{h} \qquad \text{Combine like terms and factor the numerator.}$$

$$= \frac{h(2 + h)}{h} \qquad \text{Cancel.}$$

$$= 2 + h \qquad h \neq 0$$

(C) The limit of the secant line slope from part (B) is

$$\lim_{h\to 0}\frac{f(1+h)-f(1)}{h} = \lim_{h\to 0}(2+h)$$
$$= 2$$

(D) In part (C), we saw that the limit of the slopes of the secant lines through the point $(1, f(1))$ is 2. If we graph the line through $(1, f(1))$ with slope 2 (Fig. 7), then this line is the limit of the secant lines. The slope obtained from the limit of slopes of secant lines is called the *slope of the graph* at $x = 1$. The line through the point $(1, f(1))$ with this slope is called the *tangent line.* We have solved another basic problem of calculus (see Fig. 1A on page 330).

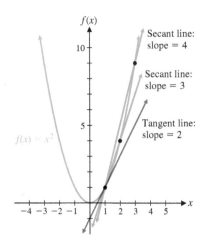

Figure 7 Tangent line

Matched Problem 3 Given $f(x) = x^2$,

(A) Find the slope of the secant line for $a = 2$ and $h = 2$ and 1, respectively.

(B) Find and simplify the slope of the secant line for $a = 2$ and h any nonzero number.

(C) Find the limit of the expression in part (B).

(D) Find the slope of the graph and the slope of the tangent line at $a = 2$.

The ideas introduced in the preceding example are summarized next:

DEFINITION Slope of a Graph and Tangent Line

Given $y = f(x)$, the **slope of the graph** at the point $(a, f(a))$ is given by

$$\lim_{h\to 0}\frac{f(a+h)-f(a)}{h} \qquad (3)$$

provided the limit exists. In this case, the **tangent line** to the graph is the line through $(a, f(a))$ with slope given by (3).

CONCEPTUAL INSIGHT

If the function f is continuous at a, then

$$\lim_{h\to 0} f(a+h) = f(a)$$

and limit (3) will be a $0/0$ indeterminate form. As we saw in Examples 2 and 3, evaluating this type of limit typically involves algebraic simplification.

The Derivative

We have seen that the limit of a difference quotient can be interpreted as a rate of change, as a velocity, or as the slope of a tangent line. In addition, this limit provides solutions to the two basic problems stated at the beginning of this section. We are now ready to introduce some terms that refer to that limit. To follow customary practice, we use x in place of a and think of the difference quotient

$$\frac{f(x+h)-f(x)}{h}$$

as a function of h, with x held fixed as h tends to 0. This allows us to find a single general limit instead of finding many individual limits.

DEFINITION The Derivative

For $y = f(x)$, we define the **derivative of f at x**, denoted $f'(x)$, by

$$f'(x) = \lim_{h \to 0} \frac{f(x+h) - f(x)}{h} \quad \text{if the limit exists.}$$

If $f'(x)$ exists for each x in the open interval (a, b), then f is said to be **differentiable** over (a, b).

The process of finding the derivative of a function is called **differentiation**. The derivative of a function is obtained by **differentiating** the function.

SUMMARY Interpretations of the Derivative

The derivative of a function f is a new function f'. The domain of f' is a subset of the domain of f. The derivative has various applications and interpretations, including the following:

1. *Slope of the tangent line.* For each x in the domain of $f', f'(x)$ is the slope of the line tangent to the graph of f at the point $(x, f(x))$.
2. *Instantaneous rate of change.* For each x in the domain of $f', f'(x)$ is the instantaneous rate of change of $y = f(x)$ with respect to x.
3. *Velocity.* If $f(x)$ is the position of a moving object at time x, then $v = f'(x)$ is the velocity of the object at that time.

Example 4 illustrates the *four-step process* that we use to find derivatives in this section. The four-step process makes it easier to compute the limit in the definition of the derivative by breaking the process into smaller steps. In subsequent sections, we develop rules for finding derivatives that do not involve limits. However, it is important that you master the limit process in order to fully comprehend and appreciate the various applications we will consider.

EXAMPLE 4 **Finding a Derivative** Find $f'(x)$, the derivative of f at x, for $f(x) = 4x - x^2$.

SOLUTION To find $f'(x)$, we use a four-step process.

Step 1 Find $f(x + h)$.

$$\begin{aligned} f(x+h) &= 4(x+h) - (x+h)^2 \\ &= 4x + 4h - x^2 - 2xh - h^2 \end{aligned}$$

Step 2 Find $f(x + h) - f(x)$.

$$\begin{aligned} f(x+h) - f(x) &= 4x + 4h - x^2 - 2xh - h^2 - (4x - x^2) \\ &= 4h - 2xh - h^2 \end{aligned}$$

Step 3 Find $\dfrac{f(x+h) - f(x)}{h}$.

$$\begin{aligned} \frac{f(x+h) - f(x)}{h} &= \frac{4h - 2xh - h^2}{h} = \frac{h(4 - 2x - h)}{h} \\ &= 4 - 2x - h, \quad h \neq 0 \end{aligned}$$

Step 4 Find $f'(x) = \lim_{h\to 0} \frac{f(x+h) - f(x)}{h}$.

$$f'(x) = \lim_{h\to 0} \frac{f(x+h) - f(x)}{h} = \lim_{h\to 0}(4 - 2x - h) = 4 - 2x$$

So if $f(x) = 4x - x^2$, then $f'(x) = 4 - 2x$. The function f' is a new function derived from the function f.

Matched Problem 4 Find $f'(x)$, the derivative of f at x, for $f(x) = 8x - 2x^2$.

The four-step process used in Example 4 is summarized as follows for easy reference:

PROCEDURE The four-step process for finding the derivative of a function f:

Step 1 Find $f(x + h)$.

Step 2 Find $f(x + h) - f(x)$.

Step 3 Find $\frac{f(x+h) - f(x)}{h}$.

Step 4 Find $\lim_{h\to 0} \frac{f(x+h) - f(x)}{h}$.

EXAMPLE 5 **Finding Tangent Line Slopes** In Example 4, we started with the function $f(x) = 4x - x^2$ and found the derivative of f at x to be $f'(x) = 4 - 2x$. So the slope of a line tangent to the graph of f at any point $(x, f(x))$ on the graph is

$$m = f'(x) = 4 - 2x$$

(A) Find the slope of the graph of f at $x = 0$, $x = 2$, and $x = 3$.

(B) Graph $y = f(x) = 4x - x^2$ and use the slopes found in part (A) to make a rough sketch of the lines tangent to the graph at $x = 0$, $x = 2$, and $x = 3$.

SOLUTION

(A) Using $f'(x) = 4 - 2x$, we have

$$f'(0) = 4 - 2(0) = 4 \quad \text{Slope at } x = 0$$
$$f'(2) = 4 - 2(2) = 0 \quad \text{Slope at } x = 2$$
$$f'(3) = 4 - 2(3) = -2 \quad \text{Slope at } x = 3$$

(B)

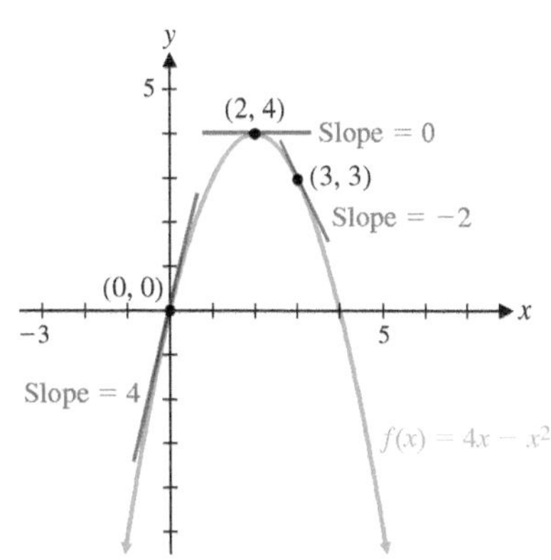

Matched Problem 5 In Matched Problem 4, we started with the function $f(x) = 8x - 2x^2$. Using the derivative found there,

(A) Find the slope of the graph of f at $x = 1, x = 2$, and $x = 4$.

(B) Graph $y = f(x) = 8x - 2x^2$, and use the slopes from part (A) to make a rough sketch of the lines tangent to the graph at $x = 1, x = 2$, and $x = 4$.

Explore and Discuss 1

In Example 4, we found that the derivative of $f(x) = 4x - x^2$ is $f'(x) = 4 - 2x$. In Example 5, we graphed $f(x)$ and several tangent lines.

(A) Graph f and f' on the same set of axes.

(B) The graph of f' is a straight line. Is it a tangent line for the graph of f? Explain.

(C) Find the x intercept for the graph of f'. What is the slope of the line tangent to the graph of f for this value of x? Write a verbal description of the relationship between the slopes of the tangent lines of a function and the x intercepts of the derivative of the function.

EXAMPLE 6 **Finding a Derivative** Find $f'(x)$, the derivative of f at x, for $f(x) = \frac{1}{x}$.

SOLUTION

Step 1 Find $f(x + h)$.

$$f(x+h) = \frac{1}{x+h}$$

Step 2 Find $f(x + h) - f(x)$.

$$f(x+h) - f(x) = \frac{1}{x+h} - \frac{1}{x} \qquad \text{Add fractions. (Section A.4)}$$

$$= \frac{x - (x+h)}{x(x+h)} \qquad \text{Simplify.}$$

$$= \frac{-h}{x(x+h)}$$

Step 3 Find $\frac{f(x+h) - f(x)}{h}$.

$$\frac{f(x+h) - f(x)}{h} = \frac{\frac{-h}{x(x+h)}}{h} \qquad \text{Simplify.}$$

$$= \frac{-1}{x(x+h)} \qquad h \neq 0$$

Step 4 Find $\lim_{h \to 0} \frac{f(x+h) - f(x)}{h}$.

$$\lim_{h \to 0} \frac{f(x+h) - f(x)}{h} = \lim_{h \to 0} \frac{-1}{x(x+h)}$$

$$= \frac{-1}{x^2} \qquad x \neq 0$$

So the derivative of $f(x) = \frac{1}{x}$ is $f'(x) = \frac{-1}{x^2}$, a new function. The domain of f is the set of all nonzero real numbers. The domain of f' is also the set of all nonzero real numbers.

Matched Problem 6 Find $f'(x)$ for $f(x) = \frac{1}{x + 2}$.

EXAMPLE 7 **Finding a Derivative** Find $f'(x)$, the derivative of f at x, for $f(x) = \sqrt{x} + 2$.

SOLUTION We use the four-step process to find $f'(x)$.

Step 1 Find $f(x + h)$.

$$f(x + h) = \sqrt{x + h} + 2$$

Step 2 Find $f(x + h) - f(x)$.

$$\begin{aligned} f(x + h) - f(x) &= \sqrt{x + h} + 2 - (\sqrt{x} + 2) && \text{Combine like terms.} \\ &= \sqrt{x + h} - \sqrt{x} \end{aligned}$$

Step 3 Find $\frac{f(x + h) - f(x)}{h}$.

$$\begin{aligned} \frac{f(x + h) - f(x)}{h} &= \frac{\sqrt{x + h} - \sqrt{x}}{h} && \text{We rationalize the numerator (Appendix A, Section A.6) to change the form of this fraction.} \\ &= \frac{\sqrt{x + h} - \sqrt{x}}{h} \cdot \frac{\sqrt{x + h} + \sqrt{x}}{\sqrt{x + h} + \sqrt{x}} \\ &= \frac{x + h - x}{h(\sqrt{x + h} + \sqrt{x})} && \text{Combine like terms.} \\ &= \frac{h}{h(\sqrt{x + h} + \sqrt{x})} && \text{Cancel.} \\ &= \frac{1}{\sqrt{x + h} + \sqrt{x}} \qquad h \neq 0 \end{aligned}$$

Step 4 Find $f'(x) = \lim_{h \to 0} \frac{f(x + h) - f(x)}{h}$.

$$\begin{aligned} \lim_{h \to 0} \frac{f(x + h) - f(x)}{h} &= \lim_{h \to 0} \frac{1}{\sqrt{x + h} + \sqrt{x}} \\ &= \frac{1}{\sqrt{x} + \sqrt{x}} = \frac{1}{2\sqrt{x}} \qquad x > 0 \end{aligned}$$

So the derivative of $f(x) = \sqrt{x} + 2$ is $f'(x) = 1/(2\sqrt{x})$, a new function. The domain of f is $[0, \infty)$. Since $f'(0)$ is not defined, the domain of f' is $(0, \infty)$, a subset of the domain of f.

Matched Problem 7 Find $f'(x)$ for $f(x) = \sqrt{x} + 4$.

EXAMPLE 8 **Sales Analysis** A company's total sales (in millions of dollars) t months from now are given by $S(t) = \sqrt{t} + 2$. Find and interpret $S(25)$ and $S'(25)$. Use these results to estimate the total sales after 26 months and after 27 months.

SOLUTION The total sales function S has the same form as the function f in Example 7. Only the letters used to represent the function and the independent variable have been changed. It follows that S' and f' also have the same form:

$$S(t) = \sqrt{t} + 2 \qquad f(x) = \sqrt{x} + 2$$

$$S'(t) = \frac{1}{2\sqrt{t}} \qquad f'(x) = \frac{1}{2\sqrt{x}}$$

Evaluating S and S' at $t = 25$, we have

$$S(25) = \sqrt{25} + 2 = 7 \qquad S'(25) = \frac{1}{2\sqrt{25}} = 0.1$$

So 25 months from now, the total sales will be \$7 million and will be increasing at the rate of \$0.1 million (\$100,000) per month. If this instantaneous rate of change of sales remained constant, the sales would grow to \$7.1 million after 26 months, \$7.2 million after 27 months, and so on. Even though $S'(t)$ is not a constant function in this case, these values provide useful estimates of the total sales.

Matched Problem 8 A company's total sales (in millions of dollars) t months from now are given by $S(t) = \sqrt{t+4}$. Find and interpret $S(12)$ and $S'(12)$. Use these results to estimate the total sales after 13 months and after 14 months. (Use the derivative found in Matched Problem 7.)

In Example 8, we can compare the estimates of total sales obtained by using the derivative with the corresponding exact values of $S(t)$:

	Exact values	Estimated values
$S(26) = \sqrt{26} + 2 = 7.099\ldots$		≈ 7.1
$S(27) = \sqrt{27} + 2 = 7.196\ldots$		≈ 7.2

For this function, the estimated values provide very good approximations to the exact values of $S(t)$. For other functions, the approximation might not be as accurate.

Using the instantaneous rate of change of a function at a point to estimate values of the function at nearby points is an important application of the derivative.

Nonexistence of the Derivative

The existence of a derivative at $x = a$ depends on the existence of a limit at $x = a$, that is, on the existence of

$$f'(a) = \lim_{h \to 0} \frac{f(a+h) - f(a)}{h} \tag{4}$$

If the limit does not exist at $x = a$, we say that the function f is **nondifferentiable at** $\boldsymbol{x = a}$, or $\boldsymbol{f'(a)}$ **does not exist.**

Explore and Discuss 2

Let $f(x) = |x - 1|$.

(A) Graph f.

(B) Complete the following table:

h	-0.1	-0.01	-0.001	$\to 0 \leftarrow$	0.001	0.01	0.1
$\dfrac{f(1+h) - f(1)}{h}$	?	?	?	$\to ? \leftarrow$	?	?	?

(C) Find the following limit if it exists:

$$\lim_{h\to 0}\frac{f(1+h)-f(1)}{h}$$

(D) Use the results of parts (A)–(C) to discuss the existence of $f'(1)$.

(E) Repeat parts (A)–(D) for $\sqrt[3]{x-1}$.

How can we recognize the points on the graph of f where $f'(a)$ does not exist? It is impossible to describe all the ways that the limit of a difference quotient can fail to exist. However, we can illustrate some common situations where $f'(a)$ fails to exist (see Fig. 8):

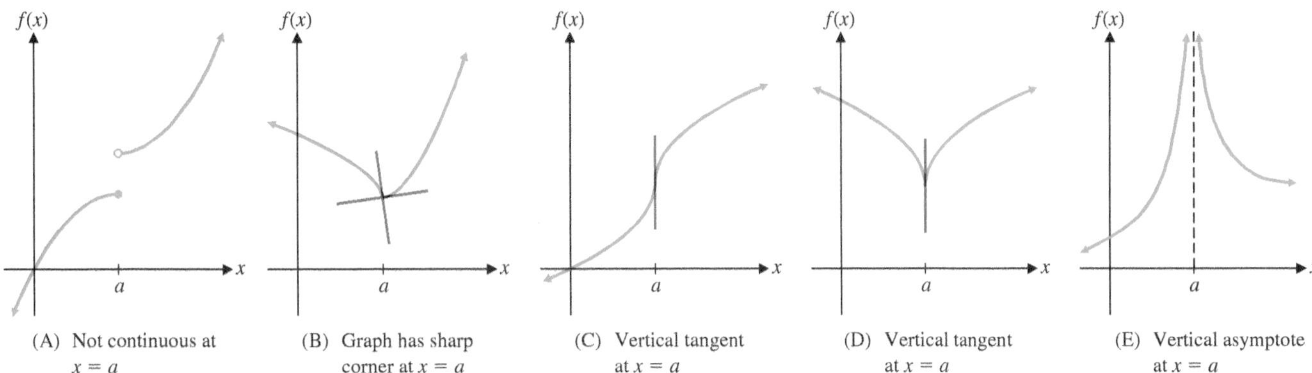

Figure 8 The function f is nondifferentiable at $x = a$.

1. If the graph of f has a hole or a break at $x = a$, then $f'(a)$ does not exist (Fig. 8A and Fig. 8E).
2. If the graph of f has a sharp corner at $x = a$, then $f'(a)$ does not exist, and the graph has no tangent line at $x = a$ (Fig. 8B and Fig. 8D). (In Fig. 8B, the left- and right-hand derivatives exist but are not equal.)
3. If the graph of f has a vertical tangent line at $x = a$, then $f'(a)$ does not exist (Fig. 8C and Fig. 8D).

Exercises 6.4

Skills Warm-up Exercises

W *In Problems 1–4, find the slope of the line through the given points. Write the slope as a reduced fraction, and also give its decimal form.*

1. $(2,7)$ and $(6,16)$
2. $(-1,11)$ and $(1,8)$
3. $(10,14)$ and $(0,68)$
4. $(-12,-3)$ and $(4,3)$

In Problems 5–8, write the expression in the form $a + b\sqrt{n}$ where a and b are reduced fractions and n is an integer. (If necessary, review Section A.6.)

5. $\dfrac{1}{\sqrt{3}}$
6. $\dfrac{2}{\sqrt{5}}$
7. $\dfrac{5}{3+\sqrt{7}}$
8. $\dfrac{4+\sqrt{3}}{2+\sqrt{3}}$

A *In Problems 9 and 10, find the indicated quantity for $y = f(x) = 5 - x^2$ and interpret that quantity in terms of the following graph.*

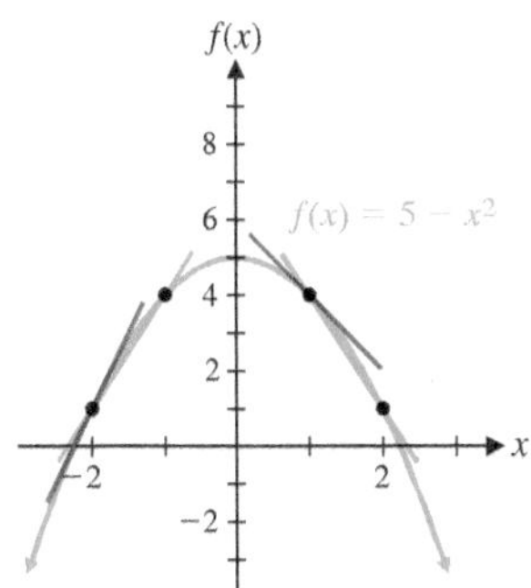

9. (A) $\dfrac{f(2) - f(1)}{2 - 1}$

(B) $\dfrac{f(1 + h) - f(1)}{h}$

(C) $\lim_{h \to 0} \dfrac{f(1 + h) - f(1)}{h}$

10. (A) $\dfrac{f(-1) - f(-2)}{-1 - (-2)}$

(B) $\dfrac{f(-2 + h) - f(-2)}{h}$

(C) $\lim_{h \to 0} \dfrac{f(-2 + h) - f(-2)}{h}$

11. Find the indicated quantities for $f(x) = 3x^2$.

(A) The slope of the secant line through the points $(1, f(1))$ and $(4, f(4))$ on the graph of $y = f(x)$.

(B) The slope of the secant line through the points $(1, f(1))$ and $(1 + h, f(1 + h)), h \neq 0$. Simplify your answer.

(C) The slope of the graph at $(1, f(1))$.

12. Find the indicated quantities for $f(x) = 3x^2$.

(A) The slope of the secant line through the points $(-1, f(-1))$ and $(3, f(3))$ on the graph of $y = f(x)$.

(B) The slope of the secant line through the points $(-1, f(-1))$ and $(-1 + h, f(-1 + h)), h \neq 0$. Simplify your answer.

(C) The slope of the graph at $(-1, f(-1))$.

13. Two hours after the start of a 100-kilometer bicycle race, a cyclist passes the 80-kilometer mark while riding at a velocity of 45 kilometers per hour.

(A) Find the cyclist's average velocity during the first two hours of the race.

(B) Let $f(x)$ represent the distance traveled (in kilometers) from the start of the race ($x = 0$) to time x (in hours). Find the slope of the secant line through the points $(0, f(0))$ and $(2, f(2))$ on the graph of $y = f(x)$.

(C) Find the equation of the tangent line to the graph of $y = f(x)$ at the point $(2, f(2))$.

14. Four hours after the start of a 600-mile auto race, a driver's velocity is 150 miles per hour as she completes the 352nd lap on a 1.5-mile track.

(A) Find the driver's average velocity during the first four hours of the race.

(B) Let $f(x)$ represent the distance traveled (in miles) from the start of the race ($x = 0$) to time x (in hours). Find the slope of the secant line through the points $(0, f(0))$ and $(4, f(4))$ on the graph of $y = f(x)$.

(C) Find the equation of the tangent line to the graph of $y = f(x)$ at the point $(4, f(4))$.

15. For $f(x) = \frac{1}{1 + x^2}$, the slope of the graph of $y = f(x)$ is known to be $-\frac{1}{2}$ at the point with x coordinate 1. Find the equation of the tangent line at that point.

16. For $f(x) = \frac{1}{1 + x^2}$, the slope of the graph of $y = f(x)$ is known to be -0.16 at the point with x coordinate 2. Find the equation of the tangent line at that point.

17. For $f(x) = x^4$, the instantaneous rate of change is known to be -32 at $x = -2$. Find the equation of the tangent line to the graph of $y = f(x)$ at the point with x coordinate -2.

18. For $f(x) = x^4$, the instantaneous rate of change is known to be -108 at $x = -3$. Find the equation of the tangent line to the graph of $y = f(x)$ at the point with x coordinate -3.

In Problems 19–44, use the four-step process to find $f'(x)$ and then find $f'(1)$, $f'(2)$, and $f'(3)$.

19. $f(x) = -5$

20. $f(x) = 9$

21. $f(x) = 3x - 7$

22. $f(x) = 4 - 6x$

23. $f(x) = 2 - 3x^2$

24. $f(x) = 7x^2 + 11$

25. $f(x) = x^2 - 2x + 3$

26. $f(x) = 3x^2 + 2x - 10$

27. $f(x) = 4x^2 + 3x - 8$

28. $f(x) = x^2 - 4x + 7$

29. $f(x) = -x^2 + 5x + 1$

30. $f(x) = 6x^2 - 3x + 4$

31. $f(x) = 10x^2 - 9x + 5$

32. $f(x) = -x^2 + 3x + 2$

33. $f(x) = 2x^3 + 1$

34. $f(x) = -2x^3 + 5$

35. $f(x) = 4 + \dfrac{4}{x}$

36. $f(x) = \dfrac{6}{x} - 2$

37. $f(x) = 5 + 3\sqrt{x}$

38. $f(x) = 3 - 7\sqrt{x}$

39. $f(x) = 10\sqrt{x + 5}$

40. $f(x) = 16\sqrt{x + 9}$

41. $f(x) = \dfrac{1}{x - 4}$

42. $f(x) = \dfrac{1}{x + 4}$

43. $f(x) = \dfrac{x}{x + 1}$

44. $f(x) = \dfrac{x}{x - 4}$

B *Problems 45 and 46 refer to the graph of $y = f(x) = x^2 + x$ shown.*

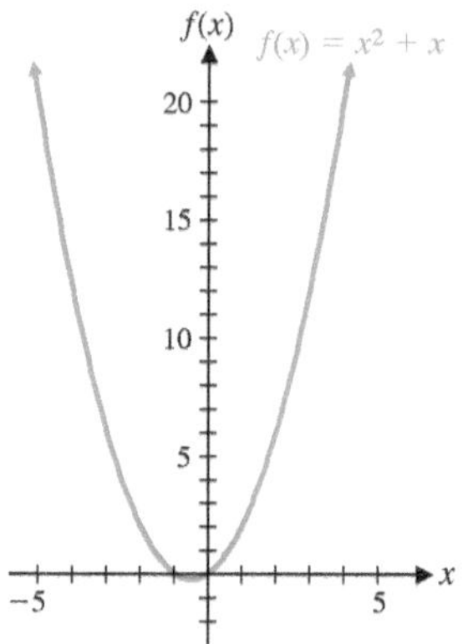

45. (A) Find the slope of the secant line joining $(1, f(1))$ and $(3, f(3))$.

(B) Find the slope of the secant line joining $(1, f(1))$ and $(1 + h, f(1 + h))$.

(C) Find the slope of the tangent line at $(1, f(1))$.

(D) Find the equation of the tangent line at $(1, f(1))$.

46. (A) Find the slope of the secant line joining $(3, f(3))$ and $(5, f(5))$.

(B) Find the slope of the secant line joining $(3, f(3))$ and $(3 + h, f(3 + h))$.

(C) Find the slope of the tangent line at $(3, f(3))$.

(D) Find the equation of the tangent line at $(3, f(3))$.

In Problems 47 and 48, suppose an object moves along the y axis so that its location is $y = f(x) = x^2 + x$ at time x (y is in meters and x is in seconds). Find

47. (A) The average velocity (the average rate of change of y with respect to x) for x changing from 1 to 3 seconds

(B) The average velocity for x changing from 1 to $1 + h$ seconds

(C) The instantaneous velocity at $x = 1$ second

48. (A) The average velocity (the average rate of change of y with respect to x) for x changing from 2 to 4 seconds

(B) The average velocity for x changing from 2 to $2 + h$ seconds

(C) The instantaneous velocity at $x = 2$ seconds

Problems 49–56 refer to the function F in the graph shown. Use the graph to determine whether $F'(x)$ exists at each indicated value of x.

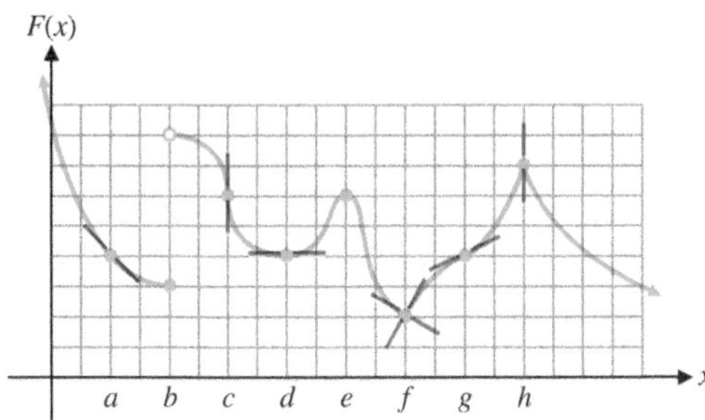

49. $x = a$ **50.** $x = b$

51. $x = c$ **52.** $x = d$

53. $x = e$ **54.** $x = f$

55. $x = g$ **56.** $x = h$

For Problems 57–58,

(A) *Find $f'(x)$.*

(B) *Find the slopes of the lines tangent to the graph of f at $x = 0, 2,$ and 4.*

(C) *Graph f and sketch in the tangent lines at $x = 0, 2,$ and 4.*

57. $f(x) = x^2 - 4x$

58. $f(x) = 4x - x^2 + 1$

59. If an object moves along a line so that it is at $y = f(x) = 4x^2 - 2x$ at time x (in seconds), find the instantaneous velocity function $v = f'(x)$ and find the velocity at times $x = 1, 3,$ and 5 seconds (y is measured in feet).

60. Repeat Problem 59 with $f(x) = 8x^2 - 4x$.

61. Let $f(x) = x^2$, $g(x) = x^2 - 1$, and $h(x) = x^2 + 2$.

(A) How are the graphs of these functions related? How would you expect the derivatives of these functions to be related?

(B) Use the four-step process to find the derivative of $m(x) = x^2 + C$, where C is any real constant.

62. Let $f(x) = -x^2$, $g(x) = -x^2 - 1$, and $h(x) = -x^2 + 2$.

(A) How are the graphs of these functions related? How would you expect the derivatives of these functions to be related?

(B) Use the four-step process to find the derivative of $m(x) = -x^2 + C$, where C is any real constant.

In Problems 63–68, discuss the validity of each statement. If the statement is always true, explain why. If not, give a counterexample.

63. If $f(x) = C$ is a constant function, then $f'(x) = 0$.

64. If $f(x) = mx + b$ is a linear function, then $f'(x) = m$.

65. If a function f is continuous on the interval (a, b), then f is differentiable on (a, b).

66. If a function f is differentiable on the interval (a, b), then f is continuous on (a, b).

67. The average rate of change of a function f from $x = a$ to $x = a + h$ is less than the instantaneous rate of change at $x = a + \frac{h}{2}$.

68. If the graph of f has a sharp corner at $x = a$, then f is not continuous at $x = a$.

In Problems 69–72, sketch the graph of f and determine where f is nondifferentiable.

69. $f(x) = \begin{cases} 2x & \text{if } x < 1 \\ 2 & \text{if } x \geq 1 \end{cases}$

70. $f(x) = \begin{cases} 2x & \text{if } x < 2 \\ 6 - x & \text{if } x \geq 2 \end{cases}$

71. $f(x) = \begin{cases} x^2 + 1 & \text{if } x < 0 \\ 1 & \text{if } x \geq 0 \end{cases}$

72. $f(x) = \begin{cases} 2 - x^2 & \text{if } x \leq 0 \\ 2 & \text{if } x > 0 \end{cases}$

C *In Problems 73–78, determine whether f is differentiable at $x = 0$ by considering*

$$\lim_{h \to 0} \frac{f(0 + h) - f(0)}{h}$$

73. $f(x) = |x|$ **74.** $f(x) = 1 - |x|$

75. $f(x) = x^{1/3}$ **76.** $f(x) = x^{2/3}$

77. $f(x) = \sqrt{1 - x^2}$ **78.** $f(x) = \sqrt{9 + x^2}$

79. A ball dropped from a balloon falls $y = 16x^2$ feet in x seconds. If the balloon is 576 feet above the ground when the ball is dropped, when does the ball hit the ground? What is the velocity of the ball at the instant it hits the ground?

80. Repeat Problem 79 if the balloon is 1,296 feet above the ground when the ball is dropped.

Applications

81. Revenue. The revenue (in dollars) from the sale of x infant car seats is given by

$$R(x) = 60x - 0.025x^2 \qquad 0 \le x \le 2{,}400$$

(A) Find the average change in revenue if production is changed from 1,000 car seats to 1,050 car seats.

(B) Use the four-step process to find $R'(x)$.

(C) Find the revenue and the instantaneous rate of change of revenue at a production level of 1,000 car seats, and write a brief verbal interpretation of these results.

82. Profit. The profit (in dollars) from the sale of x infant car seats is given by

$$P(x) = 45x - 0.025x^2 - 5{,}000 \qquad 0 \le x \le 2{,}400$$

(A) Find the average change in profit if production is changed from 800 car seats to 850 car seats.

(B) Use the four-step process to find $P'(x)$.

(C) Find the profit and the instantaneous rate of change of profit at a production level of 800 car seats, and write a brief verbal interpretation of these results.

83. Sales analysis. A company's total sales (in millions of dollars) t months from now are given by

$$S(t) = \sqrt{t} + 4$$

(A) Use the four-step process to find $S'(t)$.

(B) Find $S(4)$ and $S'(4)$. Write a brief verbal interpretation of these results.

(C) Use the results in part (B) to estimate the total sales after 5 months and after 6 months.

84. Sales analysis. A company's total sales (in millions of dollars) t months from now are given by

$$S(t) = \sqrt{t} + 8$$

(A) Use the four-step process to find $S'(t)$.

(B) Find $S(9)$ and $S'(9)$. Write a brief verbal interpretation of these results.

(C) Use the results in part (B) to estimate the total sales after 10 months and after 11 months.

85. Mineral production. Argentina's production of zinc (in tons) is given approximately by

$$p(t) = 317t^2 + 4{,}067t + 32{,}600$$

where t is time in years and $t = 0$ corresponds to 2010.

(A) Use the four-step process to find $p'(t)$.

(B) Find the annual production in 2020 and the instantaneous rate of change of consumption in 2020, and write a brief verbal interpretation of these results.

86. Mineral production. Spain's production of tungsten (in tons) is given approximately by

$$p(t) = 20t^2 + 102t + 303$$

where t is time in years and $t = 0$ corresponds to 2010.

(A) Use the four-step process to find $p'(t)$.

(B) Find the annual production in 2020 and the instantaneous rate of change of consumption in 2020, and write a brief verbal interpretation of these results.

87. Electricity consumption. Table 1 gives the retail sales of electricity (in billions of kilowatt-hours) for the residential and commercial sectors in the United States. (*Source:* Energy Information Administration)

Table 1 **Electricity Sales**

Year	Residential	Commercial
2000	1,192	1,055
2003	1,276	1,199
2006	1,352	1,300
2009	1,365	1,307
2012	1,375	1,327
2015	1,400	1,358

(A) Let x represent time (in years) with $x = 0$ corresponding to 2000, and let y represent the corresponding residential sales. Enter the appropriate data set in a graphing calculator and find a quadratic regression equation for the data.

(B) If $y = R(x)$ denotes the regression equation found in part (A), find $R(30)$ and $R'(30)$, and write a brief verbal interpretation of these results. Round answers to the nearest tenth of a billion.

88. Electricity consumption. Refer to the data in Table 1.

(A) Let x represent time (in years) with $x = 0$ corresponding to 2000, and let y represent the corresponding commercial sales. Enter the appropriate data set in a graphing calculator and find a quadratic regression equation for the data.

(B) If $y = C(x)$ denotes the regression equation found in part (A), find $C(30)$ and $C'(30)$, and write a brief verbal interpretation of these results. Round answers to the nearest tenth of a billion.

89. Air pollution. The ozone level (in parts per billion) on a summer day in a metropolitan area is given by

$$P(t) = 80 + 12t - t^2$$

where t is time in hours and $t = 0$ corresponds to 9 A.M.

(A) Use the four-step process to find $P'(t)$.

(B) Find $P(3)$ and $P'(3)$. Write a brief verbal interpretation of these results.

90. Medicine. The body temperature (in degrees Fahrenheit) of a patient t hours after taking a fever-reducing drug is given by

$$F(t) = 98 + \frac{4}{t+1}$$

(A) Use the four-step process to find $F'(t)$.

(B) Find $F(3)$ and $F'(3)$. Write a brief verbal interpretation of these results.

Answers to Matched Problems

1. (A) $-\$1,600$ (B) $-\$8$ per planter
2. (A) 48 ft/s (B) $32 + 16h$ (C) 32 ft/s
3. (A) 6, 5 (B) $4 + h$ (C) 4 (D) Both are 4
4. $f'(x) = 8 - 4x$
5. (A) $f'(1) = 4, f'(2) = 0, f'(4) = -8$

(B)

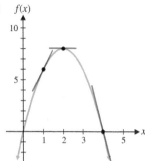

6. $f'(x) = -1/(x+2)^2, x \neq -2$
7. $f'(x) = 1/(2\sqrt{x+4}), x \geq -4$
8. $S(12) = 4, S'(12) = 0.125$; 12 months from now, the total sales will be \$4 million and will be increasing at the rate of \$0.125 million (\$125,000) per month. The estimated total sales are \$4.125 million after 13 months and \$4.25 million after 14 months.

6.5 Basic Differentiation Properties

- Constant Function Rule
- Power Rule
- Constant Multiple Property
- Sum and Difference Properties
- Applications

In Section 6.4, we defined the derivative of f at x as

$$f'(x) = \lim_{h \to 0} \frac{f(x+h) - f(x)}{h}$$

if the limit exists, and we used this definition and a four-step process to find the derivatives of several functions. Now we want to develop some rules of differentiation. These rules will enable us to find the derivative of many functions without using the four-step process.

Before exploring these rules, we list some symbols that are often used to represent derivatives.

NOTATION The Derivative

If $y = f(x)$, then

$$f'(x) \qquad y' \qquad \frac{dy}{dx} \qquad \frac{d}{dx}f(x)$$

all represent the derivative of f at x.

Each of these derivative symbols has its particular advantage in certain situations. All of them will become familiar to you after a little experience.

Constant Function Rule

If $f(x) = C$ is a constant function, then the four-step process can be used to show that $f'(x) = 0$. Therefore,

The derivative of any constant function is 0.

THEOREM 1 Constant Function Rule

If $y = f(x) = C$, then

$$f'(x) = 0$$

Also, $y' = 0$ and $dy/dx = 0$.

Note: When we write $C' = 0$ or $\frac{d}{dx}C = 0$, we mean that $y' = \frac{dy}{dx} = 0$ when $y = C$.

CONCEPTUAL INSIGHT

The graph of $f(x) = C$ is a horizontal line with slope 0 (Fig. 1), so we would expect that $f'(x) = 0$.

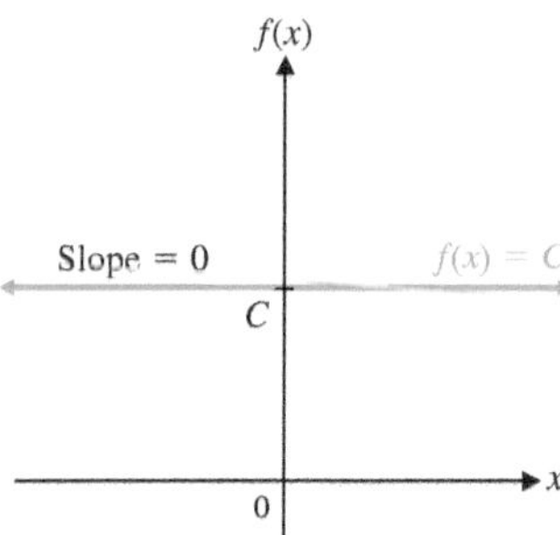

Figure 1

EXAMPLE 1 Differentiating Constant Functions

(A) Find $f'(x)$ for $f(x) = 3$.

(B) Find y' for $y = -1.4$.

(C) Find $\frac{dy}{dx}$ for $y = \pi$.

(D) Find $\frac{d}{dx}23$.

SOLUTION

(A) $f'(x) = 0$

(B) $y' = 0$

(C) $\frac{dy}{dx} = 0$

(D) $\frac{d}{dx}23 = 0$

Matched Problem 1 Find

(A) $f'(x)$ for $f(x) = -24$

(B) y' for $y = 12$

(C) $\frac{dy}{dx}$ for $y = -\sqrt{7}$

(D) $\frac{d}{dx}(-\pi)$

Power Rule

A function of the form $f(x) = x^k$, where k is a real number, is called a **power function**. The following elementary functions are examples of power functions:

$$f(x) = x \qquad h(x) = x^2 \qquad m(x) = x^3 \tag{1}$$
$$n(x) = \sqrt{x} \qquad p(x) = \sqrt[3]{x} \qquad q(x) = x^{-3}$$

Explore and Discuss 1

(A) It is clear that the functions f, h, and m in (1) are power functions. Explain why the functions n, p, and q are also power functions.

(B) The domain of a power function depends on the power. Discuss the domain of each of the following power functions:

$$r(x) = x^4 \qquad s(x) = x^{-4} \qquad t(x) = x^{1/4}$$
$$u(x) = x^{-1/4} \qquad v(x) = x^{1/5} \qquad w(x) = x^{-1/5}$$

The definition of the derivative and the four-step process introduced in Section 6.4 can be used to find the derivatives of many power functions. For example, it can be shown that

$$\begin{aligned}
&\text{If} \quad f(x) = x^2, \quad \text{then} \quad f'(x) = 2x.\\
&\text{If} \quad f(x) = x^3, \quad \text{then} \quad f'(x) = 3x^2.\\
&\text{If} \quad f(x) = x^4, \quad \text{then} \quad f'(x) = 4x^3.\\
&\text{If} \quad f(x) = x^5, \quad \text{then} \quad f'(x) = 5x^4.
\end{aligned}$$

Notice the pattern in these derivatives. In each case, the power in f becomes the coefficient in f' and the power in f' is 1 less than the power in f. In general, for any positive integer n,

$$\text{If} \quad f(x) = x^n, \quad \text{then} \quad f'(x) = nx^{n-1}. \tag{2}$$

In fact, more advanced techniques can be used to show that (2) holds for *any* real number n. We will assume this general result for the remainder of the book.

THEOREM 2 Power Rule

If $y = f(x) = x^n$, where n is a real number, then

$$f'(x) = nx^{n-1}$$

Also, $y' = nx^{n-1}$ and $dy/dx = nx^{n-1}$.

EXAMPLE 2 **Differentiating Power Functions**

(A) Find $f'(x)$ for $f(x) = x^5$.

(B) Find y' for $y = x^{25}$.

(C) Find $\frac{dy}{dt}$ for $y = t^{-3}$.

(D) Find $\frac{d}{dx}x^{5/3}$.

SOLUTION

(A) $f'(x) = 5x^{5-1} = 5x^4$

(B) $y' = 25x^{25-1} = 25x^{24}$

(C) $\frac{dy}{dt} = -3t^{-3-1} = -3t^{-4}$

(D) $\frac{d}{dx}x^{5/3} = \frac{5}{3}x^{(5/3)-1} = \frac{5}{3}x^{2/3}$

Matched Problem 2 Find

(A) $f'(x)$ for $f(x) = x^6$

(B) y' for $y = x^{30}$

(C) $\frac{dy}{dt}$ for $y = t^{-2}$

(D) $\frac{d}{dx}x^{3/2}$

In some cases, properties of exponents must be used to rewrite an expression before the power rule is applied.

EXAMPLE 3 **Differentiating Power Functions**

(A) Find $f'(x)$ for $f(x) = \frac{1}{x^4}$.

(B) Find y' for $y = \sqrt{u}$.

(C) Find $\frac{d}{dx}\frac{1}{\sqrt[3]{x}}$.

SOLUTION

(A) We can write $f(x) = x^{-4}$ to get

$$f'(x) = -4x^{-4-1} = -4x^{-5} = -\frac{4}{x^5}.$$

(B) We can write $y = u^{1/2}$ to get

$$y' = \frac{1}{2}u^{(1/2)-1} = \frac{1}{2}u^{-1/2} = \frac{1}{2\sqrt{u}}.$$

(C) $$\frac{d}{dx}\frac{1}{\sqrt[3]{x}} = \frac{d}{dx}x^{-1/3} = -\frac{1}{3}x^{(-1/3)-1} = -\frac{1}{3}x^{-4/3}, \text{ or } \frac{-1}{3\sqrt[3]{x^4}}$$

Matched Problem 3 Find

(A) $f'(x)$ for $f(x) = \frac{1}{x}$

(B) y' for $y = \sqrt[3]{u^2}$

(C) $\frac{d}{dx}\frac{1}{\sqrt{x}}$

Constant Multiple Property

Let $f(x) = ku(x)$, where k is a constant and u is differentiable at x. Using the four-step process, we have the following:

Step 1 $f(x + h) = ku(x + h)$

Step 2 $f(x + h) - f(x) = ku(x + h) - ku(x) = k[u(x + h) - u(x)]$

Step 3 $$\frac{f(x + h) - f(x)}{h} = \frac{k[u(x + h) - u(x)]}{h} = k\left[\frac{u(x + h) - u(x)}{h}\right]$$

Step 4 $$\begin{aligned} f'(x) &= \lim_{h\to 0}\frac{f(x + h) - f(x)}{h} \\ &= \lim_{h\to 0} k\left[\frac{u(x + h) - u(x)}{h}\right] && \lim_{x\to c} kg(x) = k\lim_{x\to c} g(x) \\ &= k\lim_{h\to 0}\left[\frac{u(x + h) - u(x)}{h}\right] && \text{Definition of } u'(x) \\ &= ku'(x) \end{aligned}$$

Therefore,

The derivative of a constant times a differentiable function is the constant times the derivative of the function.

THEOREM 3 Constant Multiple Property

If $y = f(x) = ku(x)$, then

$$f'(x) = ku'(x)$$

Also,

$$y' = ku' \qquad \frac{dy}{dx} = k\frac{du}{dx}$$

EXAMPLE 4 **Differentiating a Constant Times a Function**

(A) Find $f'(x)$ for $f(x) = 3x^2$. (B) Find $\frac{dy}{dt}$ for $y = \frac{t^3}{6}$.

(C) Find y' for $y = \frac{1}{2x^4}$. (D) Find $\frac{d}{dx}\frac{0.4}{\sqrt{x^3}}$.

SOLUTION

(A) $f'(x) = 3 \cdot 2x^{2-1} = 6x$

(B) We can write $y = \frac{1}{6}t^3$ to get $\frac{dy}{dt} = \frac{1}{6} \cdot 3t^{3-1} = \frac{1}{2}t^2$.

(C) We can write $y = \frac{1}{2}x^{-4}$ to get

$$y' = \frac{1}{2}(-4x^{-4-1}) = -2x^{-5}, \text{ or } \frac{-2}{x^5}.$$

(D) $$\frac{d}{dx}\frac{0.4}{\sqrt{x^3}} = \frac{d}{dx}\frac{0.4}{x^{3/2}} = \frac{d}{dx}0.4x^{-3/2} = 0.4\left[-\frac{3}{2}x^{(-3/2)-1}\right]$$

$$= -0.6x^{-5/2}, \quad \text{or} \quad -\frac{0.6}{\sqrt{x^5}}$$

Matched Problem 4 Find

(A) $f'(x)$ for $f(x) = 4x^5$ (B) $\frac{dy}{dt}$ for $y = \frac{t^4}{12}$

(C) y' for $y = \frac{1}{3x^3}$ (D) $\frac{d}{dx}\frac{0.9}{\sqrt[3]{x}}$

Sum and Difference Properties

Let $f(x) = u(x) + v(x)$, where $u'(x)$ and $v'(x)$ exist. Using the four-step process (see Problems 87 and 88 in Exercises 6.5):

$$f'(x) = u'(x) + v'(x)$$

Therefore,

The derivative of the sum of two differentiable functions is the sum of the derivatives of the functions.

Similarly, we can show that

The derivative of the difference of two differentiable functions is the difference of the derivatives of the functions.

Together, we have the **sum and difference property** for differentiation:

THEOREM 4 Sum and Difference Property

If $y = f(x) = u(x) \pm v(x)$, then

$$f'(x) = u'(x) \pm v'(x)$$

Also,

$$y' = u' \pm v' \qquad \frac{dy}{dx} = \frac{du}{dx} \pm \frac{dv}{dx}$$

Note: This rule generalizes to the sum and difference of any given number of functions.

With Theorems 1 through 4, we can compute the derivatives of all polynomials and a variety of other functions.

EXAMPLE 5 **Differentiating Sums and Differences**

(A) Find $f'(x)$ for $f(x) = 3x^2 + 2x$. (B) Find y' for $y = 4 + 2x^3 - 3x^{-1}$.

(C) Find $\frac{dy}{dw}$ for $y = \sqrt[3]{w} - 3w$. (D) Find $\frac{d}{dx}\left(\frac{5}{3x^2} - \frac{2}{x^4} + \frac{x^3}{9}\right)$.

SOLUTION

(A) $f'(x) = (3x^2)' + (2x)' = 3(2x) + 2(1) = 6x + 2$

(B) $y' = (4)' + (2x^3)' - (3x^{-1})' = 0 + 2(3x^2) - 3(-1)x^{-2} = 6x^2 + 3x^{-2}$

(C) $\frac{dy}{dw} = \frac{d}{dw}w^{1/3} - \frac{d}{dw}3w = \frac{1}{3}w^{-2/3} - 3 = \frac{1}{3w^{2/3}} - 3$

(D) $$\frac{d}{dx}\left(\frac{5}{3x^2} - \frac{2}{x^4} + \frac{x^3}{9}\right) = \frac{d}{dx}\frac{5}{3}x^{-2} - \frac{d}{dx}2x^{-4} + \frac{d}{dx}\frac{1}{9}x^3$$

$$= \frac{5}{3}(-2)x^{-3} - 2(-4)x^{-5} + \frac{1}{9}\cdot 3x^2$$

$$= -\frac{10}{3x^3} + \frac{8}{x^5} + \frac{1}{3}x^2$$

Matched Problem 5 Find

(A) $f'(x)$ for $f(x) = 3x^4 - 2x^3 + x^2 - 5x + 7$

(B) y' for $y = 3 - 7x^{-2}$

(C) $\frac{dy}{dv}$ for $y = 5v^3 - \sqrt[4]{v}$

(D) $\frac{d}{dx}\left(-\frac{3}{4x} + \frac{4}{x^3} - \frac{x^4}{8}\right)$

Some algebraic rewriting of a function is sometimes required before we can apply the rules for differentiation.

EXAMPLE 6 **Rewrite before Differentiating** Find the derivative of $f(x) = \frac{1 + x^2}{x^4}$.

SOLUTION It is helpful to rewrite $f(x) = \frac{1 + x^2}{x^4}$, expressing $f(x)$ as the sum of terms, each of which can be differentiated by applying the power rule.

$$f(x) = \frac{1 + x^2}{x^4} \qquad \text{Write as a sum of two terms}$$

$$= \frac{1}{x^4} + \frac{x^2}{x^4} \qquad \text{Write each term as a power of } x$$

$$= x^{-4} + x^{-2}$$

Note that we have rewritten $f(x)$, but we have not used any rules of differentiation. Now, however, we can apply those rules to find the derivative:

$$f'(x) = -4x^{-5} - 2x^{-3}$$

Matched Problem 6 Find the derivative of $f(x) = \dfrac{5 - 3x + 4x^2}{x}$.

Applications

EXAMPLE 7 **Instantaneous Velocity** An object moves along the y axis (marked in feet) so that its position at time x (in seconds) is

$$f(x) = x^3 - 6x^2 + 9x$$

(A) Find the instantaneous velocity function v.

(B) Find the velocity at $x = 2$ and $x = 5$ seconds.

(C) Find the time(s) when the velocity is 0.

SOLUTION

(A) $v = f'(x) = (x^3)' - (6x^2)' + (9x)' = 3x^2 - 12x + 9$

(B) $f'(2) = 3(2)^2 - 12(2) + 9 = -3$ feet per second

$f'(5) = 3(5)^2 - 12(5) + 9 = 24$ feet per second

(C) $v = f'(x) = 3x^2 - 12x + 9 = 0$ Factor 3 out of each term.

$3(x^2 - 4x + 3) = 0$ Factor the quadratic term.

$3(x - 1)(x - 3) = 0$ Use the zero property.

$x = 1, 3$

So, $v = 0$ at $x = 1$ and $x = 3$ seconds.

Matched Problem 7 Repeat Example 7 for $f(x) = x^3 - 15x^2 + 72x$.

EXAMPLE 8 **Tangents** Let $f(x) = x^4 - 6x^2 + 10$.

(A) Find $f'(x)$.

(B) Find the equation of the tangent line at $x = 1$.

(C) Find the values of x where the tangent line is horizontal.

SOLUTION

(A) $f'(x) = (x^4)' - (6x^2)' + (10)'$

$= 4x^3 - 12x$

(B) We use the point-slope form. (Section 1.2)

$y - y_1 = m(x - x_1)$ $\quad y_1 = f(x_1) = f(1) = (1)^4 - 6(1)^2 + 10 = 5$

$y - 5 = -8(x - 1)$ $\quad m = f'(x_1) = f'(1) = 4(1)^3 - 12(1) = -8$

$y = -8x + 13$ $\quad$ Tangent line at $x = 1$

(C) Since a horizontal line has 0 slope, we must solve $f'(x) = 0$ for x:

$$f'(x) = 4x^3 - 12x = 0 \quad \text{Factor } 4x \text{ out of each term.}$$
$$4x(x^2 - 3) = 0 \quad \text{Factor the difference of two squares.}$$
$$4x(x + \sqrt{3})(x - \sqrt{3}) = 0 \quad \text{Use the zero property.}$$
$$x = 0, -\sqrt{3}, \sqrt{3}$$

Matched Problem 8 Repeat Example 8 for $f(x) = x^4 - 8x^3 + 7$.

Exercises 6.5

Skills Warm-up Exercises

W *In Problems 1–8, write the expression in the form x^n. (If necessary, review Section A.6.)*

1. $\sqrt{x}$ **2.** $\sqrt[3]{x}$ **3.** $\frac{1}{x^5}$ **4.** $\frac{1}{x}$

5. $(x^4)^3$ **6.** $\frac{1}{(x^7)^8}$ **7.** $\frac{1}{\sqrt[4]{x}}$ **8.** $\frac{1}{\sqrt[5]{x}}$

A *Find the indicated derivatives in Problems 9–26.*

9. $f'(x)$ for $f(x) = 4$ **10.** $\frac{d}{dx}5$

11. $\frac{dy}{dx}$ for $y = x^7$ **12.** y' for $y = x^8$

13. $\frac{d}{dx}x^4$ **14.** $g'(x)$ for $g(x) = x^9$

15. y' for $y = x^{-3}$ **16.** $\frac{dy}{dx}$ for $y = x^{-9}$

17. $g'(x)$ for $g(x) = x^{4/3}$ **18.** $f'(x)$ for $f(x) = x^{5/2}$

19. $\frac{dy}{dx}$ for $y = \frac{1}{x^9}$ **20.** y' for $y = \frac{1}{x^7}$

21. $f'(x)$ for $f(x) = 2x^3$ **22.** $\frac{d}{dx}(-3x^2)$

23. y' for $y = 0.3x^6$ **24.** $f'(x)$ for $f(x) = 0.7x^3$

25. $\frac{d}{dx}\left(\frac{x^4}{12}\right)$ **26.** $\frac{dy}{dx}$ for $y = \frac{x^7}{28}$

Problems 27–32 refer to functions f and g that satisfy $f'(2) = 3$ and $g'(2) = -1$. In each problem, find $h'(2)$ for the indicated function h.

27. $h(x) = 4f(x)$ **28.** $h(x) = 5g(x)$

29. $h(x) = f(x) + g(x)$ **30.** $h(x) = g(x) - f(x)$

31. $h(x) = 4f(x) - 5g(x) + 6$

32. $h(x) = -4f(x) + 5g(x) - 9$

B *Find the indicated derivatives in Problems 33–56.*

33. $\frac{d}{dx}(2x - 5)$

34. $\frac{d}{dx}(-4x + 9)$

35. $f'(t)$ if $f(t) = 3t^2 - 5t + 7$

36. $\frac{dy}{dt}$ if $y = 2 + 5t - 8t^3$

37. y' for $y = 5x^{-2} + 9x^{-1}$

38. $g'(x)$ if $g(x) = 5x^{-7} - 2x^{-4}$

39. $\frac{d}{du}(5u^{0.3} - 4u^{2.2})$

40. $\frac{d}{du}(2u^{4.5} - 3.1u + 13.2)$

41. $h'(t)$ if $h(t) = 2.1 + 0.5t - 1.1t^3$

42. $F'(t)$ if $F(t) = 0.4t^5 - 6.7t + 8.9$

43. y' if $y = \frac{2}{5x^4}$

44. w' if $w = \frac{7}{5u^2}$

45. $\frac{d}{dx}\left(\frac{3x^2}{2} - \frac{7}{5x^2}\right)$

46. $\frac{d}{dx}\left(\frac{3x^4}{5} - \frac{5}{3x^4}\right)$

47. $G'(w)$ if $G(w) = \frac{5}{9w^4} + 5\sqrt[3]{w}$

48. $H'(w)$ if $H(w) = \frac{5}{w^6} - 2\sqrt{w}$

49. $\frac{d}{du}(3u^{2/3} - 5u^{1/3})$

50. $\frac{d}{du}(8u^{3/4} + 4u^{-1/4})$

51. $h'(t)$ if $h(t) = \frac{3}{t^{3/5}} - \frac{6}{t^{1/2}}$

52. $F'(t)$ if $F(t) = \frac{5}{t^{1/5}} - \frac{8}{t^{3/2}}$

53. y' if $y = \frac{1}{\sqrt[3]{x}}$

54. w' if $w = \frac{24}{\sqrt[4]{u}}$

55. $\frac{d}{dx}\left(\frac{1.2}{\sqrt{x}} - 3.2x^{-2} + x\right)$

56. $\frac{d}{dx}\left(2.8x^{-3} - \frac{0.6}{\sqrt[3]{x^2}} + 7\right)$

For Problems 57–60, find

(A) $f'(x)$

(B) *The slope of the graph of f at $x = 2$ and $x = 4$*

(C) *The equations of the tangent lines at $x = 2$ and $x = 4$*

(D) *The value(s) of x where the tangent line is horizontal*

57. $f(x) = 6x - x^2$

58. $f(x) = 2x^2 + 8x$

59. $f(x) = 3x^4 - 6x^2 - 7$

60. $f(x) = x^4 - 32x^2 + 10$

If an object moves along the y axis (marked in feet) so that its position at time x (in seconds) is given by the indicated functions in Problems 61–64, find

(A) *The instantaneous velocity function $v = f'(x)$*

(B) *The velocity when $x = 0$ and $x = 3$ seconds*

(C) *The time(s) when $v = 0$*

61. $f(x) = 176x - 16x^2$

62. $f(x) = 80x - 10x^2$

63. $f(x) = x^3 - 9x^2 + 15x$

64. $f(x) = x^3 - 9x^2 + 24x$

Problems 65–72 require the use of a graphing calculator. For each problem, find $f'(x)$ and approximate (to four decimal places) the value(s) of x where the graph of f has a horizontal tangent line.

65. $f(x) = x^2 - 3x - 4\sqrt{x}$

66. $f(x) = x^2 + x - 10\sqrt{x}$

67. $f(x) = 3\sqrt[3]{x^4} - 1.5x^2 - 3x$

68. $f(x) = 3\sqrt[3]{x^4} - 2x^2 + 4x$

69. $f(x) = 0.05x^4 + 0.1x^3 - 1.5x^2 - 1.6x + 3$

70. $f(x) = 0.02x^4 - 0.06x^3 - 0.78x^2 + 0.94x + 2.2$

71. $f(x) = 0.2x^4 - 3.12x^3 + 16.25x^2 - 28.25x + 7.5$

72. $f(x) = 0.25x^4 - 2.6x^3 + 8.1x^2 - 10x + 9$

73. Let $f(x) = ax^2 + bx + c$, $a \neq 0$. Recall that the graph of $y = f(x)$ is a parabola. Use the derivative $f'(x)$ to derive a formula for the x coordinate of the vertex of this parabola.

74. Now that you know how to find derivatives, explain why it is no longer necessary for you to memorize the formula for the x coordinate of the vertex of a parabola.

75. Give an example of a cubic polynomial function that has

(A) No horizontal tangents

(B) One horizontal tangent

(C) Two horizontal tangents

76. Can a cubic polynomial function have more than two horizontal tangents? Explain.

C *Find the indicated derivatives in Problems 77–82.*

77. $f'(x)$ if $f(x) = (2x - 1)^2$

78. y' if $y = (4x - 3)^2$

79. $\dfrac{d}{dx}\dfrac{10x + 20}{x}$

80. $\dfrac{dy}{dx}$ if $y = \dfrac{x^2 + 25}{x^2}$

81. $\dfrac{dy}{dx}$ if $y = \dfrac{4x - 5}{20x^2}$

82. $f'(x)$ if $f(x) = \dfrac{2x^5 - 4x^3 + 2x}{x^3}$

In Problems 83–86, discuss the validity of each statement. If the statement is always true, explain why. If not, give a counterexample.

83. The derivative of a product is the product of the derivatives.

84. The derivative of a quotient is the quotient of the derivatives.

85. The derivative of a constant is 0.

86. The derivative of a constant times a function is 0.

87. Let $f(x) = u(x) + v(x)$, where $u'(x)$ and $v'(x)$ exist. Use the four-step process to show that $f'(x) = u'(x) + v'(x)$.

88. Let $f(x) = u(x) - v(x)$, where $u'(x)$ and $v'(x)$ exist. Use the four-step process to show that $f'(x) = u'(x) - v'(x)$.

Applications

89. Sales analysis. A company's total sales (in millions of dollars) t months from now are given by

$$S(t) = 0.03t^3 + 0.5t^2 + 2t + 3$$

(A) Find $S'(t)$.

(B) Find $S(5)$ and $S'(5)$ (to two decimal places). Write a brief verbal interpretation of these results.

(C) Find $S(10)$ and $S'(10)$ (to two decimal places). Write a brief verbal interpretation of these results.

90. Sales analysis. A company's total sales (in millions of dollars) t months from now are given by

$$S(t) = 0.015t^4 + 0.4t^3 + 3.4t^2 + 10t - 3$$

(A) Find $S'(t)$.

(B) Find $S(4)$ and $S'(4)$ (to two decimal places). Write a brief verbal interpretation of these results.

(C) Find $S(8)$ and $S'(8)$ (to two decimal places). Write a brief verbal interpretation of these results.

91. Advertising. A marine manufacturer will sell $N(x)$ power boats after spending $\$x$ thousand on advertising, as given by

$$N(x) = 1{,}000 - \frac{3{,}780}{x} \qquad 5 \le x \le 30$$

(see figure).

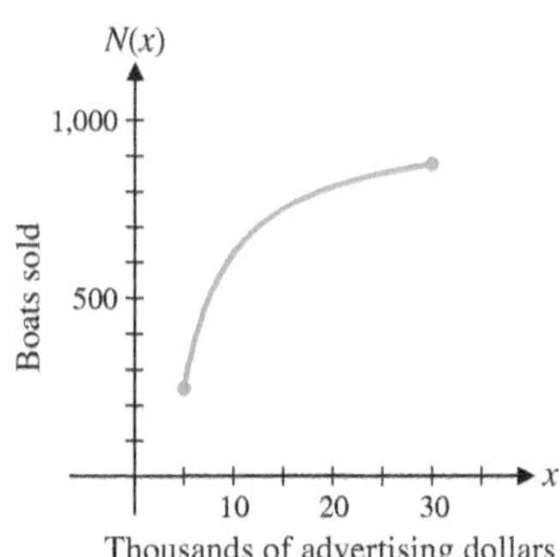

(A) Find $N'(x)$.

(B) Find $N'(10)$ and $N'(20)$. Write a brief verbal interpretation of these results.

92. Price–demand equation. Suppose that, in a given gourmet food store, people are willing to buy x pounds of chocolate candy per day at $\$p$ per quarter pound, as given by the price–demand equation

$$x = 10 + \frac{180}{p} \qquad 2 \le p \le 10$$

This function is graphed in the figure. Find the demand and the instantaneous rate of change of demand with respect to price when the price is \$5. Write a brief verbal interpretation of these results.

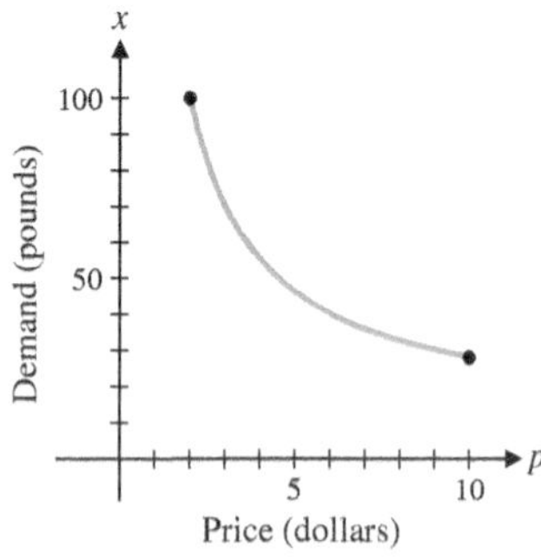

93. College enrollment. The percentages of male high school graduates who enrolled in college are given in the second column of Table 1. (*Source:* NCES)

Table 1 **College enrollment percentages**

Year	Male	Female
1970	41.0	25.5
1980	33.5	30.3
1990	40.0	38.3
2000	40.8	45.6
2010	45.9	50.5

(A) Let x represent time (in years) since 1970, and let y represent the corresponding percentage of male high school graduates who enrolled in college. Enter the data in a graphing calculator and find a cubic regression equation for the data.

(B) If $y = M(x)$ denotes the regression equation found in part (A), find $M(55)$ and $M'(55)$ (to the nearest tenth), and write a brief verbal interpretation of these results.

94. College enrollment. The percentages of female high school graduates who enrolled in college are given in the third column of Table 1.

(A) Let x represent time (in years) since 1970, and let y represent the corresponding percentage of female high school graduates who enrolled in college. Enter the data in a graphing calculator and find a cubic regression equation for the data.

(B) If $y = F(x)$ denotes the regression equation found in part (A), find $F(55)$ and $F'(55)$ (to the nearest tenth), and write a brief verbal interpretation of these results.

95. Medicine. A person x inches tall has a pulse rate of y beats per minute, as given approximately by

$$y = 590x^{-1/2} \qquad 30 \le x \le 75$$

What is the instantaneous rate of change of pulse rate at the

(A) 36-inch level?

(B) 64-inch level?

96. Ecology. A coal-burning electrical generating plant emits sulfur dioxide into the surrounding air. The concentration $C(x)$, in parts per million, is given approximately by

$$C(x) = \frac{0.1}{x^2}$$

where x is the distance from the plant in miles. Find the instantaneous rate of change of concentration at

(A) $x = 1$ mile

(B) $x = 2$ miles

97. Learning. Suppose that a person learns y items in x hours, as given by

$$y = 50\sqrt{x} \qquad 0 \le x \le 9$$

(see figure). Find the rate of learning at the end of

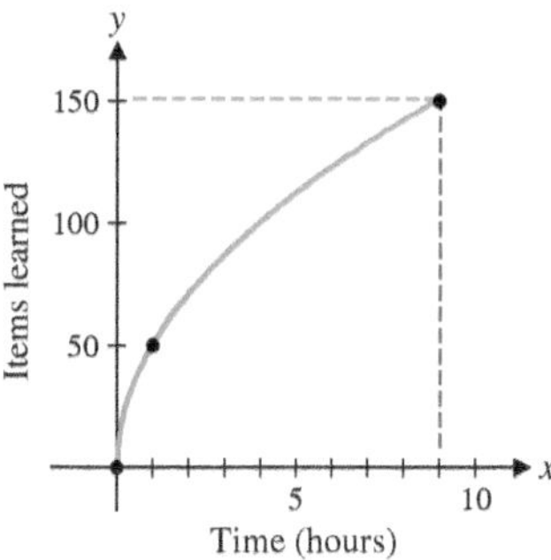

(A) 1 hour

(B) 9 hours

98. Learning. If a person learns y items in x hours, as given by

$$y = 21\sqrt[3]{x^2} \qquad 0 \le x \le 8$$

find the rate of learning at the end of

(A) 1 hour

(B) 8 hours

Answers to Matched Problems

1. All are 0.
2. (A) $6x^5$ (B) $30x^{29}$
   (C) $-2t^{-3} = -2/t^3$ (D) $\frac{3}{2}x^{1/2}$
3. (A) $-x^{-2}$, or $-1/x^2$ (B) $\frac{2}{3}u^{-1/3}$, or $2/(3\sqrt[3]{u})$
   (C) $-\frac{1}{2}x^{-3/2}$, or $-1/(2\sqrt{x^3})$
4. (A) $20x^4$ (B) $t^3/3$
   (C) $-x^{-4}$, or $-1/x^4$ (D) $-0.3x^{-4/3}$, or $-0.3/\sqrt[3]{x^4}$
5. (A) $12x^3 - 6x^2 + 2x - 5$ (B) $14x^{-3}$, or $14/x^3$
   (C) $15v^2 - \frac{1}{4}v^{-3/4}$, or $15v^2 - 1/(4v^{3/4})$
   (D) $3/(4x^2) - (12/x^4) - (x^3/2)$
6. $f'(x) = -5x^{-2} + 4$
7. (A) $v = 3x^2 - 30x + 72$
   (B) $f'(2) = 24$ ft/s; $f'(5) = -3$ ft/s
   (C) $x = 4$ and $x = 6$ seconds
8. (A) $f'(x) = 4x^3 - 24x^2$ (B) $y = -20x + 20$
   (C) $x = 0$ and $x = 6$

6.6 Differentials

- Increments
- Differentials
- Approximations Using Differentials

In this section, we introduce increments and differentials. Increments are useful and they provide an alternative notation for defining the derivative. Differentials are often easier to compute than increments and can be used to approximate increments.

Increments

In Section 6.4, we defined the derivative of f at x as the limit of the difference quotient

$$f'(x) = \lim_{h \to 0} \frac{f(x + h) - f(x)}{h}$$

We considered various interpretations of this limit, including slope, velocity, and instantaneous rate of change. Increment notation enables us to interpret the numerator and denominator of the difference quotient separately.

Given $y = f(x) = x^3$, if x changes from 2 to 2.1, then y will change from $y = f(2) = 2^3 = 8$ to $y = f(2.1) = 2.1^3 = 9.261$. The change in x is called the *increment in x* and is denoted by Δx (read as "delta x").* Similarly, the change in y is called the *increment in y* and is denoted by Δy. In terms of the given example, we write

$$\Delta x = 2.1 - 2 = 0.1 \quad \text{Change in } x$$

$$\begin{aligned} \Delta y &= f(2.1) - f(2) && f(x) = x^3 \\ &= 2.1^3 - 2^3 && \text{Use a calculator.} \\ &= 9.261 - 8 \\ &= 1.261 && \text{Corresponding change in } y \end{aligned}$$

CONCEPTUAL INSIGHT

The symbol Δx does not represent the product of Δ and x but is the symbol for a single quantity: the *change in x*. Likewise, the symbol Δy represents a single quantity: the *change in y*.

*Δ is the uppercase Greek letter delta.

DEFINITION Increments

For $y = f(x)$, $\Delta x = x_2 - x_1$, so $x_2 = x_1 + \Delta x$, and

$$\begin{aligned}\Delta y &= y_2 - y_1\\ &= f(x_2) - f(x_1)\\ &= f(x_1 + \Delta x) - f(x_1)\end{aligned}$$

Δy represents the change in y corresponding to a change Δx in x.
Δx can be either positive or negative.

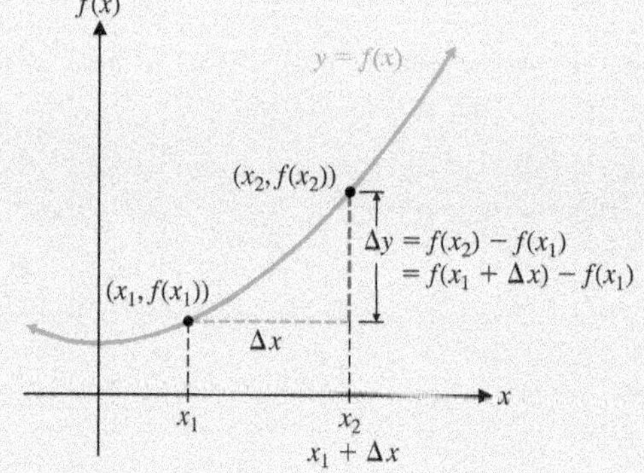

Note: Δy depends on the function f, the input x_1, and the increment Δx.

EXAMPLE 1 **Increments** Given the function $y = f(x) = \dfrac{x^2}{2}$,

(A) Find Δx, Δy, and $\Delta y/\Delta x$ for $x_1 = 1$ and $x_2 = 2$.

(B) Find $\dfrac{f(x_1 + \Delta x) - f(x_1)}{\Delta x}$ for $x_1 = 1$ and $\Delta x = 2$.

SOLUTION

(A) $\Delta x = x_2 - x_1 = 2 - 1 = 1$

$$\begin{aligned}\Delta y &= f(x_2) - f(x_1)\\ &= f(2) - f(1) = \frac{4}{2} - \frac{1}{2} = \frac{3}{2}\end{aligned}$$

$$\frac{\Delta y}{\Delta x} = \frac{f(x_2) - f(x_1)}{x_2 - x_1} = \frac{\frac{3}{2}}{1} = \frac{3}{2}$$

(B) $$\frac{f(x_1 + \Delta x) - f(x_1)}{\Delta x} = \frac{f(1 + 2) - f(1)}{2}$$

$$= \frac{f(3) - f(1)}{2} = \frac{\frac{9}{2} - \frac{1}{2}}{2} = \frac{4}{2} = 2$$

Matched Problem 1 Given the function $y = f(x) = x^2 + 1$,

(A) Find Δx, Δy, and $\Delta y/\Delta x$ for $x_1 = 2$ and $x_2 = 3$.

(B) Find $\dfrac{f(x_1 + \Delta x) - f(x_1)}{\Delta x}$ for $x_1 = 1$ and $\Delta x = 2$.

In Example 1, we observe another notation for the difference quotient

$$\frac{f(x + h) - f(x)}{h} \tag{1}$$

It is common to refer to h, the change in x, as Δx. Then the difference quotient (1) takes on the form

$$\frac{f(x + \Delta x) - f(x)}{\Delta x} \quad \text{or} \quad \frac{\Delta y}{\Delta x} \qquad \Delta y = f(x + \Delta x) - f(x)$$

and the derivative is defined by

$$f'(x) = \lim_{\Delta x \to 0} \frac{f(x + \Delta x) - f(x)}{\Delta x}$$

or

$$f'(x) = \lim_{\Delta x \to 0} \frac{\Delta y}{\Delta x} \tag{2}$$

if the limit exists.

Explore and Discuss 1

Suppose that $y = f(x)$ defines a function whose domain is the set of all real numbers. If every increment Δy is equal to 0, then what is the range of f?

Differentials

Assume that the limit in equation (2) exists. Then, for small Δx, the difference quotient $\Delta y / \Delta x$ provides a good approximation for $f'(x)$. Also, $f'(x)$ provides a good approximation for $\Delta y / \Delta x$. We write

$$\frac{\Delta y}{\Delta x} \approx f'(x) \qquad \Delta x \text{ is small, but } \neq 0 \tag{3}$$

Multiplying both sides of (3) by Δx gives us

$$\Delta y \approx f'(x)\, \Delta x \qquad \Delta x \text{ is small, but } \neq 0 \tag{4}$$

From equation (4), we see that $f'(x)\Delta x$ provides a good approximation for Δy when Δx is small.

Because of the practical and theoretical importance of $f'(x)\, \Delta x$, we give it the special name **differential** and represent it with the special symbol ***dy*** or ***df***:

$$dy = f'(x)\Delta x \qquad \text{or} \qquad df = f'(x)\Delta x$$

For example,

$$d(2x^3) = (2x^3)'\, \Delta x = 6x^2\, \Delta x$$
$$d(x) = (x)'\, \Delta x = 1\, \Delta x = \Delta x$$

In the second example, we usually drop the parentheses in $d(x)$ and simply write

$$dx = \Delta x$$

In summary, we have the following:

DEFINITION Differentials

If $y = f(x)$ defines a differentiable function, then the **differential *dy*, or *df***, is defined as the product of $f'(x)$ and dx, where $dx = \Delta x$. Symbolically,

$$dy = f'(x)\, dx, \qquad \text{or} \qquad df = f'(x)\, dx$$

where

$$dx = \Delta x$$

Note: The differential dy (or df) is actually a function involving two independent variables, x and dx. A change in either one or both will affect dy (or df).

EXAMPLE 2 **Differentials** Find dy for $f(x) = x^2 + 3x$. Evaluate dy for

(A) $x = 2$ and $dx = 0.1$

(B) $x = 3$ and $dx = 0.1$

(C) $x = 1$ and $dx = 0.02$

SOLUTION

$$dy = f'(x)\,dx$$
$$= (2x + 3)\,dx$$

(A) When $x = 2$ and $dx = 0.1$,
$$dy = [2(2) + 3]0.1 = 0.7$$

(B) When $x = 3$ and $dx = 0.1$,
$$dy = [2(3) + 3]0.1 = 0.9$$

(C) When $x = 1$ and $dx = 0.02$,
$$dy = [2(1) + 3]0.02 = 0.1$$

Matched Problem 2 Find dy for $f(x) = \sqrt{x} + 3$. Evaluate dy for

(A) $x = 4$ and $dx = 0.1$

(B) $x = 9$ and $dx = 0.12$

(C) $x = 1$ and $dx = 0.01$

We now have two interpretations of the symbol dy/dx. Referring to the function $y = f(x) = x^2 + 3x$ in Example 2 with $x = 2$ and $dx = 0.1$, we have

$$\frac{dy}{dx} = f'(2) = 7 \qquad \text{Derivative}$$

and

$$\frac{dy}{dx} = \frac{0.7}{0.1} = 7 \qquad \text{Ratio of differentials}$$

Approximations Using Differentials

Earlier, we noted that for small Δx,

$$\frac{\Delta y}{\Delta x} \approx f'(x) \qquad \text{and} \qquad \Delta y \approx f'(x)\Delta x$$

Also, since

$$dy = f'(x)\,dx$$

it follows that

$$\Delta y \approx dy$$

and dy can be used to approximate Δy.

To interpret this result geometrically, we need to recall a basic property of the slope. The vertical change in a line is equal to the product of the slope and the horizontal change, as shown in Figure 1.

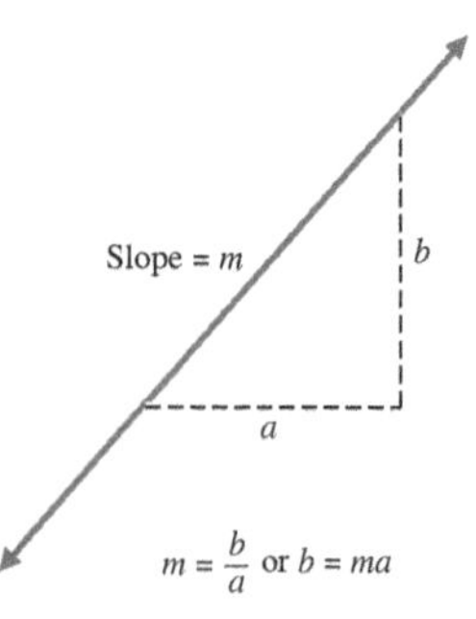

Figure 1

Now consider the line tangent to the graph of $y = f(x)$, as shown in Figure 2 on page 359. Since $f'(x)$ is the slope of the tangent line and dx is the horizontal change in the tangent line, it follows that the vertical change in the tangent line is given by $dy = f'(x)\,dx$, as indicated in Figure 2.

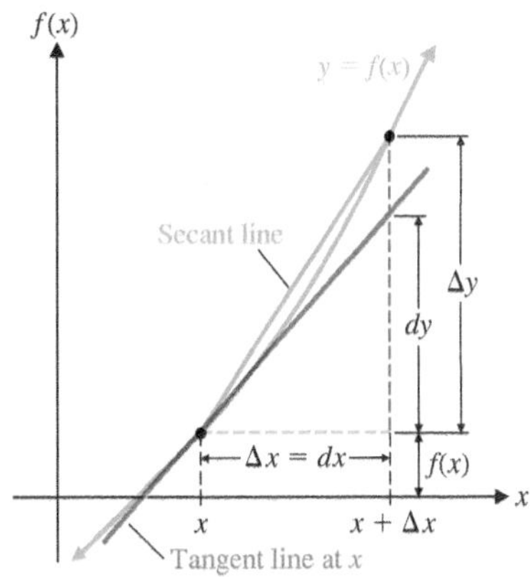

Figure 2

EXAMPLE 3 **Comparing Increments and Differentials** Let $y = f(x) = 6x - x^2$.

(A) Find Δy and dy when $x = 2$.

(B) Compare Δy and dy from part (A) for $\Delta x = 0.1, 0.2$, and 0.3.

SOLUTION

(A)
$$\begin{aligned}\Delta y &= f(2 + \Delta x) - f(2)\\ &= 6(2 + \Delta x) - (2 + \Delta x)^2 - (6 \cdot 2 - 2^2) && \text{Remove parentheses.}\\ &= 12 + 6\Delta x - 4 - 4\Delta x - \Delta x^2 - 12 + 4 && \text{Collect like terms.}\\ &= 2\Delta x - \Delta x^2\end{aligned}$$

Since $f'(x) = 6 - 2x, f'(2) = 2$, and $dx = \Delta x, dy = f'(2)\,dx = 2\Delta x$

(B) Table 1 compares the values of Δy and dy for the indicated values of Δx.

Table 1

Δx	Δy	dy
0.1	0.19	0.2
0.2	0.36	0.4
0.3	0.51	0.6

Matched Problem 3 Repeat Example 3 for $x = 4$ and $\Delta x = dx = -0.1, -0.2$, and -0.3.

EXAMPLE 4 **Cost–Revenue** A company manufactures and sells x microprocessors per week. If the weekly cost and revenue equations are

$$C(x) = 5{,}000 + 2x \qquad R(x) = 10x - \frac{x^2}{1{,}000} \qquad 0 \le x \le 8{,}000$$

then use differentials to approximate the changes in revenue and profit if production is increased from 2,000 to 2,010 units per week.

SOLUTION We will approximate ΔR and ΔP with dR and dP, respectively, using $x = 2{,}000$ and $dx = 2{,}010 - 2{,}000 = 10$.

$$R(x) = 10x - \frac{x^2}{1{,}000} \qquad P(x) = R(x) - C(x) = 10x - \frac{x^2}{1{,}000} - 5{,}000 - 2x$$

$$dR = R'(x)\,dx \qquad\qquad = 8x - \frac{x^2}{1{,}000} - 5{,}000$$

$$= \left(10 - \frac{x}{500}\right)dx \qquad\qquad dP = P'(x)\,dx$$

$$= \left(10 - \frac{2{,}000}{500}\right)10 \qquad\qquad = \left(8 - \frac{x}{500}\right)dx$$

$$= \$60 \text{ per week} \qquad\qquad = \left(8 - \frac{2{,}000}{500}\right)10$$

$$= \$40 \text{ per week}$$

Matched Problem 4 Repeat Example 4 with production increasing from 6,000 to 6,010.

Comparing the results in Example 4 and Matched Problem 4, we see that an increase in production results in a revenue and profit increase at the 2,000 production level but a revenue and profit loss at the 6,000 production level.

Exercises 6.6

Skills Warm-up Exercises

W *In Problems 1–4, let $f(x) = 0.1x + 3$ and find the given values without using a calculator.*

1. $f(0)$; $f(0.1)$

2. $f(2)$; $f(2.1)$

3. $f(-2)$; $f(-2.01)$

4. $f(-10)$; $f(-10.01)$

In Problems 5–8, let $g(x) = x^2$ and find the given values without using a calculator.

5. $g(0)$; $g(0.1)$

6. $g(1)$; $g(1.1)$

7. $g(10)$; $g(10.1)$

8. $g(-5)$; $g(-5.1)$

A *In Problems 9–14, find the indicated quantities for $y = f(x) = 5x^2$.*

9. Δx, Δy, and $\Delta y/\Delta x$; given $x_1 = 1$ and $x_2 = 4$

10. Δx, Δy, and $\Delta y/\Delta x$; given $x_1 = 3$ and $x_2 = 8$

11. $\dfrac{f(x_1 + \Delta x) - f(x_1)}{\Delta x}$; given $x_1 = 1$ and $\Delta x = 2$

12. $\dfrac{f(x_1 + \Delta x) - f(x_1)}{\Delta x}$; given $x_1 = 2$ and $\Delta x = 1$

13. $\Delta y/\Delta x$; given $x_1 = 1$ and $x_2 = 3$

14. $\Delta y/\Delta x$; given $x_1 = 2$ and $x_2 = 3$

In Problems 15–20, find dy for each function.

15. $y = 30 + 12x^2 - x^3$

16. $y = 200x - \dfrac{x^2}{30}$

17. $y = x^2\left(1 - \dfrac{x}{9}\right)$

18. $y = x^4(150 - x^3)$

19. $y = \dfrac{590}{\sqrt{x}}$

20. $y = 84\sqrt[3]{x}$

B *In Problems 21 and 22, find the indicated quantities for $y = f(x) = 3x^2$.*

21. (A) $\dfrac{f(2 + \Delta x) - f(2)}{\Delta x}$ (simplify)

(B) What does the quantity in part (A) approach as Δx approaches 0?

22. (A) $\dfrac{f(5 + \Delta x) - f(5)}{\Delta x}$ (simplify)

(B) What does the quantity in part (A) approach as Δx approaches 0?

In Problems 23–26, find dy for each function.

23. $y = (3x - 1)^2$

24. $y = (2x + 3)^2$

25. $y = \dfrac{x^2 - 9}{x}$

26. $y = \dfrac{x^2 - 9}{x^2}$

In Problems 27–30, evaluate dy and Δy for each function for the indicated values.

27. $y = f(x) = x^2 - 3x + 2$; $x = 5$, $dx = \Delta x = 0.2$

28. $y = f(x) = 30 + 12x^2 - x^3$; $x = 2$, $dx = \Delta x = 0.1$

29. $y = f(x) = 125\left(1 - \dfrac{8}{x}\right)$; $x = 5$, $dx = \Delta x = -0.3$

30. $y = f(x) = 100\left(x - \dfrac{4}{x^2}\right)$; $x = 2$, $dx = \Delta x = -0.1$

31. A cube with 10-inch sides is covered with a coat of fiberglass 0.2 inch thick. Use differentials to estimate the volume of the fiberglass shell.

32. A sphere with a radius of 5 centimeters is coated with ice 0.1 centimeter thick. Use differentials to estimate the volume of the ice. $\left[\text{Recall that } V = \frac{4}{3}\pi r^3.\right]$

C *In Problems 33–36,*

(A) *Find Δy and dy for the function f at the indicated value of x.*

(B) *Graph Δy and dy from part (A) as functions of Δx.*

(C) *Compare the values of Δy and dy from part (A) at the indicated values of Δx.*

33. $f(x) = x^2 + 2x + 3;\ x = -0.5,\ \Delta x = dx = 0.1, 0.2, 0.3$

34. $f(x) = x^2 + 2x + 3;\ x = -2,\ \Delta x = dx = -0.1, -0.2, -0.3$

35. $f(x) = x^3 - 2x^2;\ x = 1,\ \Delta x = dx = 0.05, 0.10, 0.15$

36. $f(x) = x^3 - 2x^2;\ x = 2,\ \Delta x = dx = -0.05, -0.10, -0.15$

In Problems 37–40, discuss the validity of each statement. If the statement is always true, explain why. If not, give a counterexample.

37. If the graph of the function $y = f(x)$ is a line, then the functions Δy and dy (of the independent variable $\Delta x = dx$) for $f(x)$ at $x = 3$ are identical.

38. If the graph of the function $y = f(x)$ is a parabola, then the functions Δy and dy (of the independent variable $\Delta x = dx$) for $f(x)$ at $x = 0$ are identical.

39. Suppose that $y = f(x)$ defines a differentiable function whose domain is the set of all real numbers. If every differential dy at $x = 2$ is equal to 0, then $f(x)$ is a constant function.

40. Suppose that $y = f(x)$ defines a function whose domain is the set of all real numbers. If every increment at $x = 2$ is equal to 0, then $f(x)$ is a constant function.

41. Find dy if $y = (1 - 2x)\sqrt[3]{x^2}$.

42. Find dy if $y = (4x^3 - 2)\sqrt{x^3}$.

43. Find dy and Δy for $y = 52\sqrt{x}$, $x = 4$, and $\Delta x = dx = 0.3$.

44. Find dy and Δy for $y = 780/\sqrt{x}$, $x = 100$, and $\Delta x = dx = 1$.

Applications

Use differential approximations in the following problems.

45. **Advertising.** A company will sell N units of a product after spending \$$x$ thousand in advertising, as given by

$$N = 60x - x^2 \qquad 5 \le x \le 30$$

Approximately what increase in sales will result by increasing the advertising budget from \$10,000 to \$11,000? From \$20,000 to \$21,000?

46. **Price–demand.** Suppose that the daily demand (in pounds) for chocolate candy at \$$x$ per pound is given by

$$D = 1{,}000 - 40x^2 \qquad 1 \le x \le 5$$

If the price is increased from \$3.00 per pound to \$3.20 per pound, what is the approximate change in demand?

47. **Average cost.** For a company that manufactures tennis rackets, the average cost per racket $\overline{C}$ is

$$\overline{C} = \frac{400}{x} + 5 + \frac{1}{2}x \qquad x \ge 1$$

where x is the number of rackets produced per hour. What will the approximate change in average cost per racket be if production is increased from 20 per hour to 25 per hour? From 40 per hour to 45 per hour?

48. **Revenue and profit.** A company manufactures and sells x televisions per month. If the cost and revenue equations are

$$C(x) = 72{,}000 + 60x$$

$$R(x) = 200x - \frac{x^2}{30} \qquad 0 \le x \le 6{,}000$$

what will the approximate changes in revenue and profit be if production is increased from 1,500 to 1,510? From 4,500 to 4,510?

49. **Pulse rate.** The average pulse rate y (in beats per minute) of a healthy person x inches tall is given approximately by

$$y = \frac{590}{\sqrt{x}} \qquad 30 \le x \le 75$$

Approximately how will the pulse rate change for a change in height from 36 to 37 inches? From 64 to 65 inches?

50. **Measurement.** An egg of a particular bird is nearly spherical. If the radius to the inside of the shell is 5 millimeters and the radius to the outside of the shell is 5.3 millimeters, approximately what is the volume of the shell? [Remember that $V = \frac{4}{3}\pi r^3$.]

51. **Medicine.** A drug is given to a patient to dilate her arteries. If the radius of an artery is increased from 2 to 2.1 millimeters, approximately how much is the cross-sectional area increased? $\left[\text{Assume that the cross section of the artery is circular; that is, } A = \pi r^2.\right]$

52. **Drug sensitivity.** One hour after x milligrams of a particular drug are given to a person, the change in body temperature T (in degrees Fahrenheit) is given by

$$T = x^2\left(1 - \frac{x}{9}\right) \qquad 0 \le x \le 6$$

Approximate the changes in body temperature produced by the following changes in drug dosages:

(A) From 2 to 2.1 milligrams

(B) From 3 to 3.1 milligrams

(C) From 4 to 4.1 milligrams

53. **Learning.** A particular person learning to type has an achievement record given approximately by

$$N = 75\left(1 - \frac{2}{t}\right) \qquad 3 \le t \le 20$$

where N is the number of words per minute typed after t weeks of practice. What is the approximate improvement from 5 to 5.5 weeks of practice?

54. **Learning.** If a person learns y items in x hours, as given approximately by

$$y = 52\sqrt{x} \qquad 0 \le x \le 9$$

what is the approximate increase in the number of items learned when x changes from 1 to 1.1 hours? From 4 to 4.1 hours?

55. **Politics.** In a new city, the voting population (in thousands) is given by

$$N(t) = 30 + 12t^2 - t^3 \qquad 0 \le t \le 8$$

where t is time in years. Find the approximate change in votes for the following changes in time:

(A) From 1 to 1.1 years

(B) From 4 to 4.1 years

(C) From 7 to 7.1 years

Answers to Matched Problems

1. (A) $\Delta x = 1, \Delta y = 5, \Delta y/\Delta x = 5$ (B) 4

2. $dy = \dfrac{1}{2\sqrt{x}}\,dx$

(A) 0.025 (B) 0.02 (C) 0.005

3. (A) $\Delta y = -2\Delta x - \Delta x^2;\ dy = -2\Delta x$

(B)

Δx	Δy	dy
−0.1	0.19	0.2
−0.2	0.36	0.4
−0.3	0.51	0.6

4. $dR = -\$20/\text{wk};\ dP = -\$40/\text{wk}$

6.7 Marginal Analysis in Business and Economics

- Marginal Cost, Revenue, and Profit
- Application
- Marginal Average Cost, Revenue, and Profit

Marginal Cost, Revenue, and Profit

One important application of calculus to business and economics involves *marginal analysis.* In economics, the word *marginal* refers to a rate of change—that is, to a derivative. Thus, if $C(x)$ is the total cost of producing x items, then $C'(x)$ is called the *marginal cost* and represents the instantaneous rate of change of total cost with respect to the number of items produced. Similarly, the *marginal revenue* is the derivative of the total revenue function, and the *marginal profit* is the derivative of the total profit function.

DEFINITION Marginal Cost, Revenue, and Profit

If x is the number of units of a product produced in some time interval, then

$$\begin{aligned}
\text{total cost} &= C(x)\\
\textbf{marginal cost} &= C'(x)\\
\text{total revenue} &= R(x)\\
\textbf{marginal revenue} &= R'(x)\\
\text{total profit} &= P(x) = R(x) - C(x)\\
\textbf{marginal profit} &= P'(x) = R'(x) - C'(x)\\
&= (\text{marginal revenue}) - (\text{marginal cost})
\end{aligned}$$

Marginal cost (or revenue or profit) is the instantaneous rate of change of cost (or revenue or profit) relative to production at a given production level.

To begin our discussion, we consider a cost function $C(x)$. It is important to remember that $C(x)$ represents the *total* cost of producing x items, not the cost of producing a *single* item. To find the cost of producing a single item, we use the difference of two successive values of $C(x)$:

$$\begin{aligned}
\text{Total cost of producing } x + 1 \text{ items} &= C(x + 1)\\
\text{Total cost of producing } x \text{ items} &= C(x)\\
\text{Exact cost of producing the } (x + 1)\text{st item} &= C(x + 1) - C(x)
\end{aligned}$$

EXAMPLE 1 **Cost Analysis** A company manufactures fuel tanks for cars. The total weekly cost (in dollars) of producing x tanks is given by

$$C(x) = 10{,}000 + 90x - 0.05x^2$$

(A) Find the marginal cost function.

(B) Find the marginal cost at a production level of 500 tanks per week.

(C) Interpret the results of part (B).

(D) Find the exact cost of producing the 501st item.

SOLUTION

(A) $C'(x) = 90 - 0.1x$

(B) $C'(500) = 90 - 0.1(500) = \$40$ Marginal cost

(C) At a production level of 500 tanks per week, the total production costs are increasing at the rate of \$40 per tank. We expect the 501st tank to cost about \$40.

(D)
$$\begin{aligned} C(501) &= 10{,}000 + 90(501) - 0.05(501)^2 \\ &= \$42{,}539.95 && \text{Total cost of producing 501 tanks per week} \\ C(500) &= 10{,}000 + 90(500) - 0.05(500)^2 \\ &= \$42{,}500.00 && \text{Total cost of producing 500 tanks per week} \\ C(501) - C(500) &= 42{,}539.95 - 42{,}500.00 \\ &= \$39.95 && \text{Exact cost of producing the 501st tank} \end{aligned}$$

Matched Problem 1 A company manufactures automatic transmissions for cars. The total weekly cost (in dollars) of producing x transmissions is given by

$$C(x) = 50{,}000 + 600x - 0.75x^2$$

(A) Find the marginal cost function.

(B) Find the marginal cost at a production level of 200 transmissions per week.

(C) Interpret the results of part (B).

(D) Find the exact cost of producing the 201st transmission.

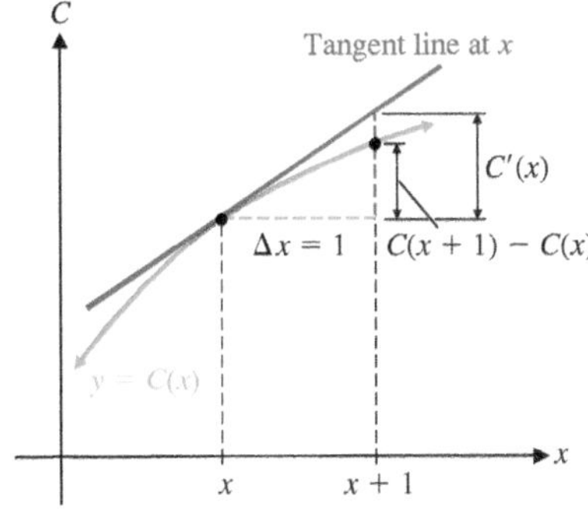

Figure 1 $C'(x) \approx C(x+1) - C(x)$

In Example 1, we found that the cost of the 501st tank and the marginal cost at a production level of 500 tanks differ by only a nickel. Increments and differentials will help us understand the relationship between marginal cost and the cost of a single item. If $C(x)$ is any total cost function, then

$$C'(x) \approx \frac{C(x + \Delta x) - C(x)}{\Delta x} \qquad \text{See Section 6.6}$$

$$C'(x) \approx C(x + 1) - C(x) \qquad \Delta x = 1$$

We see that the marginal cost $C'(x)$ approximates $C(x + 1) - C(x)$, the exact cost of producing the $(x + 1)$st item. These observations are summarized next and are illustrated in Figure 1.

THEOREM 1 Marginal Cost and Exact Cost

If $C(x)$ is the total cost of producing x items, then the marginal cost function approximates the exact cost of producing the $(x + 1)$st item:

$$\underset{\text{Marginal cost}}{C'(x)} \approx \underset{\text{Exact cost}}{C(x + 1) - C(x)}$$

Similar statements can be made for total revenue functions and total profit functions.

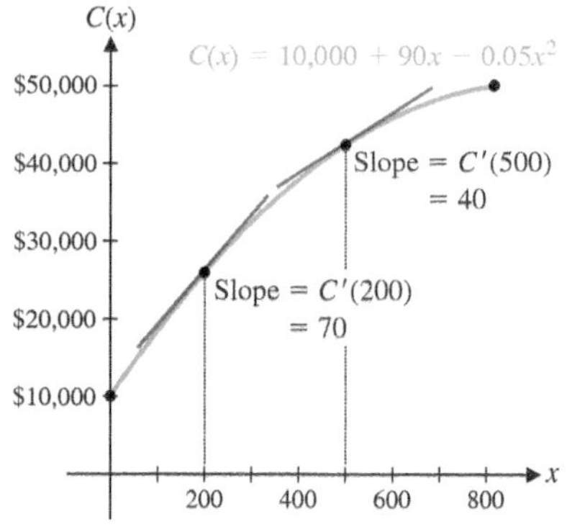

Figure 2

CONCEPTUAL INSIGHT

Theorem 1 states that the marginal cost at a given production level x approximates the cost of producing the $(x + 1)$st, or *next*, item. In practice, the marginal cost is used more frequently than the exact cost. One reason for this is that the marginal cost is easily visualized when one is examining the graph of the total cost function. Figure 2 shows the graph of the cost function discussed in Example 1, with tangent lines added at $x = 200$ and $x = 500$. The graph clearly shows that as production increases, the slope of the tangent line decreases. Thus, the cost of producing the next tank also decreases, a desirable characteristic of a total cost function. We will have much more to say about graphical analysis in Chapter 8.

EXAMPLE 2 **Exact Cost and Marginal Cost** The total cost of producing x bicycles is given by the cost function

$$C(x) = 10{,}000 + 150x - 0.2x^2$$

(A) Find the exact cost of producing the 121st bicycle.

(B) Use marginal cost to approximate the cost of producing the 121st bicycle.

SOLUTION

(A) The cost of producing 121 bicycles is

$$C(121) = 10{,}000 + 150(121) - 0.2(121)^2 = \$25{,}221.80$$

and the cost of producing 120 bicycles is

$$C(120) = 10{,}000 + 150(120) - 0.2(120)^2 = \$25{,}120.00$$

So the exact cost of producing the 121st bicycle is

$$C(121) - C(120) = \$25{,}221.80 - 25{,}120.00 = \$101.80$$

(B) By Theorem 1, the marginal cost function $C'(x)$, evaluated at $x = 120$, approximates the cost of producing the 121st bicycle:

$$C'(x) = 150 - 0.4x$$
$$C'(120) = 150 - 0.4(120) = \$102.00$$

Note that the marginal cost, \$102.00, at a production level of 120 bicycles, is a good approximation to the exact cost, \$101.80, of producing the 121st bicycle.

Matched Problem 2 For the cost function $C(x)$ in Example 2

(A) Find the exact cost of producing the 141st bicycle.

(B) Use marginal cost to approximate the cost of producing the 141st bicycle.

Application

Now we discuss how price, demand, revenue, cost, and profit are tied together in typical applications. Although either price or demand can be used as the independent variable in a price–demand equation, it is common to use demand as the independent variable when marginal revenue, cost, and profit are also involved.

EXAMPLE 3 **Production Strategy** A company's market research department recommends the manufacture and marketing of a new headphone. After suitable test marketing, the research department presents the following **price–demand equation**:

$$x = 10{,}000 - 1{,}000p \quad x \text{ is demand at price } p. \qquad (1)$$

In the price–demand equation (1), the demand x is given as a function of price p. By solving (1) for p (add $1{,}000p$ to both sides of the equation, subtract x from both sides, and divide both sides by 1,000), we obtain equation (2), in which the price p is given as a function of demand x:

$$p = 10 - 0.001x \qquad (2)$$

where x is the number of headphones that retailers are likely to buy at $\$p$ per set.

The financial department provides the **cost function**

$$C(x) = 7{,}000 + 2x \qquad (3)$$

where \$7,000 is the estimate of fixed costs (tooling and overhead) and \$2 is the estimate of variable costs per headphone (materials, labor, marketing, transportation, storage, etc.).

(A) Find the domain of the function defined by the price–demand equation (2).

(B) Find and interpret the marginal cost function $C'(x)$.

(C) Find the revenue function as a function of x and find its domain.

(D) Find the marginal revenue at $x = 2{,}000$, 5,000, and 7,000. Interpret these results.

(E) Graph the cost function and the revenue function in the same coordinate system. Find the intersection points of these two graphs and interpret the results.

(F) Find the profit function and its domain and sketch the graph of the function.

(G) Find the marginal profit at $x = 1{,}000$, 4,000, and 6,000. Interpret these results.

SOLUTION

(A) Since price p and demand x must be nonnegative, we have $x \geq 0$ and

$$\begin{aligned} p = 10 - 0.001x &\geq 0 \\ 10 &\geq 0.001x \\ 10{,}000 &\geq x \end{aligned}$$

Thus, the permissible values of x are $0 \leq x \leq 10{,}000$.

(B) The marginal cost is $C'(x) = 2$. Since this is a constant, it costs an additional \$2 to produce one more headphone at any production level.

(C) The **revenue** is the amount of money R received by the company for manufacturing and selling x headphones at $\$p$ per set and is given by

$$R = (\text{number of headphones sold})(\text{price per headphone}) = xp$$

In general, the revenue R can be expressed as a function of p using equation (1) or as a function of x using equation (2). As we mentioned earlier, when using marginal functions, we will always use the number of items x as the independent variable. Thus, the **revenue function** is

$$\begin{aligned} R(x) &= xp = x(10 - 0.001x) \quad \text{Using equation (2)} \qquad (4) \\ &= 10x - 0.001x^2 \end{aligned}$$

Since equation (2) is defined only for $0 \leq x \leq 10{,}000$, it follows that the domain of the revenue function is $0 \leq x \leq 10{,}000$.

CONCEPTUAL INSIGHT

In order to sell an increasing number of headphones, the price per headphone must decrease. At $x = 10{,}000$ the price–demand equation (2) requires a price of $p = \$0$ to sell 10,000 headphones. It is not possible to further increase demand without paying retailers to take the headphones.

(D) The **marginal revenue** is

$$R'(x) = 10 - 0.002x$$

For production levels of $x = 2{,}000$, 5,000, and 7,000, we have

$$R'(2{,}000) = 6 \qquad R'(5{,}000) = 0 \qquad R'(7{,}000) = -4$$

This means that at production levels of 2,000, 5,000, and 7,000, the respective approximate changes in revenue per unit change in production are \$6, \$0, and −\$4. That is, at the 2,000 output level, revenue increases as production increases; at the 5,000 output level, revenue does not change with a "small" change in production; and at the 7,000 output level, revenue decreases with an increase in production.

(E) Graphing $R(x)$ and $C(x)$ in the same coordinate system results in Figure 3 on page 367. The intersection points are called the **break-even points**, because revenue equals cost at these production levels. The company neither makes nor loses money, but just breaks even. The break-even points are obtained as follows:

$$\begin{aligned} C(x) &= R(x) \\ 7{,}000 + 2x &= 10x - 0.001x^2 \\ 0.001x^2 - 8x + 7{,}000 &= 0 \qquad \text{Solve by the quadratic formula} \\ x^2 - 8{,}000x + 7{,}000{,}000 &= 0 \qquad \text{(see Appendix A.7).} \\ x &= \frac{8{,}000 \pm \sqrt{8{,}000^2 - 4(7{,}000{,}000)}}{2} \\ &= \frac{8{,}000 \pm \sqrt{36{,}000{,}000}}{2} \\ &= \frac{8{,}000 \pm 6{,}000}{2} \\ &= 1{,}000, \quad 7{,}000 \end{aligned}$$

$$\begin{aligned} R(1{,}000) &= 10(1{,}000) - 0.001(1{,}000)^2 = 9{,}000 \\ C(1{,}000) &= 7{,}000 + 2(1{,}000) = 9{,}000 \\ R(7{,}000) &= 10(7{,}000) - 0.001(7{,}000)^2 = 21{,}000 \\ C(7{,}000) &= 7{,}000 + 2(7{,}000) = 21{,}000 \end{aligned}$$

The break-even points are (1,000, 9,000) and (7,000, 21,000), as shown in Figure 3. Further examination of the figure shows that cost is greater than revenue for production levels between 0 and 1,000 and also between 7,000 and 10,000. Consequently, the company incurs a loss at these levels. By contrast, for production levels between 1,000 and 7,000, revenue is greater than cost, and the company makes a profit.

(F) The **profit function** is

$$\begin{aligned} P(x) &= R(x) - C(x) \\ &= (10x - 0.001x^2) - (7{,}000 + 2x) \\ &= -0.001x^2 + 8x - 7{,}000 \end{aligned}$$

The domain of the cost function is $x \geq 0$, and the domain of the revenue function is $0 \leq x \leq 10{,}000$. The domain of the profit function is the set of x values for which both functions are defined—that is, $0 \leq x \leq 10{,}000$. The graph of the profit function is shown in Figure 4 on page 367. Notice that the x coordinates of the break-even points in Figure 3 are the x intercepts of the profit function. Furthermore, the intervals on which cost is greater than revenue and

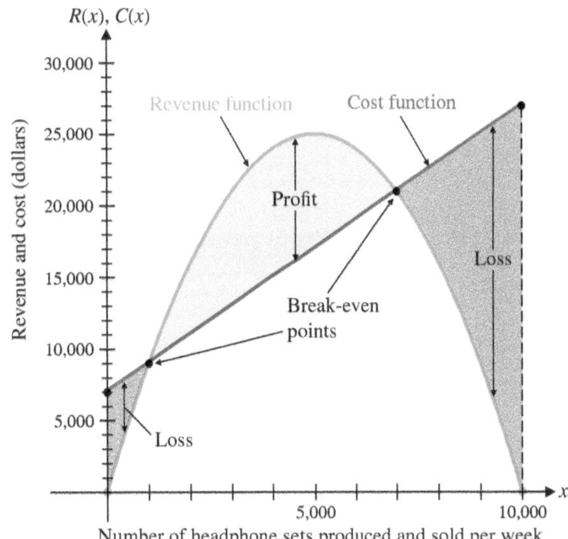

Figure 3

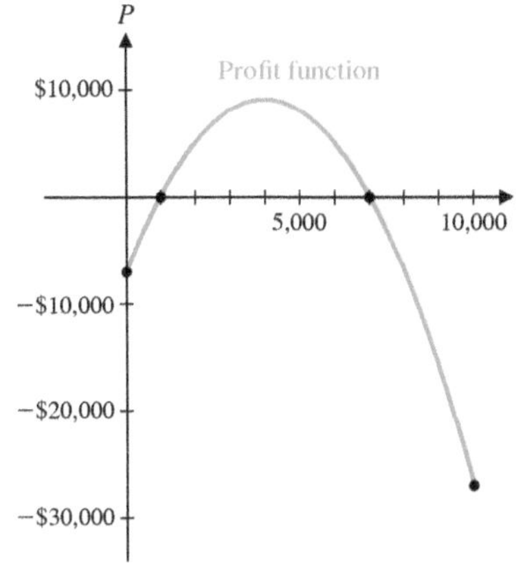

Figure 4

on which revenue is greater than cost correspond, respectively, to the intervals on which profit is negative and on which profit is positive.

(G) The **marginal profit** is

$$P'(x) = -0.002x + 8$$

For production levels of 1,000, 4,000, and 6,000, we have

$$P'(1{,}000) = 6 \qquad P'(4{,}000) = 0 \qquad P'(6{,}000) = -4$$

This means that at production levels of 1,000, 4,000, and 6,000, the respective approximate changes in profit per unit change in production are \$6, \$0, and −\$4. That is, at the 1,000 output level, profit will be increased if production is increased; at the 4,000 output level, profit does not change for "small" changes in production; and at the 6,000 output level, profits will decrease if production is increased. It seems that the best production level to produce a maximum profit is 4,000.

Example 3 requires careful study since a number of important ideas in economics and calculus are involved. In the next chapter, we will develop a systematic procedure for finding the production level (and, using the demand equation, the selling price) that will maximize profit.

Matched Problem 3 Refer to the revenue and profit functions in Example 3.

(A) Find $R'(3{,}000)$ and $R'(6{,}000)$. Interpret the results.

(B) Find $P'(2{,}000)$ and $P'(7{,}000)$. Interpret the results.

Marginal Average Cost, Revenue, and Profit

Sometimes it is desirable to carry out marginal analysis relative to **average cost (cost per unit), average revenue (revenue per unit),** and **average profit (profit per unit).**

DEFINITION Marginal Average Cost, Revenue, and Profit

If x is the number of units of a product produced in some time interval, then

Cost per unit: $\quad$ **average cost** $= \overline{C}(x) = \dfrac{C(x)}{x}$

marginal average cost $= \overline{C}'(x) = \dfrac{d}{dx}\overline{C}(x)$

Revenue per unit: **average revenue** $= \overline{R}(x) = \dfrac{R(x)}{x}$

marginal average revenue $= \overline{R}'(x) = \dfrac{d}{dx}\overline{R}(x)$

Profit per unit: **average profit** $= \overline{P}(x) = \dfrac{P(x)}{x}$

marginal average profit $= \overline{P}'(x) = \dfrac{d}{dx}\overline{P}(x)$

EXAMPLE 4 **Cost Analysis** A small machine shop manufactures drill bits used in the petroleum industry. The manager estimates that the total daily cost (in dollars) of producing x bits is

$$C(x) = 1{,}000 + 25x - 0.1x^2$$

(A) Find $\overline{C}(x)$ and $\overline{C}'(x)$.

(B) Find $\overline{C}(10)$ and $\overline{C}'(10)$. Interpret these quantities.

(C) Use the results in part (B) to estimate the average cost per bit at a production level of 11 bits per day.

SOLUTION

(A) $$\overline{C}(x) = \frac{C(x)}{x} = \frac{1{,}000 + 25x - 0.1x^2}{x}$$

$$= \frac{1{,}000}{x} + 25 - 0.1x \qquad \text{Average cost function}$$

$$\overline{C}'(x) = \frac{d}{dx}\overline{C}(x) = -\frac{1{,}000}{x^2} - 0.1 \qquad \text{Marginal average cost function}$$

(B) $$\overline{C}(10) = \frac{1{,}000}{10} + 25 - 0.1(10) = \$124$$

$$\overline{C}'(10) = -\frac{1{,}000}{10^2} - 0.1 = -\$10.10$$

At a production level of 10 bits per day, the average cost of producing a bit is \$124. This cost is decreasing at the rate of \$10.10 per bit.

(C) If production is increased by 1 bit, then the average cost per bit will decrease by approximately \$10.10. So, the average cost per bit at a production level of 11 bits per day is approximately $\$124 - \$10.10 = \$113.90$.

Matched Problem 4 Consider the cost function for the production of headphones from Example 3:

$$C(x) = 7{,}000 + 2x$$

(A) Find $\overline{C}(x)$ and $\overline{C}'(x)$.

(B) Find $\overline{C}(100)$ and $\overline{C}'(100)$. Interpret these quantities.

(C) Use the results in part (B) to estimate the average cost per headphone at a production level of 101 headphones.

Explore and Discuss 1

A student produced the following solution to Matched Problem 4:

$$C(x) = 7{,}000 + 2x \quad \text{Cost}$$
$$C'(x) = 2 \quad \text{Marginal cost}$$
$$\frac{C'(x)}{x} = \frac{2}{x} \quad \text{"Average" of the marginal cost}$$

Explain why the last function is not the same as the marginal average cost function.

CAUTION

1. The marginal average cost function is computed by first finding the average cost function and then finding its derivative. As Explore and Discuss 1 illustrates, reversing the order of these two steps produces a different function that does not have any useful economic interpretations.
2. Recall that the marginal cost function has two interpretations: the usual interpretation of any derivative as an instantaneous rate of change and the special interpretation as an approximation to the exact cost of the $(x + 1)$st item. This special interpretation does not apply to the marginal average cost function. Referring to Example 4, we would be incorrect to interpret $\overline{C}'(10) = -\$10.10$ to mean that the average cost of the next bit is approximately $-\$10.10$. In fact, the phrase "average cost of the next bit" does not even make sense. Averaging is a concept applied to a collection of items, not to a single item.

These remarks also apply to revenue and profit functions. ▲

Exercises 6.7

Skills Warm-up Exercises

W *In Problems 1–8, let $C(x) = 10{,}000 + 150x - 0.2x^2$ be the total cost in dollars of producing x bicycles.*

1. Find the total cost of producing 99 bicycles.
2. Find the total cost of producing 100 bicycles.
3. Find the cost of producing the 100th bicycle.
4. Find the total cost of producing 199 bicycles.
5. Find the total cost of producing 200 bicycles.
6. Find the cost of producing the 200th bicycle.
7. Find the average cost per bicycle of producing 100 bicycles.
8. Find the average cost per bicycle of producing 200 bicycles.

A *In Problems 9–12, find the marginal cost function.*

9. $C(x) = 150 + 0.7x$ **10.** $C(x) = 2{,}700 + 6x$

11. $C(x) = -(0.1x - 23)^2$

12. $C(x) = 640 + 12x - 0.1x^2$

In Problems 13–16, find the marginal revenue function.

13. $R(x) = 4x - 0.01x^2$ **14.** $R(x) = 36x - 0.03x^2$

15. $R(x) = x(12 - 0.04x)$ **16.** $R(x) = x(25 - 0.05x)$

In Problems 17–20, find the marginal profit function if the cost and revenue, respectively, are those in the indicated problems.

17. Problem 9 and Problem 13
18. Problem 10 and Problem 14
19. Problem 11 and Problem 15
20. Problem 12 and Problem 16

B *In Problems 21–28, find the indicated function if cost and revenue are given by $C(x) = 408 + 1.5x$ and $R(x) = 9x - 0.03x^2$, respectively.*

21. Average cost function
22. Average revenue function
23. Marginal average cost function
24. Marginal average revenue function

25. Profit function

26. Marginal profit function

27. Average profit function

28. Marginal average profit function

C *In Problems 29–32, discuss the validity of each statement. If the statement is always true, explain why. If not, give a counterexample.*

29. If a cost function is linear, then the marginal cost is a constant.

30. If a price–demand equation is linear, then the marginal revenue function is linear.

31. Marginal profit is equal to marginal cost minus marginal revenue.

32. Marginal average cost is equal to average marginal cost.

Applications

33. **Cost analysis.** The total cost (in dollars) of producing x food processors is

$$C(x) = 2{,}000 + 50x - 0.5x^2$$

(A) Find the exact cost of producing the 21st food processor.

(B) Use marginal cost to approximate the cost of producing the 21st food processor.

34. **Cost analysis.** The total cost (in dollars) of producing x electric guitars is

$$C(x) = 1{,}000 + 100x - 0.25x^2$$

(A) Find the exact cost of producing the 51st guitar.

(B) Use marginal cost to approximate the cost of producing the 51st guitar.

35. **Cost analysis.** The total cost (in dollars) of manufacturing x auto body frames is

$$C(x) = 60{,}000 + 300x$$

(A) Find the average cost per unit if 500 frames are produced.

(B) Find the marginal average cost at a production level of 500 units and interpret the results.

(C) Use the results from parts (A) and (B) to estimate the average cost per frame if 501 frames are produced.

36. **Cost analysis.** The total cost (in dollars) of printing x board games is

$$C(x) = 10{,}000 + 20x$$

(A) Find the average cost per unit if 1,000 board games are produced.

(B) Find the marginal average cost at a production level of 1,000 units and interpret the results.

(C) Use the results from parts (A) and (B) to estimate the average cost per board game if 1,001 board games are produced.

37. **Profit analysis.** The total profit (in dollars) from the sale of x skateboards is

$$P(x) = 30x - 0.3x^2 - 250 \qquad 0 \le x \le 100$$

(A) Find the exact profit from the sale of the 26th skateboard.

(B) Use marginal profit to approximate the profit from the sale of the 26th skateboard.

38. **Profit analysis.** The total profit (in dollars) from the sale of x calendars is

$$P(x) = 22x - 0.2x^2 - 400 \qquad 0 \le x \le 100$$

(A) Find the exact profit from the sale of the 41st calendar.

(B) Use the marginal profit to approximate the profit from the sale of the 41st calendar.

39. **Profit analysis.** The total profit (in dollars) from the sale of x sweatshirts is

$$P(x) = 5x - 0.005x^2 - 450 \qquad 0 \le x \le 1{,}000$$

Evaluate the marginal profit at the given values of x, and interpret the results.

(A) $x = 450$ (B) $x = 750$

40. **Profit analysis.** The total profit (in dollars) from the sale of x cameras is

$$P(x) = 12x - 0.02x^2 - 1{,}000 \qquad 0 \le x \le 600$$

Evaluate the marginal profit at the given values of x, and interpret the results.

(A) $x = 200$ (B) $x = 350$

41. **Profit analysis.** The total profit (in dollars) from the sale of x lawn mowers is

$$P(x) = 30x - 0.03x^2 - 750 \qquad 0 \le x \le 1{,}000$$

(A) Find the average profit per mower if 50 mowers are produced.

(B) Find the marginal average profit at a production level of 50 mowers and interpret the results.

(C) Use the results from parts (A) and (B) to estimate the average profit per mower if 51 mowers are produced.

42. **Profit analysis.** The total profit (in dollars) from the sale of x gas grills is

$$P(x) = 20x - 0.02x^2 - 320 \qquad 0 \le x \le 1{,}000$$

(A) Find the average profit per grill if 40 grills are produced.

(B) Find the marginal average profit at a production level of 40 grills and interpret the results.

(C) Use the results from parts (A) and (B) to estimate the average profit per grill if 41 grills are produced.

43. **Revenue analysis.** The price p (in dollars) and the demand x for a brand of running shoes are related by the equation

$$x = 4{,}000 - 40p$$

(A) Express the price p in terms of the demand x, and find the domain of this function.

(B) Find the revenue $R(x)$ from the sale of x pairs of running shoes. What is the domain of R?

(C) Find the marginal revenue at a production level of 1,600 pairs and interpret the results.

(D) Find the marginal revenue at a production level of 2,500 pairs, and interpret the results.

44. **Revenue analysis.** The price p (in dollars) and the demand x for a particular steam iron are related by the equation

$$x = 1{,}000 - 20p$$

(A) Express the price p in terms of the demand x, and find the domain of this function.

(B) Find the revenue $R(x)$ from the sale of x steam irons. What is the domain of R?

(C) Find the marginal revenue at a production level of 400 steam irons and interpret the results.

(D) Find the marginal revenue at a production level of 650 steam irons and interpret the results.

45. **Revenue, cost, and profit.** The price–demand equation and the cost function for the production of table saws are given, respectively, by

$$x = 6{,}000 - 30p \quad \text{and} \quad C(x) = 72{,}000 + 60x$$

where x is the number of saws that can be sold at a price of $\$p$ per saw and $C(x)$ is the total cost (in dollars) of producing x saws.

(A) Express the price p as a function of the demand x, and find the domain of this function.

(B) Find the marginal cost.

(C) Find the revenue function and state its domain.

(D) Find the marginal revenue.

(E) Find $R'(1{,}500)$ and $R'(4{,}500)$ and interpret these quantities.

(F) Graph the cost function and the revenue function on the same coordinate system for $0 \le x \le 6{,}000$. Find the break-even points, and indicate regions of loss and profit.

(G) Find the profit function in terms of x.

(H) Find the marginal profit.

(I) Find $P'(1{,}500)$ and $P'(3{,}000)$ and interpret these quantities.

46. **Revenue, cost, and profit.** The price–demand equation and the cost function for the production of HDTVs are given, respectively, by

$$x = 9{,}000 - 30p \quad \text{and} \quad C(x) = 150{,}000 + 30x$$

where x is the number of HDTVs that can be sold at a price of $\$p$ per TV and $C(x)$ is the total cost (in dollars) of producing x TVs.

(A) Express the price p as a function of the demand x, and find the domain of this function.

(B) Find the marginal cost.

(C) Find the revenue function and state its domain.

(D) Find the marginal revenue.

(E) Find $R'(3{,}000)$ and $R'(6{,}000)$ and interpret these quantities.

(F) Graph the cost function and the revenue function on the same coordinate system for $0 \le x \le 9{,}000$. Find the break-even points and indicate regions of loss and profit.

(G) Find the profit function in terms of x.

(H) Find the marginal profit.

(I) Find $P'(1{,}500)$ and $P'(4{,}500)$ and interpret these quantities.

47. **Revenue, cost, and profit.** A company is planning to manufacture and market a new two-speed electric mixer. After conducting extensive market surveys, the research department provides the following estimates: a weekly demand of 400 mixers at a price of \$40 per mixer and a weekly demand of 600 mixers at a price of \$35 per mixer. The financial department estimates that weekly fixed costs will be \$7,000 and variable costs (cost per unit) will be \$10.

(A) Assume that the relationship between price p and demand x is linear. Use the research department's estimates to express p as a function of x and find the domain of this function.

(B) Find the revenue function in terms of x and state its domain.

(C) Assume that the cost function is linear. Use the financial department's estimates to express the cost function in terms of x.

(D) Graph the cost function and revenue function on the same coordinate system for $0 \le x \le 2{,}000$. Find the break-even points and indicate regions of loss and profit.

(E) Find the profit function in terms of x.

(F) Evaluate the marginal profit at $x = 500$ and $x = 900$ and interpret the results.

48. **Revenue, cost, and profit.** The company in Problem 47 is also planning to manufacture and market a four-speed mixer. For this mixer, the research department's estimates are a weekly demand of 200 mixers at a price of \$80 per mixer and a weekly demand of 300 mixers at a price of \$70. The financial department's estimates are fixed weekly costs of \$6,500 and variable costs of \$25 per mixer.

(A) Assume that the relationship between price p and demand x is linear. Use the research department's estimates to express p as a function of x and find the domain of this function.

(B) Find the revenue function in terms of x and state its domain.

(C) Assume that the cost function is linear. Use the financial department's estimates to express the cost function in terms of x.

(D) Graph the cost function and revenue function on the same coordinate system for $0 \le x \le 1{,}000$. Find the break-even points and indicate regions of loss and profit.

(E) Find the profit function in terms of x.

(F) Evaluate the marginal profit at $x = 320$ and $x = 420$ and interpret the results.

49. Revenue, cost, and profit. The total cost and the total revenue (in dollars) for the production and sale of x ski jackets are given, respectively, by

$$C(x) = 24x + 21{,}900 \quad \text{and} \quad R(x) = 200x - 0.2x^2 \quad 0 \le x \le 1{,}000$$

(A) Find the value of x where the graph of $R(x)$ has a horizontal tangent line.

(B) Find the profit function $P(x)$.

(C) Find the value of x where the graph of $P(x)$ has a horizontal tangent line.

(D) Graph $C(x)$, $R(x)$, and $P(x)$ on the same coordinate system for $0 \le x \le 1{,}000$. Find the break-even points. Find the x intercepts of the graph of $P(x)$.

50. Revenue, cost, and profit. The total cost and the total revenue (in dollars) for the production and sale of x hair dryers are given, respectively, by

$$C(x) = 5x + 2{,}340 \quad \text{and} \quad R(x) = 40x - 0.1x^2 \quad 0 \le x \le 400$$

(A) Find the value of x where the graph of $R(x)$ has a horizontal tangent line.

(B) Find the profit function $P(x)$.

(C) Find the value of x where the graph of $P(x)$ has a horizontal tangent line.

(D) Graph $C(x)$, $R(x)$, and $P(x)$ on the same coordinate system for $0 \le x \le 400$. Find the break-even points. Find the x intercepts of the graph of $P(x)$.

51. Break-even analysis. The price–demand equation and the cost function for the production of garden hoses are given, respectively, by

$$p = 20 - \sqrt{x} \quad \text{and} \quad C(x) = 500 + 2x$$

where x is the number of garden hoses that can be sold at a price of $\$p$ per unit and $C(x)$ is the total cost (in dollars) of producing x garden hoses.

(A) Express the revenue function in terms of x.

(B) Graph the cost function and revenue function in the same viewing window for $0 \le x \le 400$. Use approximation techniques to find the break-even points correct to the nearest unit.

52. Break-even analysis. The price–demand equation and the cost function for the production of handwoven silk scarves are given, respectively, by

$$p = 60 - 2\sqrt{x} \quad \text{and} \quad C(x) = 3{,}000 + 5x$$

where x is the number of scarves that can be sold at a price of $\$p$ per unit and $C(x)$ is the total cost (in dollars) of producing x scarves.

(A) Express the revenue function in terms of x.

(B) Graph the cost function and the revenue function in the same viewing window for $0 \le x \le 900$. Use approximation techniques to find the break-even points correct to the nearest unit.

53. Break-even analysis. Table 1 contains price–demand and total cost data for the production of projectors, where p is the wholesale price (in dollars) of a projector for an annual demand of x projectors and C is the total cost (in dollars) of producing x projectors.

Table 1

x	p($)	C($)
3,190	581	1,130,000
4,570	405	1,241,000
5,740	181	1,410,000
7,330	85	1,620,000

(A) Find a quadratic regression equation for the price–demand data, using x as the independent variable.

(B) Find a linear regression equation for the cost data, using x as the independent variable. Use this equation to estimate the fixed costs and variable costs per projector. Round answers to the nearest dollar.

(C) Find the break-even points. Round answers to the nearest integer.

(D) Find the price range for which the company will make a profit. Round answers to the nearest dollar.

54. Break-even analysis. Table 2 contains price–demand and total cost data for the production of treadmills, where p is the wholesale price (in dollars) of a treadmill for an annual demand of x treadmills and C is the total cost (in dollars) of producing x treadmills.

Table 2

x	p($)	C($)
2,910	1,435	3,650,000
3,415	1,280	3,870,000
4,645	1,125	4,190,000
5,330	910	4,380,000

(A) Find a linear regression equation for the price–demand data, using x as the independent variable.

(B) Find a linear regression equation for the cost data, using x as the independent variable. Use this equation to estimate the fixed costs and variable costs per treadmill. Round answers to the nearest dollar.

(C) Find the break-even points. Round answers to the nearest integer.

(D) Find the price range for which the company will make a profit. Round answers to the nearest dollar.

Answers to Matched Problems

1. (A) $C'(x) = 600 - 1.5x$
   (B) $C'(200) = 300$.
   (C) At a production level of 200 transmissions, total costs are increasing at the rate of \$300 per transmission.
   (D) $C(201) - C(200) = \$299.25$
2. (A) \$93.80 (B) \$94.00
3. (A) $R'(3{,}000) = 4$. At a production level of 3,000, a unit increase in production will increase revenue by approximately \$4.
   $R'(6{,}000) = -2$. At a production level of 6,000, a unit increase in production will decrease revenue by approximately \$2.
   (B) $P'(2{,}000) = 4$. At a production level of 2,000, a unit increase in production will increase profit by approximately \$4.
   $P'(7{,}000) = -6$. At a production level of 7,000, a unit increase in production will decrease profit by approximately \$6.
4. (A) $\overline{C}(x) = \frac{7{,}000}{x} + 2$; $\overline{C}'(x) = -\frac{7{,}000}{x^2}$
   (B) $\overline{C}(100) = \$72$; $\overline{C}'(100) = -\$0.70$. At a production level of 100 headphones, the average cost per headphone is \$72. This average cost is decreasing at a rate of \$0.70 per headphone.
   (C) Approx. \$71.30.

Chapter 6 Summary and Review

Important Terms, Symbols, and Concepts

6.1 Introduction to Limits

EXAMPLES

- The graph of the function $y = f(x)$ is the graph of the set of all ordered pairs $(x, f(x))$. Ex. 1, p. 292
- The limit of the function $y = f(x)$ as x approaches c is L, written as $\lim_{x\to c} f(x) = L$, if the functional value $f(x)$ is close to the single real number L whenever x is close, but not equal, to c (on either side of c). Ex. 2, p. 293; Ex. 3, p. 294; Ex. 4, p. 295
- The limit of the function $y = f(x)$ as x approaches c from the left is K, written as $\lim_{x\to c^-} f(x) = K$, if $f(x)$ is close to K whenever x is close to, but to the left of, c on the real-number line. Ex. 5, p. 297; Ex. 6, p. 298; Ex. 7, p. 299
- The limit of the function $y = f(x)$ as x approaches c from the right is L, written as $\lim_{x\to c^+} f(x) = L$, if $f(x)$ is close to L whenever x is close to, but to the right of, c on the real-number line. Ex. 8, p. 299; Ex. 9, p. 300
- The limit of the difference quotient $[f(a + h) - f(a)]/h$ is often a $0/0$ indeterminate form. Algebraic simplification is often required to evaluate this type of limit. Ex. 10, p. 301

6.2 Infinite Limits and Limits at Infinity

- If $f(x)$ increases or decreases without bound as x approaches a from either side of a, then the line $x = a$ is a **vertical asymptote** of the graph of $y = f(x)$. Ex. 1, p. 307; Ex. 2, p. 308
- If $f(x)$ gets close to L as x increases without bound or decreases without bound, then L is called the limit of f at ∞ or $-\infty$. Ex. 3, p. 310
- The **end behavior** of a function is described by its limits at infinity. Ex. 4, p. 311; Ex. 5, p. 312
- If $f(x)$ approaches L as $x \to \infty$ or as $x \to -\infty$, then the line $y = L$ is a **horizontal asymptote** of the graph of $y = f(x)$. Polynomial functions never have horizontal asymptotes. A rational function can have at most one. Ex. 6, p. 313; Ex. 7, p. 314

6.3 Continuity

- Intuitively, the graph of a continuous function can be drawn without lifting a pen off the paper. By definition, a function f is **continuous at c** if Ex. 1, p. 320; Ex. 2, p. 321

  1. $\lim_{x\to c} f(x)$ exists, **2.** $f(c)$ exists, and **3.** $\lim_{x\to c} f(x) = f(c)$
- Continuity properties are useful for determining where a function is continuous and where it is discontinuous. Ex. 3, p. 323
- Continuity properties are also useful for solving inequalities. Ex. 4, p. 324; Ex. 5, p. 325

6.4 The Derivative

- Given a function $y = f(x)$, the **average rate of change** is the ratio of the change in y to the change in x. Ex. 1, p. 331
- The **instantaneous rate of change** is the limit of the average rate of change as the change in x approaches 0. Ex. 2, p. 331; Ex. 3, p. 334
- The slope of the secant line through two points on the graph of a function $y = f(x)$ is the ratio of the change in y to the change in x. The **slope of the graph** at the point $(a, f(a))$ is the limit of the slope of the secant line through the points $(a, f(a))$ and $(a + h, f(a + h))$ as h approaches 0, provided the limit exists. In this case, the **tangent line** to the graph is the line through $(a, f(a))$ with slope equal to the limit.
- The **derivative of $y = f(x)$ at x**, denoted $f'(x)$, is the limit of the difference quotient $[f(x + h) - f(x)]/h$ as $h \to 0$ (if the limit exists). Ex. 4, p. 336
- The four-step process is used to find derivatives. Ex. 5, p. 337
- If the limit of the difference quotient does not exist at $x = a$, then f is **nondifferentiable at a** and $f'(a)$ does not exist. Ex. 6, p. 338; Ex. 7, p. 339; Ex. 8, p. 339

6.5 Basic Differentiation Properties

- The derivative of a constant function is 0. Ex. 1, p. 346
- For any real number n, the derivative of $f(x) = x^n$ is nx^{n-1}. Ex. 2, p. 347; Ex. 3, p. 347
- If f is a differentiable function, then the derivative of $kf(x)$ is $kf'(x)$. Ex. 4, p. 349
- The derivative of the sum or difference of two differentiable functions is the sum or difference of the derivatives of the functions. Ex. 5, p. 350; Ex. 6, p. 350; Ex. 7, p. 351; Ex. 8, p. 351

6.6 Differentials

- Given the function $y = f(x)$, the change in x is also called the **increment of x** and is denoted as Δx. The corresponding change in y is called the **increment of y** and is given by $\Delta y = f(x + \Delta x) - f(x)$. Ex. 1, p. 356
- If $y = f(x)$ is differentiable at x, then the **differential of x** is $dx = \Delta x$ and the **differential of $y = f(x)$** is $dy = f'(x)dx$, or $df = f'(x)dx$. In this context, x and dx are both independent variables. Ex. 2, p. 358; Ex. 3, p. 359; Ex. 4, p. 359

6.7 Marginal Analysis in Business and Economics

- If $y = C(x)$ is the total cost of producing x items, then $y = C'(x)$ is the **marginal cost** and $C(x + 1) - C(x)$ is the exact cost of producing item $x + 1$. Furthermore, $C'(x) \approx C(x + 1) - C(x)$. Similar statements can be made regarding total revenue and total profit functions. Ex. 1, p. 363; Ex. 2, p. 364; Ex. 3, p. 364
- If $y = C(x)$ is the total cost of producing x items, then the **average cost**, or cost per unit, is $\overline{C}(x) = \frac{C(x)}{x}$ and the **marginal average cost** is $\overline{C}'(x) = \frac{d}{dx}\overline{C}(x)$. Similar statements can be made regarding total revenue and total profit functions. Ex. 4, p. 368

Review Exercises

Work through all the problems in this chapter review, and check your answers in the back of the book. Answers to all review problems are there, along with section numbers in italics to indicate where each type of problem is discussed. Where weaknesses show up, review appropriate sections of the text.

Many of the problems in this exercise set ask you to find a derivative. Most of the answers to these problems contain both an unsimplified form and a simplified form of the derivative. When checking your work, first check that you applied the rules correctly, and then check that you performed the algebraic simplification correctly.

1. Find the indicated quantities for $f(x) = 3x^2 + 2x + 7$:

(A) The change in y if x changes from 2 to 4

(B) The average rate of change of y with respect to x if x changes from 2 to 4

(C) The slope of the secant line through the points $(2, f(2))$ and $(4, f(4))$

(D) The instantaneous rate of change of y with respect to x at $x = 2$

(E) The slope of the line tangent to the graph of $y = f(x)$ at $x = 2$

(F) $f'(2)$

2. Use the four-step process to find $f'(x)$ for $f(x) = 4x - 5$.

3. If $\lim_{x\to2} f(x) = 4$ and $\lim_{x\to2} g(x) = 11$ find

(A) $\lim_{x\to2}(-3f(x) + 7g(x))$ (B) $\lim_{x\to2}(f(x)g(x))$

(C) $\lim_{x\to2}\left(\dfrac{f(x)}{g(x)}\right)$ (D) $\lim_{x\to2}(10 - x + 8g(x))$

In Problems 4–10, use the graph of f to estimate the indicated limits and function values.

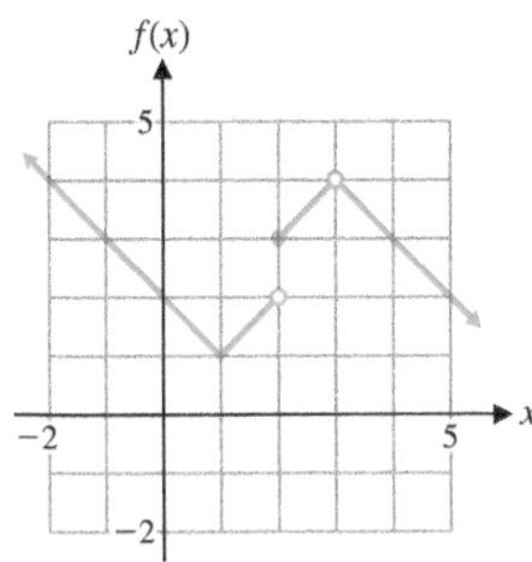

Figure for 4–10

4. $f(1.5)$ **5.** $f(2.5)$ **6.** $f(2.75)$ **7.** $f(3.25)$

8. (A) $\lim_{x\to1^-} f(x)$ (B) $\lim_{x\to1^+} f(x)$

(C) $\lim_{x\to1} f(x)$ (D) $f(1)$

9. (A) $\lim_{x\to2^-} f(x)$ (B) $\lim_{x\to2^+} f(x)$

(C) $\lim_{x\to2} f(x)$ (D) $f(2)$

10. (A) $\lim_{x\to3^-} f(x)$ (B) $\lim_{x\to3^+} f(x)$

(C) $\lim_{x\to3} f(x)$ (D) $f(3)$

In Problems 11–13, use the graph of the function f shown in the figure to answer each question.

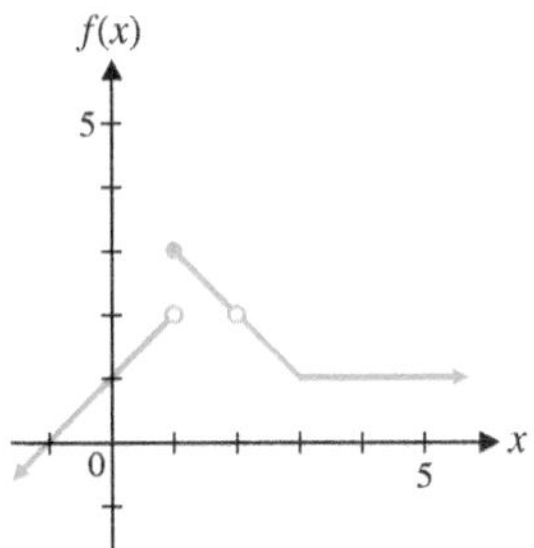

Figure for 11–13

11. (A) $\lim_{x\to1} f(x) = ?$ (B) $f(1) = ?$

(C) Is f continuous at $x = 1$?

12. (A) $\lim_{x\to2} f(x) = ?$ (B) $f(2) = ?$

(C) Is f continuous at $x = 2$?

13. (A) $\lim_{x\to3} f(x) = ?$ (B) $f(3) = ?$

(C) Is f continuous at $x = 3$?

In Problems 14–23, refer to the following graph of $y = f(x)$:

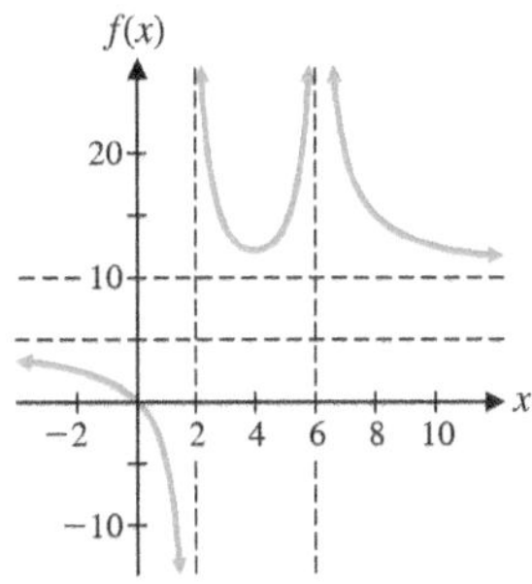

Figure for 14–23

14. $\lim_{x\to\infty} f(x) = ?$ **15.** $\lim_{x\to-\infty} f(x) = ?$

16. $\lim_{x\to2^+} f(x) = ?$ **17.** $\lim_{x\to2^-} f(x) = ?$

18. $\lim_{x\to6^-} f(x) = ?$ **19.** $\lim_{x\to6^+} f(x) = ?$

20. $\lim_{x\to6} f(x) = ?$

21. Identify any vertical asymptotes.

22. Identify any horizontal asymptotes.

23. Where is $y = f(x)$ discontinuous?

24. Use the four-step process to find $f'(x)$ for $f(x) = 4x^3$.

25. If $f(3) = 2, f'(3) = -3, g(3) = 5$, and $g'(3) = -1$, then find $h'(3)$ for each of the following functions:

(A) $h(x) = -2f(x)$

(B) $h(x) = 4g(x)$

(C) $h(x) = 3f(x) + 7$

(D) $h(x) = -g(x) + 5$

(E) $h(x) = 5f(x) - 3g(x)$

In Problems 26–31, find $f'(x)$ and simplify.

26. $f(x) = \dfrac{1}{2}x^2 + 2x + 3$ **27.** $f(x) = 3x^{1/3} + 4x + 7$

28. $f(x) = 5$ **29.** $f(x) = \dfrac{3}{2x} + \dfrac{5x^3}{4}$

30. $f(x) = \dfrac{0.5}{x^4} + 0.25x^4$

31. $f(x) = (3x^3 - 2)(x + 1)$ [*Hint:* Multiply and then differentiate.]

In Problems 32–35, find the indicated quantities for $y = f(x) = x^2 + x$.

32. Δx, Δy, and $\Delta y/\Delta x$ for $x_1 = 2$ and $x_2 = 5$.

33. $[f(x_1 + \Delta x) - f(x_1)]/\Delta x$ for $x_1 = 2$ and $\Delta x = 3$.

34. dy for $x_1 = 2$ and $x_2 = 5$.

35. Δy and dy for $x = 2$, and $\Delta x = dx = 0.1$.

Problems 36–38 refer to the function.

$$f(x) = \begin{cases} x^2 & \text{if } 0 \le x < 2 \\ 8 - x & \text{if } x \ge 2 \end{cases}$$

which is graphed in the figure.

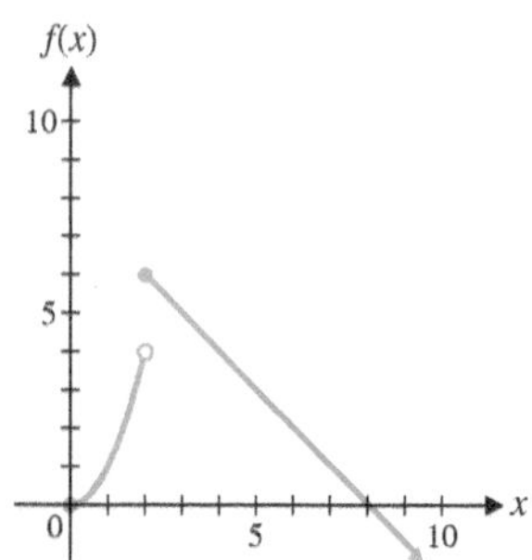

Figure for 36–38

36. (A) $\lim_{x\to 2^-} f(x) = ?$ (B) $\lim_{x\to 2^+} f(x) = ?$

(C) $\lim_{x\to 2} f(x) = ?$ (D) $f(2) = ?$

(E) Is f continuous at $x = 2$?

37. (A) $\lim_{x\to 5^-} f(x) = ?$ (B) $\lim_{x\to 5^+} f(x) = ?$

(C) $\lim_{x\to 5} f(x) = ?$ (D) $f(5) = ?$

(E) Is f continuous at $x = 5$?

38. Solve each inequality. Express answers in interval notation.

(A) $f(x) < 0$ (B) $f(x) \ge 0$

In Problems 39–41, solve each inequality. Express the answer in interval notation. Use a graphing calculator in Problem 41 to approximate partition numbers to four decimal places.

39. $x^2 - x < 12$

40. $\dfrac{x-5}{x^2+3x} > 0$

41. $x^3 + x^2 - 4x - 2 > 0$

42. Let $f(x) = 0.5x^2 - 5$.

(A) Find the slope of the secant line through $(2, f(2))$ and $(4, f(4))$.

(B) Find the slope of the secant line through $(2, f(2))$ and $(2+h, f(2+h)), h \neq 0$.

(C) Find the slope of the tangent line at $x = 2$.

In Problems 43–46, find the indicated derivative and simplify.

43. $\dfrac{dy}{dx}$ for $y = \dfrac{x^{-4}}{4} - 2x^{-2} + 3$

44. y' for $y = \dfrac{3\sqrt{x}}{2} + \dfrac{5}{3\sqrt{x}}$

45. $g'(x)$ for $g(x) = 1.8\sqrt[3]{x} + \dfrac{0.9}{\sqrt[3]{x}}$

46. $\dfrac{dy}{dx}$ for $y = \dfrac{6x^4+5}{7x^4}$

47. For $y = f(x) = 5 + (x-3)^2$, find

(A) The slope of the graph at $x = 4$

(B) The equation of the tangent line at $x = 4$ in the form $y = mx + b$

In Problems 48 and 49, find the value(s) of x where the tangent line is horizontal.

48. $f(x) = 12 + 3x^2$

49. $f(x) = \dfrac{2}{3}x^3 - 5x^2 - 12x + 101$

In Problems 50 and 51, approximate (to four decimal places) the value(s) of x where the graph of f has a horizontal tangent line.

50. $f(x) = x^4 - 2x^3 - 5x^2 + 7x$

51. $f(x) = x^5 - 10x^3 - 5x + 10$

52. If an object moves along the y axis (scale in feet) so that it is at $y = f(t) = 10 + 30t + 8t^2$ at time t (in seconds), find

(A) The instantaneous velocity function

(B) The velocity at time $t = 2$ seconds

53. A rat moves along a wall (scale in feet) so that at time x (in seconds) it is at height $y = -3x^2 + 50x + 10$. Find

(A) The instantaneous velocity function

(B) The velocity at time $x = 2$ seconds

54. Let $f(x) = x^3$, $g(x) = (x-4)^3$, and $h(x) = x^3 - 4$.

(A) How are the graphs of f, g, and h related? Illustrate your conclusion by graphing f, g, and h on the same coordinate axes.

(B) How would you expect the graphs of the derivatives of these functions to be related? Illustrate your conclusion by graphing f', g', and h' on the same coordinate axes.

In Problems 55–59, determine where f is continuous. Express the answer in interval notation.

55. $f(x) = x^2 - 4$

56. $f(x) = \dfrac{x+1}{x-2}$

57. $f(x) = \dfrac{x+4}{x^2+3x-4}$

58. $f(x) = \sqrt[3]{4-x^2}$

59. $f(x) = \sqrt{4-x^2}$

In Problems 60–69, evaluate the indicated limits if they exist.

60. Let $f(x) = \dfrac{3x}{x^2-7x}$. Find

(A) $\lim_{x\to 2} f(x)$ (B) $\lim_{x\to 7} f(x)$ (C) $\lim_{x\to 0} f(x)$

61. Let $f(x) = \dfrac{x+1}{(3-x)^2}$. Find

(A) $\lim_{x\to 1} f(x)$ (B) $\lim_{x\to -1} f(x)$ (C) $\lim_{x\to 3} f(x)$

62. Let $f(x) = \dfrac{|x-4|}{x-4}$. Find

(A) $\lim_{x\to 4^-} f(x)$ (B) $\lim_{x\to 4^+} f(x)$ (C) $\lim_{x\to 4} f(x)$

63. Let $f(x) = \dfrac{x-3}{9-x^2}$. Find

(A) $\lim_{x\to 3} f(x)$ (B) $\lim_{x\to -3} f(x)$ (C) $\lim_{x\to 0} f(x)$

64. Let $f(x) = \dfrac{x^2 - x - 2}{x^2 - 7x + 10}$. Find

(A) $\lim_{x\to -1} f(x)$ (B) $\lim_{x\to 2} f(x)$ (C) $\lim_{x\to 5} f(x)$

65. Let $f(x) = \dfrac{2x}{3x - 6}$. Find

(A) $\lim_{x\to \infty} f(x)$ (B) $\lim_{x\to -\infty} f(x)$ (C) $\lim_{x\to 2} f(x)$

66. Let $f(x) = \dfrac{2x^3}{3(x-2)^2}$. Find

(A) $\lim_{x\to \infty} f(x)$ (B) $\lim_{x\to -\infty} f(x)$ (C) $\lim_{x\to 2} f(x)$

67. Let $f(x) = \dfrac{2x}{3(x-2)^3}$. Find

(A) $\lim_{x\to \infty} f(x)$ (B) $\lim_{x\to -\infty} f(x)$ (C) $\lim_{x\to 2} f(x)$

68. $\lim_{h\to 0} \dfrac{f(1+h) - f(1)}{h}$ for $f(x) = x^2 - 1$

69. $\lim_{h\to 0} \dfrac{f(x+h) - f(x)}{h}$ for $f(x) = \dfrac{4x^2 + 3}{x^2}$

In Problems 70 and 71, use the definition of the derivative and the four-step process to find $f'(x)$.

70. $f(x) = x^2 - x$ **71.** $f(x) = \sqrt{x} - 3$

Problems 72–77 refer to the function f in the figure. Determine whether f is differentiable at the indicated value of x.

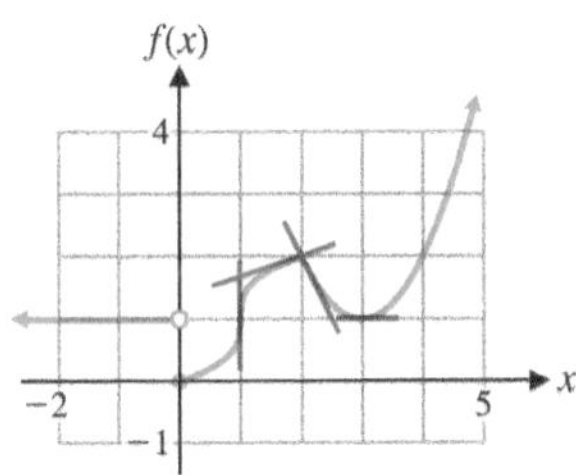

72. $x = -1$ **73.** $x = 0$ **74.** $x = 1$

75. $x = 2$ **76.** $x = 3$ **77.** $x = 4$

In Problems 78–82, find all horizontal and vertical asymptotes.

78. $f(x) = \dfrac{11x}{x - 5}$ **79.** $f(x) = \dfrac{-2x + 5}{(x-4)^2}$

80. $f(x) = \dfrac{x^2 + 9}{x - 3}$ **81.** $f(x) = \dfrac{x^2 - 9}{x^2 + x - 2}$

82. $f(x) = \dfrac{x^3 - 1}{x^3 - x^2 - x + 1}$

83. The domain of the power function $f(x) = x^{1/3}$ is the set of all real numbers. Find the domain of the derivative $f'(x)$. Discuss the nature of the graph of $y = f(x)$ for any x values excluded from the domain of $f'(x)$.

84. Let f be defined by

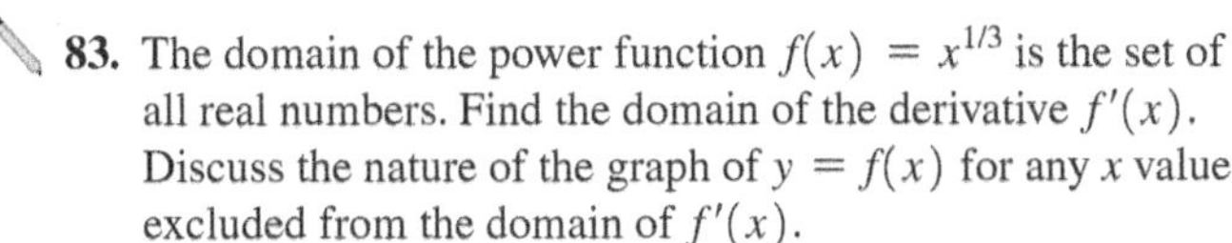

$$f(x) = \begin{cases} x^2 - m & \text{if } x \le 1 \\ -x^2 + m & \text{if } x > 1 \end{cases}$$

where m is a constant.

(A) Graph f for $m = 0$, and find

$$\lim_{x\to 1^-} f(x) \quad \text{and} \quad \lim_{x\to 1^+} f(x)$$

(B) Graph f for $m = 2$, and find

$$\lim_{x\to 1^-} f(x) \quad \text{and} \quad \lim_{x\to 1^+} f(x)$$

(C) Find m so that

$$\lim_{x\to 1^-} f(x) = \lim_{x\to 1^+} f(x)$$

and graph f for this value of m.

(D) Write a brief verbal description of each graph. How does the graph in part (C) differ from the graphs in parts (A) and (B)?

85. Let $f(x) = 1 - |x - 1|, 0 \le x \le 2$ (see figure).

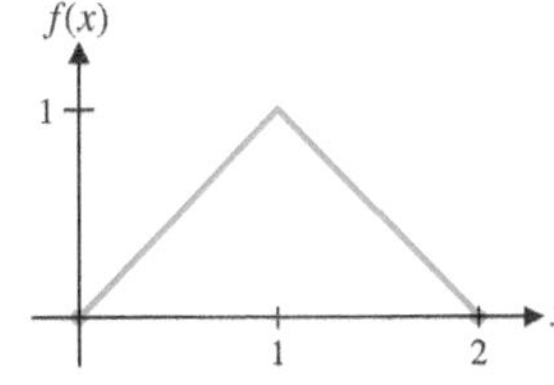

(A) $\lim_{h\to 0^-} \dfrac{f(1+h) - f(1)}{h} = ?$

(B) $\lim_{h\to 0^+} \dfrac{f(1+h) - f(1)}{h} = ?$

(C) $\lim_{h\to 0} \dfrac{f(1+h) - f(1)}{h} = ?$

(D) Does $f'(1)$ exist?

Applications

86. Natural-gas rates. Table 1 shows the winter rates for natural gas charged by the Bay State Gas Company. The base charge is a fixed monthly charge, independent of the amount of gas used per month.

Table 1 **Natural Gas Rates**

Base charge	\$7.47
First 90 therms	\$0.4000 per therm
All usage over 90 therms	\$0.2076 per therm

(A) Write a piecewise definition of the monthly charge $S(x)$ for a customer who uses x therms in a winter month.

(B) Graph $S(x)$.

(C) Is $S(x)$ continuous at $x = 90$? Explain.

87. Cost analysis. The total cost (in dollars) of producing x mobile phones is

$$C(x) = 12{,}500 + 100x + x^2$$

(A) Find the exact cost of producing the 11th mobile phone.

(B) Use the marginal cost to approximate the cost of producing the 11th mobile phone.

88. Cost analysis. The total cost (in dollars) of producing x motorcycles is

$$C(x) = 10{,}000 + 500x + 0.03x^2$$

(A) Find the total cost and the marginal cost at a production level of 200 motorcycles and interpret the results.

(B) Find the average cost and the marginal average cost at a manufacturing level of 200 motorcycles and interpret the results.

89. Cost analysis. The total cost (in dollars) of producing x laser printers per week is shown in the figure. Which is greater, the approximate cost of producing the 201st printer or the approximate cost of producing the 601st printer? Does this graph represent a manufacturing process that is becoming more efficient or less efficient as production levels increase? Explain.

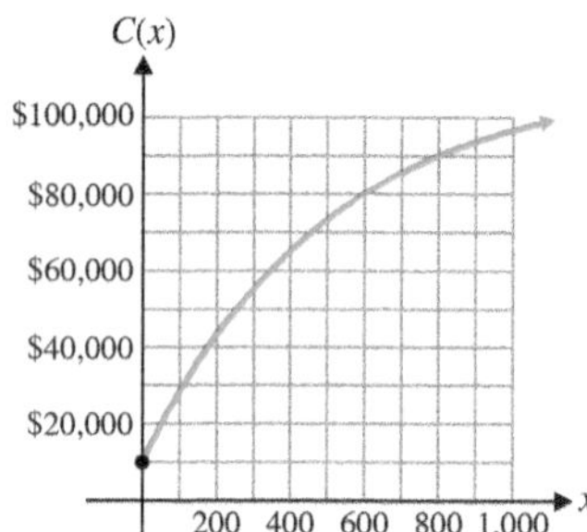

90. Cost analysis. Let

$$p = 25 - 0.01x \quad \text{and} \quad C(x) = 2x + 9{,}000$$
$$0 \le x \le 2{,}500$$

be the price–demand equation and cost function, respectively, for the manufacture of umbrellas.

(A) Find the marginal cost, average cost, and marginal average cost functions.

(B) Express the revenue in terms of x, and find the marginal revenue, average revenue, and marginal average revenue functions.

(C) Find the profit, marginal profit, average profit, and marginal average profit functions.

(D) Find the break-even point(s).

(E) Evaluate the marginal profit at $x = 1{,}000$, 1,150, and 1,400, and interpret the results.

(F) Graph $R = R(x)$ and $C = C(x)$ on the same coordinate system, and locate regions of profit and loss.

91. Employee training. A company producing computer components has established that, on average, a new employee can assemble $N(t)$ components per day after t days of on-the-job training, as given by

$$N(t) = \frac{40t - 80}{t}, t \ge 2$$

(A) Find the average rate of change of $N(t)$ from 2 days to 5 days.

(B) Find the instantaneous rate of change of $N(t)$ at 2 days.

92. Sales analysis. The total number of swimming pools, N (in thousands), sold during a year is given by

$$N(t) = 2t + \frac{1}{3}t^{3/2}$$

where t is the number of months since the beginning of the year. Find $N(9)$ and $N'(9)$, and interpret these quantities.

93. Natural-gas consumption. The data in Table 2 give the U.S. consumption of natural gas in trillions of cubic feet. (*Source:* Energy Information Administration)

Table 2

Year	Natural-Gas Consumption
1960	12.0
1970	21.1
1980	19.9
1990	18.7
2000	21.9
2010	24.1

(A) Let x represent time (in years), with $x = 0$ corresponding to 1960, and let y represent the corresponding U.S. consumption of natural gas. Enter the data set in a graphing calculator and find a cubic regression equation for the data.

(B) If $y = N(x)$ denotes the regression equation found in part (A), find $N(60)$ and $N'(60)$, and write a brief verbal interpretation of these results.

94. Break-even analysis. Table 3 contains price–demand and total cost data from a bakery for the production of kringles (a Danish pastry), where p is the price (in dollars) of a kringle for a daily demand of x kringles and C is the total cost (in dollars) of producing x kringles.

Table 3

x	p($)	C($)
125	9	740
140	8	785
170	7	850
200	6	900

(A) Find a linear regression equation for the price–demand data, using x as the independent variable.

(B) Find a linear regression equation for the cost data, using x as the independent variable. Use this equation to estimate the fixed costs and variable costs per kringle.

(C) Find the break-even points.

(D) Find the price range for which the bakery will make a profit.

95. Pollution. A sewage treatment plant uses a pipeline that extends 1 mile toward the center of a large lake. The concentration of sewage $C(x)$ in parts per million, x meters from the end of the pipe is given approximately by

$$C(x) = \frac{500}{x^2}, x \ge 1$$

What is the instantaneous rate of change of concentration at 10 meters? At 100 meters?

96. Medicine. The body temperature (in degrees Fahrenheit) of a patient t hours after taking a fever-reducing drug is given by

$$F(t) = 0.16t^2 - 1.6t + 102$$

Find $F(4)$ and $F'(4)$. Write a brief verbal interpretation of these quantities.

97. Learning. If a person learns N items in t hours, as given by

$$N(t) = 20\sqrt{t}$$

find the rate of learning after

(A) 1 hour (B) 4 hours

98. Physics. The coefficient of thermal expansion (CTE) is a measure of the expansion of an object subjected to extreme temperatures. We want to use a Michaelis–Menten function of the form

$$C(T) = \frac{C_{max}T}{M + T}$$

where C = CTE, T is temperature in K (degrees Kelvin), and C_{max} and M are constants. Table 4 lists the coefficients of thermal expansion for titanium at various temperatures.

Table 4 **Coefficients of Thermal Expansion**

T(K)	Titanium
100	4.5
200	7.4
293	8.6
500	9.9
800	11.1
1100	11.7

(A) Plot the points in columns 1 and 2 of Table 4 on graph paper and estimate C_{max} to the nearest integer. To estimate M, add the horizontal line CTE $= \frac{C_{max}}{2}$ to your graph, connect successive points on the graph with straight-line segments, and estimate the value of T (to the nearest multiple of fifty) that satisfies

$$C(T) = \frac{C_{max}}{2}.$$

(B) Use the constants $\frac{C_{max}}{2}$ and M from part (A) to form a Michaelis–Menten function for the CTE of titanium.

(C) Use the function from part (B) to estimate the CTE of titanium at 600 K and to estimate the temperature when the CTE of titanium is 10.

7 Additional Derivative Topics

Introduction

In this chapter, we develop techniques for finding derivatives of a wide variety of functions, including exponential and logarithmic functions. There are straightforward procedures—the product rule, quotient rule, and chain rule—for writing down the derivative of any function that is the product, quotient, or composite of functions whose derivatives are known. With the ability to calculate derivatives easily, we consider a wealth of applications involving rates of change. For example, we apply the derivative to determine how the demand for bicycle helmets is affected by a change in price (see Problem 94 in Section 7.4). Before starting this chapter, you may find it helpful to review the basic properties of exponential and logarithmic functions in Sections 2.5 and 2.6.

7.1 The Constant e and Continuous Compound Interest

- The Constant *e*
- Continuous Compound Interest

In Chapter 2, both the exponential function with base e and continuous compound interest were introduced informally. Now, with an understanding of limit concepts, we can give precise definitions of e and continuous compound interest.

The Constant e

The irrational number e is a particularly suitable base for both exponential and logarithmic functions. The reasons for choosing this number as a base will become clear as we develop differentiation formulas for the exponential function e^x and the natural logarithmic function $\ln x$.

In precalculus treatments (Chapter 2), the number e is defined informally as the irrational number that can be approximated by the expression $[1 + (1/n)]^n$ for n sufficiently large. Now we will use the limit concept to formally define e as either of the following two limits. [*Note:* If $s = 1/n$, then as $n \to \infty$, $s \to 0$.]

DEFINITION The Number e

$$e = \lim_{n\to\infty}\left(1 + \frac{1}{n}\right)^n \quad \text{or, alternatively,} \quad e = \lim_{s\to 0}(1 + s)^{1/s}$$

Both limits are equal to $e = 2.718\,281\,828\,459\ldots$

Proof that the indicated limits exist and represent an irrational number between 2 and 3 is not easy and is omitted.

CONCEPTUAL INSIGHT

The two limits used to define e are unlike any we have encountered so far. Some people reason (incorrectly) that both limits are 1 because $1 + s \to 1$ as $s \to 0$ and 1 to any power is 1. An ordinary scientific calculator with a y^x key can convince you otherwise. Consider the following table of values for s and $f(s) = (1 + s)^{1/s}$ and Figure 1 for s close to 0. Compute the table values with a calculator yourself, and try several values of s even closer to 0. Note that the function is discontinuous at $s = 0$.

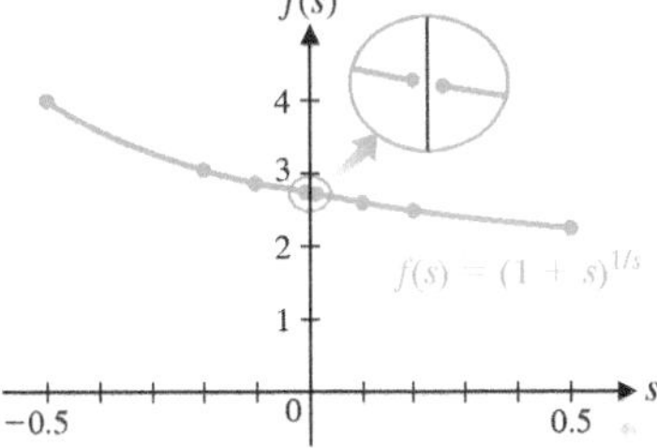

Figure 1

s approaches 0 from the left → 0 ← s approaches 0 from the right

s	−0.5	−0.2	−0.1	−0.01 → 0 ← 0.01	0.1	0.2	0.5
$(1 + s)^{1/s}$	4.0000	3.0518	2.8680	2.7320 → e ← 2.7048	2.5937	2.4883	2.2500

Continuous Compound Interest

Now we can see how e appears quite naturally in the important application of compound interest. Let us start with simple interest, move on to compound interest, and then proceed on to continuous compound interest.

On one hand, if a principal P is borrowed at an annual rate r, then after t years at simple interest, the borrower will owe the lender an amount A given by

$$A = P + Prt = P(1 + rt) \qquad \text{Simple interest} \qquad (1)$$

If r is the interest rate written as a decimal, then $100r\%$ is the rate in percent. For example, if $r = 0.12$, then $100r\% = 100(0.12)\% = 12\%$. The expressions 0.12 and 12% are equivalent. Unless stated otherwise, all formulas in this book use r in decimal form.

On the other hand, if interest is compounded m times a year, then the borrower will owe the lender an amount A given by

$$A = P\left(1 + \frac{r}{m}\right)^{mt} \qquad \text{Compound interest} \qquad (2)$$

where r/m is the interest rate per compounding period and mt is the number of compounding periods. Suppose that P, r, and t in equation (2) are held fixed and m is increased. Will the amount A increase without bound, or will it tend to approach some limiting value?

Let us perform a calculator experiment before we attack the general limit problem. If $P = \$100$, $r = 0.06$, and $t = 2$ years, then

$$A = 100\left(1 + \frac{0.06}{m}\right)^{2m}$$

We compute A for several values of m in Table 1. The biggest gain appears in the first step, then the gains slow down as m increases. The amount A appears to approach $112.75 as m gets larger and larger.

Table 1

Compounding Frequency	m	$A = 100\left(1 + \frac{0.06}{m}\right)^{2m}$
Annually	1	$112.3600
Semiannually	2	112.5509
Quarterly	4	112.6493
Monthly	12	112.7160
Weekly	52	112.7419
Daily	365	112.7486
Hourly	8,760	112.7496

Keeping P, r, and t fixed in equation (2), we pull P outside the limit using a property of limits (see Theorem 2, property 5, Section 6.1):

$$\begin{aligned}
\lim_{m\to\infty} P\left(1 + \frac{r}{m}\right)^{mt} &= P \lim_{m\to\infty}\left(1 + \frac{r}{m}\right)^{mt} && \text{Let } s = r/m, \text{ so } mt = rt/s \text{ and } s \to 0 \text{ as } m \to \infty. \\
&= P \lim_{s\to 0}(1 + s)^{rt/s} && \text{Use a new limit property.} \\
&= P\left[\lim_{s\to 0}(1 + s)^{1/s}\right]^{rt} && \text{Use the definition of } e. \\
&= Pe^{rt}
\end{aligned}$$

(The new limit property that is used in the derivation is: If $\lim_{x\to c} f(x)$ exists, then $\lim_{x\to c}[f(x)]^p = [\lim_{x\to c} f(x)]^p$, provided that the last expression names a real number.)

The resulting formula is called the **continuous compound interest formula**, a widely used formula in business and economics.

THEOREM 1 Continuous Compound Interest Formula

If a principal P is invested at an annual rate r (expressed as a decimal) compounded continuously, then the amount A in the account at the end of t years is given by

$$A = Pe^{rt}$$

EXAMPLE 1 **Computing Continuously Compounded Interest** If $100 is invested at 6% compounded continuously, what amount will be in the account after 2 years? How much interest will be earned?

Reminder

Following common usage, we will often write "at 6% compounded continuously," understanding that this means "at an annual rate of 6% compounded continuously."

SOLUTION

$$\begin{aligned} A &= Pe^{rt} \\ &= 100e^{(0.06)(2)} \qquad \text{6\% is equivalent to } r = 0.06. \\ &\approx \$112.7497 \end{aligned}$$

Compare this result with the values calculated in Table 1. The interest earned is $\$112.7497 - \$100 = \$12.7497$.

Matched Problem 1 What amount (to the nearest cent) will be in an account after 5 years if $100 is invested at an annual nominal rate of 8% compounded annually? Semiannually? Continuously?

EXAMPLE 2 **Graphing the Growth of an Investment** Union Savings Bank offers a 5-year certificate of deposit (CD) that earns 5.75% compounded continuously. If $1,000 is invested in one of these CDs, graph the amount in the account as a function of time for a period of 5 years.

SOLUTION We want to graph

$$A = 1{,}000e^{0.0575t} \qquad 0 \le t \le 5$$

If $t = 2$, then $A = 1{,}000\,e^{0.0575(2)} = 1{,}121.87$, which we round to the nearest dollar, 1,122. Similarly, using a calculator, we find A for $t = 0, 1, 3, 4,$ and 5 (Table 2). Then we graph the points from the table and join the points with a smooth curve (Fig. 2).

Table 2

t	A ($)
0	1,000
1	1,059
2	1,122
3	1,188
4	1,259
5	1,333

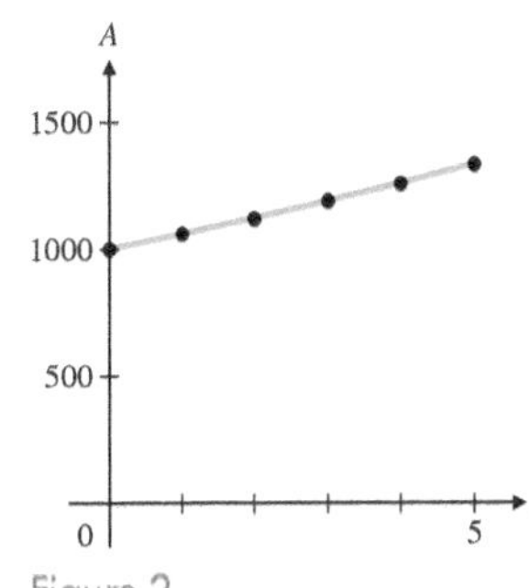

Figure 2

CONCEPTUAL INSIGHT

Depending on the domain, the graph of an exponential function can appear to be linear. Table 2 shows that the graph in Figure 2 is *not* linear. The slope determined by the first two points (for $t = 0$ and $t = 1$) is 59 but the slope determined by the first and third points (for $t = 0$ and $t = 2$) is 61. For a linear graph, the slope determined by any two points is constant.

Matched Problem 2 If \$5,000 is invested in a Union Savings Bank 4-year CD that earns 5.61% compounded continuously, graph the amount in the account as a function of time for a period of 4 years.

EXAMPLE 3 **Computing Growth Time** How long will it take an investment of \$5,000 to grow to \$8,000 if it is invested at 5% compounded continuously?

SOLUTION Starting with the continous compound interest formula $A = Pe^{rt}$, we must solve for t:

$$A = Pe^{rt}$$

$$8{,}000 = 5{,}000e^{0.05t} \quad \text{Divide both sides by 5,000 and reverse the equation.}$$

$$e^{0.05t} = 1.6$$

$$\ln e^{0.05t} = \ln 1.6 \quad \text{Take the natural logarithm of both sides—recall that } \log_b b^x = x.$$

$$0.05t = \ln 1.6$$

$$t = \frac{\ln 1.6}{0.05}$$

$$t \approx 9.4 \text{ years}$$

Figure 3 shows an alternative method for solving Example 3 on a graphing calculator.

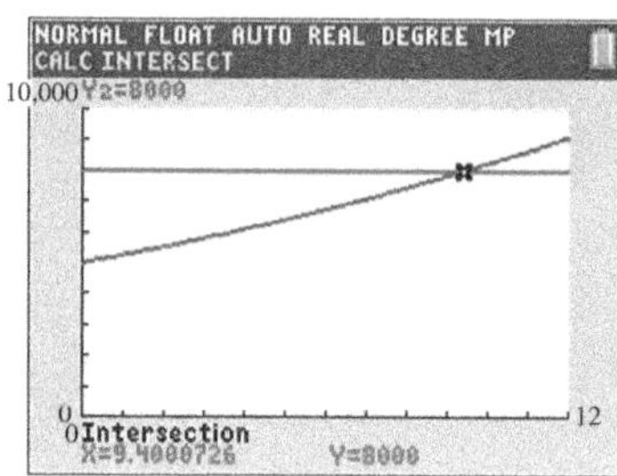

Figure 3

$y_1 = 5{,}000e^{0.05x}$
$y_2 = 8{,}000$

Matched Problem 3 How long will it take an investment of \$10,000 to grow to \$15,000 if it is invested at 9% compounded continuously?

EXAMPLE 4 **Computing Doubling Time** How long will it take money to double if it is invested at 6.5% compounded continuously?

SOLUTION Money has doubled when the amount A is twice the principal P, that is, when $A = 2P$. So we substitute $A = 2P$ and $r = 0.065$ in the continuous compound interest formula $A = Pe^{rt}$, and solve for t:

$$2P = Pe^{0.065t} \quad \text{Divide both sides by } P \text{ and reverse the equation.}$$

$$e^{0.065t} = 2 \quad \text{Take the natural logarithm of both sides.}$$

$$\ln e^{0.065t} = \ln 2 \quad \text{Simplify.}$$

$$0.065t = \ln 2$$

$$t = \frac{\ln 2}{0.065}$$

$$t \approx 10.66 \text{ years}$$

Matched Problem 4 How long will it take money to triple if it is invested at 5.5% compounded continuously?

Explore and Discuss 1

You are considering three options for investing \$10,000: at 7% compounded annually, at 6% compounded monthly, and at 5% compounded continuously.

(A) Which option would be the best for investing \$10,000 for 8 years?

(B) How long would you need to invest your money for the third option to be the best?

Exercises 7.1

Skills Warm-up Exercise

W *In Problems 1–8, solve for the variable to two decimal places. (If necessary, review Sections 2.5 and 2.6.)*

1. $A = 1{,}200e^{0.04(5)}$

2. $A = 3{,}000e^{0.07(10)}$

3. $9827.30 = Pe^{0.025(3)}$

4. $50{,}000 = Pe^{0.054(7)}$

5. $6{,}000 = 5{,}000e^{0.0325t}$

6. $10{,}000 = 7{,}500e^{0.085t}$

7. $956 = 900e^{1.5r}$

8. $4{,}660 = 3{,}450e^{3.75r}$

A *Use a calculator to evaluate A to the nearest cent in Problems 9 and 10.*

9. $A = \$10{,}000e^{0.1t}$ for $t = 1, 2,$ and 3

10. $A = \$10{,}000e^{0.1t}$ for $t = 10, 20,$ and 30

11. If \$6,000 is invested at 10% compounded continuously, graph the amount in the account as a function of time for a period of 8 years.

12. If \$4,000 is invested at 8% compounded continuously, graph the amount in the account as a function of time for a period of 6 years.

B *In Problems 13–20, solve for t or r to two decimal places.*

13. $2 = e^{0.07t}$

14. $2 = e^{0.09t}$

15. $2 = e^{9r}$

16. $2 = e^{18r}$

17. $3 = e^{0.03t}$

18. $3 = e^{0.08t}$

19. $3 = e^{10r}$

20. $3 = e^{20r}$

C *In Problems 21 and 22, use a calculator to complete each table to five decimal places.*

21.

n	$[1 + (1/n)]^n$
10	2.593 74
100	
1,000	
10,000	
100,000	
1,000,000	
10,000,000	
↓	↓
∞	$e = 2.718\,281\,828\,459\ldots$

22.

s	$(1 + s)^{1/s}$
0.01	2.704 81
−0.01	
0.001	
−0.001	
0.000 1	
−0.000 1	
0.000 01	
−0.000 01	
↓	↓
0	$e = 2.718\,281\,828\,459\ldots$

23. Use a calculator and a table of values to investigate

$$\lim_{n\to\infty} (1 + n)^{1/n}$$

Do you think this limit exists? If so, what do you think it is?

24. Use a calculator and a table of values to investigate

$$\lim_{s\to 0^+} \left(1 + \frac{1}{s}\right)^s$$

Do you think this limit exists? If so, what do you think it is?

25. It can be shown that the number e satisfies the inequality

$$\left(1 + \frac{1}{n}\right)^n < e < \left(1 + \frac{1}{n}\right)^{n+1} \qquad n \ge 1$$

Illustrate this condition by graphing

$$y_1 = (1 + 1/n)^n$$
$$y_2 = 2.718\,281\,828 \approx e$$
$$y_3 = (1 + 1/n)^{n+1}$$

in the same viewing window, for $1 \le n \le 20$.

26. It can be shown that

$$e^s = \lim_{n\to\infty} \left(1 + \frac{s}{n}\right)^n$$

for any real number s. Illustrate this equation graphically for $s = 2$ by graphing

$$y_1 = (1 + 2/n)^n$$
$$y_2 = 7.389\,056\,099 \approx e^2$$

in the same viewing window, for $1 \le n \le 50$.

Applications

27. **Continuous compound interest.** Provident Bank offers a 10-year CD that earns 2.15% compounded continuously.
    (A) If $10,000 is invested in this CD, how much will it be worth in 10 years?
    (B) How long will it take for the account to be worth $18,000?
28. **Continuous compound interest.** Provident Bank also offers a 3-year CD that earns 1.64% compounded continuously.
    (A) If $10,000 is invested in this CD, how much will it be worth in 3 years?
    (B) How long will it take for the account to be worth $11,000?
29. **Present value.** A note will pay $25,000 at maturity 10 years from now. How much should you be willing to pay for the note now if money is worth 4.6% compounded continuously?
30. **Present value.** A note will pay $35,000 at maturity 5 years from now. How much should you be willing to pay for the note now if money is worth 5.7% compounded continuously?
31. **Continuous compound interest.** An investor bought stock for $20,000. Five years later, the stock was sold for $30,000. If interest is compounded continuously, what annual nominal rate of interest did the original $20,000 investment earn?
32. **Continuous compound interest.** A family paid $99,000 cash for a house. Fifteen years later, the house was sold for $195,000. If interest is compounded continuously, what annual nominal rate of interest did the original $99,000 investment earn?
33. **Present value.** Solving $A = Pe^{rt}$ for P, we obtain

$$P = Ae^{-rt}$$

which is the present value of the amount A due in t years if money earns interest at an annual nominal rate r compounded continuously.
    (A) Graph $P = 10{,}000e^{-0.08t}$, $0 \le t \le 50$.
    (B) $\lim_{t\to\infty} 10{,}000e^{-0.08t} = ?$ [Guess, using part (A).]
    [*Conclusion:* The longer the time until the amount A is due, the smaller is its present value, as we would expect.]
34. **Present value.** Referring to Problem 33, in how many years will the $10,000 be due in order for its present value to be $5,000?
35. **Doubling time.** How long will it take money to double if it is invested at 3.5% compounded continuously?
36. **Doubling time.** How long will it take money to double if it is invested at 7% compounded continuously?
37. **Doubling rate.** At what nominal rate compounded continuously must money be invested to double in 14 years?
38. **Doubling rate.** At what nominal rate compounded continuously must money be invested to double in 21 years?
39. **Growth time.** A man with $20,000 to invest decides to diversify his investments by placing $10,000 in an account that earns 7.2% compounded continuously and $10,000 in an account that earns 8.4% compounded annually. Use graphical approximation methods to determine how long it will take for his total investment in the two accounts to grow to $35,000.
40. **Growth time.** A woman invests $5,000 in an account that earns 8.8% compounded continuously and $7,000 in an account that earns 9.6% compounded annually. Use graphical approximation methods to determine how long it will take for her total investment in the two accounts to grow to $20,000.
41. **Doubling times.**
    (A) Show that the doubling time t (in years) at an annual rate r compounded continuously is given by

$$t = \frac{\ln 2}{r}$$

    (B) Graph the doubling-time equation from part (A) for $0.02 \le r \le 0.30$. Is this restriction on r reasonable? Explain.
    (C) Determine the doubling times (in years, to two decimal places) for $r =$ 5%, 10%, 15%, 20%, 25%, and 30%.
42. **Doubling rates.**
    (A) Show that the rate r that doubles an investment at continuously compounded interest in t years is given by

$$r = \frac{\ln 2}{t}$$

    (B) Graph the doubling-rate equation from part (A) for $1 \le t \le 20$. Is this restriction on t reasonable? Explain.
    (C) Determine the doubling rates for $t = 2, 4, 6, 8, 10$, and 12 years.
43. **Radioactive decay.** A mathematical model for the decay of radioactive substances is given by

$$Q = Q_0e^{rt}$$

where

Q_0 = amount of the substance at time $t = 0$
r = continuous compound rate of decay
t = time in years
Q = amount of the substance at time t

If the continuous compound rate of decay of radium per year is $r = -0.000\,433\,2$, how long will it take a certain amount of radium to decay to half the original amount? (This period is the *half-life* of the substance.)
44. **Radioactive decay.** The continuous compound rate of decay of carbon-14 per year is $r = -0.000\,123\,8$. How long will it take a certain amount of carbon-14 to decay to half the original amount? (Use the radioactive decay model in Problem 43.)
45. **Radioactive decay.** A cesium isotope has a half-life of 30 years. What is the continuous compound rate of decay? (Use the radioactive decay model in Problem 43.)
46. **Radioactive decay.** A strontium isotope has a half-life of 90 years. What is the continuous compound rate of decay? (Use the radioactive decay model in Problem 43.)

47. World population. A mathematical model for world population growth over short intervals is given by

$$P = P_0e^{rt}$$

where

P_0 = population at time $t = 0$
r = continuous compound rate of growth
t = time in years
P = population at time t

How long will it take the world population to double if it continues to grow at its current continuous compound rate of 1.13% per year?

48. Australian population. In 2017, Australia's population grew by 1.6%. If the rate of growth remains constant, how long will it take for the Australian population to double?

49. Population growth. Some underdeveloped nations have population doubling times of 50 years. At what continuous compound rate is the population growing? (Use the population growth model in Problem 47.)

50. Population growth. Some developed nations have population doubling times of 200 years. At what continuous compound rate is the population growing? (Use the population growth model in Problem 47.)

Answers to Matched Problems

1. \$146.93; \$148.02; \$149.18
2. $A = 5{,}000e^{0.0561t}$

t	A(\$)
0	5,000
1	5,289
2	5,594
3	5,916
4	6,258

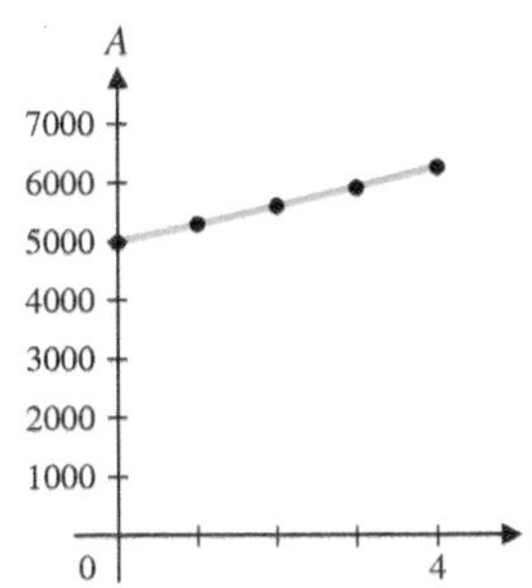

3. 4.51 yr
4. 19.97 yr

7.2 Derivatives of Exponential and Logarithmic Functions

- The Derivative of e^x
- The Derivative of ln x
- Other Logarithmic and Exponential Functions
- Exponential and Logarithmic Models

In this section, we find formulas for the derivatives of logarithmic and exponential functions. A review of Sections 2.5 and 2.6 may prove helpful. In particular, recall that $f(x) = e^x$ is the exponential function with base $e \approx 2.718$, and the inverse of the function e^x is the natural logarithm function $\ln x$. More generally, if b is a positive real number, $b \neq 1$, then the exponential function b^x with base b, and the logarithmic function $\log_b x$ with base b, are inverses of each other.

The Derivative of e^x

In the process of finding the derivative of e^x, we use (without proof) the fact that

$$\lim_{h \to 0} \frac{e^h - 1}{h} = 1 \qquad (1)$$

Explore and Discuss 1

Complete Table 1.

Table 1

h	−0.1	−0.01	−0.001	→ 0 ←	0.001	0.01	0.1
$\frac{e^h - 1}{h}$							

Do your calculations make it reasonable to conclude that

$$\lim_{h \to 0} \frac{e^h - 1}{h} = 1?$$

Discuss.

We now apply the four-step process (Section 6.4) to the exponential function $f(x) = e^x$.

Step 1 Find $f(x + h)$.

$$f(x + h) = e^{x+h} = e^x e^h$$ See Section 2.5.

Step 2 Find $f(x + h) - f(x)$.

$$f(x + h) - f(x) = e^x e^h - e^x$$ Factor out e^x.

$$= e^x(e^h - 1)$$

Step 3 Find $\dfrac{f(x + h) - f(x)}{h}$.

$$\frac{f(x + h) - f(x)}{h} = \frac{e^x(e^h - 1)}{h} = e^x\left(\frac{e^h - 1}{h}\right)$$

Step 4 Find $f'(x) = \lim_{h \to 0} \dfrac{f(x + h) - f(x)}{h}$.

$$f'(x) = \lim_{h \to 0} \frac{f(x + h) - f(x)}{h}$$

$$= \lim_{h \to 0} e^x\left(\frac{e^h - 1}{h}\right)$$

$$= e^x \lim_{h \to 0}\left(\frac{e^h - 1}{h}\right)$$ Use the limit in (1).

$$= e^x \cdot 1 = e^x$$

Therefore,

$$\frac{d}{dx}e^x = e^x$$ The derivative of the exponential function is the exponential function.

EXAMPLE 1 **Finding Derivatives** Find $f'(x)$ for

(A) $f(x) = 5e^x - 3x^4 + 9x + 16$ (B) $f(x) = -7x^e + 2e^x + e^2$

SOLUTION

(A) $f'(x) = 5e^x - 12x^3 + 9$ (B) $f'(x) = -7ex^{e-1} + 2e^x$

Remember that e is a real number, so the power rule (Section 6.5) is used to find the derivative of x^e. The derivative of the exponential function e^x, however, is e^x. Note that $e^2 \approx 7.389$ is a constant, so its derivative is 0.

Matched Problem 1 Find $f'(x)$ for

(A) $f(x) = 4e^x + 8x^2 + 7x - 14$ (B) $f(x) = x^7 - x^5 + e^3 - x + e^x$

CAUTION $\dfrac{d}{dx}e^x \neq xe^{x-1}$ $\dfrac{d}{dx}e^x = e^x$

The power rule cannot be used to differentiate the exponential function. The power rule applies to exponential forms x^n, where the exponent is a constant and the base is a variable. In the exponential form e^x, the base is a constant and the exponent is a variable.

The Derivative of ln *x*

We summarize some important facts about logarithmic functions from Section 2.6:

SUMMARY

Recall that the inverse of an exponential function is called a **logarithmic function**. For $b > 0$ and $b \neq 1$,

Logarithmic form		Exponential form
$y = \log_b x$	is equivalent to	$x = b^y$
Domain: $(0, \infty)$		Domain: $(-\infty, \infty)$
Range: $(-\infty, \infty)$		Range: $(0, \infty)$

The graphs of $y = \log_b x$ and $y = b^x$ are symmetric with respect to the line $y = x$. (See Fig. 1.)

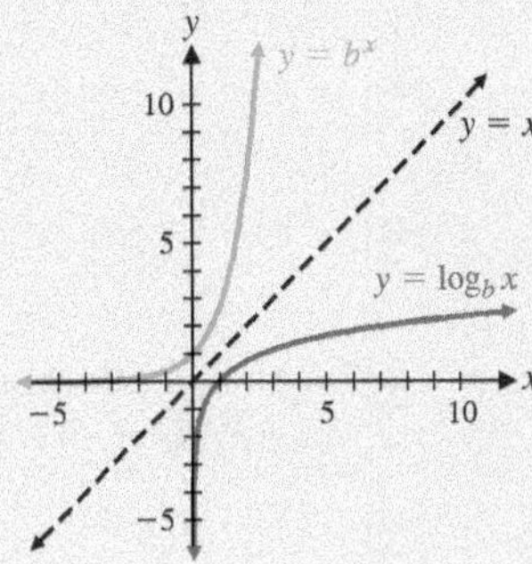

Figure 1

Of all the possible bases for logarithmic functions, the two most widely used are

$$\log x = \log_{10} x \qquad \text{Common logarithm (base 10)}$$
$$\ln x = \log_e x \qquad \text{Natural logarithm (base } e\text{)}$$

We are now ready to use the definition of the derivative and the four-step process discussed in Section 6.4 to find a formula for the derivative of $\ln x$. Later we will extend this formula to include $\log_b x$ for any base b.

Let $f(x) = \ln x, x > 0$.

Step 1 Find $f(x + h)$.

$$f(x + h) = \ln(x + h) \qquad \ln(x + h) \text{ cannot be simplified.}$$

Step 2 Find $f(x + h) - f(x)$.

$$f(x + h) - f(x) = \ln(x + h) - \ln x \qquad \text{Use } \ln A - \ln B = \ln\frac{A}{B}.$$
$$= \ln\frac{x + h}{x}$$

Step 3 Find $\dfrac{f(x + h) - f(x)}{h}$.

$$\frac{f(x + h) - f(x)}{h} = \frac{\ln(x + h) - \ln x}{h}$$
$$= \frac{1}{h}\ln\frac{x + h}{x} \qquad \text{Multiply by } 1 = x/x \text{ to change form.}$$
$$= \frac{x}{x}\cdot\frac{1}{h}\ln\frac{x + h}{x}$$
$$= \frac{1}{x}\left[\frac{x}{h}\ln\left(1 + \frac{h}{x}\right)\right] \qquad \text{Use } p\ln A = \ln A^p.$$
$$= \frac{1}{x}\ln\left(1 + \frac{h}{x}\right)^{x/h}$$

Step 4 Find $f'(x) = \lim_{h \to 0} \frac{f(x+h) - f(x)}{h}$.

$$f'(x) = \lim_{h \to 0} \frac{f(x+h) - f(x)}{h}$$

$$= \lim_{h \to 0} \left[\frac{1}{x} \ln\left(1 + \frac{h}{x}\right)^{x/h} \right] \quad \text{Let } s = h/x. \text{ Note that } h \to 0 \text{ implies } s \to 0.$$

$$= \frac{1}{x} \lim_{s \to 0} \left[\ln(1+s)^{1/s} \right] \quad \text{Use a new limit property.}$$

$$= \frac{1}{x} \ln\left[\lim_{s \to 0} (1+s)^{1/s} \right] \quad \text{Use the definition of } e.$$

$$= \frac{1}{x} \ln e \quad \ln e = \log_e e = 1.$$

$$= \frac{1}{x}$$

The new limit property used in the derivation is: If $\lim_{x \to c} f(x)$ exists and is positive, then $\lim_{x \to c} [\ln f(x)] = \ln[\lim_{x \to c} f(x)]$. Therefore,

$$\frac{d}{dx} \ln x = \frac{1}{x} \quad (x > 0)$$

CONCEPTUAL INSIGHT

In finding the derivative of $\ln x$, we used the following properties of logarithms:

$$\ln \frac{A}{B} = \ln A - \ln B \qquad \ln A^p = p \ln A$$

We also noted that there is no property that simplifies $\ln(A + B)$. (See Theorem 1 in Section 2.6 for a list of properties of logarithms.)

EXAMPLE 2 **Finding Derivatives** Find y' for

(A) $y = 3e^x + 5 \ln x$ (B) $y = x^4 - \ln x^4$

SOLUTION

(A) $y' = 3e^x + \frac{5}{x}$

(B) Before taking the derivative, we use a property of logarithms (see Theorem 1, Section 2.6) to rewrite y.

$$y = x^4 - \ln x^4 \quad \text{Use } \ln M^p = p \ln M.$$

$$y = x^4 - 4 \ln x \quad \text{Now take the derivative of both sides.}$$

$$y' = 4x^3 - \frac{4}{x}$$

Matched Problem 2 Find y' for

(A) $y = 10x^3 - 100 \ln x$ (B) $y = \ln x^5 + e^x - \ln e^2$

Other Logarithmic and Exponential Functions

In most applications involving logarithmic or exponential functions, the number e is the preferred base. However, in some situations it is convenient to use a base other than e. Derivatives of $y = \log_b x$ and $y = b^x$ can be obtained by expressing these functions in terms of the natural logarithmic and exponential functions.

We begin by finding a relationship between $\log_b x$ and $\ln x$ for any base b such that $b > 0$ and $b \neq 1$.

$$
\begin{aligned}
y &= \log_b x && \text{Change to exponential form.}\\
b^y &= x && \text{Take the natural logarithm of both sides.}\\
\ln b^y &= \ln x && \text{Recall that } \ln b^y = y \ln b.\\
y \ln b &= \ln x && \text{Solve for y.}\\
y &= \frac{1}{\ln b} \ln x
\end{aligned}
$$

Therefore,

$$\log_b x = \frac{1}{\ln b} \ln x \quad \text{Change-of-base formula for logarithms.} \qquad (2)$$

Equation (2) is a special case of the **general change-of-base formula** for logarithms (which can be derived in the same way):

$$\log_b x = (\log_a x)/(\log_a b).$$

Similarly, we can find a relationship between b^x and e^x for any base b such that $b > 0, b \neq 1$.

$$
\begin{aligned}
y &= b^x && \text{Take the natural logarithm of both sides.}\\
\ln y &= \ln b^x && \text{Recall that } \ln b^x = x \ln b.\\
\ln y &= x \ln b && \text{Take the exponential function of both sides.}\\
y &= e^{x \ln b}
\end{aligned}
$$

Therefore,

$$b^x = e^{x \ln b} \quad \text{Change-of-base formula for exponential functions.} \qquad (3)$$

Differentiating both sides of equation (2) gives

$$\frac{d}{dx} \log_b x = \frac{1}{\ln b} \frac{d}{dx} \ln x = \frac{1}{\ln b}\left(\frac{1}{x}\right) \quad (x > 0)$$

It can be shown that the derivative of the function e^{cx}, where c is a constant, is the function ce^{cx} (see Problems 65–66 in Exercise 7.2 or the more general results of Section 7.4). Therefore, differentiating both sides of equation (3), we have

$$\frac{d}{dx} b^x = e^{x \ln b} \ln b = b^x \ln b$$

For convenience, we list the derivative formulas for exponential and logarithmic functions:

Derivatives of Exponential and Logarithmic Functions

For $b > 0, b \neq 1$,

$$\frac{d}{dx} e^x = e^x \qquad \frac{d}{dx} b^x = b^x \ln b$$

For $b > 0, b \neq 1$, and $x > 0$,

$$\frac{d}{dx} \ln x = \frac{1}{x} \qquad \frac{d}{dx} \log_b x = \frac{1}{\ln b}\left(\frac{1}{x}\right)$$

EXAMPLE 3 **Finding Derivatives** Find $g'(x)$ for

(A) $g(x) = 2^x - 3^x$ (B) $g(x) = \log_4 x^5$

SOLUTION

(A) $g'(x) = 2^x \ln 2 - 3^x \ln 3$

(B) First, use a property of logarithms to rewrite $g(x)$.

$$g(x) = \log_4 x^5 \qquad \text{Use } \log_b M^p = p \log_b M.$$

$$g(x) = 5 \log_4 x \qquad \text{Take the derivative of both sides.}$$

$$g'(x) = \frac{5}{\ln 4}\left(\frac{1}{x}\right)$$

Matched Problem 3 Find $g'(x)$ for

(A) $g(x) = x^{10} + 10^x$ (B) $g(x) = \log_2 x - 6 \log_5 x$

Explore and Discuss 2

(A) The graphs of $f(x) = \log_2 x$ and $g(x) = \log_4 x$ are shown in Figure 2. Which graph belongs to which function?

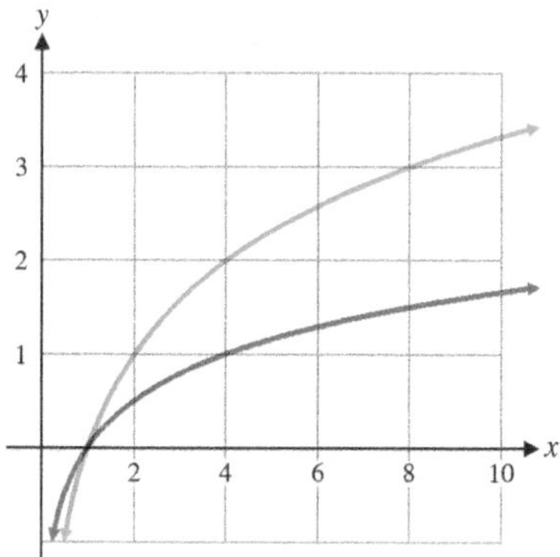

Figure 2

(B) Sketch graphs of $f'(x)$ and $g'(x)$.

(C) The function $f(x)$ is related to $g(x)$ in the same way that $f'(x)$ is related to $g'(x)$. What is that relationship?

Exponential and Logarithmic Models

EXAMPLE 4 **Price–Demand Model** An Internet store sells Australian wool blankets. If the store sells x blankets at a price of $\$p$ per blanket, then the price–demand equation is $p = 350(0.999)^x$. Find the rate of change of price with respect to demand when the demand is 800 blankets and interpret the result.

SOLUTION

$$\frac{dp}{dx} = 350(0.999)^x \ln 0.999$$

If $x = 800$, then

$$\frac{dp}{dx} = 350(0.999)^{800} \ln 0.999 \approx -0.157, \text{ or } -\$0.16$$

When the demand is 800 blankets, the price is decreasing by $0.16 per blanket.

Matched Problem 4 The store in Example 4 also sells a reversible fleece blanket. If the price–demand equation for reversible fleece blankets is $p = 200(0.998)^x$, find the rate of change of price with respect to demand when the demand is 400 blankets and interpret the result.

EXAMPLE 5 **Continuous Compound Interest** An investment of \$1,000 earns interest at an annual rate of 4% compounded continuously.

(A) Find the instantaneous rate of change of the amount in the account after 2 years.

(B) Find the instantaneous rate of change of the amount in the account at the time the amount is equal to \$2,000.

SOLUTION

(A) The amount $A(t)$ at time t (in years) is given by $A(t) = 1{,}000e^{0.04t}$. Note that $A(t) = 1{,}000b^t$, where $b = e^{0.04}$. The instantaneous rate of change is the derivative $A'(t)$, which we find by using the formula for the derivative of the exponential function with base b:

$$A'(t) = 1{,}000b^t \ln b = 1{,}000e^{0.04t}(0.04) = 40e^{0.04t}$$

After 2 years, $A'(2) = 40e^{0.04(2)} = \$43.33$ per year.

(B) From the calculation of the derivative in part (A), we note that $A'(t) = (0.04)1{,}000e^{0.04t} = 0.04A(t)$. In other words, the instantaneous rate of change of the amount is always equal to 4% of the amount. So if the amount is \$2,000, then the instantaneous rate of change is $(0.04)\$2{,}000 = \$80$ per year.

Matched Problem 5 An investment of \$5,000 earns interest at an annual rate of 6% compounded continuously.

(A) Find the instantaneous rate of change of the amount in the account after 3 years.

(B) Find the instantaneous rate of change of the amount in the account at the time the amount is equal to \$8,000.

EXAMPLE 6 **Franchise Locations** A model for the growth of a sandwich shop franchise is

$$N(t) = -765 + 482 \ln t$$

where $N(t)$ is the number of locations in year t ($t = 0$ corresponds to 1980). Use this model to estimate the number of locations in 2028 and the rate of change of the number of locations in 2028. Round both to the nearest integer. Interpret these results.

SOLUTION Because 2028 corresponds to $t = 48$, we must find $N(48)$ and $N'(48)$.

$$N(48) = -765 + 482 \ln 48 \approx 1{,}101$$

$$N'(t) = 482\frac{1}{t} = \frac{482}{t}$$

$$N'(48) = \frac{482}{48} \approx 10$$

In 2028 there will be approximately 1,101 locations, and this number will be growing at the rate of 10 locations per year.

Matched Problem 6 A model for a newspaper's circulation is

$$C(t) = 83 - 9 \ln t$$

where $C(t)$ is the circulation (in thousands) in year t ($t = 0$ corresponds to 1980). Use this model to estimate the circulation and the rate of change of circulation in 2026. Round both to the nearest hundred. Interpret these results.

CONCEPTUAL INSIGHT

On most graphing calculators, exponential regression produces a function of the form $y = a \cdot b^x$. Formula (3) on page 391 allows you to change the base b (chosen by the graphing calculator) to the more familiar base e:

$$y = a \cdot b^x = a \cdot e^{x \ln b}$$

On most graphing calculators, logarithmic regression produces a function of the form $y = a + b \ln x$. Formula (2) on page 391 allows you to write the function in terms of logarithms to any base d that you may prefer:

$$y = a + b \ln x = a + b(\ln d) \log_d x$$

Exercises 7.2

Skills Warm-up Exercises

W *In Problems 1–6, solve for the variable without using a calculator. (If necessary, review Section 2.6.)*

1. $y = \log_3 81$

2. $y = \log_4 64$

3. $\log_5 x = -1$

4. $\log_{10} x = -3$

5. $y = \ln \sqrt[3]{e}$

6. $\ln x = 4$

In Problems 7–12, use logarithmic properties to write in simpler form. (If necessary, review Section 2.6.)

7. $\ln \dfrac{x}{y}$

8. $\ln e^x$

9. $\ln x^5$

10. $\ln xy$

11. $\ln \dfrac{uv^2}{w}$

12. $\ln \dfrac{u^4}{v^3 w^2}$

A *In Problems 13–30, find $f'(x)$.*

13. $f(x) = 5e^x + 3x + 1$

14. $f(x) = -7e^x - 2x + 5$

15. $f(x) = -2 \ln x + x^2 - 4$

16. $f(x) = 6 \ln x - x^3 + 2$

17. $f(x) = x^3 - 6e^x$

18. $f(x) = 8e^x + 7x^6$

19. $f(x) = e^x + x - \ln x$

20. $f(x) = \ln x + 2e^x - 3x^2$

21. $f(x) = \ln x^3$

22. $f(x) = \ln x^8$

23. $f(x) = 5x - \ln x^5$

24. $f(x) = 4 + \ln x^9$

25. $f(x) = \ln x^2 + 4e^x$

26. $f(x) = \ln x^{12} - 3 \ln x$

27. $f(x) = e^x + x^e$

28. $f(x) = 3x^e - 2e^x$

29. $f(x) = xx^e$

30. $f(x) = ee^x$

B *In Problems 31–38, find the equation of the line tangent to the graph of f at the indicated value of x.*

31. $f(x) = 3 + \ln x; x = 1$

32. $f(x) = 2 \ln x; x = 1$

33. $f(x) = 3e^x; x = 0$

34. $f(x) = e^x + 1; x = 0$

35. $f(x) = \ln x^3; x = e$

36. $f(x) = 1 + \ln x^4; x = e$

37. $f(x) = 4 + 3e^x; x = 1$

38. $f(x) = 5e^x; x = 1$

39. A student claims that the line tangent to the graph of $f(x) = e^x$ at $x = 3$ passes through the point $(2, 0)$ (see the figure). Is she correct? Will the line tangent at $x = 4$ pass through $(3, 0)$? Explain.

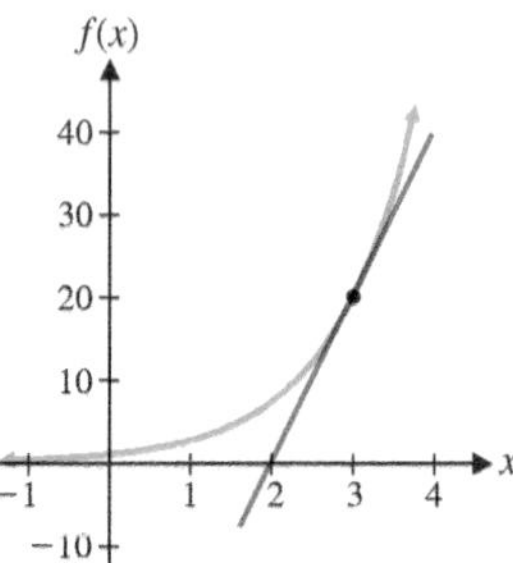

40. Refer to Problem 39. Does the line tangent to the graph of $f(x) = e^x$ at $x = 1$ pass through the origin? Are there any other lines tangent to the graph of f that pass through the origin? Explain.

41. A student claims that the line tangent to the graph of $g(x) = \ln x$ at $x = 3$ passes through the origin (see the figure). Is he correct? Will the line tangent at $x = 4$ pass through the origin? Explain.

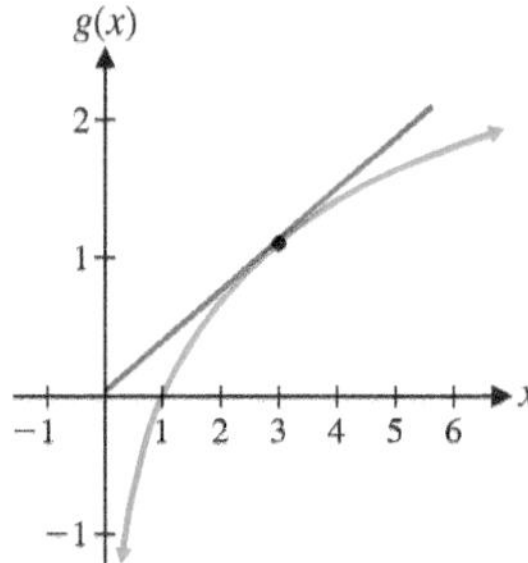

42. Refer to Problem 41. Does the line tangent to the graph of $f(x) = \ln x$ at $x = e$ pass through the origin? Are there any other lines tangent to the graph of f that pass through the origin? Explain.

In Problems 43–46, first use appropriate properties of logarithms to rewrite $f(x)$, and then find $f'(x)$.

43. $f(x) = 10x + \ln 10x$

44. $f(x) = 2 + 3\ln\frac{1}{x}$

45. $f(x) = \ln\frac{4}{x^3}$

46. $f(x) = 8x - 7\ln 6x$

C *In Problems 47–58, find $\frac{dy}{dx}$ for the indicated function y.*

47. $y = \log_2 x$

48. $y = 3\log_5 x$

49. $y = 3^x$

50. $y = 4^x$

51. $y = 2x - \log x$

52. $y = \log x + 4x^2 + 1$

53. $y = 10 + x + 10^x$

54. $y = 8^x - x^8$

55. $y = 3\ln x + 2\log_3 x$

56. $y = -\log_2 x + 10\ln x$

57. $y = 2^x + e^2$

58. $y = e^3 - 3^x$

In Problems 59–64, use graphical approximation methods to find the points of intersection of $f(x)$ and $g(x)$ (to two decimal places).

59. $f(x) = e^x$; $g(x) = x^4$

[Note that there are three points of intersection and that e^x is greater than x^4 for large values of x.]

60. $f(x) = e^x$; $g(x) = x^5$

[Note that there are two points of intersection and that e^x is greater than x^5 for large values of x.]

61. $f(x) = (\ln x)^2$; $g(x) = x$

62. $f(x) = (\ln x)^4$; $g(x) = 4x$

63. $f(x) = \ln x$; $g(x) = x^{1/5}$

64. $f(x) = \ln x$; $g(x) = x^{1/3}$

65. Explain why $\lim_{h\to 0}\frac{e^{ch} - 1}{h} = c$.

66. Use the result of Problem 65 and the four-step process to show that if $f(x) = e^{cx}$, then $f'(x) = ce^{cx}$.

Applications

67. Salvage value. The estimated salvage value S (in dollars) of a company airplane after t years is given by

$$S(t) = 300{,}000(0.9)^t$$

What is the rate of depreciation (in dollars per year) after 1 year? 5 years? 10 years?

68. Resale value. The estimated resale value R (in dollars) of a company car after t years is given by

$$R(t) = 20{,}000(0.86)^t$$

What is the rate of depreciation (in dollars per year) after 1 year? 2 years? 3 years?

69. Bacterial growth. A single cholera bacterium divides every 0.5 hour to produce two complete cholera bacteria. If we start with a colony of 5,000 bacteria, then after t hours, there will be

$$A(t) = 5{,}000 \cdot 2^{2t} = 5{,}000 \cdot 4^t$$

bacteria. Find $A'(t)$, $A'(1)$, and $A'(5)$, and interpret the results.

70. Bacterial growth. Repeat Problem 69 for a starting colony of 2,000 bacteria such that a single bacterium divides every 20 minutes.

71. Blood pressure. An experiment was set up to find a relationship between weight and systolic blood pressure in children. Using hospital records for 5,000 children, the experimenters found that the systolic blood pressure was given approximately by

$$P(x) = 17.5(1 + \ln x) \qquad 10 \le x \le 100$$

where $P(x)$ is measured in millimeters of mercury and x is measured in pounds. What is the rate of change of blood pressure with respect to weight at the 40-pound weight level? At the 90-pound weight level?

72. Blood pressure. Refer to Problem 71. Find the weight (to the nearest pound) at which the rate of change of blood pressure with respect to weight is 0.3 millimeter of mercury per pound.

73. Psychology: stimulus/response. In psychology, the Weber–Fechner law for the response to a stimulus is

$$R = k\ln\frac{S}{S_0}$$

where R is the response, S is the stimulus, and S_0 is the lowest level of stimulus that can be detected. Find dR/dS.

74. Psychology: learning. A mathematical model for the average of a group of people learning to type is given by

$$N(t) = 10 + 6\ln t \qquad t \ge 1$$

where $N(t)$ is the number of words per minute typed after t hours of instruction and practice (2 hours per day, 5 days per week). What is the rate of learning after 10 hours of instruction and practice? After 100 hours?

75. Continuous compound interest. An investment of \$10,000 earns interest at an annual rate of 7.5% compounded continuously.

(A) Find the instantaneous rate of change of the amount in the account after 1 year.

(B) Find the instantaneous rate of change of the amount in the account at the time the amount is equal to \$12,500.

76. Continuous compound interest. An investment of \$25,000 earns interest at an annual rate of 8.4% compounded continuously.

(A) Find the instantaneous rate of change of the amount in the account after 2 years.

(B) Find the instantaneous rate of change of the amount in the account at the time the amount is equal to \$30,000.

Answers to Matched Problems

1. (A) $4e^x + 16x + 7$ (B) $7x^6 - 5x^4 - 1 + e^x$

2. (A) $30x^2 - \frac{100}{x}$ (B) $\frac{5}{x} + e^x$

3. (A) $10x^9 + 10^x \ln 10$ (B) $\left(\frac{1}{\ln 2} - \frac{6}{\ln 5}\right)\frac{1}{x}$

4. The price is decreasing at the rate of \$0.18 per blanket.

5. (A) \$359.17 per year (B) \$480 per year

6. The circulation in 2026 is approximately 48,500 and is decreasing at the rate of 200 per year.

7.3 Derivatives of Products and Quotients

- Derivatives of Products
- Derivatives of Quotients

The derivative properties discussed in Section 6.5 add substantially to our ability to compute and apply derivatives to many practical problems. In this and the next two sections, we add a few more properties that will increase this ability even further.

Derivatives of Products

In Section 6.5, we found that the derivative of a sum is the sum of the derivatives. Is the derivative of a product the product of the derivatives?

Explore and Discuss 1

Let $F(x) = x^2$, $S(x) = x^3$, and $f(x) = F(x)S(x) = x^5$. Which of the following is $f'(x)$?

(A) $F'(x)S'(x)$

(B) $F(x)S'(x)$

(C) $F'(x)S(x)$

(D) $F(x)S'(x) + F'(x)S(x)$

Comparing the various expressions computed in Explore and Discuss 1, we see that the derivative of a product is not the product of the derivatives.

Using the definition of the derivative and the four-step process, we can show that

The derivative of the product of two functions is the first times the derivative of the second, plus the second times the derivative of the first.

This **product rule** is expressed more compactly in Theorem 1, with notation chosen to aid memorization (F for "first", S for "second").

THEOREM 1 Product Rule

If

$$y = f(x) = F(x)S(x)$$

and if $F'(x)$ and $S'(x)$ exist, then

$$f'(x) = F(x)S'(x) + S(x)F'(x)$$

Using simplified notation,

$$y' = FS' + SF' \quad \text{or} \quad \frac{dy}{dx} = F\frac{dS}{dx} + S\frac{dF}{dx}$$

EXAMPLE 1 **Differentiating a Product** Use two different methods to find $f'(x)$ for

$$f(x) = 2x^2(3x^4 - 2).$$

SOLUTION

Method 1. Use the product rule with $F(x) = 2x^2$ and $S(x) = 3x^4 - 2$:

$$f'(x) = 2x^2(3x^4 - 2)' + (3x^4 - 2)(2x^2)'$$ First times derivative of second, plus second times derivative of first

$$= 2x^2(12x^3) + (3x^4 - 2)(4x)$$

$$= 24x^5 + 12x^5 - 8x$$

$$= 36x^5 - 8x$$

Method 2. Multiply first; then find the derivative:

$$f(x) = 2x^2(3x^4 - 2) = 6x^6 - 4x^2$$
$$f'(x) = 36x^5 - 8x$$

Matched Problem 1 Use two different methods to find $f'(x)$ for $f(x) = 3x^3(2x^2 - 3x + 1)$.

Some products we encounter can be differentiated by either method illustrated in Example 1. In other situations, the product rule *must* be used. Unless instructed otherwise, you should use the product rule to differentiate all products in this section in order to gain experience with this important differentiation rule.

EXAMPLE 2 **Tangent Lines** Let $f(x) = (2x - 9)(x^2 + 6)$.

(A) Find the equation of the line tangent to the graph of $f(x)$ at $x = 3$.

(B) Find the value(s) of x where the tangent line is horizontal.

SOLUTION

(A) First, find $f'(x)$:

$$f'(x) = (2x - 9)(x^2 + 6)' + (x^2 + 6)(2x - 9)'$$
$$= (2x - 9)(2x) + (x^2 + 6)(2)$$

Then, find $f(3)$ and $f'(3)$:

$$f(3) = [2(3) - 9](3^2 + 6) = (-3)(15) = -45$$
$$f'(3) = [2(3) - 9]2(3) + (3^2 + 6)(2) = -18 + 30 = 12$$

Now, find the equation of the tangent line at $x = 3$:

$$y - y_1 = m(x - x_1) \qquad y_1 = f(x_1) = f(3) = -45$$
$$y - (-45) = 12(x - 3) \qquad m = f'(x_1) = f'(3) = 12$$
$$y = 12x - 81 \qquad \text{Tangent line at } x = 3$$

(B) The tangent line is horizontal at any value of x such that $f'(x) = 0$, so

$$f'(x) = (2x - 9)2x + (x^2 + 6)2 = 0$$
$$6x^2 - 18x + 12 = 0$$
$$x^2 - 3x + 2 = 0$$
$$(x - 1)(x - 2) = 0$$
$$x = 1, 2$$

The tangent line is horizontal at $x = 1$ and at $x = 2$.

Matched Problem 2 Repeat Example 2 for $f(x) = (2x + 9)(x^2 - 12)$.

CONCEPTUAL INSIGHT

As Example 2 illustrates, the way we write $f'(x)$ depends on what we want to do. If we are interested only in evaluating $f'(x)$ at specified values of x, then the form in part (A) is sufficient. However, if we want to solve $f'(x) = 0$, we must multiply and collect like terms, as we did in part (B).

EXAMPLE 3 **Finding Derivatives** Find $f'(x)$ for

(A) $f(x) = 2x^3e^x$ (B) $f(x) = 6x^4 \ln x$

SOLUTION

(A) $f'(x) = 2x^3(e^x)' + e^x(2x^3)'$
$= 2x^3e^x + e^x(6x^2)$
$= 2x^2e^x(x + 3)$

(B) $f'(x) = 6x^4 (\ln x)' + (\ln x)(6x^4)'$
$= 6x^4 \dfrac{1}{x} + (\ln x)(24x^3)$
$= 6x^3 + 24x^3 \ln x$
$= 6x^3(1 + 4 \ln x)$

Matched Problem 3 Find $f'(x)$ for

(A) $f(x) = 5x^8 e^x$ (B) $f(x) = x^7 \ln x$

Derivatives of Quotients

The derivative of a quotient of two functions is not the quotient of the derivatives of the two functions.

Explore and Discuss 2

Let $T(x) = x^5$, $B(x) = x^2$, and

$$f(x) = \frac{T(x)}{B(x)} = \frac{x^5}{x^2} = x^3$$

Which of the following is $f'(x)$?

(A) $\dfrac{T'(x)}{B'(x)}$ (B) $\dfrac{T'(x)B(x)}{[B(x)]^2}$ (C) $\dfrac{T(x)B'(x)}{[B(x)]^2}$

(D) $\dfrac{T'(x)B(x)}{[B(x)]^2} - \dfrac{T(x)B'(x)}{[B(x)]^2} = \dfrac{B(x)T'(x) - T(x)B'(x)}{[B(x)]^2}$

The expressions in Explore and Discuss 2 suggest that the derivative of a quotient leads to a more complicated quotient than expected.

If $T(x)$ and $B(x)$ are any two differentiable functions and

$$f(x) = \frac{T(x)}{B(x)}$$

then

$$f'(x) = \frac{B(x)T'(x) - T(x)B'(x)}{[B(x)]^2}$$

Therefore,

The derivative of the quotient of two functions is the denominator times the derivative of the numerator, minus the numerator times the derivative of the denominator, divided by the denominator squared.

This **quotient rule** is expressed more compactly in Theorem 2, with notation chosen to aid memorization (T for "top", B for "bottom").

THEOREM 2 Quotient Rule

If

$$y = f(x) = \frac{T(x)}{B(x)}$$

and if $T'(x)$ and $B'(x)$ exist, then

$$f'(x) = \frac{B(x)T'(x) - T(x)B'(x)}{[B(x)]^2}$$

Using simplified notation,

$$y' = \frac{BT' - TB'}{B^2} \quad \text{or} \quad \frac{dy}{dx} = \frac{B\frac{dT}{dx} - T\frac{dB}{dx}}{B^2}$$

EXAMPLE 4 **Differentiating Quotients**

(A) If $f(x) = \dfrac{x^2}{2x - 1}$, find $f'(x)$. (B) If $y = \dfrac{t^2 - t}{t^3 + 1}$, find y'.

(C) Find $\dfrac{d}{dx}\dfrac{x^2 - 3}{x^2}$ by using the quotient rule and also by splitting the fraction into two fractions.

SOLUTION

(A) Use the quotient rule with $T(x) = x^2$ and $B(x) = 2x - 1$;

$$\begin{aligned} f'(x) &= \frac{(2x - 1)(x^2)' - x^2(2x - 1)'}{(2x - 1)^2} \\ &= \frac{(2x - 1)(2x) - x^2(2)}{(2x - 1)^2} \\ &= \frac{4x^2 - 2x - 2x^2}{(2x - 1)^2} \\ &= \frac{2x^2 - 2x}{(2x - 1)^2} \end{aligned}$$

The denominator times the derivative of the numerator, minus the numerator times the derivative of the denominator, divided by the square of the denominator

(B)
$$\begin{aligned} y' &= \frac{(t^3 + 1)(t^2 - t)' - (t^2 - t)(t^3 + 1)'}{(t^3 + 1)^2} \\ &= \frac{(t^3 + 1)(2t - 1) - (t^2 - t)(3t^2)}{(t^3 + 1)^2} \\ &= \frac{2t^4 - t^3 + 2t - 1 - 3t^4 + 3t^3}{(t^3 + 1)^2} \\ &= \frac{-t^4 + 2t^3 + 2t - 1}{(t^3 + 1)^2} \end{aligned}$$

(C) Method 1. Use the quotient rule:

$$\frac{d}{dx}\frac{x^2-3}{x^2} = \frac{x^2\frac{d}{dx}(x^2-3) - (x^2-3)\frac{d}{dx}x^2}{(x^2)^2}$$

$$= \frac{x^2(2x) - (x^2-3)2x}{x^4}$$

$$= \frac{2x^3 - 2x^3 + 6x}{x^4} = \frac{6x}{x^4} = \frac{6}{x^3}$$

Method 2. Split into two fractions:

$$\frac{x^2-3}{x^2} = \frac{x^2}{x^2} - \frac{3}{x^2} = 1 - 3x^{-2}$$

$$\frac{d}{dx}(1 - 3x^{-2}) = 0 - 3(-2)x^{-3} = \frac{6}{x^3}$$

Comparing methods 1 and 2, we see that it often pays to change an expression algebraically before choosing a differentiation formula.

Matched Problem 4 Find

(A) $f'(x)$ for $f(x) = \frac{2x}{x^2+3}$ (B) y' for $y = \frac{t^3-3t}{t^2-4}$

(C) $\frac{d}{dx}\frac{2+x^3}{x^3}$ in two ways

EXAMPLE 5 **Finding Derivatives** Find $f'(x)$ for

(A) $f(x) = \frac{3e^x}{1+e^x}$ (B) $f(x) = \frac{\ln x}{2x+5}$

SOLUTION

(A) $$f'(x) = \frac{(1+e^x)(3e^x)' - 3e^x(1+e^x)'}{(1+e^x)^2}$$

$$= \frac{(1+e^x)3e^x - 3e^xe^x}{(1+e^x)^2}$$

$$= \frac{3e^x}{(1+e^x)^2}$$

(B) $$f'(x) = \frac{(2x+5)(\ln x)' - (\ln x)(2x+5)'}{(2x+5)^2}$$

$$= \frac{(2x+5)\cdot\frac{1}{x} - (\ln x)(2)}{(2x+5)^2}$$ Multiply by $\frac{x}{x}$

$$= \frac{2x+5-2x\ln x}{x(2x+5)^2}$$

Matched Problem 5 Find $f'(x)$ for

(A) $f(x) = \dfrac{x^3}{e^x + 2}$ (B) $f(x) = \dfrac{4x}{1 + \ln x}$

EXAMPLE 6 **Sales Analysis** The total sales S (in thousands of games) of a video game t months after the game is introduced are given by

$$S(t) = \frac{125t^2}{t^2 + 100}$$

(A) Find $S'(t)$.

(B) Find $S(10)$ and $S'(10)$. Write a brief interpretation of these results.

(C) Use the results from part (B) to estimate the total sales after 11 months.

SOLUTION

(A)
$$S'(t) = \frac{(t^2 + 100)(125t^2)' - 125t^2(t^2 + 100)'}{(t^2 + 100)^2}$$
$$= \frac{(t^2 + 100)(250t) - 125t^2(2t)}{(t^2 + 100)^2}$$
$$= \frac{250t^3 + 25{,}000t - 250t^3}{(t^2 + 100)^2}$$
$$= \frac{25{,}000t}{(t^2 + 100)^2}$$

(B) $S(10) = \dfrac{125(10)^2}{10^2 + 100} = 62.5$ and $S'(10) = \dfrac{25{,}000(10)}{(10^2 + 100)^2} = 6.25.$

Total sales after 10 months are 62,500 games, and sales are increasing at the rate of 6,250 games per month.

(C) Total sales will increase by approximately 6,250 games during the next month, so the estimated total sales after 11 months are $62{,}500 + 6{,}250 = 68{,}750$ games.

Matched Problem 6 Refer to Example 6. Suppose that the total sales S (in thousands of games) t months after the game is introduced are given by

$$S(t) = \frac{150t}{t + 3}$$

(A) Find $S'(t)$.

(B) Find $S(12)$ and $S'(12)$. Write a brief interpretation of these results.

(C) Use the results from part (B) to estimate the total sales after 13 months.

Exercises 7.3

Skills Warm-up Exercises

W *In Problems 1–4, find (A) the derivative of $F(x)S(x)$ without using the product rule, and (B) $F'(x)S'(x)$. Note that the answer to part (B) is different from the answer to part (A).*

1. $F(x) = x^4, S(x) = x$ **2.** $F(x) = x^3, S(x) = x^3$

3. $F(x) = x^5, S(x) = x^{10}$ **4.** $F(x) = x + 1, S(x) = x^8$

In Problems 5–8, find (A) the derivative of $T(x)/B(x)$ without using the quotient rule, and (B) $T'(x)/B'(x)$. Note that the answer to part (B) is different from the answer to part (A).

5. $T(x) = x^6, B(x) = x^3$ **6.** $T(x) = x^8, B(x) = x^2$

7. $T(x) = x^2, B(x) = x^7$ **8.** $T(x) = 1, B(x) = x^9$

Answers to most of the following problems in this exercise set contain both an unsimplified form and a simplified form of the derivative. When checking your work, first check that you applied the rules correctly and then check that you performed the algebraic simplification correctly. Unless instructed otherwise, when differentiating a product, use the product rule rather than performing the multiplication first.

A *In Problems 9–34, find $f'(x)$ and simplify.*

9. $f(x) = 2x^3(x^2 - 2)$ **10.** $f(x) = 5x^2(x^3 + 2)$

11. $f(x) = (x - 3)(2x - 1)$

12. $f(x) = (4x - 5)(6x + 7)$

13. $f(x) = \dfrac{x}{x - 3}$ **14.** $f(x) = \dfrac{3x}{2x + 1}$

15. $f(x) = \dfrac{2x + 3}{x - 2}$ **16.** $f(x) = \dfrac{3x - 4}{2x + 3}$

17. $f(x) = 3xe^x$ **18.** $f(x) = x^2e^x$

19. $f(x) = x^3 \ln x$ **20.** $f(x) = 5x \ln x$

21. $f(x) = (x^2 + 1)(2x - 3)$

22. $f(x) = (3x + 5)(x^2 - 3)$

23. $f(x) = (0.4x + 2)(0.5x - 5)$

24. $f(x) = (0.5x - 4)(0.2x + 1)$

25. $f(x) = \dfrac{x^2 + 1}{2x - 3}$ **26.** $f(x) = \dfrac{3x + 5}{x^2 - 3}$

27. $f(x) = (x^2 + 3)(x^2 - 5)$

28. $f(x) = (x^2 - 4)(x^2 + 5)$

29. $f(x) = \dfrac{x^2 + 3}{x^2 - 5}$ **30.** $f(x) = \dfrac{x^2 - 4}{x^2 + 5}$

31. $f(x) = \dfrac{e^x}{x^2 + 1}$ **32.** $f(x) = \dfrac{1 - e^x}{1 + e^x}$

33. $f(x) = \dfrac{\ln x}{1 + x}$ **34.** $f(x) = \dfrac{2x}{1 + \ln x}$

In Problems 35–46, find $h'(x)$, where $f(x)$ is an unspecified differentiable function.

35. $h(x) = xf(x)$ **36.** $h(x) = x^2f(x)$

37. $h(x) = x^4f(x)$ **38.** $h(x) = \dfrac{f(x)}{x}$

39. $h(x) = \dfrac{f(x)}{x^2}$ **40.** $h(x) = \dfrac{f(x)}{x^4}$

41. $h(x) = \dfrac{x}{f(x)}$ **42.** $h(x) = \dfrac{x^2}{f(x)}$

43. $h(x) = e^xf(x)$ **44.** $h(x) = \dfrac{e^x}{f(x)}$

45. $h(x) = \dfrac{\ln x}{f(x)}$ **46.** $h(x) = \dfrac{f(x)}{\ln x}$

B *In Problems 47–56, find the indicated derivatives and simplify.*

47. $f'(x)$ for $f(x) = (2x + 1)(x^2 - 3x)$

48. y' for $y = (x^3 + 2x^2)(3x - 1)$

49. $\dfrac{dy}{dt}$ for $y = (1.5t - t^2)(6t - 5.4)$

50. $\dfrac{d}{dt}[(3 - 0.4t^3)(0.5t^2 - 2t)]$

51. y' for $y = \dfrac{5x - 3}{x^2 + 2x}$

52. $f'(x)$ for $f(x) = \dfrac{3x^2}{2x - 1}$

53. $\dfrac{d}{dw}\dfrac{w^2 - 3w + 1}{w^2 - 1}$

54. $\dfrac{dy}{dw}$ for $y = \dfrac{w^4 - w^3}{3w - 1}$

55. y' for $y = (3 - 2x + x^2)e^x$

56. $\dfrac{dy}{dt}$ for $y = (1 + e^t) \ln t$

In Problems 57–60:

(A) Find $f'(x)$ using the quotient rule, and

(B) Explain how $f'(x)$ can be found easily without using the quotient rule.

57. $f(x) = \dfrac{1}{x}$ **58.** $f(x) = \dfrac{-1}{x^2}$

59. $f(x) = \dfrac{-3}{x^4}$ **60.** $f(x) = \dfrac{2}{x^3}$

In Problems 61–66, find $f'(x)$ and find the equation of the line tangent to the graph of f at $x = 2$.

61. $f(x) = (1 + 3x)(5 - 2x)$

62. $f(x) = (7 - 3x)(1 + 2x)$

63. $f(x) = \dfrac{x - 8}{3x - 4}$ **64.** $f(x) = \dfrac{2x - 5}{2x - 3}$

65. $f(x) = \dfrac{x}{2^x}$ **66.** $f(x) = (x - 2) \ln x$

In Problems 67–70, find $f'(x)$ and find the value(s) of x where $f'(x) = 0$.

67. $f(x) = (2x - 15)(x^2 + 18)$

68. $f(x) = (2x + 9)(x^2 - 54)$

69. $f(x) = \dfrac{x}{x^2 + 1}$ **70.** $f(x) = \dfrac{x}{x^2 + 9}$

In Problems 71–74, find $f'(x)$ in two ways: (1) using the product or quotient rule and (2) simplifying first.

71. $f(x) = x^3(x^4 - 1)$ **72.** $f(x) = x^4(x^3 - 1)$

73. $f(x) = \dfrac{x^3 + 9}{x^3}$ **74.** $f(x) = \dfrac{x^4 + 4}{x^4}$

C *In Problems 75–92, find each indicated derivative and simplify.*

75. $f'(w)$ for $f(w) = (w - 4)3^w$

76. $g'(w)$ for $g(w) = (w - 5)\log_3 w$

77. $\dfrac{dy}{dx}$ for $y = 9x^{1/3}(x^3 + 5)$

78. $\dfrac{d}{dx}[(4x^{1/2} - 1)(3x^{1/3} + 2)]$

79. y' for $y = \dfrac{\log_2 x}{1 + x^2}$ **80.** $\dfrac{dy}{dx}$ for $y = \dfrac{10^x}{1 + x^4}$

81. $f'(x)$ for $f(x) = \dfrac{6\sqrt[3]{x}}{x^2 - 3}$

82. y' for $y = \dfrac{2\sqrt{x}}{x^2 - 3x + 1}$

83. $g'(t)$ if $g(t) = \dfrac{0.2t}{3t^2 - 1}$

84. $h'(t)$ if $h(t) = \dfrac{-0.05t^2}{2t + 1}$

85. $\dfrac{d}{dx}[4x \log x^5]$ **86.** $\dfrac{d}{dt}[10^t \log t]$

87. $\dfrac{dy}{dx}$ for $y = (x + 3)(x^2 - 3x + 5)$

88. $f'(x)$ for $f(x) = (x^4 + x^2 + 1)(x^2 - 1)$

89. y' for $y = (x^2 + x + 1)(x^2 - x + 1)$

90. $g'(t)$ for $g(t) = (t + 1)(t^4 - t^3 + t^2 - t + 1)$

91. $\dfrac{dy}{dt}$ for $y = \dfrac{t \ln t}{e^t}$ **92.** $\dfrac{dy}{du}$ for $y = \dfrac{u^2 e^u}{1 + \ln u}$

Applications

93. Sales analysis. The total sales S (in thousands) of a video game are given by

$$S(t) = \frac{90t^2}{t^2 + 50}$$

where t is the number of months since the release of the game.

(A) Find $S'(t)$.

(B) Find $S(10)$ and $S'(10)$. Write a brief interpretation of these results.

(C) Use the results from part (B) to estimate the total sales after 11 months.

94. Sales analysis. A communications company has installed a new cable television system in a city. The total number N (in thousands) of subscribers t months after the installation of the system is given by

$$N(t) = \frac{180t}{t + 4}$$

(A) Find $N'(t)$.

(B) Find $N(16)$ and $N'(16)$. Write a brief interpretation of these results.

(C) Use the results from part (B) to estimate the total number of subscribers after 17 months.

95. Price–demand equation. According to economic theory, the demand x for a quantity in a free market decreases as the price p increases (see the figure). Suppose that the number x of DVD players people are willing to buy per week from a retail chain at a price of \$$p$ is given by

$$x = \frac{4{,}000}{0.1p + 1} \qquad 10 \le p \le 70$$

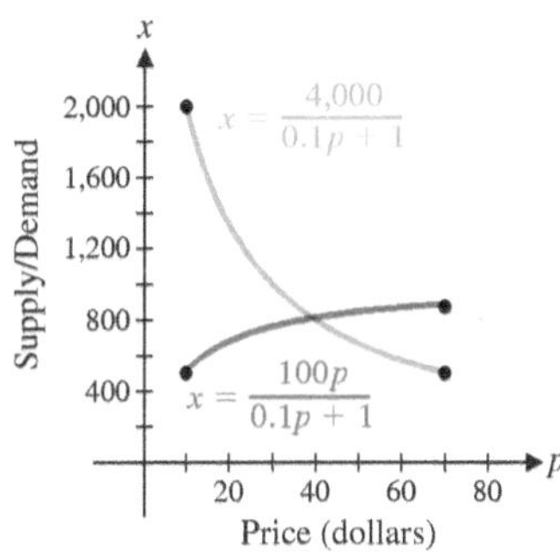

Figure for 95 and 96

(A) Find dx/dp.

(B) Find the demand and the instantaneous rate of change of demand with respect to price when the price is \$40. Write a brief interpretation of these results.

(C) Use the results from part (B) to estimate the demand if the price is increased to \$41.

96. Price–supply equation. According to economic theory, the supply x of a quantity in a free market increases as the price p increases (see the figure). Suppose that the number x of DVD players a retail chain is willing to sell per week at a price of \$$p$ is given by

$$x = \frac{100p}{0.1p + 1} \qquad 10 \le p \le 70$$

(A) Find dx/dp.

(B) Find the supply and the instantaneous rate of change of supply with respect to price when the price is $40. Write a brief verbal interpretation of these results.

(C) Use the results from part (B) to estimate the supply if the price is increased to $41.

97. Medicine. A drug is injected into a patient's bloodstream through her right arm. The drug concentration (in milligrams per cubic centimeter) in the bloodstream of the left arm t hours after the injection is given by

$$C(t) = \frac{0.14t}{t^2 + 1}$$

(A) Find $C'(t)$.

(B) Find $C'(0.5)$ and $C'(3)$, and interpret the results.

98. Drug sensitivity. One hour after a dose of x milligrams of a particular drug is administered to a person, the change in body temperature $T(x)$, in degrees Fahrenheit, is given approximately by

$$T(x) = x^2\left(1 - \frac{x}{9}\right) \qquad 0 \le x \le 7$$

The rate $T'(x)$ at which T changes with respect to the size of the dosage x is called the *sensitivity* of the body to the dosage.

(A) Use the product rule to find $T'(x)$.

(B) Find $T'(1)$, $T'(3)$, and $T'(6)$.

Answers to Matched Problems

1. $30x^4 - 36x^3 + 9x^2$
2. (A) $y = 84x - 297$
   (B) $x = -4, x = 1$
3. (A) $5x^8e^x + e^x(40x^7) = 5x^7(x + 8)e^x$
   (B) $x^7 \cdot \frac{1}{x} + \ln x\,(7x^6) = x^6\,(1 + 7\ln x)$
4. (A) $\dfrac{(x^2 + 3)2 - (2x)(2x)}{(x^2 + 3)^2} = \dfrac{6 - 2x^2}{(x^2 + 3)^2}$
   (B) $\dfrac{(t^2 - 4)(3t^2 - 3) - (t^3 - 3t)(2t)}{(t^2 - 4)^2} = \dfrac{t^4 - 9t^2 + 12}{(t^2 - 4)^2}$
   (C) $-\dfrac{6}{x^4}$
5. (A) $\dfrac{(e^x + 2)\,3x^2 - x^3e^x}{(e^x + 2)^2}$
   (B) $\dfrac{(1 + \ln x)\,4 - 4x\frac{1}{x}}{(1 + \ln x)^2} = \dfrac{4\ln x}{(1 + \ln x)^2}$
6. (A) $S'(t) = \dfrac{450}{(t + 3)^2}$
   (B) $S(12) = 120$; $S'(12) = 2$. After 12 months, the total sales are 120,000 games, and sales are increasing at the rate of 2,000 games per month.
   (C) 122,000 games

7.4 The Chain Rule

- Composite Functions
- General Power Rule
- The Chain Rule

The word *chain* in the name "chain rule" comes from the fact that a function formed by composition involves a chain of functions—that is, a function of a function. The *chain rule* enables us to compute the derivative of a composite function in terms of the derivatives of the functions making up the composite. In this section, we review composite functions, introduce the chain rule by means of a special case known as the *general power rule,* and then discuss the chain rule itself.

Composite Functions

The function $m(x) = (x^2 + 4)^3$ is a combination of a quadratic function and a cubic function. To see this more clearly, let

$$y = f(u) = u^3 \qquad \text{and} \qquad u = g(x) = x^2 + 4$$

We can express y as a function of x:

$$y = f(u) = f[g(x)] = [x^2 + 4]^3 = m(x)$$

The function m is the *composite* of the two functions f and g.

DEFINITION Composite Functions

A function m is a **composite** of functions f and g if

$$m(x) = f[g(x)]$$

The domain of m is the set of all numbers x such that x is in the domain of g, and $g(x)$ is in the domain of f.

The composite m of functions f and g is pictured in Figure 1. The domain of m is the shaded subset of the domain of g (Fig. 1); it consists of all numbers x such that x is in the domain of g and $g(x)$ is in the domain of f. Note that the functions f and g play different roles. The function g, which is on the *inside* or *interior* of the square brackets in $f[g(x)]$, is applied first to x. Then function f, which appears on the *outside* or *exterior* of the square brackets, is applied to $g(x)$, provided $g(x)$ is in the domain of f. Because f and g play different roles, the composite of f and g is usually a different function than the composite of g and f, as illustrated by Example 1.

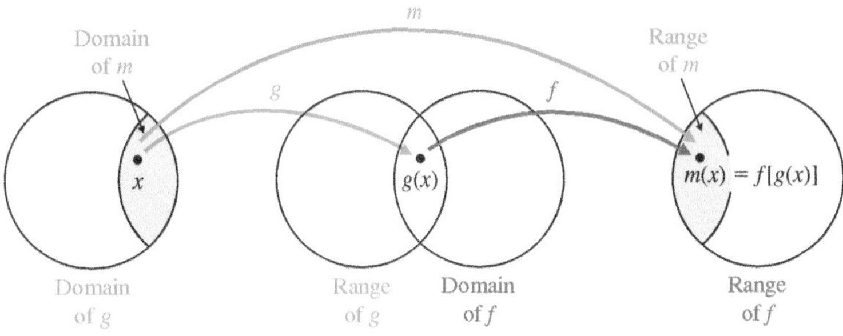

Figure 1 **The composite m of f and g**

EXAMPLE 1 **Composite Functions** Let $f(u) = e^u$ and $g(x) = -3x$. Find $f[g(x)]$ and $g[f(u)]$.

SOLUTION

$$f[g(x)] = f(-3x) = e^{-3x}$$

$$g[f(u)] = g(e^u) = -3e^u$$

Matched Problem 1 Let $f(u) = 2u$ and $g(x) = e^x$. Find $f[g(x)]$ and $g[f(u)]$.

EXAMPLE 2 **Composite Functions** Write each function as a composite of two simpler functions.

(A) $y = 100e^{0.04x}$ (B) $y = \sqrt{4 - x^2}$

SOLUTION

(A) Let

$$y = f(u) = 100e^u$$

$$u = g(x) = 0.04x$$

Check: $y = f[g(x)] = f(0.04x) = 100e^{0.04x}$

(B) Let

$$y = f(u) = \sqrt{u}$$
$$u = g(x) = 4 - x^2$$

Check: $y = f[g(x)] = f(4 - x^2) = \sqrt{4 - x^2}$

Matched Problem 2 Write each function as a composite of two simpler functions.

(A) $y = 50e^{-2x}$ (B) $y = \sqrt[3]{1 + x^3}$

CONCEPTUAL INSIGHT

There can be more than one way to express a function as a composite of simpler functions. Choosing $y = f(u) = 100u$ and $u = g(x) = e^{0.04x}$ in Example 2A produces the same result:

$$y = f[g(x)] = 100g(x) = 100e^{0.04x}$$

Since we will be using composition as a means to an end (finding a derivative), usually it will not matter which functions you choose for the composition.

General Power Rule

We have already made extensive use of the power rule,

$$\frac{d}{dx}x^n = nx^{n-1} \tag{1}$$

Can we apply rule (1) to find the derivative of the composite function $m(x) = p[u(x)] = [u(x)]^n$, where p is the power function $p(u) = u^n$ and $u(x)$ is a differentiable function? In other words, is rule (1) valid if x is replaced by $u(x)$?

Explore and Discuss 1

Let $u(x) = 2x^2$ and $m(x) = [u(x)]^3 = 8x^6$. Which of the following is $m'(x)$?

(A) $3[u(x)]^2$ (B) $3[u'(x)]^2$ (C) $3[u(x)]^2u'(x)$

The calculations in Explore and Discuss 1 show that we cannot find the derivative of $[u(x)]^n$ simply by replacing x with $u(x)$ in equation (1).

How can we find a formula for the derivative of $[u(x)]^n$, where $u(x)$ is an arbitrary differentiable function? Let's begin by considering the derivatives of $[u(x)]^2$ and $[u(x)]^3$ to see if a general pattern emerges. Since $[u(x)]^2 = u(x)u(x)$, we use the product rule to write

$$\begin{aligned}\frac{d}{dx}[u(x)]^2 &= \frac{d}{dx}[u(x)u(x)] \\ &= u(x)u'(x) + u(x)u'(x) \\ &= 2u(x)u'(x) \end{aligned} \tag{2}$$

Because $[u(x)]^3 = [u(x)]^2u(x)$, we use the product rule and the result in equation (2) to write

$$\begin{aligned}\frac{d}{dx}[u(x)]^3 &= \frac{d}{dx}\{[u(x)]^2u(x)\} \\ &= [u(x)]^2\frac{d}{dx}u(x) + u(x)\frac{d}{dx}[u(x)]^2 \\ &= [u(x)]^2u'(x) + u(x)[2u(x)u'(x)] \\ &= 3[u(x)]^2u'(x)\end{aligned}$$

Use equation (2) to substitute for $\frac{d}{dx}[u(x)]^2$.

Continuing in this fashion, we can show that

$$\frac{d}{dx}[u(x)]^n = n[u(x)]^{n-1}u'(x) \qquad n \text{ a positive integer} \qquad (3)$$

Using more advanced techniques, we can establish formula (3) for all real numbers n, obtaining the **general power rule**.

THEOREM 1 General Power Rule

If $u(x)$ is a differentiable function, n is any real number, and

$$y = f(x) = [u(x)]^n$$

then

$$f'(x) = n[u(x)]^{n-1}u'(x)$$

Using simplified notation,

$$y' = nu^{n-1}u' \qquad \text{or} \qquad \frac{d}{dx}u^n = nu^{n-1}\frac{du}{dx} \qquad \text{where } u = u(x)$$

EXAMPLE 3 **Using the General Power Rule** Find the indicated derivatives:

(A) $f'(x)$ if $f(x) = (3x + 1)^4$

(B) y' if $y = (x^3 + 4)^7$

(C) $\frac{d}{dt}\frac{1}{(t^2 + t + 4)^3}$

(D) $\frac{dh}{dw}$ if $h(w) = \sqrt{3 - w}$

SOLUTION

(A) $f(x) = (3x + 1)^4$ — Apply general power rule.

$f'(x) = 4(3x + 1)^3(3x + 1)'$ — Substitute $(3x + 1)' = 3$.

$= 4(3x + 1)^3\,3$ — Simplify.

$= 12(3x + 1)^3$

(B) $y = (x^3 + 4)^7$ — Apply general power rule.

$y' = 7(x^3 + 4)^6(x^3 + 4)'$ — Substitute $(x^3 + 4)' = 3x^2$.

$= 7(x^3 + 4)^6\,3x^2$ — Simplify.

$= 21x^2(x^3 + 4)^6$

(C) $\frac{d}{dt}\frac{1}{(t^2 + t + 4)^3}$

$= \frac{d}{dt}(t^2 + t + 4)^{-3}$ Apply general power rule.

$= -3(t^2 + t + 4)^{-4}(t^2 + t + 4)'$ Substitute $(t^2 + t + 4)' = 2t + 1$.

$= -3(t^2 + t + 4)^{-4}(2t + 1)$ Simplify.

$= \frac{-3(2t + 1)}{(t^2 + t + 4)^4}$

(D) $h(w) = \sqrt{3 - w} = (3 - w)^{1/2}$ Apply general power rule.

$\frac{dh}{dw} = \frac{1}{2}(3 - w)^{-1/2}(3 - w)'$ Substitute $(3 - w)' = -1$.

$= \frac{1}{2}(3 - w)^{-1/2}(-1)$ Simplify.

$= -\frac{1}{2(3 - w)^{1/2}}$ or $-\frac{1}{2\sqrt{3 - w}}$

Matched Problem 3 Find the indicated derivatives:

(A) $h'(x)$ if $h(x) = (5x + 2)^3$

(B) y' if $y = (x^4 - 5)^5$

(C) $\frac{d}{dt}\frac{1}{(t^2 + 4)^2}$

(D) $\frac{dg}{dw}$ if $g(w) = \sqrt{4 - w}$

Notice that we used two steps to differentiate each function in Example 3. First, we applied the general power rule, and then we found du/dx. As you gain experience with the general power rule, you may want to combine these two steps. If you do this, be certain to multiply by du/dx. For example,

$$\frac{d}{dx}(x^5 + 1)^4 = 4(x^5 + 1)^3 5x^4 \quad \text{Correct}$$

$$\frac{d}{dx}(x^5 + 1)^4 \neq 4(x^5 + 1)^3 \quad du/dx = 5x^4 \text{ is missing}$$

CONCEPTUAL INSIGHT

If we let $u(x) = x$, then $du/dx = 1$, and the general power rule reduces to the (ordinary) power rule discussed in Section 6.5. Compare the following:

$$\frac{d}{dx}x^n = nx^{n-1} \quad \text{Yes—power rule}$$

$$\frac{d}{dx}u^n = nu^{n-1}\frac{du}{dx} \quad \text{Yes—general power rule}$$

$$\frac{d}{dx}u^n \neq nu^{n-1} \quad \text{Unless } u(x) = x + k, \text{ so that } du/dx = 1$$

The Chain Rule

We have used the general power rule to find derivatives of composite functions of the form $f[g(x)]$, where $f(u) = u^n$ is a power function. But what if f is not a power function? Then a more general rule, the *chain rule,* enables us to compute the derivatives of many composite functions of the form $f[g(x)]$.

Suppose that

$$y = m(x) = f[g(x)]$$

is a composite of f and g, where

$$y = f(u) \qquad \text{and} \qquad u = g(x)$$

To express the derivative dy/dx in terms of the derivatives of f and g, we use the definition of a derivative (see Section 6.4).

$$m'(x) = \lim_{h\to 0} \frac{m(x+h) - m(x)}{h} \qquad \text{Substitute } m(x+h) = f[g(x+h)] \text{ and } m(x) = f[g(x)].$$

$$= \lim_{h\to 0} \frac{f[g(x+h)] - f[g(x)]}{h} \qquad \text{Multiply by } 1 = \frac{g(x+h)-g(x)}{g(x+h)-g(x)}.$$

$$= \lim_{h\to 0} \left[\frac{f[g(x+h)] - f[g(x)]}{h} \cdot \frac{g(x+h) - g(x)}{g(x+h) - g(x)}\right]$$

$$= \lim_{h\to 0} \left[\frac{f[g(x+h)] - f[g(x)]}{g(x+h) - g(x)} \cdot \frac{g(x+h) - g(x)}{h}\right] \qquad (4)$$

We recognize the second factor in equation (4) as the difference quotient for $g(x)$. To interpret the first factor as the difference quotient for $f(u)$, we let $k = g(x+h) - g(x)$. Since $u = g(x)$, we write

$$u + k = g(x) + g(x+h) - g(x) = g(x+h)$$

Substituting in equation (4), we have

$$m'(x) = \lim_{h\to 0} \left[\frac{f(u+k) - f(u)}{k} \cdot \frac{g(x+h) - g(x)}{h}\right] \qquad (5)$$

If we assume that $k = [g(x+h) - g(x)] \to 0$ as $h \to 0$, we can find the limit of each difference quotient in equation (5):

$$m'(x) = \left[\lim_{k\to 0} \frac{f(u+k) - f(u)}{k}\right]\left[\lim_{h\to 0} \frac{g(x+h) - g(x)}{h}\right]$$

$$= f'(u)g'(x)$$

$$= f'[g(x)]g'(x)$$

Therefore, referring to f and g in the composite function $f[g(x)]$ as the exterior function and interior function, respectively,

The derivative of the composite of two functions is the derivative of the exterior, evaluated at the interior, times the derivative of the interior.

This **chain rule** is expressed more compactly in Theorem 2, with notation chosen to aid memorization (E for "exterior", I for "interior").

THEOREM 2 Chain Rule

If $m(x) = E[I(x)]$ is a composite function, then

$$m'(x) = E'[I(x)]I'(x)$$

provided that $E'[I(x)]$ and $I'(x)$ exist.
Equivalently, if $y = E(u)$ and $u = I(x)$, then

$$\frac{dy}{dx} = \frac{dy}{du}\frac{du}{dx}$$

provided that $\frac{dy}{du}$ and $\frac{du}{dx}$ exist.

EXAMPLE 4 **Using the Chain Rule** Find the derivative $m'(x)$ of the composite function $m(x)$.

(A) $m(x) = (3x^2 + 1)^{3/2}$ (B) $m(x) = e^{2x^3+5}$ (C) $m(x) = \ln(x^2 - 4x + 2)$

SOLUTION

(A) The function m is the composite of $E(u) = u^{3/2}$ and $I(x) = 3x^2 + 1$. Then $E'(u) = \frac{3}{2}u^{1/2}$ and $I'(x) = 6x$; so by the chain rule,
$m'(x) = \frac{3}{2}(3x^2 + 1)^{1/2}(6x) = 9x(3x^2 + 1)^{1/2}$.

(B) The function m is the composite of $E(u) = e^u$ and $I(x) = 2x^3 + 5$. Then $E'(u) = e^u$ and $I'(x) = 6x^2$; so by the chain rule,
$m'(x) = e^{2x^3+5}(6x^2) = 6x^2e^{2x^3+5}$.

(C) The function m is the composite of $E(u) = \ln u$ and $I(x) = x^2 - 4x + 2$. Then $E'(u) = \frac{1}{u}$ and $I'(x) = 2x - 4$; so by the chain rule,
$m'(x) = \frac{1}{x^2 - 4x + 2}(2x - 4) = \frac{2x - 4}{x^2 - 4x + 2}$.

Matched Problem 4 Find the derivative $m'(x)$ of the composite function $m(x)$.

(A) $m(x) = (2x^3 + 4)^{-5}$ (B) $m(x) = e^{3x^4+6}$ (C) $m(x) = \ln(x^2 + 9x + 4)$

Explore and Discuss 2

Let $m(x) = f[g(x)]$. Use the chain rule and Figures 2 and 3 to find

(A) $f(4)$ (B) $g(6)$ (C) $m(6)$
(D) $f'(4)$ (E) $g'(6)$ (F) $m'(6)$

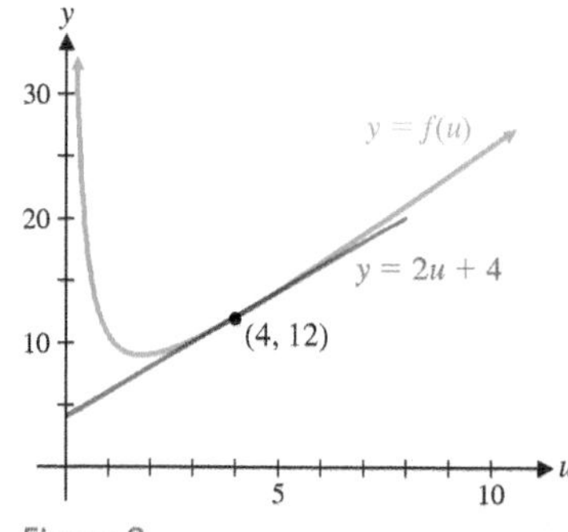

Figure 2

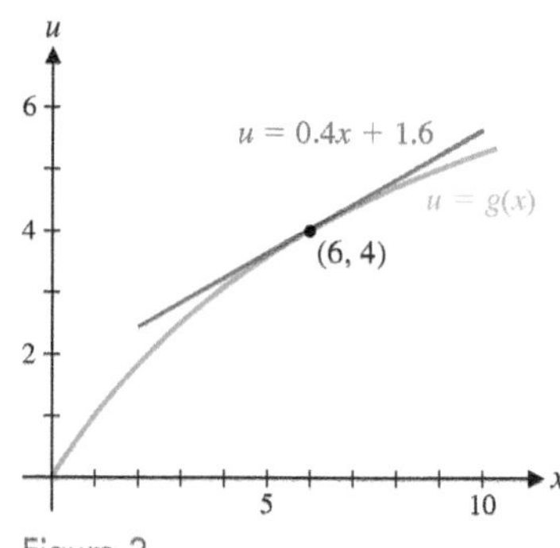

Figure 3

The chain rule can be extended to compositions of three or more functions. For example, if $y = f(w)$, $w = g(u)$, and $u = h(x)$, then

$$\frac{dy}{dx} = \frac{dy}{dw}\frac{dw}{du}\frac{du}{dx}$$

EXAMPLE 5 **Using the Chain Rule** For $y = h(x) = e^{1+(\ln x)^2}$, find dy/dx.

SOLUTION Note that h is of the form $y = e^w$, where $w = 1 + u^2$ and $u = \ln x$.

$$\frac{dy}{dx} = \frac{dy}{dw}\frac{dw}{du}\frac{du}{dx}$$

$$= e^w(2u)\left(\frac{1}{x}\right) \qquad \text{Substitute } w = 1 + u^2.$$

$$= e^{1+u^2}(2u)\left(\frac{1}{x}\right) \qquad \text{Substitute } u = \ln x \text{ (twice).}$$

$$= e^{1+(\ln x)^2}(2\ln x)\left(\frac{1}{x}\right) \qquad \text{Simplify.}$$

$$= \frac{2}{x}(\ln x)e^{1+(\ln x)^2}$$

Matched Problem 5 For $y = h(x) = [\ln(1 + e^x)]^3$, find dy/dx.

The chain rule generalizes basic derivative rules. We list three general derivative rules here for convenient reference [the first, equation (6), is the general power rule of Theorem 1].

General Derivative Rules

$$\frac{d}{dx}[f(x)]^n = n[f(x)]^{n-1}f'(x) \tag{6}$$

$$\frac{d}{dx}\ln[f(x)] = \frac{1}{f(x)}f'(x) \tag{7}$$

$$\frac{d}{dx}e^{f(x)} = e^{f(x)}f'(x) \tag{8}$$

Unless directed otherwise, you now have a choice between the chain rule and the general derivative rules. However, practicing with the chain rule will help prepare you for concepts that appear later in the text. Examples 4 and 5 illustrate the chain rule method, and the next example illustrates the general derivative rules method.

EXAMPLE 6 **Using General Derivative Rules** Find the derivatives:

(A) $\frac{d}{dx}e^{2x}$ (B) $\frac{d}{dx}\ln(x^2 + 9)$ (C) $\frac{d}{dx}(1 + e^{x^2})^3$

SOLUTION

(A) $\frac{d}{dx}e^{2x}$ Apply equation (8).

$= e^{2x}\frac{d}{dx}2x$

$= e^{2x}(2) = 2e^{2x}$

(B) $\frac{d}{dx}\ln(x^2 + 9)$ Apply equation (7).

$= \frac{1}{x^2 + 9}\frac{d}{dx}(x^2 + 9)$

$= \frac{1}{x^2 + 9}2x = \frac{2x}{x^2 + 9}$

(C) $\frac{d}{dx}(1 + e^{x^2})^3$ Apply equation (6).

$= 3(1 + e^{x^2})^2\frac{d}{dx}(1 + e^{x^2})$ Apply equation (8).

$= 3(1 + e^{x^2})^2 e^{x^2}\frac{d}{dx}x^2$

$= 3(1 + e^{x^2})^2 e^{x^2}(2x)$

$= 6xe^{x^2}(1 + e^{x^2})^2$

Matched Problem 6 Find

(A) $\frac{d}{dx}\ln(x^3 + 2x)$ (B) $\frac{d}{dx}e^{3x^2+2}$ (C) $\frac{d}{dx}(2 + e^{-x^2})^4$

Exercises 7.4

For many of the problems in this exercise set, the answers in the back of the book include both an unsimplified form and a simplified form. When checking your work, first check that you applied the rules correctly, and then check that you performed the algebraic simplification correctly.

Skills Warm-up Exercises

W *In Problems 1–8, find $f'(x)$. (If necessary, review Section 6.5 and 7.2.)*

1. $f(x) = x^9 + 10x$

2. $f(x) = 5 - 6x^5$

3. $f(x) = 7\sqrt{x} + \frac{3}{x^2}$

4. $f(x) = 15x^{-3} + 4\sqrt[3]{x}$

5. $f(x) = 8e^x + e$

6. $f(x) = 12e^x - 11x^e$

7. $f(x) = 4\ln x + 4x^2$

8. $f(x) = 5\ln x - x\ln 5$

A *In Problems 9–16, replace ? with an expression that will make the indicated equation valid.*

9. $\frac{d}{dx}(3x + 4)^4 = 4(3x + 4)^3$ __?__

10. $\frac{d}{dx}(5 - 2x)^6 = 6(5 - 2x)^5$ __?__

11. $\frac{d}{dx}(4 - 5x^6)^7 = 7(4 - 5x^6)^6$ __?__

12. $\frac{d}{dx}(3x^2 + 7)^5 = 5(3x^2 + 7)^4$ __?__

13. $\frac{d}{dx}e^{x^2+1} = e^{x^2+1}$ __?__

14. $\frac{d}{dx}e^{4x-2} = e^{4x-2}$ __?__

15. $\dfrac{d}{dx}\ln(x^4 + 1) = \dfrac{1}{x^4 + 1}$ ___?___

16. $\dfrac{d}{dx}\ln(x - x^3) = \dfrac{1}{x - x^3}$ ___?___

In Problems 17–34, find $f'(x)$ and simplify.

17. $f(x) = (5 - 2x)^4$
18. $f(x) = (9 - 5x)^2$
19. $f(x) = (4 + 0.2x)^5$
20. $f(x) = (6 - 0.5x)^4$
21. $f(x) = (3x^2 + 5)^5$
22. $f(x) = (5x^2 - 3)^6$
23. $f(x) = e^{5x}$
24. $f(x) = 18e^{-3x}$
25. $f(x) = 3e^{-6x}$
26. $f(x) = e^{x^2 + 3x + 1}$
27. $f(x) = (2x - 5)^{1/2}$
28. $f(x) = (4x + 3)^{1/2}$
29. $f(x) = (x^4 + 1)^{-2}$
30. $f(x) = (x^5 + 2)^{-3}$
31. $f(x) = 3\ln(1 + x^2)$
32. $f(x) = 2\ln(x^2 - 3x + 4)$
33. $f(x) = (1 + \ln x)^3$
34. $f(x) = (x - 2\ln x)^4$

In Problems 35–40, find $f'(x)$ and the equation of the line tangent to the graph of f at the indicated value of x. Find the value(s) of x where the tangent line is horizontal.

35. $f(x) = (2x - 1)^3;\quad x = 1$
36. $f(x) = (7x + 6)^5;\quad x = -1$
37. $f(x) = (4x - 3)^{1/2};\quad x = 3$
38. $f(x) = (2x + 8)^{1/2};\quad x = 4$
39. $f(x) = 5e^{x^2 - 4x + 1};\quad x = 0$
40. $f(x) = \ln(1 - x^2 + 2x^4);\quad x = 1$

B *In Problems 41–56, find the indicated derivative and simplify.*

41. y' if $y = 3(x^2 - 2)^4$
42. y' if $y = 2(x^3 + 6)^5$
43. $\dfrac{d}{dt}2(t^2 + 3t)^{-3}$
44. $\dfrac{d}{dt}3(t^3 + t^2)^{-2}$
45. $\dfrac{dh}{dw}$ if $h(w) = \sqrt{w^2 + 8}$
46. $\dfrac{dg}{dw}$ if $g(w) = \sqrt[3]{3w - 7}$
47. $g'(x)$ if $g(x) = 6xe^{-7x}$
48. $h'(x)$ if $h(x) = \dfrac{e^{2x}}{x^2 + 9}$
49. $\dfrac{d}{dx}\dfrac{\ln(1 + x^2)}{3x}$
50. $\dfrac{d}{dx}[x\ln(1 + e^x)]$
51. $F'(t)$ if $F(t) = (e^{t^2+1})^3$
52. $G'(t)$ if $G(t) = (1 - e^{2t})^2$
53. y' if $y = \ln(x^2 + 3)^{3/2}$
54. y' if $y = [\ln(x^2 + 3)]^{3/2}$
55. $\dfrac{d}{dw}\dfrac{1}{(w^3 + 4)^5}$
56. $\dfrac{d}{dw}\dfrac{1}{(w^6 - 5)^4}$

C *In Problems 57–62, find $f'(x)$ and find the equation of the line tangent to the graph of f at the indicated value of x.*

57. $f(x) = x(4 - x)^3;\quad x = 2$
58. $f(x) = x^2(1 - x)^4;\quad x = 2$
59. $f(x) = \dfrac{x}{(4x - 7)^5};\quad x = 2$
60. $f(x) = \dfrac{x^4}{(3x - 8)^2};\quad x = 4$
61. $f(x) = \sqrt{\ln x};\quad x = e$
62. $f(x) = e^{\sqrt{x}};\quad x = 1$

In Problems 63–68, find $f'(x)$ and find the value(s) of x where the tangent line is horizontal.

63. $f(x) = x^2(x - 5)^3$
64. $f(x) = x^3(x - 7)^4$
65. $f(x) = \dfrac{x}{(4x + 6)^3}$
66. $f(x) = \dfrac{x - 1}{(x - 3)^3}$
67. $f(x) = \sqrt{x^2 - 8x + 20}$
68. $f(x) = \sqrt{x^2 + 4x + 5}$

69. A student reasons that the functions $f(x) = \ln[5(x^2 + 3)^4]$ and $g(x) = 4\ln(x^2 + 3)$ must have the same derivative since he has entered $f(x)$, $g(x)$, $f'(x)$, and $g'(x)$ into a graphing calculator, but only three graphs appear (see the figure). Is his reasoning correct? Are $f'(x)$ and $g'(x)$ the same function? Explain.

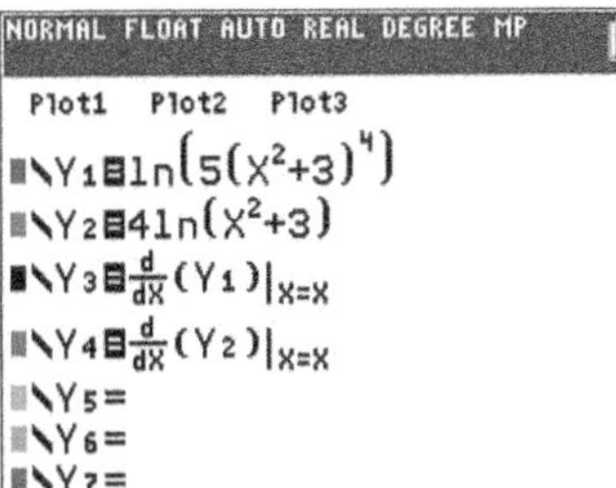

(A)

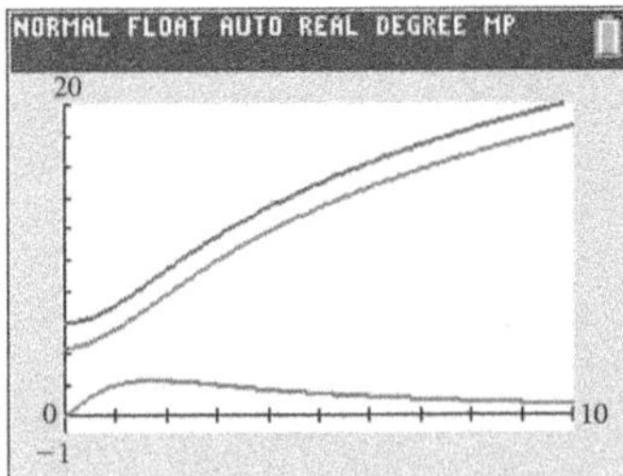

(B)

Figure for 73

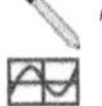

70. A student reasons that the functions $f(x) = (x + 1)\ln(x + 1) - x$ and $g(x) = (x + 1)^{1/3}$ must have the same derivative since she has entered $f(x)$, $g(x)$, $f'(x)$, and $g'(x)$ into a graphing calculator, but only three graphs appear (see the figure). Is her reasoning correct? Are $f'(x)$ and $g'(x)$ the same function? Explain.

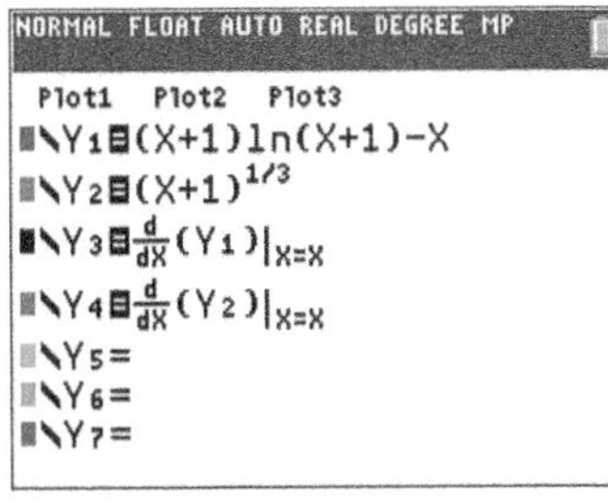

(A)

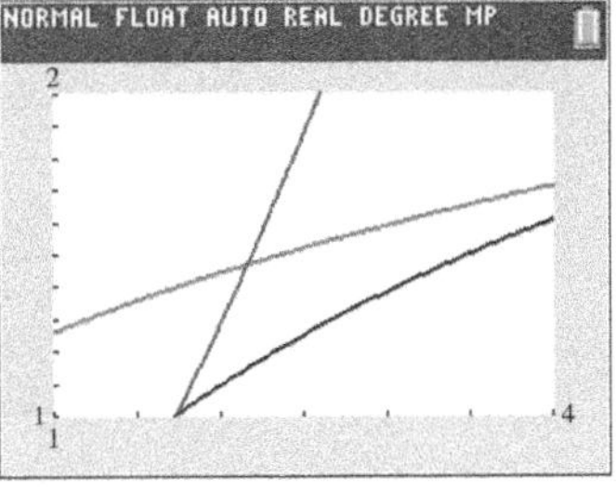

(B)

In Problems 71–78, give the domain of f, the domain of g, and the domain of m, where $m(x) = f[g(x)]$.

71. $f(u) = \ln u;\ g(x) = \sqrt{x}$

72. $f(u) = e^u;\ g(x) = \sqrt{x}$

73. $f(u) = \sqrt{u};\ g(x) = \ln x$

74. $f(u) = \sqrt{u};\ g(x) = e^x$

75. $f(u) = \ln u;\ g(x) = 4 - x^2$

76. $f(u) = \ln u;\ g(x) = 3x + 12$

77. $f(u) = \dfrac{1}{u^2 - 1};\ g(x) = \ln x$

78. $f(u) = \dfrac{1}{u};\ g(x) = x^2 - 9$

In Problems 79–90, find each derivative and simplify.

79. $\dfrac{d}{dx}[3x(x^2 + 1)^3]$

80. $\dfrac{d}{dx}[2x^2(x^3 - 3)^4]$

81. $\dfrac{d}{dx}\dfrac{(x^3 - 7)^4}{2x^3}$

82. $\dfrac{d}{dx}\dfrac{3x^2}{(x^2 + 5)^3}$

83. $\dfrac{d}{dx}\log_2(5x^4 + 3)$

84. $\dfrac{d}{dx}\log(x^3 - 1)$

85. $\dfrac{d}{dx}10^{x^2+x}$

86. $\dfrac{d}{dx}8^{1-2x^2}$

87. $\dfrac{d}{dx}\log_3(4x^3 + 5x + 7)$

88. $\dfrac{d}{dx}\log_5(5^{x^2-1})$

89. $\dfrac{d}{dx}2^{x^3-x^2+4x+1}$

90. $\dfrac{d}{dx}10^{\ln x}$

Applications

91. Cost function. The total cost (in hundreds of dollars) of producing x cell phones per day is

$$C(x) = 10 + \sqrt{2x + 16} \qquad 0 \le x \le 50$$

(see the figure).

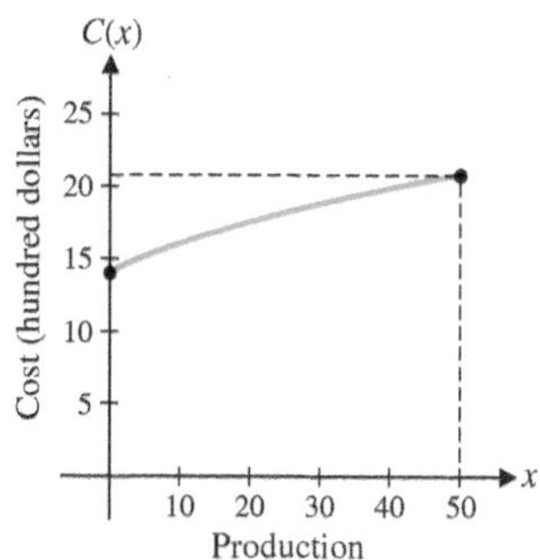

Figure for 91

(A) Find $C'(x)$.

(B) Find $C'(24)$ and $C'(42)$. Interpret the results.

92. Cost function. The total cost (in hundreds of dollars) of producing x cameras per week is

$$C(x) = 6 + \sqrt{4x + 4} \qquad 0 \le x \le 30$$

(A) Find $C'(x)$.

(B) Find $C'(15)$ and $C'(24)$. Interpret the results.

93. Price–supply equation. The number x of bicycle helmets a retail chain is willing to sell per week at a price of \$$p$ is given by

$$x = 80\sqrt{p + 25} - 400 \qquad 20 \le p \le 100$$

(see the figure).

(A) Find dx/dp.

(B) Find the supply and the instantaneous rate of change of supply with respect to price when the price is \$75. Write a brief interpretation of these results.

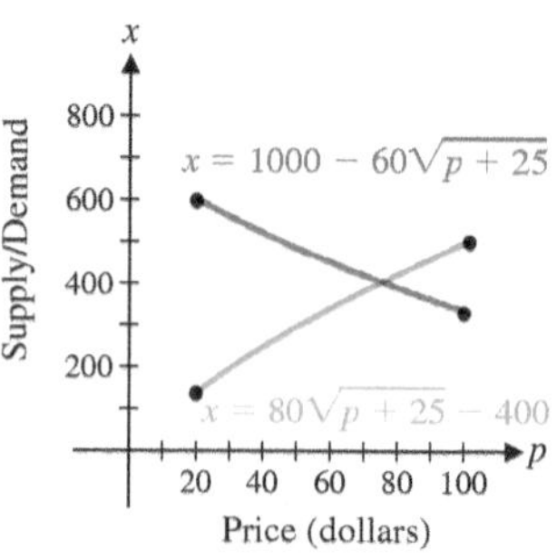

Figure for 93 and 94

94. Price–demand equation. The number x of bicycle helmets people are willing to buy per week from a retail chain at a price of \$$p$ is given by

$$x = 1{,}000 - 60\sqrt{p + 25} \qquad 20 \le p \le 100$$

(see the figure).

(A) Find dx/dp.

(B) Find the demand and the instantaneous rate of change of demand with respect to price when the price is \$75. Write a brief interpretation of these results.

95. Drug concentration. The drug concentration in the bloodstream t hours after injection is given approximately by

$$C(t) = 4.35e^{-t} \qquad 0 \le t \le 5$$

where $C(t)$ is concentration in milligrams per milliliter.

(A) What is the rate of change of concentration after 1 hour? After 4 hours?

(B) Graph C.

96. Water pollution. The use of iodine crystals is a popular way of making small quantities of water safe to drink. Crystals placed in a 1-ounce bottle of water will dissolve until the solution is saturated. After saturation, half of the solution is poured into a quart container of water, and after about an hour, the water is usually safe to drink. The half-empty 1-ounce bottle is then refilled, to be used again in the same way. Suppose that the concentration of iodine in the 1-ounce bottle t minutes after the crystals are introduced can be approximated by

$$C(t) = 250(1 - e^{-t}) \qquad t \ge 0$$

where $C(t)$ is the concentration of iodine in micrograms per milliliter.

(A) What is the rate of change of the concentration after 1 minute? After 4 minutes?

(B) Graph C for $0 \le t \le 5$.

97. Blood pressure and age. A research group using hospital records developed the following mathematical model relating systolic blood pressure and age:

$$P(x) = 40 + 25\ln(x + 1) \qquad 0 \le x \le 65$$

$P(x)$ is pressure, measured in millimeters of mercury, and x is age in years. What is the rate of change of pressure at the end of 10 years? At the end of 30 years? At the end of 60 years?

98. Biology. A yeast culture at room temperature (68°F) is placed in a refrigerator set at a constant temperature of 38°F. After t hours, the temperature T of the culture is given approximately by

$$T = 30e^{-0.58t} + 38 \qquad t \ge 0$$

What is the rate of change of temperature of the culture at the end of 1 hour? At the end of 4 hours?

Answers to Matched Problems

1. $f[g(x)] = 2e^x$, $g[f(u)] = e^{2u}$

2. (A) $f(u) = 50e^u$, $u = -2x$

(B) $f(u) = \sqrt[3]{u}$, $u = 1 + x^3$

[Note: There are other correct answers.]

3. (A) $15(5x + 2)^2$

(B) $20x^3(x^4 - 5)^4$

(C) $-4t/(t^2 + 4)^3$

(D) $-1/(2\sqrt{4 - w})$

4. (A) $m'(x) = -30x^2(2x^3 + 4)^{-6}$

(B) $m'(x) = 12x^3e^{3x^4+6}$

(C) $m'(x) = \dfrac{2x + 9}{x^2 + 9x + 4}$

5. $\dfrac{3e^x[\ln(1 + e^x)]^2}{1 + e^x}$

6. (A) $\dfrac{3x^2 + 2}{x^3 + 2x}$ (B) $6xe^{3x^2+2}$

(C) $-8xe^{-x^2}(2 + e^{-x^2})^3$

7.5 Implicit Differentiation

- Special Function Notation
- Implicit Differentiation

Special Function Notation

The equation

$$y = 2 - 3x^2 \tag{1}$$

defines a function f with y as a dependent variable and x as an independent variable. Using function notation, we would write

$$y = f(x) \quad \text{or} \quad f(x) = 2 - 3x^2$$

In order to minimize the number of symbols, we will often write equation (1) in the form

$$y = 2 - 3x^2 = y(x)$$

where y is *both* a dependent variable and a function symbol. This is a convenient notation, and no harm is done as long as one is aware of the double role of y. Other examples are

$$x = 2t^2 - 3t + 1 = x(t)$$

$$z = \sqrt{u^2 - 3u} = z(u)$$

$$r = \frac{1}{(s^2 - 3s)^{2/3}} = r(s)$$

Until now, we have considered functions involving only one independent variable. There is no reason to stop there: The concept can be generalized to functions involving two or more independent variables. For now, we will "borrow" the notation for a function involving two independent variables. For example,

$$f(x, y) = x^2 - 2xy + 3y^2 - 5$$

specifies a function F involving two independent variables.

Implicit Differentiation

Consider the equation

$$3x^2 + y - 2 = 0 \tag{2}$$

and the equation obtained by solving equation (2) for y in terms of x,

$$y = 2 - 3x^2 \tag{3}$$

Both equations define the same function with x as the independent variable and y as the dependent variable. For equation (3), we write

$$y = f(x)$$

where

$$f(x) = 2 - 3x^2 \tag{4}$$

and we have an **explicit** (directly stated) rule that enables us to determine y for each value of x. On the other hand, the y in equation (2) is the same y as in equation (3), and equation (2) **implicitly** gives (implies, though does not directly express) y as a function of x. We say that equations (3) and (4) define the function f explicitly and equation (2) defines f implicitly.

Using an equation that defines a function implicitly to find the derivative of the function is called **implicit differentiation**. Let's differentiate equation (2) implicitly and equation (3) directly, and compare results.

Starting with

$$3x^2 + y - 2 = 0$$

we think of y as a function of x and write

$$3x^2 + y(x) - 2 = 0$$

Then we differentiate both sides with respect to x:

$$\frac{d}{dx}[(3x^2 + y(x) - 2)] = \frac{d}{dx}0$$

$$\frac{d}{dx}3x^2 + \frac{d}{dx}y(x) - \frac{d}{dx}2 = 0$$

$$6x + y' - 0 = 0$$

Since y is a function of x, but is not explicitly given, simply write y' to denote $\frac{d}{dx}y(x)$.

Now we solve for y':

$$y' = -6x$$

Note that we get the same result if we start with equation (3) and differentiate directly:

$$y = 2 - 3x^2$$

$$y' = -6x$$

Why are we interested in implicit differentiation? Why not solve for y in terms of x and differentiate directly? The answer is that there are many equations of the form

$$f(x, y) = 0 \tag{5}$$

that are either difficult or impossible to solve for y explicitly in terms of x (try it for $x^2y^5 - 3xy + 5 = 0$ or for $e^y - y = 3x$, for example). But it can be shown that, under fairly general conditions on F, equation (5) will define one or more functions in which y is a dependent variable and x is an independent variable. To find y' under these conditions, we differentiate equation (5) implicitly.

Explore and Discuss 1

(A) How many tangent lines are there to the graph in Figure 1 when $x = 0$? When $x = 1$? When $x = 2$? When $x = 4$? When $x = 6$?

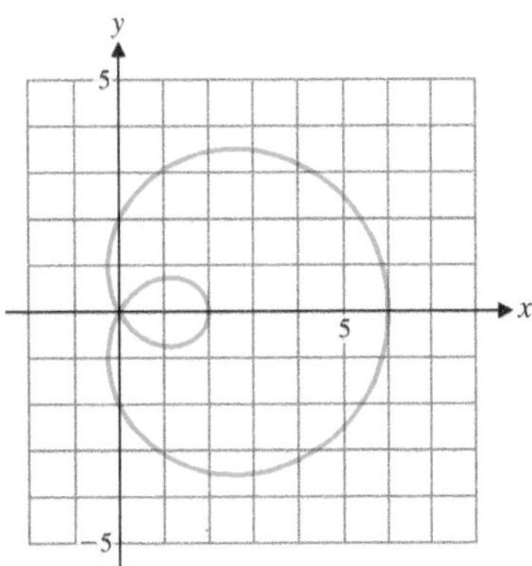

Figure 1

(B) Sketch the tangent lines referred to in part (A), and estimate each of their slopes.

(C) Explain why the graph in Figure 1 is not the graph of a function.

EXAMPLE 1 **Differentiating Implicitly** Given

$$f(x, y) = x^2 + y^2 - 25 = 0 \tag{6}$$

find y' and the slope of the graph at $x = 3$.

SOLUTION We start with the graph of $x^2 + y^2 - 25 = 0$ (a circle, as shown in Fig. 2) so that we can interpret our results geometrically. From the graph, it is clear that equation (6) does not define a function. But with a suitable restriction on the variables, equation (6) can define two or more functions. For example, the upper half and the lower half of the circle each define a function. On each half-circle, a point that corresponds to $x = 3$ is found by substituting $x = 3$ into equation (6) and solving for y:

$$\begin{aligned} x^2 + y^2 - 25 &= 0 \\ (3)^2 + y^2 &= 25 \\ y^2 &= 16 \\ y &= \pm 4 \end{aligned}$$

The point (3, 4) is on the upper half-circle, and the point $(3, -4)$ is on the lower half-circle. We will use these results in a moment. We now differentiate equation (6) implicitly, treating y as a function of x [i.e., $y = y(x)$]:

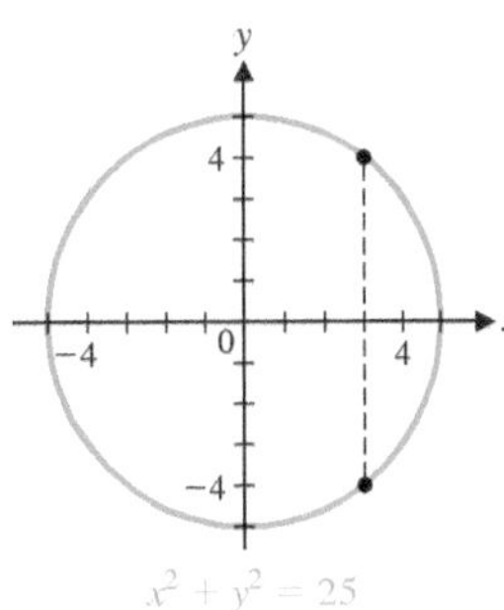

Figure 2

$$x^2 + y^2 - 25 = 0$$

$$x^2 + [y(x)]^2 - 25 = 0$$

$$\frac{d}{dx}\{x^2 + [y(x)]^2 - 25\} = \frac{d}{dx}0$$

$$\frac{d}{dx}x^2 + \frac{d}{dx}[y(x)]^2 - \frac{d}{dx}25 = 0 \quad \text{Use the chain rule.}$$

$$2x + 2[y(x)]^{2-1}y'(x) - 0 = 0$$

$$2x + 2yy' = 0 \quad \text{Solve for } y' \text{ in terms of } x \text{ and } y.$$

$$y' = -\frac{2x}{2y}$$

$$y' = -\frac{x}{y} \quad \text{Leave the answer in terms of } x \text{ and } y.$$

We have found y' without first solving $x^2 + y^2 - 25 = 0$ for y in terms of x. And by leaving y' in terms of x and y, we can use $y' = -x/y$ to find y' for *any* point on the graph of $x^2 + y^2 - 25 = 0$ (except where $y = 0$). In particular, for $x = 3$, we found that (3, 4) and $(3, -4)$ are on the graph. The slope of the graph at (3, 4) is

$$y'|_{(3,4)} = -\tfrac{3}{4} \quad \text{The slope of the graph at } (3, 4)$$

and the slope at $(3, -4)$ is

$$y'|_{(3,-4)} = -\tfrac{3}{-4} = \tfrac{3}{4} \quad \text{The slope of the graph at } (3, -4)$$

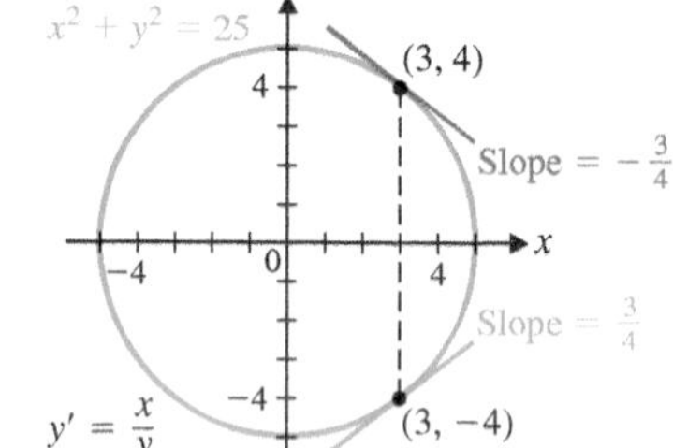

Figure 3

The symbol

$$y'|_{(a,b)}$$

is used to indicate that we are evaluating y' at $x = a$ and $y = b$.

The results are interpreted geometrically in Figure 3 on the original graph.

Matched Problem 1 Graph $x^2 + y^2 - 169 = 0$, find y' by implicit differentiation, and find the slope of the graph when $x = 5$.

CONCEPTUAL INSIGHT

When differentiating implicitly, the derivative of y^2 is $2yy'$, not just $2y$. This is because y represents a function of x, so the chain rule applies. Suppose, for example, that y represents the function $y = 5x + 4$. Then

$$(y^2)' = [(5x + 4)^2]' = 2(5x + 4) \cdot 5 = 2yy'$$

So, when differentiating implicitly, the derivative of y is y', the derivative of y^2 is $2yy'$, the derivative of y^3 is $3y^2y'$, and so on.

EXAMPLE 2 **Differentiating Implicitly** Find the equation(s) of the tangent line(s) to the graph of

$$y - xy^2 + x^2 + 1 = 0 \tag{7}$$

at the point(s) where $x = 1$.

SOLUTION We first find y when $x = 1$:

$$\begin{aligned} y - xy^2 + x^2 + 1 &= 0 \\ y - (1)y^2 + (1)^2 + 1 &= 0 \\ y - y^2 + 2 &= 0 \\ y^2 - y - 2 &= 0 \\ (y - 2)(y + 1) &= 0 \\ y &= -1 \quad \text{or} \quad 2 \end{aligned}$$

So there are two points on the graph of (7) where $x = 1$, namely, $(1, -1)$ and $(1, 2)$. We next find the slope of the graph at these two points by differentiating equation (7) implicitly:

$$\begin{aligned} y - xy^2 + x^2 + 1 &= 0 \\ \frac{d}{dx}y - \frac{d}{dx}xy^2 + \frac{d}{dx}x^2 + \frac{d}{dx}1 &= \frac{d}{dx}0 \\ y' - (x \cdot 2yy' + y^2) + 2x &= 0 \\ y' - 2xyy' - y^2 + 2x &= 0 \\ y' - 2xyy' &= y^2 - 2x \\ (1 - 2xy)y' &= y^2 - 2x \\ y' &= \frac{y^2 - 2x}{1 - 2xy} \end{aligned}$$

Use the product rule and the chain rule for $\frac{d}{dx}xy^2$.

Solve for y' by getting all terms involving y' on one side.

Factor out y'.

Now find the slope at each point:

$$y'\big|_{(1,-1)} = \frac{(-1)^2 - 2(1)}{1 - 2(1)(-1)} = \frac{1 - 2}{1 + 2} = \frac{-1}{3} = -\frac{1}{3}$$

$$y'\big|_{(1,2)} = \frac{(2)^2 - 2(1)}{1 - 2(1)(2)} = \frac{4 - 2}{1 - 4} = \frac{2}{-3} = -\frac{2}{3}$$

Equation of tangent line at $(1, -1)$:

$$\begin{aligned} y - y_1 &= m(x - x_1) \\ y + 1 &= -\tfrac{1}{3}(x - 1) \\ y + 1 &= -\tfrac{1}{3}x + \tfrac{1}{3} \\ y &= -\tfrac{1}{3}x - \tfrac{2}{3} \end{aligned}$$

Equation of tangent line at $(1, 2)$:

$$\begin{aligned} y - y_1 &= m(x - x_1) \\ y - 2 &= -\tfrac{2}{3}(x - 1) \\ y - 2 &= -\tfrac{2}{3}x + \tfrac{2}{3} \\ y &= -\tfrac{2}{3}x + \tfrac{8}{3} \end{aligned}$$

Matched Problem 2 Repeat Example 2 for $x^2 + y^2 - xy - 7 = 0$ at $x = 1$.

EXAMPLE 3 **Differentiating Implicitly** Find x' for $x = x(t)$ defined implicitly by

$$t \ln x = xe^t - 1$$

and evaluate x' at $(t, x) = (0, 1)$.

SOLUTION It is important to remember that x is the dependent variable and t is the independent variable. Therefore, we differentiate both sides of the equation with respect to t (using product and chain rules where appropriate) and then solve for x':

$$t \ln x = xe^t - 1 \qquad \text{Differentiate implicitly with respect to } t.$$

$$\frac{d}{dt}(t \ln x) = \frac{d}{dt}(xe^t) - \frac{d}{dt}1 \qquad \text{Use the product rule twice.}$$

$$t\frac{x'}{x} + \ln x = xe^t + e^t x' \qquad \text{Clear fractions.}$$

$$\mathbf{x} \cdot t\frac{x'}{x} + \mathbf{x} \cdot \ln x = \mathbf{x} \cdot xe^t + \mathbf{x} \cdot e^t x' \qquad x \neq 0$$

$$tx' + x \ln x = x^2 e^t + xe^t x' \qquad \text{Subtract to collect } x' \text{ terms.}$$

$$tx' - xe^t x' = x^2 e^t - x \ln x \qquad \text{Factor out } x'.$$

$$(t - xe^t)x' = x^2 e^t - x \ln x \qquad \text{Solve for } x'.$$

$$x' = \frac{x^2 e^t - x \ln x}{t - xe^t}$$

Now we evaluate x' at $(t, x) = (0, 1)$, as requested:

$$x'\big|_{(0,1)} = \frac{(1)^2 e^0 - 1 \ln 1}{0 - 1e^0} = \frac{1}{-1} = -1$$

Matched Problem 3 Find x' for $x = x(t)$ defined implicitly by

$$1 + x \ln t = te^x$$

and evaluate x' at $(t, x) = (1, 0)$.

Exercises 7.5

Skills Warm-up Exercises

W *In Problems 1–8, if it is possible to solve for y in terms of x, do so. If not, write "Impossible." (If necessary, review Section 1.1.)*

1. $3x + 2y - 20 = 0$

2. $-4x^2 + 3y + 12 = 0$

3. $\frac{x^2}{36} + \frac{y^2}{25} = 1$

4. $4y^2 - x^2 = 36$

5. $x^2 + xy + y^2 = 1$

6. $2 \ln y + y \ln x = 3x$

7. $5x + 3y = e^y$

8. $y^2 + e^x y + x^3 = 0$

A *In Problems 9–16, find y′ in two ways:*

(A) Differentiate the given equation implicitly and then solve for y'.

(B) Solve the given equation for y and then differentiate directly.

9. $-4x + 3y = 10$

10. $2x + 9y = 12$

11. $6x^2 + y^3 = 36$

12. $x^5 + y^5 = 1$

13. $3x + e^y = 7$

14. $4x^2 - e^y = 10$

15. $x^2 - \ln y = 0$

16. $x^3 + \ln y = 2$

B *In Problems 17–34, use implicit differentiation to find y′ and evaluate y′ at the indicated point.*

17. $y - 5x^2 + 3 = 0$; $(1, 2)$

18. $5x^3 - y - 1 = 0$; $(1, 4)$

19. $x^2 - y^3 - 3 = 0$; $(2, 1)$

20. $y^2 + x^3 + 4 = 0$; $(-2, 2)$

21. $y^2 - 5y + 6x = 0$; $(1, 2)$

22. $y^2 - y - 4x = 0$; $(0, 1)$

23. $xy - 6 = 0$; $(2, 3)$

24. $3xy - 2x - 2 = 0$; $(2, 1)$

25. $2xy + y + 2 = 0$; $(-1, 2)$

26. $2y + xy - 1 = 0$; $(-1, 1)$

27. $x^2 y - 3x^2 - 4 = 0$; $(2, 4)$

28. $4x^4 y - 3x^4 - 5 = 0$; $(-1, 2)$

29. $e^y = x^2 + y^2$; $(1, 0)$

30. $x^2 - y = 4e^y$; $(2, 0)$

31. $x^3 - y = \ln y$; $(1, 1)$

32. $\ln y = 2y^2 - x$; $(2, 1)$

33. $x \ln y + 3y = 3x^4$; $(-1, 1)$

34. $xe^y - y = x^2 - 2$; $(2, 0)$

In Problems 35 and 36, find x' for $x = x(t)$ defined implicitly by the given equation. Evaluate x' at the indicated point.

35. $x^2 - t^2x + t^3 + 11 = 0$; $(-2, 1)$

36. $x^3 - tx^2 - 4 = 0$; $(-3, -2)$

C *Problems 37 and 38 refer to the equation and graph shown in the figure.*

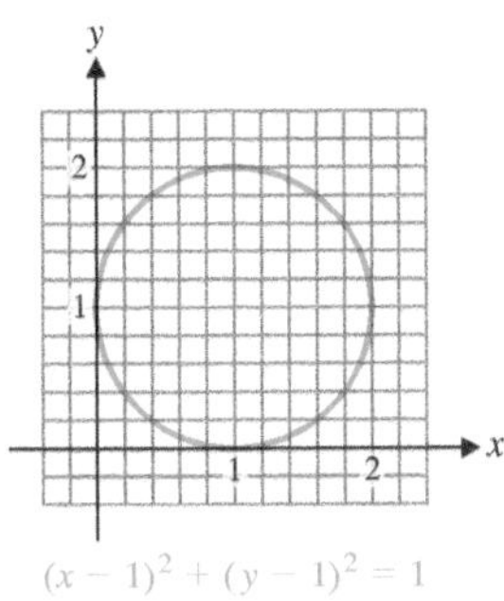

Figure for 37 and 38

37. Use implicit differentiation to find the slopes of the tangent lines at the points on the graph where $x = 1.6$. Check your answers by visually estimating the slopes on the graph in the figure.

38. Find the slopes of the tangent lines at the points on the graph where $x = 0.2$. Check your answers by visually estimating the slopes on the graph in the figure.

In Problems 39–42, find the equation(s) of the tangent line(s) to the graphs of the indicated equations at the point(s) with the given value of x.

39. $xy - 2x - 9 = 0$; $x = -3$

40. $3x + xy + 1 = 0$; $x = -1$

41. $y^2 - xy - 6 = 0$; $x = 1$

42. $xy^2 - y - 2 = 0$; $x = 1$

43. If $xe^y = 1$, find y' in two ways, first by differentiating implicitly and then by solving for y explicitly in terms of x. Which method do you prefer? Explain.

44. Explain the difficulty that arises in solving $x^3 + y + xe^y = 1$ for y as an explicit function of x. Find the slope of the tangent line to the graph of the equation at the point (0, 1).

In Problems 45–52, find y' and the slope of the tangent line to the graph of each equation at the indicated point.

45. $(1 + y)^3 + y = x + 7$; $(2, 1)$

46. $(y - 3)^4 - x = y$; $(-3, 4)$

47. $(x - 3y)^3 = 4y^3 - 5$; $(2, 1)$

48. $(2x - y)^4 - y^3 = 8$; $(-1, -2)$

49. $\sqrt{7 + y^2} - x^3 + 4 = 0$; $(2, 3)$

50. $6\sqrt{y^3 + 1} - 2x^{3/2} - 2 = 0$; $(4, 2)$

51. $\ln(xy) = y^2 - 1$; $(1, 1)$

52. $e^{xy} - 6x = 2y - 5$; $(1, 0)$

53. Find the equation(s) of the tangent line(s) at the point(s) on the graph of the equation

$$y^3 - xy - x^3 = 2$$

where $x = 1$. Round all approximate values to two decimal places.

54. Refer to the equation in Problem 53. Find the equation(s) of the tangent line(s) at the point(s) on the graph where $y = -1$. Round all approximate values to two decimal places.

Applications

55. **Price–supply equation.** The number x of fitness watches that an online retailer is willing to sell per week at a price of $\$p$ is given by

$$x = 0.5p^2 - 3p + 200$$

Use implicit differentiation to find dp/dx.

56. **Price–demand equation.** The number x of fitness watches that people are willing to buy per week from an online retailer at a price of $\$p$ is given by

$$x = 5{,}000 - 0.1p^2$$

Use implicit differentiation to find dp/dx.

57. **Price–demand equation.** The number x of compact refrigerators that people are willing to buy per week from an appliance chain at a price of $\$p$ is given by

$$x = 900 - 30\sqrt{p + 25}$$

Use implicit differentiation to find dp/dx.

58. **Price–supply equation.** The number x of compact refrigerators that an appliance chain is willing to sell per week at a price of $\$p$ is given by

$$x = 60\sqrt{p + 50} - 300$$

Use implicit differentiation to find dp/dx.

59. **Biophysics.** In biophysics, the equation

$$(L + m)(V + n) = k$$

is called the *fundamental equation of muscle contraction,* where m, n, and k are constants and V is the velocity of the shortening of muscle fibers for a muscle subjected to a load L. Find dL/dV by implicit differentiation.

60. **Biophysics.** In Problem 59, find dV/dL by implicit differentiation.

61. **Speed of sound.** The speed of sound in air is given by the formula

$$v = k\sqrt{T}$$

where v is the velocity of sound, T is the temperature of the air, and k is a constant. Use implicit differentiation to find $\frac{dT}{dv}$.

62. **Gravity.** The equation

$$F = G\frac{m_1 m_2}{r^2}$$

is Newton's law of universal gravitation. G is a constant and F is the gravitational force between two objects having masses m_1 and m_2 that are a distance r from each other.

Use implicit differentiation to find $\frac{dr}{dF}$. Assume that m_1 and m_2 are constant.

63. **Speed of sound.** Refer to Problem 61. Find $\frac{dv}{dT}$ and discuss the connection between $\frac{dv}{dT}$ and $\frac{dT}{dv}$.

64. **Gravity.** Refer to Problem 62. Find $\frac{dF}{dr}$ and discuss the connection between $\frac{dF}{dr}$ and $\frac{dr}{dF}$.

Answers to Matched Problems

1. $y' = -x/y$. When $x = 5, y = \pm 12$; thus, $y'|_{(5,12)} = -\frac{5}{12}$ and $y'|_{(5,-12)} = \frac{5}{12}$

2. $y' = \frac{y - 2x}{2y - x}$; $y = \frac{4}{5}x - \frac{14}{5}, y = \frac{1}{5}x + \frac{14}{5}$

3. $x' = \frac{te^x - x}{t \ln t - t^2 e^x}$; $x'|_{(1,0)} = -1$

7.6 Related Rates

Union workers are concerned that the rate at which wages are increasing is lagging behind the rate of increase in the company's profits. An automobile dealer wants to predict how much an anticipated increase in interest rates will decrease his rate of sales. An investor is studying the connection between the rate of increase in the Dow Jones average and the rate of increase in the gross domestic product over the past 50 years.

In each of these situations, there are two quantities—wages and profits, for example—that are changing with respect to time. We would like to discover the precise relationship between the rates of increase (or decrease) of the two quantities. We begin our discussion of such *related rates* by considering familiar situations in which the two quantities are distances and the two rates are velocities.

EXAMPLE 1 **Related Rates and Motion** A 26-foot ladder is placed against a wall (Fig. 1). If the top of the ladder is sliding down the wall at 2 feet per second, at what rate is the bottom of the ladder moving away from the wall when the bottom of the ladder is 10 feet away from the wall?

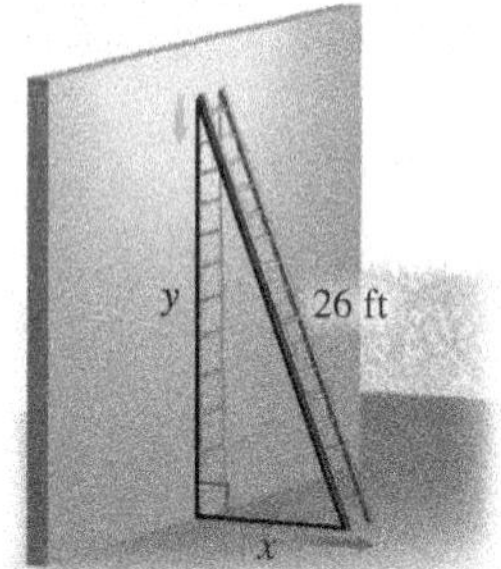

Figure 1

SOLUTION Many people think that since the ladder is a constant length, the bottom of the ladder will move away from the wall at the rate that the top of the ladder is moving down the wall. This is not the case, however.

At any moment in time, let x be the distance of the bottom of the ladder from the wall and let y be the distance of the top of the ladder from the ground (see Fig. 1). Both x and y are changing with respect to time and can be thought of as functions of time; that is, $x = x(t)$ and $y = y(t)$. Furthermore, x and y are related by the Pythagorean relationship:

$$x^2 + y^2 = 26^2 \tag{1}$$

Differentiating equation (1) implicitly with respect to time t and using the chain rule where appropriate, we obtain

$$2x\frac{dx}{dt} + 2y\frac{dy}{dt} = 0 \tag{2}$$

The rates dx/dt and dy/dt are related by equation (2). This is a **related-rates problem.**

Our problem is to find dx/dt when $x = 10$ feet, given that $dy/dt = -2$ (y is decreasing at a constant rate of 2 feet per second). We have all the quantities we need in equation (2) to solve for dx/dt, except y. When $x = 10$, y can be found from equation (1):

$$10^2 + y^2 = 26^2$$

$$y = \sqrt{26^2 - 10^2} = 24 \text{ feet}$$

Substitute $dy/dt = -2$, $x = 10$, and $y = 24$ into (2). Then solve for dx/dt:

$$2(10)\frac{dx}{dt} + 2(24)(-2) = 0$$

$$\frac{dx}{dt} = \frac{-2(24)(-2)}{2(10)} = 4.8 \text{ feet per second}$$

The bottom of the ladder is moving away from the wall at a rate of 4.8 feet per second.

CONCEPTUAL INSIGHT

In the solution to Example 1, we used equation (1) in two ways: first, to find an equation relating dy/dt and dx/dt, and second, to find the value of y when $x = 10$. These steps must be done in this order. Substituting $x = 10$ and then differentiating does not produce any useful results:

$$x^2 + y^2 = 26^2$$

$$100 + y^2 = 26^2$$

$$0 + 2yy' = 0$$

$$y' = 0$$

Substituting 10 for x has the effect of stopping the ladder.

The rate of change of a stationary object is always 0, but that is not the rate of change of the moving ladder.

Matched Problem 1 Again, a 26-foot ladder is placed against a wall (Fig. 1). If the bottom of the ladder is moving away from the wall at 3 feet per second, at what rate is the top moving down when the top of the ladder is 24 feet above ground?

Explore and Discuss 1

(A) For which values of x and y in Example 1 is dx/dt equal to 2 (i.e., the same rate that the ladder is sliding down the wall)?

(B) When is dx/dt greater than 2? Less than 2?

DEFINITION Suggestions for Solving Related-Rates Problems

Step 1 Sketch a figure if helpful.

Step 2 Identify all relevant variables, including those whose rates are given and those whose rates are to be found.

Step 3 Express all given rates and rates to be found as derivatives.

Step 4 Find an equation connecting the variables identified in step 2.

Step 5 Implicitly differentiate the equation found in step 4, using the chain rule where appropriate, and substitute in all given values.

Step 6 Solve for the derivative that will give the unknown rate.

EXAMPLE 2 **Related Rates and Motion** Suppose that two motorboats leave from the same point at the same time. If one travels north at 15 miles per hour and the other travels east at 20 miles per hour, how fast will the distance between them be changing after 2 hours?

SOLUTION First, draw a picture, as shown in Figure 2.

All variables, x, y, and z, are changing with time. They can be considered as functions of time: $x = x(t)$, $y = y(t)$, and $z = z(t)$, given implicitly. It now makes

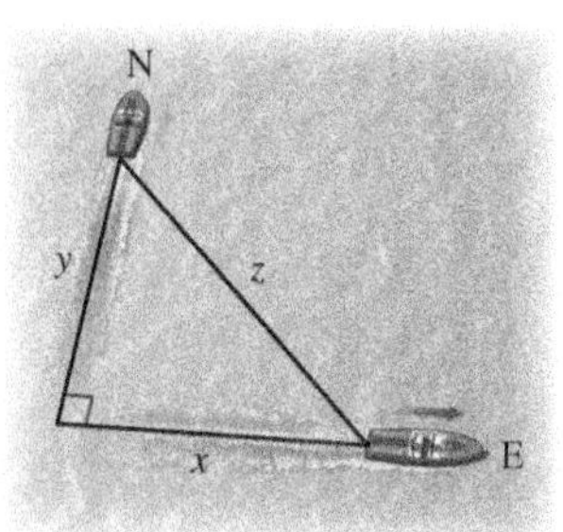

Figure 2

sense to find derivatives of each variable with respect to time. From the Pythagorean theorem,

$$z^2 = x^2 + y^2 \tag{3}$$

We also know that

$$\frac{dx}{dt} = 20 \text{ miles per hour} \quad \text{and} \quad \frac{dy}{dt} = 15 \text{ miles per hour}$$

We want to find dz/dt at the end of 2 hours—that is, when $x = 40$ miles and $y = 30$ miles. To do this, we differentiate both sides of equation (3) with respect to t and solve for dz/dt:

$$2z\frac{dz}{dt} = 2x\frac{dx}{dt} + 2y\frac{dy}{dt} \tag{4}$$

We have everything we need except z. From equation (3), when $x = 40$ and $y = 30$, we find z to be 50. Substituting the known quantities into equation (4), we obtain

$$2(50)\frac{dz}{dt} = 2(40)(20) + 2(30)(15)$$

$$\frac{dz}{dt} = 25 \text{ miles per hour}$$

The boats will be separating at a rate of 25 miles per hour.

Matched Problem 2 Repeat Example 2 for the same situation at the end of 3 hours.

EXAMPLE 3 **Related Rates and Motion** Suppose that a point is moving along the graph of $x^2 + y^2 = 25$ (Fig. 3). When the point is at $(-3, 4)$, its x coordinate is increasing at the rate of 0.4 unit per second. How fast is the y coordinate changing at that moment?

Figure 3

SOLUTION Since both x and y are changing with respect to time, we can consider each as a function of time, namely,

$$x = x(t) \quad \text{and} \quad y = y(t)$$

but restricted so that

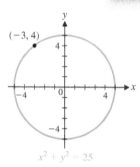

$$x^2 + y^2 = 25 \tag{5}$$

We want to find dy/dt, given $x = -3$, $y = 4$, and $dx/dt = 0.4$. Implicitly differentiating both sides of equation (5) with respect to t, we have

$$x^2 + y^2 = 25$$

$$2x\frac{dx}{dt} + 2y\frac{dy}{dt} = 0 \qquad \text{Divide both sides by 2.}$$

$$x\frac{dx}{dt} + y\frac{dy}{dt} = 0 \qquad \text{Substitute } x = -3,\ y = 4, \text{ and } dx/dt = 0.4, \text{ and solve for } dy/dt.$$

$$(-3)(0.4) + 4\frac{dy}{dt} = 0$$

$$\frac{dy}{dt} = 0.3 \text{ unit per second}$$

Matched Problem 3 A point is moving on the graph of $y^3 = x^2$. When the point is at $(-8, 4)$, its y coordinate is decreasing by 2 units per second. How fast is the x coordinate changing at that moment?

EXAMPLE 4 **Related Rates and Business** Suppose that for a company manufacturing flash drives, the cost, revenue, and profit equations are given by

$$C = 5{,}000 + 2x \qquad \text{Cost equation}$$

$$R = 10x - 0.001x^2 \qquad \text{Revenue equation}$$

$$P = R - C \qquad \text{Profit equation}$$

where the production output in 1 week is x flash drives. If production is increasing at the rate of 500 flash drives per week when production is 2,000 flash drives, find the rate of increase in

(A) Cost (B) Revenue (C) Profit

SOLUTION If production x is a function of time (it must be, since it is changing with respect to time), then C, R, and P must also be functions of time. These functions are given implicitly (rather than explicitly). Letting t represent time in weeks, we differentiate both sides of each of the preceding three equations with respect to t and then substitute $x = 2{,}000$ and $dx/dt = 500$ to find the desired rates.

(A) $C = 5{,}000 + 2x$ Think: $C = C(t)$ and $x = x(t)$.

$$\frac{dC}{dt} = \frac{d}{dt}(5{,}000) + \frac{d}{dt}(2x) \qquad \text{Differentiate both sides with respect to } t.$$

$$\frac{dC}{dt} = 0 + 2\frac{dx}{dt} = 2\frac{dx}{dt}$$

Since $dx/dt = 500$ when $x = 2{,}000$,

$$\frac{dC}{dt} = 2(500) = \$1{,}000 \text{ per week}$$

Cost is increasing at a rate of \$1,000 per week.

(B) $R = 10x - 0.001x^2$

$$\frac{dR}{dt} = \frac{d}{dt}(10x) - \frac{d}{dt}0.001x^2$$

$$\frac{dR}{dt} = 10\frac{dx}{dt} - 0.002x\frac{dx}{dt}$$

$$\frac{dR}{dt} = (10 - 0.002x)\frac{dx}{dt}$$

Since $dx/dt = 500$ when $x = 2{,}000$,

$$\frac{dR}{dt} = [10 - 0.002(2{,}000)](500) = \$3{,}000 \text{ per week}$$

Revenue is increasing at a rate of \$3,000 per week.

(C) $P = R - C$

$$\frac{dP}{dt} = \frac{dR}{dt} - \frac{dC}{dt} \qquad \text{Results from parts (A) and (B)}$$

$$= \$3{,}000 - \$1{,}000$$

$$= \$2{,}000 \text{ per week}$$

Profit is increasing at a rate of \$2,000 per week.

Matched Problem 4 Repeat Example 4 for a production level of 6,000 flash drives per week.

Exercises 7.6

Skills Warm-up Exercises

W *For Problems 1–8, review the geometric formulas in A Library of Elementary Functions at the back of the book, if necessary.*

1. A circular flower bed has an area of 300 square feet. Find its diameter to the nearest tenth of a foot.
2. A central pivot irrigation system covers a circle of radius 400 meters. Find the area of the circle to the nearest square meter.
3. The hypotenuse of a right triangle has length 60 meters, and another side has length 30 meters. Find the length of the third side to the nearest meter.
4. The legs of a right triangle have lengths 54 feet and 69 feet. Find the length of the hypotenuse to the nearest foot.
5. A person 69 inches tall stands 40 feet from the base of a streetlight. The streetlight casts a shadow of length 96 inches. How far above the ground is the streetlight?
6. The radius of a spherical balloon is 3 meters. Find its volume to the nearest tenth of a cubic meter.
7. A right circular cylinder and a sphere both have radius 12 feet. If the volume of the cylinder is twice the volume of the sphere, find the height of the cylinder.
8. The radius of a right circular cylinder is twice its height. If the volume is 375 cubic meters, find the radius and height to the nearest hundredth of a meter.

A *In Problems 9–14, assume that $x = x(t)$ and $y = y(t)$. Find the indicated rate, given the other information.*

9. $y = x^2 + 2$; $dx/dt = 3$ when $x = 5$; find dy/dt
10. $y = x^3 - 5$; $dx/dt = -1$ when $x = 4$; find dy/dt
11. $x^2 + y^2 = 1$; $dy/dt = -4$ when $x = -0.6$ and $y = 0.8$; find dx/dt
12. $x^2 + y^2 = 4$; $dy/dt = 5$ when $x = 1.2$ and $y = -1.6$; find dx/dt
13. $x^2 + 3xy + y^2 = 11$; $dx/dt = 2$ when $x = 1$ and $y = 2$; find dy/dt
14. $x^2 - 4xy - y^2 = 4$; $dy/dt = -2$ when $x = 1$ and $y = -3$; find dx/dt

B 15. A point is moving on the graph of $xy = 24$. When the point is at (4, 6), its x coordinate is increasing by 2 units per second. How fast is its y coordinate changing at that moment?

16. A point is moving on the graph of $16x^2 + 9y^2 = 160$. When the point is at (1, 4), its x coordinate is decreasing by 18 units per second. How fast is its y coordinate changing at that moment?

17. A boat is being pulled toward a dock as shown in the figure. If the rope is being pulled in at 3 feet per second, how fast is the distance between the dock and the boat decreasing when it is 30 feet from the dock?

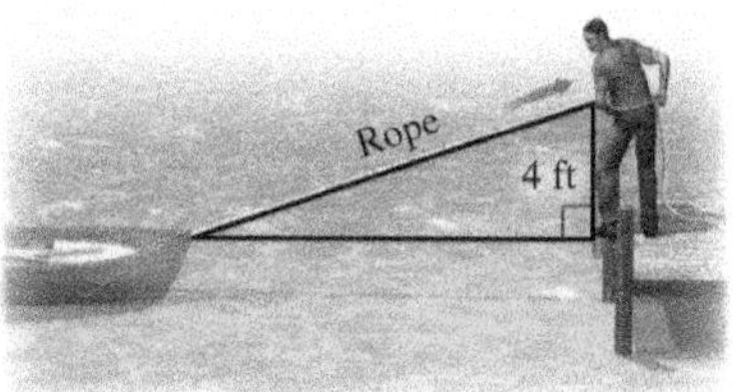

Figure for 17 and 18

18. Refer to Problem 17. Suppose that the distance between the boat and the dock is decreasing by 3.05 feet per second. How fast is the rope being pulled in when the boat is 10 feet from the dock?

19. A rock thrown into a still pond causes a circular ripple. If the radius of the ripple is increasing by 2 feet per second, how fast is the area changing when the radius is 10 feet?

20. Refer to Problem 19. How fast is the circumference of a circular ripple changing when the radius is 10 feet?

21. The radius of a spherical balloon is increasing at the rate of 6 centimeters per minute. How fast is the volume changing when the radius is 25 centimeters?

22. Refer to Problem 21. How fast is the surface area of the sphere increasing when the radius is 25 centimeters?

23. Boyle's law for enclosed gases states that if the volume is kept constant, the pressure P and temperature T are related by the equation

$$\frac{P}{T} = k$$

where k is a constant. If the temperature is increasing at 3 kelvins per hour, what is the rate of change of pressure when the temperature is 250 kelvins and the pressure is 500 pounds per square inch?

24. Boyle's law for enclosed gases states that if the temperature is kept constant, the pressure P and volume V of a gas are related by the equation

$$VP = k$$

where k is a constant. If the volume is decreasing by 5 cubic inches per second, what is the rate of change of pressure when the volume is 1,000 cubic inches and the pressure is 40 pounds per square inch?

25. A 10-foot ladder is placed against a vertical wall. Suppose that the bottom of the ladder slides away from the wall at a constant rate of 3 feet per second. How fast is the top of the ladder sliding down the wall when the bottom is 6 feet from the wall?

26. A weather balloon is rising vertically at the rate of 5 meters per second. An observer is standing on the ground 300 meters from where the balloon was released. At what rate is the

distance between the observer and the balloon changing when the balloon is 400 meters high?

C 27. A streetlight is on top of a 20-foot pole. A person who is 5 feet tall walks away from the pole at the rate of 5 feet per second. At what rate is the tip of the person's shadow moving away from the pole when he is 20 feet from the pole?

28. Refer to Problem 27. At what rate is the person's shadow growing when he is 20 feet from the pole?

29. Helium is pumped into a spherical balloon at a constant rate of 4 cubic feet per second. How fast is the radius increasing after 1 minute? After 2 minutes? Is there any time at which the radius is increasing at a rate of 100 feet per second? Explain.

30. A point is moving along the x axis at a constant rate of 5 units per second. At which point is its distance from (0, 1) increasing at a rate of 2 units per second? At 4 units per second? At 5 units per second? At 10 units per second? Explain.

31. A point is moving on the graph of $y = e^x + x + 1$ in such a way that its x coordinate is always increasing at a rate of 3 units per second. How fast is the y coordinate changing when the point crosses the x axis?

32. A point is moving on the graph of $x^3 + y^2 = 1$ in such a way that its y coordinate is always increasing at a rate of 2 units per second. At which point(s) is the x coordinate increasing at a rate of 1 unit per second?

Applications

33. **Cost, revenue, and profit rates.** Suppose that for a company manufacturing calculators, the cost, revenue, and profit equations are given by

$$C = 90{,}000 + 30x \qquad R = 300x - \frac{x^2}{30}$$

$$P = R - C$$

where the production output in 1 week is x calculators. If production is increasing at a rate of 500 calculators per week when production output is 6,000 calculators, find the rate of increase (decrease) in

(A) Cost (B) Revenue (C) Profit

34. **Cost, revenue, and profit rates.** Repeat Problem 33 for

$$C = 72{,}000 + 60x \qquad R = 200x - \frac{x^2}{30}$$

$$P = R - C$$

where production is increasing at a rate of 500 calculators per week at a production level of 1,500 calculators.

35. **Advertising.** A retail store estimates that weekly sales s and weekly advertising costs x (both in dollars) are related by

$$s = 60{,}000 - 40{,}000e^{-0.0005x}$$

The current weekly advertising costs are $2,000, and these costs are increasing at the rate of $300 per week. Find the current rate of change of sales.

36. **Advertising.** Repeat Problem 35 for

$$s = 50{,}000 - 20{,}000e^{-0.0004x}$$

37. **Price–demand.** The price p (in dollars) and demand x for wireless headphones are related by

$$x = 6{,}000 - 0.15p^2$$

If the current price of $110 is decreasing at a rate of $5 per week, find the rate of change (in headphones per week) of the demand.

38. **Price–demand.** The price p (in dollars) and demand x for microwave ovens are related by

$$x = 800 - 36\sqrt{p + 20}$$

If the current price of $124 is increasing at a rate of $3 per week, find the rate of change (in ovens per week) of the demand.

39. **Revenue.** Refer to Problem 37. Find the associated revenue function $R(p)$ and the rate of change (in dollars per week) of the revenue.

40. **Revenue.** Refer to Problem 38. Find the associated revenue function $R(p)$ and the rate of change (in dollars per week) of the revenue.

41. **Price–supply equation.** The price p (in dollars per pound) and demand x (in pounds) for almonds are related by

$$x = 5{,}600\sqrt{p + 10} - 3{,}000$$

If the current price of $2.25 per pound is increasing at a rate of $0.20 per week, find the rate of change (in pounds per week) of the supply.

42. **Price–supply equation.** The price p (in dollars) and demand x (in bushels) for peaches are related by

$$x = 3p^2 - 2p + 500$$

If the current price of $38 per bushel is decreasing at a rate of $1.50 per week, find the rate of change (in bushels per week) of the supply.

43. **Political campaign.** A political campaign estimates that the candidate's polling percentage y and the amount x (in millions of dollars) that is spent on television advertising are related by

$$y = 20 + 5\ln x$$

If $10 million has been spent on television advertising, find the rate of spending (in millions of dollars per week) that will increase the polling percentage by 1 percentage point per week.

44. **Political campaign.** Refer to Problem 43. If $12 million has been spent on television advertising and the rate of spending is $3 million per week, at what rate (in percentage points per week) will the polling percentage increase?

45. **Price–demand.** The price p (in dollars) and demand x for a product are related by

$$2x^2 + 5xp + 50p^2 = 80{,}000$$

(A) If the price is increasing at a rate of $2 per month when the price is $30, find the rate of change of the demand.

(B) If the demand is decreasing at a rate of 6 units per month when the demand is 150 units, find the rate of change of the price.

46. **Price–demand.** Repeat Problem 45 for

$$x^2 + 2xp + 25p^2 = 74{,}500$$

47. Pollution. An oil tanker aground on a reef is forming a circular oil slick about 0.1 foot thick (see the figure). To estimate the rate dV/dt (in cubic feet per minute) at which the oil is leaking from the tanker, it was found that the radius of the slick was increasing at 0.32 foot per minute $(dR/dt = 0.32)$ when the radius R was 500 feet. Find dV/dt.

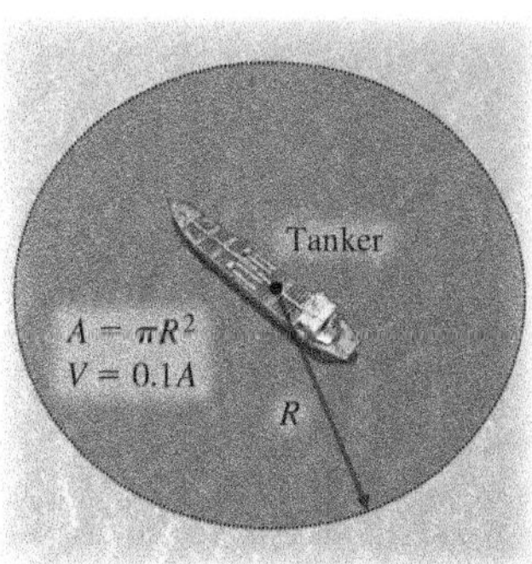

48. Learning. A person who is new on an assembly line performs an operation in T minutes after x performances of the operation, as given by

$$T = 6\left(1 + \frac{1}{\sqrt{x}}\right)$$

If $dx/dt = 6$ operations per hours, where t is time in hours, find dT/dt after 36 performances of the operation.

Answers to Matched Problems

1. $dy/dt = -1.25$ ft/sec
2. $dz/dt = 25$ mi/hr
3. $dx/dt = 6$ units/sec
4. (A) $dC/dt = \$1{,}000/\text{wk}$
   (B) $dR/dt = -\$1{,}000/\text{wk}$
   (C) $dP/dt = -\$2{,}000/\text{wk}$

7.7 Elasticity of Demand

- Relative Rate of Change
- Elasticity of Demand

When will a price increase lead to an increase in revenue? To answer this question and study relationships among price, demand, and revenue, economists use the notion of *elasticity of demand.* In this section, we define the concepts of *relative rate of change*, *percentage rate of change*, and *elasticity of demand.*

Relative Rate of Change

Explore and Discuss 1

A broker is trying to sell you two stocks: Biotech and Comstat. The broker estimates that Biotech's price per share will increase \$2 per year over the next several years, while Comstat's price per share will increase only \$1 per year. Is this sufficient information for you to choose between the two stocks? What other information might you request from the broker to help you decide?

Interpreting rates of change is a fundamental application of calculus. In Explore and Discuss 1, Biotech's price per share is increasing at twice the rate of Comstat's, but that does not automatically make Biotech the better buy. The obvious information that is missing is the current price of each stock. If Biotech costs \$100 a share and Comstat costs \$25 a share, then which stock is the better buy? To answer this question, we introduce two new concepts: *relative rate of change* and *percentage rate of change.*

DEFINITION Relative and Percentage Rates of Change

The **relative rate of change** of a function $f(x)$ is $\frac{f'(x)}{f(x)}$, or equivalently, $\frac{d}{dx}\ln f(x)$.

The **percentage rate of change** is $100 \times \frac{f'(x)}{f(x)}$, or equivalently, $100 \times \frac{d}{dx}\ln f(x)$.

The alternative form for the relative rate of change, $\frac{d}{dx}\ln f(x)$, is called the **logarithmic derivative** of $f(x)$.

Note that

$$\frac{d}{dx}\ln f(x) = \frac{f'(x)}{f(x)}$$

by the chain rule. So the relative rate of change of a function $f(x)$ is its logarithmic derivative, and the percentage rate of change is 100 times the logarithmic derivative.

Returning to Explore and Discuss 1, the table shows the relative rate of change and percentage rate of change for Biotech and Comstat. We conclude that Comstat is the better buy.

	Relative rate of change	Percentage rate of change
Biotech	$\frac{2}{100} = 0.02$	2%
Comstat	$\frac{1}{25} = 0.04$	4%

EXAMPLE 1 **Percentage Rate of Change** Table 1 lists the GDP (gross domestic product expressed in billions of 2005 dollars) and U.S. population from 2000 to 2012. A model for the GDP is

$$f(t) = 209.5t + 11{,}361$$

where t is years since 2000. Find and graph the percentage rate of change of $f(t)$ for $0 \le t \le 12$.

Table 1

Year	Real GDP (billions of 2005 dollars)	Population (in millions)
2000	\$11,226	282.2
2004	\$12,264	292.9
2008	\$13,312	304.1
2012	\$13,670	313.9

SOLUTION If $p(t)$ is the percentage rate of change of $f(t)$, then

$$p(t) = 100 \times \frac{d}{dt}\ln(209.5t + 11{,}361)$$

$$= \frac{20{,}950}{209.5t + 11{,}361}$$

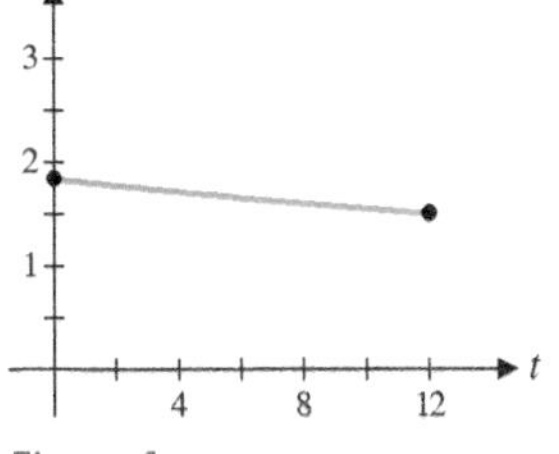

Figure 1

The graph of $p(t)$ is shown in Figure 1 (graphing details omitted). Notice that $p(t)$ is decreasing, even though the GDP is increasing.

Matched Problem 1 A model for the population data in Table 1 is

$$f(t) = 2.7t + 282$$

where t is years since 2000. Find and graph $p(t)$, the percentage rate of change of $f(t)$ for $0 \le t \le 12$.

CONCEPTUAL INSIGHT

If \$10,000 is invested at an annual rate of 4.5% compounded continuously, what is the relative rate of change of the amount in the account? The answer is the logarithmic derivative of $A(t) = 10{,}000e^{0.045t}$, namely

$$\frac{d}{dx}\ln\left(10{,}000e^{0.045t}\right) = \frac{10{,}000e^{0.045t}(0.045)}{10{,}000e^{0.045t}} = 0.045$$

So the relative rate of change of $A(t)$ is 0.045, and the percentage rate of change is just the annual interest rate, 4.5%.

Elasticity of Demand

Explore and Discuss 2

In both parts below, assume that increasing the price per unit by \$1 will decrease the demand by 500 units. If your objective is to increase revenue, should you increase the price by \$1 per unit?

(A) At the current price of \$8.00 per baseball cap, there is a demand for 6,000 caps.

(B) At the current price of \$12.00 per baseball cap, there is a demand for 4,000 caps.

In Explore and Discuss 2, the rate of change of demand with respect to price was assumed to be −500 units per dollar. But in one case, part (A), you should increase the price, and in the other, part (B), you should not. Economists use the concept of *elasticity of demand* to answer the question "When does an increase in price lead to an increase in revenue?"

DEFINITION Elasticity of Demand

Let the price p and demand x for a product be related by a price–demand equation of the form $x = f(p)$. Then the **elasticity of demand at price p**, denoted by $E(p)$, is

$$E(p) = -\frac{\text{relative rate of change of demand}}{\text{relative rate of change of price}}$$

Using the definition of relative rate of change, we can find a formula for $E(p)$:

$$E(p) = -\frac{\text{relative rate of change of demand}}{\text{relative rate of change of price}} = -\frac{\frac{d}{dp}\ln f(p)}{\frac{d}{dp}\ln p}$$

$$= -\frac{\frac{f'(p)}{f(p)}}{\frac{1}{p}}$$

$$= -\frac{pf'(p)}{f(p)}$$

THEOREM 1 Elasticity of Demand

If price and demand are related by $x = f(p)$, then the elasticity of demand is given by

$$E(p) = -\frac{pf'(p)}{f(p)}$$

CONCEPTUAL INSIGHT

Since p and $f(p)$ are nonnegative and $f'(p)$ is negative (demand is usually a decreasing function of price), $E(p)$ is nonnegative. This is why elasticity of demand is defined as the negative of a ratio.

EXAMPLE 2 **Elasticity of Demand** The price p and the demand x for a product are related by the price–demand equation

$$x + 500p = 10{,}000 \qquad (1)$$

Find the elasticity of demand, $E(p)$, and interpret each of the following:

(A) $E(4)$ (B) $E(16)$ (C) $E(10)$

SOLUTION To find $E(p)$, we first express the demand x as a function of the price p by solving (1) for x:

$$\begin{aligned} x &= 10{,}000 - 500p \\ &= 500(20 - p) \qquad \text{Demand as a function of price} \end{aligned}$$

or

$$x = f(p) = 500(20 - p) \qquad 0 \le p \le 20 \qquad (2)$$

Since x and p both represent nonnegative quantities, we must restrict p so that $0 \le p \le 20$. Note that the demand is a decreasing function of price. That is, a price increase results in lower demand, and a price decrease results in higher demand (see Fig. 2).

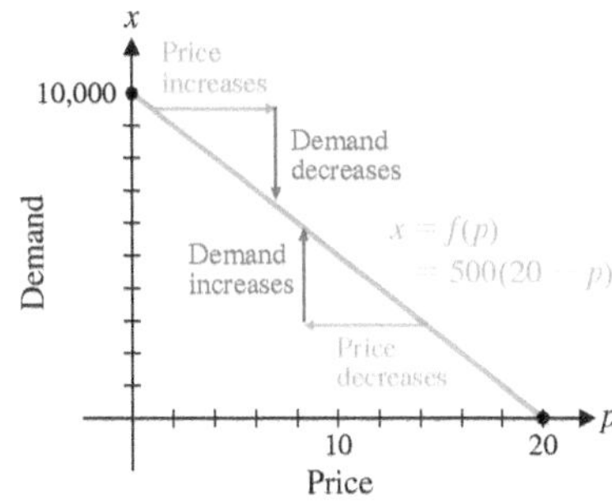

Figure 2

$$E(p) = -\frac{pf'(p)}{f(p)} = -\frac{p(-500)}{500(20 - p)} = \frac{p}{20 - p}$$

In order to interpret values of $E(p)$, we must recall the definition of elasticity:

$$E(p) = -\frac{\text{relative rate of change of demand}}{\text{relative rate of change of price}}$$

or

$$-\begin{pmatrix}\text{relative rate of}\\ \text{change of demand}\end{pmatrix} \approx E(p)\begin{pmatrix}\text{relative rate of}\\ \text{change of price}\end{pmatrix}$$

(A) $E(4) = \frac{4}{16} = 0.25 < 1$. If the \$4 price changes by 10%, then the demand will change by approximately $0.25(10\%) = 2.5\%$.

(B) $E(16) = \frac{16}{4} = 4 > 1$. If the \$16 price changes by 10%, then the demand will change by approximately $4(10\%) = 40\%$.

(C) $E(10) = \frac{10}{10} = 1$. If the \$10 price changes by 10%, then the demand will also change by approximately 10%.

Matched Problem 2 Find $E(p)$ for the price–demand equation

$$x = f(p) = 1{,}000(40 - p)$$

Find and interpret each of the following:

(A) $E(8)$ (B) $E(30)$ (C) $E(20)$

The three cases illustrated in the solution to Example 2 are referred to as **inelastic demand, elastic demand**, and **unit elasticity**, as indicated in Table 2.

Table 2

$E(p)$	Demand	Interpretation	Revenue
$0 < E(p) < 1$	Inelastic	Demand is not sensitive to changes in price; that is, percentage change in price produces a smaller percentage change in demand.	A price increase will increase revenue.
$E(p) > 1$	Elastic	Demand is sensitive to changes in price; that is, a percentage change in price produces a larger percentage change in demand.	A price increase will decrease revenue.
$E(p) = 1$	Unit	A percentage change in price produces the same percentage change in demand.	

To justify the connection between elasticity of demand and revenue as given in the fourth column of Table 2, we recall that revenue R is the demand x (number of items sold) multiplied by p (price per item). Assume that the price–demand equation is written in the form $x = f(p)$. Then

$$R(p) = xp = f(p)p \quad \text{Use the product rule.}$$

$$R'(p) = f(p)\cdot 1 + pf'(p) \quad \text{Multiply and divide by } f(p).$$

$$R'(p) = f(p) + pf'(p)\frac{f(p)}{f(p)} \quad \text{Factor out } f(p).$$

$$R'(p) = f(p)\left[1 + \frac{pf'(p)}{f(p)}\right] \quad \text{Use Theorem 1.}$$

$$R'(p) = f(p)[1 - E(p)]$$

Since $x = f(p) > 0$, it follows that $R'(p)$ and $1 - E(p)$ have the same sign. So if $E(p) < 1$, then $R'(p)$ is positive and revenue is increasing (Fig. 3). Similarly, if $E(p) > 1$, then $R'(p)$ is negative, and revenue is decreasing (Fig. 3).

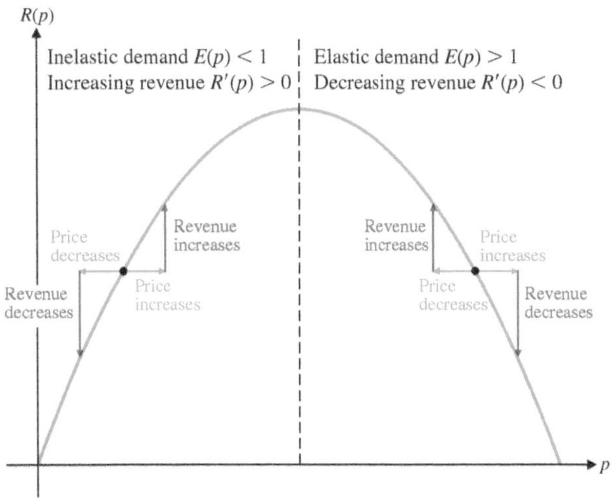

R(p)
Inelastic demand $E(p) < 1$
Increasing revenue $R'(p) > 0$
Elastic demand $E(p) > 1$
Decreasing revenue $R'(p) < 0$
Price decreases
Revenue increases
Revenue decreases
Price increases
Revenue increases
Price increases
Price decreases
Revenue decreases
p

Figure 3 **Revenue and elasticity**

EXAMPLE 3 **Elasticity and Revenue** A manufacturer of sunglasses currently sells one type for \$15 a pair. The price p and the demand x for these glasses are related by

$$x = f(p) = 9{,}500 - 250p$$

If the current price is increased, will revenue increase or decrease?

SOLUTION

$$E(p) = -\frac{pf'(p)}{f(p)}$$

$$= -\frac{p(-250)}{9{,}500 - 250p}$$

$$= \frac{p}{38 - p}$$

$$E(15) = \frac{15}{23} \approx 0.65$$

At the \$15 price level, demand is inelastic and a price increase will increase revenue.

Matched Problem 3 Repeat Example 3 if the current price for sunglasses is \$21 a pair.

In summary, if demand is inelastic, then a price increase will increase revenue. But if demand is elastic, then a price increase will decrease revenue.

Exercises 7.7

Skills Warm-up Exercises

W *In Problems 1–8, use the given equation, which expresses price p as a function of demand x, to find a function f(p) that expresses demand x as a function of price p. Give the domain of f(p). (If necessary, review Section 1.6.)*

1. $p = 42 - 0.4x, 0 \le x \le 105$

2. $p = 125 - 0.02x, 0 \le x \le 6{,}250$

3. $p = 50 - 0.5x^2, 0 \le x \le 10$

4. $p = 180 - 0.8x^2, 0 \le x \le 15$

5. $p = 25e^{-x/20}, 0 \le x \le 20$

6. $p = 45 - e^{x/4}, 0 \le x \le 12$

7. $p = 80 - 10 \ln x, 1 \le x \le 30$

8. $p = \ln(500 - 5x), 0 \le x \le 90$

A *In Problems 9–14, find the relative rate of change of f(x).*

9. $f(x) = 35x - 0.4x^2$

10. $f(x) = 60x - 1.2x^2$

11. $f(x) = 9 + 8e^{-x}$

12. $f(x) = 15 - 3e^{-0.5x}$

13. $f(x) = 12 + 5 \ln x$

14. $f(x) = 25 - 2 \ln x$

In Problems 15–24, find the relative rate of change of $f(x)$ at the indicated value of x. Round to three decimal places.

15. $f(x) = 45; x = 100$

16. $f(x) = 580; x = 300$

17. $f(x) = 420 - 5x; x = 25$

18. $f(x) = 500 - 6x; x = 40$

19. $f(x) = 420 - 5x; x = 55$

20. $f(x) = 500 - 6x; x = 75$

21. $f(x) = 4x^2 - \ln x; x = 2$

22. $f(x) = 5x^3 - 4 \ln x; x = 4$

23. $f(x) = 4x^2 - \ln x; x = 5$

24. $f(x) = 5x^3 - 4 \ln x; x = 10$

In Problems 25–32, find the percentage rate of change of $f(x)$ at the indicated value of x. Round to the nearest tenth of a percent.

25. $f(x) = 225 + 65x; x = 5$

26. $f(x) = 75 + 110x; x = 4$

27. $f(x) = 225 + 65x; x = 15$

28. $f(x) = 75 + 110x; x = 16$

29. $f(x) = 5{,}100 - 3x^2; x = 35$

30. $f(x) = 3{,}000 - 8x^2; x = 12$

31. $f(x) = 5{,}100 - 3x^2; x = 41$

32. $f(x) = 3{,}000 - 8x^2; x = 18$

In Problems 33–38, use the price–demand equation to find $E(p)$, the elasticity of demand.

33. $x = f(p) = 25{,}000 - 450p$

34. $x = f(p) = 10{,}000 - 190p$

35. $x = f(p) = 4{,}800 - 4p^2$

36. $x = f(p) = 8{,}400 - 7p^2$

37. $x = f(p) = 98 - 0.6e^p$

38. $x = f(p) = 160 - 35 \ln p$

B *In Problems 39–46, find the logarithmic derivative.*

39. $A(t) = 500e^{0.07t}$ **40.** $A(t) = 2{,}000e^{0.052t}$

41. $A(t) = 3{,}500e^{0.15t}$ **42.** $A(t) = 900e^{0.24t}$

43. $f(x) = xe^x$ **44.** $f(x) = x^3e^x$

45. $f(x) = \ln x$ **46.** $f(x) = x \ln x$

In Problems 47–50, use the price–demand equation to determine whether demand is elastic, is inelastic, or has unit elasticity at the indicated values of p.

47. $x = f(p) = 12{,}000 - 10p^2$

(A) $p = 10$ (B) $p = 20$ (C) $p = 30$

48. $x = f(p) = 1{,}875 - p^2$

(A) $p = 15$ (B) $p = 25$ (C) $p = 40$

49. $x = f(p) = 950 - 2p - 0.1p^2$

(A) $p = 30$ (B) $p = 50$ (C) $p = 70$

50. $x = f(p) = 875 - p - 0.05p^2$

(A) $p = 50$ (B) $p = 70$ (C) $p = 100$

In Problems 51–58, use the price–demand equation $p + 0.004x = 32, 0 \le p \le 32$.

51. Find the elasticity of demand when $p = \$12$. If the \$12 price is increased by 4%, what is the approximate percentage change in demand?

52. Find the elasticity of demand when $p = \$28$. If the \$28 price is decreased by 6%, what is the approximate percentage change in demand?

53. Find the elasticity of demand when $p = \$22$. If the \$22 price is decreased by 5%, what is the approximate percentage change in demand?

54. Find the elasticity of demand when $p = \$16$. If the \$16 price is increased by 9%, what is the approximate percentage change in demand?

55. Find all values of p for which demand is elastic.

56. Find all values of p for which demand is inelastic.

57. If $p = \$14$ and the price is increased, will revenue increase or decrease?

58. If $p = \$21$ and the price is decreased, will revenue increase or decrease?

In Problems 59–66, use the price–demand equation to find the values of p for which demand is elastic and the values for which demand is inelastic. Assume that price and demand are both positive.

59. $x = f(p) = 210 - 30p$ **60.** $x = f(p) = 480 - 8p$

61. $x = f(p) = 3{,}125 - 5p^2$ **62.** $x = f(p) = 2{,}400 - 6p^2$

63. $x = f(p) = \sqrt{144 - 2p}$ **64.** $x = f(p) = \sqrt{324 - 2p}$

65. $x = f(p) = \sqrt{2{,}500 - 2p^2}$

66. $x = f(p) = \sqrt{3{,}600 - 2p^2}$

In Problems 67–72, use the demand equation to find the revenue function. Sketch the graph of the revenue function, and indicate the regions of inelastic and elastic demand on the graph.

67. $x = f(p) = 20(10 - p)$ **68.** $x = f(p) = 10(16 - p)$

69. $x = f(p) = 40(p - 15)^2$ **70.** $x = f(p) = 10(p - 9)^2$

71. $x = f(p) = 30 - 10\sqrt{p}$ **72.** $x = f(p) = 30 - 5\sqrt{p}$

C *If a price–demand equation is solved for p, then price is expressed as $p = g(x)$ and x becomes the independent variable. In this case, it can be shown that the elasticity of demand is given by*

$$E(x) = -\frac{g(x)}{xg'(x)}$$

In Problems 73–76, use the price–demand equation to find $E(x)$ at the indicated value of x.

73. $p = g(x) = 50 - 0.1x, x = 200$

74. $p = g(x) = 70 - 0.2x, x = 250$

75. $p = g(x) = 50 - 2\sqrt{x}, x = 400$

76. $p = g(x) = 20 - \sqrt{x}, x = 100$

In Problems 77–80, use the price–demand equation to find the values of x for which demand is elastic and for which demand is inelastic.

77. $p = g(x) = 180 - 0.3x$ **78.** $p = g(x) = 640 - 0.4x$

79. $p = g(x) = 90 - 0.1x^2$ **80.** $p = g(x) = 540 - 0.2x^2$

81. Find $E(p)$ for $x = f(p) = Ap^{-k}$, where A and k are positive constants.

82. Find $E(p)$ for $x = f(p) = Ae^{-kp}$, where A and k are positive constants.

Applications

83. Rate of change of cost. A fast-food restaurant can produce a hamburger for \$2.50. If the restaurant's daily sales are increasing at the rate of 30 hamburgers per day, how fast is its daily cost for hamburgers increasing?

84. Rate of change of cost. The fast-food restaurant in Problem 83 can produce an order of fries for \$0.80. If the restaurant's daily sales are increasing at the rate of 45 orders of fries per day, how fast is its daily cost for fries increasing?

85. Revenue and elasticity. The price–demand equation for hamburgers at a fast-food restaurant is

$$x + 400p = 3{,}000$$

Currently, the price of a hamburger is \$3.00. If the price is increased by 10%, will revenue increase or decrease?

86. Revenue and elasticity. Refer to Problem 85. If the current price of a hamburger is \$4.00, will a 10% price increase cause revenue to increase or decrease?

87. Revenue and elasticity. The price–demand equation for an order of fries at a fast-food restaurant is

$$x + 1{,}000p = 2{,}500$$

Currently, the price of an order of fries is \$0.99. If the price is decreased by 10%, will revenue increase or decrease?

88. Revenue and elasticity. Refer to Problem 87. If the current price of an order of fries is \$1.49, will a 10% price decrease cause revenue to increase or decrease?

89. Maximum revenue. Refer to Problem 85. What price will maximize the revenue from selling hamburgers?

90. Maximum revenue. Refer to Problem 87. What price will maximize the revenue from selling fries?

91. Population growth. A model for Australia's population (Table 3) is

$$f(t) = 0.23t + 10.3$$

where t is years since 1960. Find and graph the percentage rate of change of $f(t)$ for $0 \le t \le 50$.

Table 3 Population

Year	Australia (millions)	Vietnam (millions)
1960	10	33
1970	13	43
1980	15	54
1990	17	68
2000	19	80
2010	22	88

92. Population growth. A model for Vietnam's population (Table 3) is

$$f(t) = 1.14t + 32.4$$

where t is years since 1960. Find and graph the percentage rate of change of $f(t)$ for $0 \le t \le 50$.

93. Crime. A model for the number of robberies of personal properties in England and Wales (Table 4) is

$$p(t) = 138.7 - 31.3 \ln t$$

where t is years since the financial year 1999/00. Find the relative rate of change for robberies of personal properties in the financial year 2019/20.

Table 4 Number of Robberies (thousands)

	Personal Property	Business Property
2002/03	99.21	11.07
2005/06	89.44	8.76
2008/09	70.78	9.35
2011/12	67.92	6.77
2014/15	44.48	5.75

Source: Home Office Crime and Policing Analysis

94. Crime. A model for the number of robberies of business properties in England and Wales (Table 4) is

$$b(t) = 14.63 - 3.06 \ln t$$

where t is years since the financial year 1999/00. Find the relative rate of change for robberies of business properties in the financial year 2019/20.

Answers to Matched Problems

1. $p(t) = \dfrac{270}{2.7t + 282}$

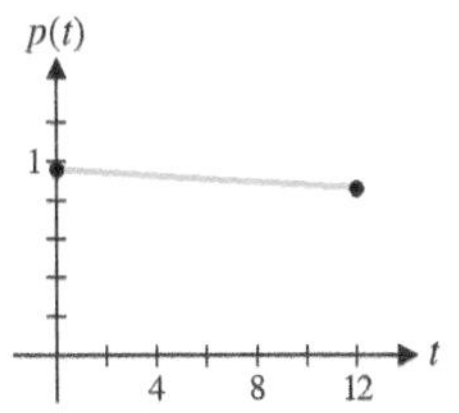

2. $E(p) = \dfrac{p}{40 - p}$

(A) $E(8) = 0.25$; demand is inelastic.

(B) $E(30) = 3$; demand is elastic.

(C) $E(20) = 1$; demand has unit elasticity.

3. $E(21) = \dfrac{21}{17} \approx 1.2$; demand is elastic. Increasing price will decrease revenue.

Chapter 7 Summary and Review

Important Terms, Symbols, and Concepts

7.1 The Constant e and Continuous Compound Interest

EXAMPLES

- The number e is defined as

$$\lim_{x\to\infty}\left(1+\frac{1}{n}\right)^n = \lim_{x\to 0}(1+s)^{1/s} = 2.718\,281\,828\,459\ldots$$

- If a principal P is invested at an annual rate r (expressed as a decimal) compounded continuously, then the amount A in the account at the end of t years is given by the **compound interest formula**

$$A = Pe^{rt}$$

Ex. 1, p. 383
Ex. 2, p. 383
Ex. 3, p. 384
Ex. 4, p. 384

7.2 Derivatives of Exponential and Logarithmic Functions

- For $b > 0, b \neq 1$,

$$\frac{d}{dx}e^x = e^x \qquad \frac{d}{dx}b^x = b^x \ln b$$

For $b > 0, b \neq 1$, and $x > 0$,

$$\frac{d}{dx}\ln x = \frac{1}{x} \qquad \frac{d}{dx}\log_b x = \frac{1}{\ln b}\left(\frac{1}{x}\right)$$

Ex. 1, p. 388
Ex. 2, p. 390
Ex. 3, p. 392
Ex. 4, p. 392
Ex. 5, p. 393
Ex. 6, p. 393

- The **change-of-base formulas** allow conversion from base e to any base b, $b > 0, b \neq 1$:

$$b^x = e^{x \ln b} \qquad \log_b x = \frac{\ln x}{\ln b}$$

7.3 Derivatives of Products and Quotients

- Product rule. If $y = f(x) = F(x)\,S(x)$, then $f'(x) = F(x)S'(x) + S(x)F'(x)$, provided that both $F'(x)$ and $S'(x)$ exist.

- Quotient rule. If $y = f(x) = \dfrac{T(x)}{B(x)}$, then $f'(x) = \dfrac{B(x)\,T'(x) - T(x)\,B'(x)}{[B(x)]^2}$ provided that both $T'(x)$ and $B'(x)$ exist.

Ex. 1, p. 396
Ex. 2, p. 397
Ex. 3, p. 398
Ex. 4, p. 399
Ex. 5, p. 400
Ex. 6, p. 401

7.4 The Chain Rule

- A function m is a **composite** of functions f and g if $m(x) = f[g(x)]$.
- The **chain rule** gives a formula for the derivative of the composite function $m(x) = E[I(x)]$:

$$m'(x) = E'[I(x)]I'(x)$$

Ex. 1, p. 405
Ex. 2, p. 405
Ex. 4, p. 410
Ex. 5, p. 411

- A special case of the chain rule is called the **general power rule:**

Ex. 3, p. 407

$$\frac{d}{dx}[f(x)]^n = n[f(x)]^{n-1}f'(x)$$

- Other special cases of the chain rule are the following **general derivative rules:**

Ex. 6, p. 411

$$\frac{d}{dx}\ln[f(x)] = \frac{1}{f(x)}f'(x)$$

$$\frac{d}{dx}e^{f(x)} = e^{f(x)}f'(x)$$

7.5 Implicit Differentiation

- If $y = y(x)$ is a function defined implicitly by the equation $f(x, y) = 0$, then we use **implicit differentiation** to find an equation in x, y, and y'.

Ex. 1, p. 417
Ex. 2, p. 418
Ex. 3, p. 419

7.6 Related Rates

- If x and y represent quantities that are changing with respect to time and are related by the equation $F(x, y) = 0$, then implicit differentiation produces an equation that relates x, y, dy/dt, and dx/dt. Problems of this type are called **related-rates problems**.
- Suggestions for solving related-rates problems are given on page 423.

Ex. 1, p. 422
Ex. 2, p. 423
Ex. 3, p. 425
Ex. 4, p. 425

7.7 Elasticity of Demand

- The **relative rate of change**, or the **logarithmic derivative**, of a function $f(x)$ is $f'(x)/f(x)$, and the **percentage rate of change** is $100 \times [f'(x)/f(x)]$. Ex. 1, p. 429
- If price and demand are related by $x = f(p)$, then the **elasticity of demand** is given by Ex. 2, p. 431

$$E(p) = -\frac{pf'(p)}{f(p)} = -\frac{\text{relative rate of change of demand}}{\text{relative rate of change of price}}$$

- **Demand is inelastic** if $0 < E(p) < 1$. (Demand is not sensitive to changes in price; a percentage change in price produces a smaller percentage change in demand.) **Demand is elastic** if $E(p) > 1$. (Demand is sensitive to changes in price; a percentage change in price produces a larger percentage change in demand.) **Demand has unit elasticity** if $E(p) = 1$. (A percentage change in price produces the same percentage change in demand.) Ex. 3, p. 433
- If $R(p) = pf(p)$ is the revenue function, then $R'(p)$ and $[1 - E(p)]$ always have the same sign. If demand is inelastic, then a price increase will increase revenue. If demand is elastic, then a price increase will decrease revenue.

Review Exercises

Work through all the problems in this chapter review, and check your answers in the back of the book. Answers to all review problems are there, along with section numbers in italics to indicate where each type of problem is discussed. Where weaknesses show up, review appropriate sections of the text.

1. Use a calculator to evaluate $A = 2{,}000e^{0.09t}$ to the nearest cent for $t = 5$, 10, and 20.

In Problems 2–5, find the indicated derivative.

2. $\frac{d}{dx}(\ln x^3 + 2e^{-x})$
3. $\frac{d}{dx}e^{2x-3}$
4. y' for $y = \ln(3x + 4)$
5. $f'(x)$ for $f(x) = \ln(e^{2x} + e^x + 4)$
6. Find y' for $y = y(x)$ defined implicitly by the equation $y^4 - \ln x + 2x + 8 = 0$, and evaluate at $(x, y) = (1, 1)$.
7. For $y = 4x^3 + 5$, where $x = x(t)$ and $y = y(t)$, find dy/dt if $dx/dt = 3$ when $x = 4$.

In Problems 8–12, use the price–demand equation $2p + 0.01x = 50, 0 \le p \le 25$.

8. Express the demand x as a function of the price p.
9. Find the elasticity of demand $E(p)$.
10. Find the elasticity of demand when $p = \$15$. If the \$15 price is increased by 5%, what is the approximate percentage change in demand?
11. Find all values of p for which demand is elastic.
12. If $p = \$9$ and the price is increased, will revenue increase or decrease?

B

13. Find the slope of the line tangent to $y = \ln x^5$ when $x = 1$.
14. Use a calculator and a table of values to investigate

$$\lim_{n\to\infty}\left(1 + \frac{2}{n}\right)^n$$

Do you think the limit exists? If so, what do you think it is?

Find the indicated derivatives in Problems 15–20.

15. $\frac{d}{dz}[(\ln z)^7 + \ln z^7]$
16. $\frac{d}{dx}(x^6 \ln x)$
17. $\frac{d}{dx}\frac{e^x}{x^6}$
18. y' for $y = \ln(2x^6 + e^x)$
19. $f'(x)$ for $f(x) = e^{x^3 - x^2}$
20. dy/dx for $y = e^{-2x}\ln 5x$
21. Find the equation of the line tangent to the graph of $y = f(x) = 1 + e^{-x}$ at $x = 0$. At $x = -1$.

22. Find y' for $y = y(x)$ defined implicitly by the equation $x^2 - 3xy + 4y^2 = 23$, and find the slope of the graph at $(-1, 2)$.

23. Find x' for $x(t)$ defined implicitly by $4t^3x^2 - x^2 + 100 = 0$, and evaluate at $(t, x) = (-1, -1)$.

24. Find y' for $y = y(x)$ defined implicitly by $x - y^2 = e^y$, and evaluate at $(1, 0)$.

25. Find y' for $y = y(x)$ defined implicitly by $\ln y = x^2 - y^2$, and evaluate at $(1, 1)$.

In Problems 26–28, find the logarithmic derivatives.

26. $A(t) = 400e^{0.049t}$

27. $f(p) = 100 - 3p$

28. $f(x) = 4 + x^2 + e^x$

29. A point is moving on the graph of $3y^2 + 40x^2 = 16$ so that its y coordinate is increasing by 2 units per second when $(x, y) = (2, 2)$. Find the rate of change of the x coordinate.

30. A 17-foot ladder is placed against a wall. If the foot of the ladder is pushed toward the wall at 0.5 foot per second, how fast is the top of the ladder rising when the foot is 8 feet from the wall?

31. Water is leaking onto a floor. The resulting circular pool has an area that is increasing at the rate of 30 square inches per minute. How fast is the circumference C of the pool increasing when the radius R is 10 inches?

B 32. Find the values of p for which demand is elastic and the values for which demand is inelastic if the price–demand equation is

$$x = f(p) = 20(p - 15)^2 \qquad 0 \le p \le 15$$

33. Graph the revenue function as a function of price p, and indicate the regions of inelastic and elastic demand if the price–demand equation is

$$x = f(p) = 5(20 - p) \qquad 0 \le p \le 20$$

34. Let $y = w^2$, $w = e^{2u}$, and $u = \ln x$.
   (A) Express y in terms of x.
   (B) Use the chain rule to find $\frac{dy}{dx}$.

Find the indicated derivatives in Problems 34–36.

35. y' for $y = 7^{2x^2+4}$

36. $\frac{d}{dx}\log_5(x^2 - x)$

37. $\frac{d}{dx}\sqrt{\ln(e^{2x} + 4x^2 + 3)}$

38. Find y' for $y = y(x)$ defined implicitly by the equation $e^{xy} = x^2 + y + 1$, and evaluate at $(0, 0)$.

39. A rock thrown into a still pond causes a circular ripple. The radius is increasing at a constant rate of 3 feet per second. Show that the area does not increase at a constant rate. When is the rate of increase of the area the smallest? The largest? Explain.

40. An ant moves along a hillock given by the equation $y = 4x^{1/2}$ (where the x and y axes are along the horizontal and vertical directions, respectively) in such a way that its y coordinate is increasing at a constant rate of 3 units per second. Does the horizontal distance (x) ever increase at a faster rate than the height (y)? Explain.

Applications

41. **Doubling time.** How long will it take money to double if it is invested at 5% interest compounded
   (A) Annually? (B) Continuously?

42. **Continuous compound interest.** If \$100 is invested at 10% interest compounded continuously, then the amount (in dollars) at the end of t years is given by

$$A = 100e^{0.1t}$$

Find $A'(t)$, $A'(1)$, and $A'(10)$.

43. **Continuous compound interest.** If \$12,000 is invested in an account that earns 3.95% compounded continuously, find the instantaneous rate of change of the amount when the account is worth \$25,000.

44. **Marginal analysis.** The price-demand equation for 32-inch LCD televisions at an appliance store is

$$P(x) = 3{,}000(0.998)^x$$

where x is the daily demand and P is the price in dollars. Find the marginal revenue equation.

45. **Demand equation.** Given the demand equation

$$x = (3{,}000 - 4p^5)^{1/2}$$

find the rate of change of p with respect to x by implicit differentiation (x is the number of items that can be sold at a price of \$$p$ per item).

46. **Rate of change of revenue.** A company is manufacturing kayaks and can sell all that it manufactures. The revenue (in dollars) is given by

$$R = 750x - \frac{x^2}{30}$$

where the production output in 1 day is x kayaks. If production is increasing at 3 kayaks per day when production is 40 kayaks per day, find the rate of increase in revenue.

47. **Revenue and elasticity.** The price–demand equation for home-delivered large pizzas is

$$p = 38.2 - 0.002x$$

where x is the number of pizzas delivered weekly. The current price of one pizza is \$21. In order to generate additional revenue from the sale of large pizzas, would you recommend a price increase or a price decrease? Explain.

48. **Average income.** A model for the average income per household before taxes are paid is

$$f(t) = 1{,}700t + 20{,}500$$

where t is years since 1980. Find the relative rate of change of household income in 2015.

49. Drug concentration. The drug concentration in the bloodstream t hours after injection is given approximately by

$$C(t) = 5e^{-0.3t}$$

where $C(t)$ is concentration in milligrams per milliliter. What is the rate of change of concentration after 1 hour? After 5 hours?

50. Wound healing. A circular wound on an arm is healing at the rate of 45 square millimeters per day (the area of the wound is decreasing at this rate). How fast is the radius R of the wound decreasing when $R = 15$ millimeters?

51. Learning. A new secretary types a 10-page document in T minutes after typing x similar documents, as given by

$$T = 4\left(2 + \frac{1}{\sqrt{x}}\right)$$

If, after typing 10 similar documents, the rate of improvement is $dx/dt = 2$ documents per hour, find the rate of improvement in time dT/dt in typing each document.

52. Learning. A new worker on the production line performs an operation in T minutes after x performances of the operation, as given by

$$T = 2\left(1 + \frac{1}{x^{3/2}}\right)$$

If, after performing the operation 9 times, the rate of improvement is $dx/dt = 3$ operations per hour, find the rate of improvement in time dT/dt in performing each operation.

8 Graphing and Optimization

Introduction

Since the derivative is associated with the slope of the graph of a function at a point, we might expect that it is also related to other properties of a graph. As we will see in this chapter, the derivative can tell us a great deal about the shape of the graph of a function. In particular, we will study methods for finding absolute maximum and minimum values. These methods have many applications. For example, a company that manufactures backpacks can use them to calculate the price per backpack that should be charged to realize the maximum profit (see Problems 23 and 24 in Section 8.6). A pharmacologist can use them to determine drug dosages that produce maximum sensitivity, and advertisers can use them to find the number of ads that will maximize the rate of change of sales.

8.1 First Derivative and Graphs

- Increasing and Decreasing Functions
- Local Extrema
- First-Derivative Test
- Economics Applications

Increasing and Decreasing Functions

Sign charts will be used throughout this chapter. You may find it helpful to review the terminology and techniques for constructing sign charts in Section 8.3.

Explore and Discuss 1

Figure 1 shows the graph of $y = f(x)$ and a sign chart for $f'(x)$, where

$$f(x) = x^3 - 3x$$

and

$$f'(x) = 3x^2 - 3 = 3(x + 1)(x - 1)$$

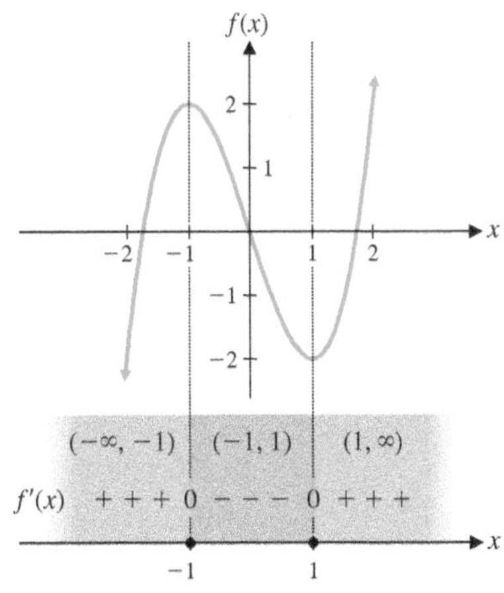

Figure 1

Discuss the relationship between the graph of f and the sign of $f'(x)$ over each interval on which $f'(x)$ has a constant sign. Also, describe the behavior of the graph of f at each partition number for f'.

As they are scanned from left to right, graphs of functions generally have rising and falling sections. If you scan the graph of $f(x) = x^3 - 3x$ in Figure 1 from left to right, you will observe the following:

- On the interval $(-\infty, -1)$, the graph of f is rising, $f(x)$ is increasing, and tangent lines have positive slope $[f'(x) > 0]$.
- On the interval $(-1, 1)$, the graph of f is falling, $f(x)$ is decreasing, and tangent lines have negative slope $[f'(x) < 0]$.
- On the interval $(1, \infty)$, the graph of f is rising, $f(x)$ is increasing, and tangent lines have positive slope $[f'(x) > 0]$.
- At $x = -1$ and $x = 1$, the slope of the graph is 0 $[f'(x) = 0]$.

If $f'(x) > 0$ (is positive) on the interval (a, b) (Fig. 2), then $f(x)$ increases ($\nearrow$) and the graph of f rises as we move from left to right over the interval. If $f'(x) < 0$ (is negative) on an interval (a, b), then $f(x)$ decreases ($\searrow$) and the graph of f falls as we move from left to right over the interval. We summarize these important results in Theorem 1.

Reminder

We say that the function f is **increasing** on an interval (a, b) if $f(x_2) > f(x_1)$ whenever $a < x_1 < x_2 < b$, and f is **decreasing** on (a, b) if $f(x_2) < f(x_1)$ whenever $a < x_1 < x_2 < b$.

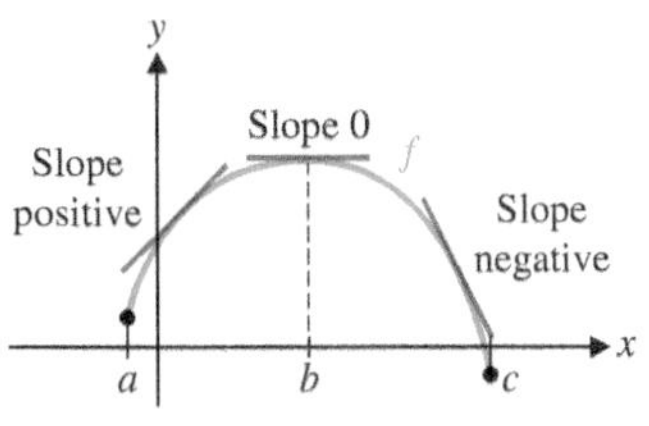

Figure 2

THEOREM 1 Increasing and Decreasing Functions

For the interval (a, b), if $f' > 0$, then f is increasing, and if $f' < 0$, then f is decreasing.

$f'(x)$	$f(x)$	Graph of f	Examples
+	Increases ↗	Rises ↗	
−	Decreases ↘	Falls ↘	

EXAMPLE 1 **Finding Intervals on Which a Function Is Increasing or Decreasing** Given the function $f(x) = 8x - x^2$,

(A) Which values of x correspond to horizontal tangent lines?

(B) For which values of x is $f(x)$ increasing? Decreasing?

(C) Sketch a graph of f. Add any horizontal tangent lines.

SOLUTION

(A) $f'(x) = 8 - 2x = 0$

$$x = 4$$

So a horizontal tangent line exists at $x = 4$ only.

(B) We will construct a sign chart for $f'(x)$ to determine which values of x make $f'(x) > 0$ and which values make $f'(x) < 0$. Recall from Section 8.3 that the partition numbers for a function are the numbers at which the function is 0 or discontinuous. When constructing a sign chart for $f'(x)$, we must locate all points where $f'(x) = 0$ or $f'(x)$ is discontinuous. From part (A), we know that $f'(x) = 8 - 2x = 0$ at $x = 4$. Since $f'(x) = 8 - 2x$ is a polynomial, it is continuous for all x. So 4 is the only partition number for f'. We construct a sign chart for the intervals $(-\infty, 4)$ and $(4, \infty)$, using test numbers 3 and 5:

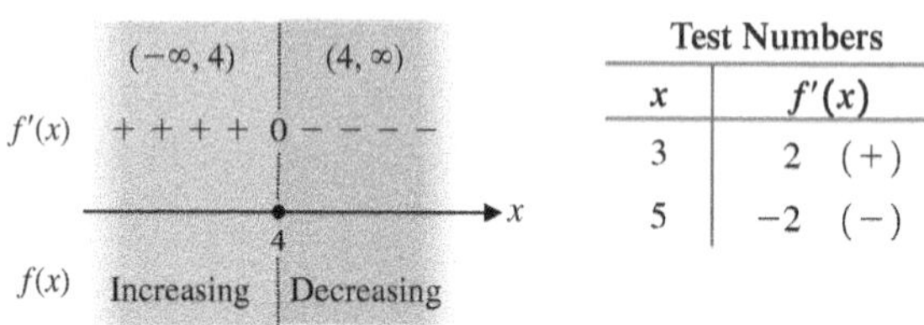

Test Numbers

x	$f'(x)$
3	2 (+)
5	−2 (−)

Therefore, $f(x)$ is increasing on $(-\infty, 4)$ and decreasing on $(4, \infty)$.

(C)

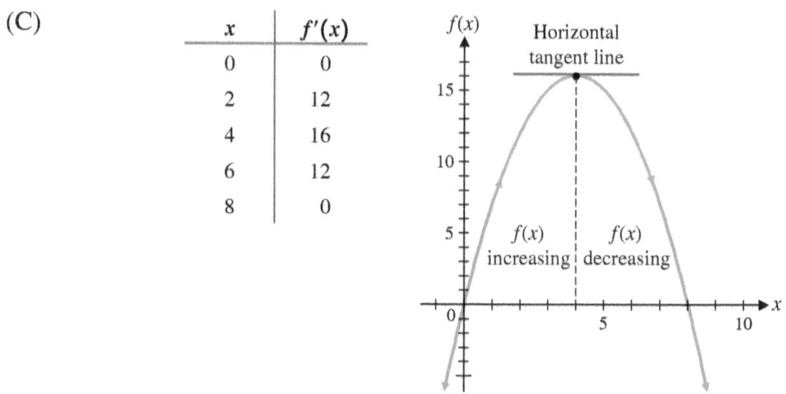

x	$f'(x)$
0	0
2	12
4	16
6	12
8	0

Matched Problem 1 Repeat Example 1 for $f(x) = x^2 - 6x + 10$.

As Example 1 illustrates, the construction of a sign chart will play an important role in using the derivative to analyze and sketch the graph of a function *f*. The partition numbers for f' are central to the construction of these sign charts and also to the analysis of the graph of $y = f(x)$. The partition numbers for f' that belong to the domain of *f* are called **critical numbers** of *f*. We are assuming that $f'(c)$ does not exist at any point of discontinuity of f'. There do exist functions *f* such that f' is discontinuous at $x = c$, yet $f'(c)$ exists. However, we do not consider such functions in this book.

DEFINITION Critical Numbers

A real number x in the domain of *f* such that $f'(x) = 0$ or $f'(x)$ does not exist is called a **critical number** of *f*.

CONCEPTUAL INSIGHT

The critical numbers of *f* belong to the domain of *f* and are partition numbers for f'. But f' may have partition numbers that do not belong to the domain of *f* so are not critical numbers of *f*. We need all partition numbers of f' when building a sign chart for f'.

If *f* is a polynomial, then both the partition numbers for f' and the critical numbers of *f* are the solutions of $f'(x) = 0$.

EXAMPLE 2 **Partition Numbers for f' and Critical Numbers of f** Find the critical numbers of *f*, the intervals on which *f* is increasing, and those on which *f* is decreasing, for $f(x) = 1 + x^3$.

SOLUTION Begin by finding the partition numbers for $f'(x)$ [since $f'(x) = 3x^2$ is continuous we just need to solve $f'(x) = 0$]

$$f'(x) = 3x^2 = 0 \quad \text{only if } x = 0$$

The partition number 0 for f' is in the domain of *f*, so 0 is the only critical number of *f*.

The sign chart for $f'(x) = 3x^2$ (partition number is 0) is

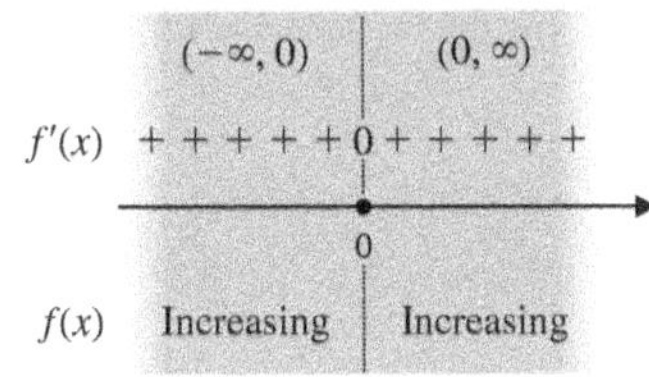

Test Numbers

x	$f'(x)$
−1	3 (+)
1	3 (+)

The sign chart indicates that $f(x)$ is increasing on $(-\infty, 0)$ and $(0, \infty)$. Since *f* is continuous at $x = 0$, it follows that $f(x)$ is increasing for all x. The graph of *f* is shown in Figure 3.

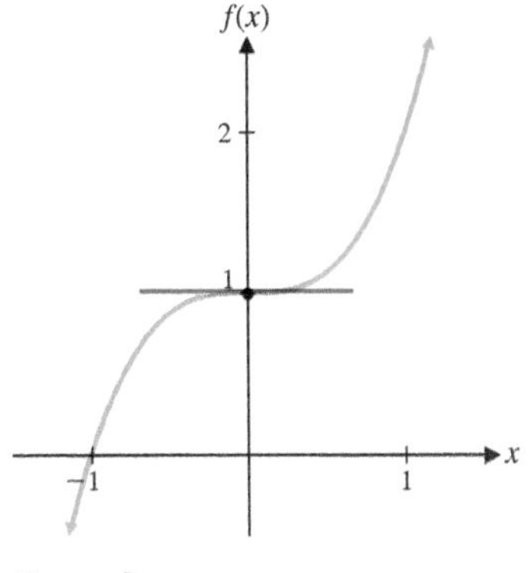

Figure 3

Matched Problem 2 Find the critical numbers of *f*, the intervals on which *f* is increasing, and those on which *f* is decreasing, for $f(x) = 1 - x^3$.

EXAMPLE 3 **Partition Numbers for f' and Critical Numbers of f** Find the critical numbers of *f*, the intervals on which *f* is increasing, and those on which *f* is decreasing, for $f(x) = (1 - x)^{1/3}$.

SOLUTION

$$f'(x) = -\frac{1}{3}(1 - x)^{-2/3} = \frac{-1}{3(1 - x)^{2/3}}$$

To find the partition numbers for f', we note that f' is continuous for all x, except for values of x for which the denominator is 0; that is, $f'(1)$ does not exist and f' is discontinuous at $x = 1$. Since the numerator of f' is the constant -1, $f'(x) \neq 0$ for any value of x. Thus, $x = 1$ is the only partition number for f'. Since 1 is in the domain of f, $x = 1$ is also the only critical number of f. When constructing the sign chart for f' we use the abbreviation ND to note the fact that $f'(x)$ is *not defined* at $x = 1$.

The sign chart for $f'(x) = -1/[3(1 - x)^{2/3}]$ (partition number for f' is 1) is as follows:

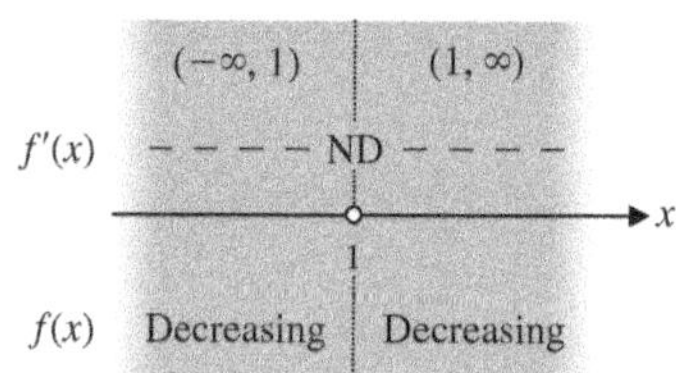

Test Numbers

x	$f'(x)$
0	$-\frac{1}{3}$ (−)
2	$-\frac{1}{3}$ (−)

Figure 4

The sign chart indicates that f is decreasing on $(-\infty, 1)$ and $(1, \infty)$. Since f is continuous at $x = 1$, it follows that $f(x)$ is decreasing for all x. **A continuous function can be decreasing (or increasing) on an interval containing values of x where $f'(x)$ does not exist.** The graph of f is shown in Figure 4. Notice that the undefined derivative at $x = 1$ results in a vertical tangent line at $x = 1$. **A vertical tangent will occur at $x = c$ if f is continuous at $x = c$ and if $|f'(x)|$ becomes larger and larger as x approaches c.**

Matched Problem 3 Find the critical numbers of f, the intervals on which f is increasing, and those on which f is decreasing, for $f(x) = (1 + x)^{1/3}$.

EXAMPLE 4 **Partition Numbers for f' and Critical Numbers of f** Find the critical numbers of f, the intervals on which f is increasing, and those on which f is decreasing, for $f(x) = \dfrac{1}{x - 2}$.

SOLUTION

$$f(x) = \frac{1}{x - 2} = (x - 2)^{-1}$$

$$f'(x) = -(x - 2)^{-2} = \frac{-1}{(x - 2)^2}$$

To find the partition numbers for f', note that $f'(x) \neq 0$ for any x and f' is not defined at $x = 2$. Thus, $x = 2$ is the only partition number for f'. However, $x = 2$ is *not* in the domain of f. Consequently, $x = 2$ is *not* a critical number of f. The function f has no critical numbers.

The sign chart for $f'(x) = -1/(x-2)^2$ (partition number for f' is 2) is as follows:

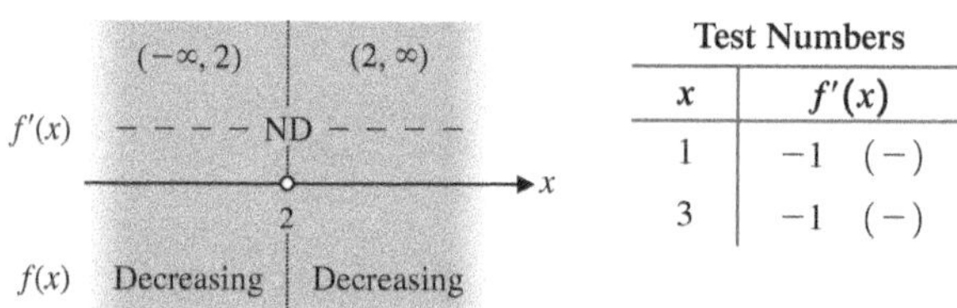

Test Numbers

x	$f'(x)$
1	−1 (−)
3	−1 (−)

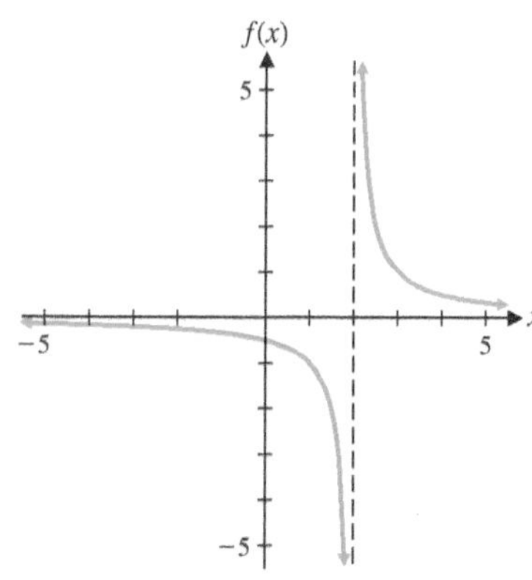

Figure 5

Therefore, f is decreasing on $(-\infty, 2)$ and $(2, \infty)$. The graph of f is shown in Figure 5.

Matched Problem 4 Find the critical numbers of f, the intervals on which f is increasing, and those on which f is decreasing, for $f(x) = \dfrac{1}{x}$.

EXAMPLE 5 **Partition Numbers for f' and Critical Numbers of f** Find the critical numbers of f, the intervals on which f is increasing, and those on which f is decreasing, for $f(x) = 8 \ln x - x^2$.

SOLUTION The natural logarithm function $\ln x$ is defined on $(0, \infty)$, or $x > 0$, so $f(x)$ is defined only for $x > 0$.

$$f(x) = 8 \ln x - x^2, x > 0$$

$$f'(x) = \frac{8}{x} - 2x \qquad \text{Find a common denominator.}$$

$$= \frac{8}{x} - \frac{2x^2}{x} \qquad \text{Subtract numerators.}$$

$$= \frac{8 - 2x^2}{x} \qquad \text{Factor numerator.}$$

$$= \frac{2(2 - x)(2 + x)}{x}, \quad x > 0$$

The only partition number for f' that is positive, and therefore belongs to the domain of f, is 2. So 2 is the only critical number of f.

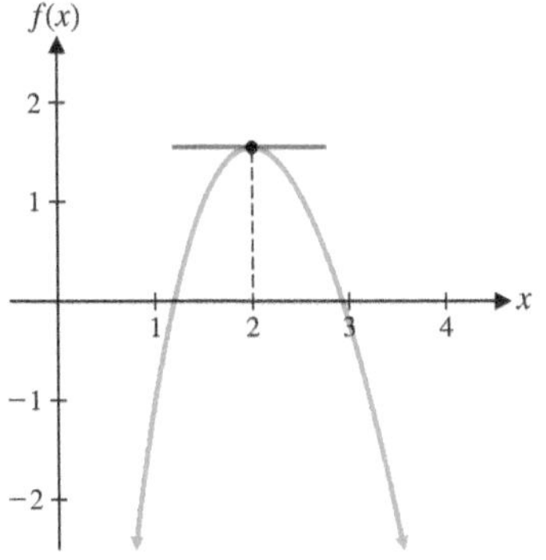

Figure 6

The sign chart for $f'(x) = \dfrac{2(2 - x)(2 + x)}{x}$, $x > 0$ (partition number for f' is 2), is as follows:

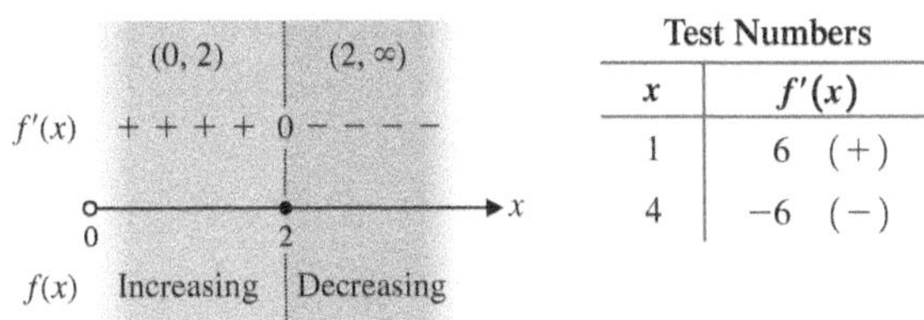

Test Numbers

x	$f'(x)$
1	6 (+)
4	−6 (−)

Therefore, f is increasing on $(0, 2)$ and decreasing on $(2, \infty)$. The graph of f is shown in Figure 6.

Matched Problem 5 Find the critical numbers of f, the intervals on which f is increasing, and those on which f is decreasing, for $f(x) = 5 \ln x - x$.

CONCEPTUAL INSIGHT

Examples 4 and 5 illustrate two important ideas:

1. Do not assume that all partition numbers for the derivative f' are critical numbers of the function f. To be a critical number of f, a partition number for f' must also be in the domain of f.
2. The intervals on which a function f is increasing or decreasing must always be expressed in terms of open intervals that are subsets of the domain of f.

Local Extrema

When the graph of a continuous function changes from rising to falling, a high point, or *local maximum,* occurs. When the graph changes from falling to rising, a low point, or *local minimum,* occurs. In Figure 7, high points occur at c_3 and c_6, and low points occur at c_2 and c_4. In general, we call $f(c)$ a **local maximum** if there exists an interval (m, n) containing c such that

$$f(x) \le f(c) \qquad \text{for all } x \text{ in } (m, n)$$

Note that this inequality need hold only for numbers x near c, which is why we use the term *local.* So the y coordinate of the high point $(c_3, f(c_3))$ in Figure 7 is a local maximum, as is the y coordinate of $(c_6, f(c_6))$.

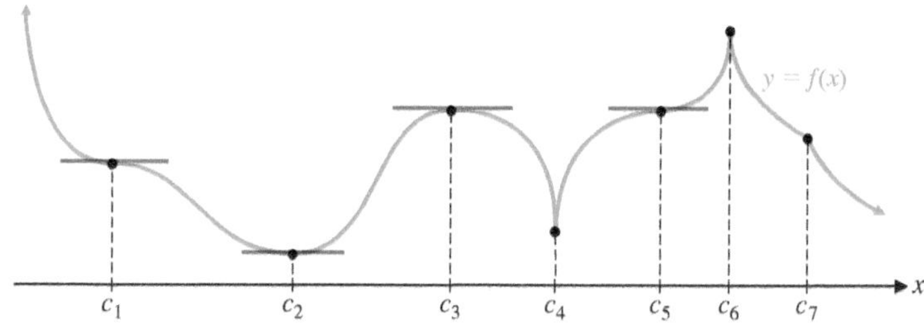

Figure 7

The value $f(c)$ is called a **local minimum** if there exists an interval (m, n) containing c such that

$$f(x) \geq f(c) \qquad \text{for all } x \text{ in } (m, n)$$

The value $f(c)$ is called a **local extremum** if it is either a local maximum or a local minimum. A point on a graph where a local extremum occurs is also called a **turning point**. In Figure 7 we see that local maxima occur at c_3 and c_6, local minima occur at c_2 and c_4, and all four values produce local extrema. The points c_1, c_5, and c_7 are critical numbers but do not produce local extrema. Also, the local maximum $f(c_3)$ is not the largest y coordinate of points on the graph in Figure 7. Later in this chapter, we consider the problem of finding *absolute extrema,* the y coordinates of the highest and lowest points on a graph. For now, we are concerned only with locating *local* extrema.

EXAMPLE 6 **Analyzing a Graph** Use the graph of f in Figure 8 to find the intervals on which f is increasing, those on which f is decreasing, any local maxima, and any local minima.

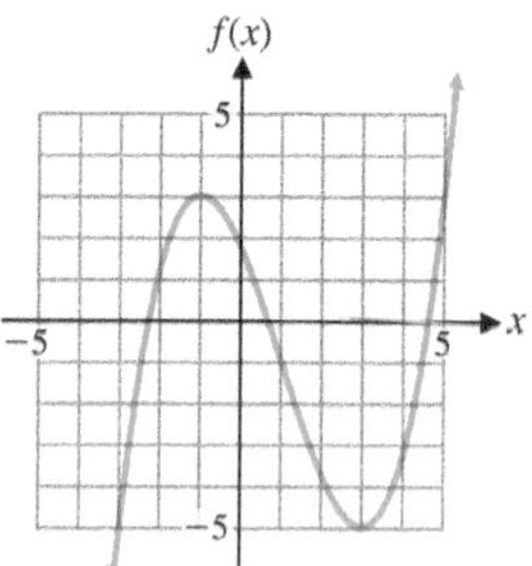

Figure 8

SOLUTION The function f is increasing (the graph is rising) on $(-\infty, -1)$ and on $(3, \infty)$ and is decreasing (the graph is falling) on $(-1, 3)$. Because the graph changes from rising to falling at $x = -1$, $f(-1) = 3$ is a local maximum. Because the graph changes from falling to rising at $x = 3$, $f(3) = -5$ is a local minimum.

Matched Problem 6 Use the graph of g in Figure 9 to find the intervals on which g is increasing, those on which g is decreasing, any local maxima, and any local minima.

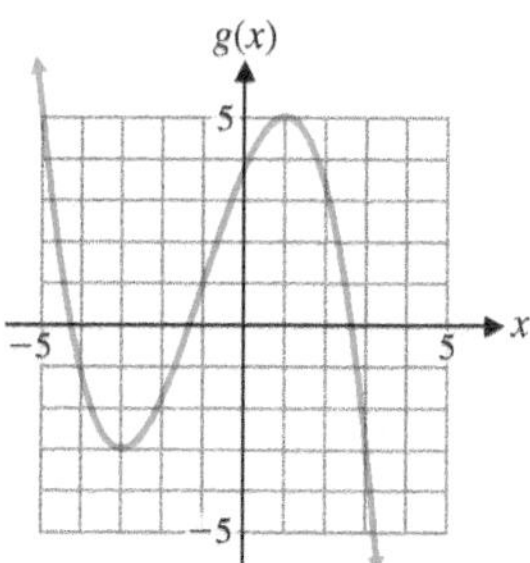

Figure 9

How can we locate local maxima and minima if we are given the equation of a function and not its graph? The key is to examine the critical numbers of the function. The local extrema of the function f in Figure 7 occur either at points where the derivative is 0 $(c_2$ and $c_3)$ or at points where the derivative does not exist $(c_4$ and $c_6)$. In other words, local extrema occur only at critical numbers of f.

Explore and Discuss 1

Suppose that f is a function such that $f'(c) = 2$. Explain why f does not have a local extremum at $x = c$. What if $f'(c) = -1$?

THEOREM 2 Local Extrema and Critical Numbers

If $f(c)$ is a local extremum of the function f, then c is a critical number of f.

Theorem 2 states that a local extremum can occur only at a critical number, but it does not imply that every critical number produces a local extremum. In Figure 7, c_1 and c_5 are critical numbers (the slope is 0), but the function does not have a local maximum or local minimum at either of these numbers.

Our strategy for finding local extrema is now clear: We find all critical numbers of f and test each one to see if it produces a local maximum, a local minimum, or neither.

First-Derivative Test

If $f'(x)$ exists on both sides of a critical number c, the sign of $f'(x)$ can be used to determine whether the point $(c, f(c))$ is a local maximum, a local minimum, or neither. The various possibilities are summarized in the following box and are illustrated in Figure 10:

PROCEDURE First-Derivative Test for Local Extrema

Let c be a critical number of f $[f(c)$ is defined and either $f'(c) = 0$ or $f'(c)$ is not defined$]$. Construct a sign chart for $f'(x)$ close to and on either side of c.

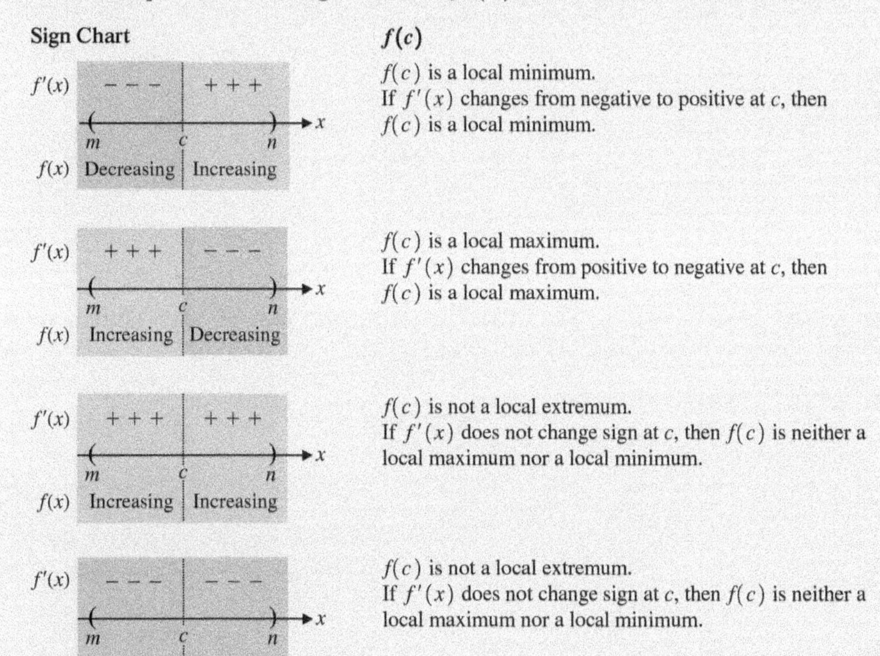

Sign Chart
f(c)
f'(x) − − − + + +
m c n x
f(x) Decreasing Increasing
f(c) is a local minimum.
If f'(x) changes from negative to positive at c, then f(c) is a local minimum.
f'(x) + + + − − −
m c n x
f(x) Increasing Decreasing
f(c) is a local maximum.
If f'(x) changes from positive to negative at c, then f(c) is a local maximum.
f'(x) + + + + + +
m c n x
f(x) Increasing Increasing
f(c) is not a local extremum.
If f'(x) does not change sign at c, then f(c) is neither a local maximum nor a local minimum.
f'(x) − − − − − −
m c n x
f(x) Decreasing Decreasing
f(c) is not a local extremum.
If f'(x) does not change sign at c, then f(c) is neither a local maximum nor a local minimum.

$f'(c) = 0$: Horizontal tangent

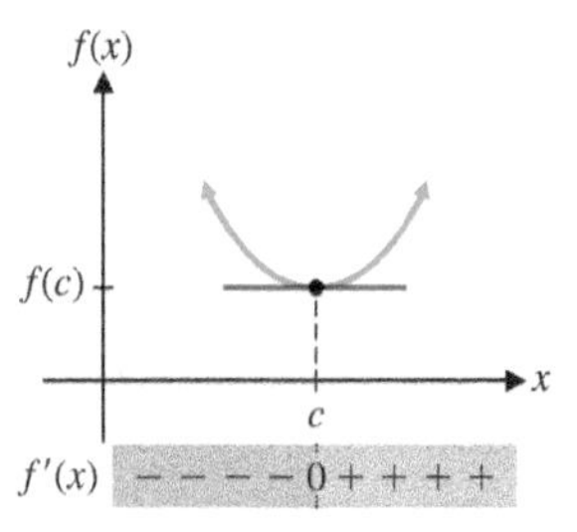

(A) $f(c)$ is a local minimum

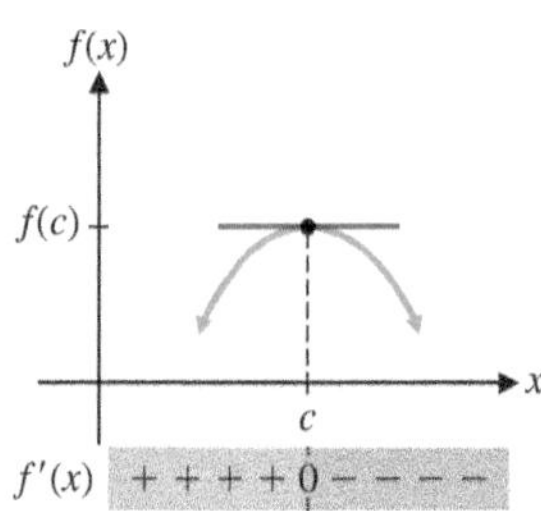

(B) $f(c)$ is a local maximum

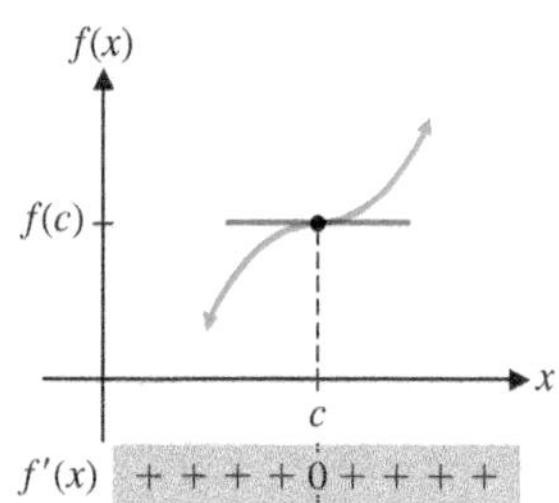

(C) $f(c)$ is neither a local maximum nor a local minimum

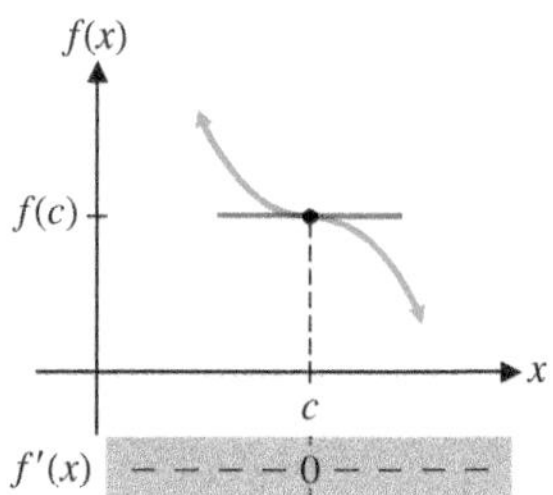

(D) $f(c)$ is neither a local maximum nor a local minimum

$f'(c)$ is not defined but $f(c)$ is defined

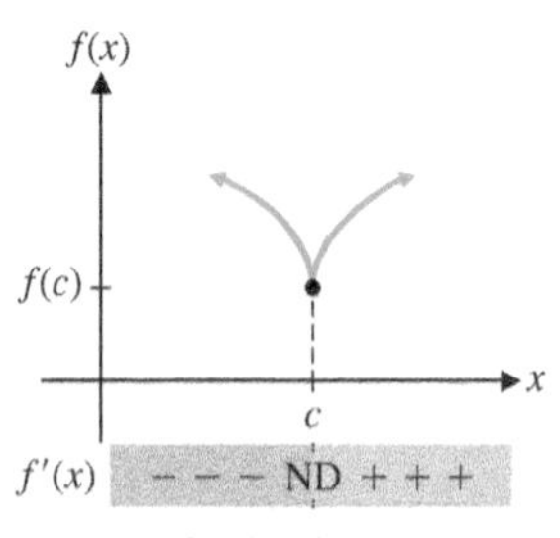

(E) $f(c)$ is a local minimum

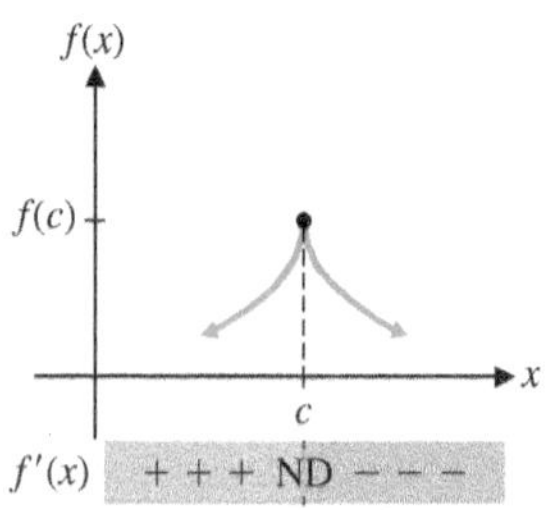

(F) $f(c)$ is a local maximum

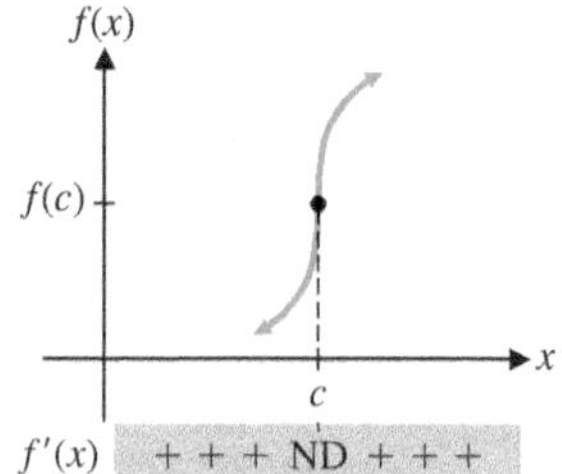

(G) $f(c)$ is neither a local maximum nor a local minimum

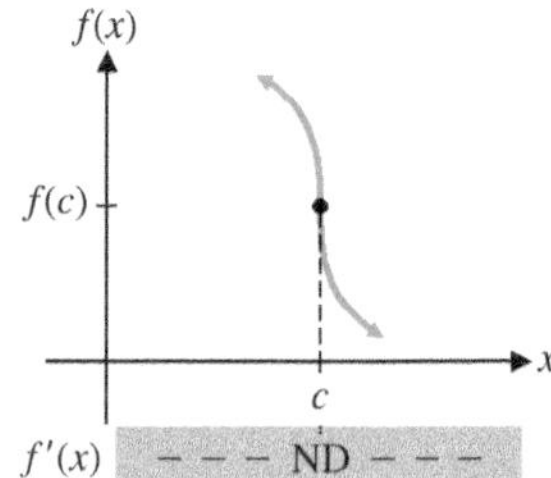

(H) $f(c)$ is neither a local maximum nor a local minimum

Figure 10 Local extrema

EXAMPLE 7 **Locating Local Extrema** Given $f(x) = x^3 - 6x^2 + 9x + 1$,

(A) Find the critical numbers of f.

(B) Find the local maxima and local minima of f.

(C) Sketch the graph of f.

SOLUTION

(A) Find all numbers x in the domain of f where $f'(x) = 0$ or $f'(x)$ does not exist.

$$
\begin{aligned}
f'(x) &= 3x^2 - 12x + 9 = 0 \\
3(x^2 - 4x + 3) &= 0 \\
3(x - 1)(x - 3) &= 0 \\
x = 1 \quad &\text{or} \quad x = 3
\end{aligned}
$$

$f'(x)$ exists for all x; the critical numbers of f are $x = 1$ and $x = 3$.

(B) The easiest way to apply the first-derivative test for local maxima and minima is to construct a sign chart for $f'(x)$ for all x. Partition numbers for $f'(x)$ are $x = 1$ and $x = 3$ (which also happen to be critical numbers of f).

Sign chart for $f'(x) = 3(x - 1)(x - 3)$:

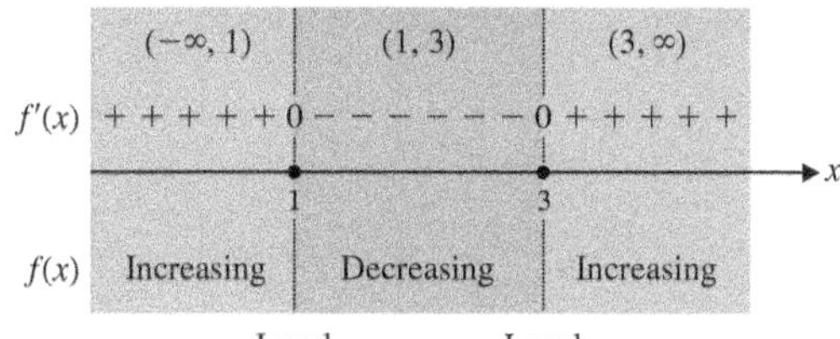

Test Numbers

x	$f'(x)$
0	9 (+)
2	−3 (−)
4	9 (+)

The sign chart indicates that f increases on $(-\infty, 1)$, has a local maximum at $x = 1$, decreases on $(1, 3)$, has a local minimum at $x = 3$, and increases on $(3, \infty)$. These facts are summarized in the following table:

x	$f'(x)$	$f(x)$	Graph of f
$(-\infty, 1)$	+	Increasing	Rising
$x = 1$	0	Local maximum	Horizontal tangent
$(1, 3)$	–	Decreasing	Falling
$x = 3$	0	Local minimum	Horizontal tangent
$(3, \infty)$	+	Increasing	Rising

The local maximum is $f(1) = 5$; the local minimum is $f(3) = 1$.

(C) We sketch a graph of f, using the information from part (B) and point-by-point plotting.

x	$f(x)$
0	1
1	5
2	3
3	1
4	5

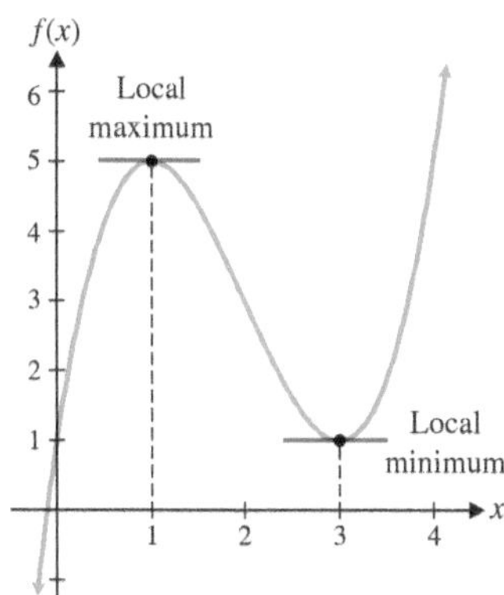

Matched Problem 7 Given $f(x) = x^3 - 9x^2 + 24x - 10$,

(A) Find the critical numbers of f.

(B) Find the local maxima and local minima of f.

(C) Sketch a graph of f.

How can you tell if you have found all the local extrema of a function? In general, this can be a difficult question to answer. However, in the case of a polynomial function, there is an easily determined upper limit on the number of local extrema. Since the local extrema are the x intercepts of the derivative, this limit is a consequence of the number of x intercepts of a polynomial. The relevant information is summarized in the following theorem, which is stated without proof:

THEOREM 3 Intercepts and Local Extrema of Polynomial Functions

If $f(x) = a_n x^n + a_{n-1}x^{n-1} + \cdots + a_1 x + a_0$, $a_n \neq 0$, is a polynomial function of degree $n \geq 1$, then f has at most n x intercepts and at most $n - 1$ local extrema.

Theorem 3 does not guarantee that every nth-degree polynomial has exactly $n - 1$ local extrema; it says only that there can never be more than $n - 1$ local extrema. For example, the third-degree polynomial in Example 7 has two local extrema, while the third-degree polynomial in Example 2 does not have any.

Economics Applications

In addition to providing information for hand-sketching graphs, the derivative is an important tool for analyzing graphs and discussing the interplay between a function and its rate of change. The next two examples illustrate this process in the context of economics.

EXAMPLE 8 **Agricultural Exports and Imports** Over the past few decades, the United States has exported more agricultural products than it has imported, maintaining a positive balance of trade in this area. However, the trade balance fluctuated considerably during that period. The graph in Figure 11 approximates the rate of change of the balance of trade over a 15-year period, where $B(t)$ is the balance of trade (in billions of dollars) and t is time (in years).

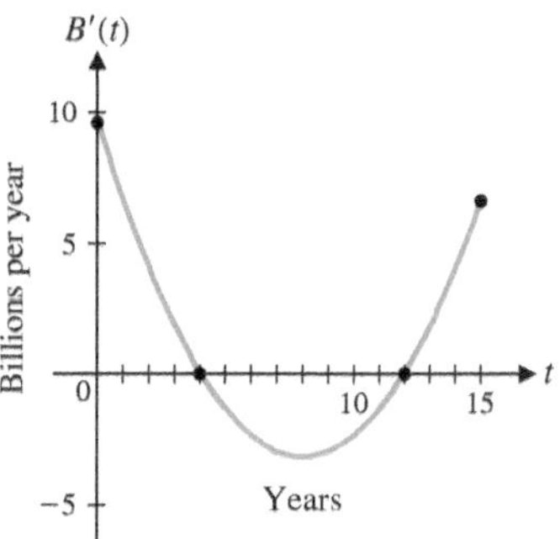

Figure 11 Rate of change of the balance of trade

(A) Write a brief description of the graph of $y = B(t)$, including a discussion of any local extrema.

(B) Sketch a possible graph of $y = B(t)$.

SOLUTION

(A) The graph of the derivative $y = B'(t)$ contains the same essential information as a sign chart. That is, we see that $B'(t)$ is positive on $(0, 4)$, 0 at $t = 4$, negative on $(4, 12)$, 0 at $t = 12$, and positive on $(12, 15)$. The trade balance increases for the first 4 years to a local maximum, decreases for the next 8 years to a local minimum, and then increases for the final 3 years.

(B) Without additional information concerning the actual values of $y = B(t)$, we cannot produce an accurate graph. However, we can sketch a possible graph that illustrates the important features, as shown in Figure 12. The absence of a scale on the vertical axis is a consequence of the lack of information about the values of $B(t)$.

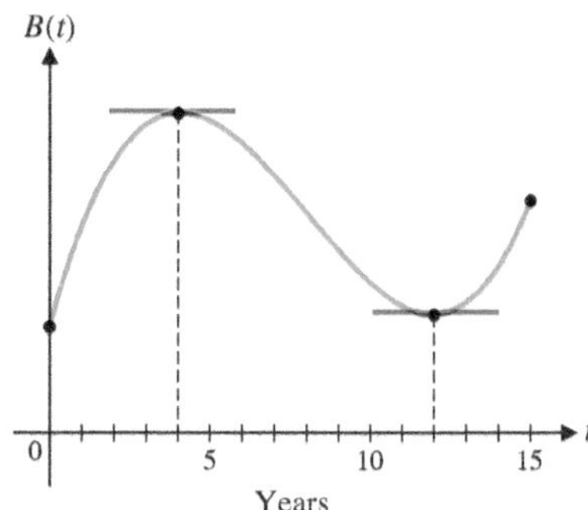

Figure 12 Balance of trade

Matched Problem 8 The graph in Figure 13 approximates the rate of change of the U.S. share of the total world production of motor vehicles over a 20-year period, where $S(t)$ is the U.S. share (as a percentage) and t is time (in years).

(A) Write a brief description of the graph of $y = S(t)$, including a discussion of any local extrema.

(B) Sketch a possible graph of $y = S(t)$.

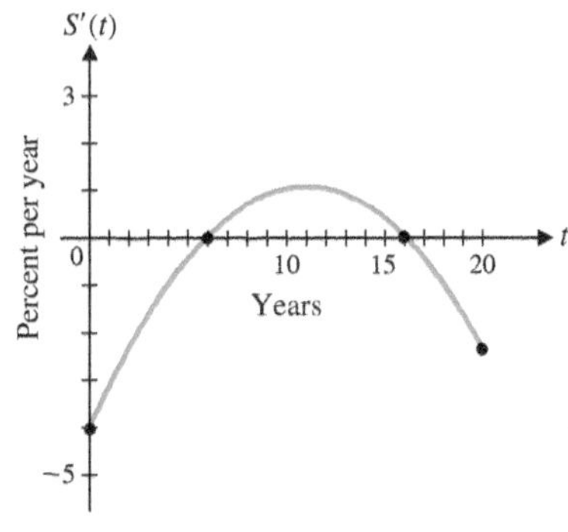

Figure 13

EXAMPLE 9 **Revenue Analysis** The graph of the total revenue $R(x)$ (in dollars) from the sale of x bookcases is shown in Figure 14.

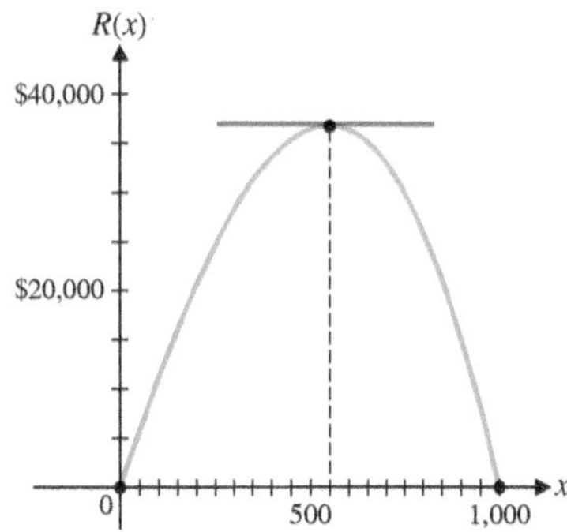

Figure 14 Revenue

(A) Write a brief description of the graph of the marginal revenue function $y = R'(x)$, including a discussion of any x intercepts.

(B) Sketch a possible graph of $y = R'(x)$.

SOLUTION

(A) The graph of $y = R(x)$ indicates that $R(x)$ increases on $(0, 550)$, has a local maximum at $x = 550$, and decreases on $(550, 1{,}000)$. Consequently, the marginal revenue function $R'(x)$ must be positive on $(0, 550)$, 0 at $x = 550$, and negative on $(550, 1{,}000)$.

(B) A possible graph of $y = R'(x)$ illustrating the information summarized in part (A) is shown in Figure 15.

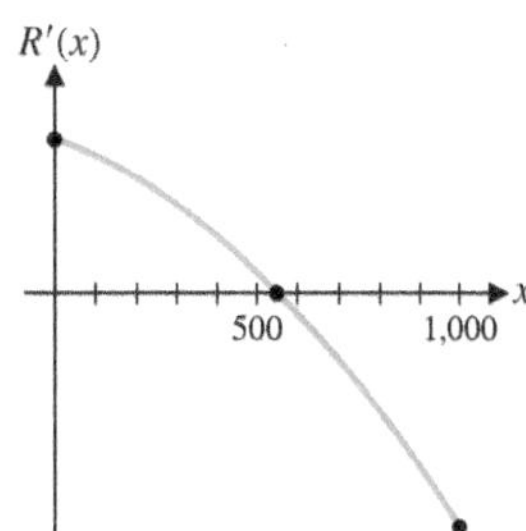

Figure 15 Marginal revenue

Matched Problem 9 The graph of the total revenue $R(x)$ (in dollars) from the sale of x desks is shown in Figure 16.

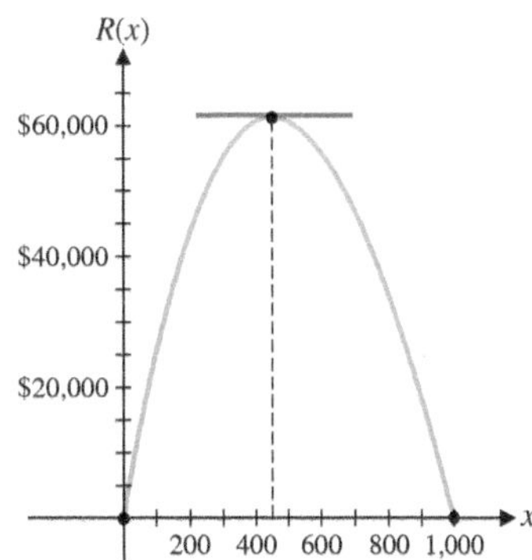

Figure 16

(A) Write a brief description of the graph of the marginal revenue function $y = R'(x)$, including a discussion of any x intercepts.

(B) Sketch a possible graph of $y = R'(x)$.

Comparing Examples 8 and 9, we see that we were able to obtain more information about the function from the graph of its derivative (Example 8) than we were when the process was reversed (Example 9). In the next section, we introduce some ideas that will help us obtain additional information about the derivative from the graph of the function.

Exercises 8.1

Skills Warm-up Exercises

W *In Problems 1–8, inspect the graph of the function to determine whether it is increasing or decreasing on the given interval. (If necessary, review Section 1.2.)*

1. $g(x) = |x|$ on $(-\infty, 0)$
2. $m(x) = x^3$ on $(0, \infty)$
3. $f(x) = x$ on $(-\infty, \infty)$
4. $k(x) = -x^2$ on $(0, \infty)$
5. $p(x) = \sqrt[3]{x}$ on $(-\infty, 0)$
6. $h(x) = x^3$ on $(-\infty, 0)$
7. $r(x) = 4 - \sqrt{x}$ on $(0, \infty)$
8. $g(x) = |x|$ on $(0, \infty)$

A *Problems 9–16 refer to the following graph of $y = f(x)$:*

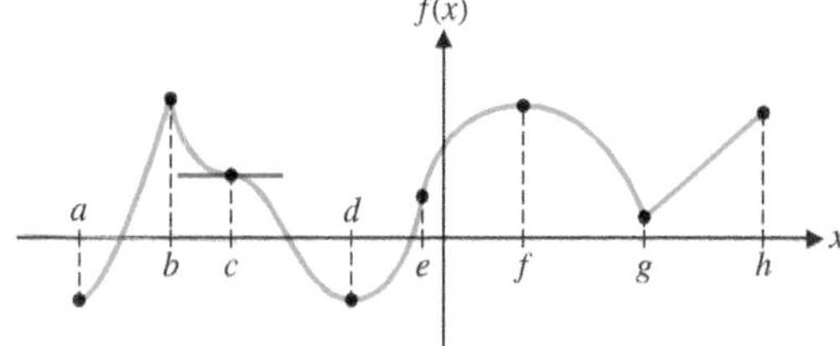

Figure for 9–16

9. Identify the intervals on which $f(x)$ is increasing.
10. Identify the intervals on which $f(x)$ is decreasing.
11. Identify the intervals on which $f'(x) < 0$.
12. Identify the intervals on which $f'(x) > 0$.
13. Identify the x coordinates of the points where $f'(x) = 0$.
14. Identify the x coordinates of the points where $f'(x)$ does not exist.
15. Identify the x coordinates of the points where $f(x)$ has a local maximum.
16. Identify the x coordinates of the points where $f(x)$ has a local minimum.

In Problems 17 and 18, $f(x)$ is continuous on $(-\infty, \infty)$ and has critical numbers at $x = a, b, c$, and d. Use the sign chart for $f'(x)$ to determine whether f has a local maximum, a local minimum, or neither at each critical number.

17.

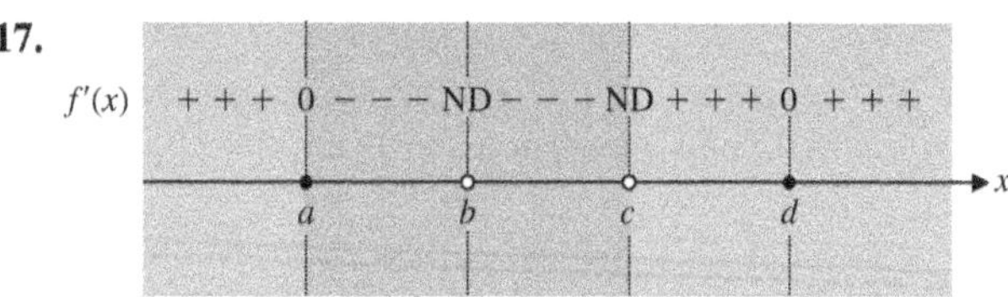

18.

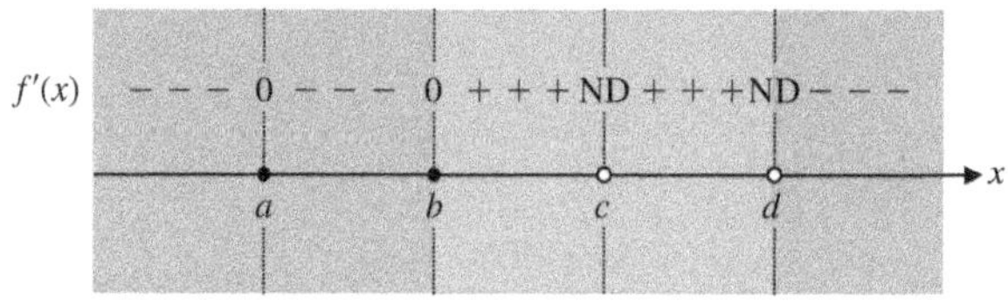

In Problems 19–26, give the local extrema of f and match the graph of f with one of the sign charts a–h in the figure on page 453.

19.

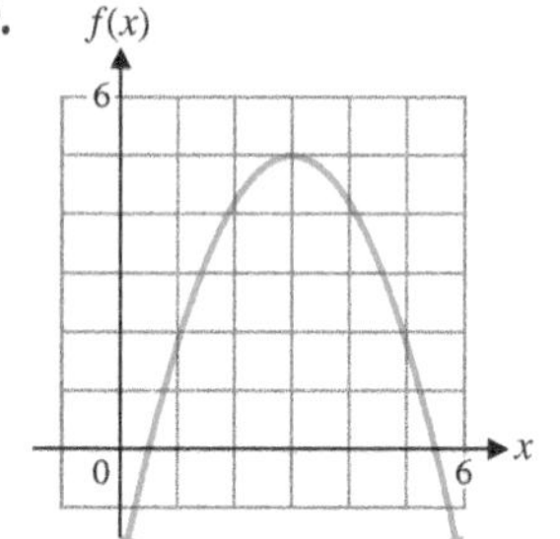

20.

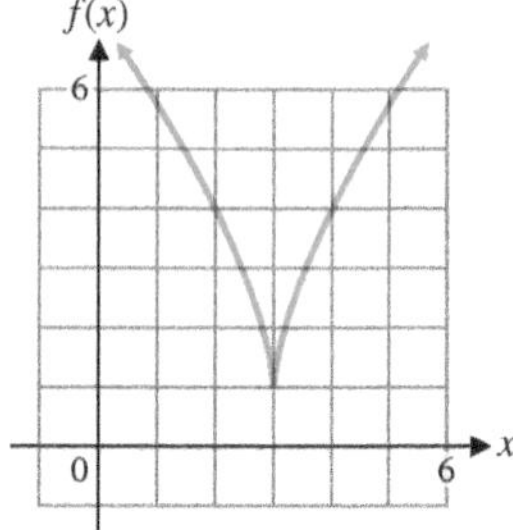

21.

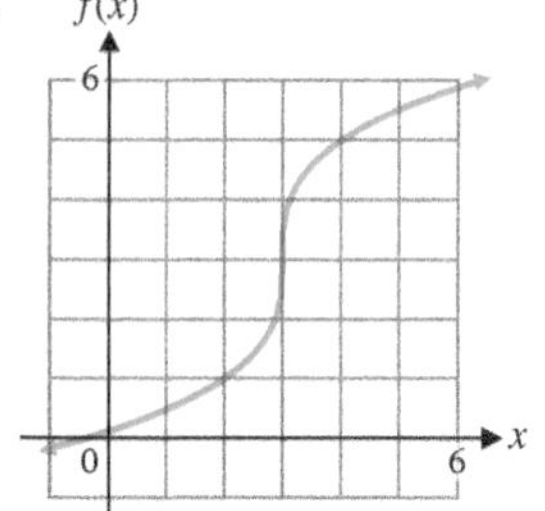

22.

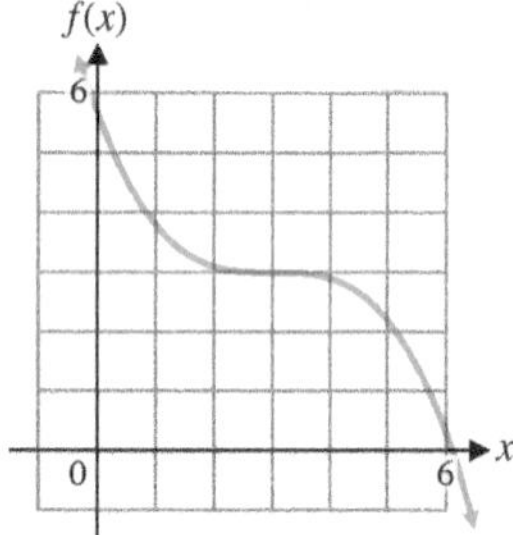

23.

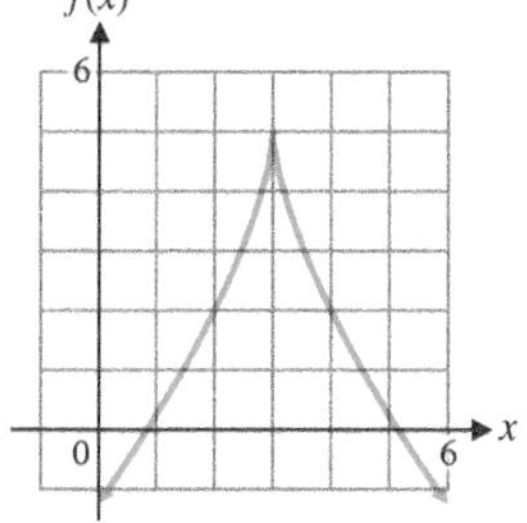

24.

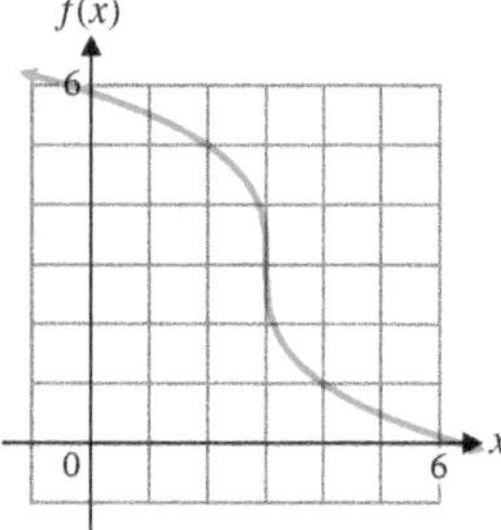

25.

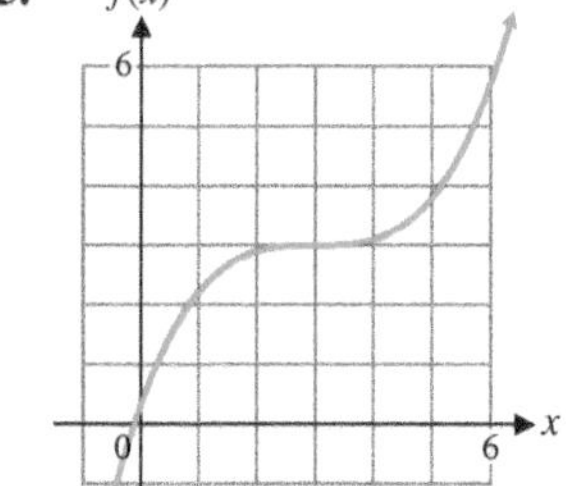

26.

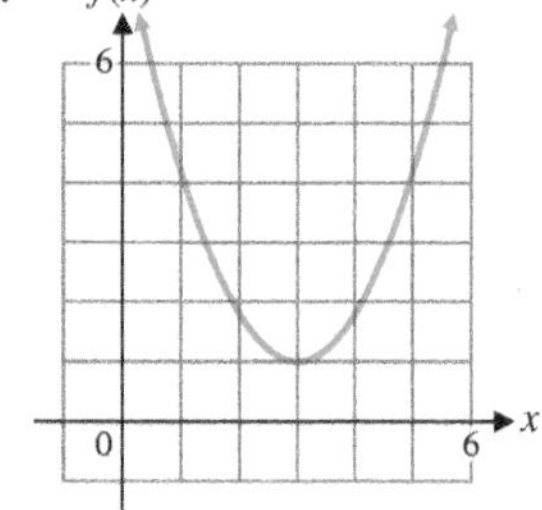

(a)

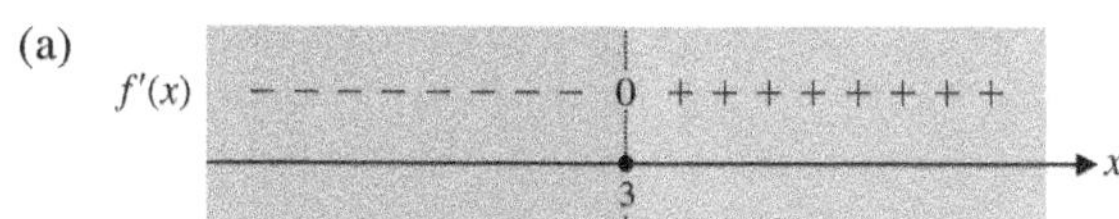

(b)

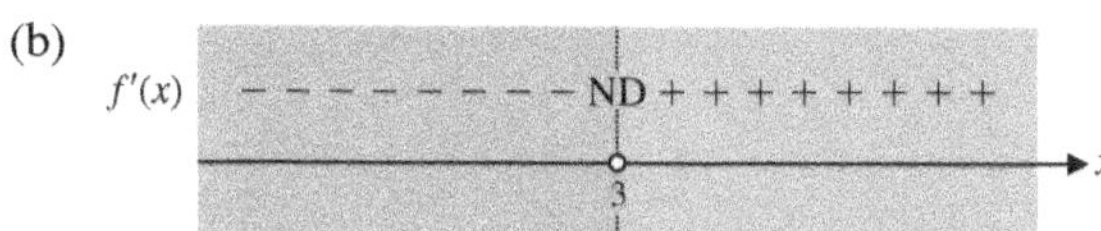

(c)

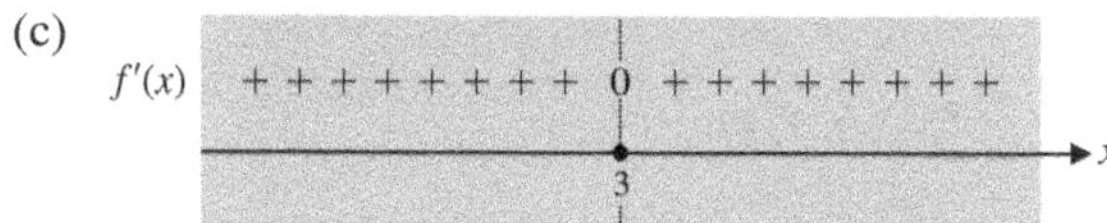

(d)

f′(x) + + + + + + + + ND + + + + + + + +

x

3

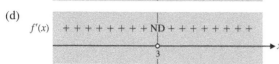

(e)

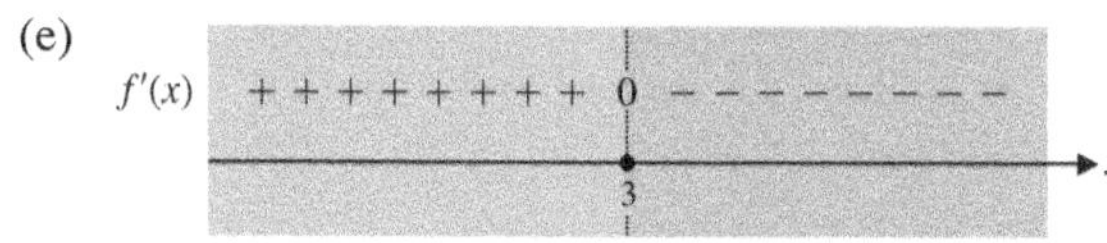

(f)

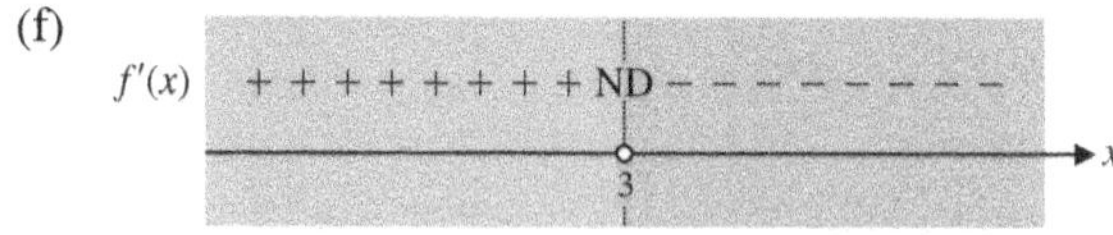

(g)

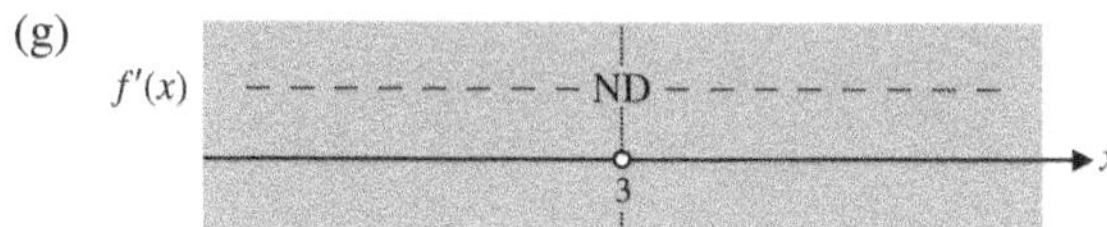

(h)

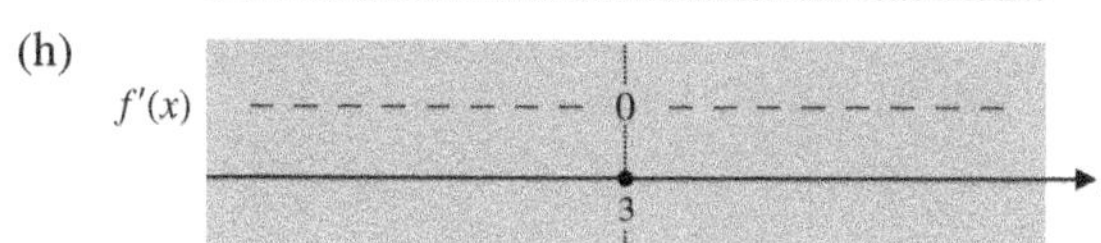

B *In Problems 27–32, find (A) $f'(x)$, (B) the partition numbers for f', and (C) the critical numbers of f.*

27. $f(x) = x^3 - 3x + 5$

28. $f(x) = x^3 - 48x + 96$

29. $f(x) = \dfrac{4}{x + 3}$

30. $f(x) = \dfrac{8}{x - 9}$

31. $f(x) = x^{1/4}$

32. $f(x) = x^{3/4}$

In Problems 33–48, find the intervals on which $f(x)$ is increasing, the intervals on which $f(x)$ is decreasing, and the local extrema.

33. $f(x) = 3x^2 - 12x + 2$

34. $f(x) = 5x^2 - 10x - 3$

35. $f(x) = -2x^2 - 16x - 25$

36. $f(x) = -3x^2 + 12x - 5$

37. $f(x) = x^3 + 5x + 2$

38. $f(x) = -x^3 - 2x - 5$

39. $f(x) = x^3 - 3x + 5$

40. $f(x) = -x^3 + 3x + 7$

41. $f(x) = -3x^3 - 9x^2 + 72x + 20$

42. $f(x) = 3x^3 + 9x^2 - 720x - 15$

43. $f(x) = x^4 + 4x^3 + 30$

44. $f(x) = x^4 - 8x^3 + 32$

45. $f(x) = (x + 3)e^x$

46. $f(x) = (x - 3)e^x$

47. $f(x) = (x^2 - 4)^{2/3}$

48. $f(x) = (x^2 - 4)^{1/3}$

In Problems 49–56, find the intervals on which $f(x)$ is increasing and the intervals on which $f(x)$ is decreasing. Then sketch the graph. Add horizontal tangent lines.

49. $f(x) = 4 + 8x - x^2$

50. $f(x) = 2x^2 - 8x + 9$

51. $f(x) = x^3 - 3x + 1$

52. $f(x) = x^3 - 12x + 2$

53. $f(x) = 10 - 12x + 6x^2 - x^3$

54. $f(x) = x^3 + 3x^2 + 3x$

55. $f(x) = x^4 - 18x^2$

56. $f(x) = -x^4 + 50x^2$

In Problems 57–60, use a graphing calculator to approximate the critical numbers of $f(x)$ to two decimal places. Find the intervals on which $f(x)$ is increasing, the intervals on which $f(x)$ is decreasing, and the local extrema.

57. $f(x) = x^4 - 4x^3 + 9x$

58. $f(x) = x^4 + 5x^3 - 15x$

59. $f(x) = e^{-x} - 3x^2$

60. $f(x) = e^x - 2x^2$

In Problems 61–68, $f(x)$ is continuous on $(-\infty, \infty)$. Use the given information to sketch the graph of f.

61.

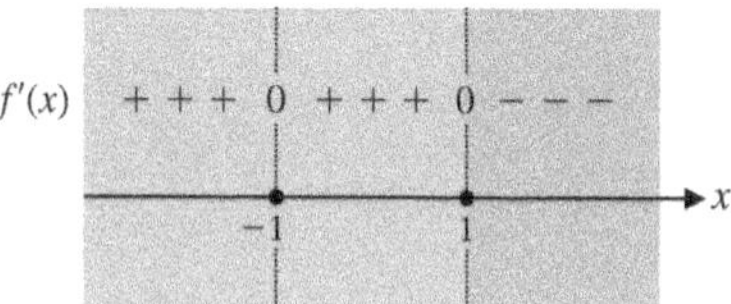

x	−2	−1	0	1	2
$f(x)$	−1	1	2	3	1

62.

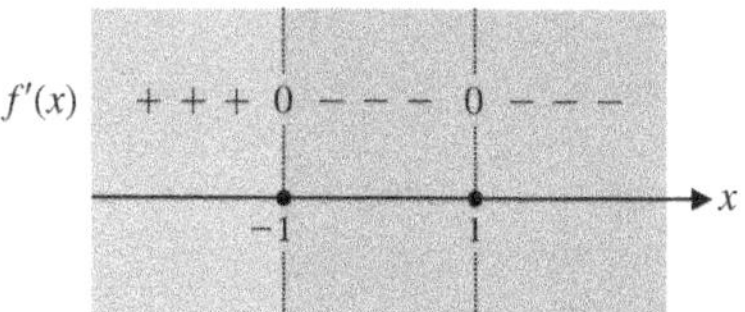

x	−2	−1	0	1	2
$f(x)$	1	3	2	1	−1

63.

f′(x) - - - 0 + + + ND - - - - - - - - 0 - - -

x

−1 0 2

x	−2	−1	0	2	4
$f(x)$	2	1	2	1	0

64.

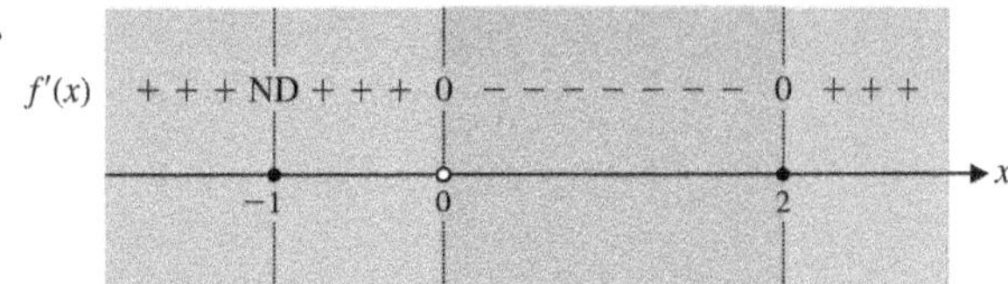

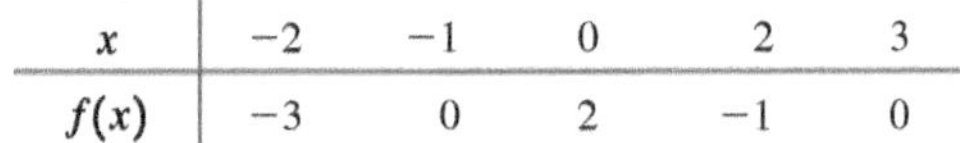

x	−2	−1	0	2	3
$f(x)$	−3	0	2	−1	0

65. $f(-2) = 4, f(0) = 0, f(2) = -4;$
$f'(-2) = 0, f'(0) = 0, f'(2) = 0;$
$f'(x) > 0$ on $(-\infty, -2)$ and $(2, \infty)$;
$f'(x) < 0$ on $(-2, 0)$ and $(0, 2)$

66. $f(-2) = -1, f(0) = 0, f(2) = 1;$
$f'(-2) = 0, f'(2) = 0;$
$f'(x) > 0$ on $(-\infty, -2)$, $(-2, 2)$, and $(2, \infty)$

67. $f(-1) = 2, f(0) = 0, f(1) = -2;$
$f'(-1) = 0, f'(1) = 0, f'(0)$ is not defined;
$f'(x) > 0$ on $(-\infty, -1)$ and $(1, \infty)$;
$f'(x) < 0$ on $(-1, 0)$ and $(0, 1)$

68. $f(-1) = 2, f(0) = 0, f(1) = 2;$
$f'(-1) = 0, f'(1) = 0, f'(0)$ is not defined;
$f'(x) > 0$ on $(-\infty, -1)$ and $(0, 1)$;
$f'(x) < 0$ on $(-1, 0)$ and $(1, \infty)$

Problems 69–74 involve functions f_1–f_6 and their derivatives, g_1–g_6. Use the graphs shown in figures (A) and (B) to match each function f_i with its derivative g_j.

69. f_1 **70.** f_2 **71.** f_3

72. f_4 **73.** f_5 **74.** f_6

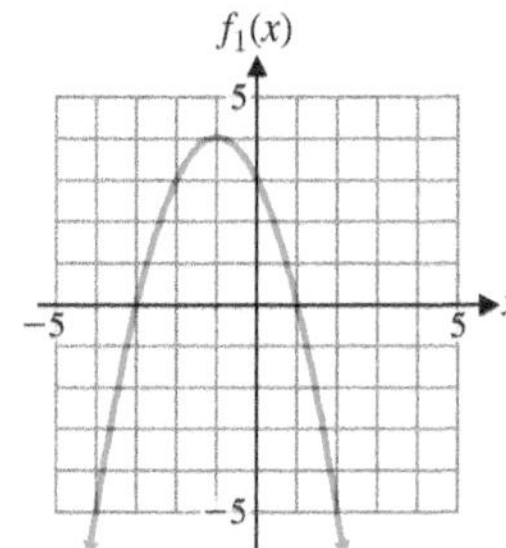

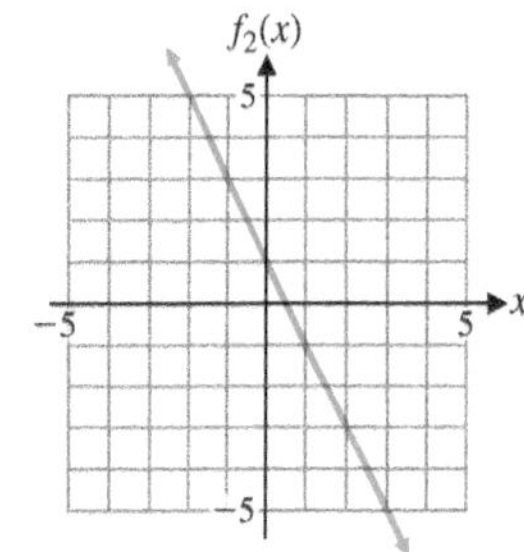

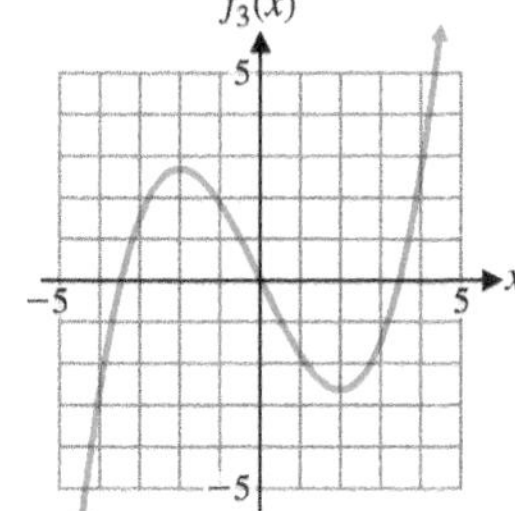

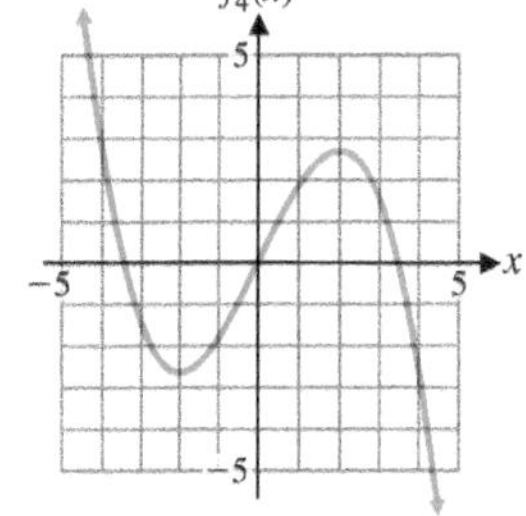

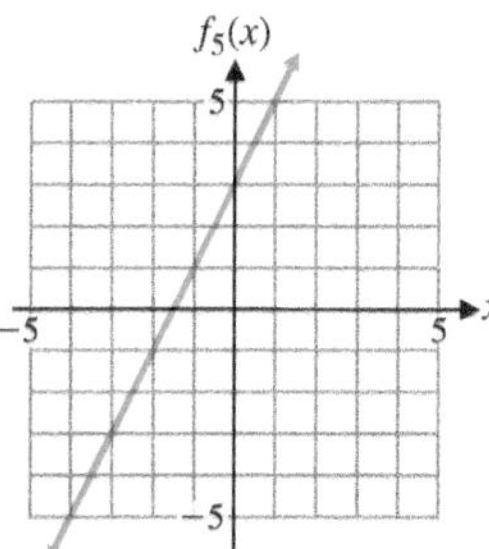

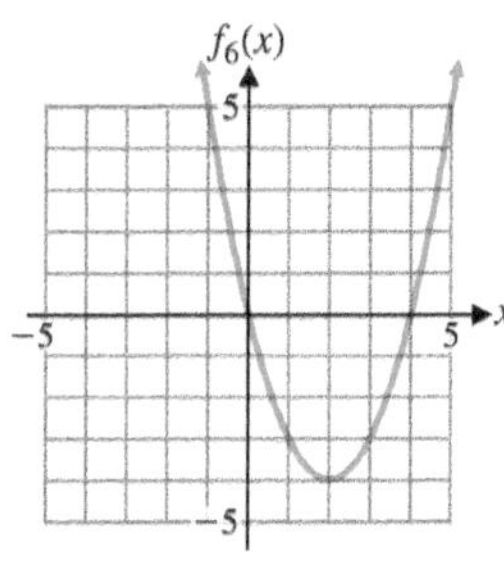

Figure (A) for 69–74

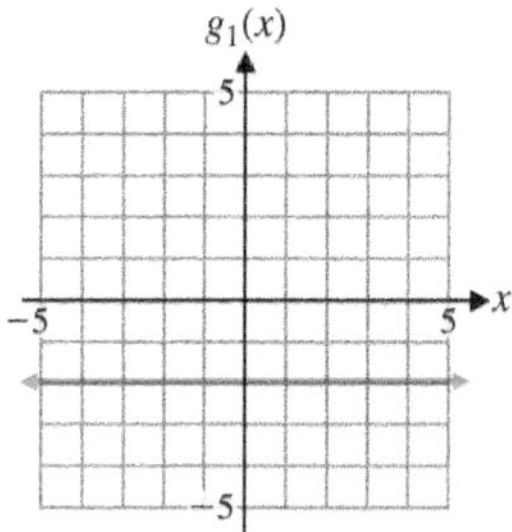

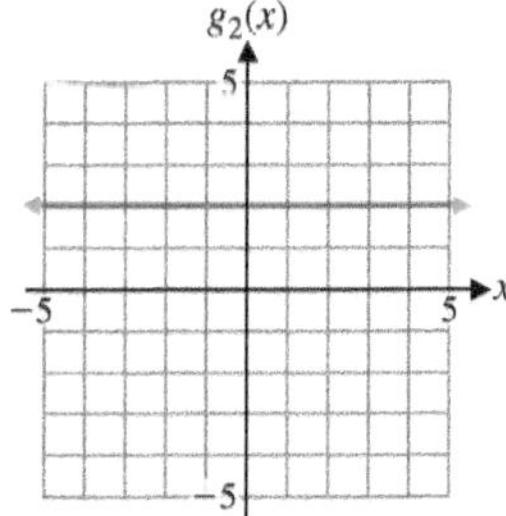

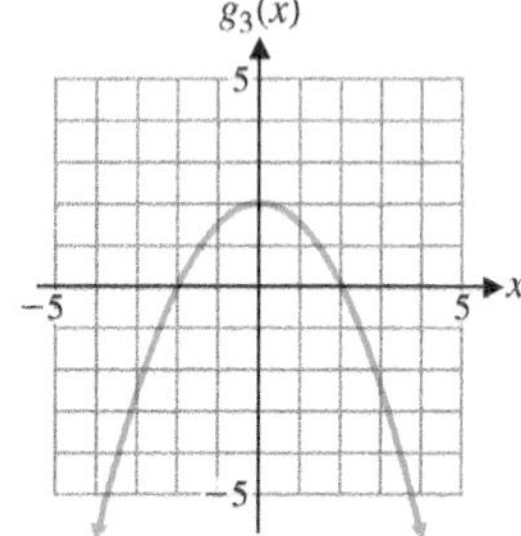

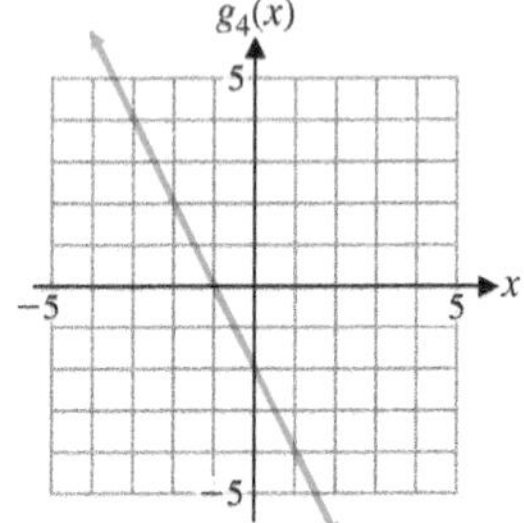

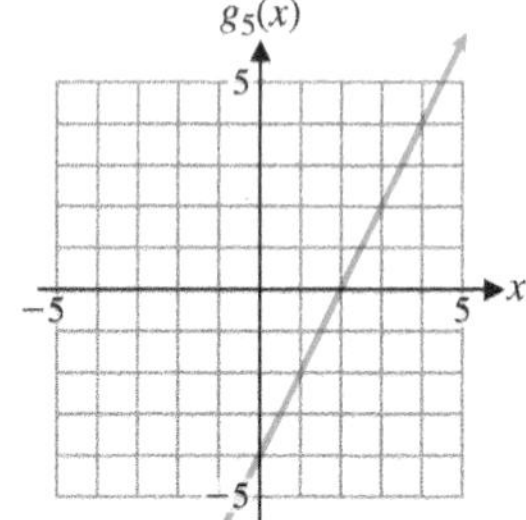

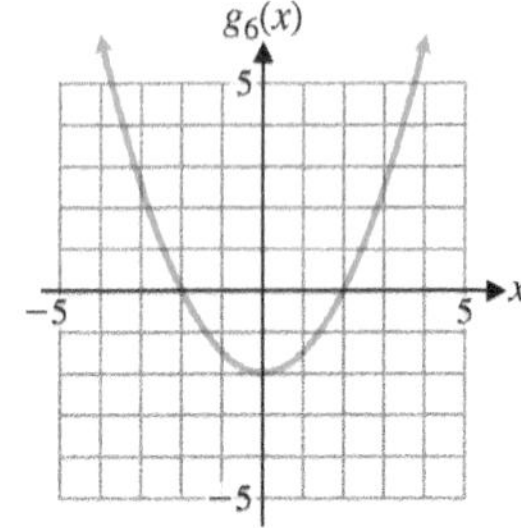

Figure (B) for 69–74

C *In Problems 75–80, use the given graph of $y = f'(x)$ to find the intervals on which f is increasing, the intervals on which f is decreasing, and the x coordinates of the local extrema of f. Sketch a possible graph of $y = f(x)$.*

75.

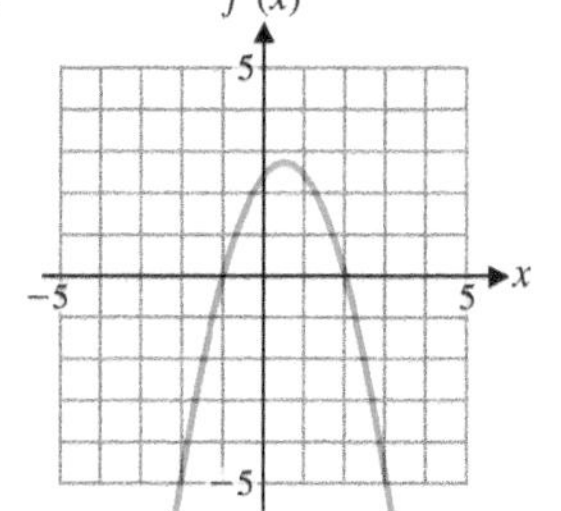

76.

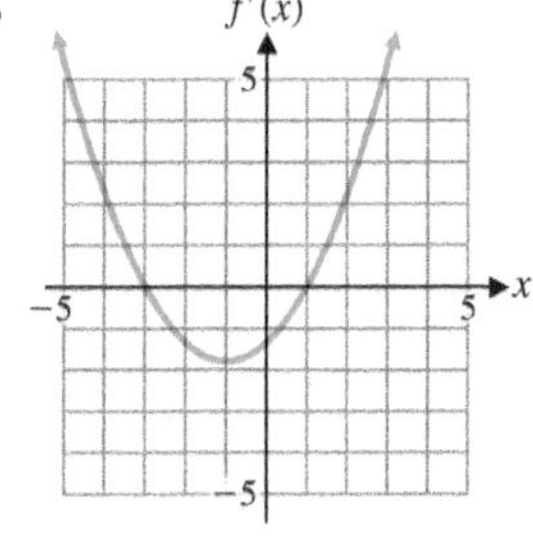

77.

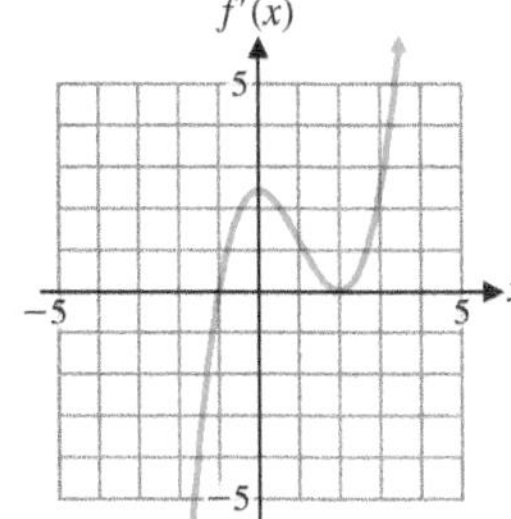

78.

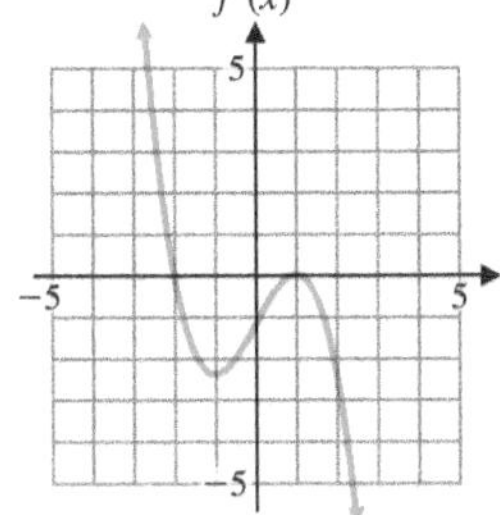

79.

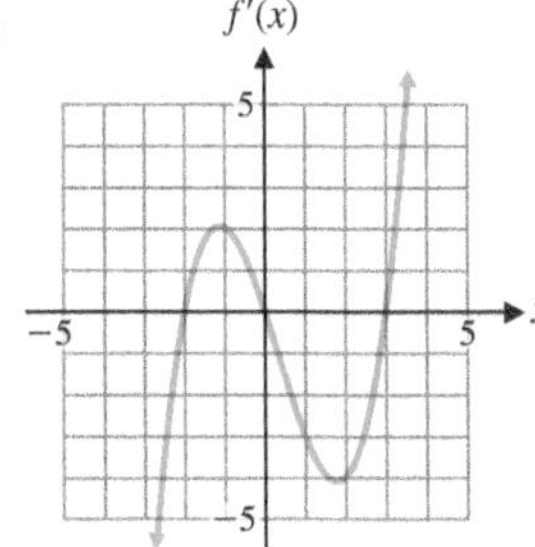

80.

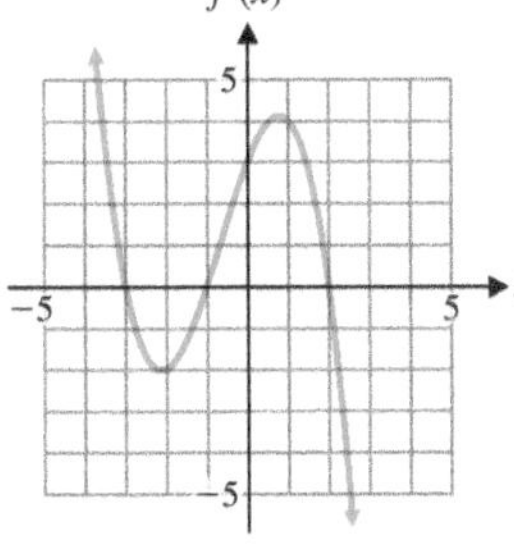

In Problems 81–84, use the given graph of $y = f(x)$ to find the intervals on which $f'(x) > 0$, the intervals on which $f'(x) < 0$, and the values of x for which $f'(x) = 0$. Sketch a possible graph of $y = f'(x)$.

81.

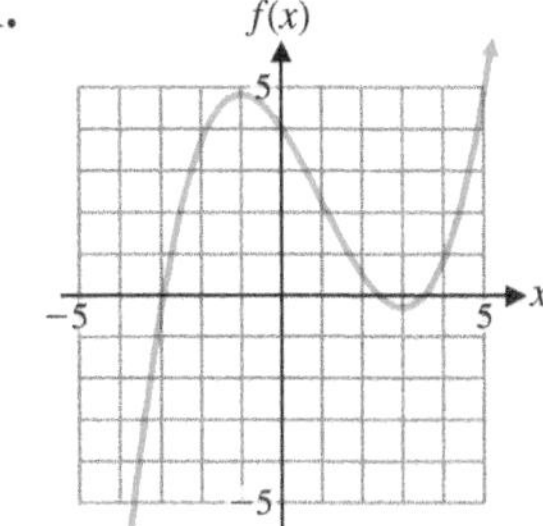

82.

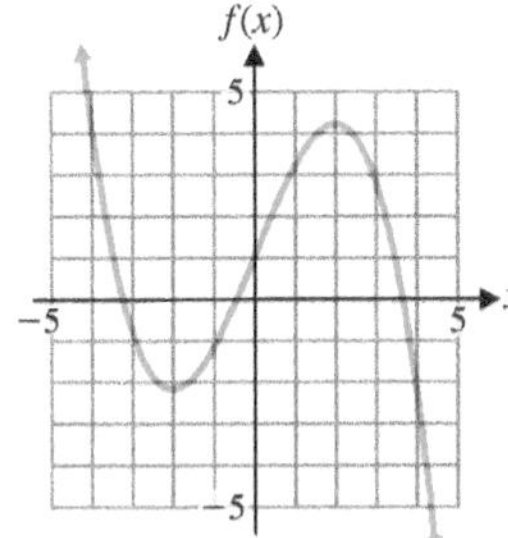

83.

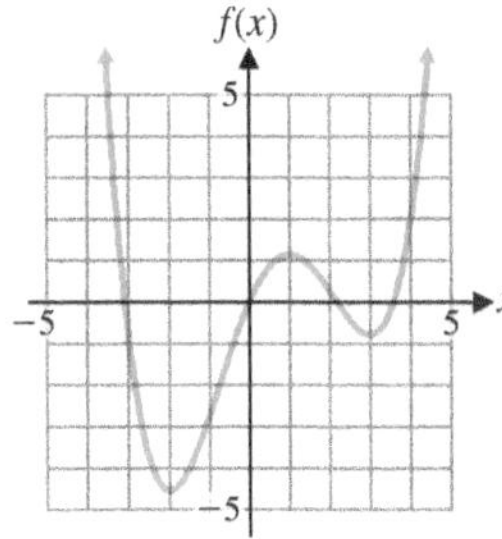

84.

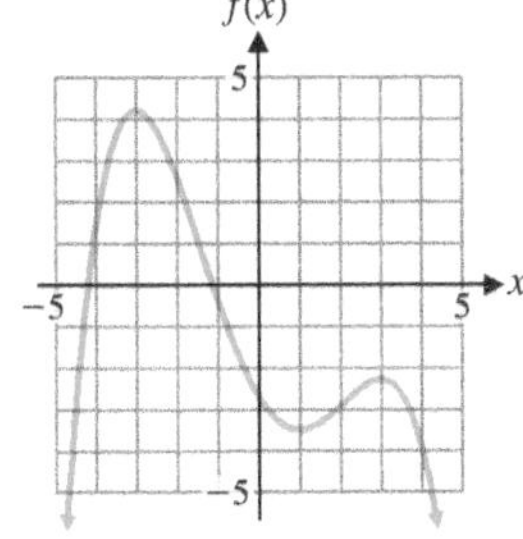

In Problems 85–90, find the critical numbers, the intervals on which $f(x)$ is increasing, the intervals on which $f(x)$ is decreasing, and the local extrema. Do not graph.

85. $f(x) = x + \frac{4}{x}$

86. $f(x) = \frac{9}{x} + x$

87. $f(x) = \ln(x^2 + 1)$

88. $f(x) = \ln(x^4 + 5)$

89. $f(x) = \frac{x^2}{x - 2}$

90. $f(x) = \frac{x^2}{x + 1}$

Applications

91. Profit analysis. The graph of the total profit $P(x)$ (in dollars) from the sale of x cordless electric screwdrivers is shown in the figure.

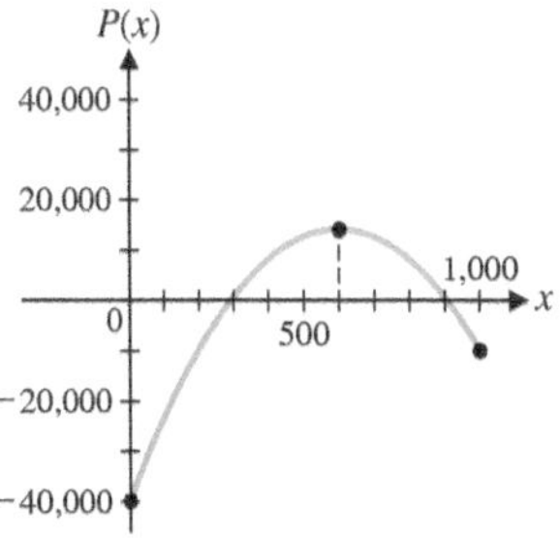

(A) Write a brief description of the graph of the marginal profit function $y = P'(x)$, including a discussion of any x intercepts.

(B) Sketch a possible graph of $y = P'(x)$.

92. Revenue analysis. The graph of the total revenue $R(x)$ (in dollars) from the sale of x cordless electric screwdrivers is shown in the figure.

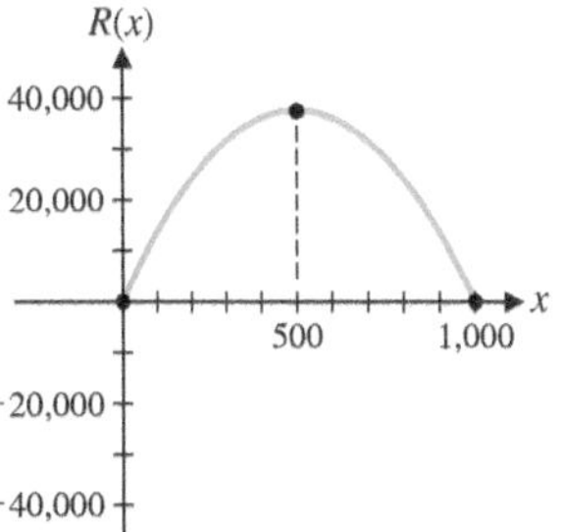

(A) Write a brief description of the graph of the marginal revenue function $y = R'(x)$, including a discussion of any x intercepts.

(B) Sketch a possible graph of $y = R'(x)$.

93. Price analysis. The figure approximates the rate of change of the price of beetroot over a 60-month period, where $B(t)$ is the price of a pound of beetroots (in dollars) and t is time (in months).

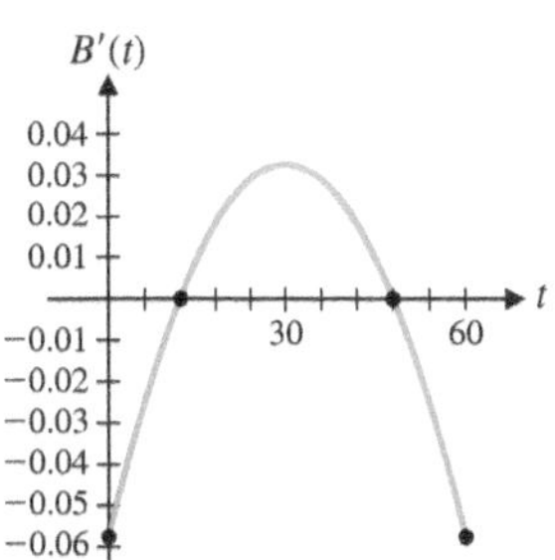

(A) Write a brief description of the graph of $y = B(t)$, including a discussion of any local extrema.

(B) Sketch a possible graph of $y = B(t)$.

94. Price analysis. The figure approximates the rate of change of the price of carrots over a 60-month period, where $C(t)$ is the price of a pound of carrots (in dollars) and t is time (in months).

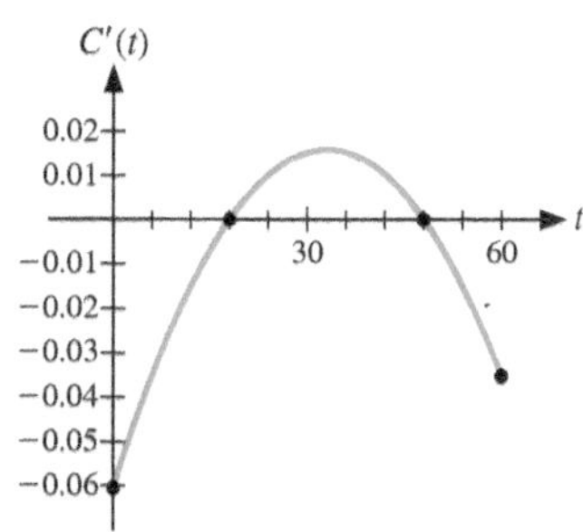

(A) Write a brief description of the graph of $y = C(t)$, including a discussion of any local extrema.

(B) Sketch a possible graph of $y = C(t)$.

95. Average cost. A manufacturer incurs the following costs in producing x water ski vests in one day, for $0 < x < 150$: fixed costs, \$320; unit production cost, \$20 per vest; equipment maintenance and repairs, $0.05x^2$ dollars. So the cost of manufacturing x vests in one day is given by

$$C(x) = 0.05x^2 + 20x + 320 \qquad 0 < x < 150$$

(A) What is the average cost $\overline{C}(x)$ per vest if x vests are produced in one day?

(B) Find the critical numbers of $\overline{C}(x)$, the intervals on which the average cost per vest is decreasing, the intervals on which the average cost per vest is increasing, and the local extrema. Do not graph.

96. Average cost. A manufacturer incurs the following costs in producing x rain jackets in one day for $0 < x < 200$: fixed costs, \$450; unit production cost, \$30 per jacket; equipment maintenance and repairs, $0.08x^2$ dollars.

(A) What is the average cost $\overline{C}(x)$ per jacket if x jackets are produced in one day?

(B) Find the critical numbers of $\overline{C}(x)$, the intervals on which the average cost per jacket is decreasing, the intervals on which the average cost per jacket is increasing, and the local extrema. Do not graph.

97. Medicine. A drug is injected into the bloodstream of a patient through the right arm. The drug concentration in the bloodstream of the left arm t hours after the injection is approximated by

$$C(t) = \frac{0.28t}{t^2 + 4} \qquad 0 < t < 24$$

Find the critical numbers of $C(t)$, the intervals on which the drug concentration is increasing, the intervals on which the concentration of the drug is decreasing, and the local extrema. Do not graph.

98. Medicine. The concentration $C(t)$, in milligrams per cubic centimeter, of a particular drug in a patient's bloodstream is given by

$$C(t) = \frac{0.3t}{t^2 + 6t + 9} \qquad 0 < t < 12$$

where t is the number of hours after the drug is taken orally. Find the critical numbers of $C(t)$, the intervals on which the drug concentration is increasing, the intervals on which the drug concentration is decreasing, and the local extrema. Do not graph.

Answers to Matched Problems

1. (A) Horizontal tangent line at $x = 3$.

   (B) Decreasing on $(-\infty, 3)$; increasing on $(3, \infty)$

   (C)

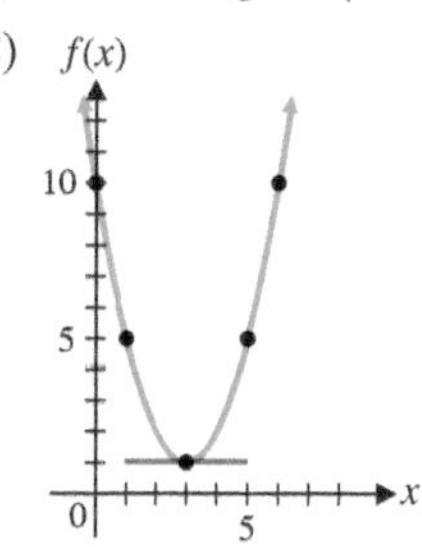

2. Partition number for f': $x = 0$; critical number of f: $x = 0$; decreasing for all x
3. Partition number for f': $x = -1$; critical number of f: $x = -1$; increasing for all x
4. Partition number for f': $x = 0$; no critical number of f; decreasing on $(-\infty, 0)$ and $(0, \infty)$
5. Partition number for f': $x = 5$; critical number of f: $x = 5$; increasing on $(0, 5)$; decreasing on $(5, \infty)$
6. Increasing on $(-3, 1)$; decreasing on $(-\infty, -3)$ and $(1, \infty)$; $f(1) = 5$ is a local maximum; $f(-3) = -3$ is a local minimum
7. (A) Critical numbers of f: $x = 2, x = 4$

   (B) $f(2) = 10$ is a local maximum; $f(4) = 6$ is a local minimum

   (C)

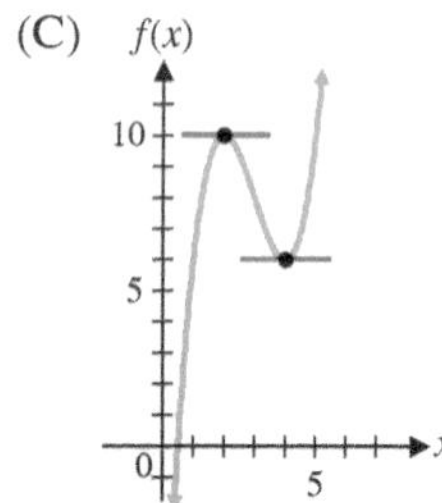

8. (A) The U.S. share of the world market decreases for 6 years to a local minimum, increases for the next 10 years to a local maximum, and then decreases for the final 4 years.

   (B)

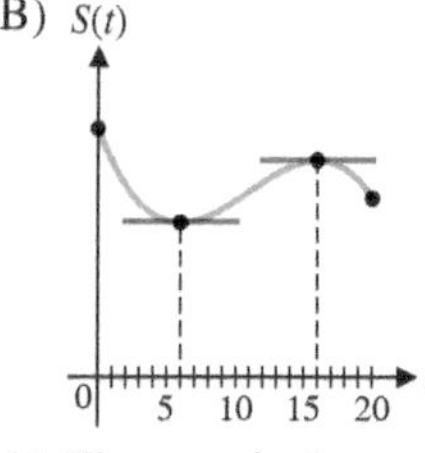

9. (A) The marginal revenue is positive on $(0, 450)$, 0 at $x = 450$, and negative on $(450, 1{,}000)$.

   (B)

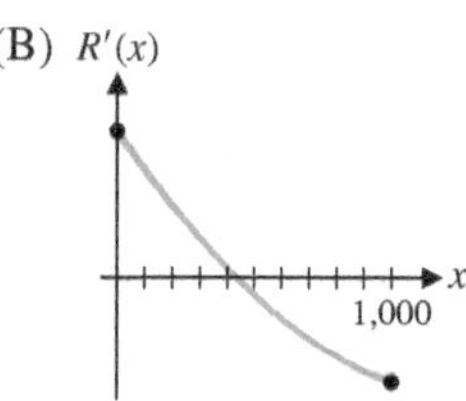

8.2 Second Derivative and Graphs

- Using Concavity as a Graphing Tool
- Finding Inflection Points
- Analyzing Graphs
- Curve Sketching
- Point of Diminishing Returns

In Section 8.1, we saw that the derivative can be used to determine when a graph is rising or falling. Now we want to see what the *second derivative* (the derivative of the derivative) can tell us about the shape of a graph.

Using Concavity as a Graphing Tool

Consider the functions

$$f(x) = x^2 \quad \text{and} \quad g(x) = \sqrt{x}$$

for x in the interval $(0, \infty)$. Since

$$f'(x) = 2x > 0 \quad \text{for } 0 < x < \infty$$

and

$$g'(x) = \frac{1}{2\sqrt{x}} > 0 \quad \text{for } 0 < x < \infty$$

both functions are increasing on $(0, \infty)$.

Explore and Discuss 1

(A) Discuss the difference in the shapes of the graphs of f and g shown in Figure 1.

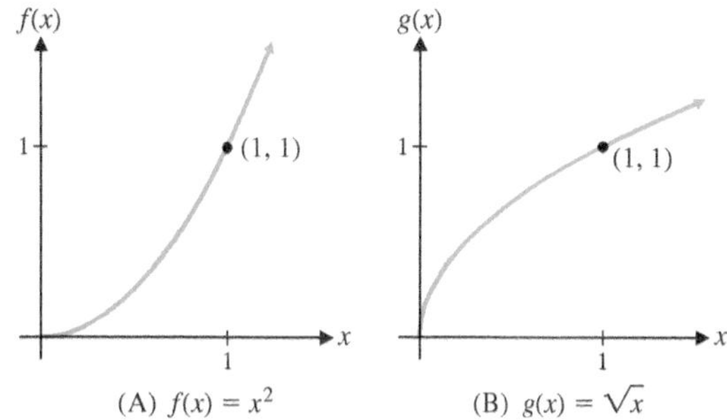

Figure 1

(B) Complete the following table, and discuss the relationship between the values of the derivatives of f and g and the shapes of their graphs:

x	0.25	0.5	0.75	1
$f'(x)$				
$g'(x)$				

We use the term *concave upward* to describe a graph that opens upward and *concave downward* to describe a graph that opens downward. Thus, the graph of f in Figure 1A is concave upward, and the graph of g in Figure 1B is concave downward. Finding a mathematical formulation of concavity will help us sketch and analyze graphs.

We examine the slopes of f and g at various points on their graphs (see Fig. 2) and make two observations about each graph:

1. Looking at the graph of f in Figure 2A, we see that $f'(x)$ (the slope of the tangent line) is *increasing* and that the graph lies *above* each tangent line.
2. Looking at Figure 2B, we see that $g'(x)$ is *decreasing* and that the graph lies *below* each tangent line.

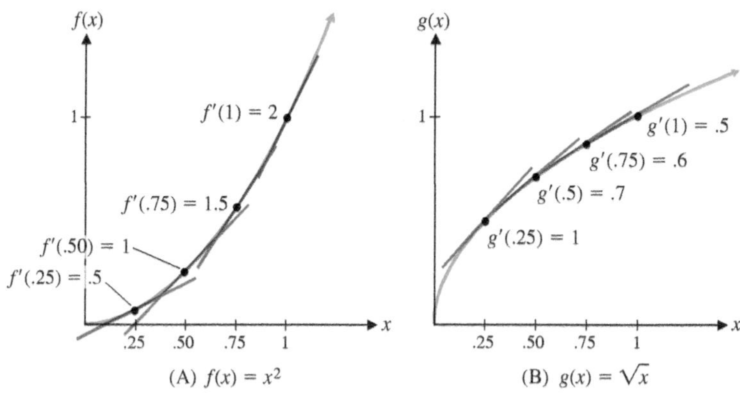

Figure 2

DEFINITION Concavity

The graph of a function f is **concave upward** on the interval (a, b) if $f'(x)$ is *increasing* on (a, b) and is **concave downward** on the interval (a, b) if $f'(x)$ is *decreasing* on (a, b).

Geometrically, the graph is concave upward on (a, b) if it lies above its tangent lines in (a, b) and is concave downward on (a, b) if it lies below its tangent lines in (a, b).

How can we determine when $f'(x)$ is increasing or decreasing? In Section 8.1, we used the derivative to determine when a function is increasing or decreasing. To determine when the function $f'(x)$ is increasing or decreasing, we use the derivative of $f'(x)$. The derivative of the derivative of a function is called the *second derivative* of the function. Various notations for the second derivative are given in the following box:

NOTATION Second Derivative

For $y = f(x)$, the **second derivative** of f, provided that it exists, is

$$f''(x) = \frac{d}{dx}f'(x)$$

Other notations for $f''(x)$ are

$$\frac{d^2y}{dx^2} \quad \text{and} \quad y''$$

Returning to the functions f and g discussed at the beginning of this section, we have

$$f(x) = x^2 \qquad g(x) = \sqrt{x} = x^{1/2}$$

$$f'(x) = 2x \qquad g'(x) = \frac{1}{2}x^{-1/2} = \frac{1}{2\sqrt{x}}$$

$$f''(x) = \frac{d}{dx}2x = 2 \qquad g''(x) = \frac{d}{dx}\frac{1}{2}x^{-1/2} = -\frac{1}{4}x^{-3/2} = -\frac{1}{4\sqrt{x^3}}$$

For $x > 0$, we see that $f''(x) > 0$; so $f'(x)$ is increasing, and the graph of f is concave upward (see Fig. 2A). For $x > 0$, we also see that $g''(x) < 0$; so $g'(x)$ is decreasing, and the graph of g is concave downward (see Fig. 2B). These ideas are summarized in the following box:

SUMMARY Concavity

For the interval (a, b), if $f'' > 0$, then f is concave upward, and if $f'' < 0$, then f is concave downward.

$f''(x)$	$f'(x)$	Graph of $y = f(x)$	Examples
+	Increasing	Concave upward	
–	Decreasing	Concave downward	

CONCEPTUAL INSIGHT

Be careful not to confuse concavity with falling and rising. A graph that is concave upward on an interval may be falling, rising, or both falling and rising on that interval. A similar statement holds for a graph that is concave downward. See Figure 3.

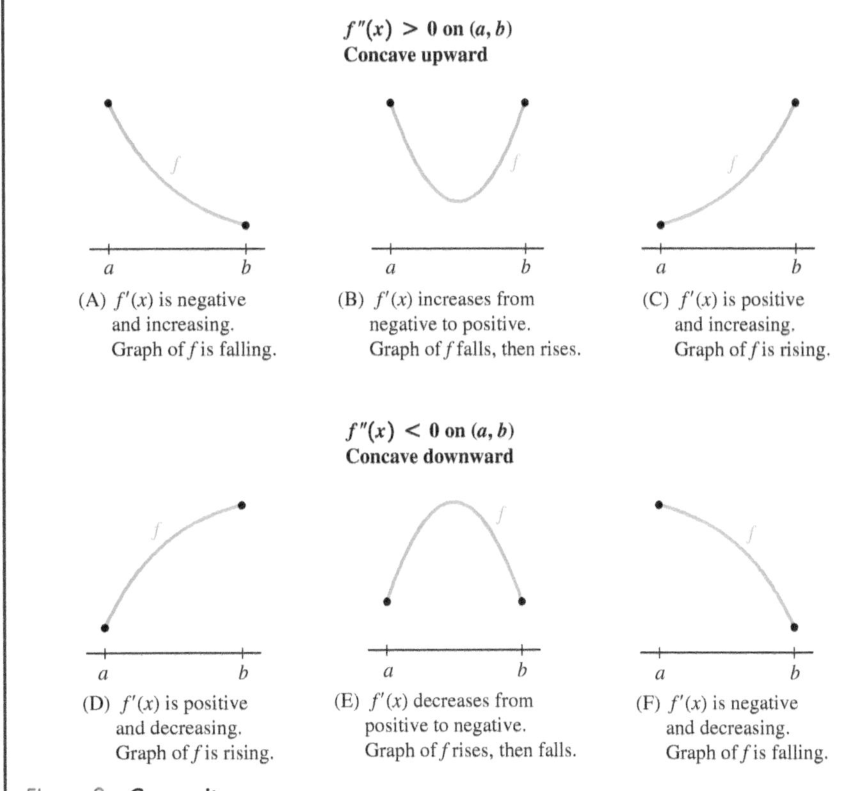

Figure 3 Concavity

EXAMPLE 1 **Concavity of Graphs** Determine the intervals on which the graph of each function is concave upward and the intervals on which it is concave downward. Sketch a graph of each function.

(A) $f(x) = e^x$

(B) $g(x) = \ln x$

(C) $h(x) = x^3$

SOLUTION

(A) $f(x) = e^x$

$f'(x) = e^x$

$f''(x) = e^x$

Since $f''(x) > 0$ on $(-\infty, \infty)$, the graph of $f(x) = e^x$ [Fig. 4(A)] is concave upward on $(-\infty, \infty)$.

(B) $g(x) = \ln x$

$g'(x) = \frac{1}{x}$

$g''(x) = -\frac{1}{x^2}$

The domain of $g(x) = \ln x$ is $(0, \infty)$ and $g''(x) < 0$ on this interval, so the graph of $g(x) = \ln x$ [Fig. 4(B)] is concave downward on $(0, \infty)$.

(C) $h(x) = x^3$

$h'(x) = 3x^2$

$h''(x) = 6x$

Since $h''(x) < 0$ when $x < 0$ and $h''(x) > 0$ when $x > 0$, the graph of $h(x) = x^3$ [Fig. 4(C)] is concave downward on $(-\infty, 0)$ and concave upward on $(0, \infty)$.

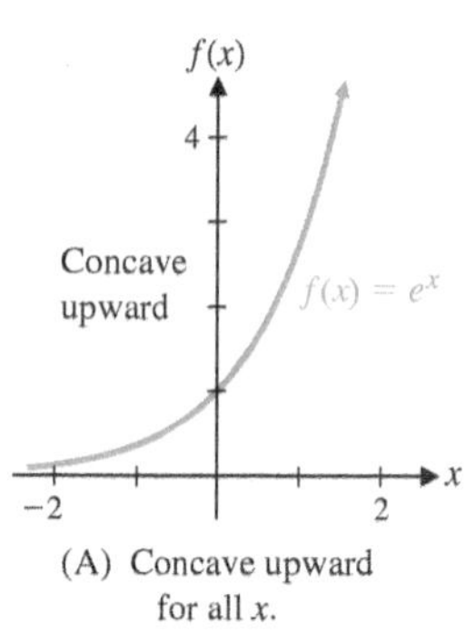

(A) Concave upward for all x.

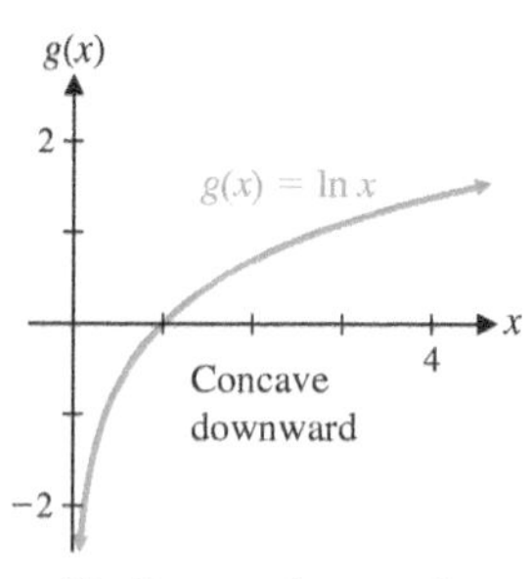

(B) Concave downward for $x > 0$.

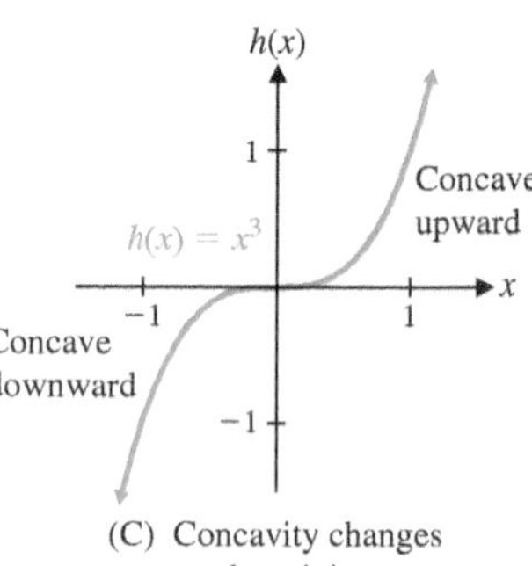

(C) Concavity changes at the origin.

Figure 4

Matched Problem 1 Determine the intervals on which the graph of each function is concave upward and the intervals on which it is concave downward. Sketch a graph of each function.

(A) $f(x) = -e^{-x}$ (B) $g(x) = \ln \frac{1}{x}$ (C) $h(x) = x^{1/3}$

Refer to Example 1. The graphs of $f(x) = e^x$ and $g(x) = \ln x$ never change concavity. But the graph of $h(x) = x^3$ changes concavity at $(0, 0)$. This point is called an *inflection point.*

Finding Inflection Points

An **inflection point** is a point on the graph of a function where the function is continuous and the concavity changes (from upward to downward or from downward to upward). For the concavity to change at a point, $f''(x)$ must change sign at that point. But in Section 8.2, we saw that the partition numbers identify the points where a function can change sign.

THEOREM 1 Inflection Points

If $(c, f(c))$ is an inflection point of f, then c is a partition number for f''.

If f is continuous at a partition number c of $f''(x)$ and $f''(x)$ exists on both sides of c, the sign chart of $f''(x)$ can be used to determine whether the point $(c, f(c))$ is an inflection point. The procedure is summarized in the following box and illustrated in Figure 5:

PROCEDURE Testing for Inflection Points

Step 1 Find all partition numbers c of f'' such that f is continuous at c.

Step 2 For each of these partition numbers c, construct a sign chart of f'' near $x = c$.

Step 3 If the sign chart of f'' changes sign at c, then $(c, f(c))$ is an inflection point of f. If the sign chart does not change sign at c, then there is no inflection point at $x = c$.

If $f'(c)$ exists and $f''(x)$ changes sign at $x = c$, then the tangent line at an inflection point $(c, f(c))$ will always lie below the graph on the side that is concave upward and above the graph on the side that is concave downward (see Fig. 5A, B, and C).

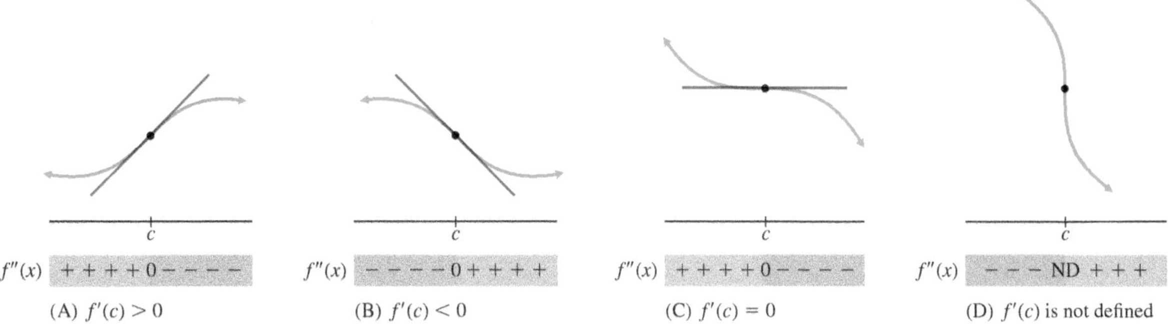

Figure 5 Inflection points

EXAMPLE 2 **Locating Inflection Points** Find the inflection point(s) of

$$f(x) = x^3 - 6x^2 + 9x + 1$$

SOLUTION Since inflection points occur at values of x where $f''(x)$ changes sign, we construct a sign chart for $f''(x)$.

$$f(x) = x^3 - 6x^2 + 9x + 1$$
$$f'(x) = 3x^2 - 12x + 9$$
$$f''(x) = 6x - 12 = 6(x - 2)$$

The sign chart for $f''(x) = 6(x - 2)$ (partition number is 2) is as follows:

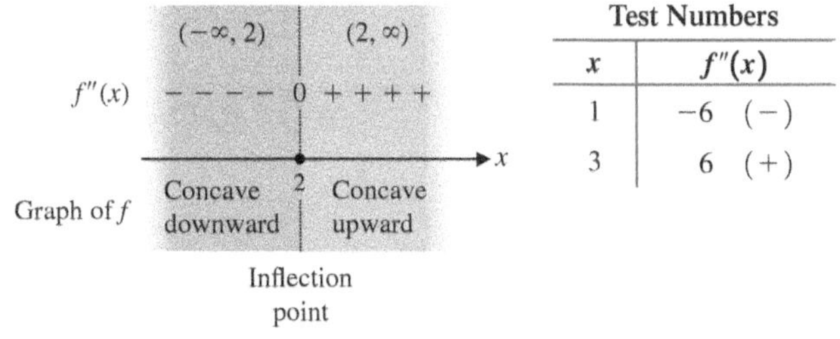

Test Numbers

x	$f''(x)$
1	$-6\ (-)$
3	$6\ (+)$

From the sign chart, we see that the graph of f has an inflection point at $x = 2$. That is, the point

$$(2, f(2)) = (2, 3) \quad f(2) = 2^3 - 6 \cdot 2^2 + 9 \cdot 2 + 1 = 3$$

is an inflection point on the graph of f.

Matched Problem 2 Find the inflection point(s) of

$$f(x) = x^3 - 9x^2 + 24x - 10$$

EXAMPLE 3 **Locating Inflection Points** Find the inflection point(s) of

$$f(x) = \ln(x^2 - 4x + 5)$$

SOLUTION First we find the domain of f. Since $\ln x$ is defined only for $x > 0$, f is defined only for

$$x^2 - 4x + 5 > 0 \quad \text{Complete the square (Section B.7).}$$
$$(x-2)^2 + 1 > 0 \quad \text{True for all } x \text{ (the square of any number is } \geq 0).$$

So the domain of f is $(-\infty, \infty)$. Now we find $f''(x)$ and construct a sign chart for it.

$$f(x) = \ln(x^2 - 4x + 5)$$
$$f'(x) = \frac{2x - 4}{x^2 - 4x + 5}$$
$$f''(x) = \frac{(x^2 - 4x + 5)(2x - 4)' - (2x - 4)(x^2 - 4x + 5)'}{(x^2 - 4x + 5)^2}$$
$$= \frac{(x^2 - 4x + 5)2 - (2x - 4)(2x - 4)}{(x^2 - 4x + 5)^2}$$
$$= \frac{2x^2 - 8x + 10 - 4x^2 + 16x - 16}{(x^2 - 4x + 5)^2}$$
$$= \frac{-2x^2 + 8x - 6}{(x^2 - 4x + 5)^2}$$
$$= \frac{-2(x-1)(x-3)}{(x^2 - 4x + 5)^2}$$

The partition numbers for $f''(x)$ are $x = 1$ and $x = 3$.
Sign chart for $f''(x)$:

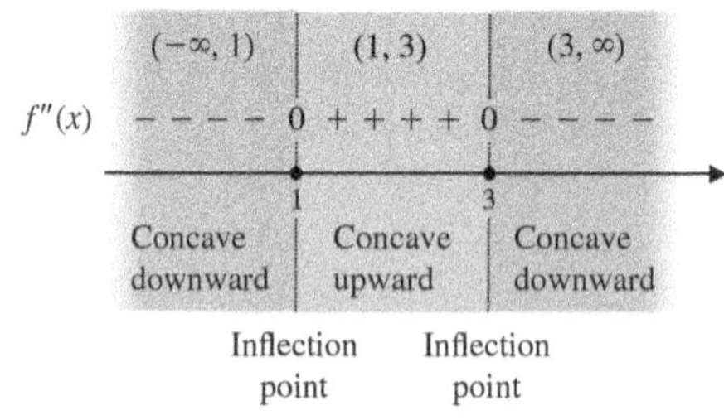

Test Numbers

x	$f''(x)$
0	$-\frac{6}{25}$ (−)
2	2 (+)
4	$-\frac{6}{25}$ (−)

The sign chart shows that the graph of f has inflection points at $x = 1$ and $x = 3$. Since $f(1) = \ln 2$ and $f(3) = \ln 2$, the inflection points are $(1, \ln 2)$ and $(3, \ln 2)$.

Matched Problem 3 Find the inflection point(s) of

$$f(x) = \ln(x^2 - 2x + 5)$$

CONCEPTUAL INSIGHT

It is important to remember that the partition numbers for f'' are only *candidates* for inflection points. The function f must be defined at $x = c$, and the second derivative must change sign at $x = c$ in order for the graph to have an inflection point at $x = c$. For example, consider

$$f(x) = x^4 \qquad g(x) = \frac{1}{x}$$
$$f'(x) = 4x^3 \qquad g'(x) = -\frac{1}{x^2}$$
$$f''(x) = 12x^2 \qquad g''(x) = \frac{2}{x^3}$$

In each case, $x = 0$ is a partition number for the second derivative, but neither the graph of $f(x)$ nor the graph of $g(x)$ has an inflection point at $x = 0$. Function f does not have an inflection point at $x = 0$ because $f''(x)$ does not change sign at $x = 0$ (see Fig. 6A). Function g does not have an inflection point at $x = 0$ because $g(0)$ is not defined (see Fig. 6B).

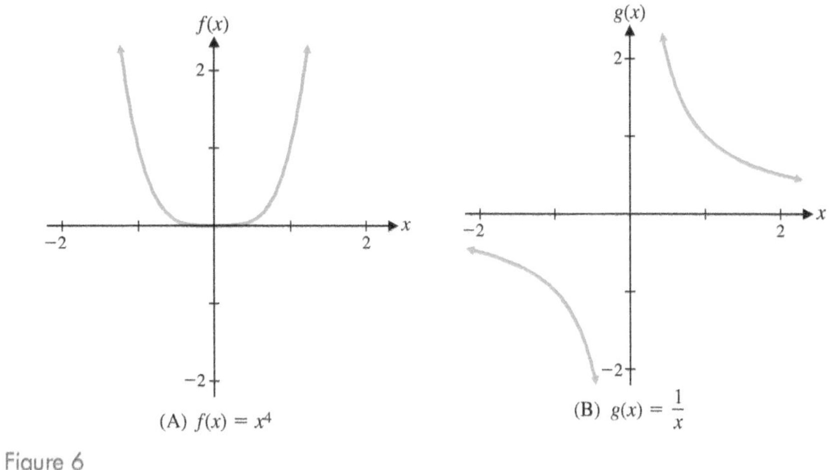

Figure 6

Analyzing Graphs

In the next example, we combine increasing/decreasing properties with concavity properties to analyze the graph of a function.

EXAMPLE 4 **Analyzing a Graph** Figure 7 shows the graph of the derivative of a function f. Use this graph to discuss the graph of f. Include a sketch of a possible graph of f.

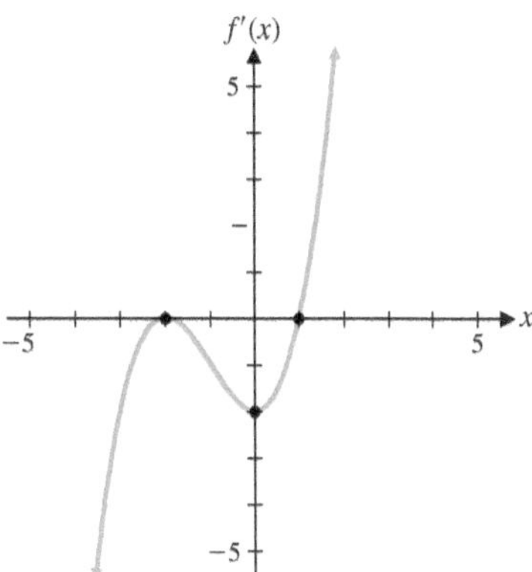

Figure 7

SOLUTION The sign of the derivative determines where the original function is increasing and decreasing, and the increasing/decreasing properties of the derivative determine the concavity of the original function. The relevant information obtained from the graph of f' is summarized in Table 1, and a possible graph of f is shown in Figure 8.

Table 1

x	$f'(x)$ (Fig. 7)	$f(x)$ (Fig. 8)
$-\infty < x < -2$	Negative and increasing	Decreasing and concave upward
$x = -2$	Local maximum	Inflection point
$-2 < x < 0$	Negative and decreasing	Decreasing and concave downward
$x = 0$	Local minimum	Inflection point
$0 < x < 1$	Negative and increasing	Decreasing and concave upward
$x = 1$	x intercept	Local minimum
$1 < x < \infty$	Positive and increasing	Increasing and concave upward

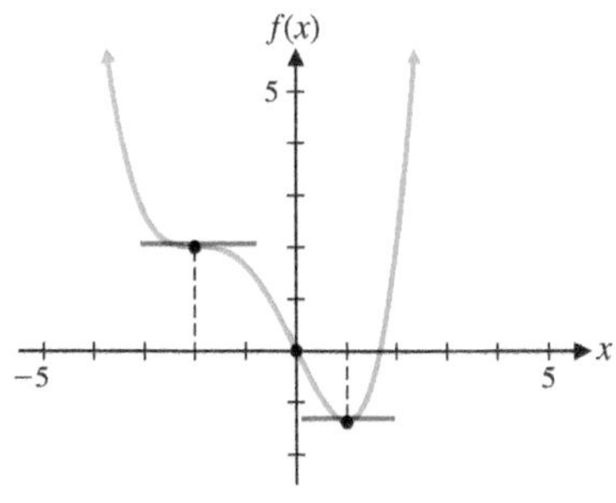

Figure 8

Matched Problem 4 Figure 9 shows the graph of the derivative of a function f. Use this graph to discuss the graph of f. Include a sketch of a possible graph of f.

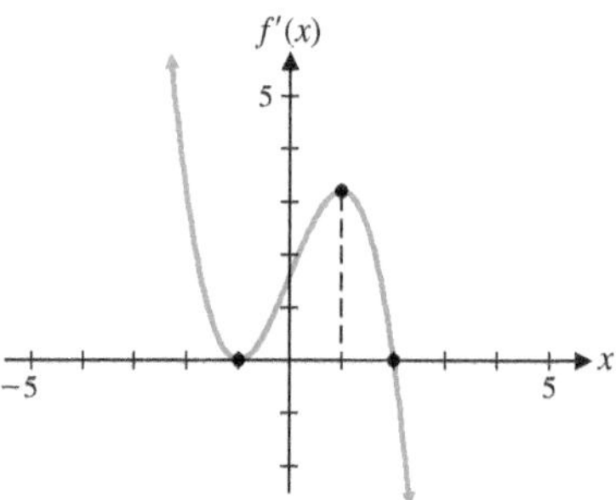

Figure 9

Curve Sketching

Graphing calculators and computers produce the graph of a function by plotting many points. However, key points on a plot many be difficult to identify. Using information gained from the function $f(x)$ and its derivatives, and plotting the key points—intercepts, local extrema, and inflection points—we can sketch by hand a very good representation of the graph of $f(x)$. This graphing process is called **curve sketching**.

PROCEDURE Graphing Strategy (First Version)*

Step 1 *Analyze* $f(x)$. Find the domain and the intercepts. The x intercepts are the solutions of $f(x) = 0$, and the y intercept is $f(0)$.

Step 2 *Analyze* $f'(x)$. Find the partition numbers for f' and the critical numbers of f. Construct a sign chart for $f'(x)$, determine the intervals on which f is increasing and decreasing, and find the local maxima and minima of f.

Step 3 *Analyze* $f''(x)$. Find the partition numbers for $f''(x)$. Construct a sign chart for $f''(x)$, determine the intervals on which the graph of f is concave upward and concave downward, and find the inflection points of f.

Step 4 *Sketch the graph of* f. Locate intercepts, local maxima and minima, and inflection points. Sketch in what you know from steps 1–3. Plot additional points as needed and complete the sketch.

EXAMPLE 5 **Using the Graphing Strategy** Follow the graphing strategy and analyze the function

$$f(x) = x^4 - 2x^3$$

State all the pertinent information and sketch the graph of f.

SOLUTION

Step 1 *Analyze* $f(x)$. Since f is a polynomial, its domain is $(-\infty, \infty)$.

$$\begin{aligned} x \text{ intercept:} \quad f(x) &= 0 \\ x^4 - 2x^3 &= 0 \\ x^3(x - 2) &= 0 \\ x &= 0, 2 \\ y \text{ intercept:} \quad f(0) &= 0 \end{aligned}$$

*We will modify this summary in Section 8.4 to include additional information about the graph of f.

Step 2 *Analyze* $f'(x)$. $f'(x) = 4x^3 - 6x^2 = 4x^2(x - \frac{3}{2})$
Partition numbers for $f'(x)$: 0 and $\frac{3}{2}$
Critical numbers of $f(x)$: 0 and $\frac{3}{2}$
Sign chart for $f'(x)$:

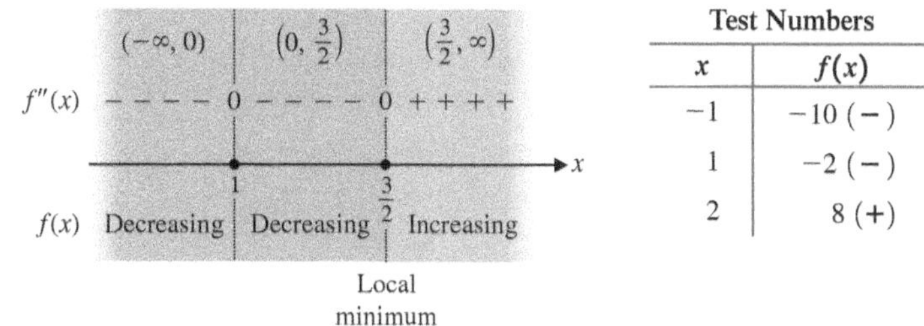

Test Numbers

x	$f(x)$
-1	$-10\ (-)$
1	$-2\ (-)$
2	$8\ (+)$

So $f(x)$ is decreasing on $(-\infty, \frac{3}{2})$, is increasing on $(\frac{3}{2}, \infty)$, and has a local minimum at $x = \frac{3}{2}$. The local minimum is $f(\frac{3}{2}) = -\frac{27}{16}$.

Step 3 *Analyze* $f''(x)$. $f''(x) = 12x^2 - 12x = 12x(x - 1)$
Partition numbers for $f''(x)$: 0 and 1
Sign chart for $f''(x)$:

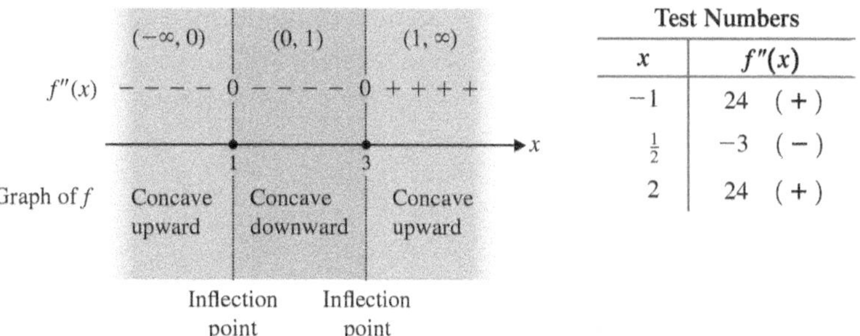

Test Numbers

x	$f''(x)$
-1	$24\ (+)$
$\frac{1}{2}$	$-3\ (-)$
2	$24\ (+)$

So the graph of f is concave upward on $(-\infty, 0)$ and $(1, \infty)$, is concave downward on $(0, 1)$, and has inflection points at $x = 0$ and $x = 1$. Since $f(0) = 0$ and $f(1) = -1$, the inflection points are $(0, 0)$ and $(1, -1)$.

Step 4 *Sketch the graph of f.*

Key Points

x	$f(x)$
0	0
1	-1
$\frac{3}{2}$	$-\frac{27}{16}$
2	0

Matched Problem 5 Follow the graphing strategy and analyze the function $f(x) = x^4 + 4x^3$. State all the pertinent information and sketch the graph of f.

CONCEPTUAL INSIGHT

Refer to the solution of Example 5. Combining the sign charts for $f'(x)$ and $f''(x)$ (Fig. 10) partitions the real-number line into intervals on which neither $f'(x)$ nor $f''(x)$ changes sign. On each of these intervals, the graph of $f(x)$ must have one of four basic shapes (see also Fig. 3, parts A, C, D, and F on page 460). This reduces sketching the graph of a function to plotting the points identified in the graphing strategy and connecting them with one of the basic shapes.

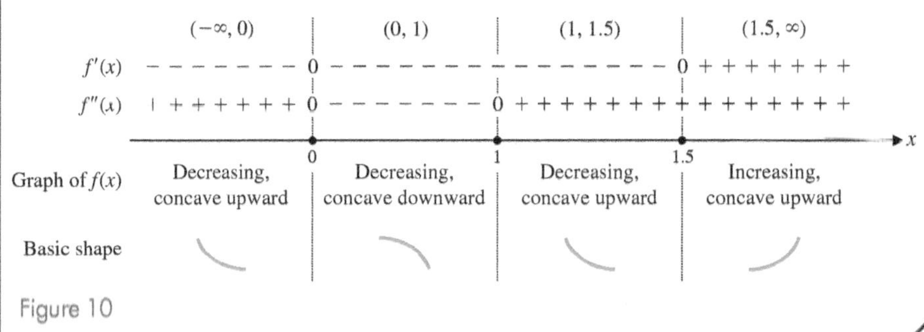

Figure 10

EXAMPLE 6 **Using the Graphing Strategy** Follow the graphing strategy and analyze the function

$$f(x) = 3x^{5/3} - 20x$$

State all the pertinent information and sketch the graph of f. Round any decimal values to two decimal places.

SOLUTION

Step 1 *Analyze* $f(x)$. $f(x) = 3x^{5/3} - 20x$

Since x^p is defined for any x and any positive p, the domain of f is $(-\infty, \infty)$.

$$x \text{ intercepts: Solve } f(x) = 0$$

$$3x^{5/3} - 20x = 0$$

$$3x\left(x^{2/3} - \frac{20}{3}\right) = 0 \qquad (a^2 - b^2) = (a - b)(a + b)$$

$$3x\left(x^{1/3} - \sqrt{\frac{20}{3}}\right)\left(x^{1/3} + \sqrt{\frac{20}{3}}\right) = 0$$

The x intercepts of f are

$$x = 0, \quad x = \left(\sqrt{\frac{20}{3}}\right)^3 \approx 17.21, \quad x = \left(-\sqrt{\frac{20}{3}}\right)^3 \approx -17.21$$

y intercept: $f(0) = 0$.

Step 2 Analyze $f'(x)$.

$$\begin{aligned} f'(x) &= 5x^{2/3} - 20 \\ &= 5(x^{2/3} - 4) \qquad \text{Again, } a^2 - b^2 = (a - b)(a + b) \\ &= 5(x^{1/3} - 2)(x^{1/3} + 2) \end{aligned}$$

Partition numbers for f': $x = 2^3 = 8$ and $x = (-2)^3 = -8$.
Critical numbers of f: $-8, 8$

Sign chart for $f'(x)$:

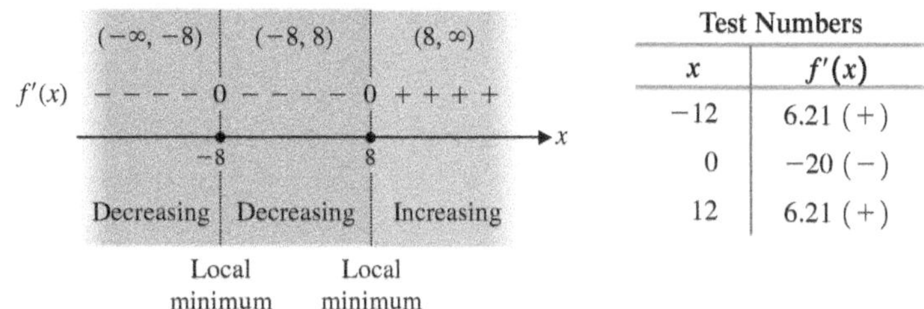

Test Numbers

x	$f'(x)$
−12	6.21 (+)
0	−20 (−)
12	6.21 (+)

So f is increasing on $(-\infty, -8)$ and $(8, \infty)$ and decreasing on $(-8, 8)$. Therefore, $f(-8) = 64$ is a local maximum, and $f(8) = -64$ is a local minimum.

Step 3 *Analyze $f''(x)$.*

$$f'(x) = 5x^{2/3} - 20$$

$$f''(x) = \frac{10}{3}x^{-1/3} = \frac{10}{3x^{1/3}}$$

Partition number for f'': 0

Sign chart for $f''(x)$:

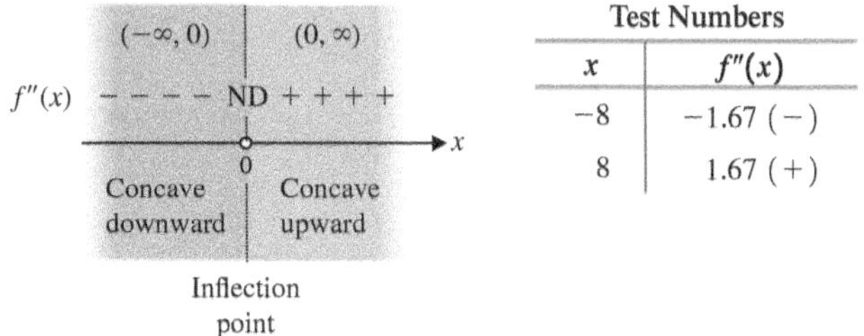

Test Numbers

x	$f''(x)$
−8	−1.67 (−)
8	1.67 (+)

So f is concave downward on $(-\infty, 0)$, is concave upward on $(0, \infty)$, and has an inflection point at $x = 0$. Since $f(0) = 0$, the inflection point is $(0, 0)$.

Step 4 *Sketch the graph of f.*

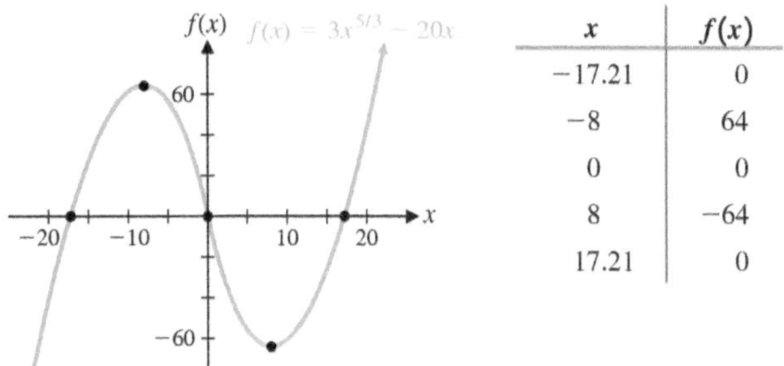

x	$f(x)$
−17.21	0
−8	64
0	0
8	−64
17.21	0

Matched Problem 6 Follow the graphing strategy and analyze the function $f(x) = 3x^{2/3} - x$. State all the pertinent information and sketch the graph of f. Round any decimal values to two decimal places.

Point of Diminishing Returns

If a company decides to increase spending on advertising, it would expect sales to increase. At first, sales will increase at an increasing rate and then increase at a decreasing rate. The dollar amount x at which the rate of change of sales goes from increasing to decreasing is called the **point of diminishing returns**. This is also the amount at which the rate of change has a maximum value. Money spent beyond this amount may increase sales but at a lower rate.

EXAMPLE 7 **Maximum Rate of Change** Currently, a discount appliance store is selling 200 large-screen TVs monthly. If the store invests $\$x$ thousand in an advertising campaign, the ad company estimates that monthly sales will be given by

$$N(x) = 3x^3 - 0.25x^4 + 200 \qquad 0 \le x \le 9$$

When is the rate of change of sales increasing and when is it decreasing? What is the point of diminishing returns and the maximum rate of change of sales? Graph N and N' on the same coordinate system.

SOLUTION The rate of change of sales with respect to advertising expenditures is

$$N'(x) = 9x^2 - x^3 = x^2(9 - x)$$

To determine when $N'(x)$ is increasing and decreasing, we find $N''(x)$, the derivative of $N'(x)$:

$$N''(x) = 18x - 3x^2 = 3x(6 - x)$$

The information obtained by analyzing the signs of $N'(x)$ and $N''(x)$ is summarized in Table 2 (sign charts are omitted).

Table 2

x	$N''(x)$	$N'(x)$	$N'(x)$	$N(x)$
$0 < x < 6$	+	+	Increasing	Increasing, concave upward
$x = 6$	0	+	Local maximum	Inflection point
$6 < x < 9$	−	+	Decreasing	Increasing, concave downward

Examining Table 2, we see that $N'(x)$ is increasing on $(0, 6)$ and decreasing on $(6, 9)$. The point of diminishing returns is $x = 6$ and the maximum rate of change is $N'(6) = 108$. Note that $N'(x)$ has a local maximum and $N(x)$ has an inflection point at $x = 6$ [the inflection point of $N(x)$ is $(6, 524)$].

So if the store spends \$6,000 on advertising, monthly sales are expected to be 524 TVs, and sales are expected to increase at a rate of 108 TVs per thousand dollars spent on advertising. Money spent beyond the \$6,000 would increase sales, but at a lower rate.

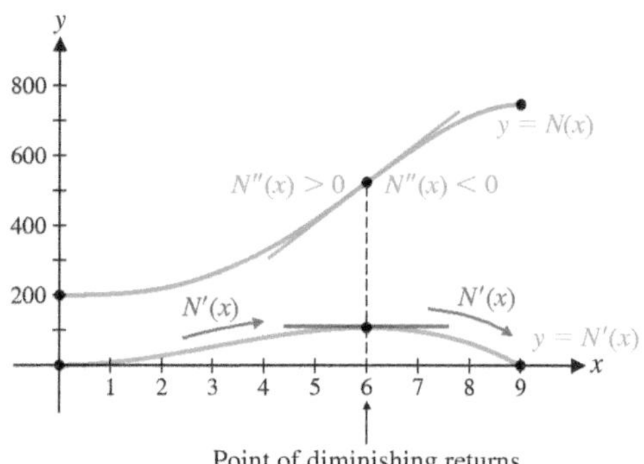

Matched Problem 7 Repeat Example 7 for

$$N(x) = 4x^3 - 0.25x^4 + 500 \qquad 0 \le x \le 12$$

Exercises 8.2

Skills Warm-up Exercises

W *In Problems 1–8, inspect the graph of the function to determine whether it is concave up, concave down, or neither, on the given interval. (If necessary, review Section 1.2.)*

1. The square function, $h(x) = x^2$, on $(-\infty, \infty)$
2. The identity function, $f(x) = x$, on $(-\infty, \infty)$
3. The cube function, $m(x) = x^3$, on $(-\infty, 0)$
4. The cube function, $m(x) = x^3$, on $(0, \infty)$
5. The square root function, $n(x) = \sqrt{x}$, on $(0, \infty)$
6. The cube root function, $p(x) = \sqrt[3]{x}$, on $(-\infty, 0)$
7. The absolute value function, $g(x) = |x|$, on $(-\infty, 0)$
8. The cube root function, $p(x) = \sqrt[3]{x}$, on $(0, \infty)$

A

9. Use the graph of $y = f(x)$, assuming $f''(x) > 0$ if $x = b$ or f, to identify
   (A) Intervals on which the graph of f is concave upward
   (B) Intervals on which the graph of f is concave downward
   (C) Intervals on which $f''(x) < 0$
   (D) Intervals on which $f''(x) > 0$
   (E) Intervals on which $f'(x)$ is increasing
   (F) Intervals on which $f'(x)$ is decreasing

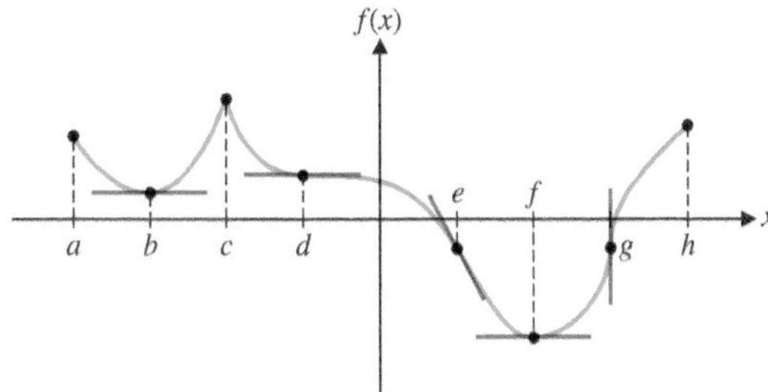

10. Use the graph of $y = g(x)$, assuming $g''(x) > 0$ if $x = c$ or g, to identify
    (A) Intervals on which the graph of g is concave upward
    (B) Intervals on which the graph of g is concave downward
    (C) Intervals on which $g''(x) < 0$
    (D) Intervals on which $g''(x) > 0$
    (E) Intervals on which $g'(x)$ is increasing
    (F) Intervals on which $g'(x)$ is decreasing

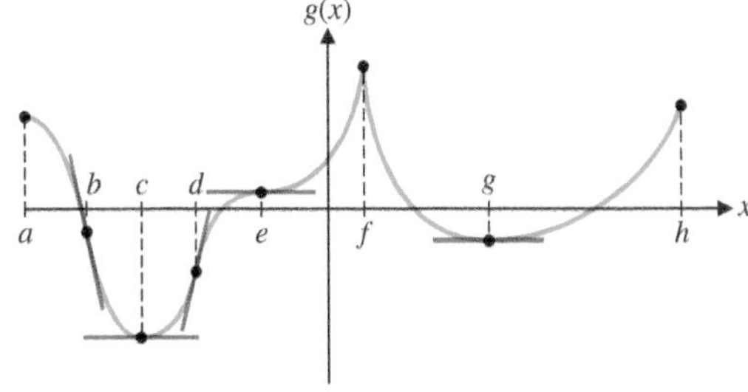

11. Use the graph of $y = f(x)$ to identify
    (A) The local extrema of $f(x)$.
    (B) The inflection points of $f(x)$.
    (C) The numbers u for which $f'(u)$ is a local extremum of $f'(x)$.

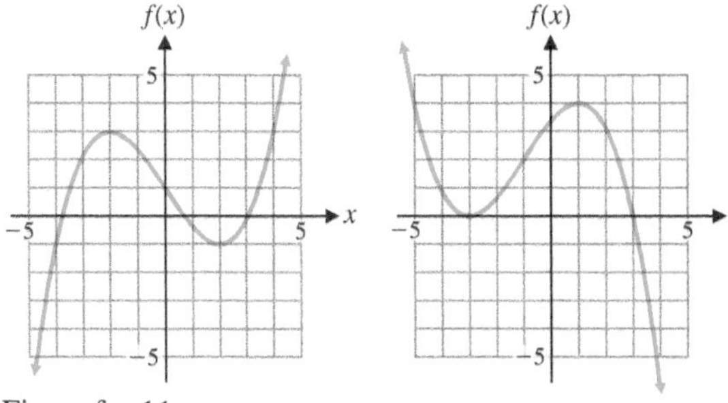

Figure for 11

Figure for 12

12. Use the graph of $y = f(x)$ to identify
    (A) The local extrema of $f(x)$.
    (B) The inflection points of $f(x)$.
    (C) The numbers u for which $f'(u)$ is a local extremum of $f'(x)$.

In Problems 13–16, match the indicated conditions with one of the graphs (A)–(D) shown in the figure.

13. $f'(x) > 0$ and $f''(x) > 0$ on (a, b)
14. $f'(x) > 0$ and $f''(x) < 0$ on (a, b)
15. $f'(x) < 0$ and $f''(x) > 0$ on (a, b)
16. $f'(x) < 0$ and $f''(x) < 0$ on (a, b)

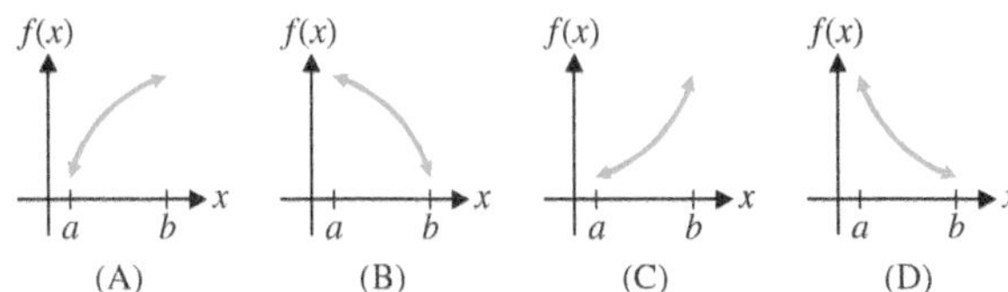

In Problems 17–24, find the indicated derivative for each function.

17. $f''(x)$ for $f(x) = 2x^3 - 4x^2 + 5x - 6$
18. $g''(x)$ for $g(x) = -4x^3 + 3x^2 - 2x + 1$
19. $h''(x)$ for $h(x) = 2x^{-1} - 3x^{-2}$
20. $k''(x)$ for $k(x) = -6x^{-2} + 12x^{-3}$
21. d^2y/dx^2 for $y = x^2 - 18x^{1/2}$
22. d^2y/dx^2 for $y = x^4 - 32x^{1/4}$
23. y'' for $y = (x^2 + 9)^4$
24. y'' for $y = (x^2 - 25)^6$

In Problems 25–30, find the x and y coordinates of all inflection points.

25. $f(x) = x^3 + 30x^2$
26. $f(x) = x^3 - 36x^2$
27. $f(x) = x^{5/3} + 2$
28. $f(x) = 5 - x^{4/3}$

29. $f(x) = 1 + x + x^{2/5}$

30. $f(x) = x^{5/6} + 7x - 8$

B *In Problems 31–40, find the intervals on which the graph of f is concave upward, the intervals on which the graph of f is concave downward, and the x, y coordinates of the inflection points.*

31. $f(x) = x^4 - 24x^2$

32. $f(x) = 3x^4 - 18x^2$

33. $f(x) = x^3 - 3x^2 + 7x + 2$

34. $f(x) = -x^3 + 3x^2 + 5x - 4$

35. $f(x) = -x^4 + 12x^3 - 7x + 10$

36. $f(x) = x^4 - 2x^3 - 5x + 3$

37. $f(x) = \ln(x^2 + 4x + 5)$

38. $f(x) = \ln(x^2 - 6x + 10)$

39. $f(x) = 4e^{3x} - 9e^{2x}$

40. $f(x) = 36e^{4x} - 16e^{6x}$

In Problems 41–44, use the given sign chart to sketch a possible graph of f.

41.

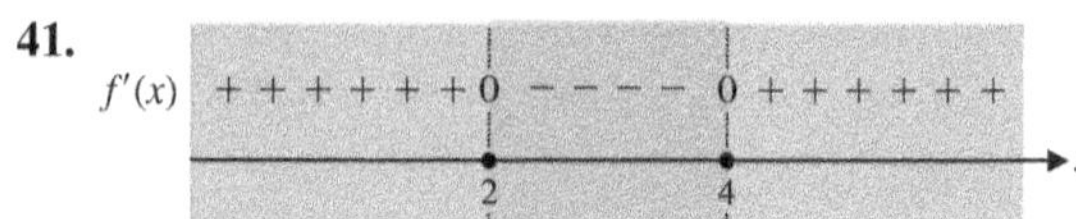

42.

43.

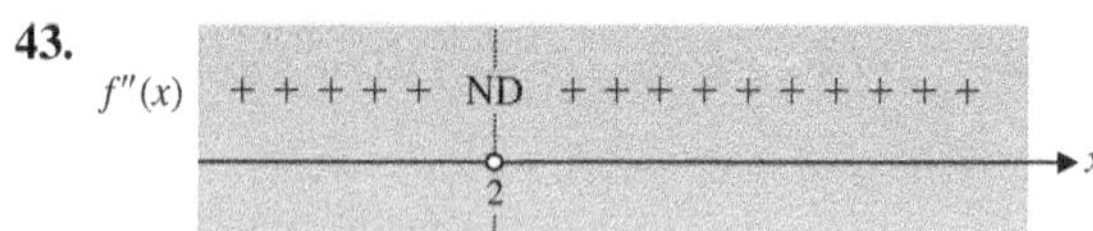

44.

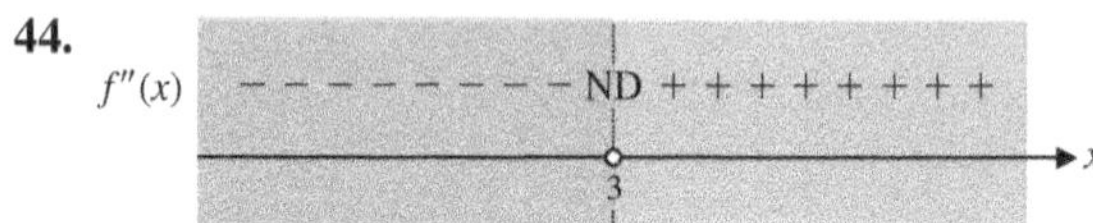

In Problems 45–52, $f(x)$ is continuous on $(-\infty, \infty)$. Use the given information to sketch the graph of f.

45.

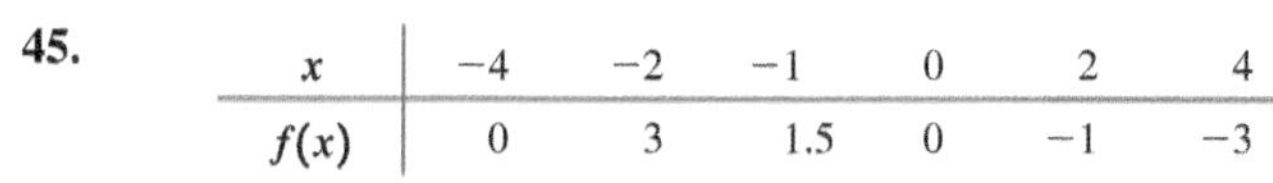

x	−4	−2	−1	0	2	4
$f(x)$	0	3	1.5	0	−1	−3

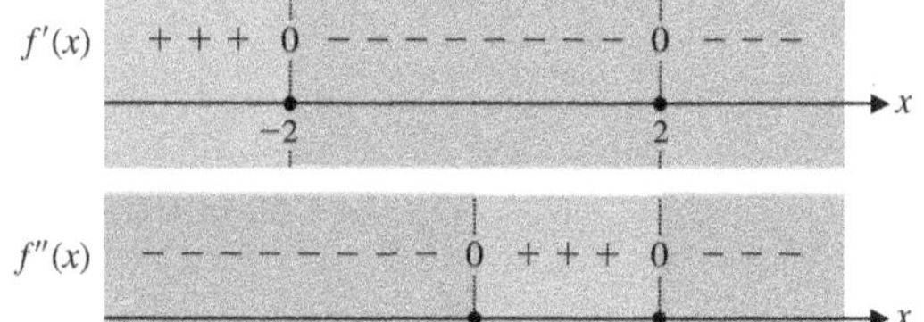

46.

x	−4	−2	−1	0	2	4
$f(x)$	0	−2	−1	0	1	3

f'(x): - - - 0 + + + + + + + + + 0 + + + (x; −2, 2)

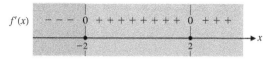

f''(x): + + + + + + + + + 0 - - - 0 + + + (x; −1, 2)

47.

x	−3	0	1	2	4	5
$f(x)$	−4	0	2	1	−1	0

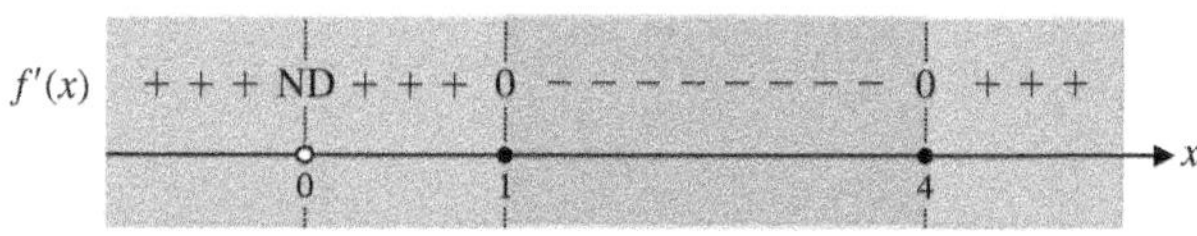

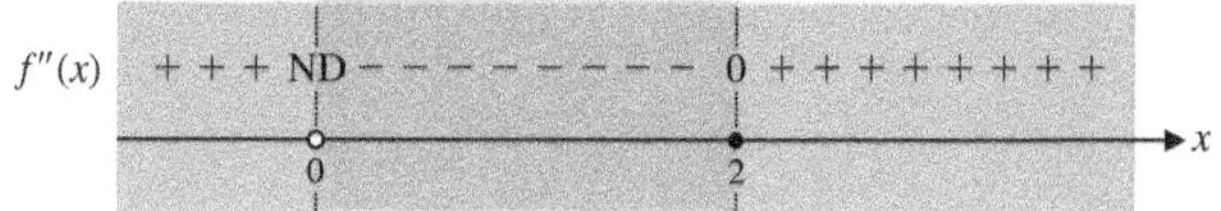

48.

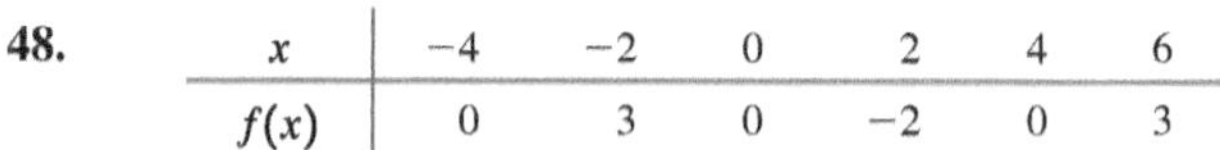

x	−4	−2	0	2	4	6
$f(x)$	0	3	0	−2	0	3

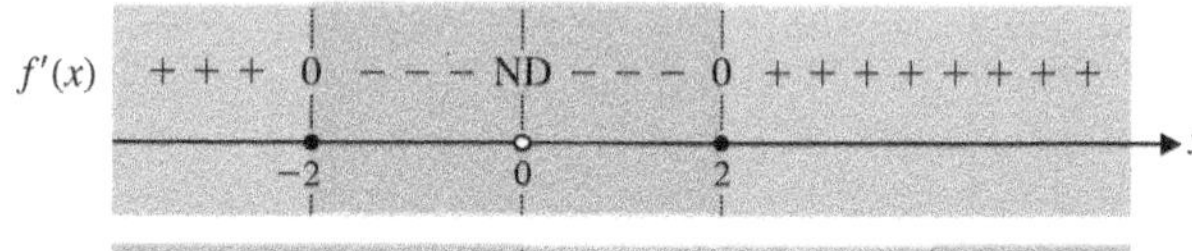

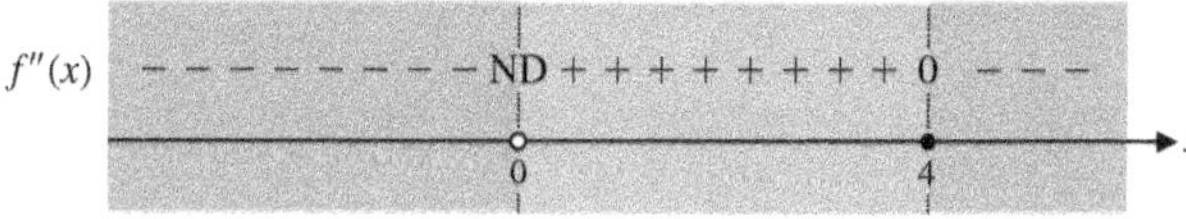

49. $f(0) = 2, f(1) = 0, f(2) = -2;$
$f'(0) = 0, f'(2) = 0;$
$f'(x) > 0$ on $(-\infty, 0)$ and $(2, \infty);$
$f'(x) < 0$ on $(0, 2);$
$f''(1) = 0;$
$f''(x) > 0$ on $(1, \infty);$
$f''(x) < 0$ on $(-\infty, 1)$

50. $f(-2) = -2, f(0) = 1, f(2) = 4;$
$f'(-2) = 0, f'(2) = 0;$
$f'(x) > 0$ on $(-2, 2);$
$f'(x) < 0$ on $(-\infty, -2)$ and $(2, \infty);$
$f''(0) = 0;$
$f''(x) > 0$ on $(-\infty, 0);$
$f''(x) < 0$ on $(0, \infty)$

51. $f(-1) = 0, f(0) = -2, f(1) = 0;$
$f'(0) = 0, f'(-1)$ and $f'(1)$ are not defined;
$f'(x) > 0$ on $(0, 1)$ and $(1, \infty);$

$f'(x) < 0$ on $(-\infty, -1)$ and $(-1, 0)$;

$f''(-1)$ and $f''(1)$ are not defined;

$f''(x) > 0$ on $(-1, 1)$;

$f''(x) < 0$ on $(-\infty, -1)$ and $(1, \infty)$

52. $f(0) = -2, f(1) = 0, f(2) = 4$;

$f'(0) = 0, f'(2) = 0, f'(1)$ is not defined

$f'(x) > 0$ on $(0, 1)$ and $(1, 2)$;

$f'(x) < 0$ on $(-\infty, 0)$ and $(2, \infty)$;

$f''(1)$ is not defined;

$f''(x) > 0$ on $(-\infty, 1)$;

$f''(x) < 0$ on $(1, \infty)$

C *In Problems 53–74, summarize the pertinent information obtained by applying the graphing strategy and sketch the graph of $y = f(x)$.*

53. $f(x) = (x - 2)(x^2 - 4x - 8)$

54. $f(x) = (x - 3)(x^2 - 6x - 3)$

55. $f(x) = (x + 1)(x^2 - x + 2)$

56. $f(x) = (1 - x)(x^2 + x + 4)$

57. $f(x) = -0.25x^4 + x^3$

58. $f(x) = 0.25x^4 - 2x^3$

59. $f(x) = 16x(x - 1)^3$

60. $f(x) = -4x(x + 2)^3$

61. $f(x) = (x^2 + 3)(9 - x^2)$

62. $f(x) = (x^2 + 3)(x^2 - 1)$

63. $f(x) = (x^2 - 4)^2$

64. $f(x) = (x^2 - 1)(x^2 - 5)$

65. $f(x) = 2x^6 - 3x^5$

66. $f(x) = 3x^5 - 5x^4$

67. $f(x) = 1 - e^{-x}$

68. $f(x) = 2 - 3e^{-2x}$

69. $f(x) = e^{0.5x} + 4e^{-0.5x}$

70. $f(x) = 2e^{0.5x} + e^{-0.5x}$

71. $f(x) = -4 + 2\ln x$

72. $f(x) = 5 - 3\ln x$

73. $f(x) = \ln(x + 4) - 2$

74. $f(x) = 1 - \ln(x - 3)$

In Problems 75–78, use the graph of $y = f'(x)$ to discuss the graph of $y = f(x)$. Organize your conclusions in a table (see Example 4), and sketch a possible graph of $y = f(x)$.

75.

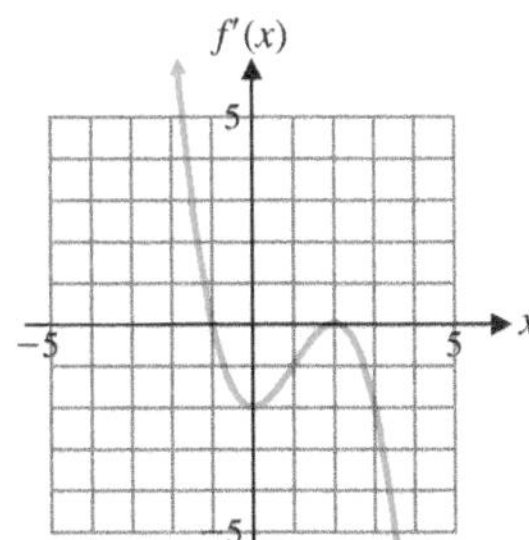

76.

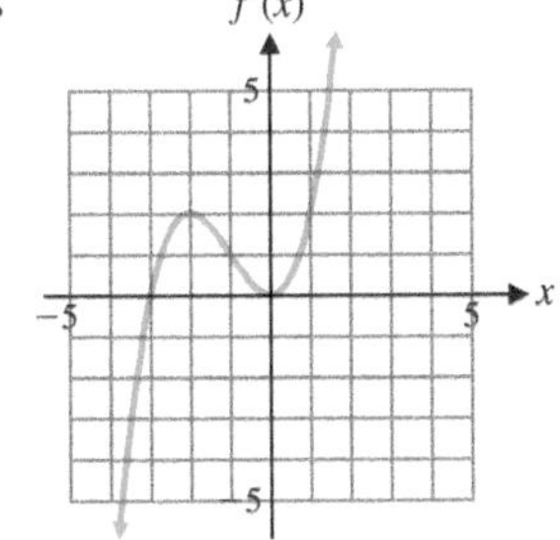

77.

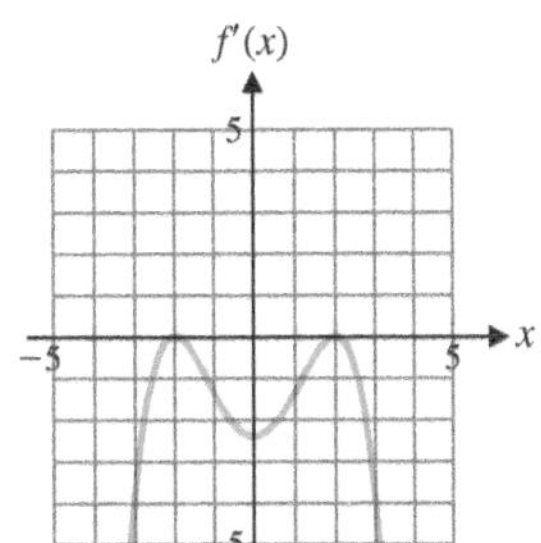

78.

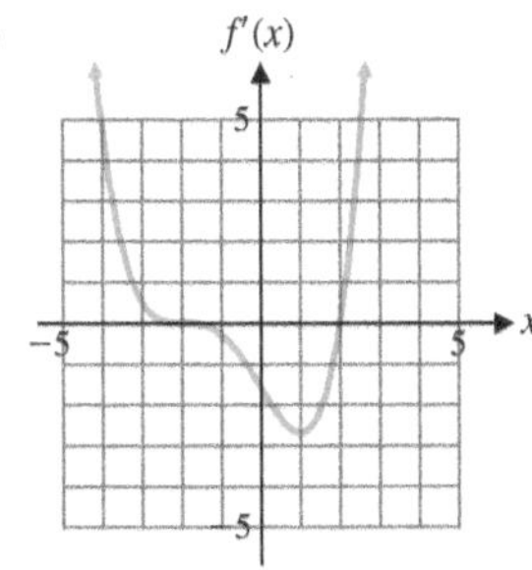

In Problems 79–82, apply steps 1–3 of the graphing strategy to $f(x)$. Use a graphing calculator to approximate (to two decimal places) x intercepts, critical numbers, and inflection points. Summarize all the pertinent information.

79. $f(x) = x^4 - 5x^3 + 3x^2 + 8x - 5$

80. $f(x) = x^4 + 4x^3 - 3x^2 - 2x + 1$

81. $f(x) = -x^4 - x^3 + 2x^2 - 2x + 3$

82. $f(x) = -x^4 + 4x^3 + 3x^2 + 2$

Applications

83. Inflation. One commonly used measure of inflation is the annual rate of change of the Consumer Price Index (CPI). A TV news story says that the annual rate of change of the CPI is increasing. What does this say about the shape of the graph of the CPI?

84. Inflation. Another commonly used measure of inflation is the annual rate of change of the Producer Price Index (PPI). A government report states that the annual rate of change of the PPI is decreasing. What does this say about the shape of the graph of the PPI?

85. Cost analysis. A company manufactures a variety of camp stoves at different locations. The total cost $C(x)$ (in dollars) of producing x camp stoves per week at plant A is shown in the figure. Discuss the graph of the marginal cost function $C'(x)$ and interpret the graph of $C'(x)$ in terms of the efficiency of the production process at this plant.

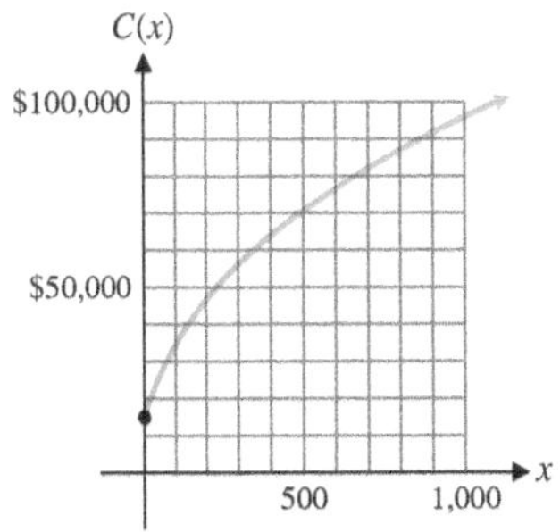

Production costs at plant A

86. Cost analysis. The company in Problem 85 produces the same camp stove at another plant. The total cost $C(x)$ (in dollars) of producing x camp stoves per week at plant B is shown in the figure. Discuss the graph of the marginal cost function $C'(x)$ and interpret the graph of $C'(x)$ in terms of the efficiency of the production process at plant B. Compare the production processes at the two plants.

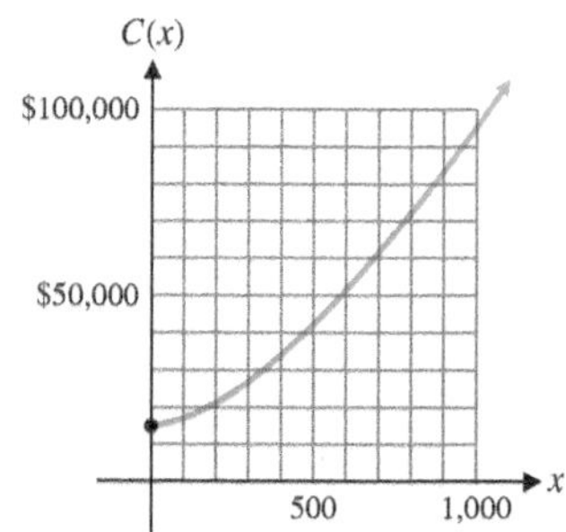

Production costs at plant *B*

87. **Revenue.** The marketing research department of a computer company used a large city to test market the firm's new laptop. The department found that the relationship between price p (dollars per unit) and the demand x (units per week) was given approximately by

$$p = 1{,}296 - 0.12x^2 \qquad 0 < x < 80$$

So weekly revenue can be approximated by

$$R(x) = xp = 1{,}296x - 0.12x^3 \qquad 0 < x < 80$$

(A) Find the local extrema for the revenue function.

(B) On which intervals is the graph of the revenue function concave upward? Concave downward?

88. **Profit.** Suppose that the cost equation for the company in Problem 87 is

$$C(x) = 830 + 396x$$

(A) Find the local extrema for the profit function.

(B) On which intervals is the graph of the profit function concave upward? Concave downward?

89. **Revenue.** A dairy is planning to introduce and promote a new line of organic ice cream. After test marketing the new line in a large city, the marketing research department found that the demand in that city is given approximately by

$$p = 10e^{-x} \qquad 0 \le x \le 5$$

where x thousand quarts were sold per week at a price of $\$p$ each.

(A) Find the local extrema for the revenue function.

(B) On which intervals is the graph of the revenue function concave upward? Concave downward?

90. **Revenue.** A national food service runs food concessions for sporting events throughout the country. The company's marketing research department chose a particular football stadium to test market a new jumbo hot dog. It was found that the demand for the new hot dog is given approximately by

$$p = 8 - 2\ln x \qquad 5 \le x \le 50$$

where x is the number of hot dogs (in thousands) that can be sold during one game at a price of $\$p$.

(A) Find the local extrema for the revenue function.

(B) On which intervals is the graph of the revenue function concave upward? Concave downward?

91. **Production: point of diminishing returns.** A T-shirt manufacturer is planning to expand its workforce. It estimates that the number of T-shirts produced by hiring x new workers is given by

$$T(x) = -0.25x^4 + 5x^3 \qquad 0 \le x \le 15$$

When is the rate of change of T-shirt production increasing and when is it decreasing? What is the point of diminishing returns and the maximum rate of change of T-shirt production? Graph T and T' on the same coordinate system.

92. **Production: point of diminishing returns.** A soccer ball manufacturer is planning to expand its workforce. It estimates that the number of soccer balls produced by hiring x new workers is given by

$$T(x) = -0.25x^4 + 4x^3 \qquad 0 \le x \le 12$$

When is the rate of change of soccer ball production increasing and when is it decreasing? What is the point of diminishing returns and the maximum rate of change of soccer ball production? Graph T and T' on the same coordinate system.

93. **Advertising: point of diminishing returns.** A company estimates that it will sell $N(x)$ units of a product after spending $\$x$ thousand on advertising, as given by

$$N(x) = -0.5x^4 + 46x^3 - 1{,}080x^2 + 160{,}000 \qquad 24 \le x \le 45$$

When is the rate of change of sales increasing and when is it decreasing? What is the point of diminishing returns and the maximum rate of change of sales? Graph N and N' on the same coordinate system.

94. **Advertising: point of diminishing returns.** A company estimates that it will sell $N(x)$ units of a product after spending $\$x$ thousand on advertising, as given by

$$N(x) = -0.5x^4 + 26x^3 - 360x^2 + 20{,}000 \qquad 15 \le x \le 24$$

When is the rate of change of sales increasing and when is it decreasing? What is the point of diminishing returns and the maximum rate of change of sales? Graph N and N' on the same coordinate system.

95. **Advertising.** An automobile dealer uses TV advertising to promote car sales. On the basis of past records, the dealer arrived at the following data, where x is the number of ads placed monthly and y is the number of cars sold that month:

Number of Ads x	Number of Cars y
10	325
12	339
20	417
30	546
35	615
40	682
50	795

(A) Enter the data in a graphing calculator and find a cubic regression equation for the number of cars sold monthly as a function of the number of ads.

(B) How many ads should the dealer place each month to maximize the rate of change of sales with respect to the number of ads, and how many cars can the dealer expect to sell with this number of ads? Round answers to the nearest integer.

96. **Advertising.** A sporting goods chain places TV ads to promote golf club sales. The marketing director used past records to determine the following data, where x is the number of ads placed monthly and y is the number of golf clubs sold that month.

Number of Ads x	Number of Golf Clubs y
10	345
14	488
20	746
30	1,228
40	1,671
50	1,955

(A) Enter the data in a graphing calculator and find a cubic regression equation for the number of golf clubs sold monthly as a function of the number of ads.

(B) How many ads should the store manager place each month to maximize the rate of change of sales with respect to the number of ads, and how many golf clubs can the manager expect to sell with this number of ads? Round answers to the nearest integer.

97. **Population growth: bacteria.** A drug that stimulates reproduction is introduced into a colony of bacteria. After t minutes, the number of bacteria is given approximately by

$$N(t) = 1{,}000 + 30t^2 - t^3 \qquad 0 \le t \le 20$$

(A) When is the rate of growth, $N'(t)$, increasing? Decreasing?

(B) Find the inflection points for the graph of N.

(C) Sketch the graphs of N and N' on the same coordinate system.

(D) What is the maximum rate of growth?

98. **Drug sensitivity.** One hour after x milligrams of a particular drug are given to a person, the change in body temperature $T(x)$, in degrees Fahrenheit, is given by

$$T(x) = x^2\left(1 - \frac{x}{9}\right) \qquad 0 \le x \le 6$$

The rate $T'(x)$ at which $T(x)$ changes with respect to the size of the dosage x is called the *sensitivity* of the body to the dosage.

(A) When is $T'(x)$ increasing? Decreasing?

(B) Where does the graph of T have inflection points?

(C) Sketch the graphs of T and T' on the same coordinate system.

(D) What is the maximum value of $T'(x)$?

99. **Learning.** The time T (in minutes) it takes a person to learn a list of length n is

$$T(n) = 0.08n^3 - 1.2n^2 + 6n \qquad n \ge 0$$

(A) When is the rate of change of T with respect to the length of the list increasing? Decreasing?

(B) Where does the graph of T have inflection points?

(C) Graph T and T' on the same coordinate system.

(D) What is the minimum value of $T'(n)$?

Answers to Matched Problems

1. (A) Concave downward on $(-\infty, \infty)$

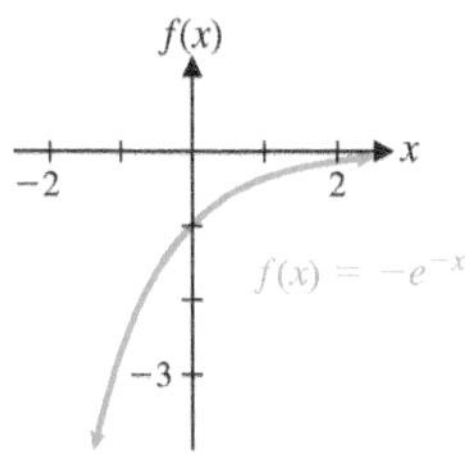

(B) Concave upward on $(0, \infty)$

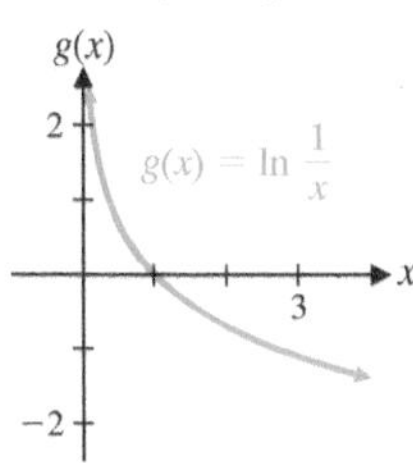

(C) Concave upward on $(-\infty, 0)$ and concave downward on $(0, \infty)$

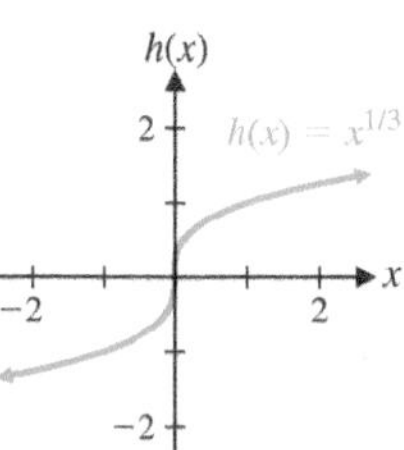

2. The only inflection point is $(3, f(3)) = (3, 8)$.
3. The inflection points are $(-1, f(-1)) = (-1, \ln 8)$ and $(3, f(3)) = (3, \ln 8)$.
4.

x	$f'(x)$	$f(x)$
$-\infty < x < -1$	Positive and decreasing	Increasing and concave downward
$x = -1$	Local minimum	Inflection point
$-1 < x < 1$	Positive and increasing	Increasing and concave upward
$x = 1$	Local maximum	Inflection point
$1 < x < 2$	Positive and decreasing	Increasing and concave downward
$x = 2$	x intercept	Local maximum
$2 < x < \infty$	Negative and decreasing	Decreasing and concave downward

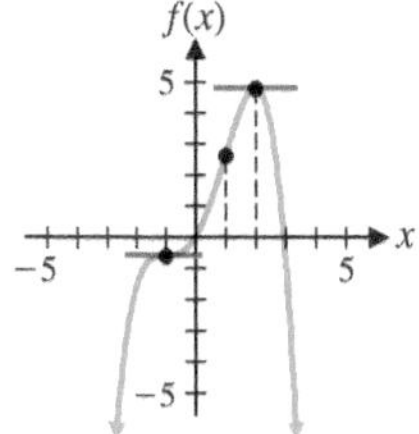

5. Domain: All real numbers
x intercepts: -4, 0; y intercept: $f(0) = 0$
Decreasing on $(-\infty, -3)$; increasing on $(-3, \infty)$; local minimum: $f(-3) = -27$
Concave upward on $(-\infty, -2)$ and $(0, \infty)$; concave downward on $(-2, 0)$
Inflection points: $(-2, -16)$, $(0, 0)$

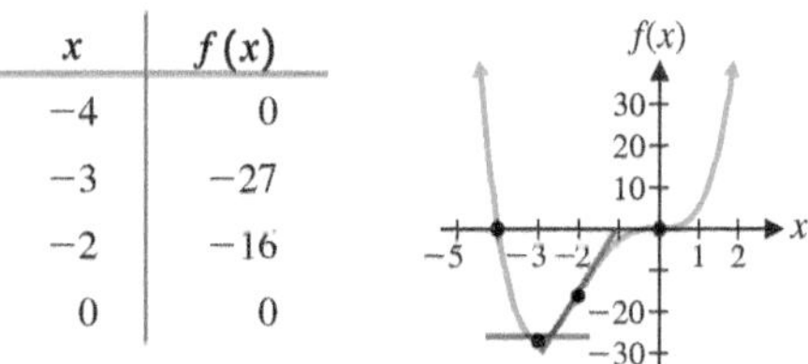

x	$f(x)$
-4	0
-3	-27
-2	-16
0	0

6. Domain: All real numbers
x intercepts: 0, 27; y intercept: $f(0) = 0$
Decreasing on $(-\infty, 0)$ and $(8, \infty)$; increasing on $(0, 8)$; local minimum: $f(0) = 0$; local maximum: $f(8) = 4$
Concave downward on $(-\infty, 0)$ and $(0, \infty)$; no inflection points

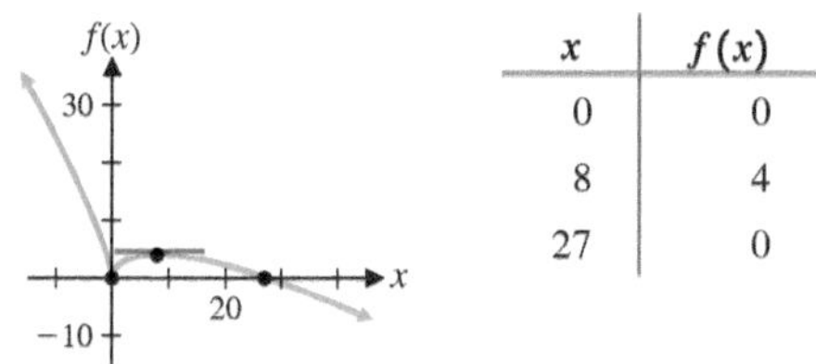

x	$f(x)$
0	0
8	4
27	0

7. $N'(x)$ is increasing on $(0, 8)$ and decreasing on $(8, 12)$. The point of diminishing returns is $x = 8$ and the maximum rate of change is $N'(8) = 256$.

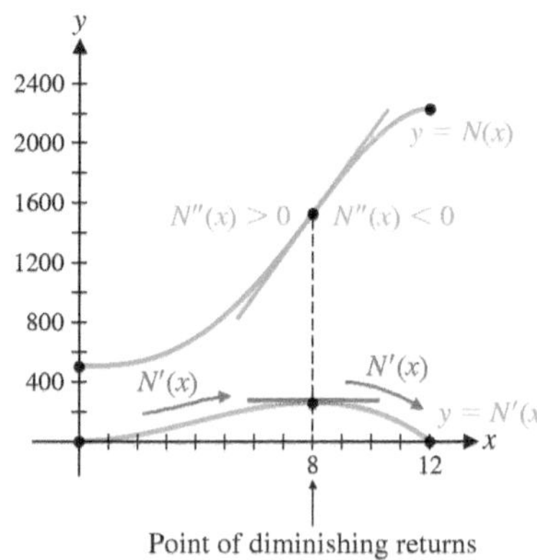

8.3 L'Hôpital's Rule

- Introduction
- L'Hôpital's Rule and the Indeterminate Form 0/0
- One-Sided Limits and Limits at ∞
- L'Hôpital's Rule and the Indeterminate Form ∞/∞

Introduction

The ability to evaluate a wide variety of different types of limits is one of the skills that are necessary to apply the techniques of calculus successfully. Limits play a fundamental role in the development of the derivative and are an important graphing tool. In order to deal effectively with graphs, we need to develop some more methods for evaluating limits.

In this section, we discuss a powerful technique for evaluating limits of quotients called *L'Hôpital's rule.* The rule is named after a French mathematician, the Marquis de L'Hôpital (1661–1704). To use L'Hôpital's rule, it is necessary to be familiar with the limit properties of some basic functions. Figure 1 reviews some limits involving powers of x that were discussed earlier.

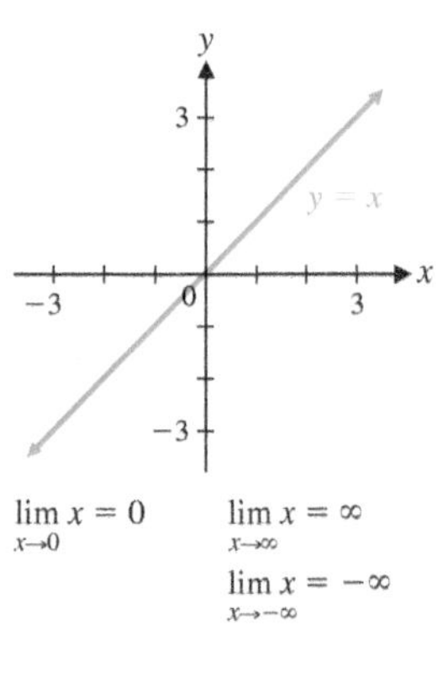

(A) $y = x$

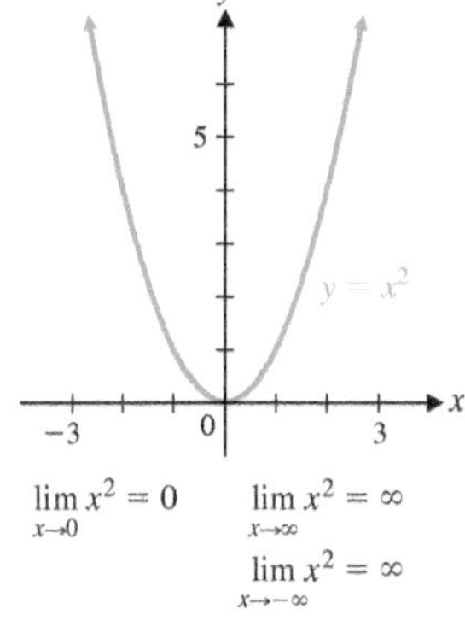

(B) $y = x^2$

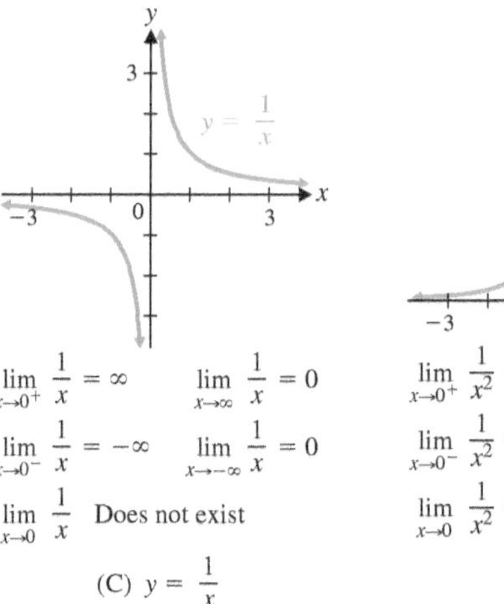

y
3
$y = \frac{1}{x}$
x
-3
0
3
$\lim_{x\to 0^+} \frac{1}{x} = \infty$
$\lim_{x\to\infty} \frac{1}{x} = 0$
$\lim_{x\to 0^-} \frac{1}{x} = -\infty$
$\lim_{x\to-\infty} \frac{1}{x} = 0$
$\lim_{x\to 0} \frac{1}{x}$ Does not exist

(C) $y = \frac{1}{x}$

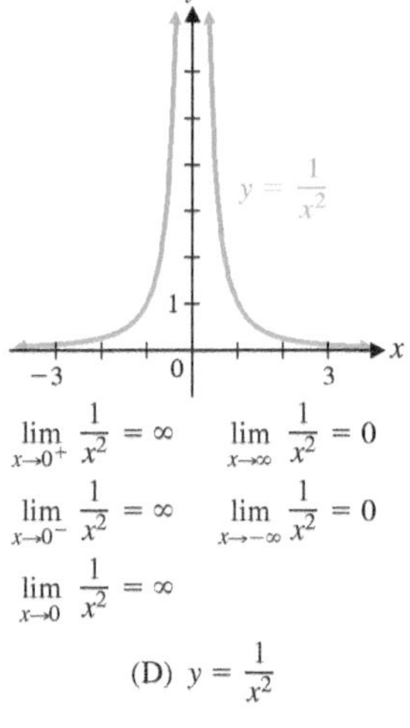

(D) $y = \frac{1}{x^2}$

Figure 1 Limits involving powers of x

The limits in Figure 1 are easily extended to functions of the form $f(x) = (x - c)^n$ and $g(x) = 1/(x - c)^n$. In general, if n is an odd integer, then limits involving $(x - c)^n$ or $1/(x - c)^n$ as x approaches c (or $\pm\infty$) behave, respectively, like the limits of x and $1/x$ as x approaches 0 (or $\pm\infty$). If n is an even integer, then limits involving these expressions behave, respectively, like the limits of x^2 and $1/x^2$ as x approaches 0 (or $\pm\infty$).

EXAMPLE 1 **Limits Involving Powers of $x - c$**

(A) $\lim_{x\to 2} \frac{5}{(x-2)^4} = \infty$ Compare with $\lim_{x\to 0} \frac{1}{x^2}$ in Figure 1.

(B) $\lim_{x\to -1^-} \frac{4}{(x+1)^3} = -\infty$ Compare with $\lim_{x\to 0^-} \frac{1}{x}$ in Figure 1.

(C) $\lim_{x\to\infty} \frac{4}{(x-9)^6} = 0$ Compare with $\lim_{x\to\infty} \frac{1}{x^2}$ in Figure 1.

(D) $\lim_{x\to -\infty} 3x^3 = -\infty$ Compare with $\lim_{x\to -\infty} x$ in Figure 1.

Matched Problem 1 Evaluate each limit.

(A) $\lim_{x\to 3^+} \frac{7}{(x-3)^5}$ (B) $\lim_{x\to -4} \frac{6}{(x+4)^6}$

(C) $\lim_{x\to -\infty} \frac{3}{(x+2)^3}$ (D) $\lim_{x\to\infty} 5x^4$

Figure 2 reviews limits of exponential and logarithmic functions.

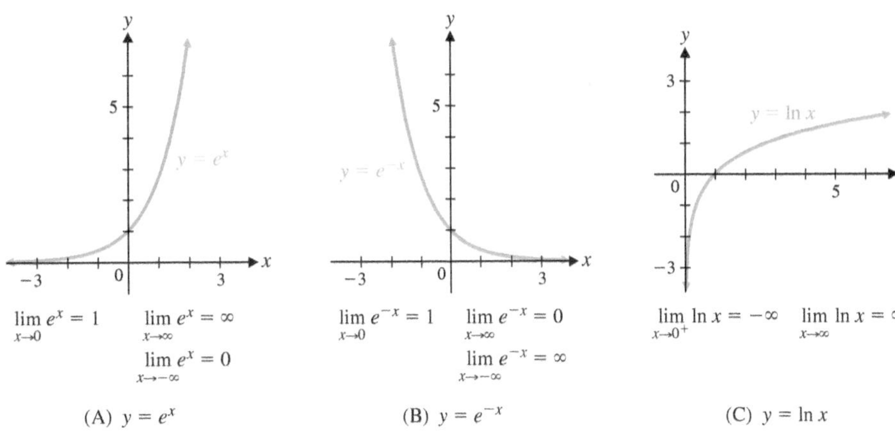

Figure 2 Limits involving exponential and logarithmic functions

The limits in Figure 2 also generalize to other simple exponential and logarithmic forms.

EXAMPLE 2 **Limits Involving Exponential and Logarithmic Forms**

(A) $\lim_{x\to\infty} 2e^{3x} = \infty$ Compare with $\lim_{x\to\infty} e^x$ in Figure 2.

(B) $\lim_{x\to\infty} 4e^{-5x} = 0$ Compare with $\lim_{x\to\infty} e^{-x}$ in Figure 2.

(C) $\lim_{x\to\infty} \ln(x+4) = \infty$ Compare with $\lim_{x\to\infty} \ln x$ in Figure 2.

(D) $\lim_{x\to 2^+} \ln(x-2) = -\infty$ Compare with $\lim_{x\to 0^+} \ln x$ in Figure 2.

Matched Problem 2 Evaluate each limit.

(A) $\lim_{x \to -\infty} 2e^{-6x}$ (B) $\lim_{x \to -\infty} 3e^{2x}$

(C) $\lim_{x \to -4^+} \ln(x + 4)$ (D) $\lim_{x \to \infty} \ln(x - 10)$

Now that we have reviewed the limit properties of some basic functions, we are ready to consider the main topic of this section: L'Hôpital's rule.

L'Hôpital's Rule and the Indeterminate Form 0/0

Recall that the limit

$$\lim_{x \to c} \frac{f(x)}{g(x)}$$

is a $0/0$ indeterminate form if

$$\lim_{x \to c} f(x) = 0 \quad \text{and} \quad \lim_{x \to c} g(x) = 0$$

The quotient property for limits in Section 8.1 does not apply since $\lim_{x \to c} g(x) = 0$.

If we are dealing with a $0/0$ indeterminate form, the limit may or may not exist, and we cannot tell which is true without further investigation.

Each of the following is a $0/0$ indeterminate form:

$$\lim_{x \to 2} \frac{x^2 - 4}{x - 2} \quad \text{and} \quad \lim_{x \to 1} \frac{e^x - e}{x - 1} \qquad (1)$$

The first limit can be evaluated by performing an algebraic simplification:

$$\lim_{x \to 2} \frac{x^2 - 4}{x - 2} = \lim_{x \to 2} \frac{(x - 2)(x + 2)}{x - 2} = \lim_{x \to 2} (x + 2) = 4$$

The second cannot. Instead, we turn to the powerful **L'Hôpital's rule**, which we state without proof. This rule can be used whenever a limit is a $0/0$ indeterminate form, so it can be used to evaluate both of the limits in (1).

THEOREM 1 L'Hôpital's Rule for 0/0 Indeterminate Forms:

For c a real number,
if $\lim_{x \to c} f(x) = 0$ and $\lim_{x \to c} g(x) = 0$, then

$$\lim_{x \to c} \frac{f(x)}{g(x)} = \lim_{x \to c} \frac{f'(x)}{g'(x)}$$

provided that the second limit exists or is ∞ or $-\infty$. The theorem remains valid if the symbol $x \to c$ is replaced everywhere it occurs with one of the following symbols:

$$x \to c^- \qquad x \to c^+ \qquad x \to \infty \qquad x \to -\infty$$

By L'Hôpital's rule,

$$\lim_{x \to 2} \frac{x^2 - 4}{x - 2} = \lim_{x \to 2} \frac{2x}{1} = 4$$

which agrees with the result obtained by algebraic simplification.

EXAMPLE 3 **L'Hôpital's Rule** Evaluate $\lim_{x \to 1} \frac{e^x - e}{x - 1}$.

SOLUTION

Step 1 *Check to see if L'Hôpital's rule applies:*

$$\lim_{x \to 1} (e^x - e) = e^1 - e = 0 \quad \text{and} \quad \lim_{x \to 1} (x - 1) = 1 - 1 = 0$$

L'Hôpital's rule does apply.

Step 2 *Apply L'Hôpital's rule:*

0/0 form

$$\lim_{x\to 1}\frac{e^x - e}{x - 1} = \lim_{x\to 1}\frac{\frac{d}{dx}(e^x - e)}{\frac{d}{dx}(x - 1)}$$

$$= \lim_{x\to 1}\frac{e^x}{1}$$ e^x is continuous at $x = 1$.

$$= \frac{e^1}{1} = e$$

Matched Problem 3 Evaluate $\lim_{x\to 4}\frac{e^x - e^4}{x - 4}$.

CAUTION In L'Hôpital's rule, the symbol $f'(x)/g'(x)$ represents the derivative of $f(x)$ divided by the derivative of $g(x)$, not the derivative of the quotient $f(x)/g(x)$.

When applying L'Hôpital's rule to a 0/0 indeterminate form, do not use the quotient rule. Instead, evaluate the limit of the derivative of the numerator divided by the derivative of the denominator.

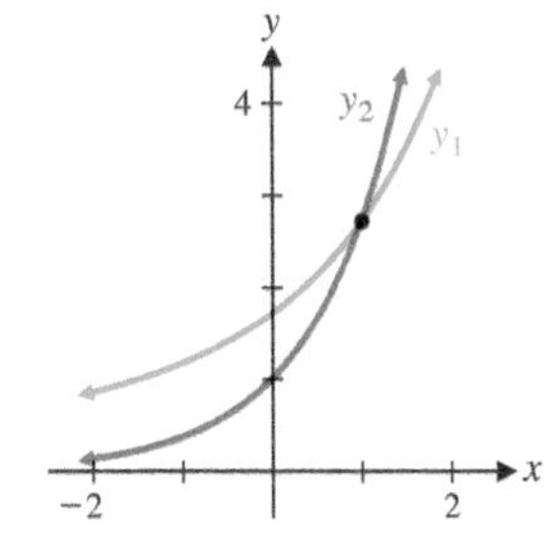

Figure 3

The functions

$$y_1 = \frac{e^x - e}{x - 1} \quad \text{and} \quad y_2 = \frac{e^x}{1}$$

of Example 3 are different functions (see Fig. 3), but both functions have the same limit e as x approaches 1. Although y_1 is undefined at $x = 1$, the graph of y_1 provides a check of the answer to Example 3.

EXAMPLE 4 **L'Hôpital's Rule** Evaluate $\lim_{x\to 0}\frac{\ln(1 + x^2)}{x^4}$.

SOLUTION

Step 1 *Check to see if L'Hôpital's rule applies:*

$$\lim_{x\to 0}\ln(1 + x^2) = \ln 1 = 0 \quad \text{and} \quad \lim_{x\to 0}x^4 = 0$$

L'Hôpital's rule does apply.

Step 2 *Apply L'Hôpital's rule:*

0/0 form

$$\lim_{x\to 0}\frac{\ln(1 + x^2)}{x^4} = \lim_{x\to 0}\frac{\frac{d}{dx}\ln(1 + x^2)}{\frac{d}{dx}x^4}$$

$$\lim_{x\to 0}\frac{\ln(1 + x^2)}{x^4} = \lim_{x\to 0}\frac{\frac{2x}{1 + x^2}}{4x^3}$$ Multiply numerator and denominator by $1/4x^3$.

$$= \lim_{x\to 0}\frac{\frac{2x}{1 + x^2}\frac{1}{4x^3}}{4x^3\frac{1}{4x^3}}$$ Simplify.

$$= \lim_{x\to 0} \frac{1}{2x^2(1+x^2)}$$ Apply Theorem 1 in Section 8.2 and compare with Fig. 1(D).

$$= \infty$$

Matched Problem 4 Evaluate $\lim_{x\to 1} \frac{\ln x}{(x-1)^3}$.

EXAMPLE 5 **L'Hôpital's Rule May Not Be Applicable** Evaluate $\lim_{x\to 1} \frac{\ln x}{x}$.

SOLUTION

Step 1 *Check to see if L'Hôpital's rule applies:*

$$\lim_{x\to 1} \ln x = \ln 1 = 0, \quad \text{but} \quad \lim_{x\to 1} x = 1 \neq 0$$

L'Hôpital's rule does not apply.

Step 2 *Evaluate by another method.* The quotient property for limits from Section 8.1 does apply, and we have

$$\lim_{x\to 1} \frac{\ln x}{x} = \frac{\lim_{x\to 1} \ln x}{\lim_{x\to 1} x} = \frac{\ln 1}{1} = \frac{0}{1} = 0$$

Note that applying L'Hôpital's rule would give us an incorrect result:

$$\lim_{x\to 1} \frac{\ln x}{x} \neq \lim_{x\to 1} \frac{\frac{d}{dx}\ln x}{\frac{d}{dx}x} = \lim_{x\to 1} \frac{1/x}{1} = 1$$

Matched Problem 5 Evaluate $\lim_{x\to 0} \frac{x}{e^x}$.

⚠ CAUTION As Example 5 illustrates, some limits involving quotients are not $0/0$ indeterminate forms.

You must always check to see if L'Hôpital's rule applies before you use it. ▲

EXAMPLE 6 **Repeated Application of L'Hôpital's Rule** Evaluate

$$\lim_{x\to 0} \frac{x^2}{e^x - 1 - x}$$

SOLUTION

Step 1 *Check to see if L'Hôpital's rule applies:*

$$\lim_{x\to 0} x^2 = 0 \quad \text{and} \quad \lim_{x\to 0}(e^x - 1 - x) = 0$$

L'Hôpital's rule does apply.

Step 2 *Apply L'Hôpital's rule:*

0/0 form

$$\lim_{x\to 0} \frac{x^2}{e^x - 1 - x} = \lim_{x\to 0} \frac{\frac{d}{dx}x^2}{\frac{d}{dx}(e^x - 1 - x)} = \lim_{x\to 0} \frac{2x}{e^x - 1}$$

Since $\lim_{x\to 0} 2x = 0$ and $\lim_{x\to 0}(e^x - 1) = 0$, the new limit obtained is also a $0/0$ indeterminate form, and L'Hôpital's rule can be applied again.

Step 3 *Apply L'Hôpital's rule again:*

0/0 form

$$\lim_{x\to 0}\frac{2x}{e^x-1} = \lim_{x\to 0}\frac{\frac{d}{dx}2x}{\frac{d}{dx}(e^x-1)} = \lim_{x\to 0}\frac{2}{e^x} = \frac{2}{e^0} = 2$$

Therefore,

$$\lim_{x\to 0}\frac{x^2}{e^x-1-x} = \lim_{x\to 0}\frac{2x}{e^x-1} = \lim_{x\to 0}\frac{2}{e^x} = 2$$

Matched Problem 6 Evaluate $\lim_{x\to 0}\frac{e^{2x}-1-2x}{x^2}$

One-Sided Limits and Limits at ∞

In addition to examining the limit as x approaches c, we have discussed one-sided limits and limits at ∞ in Chapter 7. L'Hôpital's rule is valid in these cases also.

EXAMPLE 7 **L'Hôpital's Rule for One-Sided Limits** Evaluate $\lim_{x\to 1^+}\frac{\ln x}{(x-1)^2}$.

SOLUTION

Step 1 *Check to see if L'Hôpital's rule applies:*

$$\lim_{x\to 1^+}\ln x = 0 \quad\text{and}\quad \lim_{x\to 1^+}(x-1)^2 = 0$$

L'Hôpital's rule does apply.

Step 2 *Apply L'Hôpital's rule:*

0/0 form

$$\begin{aligned}\lim_{x\to 1^+}\frac{\ln x}{(x-1)^2} &= \lim_{x\to 1^+}\frac{\frac{d}{dx}(\ln x)}{\frac{d}{dx}(x-1)^2}\\ &= \lim_{x\to 1^+}\frac{1/x}{2(x-1)} \quad \text{Simplify.}\\ &= \lim_{x\to 1^+}\frac{1}{2x(x-1)}\\ &= \infty\end{aligned}$$

The limit as $x\to 1^+$ is ∞ because $1/2x(x-1)$ has a vertical asymptote at $x = 1$ (Theorem 1, Section 8.2) and $x(x-1) > 0$ for $x > 1$.

Matched Problem 7 Evaluate $\lim_{x\to 1^-}\frac{\ln x}{(x-1)^2}$.

EXAMPLE 8 **L'Hôpital's Rule for Limits at Infinity** Evaluate $\lim_{x\to\infty}\frac{\ln(1+e^{-x})}{e^{-x}}$.

SOLUTION

Step 1 *Check to see if L'Hôpital's rule applies:*

$$\lim_{x\to\infty}\ln(1+e^{-x}) = \ln(1+0) = \ln 1 = 0 \text{ and } \lim_{x\to\infty}e^{-x} = 0$$

L'Hôpital's rule does apply.

Step 2 *Apply L'Hôpital's rule:*

$$\lim_{x\to\infty} \frac{\ln(1 + e^{-x})}{e^{-x}} \quad (0/0 \text{ form}) = \lim_{x\to\infty} \frac{\frac{d}{dx}[\ln(1 + e^{-x})]}{\frac{d}{dx}e^{-x}}$$

$$= \lim_{x\to\infty} \frac{-e^{-x}/(1 + e^{-x})}{-e^{-x}}$$

Multiply numerator and denominator by $-e^{x}$.

$$= \lim_{x\to\infty} \frac{1}{1 + e^{-x}}$$

$\lim_{x\to\infty} e^{-x} = 0$

$$= \frac{1}{1 + 0} = 1$$

Matched Problem 8 Evaluate $\lim_{x\to-\infty} \frac{\ln(1 + 2e^{x})}{e^{x}}$.

L'Hôpital's Rule and the Indeterminate Form ∞/∞

In Section 8.2, we discussed techniques for evaluating limits of rational functions such as

$$\lim_{x\to\infty} \frac{2x^2}{x^3 + 3} \qquad \lim_{x\to\infty} \frac{4x^3}{2x^2 + 5} \qquad \lim_{x\to\infty} \frac{3x^3}{5x^3 + 6} \tag{2}$$

Each of these limits is an ∞/∞ *indeterminate form.* In general, if $\lim_{x\to c} f(x) = \pm\infty$ and $\lim_{x\to c} g(x) = \pm\infty$, then

$$\lim_{x\to c} \frac{f(x)}{g(x)}$$

is called an **∞/∞ indeterminate form**. Furthermore, $x \to c$ can be replaced in all three limits above with $x \to c^{+}, x \to c^{-}, x \to \infty$, or $x \to -\infty$. It can be shown that L'Hôpital's rule also applies to these ∞/∞ indeterminate forms.

THEOREM 2 L'Hôpital's Rule for the Indeterminate Form ∞/∞

L'Hôpital's rule for the indeterminate form 0/0 is also valid if the limit of *f* and the limit of *g* are both infinite; that is, both $+\infty$ and $-\infty$ are permissible for either limit.

For example, if $\lim_{x\to c^{+}} f(x) = \infty$ and $\lim_{x\to c^{+}} g(x) = -\infty$, then L'Hôpital's rule can be applied to $\lim_{x\to c^{+}} [f(x)/g(x)]$.

Explore and Discuss 1

Evaluate each of the limits in (2) in two ways:

1. Use Theorem 4 in Section 8.2.
2. Use L'Hôpital's rule.

Given a choice, which method would you choose? Why?

EXAMPLE 9 **L'Hôpital's Rule for the Indeterminate Form ∞/∞** Evaluate $\lim_{x\to\infty} \frac{\ln x}{x^2}$.

SOLUTION

Step 1 *Check to see if L'Hôpital's rule applies:*

$$\lim_{x\to\infty} \ln x = \infty \quad \text{and} \quad \lim_{x\to\infty} x^2 = \infty$$

L'Hôpital's rule does apply.

Step 2 *Apply L'Hôpital's rule:*

$$\lim_{x\to\infty} \frac{\ln x}{x^2} = \lim_{x\to\infty} \frac{\frac{d}{dx}(\ln x)}{\frac{d}{dx}x^2} \quad \text{(∞/∞ form) Apply L'Hôpital's rule.}$$

$$= \lim_{x\to\infty} \frac{1/x}{2x} \quad \text{Simplify.}$$

$$\lim_{x\to\infty} \frac{\ln x}{x^2} = \lim_{x\to\infty} \frac{1}{2x^2} \quad \text{See Figure 1(D).}$$

$$= 0$$

Matched Problem 9 Evaluate $\lim_{x\to\infty} \frac{\ln x}{x}$.

EXAMPLE 10 **Horizontal Asymptotes and L'Hôpital's Rule** Find all horizontal asymptotes of $f(x) = \frac{x^2}{e^x}$.

SOLUTION

Step 1 *Consider the limit at $-\infty$:*

Since $\lim_{x\to-\infty} x^2 = \infty$ and $\lim_{x\to-\infty} e^x = 0$, L'Hôpital's rule does not apply. Rewriting f as $f(x) = x^2e^{-x}$ we see that as $x \to -\infty$, $x^2 \to \infty$ and $e^{-x} \to \infty$, so $\lim_{x\to-\infty} f(x) = \infty$, which does not give a horizontal asymptote.

Step 2 *Consider the limit at ∞:*

Since $\lim_{x\to\infty} x^2 = \infty$ and $\lim_{x\to\infty} e^x = \infty$, we may apply L'Hôpital's rule to get

$$\lim_{x\to\infty} \frac{x^2}{e^x} = \lim_{x\to\infty} \frac{\frac{d}{dx}x^2}{\frac{d}{dx}e^x} = \lim_{x\to\infty} \frac{2x}{e^x} \quad \text{(∞/∞ form) } \frac{\infty}{\infty} \text{ form: Apply L'Hôpital's Rule again}$$

$$= \lim_{x\to\infty} \frac{\frac{d}{dx}2x}{\frac{d}{dx}e^x} = \lim_{x\to\infty} \frac{2}{e^x} = 0.$$

This gives a horizontal asymptote of $y = 0$.

Matched Problem 10 Find all horizontal asymptotes of $f(x) = \frac{x^2}{e^{-x}}$.

CONCEPTUAL INSIGHT

Theorems 1 and 2 on L'Hôpital's rule cover a multitude of limits—far too many to remember case by case. Instead, we suggest you use the following pattern, common to both theorems, as a memory aid:

1. All cases involve three limits: $\lim\,[f(x)/g(x)]$, $\lim f(x)$, and $\lim g(x)$.
2. The independent variable x must behave the same way in all three limits. The acceptable behaviors are $x \to c$, $x \to c^+$, $x \to c^-$, $x \to \infty$, or $x \to -\infty$.
3. The form of $\lim\,[f(x)/g(x)]$ must be $\frac{0}{0}$ or $\frac{\pm\infty}{\pm\infty}$ and both $\lim f(x)$ and $\lim g(x)$ must approach 0 or both must approach $\pm\infty$.

Exercises 8.3

Skills Warm-up Exercises

W *In Problems 1–8, round each expression to the nearest integer without using a calculator. (If necessary, review Section B.1.)*

1. $\dfrac{5}{0.01}$
2. $\dfrac{8}{0.002}$
3. $\dfrac{3}{1{,}000}$
4. $\dfrac{2^8}{8}$
5. $\dfrac{1}{2(1.01 - 1)}$
6. $\dfrac{47}{106}$
7. $\dfrac{\ln 100}{100}$
8. $\dfrac{5e^6}{e^6 + 3^2}$

A *In Problems 9–16, even though the limit can be found using algebraic simplification as in Section 8.1, use L'Hôpital's rule to find the limit.*

9. $\lim\limits_{x \to 3} \dfrac{x^2 - 9}{x - 3}$
10. $\lim\limits_{x \to -3} \dfrac{x^2 - 9}{x + 3}$
11. $\lim\limits_{x \to -5} \dfrac{x + 5}{x^2 - 25}$
12. $\lim\limits_{x \to 7} \dfrac{x - 7}{x^2 - 49}$
13. $\lim\limits_{x \to 1} \dfrac{x^2 + 5x - 6}{x - 1}$
14. $\lim\limits_{x \to 10} \dfrac{x^2 - 5x - 50}{x - 10}$
15. $\lim\limits_{x \to -8} \dfrac{x + 8}{x^2 + 14x + 48}$
16. $\lim\limits_{x \to -1} \dfrac{x + 1}{x^2 - 7x - 8}$

In Problems 17–24, even though the limit can be found using Theorem 4 of Section 8.2, use L'Hôpital's rule to find the limit.

17. $\lim\limits_{x \to \infty} \dfrac{2x + 3}{5x - 1}$
18. $\lim\limits_{x \to \infty} \dfrac{6x - 7}{7x - 6}$
19. $\lim\limits_{x \to \infty} \dfrac{3x^2 - 1}{x^3 + 4}$
20. $\lim\limits_{x \to \infty} \dfrac{5x^2 + 10x + 1}{x^4 + x^2 + 1}$
21. $\lim\limits_{x \to -\infty} \dfrac{x^2 - 9}{x - 3}$
22. $\lim\limits_{x \to -\infty} \dfrac{x^4 - 16}{x^2 + 4}$
23. $\lim\limits_{x \to \infty} \dfrac{3x^2 + 4x - 5}{4x^2 - 3x + 2}$
24. $\lim\limits_{x \to \infty} \dfrac{5 - 4x^3}{1 + 7x^3}$

In Problems 25–32, use L'Hôpital's rule to find the limit. Note that in these problems, neither algebraic simplification nor Theorem 4 of Section 8.2 provides an alternative to L'Hôpital's rule.

25. $\lim\limits_{x \to 0} \dfrac{e^x - 1}{4x}$
26. $\lim\limits_{x \to 1} \dfrac{x - 1}{\ln x^3}$
27. $\lim\limits_{x \to 1} \dfrac{x - 1}{\ln x^5}$
28. $\lim\limits_{x \to 0} \dfrac{3x}{e^x - 1}$
29. $\lim\limits_{x \to \infty} \dfrac{e^x}{x^2}$
30. $\lim\limits_{x \to \infty} \dfrac{x^2}{\ln x}$
31. $\lim\limits_{x \to \infty} \dfrac{x}{\ln x^2}$
32. $\lim\limits_{x \to \infty} \dfrac{e^{2x}}{x^2}$

In Problems 33–36, explain why L'Hôpital's rule does not apply. If the limit exists, find it by other means.

33. $\lim\limits_{x \to -2} \dfrac{x^2 + 8x - 20}{x^3 - 8}$
34. $\lim\limits_{x \to \infty} \dfrac{e^{-x}}{\ln x}$
35. $\lim\limits_{x \to 2} \dfrac{x + 2}{(x - 2)^4}$
36. $\lim\limits_{x \to -3} \dfrac{x^2}{(x + 3)^5}$

B *Find each limit in Problems 37–60. Note that L'Hôpital's rule does not apply to every problem, and some problems will require more than one application of L'Hôpital's rule.*

37. $\lim\limits_{x \to 0} \dfrac{e^{4x} - 1 - 4x}{x^2}$
38. $\lim\limits_{x \to 0} \dfrac{6x - 1 + e^{-6x}}{x^2}$
39. $\lim\limits_{x \to 2} \dfrac{\ln(x - 1)}{x - 1}$
40. $\lim\limits_{x \to -1} \dfrac{\ln(x + 2)}{x + 2}$
41. $\lim\limits_{x \to 0^+} \dfrac{\ln(1 + x^2)}{x^3}$
42. $\lim\limits_{x \to 0^-} \dfrac{\ln(1 + 2x)}{x^2}$
43. $\lim\limits_{x \to 0^+} \dfrac{\ln(1 + \sqrt{x})}{x}$
44. $\lim\limits_{x \to 0^+} \dfrac{\ln(1 + x)}{\sqrt{x}}$
45. $\lim\limits_{x \to -2} \dfrac{x^2 + 2x + 1}{x^2 + x + 1}$
46. $\lim\limits_{x \to 1} \dfrac{2x^3 - 3x^2 + 1}{x^3 - 3x + 2}$

47. $\lim_{x \to -1} \frac{x^3 + x^2 - x - 1}{x^3 + 4x^2 + 5x + 2}$

48. $\lim_{x \to -2} \frac{x^3 - 4x^2 - 5x + 6}{x^2 - 7x - 8}$

49. $\lim_{x \to 2^-} \frac{x^3 - 12x + 16}{x^3 - 6x^2 + 12x - 8}$

50. $\lim_{x \to 1^+} \frac{x^3 + x^2 - x + 1}{x^3 + 3x^2 + 3x - 1}$

51. $\lim_{x \to \infty} \frac{3x^2 + 5x}{4x^3 + 7}$

52. $\lim_{x \to \infty} \frac{4x^2 + 9x}{5x^2 + 8}$

53. $\lim_{x \to \infty} \frac{x^2}{e^{2x}}$

54. $\lim_{x \to \infty} \frac{e^{3x}}{x^3}$

55. $\lim_{x \to \infty} \frac{1 + e^{-x}}{1 + x^2}$

56. $\lim_{x \to -\infty} \frac{1 + e^{-x}}{1 + x^2}$

57. $\lim_{x \to \infty} \frac{e^{-x}}{\ln(1 + 4e^{-x})}$

58. $\lim_{x \to \infty} \frac{\ln(1 + 2e^{-x})}{\ln(1 + e^{-x})}$

59. $\lim_{x \to 0} \frac{e^x - e^{-x} - 2x}{x^3}$

60. $\lim_{x \to 0} \frac{e^{2x} - 1 - 2x - 2x^2}{x^3}$

C 61. Find $\lim_{x \to 0^+} (x \ln x)$.
[*Hint*: Write $x \ln x = (\ln x)/x^{-1}$.]

62. Find $\lim_{x \to 0^+} (\sqrt{x} \ln x)$.
[*Hint*: Write $\sqrt{x} \ln x = (\ln x)/x^{-1/2}$.]

In Problems 63–66, n is a positive integer. Find each limit.

63. $\lim_{x \to \infty} \frac{\ln x}{x^n}$

64. $\lim_{x \to \infty} \frac{x^n}{\ln x}$

65. $\lim_{x \to \infty} \frac{e^x}{x^n}$

66. $\lim_{x \to \infty} \frac{x^n}{e^x}$

Find all horizontal asymptotes for each function in Problems 67–70.

67. $f(x) = \frac{e^{2x} + 10}{e^x - 1}$

68. $f(x) = \frac{12 + e^{-x}}{4 + e^{-3x}}$

69. $f(x) = \frac{3e^x + 1}{5e^x - 1}$

70. $f(x) = \frac{9e^x - 12}{3e^x + 4}$

Answers to Matched Problems

1. (A) ∞ (B) ∞ (C) 0 (D) ∞
2. (A) ∞ (B) 0 (C) $-\infty$ (D) ∞
3. e^4
4. ∞
5. 0
6. 2
7. $-\infty$
8. 2
9. 0
10. $y = 0$

8.4 Curve-Sketching Techniques

- Modifying the Graphing Strategy
- Using the Graphing Strategy
- Modeling Average Cost

When we summarized the graphing strategy in Section 8.2, we omitted one important topic: asymptotes. Polynomial functions do not have any asymptotes. Asymptotes of rational functions were discussed in Section 8.2, but what about all the other functions, such as logarithmic and exponential functions? Since investigating asymptotes always involves limits, we can now use L'Hôpital's rule (Section 8.3) as a tool for finding asymptotes of many different types of functions.

Modifying the Graphing Strategy

The first version of the graphing strategy in Section 8.2 made no mention of asymptotes. Including information about asymptotes produces the following (and final) version of the graphing strategy.

PROCEDURE Graphing Strategy (Final Version)

Step 1 *Analyze* $f(x)$.
(A) Find the domain of f.
(B) Find the intercepts.
(C) Find asymptotes.

Step 2 *Analyze* $f'(x)$. Find the partition numbers for f' and the critical numbers of f. Construct a sign chart for $f'(x)$, determine the intervals on which f is increasing and decreasing, and find local maxima and minima of f.

Step 3 *Analyze $f''(x)$.* Find the partition numbers for $f''(x)$. Construct a sign chart for $f''(x)$, determine the intervals on which the graph of f is concave upward and concave downward, and find the inflection points of f.

Step 4 *Sketch the graph of f.* Draw asymptotes and locate intercepts, local maxima and minima, and inflection points. Sketch in what you know from steps 1–3. Plot additional points as needed and complete the sketch.

Using the Graphing Strategy

We will illustrate the graphing strategy with several examples. From now on, you should always use the final version of the graphing strategy. If a function does not have any asymptotes, simply state this fact.

EXAMPLE 1 **Using the Graphing Strategy** Use the graphing strategy to analyze the function $f(x) = (x - 1)/(x - 2)$. State all the pertinent information and sketch the graph of f.

SOLUTION

Step 1 *Analyze $f(x)$.* $f(x) = \dfrac{x - 1}{x - 2}$

(A) Domain: All real x, except $x = 2$

(B) y intercept: $f(0) = \dfrac{0 - 1}{0 - 2} = \dfrac{1}{2}$

x intercepts: Since a fraction is 0 when its numerator is 0 and its denominator is not 0, the x intercept is $x = 1$.

(C) Horizontal asymptote: $\dfrac{a_m x^m}{b_n x^n} = \dfrac{x}{x} = 1$

So the line $y = 1$ is a horizontal asymptote.
Vertical asymptote: The denominator is 0 for $x = 2$, and the numerator is not 0 for this value. Therefore, the line $x = 2$ is a vertical asymptote.

Step 2 *Analyze $f'(x)$.* $f'(x) = \dfrac{(x - 2)(1) - (x - 1)(1)}{(x - 2)^2} = \dfrac{-1}{(x - 2)^2}$

Partition number for $f'(x)$: $x = 2$
Critical numbers of $f(x)$: None
Sign chart for $f'(x)$:

	$(-\infty, 2)$		$(2, \infty)$
$f'(x)$	- - - -	ND (2)	- - - -
$f(x)$	Decreasing		Decreasing

Test Numbers

x	$f'(x)$
1	-1 $(-)$
3	-1 $(-)$

So $f(x)$ is decreasing on $(-\infty, 2)$ and $(2, \infty)$. There are no local extrema.

Step 3 *Analyze $f''(x)$.* $f''(x) = \dfrac{2}{(x - 2)^3}$

Partition number for $f''(x)$: $x = 2$
Sign chart for $f''(x)$:

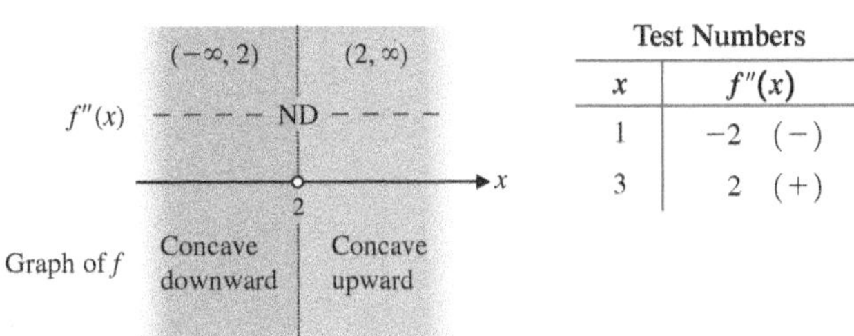

Test Numbers

x	$f''(x)$
1	−2 (−)
3	2 (+)

The graph of f is concave downward on $(-\infty, 2)$ and concave upward on $(2, \infty)$. Since $f(2)$ is not defined, there is no inflection point at $x = 2$, even though $f''(x)$ changes sign at $x = 2$.

Step 4 *Sketch the graph of f.* Insert intercepts and asymptotes, and plot a few additional points (for functions with asymptotes, plotting additional points is often helpful). Then sketch the graph.

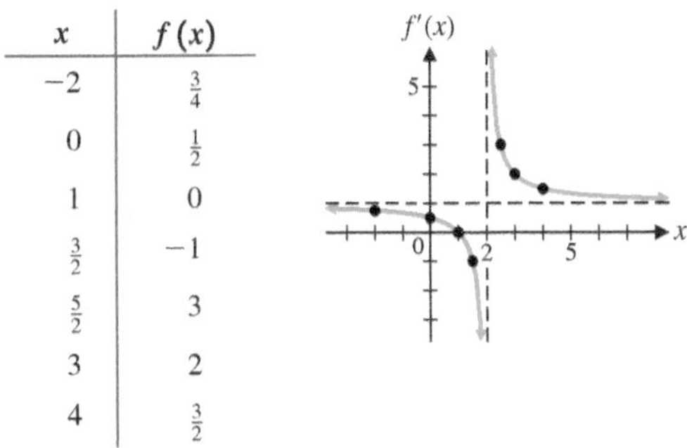

x	$f(x)$
−2	$\frac{3}{4}$
0	$\frac{1}{2}$
1	0
$\frac{3}{2}$	−1
$\frac{5}{2}$	3
3	2
4	$\frac{3}{2}$

Matched Problem 1 Follow the graphing strategy and analyze the function $f(x) = 2x/(1 - x)$. State all the pertinent information and sketch the graph of f.

EXAMPLE 2 **Using the Graphing Strategy** Use the graphing strategy to analyze the function

$$g(x) = \frac{2x - 1}{x^2}$$

State all pertinent information and sketch the graph of g.

SOLUTION

Step 1 *Analyze $g(x)$.*

(A) Domain: All real x, except $x = 0$

(B) x intercept: $x = \frac{1}{2} = 0.5$

y intercept: Since 0 is not in the domain of g, there is no y intercept.

(C) Horizontal asymptote: $y = 0$ (the x axis)

Vertical asymptote: The denominator of $g(x)$ is 0 at $x = 0$ and the numerator is not. So the line $x = 0$ (the y axis) is a vertical asymptote.

Step 2 *Analyze $g'(x)$.*

$$g(x) = \frac{2x - 1}{x^2} = \frac{2}{x} - \frac{1}{x^2} = 2x^{-1} - x^{-2}$$

$$g'(x) = -2x^{-2} + 2x^{-3} = -\frac{2}{x^2} + \frac{2}{x^3} = \frac{-2x + 2}{x^3}$$

$$= \frac{2(1 - x)}{x^3}$$

Partition numbers for $g'(x)$: $x = 0, x = 1$
Critical number of $g(x)$: $x = 1$
Sign chart for $g'(x)$:

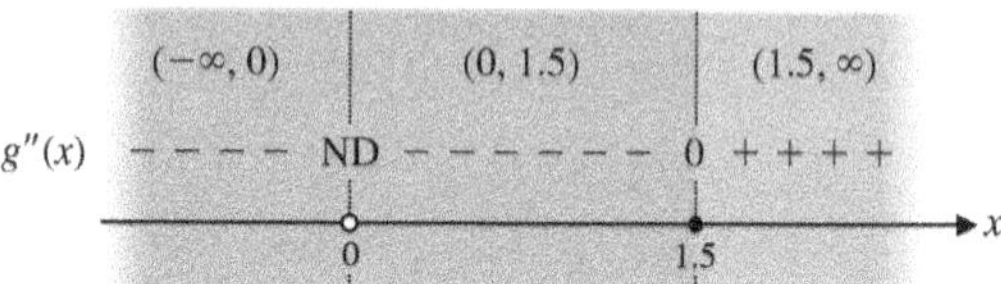

Function $f(x)$ is decreasing on $(-\infty, 0)$ and $(1, \infty)$, is increasing on (0, 1), and has a local maximum at $x = 1$. The local maximum is $g(1) = 1$.

Step 3 *Analyze* $g''(x)$.

$$g'(x) = -2x^{-2} + 2x^{-3}$$

$$g''(x) = 4x^{-3} - 6x^{-4} = \frac{4}{x^3} - \frac{6}{x^4} = \frac{4x - 6}{x^4} = \frac{2(2x - 3)}{x^4}$$

Partition numbers for $g''(x)$: $x = 0, x = \frac{3}{2} = 1.5$

Sign chart for $g''(x)$:

(−∞, 0) | (0, 1.5) | (1.5, ∞)

$g''(x)$ − − − − ND − − − − − − − 0 + + + +

0   1.5 x

Function $g(x)$ is concave downward on $(-\infty, 0)$ and (0, 1.5), is concave upward on $(1.5, \infty)$, and has an inflection point at $x = 1.5$. Since $g(1.5) = 0.89$, the inflection point is $(1.5, 0.89)$.

Step 4 *Sketch the graph of g.* Plot key points, note that the coordinate axes are asymptotes, and sketch the graph.

x	$g(x)$
−10	−0.21
−1	−3
0.5	0
1	1
1.5	0.89
10	0.19

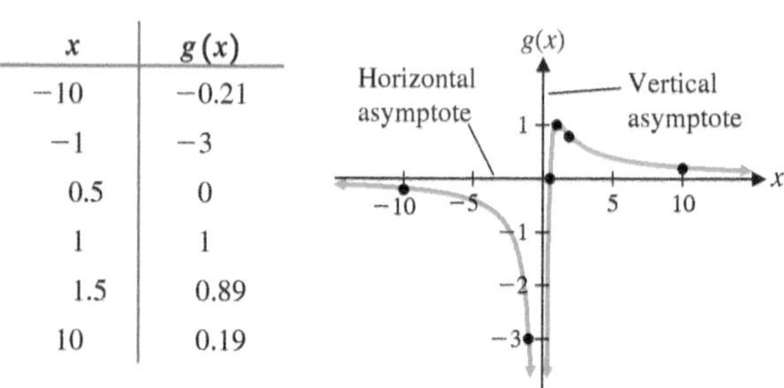

Matched Problem 2 Use the graphing strategy to analyze the function

$$h(x) = \frac{4x + 3}{x^2}$$

State all pertinent information and sketch the graph of h.

EXAMPLE 3 **Graphing Strategy** Follow the steps of the graphing strategy and analyze the function $f(x) = xe^x$. State all the pertinent information and sketch the graph of f.

SOLUTION

Step 1 *Analyze* $f(x)$: $f(x) = xe^x$.

(A) Domain: All real numbers

(B) y intercept: $f(0) = 0$
x intercept: $xe^x = 0$ for $x = 0$ only, since $e^x > 0$ for all x.

(C) Vertical asymptotes: None

(D) Horizontal asymptotes: We use tables to determine the nature of the graph of f as $x \to \infty$ and $x \to -\infty$:

x	1	5	10	$\to \infty$
$f(x)$	2.72	742.07	220,264.66	$\to \infty$

x	-1	-5	-10	$\to -\infty$
$f(x)$	-0.37	-0.03	$-0.000\,45$	$\to 0$

Step 2 *Analyze* $f'(x)$:

$$f'(x) = x\frac{d}{dx}e^x + e^x\frac{d}{dx}x$$

$$= xe^x + e^x = e^x(x + 1)$$

Partition number for $f'(x)$: -1
Critical number of $f(x)$: -1
Sign chart for $f'(x)$:

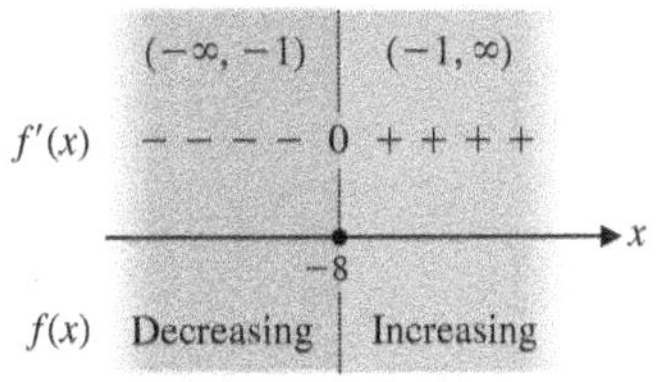

$(-\infty, -1)$ | $(-1, \infty)$
$f'(x)$ − − − − 0 + + + +
-8 x
$f(x)$ Decreasing | Increasing

Test Numbers

x	$f'(x)$
-2	$-e^{-2}$ $(-)$
0	1 $(+)$

So $f(x)$ decreases on $(-\infty, -1)$, has a local minimum at $x = -1$, and increases on $(-1, \infty)$. The local minimum is $f(-1) = -0.37$.

Step 3 *Analyze* $f''(x)$:

$$f''(x) = e^x\frac{d}{dx}(x + 1) + (x + 1)\frac{d}{dx}e^x$$

$$= e^x + (x + 1)e^x = e^x(x + 2)$$

Sign chart for $f''(x)$ (partition number is -2):

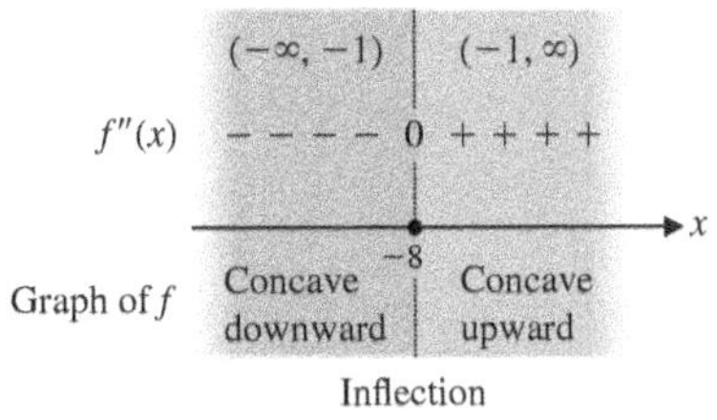

$(-\infty, -1)$ | $(-1, \infty)$
$f''(x)$ − − − − 0 + + + +
-8 x
Graph of f Concave downward | Concave upward
Inflection

Test Numbers

x	$f'(x)$
-3	$-e^{-3}$ $(-)$
-1	e^{-1} $(+)$

The graph of f is concave downward on $(-\infty, -2)$, has an inflection point at $x = -2$, and is concave upward on $(-2, \infty)$. Since $f(-2) = -0.27$, the inflection point is $(-2, -0.27)$.

Step 4 *Sketch the graph of f, using the information from steps 1 to 3:*

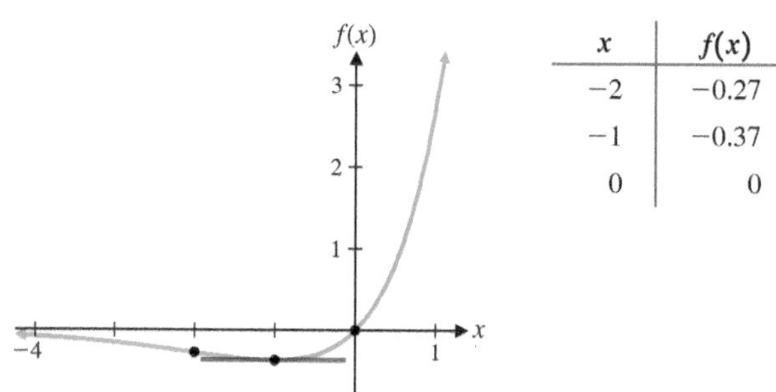

x	$f(x)$
−2	−0.27
−1	−0.37
0	0

Matched Problem 3 Analyze the function $f(x) = xe^{-0.5x}$. State all the pertinent information and sketch the graph of f.

Explore and Discuss 1

Refer to the discussion of asymptotes in the solution of Example 3. We used tables of values to estimate limits at infinity and determine horizontal asymptotes. In some cases, the functions involved in these limits can be written in a form that allows us to use L'Hôpital's rule.

$$\begin{aligned}
\lim_{x\to-\infty} f(x) &= \overset{-\infty\cdot 0 \text{ form}}{\lim_{x\to-\infty} xe^{x}} && \text{Rewrite as a fraction.}\\
&= \overset{-\infty/\infty \text{ form}}{\lim_{x\to-\infty} \frac{x}{e^{-x}}} && \text{Apply L'Hôpital's rule.}\\
&= \lim_{x\to-\infty} \frac{1}{-e^{-x}} && \text{Simplify.}\\
&= \lim_{x\to-\infty} (-e^{x}) && \text{Property of } e^{x}\\
&= 0
\end{aligned}$$

Use algebraic manipulation and L'Hôpital's rule to verify the value of each of the following limits:

(A) $\lim_{x\to\infty} xe^{-0.5x} = 0$

(B) $\lim_{x\to0^+} x^2(\ln x - 0.5) = 0$

(C) $\lim_{x\to0^+} x \ln x = 0$

EXAMPLE 4 **Graphing Strategy** Let $f(x) = x^2 \ln x - 0.5x^2$. Follow the steps in the graphing strategy and analyze this function. State all the pertinent information and sketch the graph of f.

SOLUTION

Step 1 *Analyze $f(x)$:* $f(x) = x^2 \ln x - 0.5x^2 = x^2(\ln x - 0.5)$.

(A) Domain: $(0, \infty)$

(B) y intercept: None [$f(0)$ is not defined.]

x intercept: Solve $x^2(\ln x - 0.5) = 0$

$$\begin{aligned}
\ln x - 0.5 = 0 \quad \text{or} \quad x^2 &= 0 && \text{Discard, since 0 is not in the domain of } f.\\
\ln x &= 0.5 && \ln x = a \text{ if and only if } x = e^{a}.\\
x &= e^{0.5} && x \text{ intercept}
\end{aligned}$$

(C) Asymptotes: None. The following tables suggest the nature of the graph as $x \to 0^+$ and as $x \to \infty$:

x	0.1	0.01	0.001	$\to 0^+$
$f(x)$	−0.0280	−0.00051	−0.000007	$\to 0$

See Explore and Discuss 1(B).

x	10	100	1,000	$\to \infty$
$f(x)$	180	41,000	6,400,000	$\to \infty$

Step 2 *Analyze $f'(x)$:*

$$f'(x) = x^2 \frac{d}{dx} \ln x + (\ln x)\frac{d}{dx}x^2 - 0.5\frac{d}{dx}x^2$$

$$= x^2\frac{1}{x} + (\ln x)\,2x - 0.5(2x)$$

$$= x + 2x \ln x - x$$

$$= 2x \ln x$$

Partition number for $f'(x)$: 1
Critical number of $f(x)$: 1
Sign chart for $f'(x)$:

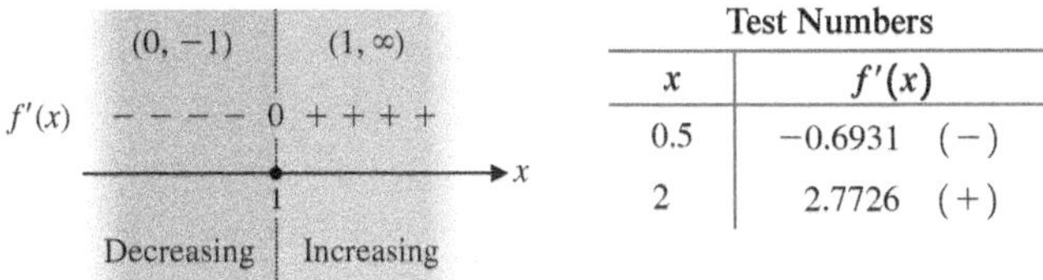

Test Numbers

x	$f'(x)$
0.5	−0.6931 (−)
2	2.7726 (+)

The function $f(x)$ decreases on (0, 1), has a local minimum at $x = 1$, and increases on $(1, \infty)$. The local minimum is $f(1) = -0.5$.

Step 3 *Analyze $f''(x)$:*

$$f''(x) = 2x\frac{d}{dx}(\ln x) + (\ln x)\frac{d}{dx}(2x)$$

$$= 2x\frac{1}{x} + (\ln x)\,2$$

$$= 2 + 2\ln x = 0$$

$$2\ln x = -2$$

$$\ln x = -1$$

$$x = e^{-1} \approx 0.3679$$

Sign chart for $f''(x)$ (partition number is e^{-1}):

$(0, e^{-1})$ | (e^{-1}, ∞)

$f''(x)$ − − − − 0 + + + +

x ; e^{-1}

Concave downward | Concave upward

Test Numbers

x	$f''(x)$
0.2	−1.2189 (−)
1	2 (+)

The graph of $f(x)$ is concave downward on $(0, e^{-1})$, has an inflection point at $x = e^{-1}$, and is concave upward on (e^{-1}, ∞). Since $f(e^{-1}) = -1.5e^{-2} \approx -0.20$, the inflection point is $(0.37, -0.20)$.

Step 4 *Sketch the graph of f, using the information from steps 1 to 3:*

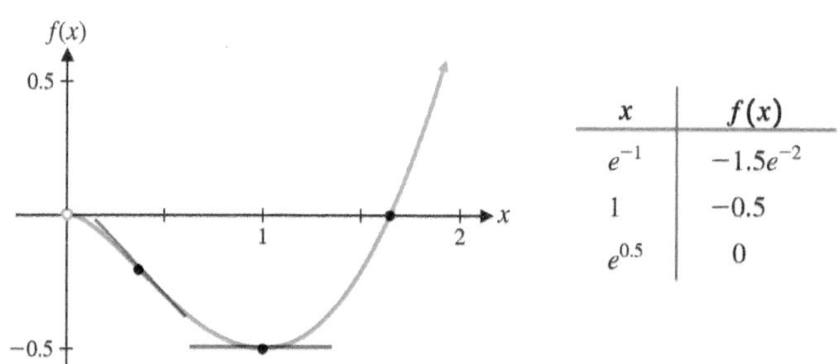

x	$f(x)$
e^{-1}	$-1.5e^{-2}$
1	−0.5
$e^{0.5}$	0

Matched Problem 4 Analyze the function $f(x) = x \ln x$. State all pertinent information and sketch the graph of f.

Modeling Average Cost

When functions approach a horizontal line as x approaches ∞ or $-\infty$, that line is a horizontal asymptote. Average cost functions often approach a nonvertical line as x approaches ∞ or $-\infty$.

DEFINITION Oblique Asymptote

If a graph approaches a line that is neither horizontal nor vertical as x approaches ∞ or $-\infty$, then that line is called an **oblique asymptote**.

If $f(x) = n(x)/d(x)$ is a rational function for which the degree of $n(x)$ is 1 more than the degree of $d(x)$, then we can use polynomial long division to write $f(x) = mx + b + r(x)/d(x)$, where the degree of $r(x)$ is less than the degree of $d(x)$. The line $y = mx + b$ is then an oblique asymptote for the graph of $y = f(x)$.

EXAMPLE 5 **Average Cost** Given the cost function $C(x) = 5{,}000 + 0.5x^2$, where x is the number of items produced, use the graphing strategy to analyze the graph of the average cost function. State all the pertinent information and sketch the graph of the average cost function. Find the marginal cost function and graph it on the same set of coordinate axes.

SOLUTION The average cost function is

$$\overline{C}(x) = \frac{5{,}000 + 0.5x^2}{x} = \frac{5{,}000}{x} + 0.5x$$

Step 1 *Analyze* $\overline{C}(x)$.

(A) Domain: Since we cannot produce a negative number of items and $\overline{C}(0)$ is not defined, the domain is the set of positive real numbers.

(B) Intercepts: None

(C) Horizontal asymptote: $\dfrac{a_m x^m}{b_n x^n} = \dfrac{0.5x^2}{x} = 0.5x$

So there is no horizontal asymptote.

Vertical asymptote: The line $x = 0$ is a vertical asymptote since the denominator is 0 and the numerator is not 0 for $x = 0$.

Oblique asymptote: If x is a large positive number, then $5{,}000/x$ is very small and

$$\overline{C}(x) = \frac{5{,}000}{x} + 0.5x \approx 0.5x$$

That is,

$$\lim_{x \to \infty} [\overline{C}(x) - 0.5x] = \lim_{x \to \infty} \frac{5{,}000}{x} = 0$$

This implies that the graph of $y = \overline{C}(x)$ approaches the line $y = 0.5x$ as x approaches ∞. That line is an oblique asymptote for the graph of $y = \overline{C}(x)$.

Step 2 *Analyze* $\overline{C}'(x)$.

$$\begin{aligned}\overline{C}'(x) &= -\frac{5{,}000}{x^2} + 0.5 \\ &= \frac{0.5x^2 - 5{,}000}{x^2} \\ &= \frac{0.5(x - 100)(x + 100)}{x^2}\end{aligned}$$

Partition numbers for $\overline{C}'(x)$: 0 and 100
Critical number of $\overline{C}(x)$: 100
Sign chart for $\overline{C}'(x)$:

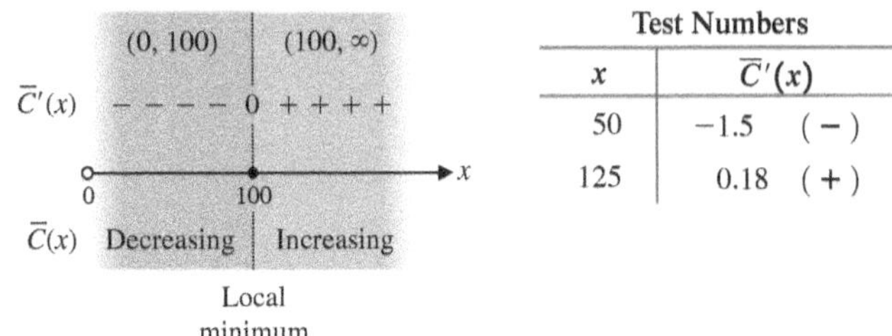

Test Numbers	
x	$\overline{C}'(x)$
50	−1.5 (−)
125	0.18 (+)

So $\overline{C}(x)$ is decreasing on (0, 100), is increasing on $(100, \infty)$, and has a local minimum at $x = 100$. The local minimum is $\overline{C}(100) = 100$.

Step 3 *Analyze* $\overline{C}''(x)$: $\overline{C}''(x) = \dfrac{10{,}000}{x^3}$.

$\overline{C}''(x)$ is positive for all positive x, so the graph of $y = \overline{C}(x)$ is concave upward on $(0, \infty)$.

Step 4 *Sketch the graph of* $\overline{C}$. The graph of $\overline{C}$ is shown in Figure 1.

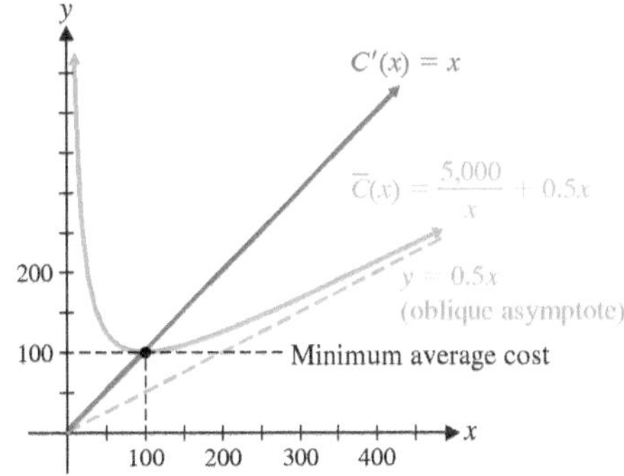

Figure 1

The marginal cost function is $C'(x) = x$. The graph of this linear function is also shown in Figure 1.

Figure 1 illustrates an important principle in economics:

The minimum average cost occurs when the average cost is equal to the marginal cost.

Matched Problem 5 Given the cost function $C(x) = 1{,}600 + 0.25x^2$, where x is the number of items produced,

(A) Use the graphing strategy to analyze the graph of the average cost function. State all the pertinent information and sketch the graph of the average cost function. Find the marginal cost function and graph it on the same set of coordinate axes. Include any oblique asymptotes.

(B) Find the minimum average cost.

Exercises 8.4

Skills Warm-up Exercises

W *In Problems 1–8, find the domain of the function and all x or y intercepts. (If necessary, review Section 1.1.)*

1. $f(x) = 3x + 36$

2. $f(x) = -4x - 28$

3. $f(x) = \sqrt{25 - x}$

4. $f(x) = \sqrt{9 - x^2}$

5. $f(x) = \dfrac{x + 1}{x - 2}$

6. $f(x) = \dfrac{x^2 - 9}{x + 9}$

7. $f(x) = \dfrac{3}{x^2 - 1}$

8. $f(x) = \dfrac{x - 6}{x^2 - 5x + 6}$

A **9.** Use the graph of f in the figure to identify the following (assume that $f''(0) < 0$, $f''(b) > 0$, and $f''(g) > 0$):

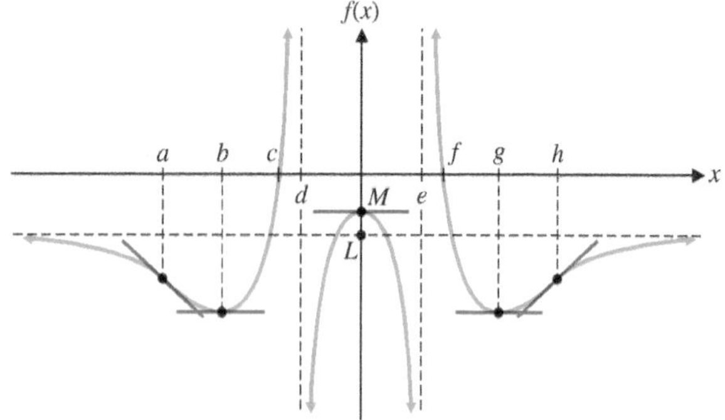

(A) the intervals on which $f'(x) < 0$

(B) the intervals on which $f'(x) > 0$

(C) the intervals on which $f(x)$ is increasing

(D) the intervals on which $f(x)$ is decreasing

(E) the x coordinate(s) of the point(s) where $f(x)$ has a local maximum

(F) the x coordinate(s) of the point(s) where $f(x)$ has a local minimum

(G) the intervals on which $f''(x) < 0$

(H) the intervals on which $f''(x) > 0$

(I) the intervals on which the graph of f is concave upward

(J) the intervals on which the graph of f is concave downward

(K) the x coordinate(s) of the inflection point(s)

(L) the horizontal asymptote(s)

(M) the vertical asymptote(s)

10. Repeat Problem 9 for the following graph of f (assume that $f''(d) < 0$):

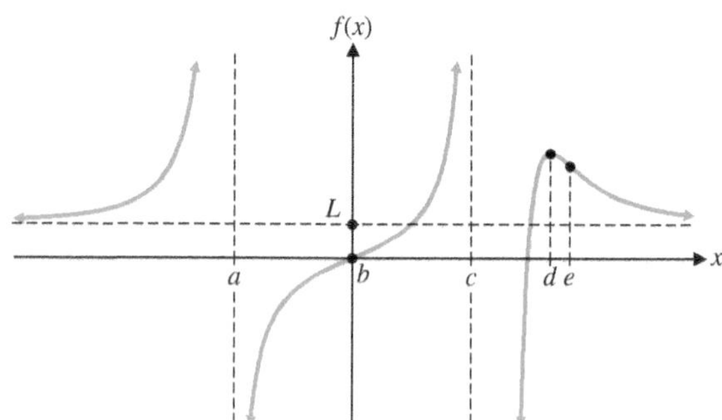

In Problems 11–14, use the given information to sketch a possible graph of f.

11. Domain: All real x, except $x = 2$;

$\lim_{x\to 2^-} f(x) = \infty$; $\lim_{x\to 2^+} f(x) = -\infty$; $\lim_{x\to\infty} f(x) = 4$

12. Domain: All real x, except $x = 4$;

$\lim_{x\to 4^-} f(x) = -\infty$; $\lim_{x\to 4^+} f(x) = -\infty$; $\lim_{x\to -\infty} f(x) = 3$

13. Domain: All real x, except $x = -1$;

$\lim_{x\to -1^-} f(x) = -\infty$; $\lim_{x\to -1^+} f(x) = -\infty$;

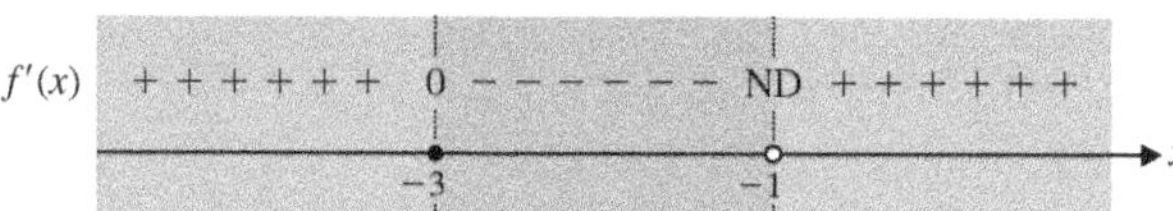

14. Domain: All real x, except $x = 7$;

$\lim_{x\to 7^-} f(x) = \infty$; $\lim_{x\to 7^+} f(x) = -\infty$;

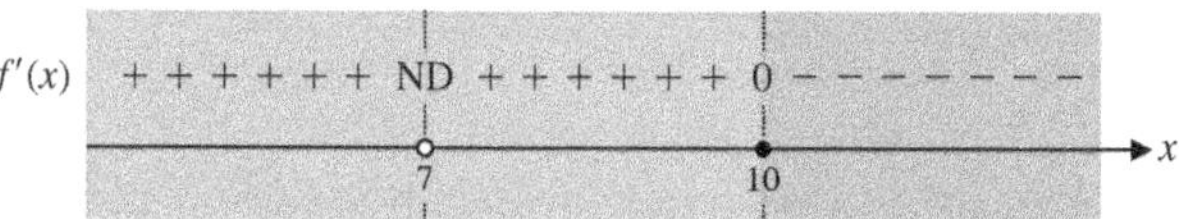

In Problems 15–22, use the given information to sketch the graph of f. Assume that f is continuous on its domain and that all intercepts are included in the table of values.

15. Domain: All real x; $\lim_{x\to\pm\infty} f(x) = 2$

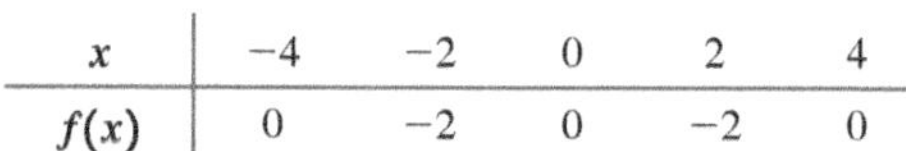

x	−4	−2	0	2	4
$f(x)$	0	−2	0	−2	0

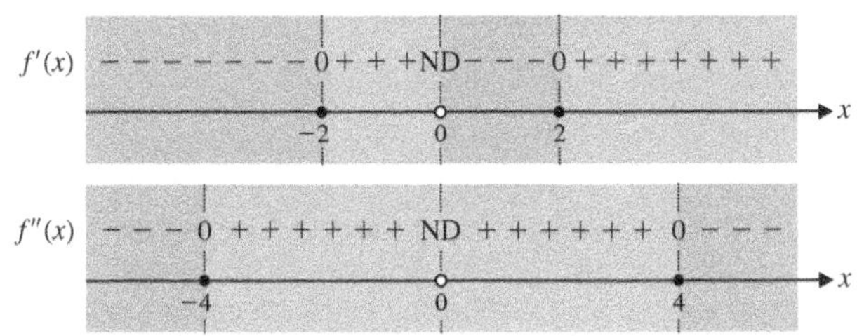

16. Domain: All real x;
$\lim_{x \to -\infty} f(x) = -3$; $\lim_{x \to \infty} f(x) = 3$

x	-2	-1	0	1	2
$f(x)$	0	2	0	-2	0

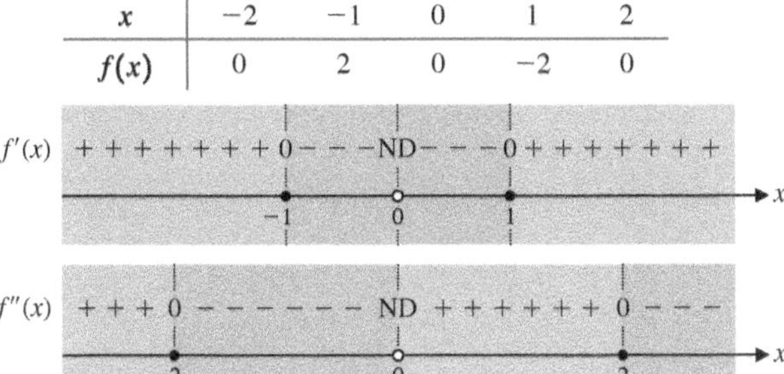

17. Domain: All real x, except $x = -2$;
$\lim_{x \to -2^-} f(x) = \infty$; $\lim_{x \to -2^+} f(x) = -\infty$; $\lim_{x \to \infty} f(x) = 1$

x	-4	0	4	6
$f(x)$	0	0	3	2

$f'(x)$: + + + ND + + + 0 – – – – – – – – (ND at -2, 0 at 4)

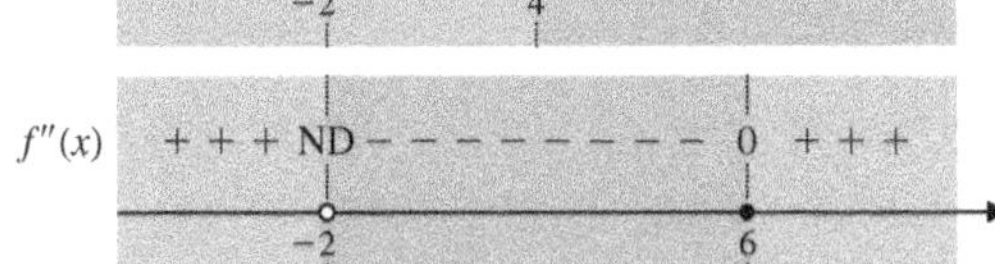

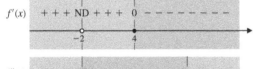

18. Domain: All real x, except $x = 1$;
$\lim_{x \to 1^-} f(x) = \infty$; $\lim_{x \to 1^+} f(x) = \infty$; $\lim_{x \to \infty} f(x) = -2$

x	-4	-2	0	2
$f(x)$	0	-2	0	0

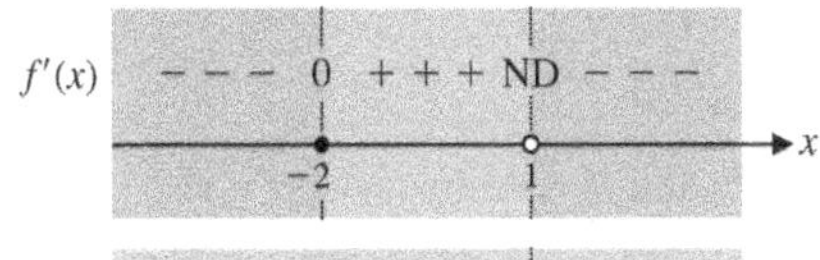

$f''(x)$: + + + + + + + + ND + + + (ND at 1)

19. Domain: All real x, except $x = -1$;
$f(-3) = 2, f(-2) = 3, f(0) = -1, f(1) = 0$;
$f'(x) > 0$ on $(-\infty, -1)$ and $(-1, \infty)$;
$f''(x) > 0$ on $(-\infty, -1)$; $f''(x) < 0$ on $(-1, \infty)$;
vertical asymptote: $x = -1$;
horizontal asymptote: $y = 1$

20. Domain: All real x, except $x = 1$;
$f(0) = -2, f(2) = 0$;
$f'(x) < 0$ on $(-\infty, 1)$ and $(1, \infty)$;
$f''(x) < 0$ on $(-\infty, 1)$;
$f''(x) > 0$ on $(1, \infty)$;
vertical asymptote: $x = 1$;
horizontal asymptote: $y = -1$

21. Domain: All real x, except $x = -2$ and $x = 2$;
$f(-3) = -1, f(0) = 0, f(3) = 1$;
$f'(x) < 0$ on $(-\infty, -2)$ and $(2, \infty)$;
$f'(x) > 0$ on $(-2, 2)$;
$f''(x) < 0$ on $(-\infty, -2)$ and $(-2, 0)$;
$f''(x) > 0$ on $(0, 2)$ and $(2, \infty)$;
vertical asymptotes: $x = -2$ and $x = 2$;
horizontal asymptote: $y = 0$

22. Domain: All real x, except $x = -1$ and $x = 1$;
$f(-2) = 1, f(0) = 0, f(2) = 1$;
$f'(x) > 0$ on $(-\infty, -1)$ and $(0, 1)$;
$f'(x) < 0$ on $(-1, 0)$ and $(1, \infty)$;
$f''(x) > 0$ on $(-\infty, -1)$, $(-1, 1)$, and $(1, \infty)$;
vertical asymptotes: $x = -1$ and $x = 1$;
horizontal asymptote: $y = 0$

B *In Problems 23–62, summarize the pertinent information obtained by applying the graphing strategy and sketch the graph of $y = f(x)$.*

23. $f(x) = \dfrac{x + 3}{x - 3}$

24. $f(x) = \dfrac{2x - 4}{x + 2}$

25. $f(x) = \dfrac{x}{x - 2}$

26. $f(x) = \dfrac{2 + x}{3 - x}$

27. $f(x) = 5 + 5e^{-0.1x}$

28. $f(x) = 4 + 5e^{-0.3x}$

29. $f(x) = 5xe^{-0.2x}$

30. $f(x) = 10xe^{-0.1x}$

31. $f(x) = \ln(1 - x)$

32. $f(x) = \ln(2x + 4)$

33. $f(x) = x - \ln x$

34. $f(x) = \ln(x^2 + 4)$

35. $f(x) = \dfrac{x}{x^2 - 4}$

36. $f(x) = \dfrac{1}{x^2 - 4}$

37. $f(x) = \dfrac{1}{1 + x^2}$

38. $f(x) = \dfrac{x^2}{1 + x^2}$

39. $f(x) = \dfrac{2x}{1 - x^2}$

40. $f(x) = \dfrac{2x}{x^2 - 9}$

41. $f(x) = \dfrac{-5x}{(x - 1)^2}$

42. $f(x) = \dfrac{x}{(x - 2)^2}$

43. $f(x) = \dfrac{x^2 + x - 2}{x^2}$

44. $f(x) = \dfrac{x^2 - 5x - 6}{x^2}$

45. $f(x) = \dfrac{x^2}{x - 1}$

46. $f(x) = \dfrac{x^2}{2 + x}$

47. $f(x) = \dfrac{3x^2 + 2}{x^2 - 9}$

48. $f(x) = \dfrac{2x^2 + 5}{4 - x^2}$

49. $f(x) = \dfrac{x^3}{x - 2}$

50. $f(x) = \dfrac{x^3}{4 - x}$

51. $f(x) = (3 - x)e^x$

52. $f(x) = (x - 2)e^x$

53. $f(x) = e^{-0.5x^2}$

54. $f(x) = e^{-2x^2}$

55. $f(x) = x^2 \ln x$

56. $f(x) = \dfrac{\ln x}{x}$

57. $f(x) = (\ln x)^2$

58. $f(x) = \dfrac{x}{\ln x}$

59. $f(x) = \dfrac{1}{x^2 + 2x - 8}$

60. $f(x) = \dfrac{1}{3 - 2x - x^2}$

61. $f(x) = \dfrac{x^3}{3 - x^2}$

62. $f(x) = \dfrac{x^3}{x^2 - 12}$

C *In Problems 63–66, show that the line $y = x$ is an oblique asymptote for the graph of $y = f(x)$, summarize all pertinent information obtained by applying the graphing strategy, and sketch the graph of $y = f(x)$.*

63. $f(x) = x + \dfrac{4}{x}$

64. $f(x) = x - \dfrac{9}{x}$

65. $f(x) = x - \dfrac{4}{x^2}$

66. $f(x) = x + \dfrac{32}{x^2}$

In Problems 67–70, for the given cost function $C(x)$, find the oblique asymptote of the average cost function $\overline{C}(x)$.

67. $C(x) = 10{,}000 + 90x + 0.02x^2$

68. $C(x) = 15{,}000 + 125x + 0.03x^2$

69. $C(x) = 95{,}000 + 210x + 0.1x^2$

70. $C(x) = 125{,}000 + 325x + 0.5x^2$

In Problems 71–78, summarize all pertinent information obtained by applying the graphing strategy and sketch the graph of $y = f(x)$. [Note: These rational functions are not reduced to lowest terms.]

71. $f(x) = \dfrac{x^2 - 1}{x^2 - x - 2}$

72. $f(x) = \dfrac{x^2 - 9}{x^2 + x - 6}$

73. $f(x) = \dfrac{x^2 + 3x + 2}{x^2 + 2x + 1}$

74. $f(x) = \dfrac{x^2 - x - 6}{x^2 + 4x + 4}$

75. $f(x) = \dfrac{2x^2 + 5x - 12}{x^2 + x - 12}$

76. $f(x) = \dfrac{2x^2 - 3x - 20}{x^2 - x - 12}$

77. $f(x) = \dfrac{x^3 + 4x^2 - 21x}{x^2 - 2x - 3}$

78. $f(x) = \dfrac{x^3 + 7x^2 - 18x}{x^2 + 8x - 9}$

Applications

79. **Revenue.** The marketing research department for a computer company used a large city to test market the firm's new laptop. The department found that the relationship between price p (dollars per unit) and demand x (units sold per week) was given approximately by

$$p = 1{,}296 - 0.12x^2 \qquad 0 \le x \le 80$$

So, weekly revenue can be approximated by

$$R(x) = xp = 1{,}296x - 0.12x^3 \qquad 0 \le x \le 80$$

Graph the revenue function R.

80. **Profit.** Suppose that the cost function $C(x)$ (in dollars) for the company in Problem 79 is

$$C(x) = 830 + 396x$$

(A) Write an equation for the profit $P(x)$.

(B) Graph the profit function P.

81. **Pollution.** In Silicon Valley, a number of computer firms were found to be contaminating underground water supplies with toxic chemicals stored in leaking underground containers. A water quality control agency ordered the companies to take immediate corrective action and contribute to a monetary pool for the testing and cleanup of the underground contamination. Suppose that the required monetary pool (in millions of dollars) is given by

$$P(x) = \frac{2x}{1 - x} \qquad 0 \le x < 1$$

where x is the percentage (expressed as a decimal fraction) of the total contaminant removed.

(A) Where is $P(x)$ increasing? Decreasing?

(B) Where is the graph of P concave upward? Downward?

(C) Find any horizontal or vertical asymptotes.

(D) Find the x and y intercepts.

(E) Sketch a graph of P.

82. **Employee training.** A company producing dive watches has established that, on average, a new employee can assemble $N(t)$ dive watches per day after t days of on-the-job training, as given by

$$N(t) = \frac{100t}{t + 9} \qquad t \ge 0$$

(A) Where is $N(t)$ increasing? Decreasing?

(B) Where is the graph of N concave upward? Downward?

(C) Find any horizontal and vertical asymptotes.

(D) Find the intercepts.

(E) Sketch a graph of N.

83. **Replacement time.** An outboard motor has an initial price of \$3,200. A service contract costs \$300 for the first year and increases \$100 per year thereafter. The total cost of the outboard motor (in dollars) after n years is given by

$$C(n) = 3{,}200 + 250n + 50n^2 \qquad n \ge 1$$

(A) Write an expression for the average cost per year, $\overline{C}(n)$, for n years.

(B) Graph the average cost function found in part (A).

(C) When is the average cost per year at its minimum? (This time is frequently referred to as the **replacement time** for this piece of equipment.)

84. **Construction costs.** The management of a manufacturing plant wishes to add a fenced-in rectangular storage yard of 20,000 square feet, using a building as one side of the yard (see the figure). If x is the distance (in feet) from the building to the fence, show that the length of the fence required for the yard is given by

$$L(x) = 2x + \frac{20{,}000}{x} \qquad x > 0$$

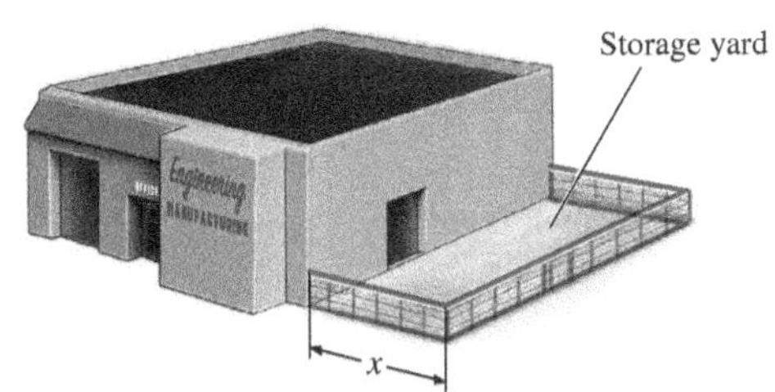

(A) Graph L.

(B) What are the dimensions of the rectangle requiring the least amount of fencing?

85. Average and marginal costs. The total daily cost (in dollars) of producing x mountain bikes is given by

$$C(x) = 1{,}000 + 5x + 0.1x^2$$

(A) Sketch the graphs of the average cost function and the marginal cost function on the same set of coordinate axes. Include any oblique asymptotes.

(B) Find the minimum average cost.

86. Average and marginal costs. The total daily cost (in dollars) of producing x city bikes is given by

$$C(x) = 500 + 2x + 0.2x^2$$

(A) Sketch the graphs of the average cost function and the marginal cost function on the same set of coordinate axes. Include any oblique asymptotes.

(B) Find the minimum average cost.

87. Medicine. A doctor prescribes a 500 mg pill every eight hours. The concentration of the drug (in parts per million) in the bloodstream t hours after ingesting the pill is

$$C(t) = \frac{t}{e^{0.75t}}.$$

(A) Graph $C(t)$.

(B) What is the concentration after 8 hours?

(C) What is the maximum concentration?

88. Medicine. A doctor prescribes a 1,000 mg pill every twelve hours. The concentration of the drug (in parts per million) in the bloodstream t hours after ingesting the pill is

$$D(t) = \frac{0.9t}{e^{0.5t}}.$$

(A) Graph $D(t)$.

(B) What is the concentration after 12 hours?

(C) What is the maximum concentration?

89. Discuss the differences between the function $C(t)$ defined in Problem 87 and the function $D(t)$ defined in Problem 88. Under what circumstances might each prescription be the better option?

90. Physiology. In a study on the speed of muscle contraction in frogs under various loads, researchers found that the speed of contraction decreases with increasing loads. More precisely, they found that the relationship between speed of contraction, S (in centimeters per second), and load w, (in grams), is given approximately by

$$S(w) = \frac{26 + 0.06w}{w} \qquad w \ge 5$$

Graph S.

91. Psychology: retention. Each student in a psychology class is given one day to memorize the same list of 30 special characters. The lists are turned in at the end of the day, and for each succeeding day for 30 days, each student is asked to turn in a list of as many of the symbols as can be recalled. Averages are taken, and it is found that

$$N(t) = \frac{5t + 20}{t} \qquad t \ge 1$$

provides a good approximation of the average number $N(t)$ of symbols retained after t days. Graph N.

Answers to Matched Problems

1. Domain: All real x, except $x = 1$
y intercept: $f(0) = 0$; x intercept: 0
Horizontal asymptote: $y = -2$
Vertical asymptote: $x = 1$
Increasing on $(-\infty, 1)$ and $(1, \infty)$
Concave upward on $(-\infty, 1)$
Concave downward on $(1, \infty)$

x	$f(x)$
-1	-1
0	0
$\frac{1}{2}$	2
$\frac{3}{2}$	-6
2	-4
5	$-\frac{5}{2}$

2. Domain: All real x, except $x = 0$
x intercept: $= -\frac{3}{4} = -0.75$
$h(0)$ is not defined
Vertical asymptote: $x = 0$ (the y axis)
Horizontal asymptote: $y = 0$ (the x axis)
Increasing on $(-1.5, 0)$
Decreasing on $(-\infty, -1.5)$ and $(0, \infty)$
Local minimum: $f(-1.5) = -1.33$
Concave upward on $(-2.25, 0)$ and $(0, \infty)$
Concave downward on $(-\infty, -2.25)$
Inflection point: $(-2.25, -1.19)$

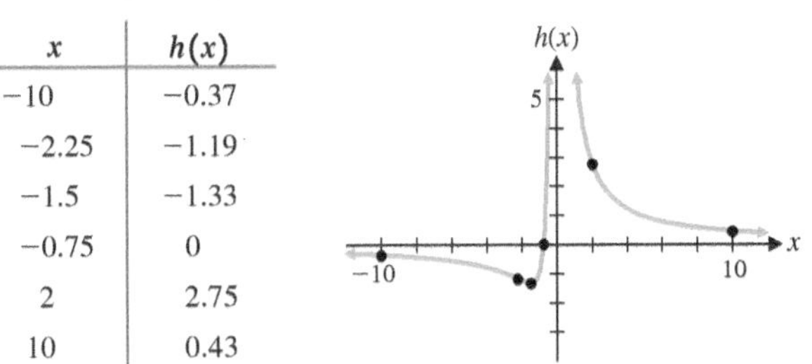

x	$h(x)$
-10	-0.37
-2.25	-1.19
-1.5	-1.33
-0.75	0
2	2.75
10	0.43

3. Domain: $(-\infty, \infty)$
   y intercept: $f(0) = 0$
   x intercept: $x = 0$
   Horizontal asymptote: $y = 0$ (the x axis)
   Increasing on $(-\infty, 2)$
   Decreasing on $(2, \infty)$
   Local maximum: $f(2) = 2e^{-1} \approx 0.736$
   Concave downward on $(-\infty, 4)$
   Concave upward on $(4, \infty)$
   Inflection point: $(4, 0.541)$

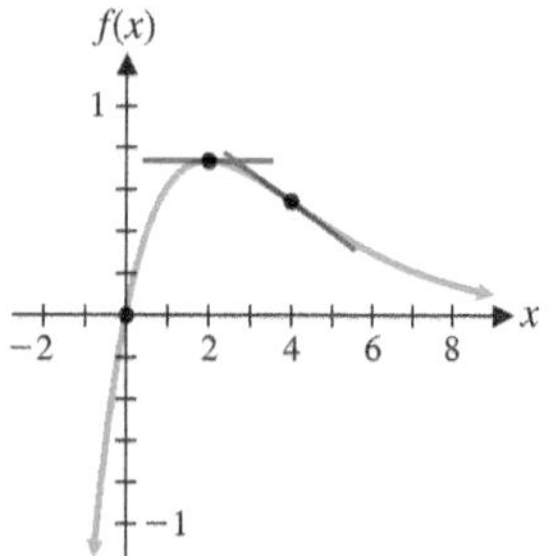

4. Domain: $(0, \infty)$
   y intercept: None [$f(0)$ is not defined]
   x intercept: $x = 1$
   Increasing on (e^{-1}, ∞)
   Decreasing on $(0, e^{-1})$
   Local minimum: $f(e^{-1}) = -e^{-1} \approx -0.368$
   Concave upward on $(0, \infty)$

x	5	10	100	$\to \infty$
$f(x)$	8.05	23.03	460.52	$\to \infty$

x	0.1	0.01	0.001	0.000 1	$\to 0$
$f(x)$	−0.23	−0.046	−0.006 9	−0.000 92	$\to 0$

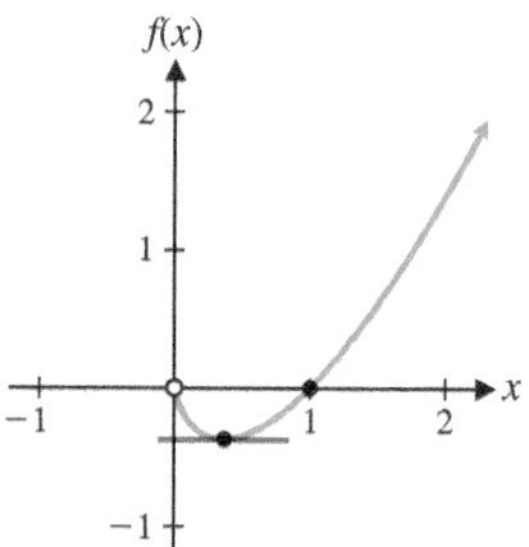

5. (A) Domain: $(0, \infty)$
   Intercepts: None
   Vertical asymptote: $x = 0$;
   oblique asymptote: $y = 0.25x$
   Decreasing on $(0, 80)$;
   increasing on $(80, \infty)$;
   local minimum at $x = 80$
   Concave upward on $(0, \infty)$

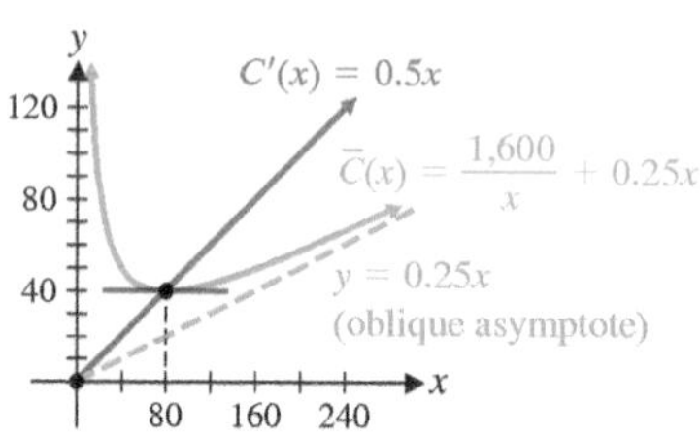

   (B) Minimum average cost is 40 at $x = 80$.

8.5 Absolute Maxima and Minima

- Absolute Maxima and Minima
- Second Derivative and Extrema

One of the most important applications of the derivative is to find the absolute maximum or minimum value of a function. An economist may be interested in the price or production level of a commodity that will bring a maximum profit, a doctor may be interested in the time it takes for a drug to reach its maximum concentration in the bloodstream after an injection, and a city planner might be interested in the location of heavy industry in a city in order to produce minimum pollution in residential and business areas. In this section, we develop the procedures needed to find the absolute maximum and absolute minimum values of a function.

Absolute Maxima and Minima

Recall that $f(c)$ is a local maximum if $f(x) \le f(c)$ for x near c and a local minimum if $f(x) \ge f(c)$ for x near c. Now we are interested in finding the largest and the smallest values of $f(x)$ throughout the domain of f.

DEFINITION Absolute Maxima and Minima

If $f(c) \ge f(x)$ for all x in the domain of f, then $f(c)$ is called the **absolute maximum** of f. If $f(c) \le f(x)$ for all x in the domain of f, then $f(c)$ is called the **absolute minimum** of f. An absolute maximum or absolute minimum is called an **absolute extremum.**

Figure 1 illustrates some typical examples.

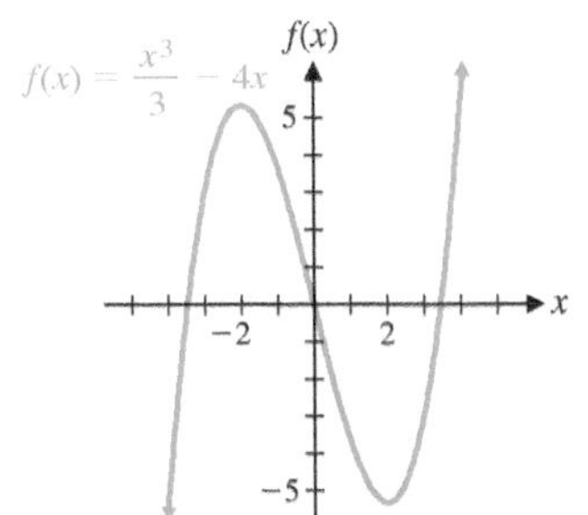

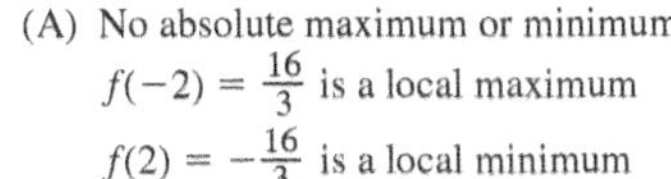
(A) No absolute maximum or minimum

$f(-2) = \frac{16}{3}$ is a local maximum

$f(2) = -\frac{16}{3}$ is a local minimum

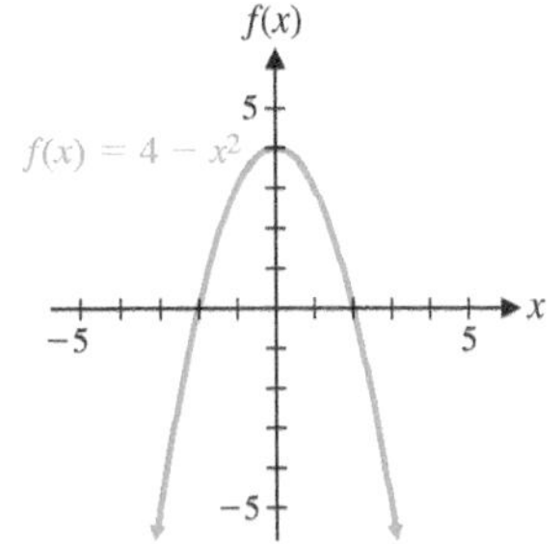

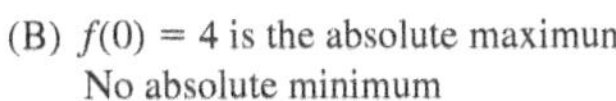
(B) $f(0) = 4$ is the absolute maximum
No absolute minimum

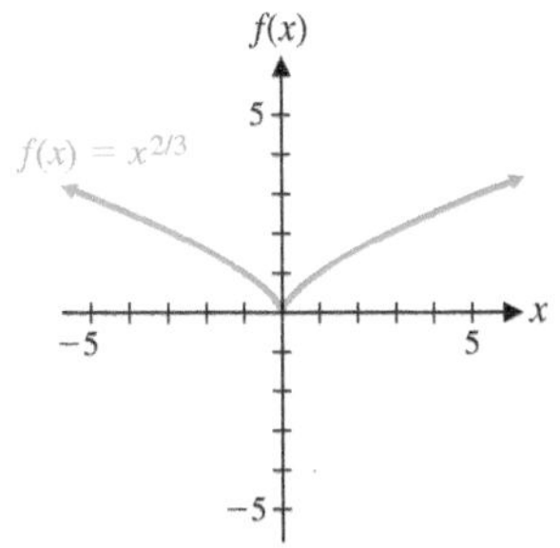

(C) $f(0) = 0$ is the absolute minimum
No absolute maximum

Figure 1

In many applications, the domain of a function is restricted because of practical or physical considerations. Prices and quantities cannot be negative. Factories cannot produce arbitrarily large numbers of goods. If the domain is restricted to some closed interval, as is often the case, then Theorem 1 applies.

THEOREM 1 Extreme Value Theorem

A function f that is continuous on a closed interval $[a, b]$ has both an absolute maximum and an absolute minimum on that interval.

It is important to understand that the absolute maximum and absolute minimum depend on both the function f and the interval $[a, b]$. Figure 2 illustrates four cases.

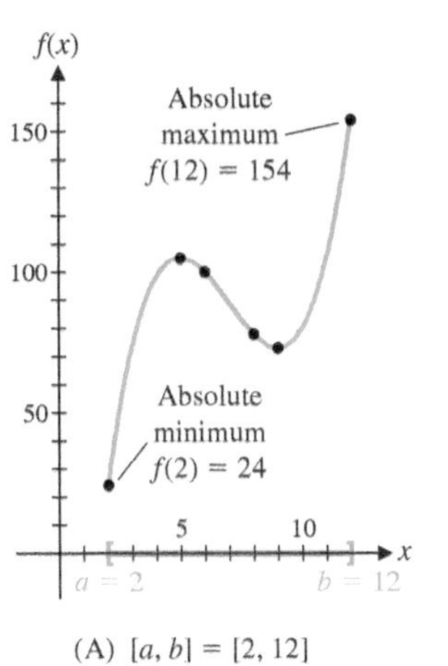

(A) $[a, b] = [2, 12]$

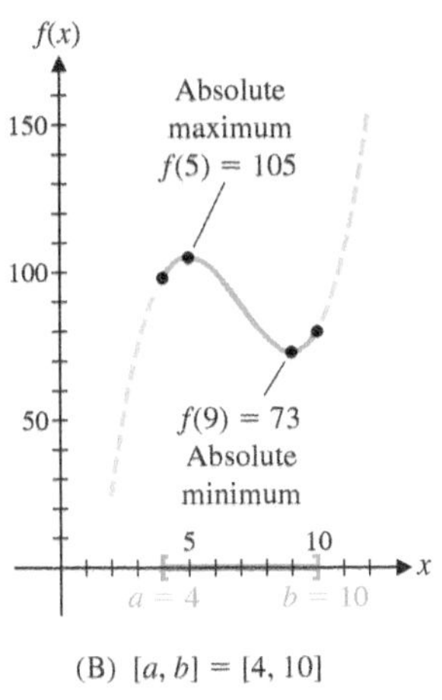

(B) $[a, b] = [4, 10]$

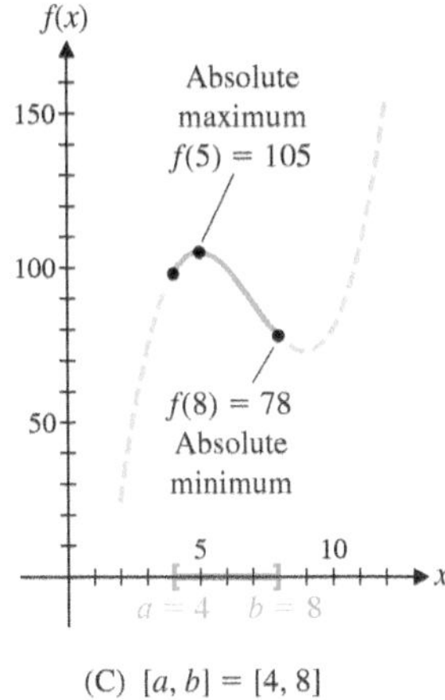

(C) $[a, b] = [4, 8]$

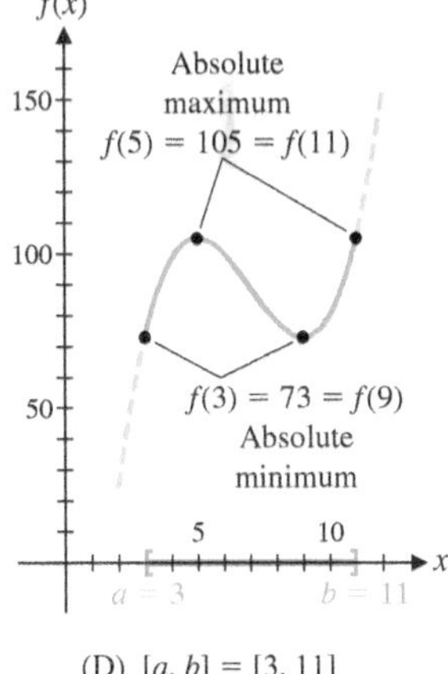

(D) $[a, b] = [3, 11]$

Figure 2 Absolute extrema for $f(x) = x^3 - 21x^2 + 135x - 170$ on various closed intervals

In all four cases illustrated in Figure 2, the absolute maximum and absolute minimum occur at a critical number or an endpoint. This property is generalized in Theorem 2. Note that both the absolute maximum and the absolute minimum are unique, but each can occur at more than one point in the interval (Fig. 2D).

Explore and Discuss 1

Suppose that f is a function such that $f'(c) = 1$ for some number c in the interval $[a, b]$. Is it possible for $f(c)$ to be an absolute extremum on $[a, b]$?

Reminder:

Critical numbers, if they exist, must lie in the domain of the function. If our function is restricted to $[a, b]$, then a number c must satisfy $a \leq c \leq b$ in order to be a critical number.

THEOREM 2 Locating Absolute Extrema

Absolute extrema (if they exist) must occur at critical numbers or at endpoints.

To find the absolute maximum and minimum of a continuous function on a closed interval, we simply identify the endpoints and critical numbers in the interval, evaluate the function at each, and choose the largest and smallest values.

PROCEDURE Finding Absolute Extrema on a Closed Interval

Step 1 Check to make certain that f is continuous over $[a, b]$.
Step 2 Find the critical numbers in the interval (a, b).
Step 3 Evaluate f at the endpoints a and b and at the critical numbers found in step 2.
Step 4 The absolute maximum of f on $[a, b]$ is the largest value found in step 3.
Step 5 The absolute minimum of f on $[a, b]$ is the smallest value found in step 3.

EXAMPLE 1 **Finding Absolute Extrema** Find the absolute maximum and absolute minimum of

$$f(x) = x^3 + 3x^2 - 9x - 7$$

on each of the following intervals:

(A) $[-6, 4]$ (B) $[-4, 2]$ (C) $[-2, 2]$

SOLUTION

(A) The function is continuous for all values of x.

$$f'(x) = 3x^2 + 6x - 9 = 3(x - 1)(x + 3)$$

So $x = -3$ and $x = 1$ are the critical numbers in the interval $(-6, 4)$. Evaluate f at the endpoints and critical numbers $(-6, -3, 1, \text{and } 4)$, and choose the largest and smallest values.

$$f(-6) = -61 \quad \text{Absolute minimum}$$

$$f(-3) = 20$$

$$f(1) = -12$$

$$f(4) = 69 \quad \text{Absolute maximum}$$

The absolute maximum of f on $[-6, 4]$ is 69, and the absolute minimum is -61.

(B) Interval: $[-4, 2]$

x	$f(x)$	
−4	13	
−3	20	Absolute maximum
1	−12	Absolute minimum
2	−5	

The absolute maximum of f on $[-4, 2]$ is 20, and the absolute minimum is -12.

(C) Interval: $[-2, 2]$

x	$f(x)$	
−2	15	Absolute maximum
1	−12	Absolute minimum
2	−5	

Note that the critical number $x = -3$ is not included in the table, because it is not in the interval $[-2, 2]$. The absolute maximum of f on $[-2, 2]$ is 15, and the absolute minimum is -12.

Matched Problem 1 Find the absolute maximum and absolute minimum of

$$f(x) = x^3 - 12x$$

on each of the following intervals:

(A) $[-5, 5]$ (B) $[-3, 3]$ (C) $[-3, 1]$

Now, suppose that we want to find the absolute maximum or minimum of a function that is continuous on an interval that is not closed. Since Theorem 1 no longer applies, we cannot be certain that the absolute maximum or minimum value exists. Figure 3 illustrates several ways that functions can fail to have absolute extrema.

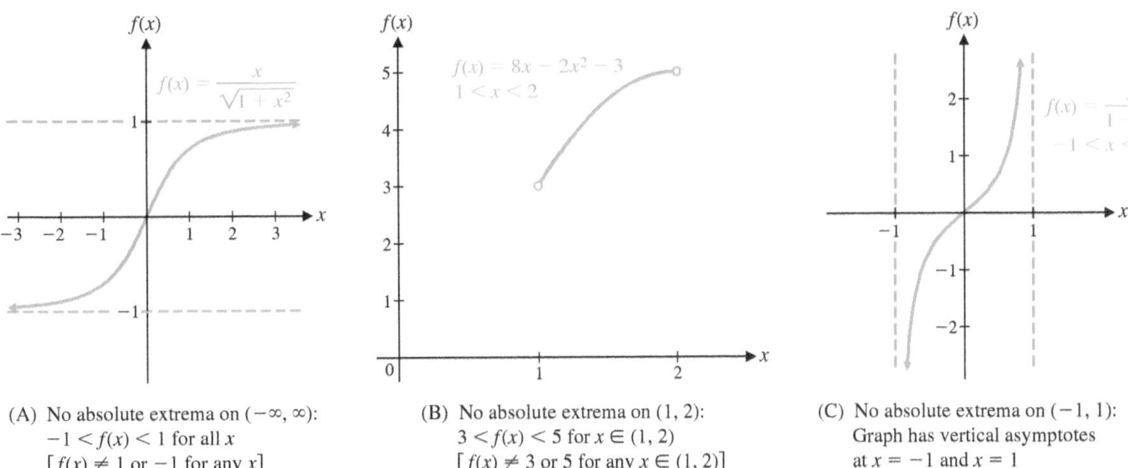

(A) No absolute extrema on $(-\infty, \infty)$: $-1 < f(x) < 1$ for all x [$f(x) \neq 1$ or -1 for any x]

(B) No absolute extrema on $(1, 2)$: $3 < f(x) < 5$ for $x \in (1, 2)$ [$f(x) \neq 3$ or 5 for any $x \in (1, 2)$]

(C) No absolute extrema on $(-1, 1)$: Graph has vertical asymptotes at $x = -1$ and $x = 1$

Figure 3 Functions with no absolute extrema

In general, the best procedure to follow in searching for absolute extrema on an interval that is not of the form $[a, b]$ is to sketch a graph of the function. However, many applications can be solved with a new tool that does not require any graphing.

Second Derivative and Extrema

The second derivative can be used to classify the local extrema of a function. Suppose that f is a function satisfying $f'(c) = 0$ and $f''(c) > 0$. First, note that if $f''(c) > 0$, then it follows from the properties of limits* that $f''(x) > 0$ in some interval (m, n) containing c. Thus, the graph of f must be concave upward in this interval. But this implies that $f'(x)$ is increasing in the interval. Since $f'(c) = 0$, $f'(x)$ must change from negative to positive at $x = c$, and $f(c)$ is a local minimum (see Fig. 4). Reasoning in the same fashion, we conclude that if $f'(c) = 0$ and $f''(c) < 0$, then $f(c)$ is a local maximum. Of course, it is possible that both $f'(c) = 0$ and $f''(c) = 0$. In this case, the second derivative cannot be used to determine the shape of the graph around $x = c$; $f(c)$ may be a local minimum, a local maximum, or neither.

The sign of the second derivative provides a simple test for identifying local maxima and minima. This test is most useful when we do not want to draw the graph of the function. If we are interested in drawing the graph and have already constructed the sign chart for $f'(x)$, then the first-derivative test can be used to identify the local extrema.

*Actually, we are assuming that $f''(x)$ is continuous in an interval containing c. It is unlikely that we will encounter a function for which $f''(c)$ exists but $f''(x)$ is not continuous in an interval containing c.

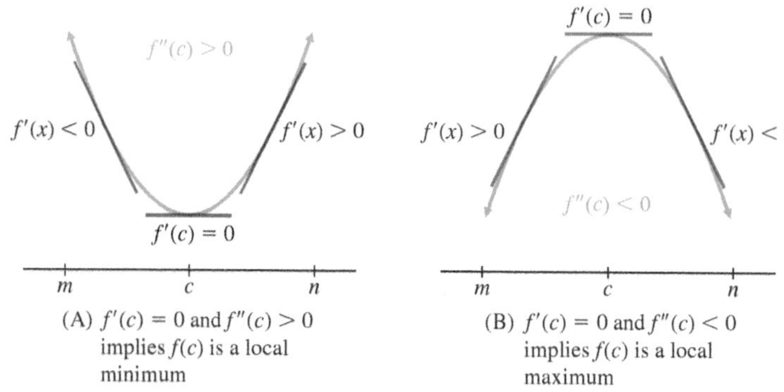

(A) $f'(c) = 0$ and $f''(c) > 0$ implies $f(c)$ is a local minimum

(B) $f'(c) = 0$ and $f''(c) < 0$ implies $f(c)$ is a local maximum

Figure 4 Second derivative and local extrema

RESULT Second-Derivative Test for Local Extrema

Let c be a critical number of $f(x)$ such that $f'(c) = 0$. If the second derivative $f''(c) > 0$, then $f(c)$ is a local minimum. If $f''(c) < 0$, then $f(c)$ is a local maximum.

$f'(c)$	$f''(c)$	Graph of f is:	$f(c)$	Example
0	+	Concave upward	Local minimum	
0	−	Concave downward	Local maximum	
0	0	?	Test does not apply	

EXAMPLE 2 **Testing Local Extrema** Find the local maxima and minima for each function. Use the second-derivative test for local extrema when it applies.

(A) $f(x) = 4x^3 + 9x^2 - 12x + 3$

(B) $f(x) = xe^{-0.2x}$

(C) $f(x) = \frac{1}{6}x^6 - 4x^5 + 25x^4$

SOLUTION

(A) Find first and second derivatives and determine critical numbers:

$$f(x) = 4x^3 + 9x^2 - 12x + 3$$
$$f'(x) = 12x^2 + 18x - 12 = 6(2x - 1)(x + 2)$$
$$f''(x) = 24x + 18 = 6(4x + 3)$$

Critical numbers are $x = -2$ and $x = 0.5$.

$$f''(-2) = -30 < 0 \qquad f \text{ has a local maximum at } x = -2.$$
$$f''(0.5) = 30 > 0 \qquad f \text{ has a local minimum at } x = 0.5.$$

Substituting $x = -2$ in the expression for $f(x)$ we find that $f(-2) = 31$ is a local maximum. Similarly, $f(0.5) = -0.25$ is a local minimum.

(B)

$$f(x) = xe^{-0.2x}$$
$$f'(x) = e^{-0.2x} + xe^{-0.2x}(-0.2)$$
$$= e^{-0.2x}(1 - 0.2x)$$
$$f''(x) = e^{-0.2x}(-0.2)(1 - 0.2x) + e^{-0.2x}(-0.2)$$
$$= e^{-0.2x}(0.04x - 0.4)$$

Critical number: $x = 1/0.2 = 5$

$$f''(5) = e^{-1}(-0.2) < 0 \qquad f \text{ has a local maximum at } x = 5.$$

So $f(5) = 5e^{-0.2(5)} \approx 1.84$ is a local maximum.

(C)

$$f(x) = \tfrac{1}{6}x^6 - 4x^5 + 25x^4$$
$$f'(x) = x^5 - 20x^4 + 100x^3 = x^3(x - 10)^2$$
$$f''(x) = 5x^4 - 80x^3 + 300x^2$$

Critical numbers are $x = 0$ and $x = 10$.

$f''(0) = 0$ — The second-derivative test fails at both critical numbers, so
$f''(10) = 0$ — the first-derivative test must be used.

Sign chart for $f'(x) = x^3(x - 10)^2$ (partition numbers for f' are 0 and 10):

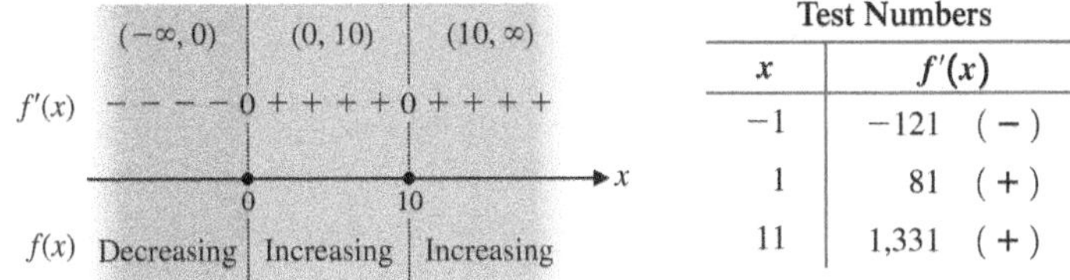

Test Numbers

x	$f'(x)$
−1	−121 (−)
1	81 (+)
11	1,331 (+)

From the chart, we see that $f(x)$ has a local minimum at $x = 0$ and does not have a local extremum at $x = 10$. So $f(0) = 0$ is a local minimum.

Matched Problem 2 Find the local maxima and minima for each function. Use the second-derivative test when it applies.

(A) $f(x) = x^3 - 9x^2 + 24x - 10$

(B) $f(x) = e^x - 5x$

(C) $f(x) = 10x^6 - 24x^5 + 15x^4$

CONCEPTUAL INSIGHT

The second-derivative test for local extrema does not apply if $f''(c) = 0$ or if $f''(c)$ is not defined. As Example 2C illustrates, if $f''(c) = 0$, then $f(c)$ may or may not be a local extremum. Some other method, such as the first-derivative test, must be used when $f''(c) = 0$ or $f''(c)$ does not exist.

The solution of many optimization problems involves searching for an absolute extremum. If the function in question has only one critical number, then the second-derivative test for local extrema not only classifies the local extremum but also guarantees that the local extremum is, in fact, the absolute extremum.

THEOREM 3 Second-Derivative Test for Absolute Extrema on an Interval

Let f be continuous on an interval I from a to b with only one critical number c in (a, b).

If $f'(c) = 0$ and $f''(c) > 0$, then $f(c)$ is the absolute minimum of f on I.

If $f'(c) = 0$ and $f''(c) < 0$, then $f(c)$ is the absolute maximum of f on I.

The function f may have additional critical numbers at one or both of a or b. Theorem 3 applies as long as I contains exactly one critical point that is not an endpoint of I. Since the second-derivative test for local extrema cannot be applied when $f''(c) = 0$ or $f''(c)$ does not exist, Theorem 3 makes no mention of these cases.

Explore and Discuss 2

Suppose that $f'(c) = 0$ and $f''(c) > 0$. What does a sign chart for $f'(x)$ look like near c? What does the first-derivative test imply?

EXAMPLE 3 **Finding Absolute Extrema on an Open Interval** Find the absolute extrema of each function on $(0, \infty)$.

(A) $f(x) = x + \frac{4}{x}$ (B) $f(x) = (\ln x)^2 - 3 \ln x$

SOLUTION

(A) $f(x) = x + \frac{4}{x}$

$$f'(x) = 1 - \frac{4}{x^2} = \frac{x^2 - 4}{x^2} = \frac{(x-2)(x+2)}{x^2}$$ Critical numbers are $x = -2$ and $x = 2$.

$$f''(x) = \frac{8}{x^3}$$

The only critical number in the interval $(0, \infty)$ is $x = 2$. Since $f''(2) = 1 > 0$, $f(2) = 4$ is the absolute minimum of f on $(0, \infty)$. Note that since $\lim_{x\to\infty} f(x) = \infty$, f has no maximum on $(0, \infty)$.

(B) $f(x) = (\ln x)^2 - 3 \ln x$

$$f'(x) = (2 \ln x)\frac{1}{x} - \frac{3}{x} = \frac{2 \ln x - 3}{x}$$ Critical number is $x = e^{3/2}$.

$$f''(x) = \frac{x\frac{2}{x} - (2 \ln x - 3)}{x^2} = \frac{5 - 2 \ln x}{x^2}$$

The only critical number in the interval $(0, \infty)$ is $x = e^{3/2}$. Since $f''(e^{3/2}) = 2/e^3 > 0$, $f(e^{3/2}) = -2.25$ is the absolute minimum of f on $(0, \infty)$. Note that since $\lim_{x\to\infty} \ln(x) = \infty$, we have $\lim_{x\to\infty} f(x) = \lim_{x\to\infty} (\ln x)(\ln x - 3) = \infty$, so f has no maximum on $(0, \infty)$.

Matched Problem 3 Find the absolute extrema of each function on $(0, \infty)$.

(A) $f(x) = 12 - x - \frac{5}{x}$ (B) $f(x) = 5 \ln x - x$

Exercises 8.5

Skills Warm-up Exercises

W *In Problems 1–8, by inspecting the graph of the function, find the absolute maximum and absolute minimum on the given interval. (If necessary, review Section 1.2.)*

1. $f(x) = x$ on $[-2, 3]$
2. $g(x) = |x|$ on $[-1, 4]$
3. $h(x) = x^2$ on $[-5, 3]$
4. $m(x) = x^3$ on $[-3, 1]$
5. $n(x) = \sqrt{x}$ on $[3, 4]$
6. $p(x) = \sqrt[3]{x}$ on $[-125, 216]$
7. $q(x) = -\sqrt[3]{x}$ on $[27, 64]$
8. $r(x) = -x^2$ on $[-10, 11]$

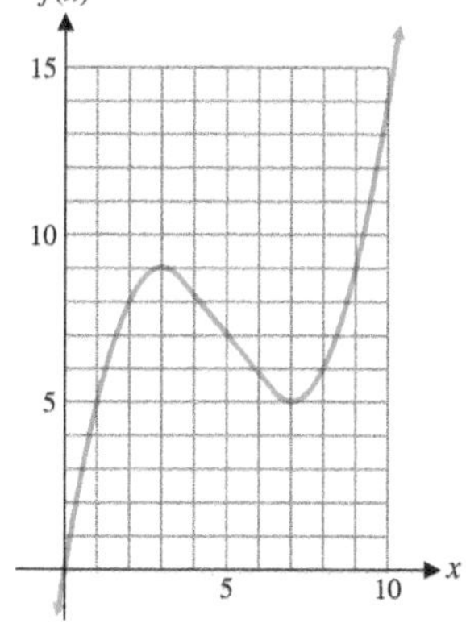

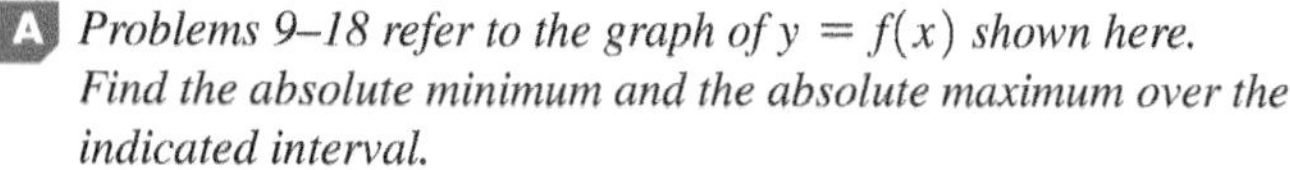

A *Problems 9–18 refer to the graph of $y = f(x)$ shown here. Find the absolute minimum and the absolute maximum over the indicated interval.*

9. $[0, 10]$ **10.** $[2, 8]$ **11.** $[0, 8]$ **12.** $[2, 10]$

13. $[1, 10]$ **14.** $[0, 9]$ **15.** $[1, 9]$ **16.** $[0, 2]$

17. $[2, 5]$ **18.** $[5, 8]$

In Problems 19–22, find the absolute maximum and absolute minimum of each function on the indicated intervals.

19. $f(x) = 2x - 5$
(A) $[0, 4]$ (B) $[0, 10]$ (C) $[-5, 10]$

20. $f(x) = 8 - x$
(A) $[0, 1]$ (B) $[-1, 1]$ (C) $[-1, 6]$

21. $f(x) = x^2$
(A) $[-1, 1]$ (B) $[1, 5]$ (C) $[-5, 5]$

22. $f(x) = 36 - x^2$
(A) $[-6, 6]$ (B) $[0, 6]$ (C) $[4, 8]$

In Problems 23–26, find the absolute maximum and absolute minimum of each function on the given interval.

23. $f(x) = e^{-x}$ on $[-1, 1]$ **24.** $f(x) = \ln x$ on $[1, 2]$

25. $f(x) = 9 - x^2$ on $[-4, 4]$

26. $f(x) = x^2 - 12x + 11$ on $[0, 10]$

B *In Problems 27–42, find the absolute extremum, if any, given by the second derivative test for each function.*

27. $f(x) = x^2 - 4x + 4$ **28.** $f(x) = x^2 + 2x + 1$

29. $f(x) = -x^2 - 4x + 6$ **30.** $f(x) = -x^2 + 6x + 1$

31. $f(x) = x^3 - 3$ **32.** $f(x) = 6 - x^3$

33. $f(x) = x^4 - 7$ **34.** $f(x) = 8 - x^4$

35. $f(x) = x + \frac{4}{x}$ **36.** $f(x) = x + \frac{9}{x}$

37. $f(x) = \frac{-3}{x^2 + 2}$ **38.** $f(x) = \frac{x}{x^2 + 4}$

39. $f(x) = \frac{1 - x}{x^2 - 4}$ **40.** $f(x) = \frac{x - 1}{x^2 - 1}$

41. $f(x) = \frac{-x^2}{x^2 + 4}$ **42.** $f(x) = \frac{x^2}{x^2 + 1}$

In Problems 43–66, find the indicated extremum of each function on the given interval.

43. Absolute minimum value on $[0, \infty)$ for
$$f(x) = 2x^2 - 8x + 6$$

44. Absolute maximum value on $[0, \infty)$ for
$$f(x) = 6x - x^2 + 4$$

45. Absolute maximum value on $[0, \infty)$ for
$$f(x) = 3x^2 - x^3$$

46. Absolute minimum value on $[0, \infty)$ for
$$f(x) = 2x^3 - 9x^2$$

47. Absolute minimum value on $[0, \infty)$ for
$$f(x) = (x + 4)(x - 2)^2$$

48. Absolute minimum value on $[0, \infty)$ for
$$f(x) = (2 - x)(x + 1)^2$$

49. Absolute maximum value on $(0, \infty)$ for
$$f(x) = 2x^4 - 8x^3$$

50. Absolute maximum value on $(0, \infty)$ for
$$f(x) = 4x^3 - 8x^4$$

51. Absolute maximum value on $(0, \infty)$ for
$$f(x) = 20 - 3x - \frac{12}{x}$$

52. Absolute minimum value on $(0, \infty)$ for
$$f(x) = 4 + x + \frac{9}{x}$$

53. Absolute minimum value on $(0, \infty)$ for
$$f(x) = 10 + 2x + \frac{64}{x^2}$$

54. Absolute maximum value on $[0, \infty)$ for
$$f(x) = 65 - 5x - \frac{540}{x^2}$$

55. Absolute minimum value on $(0, \infty)$ for
$$f(x) = x + \frac{1}{x} + \frac{30}{x^3}$$

56. Absolute minimum value on $(0, \infty)$ for
$$f(x) = 2x + \frac{5}{x} + \frac{4}{x^3}$$

57. Absolute minimum value on $(0, \infty)$ for
$$f(x) = \frac{e^x}{x^2}$$

58. Absolute maximum value on $(0, \infty)$ for
$$f(x) = \frac{x^4}{e^x}$$

59. Absolute maximum value on $(0, \infty)$ for
$$f(x) = \frac{x^3}{e^x}$$

60. Absolute minimum value on $(0, \infty)$ for
$$f(x) = \frac{e^x}{x}$$

61. Absolute maximum value on $(0, \infty)$ for
$$f(x) = 5x - 2x \ln x$$

62. Absolute minimum value on $(0, \infty)$ for
$$f(x) = 4x \ln x - 7x$$

63. Absolute maximum value on $(0, \infty)$ for
$$f(x) = x^2(3 - \ln x)$$

64. Absolute minimum value on $(0, \infty)$ for
$$f(x) = x^3(\ln x - 2)$$

65. Absolute maximum value on $(0, \infty)$ for
$$f(x) = \ln(xe^{-x})$$

66. Absolute maximum value on $(0, \infty)$ for
$$f(x) = \ln(x^2e^{-x})$$

C *In Problems 67–72, find the absolute maximum and minimum, if either exists, for each function on the indicated intervals.*

67. $f(x) = x^3 - 9x^2 + 15x + 21$
(A) $[0, 6]$ (B) $[-2, 5]$ (C) $[2, 7]$

68. $f(x) = 2x^3 - 3x^2 - 12x + 24$
(A) $[-3, 4]$ (B) $[-2, 3]$ (C) $[-2, 1]$

69. $f(x) = (x - 1)(x - 5)^3 + 1$
(A) $[0, 3]$ (B) $[1, 7]$ (C) $[3, 6]$

70. $f(x) = x^4 - 8x^2 + 16$
(A) $[-1, 3]$ (B) $[0, 2]$ (C) $[-3, 4]$

71. $f(x) = x^4 + 4x^3 + 3$
(A) $[-1, 1]$ (B) $[0, 6]$ (C) $[4, 8]$

72. $f(x) = x^4 - 18x^2 + 32$
(A) $[-4, 4]$ (B) $[-1, 1]$ (C) $[1, 3]$

In Problems 73–80, describe the graph of f at the given point relative to the existence of a local maximum or minimum with one of the following phrases: "Local maximum," "Local minimum," "Neither," or "Unable to determine from the given information." Assume that f(x) is continuous on $(-\infty, \infty)$.

73. $(3, f(3))$ if $f'(3) = 0$ and $f''(3) < 0$

74. $(4, f(4))$ if $f'(4) = 1$ and $f''(4) < 0$

75. $(-3, f(-3))$ if $f'(-3) = 0$ and $f''(-3) = 0$

76. $(-1, f(-1))$ if $f'(-1) = 0$ and $f''(-1) < 0$

77. $(6, f(6))$ if $f'(6) = 1$ and $f''(6)$ does not exist

78. $(5, f(5))$ if $f'(5) = 0$ and $f''(5)$ does not exist

79. $(-4, f(-4))$ if $f'(-4) = 0$ and $f''(-4) > 0$

80. $(1, f(1))$ if $f'(1) = 0$ and $f''(1) > 0$

Answers to Matched Problems

1. (A) Absolute maximum: $f(5) = 65$; absolute minimum: $f(-5) = -65$
(B) Absolute maximum: $f(-2) = 16$; absolute minimum: $f(2) = -16$
(C) Absolute maximum: $f(-2) = 16$; absolute minimum: $f(1) = -11$

2. (A) $f(2) = 10$ is a local maximum; $f(4) = 6$ is a local minimum.
(B) $f(\ln 5) = 5 - 5\ln 5$ is a local minimum.
(C) $f(0) = 0$ is a local minimum; there is no local extremum at $x = 1$.

3. (A) $f(\sqrt{5}) = 12 - 2\sqrt{5}$
(B) $f(5) = 5\ln 5 - 5$

8.6 Optimization

- Area and Perimeter
- Maximizing Revenue and Profit
- Inventory Control

Now we can use calculus to solve **optimization problems**—problems that involve finding the absolute maximum or the absolute minimum of a function. As you work through this section, note that the statement of the problem does not usually include the function to be optimized. Often, it is your responsibility to find the function and then to find the relevant absolute extremum.

Area and Perimeter

The techniques used to solve optimization problems are best illustrated through examples.

EXAMPLE 1 **Maximizing Area** A homeowner has \$320 to spend on building a fence around a rectangular garden. Three sides of the fence will be constructed with wire fencing at a cost of \$2 per linear foot. The fourth side will be constructed with wood fencing at a cost of \$6 per linear foot. Find the dimensions and the area of the largest garden that can be enclosed with \$320 worth of fencing.

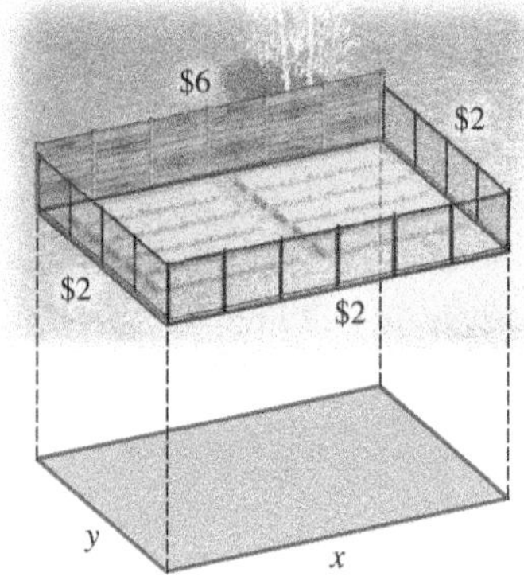

Figure 1

SOLUTION To begin, we draw a figure (Fig. 1), introduce variables, and look for relationships among the variables.

Since we don't know the dimensions of the garden, the lengths of fencing are represented by the variables x and y. The costs of the fencing materials are fixed and are represented by constants.

Now we look for relationships among the variables. The area of the garden is

$$A = xy$$

while the cost of the fencing is

$$\begin{aligned} C &= 2y + 2x + 2y + 6x \\ &= 8x + 4y \end{aligned}$$

The problem states that the homeowner has \$320 to spend on fencing. We assume that enclosing the largest area will use all the money available for fencing. The problem has now been reduced to

$$\text{Maximize} \quad A = xy \quad \text{subject to} \quad 8x + 4y = 320$$

Before we can use calculus to find the maximum area A, we must express A as a function of a single variable. We use the cost equation to eliminate one of the variables in the area expression (we choose to eliminate y—either will work).

$$\begin{aligned} 8x + 4y &= 320 \\ 4y &= 320 - 8x \\ y &= 80 - 2x \\ A = xy &= x(80 - 2x) = 80x - 2x^2 \end{aligned}$$

Now we consider the permissible values of x. Because x is one of the dimensions of a rectangle, x must satisfy

$$x \geq 0 \qquad \text{Length is always nonnegative.}$$

And because $y = 80 - 2x$ is also a dimension of a rectangle, y must satisfy

$$\begin{aligned} y = 80 - 2x &\geq 0 \qquad \text{Width is always nonnegative.} \\ 80 &\geq 2x \\ 40 &\geq x \qquad \text{or} \qquad x \leq 40 \end{aligned}$$

We summarize the preceding discussion by stating the following model for this optimization problem:

$$\text{Maximize} \quad A(x) = 80x - 2x^2 \quad \text{for } 0 \leq x \leq 40$$

Next, we find any critical numbers of A:

$$\begin{aligned} A'(x) = 80 - 4x &= 0 \\ 80 &= 4x \\ x &= \frac{80}{4} = 20 \qquad \text{Critical number} \end{aligned}$$

Table 1

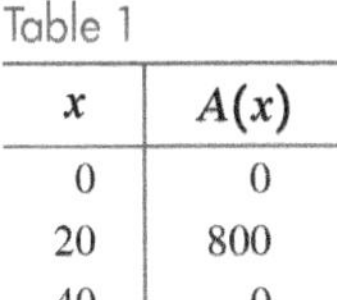

x	$A(x)$
0	0
20	800
40	0

Since $A(x)$ is continuous on [0, 40], the absolute maximum of A, if it exists, must occur at a critical number or an endpoint. Evaluating A at these numbers (Table 1), we see that the maximum area is 800 when

$$x = 20 \qquad \text{and} \qquad y = 80 - 2(20) = 40$$

Finally, we must answer the questions posed in the problem. The dimensions of the garden with the maximum area of 800 square feet are 20 feet by 40 feet, with one 20-foot side of wood fencing.

Matched Problem 1 Repeat Example 1 if the wood fencing costs \$8 per linear foot and all other information remains the same.

We summarize the steps in the solution of Example 1 in the following box:

PROCEDURE Strategy for Solving Optimization Problems

Step 1 Introduce variables, look for relationships among the variables, and construct a mathematical model of the form

$$\text{Maximize (or minimize) } f(x) \text{ on the interval } I$$

Step 2 Find the critical numbers of $f(x)$.

Step 3 Use the procedures developed in Section 8.5 to find the absolute maximum (or minimum) of $f(x)$ on the interval I and the numbers x where this occurs.

Step 4 Use the solution to the mathematical model to answer all the questions asked in the problem.

EXAMPLE 2 **Minimizing Perimeter** Refer to Example 1. The homeowner judges that an area of 800 square feet for the garden is too small and decides to increase the area to 1,250 square feet. What is the minimum cost of building a fence that will enclose a garden with an area of 1,250 square feet? What are the dimensions of this garden? Assume that the cost of fencing remains unchanged.

SOLUTION Refer to Figure 1 and the solution of Example 1. This time we want to minimize the cost of the fencing that will enclose 1,250 square feet. The problem can be expressed as

$$\text{Minimize} \quad C = 8x + 4y \quad \text{subject to} \quad xy = 1{,}250$$

Since x and y represent distances, we know that $x \geq 0$ and $y \geq 0$. But neither variable can equal 0 because their product must be 1,250.

$$xy = 1{,}250 \qquad \text{Solve the area equation for } y.$$

$$y = \frac{1{,}250}{x} \qquad \text{Substitute for } y \text{ in the cost equation.}$$

$$C(x) = 8x + 4\frac{1{,}250}{x}$$

$$= 8x + \frac{5{,}000}{x} \qquad x > 0$$

The model for this problem is

$$\text{Minimize} \quad C(x) = 8x + \frac{5{,}000}{x} \quad \text{for } x > 0$$

$$= 8x + 5{,}000x^{-1}$$

$$C'(x) = 8 - 5{,}000x^{-2}$$

$$= 8 - \frac{5{,}000}{x^2} = 0$$

$$8 = \frac{5{,}000}{x^2}$$

$$x^2 = \frac{5{,}000}{8} = 625$$

$$x = \sqrt{625} = 25 \qquad \text{The negative square root is discarded, since } x > 0.$$

We use the second derivative to determine the behavior at $x = 25$.

$$C'(x) = 8 - 5{,}000x^{-2}$$

$$C''(x) = 0 + 10{,}000x^{-3} = \frac{10{,}000}{x^3}$$

$$C''(25) = \frac{10{,}000}{25^3} = 0.64 > 0$$

⚠ CAUTION We cannot assume that a critical number gives the location of the minimum (or maximum). We still need to test the critical number. ▲

The second-derivative test for local extrema shows that $C(x)$ has a local minimum at $x = 25$, and since $x = 25$ is the only critical number of $C(x)$ for $x > 0$, then $C(25)$ must be the absolute minimum for $x > 0$. When $x = 25$, the cost is

$$C(25) = 8(25) + \frac{5{,}000}{25} = 200 + 200 = \$400$$

and

$$y = \frac{1{,}250}{25} = 50$$

The minimum cost for enclosing a 1,250-square-foot garden is \$400, and the dimensions are 25 feet by 50 feet, with one 25-foot side of wood fencing.

Matched Problem 2 Repeat Example 2 if the homeowner wants to enclose a 1,800-square-foot garden and all other data remain unchanged.

CONCEPTUAL INSIGHT

The restrictions on the variables in the solutions of Examples 1 and 2 are typical of problems involving areas or perimeters (or the cost of the perimeter):

$$8x + 4y = 320 \qquad \text{Cost of fencing (Example 1)}$$
$$xy = 1{,}250 \qquad \text{Area of garden (Example 2)}$$

The equation in Example 1 restricts the values of x to

$$0 \le x \le 40 \qquad \text{or} \qquad [0, 40]$$

The endpoints are included in the interval for our convenience (a closed interval is easier to work with than an open one). The area function is defined at each endpoint, so it does no harm to include them.

The equation in Example 2 restricts the values of x to

$$x > 0 \qquad \text{or} \qquad (0, \infty)$$

Neither endpoint can be included in this interval. We cannot include 0 because the area is not defined when $x = 0$, and we can never include ∞ as an endpoint. Remember, ∞ is not a number; it is a symbol that indicates the interval is unbounded.

Maximizing Revenue and Profit

EXAMPLE 3 **Maximizing Revenue** An office supply company sells x permanent markers per year at \$$p$ per marker. The price–demand equation for these markers is $p = 10 - 0.001x$. What price should the company charge for the markers to maximize revenue? What is the maximum revenue?

SOLUTION

$$\begin{aligned} \text{Revenue} &= \text{price} \times \text{demand} \\ R(x) &= (10 - 0.001x)x \\ &= 10x - 0.001x^2 \end{aligned}$$

Both price and demand must be nonnegative, so

$$x \ge 0 \quad \text{and} \quad p = 10 - 0.001x \ge 0$$
$$10 \ge 0.001x$$
$$10{,}000 \ge x$$

The mathematical model for this problem is

$$\text{Maximize} \quad R(x) = 10x - 0.001x^2 \qquad 0 \le x \le 10{,}000$$
$$R'(x) = 10 - 0.002x$$
$$10 - 0.002x = 0$$
$$10 = 0.002x$$
$$x = \frac{10}{0.002} = 5{,}000 \qquad \text{Critical number}$$

Use the second-derivative test for absolute extrema:

$$R''(x) = -0.002 < 0 \quad \text{for all } x$$
$$\text{Max } R(x) = R(5{,}000) = \$25{,}000$$

When the demand is $x = 5{,}000$, the price is

$$10 - 0.001(5{,}000) = \$5 \qquad p = 10 - 0.001x$$

The company will realize a maximum revenue of \$25,000 when the price of a marker is \$5.

Matched Problem 3 An office supply company sells x heavy-duty paper shredders per year at \$$p$ per shredder. The price–demand equation for these shredders is

$$p = 300 - \frac{x}{30}$$

What price should the company charge for the shredders to maximize revenue? What is the maximum revenue?

EXAMPLE 4 **Maximizing Profit** The total annual cost of manufacturing x permanent markers for the office supply company in Example 3 is

$$C(x) = 5{,}000 + 2x$$

What is the company's maximum profit? What should the company charge for each marker, and how many markers should be produced?

SOLUTION Using the revenue model in Example 3, we have

$$\begin{aligned} \text{Profit} &= \text{Revenue} - \text{Cost} \\ P(x) &= R(x) - C(x) \\ &= 10x - 0.001x^2 - 5{,}000 - 2x \\ &= 8x - 0.001x^2 - 5{,}000 \end{aligned}$$

The mathematical model for profit is

$$\text{Maximize} \quad P(x) = 8x - 0.001x^2 - 5{,}000 \qquad 0 \le x \le 10{,}000$$

The restrictions on x come from the revenue model in Example 3.

$$\begin{aligned} P'(x) = 8 - 0.002x &= 0 \\ 8 &= 0.002x \\ x &= \frac{8}{0.002} = 4{,}000 \qquad \text{Critical number} \\ P''(x) &= -0.002 < 0 \quad \text{for all } x \end{aligned}$$

Since $x = 4{,}000$ is the only critical number and $P''(x) < 0$,

$$\text{Max } P(x) = P(4{,}000) = \$11{,}000$$

Using the price–demand equation from Example 3 with $x = 4{,}000$, we find that

$$p = 10 - 0.001(4{,}000) = \$6 \qquad p = 10 - 0.001x$$

A maximum profit of \$11,000 is realized when 4,000 markers are manufactured annually and sold for \$6 each.

The results in Examples 3 and 4 are illustrated in Figure 2.

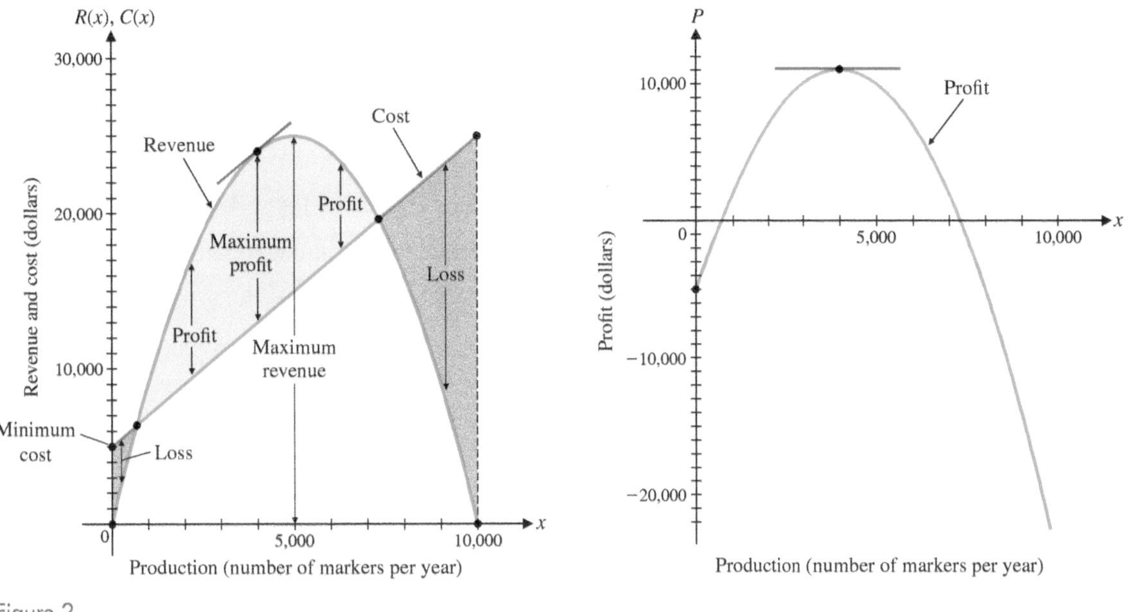

Figure 2

CONCEPTUAL INSIGHT

In Figure 2, notice that the maximum revenue and the maximum profit occur at different production levels. The maximum profit occurs when

$$P'(x) = R'(x) - C'(x) = 0$$

that is, when the marginal revenue is equal to the marginal cost. Notice that the slopes of the revenue function and the cost function are the same at this production level.

Matched Problem 4 The annual cost of manufacturing x paper shredders for the office supply company in Matched Problem 3 is $C(x) = 90{,}000 + 30x$. What is the company's maximum profit? What should it charge for each shredder, and how many shredders should it produce?

EXAMPLE 5 **Maximizing Profit** The government decides to tax the company in Example 4 \$2 for each marker produced. Taking into account this additional cost, how many markers should the company manufacture annually to maximize its profit? What is the maximum profit? How much should the company charge for the markers to realize the maximum profit?

SOLUTION The tax of \$2 per unit changes the company's cost equation:

$$\begin{aligned} C(x) &= \text{original cost} + \text{tax} \\ &= 5{,}000 + 2x + 2x \\ &= 5{,}000 + 4x \end{aligned}$$

The new profit function is

$$\begin{aligned} P(x) &= R(x) - C(x) \\ &= 10x - 0.001x^2 - 5{,}000 - 4x \\ &= 6x - 0.001x^2 - 5{,}000 \end{aligned}$$

So we must solve the following equation:

$$\begin{aligned} \text{Maximize} \quad P(x) &= 6x - 0.001x^2 - 5{,}000 \qquad 0 \le x \le 10{,}000 \\ P'(x) &= 6 - 0.002x \\ 6 - 0.002x &= 0 \\ x &= 3{,}000 \qquad \text{Critical number} \\ P''(x) &= -0.002 < 0 \quad \text{for all } x \\ \text{Max } P(x) &= P(3{,}000) = \$4{,}000 \end{aligned}$$

Using the price–demand equation (Example 3) with $x = 3{,}000$, we find that

$$p = 10 - 0.001(3{,}000) = \$7 \qquad p = 10 - 0.001x$$

The company's maximum profit is $4,000 when 3,000 markers are produced and sold annually at a price of $7.

Even though the tax caused the company's cost to increase by $2 per marker, the price that the company should charge to maximize its profit increases by only $1. The company must absorb the other $1, with a resulting decrease of $7,000 in maximum profit.

Matched Problem 5 The government decides to tax the office supply company in Matched Problem 4 $20 for each shredder produced. Taking into account this additional cost, how many shredders should the company manufacture annually to maximize its profit? What is the maximum profit? How much should the company charge for the shredders to realize the maximum profit?

EXAMPLE 6 **Maximizing Revenue** When a management training company prices its seminar on management techniques at $400 per person, 1,000 people will attend the seminar. The company estimates that for each $5 reduction in price, an additional 20 people will attend the seminar. How much should the company charge for the seminar in order to maximize its revenue? What is the maximum revenue?

SOLUTION Let x represent the number of $5 price reductions.

$$\begin{aligned} 400 - 5x &= \text{price per customer} \\ 1{,}000 + 20x &= \text{number of customers} \\ \text{Revenue} &= (\text{price per customer})(\text{number of customers}) \\ R(x) &= (400 - 5x) \times (1{,}000 + 20x) \end{aligned}$$

Since price cannot be negative, we have

$$\begin{aligned} 400 - 5x &\ge 0 \\ 400 &\ge 5x \\ 80 &\ge x \qquad \text{or} \qquad x \le 80 \end{aligned}$$

A negative value of x would result in a price increase. Since the problem is stated in terms of price reductions, we must restrict x so that $x \ge 0$. Putting all this together, we have the following model:

$$\begin{aligned} \text{Maximize} \quad R(x) &= (400 - 5x)(1{,}000 + 20x) \quad \text{for } 0 \le x \le 80 \\ R(x) &= 400{,}000 + 3{,}000x - 100x^2 \\ R'(x) &= 3{,}000 - 200x = 0 \\ 3{,}000 &= 200x \\ x &= 15 \qquad \text{Critical number} \end{aligned}$$

Since $R(x)$ is continuous on the interval [0, 80], we can determine the behavior of the graph by constructing a table. Table 2 shows that $R(15) = \$422{,}500$ is

Table 2

x	$R(x)$
0	400,000
15	422,500
80	0

the absolute maximum revenue. The price of attending the seminar at $x = 15$ is $400 - 5(15) = \$325$. The company should charge \$325 for the seminar in order to receive a maximum revenue of \$422,500.

Matched Problem 6 A walnut grower estimates from past records that if 20 trees are planted per acre, then each tree will average 60 pounds of nuts per year. If, for each additional tree planted per acre, the average yield per tree drops 2 pounds, then how many trees should be planted to maximize the yield per acre? What is the maximum yield?

EXAMPLE 7 **Maximizing Revenue** After additional analysis, the management training company in Example 6 decides that its estimate of attendance was too high. Its new estimate is that only 10 additional people will attend the seminar for each \$5 decrease in price. All other information remains the same. How much should the company charge for the seminar now in order to maximize revenue? What is the new maximum revenue?

SOLUTION Under the new assumption, the model becomes

$$\begin{aligned} \text{Maximize} \quad R(x) &= (400 - 5x)(1{,}000 + 10x) \qquad 0 \le x \le 80 \\ &= 400{,}000 - 1{,}000x - 50x^2 \\ R'(x) &= -1{,}000 - 100x = 0 \\ -1{,}000 &= 100x \\ x &= -10 \qquad \text{Critical number} \end{aligned}$$

Table 3

x	$R(x)$
0	400,000
80	0

Note that $x = -10$ is not in the interval [0, 80]. Since $R(x)$ is continuous on [0, 80], we can use a table to find the absolute maximum revenue. Table 3 shows that the maximum revenue is $R(0) = \$400{,}000$. The company should leave the price at \$400. Any \$5 decreases in price will lower the revenue.

Matched Problem 7 After further analysis, the walnut grower in Matched Problem 6 determines that each additional tree planted will reduce the average yield by 4 pounds. All other information remains the same. How many additional trees per acre should the grower plant now in order to maximize the yield? What is the new maximum yield?

CONCEPTUAL INSIGHT

The solution in Example 7 is called an **endpoint solution** because the optimal value occurs at the endpoint of an interval rather than at a critical number in the interior of the interval.

Inventory Control

EXAMPLE 8 **Inventory Control** A multimedia company anticipates that there will be a demand for 20,000 copies of a certain DVD during the next year. It costs the company \$0.50 to store a DVD for one year. Each time it must make additional DVDs, it costs \$200 to set up the equipment. How many DVDs should the company make during each production run to minimize its total storage and setup costs?

SOLUTION This type of problem is called an **inventory control problem**. One of the basic assumptions made in such problems is that the demand is uniform. For example, if there are 250 working days in a year, then the daily demand would be $20{,}000 \div 250 = 80$ DVDs. The company could decide to produce all 20,000

DVDs at the beginning of the year. This would certainly minimize the setup costs but would result in very large storage costs. At the other extreme, the company could produce 80 DVDs each day. This would minimize the storage costs but would result in very large setup costs. Somewhere between these two extremes is the optimal solution that will minimize the total storage and setup costs. Let

$$x = \text{number of DVDs manufactured during each production run}$$
$$y = \text{number of production runs}$$

It is easy to see that the total setup cost for the year is $200y$, but what is the total storage cost? If the demand is uniform, then the number of DVDs in storage between production runs will decrease from x to 0, and the average number in storage each day is $x/2$. This result is illustrated in Figure 3.

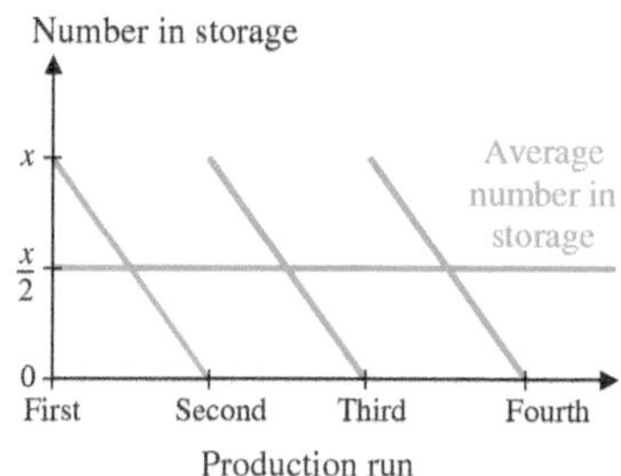

Figure 3

Since it costs \$0.50 to store a DVD for one year, the total storage cost is $0.5(x/2) = 0.25x$ and the total cost is

$$\text{total cost} = \text{setup cost} + \text{storage cost}$$
$$C = 200y + 0.25x$$

In order to write the total cost C as a function of one variable, we must find a relationship between x and y. If the company produces x DVDs in each of y production runs, then the total number of DVDs produced is xy.

$$xy = 20{,}000$$
$$y = \frac{20{,}000}{x}$$

Certainly, x must be at least 1 and cannot exceed 20,000. We must solve the following equation:

$$\text{Minimize} \quad C(x) = 200\left(\frac{20{,}000}{x}\right) + 0.25x \qquad 1 \le x \le 20{,}000$$
$$C(x) = \frac{4{,}000{,}000}{x} + 0.25x$$
$$C'(x) = -\frac{4{,}000{,}000}{x^2} + 0.25$$
$$-\frac{4{,}000{,}000}{x^2} + 0.25 = 0$$
$$x^2 = \frac{4{,}000{,}000}{0.25}$$
$$x^2 = 16{,}000{,}000$$
$$x = 4{,}000$$

$-4{,}000$ is not a critical number, since $1 \le x \le 20{,}000$.

$$C''(x) = \frac{8{,}000{,}000}{x^3} > 0 \qquad \text{for } x \in (1, 20{,}000)$$

Therefore,

$$\text{Min } C(x) = C(4{,}000) = 2{,}000$$
$$y = \frac{20{,}000}{4{,}000} = 5$$

The company will minimize its total cost by making 4,000 DVDs five times during the year.

Matched Problem 8 Repeat Example 8 if it costs \$250 to set up a production run and \$0.40 to store a DVD for one year.

Exercises 8.6

Skills Warm-up Exercises

W *In Problems 1–8, express the given quantity as a function $f(x)$ of one variable x. (If necessary, review Section 1.1.)*

1. The product of two numbers x and y whose sum is 28
2. The sum of two numbers x and y whose product is 54
3. The area of a circle of diameter x
4. The volume of a sphere of diameter x
5. The volume of a right circular cylinder of radius x and height equal to the radius
6. The volume of a right circular cylinder of diameter x and height equal to one-third of the diameter
7. The area of a rectangle of length x and width y that has a perimeter of 120 feet
8. The perimeter of a rectangle of length x and width y that has an area of 200 square meters

9. Find two numbers whose sum is 13 and whose product is a maximum.
10. Find two numbers whose sum is 27 and whose product is a maximum.
11. Find two numbers whose difference is 13 and whose product is a minimum.
12. Find two numbers whose difference is 27 and whose product is a minimum.
13. Find two positive numbers whose product is 13 and whose sum is a minimum.
14. Find two positive numbers whose product is 27 and whose sum is a minimum.
15. Find the dimensions of a rectangle with an area of 200 square feet that has the minimum perimeter.
16. Find the dimensions of a rectangle with an area of 108 square feet that has the minimum perimeter.
17. Find the dimensions of a rectangle with a perimeter of 148 feet that has the maximum area.
18. Find the dimensions of a rectangle with a perimeter of 92 feet that has the maximum area.

B 19. **Maximum revenue and profit.** A company manufactures and sells x smartphones per week. The weekly price–demand and cost equations are, respectively,

$$p = 500 - 0.4x \quad \text{and} \quad C(x) = 20{,}000 + 20x$$

(A) What price should the company charge for the phones, and how many phones should be produced to maximize the weekly revenue? What is the maximum weekly revenue?

(B) What is the maximum weekly profit? How much should the company charge for the phones, and how many phones should be produced to realize the maximum weekly profit?

20. **Maximum revenue and profit.** A company manufactures and sells x cameras per week. The weekly price–demand and cost equations are, respectively,

$$p = 400 - 0.5x \quad \text{and} \quad C(x) = 2{,}000 + 200x$$

(A) What price should the company charge for the cameras, and how many cameras should be produced to maximize the weekly revenue? What is the maximum revenue?

(B) What is the maximum weekly profit? How much should the company charge for the cameras, and how many cameras should be produced to realize the maximum weekly profit?

21. **Maximum revenue and profit.** A company manufactures and sells x television sets per month. The monthly cost and price–demand equations are

$$C(x) = 72{,}000 + 60x$$
$$p = 200 - \frac{x}{30} \qquad 0 \le x \le 6{,}000$$

(A) Find the maximum revenue.

(B) Find the maximum profit, the production level that will realize the maximum profit, and the price the company should charge for each television set.

(C) If the government decides to tax the company \$5 for each set it produces, how many sets should the company manufacture each month to maximize its profit? What is the maximum profit? What should the company charge for each set?

22. **Maximum revenue and profit.** Repeat Problem 21 for

$$C(x) = 60{,}000 + 60x$$

$$p = 200 - \frac{x}{50} \qquad 0 \le x \le 10{,}000$$

23. **Maximum profit.** The following table contains price–demand and total cost data for the production of 70-litre expedition backpacks, where p is the wholesale price (in dollars) of a backpack for an annual demand of x backpacks and C is the total cost (in dollars) of producing x backpacks:

(A) Find a quadratic regression equation for the price–demand data, using x as the independent variable.

x	p	C
900	280	115,000
1,050	260	135,000
1,400	200	165,000
1,750	140	195,000

(B) Find a linear regression equation for the cost data, using x as the independent variable.

(C) What is the maximum profit? What is the wholesale price per 70-litre expedition backpack that should be charged to realize the maximum profit? Round answers to the nearest dollar.

24. **Maximum profit.** The following table contains price–demand and total cost data for the production of lightweight backpacks, where p is the wholesale price (in dollars) of a backpack for an annual demand of x backpacks and C is the total cost (in dollars) of producing x backpacks:

x	p	C
3,100	69	115,000
4,300	59	145,000
5,400	49	160,000
6,500	29	180,000

(A) Find a quadratic regression equation for the price–demand data, using x as the independent variable.

(B) Find a linear regression equation for the cost data, using x as the independent variable.

(C) What is the maximum profit? What is the wholesale price per lightweight backpack that should be charged to realize the maximum profit? Round answers to the nearest dollar.

25. **Maximum revenue.** A deli sells 640 sandwiches per day at a price of $8 each.

(A) A market survey shows that for every $0.10 reduction in price, 40 more sandwiches will be sold. How much should the deli charge for a sandwich in order to maximize revenue?

(B) A different market survey shows that for every $0.20 reduction in the original $8 price, 15 more sandwiches will be sold. Now how much should the deli charge for a sandwich in order to maximize revenue?

26. **Maximum revenue.** A university student center sells 1,600 cups of coffee per day at a price of $2.40.

(A) A market survey shows that for every $0.05 reduction in price, 50 more cups of coffee will be sold. How much should the student center charge for a cup of coffee in order to maximize revenue?

(B) A different market survey shows that for every $0.10 reduction in the original $2.40 price, 60 more cups of coffee will be sold. Now how much should the student center charge for a cup of coffee in order to maximize revenue?

27. **Car rental.** A car rental agency rents 200 cars per day at a rate of $30 per day. For each $1 increase in rate, 5 fewer cars are rented. At what rate should the cars be rented to produce the maximum income? What is the maximum income?

28. **Rental income.** A 250-room hotel in Paris is filled to capacity every night at €100 a room. For each €1 increase in rent, 2 fewer rooms are rented. If each rented room costs €9 to service per day, how much should the management charge for each room to maximize gross profit? What is the maximum gross profit?

29. **Agriculture.** A commercial cherry grower estimates from past records that if 30 trees are planted per acre, then each tree will yield an average of 50 pounds of cherries per season. If, for each additional tree planted per acre (up to 20), the average yield per tree is reduced by 1 pound, how many trees should be planted per acre to obtain the maximum yield per acre? What is the maximum yield?

30. **Agriculture.** A commercial pear grower must decide on the optimum time to have fruit picked and sold. If the pears are picked now, they will bring 30¢ per pound, with each tree yielding an average of 60 pounds of salable pears. If the average yield per tree increases 6 pounds per tree per week for the next 4 weeks, but the price drops 2¢ per pound per week, when should the pears be picked to realize the maximum return per tree? What is the maximum return?

C 31. **Manufacturing.** A candy box is to be made out of a piece of cardboard that measures 8 by 12 inches. Squares of equal size will be cut out of each corner, and then the ends and sides will be folded up to form a rectangular box. What size square should be cut from each corner to obtain a maximum volume?

32. **Packaging.** A parcel delivery service will deliver a package only if the length plus girth (distance around) does not exceed 108 inches.

(A) Find the dimensions of a rectangular box with square ends that satisfies the delivery service's restriction and has maximum volume. What is the maximum volume?

(B) Find the dimensions (radius and height) of a cylindrical container that meets the delivery service's requirement and has maximum volume. What is the maximum volume?

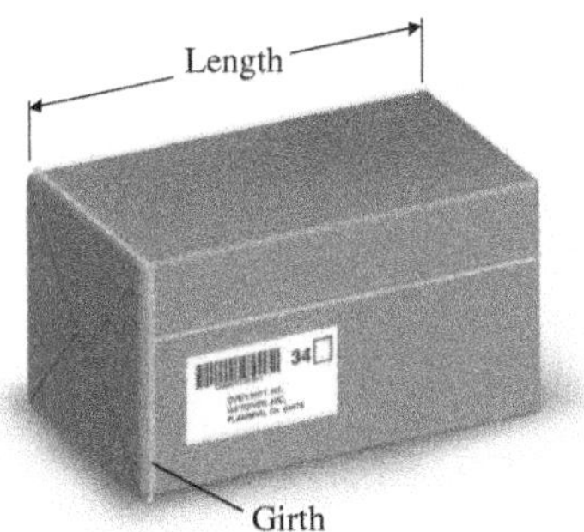

Figure for 32

33. **Construction costs.** A fence is to be built to enclose a rectangular area of 800 square feet. The fence along three sides is to be made of material that costs \$6 per foot. The material for the fourth side costs \$18 per foot. Find the dimensions of the rectangle that will allow for the most economical fence to be built.

34. **Construction costs.** If a builder has only \$864 to spend on a fence, but wants to use both \$6 and \$18 per foot fencing as in Problem 33, what is the maximum area that can be enclosed? What are its dimensions?

35. **Construction costs.** The owner of a retail lumber store wants to construct a fence to enclose an outdoor storage area adjacent to the store. The enclosure must use the full length of the store as part of one side of the area (see figure). Find the dimensions that will enclose the largest area if

    (A) 240 feet of fencing material are used.

    (B) 400 feet of fencing material are used.

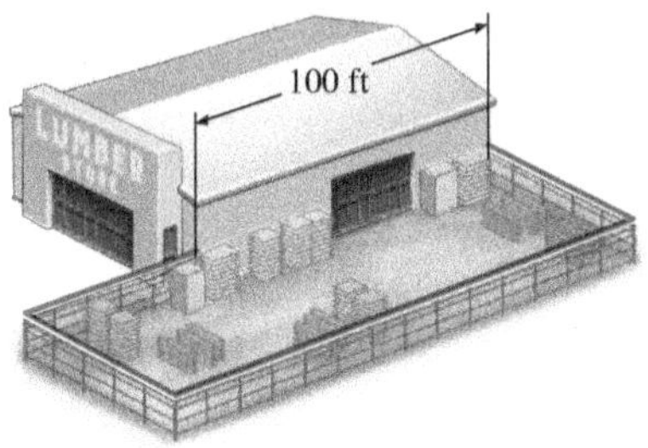

36. **Construction costs.** If the owner wants to enclose a rectangular area of 12,100 square feet as in Problem 35, what are the dimensions of the area that requires the least fencing? How many feet of fencing are required?

37. **Inventory control.** A paint manufacturer has a uniform annual demand for 16,000 cans of automobile primer. It costs \$4 to store one can of paint for one year and \$500 to set up the plant for production of the primer. How many times a year should the company produce this primer in order to minimize the total storage and setup costs?

38. **Inventory control.** A pharmacy has a uniform annual demand for 200 bottles of a certain antibiotic. It costs \$10 to store one bottle for one year and \$40 to place an order. How many times during the year should the pharmacy order the antibiotic in order to minimize the total storage and reorder costs?

39. **Inventory control.** A publishing company sells 50,000 copies of a certain book each year. It costs the company \$1 to store a book for one year. Each time that it prints additional copies, it costs the company \$1,000 to set up the presses. How many books should the company produce during each printing in order to minimize its total storage and setup costs?

40. **Inventory control.** A tool company has a uniform annual demand for 9,000 premium chainsaws. It costs \$5 to store a chainsaw for a year and \$2,500 to set up the plant for manufacture of the premium model. How many chainsaws should be manufactured in each production run in order to minimize the total storage and setup costs?

41. **Operational costs.** The cost per hour for fuel to run a train is $v^2/4$ dollars, where v is the speed of the train in miles per hour. (Note that the cost goes up as the square of the speed.) Other costs, including labor, are \$300 per hour. How fast should the train travel on a 360-mile trip to minimize the total cost for the trip?

42. **Operational costs.** The cost per hour for fuel to drive a rental truck from one city to another, a distance of 800 miles, is given by

$$f(v) = 0.03v^2 - 2.2v + 72,$$

where v is the speed of the truck in miles per hour. Other costs are \$40 per hour. How fast should you drive to minimize the total cost?

43. **Construction costs.** A freshwater pipeline is to be run from a source on the edge of a lake to a small resort community on an island 5 miles offshore, as indicated in the figure.

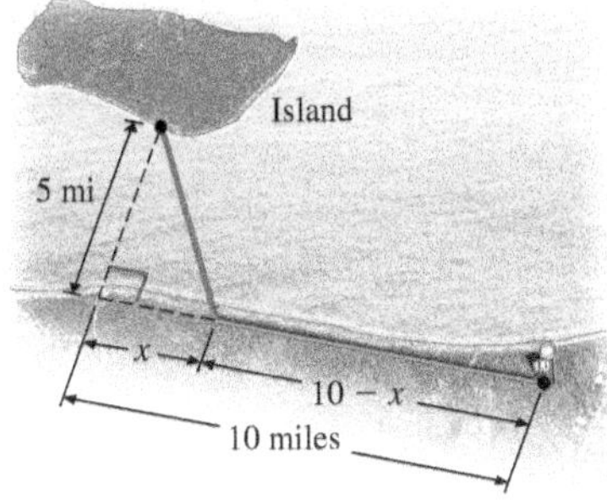

(A) If it costs 1.4 times as much to lay the pipe in the lake as it does on land, what should x be (in miles) to minimize the total cost of the project?

(B) If it costs only 1.1 times as much to lay the pipe in the lake as it does on land, what should x be to minimize the total cost of the project? [*Note:* Compare with Problem 46.]

44. Drug concentration. The concentration $C(t)$, in milligrams per cubic centimeter, of a particular drug in a patient's bloodstream is given by

$$C(t) = \frac{0.16t}{t^2 + 4t + 4}$$

where t is the number of hours after the drug is taken. How many hours after the drug is taken will the concentration be maximum? What is the maximum concentration?

45. Bacteria control. A lake used for recreational swimming is treated periodically to control harmful bacteria growth. Suppose that t days after a treatment, the concentration of bacteria per cubic centimeter is given by

$$C(t) = 30t^2 - 240t + 500 \qquad 0 \le t \le 8$$

How many days after a treatment will the concentration be minimal? What is the minimum concentration?

46. Bird flights. Some birds tend to avoid flights over large bodies of water during daylight hours. Suppose that an adult bird with this tendency is taken from its nesting area on the edge of a large lake to an island 5 miles offshore and is then released (see figure).

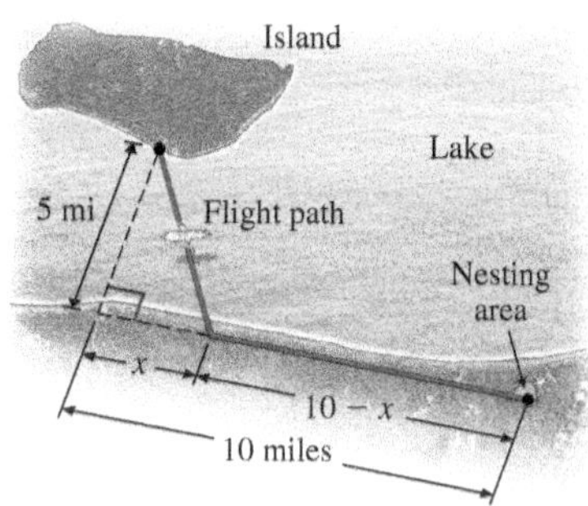

(A) If it takes 1.4 times as much energy to fly over water as land, how far up the shore (x, in miles) should the bird head to minimize the total energy expended in returning to the nesting area?

(B) If it takes only 1.1 times as much energy to fly over water as land, how far up the shore should the bird head to minimize the total energy expended in returning to the nesting area? [*Note:* Compare with Problem 43.]

47. Botany. If it is known from past experiments that the height (in feet) of a certain plant after t months is given approximately by

$$H(t) = 4t^{1/2} - 2t \qquad 0 \le t \le 2$$

then how long, on average, will it take a plant to reach its maximum height? What is the maximum height?

48. Pollution. Two heavily industrial areas are located 10 miles apart, as shown in the figure. If the concentration of particulate matter (in parts per million) decreases as the reciprocal of the square of the distance from the source, and if area A_1 emits eight times the particulate matter as A_2, then the concentration of particulate matter at any point between the two areas is given by

$$C(x) = \frac{8k}{x^2} + \frac{k}{(10 - x)^2} \qquad 0.5 \le x \le 9.5, \quad k > 0$$

How far from A_1 will the concentration of particulate matter between the two areas be at a minimum?

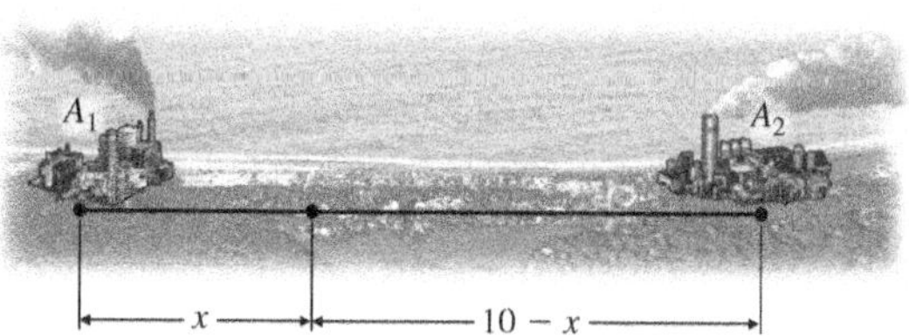

49. Politics. In a newly incorporated city, the voting population (in thousands) is estimated to be

$$N(t) = 30 + 12t^2 - t^3 \qquad 0 \le t \le 8$$

where t is time in years. When will the rate of increase of $N(t)$ be most rapid?

50. Learning. A large grocery chain found that, on average, a checker can recall $P\%$ of a given price list x hours after starting work, as given approximately by

$$P(x) = 96x - 24x^2 \qquad 0 \le x \le 3$$

At what time x does the checker recall a maximum percentage? What is the maximum?

Answers to Matched Problems

1. The dimensions of the garden with the maximum area of 640 square feet are 16 feet by 40 feet, with one 16-foot side with wood fencing.
2. The minimum cost for enclosing a 1,800-square-foot garden is \$480, and the dimensions are 30 feet by 60 feet, with one 30-foot side with wood fencing.
3. The company will realize a maximum revenue of \$675,000 when the price of a shredder is \$150.
4. A maximum profit of \$456,750 is realized when 4,050 shredders are manufactured annually and sold for \$165 each.
5. A maximum profit of \$378,750 is realized when 3,750 shredders are manufactured annually and sold for \$175 each.
6. The maximum yield is 1,250 pounds per acre when 5 additional trees are planted on each acre.
7. The maximum yield is 1,200 pounds when no additional trees are planted.
8. The company should produce 5,000 DVDs four times a year.

Chapter 8 Summary and Review

Important Terms, Symbols, and Concepts

8.1 First Derivative and Graphs

EXAMPLES

- A function f is **increasing** on an interval (a, b) if $f(x_2) > f(x_1)$ whenever $a < x_1 < x_2 < b$, and f is **decreasing** on (a, b) if $f(x_2) < f(x_1)$ whenever $a < x_1 < x_2 < b$.
- For the interval (a, b), if $f' > 0$, then f is increasing, and if $f' < 0$, then f is decreasing. So a sign chart for f' can be used to tell where f is increasing or decreasing.
- A real number x in the domain of f such that $f'(x) = 0$ or $f'(x)$ does not exist is called a **critical number** of f. So a critical number of f is a partition number for f' that also belongs to the domain of f.
- A value $f(c)$ is a **local maximum** if there is an interval (m, n) containing c such that $f(x) \le f(c)$ for all x in (m, n). A value $f(c)$ is a **local minimum** if there is an interval (m, n) containing c such that $f(x) \ge f(c)$ for all x in (m, n). A local maximum or local minimum is called a **local extremum**.
- If $f(c)$ is a local extremum, then c is a critical number of f.
- The **first-derivative test for local extrema** identifies local maxima and minima of f by means of a sign chart for f'.

Ex. 1, p. 442
Ex. 2, p. 443
Ex. 3, p. 443
Ex. 4, p. 444
Ex. 5, p. 445
Ex. 6, p. 446
Ex. 7, p. 448
Ex. 8, p. 450
Ex. 9, p. 451

8.2 Second Derivative and Graphs

- The graph of f is **concave upward** on (a, b) if f' is increasing on (a, b), and is **concave downward** on (a, b) if f' is decreasing on (a, b).

Ex. 1, p. 459

- For the interval (a, b), if $f'' > 0$, then f is concave upward, and if $f'' < 0$, then f is concave downward. So a sign chart for f'' can be used to tell where f is concave upward or concave downward.
- An **inflection point** of f is a point $(c, f(c))$ on the graph of f where the concavity changes.
- The graphing strategy on page 464 is used to organize the information obtained from f' and f'' in order to sketch the graph of f.
- If sales $N(x)$ are expressed as a function of the amount x spent on advertising, then the dollar amount at which $N'(x)$, the rate of change of sales, goes from increasing to decreasing is called the **point of diminishing returns**. If d is the point of diminishing returns, then $(d, N(d))$ is an inflection point of $N(x)$.

Ex. 2, p. 461
Ex. 3, p. 462
Ex. 4, p. 463
Ex. 5, p. 464
Ex. 6, p. 466
Ex. 7, p. 468

8.3 L'Hôpital's Rule

- L'Hôpital's rule for $0/0$ indeterminate forms: If $\lim_{x \to c} f(x) = 0$ and $\lim_{x \to c} g(x) = 0$, then

$$\lim_{x \to c} \frac{f(x)}{g(x)} = \lim_{x \to c} \frac{f'(x)}{g'(x)}$$

provided the second limit exists or is ∞ or $-\infty$.

- Always check to make sure that L'Hôpital's rule is applicable before using it.

Ex. 1, p. 475
Ex. 2, p. 475
Ex. 3, p. 476
Ex. 4, p. 477
Ex. 5, p. 478
Ex. 6, p. 478

- L'Hôpital's rule remains valid if the symbol $x \to c$ is replaced everywhere it occurs by one of

$$x \to c^+ \qquad x \to c^- \qquad x \to \infty \qquad x \to -\infty$$

Ex. 7, p. 479
Ex. 8, p. 479

- L'Hôpital's rule is also valid for indeterminate forms $\frac{\pm\infty}{\pm\infty}$.

Ex. 9, p. 481
Ex. 10, p. 481

8.4 Curve-Sketching Techniques

- The graphing strategy on pages 483 and 484 incorporates analyses of f, f', and f'' in order to sketch a graph of f, including intercepts and asymptotes.
- If $f(x) = n(x)/d(x)$ is a rational function and the degree of $n(x)$ is 1 more than the degree of $d(x)$, then the graph of $f(x)$ has an **oblique asymptote** of the form $y = mx + b$.

Ex. 1, p. 484
Ex. 2, p. 485
Ex. 3, p. 486
Ex. 4, p. 488
Ex. 5, p. 490

8.5 Absolute Maxima and Minima

- If $f(c) \geq f(x)$ for all x in the domain of f, then $f(c)$ is called the **absolute maximum** of f. If $f(c) \leq f(x)$ for all x in the domain of f, then $f(c)$ is called the **absolute minimum** of f. An absolute maximum or absolute minimum is called an **absolute extremum**.
- A function that is continuous on a closed interval $[a, b]$ has both an absolute maximum and an absolute minimum on that interval.
- Absolute extrema, if they exist, must occur at critical numbers or endpoints.
- To find the absolute maximum and absolute minimum of a continuous function f on a closed interval, identify the endpoints and critical numbers in the interval, evaluate the function f at each of them, and choose the largest and smallest values of f. Ex. 1, p. 498
- **Second-derivative test for local extrema:** If $f'(c) = 0$ and $f''(c) > 0$, then $f(c)$ is a local minimum. If $f'(c) = 0$ and $f''(c) < 0$, then $f(c)$ is a local maximum. No conclusion can be drawn if $f''(c) = 0$. Ex. 2, p. 500
- The **second-derivative test for absolute extrema on an interval** is applicable when there is only one critical number c in the interior of an interval I and $f'(c) = 0$ and $f''(c) \neq 0$. Ex. 3, p. 502

8.6 Optimization

- The procedure on pages 505 and 506 for solving optimization problems involves finding the absolute maximum or absolute minimum of a function $f(x)$ on an interval I. If the absolute maximum or absolute minimum occurs at an endpoint, not at a critical number in the interior of I, the extremum is called an **endpoint solution**. The procedure is effective in solving problems in business, including **inventory control problems**, manufacturing, construction, engineering, and many other fields.

Ex. 1, p. 504
Ex. 2, p. 506
Ex. 3, p. 507
Ex. 4, p. 508
Ex. 5, p. 509
Ex. 6, p. 510
Ex. 7, p. 511
Ex. 8, p. 511

Review Exercises

Work through all the problems in this chapter review, and check your answers in the back of the book. Answers to all review problems are there, along with section numbers in italics to indicate where each type of problem is discussed. Where weaknesses show up, review appropriate sections in the text.

Problems 1–8 refer to the following graph of $y = f(x)$. Identify the points or intervals on the x axis that produce the indicated behavior.

1. $f(x)$ is increasing. **2.** $f'(x) < 0$

3. The graph of f is concave downward.

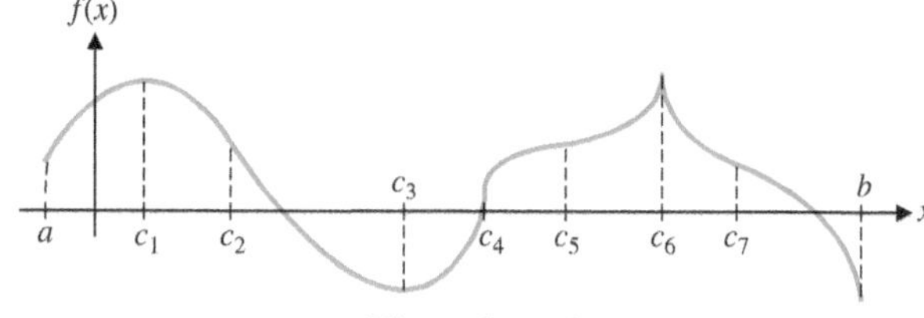

Figure for 1–8

4. Local minima **5.** Absolute maxima

6. $f'(x)$ appears to be 0.

7. $f'(x)$ does not exist.

8. Inflection points

In Problems 9 and 10, use the given information to sketch the graph of f. Assume that f is continuous on its domain and that all intercepts are included in the information given.

9. Domain: All real x

x	−3	−2	−1	0	2	3
$f(x)$	0	3	2	0	−3	0

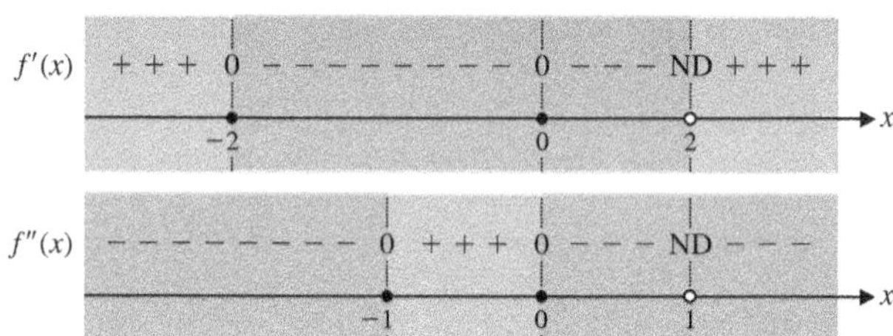

10. Domain: All real x

$f(-2) = 1, f(0) = 0, f(2) = 1;$
$f'(0) = 0; f'(x) < 0$ on $(-\infty, 0)$;
$f'(x) > 0$ on $(0, \infty)$;
$f''(-2) = 0, f''(2) = 0;$
$f''(x) < 0$ on $(-\infty, -2)$ and $(2, \infty)$;
$f''(x) > 0$ on $(-2, 2)$;
$\lim_{x \to -\infty} f(x) = 2; \lim_{x \to \infty} f(x) = 2$

11. Find $f''(x)$ for $f(x) = 3x^2 + \ln x$.

12. Find y'' for $y = 3x + \frac{4}{x}$.

In Problems 13 and 14, find the domain and intercepts.

13. $f(x) = \frac{2 + x}{1 - x^2}$ **14.** $f(x) = \ln(x + 2)$

In Problems 15 and 16, find the horizontal and vertical asymptotes.

15. $f(x) = \frac{2x + 5}{2x^2 - 32}$ **16.** $f(x) = \frac{2x - 7}{3x + 10}$

In Problems 17 and 18, find the x and y coordinates of all inflection points.

17. $f(x) = x^4 - 12x^2$ **18.** $f(x) = x^4 - 16x^3 + 10$

In Problems 19 and 20, find (A) $f'(x)$, (B) the partition numbers for f', and (C) the critical numbers of f.

19. $f(x) = 2x^{1/3} - x^{2/3}$ **20.** $f(x) = x^{-1/5}$

In Problems 21–30, summarize all the pertinent information obtained by applying the final version of the graphing strategy (Section 8.4) to f, and sketch the graph of f.

21. $f(x) = x^3 - 18x^2 + 81x$

22. $f(x) = (x + 4)(x - 2)^2$

23. $f(x) = 8x^3 - 2x^4$ **24.** $f(x) = (x - 1)^3(x + 3)$

25. $f(x) = \dfrac{3x}{x + 2}$ **26.** $f(x) = \dfrac{x^2}{x^2 + 27}$

27. $f(x) = \dfrac{x}{(x + 2)^2}$ **28.** $f(x) = \dfrac{x^3}{x^2 + 3}$

29. $f(x) = 5 - 5e^{-x}$ **30.** $f(x) = x^3 \ln x$

Find each limit in Problems 31–40.

31. $\lim\limits_{x\to 0} \dfrac{x^2 - x}{e^{2x} - 1}$ **32.** $\lim\limits_{x\to 4} \dfrac{x^2 - 3x - 4}{x^2 - 5x + 4}$

33. $\lim\limits_{x\to 0^+} \dfrac{\ln(1 + 4x)}{x^{1/4}}$ **34.** $\lim\limits_{x\to 0} \dfrac{e^x - 1}{x - 1}$

35. $\lim\limits_{x\to \infty} \dfrac{\ln(1 + x)}{x^3}$ **36.** $\lim\limits_{x\to 0} \dfrac{x^3}{e^x - x - 1}$

37. $\lim\limits_{x\to 0^+} \dfrac{\sqrt{x}}{\ln(1 + x)}$ **38.** $\lim\limits_{x\to \infty} \dfrac{e^x + e^{-x} - 5}{\ln x}$

39. $\lim\limits_{x\to \infty} \dfrac{e^x - 1}{e^{2x} - 1}$ **40.** $\lim\limits_{x\to 0} \dfrac{e^x - 1}{e^{2x} - 1}$

41. Use the graph of $y = f'(x)$ shown here to discuss the graph of $y = f(x)$. Organize your conclusions in a table (see Example 4, Section 8.2). Sketch a possible graph of $y = f(x)$.

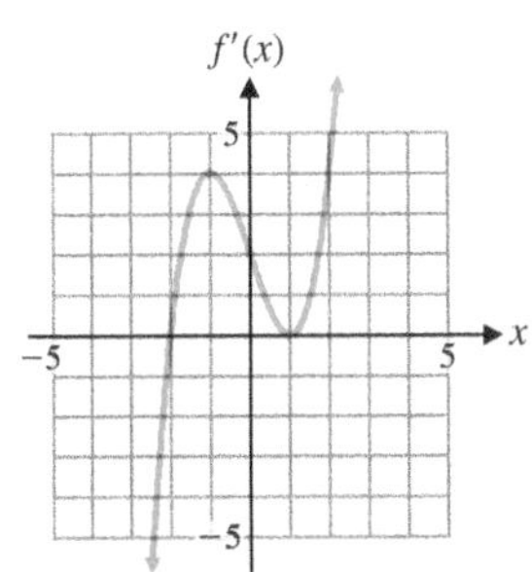

Figure for 41 and 42

42. Refer to the above graph of $y = f'(x)$. Which of the following could be the graph of $y = f''(x)$?

(A)

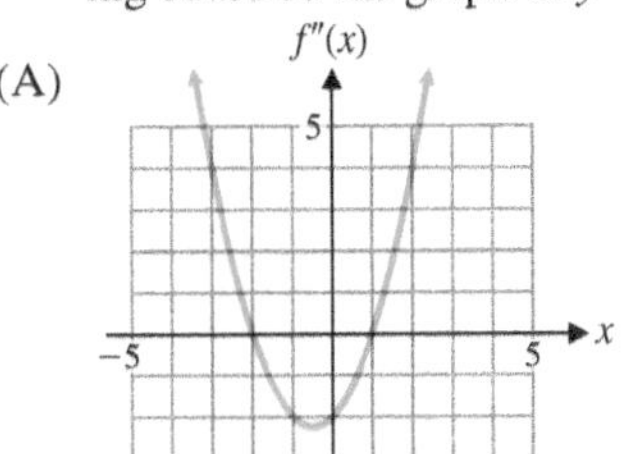

(B)

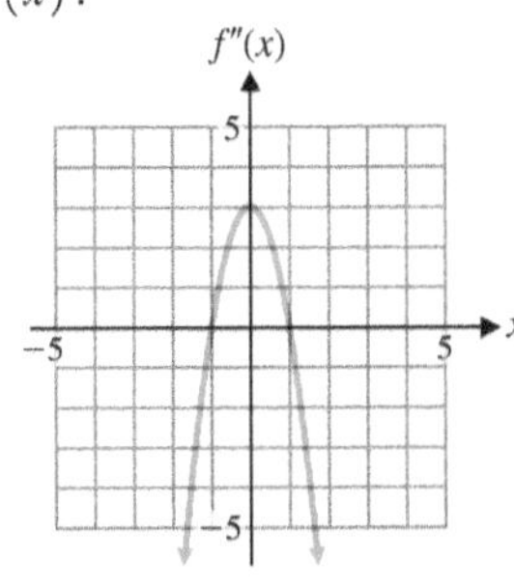

(C)

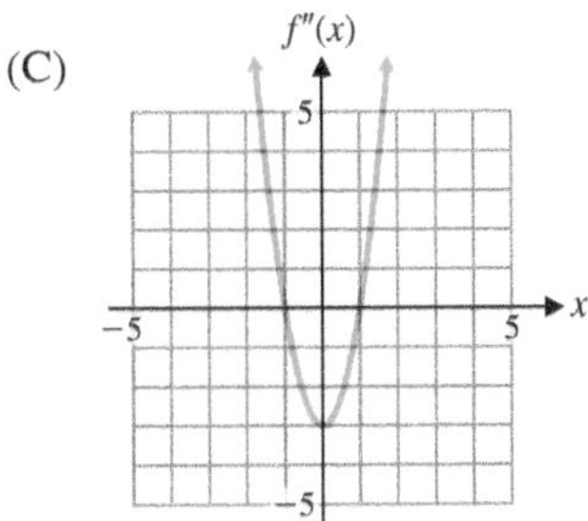

43. Use the second-derivative test to find any local extrema for

$$f(x) = \frac{1}{3}x^3 - 3x^2 - 16x + 200$$

44. Find the absolute maximum and absolute minimum, if either exists, for

$$y = f(x) = x^3 - 12x + 12 \qquad -3 \le x \le 5$$

45. Find the absolute minimum, if it exists, for

$$f(x) = \frac{3x}{(1 + x)^2} \qquad x > 0$$

46. Find the absolute maximum, if it exists, for

$$f(x) = 11x - 2x \ln x \qquad x > 0$$

47. Find the absolute maximum, if it exists, for

$$f(x) = 10xe^{-2x} \qquad x > 0$$

48. Let $y = f(x)$ be a polynomial function with local minima at $x = a$ and $x = b$, $a < b$. Must f have at least one local maximum between a and b? Justify your answer.

49. The derivative of $f(x) = x^{-1}$ is $f'(x) = -x^{-2}$. Since $f'(x) < 0$ for $x \ne 0$, is it correct to say that $f(x)$ is decreasing for all x except $x = 0$? Explain.

50. Discuss the difference between a partition number for $f'(x)$ and a critical number of $f(x)$, and illustrate with examples.

51. Find the absolute maximum for $f'(x)$ if

$$f(x) = 6x^2 - x^3 + 8$$

Graph f and f' on the same coordinate system for $0 \le x \le 4$.

52. Find two positive numbers whose product is 400 and whose sum is a minimum. What is the minimum sum?

In Problems 53 and 54, apply the graphing strategy and summarize the pertinent information. Round any approximate values to two decimal places.

53. $f(x) = x^4 + x^3 - 4x^2 - 3x + 4$

54. $f(x) = 0.25x^4 - 5x^3 + 31x^2 - 70x$

55. Find the absolute maximum, if it exists, for

$$f(x) = 3x - x^2 + e^{-x} \quad x > 0$$

56. Find the absolute maximum, if it exists, for

$$f(x) = \frac{\ln x}{e^x} \quad x > 0$$

Applications

57. **Price analysis.** The graph in the figure approximates the rate of change of the price of tomatoes over a 60-month period, where $p(t)$ is the price of a pound of tomatoes and t is time (in months).

(A) Write a brief description of the graph of $y = p(t)$, including a discussion of local extrema and inflection points.

(B) Sketch a possible graph of $y = p(t)$.

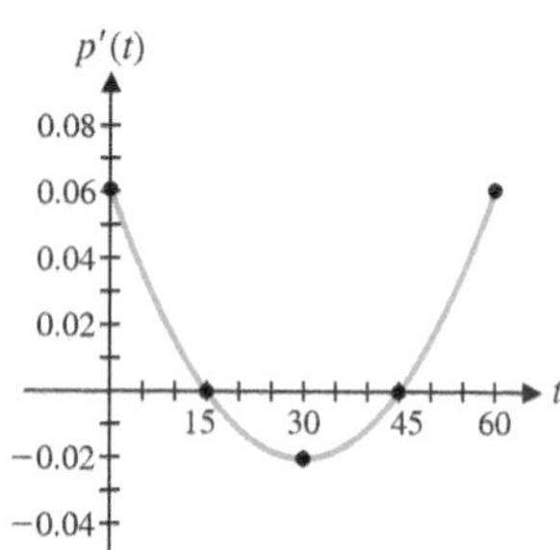

58. **Maximum revenue and profit.** A company manufactures and sells x cell phones per month. The monthly cost and price–demand equations are, respectively,

$$C(x) = 200x + 100{,}000$$
$$P = 300 - \frac{1}{80}x \quad 0 < x \le 24{,}000$$

(A) Find the maximum revenue.

(B) How many phones should the company manufacture each month to maximize its profit? What is the maximum monthly profit? How much should the company charge for each phone?

(C) If the government decides to give a tax incentive to the company of \$10 for each phone it produces, how many phones should the company manufacture each month to maximize its profit? What is the maximum monthly profit? How much should the company charge for each phone?

59. **Construction.** A fence is to be built to enclose a rectangular area. The fence along three sides is to be made of material that costs \$5 per foot. The material for the fourth side costs \$15 per foot.

(A) If the area is 5,000 square feet, find the dimensions of the rectangle that will allow for the most economical fence.

(B) If \$3,000 is available for the fencing, find the dimensions of the rectangle that will enclose the most area.

60. **Rental income.** A 100-apartment building in a city is fully occupied every month when the rent per month is \$500 per apartment. For each \$40 increase in the monthly rent, 5 fewer apartments are rented. If each rented apartment costs \$20 a month to service, how much should the management charge per apartment in order to maximize gross profit? What is the maximum gross profit?

61. **Inventory control.** A computer store sells 7,200 boxes of storage drives annually. It costs the store \$0.20 to store a box of drives for one year. Each time it reorders drives, the store must pay a \$5.00 service charge for processing the order. How many times during the year should the store order drives to minimize the total storage and reorder costs?

62. **Average cost.** The total cost of producing x dorm refrigerators per day is given by

$$C(x) = 4{,}000 + 10x + 0.1x^2$$

Find the minimum average cost. Graph the average cost and the marginal cost functions on the same coordinate system. Include any oblique asymptotes.

63. **Average cost.** The cost of producing x wheeled picnic coolers is given by

$$C(x) = 200 + 50x - 50\ln x \quad x \ge 1$$

Find the minimum average cost.

64. **Marginal analysis.** The price–demand equation for a GPS device is

$$p(x) = 1{,}000e^{-0.02x}$$

where x is the monthly demand and p is the price in dollars. Find the production level and price per unit that produce the maximum revenue. What is the maximum revenue?

65. **Maximum revenue.** Graph the revenue function from Problem 64 for $0 \le x \le 100$.

66. **Maximum profit.** Refer to Problem 64. If the GPS devices cost the store \$220 each, find the price (to the nearest cent) that maximizes the profit. What is the maximum profit (to the nearest dollar)?

67. **Maximum profit.** The data in the table show the daily demand x for cream puffs at a state fair at various price levels p. If it costs \$1 to make a cream puff, use logarithmic regression ($p = a + b\ln x$) to find the price (to the nearest cent) that maximizes profit.

Demand	Price per Cream Puff (\$)
x	p
3,125	1.99
3,879	1.89
5,263	1.79
5,792	1.69
6,748	1.59
8,120	1.49

68. Construction costs. The ceiling supports in a new discount department store are 12 feet apart. Lights are to be hung from these supports by chains in the shape of a "Y." If the lights are 10 feet below the ceiling, what is the shortest length of chain that can be used to support these lights?

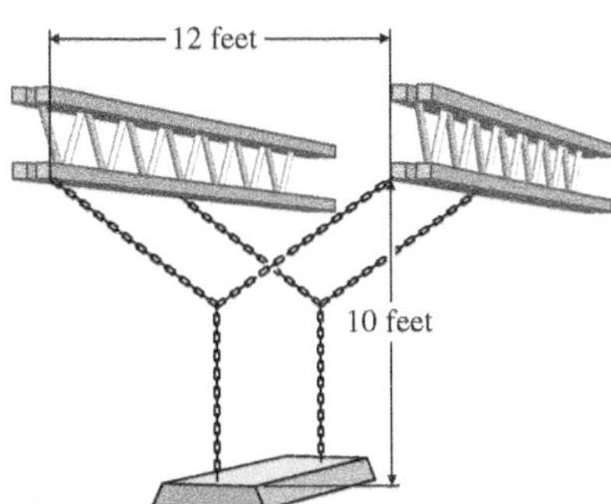

69. Average cost. The table gives the total daily cost y (in dollars) of producing x dozen chocolate chip cookies at various production levels.

Dozens of Cookies	Total Cost
x	y
50	119
100	187
150	248
200	382
250	505
300	695

(A) Enter the data into a graphing calculator and find a quadratic regression equation for the total cost.

(B) Use the regression equation from part (*A*) to find the minimum average cost (to the nearest cent) and the corresponding production level (to the nearest integer).

70. Advertising: point of diminishing returns. A company estimates that it will sell $N(x)$ units of a product after spending $\$x$ thousand on advertising, as given by

$$N(x) = -0.25x^4 + 11x^3 - 108x^2 + 3{,}000$$
$$9 \le x \le 24$$

When is the rate of change of sales increasing and when is it decreasing? What is the point of diminishing returns and the maximum rate of change of sales? Graph N and N' on the same coordinate system.

71. Advertising. A chain of appliance stores uses TV ads to promote its HDTV sales. Analyzing past records produced the data in the following table, where x is the number of ads placed monthly and y is the number of HDTVs sold that month:

Number of Ads	Number of HDTVs
x	y
10	271
20	427
25	526
30	629
45	887
48	917

(A) Enter the data into a graphing calculator, set the calculator to display two decimal places, and find a cubic regression equation for the number of HDTVs sold monthly as a function of the number of ads.

(B) How many ads should be placed each month to maximize the rate of change of sales with respect to the number of ads, and how many HDTVs can be expected to be sold with that number of ads? Round answers to the nearest integer.

72. Bacteria control. If the bacteria count per cubic centimeter in a body of water t days after treatment is given by

$$C(t) = t^3 - 15t^2 + 48t + 200 \qquad 3 \le t \le 11$$

then in how many days will the count be a minimum?

73. Politics. The number of registered voters in a town t years after the last election is estimated to be

$$N(t) = 20 + 24t^2 - t^4 \qquad 0 \le t \le 4.5$$

where N is in thousands. When will the rate of increase of $N(t)$ be at its maximum?

9 Multivariable Calculus

Introduction

In previous chapters, we have applied the key concepts of calculus, the derivative and the integral, to functions with one independent variable. The graph of such a function is a curve in the plane. In Chapter 9, we extend the key concepts of calculus to functions with two independent variables. Graphs of such functions are surfaces in a three-dimensional coordinate system. We use functions with two independent variables to study how production depends on both labor and capital, how braking distance depends on both the weight and speed of a car, how resistance in a blood vessel depends on both its length and radius. In Section 9.5, we justify the method of least squares and use the method to construct linear models (see, for example, Problem 35 in Section 9.5 on pole vaulting in the Olympic Games).

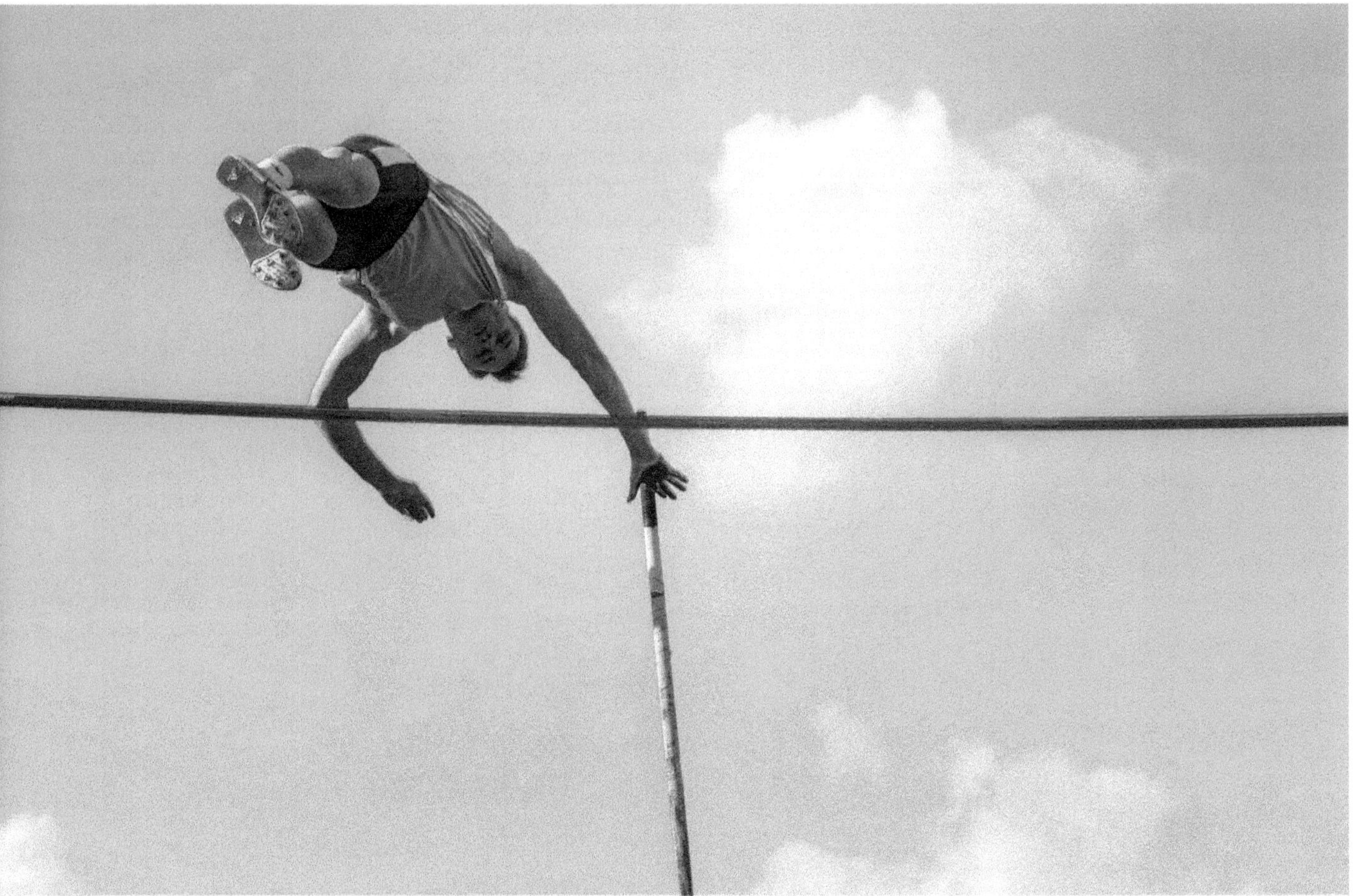

9.1 Functions of Several Variables

- Functions of Two or More Independent Variables
- Examples of Functions of Several Variables
- Three-Dimensional Coordinate Systems

Functions of Two or More Independent Variables

In Section 1.1, we introduced the concept of a function with one independent variable. Now we broaden the concept to include functions with more than one independent variable.

A small manufacturing company produces a standard type of surfboard. If fixed costs are \$500 per week and variable costs are \$70 per board produced, the weekly cost function is given by

$$C(x) = 500 + 70x \tag{1}$$

where x is the number of boards produced per week. The cost function is a function of a single independent variable x. For each value of x from the domain of C, there exists exactly one value of $C(x)$ in the range of C.

Now, suppose that the company decides to add a high-performance competition board to its line. If the fixed costs for the competition board are \$200 per week and the variable costs are \$100 per board, then the cost function (1) must be modified to

$$C(x, y) = 700 + 70x + 100y \tag{2}$$

where $C(x, y)$ is the cost for a weekly output of x standard boards and y competition boards. Equation (2) is an example of a function with two independent variables x and y. Of course, as the company expands its product line even further, its weekly cost function must be modified to include more and more independent variables, one for each new product produced.

If the domain of a function is a set of ordered pairs, then it is a **function of two independent variables**. An equation of the form

$$z = f(x, y)$$

where $f(x, y)$, is an algebraic expression in the variables x and y, specifies a function. The variables x and y are **independent variables**, and the variable z is a **dependent variable**. The **domain** is the set of all ordered pairs (x, y) such that $f(x, y)$ is a real number, and the set of all corresponding values $f(x, y)$ is the **range** of the function. It should be noted, however, that certain conditions in practical problems often lead to further restrictions on the domain of a function.

We can similarly define functions of three independent variables, $w = f(x, y, z)$, of four independent variables, $u = f(w, x, y, z)$, and so on. In this chapter, we concern ourselves primarily with functions of two independent variables.

EXAMPLE 1 **Evaluating a Function of Two Independent Variables** For the cost function $C(x, y) = 700 + 70x + 100y$ described earlier, find $C(10, 5)$.

SOLUTION

$$\begin{aligned} C(10, 5) &= 700 + 70(10) + 100(5) \\ &= \$1,900 \end{aligned}$$

Matched Problem 1 Find $C(20, 10)$ for the cost function in Example 1.

EXAMPLE 2 **Evaluating a Function of Three Independent Variables** For the function $f(x, y, z) = 2x^2 - 3xy + 3z + 1$, find $f(3, 0, -1)$.

SOLUTION

$$f(3, 0, -1) = 2(3)^2 - 3(3)(0) + 3(-1) + 1$$
$$= 18 - 0 - 3 + 1 = 16$$

Matched Problem 2 Find $f(-2, 2, 3)$ for f in Example 2.

EXAMPLE 3 **Revenue, Cost, and Profit Functions** Suppose the surfboard company discussed earlier has determined that the demand equations for its two types of boards are given by

$$p = 210 - 4x + y$$
$$q = 300 + x - 12y$$

where p is the price of the standard board, q is the price of the competition board, x is the weekly demand for standard boards, and y is the weekly demand for competition boards.

(A) Find the weekly revenue function $R(x, y)$, and evaluate $R(20, 10)$.

(B) If the weekly cost function is

$$C(x, y) = 700 + 70x + 100y$$

find the weekly profit function $P(x, y)$ and evaluate $P(20, 10)$.

SOLUTION

(A)

$$\text{Revenue} = \begin{pmatrix}\text{demand for}\\ \text{standard}\\ \text{boards}\end{pmatrix} \times \begin{pmatrix}\text{price of a}\\ \text{standard}\\ \text{board}\end{pmatrix} + \begin{pmatrix}\text{demand for}\\ \text{competition}\\ \text{boards}\end{pmatrix} \times \begin{pmatrix}\text{price of a}\\ \text{competition}\\ \text{board}\end{pmatrix}$$

$$R(x, y) = xp + yq$$
$$= x(210 - 4x + y) + y(300 + x - 12y)$$
$$= 210x + 300y - 4x^2 + 2xy - 12y^2$$
$$R(20, 10) = 210(20) + 300(10) - 4(20)^2 + 2(20)(10) - 12(10)^2$$
$$= \$4{,}800$$

(B)

$$\text{Profit} = \text{revenue} - \text{cost}$$
$$P(x, y) = R(x, y) - C(x, y)$$
$$= 210x + 300y - 4x^2 + 2xy - 12y^2 - 700 - 70x - 100y$$
$$= 140x + 200y - 4x^2 + 2xy - 12y^2 - 700$$
$$P(20, 10) = 140(20) + 200(10) - 4(20)^2 + 2(20)(10) - 12(10)^2 - 700$$
$$= \$1{,}700$$

Matched Problem 3 Repeat Example 3 if the demand and cost equations are given by

$$p = 220 - 6x + y$$
$$q = 300 + 3x - 10y$$
$$C(x, y) = 40x + 80y + 1{,}000$$

Examples of Functions of Several Variables

A number of concepts can be considered as functions of two or more variables.

Area of a rectangle	$A(x, y) = xy$	A = area; x; y
Volume of a box	$V(x, y, z) = xyz$	V = volume; x; y; z
Volume of a right circular cylinder	$V(r, h) = \pi r^2 h$	r; h
Simple interest	$A(P, r, t) = P(1 + rt)$	A = amount P = principal r = annual rate t = time in years
Compound interest	$A(P, r, t, n) = P\left(1 + \frac{r}{n}\right)^{nt}$	A = amount P = principal r = annual rate t = time in years n = number of compounding periods per year
IQ	$Q(M, C) = \frac{M}{C}(100)$	Q = IQ = intelligence quotient M = MA = mental age C = CA = chronological age
Resistance for blood flow in a vessel (Poiseuille's law)	$R(L, r) = k\frac{L}{r^4}$	R = resistance L = length of vessel r = radius of vessel k = constant

EXAMPLE 4 **Package Design** A company uses a box with a square base and an open top for a bath assortment (see Fig. 1). If x is the length (in inches) of each side of the base and y is the height (in inches), find the total amount of material $M(x, y)$ required to construct one of these boxes, and evaluate $M(5, 10)$.

$$\begin{aligned} \text{Area of base} &= x^2 \\ \text{Area of one side} &= xy \\ \text{Total material} &= (\text{area of base}) + 4(\text{area of one side}) \\ M(x, y) &= x^2 + 4xy \\ M(5, 10) &= (5)^2 + 4(5)(10) \\ &= 225 \text{ square inches} \end{aligned}$$

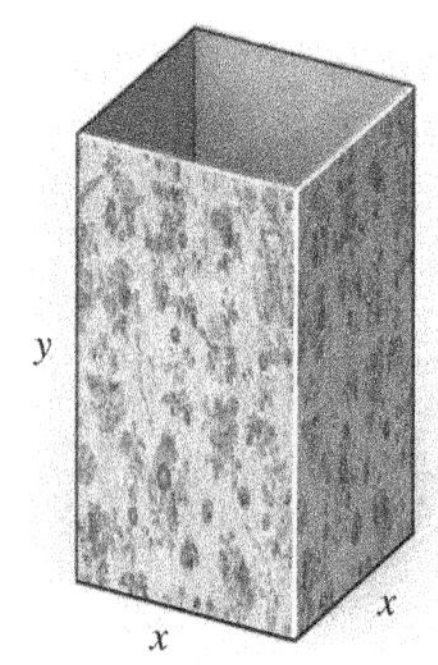

Figure 1

Matched Problem 4 For the box in Example 4, find the volume $V(x, y)$ and evaluate $V(5, 10)$.

The next example concerns the **Cobb–Douglas production function**

$$f(x, y) = kx^m y^n$$

where k, m, and n are positive constants with $m + n = 1$. Economists use this function to describe the number of units $f(x, y)$ produced from the utilization of x units of labor and y units of capital (for equipment such as tools, machinery, buildings, and so on). Cobb–Douglas production functions are also used to describe the productivity of a single industry, of a group of industries producing the same product, or even of an entire country.

EXAMPLE 5 **Productivity** The productivity of a steel-manufacturing company is given approximately by the function

$$f(x, y) = 10x^{0.2}y^{0.8}$$

with the utilization of x units of labor and y units of capital. If the company uses 3,000 units of labor and 1,000 units of capital, how many units of steel will be produced?

SOLUTION The number of units of steel produced is given by

$$f(3{,}000, 1{,}000) = 10(3{,}000)^{0.2}(1{,}000)^{0.8} \quad \text{Use a calculator.}$$
$$\approx 12{,}457 \text{ units}$$

Matched Problem 5 Refer to Example 5. Find the steel production if the company uses 1,000 units of labor and 2,000 units of capital.

Three-Dimensional Coordinate Systems

We now take a brief look at graphs of functions of two independent variables. Since functions of the form $z = f(x, y)$ involve two independent variables x and y, and one dependent variable z, we need a *three-dimensional coordinate system* for their graphs. A **three-dimensional coordinate system** is formed by three mutually perpendicular number lines intersecting at their origins (see Fig. 2). In such a system, every **ordered triplet of numbers** (x, y, z) can be associated with a unique point, and conversely.

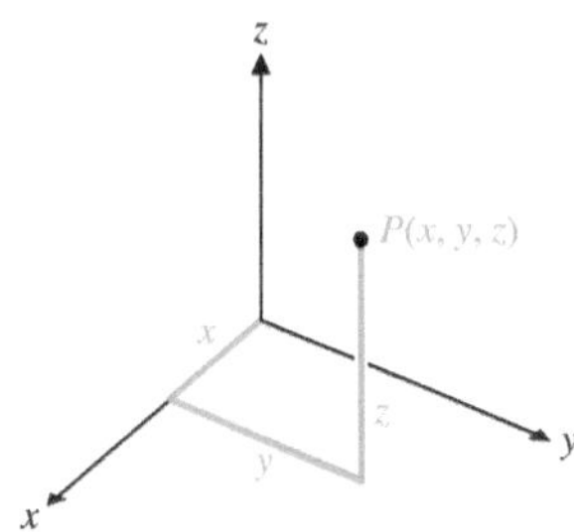

Figure 2 Rectangular coordinate system

EXAMPLE 6 **Three-Dimensional Coordinates** Locate $(-3, 5, 2)$ in a rectangular coordinate system.

SOLUTION We sketch a three-dimensional coordinate system and locate the point $(-3, 5, 2)$ (see Fig. 3).

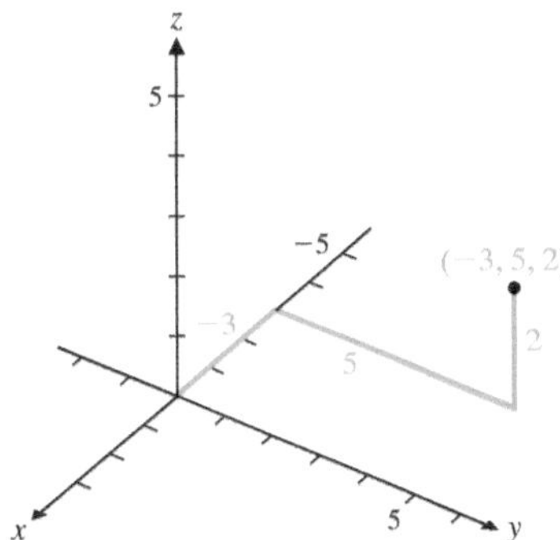

Figure 3

Matched Problem 6 Find the coordinates of the corners A, C, G, and D of the rectangular box shown in Figure 4:

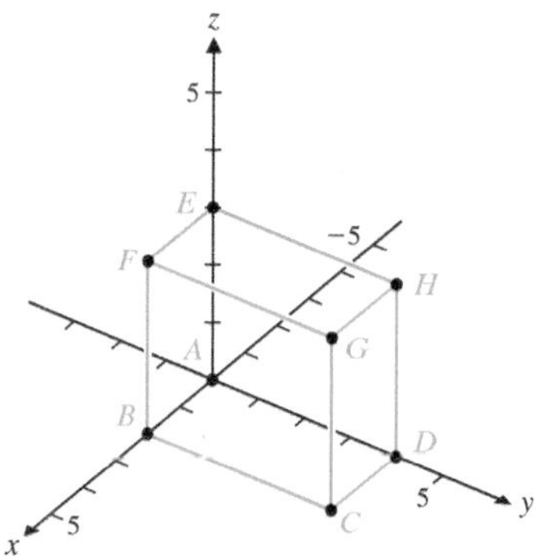

Figure 4

Explore and Discuss 1

Imagine that you are facing the front of a classroom whose rectangular walls meet at right angles. Suppose that the point of intersection of the floor, front wall, and left-side wall is the origin of a three-dimensional coordinate system in which every point in the room has nonnegative coordinates. Then the plane $z = 0$ (or, equivalently, the xy plane) can be described as "the floor," and the plane $z = 2$ can be described as "the plane parallel to, but 2 units above, the floor." Give similar descriptions of the following planes:

(A) $x = 0$ (B) $x = 3$ (C) $y = 0$ (D) $y = 4$ (E) $x = -1$

What does the graph of $z = x^2 + y^2$ look like? If we let $x = 0$ and graph $z = 0^2 + y^2 = y^2$ in the yz plane, we obtain a parabola; if we let $y = 0$ and graph $z = x^2 + 0^2 = x^2$ in the xz plane, we obtain another parabola. The graph of $z = x^2 + y^2$ is either one of these parabolas rotated around the z axis (see Fig. 5). This cup-shaped figure is a *surface* and is called a **paraboloid**.

In general, the graph of any function of the form $z = f(x, y)$ is called a **surface**. The graph of such a function is the graph of all ordered triplets of numbers (x, y, z) that satisfy the equation. Graphing functions of two independent variables is a difficult task, and the general process will not be dealt with in this book. We present only a few simple graphs to suggest extensions of earlier geometric interpretations of the derivative and local maxima and minima to functions of two variables. Note that $z = f(x, y) = x^2 + y^2$ appears (see Fig. 5) to have a local minimum at $(x, y) = (0, 0)$. Figure 6 shows a local maximum at $(x, y) = (0, 0)$.

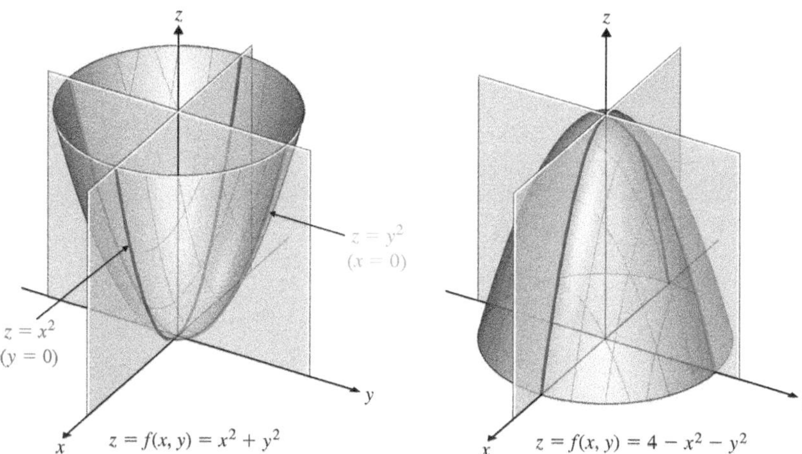

Figure 5 Paraboloid

Figure 6 Local maximum: $f(0, 0) = 4$

Figure 7 shows a point at $(x, y) = (0, 0)$, called a **saddle point**, that is neither a local minimum nor a local maximum. Note that in the cross section $x = 0$, the saddle point is a local minimum, and in the cross section $y = 0$, the saddle point is a local maximum.

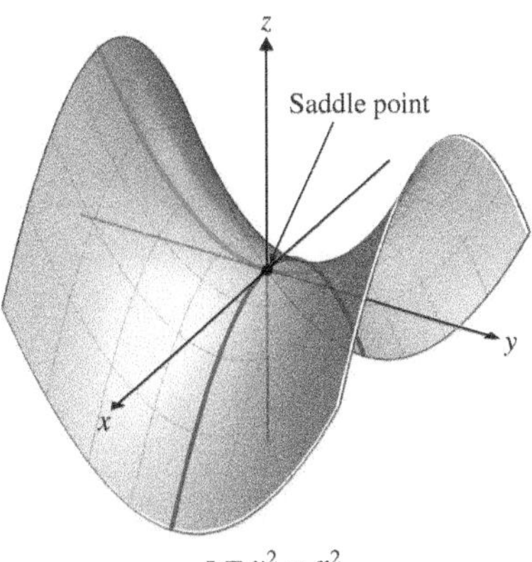

Figure 7 Saddle point at (0, 0, 0)

Some graphing calculators are designed to draw graphs (like those of Figs. 5, 6, and 7) of functions of two independent variables. Others, such as the graphing calculator used for the displays in this book, are designed to draw graphs of functions of one independent variable. When using the latter type of calculator, we can graph cross sections produced by cutting surfaces with planes parallel to the xz plane or yz plane to gain insight into the graph of a function of two independent variables.

EXAMPLE 7 Graphing Cross Sections

(A) Describe the cross sections of $f(x, y) = 2x^2 + y^2$ in the planes $y = 0$, $y = 1, y = 2, y = 3$, and $y = 4$.

(B) Describe the cross sections of $f(x, y) = 2x^2 + y^2$ in the planes $x = 0$, $x = 1, x = 2, x = 3$, and $x = 4$.

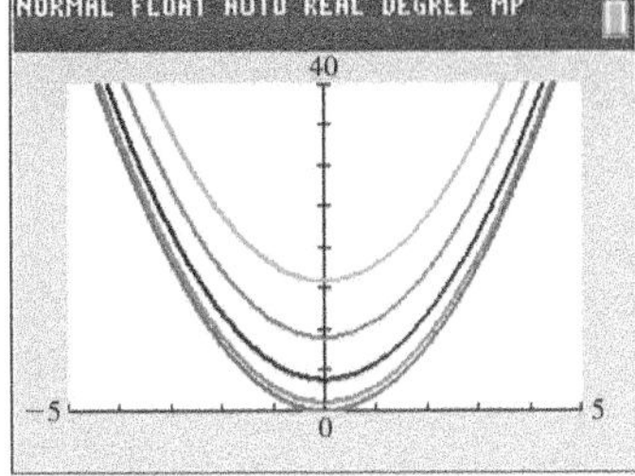

Figure 8

$y_1 = 2x^2$ $y_4 = 2x^2 + 9$
$y_2 = 2x^2 + 1$ $y_5 = 2x^2 + 16$
$y_3 = 2x^2 + 4$

SOLUTION

(A) The cross section of $f(x, y) = 2x^2 + y^2$ produced by cutting it with the plane $y = 0$ is the graph of the function $f(x, 0) = 2x^2$ in this plane. We can examine the shape of this cross section by graphing $y_1 = 2x^2$ on a graphing calculator (Fig. 8). Similarly, the graphs of $y_2 = f(x, 1) = 2x^2 + 1, y_3 = f(x, 2) = 2x^2 + 4, y_4 = f(x, 3) = 2x^2 + 9$, and $y_5 = f(x, 4) = 2x^2 + 16$ show the shapes of the other four cross sections (see Fig. 8). Each of these is a parabola that opens upward. Note the correspondence between the graphs in Figure 8 and the actual cross sections of $f(x, y) = 2x^2 + y^2$ shown in Figure 9.

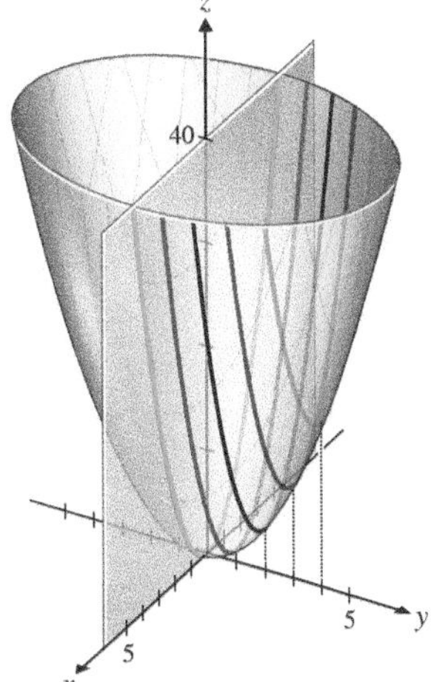

Figure 9

Figure 10

$y_1 = x^2$
$y_2 = 2 + x^2$
$y_3 = 8 + x^2$
$y_4 = 18 + x^2$
$y_5 = 32 + x^2$

(B) The five cross sections are represented by the graphs of the functions $f(0, y) = y^2$, $f(1, y) = 2 + y^2$, $f(2, y) = 8 + y^2$, $f(3, y) = 18 + y^2$, and $f(4, y) = 32 + y^2$. These five functions are graphed in Figure 10. (Note that changing the name of the independent variable from y to x for graphing purposes does not affect the graph displayed.) Each of the five cross sections is a parabola that opens upward.

Matched Problem 7

(A) Describe the cross sections of $g(x, y) = y^2 - x^2$ in the planes $y = 0$, $y = 1$, $y = 2$, $y = 3$, and $y = 4$.

(B) Describe the cross sections of $g(x, y) = y^2 - x^2$ in the planes $x = 0$, $x = 1$, $x = 2$, $x = 3$, and $x = 4$.

CONCEPTUAL INSIGHT

The graph of the *equation*

$$x^2 + y^2 + z^2 = 4 \quad (3)$$

is the graph of all ordered triplets of numbers (x, y, z) that satisfy the equation. The Pythagorean theorem can be used to show that the distance from the point (x, y, z) to the origin $(0, 0, 0)$ is equal to

$$\sqrt{x^2 + y^2 + z^2}$$

Therefore, the graph of (3) consists of all points that are at a distance 2 from the origin—that is, all points on the sphere of radius 2 and with center at the origin. Recall that a circle in the plane is *not* the graph of a function $y = f(x)$, because it fails the vertical-line test (Section 1.1). Similarly, a sphere is *not* the graph of a *function* $z = f(x, y)$ of two variables.

Exercises 9.1

Skills Warm-up Exercises

W *In Problems 1–8, find the indicated value of the function of two or three variables. (If necessary, review the basic geometric formulas at the back of the book.)*

1. The height of a trapezoid is 3 feet and the lengths of its parallel sides are 5 feet and 8 feet. Find the area.

2. The height of a trapezoid is 4 meters and the lengths of its parallel sides are 25 meters and 32 meters. Find the area.

3. The length, width, and height of a rectangular box are 12 inches, 5 inches, and 4 inches, respectively. Find the volume.

4. The length, width, and height of a rectangular box are 30 centimeters, 15 centimeters, and 10 centimeters, respectively. Find the volume.

5. The height of a right circular cylinder is 8 meters and the radius is 2 meters. Find the volume.

6. The height of a right circular cylinder is 6 feet and the diameter is also 6 feet. Find the total surface area.

7. The height of a right circular cone is 48 centimeters and the radius is 20 centimeters. Find the total surface area.

8. The height of a right circular cone is 42 inches and the radius is 7 inches. Find the volume.

A *In Problems 9–16, find the indicated values of the functions*

$$f(x, y) = 2x + 7y - 5 \quad \text{and} \quad g(x, y) = \frac{88}{x^2 + 3y}$$

9. $f(4, -1)$ **10.** $f(0, 10)$

11. $f(8, 0)$ **12.** $f(5, 6)$

13. $g(1, 7)$ **14.** $g(-2, 0)$

15. $g(3, -3)$ **16.** $g(0, 0)$

In Problems 17–20, find the indicated values of

$$f(x, y, z) = 2x - 3y^2 + 5z^3 - 1$$

17. $f(0, 0, 0)$ **18.** $f(0, 0, 2)$

19. $f(6, -5, 0)$ **20.** $f(-10, 4, -3)$

B *In Problems 21–30, find the indicated value of the given function.*

21. $P(13, 5)$ for $P(n, r) = \dfrac{n!}{(n - r)!}$

22. $C(13, 5)$ for $C(n, r) = \dfrac{n!}{r!(n - r)!}$

23. $V(4, 12)$ for $V(R, h) = \pi R^2 h$

24. $T(4, 12)$ for $T(R, h) = 2\pi R(R + h)$

25. $S(3, 10)$ for $S(R, h) = \pi R\sqrt{R^2 + h^2}$

26. $W(3, 10)$ for $W(R, h) = \frac{1}{3}\pi R^2 h$

27. $A(100, 0.06, 3)$ for $A(P, r, t) = P + Prt$

28. $A(10, 0.04, 3, 2)$ for $A(P, r, t, n) = P\left(1 + \frac{r}{n}\right)^{tn}$

29. $P(4, 2)$ for $P(r, T) = \int_1^T x^r\, dx$

30. $F(1, e)$ for $F(r, T) = \int_1^T x^{-r}\, dx$

In Problems 31–36, find the indicated function f of a single variable.

31. $f(x) = G(x, 0)$ for $G(x, y) = x^2 + 3xy + y^2 - 7$

32. $f(y) = H(0, y)$ for $H(x, y) = x^2 - 5xy - y^2 + 2$

33. $f(y) = K(4, y)$ for $K(x, y) = 10xy + 3x - 2y + 8$

34. $f(x) = L(x, -2)$ for $L(x, y) = 25 - x + 5y - 6xy$

35. $f(y) = M(y, y)$ for $M(x, y) = x^2y - 3xy^2 + 5$

36. $f(x) = N(x, 2x)$ for $N(x, y) = 3xy + x^2 - y^2 + 1$

37. Find a formula for the function $D(x, y)$ of two variables that gives the square of the distance from the point (x, y) to the origin $(0, 0)$.

38. Find a formula for the function $V(d, h)$ of two variables that gives the volume of a right circular cylinder of diameter d and height h.

39. Find a formula for the function $C(n, w)$ of two variables that gives the number of calories in n cookies, each weighing w ounces, if there are 35 calories per ounce.

40. Find a formula for the function $N(p, r)$ of two variables that gives the number of hot dogs sold at a baseball game, if p is the price per hot dog and r is the total amount received from the sale of hot dogs.

41. Find a formula for the function $S(x, y, z)$ of three variables that gives the average of three test scores x, y, and z.

42. Find a formula for the function $W(x_1, x_2, x_3, x_4)$ of four variables that gives the total volume of oil that can be carried in four oil tankers of capacities x_1, x_2, x_3, and x_4, respectively.

43. Find a formula for the function $L(d, h)$ of two variables that gives the volume of a right circular cone of diameter d and height h.

44. Find a formula for the function $T(x, y, z)$ of three variables that gives the square of the distance from the point (x, y, z) to the origin $(0, 0, 0)$.

45. Find a formula for the function $J(C, h)$ of two variables that gives the volume of a right circular cylinder of circumference C and height h.

46. Find a formula for the function $K(C, h)$ of two variables that gives the volume of a right circular cone of circumference C and height h.

47. Let $F(x, y) = 2x + 3y - 6$. Find all values of y such that $F(0, y) = 0$.

48. Let $F(x, y) = 5x - 4y + 12$. Find all values of x such that $F(x, 0) = 0$.

49. Let $F(x, y) = 2xy + 3x - 4y - 1$. Find all values of x such that $F(x, x) = 0$.

50. Let $F(x, y) = xy + 2x^2 + y^2 - 25$. Find all values of y such that $F(y, y) = 0$.

51. Let $F(x, y) = x^2 + e^x y - y^2$. Find all values of x such that $F(x, 2) = 0$.

52. Let $G(a, b, c) = a^3 + b^3 + c^3 - (ab + ac + bc) - 6$. Find all values of b such that $G(2, b, 1) = 0$.

C 53. For the function $f(x, y) = x^2 + 2y^2$, find

$$\frac{f(x + h, y) - f(x, y)}{h}$$

54. For the function $f(x, y) = x^2 + 2y^2$, find

$$\frac{f(x, y + k) - f(x, y)}{k}$$

55. For the function $f(x, y) = 2xy^2$, find

$$\frac{f(x + h, y) - f(x, y)}{h}$$

56. For the function $f(x, y) = 2xy^2$, find

$$\frac{f(x, y + k) - f(x, y)}{k}$$

57. Find the coordinates of E and F in the figure for Matched Problem 6 on page 528.

58. Find the coordinates of B and H in the figure for Matched Problem 6 on page 528.

In Problems 59–64, use a graphing calculator as necessary to explore the graphs of the indicated cross sections.

59. Let $f(x, y) = x^2$.
   (A) Explain why the cross sections of the surface $z = f(x, y)$ produced by cutting it with planes parallel to $y = 0$ are parabolas.
   (B) Describe the cross sections of the surface in the planes $x = 0$, $x = 1$, and $x = 2$.
   (C) Describe the surface $z = f(x, y)$.

60. Let $f(x, y) = \sqrt{4 - y^2}$.
   (A) Explain why the cross sections of the surface $z = f(x, y)$ produced by cutting it with planes parallel to $x = 0$ are semicircles of radius 2.
   (B) Describe the cross sections of the surface in the planes $y = 0$, $y = 2$, and $y = 3$.
   (C) Describe the surface $z = f(x, y)$.

61. Let $f(x, y) = \sqrt{36 - x^2 - y^2}$.
   (A) Describe the cross sections of the surface $z = f(x, y)$ produced by cutting it with the planes $y = 1$, $y = 2$, $y = 3$, $y = 4$, and $y = 5$.
   (B) Describe the cross sections of the surface in the planes $x = 0$, $x = 1$, $x = 2$, $x = 3$, $x = 4$, and $x = 5$.
   (C) Describe the surface $z = f(x, y)$.

62. Let $f(x, y) = 100 + 10x + 25y - x^2 - 5y^2$.
   (A) Describe the cross sections of the surface $z = f(x, y)$ produced by cutting it with the planes $y = 0$, $y = 1$, $y = 2$, and $y = 3$.
   (B) Describe the cross sections of the surface in the planes $x = 0$, $x = 1$, $x = 2$, and $x = 3$.
   (C) Describe the surface $z = f(x, y)$.

63. Let $f(x, y) = e^{-(x^2+y^2)}$.
   (A) Explain why $f(a, b) = f(c, d)$ whenever (a, b) and (c, d) are points on the same circle centered at the origin in the xy plane.
   (B) Describe the cross sections of the surface $z = f(x, y)$ produced by cutting it with the planes $x = 0$, $y = 0$, and $x = y$.
   (C) Describe the surface $z = f(x, y)$.

64. Let $f(x, y) = 4 - \sqrt{x^2 + y^2}$.
   (A) Explain why $f(a, b) = f(c, d)$ whenever (a, b) and (c, d) are points on the same circle with center at the origin in the xy plane.
   (B) Describe the cross sections of the surface $z = f(x, y)$ produced by cutting it with the planes $x = 0$, $y = 0$, and $x = y$.
   (C) Describe the surface $z = f(x, y)$.

Applications

65. **Cost function.** A small manufacturing company produces two models of a surfboard: a standard model and a competition model. If the standard model is produced at a variable cost of \$210 each and the competition model at a variable cost of \$300 each, and if the total fixed costs per month are \$6,000, then the monthly cost function is given by

$$C(x, y) = 6{,}000 + 210x + 300y$$

where x and y are the numbers of standard and competition models produced per month, respectively. Find $C(20, 10)$, $C(50, 5)$, and $C(30, 30)$.

66. **Advertising and sales.** A company spends \$$x$ thousand per week on online advertising and \$$y$ thousand per week on TV advertising. Its weekly sales are found to be given by

$$S(x, y) = 5x^2y^3$$

Find $S(3, 2)$ and $S(2, 3)$.

67. **Revenue function.** A supermarket sells two brands of coffee: brand A at \$$p$ per pound and brand B at \$$q$ per pound. The daily demand equations for brands A and B are, respectively,

$$x = 200 - 5p + 4q$$
$$y = 300 + 2p - 4q$$

(both in pounds). Find the daily revenue function $R(p, q)$. Evaluate $R(2, 3)$ and $R(3, 2)$.

68. **Revenue, cost, and profit functions.** A company manufactures 10- and 3-speed bicycles. The weekly demand and cost equations are

$$p = 230 - 9x + y$$
$$q = 130 + x - 4y$$
$$C(x, y) = 200 + 80x + 30y$$

where \$$p$ is the price of a 10-speed bicycle, \$$q$ is the price of a 3-speed bicycle, x is the weekly demand for 10-speed bicycles, y is the weekly demand for 3-speed bicycles, and $C(x, y)$ is the cost function. Find the weekly revenue function $R(x, y)$ and the weekly profit function $P(x, y)$. Evaluate $R(10, 15)$ and $P(10, 15)$.

69. **Productivity.** The Cobb–Douglas production function for a petroleum company is given by

$$f(x, y) = 20x^{0.4}y^{0.6}$$

where x is the utilization of labor and y is the utilization of capital. If the company uses 1,250 units of labor and 1,700 units of capital, how many units of petroleum will be produced?

70. **Productivity.** The petroleum company in Problem 69 is taken over by another company that decides to double both the units of labor and the units of capital utilized in the production of petroleum. Use the Cobb–Douglas production function given in Problem 69 to find the amount of petroleum that will be produced by this increased utilization of labor and capital. What is the effect on productivity of doubling both the units of labor and the units of capital?

71. **Future value.** At the end of each year, \$5,000 is invested into an IRA earning 3% compounded annually.
   (A) How much will be in the account at the end of 30 years? Use the annuity formula

$$F(P, i, n) = P\frac{(1 + i)^n - 1}{i}$$

where

P = periodic payment
i = rate per period
n = number of payments (periods)
F = FV = future value

   (B) Use graphical approximation methods to determine the rate of interest that would produce \$300,000 in the account at the end of 30 years.

72. **Package design.** The packaging department in a company has been asked to design a rectangular box with no top and a partition down the middle (see the figure). Let x, y, and z be the dimensions of the box (in inches). Ignore the thickness of the material from which the box will be made.

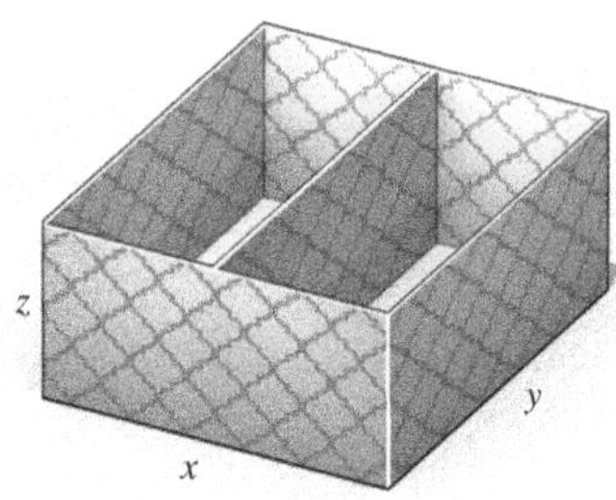

(A) Explain why $M(x, y, z) = xy + 2xz + 3yz$ gives the total area of the material used in constructing one of the boxes.

(B) Evaluate $M(10, 12, 6)$.

(C) Suppose that the box will have a square base and a volume of 720 cubic inches. Use graphical approximation methods to determine the dimensions that require the least material.

73. Marine biology. For a diver using scuba-diving gear, a marine biologist estimates the time (duration) of a dive according to the equation

$$T(V, x) = \frac{33V}{x + 33}$$

where

T = time of dive in minutes
V = volume of air, at sea level pressure, compressed into tanks
x = depth of dive in feet

Find $T(70, 47)$ and $T(60, 27)$.

74. Blood flow. Poiseuille's law states that the resistance R for blood flowing in a blood vessel varies directly as the length L of the vessel and inversely as the fourth power of its radius r. Stated as an equation,

$$R(L, r) = k\frac{L}{r^4} \qquad k \text{ a constant}$$

Find $R(8, 1)$ and $R(4, 0.2)$.

75. Physical anthropology. Anthropologists use an index called the *cephalic index*. The cephalic index C varies directly as the width W of the head and inversely as the length L of the head (both viewed from the top). In terms of an equation,

$$C(W, L) = 100\frac{W}{L}$$

where

W = width in inches
L = length in inches

Find $C(6, 8)$ and $C(8.1, 9)$.

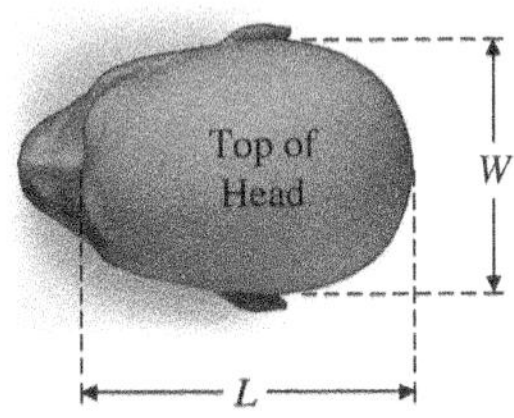

76. Safety research. Under ideal conditions, if a person driving a car slams on the brakes and skids to a stop, the length of the skid marks (in feet) is given by the formula

$$L(w, v) = kwv^2$$

where

k = constant
w = weight of car in pounds
v = speed of car in miles per hour

For $k = 0.000\,013\,3$, find $L(2{,}000, 40)$ and $L(3{,}000, 60)$.

77. Psychology. The intelligence quotient (IQ) is defined to be the ratio of mental age (MA), as determined by certain tests, to chronological age (CA), multiplied by 100. Stated as an equation,

$$Q(M, C) = \frac{M}{C} \cdot 100$$

where

Q = IQ $\quad M$ = MA $\quad C$ = CA

Find $Q(12, 10)$ and $Q(10, 12)$.

78. Space travel. The force F of attraction between two masses m_1 and m_2 at distance r is given by Newton's law of universal gravitation

$$F(m_1, m_2, r) = G\frac{m_1 m_2}{r^2}$$

where G is a constant. Evaluate $F(50, 100, 20)$ and $F(50, 100, 40)$.

Answers to Matched Problems

1. \$3,100
2. 30
3. (A) $R(x, y) = 220x + 300y - 6x^2 + 4xy - 10y^2$; $R(20, 10) = \$4{,}800$
   (B) $P(x, y) = 180x + 220y - 6x^2 + 4xy - 10y^2 - 1{,}000$; $P(20, 10) = \$2{,}200$
4. $V(x, y) = x^2y$; $V(5, 10) = 250$ in.^{3}
5. 17,411 units
6. $A\ (0, 0, 0)$; $C\ (2, 4, 0)$; $G\ (2, 4, 3)$; $D\ (0, 4, 0)$
7. (A) Each cross section is a parabola that opens downward.
   (B) Each cross section is a parabola that opens upward.

9.2 Partial Derivatives

- Partial Derivatives
- Second-Order Partial Derivatives

Partial Derivatives

We know how to differentiate many kinds of functions of one independent variable and how to interpret the derivatives that result. What about functions with two or more independent variables? Let's return to the surfboard example considered at the beginning of Section 9.1 on page 524.

For the company producing only the standard board, the cost function was

$$C(x) = 500 + 70x$$

Differentiating with respect to x, we obtain the marginal cost function

$$C'(x) = 70$$

Since the marginal cost is constant, \$70 is the change in cost for a 1-unit increase in production at any output level.

For the company producing two types of boards—a standard model and a competition model—the cost function was

$$C(x, y) = 700 + 70x + 100y$$

Now suppose that we differentiate with respect to x, holding y fixed, and denote the resulting function by $C_x(x, y)$, or suppose we differentiate with respect to y, holding x fixed, and denote the resulting function by $C_y(x, y)$. Differentiating in this way, we obtain

$$C_x(x, y) = 70 \qquad C_y(x, y) = 100$$

Each of these functions is called a **partial derivative**, and, in this example, each represents marginal cost. The first is the change in cost due to a 1-unit increase in production of the standard board with the production of the competition model held fixed. The second is the change in cost due to a 1-unit increase in production of the competition board with the production of the standard board held fixed.

In general, if $z = f(x, y)$, then the **partial derivative of f with respect to x**, denoted $\partial z/\partial x$, f_x, or $f_x(x, y)$, is defined by

$$\frac{\partial z}{\partial x} = \lim_{h \to 0} \frac{f(x + h, y) - f(x, y)}{h}$$

provided that the limit exists. We recognize this formula as the ordinary derivative of f with respect to x, holding y constant. We can continue to use all the derivative rules and properties discussed in Chapters 6 to 8 and apply them to partial derivatives.

Similarly, the **partial derivative of f with respect to y**, denoted $\partial z/\partial y$, f_y, or $f_y(x, y)$, is defined by

$$\frac{\partial z}{\partial y} = \lim_{k \to 0} \frac{f(x, y + k) - f(x, y)}{k}$$

which is the ordinary derivative with respect to y, holding x constant.

Parallel definitions and interpretations hold for functions with three or more independent variables.

Reminder

If $y = f(x)$ is a function of a single variable x, then

$$f'(x) = \lim_{h \to 0} \frac{f(x + h) - f(x)}{h}$$

if the limit exists.

EXAMPLE 1 **Partial Derivatives** For $z = f(x, y) = 2x^2 - 3x^2y + 5y + 1$, find

(A) $\partial z/\partial x$ (B) $f_x(2, 3)$

SOLUTION

(A) $z = 2x^2 - 3x^2y + 5y + 1$

Differentiating with respect to x, holding y constant (that is, treating y as a constant), we obtain

$$\frac{\partial z}{\partial x} = 4x - 6xy$$

(B) $f(x, y) = 2x^2 - 3x^2y + 5y + 1$

First, differentiate with respect to x. From part (A), we have

$$f_x(x, y) = 4x - 6xy$$

Then evaluate this equation at $(2, 3)$:

$$f_x(2, 3) = 4(2) - 6(2)(3) = -28$$

In Example 1B, an alternative approach would be to substitute $y = 3$ into $f(x, y)$ and graph the function $f(x, 3) = -7x^2 + 16$, which represents the cross section of the surface $z = f(x, y)$ produced by cutting it with the plane $y = 3$. Then determine the slope of the tangent line when $x = 2$. Again, we conclude that $f_x(2, 3) = -28$ (see Fig. 1).

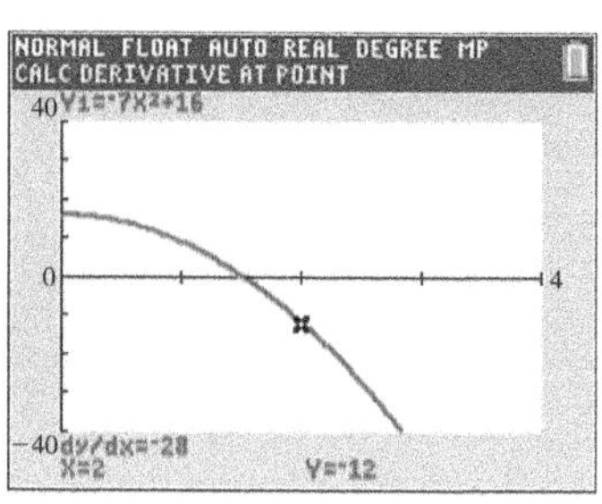

Figure 1 $y_1 = -7x^2 + 16$

Matched Problem 1 For f in Example 1, find

(A) $\partial z/\partial y$ (B) $f_y(2, 3)$

EXAMPLE 2 **Partial Derivatives Using the Chain Rule** For $z = f(x, y) = e^{x^2+y^2}$, find

(A) $\partial z/\partial x$ (B) $f_y(2, 1)$

SOLUTION

(A) Using the chain rule [thinking of $z = e^u$, $u = u(x)$; y is held constant], we obtain

$$\frac{\partial z}{\partial x} = e^{x^2+y^2}\frac{\partial(x^2 + y^2)}{\partial x}$$
$$= 2xe^{x^2+y^2}$$

(B) $$f_y(x, y) = e^{x^2+y^2}\frac{\partial(x^2 + y^2)}{\partial y} = 2ye^{x^2+y^2}$$
$$f_y(2, 1) = 2(1)e^{(2)^2+(1)^2}$$
$$= 2e^5$$

Matched Problem 2 For $z = f(x, y) = (x^2 + 2xy)^5$, find

(A) $\partial z/\partial y$ (B) $f_x(1, 0)$

EXAMPLE 3 **Profit** The profit function for the surfboard company in Example 3 of Section 9.1 was

$$P(x, y) = 140x + 200y - 4x^2 + 2xy - 12y^2 - 700$$

Find $P_x(15, 10)$ and $P_x(30, 10)$, and interpret the results.

SOLUTION

$$P_x(x, y) = 140 - 8x + 2y$$
$$P_x(15, 10) = 140 - 8(15) + 2(10) = 40$$
$$P_x(30, 10) = 140 - 8(30) + 2(10) = -80$$

At a production level of 15 standard and 10 competition boards per week, increasing the production of standard boards by 1 unit and holding the production of competition boards fixed at 10 will increase profit by approximately \$40. At a production level of 30 standard and 10 competition boards per week, increasing the production of standard boards by 1 unit and holding the production of competition boards fixed at 10 will decrease profit by approximately \$80.

Matched Problem 3 For the profit function in Example 3, find $P_y(25, 10)$ and $P_y(25, 15)$, and interpret the results.

EXAMPLE 4 **Productivity** The productivity of a major computer manufacturer is given approximately by the Cobb–Douglas production function

$$f(x, y) = 15x^{0.4}y^{0.6}$$

with the utilization of x units of labor and y units of capital. The partial derivative $f_x(x, y)$ represents the rate of change of productivity with respect to labor and is called the **marginal productivity of labor**. The partial derivative $f_y(x, y)$ represents the rate of change of productivity with respect to capital and is called the **marginal productivity of capital**. If the company is currently utilizing 4,000 units of labor and 2,500 units of capital, find the marginal productivity of labor and the marginal productivity of capital. For the greatest increase in productivity, should the management of the company encourage increased use of labor or increased use of capital?

SOLUTION

$$\begin{aligned} f_x(x, y) &= 6x^{-0.6}y^{0.6} \\ f_x(4{,}000, 2{,}500) &= 6(4{,}000)^{-0.6}(2{,}500)^{0.6} \\ &\approx 4.53 \quad \text{Marginal productivity of labor} \\ f_y(x, y) &= 9x^{0.4}y^{-0.4} \\ f_y(4{,}000, 2{,}500) &= 9(4{,}000)^{0.4}(2{,}500)^{-0.4} \\ &\approx 10.86 \quad \text{Marginal productivity of capital} \end{aligned}$$

At the current level of utilization of 4,000 units of labor and 2,500 units of capital, each 1-unit increase in labor utilization (keeping capital utilization fixed at 2,500 units) will increase production by approximately 4.53 units, and each 1-unit increase in capital utilization (keeping labor utilization fixed at 4,000 units) will increase production by approximately 10.86 units. The management of the company should encourage increased use of capital.

Matched Problem 4 The productivity of an airplane-manufacturing company is given approximately by the Cobb–Douglas production function

$$f(x, y) = 40x^{0.3}y^{0.7}$$

(A) Find $f_x(x, y)$ and $f_y(x, y)$.

(B) If the company is currently using 1,500 units of labor and 4,500 units of capital, find the marginal productivity of labor and the marginal productivity of capital.

(C) For the greatest increase in productivity, should the management of the company encourage increased use of labor or increased use of capital?

Partial derivatives have simple geometric interpretations, as shown in Figure 2. If we hold x fixed at $x = a$, then $f_y(a, y)$ is the slope of the curve obtained by intersecting the surface $z = f(x, y)$ with the plane $x = a$. A similar interpretation is given to $f_x(x, b)$.

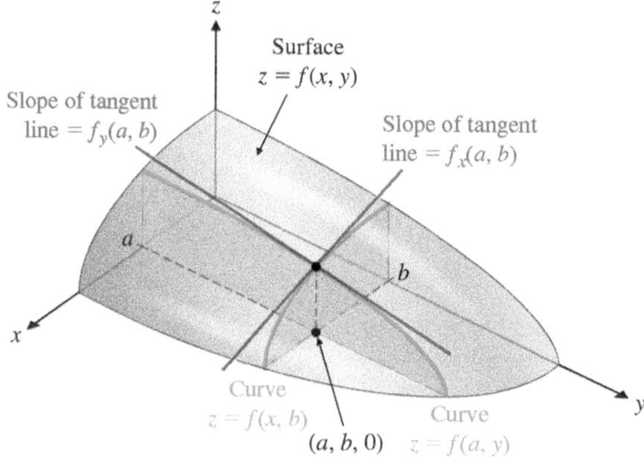

Figure 2

Second-Order Partial Derivatives

The function

$$z = f(x, y) = x^4y^7$$

has two **first-order partial derivatives**:

$$\frac{\partial z}{\partial x} = f_x = f_x(x, y) = 4x^3y^7 \quad \text{and} \quad \frac{\partial z}{\partial y} = f_y = f_y(x, y) = 7x^4y^6$$

Each of these partial derivatives, in turn, has two partial derivatives called **second-order partial derivatives** of $z = f(x, y)$. Generalizing the various notations we have for first-order partial derivatives, we write the four second-order partial derivatives of $z = f(x, y) = x^4y^7$ as

Equivalent notations

$$f_{xx} = f_{xx}(x, y) = \frac{\partial^2 z}{\partial x^2} = \frac{\partial}{\partial x}\left(\frac{\partial z}{\partial x}\right) = \frac{\partial}{\partial x}(4x^3y^7) = 12x^2y^7$$

$$f_{xy} = f_{xy}(x, y) = \frac{\partial^2 z}{\partial y\,\partial x} = \frac{\partial}{\partial y}\left(\frac{\partial z}{\partial x}\right) = \frac{\partial}{\partial y}(4x^3y^7) = 28x^3y^6$$

$$f_{yx} = f_{yx}(x, y) = \frac{\partial^2 z}{\partial x\,\partial y} = \frac{\partial}{\partial x}\left(\frac{\partial z}{\partial y}\right) = \frac{\partial}{\partial x}(7x^4y^6) = 28x^3y^6$$

$$f_{yy} = f_{yy}(x, y) = \frac{\partial^2 z}{\partial y^2} = \frac{\partial}{\partial y}\left(\frac{\partial z}{\partial y}\right) = \frac{\partial}{\partial y}(7x^4y^6) = 42x^4y^5$$

In the mixed partial derivative $\partial^2 z/\partial y\,\partial x = f_{xy}$, we started with $z = f(x, y)$ and first differentiated with respect to x (holding y constant). Then we differentiated with respect to y (holding x constant). In the other mixed partial derivative, $\partial^2 z/\partial x\,\partial y = f_{yx}$, the order of differentiation was reversed; however, the final result was the same—that is, $f_{xy} = f_{yx}$. Although it is possible to find functions for which $f_{xy} \neq f_{yx}$, such functions rarely occur in applications involving partial derivatives. For all the functions in this book, we will assume that $f_{xy} = f_{yx}$.

In general, we have the following definitions:

DEFINITION Second-Order Partial Derivatives

If $z = f(x, y)$, then

$$f_{xx} = f_{xx}(x, y) = \frac{\partial^2 z}{\partial x^2} = \frac{\partial}{\partial x}\left(\frac{\partial z}{\partial x}\right)$$

$$f_{xy} = f_{xy}(x, y) = \frac{\partial^2 z}{\partial y\,\partial x} = \frac{\partial}{\partial y}\left(\frac{\partial z}{\partial x}\right)$$

$$f_{yx} = f_{yx}(x, y) = \frac{\partial^2 z}{\partial x\,\partial y} = \frac{\partial}{\partial x}\left(\frac{\partial z}{\partial y}\right)$$

$$f_{yy} = f_{yy}(x, y) = \frac{\partial^2 z}{\partial y^2} = \frac{\partial}{\partial y}\left(\frac{\partial z}{\partial y}\right)$$

EXAMPLE 5 **Second-Order Partial Derivatives** For $z = f(x, y) = 3x^2 - 2xy^3 + 1$, find

(A) $\dfrac{\partial^2 z}{\partial x\,\partial y}, \dfrac{\partial^2 z}{\partial y\,\partial x}$ (B) $\dfrac{\partial^2 z}{\partial x^2}$ (C) $f_{yx}(2, 1)$

SOLUTION

(A) First differentiate with respect to y and then with respect to x:

$$\frac{\partial z}{\partial y} = -6xy^2 \qquad \frac{\partial^2 z}{\partial x\, \partial y} = \frac{\partial}{\partial x}\left(\frac{\partial z}{\partial y}\right) = \frac{\partial}{\partial x}(-6xy^2) = -6y^2$$

Now differentiate with respect to x and then with respect to y:

$$\frac{\partial z}{\partial x} = 6x - 2y^3 \qquad \frac{\partial^2 z}{\partial y\, \partial x} = \frac{\partial}{\partial y}\left(\frac{\partial z}{\partial x}\right) = \frac{\partial}{\partial y}(6x - 2y^3) = -6y^2$$

(B) Differentiate with respect to x twice:

$$\frac{\partial z}{\partial x} = 6x - 2y^3 \qquad \frac{\partial^2 z}{\partial x^2} = \frac{\partial}{\partial x}\left(\frac{\partial z}{\partial x}\right) = 6$$

(C) First find $f_{yx}(x, y)$; then evaluate the resulting equation at (2, 1). Again, remember that f_{yx} signifies differentiation first with respect to y and then with respect to x.

$$f_y(x, y) = -6xy^2 \qquad f_{yx}(x, y) = -6y^2$$

and

$$f_{yx}(2, 1) = -6(1)^2 = -6$$

Matched Problem 5 For $z = f(x, y) = x^3y - 2y^4 + 3$, find

(A) $\dfrac{\partial^2 z}{\partial y\, \partial x}$ (B) $\dfrac{\partial^2 z}{\partial y^2}$

(C) $f_{xy}(2, 3)$ (D) $f_{yx}(2, 3)$

CONCEPTUAL INSIGHT

Although the mixed second-order partial derivatives f_{xy} and f_{yx} are equal for all functions considered in this book, it is a good idea to compute both of them, as in Example 5A, as a check on your work. By contrast, the other two second-order partial derivatives, f_{xx} and f_{yy}, are generally not equal to each other. For example, for the function

$$f(x, y) = 3x^2 - 2xy^3 + 1$$

of Example 5,

$$f_{xx} = 6 \qquad \text{and} \qquad f_{yy} = -12xy$$

Exercises 9.2

Skills Warm-up Exercises

W *In Problems 1–16, find the indicated derivative. (If necessary, review Sections 7.3 and 7.4).*

1. $f'(x)$ if $f(x) = 6x - 7\pi + 2$

2. $f'(x)$ if $f(x) = 4\pi - 9x + 10$

3. $f'(x)$ if $f(x) = 2e^2 - 5ex + 7x^2$

4. $f'(x)$ if $f(x) = 3x^2 + 4ex + e^2$

5. $f'(x)$ if $f(x) = x^3 - 8\pi^2x + \pi^3$

6. $f'(x)$ if $f(x) = 2\pi^3 + \pi x^2 - 3x^4$

7. $f'(x)$ if $f(x) = (e^2 + 5x^2)^7$

8. $f'(x)$ if $f(x) = (4x - 3e)^5$

9. $\dfrac{dz}{dx}$ if $z = e^x - 3ex + x^e$

10. $\dfrac{dz}{dx}$ if $z = x \ln \pi - \pi \ln x$

11. $\dfrac{dz}{dx}$ if $z = \ln(x^2 + \pi^2)$

12. $\dfrac{dz}{dx}$ if $z = e^{\pi x^2}$

13. $\dfrac{dz}{dx}$ if $z = (x + e)\ln x$

14. $\dfrac{dz}{dx}$ if $z = exe^x$

15. $\frac{dz}{dx}$ if $z = \frac{5x}{x^2 + \pi^2}$

16. $\frac{dz}{dx}$ if $z = \frac{\pi x}{1 + x}$

A *In Problems 17–24, find the indicated first-order partial derivative for each function $z = f(x, y)$.*

17. $f_x(x, y)$ if $f(x, y) = 4x - 3y + 6$

18. $f_x(x, y)$ if $f(x, y) = 7x + 8y - 2$

19. $f_y(x, y)$ if $f(x, y) = x^2 - 3xy + 2y^2$

20. $f_y(x, y)$ if $f(x, y) = 3x^2 + 2xy - 7y^2$

21. $\frac{\partial z}{\partial x}$ if $z = x^3 + 4x^2y + 2y^3$

22. $\frac{\partial z}{\partial y}$ if $z = 4x^2y - 5xy^2$

23. $\frac{\partial z}{\partial y}$ if $z = (5x + 2y)^{10}$

24. $\frac{\partial z}{\partial x}$ if $z = (2x - 3y)^8$

In Problems 25–32, find the indicated value.

25. $f_x(1, 3)$ if $f(x, y) = 5x^3y - 4xy^2$

26. $f_x(4, 1)$ if $f(x, y) = x^2y^2 - 5xy^3$

27. $f_y(1, 0)$ if $f(x, y) = 3xe^y$

28. $f_y(2, 4)$ if $f(x, y) = x^4 \ln y$

29. $f_y(2, 1)$ if $f(x, y) = e^{x^2} - 4y$

30. $f_y(3, 3)$ if $f(x, y) = e^{3x} - y^2$

31. $f_x(1, -1)$ if $f(x, y) = \frac{2xy}{1 + x^2y^2}$

32. $f_x(-1, 2)$ if $f(x, y) = \frac{x^2 - y^2}{1 + x^2}$

In Problems 33–38, $M(x, y) = 68 + 0.3x - 0.8y$ gives the mileage (in mpg) of a new car as a function of tire pressure x (in psi) and speed (in mph). Find the indicated quantity (include the appropriate units) and explain what it means.

33. $M(32, 40)$
34. $M(22, 40)$
35. $M(32, 50)$
36. $M(22, 50)$
37. $M_x(32, 50)$
38. $M_y(32, 50)$

B *In Problems 39–50, find the indicated second-order partial derivative for each function $f(x, y)$.*

39. $f_{xx}(x, y)$ if $f(x, y) = 6x - 5y + 3$

40. $f_{yx}(x, y)$ if $f(x, y) = -2x + y + 8$

41. $f_{xy}(x, y)$ if $f(x, y) = 4x^2 + 6y^2 - 10$

42. $f_{yy}(x, y)$ if $f(x, y) = x^2 + 9y^2 - 4$

43. $f_{xy}(x, y)$ if $f(x, y) = e^{xy^2}$

44. $f_{yx}(x, y)$ if $f(x, y) = e^{3x+2y}$

45. $f_{yy}(x, y)$ if $f(x, y) = \frac{\ln x}{y}$

46. $f_{xx}(x, y)$ if $f(x, y) = \frac{3 \ln x}{y^2}$

47. $f_{xx}(x, y)$ if $f(x, y) = (2x + y)^5$

48. $f_{yx}(x, y)$ if $f(x, y) = (3x - 8y)^6$

49. $f_{xy}(x, y)$ if $f(x, y) = (x^2 + y^4)^{10}$

50. $f_{yy}(x, y)$ if $f(x, y) = (1 + 2xy^2)^8$

In Problems 51–60, find the indicated function or value if $C(x, y) = 3x^2 + 10xy - 8y^2 + 4x - 15y - 120$.

51. $C_x(x, y)$
52. $C_y(x, y)$
53. $C_x(3, -2)$
54. $C_y(3, -2)$
55. $C_{xx}(x, y)$
56. $C_{yy}(x, y)$
57. $C_{xy}(x, y)$
58. $C_{yx}(x, y)$
59. $C_{xx}(3, -2)$
60. $C_{yy}(3, -2)$

In Problems 61–66, $S(T, r) = 50(T - 40)(5 - r)$ gives an ice cream shop's daily sales as a function of temperature T (in °F) and rain r (in inches). Find the indicated quantity (include the appropriate units) and explain what it means.

61. $S(60, 2)$
62. $S(80, 0)$
63. $S_r(90, 1)$
64. $S_T(90, 1)$
65. $S_{Tr}(90, 1)$
66. $S_{rT}(90, 1)$

67. (A) Let $f(x, y) = y^3 + 4y^2 - 5y + 3$. Show that $\partial f/\partial x = 0$.
    (B) Explain why there are an infinite number of functions $g(x, y)$ such that $\partial g/\partial x = 0$.

68. (A) Find an example of a function $f(x, y)$ such that $\partial f/\partial x = 3$ and $\partial f/\partial y = 2$.
    (B) How many such functions are there? Explain.

In Problems 69–74, find $f_{xx}(x, y)$, $f_{xy}(x, y)$, $f_{yx}(x, y)$, and $f_{yy}(x, y)$ for each function f.

69. $f(x, y) = x^2y^2 + x^3 + y$

70. $f(x, y) = x^3y^3 + x + y^2$

71. $f(x, y) = \frac{x}{y} - \frac{y}{x}$
72. $f(x, y) = \frac{x^2}{y} - \frac{y^2}{x}$

73. $f(x, y) = xe^{xy}$
74. $f(x, y) = x \ln(xy)$

C 75. For

$$P(x, y) = -x^2 + 2xy - 2y^2 - 4x + 12y - 5$$

find all values of x and y such that

$$P_x(x, y) = 0 \quad \text{and} \quad P_y(x, y) = 0$$

simultaneously.

76. For

$$C(x, y) = 2x^2 + 2xy + 3y^2 - 16x - 18y + 54$$

find all values of x and y such that

$$C_x(x, y) = 0 \quad \text{and} \quad C_y(x, y) = 0$$

simultaneously.

77. For

$$F(x, y) = x^3 - 2x^2y^2 - 2x - 4y + 10$$

find all values of x and y such that

$$F_x(x, y) = 0 \quad \text{and} \quad F_y(x, y) = 0$$

simultaneously.

78. For

$$G(x, y) = x^2 \ln y - 3x - 2y + 1$$

find all values of x and y such that

$$G_x(x, y) = 0 \quad \text{and} \quad G_y(x, y) = 0$$

simultaneously.

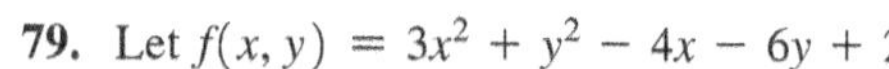

79. Let $f(x, y) = 3x^2 + y^2 - 4x - 6y + 2$.

(A) Find the minimum value of $f(x, y)$ when $y = 1$.

(B) Explain why the answer to part (A) is not the minimum value of the function $f(x, y)$.

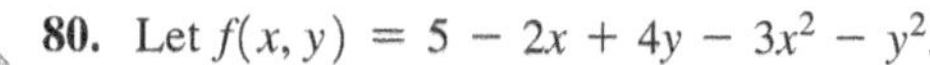

80. Let $f(x, y) = 5 - 2x + 4y - 3x^2 - y^2$.

(A) Find the maximum value of $f(x, y)$ when $x = 2$.

(B) Explain why the answer to part (A) is not the maximum value of the function $f(x, y)$.

81. Let $f(x, y) = 4 - x^4y + 3xy^2 + y^5$.

(A) Use graphical approximation methods to find c (to three decimal places) such that $f(c, 2)$ is the maximum value of $f(x, y)$ when $y = 2$.

(B) Find $f_x(c, 2)$ and $f_y(c, 2)$.

82. Let $f(x, y) = e^x + 2e^y + 3xy^2 + 1$.

(A) Use graphical approximation methods to find d (to three decimal places) such that $f(1, d)$ is the minimum value of $f(x, y)$ when $x = 1$.

(B) Find $f_x(1, d)$ and $f_y(1, d)$.

83. For $f(x, y) = x^2 + 2y^2$, find

(A) $\lim_{h \to 0} \frac{f(x + h, y) - f(x, y)}{h}$

(B) $\lim_{k \to 0} \frac{f(x, y + k) - f(x, y)}{k}$

84. For $f(x, y) = 2xy^2$, find

(A) $\lim_{h \to 0} \frac{f(x + h, y) - f(x, y)}{h}$

(B) $\lim_{k \to 0} \frac{f(x, y + k) - f(x, y)}{k}$

Applications

85. Profit function. A firm produces two types of calculators each week, x of type A and y of type B. The weekly revenue and cost functions (in dollars) are

$$R(x, y) = 80x + 90y + 0.04xy - 0.05x^2 - 0.05y^2$$

$$C(x, y) = 8x + 6y + 20{,}000$$

Find $P_x(1{,}200, 1{,}800)$ and $P_y(1{,}200, 1{,}800)$, and interpret the results.

86. Advertising and sales. A company spends \$$x$ per week on online advertising and \$$y$ per week on TV advertising. Its weekly sales were found to be given by

$$S(x, y) = 10x^{0.4}y^{0.8}$$

Find $S_x(3{,}000, 2{,}000)$ and $S_y(3{,}000, 2{,}000)$, and interpret the results.

87. Demand equations. A supermarket sells two brands of coffee: brand A at \$$p$ per pound and brand B at \$$q$ per pound. The daily demands x and y (in pounds) for brands A and B, respectively, are given by

$$x = 200 - 5p + 4q$$

$$y = 300 + 2p - 4q$$

Find $\partial x/\partial p$ and $\partial y/\partial p$, and interpret the results.

88. Revenue and profit functions. A company manufactures 10- and 3-speed bicycles. The weekly demand and cost functions are

$$p = 230 - 9x + y$$

$$q = 130 + x - 4y$$

$$C(x, y) = 200 + 80x + 30y$$

where \$$p$ is the price of a 10-speed bicycle, \$$q$ is the price of a 3-speed bicycle, x is the weekly demand for 10-speed bicycles, y is the weekly demand for 3-speed bicycles, and $C(x, y)$ is the cost function. Find $R_x(10, 5)$ and $P_x(10, 5)$, and interpret the results.

89. Productivity. The productivity of a certain third-world country is given approximately by the function

$$f(x, y) = 10x^{0.75}y^{0.25}$$

with the utilization of x units of labor and y units of capital.

(A) Find $f_x(x, y)$ and $f_y(x, y)$.

(B) If the country is now using 600 units of labor and 100 units of capital, find the marginal productivity of labor and the marginal productivity of capital.

(C) For the greatest increase in the country's productivity, should the government encourage increased use of labor or increased use of capital?

90. Productivity. The productivity of an automobile-manufacturing company is given approximately by the function

$$f(x, y) = 50\sqrt{xy} = 50x^{0.5}y^{0.5}$$

with the utilization of x units of labor and y units of capital.

(A) Find $f_x(x, y)$ and $f_y(x, y)$.

(B) If the company is now using 250 units of labor and 125 units of capital, find the marginal productivity of labor and the marginal productivity of capital.

(C) For the greatest increase in the company's productivity, should the management encourage increased use of labor or increased use of capital?

Problems 91–94 refer to the following: If a decrease in demand for one product results in an increase in demand for another product, the two products are said to be **competitive**, *or* **substitute**,

products. *(Real whipping cream and imitation whipping cream are examples of competitive, or substitute, products.) If a decrease in demand for one product results in a decrease in demand for another product, the two products are said to be* **complementary products**. *(Fishing boats and outboard motors are examples of complementary products.) Partial derivatives can be used to test whether two products are competitive, complementary, or neither. We start with demand functions for two products such that the demand for either depends on the prices for both:*

$$x = f(p, q) \quad \text{Demand function for product } A$$

$$y = g(p, q) \quad \text{Demand function for product } B$$

The variables x and y represent the number of units demanded of products A and B, respectively, at a price p for 1 unit of product A and a price q for 1 unit of product B. Normally, if the price of A increases while the price of B is held constant, then the demand for A will decrease; that is, $f_p(p, q) < 0$. *Then, if A and B are competitive products, the demand for B will increase; that is,* $g_p(p, q) > 0$. *Similarly, if the price of B increases while the price of A is held constant, the demand for B will decrease; that is,* $g_q(p, q) < 0$. *Then, if A and B are competitive products, the demand for A will increase; that is,* $f_q(p, q) > 0$. *Reasoning similarly for complementary products, we arrive at the following test:*

Test for Competitive and Complementary Products

Partial Derivatives	Products A and B
$f_q(p, q) > 0$ and $g_p(p, q) > 0$	Competitive (substitute)
$f_q(p, q) < 0$ and $g_p(p, q) < 0$	Complementary
$f_q(p, q) \geq 0$ and $g_p(p, q) \leq 0$	Neither
$f_q(p, q) \leq 0$ and $g_p(p, q) \geq 0$	Neither

Use this test in Problems 91–94 to determine whether the indicated products are competitive, complementary, or neither.

91. Product demand. The weekly demand equations for the sale of butter and margarine in a supermarket are

$$x = f(p, q) = 8{,}000 - 0.09p^2 + 0.08q^2 \quad \text{Butter}$$

$$y = g(p, q) = 15{,}000 + 0.04p^2 - 0.3q^2 \quad \text{Margarine}$$

92. Product demand. The daily demand equations for the sale of brand *A* coffee and brand *B* coffee in a supermarket are

$$x = f(p, q) = 200 - 5p + 4q \quad \text{Brand } A \text{ coffee}$$

$$y = g(p, q) = 300 + 2p - 4q \quad \text{Brand } B \text{ coffee}$$

93. Product demand. The monthly demand equations for the sale of skis and ski boots in a sporting goods store are

$$x = f(p, q) = 800 - 0.004p^2 - 0.003q^2 \quad \text{Skis}$$

$$y = g(p, q) = 600 - 0.003p^2 - 0.002q^2 \quad \text{Ski boots}$$

94. Product demand. The monthly demand equations for the sale of tennis rackets and tennis balls in a sporting goods store are

$$x = f(p, q) = 500 - 0.5p - q^2 \quad \text{Tennis rackets}$$

$$y = g(p, q) = 10{,}000 - 8p - 100q^2 \quad \text{Tennis balls (cans)}$$

95. Medicine. The following empirical formula relates the surface area *A* (in square inches) of an average human body to its weight *w* (in pounds) and its height *h* (in inches):

$$A = f(w, h) = 15.64w^{0.425}h^{0.725}$$

(A) Find $f_w(w, h)$ and $f_h(w, h)$.

(B) For a 65-pound child who is 57 inches tall, find $f_w(65, 57)$ and $f_h(65, 57)$, and interpret the results.

96. Blood flow. Poiseuille's law states that the resistance *R* for blood flowing in a blood vessel varies directly as the length *L* of the vessel and inversely as the fourth power of its radius *r*. Stated as an equation,

$$R(L, r) = k\frac{L}{r^4} \quad k \text{ a constant}$$

Find $R_L(4, 0.2)$ and $R_r(4, 0.2)$, and interpret the results.

97. Physical anthropology. Anthropologists use the cephalic index *C*, which varies directly as the width *W* of the head and inversely as the length *L* of the head (both viewed from the top). In terms of an equation,

$$C(W, L) = 100\frac{W}{L}$$

where

W = width in inches

L = length in inches

Find $C_W(6, 8)$ and $C_L(6, 8)$, and interpret the results.

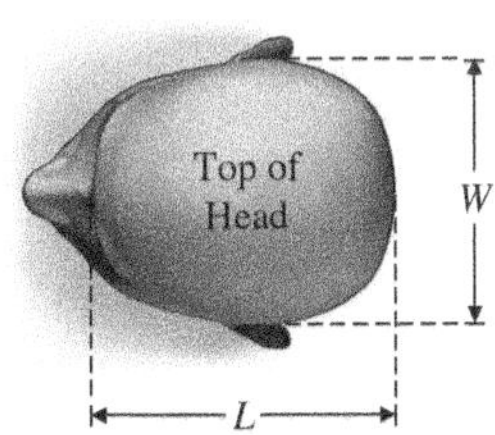

98. Safety research. Under ideal conditions, if a person driving a car slams on the brakes and skids to a stop, the length of the skid marks (in feet) is given by the formula

$$L(w, v) = kwv^2$$

where

k = constant

w = weight of car in pounds

v = speed of car in miles per hour

For $k = 0.000\,013\,3$, find $L_w(2{,}500, 60)$ and $L_v(2{,}500, 60)$, and interpret the results.

Answers to Matched Problems

1. (A) $\partial z/\partial y = -3x^2 + 5$ (B) $f_y(2, 3) = -7$
2. (A) $10x(x^2 + 2xy)^4$ (B) 10
3. $P_y(25, 10) = 10$: At a production level of $x = 25$ and $y = 10$, increasing *y* by 1 unit and holding *x* fixed at 25 will increase profit by approximately \$10; $P_y(25, 15) = -110$; at a production level of $x = 25$ and $y = 15$, increasing *y* by 1 unit and holding *x* fixed at 25 will decrease profit by approximately \$110
4. (A) $f_x(x, y) = 12x^{-0.7}y^{0.7}$; $f_y(x, y) = 28x^{0.3}y^{-0.3}$
   (B) Marginal productivity of labor ≈ 25.89; marginal productivity of capital ≈ 20.14
   (C) Labor
5. (A) $3x^2$ (B) $-24y^2$ (C) 12 (D) 12

9.3 Maxima and Minima

We are now ready to undertake a brief, but useful, analysis of local maxima and minima for functions of the type $z = f(x, y)$. We will extend the second-derivative test developed for functions of a single independent variable. We assume that all second-order partial derivatives exist for the function f in some circular region in the xy plane. This guarantees that the surface $z = f(x, y)$ has no sharp points, breaks, or ruptures. In other words, we are dealing only with smooth surfaces with no edges (like the edge of a box), breaks (like an earthquake fault), or sharp points (like the bottom point of a golf tee). (See Fig. 1.)

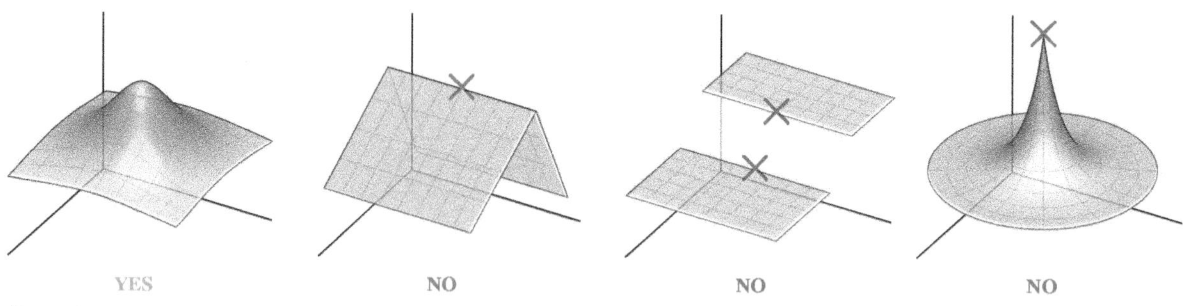

Figure 1

In addition, we will not concern ourselves with boundary points or absolute maxima–minima theory. Despite these restrictions, the procedure we will describe will help us solve a large number of useful problems.

Reminder

If $y = f(x)$ is a function of a single variable x, then $f(c)$ is a **local maximum** if there exists an interval (m, n) containing c such that $f(c) \geq f(x)$ for all x in (m, n).

What does it mean for $f(a, b)$ to be a local maximum or a local minimum? We say that **$f(a, b)$ is a local maximum** if there exists a circular region in the domain of f with (a, b) as the center, such that

$$f(a, b) \geq f(x, y)$$

for all (x, y) in the region. Similarly, we say that **$f(a, b)$ is a local minimum** if there exists a circular region in the domain of f with (a, b) as the center, such that

$$f(a, b) \leq f(x, y)$$

for all (x, y) in the region. Figure 2A illustrates a local maximum, Figure 2B a local minimum, and Figure 2C a **saddle point**, which is neither a local maximum nor a local minimum.

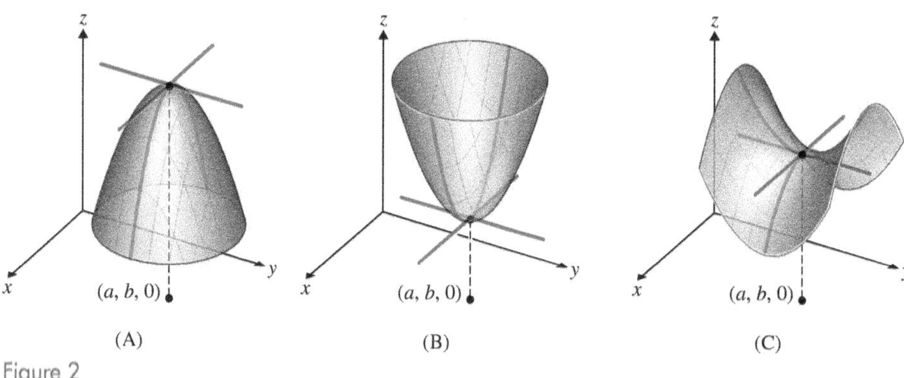

Figure 2

What happens to $f_x(a, b)$ and $f_y(a, b)$ if $f(a, b)$ is a local minimum or a local maximum and the partial derivatives of f exist in a circular region containing (a, b)? Figure 2 suggests that $f_x(a, b) = 0$ and $f_y(a, b) = 0$, since the tangent lines to the given curves are horizontal. Theorem 1 indicates that our intuitive reasoning is correct.

THEOREM 1 Local Extrema and Partial Derivatives

Let $f(a, b)$ be a local extremum (a local maximum or a local minimum) for the function f. If both f_x and f_y exist at (a, b), then

$$f_x(a, b) = 0 \quad \text{and} \quad f_y(a, b) = 0 \tag{1}$$

The converse of this theorem is false. If $f_x(a, b) = 0$ and $f_y(a, b) = 0$, then $f(a, b)$ may or may not be a local extremum; for example, the point $(a, b, f(a, b))$ may be a saddle point (see Fig. 2C).

Theorem 1 gives us *necessary* (but not *sufficient*) conditions for $f(a, b)$ to be a local extremum. We find all points (a, b) such that $f_x(a, b) = 0$ and $f_y(a, b) = 0$ and test these further to determine whether $f(a, b)$ is a local extremum or a saddle point. Points (a, b) such that conditions (1) hold are called **critical points**.

Explore and Discuss 1

(A) Let $f(x, y) = y^2 + 1$. Explain why $f(x, y)$ has a local minimum at every point on the x axis. Verify that every point on the x axis is a critical point. Explain why the graph of $z = f(x, y)$ could be described as a trough.

(B) Let $g(x, y) = x^3$. Show that every point on the y axis is a critical point. Explain why no point on the y axis is a local extremum. Explain why the graph of $z = g(x, y)$ could be described as a slide.

The next theorem, using second-derivative tests, gives us *sufficient* conditions for a critical point to produce a local extremum or a saddle point.

THEOREM 2 Second-Derivative Test for Local Extrema

If

1. $z = f(x, y)$
2. $f_x(a, b) = 0$ and $f_y(a, b) = 0$ [(a, b) is a critical point]
3. All second-order partial derivatives of f exist in some circular region containing (a, b) as center.
4. $A = f_{xx}(a, b), \quad B = f_{xy}(a, b), \quad C = f_{yy}(a, b)$

Then

Case 1. If $AC - B^2 > 0$ and $A < 0$, then $f(a, b)$ is a local maximum.

Case 2. If $AC - B^2 > 0$ and $A > 0$, then $f(a, b)$ is a local minimum.

Case 3. If $AC - B^2 < 0$, then f has a saddle point at (a, b).

Case 4. If $AC - B^2 = 0$, the test fails.

CONCEPTUAL INSIGHT

The condition $A = f_{xx}(a, b) < 0$ in case 1 of Theorem 2 is analogous to the condition $f''(c) < 0$ in the second-derivative test for local extrema for a function of one variable (Section 8.5), which implies that the function is concave downward and therefore has a local maximum. Similarly, the condition $A = f_{xx}(a, b) > 0$ in case 2 is analogous to the condition $f''(c) > 0$ in the earlier second-derivative test, which implies that the function is concave upward and therefore has a local minimum.

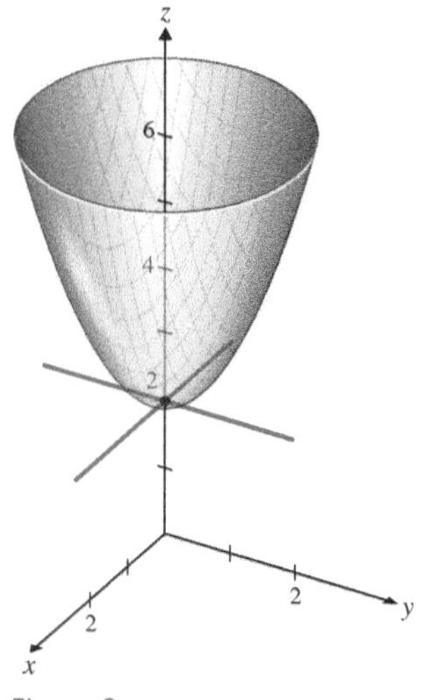

Figure 3

To illustrate the use of Theorem 2, we find the local extremum for a very simple function whose solution is almost obvious: $z = f(x, y) = x^2 + y^2 + 2$. From the function f itself and its graph (Fig. 3), it is clear that a local minimum is found at $(0, 0)$. Let us see how Theorem 2 confirms this observation.

Step 1 Find critical points: Find (x, y) such that $f_x(x, y) = 0$ and $f_y(x, y) = 0$ simultaneously:

$$f_x(x, y) = 2x = 0 \qquad f_y(x, y) = 2y = 0$$
$$x = 0 \qquad y = 0$$

The only critical point is $(a, b) = (0, 0)$.

Step 2 Compute $A = f_{xx}(0, 0)$, $B = f_{xy}(0, 0)$, and $C = f_{yy}(0, 0)$:

$$f_{xx}(x, y) = 2; \quad \text{so} \quad A = f_{xx}(0, 0) = 2$$
$$f_{xy}(x, y) = 0; \quad \text{so} \quad B = f_{xy}(0, 0) = 0$$
$$f_{yy}(x, y) = 2; \quad \text{so} \quad C = f_{yy}(0, 0) = 2$$

Step 3 Evaluate $AC - B^2$ and try to classify the critical point $(0, 0)$ by using Theorem 2:

$$AC - B^2 = (2)(2) - (0)^2 = 4 > 0 \quad \text{and} \quad A = 2 > 0$$

Therefore, case 2 in Theorem 2 holds. That is, $f(0, 0) = 2$ is a local minimum.

We will now use Theorem 2 to analyze extrema without the aid of graphs.

EXAMPLE 1 **Finding Local Extrema** Use Theorem 2 to find local extrema of

$$f(x, y) = -x^2 - y^2 + 6x + 8y - 21$$

SOLUTION

Step 1 Find critical points: Find (x, y) such that $f_x(x, y) = 0$ and $f_y(x, y) = 0$ simultaneously:

$$f_x(x, y) = -2x + 6 = 0 \qquad f_y(x, y) = -2y + 8 = 0$$
$$x = 3 \qquad y = 4$$

The only critical point is $(a, b) = (3, 4)$.

Step 2 Compute $A = f_{xx}(3, 4)$, $B = f_{xy}(3, 4)$, and $C = f_{yy}(3, 4)$:

$$f_{xx}(x, y) = -2; \quad \text{so} \quad A = f_{xx}(3, 4) = -2$$
$$f_{xy}(x, y) = 0; \quad \text{so} \quad B = f_{xy}(3, 4) = 0$$
$$f_{yy}(x, y) = -2; \quad \text{so} \quad C = f_{yy}(3, 4) = -2$$

Step 3 Evaluate $AC - B^2$ and try to classify the critical point $(3, 4)$ by using Theorem 2:

$$AC - B^2 = (-2)(-2) - (0)^2 = 4 > 0 \quad \text{and} \quad A = -2 < 0$$

Therefore, case 1 in Theorem 2 holds, and $f(3, 4) = 4$ is a local maximum.

Matched Problem 1 Use Theorem 2 to find local extrema of

$$f(x, y) = x^2 + y^2 - 10x - 2y + 36$$

EXAMPLE 2 **Finding Local Extrema: Multiple Critical Points** Use Theorem 2 to find local extrema of

$$f(x, y) = x^3 + y^3 - 6xy$$

SOLUTION

Step 1 Find critical points of $f(x, y) = x^3 + y^3 - 6xy$:

$$f_x(x, y) = 3x^2 - 6y = 0 \qquad \text{Solve for } y.$$

$$6y = 3x^2$$

$$y = \tfrac{1}{2}x^2 \qquad (2)$$

$$f_y(x, y) = 3y^2 - 6x = 0$$

$$3y^2 = 6x \qquad \text{Use equation (2) to eliminate } y.$$

$$3\left(\tfrac{1}{2}x^2\right)^2 = 6x$$

$$\tfrac{3}{4}x^4 = 6x \qquad \text{Solve for } x.$$

$$3x^4 - 24x = 0$$

$$3x(x^3 - 8) = 0$$

$$x = 0 \quad \text{or} \quad x = 2$$

$$y = 0 \quad \text{or} \quad y = \tfrac{1}{2}(2)^2 = 2$$

The critical points are $(0, 0)$ and $(2, 2)$.

Since there are two critical points, steps 2 and 3 must be performed twice.

TEST (0, 0)

Step 2 Compute $A = f_{xx}(0, 0)$, $B = f_{xy}(0, 0)$, and $C = f_{yy}(0, 0)$:

$$f_{xx}(x, y) = 6x; \quad \text{so} \quad A = f_{xx}(0, 0) = 0$$

$$f_{xy}(x, y) = -6; \quad \text{so} \quad B = f_{xy}(0, 0) = -6$$

$$f_{yy}(x, y) = 6y; \quad \text{so} \quad C = f_{yy}(0, 0) = 0$$

Step 3 Evaluate $AC - B^2$ and try to classify the critical point $(0, 0)$ by using Theorem 2:

$$AC - B^2 = (0)(0) - (-6)^2 = -36 < 0$$

Therefore, case 3 in Theorem 2 applies. That is, f has a saddle point at $(0, 0)$.

Now we will consider the second critical point, $(2, 2)$:

TEST (2, 2)

Step 2 Compute $A = f_{xx}(2, 2)$, $B = f_{xy}(2, 2)$, and $C = f_{yy}(2, 2)$:

$$f_{xx}(x, y) = 6x; \quad \text{so} \quad A = f_{xx}(2, 2) = 12$$

$$f_{xy}(x, y) = -6; \quad \text{so} \quad B = f_{xy}(2, 2) = -6$$

$$f_{yy}(x, y) = 6y; \quad \text{so} \quad C = f_{yy}(2, 2) = 12$$

Step 3 Evaluate $AC - B^2$ and try to classify the critical point $(2, 2)$ by using Theorem 2:

$$AC - B^2 = (12)(12) - (-6)^2 = 108 > 0 \quad \text{and} \quad A = 12 > 0$$

So case 2 in Theorem 2 applies, and $f(2, 2) = -8$ is a local minimum.

Our conclusions in Example 2 may be confirmed geometrically by graphing cross sections of the function f. The cross sections of f in the planes $y = 0$, $x = 0$, $y = x$, and $y = -x$ [each of these planes contains $(0, 0)$] are represented by the graphs of the functions $f(x, 0) = x^3$, $f(0, y) = y^3$, $f(x, x) = 2x^3 - 6x^2$, and $f(x, -x) = 6x^2$, respectively, as shown in Figure 4A (note that the first two functions have the same graph). The cross sections of f in the planes $y = 2$, $x = 2$, $y = x$, and $y = 4 - x$ [each of these planes contains $(2, 2)$] are represented by the graphs of $f(x, 2) = x^3 - 12x + 8$, $f(2, y) = y^3 - 12y + 8$, $f(x, x) = 2x^3 - 6x^2$, and $f(x, 4 - x) = x^3 + (4 - x)^3 + 6x^2 - 24x$, respectively, as shown in Figure 4B (the first two functions have the same graph). Figure 4B illustrates the fact that since

f has a local minimum at $(2, 2)$, each of the cross sections of f through $(2, 2)$ has a local minimum of -8 at $(2, 2)$. Figure 4A, by contrast, indicates that some cross sections of f through $(0, 0)$ have a local minimum, some a local maximum, and some neither one, at $(0, 0)$.

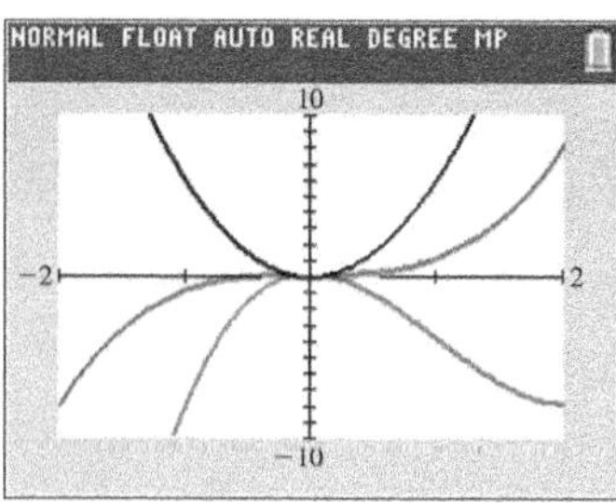

(A) $y_1 = x^3$
$y_2 = 2x^3 - 6x^2$
$y_3 = 6x^2$

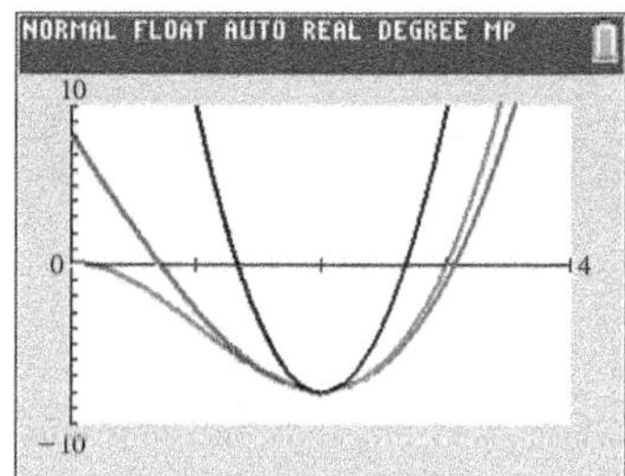

(B) $y_1 = x^3 - 12x + 8$
$y_2 = 2x^3 - 6x^2$
$y_3 = x^3 + (4 - x)^3 + 6x^2 - 24x$

Figure 4

Matched Problem 2 Use Theorem 2 to find local extrema for $f(x, y) = x^3 + y^2 - 6xy$.

EXAMPLE 3 **Profit** Suppose that the surfboard company discussed earlier has developed the yearly profit equation

$$P(x, y) = -22x^2 + 22xy - 11y^2 + 110x - 44y - 23$$

where x is the number (in thousands) of standard surfboards produced per year, y is the number (in thousands) of competition surfboards produced per year, and P is profit (in thousands of dollars). How many of each type of board should be produced per year to realize a maximum profit? What is the maximum profit?

SOLUTION

Step 1 Find critical points:

$$P_x(x, y) = -44x + 22y + 110 = 0$$
$$P_y(x, y) = 22x - 22y - 44 = 0$$

Solving this system, we obtain $(3, 1)$ as the only critical point.

Step 2 Compute $A = P_{xx}(3, 1)$, $B = P_{xy}(3, 1)$, and $C = P_{yy}(3, 1)$:

$$P_{xx}(x, y) = -44; \quad \text{so} \quad A = P_{xx}(3, 1) = -44$$
$$P_{xy}(x, y) = 22; \quad \text{so} \quad B = P_{xy}(3, 1) = 22$$
$$P_{yy}(x, y) = -22; \quad \text{so} \quad C = P_{yy}(3, 1) = -22$$

Step 3 Evaluate $AC - B^2$ and try to classify the critical point $(3, 1)$ by using Theorem 2:

$$AC - B^2 = (-44)(-22) - 22^2 = 484 > 0 \quad \text{and} \quad A = -44 < 0$$

Therefore, case 1 in Theorem 2 applies. That is, $P(3, 1) = 120$ is a local maximum. A maximum profit of \$120,000 is obtained by producing and selling 3,000 standard boards and 1,000 competition boards per year.

Matched Problem 3 Repeat Example 3 with

$$P(x, y) = -66x^2 + 132xy - 99y^2 + 132x - 66y - 19$$

EXAMPLE 4 **Package Design** The packaging department in a company is to design a rectangular box with no top and a partition down the middle. The box must have a volume of 48 cubic inches. Find the dimensions that will minimize the area of material used to construct the box.

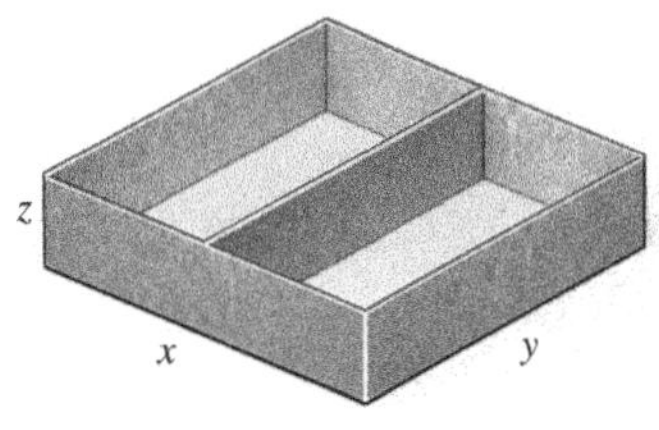

Figure 5

SOLUTION Refer to Figure 5. The area of material used in constructing this box is

$$M = \underset{\text{Base}}{xy} + \underset{\substack{\text{Front,}\\ \text{back}}}{2xz} + \underset{\substack{\text{Sides,}\\ \text{partition}}}{3yz} \tag{3}$$

The volume of the box is

$$V = xyz = 48 \tag{4}$$

Since Theorem 2 applies only to functions with two independent variables, we must use equation (4) to eliminate one of the variables in equation (3):

$$\begin{aligned} M &= xy + 2xz + 3yz && \text{Substitute } z = 48/xy. \\ &= xy + 2x\left(\frac{48}{xy}\right) + 3y\left(\frac{48}{xy}\right) \\ &= xy + \frac{96}{y} + \frac{144}{x} \end{aligned}$$

So we must find the minimum value of

$$M(x, y) = xy + \frac{96}{y} + \frac{144}{x} \qquad x > 0 \quad \text{and} \quad y > 0$$

Step 1 Find critical points:

$$M_x(x, y) = y - \frac{144}{x^2} = 0$$

$$y = \frac{144}{x^2} \tag{5}$$

$$\begin{aligned} M_y(x, y) = x - \frac{96}{y^2} &= 0 \\ x &= \frac{96}{y^2} && \text{Solve for } y^2. \\ y^2 &= \frac{96}{x} && \text{Use equation (5) to eliminate } y \text{ and solve for } x. \\ \left(\frac{144}{x^2}\right)^2 &= \frac{96}{x} \\ \frac{20{,}736}{x^4} &= \frac{96}{x} && \text{Multiply both sides by } x^4/96 \text{ (recall that } x > 0). \\ x^3 &= \frac{20{,}736}{96} = 216 \\ x &= 6 && \text{Use equation (5) to find } y. \\ y &= \frac{144}{36} = 4 \end{aligned}$$

Therefore, $(6, 4)$ is the only critical point.

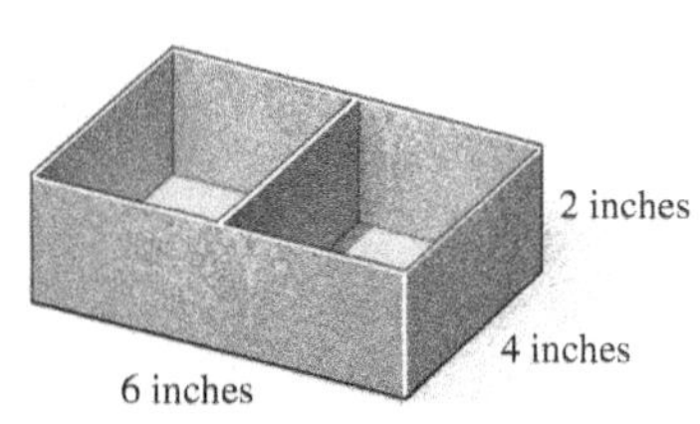

Figure 6

Step 2 Compute $A = M_{xx}(6, 4)$, $B = M_{xy}(6, 4)$, and $C = M_{yy}(6, 4)$:

$$M_{xx}(x, y) = \frac{288}{x^3}; \quad \text{so} \quad A = M_{xx}(6, 4) = \tfrac{288}{216} = \tfrac{4}{3}$$

$$M_{xy}(x, y) = 1; \quad \text{so} \quad B = M_{xy}(6, 4) = 1$$

$$M_{yy}(x, y) = \frac{192}{y^3}; \quad \text{so} \quad C = M_{yy}(6, 4) = \tfrac{192}{64} = 3$$

Step 3 Evaluate $AC - B^2$ and try to classify the critical point $(6, 4)$ by using Theorem 2:

$$AC - B^2 = \left(\tfrac{4}{3}\right)(3) - (1)^2 = 3 > 0 \quad \text{and} \quad A = \tfrac{4}{3} > 0$$

Case 2 in Theorem 2 applies, and $M(x, y)$ has a local minimum at $(6, 4)$. If $x = 6$ and $y = 4$, then

$$z = \frac{48}{xy} = \frac{48}{(6)(4)} = 2$$

The dimensions that will require the least material are 6 inches by 4 inches by 2 inches (see Fig. 6).

Matched Problem 4 If the box in Example 4 must have a volume of 384 cubic inches, find the dimensions that will require the least material.

Exercises 9.3

Skills Warm-up Exercises

W *In Problems 1–8, find $f'(0)$, $f''(0)$, and determine whether f has a local minimum, local maximum, or neither at $x = 0$. (If necessary, review the second derivative test for local extrema in Section 8.5.)*

1. $f(x) = 2x^3 - 9x^2 + 4$
2. $f(x) = 4x^3 + 6x^2 + 100$
3. $f(x) = \dfrac{1}{1 - x^2}$
4. $f(x) = \dfrac{1}{1 + x^2}$
5. $f(x) = e^{-x^2}$
6. $f(x) = e^{x^2}$
7. $f(x) = x^3 - x^2 + x - 1$
8. $f(x) = (3x + 1)^2$

A *In Problems 9–16, find $f_x(x, y)$ and $f_y(x, y)$, and explain, using Theorem 1, why $f(x, y)$ has no local extrema.*

9. $f(x, y) = 4x + 5y - 6$
10. $f(x, y) = 10 - 2x - 3y + x^2$
11. $f(x, y) = 3.7 - 1.2x + 6.8y + 0.2y^3 + x^4$
12. $f(x, y) = x^3 - y^2 + 7x + 3y + 1$
13. $f(x, y) = -x^2 + 2xy - y^2 - 4x + 5y$
14. $f(x, y) = 3x^2 - 12xy + 12y^2 + 8x + 9y - 15$
15. $f(x, y) = ye^x - 3x + 4y$
16. $f(x, y) = y + y^2 \ln x$

B *In Problems 17–36, use Theorem 2 to find the local extrema.*

17. $f(x, y) = x^2 + 8x + y^2 + 25$
18. $f(x, y) = 15x^2 - y^2 - 10y$
19. $f(x, y) = 8 - x^2 + 12x - y^2 - 2y$
20. $f(x, y) = x^2 + y^2 + 6x - 8y + 10$
21. $f(x, y) = x^2 + 3xy + 2y^2 + 5$
22. $f(x, y) = 4x^2 - xy + y^2 + 12$
23. $f(x, y) = 100 + 6xy - 4x^2 - 3y^2$
24. $f(x, y) = 5x^2 - y^2 + 2y + 6$
25. $f(x, y) = x^2 + xy + y^2 - 7x + 4y + 9$
26. $f(x, y) = -x^2 + 2xy - 2y^2 - 20x + 34y + 40$

C

27. $f(x, y) = e^{xy}$
28. $f(x, y) = x^2y - xy^2$
29. $f(x, y) = x^3 + y^3 - 3xy$
30. $f(x, y) = 2y^3 - 6xy - x^2$
31. $f(x, y) = 2x^4 + y^2 - 12xy$
32. $f(x, y) = 16xy - x^4 - 2y^2$
33. $f(x, y) = x^3 - 3xy^2 + 6y^2$
34. $f(x, y) = 2x^2 - 2x^2y + 6y^3$
35. $f(x, y) = xe^y + xy + 1$
36. $f(x, y) = y \ln x + 3xy$
37. Explain why $f(x, y) = x^2$ has a local extremum at infinitely many points.

38. (A) Find the local extrema of the functions $f(x, y) = x + y, g(x, y) = x^2 + y^2$, and $h(x, y) = x^3 + y^3$.

(B) Discuss the local extrema of the function $k(x, y) = x^n + y^n$, where n is a positive integer.

39. (A) Show that (0, 0) is a critical point of the function $f(x, y) = x^4e^y + x^2y^4 + 1$, but that the second-derivative test for local extrema fails.

(B) Use cross sections, as in Example 2, to decide whether f has a local maximum, a local minimum, or a saddle point at (0, 0).

40. (A) Show that (0, 0) is a critical point of the function $g(x, y) = e^{xy^2} + x^2y^3 + 2$, but that the second-derivative test for local extrema fails.

(B) Use cross sections, as in Example 2, to decide whether g has a local maximum, a local minimum, or a saddle point at (0, 0).

Applications

41. **Product mix for maximum profit.** A firm produces two types of earphones per year: x thousand of type A and y thousand of type B. If the revenue and cost equations for the year are (in millions of dollars)

$$R(x, y) = 2x + 3y$$

$$C(x, y) = x^2 - 2xy + 2y^2 + 6x - 9y + 5$$

determine how many of each type of earphone should be produced per year to maximize profit. What is the maximum profit?

42. **Automation–labor mix for minimum cost.** The annual labor and automated equipment cost (in millions of dollars) for a company's production of HDTVs is given by

$$C(x, y) = 2x^2 + 2xy + 3y^2 - 16x - 18y + 54$$

where x is the amount spent per year on labor and y is the amount spent per year on automated equipment (both in millions of dollars). Determine how much should be spent on each per year to minimize this cost. What is the minimum cost?

43. **Maximizing profit.** A store sells two brands of camping chairs. The store pays \$60 for each brand A chair and \$80 for each brand B chair. The research department has estimated the weekly demand equations for these two competitive products to be

$$x = 260 - 3p + q \quad \text{Demand equation for brand } A$$

$$y = 180 + p - 2q \quad \text{Demand equation for brand } B$$

where p is the selling price for brand A and q is the selling price for brand B.

(A) Determine the demands x and y when $p = \$100$ and $q = \$120$; when $p = \$110$ and $q = \$110$.

(B) How should the store price each chair to maximize weekly profits? What is the maximum weekly profit? [*Hint:* $C = 60x + 80y, R = px + qy$, and $P = R - C$.]

44. **Maximizing profit.** A store sells two brands of laptop sleeves. The store pays \$25 for each brand A sleeve and \$30 for each brand B sleeve. A consulting firm has estimated the daily demand equations for these two competitive products to be

$$x = 130 - 4p + q \quad \text{Demand equation for brand } A$$

$$y = 115 + 2p - 3q \quad \text{Demand equation for brand } B$$

where p is the selling price for brand A and q is the selling price for brand B.

(A) Determine the demands x and y when $p = \$40$ and $q = \$50$; when $p = \$45$ and $q = \$55$.

(B) How should the store price each brand of sleeve to maximize daily profits? What is the maximum daily profit? [*Hint:* $C = 25x + 30y, R = px + qy$, and $P = R - C$.]

45. **Minimizing cost.** A satellite TV station is to be located at $P(x, y)$ so that the sum of the squares of the distances from P to the three towns A, B, and C is a minimum (see the figure). Find the coordinates of P, the location that will minimize the cost of providing satellite TV for all three towns.

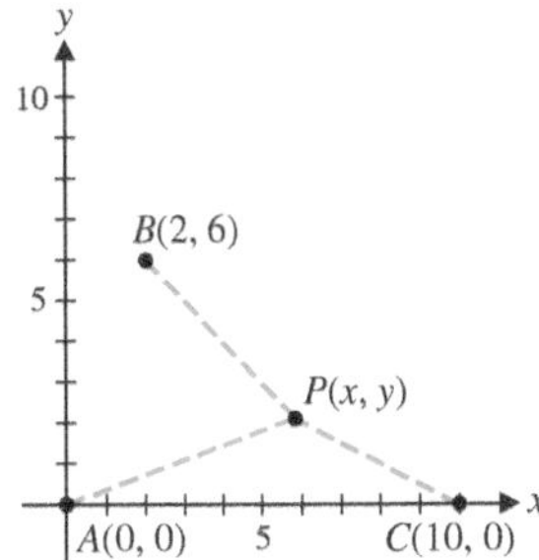

46. **Minimizing cost.** Repeat Problem 45, replacing the coordinates of B with $B(6, 9)$ and the coordinates of C with $C(9, 0)$.

47. **Minimum material.** A rectangular box with no top and two parallel partitions (see the figure) must hold a volume of 64 cubic inches. Find the dimensions that will require the least material.

48. **Minimum material.** A rectangular box with no top and two intersecting partitions (see the figure) must hold a volume of 72 cubic inches. Find the dimensions that will require the least material.

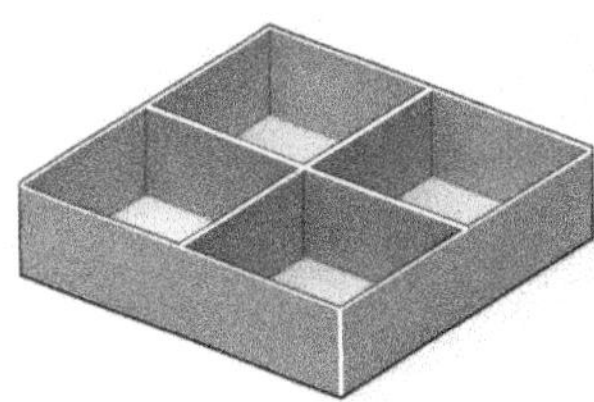

49. **Maximum volume.** A mailing service states that a rectangular package cannot have the sum of its length and girth exceed 120 inches (see the figure). What are the dimensions of the largest (in volume) mailing carton that can be constructed to meet these restrictions?

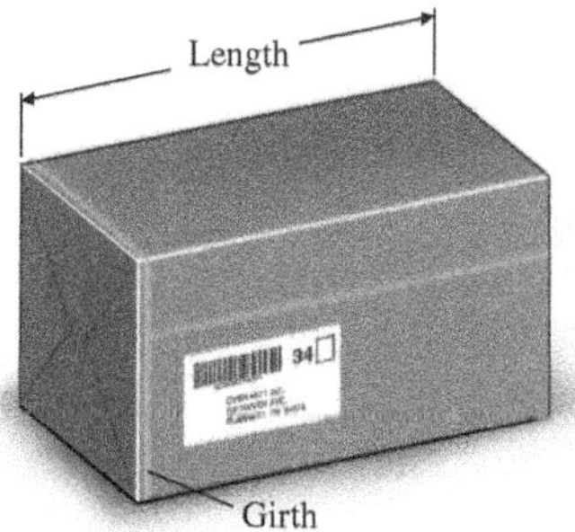

50. **Maximum shipping volume.** A shipping box is to be reinforced with steel bands in all three directions, as shown in the figure. A total of 150 inches of steel tape is to be used, with 6 inches of waste because of a 2-inch overlap in each direction. Find the dimensions of the box with maximum volume that can be taped as described.

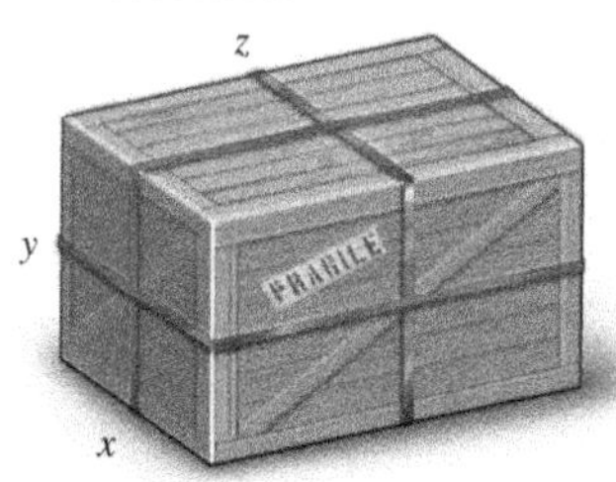

Answers to Matched Problems

1. $f(5, 1) = 10$ is a local minimum
2. f has a saddle point at (0, 0); $f(6, 18) = -108$ is a local minimum
3. Local maximum for $x = 2$ and $y = 1$; $P(2, 1) = 80$; a maximum profit of $80,000 is obtained by producing and selling 2,000 standard boards and 1,000 competition boards
4. 12 in. by 8 in. by 4 in.

9.4 Maxima and Minima Using Lagrange Multipliers

- Functions of Two Independent Variables
- Functions of Three Independent Variables

Functions of Two Independent Variables

We now consider a powerful method of solving a certain class of maxima–minima problems. Joseph Louis Lagrange (1736–1813), an eighteenth-century French mathematician, discovered this method, called the **method of Lagrange multipliers**. We introduce the method through an example.

A rancher wants to construct two feeding pens of the same size along an existing fence (see Fig. 1). If the rancher has 720 feet of fencing materials available, how long should x and y be in order to obtain the maximum total area? What is the maximum area?

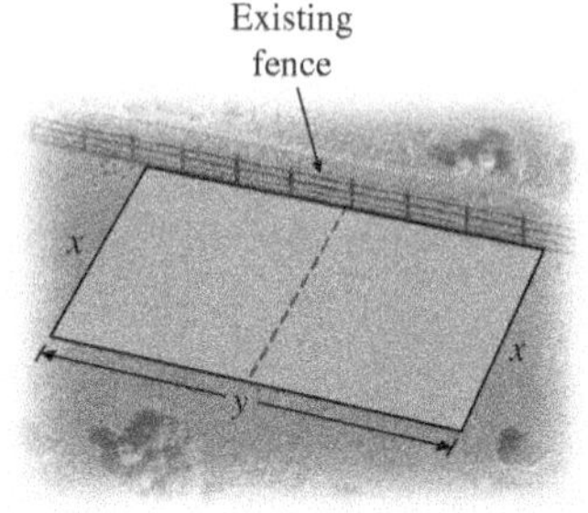

Figure 1

The total area is given by

$$f(x, y) = xy$$

which can be made as large as we like, provided that there are no restrictions on x and y. But there are restrictions on x and y, since we have only 720 feet of fencing. The variables x and y must be chosen so that

$$3x + y = 720$$

This restriction on x and y, called a **constraint**, leads to the following maxima–minima problem:

$$\text{Maximize } f(x, y) = xy \tag{1}$$

$$\text{subject to } 3x + y = 720, \quad \text{or} \quad 3x + y - 720 = 0 \tag{2}$$

This problem is one of a general class of problems of the form

$$\text{Maximize (or minimize) } z = f(x, y) \tag{3}$$

$$\text{subject to } g(x, y) = 0 \tag{4}$$

Of course, we could try to solve equation (4) for y in terms of x, or for x in terms of y, then substitute the result into equation (3), and use methods developed in Section 8.5 for functions of a single variable. But what if equation (4) is more complicated than equation (2), and solving for one variable in terms of the other is either very difficult or impossible?

In the method of Lagrange multipliers, we will work with $g(x, y)$ directly and avoid solving equation (4) for one variable in terms of the other. In addition, the method generalizes to functions of arbitrarily many variables subject to one or more constraints.

Now to the method: We form a new function F, using functions f and g in equations (3) and (4), as follows:

$$F(x, y, \lambda) = f(x, y) + \lambda g(x, y) \tag{5}$$

Here, λ (the Greek lowercase letter lambda) is called a **Lagrange multiplier**. Theorem 1 gives the basis for the method.

THEOREM 1 Method of Lagrange Multipliers for Functions of Two Variables

Any local maxima or minima of the function $z = f(x, y)$ subject to the constraint $g(x, y) = 0$ will be among those points (x_0, y_0) for which (x_0, y_0, λ_0) is a solution of the system

$$F_x(x, y, \lambda) = 0$$
$$F_y(x, y, \lambda) = 0$$
$$F_\lambda(x, y, \lambda) = 0$$

where $F(x, y, \lambda) = f(x, y) + \lambda g(x, y)$, provided that all the partial derivatives exist.

We now use the method of Lagrange multipliers to solve the fence problem.

Step 1 Formulate the problem in the form of equations (3) and (4):

$$\text{Maximize } f(x, y) = xy$$
$$\text{subject to } g(x, y) = 3x + y - 720 = 0$$

Step 2 Form the function F, introducing the Lagrange multiplier λ:

$$\begin{aligned} F(x, y, \lambda) &= f(x, y) + \lambda g(x, y) \\ &= xy + \lambda(3x + y - 720) \end{aligned}$$

Step 3 Solve the system $F_x = 0, F_y = 0, F_\lambda = 0$ (the solutions are **critical points** of F):

$$F_x = y + 3\lambda = 0$$
$$F_y = x + \lambda = 0$$
$$F_\lambda = 3x + y - 720 = 0$$

From the first two equations, we see that

$$y = -3\lambda$$
$$x = -\lambda$$

Substitute these values for x and y into the third equation and solve for λ:

$$\begin{aligned} -3\lambda - 3\lambda &= 720 \\ -6\lambda &= 720 \\ \lambda &= -120 \end{aligned}$$

So

$$y = -3(-120) = 360 \text{ feet}$$
$$x = -(-120) = 120 \text{ feet}$$

and $(x_0, y_0, \lambda_0) = (120, 360, -120)$ is the only critical point of F.

Step 4 According to Theorem 1, if the function $f(x, y)$, subject to the constraint $g(x, y) = 0$, has a local maximum or minimum, that maximum or minimum must occur at $x = 120, y = 360$. Although it is possible to develop a test similar to Theorem 2 in Section 9.3 to determine the nature of this local extremum, we will not do so. [Note that Theorem 2 cannot be applied to $f(x, y)$ at (120, 360), since this point is not a critical point of the unconstrained function $f(x, y)$.] We simply assume that the maximum value of $f(x, y)$ must occur for $x = 120, y = 360$.

$$\begin{aligned} \text{Max } f(x, y) &= f(120, 360) \\ &= (120)(360) = 43{,}200 \text{ square feet} \end{aligned}$$

The key steps in applying the method of Lagrange multipliers are as follows:

PROCEDURE Method of Lagrange Multipliers: Key Steps

Step 1 Write the problem in the form

$$\begin{aligned} &\text{Maximize (or minimize)} && z = f(x, y) \\ &\text{subject to} && g(x, y) = 0 \end{aligned}$$

Step 2 Form the function F:

$$F(x, y, \lambda) = f(x, y) + \lambda g(x, y)$$

Step 3 Find the critical points of F; that is, solve the system

$$\begin{aligned} F_x(x, y, \lambda) &= 0 \\ F_y(x, y, \lambda) &= 0 \\ F_\lambda(x, y, \lambda) &= 0 \end{aligned}$$

Step 4 If (x_0, y_0, λ_0) is the only critical point of F, we assume that (x_0, y_0) will always produce the solution to the problems we consider. If F has more than one critical point, we evaluate $z = f(x, y)$ at (x_0, y_0) for each critical point (x_0, y_0, λ_0) of F. For the problems we consider, we assume that the largest of these values is the maximum value of $f(x, y)$, subject to the constraint $g(x, y) = 0$, and the smallest is the minimum value of $f(x, y)$, subject to the constraint $g(x, y) = 0$.

EXAMPLE 1 **Minimization Subject to a Constraint** Minimize $f(x, y) = x^2 + y^2$ subject to $x + y = 10$.

SOLUTION

Step 1

$$\begin{aligned} &\text{Minimize} && f(x, y) = x^2 + y^2 \\ &\text{subject to} && g(x, y) = x + y - 10 = 0 \end{aligned}$$

Step 2

$$F(x, y, \lambda) = x^2 + y^2 + \lambda(x + y - 10)$$

Step 3

$$\begin{aligned} F_x &= 2x + \lambda = 0 \\ F_y &= 2y + \lambda = 0 \\ F_\lambda &= x + y - 10 = 0 \end{aligned}$$

From the first two equations, $x = -\lambda/2$ and $y = -\lambda/2$. Substituting these values into the third equation, we obtain

$$\begin{aligned} -\frac{\lambda}{2} - \frac{\lambda}{2} &= 10 \\ -\lambda &= 10 \\ \lambda &= -10 \end{aligned}$$

The only critical point is $(x_0, y_0, \lambda_0) = (5, 5, -10)$.

Step 4 Since $(5, 5, -10)$ is the only critical point of F, we conclude that (see step 4 in the box)

$$\text{Min} f(x, y) = f(5, 5) = (5)^2 + (5)^2 = 50$$

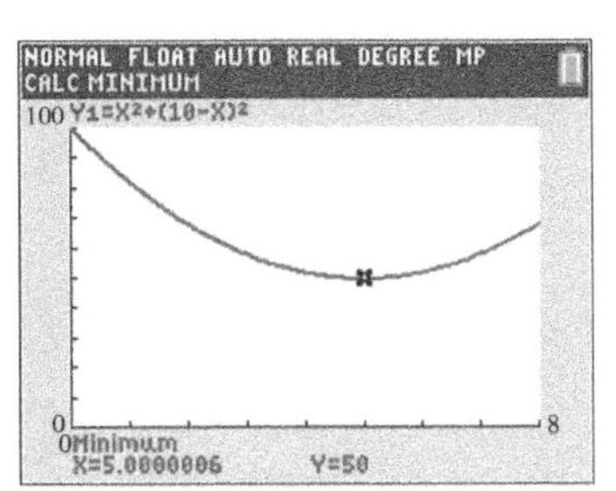

Figure 2 $h(x) = x^2 + (10 - x)^2$

Since $g(x, y)$ in Example 1 has a relatively simple form, an alternative to the method of Lagrange multipliers is to solve $g(x, y) = 0$ for y and then substitute into $f(x, y)$ to obtain the function $h(x) = f(x, 10 - x) = x^2 + (10 - x)^2$ in the single variable x. Then we minimize h (see Fig. 2). From Figure 2, we conclude that $\min f(x, y) = f(5, 5) = 50$. This technique depends on being able to solve the constraint for one of the two variables and so is not always available as an alternative to the method of Lagrange multipliers.

Matched Problem 1 Maximize $f(x, y) = 25 - x^2 - y^2$ subject to $x + y = 4$.

Figures 3 and 4 illustrate the results obtained in Example 1 and Matched Problem 1, respectively.

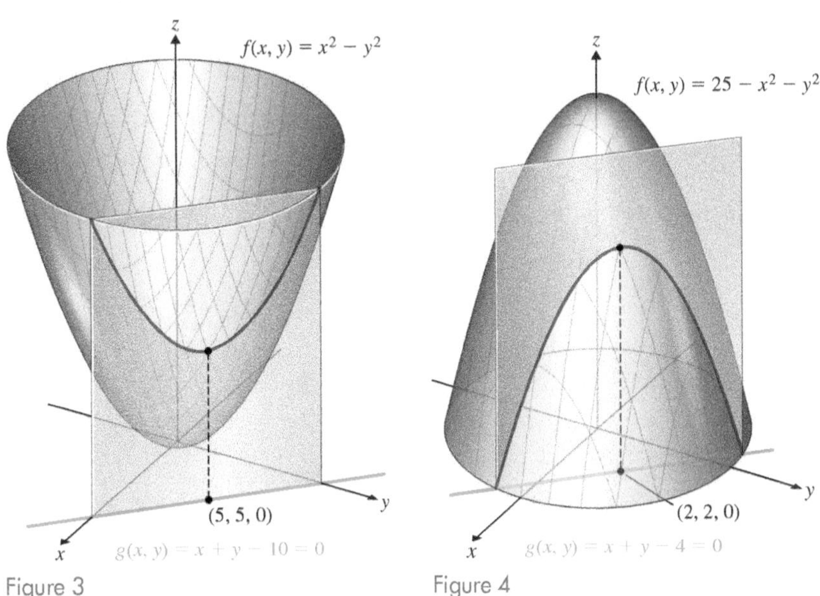

Figure 3 Figure 4

Explore and Discuss 1

Consider the problem of minimizing $f(x, y) = 3x^2 + 5y^2$ subject to the constraint $g(x, y) = 2x + 3y - 6 = 0$.

(A) Compute the value of $f(x, y)$ when x and y are integers, $0 \le x \le 3$, $0 \le y \le 2$. Record your answers in the empty boxes next to the points (x, y) in Figure 5.

(B) Graph the constraint $g(x, y) = 0$.

(C) Estimate the minimum value of f on the basis of your graph and the computations from part (A).

(D) Use the method of Lagrange multipliers to solve the minimization problem.

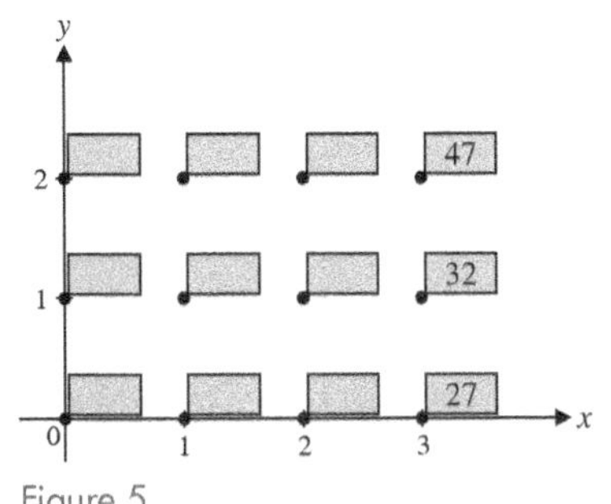

Figure 5

EXAMPLE 2 **Productivity** The Cobb–Douglas production function for a new product is given by

$$N(x, y) = 16x^{0.25}y^{0.75}$$

where x is the number of units of labor and y is the number of units of capital required to produce $N(x, y)$ units of the product. Each unit of labor costs \$50 and each unit of capital costs \$100. If \$500,000 has been budgeted for the production of this product, how should that amount be allocated between labor and capital in order to maximize production? What is the maximum number of units that can be produced?

SOLUTION The total cost of using x units of labor and y units of capital is $50x + 100y$. Thus, the constraint imposed by the $500,000 budget is

$$50x + 100y = 500{,}000$$

Step 1 Maximize $N(x, y) = 16x^{0.25}y^{0.75}$

subject to $g(x, y) = 50x + 100y - 500{,}000 = 0$

Step 2 $F(x, y, \lambda) = 16x^{0.25}y^{0.75} + \lambda(50x + 100y - 500{,}000)$

Step 3

$$F_x = 4x^{-0.75}y^{0.75} + 50\lambda = 0$$

$$F_y = 12x^{0.25}y^{-0.25} + 100\lambda = 0$$

$$F_\lambda = 50x + 100y - 500{,}000 = 0$$

From the first two equations,

$$\lambda = -\tfrac{2}{25}x^{-0.75}y^{0.75} \quad \text{and} \quad \lambda = -\tfrac{3}{25}x^{0.25}y^{-0.25}$$

Therefore,

$$-\tfrac{2}{25}x^{-0.75}y^{0.75} = -\tfrac{3}{25}x^{0.25}y^{-0.25}$$ Multiply both sides by $x^{0.75}y^{0.25}$.

$$-\tfrac{2}{25}y = -\tfrac{3}{25}x$$ (We can assume that $x \neq 0$ and $y \neq 0$.)

$$y = \tfrac{3}{2}x$$

Now substitute for y in the third equation and solve for x:

$$50x + 100\left(\tfrac{3}{2}x\right) - 500{,}000 = 0$$

$$200x = 500{,}000$$

$$x = 2{,}500$$

So

$$y = \tfrac{3}{2}(2{,}500) = 3{,}750$$

and

$$\lambda = -\tfrac{2}{25}(2{,}500)^{-0.75}(3{,}750)^{0.75} \approx -0.1084$$

The only critical point of F is $(2{,}500, 3{,}750, -0.1084)$.

Step 4 Since F has only one critical point, we conclude that maximum productivity occurs when 2,500 units of labor and 3,750 units of capital are used (see step 4 in the method of Lagrange multipliers).

$$\begin{aligned}\text{Max } N(x, y) &= N(2{,}500, 3{,}750)\\ &= 16(2{,}500)^{0.25}(3{,}750)^{0.75}\\ &\approx 54{,}216 \text{ units}\end{aligned}$$

The negative of the value of the Lagrange multiplier found in step 3 is called the **marginal productivity of money** and gives the approximate increase in production for each additional dollar spent on production. In Example 2, increasing the production budget from $500,000 to $600,000 would result in an approximate increase in production of

$$0.1084(100{,}000) = 10{,}840 \text{ units}$$

Note that simplifying the constraint equation

$$50x + 100y - 500{,}000 = 0$$

to

$$x + 2y - 10{,}000 = 0$$

before forming the function $F(x, y, \lambda)$ would make it difficult to interpret $-\lambda$ correctly. **In marginal productivity problems, the constraint equation should not be simplified.**

Matched Problem 2 The Cobb–Douglas production function for a new product is given by

$$N(x, y) = 20x^{0.5}y^{0.5}$$

where x is the number of units of labor and y is the number of units of capital required to produce $N(x, y)$ units of the product. Each unit of labor costs \$40 and each unit of capital costs \$120.

(A) If \$300,000 has been budgeted for the production of this product, how should that amount be allocated in order to maximize production? What is the maximum production?

(B) Find the marginal productivity of money in this case, and estimate the increase in production if an additional \$40,000 is budgeted for production.

Explore and Discuss 2

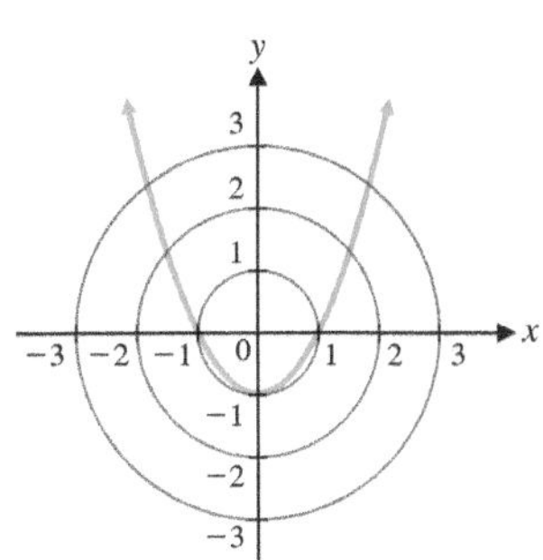

Figure 6

Consider the problem of maximizing $f(x, y) = 4 - x^2 - y^2$ subject to the constraint $g(x, y) = y - x^2 + 1 = 0$.

(A) Explain why $f(x, y) = 3$ whenever (x, y) is a point on the circle of radius 1 centered at the origin. What is the value of $f(x, y)$ when (x, y) is a point on the circle of radius 2 centered at the origin? On the circle of radius 3 centered at the origin? (See Fig. 6.)

(B) Explain why some points on the parabola $y - x^2 + 1 = 0$ lie inside the circle $x^2 + y^2 = 1$.

(C) In light of part (B), would you guess that the maximum value of $f(x, y)$ subject to the constraint is greater than 3? Explain.

(D) Use Lagrange multipliers to solve the maximization problem.

Functions of Three Independent Variables

The method of Lagrange multipliers can be extended to functions with arbitrarily many independent variables with one or more constraints. We now state a theorem for functions with three independent variables and one constraint, and we consider an example that demonstrates the advantage of the method of Lagrange multipliers over the method used in Section 9.3.

THEOREM 2 Method of Lagrange Multipliers for Functions of Three Variables

Any local maxima or minima of the function $w = f(x, y, z)$, subject to the constraint $g(x, y, z) = 0$, will be among the set of points (x_0, y_0, z_0) for which $(x_0, y_0, z_0, \lambda_0)$ is a solution of the system

$$F_x(x, y, z, \lambda) = 0$$

$$F_y(x, y, z, \lambda) = 0$$

$$F_z(x, y, z, \lambda) = 0$$

$$F_\lambda(x, y, z, \lambda) = 0$$

where $F(x, y, z, \lambda) = f(x, y, z) + \lambda g(x, y, z)$, provided that all the partial derivatives exist.

EXAMPLE 3 **Package Design** A rectangular box with an open top and one partition is to be constructed from 162 square inches of cardboard (Fig. 7). Find the dimensions that result in a box with the largest possible volume.

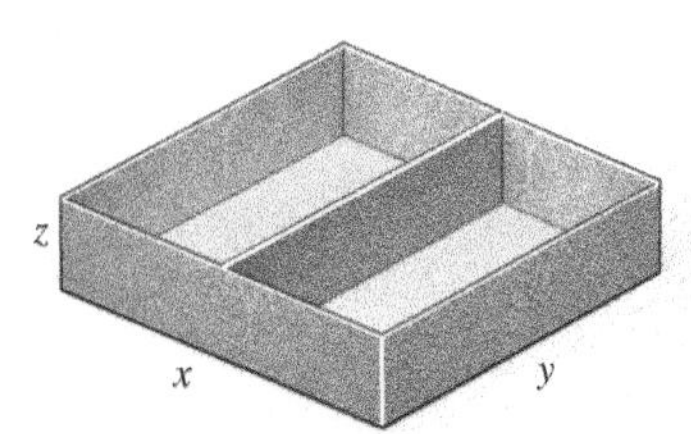

Figure 7

SOLUTION We must maximize

$$V(x, y, z) = xyz$$

subject to the constraint that the amount of material used is 162 square inches. So x, y, and z must satisfy

$$xy + 2xz + 3yz = 162$$

Step 1 Maximize $V(x, y, z) = xyz$

subject to $g(x, y, z) = xy + 2xz + 3yz - 162 = 0$

Step 2 $F(x, y, z, \lambda) = xyz + \lambda(xy + 2xz + 3yz - 162)$

Step 3

$$F_x = yz + \lambda(y + 2z) = 0$$
$$F_y = xz + \lambda(x + 3z) = 0$$
$$F_z = xy + \lambda(2x + 3y) = 0$$
$$F_\lambda = xy + 2xz + 3yz - 162 = 0$$

From the first two equations, we can write

$$\lambda = \frac{-yz}{y + 2z} \qquad \lambda = \frac{-xz}{x + 3z}$$

Eliminating λ, we have

$$\frac{-yz}{y + 2z} = \frac{-xz}{x + 3z}$$
$$-xyz - 3yz^2 = -xyz - 2xz^2$$
$$3yz^2 = 2xz^2 \qquad \text{We can assume that } z \neq 0.$$
$$3y = 2x$$
$$x = \tfrac{3}{2}y$$

From the second and third equations,

$$\lambda = \frac{-xz}{x + 3z} \qquad \lambda = \frac{-xy}{2x + 3y}$$

Eliminating λ, we have

$$\frac{-xz}{x + 3z} = \frac{-xy}{2x + 3y}$$
$$-2x^2z - 3xyz = -x^2y - 3xyz$$
$$2x^2z = x^2y \qquad \text{We can assume that } x \neq 0.$$
$$2z = y$$
$$z = \tfrac{1}{2}y$$

Substituting $x = \frac{3}{2}y$ and $z = \frac{1}{2}y$ into the fourth equation, we have

$$\left(\tfrac{3}{2}y\right)y + 2\left(\tfrac{3}{2}y\right)\left(\tfrac{1}{2}y\right) + 3y\left(\tfrac{1}{2}y\right) - 162 = 0$$
$$\tfrac{3}{2}y^2 + \tfrac{3}{2}y^2 + \tfrac{3}{2}y^2 = 162$$
$$y^2 = 36 \qquad \text{We can assume that } y > 0.$$
$$y = 6$$
$$x = \tfrac{3}{2}(6) = 9 \qquad \text{Using } x = \tfrac{3}{2}y$$
$$z = \tfrac{1}{2}(6) = 3 \qquad \text{Using } z = \tfrac{1}{2}y$$

and finally,

$$\lambda = \frac{-(6)(3)}{6 + 2(3)} = -\frac{3}{2} \qquad \text{Using } \lambda = \frac{-yz}{y + 2z}$$

The only critical point of F with x, y, and z all positive is $(9, 6, 3, -\frac{3}{2})$.

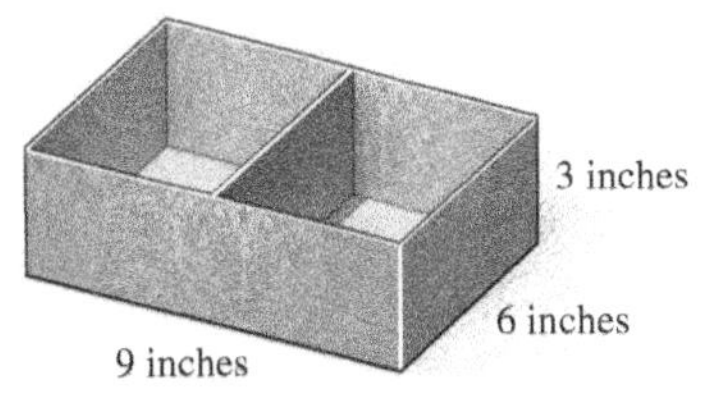

Figure 8

Step 4 The box with the maximum volume has dimensions 9 inches by 6 inches by 3 inches (see Fig. 8).

Matched Problem 3 A box of the same type as in Example 3 is to be constructed from 288 square inches of cardboard. Find the dimensions that result in a box with the largest possible volume.

CONCEPTUAL INSIGHT

An alternative to the method of Lagrange multipliers would be to solve Example 3 by means of Theorem 2 (the second-derivative test for local extrema) in Section 9.3. That approach involves solving the material constraint for one of the variables, say, z:

$$z = \frac{162 - xy}{2x + 3y}$$

Then we would eliminate z in the volume function to obtain a function of two variables:

$$V(x, y) = xy\frac{162 - xy}{2x + 3y}$$

The method of Lagrange multipliers allows us to avoid the formidable tasks of calculating the partial derivatives of V and finding the critical points of V in order to apply Theorem 2.

Exercises 9.4

Skills Warm-up Exercises

In Problems 1–6, maximize or minimize subject to the constraint without using the method of Lagrange multipliers; instead, solve the constraint for x or y and substitute into f(x, y). (If necessary, review Section 1.3.)

1. Minimize $f(x, y) = x^2 + xy + y^2$
   subject to $y = 4$
2. Maximize $f(x, y) = 64 + x^2 + 3xy - y^2$
   subject to $x = 6$
3. Minimize $f(x, y) = 4xy$
   subject to $x - y = 2$
4. Maximize $f(x, y) = 3xy$
   subject to $x + y = 1$
5. Maximize $f(x, y) = 2x + y$
   subject to $x^2 + y = 1$
6. Minimize $f(x, y) = 10x - y^2$
   subject to $x^2 + y^2 = 25$

Use the method of Lagrange multipliers in Problems 7–10.

7. Maximize $f(x, y) = 2xy$
   subject to $x + y = 6$
8. Minimize $f(x, y) = 6xy$
   subject to $y - x = 6$
9. Minimize $f(x, y) = x^2 + y^2$
   subject to $3x + 4y = 25$
10. Maximize $f(x, y) = 25 - x^2 - y^2$
    subject to $2x + y = 10$

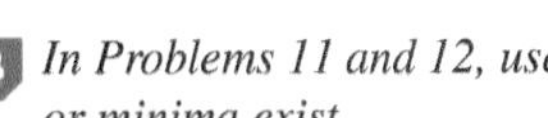

In Problems 11 and 12, use Theorem 1 to explain why no maxima or minima exist.

11. Minimize $f(x, y) = 4y - 3x$
    subject to $2x + 5y = 3$
12. Maximize $f(x, y) = 6x + 5y + 24$
    subject to $3x + 2y = 4$

Use the method of Lagrange multipliers in Problems 13–24.

13. Find the maximum and minimum of $f(x, y) = 2xy$ subject to $x^2 + y^2 = 18$.
14. Find the maximum and minimum of $f(x, y) = x^2 - y^2$ subject to $x^2 + y^2 = 25$.
15. Maximize the product of two numbers if their sum must be 10.
16. Minimize the product of two numbers if their difference must be 10.

C

17. Minimize $f(x, y, z) = x^2 + y^2 + z^2$
    subject to $x + y + 3z = 55$
18. Maximize $f(x, y, z) = 300 - x^2 - 2y^2 - z^2$
    subject to $4x + y + z = 70$
19. Maximize $f(x, y, z) = 900 - 5x^2 - y^2 - 2z^2$
    subject to $x + y + z = 34$
20. Minimize $f(x, y, z) = x^2 + 4y^2 + 2z^2$
    subject to $x + 2y + z = 10$

21. Maximize and minimize $f(x, y, z) = x + 10y + 2z$
subject to $x^2 + y^2 + z^2 = 105$
22. Maximize and minimize $f(x, y, z) = 3x + y + 2z$
subject to $2x^2 + 3y^2 + 4z^2 = 210$
23. Maximize and minimize $f(x, y, z) = x - 2y + z$
subject to $x^2 + y^2 + z^2 = 24$
24. Maximize and minimize $f(x, y, z) = x - y - 3z$
subject to $x^2 + y^2 + z^2 = 99$

In Problems 25 and 26, use Theorem 1 to explain why no maxima or minima exist.

25. Maximize $f(x, y) = e^x + 3e^y$
subject to $x - 2y = 6$
26. Minimize $f(x, y) = x^3 + 2y^3$
subject to $6x - 2y = 1$
27. Consider the problem of maximizing $f(x, y)$ subject to $g(x, y) = 0$, where $g(x, y) = y - 5$. Explain how the maximization problem can be solved without using the method of Lagrange multipliers.
28. Consider the problem of minimizing $f(x, y)$ subject to $g(x, y) = 0$, where $g(x, y) = 4x - y + 3$. Explain how the minimization problem can be solved without using the method of Lagrange multipliers.
29. Consider the problem of maximizing $f(x, y) = e^{-(x^2+y^2)}$ subject to the constraint $g(x, y) = x^2 + y - 1 = 0$.
(A) Solve the constraint equation for y, and then substitute into $f(x, y)$ to obtain a function $h(x)$ of the single variable x. Solve the original maximization problem by maximizing h (round answers to three decimal places).
(B) Confirm your answer by the method of Lagrange multipliers.
30. Consider the problem of minimizing
$$f(x, y) = x^2 + 2y^2$$
subject to the constraint $g(x, y) = ye^{x^2} - 1 = 0$.
(A) Solve the constraint equation for y, and then substitute into $f(x, y)$ to obtain a function $h(x)$ of the single variable x. Solve the original minimization problem by minimizing h (round answers to three decimal places).
(B) Confirm your answer by the method of Lagrange multipliers.

Applications

31. **Budgeting for least cost.** A manufacturing company produces two models of an HDTV per week, x units of model A and y units of model B at a cost (in dollars) of
$$C(x, y) = 6x^2 + 12y^2$$
If it is necessary (because of shipping considerations) that
$$x + y = 90$$
how many of each type of set should be manufactured per week to minimize cost? What is the minimum cost?

32. **Budgeting for maximum production.** A manufacturing firm has budgeted $60,000 per month for labor and materials. If $x thousand is spent on labor and $y thousand is spent on materials, and if the monthly output (in units) is given by
$$N(x, y) = 4xy - 8x$$
then how should the $60,000 be allocated to labor and materials in order to maximize N? What is the maximum N?

33. **Productivity.** A consulting firm for a manufacturing company arrived at the following Cobb–Douglas production function for a particular product:
$$N(x, y) = 50x^{0.8}y^{0.2}$$
In this equation, x is the number of units of labor and y is the number of units of capital required to produce $N(x, y)$ units of the product. Each unit of labor costs $40 and each unit of capital costs $80.
(A) If $400,000 is budgeted for production of the product, determine how that amount should be allocated to maximize production, and find the maximum production.
(B) Find the marginal productivity of money in this case, and estimate the increase in production if an additional $50,000 is budgeted for the production of the product.

34. **Productivity.** The research department of a manufacturing company arrived at the following Cobb–Douglas production function for a particular product:
$$N(x, y) = 10x^{0.6}y^{0.4}$$
In this equation, x is the number of units of labor and y is the number of units of capital required to produce $N(x, y)$ units of the product. Each unit of labor costs $30 and each unit of capital costs $60.
(A) If $300,000 is budgeted for production of the product, determine how that amount should be allocated to maximize production, and find the maximum production.
(B) Find the marginal productivity of money in this case, and estimate the increase in production if an additional $80,000 is budgeted for the production of the product.

35. **Maximum volume.** A rectangular box with no top and two intersecting partitions is to be constructed from 192 square inches of cardboard (see the figure). Find the dimensions that will maximize the volume.

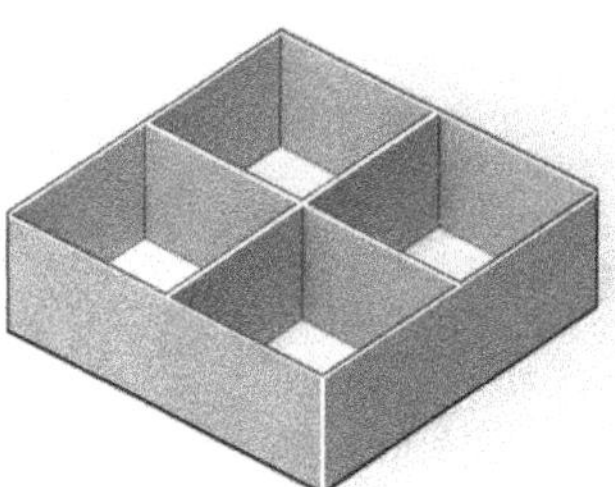

36. **Maximum volume.** A mailing service states that a rectangular package shall have the sum of its length and girth not to exceed 120 inches (see the figure on page 559). What are the dimensions of the largest (in volume) mailing carton that can be constructed to meet these restrictions?

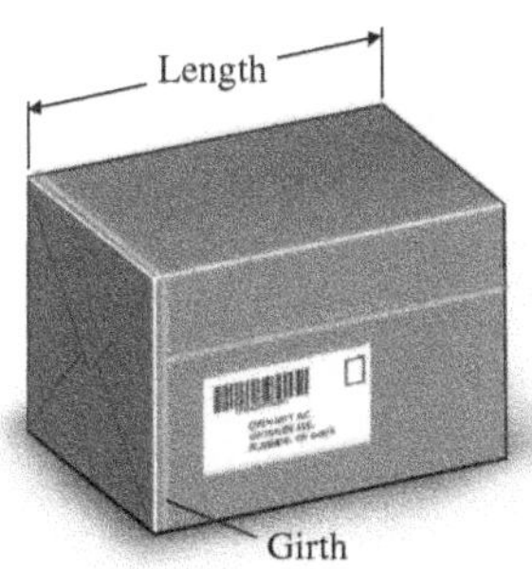

Figure for 36

37. **Agriculture.** Three pens of the same size are to be built along an existing fence (see the figure). If 400 feet of fencing is available, what length should x and y be to produce the maximum total area? What is the maximum area?

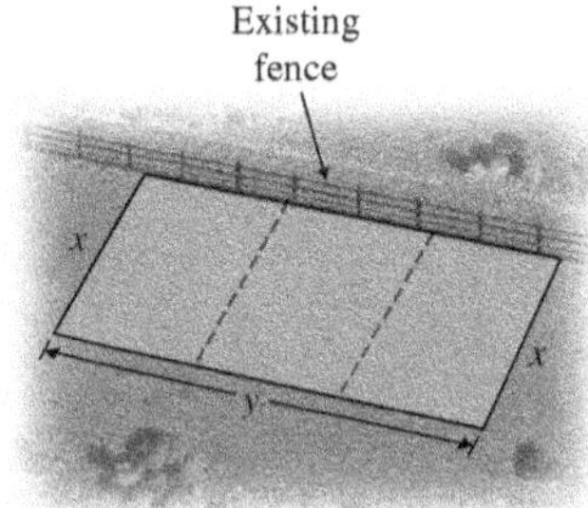

38. **Diet and minimum cost.** A group of guinea pigs is to receive 25,600 calories per week. Two available foods produce $200xy$ calories for a mixture of x kilograms of type M food and y kilograms of type N food. If type M costs \$1 per kilogram and type N costs \$2 per kilogram, how much of each type of food should be used to minimize weekly food costs? What is the minimum cost?

Note: $x \geq 0, y \geq 0$

Answers to Matched Problems

1. Max $f(x, y) = f(2, 2) = 17$ (see Fig. 4)
2. (A) 3,750 units of labor and 1,250 units of capital; Max $N(x, y) = N(3{,}750, 1{,}250) \approx 43{,}301$ units
   (B) Marginal productivity of money ≈ 0.1443; increase in production $\approx 5{,}774$ units
3. 12 in. by 8 in. by 4 in.

9.5 Method of Least Squares

- Least Squares Approximation
- Applications

Least Squares Approximation

Regression analysis is the process of fitting an elementary function to a set of data points by the **method of least squares**. The mechanics of using regression techniques were introduced in Chapter 1. Now, using the optimization techniques of Section 9.3, we can develop and explain the mathematical foundation of the method of least squares. We begin with **linear regression**, the process of finding the equation of the line that is the "best" approximation to a set of data points.

Suppose that a manufacturer wants to approximate the cost function for a product. The value of the cost function has been determined for certain levels of production, as listed in Table 1. Although these points do not all lie on a line (see Fig. 1), they are very close to being linear. The manufacturer would like to approximate the cost function by a linear function—that is, determine values a and b so that the line

$$y = ax + b$$

is, in some sense, the "best" approximation to the cost function.

Table 1

Number of Units x (hundreds)	Cost y (thousand \$)
2	4
5	6
6	7
9	8

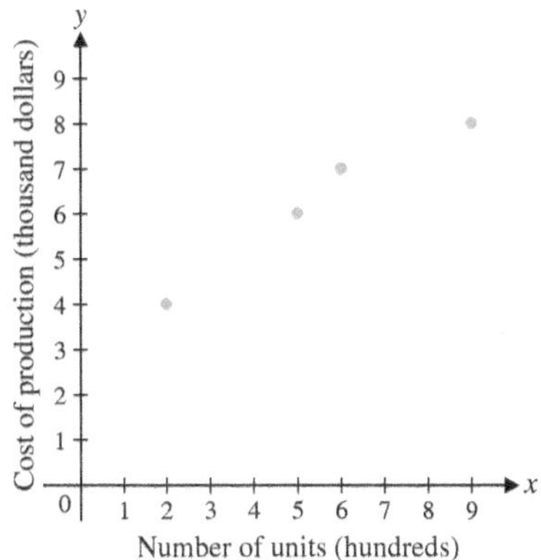

Figure 1

What do we mean by "best"? Since the line $y = ax + b$ will not go through all four points, it is reasonable to examine the differences between the y coordinates of the points listed in the table and the y coordinates of the corresponding points on the line. Each of these differences is called the **residual** at that point (see Fig. 2). For example, at $x = 2$, the point from Table 1 is (2, 4) and the point on the line is $(2, 2a + b)$, so the residual is

$$4 - (2a + b) = 4 - 2a - b$$

All the residuals are listed in Table 2.

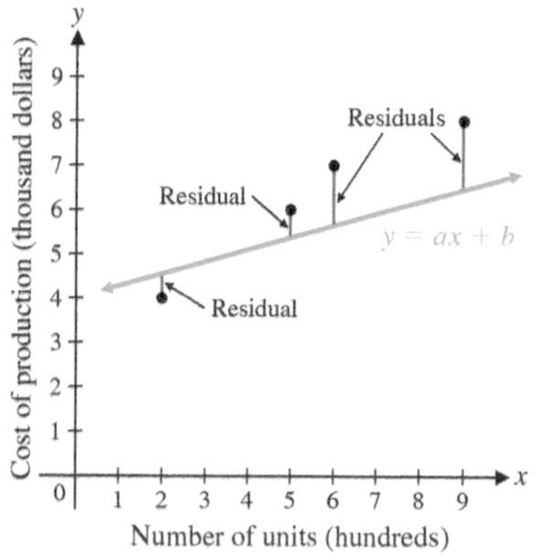

Figure 2

Table 2

x	y	$ax + b$	Residual
2	4	$2a + b$	$4 - 2a - b$
5	6	$5a + b$	$6 - 5a - b$
6	7	$6a + b$	$7 - 6a - b$
9	8	$9a + b$	$8 - 9a - b$

Our criterion for the "best" approximation is the following: Determine the values of a and b that *minimize the sum of the squares* of the residuals. The resulting line is called the **least squares line**, or the **regression line**. To this end, we minimize

$$F(a, b) = (4 - 2a - b)^2 + (6 - 5a - b)^2 + (7 - 6a - b)^2 + (8 - 9a - b)^2$$

Step 1 Find critical points:

$$\begin{aligned} F_a(a, b) &= 2(4 - 2a - b)(-2) + 2(6 - 5a - b)(-5) \\ &\quad + 2(7 - 6a - b)(-6) + 2(8 - 9a - b)(-9) \\ &= -304 + 292a + 44b = 0 \\ F_b(a, b) &= 2(4 - 2a - b)(-1) + 2(6 - 5a - b)(-1) \\ &\quad + 2(7 - 6a - b)(-1) + 2(8 - 9a - b)(-1) \\ &= -50 + 44a + 8b = 0 \end{aligned}$$

After dividing each equation by 2, we solve the system

$$\begin{aligned} 146a + 22b &= 152 \\ 22a + 4b &= 25 \end{aligned}$$

obtaining $(a, b) = (0.58, 3.06)$ as the only critical point.

Step 2 Compute $A = F_{aa}(a, b)$, $B = F_{ab}(a, b)$, and $C = F_{bb}(a, b)$:

$$\begin{aligned} F_{aa}(a, b) &= 292; \quad \text{so} \quad A = F_{aa}(0.58, 3.06) = 292 \\ F_{ab}(a, b) &= 44; \quad \text{so} \quad B = F_{ab}(0.58, 3.06) = 44 \\ F_{bb}(a, b) &= 8; \quad \text{so} \quad C = F_{bb}(0.58, 3.06) = 8 \end{aligned}$$

Step 3 Evaluate $AC - B^2$ and try to classify the critical point (a, b) by using Theorem 2 in Section 9.3:

$$AC - B^2 = (292)(8) - (44)^2 = 400 > 0 \quad \text{and} \quad A = 292 > 0$$

Therefore, case 2 in Theorem 2 applies, and $F(a, b)$ has a local minimum at the critical point (0.58, 3.06).

So the least squares line for the given data is

$$y = 0.58x + 3.06 \quad \text{Least squares line}$$

The sum of the squares of the residuals is minimized for this choice of a and b (see Fig. 3).

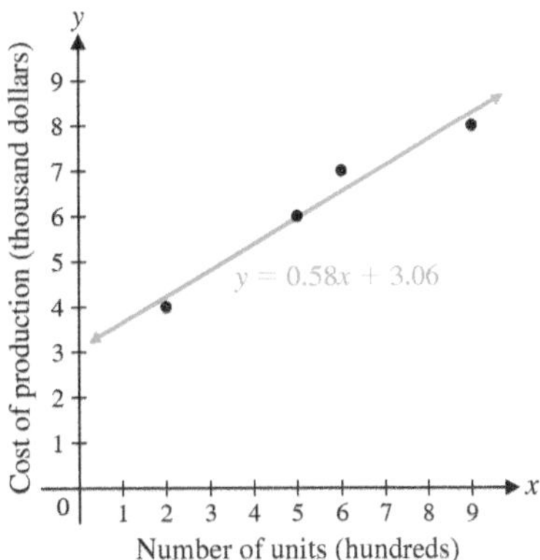

Figure 3

This linear function can now be used by the manufacturer to estimate any of the quantities normally associated with the cost function—such as costs, marginal costs, average costs, and so on. For example, the cost of producing 2,000 units is approximately

$$y = (0.58)(20) + 3.06 = 14.66, \quad \text{or} \quad \$14{,}660$$

The marginal cost function is

$$\frac{dy}{dx} = 0.58$$

The average cost function is

$$\bar{y} = \frac{0.58x + 3.06}{x}$$

In general, if we are given a set of n points $(x_1, y_1), (x_2, y_2), \ldots, (x_n, y_n)$, we want to determine the line $y = ax + b$ for which the sum of the squares of the residuals is minimized. Using summation notation, we find that the sum of the squares of the residuals is given by

$$F(a, b) = \sum_{k=1}^{n} (y_k - ax_k - b)^2$$

Note that in this expression the variables are a and b, and the x_k and y_k are all known values. To minimize $F(a, b)$, we thus compute the partial derivatives with respect to a and b and set them equal to 0:

$$F_a(a, b) = \sum_{k=1}^{n} 2(y_k - ax_k - b)(-x_k) = 0$$

$$F_b(a, b) = \sum_{k=1}^{n} 2(y_k - ax_k - b)(-1) = 0$$

Dividing each equation by 2 and simplifying, we see that the coefficients a and b of the least squares line $y = ax + b$ must satisfy the following system of *normal equations:*

$$\left(\sum_{k=1}^{n} x_k^2\right)a + \left(\sum_{k=1}^{n} x_k\right)b = \sum_{k=1}^{n} x_k y_k$$

$$\left(\sum_{k=1}^{n} x_k\right)a + nb = \sum_{k=1}^{n} y_k$$

Solving this system for a and b produces the formulas given in Theorem 1.

THEOREM 1 Least Squares Approximation

For a set of n points $(x_1, y_1), (x_2, y_2), \ldots, (x_n, y_n)$, the coefficients of the least squares line $y = ax + b$ are the solutions of the system of **normal equations**

$$\left(\sum_{k=1}^{n} x_k^2\right)a + \left(\sum_{k=1}^{n} x_k\right)b = \sum_{k=1}^{n} x_k y_k \tag{1}$$

$$\left(\sum_{k=1}^{n} x_k\right)a + nb = \sum_{k=1}^{n} y_k$$

and are given by the formulas

$$a = \frac{n\left(\sum_{k=1}^{n} x_k y_k\right) - \left(\sum_{k=1}^{n} x_k\right)\left(\sum_{k=1}^{n} y_k\right)}{n\left(\sum_{k=1}^{n} x_k^2\right) - \left(\sum_{k=1}^{n} x_k\right)^2} \tag{2}$$

$$b = \frac{\sum_{k=1}^{n} y_k - a\left(\sum_{k=1}^{n} x_k\right)}{n} \tag{3}$$

Now we return to the data in Table 1 and tabulate the sums required for the normal equations and their solution in Table 3.

Table 3

	x_k	y_k	$x_k y_k$	x_k^2
	2	4	8	4
	5	6	30	25
	6	7	42	36
	9	8	72	81
Totals	22	25	152	146

The normal equations (1) are then

$$146a + 22b = 152$$
$$22a + 4b = 25$$

The solution of the normal equations given by equations (2) and (3) is

$$a = \frac{4(152) - (22)(25)}{4(146) - (22)^2} = 0.58$$

$$b = \frac{25 - 0.58(22)}{4} = 3.06$$

Compare these results with step 1 on page 560. Note that Table 3 provides a convenient format for the computation of step 1.

Many graphing calculators have a linear regression feature that solves the system of normal equations obtained by setting the partial derivatives of the sum of squares of the residuals equal to 0. Therefore, in practice, we simply enter the given data points and use the linear regression feature to determine the line $y = ax + b$ that best fits the data (see Fig. 4). There is no need to compute partial derivatives or even to tabulate sums (as in Table 3).

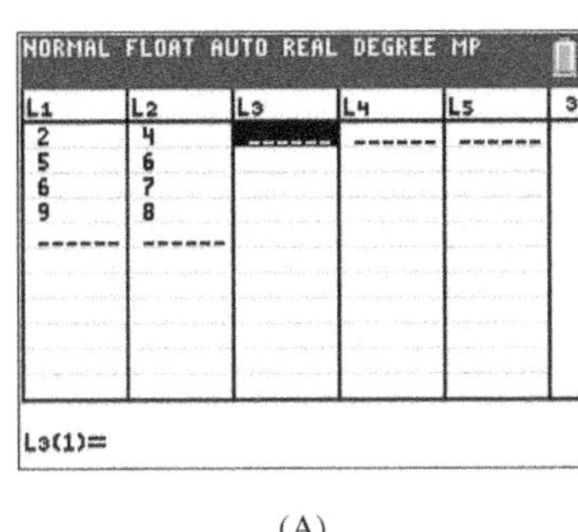

(A)

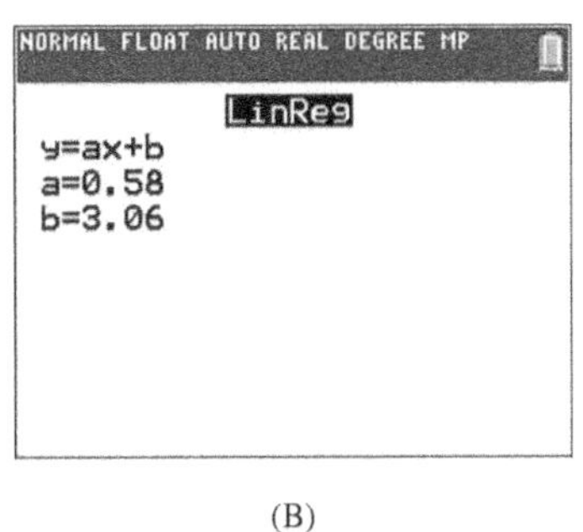

(B)

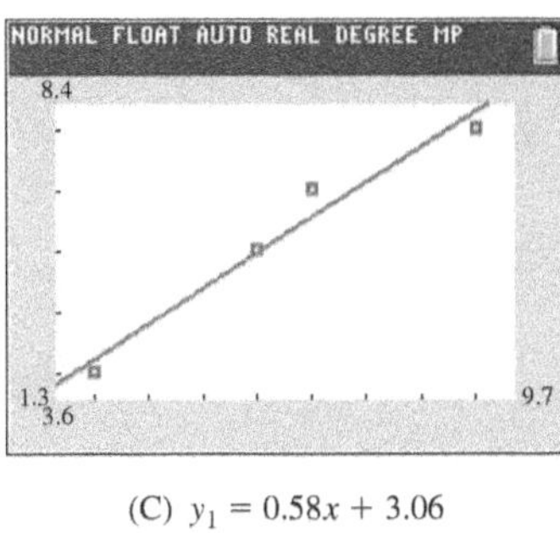

(C) $y_1 = 0.58x + 3.06$

Figure 4

Explore and Discuss 1

(A) Plot the four points (0, 0), (0, 1), (10, 0), and (10, 1). Which line would you guess "best" fits these four points? Use formulas (2) and (3) to test your conjecture.

(B) Plot the four points (0, 0), (0, 10), (1, 0) and (1, 10). Which line would you guess "best" fits these four points? Use formulas (2) and (3) to test your conjecture.

(C) If either of your conjectures was wrong, explain how your reasoning was mistaken.

CONCEPTUAL INSIGHT

Formula (2) for a is undefined if the denominator equals 0. When can this happen? Suppose $n = 3$. Then

$$\begin{aligned}
n\left(\sum_{k=1}^{n} x_k^2\right) - \left(\sum_{k=1}^{n} x_k\right)^2 \\
&= 3(x_1^2 + x_2^2 + x_3^2) - (x_1 + x_2 + x_3)^2 \\
&= 3(x_1^2 + x_2^2 + x_3^2) - (x_1^2 + x_2^2 + x_3^2 + 2x_1x_2 + 2x_1x_3 + 2x_2x_3) \\
&= 2(x_1^2 + x_2^2 + x_3^2) - (2x_1x_2 + 2x_1x_3 + 2x_2x_3) \\
&= (x_1^2 + x_2^2) + (x_1^2 + x_3^2) + (x_2^2 + x_3^2) - (2x_1x_2 + 2x_1x_3 + 2x_2x_3) \\
&= (x_1^2 - 2x_1x_2 + x_2^2) + (x_1^2 - 2x_1x_3 + x_3^2) + (x_2^2 - 2x_2x_3 + x_3^2) \\
&= (x_1 - x_2)^2 + (x_1 - x_3)^2 + (x_2 - x_3)^2
\end{aligned}$$

and the last expression is equal to 0 if and only if $x_1 = x_2 = x_3$ (i.e., if and only if the three points all lie on the same vertical line). A similar algebraic manipulation works for any integer $n > 1$, showing that, in formula (2) for a, the denominator equals 0 if and only if all n points lie on the same vertical line.

The method of least squares can also be applied to find the quadratic equation $y = ax^2 + bx + c$ that best fits a set of data points. In this case, the sum of the squares of the residuals is a function of three variables:

$$F(a, b, c) = \sum_{k=1}^{n} (y_k - ax_k^2 - bx_k - c)^2$$

There are now three partial derivatives to compute and set equal to 0:

$$F_a(a, b, c) = \sum_{k=1}^{n} 2(y_k - ax_k^2 - bx_k - c)(-x_k^2) = 0$$

$$F_b(a, b, c) = \sum_{k=1}^{n} 2(y_k - ax_k^2 - bx_k - c)(-x_k) = 0$$

$$F_c(a, b, c) = \sum_{k=1}^{n} 2(y_k - ax_k^2 - bx_k - c)(-1) = 0$$

The resulting set of three linear equations in the three variables a, b, and c is called the *set of normal equations for quadratic regression.*

A quadratic regression feature on a calculator is designed to solve such normal equations after the given set of points has been entered. Figure 5 illustrates the computation for the data of Table 1.

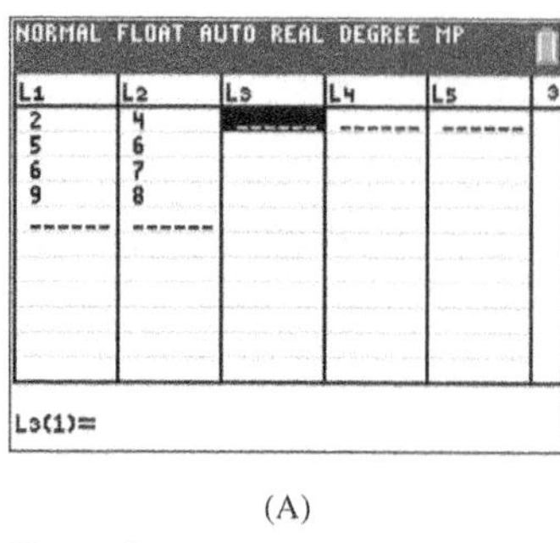

(A)

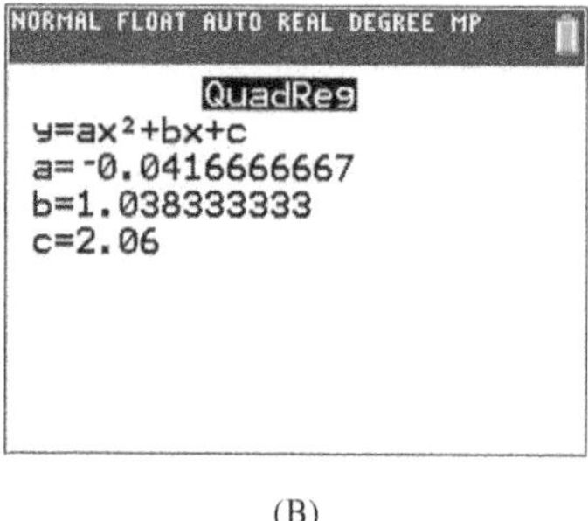

(B)

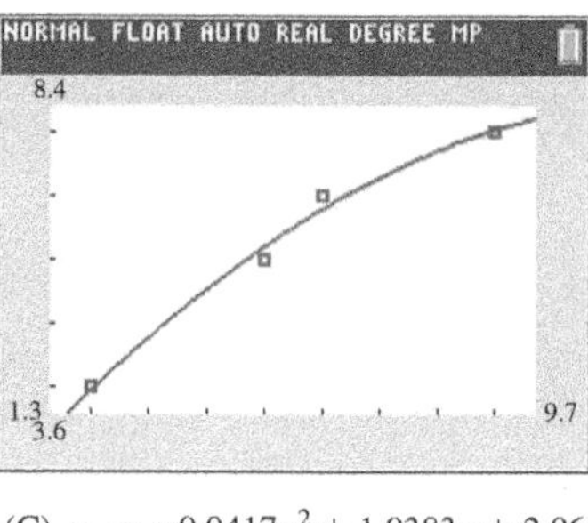

(C) $y_1 = -0.0417x^2 + 1.0383x + 2.06$

Figure 5

Explore and Discuss 2

(A) Use the graphs in Figures 4 and 5 to predict which technique, linear regression or quadratic regression, yields the smaller sum of squares of the residuals for the data of Table 1. Explain.

(B) Confirm your prediction by computing the sum of squares of the residuals in each case.

The method of least squares can also be applied to other regression equations—for example, cubic, quartic, logarithmic, exponential, and power regression models. Details are explored in some of the exercises at the end of this section.

Applications

EXAMPLE 1 **Exam Scores** Table 4 lists the midterm and final examination scores of 10 students in a calculus course.

Table 4

Midterm	Final	Midterm	Final
49	61	78	77
53	47	83	81
67	72	85	79
71	76	91	93
74	68	99	99

(A) Use formulas (1), (2), and (3) to find the normal equations and the least squares line for the data given in Table 4.

(B) Use the linear regression feature on a graphing calculator to find and graph the least squares line.

(C) Use the least squares line to predict the final examination score of a student who scored 95 on the midterm examination.

SOLUTION

(A) Table 5 shows a convenient way to compute all the sums in the formulas for a and b.

Table 5

	x_k	y_k	$x_k y_k$	x_k^2
	49	61	2,989	2,401
	53	47	2,491	2,809
	67	72	4,824	4,489
	71	76	5,396	5,041
	74	68	5,032	5,476
	78	77	6,006	6,084
	83	81	6,723	6,889
	85	79	6,715	7,225
	91	93	8,463	8,281
	99	99	9,801	9,801
Totals	750	753	58,440	58,496

From the last line in Table 5, we have

$$\sum_{k=1}^{10} x_k = 750 \qquad \sum_{k=1}^{10} y_k = 753 \qquad \sum_{k=1}^{10} x_k y_k = 58{,}440 \qquad \sum_{k=1}^{10} x_k^2 = 58{,}496$$

and the normal equations are

$$\begin{aligned} 58{,}496a + 750b &= 58{,}440 \\ 750a + \quad 10b &= 753 \end{aligned}$$

Using formulas (2) and (3), we obtain

$$a = \frac{10(58{,}440) - (750)(753)}{10(58{,}496) - (750)^2} = \frac{19{,}650}{22{,}460} \approx 0.875$$

$$b = \frac{753 - 0.875(750)}{10} = 9.675$$

The least squares line is given (approximately) by

$$y = 0.875x + 9.675$$

(B) We enter the data and use the linear regression feature, as shown in Figure 6. [The discrepancy between values of a and b in the preceding calculations and those in Figure 6B is due to rounding in part (A).]

NORMAL FLOAT AUTO REAL DEGREE MP

L1	L2	L3	L4	L5
49	61			
53	47			
67	72			
71	76			
74	68			
78	77			
83	81			
85	79			
91	93			
99	99			

L3(1)=

(A)

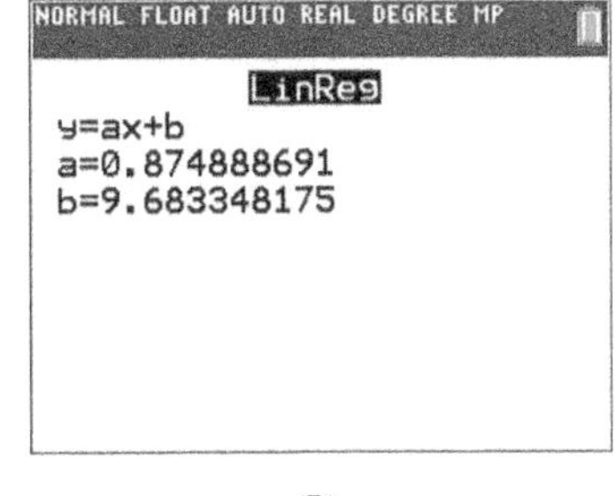

(B)

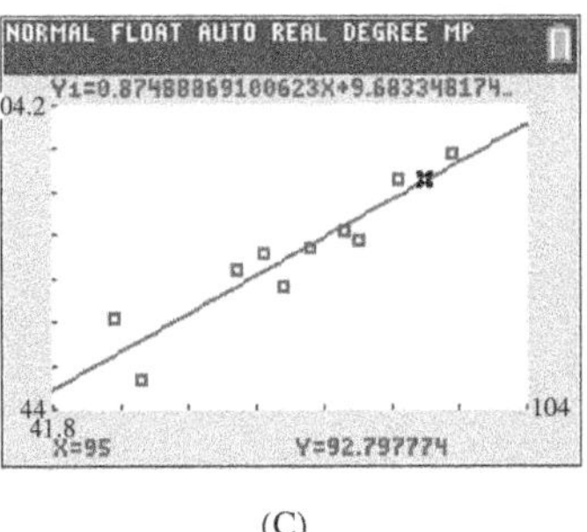

(C)

Figure 6

(C) If $x = 95$, then $y = 0.875(95) + 9.675 \approx 92.8$ is the predicted score on the final exam. This is also indicated in Figure 6C. If we assume that the exam score must be an integer, then we would predict a score of 93.

Matched Problem 1 Repeat Example 1 for the scores listed in Table 6.

Table 6

Midterm	Final	Midterm	Final
54	50	84	80
60	66	88	95
75	80	89	85
76	68	97	94
78	71	99	86

EXAMPLE 2 **Energy Consumption** The use of fuel oil for home heating in the United States has declined steadily for several decades. Table 7 lists the percentage of occupied housing units in the United States that were heated by fuel oil for various years between 1960 and 2015. Use the data in the table and linear regression to estimate the percentage of occupied housing units in the United States that were heated by fuel oil in the year 1995.

Table 7 Occupied Housing Units Heated by Fuel Oil

Year	Percent	Year	Percent
1960	32.4	1999	9.8
1970	26.0	2009	7.3
1979	19.5	2015	5.1
1989	13.3		

Source: U.S. Census Bureau

SOLUTION We enter the data, with $x = 0$ representing 1960, $x = 10$ representing 1970, and so on, and use linear regression as shown in Figure 7.

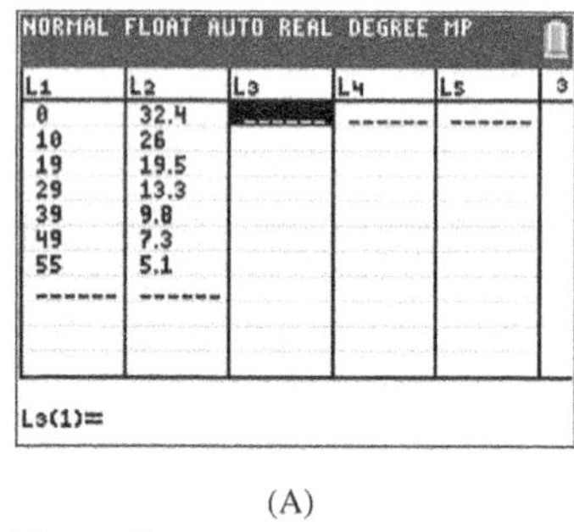

(A)

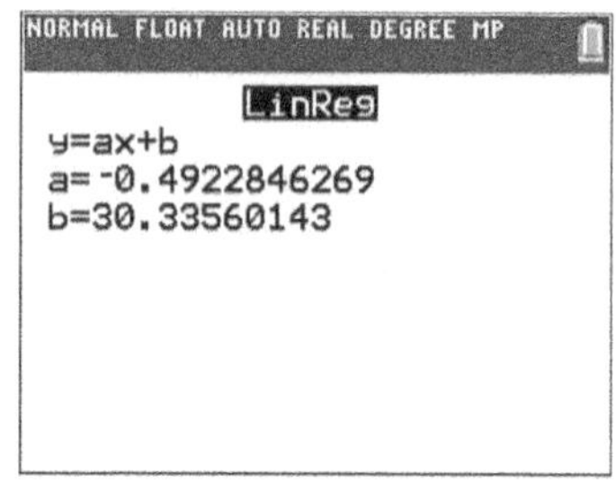

(B)

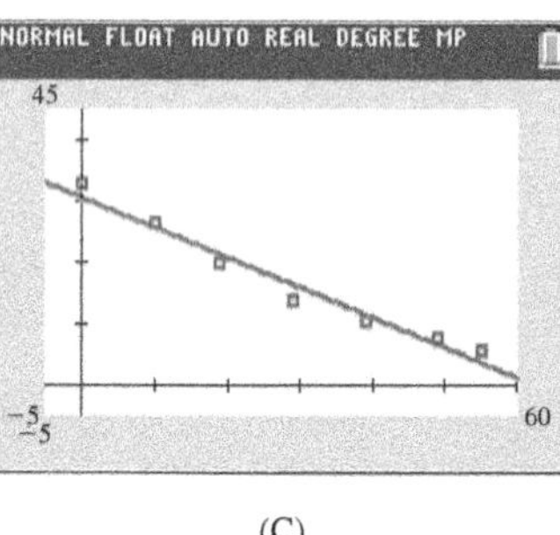

(C)

Figure 7

Figure 7 indicates that the least squares line is $y = -0.492x + 30.34$. To estimate the percentage of occupied housing units heated by fuel oil in the year 1995 (corresponding to $x = 35$), we substitute $x = 35$ in the equation of the least squares line: $-0.492(35) + 30.34 = 13.12$. The estimated percentage for 1995 is 13.12%.

Matched Problem 2 In 1950, coal was still a major source of fuel for home energy consumption, and the percentage of occupied housing units heated by fuel oil was only 22.1%. Add the data for 1950 to the data for Example 2, and compute the new least squares line and the new estimate for the percentage of occupied housing units heated by fuel oil in the year 1995. Discuss the discrepancy between the two estimates. (As in Example 2, let $x = 0$ represent 1960.)

Exercises 9.5

Skills Warm-up Exercises

W *Problems 1–6 refer to the $n = 5$ data points $(x_1, y_1) = (0, 4)$, $(x_2, y_2) = (1, 5)$, $(x_3, y_3) = (2, 7)$, $(x_4, y_4) = (3, 9)$, and $(x_5, y_5) = (4, 13)$. Calculate the indicated sum or product of sums. (If necessary, review Appendix C.1.)*

1. $\sum_{k=1}^{5} x_k$ **2.** $\sum_{k=1}^{5} y_k$ **3.** $\sum_{k=1}^{5} x_k y_k$

4. $\sum_{k=1}^{5} x_k^2$ **5.** $\sum_{k=1}^{5} x_k \sum_{k=1}^{5} y_k$ **6.** $\left(\sum_{k=1}^{5} x_k\right)^2$

A *In Problems 7–12, find the least squares line. Graph the data and the least squares line.*

7.

x	y
1	1
2	3
3	4
4	3

8.

x	y
1	−2
2	−1
3	3
4	5

9.

x	y
1	8
2	5
3	4
4	0

10.

x	y
1	20
2	14
3	11
4	3

11.

x	y
1	3
2	4
3	5
4	6

12.

x	y
1	2
2	3
3	3
4	2

B *In Problems 13–20, find the least squares line and use it to estimate y for the indicated value of x. Round answers to two decimal places.*

13.

x	y
1	3
2	1
2	2
3	0

Estimate y when $x = 2.5$.

14.

x	y
1	0
3	1
3	6
3	4

Estimate y when $x = 3$.

15.

x	y
0	10
5	22
10	31
15	46
20	51

Estimate y when $x = 25$.

16.

x	y
−5	60
0	50
5	30
10	20
15	15

Estimate y when $x = 20$.

17.

x	y
−1	14
1	12
3	8
5	6
7	5

Estimate y when $x = 2$.

18.

x	y
2	−4
6	0
10	8
14	12
18	14

Estimate y when $x = 15$.

19.

x	y	x	y
0.5	25	9.5	12
2	22	11	11
3.5	21	12.5	8
5	21	14	5
6.5	18	15.5	1

Estimate y when $x = 8$.

20.

x	y	x	y
0	−15	12	11
2	−9	14	13
4	−7	16	19
6	−7	18	25
8	−1	20	33

Estimate y when $x = 10$.

C **21.** To find the coefficients of the parabola

$$y = ax^2 + bx + c$$

that is the "best" fit to the points (1, 2), (2, 1), (3, 1), and (4, 3), minimize the sum of the squares of the residuals

$$\begin{aligned} F(a, b, c) &= (a + b + c - 2)^2 \\ &+ (4a + 2b + c - 1)^2 \\ &+ (9a + 3b + c - 1)^2 \\ &+ (16a + 4b + c - 3)^2 \end{aligned}$$

by solving the system of normal equations

$$F_a(a, b, c) = 0 \quad F_b(a, b, c) = 0 \quad F_c(a, b, c) = 0$$

for a, b, and c. Graph the points and the parabola.

22. Repeat Problem 21 for the points $(-1, -2)$, (0, 1), (1, 2), and (2, 0).

Problems 23 and 24 refer to the system of normal equations and the formulas for a and b given on page 562.

23. Verify formulas (2) and (3) by solving the system of normal equations (1) for a and b.

24. If $\bar{x} = \frac{1}{n}\sum_{k=1}^{n} x_k$ and $\bar{y} = \frac{1}{n}\sum_{k=1}^{n} y_k$ are the averages of the x and y coordinates, respectively, show that the point $(\bar{x}, \bar{y})$ satisfies the equation of the least squares line, $y = ax + b$.

25. (A) Suppose that $n = 5$ and the x coordinates of the data points $(x_1, y_1), (x_2, y_2), \ldots, (x_n, y_n)$ are $-2, -1, 0, 1, 2$. Show that system (1) in the text implies that

$$a = \frac{\sum x_k y_k}{\sum x_k^2}$$

and that b is equal to the average of the values of y_k.

(B) Show that the conclusion of part (A) holds whenever the average of the x coordinates of the data points is 0.

26. (A) Give an example of a set of six data points such that half of the points lie above the least squares line and half lie below.

(B) Give an example of a set of six data points such that just one of the points lies above the least squares line and five lie below.

27. (A) Find the linear and quadratic functions that best fit the data points (0, 1.3), (1, 0.6), (2, 1.5), (3, 3.6), and (4, 7.4). Round coefficients to two decimal places.

(B) Which of the two functions best fits the data? Explain.

28. (A) Find the linear, quadratic, and logarithmic functions that best fit the data points (1, 3.2), (2, 4.2), (3, 4.7), (4, 5.0), and (5, 5.3). (Round coefficients to two decimal places.)

(B) Which of the three functions best fits the data? Explain.

29. Describe the normal equations for cubic regression. How many equations are there? What are the variables? What techniques could be used to solve the equations?

30. Describe the normal equations for quartic regression. How many equations are there? What are the variables? What techniques could be used to solve the equations?

Applications

31. Crime rate. Data on U.S. property crimes (in number of crimes per 100,000 population) are given in the table for the years 2001 through 2015.

U.S. Property Crime Rates

Year	Rate
2001	3,658
2003	3,591
2005	3,431
2007	3,276
2009	3,041
2011	2,905
2013	2,734
2015	2,487

Source: FBI

(A) Find the least squares line for the data, using $x = 0$ for 2000.

(B) Use the least squares line to predict the property crime rate in 2025.

32. U.S. honey production. Data for U.S. honey production are given in the table for the years 1990 through 2015.

U.S. Honey Production

Year	Millions of Pounds
1990	197.8
1995	211.1
2000	220.3
2005	174.8
2010	176.5
2015	154.5

Source: USDA

(A) Find the least squares line for the data, using $x = 0$ for 1990.

(B) Use the least squares line to predict U.S. honey production in 2030.

33. Maximizing profit. The market research department for a drugstore chain chose two summer resort areas to test-market a new sunscreen lotion packaged in 4-ounce plastic bottles. After a summer of varying the selling price and recording the monthly demand, the research department arrived at the following demand table, where y is the number of bottles purchased per month (in thousands) at x dollars per bottle:

x	y
5.0	2.0
5.5	1.8
6.0	1.4
6.5	1.2
7.0	1.1

(A) Use the method of least squares to find a demand equation.

(B) If each bottle of sunscreen costs the drugstore chain \$4, how should the sunscreen be priced to achieve a maximum monthly profit? [*Hint:* Use the result of part (A), with $C = 4y$, $R = xy$, and $P = R - C$.]

34. Maximizing profit. A market research consultant for a supermarket chain chose a large city to test-market a new brand of mixed nuts packaged in 8-ounce cans. After a year of varying the selling price and recording the monthly demand, the consultant arrived at the following demand table, where y is the number of cans purchased per month (in thousands) at x dollars per can:

x	y
4.0	4.2
4.5	3.5
5.0	2.7
5.5	1.5
6.0	0.7

(A) Use the method of least squares to find a demand equation.

(B) If each can of nuts costs the supermarket chain $3, how should the nuts be priced to achieve a maximum monthly profit?

35. Olympic Games. The table gives the winning heights in the pole vault in the Olympic Games from 1980 to 2016.

Olympic Pole Vault Winning Height

Year	Height (ft)
1980	18.96
1984	18.85
1988	19.35
1992	19.02
1996	19.42
2000	19.35
2004	19.52
2008	19.56
2012	19.59
2016	19.78

Source: www.olympic.org

(A) Use a graphing calculator to find the least squares line for the data, letting $x = 0$ for 1980.

(B) Estimate the winning height in the pole vault in the Olympic Games of 2024.

36. Biology. In biology, there is an approximate rule, called the *bioclimatic rule for temperate climates*. This rule states that in spring and early summer, periodic phenomena such as the blossoming of flowers, the appearance of insects, and the ripening of fruit usually come about 4 days later for each 500 feet of altitude. Stated as a formula, the rule becomes

$$d = 8h \qquad 0 \le h \le 4$$

where d is the change in days and h is the altitude (in thousands of feet). To test this rule, an experiment was set up to record the difference in blossoming times of the same type of apple tree at different altitudes. A summary of the results is given in the following table:

h	d
0	0
1	7
2	18
3	28
4	33

(A) Use the method of least squares to find a linear equation relating h and d. Does the bioclimatic rule $d = 8h$ appear to be approximately correct?

(B) How much longer will it take this type of apple tree to blossom at 3.5 thousand feet than at sea level? [Use the linear equation found in part (A).]

37. Global warming. The global land–ocean temperature index, which measures the change in global surface temperature (in °C) relative to 1951–1980 average temperatures, is given in the table for the years 1955 through 2015.

Global Land–Ocean Temperature Index

Year	°C
1955	−0.14
1965	−0.10
1975	−0.01
1985	0.12
1995	0.46
2005	0.69
2015	0.87

Source: NASA/GISS

(A) Find the least-squares line for the data using $x = 0$ for 1950.

(B) Use the least-squares line to estimate the global land–ocean temperature index in 2030.

38. Organic food sales. Data on U.S. organic food sales (in billions of dollars) are given in the table for the years 2005 through 2015.

U.S. Organic Food Sales

Year	Billions of Dollars
2005	13.3
2007	18.2
2009	22.5
2011	26.3
2013	32.3
2015	39.7

Source: Organic Trade Association

(A) Find the least-squares line for the data using $x = 0$ for 2000.

(B) Use the least-squares line to estimate U.S. organic food sales in 2025.

Answers to Matched Problems

1. (A) $y = 0.85x + 9.47$

(B)

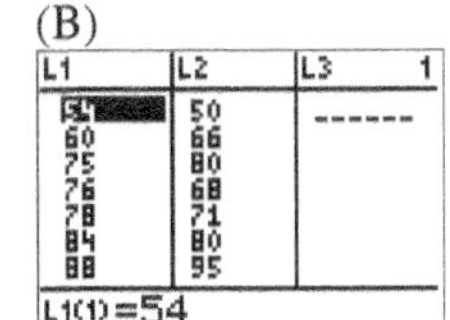

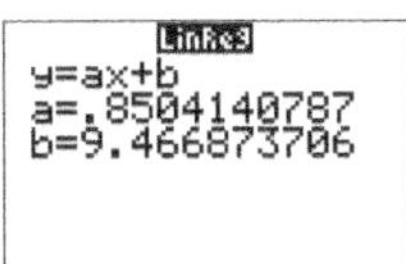

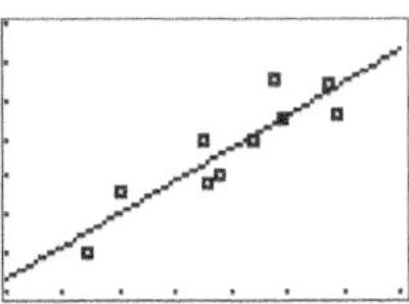

(C) 90.3

2. $y = -0.375x + 25.88$; 12.76%

9.6 Double Integrals over Rectangular Regions

- Introduction
- Definition of the Double Integral
- Average Value over Rectangular Regions
- Volume and Double Integrals

Introduction

We have generalized the concept of differentiation to functions with two or more independent variables. How can we do the same with integration, and how can we interpret the results? Let's look first at the operation of antidifferentiation. We can antidifferentiate a function of two or more variables with respect to one of the variables by treating all the other variables as though they were constants. Thus, this operation is the reverse operation of partial differentiation, just as ordinary antidifferentiation is the reverse operation of ordinary differentiation. We write $\int f(x, y)\,dx$ to indicate that we are to antidifferentiate $f(x, y)$ with respect to x, holding y fixed; we write $\int f(x, y)\,dy$ to indicate that we are to antidifferentiate $f(x, y)$ with respect to y, holding x fixed.

EXAMPLE 1 **Partial Antidifferentiation** Evaluate

(A) $\int (6xy^2 + 3x^2)\,dy$ (B) $\int (6xy^2 + 3x^2)\,dx$

SOLUTION

(A) Treating x as a constant and using the properties of antidifferentiation, we have

$$\int (6xy^2 + 3x^2)\,dy = \int 6xy^2\,dy + \int 3x^2\,dy$$

The dy tells us that we are looking for the antiderivative of $6xy^2 + 3x^2$ with respect to y only, holding x constant.

$$= 6x\int y^2\,dy + 3x^2\int dy$$

$$= 6x\left(\frac{y^3}{3}\right) + 3x^2(y) + C(x)$$

$$= 2xy^3 + 3x^2y + C(x)$$

Note that the constant of integration can be *any function of x alone* since for any such function,

$$\frac{\partial}{\partial y}C(x) = 0$$

CHECK

We can verify that our answer is correct by using partial differentiation:

$$\frac{\partial}{\partial y}[2xy^3 + 3x^2y + C(x)] = 6xy^2 + 3x^2 + 0$$

$$= 6xy^2 + 3x^2$$

(B) We treat y as a constant:

$$\int (6xy^2 + 3x^2)\,dx = \int 6xy^2\,dx + \int 3x^2\,dx$$

$$= 6y^2\int x\,dx + 3\int x^2\,dx$$

$$= 6y^2\left(\frac{x^2}{2}\right) + 3\left(\frac{x^3}{3}\right) + E(y)$$

$$= 3x^2y^2 + x^3 + E(y)$$

The antiderivative contains an arbitrary function $E(y)$ of y alone.

CHECK

$$\frac{\partial}{\partial x}[3x^2y^2 + x^3 + E(y)] = 6xy^2 + 3x^2 + 0$$
$$= 6xy^2 + 3x^2$$

Matched Problem 1 Evaluate

(A) $\int (4xy + 12x^2y^3)\, dy$ (B) $\int (4xy + 12x^2y^3)\, dx$

Now that we have extended the concept of antidifferentiation to functions with two variables, we also can evaluate definite integrals of the form

$$\int_a^b f(x, y)\, dx \quad \text{or} \quad \int_c^d f(x, y)\, dy$$

EXAMPLE 2 **Evaluating a Partial Antiderivative** Evaluate, substituting the limits of integration in y if dy is used and in x if dx is used:

(A) $\int_0^2 (6xy^2 + 3x^2)\, dy$ (B) $\int_0^1 (6xy^2 + 3x^2)\, dx$

SOLUTION

(A) From Example 1A, we know that

$$\int (6xy^2 + 3x^2)\, dy = 2xy^3 + 3x^2y + C(x)$$

According to properties of the definite integral for a function of one variable, we can use any antiderivative to evaluate the definite integral. Thus, choosing $C(x) = 0$, we have

$$\int_0^2 (6xy^2 + 3x^2)\, dy = (2xy^3 + 3x^2y)\Big|_{y=0}^{y=2}$$
$$= [2x(2)^3 + 3x^2(2)] - [2x(0)^3 + 3x^2(0)]$$
$$= 16x + 6x^2$$

(B) From Example 1B, we know that

$$\int (6xy^2 + 3x^2)\, dx = 3x^2y^2 + x^3 + E(y)$$

Choosing $E(y) = 0$, we have

$$\int_0^1 (6xy^2 + 3x^2)\, dx = (3x^2y^2 + x^3)\Big|_{x=0}^{x=1}$$
$$= [3y^2(1)^2 + (1)^3] - [3y^2(0)^2 + (0)^3]$$
$$= 3y^2 + 1$$

Matched Problem 2 Evaluate

(A) $\int_0^1 (4xy + 12x^2y^3)\, dy$ (B) $\int_0^3 (4xy + 12x^2y^3)\, dx$

Integrating and evaluating a definite integral with integrand $f(x, y)$ with respect to y produces a function of x alone (or a constant). Likewise, integrating and evaluating a definite integral with integrand $f(x, y)$ with respect to x produces a function of y alone (or a constant). Each of these results, involving at most one variable, can now be used as an integrand in a second definite integral.

EXAMPLE 3 **Evaluating Integrals** Evaluate

(A) $\int_0^1 \left[\int_0^2 (6xy^2 + 3x^2)\, dy \right] dx$ (B) $\int_0^2 \left[\int_0^1 (6xy^2 + 3x^2)\, dx \right] dy$

SOLUTION

(A) Example 2A showed that

$$\int_0^2 (6xy^2 + 3x^2)\, dy = 16x + 6x^2$$

Therefore,

$$\begin{aligned}\int_0^1 \left[\int_0^2 (6xy^2 + 3x^2)\, dy \right] dx &= \int_0^1 (16x + 6x^2)\, dx \\ &= (8x^2 + 2x^3)\Big|_{x=0}^{x=1} \\ &= [8(1)^2 + 2(1)^3] - [8(0)^2 + 2(0)^3] = 10\end{aligned}$$

(B) Example 2B showed that

$$\int_0^1 (6xy^2 + 3x^2)\, dx = 3y^2 + 1$$

Therefore,

$$\begin{aligned}\int_0^2 \left[\int_0^1 (6xy^2 + 3x^2)\, dx \right] dy &= \int_0^2 (3y^2 + 1)\, dy \\ &= (y^3 + y)\Big|_{y=0}^{y=2} \\ &= [(2)^3 + 2] - [(0)^3 + 0] = 10\end{aligned}$$

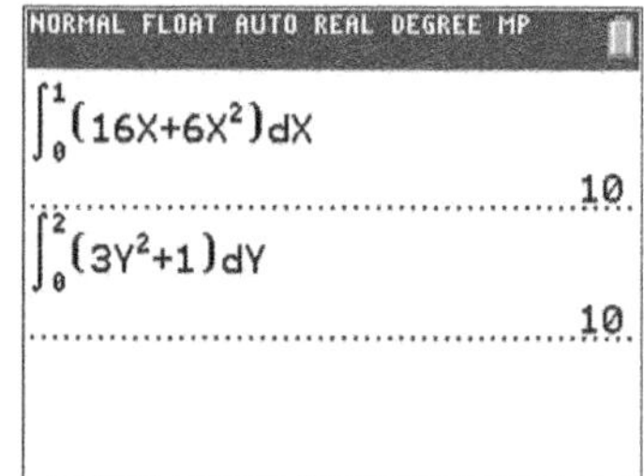

Figure 1

A numerical integration command can be used as an alternative to the fundamental theorem of calculus to evaluate the last integrals in Examples 3A and 3B, $\int_0^1 (16x + 6x^2)\, dx$ and $\int_0^2 (3y^2 + 1)\, dy$, since the integrand in each case is a function of a single variable (see Fig. 1).

Matched Problem 3 Evaluate

(A) $\int_0^3 \left[\int_0^1 (4xy + 12x^2y^3)\, dy \right] dx$ (B) $\int_0^1 \left[\int_0^3 (4xy + 12x^2y^3)\, dx \right] dy$

Definition of the Double Integral

Notice that the answers in Examples 3A and 3B are identical. This is not an accident. In fact, it is this property that enables us to define the *double integral,* as follows:

DEFINITION Double Integral

The **double integral** of a function $f(x, y)$ over a rectangle

$$R = \{(x, y) | a \le x \le b, c \le y \le d\}$$

(see Fig. 2) is

$$\begin{aligned}\iint_R f(x, y)\, dA &= \int_a^b \left[\int_c^d f(x, y)\, dy \right] dx \\ &= \int_c^d \left[\int_a^b f(x, y)\, dx \right] dy\end{aligned}$$

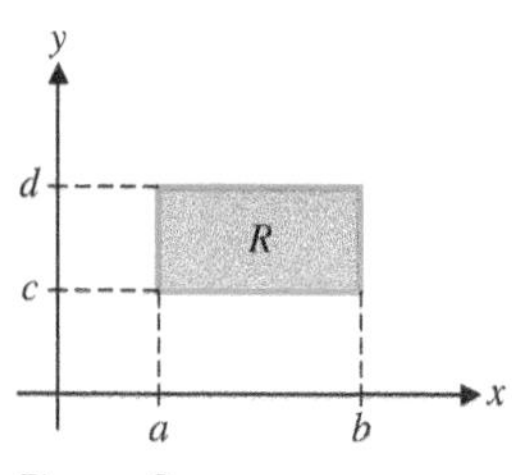

Figure 2

In the double integral $\iint_R f(x, y)\, dA$, $f(x, y)$ is called the **integrand**, and R is called the **region of integration**. The expression dA indicates that this is an integral over a two-dimensional region. The integrals

$$\int_a^b \left[\int_c^d f(x, y)\, dy \right] dx \quad \text{and} \quad \int_c^d \left[\int_a^b f(x, y)\, dx \right] dy$$

are referred to as **iterated integrals** (the brackets are often omitted), and the order in which dx and dy are written indicates the order of integration. This is not the most general definition of the double integral over a rectangular region; however, it is equivalent to the general definition for all the functions we will consider.

EXAMPLE 4 **Evaluating a Double Integral** Evaluate

$$\iint_R (x + y)\, dA \quad \text{over} \quad R = \{(x, y) \mid 1 \le x \le 3, \quad -1 \le y \le 2\}$$

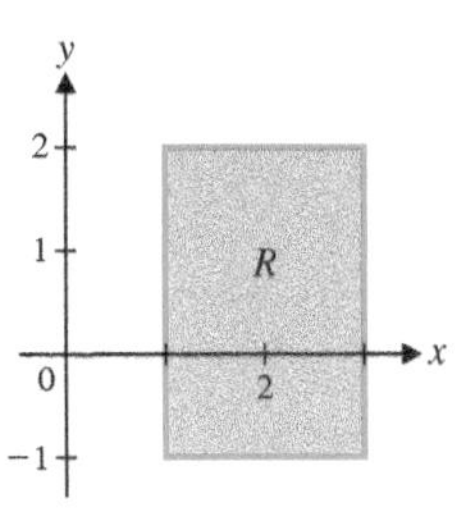

Figure 3

SOLUTION Region R is illustrated in Figure 3. We can choose either order of iteration. As a check, we will evaluate the integral both ways:

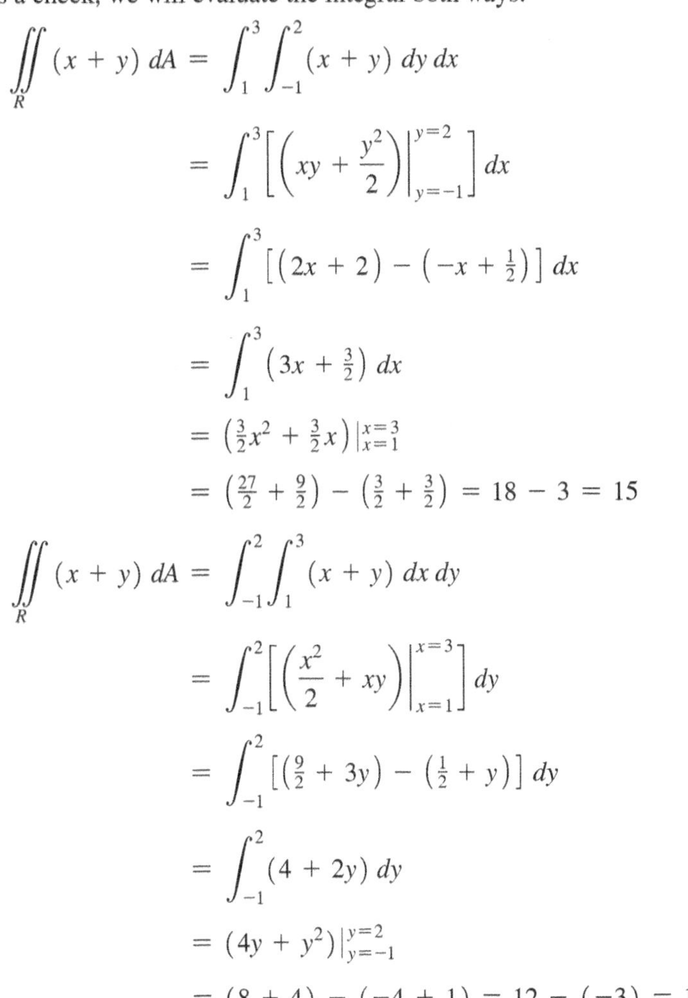

$$\iint_R (x + y)\, dA = \int_1^3 \int_{-1}^2 (x + y)\, dy\, dx$$
$$= \int_1^3 \left[\left(xy + \frac{y^2}{2} \right) \Bigg|_{y=-1}^{y=2} \right] dx$$
$$= \int_1^3 \left[(2x + 2) - \left(-x + \tfrac{1}{2}\right) \right] dx$$
$$= \int_1^3 \left(3x + \tfrac{3}{2} \right) dx$$
$$= \left(\tfrac{3}{2}x^2 + \tfrac{3}{2}x \right) \Big|_{x=1}^{x=3}$$
$$= \left(\tfrac{27}{2} + \tfrac{9}{2} \right) - \left(\tfrac{3}{2} + \tfrac{3}{2} \right) = 18 - 3 = 15$$

$$\iint_R (x + y)\, dA = \int_{-1}^2 \int_1^3 (x + y)\, dx\, dy$$
$$= \int_{-1}^2 \left[\left(\frac{x^2}{2} + xy \right) \Bigg|_{x=1}^{x=3} \right] dy$$
$$= \int_{-1}^2 \left[\left(\tfrac{9}{2} + 3y \right) - \left(\tfrac{1}{2} + y \right) \right] dy$$
$$= \int_{-1}^2 (4 + 2y)\, dy$$
$$= (4y + y^2) \Big|_{y=-1}^{y=2}$$
$$= (8 + 4) - (-4 + 1) = 12 - (-3) = 15$$

Matched Problem 4 Evaluate

$$\iint_R (2x - y)\, dA \quad \text{over} \quad R = \{(x, y) \mid -1 \le x \le 5, \quad 2 \le y \le 4\}$$

both ways.

EXAMPLE 5 **Double Integral of an Exponential Function** Evaluate

$$\iint_R 2xe^{x^2+y}\, dA \qquad \text{over} \qquad R = \{(x, y) \mid 0 \le x \le 1, \quad -1 \le y \le 1\}$$

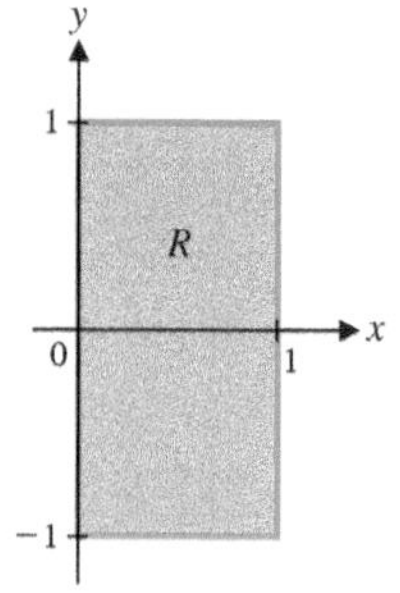

SOLUTION Region R is illustrated in Figure 4.

$$\begin{aligned} \iint_R 2xe^{x^2+y}\, dA &= \int_{-1}^{1}\int_{0}^{1} 2xe^{x^2+y}\, dx\, dy \\ &= \int_{-1}^{1}\left[\left(e^{x^2+y}\right)\Big|_{x=0}^{x=1}\right] dy \\ &= \int_{-1}^{1} (e^{1+y} - e^{y})\, dy \\ &= (e^{1+y} - e^{y})\Big|_{y=-1}^{y=1} \\ &= (e^2 - e) - (e^0 - e^{-1}) \\ &= e^2 - e - 1 + e^{-1} \end{aligned}$$

Figure 4

Matched Problem 5 Evaluate

$$\iint_R \frac{x}{y^2} e^{x/y}\, dA \qquad \text{over} \qquad R = \{(x, y) \mid 0 \le x \le 1, \quad 1 \le y \le 2\}.$$

Average Value over Rectangular Regions

The average value of a function $f(x)$ over an interval $[a, b]$ was defined as

$$\frac{1}{b - a}\int_a^b f(x)\, dx$$

This definition is easily extended to functions of two variables over rectangular regions as follows (notice that the denominator $(b - a)(d - c)$ is simply the area of the rectangle R):

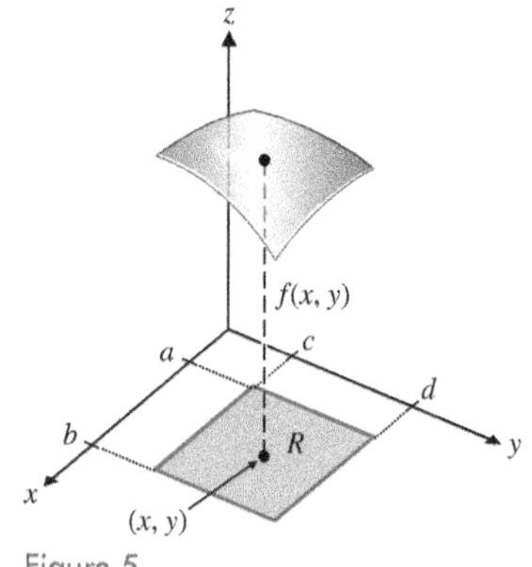

Figure 5

DEFINITION Average Value over Rectangular Regions

The **average value** of the function $f(x, y)$ over the rectangle

$$R = \{(x, y) \mid a \le x \le b, \quad c \le y \le d\}$$

(see Fig. 5) is

$$\frac{1}{(b - a)(d - c)}\iint_R f(x, y)\, dA$$

EXAMPLE 6 **Average Value** Find the average value of $f(x, y) = 4 - \frac{1}{2}x - \frac{1}{2}y$ over the rectangle $R = \{(x, y) \mid 0 \le x \le 2, \quad 0 \le y \le 2\}$.

SOLUTION Region R is illustrated in Figure 6. We have

$$\frac{1}{(b - a)(d - c)}\iint_R f(x, y)\, dA = \frac{1}{(2 - 0)(2 - 0)}\iint_R \left(4 - \frac{1}{2}x - \frac{1}{2}y\right) dA$$

$$= \frac{1}{4}\int_0^2 \int_0^2 \left(4 - \tfrac{1}{2}x - \tfrac{1}{2}y\right) dy\, dx$$

$$= \frac{1}{4}\int_0^2 \left[\left(4y - \tfrac{1}{2}xy - \tfrac{1}{4}y^2\right)\Big|_{y=0}^{y=2}\right] dx$$

$$= \frac{1}{4}\int_0^2 (7 - x)\, dx$$

$$= \tfrac{1}{4}\left(7x - \tfrac{1}{2}x^2\right)\Big|_{x=0}^{x=2}$$

$$= \tfrac{1}{4}(12) = 3$$

Figure 6

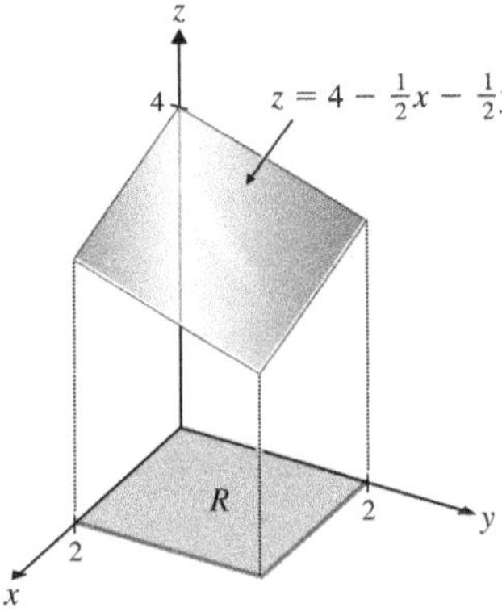

Figure 7

Figure 7 illustrates the surface $z = f(x, y)$, and our calculations show that 3 is the average of the z values over the region R.

Matched Problem 6 Find the average value of $f(x, y) = x + 2y$ over the rectangle $R = \{(x, y) \mid 0 \le x \le 2,\ \ 0 \le y \le 1\}$

Explore and Discuss 1

(A) Which of the functions $f(x, y) = 4 - x^2 - y^2$ and $g(x, y) = 4 - x - y$ would you guess has the greater average value over the rectangle $R = \{(x, y) \mid 0 \le x \le 1,\ \ 0 \le y \le 1\}$? Explain.

(B) Use double integrals to check the correctness of your guess in part (A).

Volume and Double Integrals

One application of the definite integral of a function with one variable is the calculation of areas, so it is not surprising that the definite integral of a function of two variables can be used to calculate volumes of solids.

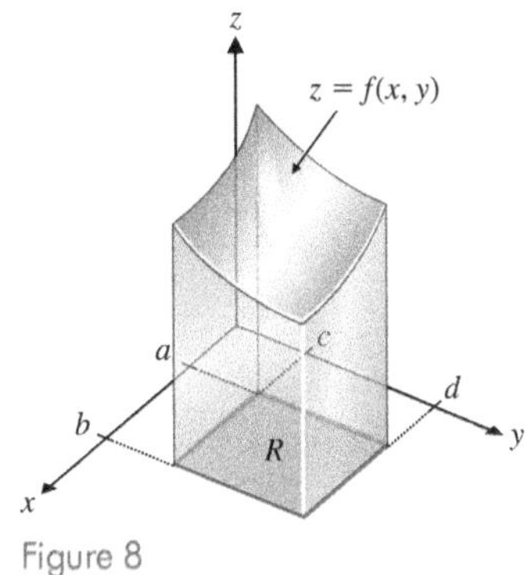

Figure 8

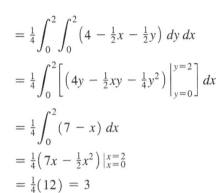

THEOREM 1 Volume under a Surface

If $f(x, y) \ge 0$ over a rectangle $R = \{(x, y) \mid a \le x \le b,\ \ c \le y \le d\}$, then the volume of the solid formed by graphing f over the rectangle R (see Fig. 8) is given by

$$V = \iint_R f(x, y)\, dA$$

EXAMPLE 7 **Volume** Find the volume of the solid under the graph of $f(x, y) = 1 + x^2 + y^2$ over the rectangle $R = \{(x, y) \mid 0 \le x \le 1,\ \ 0 \le y \le 1\}$.

SOLUTION Figure 9 shows the region R, and Figure 10 illustrates the volume under consideration.

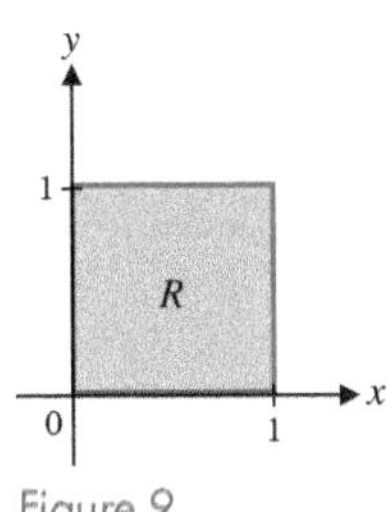

Figure 9

$$V = \iint_R (1 + x^2 + y^2)\, dA$$

$$= \int_0^1 \int_0^1 (1 + x^2 + y^2)\, dx\, dy$$

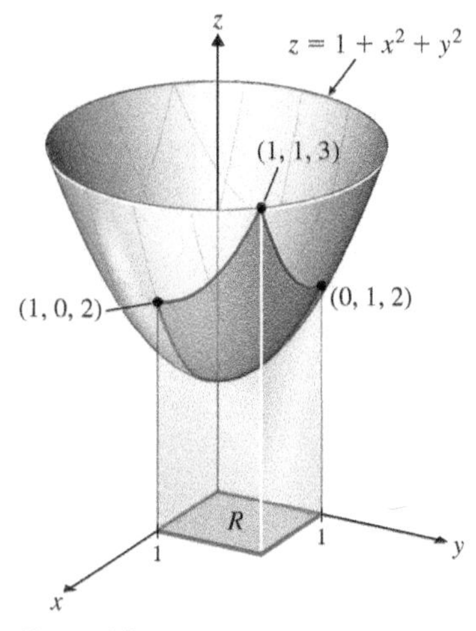

Figure 10

$$= \int_0^1 \left[\left(x + \tfrac{1}{3}x^3 + xy^2 \right) \Big|_{x=0}^{x=1} \right] dy$$

$$= \int_0^1 \left(\tfrac{4}{3} + y^2 \right) dy$$

$$= \left(\tfrac{4}{3}y + \tfrac{1}{3}y^3 \right) \Big|_{y=0}^{y=1} = \tfrac{5}{3} \text{ cubic units}$$

Matched Problem 7 Find the volume of the solid that is under the graph of

$$f(x, y) = 1 + x + y$$

and over the rectangle $R = \{(x, y) \mid 0 \le x \le 1, \quad 0 \le y \le 2\}$.

CONCEPTUAL INSIGHT

Double integrals can be defined over regions that are more general than rectangles. For example, let $R > 0$. Then the function $f(x, y) = \sqrt{R^2 - (x^2 + y^2)}$ can be integrated over the circular region $C = \{(x, y) \mid x^2 + y^2 \le R^2\}$. In fact, it can be shown that

$$\iint_C \sqrt{R^2 - (x^2 + y^2)}\, dx\, dy = \frac{2\pi R^3}{3}$$

Because $x^2 + y^2 + z^2 = R^2$ is the equation of a sphere of radius R centered at the origin, the double integral over C represents the volume of the upper hemisphere. Therefore, the volume of a sphere of radius R is given by

$$V = \frac{4\pi R^3}{3} \qquad \text{Volume of sphere of radius } R$$

Double integrals can also be used to obtain volume formulas for other geometric figures (see Table 1, Appendix C).

Exercises 9.6

Skills Warm-up Exercises

W *In Problems 1–6, find each antiderivative.*

1. $\int (\pi + x)\, dx$

2. $\int (x\pi^2 + \pi x^2)\, dx$

3. $\int \left(1 + \frac{\pi}{x}\right) dx$

4. $\int \left(1 + \frac{x}{\pi}\right) dx$

5. $\int e^{\pi x} dx$

6. $\int \frac{\ln x}{\pi x} dx$

A *In Problems 7–16, find each antiderivative. Then use the antiderivative to evaluate the definite integral.*

7. (A) $\int 12x^2y^3\, dy$ (B) $\int_0^1 12x^2y^3\, dy$

8. (A) $\int 12x^2y^3\, dx$ (B) $\int_{-1}^2 12x^2y^3\, dx$

9. (A) $\int (4x + 6y + 5)\, dx$ (B) $\int_{-2}^3 (4x + 6y + 5)\, dx$

10. (A) $\int (4x + 6y + 5)\, dy$ (B) $\int_1^4 (4x + 6y + 5)\, dy$

11. (A) $\int \frac{x}{\sqrt{y + x^2}} dx$ (B) $\int_0^2 \frac{x}{\sqrt{y + x^2}} dx$

12. (A) $\int \frac{x}{\sqrt{y + x^2}} dy$ (B) $\int_1^5 \frac{x}{\sqrt{y + x^2}} dy$

13. (A) $\int \frac{\ln x}{xy} dy$ (B) $\int_1^{e^2} \frac{\ln x}{xy} dy$

14. (A) $\int \frac{\ln x}{xy} dx$ (B) $\int_1^e \frac{\ln x}{xy} dx$

15. (A) $\int 3y^2 e^{x+y^3} dx$ (B) $\int_0^1 3y^2 e^{x+y^3} dx$

16. (A) $\int 3y^2e^{x+y^3}\,dy$ (B) $\int_0^2 3y^2e^{x+y^3}\,dy$

B *In Problems 17–26, evaluate each iterated integral. (See the indicated problem for the evaluation of the inner integral.)*

17. $\int_{-1}^{2}\int_0^1 12x^2y^3\,dy\,dx$

(See Problem 7.)

18. $\int_0^1\int_{-1}^{2} 12x^2y^3\,dx\,dy$

(See Problem 8.)

19. $\int_1^4\int_{-2}^{3}(4x + 6y + 5)\,dx\,dy$

(See Problem 9.)

20. $\int_{-2}^{3}\int_1^4(4x + 6y + 5)\,dy\,dx$

(See Problem 10.)

21. $\int_1^5\int_0^2 \frac{x}{\sqrt{y + x^2}}\,dx\,dy$

(See Problem 11.)

22. $\int_0^2\int_1^5 \frac{x}{\sqrt{y + x^2}}\,dy\,dx$

(See Problem 12.)

23. $\int_1^e\int_1^{e^2} \frac{\ln x}{xy}\,dy\,dx$

(See Problem 13.)

24. $\int_1^{e^2}\int_1^{e} \frac{\ln x}{xy}\,dx\,dy$

(See Problem 14.)

25. $\int_0^2\int_0^1 3y^2e^{x+y^3}\,dx\,dy$

(See Problem 15.)

26. $\int_0^1\int_0^2 3y^2e^{x+y^3}\,dy\,dx$

(See Problem 16.)

Use both orders of iteration to evaluate each double integral in Problems 27–30.

27. $\iint_R xy\,dA;\ R = \{(x, y)\,|\,0 \le x \le 2,\ \ 0 \le y \le 4\}$

28. $\iint_R \sqrt{xy}\,dA;\ R = \{(x, y)\,|\,1 \le x \le 4,\ \ 1 \le y \le 9\}$

29. $\iint_R (x + y)^5\,dA;\ R = \{(x, y)\,|\,-1 \le x \le 1,\ \ 1 \le y \le 2\}$

30. $\iint_R xe^y\,dA;\ R = \{(x, y)\,|\,-2 \le x \le 3,\ \ 0 \le y \le 2\}$

In Problems 31–34, find the average value of each function over the given rectangle.

31. $f(x, y) = (x + y)^2;$
$R = \{(x, y)\,|\,1 \le x \le 5,\ \ -1 \le y \le 1\}$

32. $f(x, y) = x^2 + y^2;$
$R = \{(x, y)\,|\,-1 \le x \le 2,\ \ 1 \le y \le 4\}$

33. $f(x, y) = x/y;\ R = \{(x, y)\,|\,1 \le x \le 4,\ \ 2 \le y \le 7\}$

34. $f(x, y) = x^2y^3;\ R = \{(x, y)\,|\,-1 \le x \le 1,\ \ 0 \le y \le 2\}$

In Problems 35–38, find the volume of the solid under the graph of each function over the given rectangle.

35. $f(x, y) = 2 - x^2 - y^2;$
$R = \{(x, y)\,|\,0 \le x \le 1,\ \ 0 \le y \le 1\}$

36. $f(x, y) = 5 - x;\ R = \{(x, y)\,|\,0 \le x \le 5,\ \ 0 \le y \le 5\}$

37. $f(x, y) = 4 - y^2;\ R = \{(x, y)\,|\,0 \le x \le 2,\ \ 0 \le y \le 2\}$

38. $f(x, y) = e^{-x-y};\ R = \{(x, y)\,|\,0 \le x \le 1,\ \ 0 \le y \le 1\}$

C *Evaluate each double integral in Problems 39–42. Select the order of integration carefully; each problem is easy to do one way and difficult the other.*

39. $\iint_R xe^{xy}\,dA;\ R = \{(x, y)\,|\,0 \le x \le 1,\ \ 1 \le y \le 2\}$

40. $\iint_R xye^{x^2y}\,dA;\ R = \{(x, y)\,|\,0 \le x \le 1,\ \ 1 \le y \le 2\}$

41. $\iint_R \frac{2y + 3xy^2}{1 + x^2}\,dA;$
$R = \{(x, y)\,|\,0 \le x \le 1,\ \ -1 \le y \le 1\}$

42. $\iint_R \frac{2x + 2y}{1 + 4y + y^2}\,dA;$
$R = \{(x, y)\,|\,1 \le x \le 3,\ \ 0 \le y \le 1\}$

43. Show that $\int_0^2\int_0^2(1 - y)\,dx\,dy = 0$. Does the double integral represent the volume of a solid? Explain.

44. (A) Find the average values of the functions $f(x, y) = x + y$, $g(x, y) = x^2 + y^2$, and $h(x, y) = x^3 + y^3$ over the rectangle

$$R = \{(x, y)\,|\,0 \le x \le 1,\ \ 0 \le y \le 1\}$$

(B) Does the average value of $k(x, y) = x^n + y^n$ over the rectangle

$$R_1 = \{(x, y)\,|\,0 \le x \le 1,\ \ 0 \le y \le 1\}$$

increase or decrease as n increases? Explain.

(C) Does the average value of $k(x, y) = x^n + y^n$ over the rectangle

$$R_2 = \{(x, y) | 0 \le x \le 2,\ \ 0 \le y \le 2\}$$

increase or decrease as n increases? Explain.

45. Let $f(x, y) = x^3 + y^2 - e^{-x} - 1$.

(A) Find the average value of $f(x, y)$ over the rectangle

$$R = \{(x, y) | -2 \le x \le 2,\quad -2 \le y \le 2\}.$$

(B) Graph the set of all points (x, y) in R for which $f(x, y) = 0$.

(C) For which points (x, y) in R is $f(x, y)$ greater than 0? Less than 0? Explain.

46. Find the dimensions of the square S centered at the origin for which the average value of $f(x, y) = x^2 e^y$ over S is equal to 100.

Applications

47. Multiplier principle. Suppose that Congress enacts a one-time-only 10% tax rebate that is expected to infuse \$$y$ billion, $5 \le y \le 7$, into the economy. If every person and every corporation is expected to spend a proportion x, $0.6 \le x \le 0.8$, of each dollar received, then, by the **multiplier principle** in economics, the total amount of spending S (in billions of dollars) generated by this tax rebate is given by

$$S(x, y) = \frac{y}{1 - x}$$

What is the average total amount of spending for the indicated ranges of the values of x and y? Set up a double integral and evaluate it.

48. Multiplier principle. Repeat Problem 47 if $6 \le y \le 10$ and $0.7 \le x \le 0.9$.

49. Cobb–Douglas production function. If an industry invests x thousand labor-hours, $10 \le x \le 20$, and \$$y$ million, $1 \le y \le 2$, in the production of N thousand units of a certain item, then N is given by

$$N(x, y) = x^{0.75} y^{0.25}$$

What is the average number of units produced for the indicated ranges of x and y? Set up a double integral and evaluate it.

50. Cobb–Douglas production function. Repeat Problem 49 for

$$N(x, y) = x^{0.5} y^{0.5}$$

where $10 \le x \le 30$ and $1 \le y \le 3$.

51. Population distribution. In order to study the population distribution of a certain species of insect, a biologist has constructed an artificial habitat in the shape of a rectangle 16 feet long and 12 feet wide. The only food available to the insects in this habitat is located at its center. The biologist has determined that the concentration C of insects per square foot at a point d units from the food supply (see the figure) is given approximately by

$$C = 10 - \tfrac{1}{10} d^2$$

What is the average concentration of insects throughout the habitat? Express C as a function of x and y, set up a double integral, and evaluate it.

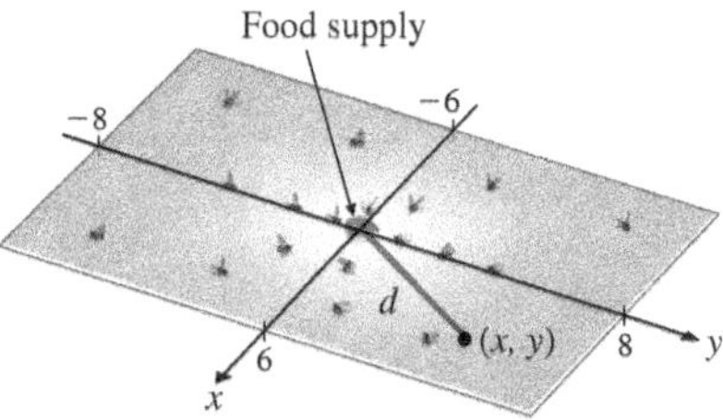

Figure for 51

52. Population distribution. Repeat Problem 51 for a square habitat that measures 12 feet on each side, where the insect concentration is given by

$$C = 8 - \tfrac{1}{10} d^2$$

53. Air quality. A heavy industrial plant located in the center of a small town emits particulate matter into the atmosphere. Suppose that the concentration of fine particulate matter (in micrograms per cubic meter) at a point d miles from the plant (see the figure) is given by

$$C = 50 - 9d^2$$

If the boundaries of the town form a rectangle 4 miles long and 2 miles wide, what is the average concentration of fine particulate matter throughout the town? Express C as a function of x and y, set up a double integral, and evaluate it.

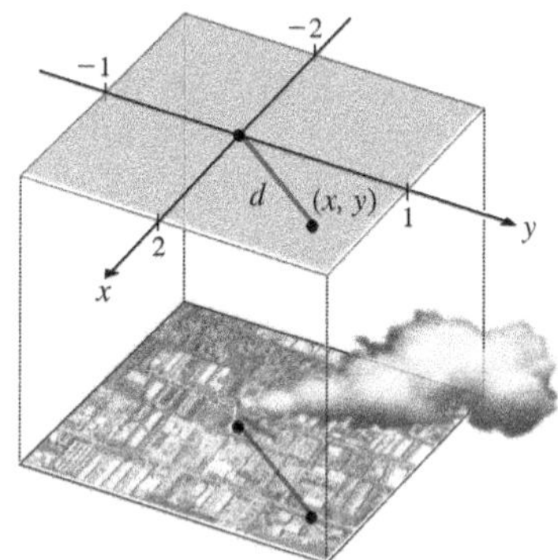

54. Air quality. Repeat Problem 53 if the boundaries of the town form a rectangle 8 miles long and 4 miles wide and the concentration of particulate matter is given by

$$C = 64 - 3d^2$$

55. Safety research. Under ideal conditions, if a person driving a car slams on the brakes and skids to a stop, the length of the skid marks (in feet) is given by the formula

$$L = 0.000\,013\,3xy^2$$

where x is the weight of the car (in pounds) and y is the speed of the car (in miles per hour). What is the average length of the skid marks for cars weighing between 2,000 and 3,000 pounds and traveling at speeds between 50 and 60 miles per hour? Set up a double integral and evaluate it.

56. Safety research. Repeat Problem 55 for cars weighing between 2,000 and 2,500 pounds and traveling at speeds between 40 and 50 miles per hour.

57. Psychology. The intelligence quotient Q for a person with mental age x and chronological age y is given by

$$Q(x, y) = 100\frac{x}{y}$$

In a group of sixth-graders, the mental age varies between 8 and 16 years and the chronological age varies between 10 and 12 years. What is the average intelligence quotient for this group? Set up a double integral and evaluate it.

58. **Psychology.** Repeat Problem 57 for a group with mental ages between 6 and 14 years and chronological ages between 8 and 10 years.

Answers to Matched Problems

1. (A) $2xy^2 + 3x^2y^4 + C(x)$
(B) $2x^2y + 4x^3y^3 + E(y)$
2. (A) $2x + 3x^2$
(B) $18y + 108y^3$
3. (A) 36
(B) 36
4. 12 **5.** $e - 2e^{1/2} + 1$ **6.** 2 **7.** 5 cubic units

9.7 Double Integrals over More General Regions

- Regular Regions
- Double Integrals over Regular Regions
- Reversing the Order of Integration
- Volume and Double Integrals

In this section, we extend the concept of double integration discussed in Section 9.6 to nonrectangular regions. We begin with an example and some new terminology.

Regular Regions

Let R be the region graphed in Figure 1. We can describe R with the following inequalities:

$$R = \{(x, y) \mid x \le y \le 6x - x^2, \quad 0 \le x \le 5\}$$

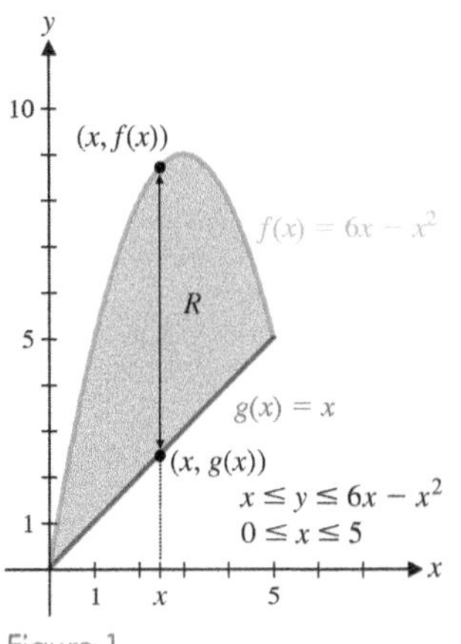

Figure 1

The region R can be viewed as a union of vertical line segments. For each x in the interval $[0, 5]$, the line segment from the point $(x, g(x))$ to the point $(x, f(x))$ lies in the region R. Any region that can be covered by vertical line segments in this manner is called a *regular x region.*

Now consider the region S in Figure 2. It can be described with the following inequalities:

$$S = \{(x, y) \mid y^2 \le x \le y + 2, \quad -1 \le y \le 2\}$$

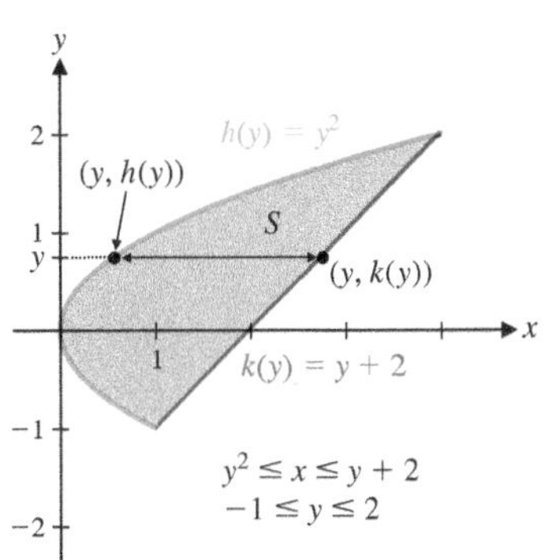

Figure 2

The region S can be viewed as a union of horizontal line segments going from the graph of $h(y) = y^2$ to the graph of $k(y) = y + 2$ on the interval $[-1, 2]$. Regions that can be described in this manner are called *regular y regions.*

In general, *regular regions* are defined as follows:

DEFINITION Regular Regions

A region R in the xy plane is a **regular x region** if there exist functions $f(x)$ and $g(x)$ and numbers a and b such that

$$R = \{(x, y) \mid g(x) \le y \le f(x), \quad a \le x \le b\}$$

A region R in the xy plane is a **regular y region** if there exist functions $h(y)$ and $k(y)$ and numbers c and d such that

$$R = \{(x, y) \mid h(y) \le x \le k(y), \quad c \le y \le d\}$$

See Figure 3 for a geometric interpretation.

CONCEPTUAL INSIGHT

If, for some region R, there is a horizontal line that has a nonempty intersection I with R, and if I is neither a closed interval nor a point, then R is *not* a regular y region. Similarly, if, for some region R, there is a vertical line that has a nonempty intersection I with R, and if I is neither a closed interval nor a point, then R is *not* a regular x region (see Fig. 3).

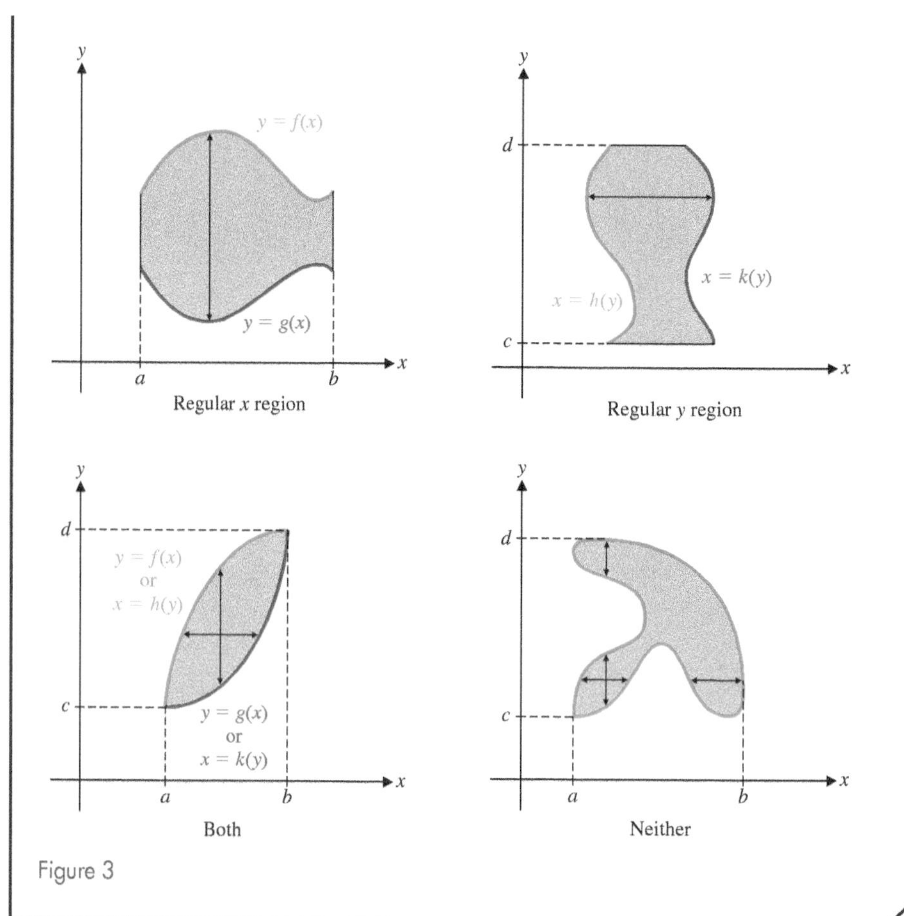

Figure 3

EXAMPLE 1 **Describing a Regular x Region** The region R is bounded by the graphs of $y = 4 - x^2$ and $y = x - 2, x \geq 0$, and the y axis. Graph R and use set notation with double inequalities to describe R as a regular x region.

SOLUTION As Figure 4 indicates, R can be covered by vertical line segments that go from the graph of $y = x - 2$ to the graph of $y = 4 - x^2$. So R is a regular x region. In terms of set notation with double inequalities, we can write

$$R = \{(x, y) \mid x - 2 \leq y \leq 4 - x^2,\ \ 0 \leq x \leq 2\}$$

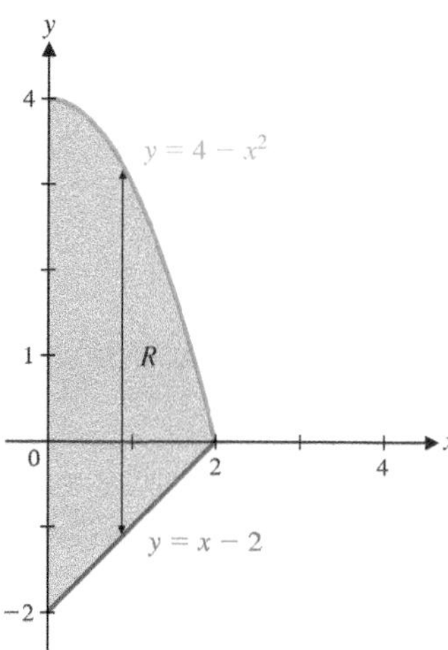

Figure 4

CONCEPTUAL INSIGHT

The region R of Example 1 is also a regular y region, since $R = \{(x, y) \mid 0 \le x \le k(y), -2 \le y \le 4\}$, where

$$k(y) = \begin{cases} 2 + y & \text{if } -2 \le y \le 0 \\ \sqrt{4 - y} & \text{if } 0 \le y \le 4 \end{cases}$$

But because $k(y)$ is piecewise defined, this description is more complicated than the description of R in Example 1 as a regular x region.

Matched Problem 1 Describe the region R bounded by the graphs of $x = 6 - y$ and $x = y^2$, $y \ge 0$, and the x axis as a regular y region (see Fig. 5).

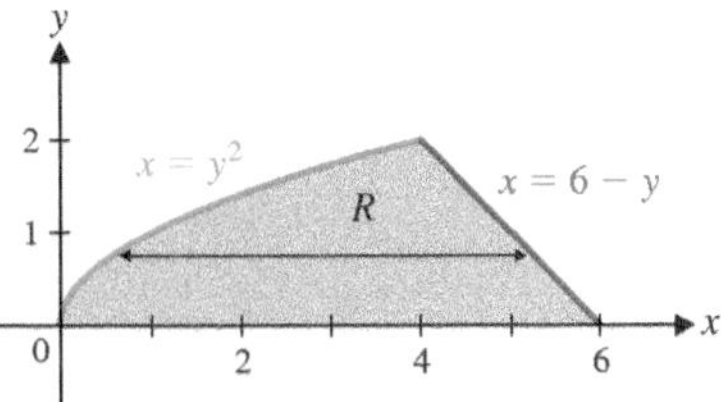

Figure 5

EXAMPLE 2 **Describing Regular Regions** The region R is bounded by the graphs of $x + y^2 = 9$ and $x + 3y = 9$. Graph R and describe R as a regular x region, a regular y region, both, or neither. Represent R in set notation with double inequalities.

SOLUTION We graph R in Figure 6.

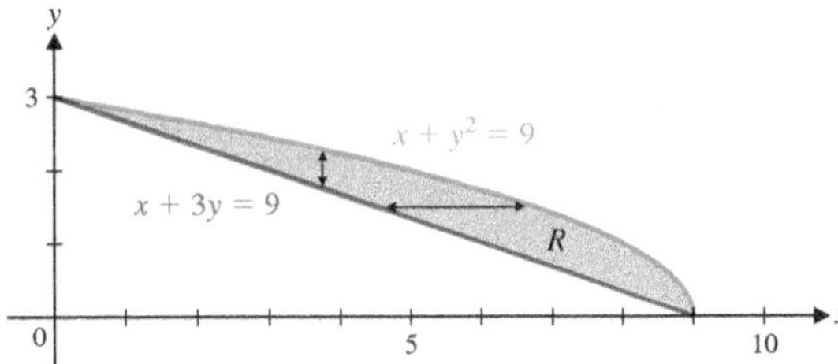

Figure 6

Region R can be covered by vertical line segments that go from the graph of $x + 3y = 9$ to the graph of $x + y^2 = 9$. Thus, R is a regular x region. In order to describe R with inequalities, we must solve each equation for y in terms of x:

$$x + 3y = 9 \qquad x + y^2 = 9$$

$$3y = 9 - x \qquad y^2 = 9 - x$$

$$y = 3 - \tfrac{1}{3}x \qquad y = \sqrt{9 - x}$$

We use the positive square root, since the graph is in the first quadrant.

So

$$R = \{(x, y) \mid 3 - \tfrac{1}{3}x \le y \le \sqrt{9 - x},\ 0 \le x \le 9\}$$

Since region R also can be covered by horizontal line segments (see Fig. 6) that go from the graph of $x + 3y = 9$ to the graph of $x + y^2 = 9$, it is a regular y region. Now we must solve each equation for x in terms of y:

$$x + 3y = 9 \qquad x + y^2 = 9$$

$$x = 9 - 3y \qquad x = 9 - y^2$$

Therefore,

$$R = \{(x, y) \mid 9 - 3y \le x \le 9 - y^2,\ 0 \le y \le 3\}$$

Matched Problem 2 Repeat Example 2 for the region bounded by the graphs of $2y - x = 4$ and $y^2 - x = 4$, as shown in Figure 7.

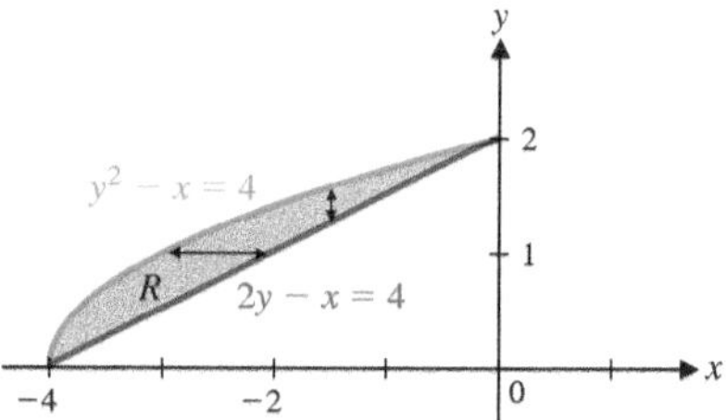

Figure 7

Explore and Discuss 1

A E I O U

Consider the vowels A, E, I, O, U, written in block letters as shown in the margin, to be regions of the plane. One of the vowels is a regular x region, but not a regular y region; one is a regular y region, but not a regular x region; one is both; two are neither. Explain.

Double Integrals over Regular Regions

Now we want to extend the definition of double integration to include regular x regions and regular y regions. The order of integration now depends on the nature of the region R. If R is a regular x region, we integrate with respect to y first, while if R is a regular y region, we integrate with respect to x first.

Note that the variable limits of integration (when present) are always on the inner integral, and the constant limits of integration are always on the outer integral.

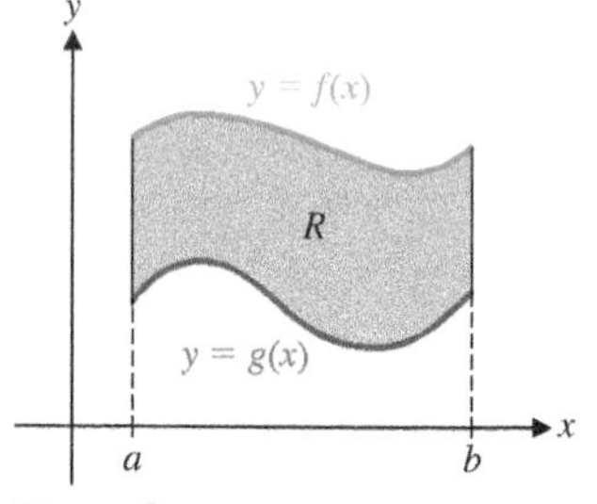

Figure 8

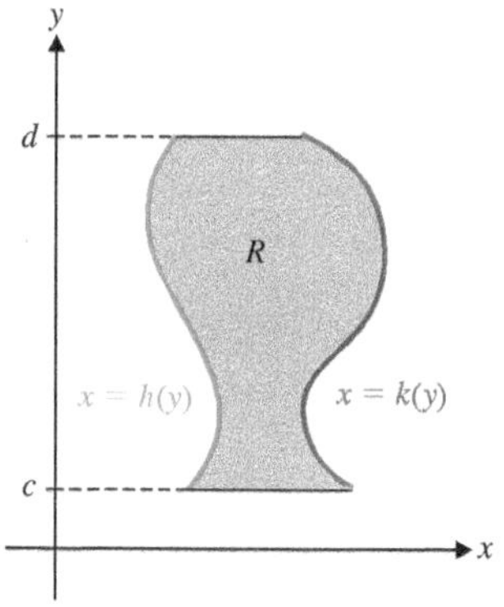

Figure 9

DEFINITION Double Integration over Regular Regions

Regular x Region

If $R = \{(x, y) | g(x) \le y \le f(x), \quad a \le x \le b\}$ (see Fig. 8), then

$$\iint_R F(x, y)\, dA = \int_a^b \left[\int_{g(x)}^{f(x)} F(x, y)\, dy \right] dx$$

Regular y Region

If $R = \{(x, y) | h(y) \le x \le k(y), \quad c \le y \le d\}$ (see Fig. 9), then

$$\iint_R F(x, y)\, dA = \int_c^d \left[\int_{h(y)}^{k(y)} F(x, y)\, dx \right] dy$$

EXAMPLE 3 **Evaluating a Double Integral** Evaluate $\iint_R 2xy\,dA$, where R is the region bounded by the graphs of $y = -x$ and $y = x^2$, $x \ge 0$, and the graph of $x = 1$.

SOLUTION From the graph (Fig. 10), we can see that R is a regular x region described by

$$R = \{(x, y) \mid -x \le y \le x^2,\ 0 \le x \le 1\}$$

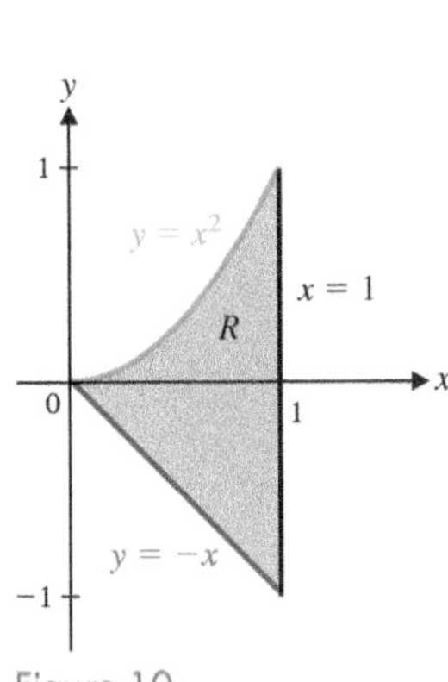

Figure 10

$$\iint_R 2xy\,dA = \int_0^1 \left[\int_{-x}^{x^2} 2xy\,dy\right] dx$$

$$= \int_0^1 \left[xy^2 \Big|_{y=-x}^{y=x^2}\right] dx$$

$$= \int_0^1 [x(x^2)^2 - x(-x)^2]\,dx$$

$$= \int_0^1 (x^5 - x^3)\,dx$$

$$= \left(\frac{x^6}{6} - \frac{x^4}{4}\right)\Big|_{x=0}^{x=1}$$

$$= \left(\tfrac{1}{6} - \tfrac{1}{4}\right) - (0 - 0) = -\tfrac{1}{12}$$

Matched Problem 3 Evaluate $\iint_R 3xy^2\,dA$, where R is the region in Example 3.

EXAMPLE 4 **Evaluating a Double Integral** Evaluate $\iint_R (2x + y)\,dA$, where R is the region bounded by the graphs of $y = \sqrt{x}$, $x + y = 2$, and $y = 0$.

SOLUTION From the graph (Fig. 11), we can see that R is a regular y region. After solving each equation for x, we can write

$$R = \{(x, y) \mid y^2 \le x \le 2 - y,\ 0 \le y \le 1\}$$

$$\iint_R (2x + y)dA = \int_0^1 \left[\int_{y^2}^{2-y} (2x + y)dx\right] dy$$

$$= \int_0^1 \left[(x^2 + yx)\Big|_{x=y^2}^{x=2-y}\right] dy$$

$$= \int_0^1 \{[(2 - y)^2 + y(2 - y)] - [(y^2)^2 + y(y^2)]\}\,dy$$

$$= \int_0^1 (4 - 2y - y^3 - y^4)\,dy$$

$$= \left(4y - y^2 - \tfrac{1}{4}y^4 - \tfrac{1}{5}y^5\right)\Big|_{y=0}^{y=1}$$

$$= \left(4 - 1 - \tfrac{1}{4} - \tfrac{1}{5}\right) - 0 = \tfrac{51}{20}$$

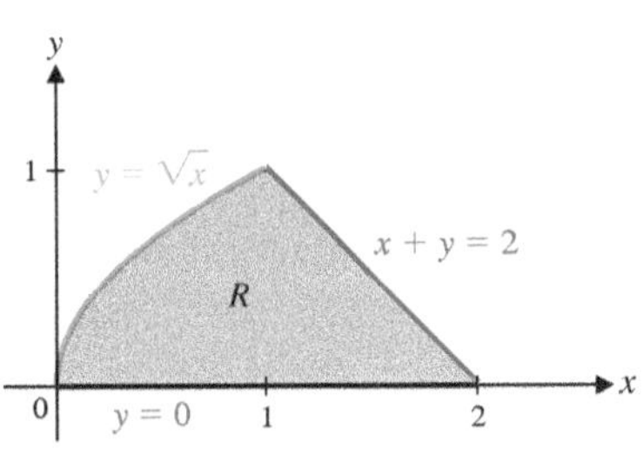

Figure 11

Matched Problem 4 Evaluate $\iint_R (y - 4x)\,dA$, where R is the region in Example 4.

EXAMPLE 5 **Evaluating a Double Integral** The region R is bounded by the graphs of $y = \sqrt{x}$ and $y = \frac{1}{2}x$. Evaluate $\iint_R 4xy^3 dA$ two different ways.

SOLUTION Region R (see Fig. 12) is both a regular x region and a regular y region:

$$R = \{(x, y) \mid \tfrac{1}{2}x \le y \le \sqrt{x},\ 0 \le x \le 4\} \qquad \text{Regular } x \text{ region}$$

$$R = \{(x, y) \mid y^2 \le x \le 2y,\ 0 \le y \le 2\} \qquad \text{Regular } y \text{ region}$$

Using the first representation (a regular x region), we obtain

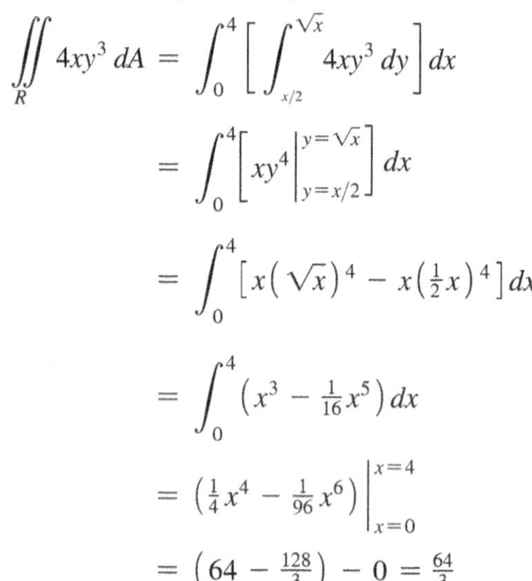

$$\iint_R 4xy^3\, dA = \int_0^4 \left[\int_{x/2}^{\sqrt{x}} 4xy^3\, dy\right] dx$$

$$= \int_0^4 \left[xy^4 \Big|_{y=x/2}^{y=\sqrt{x}}\right] dx$$

$$= \int_0^4 \left[x(\sqrt{x})^4 - x(\tfrac{1}{2}x)^4\right] dx$$

$$= \int_0^4 \left(x^3 - \tfrac{1}{16}x^5\right) dx$$

$$= \left(\tfrac{1}{4}x^4 - \tfrac{1}{96}x^6\right)\Big|_{x=0}^{x=4}$$

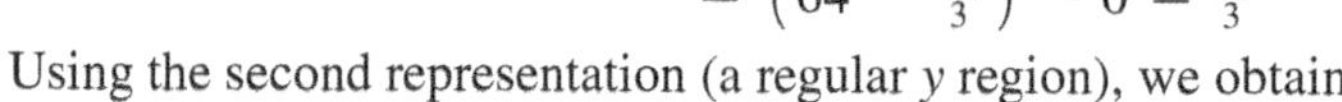

$$= \left(64 - \tfrac{128}{3}\right) - 0 = \tfrac{64}{3}$$

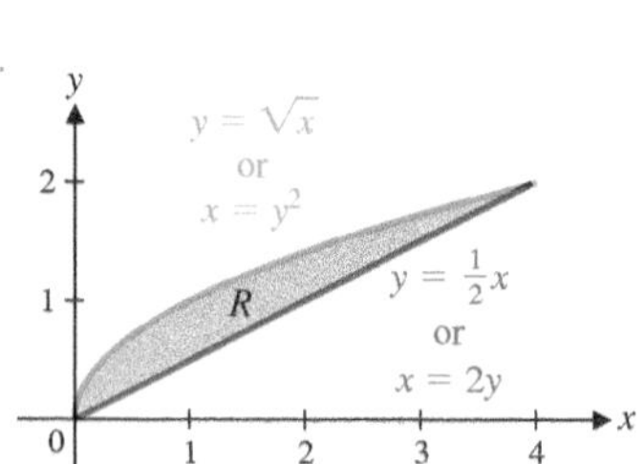

Figure 12

Using the second representation (a regular y region), we obtain

$$\iint_R 4xy^3\, dA = \int_0^2 \left[\int_{y^2}^{2y} 4xy^3\, dx\right] dy$$

$$= \int_0^2 \left[2x^2y^3 \Big|_{x=y^2}^{x=2y}\right] dy$$

$$= \int_0^2 \left[2(2y)^2y^3 - 2(y^2)^2y^3\right] dy$$

$$= \int_0^2 (8y^5 - 2y^7)\, dy$$

$$= \left(\tfrac{4}{3}y^6 - \tfrac{1}{4}y^8\right)\Big|_{y=0}^{y=2}$$

$$= \left(\tfrac{256}{3} - 64\right) - 0 = \tfrac{64}{3}$$

Matched Problem 5 The region R is bounded by the graphs of $y = x$ and $y = \frac{1}{2}x^2$. Evaluate $\iint_R 4xy^3 dA$ two different ways.

Reversing the Order of Integration

Example 5 shows that

$$\iint_R 4xy^3\, dA = \int_0^4 \left[\int_{x/2}^{\sqrt{x}} 4xy^3\, dy\right] dx = \int_0^2 \left[\int_{y^2}^{2y} 4xy^3\, dx\right] dy$$

In general, if R is both a regular x region and a regular y region, then the two iterated integrals are equal. In rectangular regions, reversing the order of integration in an iterated integral was a simple matter. As Example 5 illustrates, the process is more complicated in nonrectangular regions. The next example illustrates how to start with an iterated integral and reverse the order of integration. Since we are interested in the reversal process and not in the value of either integral, the integrand will not be specified.

EXAMPLE 6 **Reversing the Order of Integration** Reverse the order of integration in

$$\int_1^3 \left[\int_0^{x-1} f(x, y)\, dy \right] dx$$

SOLUTION The order of integration indicates that the region of integration is a regular x region:

$$R = \{(x, y) \mid 0 \le y \le x - 1,\ 1 \le x \le 3\}$$

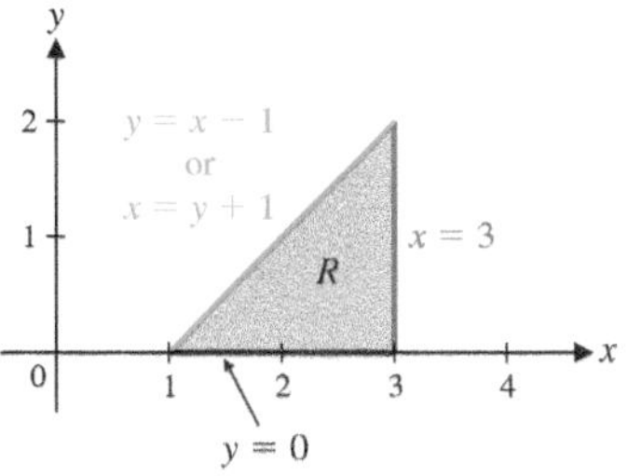

Figure 13

Graph region R to determine whether it is also a regular y region. The graph (Fig. 13) shows that R is also a regular y region, and we can write

$$R = \{(x, y) \mid y + 1 \le x \le 3,\ 0 \le y \le 2\}$$

$$\int_1^3 \left[\int_0^{x-1} f(x, y)\, dy \right] dx = \int_0^2 \left[\int_{y+1}^{3} f(x, y)\, dx \right] dy$$

Matched Problem 6 Reverse the order of integration in $\int_2^4 [\int_0^{4-x} f(x, y)\, dy]\, dx$.

Explore and Discuss 2

Explain the difficulty in evaluating $\int_0^2 \int_{x^2}^4 xe^{y^2} dy\, dx$ and how it can be overcome by reversing the order of integration.

Volume and Double Integrals

In Section 9.6, we used the double integral to calculate the volume of a solid with a rectangular base. In general, if a solid can be described by the graph of a positive function $f(x, y)$ over a regular region R (not necessarily a rectangle), then the double integral of the function f over the region R still represents the volume of the corresponding solid.

EXAMPLE 7 **Volume** The region R (see Fig. 14) is bounded by the graphs of $x + y = 1$, $y = 0$, and $x = 0$. Find the volume of the solid (see Fig. 15) under the graph of $z = 1 - x - y$ over the region R.

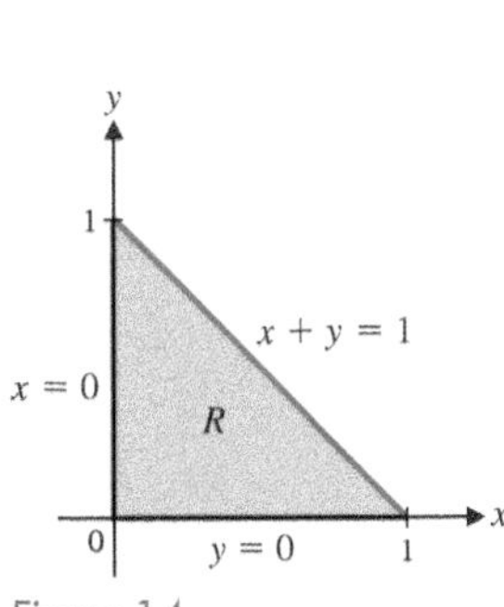

Figure 14

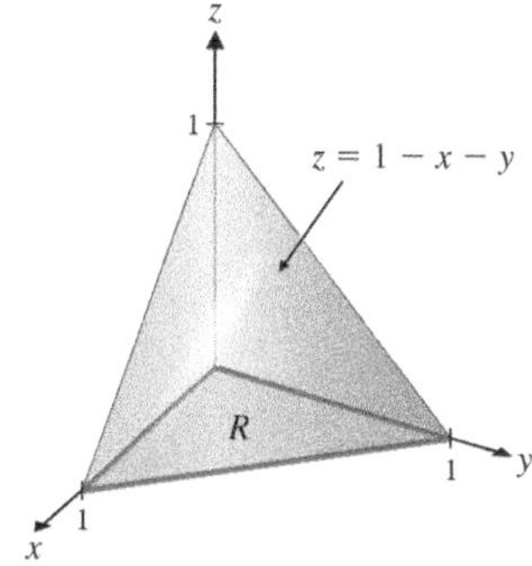

Figure 15

SOLUTION The graph of R (Fig. 14) shows that R is both a regular x region and a regular y region. We choose to use the regular x region:

$$R = \{(x, y) | 0 \le y \le 1 - x,\ \ 0 \le x \le 1\}$$

The volume of the solid is

$$V = \iint_R (1 - x - y)\, dA = \int_0^1 \left[\int_0^{1-x} (1 - x - y)\, dy \right] dx$$

$$= \int_0^1 \left[\left(y - xy - \tfrac{1}{2}y^2 \right) \Big|_{y=0}^{y=1-x} \right] dx$$

$$= \int_0^1 [(1 - x) - x(1 - x) - \tfrac{1}{2}(1 - x)^2]\, dx$$

$$= \int_0^1 \left(\tfrac{1}{2} - x + \tfrac{1}{2}x^2 \right) dx$$

$$= \left(\tfrac{1}{2}x - \tfrac{1}{2}x^2 + \tfrac{1}{6}x^3 \right) \Big|_{x=0}^{x=1}$$

$$= \left(\tfrac{1}{2} - \tfrac{1}{2} + \tfrac{1}{6} \right) - 0 = \tfrac{1}{6}$$

Matched Problem 7 The region R is bounded by the graphs of $y + 2x = 2$, $y = 0$, and $x = 0$. Find the volume of the solid under the graph of $z = 2 - 2x - y$ over the region R. [*Hint:* Sketch the region first; the solid does not have to be sketched.]

Exercises 9.7

Skills Warm-up Exercises

W *In Problems 1–6, evaluate each iterated integral. (If necessary, review Section 9.6.)*

1. $\int_0^2 \int_0^3 4\, dy\, dx$
2. $\int_0^5 \int_0^8 2\, dx\, dy$
3. $\int_0^1 \int_{-2}^2 x\, dx\, dy$
4. $\int_0^1 \int_{-2}^2 y\, dx\, dy$
5. $\int_0^1 \int_0^1 (x + y)\, dy\, dx$
6. $\int_0^1 \int_0^1 (x - y)\, dy\, dx$

A *In Problems 7–12, graph the region R bounded by the graphs of the equations. Use set notation and double inequalities to describe R as a regular x region and a regular y region in Problems 7 and 8, and as a regular x region or a regular y region, whichever is simpler, in Problems 9–12.*

7. $y = 4 - x^2, y = 0, 0 \le x \le 2$
8. $y = x^2, y = 9, 0 \le x \le 3$
9. $y = x^3, y = 12 - 2x, x = 0$
10. $y = 5 - x, y = 1 + x, y = 0$
11. $y^2 = 2x, y = x - 4$
12. $y = 4 + 3x - x^2, x + y = 4$

Evaluate each integral in Problems 13–16.

13. $\int_0^1 \int_0^x (x + y)\, dy\, dx$
14. $\int_0^2 \int_0^y xy\, dx\, dy$
15. $\int_0^1 \int_{y^3}^{\sqrt{y}} (2x + y)\, dx\, dy$
16. $\int_1^4 \int_x^{x^2} (x^2 + 2y)\, dy\, dx$

B *In Problems 17–20, give a verbal description of the region R and determine whether R is a regular x region, a regular y region, both, or neither.*

17. $R = \{(x, y) | |x| \le 2,\ \ |y| \le 3\}$
18. $R = \{(x, y) | 1 \le x^2 + y^2 \le 4\}$
19. $R = \{(x, y) | x^2 + y^2 \ge 1,\ \ |x| \le 2,\ \ 0 \le y \le 2\}$
20. $R = \{(x, y) | |x| + |y| \le 1\}$

In Problems 21–26, use the description of the region R to evaluate the indicated integral.

21. $\iint_R (x^2 + y^2)\, dA;$

$R = \{(x, y) | 0 \le y \le 2x,\ \ 0 \le x \le 2\}$

22. $\iint_R 2x^2y\, dA;$

$R = \{(x, y) | 0 \le y \le 9 - x^2,\ \ -3 \le x \le 3\}$

23. $\iint_R (x + y - 2)^3\, dA;$
$R = \{(x, y) | 0 \le x \le y + 2, \quad 0 \le y \le 1\}$

24. $\iint_R (2x + 3y)\, dA;$
$R = \{(x, y) | y^2 - 4 \le x \le 4 - 2y, \quad 0 \le y \le 2\}$

25. $\iint_R e^{x+y}\, dA;$
$R = \{(x, y) | -x \le y \le x, \quad 0 \le x \le 2\}$

26. $\iint_R \frac{x}{\sqrt{x^2 + y^2}}\, dA;$
$R = \{(x, y) | 0 \le x \le \sqrt{4y - y^2}, \quad 0 \le y \le 2\}$

In Problems 27–32, graph the region R bounded by the graphs of the indicated equations. Describe R in set notation with double inequalities, and evaluate the indicated integral.

27. $y = x + 1, y = 0, x = 0, x = 1; \quad \iint_R \sqrt{1 + x + y}\, dA$

28. $y = x^2, \quad y = \sqrt{x}; \quad \iint_R 12xy\, dA$

29. $y = 4x - x^2, \quad y = 0; \quad \iint_R \sqrt{y + x^2}\, dA$

30. $x = 1 + 3y, \quad x = 1 - y, \quad y = 1; \quad \iint_R (x + y + 1)^3\, dA$

31. $y = 1 - \sqrt{x}, \; y = 1 + \sqrt{x}, \; x = 4; \quad \iint_R x(y - 1)^2\, dA$

32. $y = \frac{1}{2}x, y = 6 - x, \quad y = 1; \quad \iint_R \frac{1}{x + y}\, dA$

In Problems 33–38, evaluate each integral. Graph the region of integration, reverse the order of integration, and then evaluate the integral with the order reversed.

33. $\int_0^3 \int_0^{3-x} (x + 2y)\, dy\, dx$
34. $\int_0^2 \int_0^y (y - x)^4\, dx\, dy$
35. $\int_0^1 \int_0^{1-x^2} x\sqrt{y}\, dy\, dx$
36. $\int_0^2 \int_{x^3}^{4x} (1 + 2y)\, dy\, dx$
37. $\int_0^4 \int_{x/4}^{\sqrt{x}/2} x\, dy\, dx$
38. $\int_0^4 \int_{y^2/4}^{2\sqrt{y}} (1 + 2xy)\, dx\, dy$

In Problems 39–42, find the volume of the solid under the graph of f(x, y) over the region R bounded by the graphs of the indicated equations. Sketch the region R; the solid does not have to be sketched.

39. $f(x, y) = 4 - x - y$; R is the region bounded by the graphs of $x + y = 4, y = 0, x = 0$

40. $f(x, y) = (x - y)^2$; R is the region bounded by the graphs of $y = x, y = 2, x = 0$

41. $f(x, y) = 4$; R is the region bounded by the graphs of $y = 1 - x^2$ and $y = 0$ for $0 \le x \le 1$

42. $f(x, y) = 4xy$; R is the region bounded by the graphs of $y = \sqrt{1 - x^2}$ and $y = 0$ for $0 \le x \le 1$

C *In Problems 43–46, reverse the order of integration for each integral. Evaluate the integral with the order reversed. Do not attempt to evaluate the integral in the original form.*

43. $\int_0^2 \int_{x^2}^4 \frac{4x}{1 + y^2}\, dy\, dx$
44. $\int_0^1 \int_y^1 \sqrt{1 - x^2}\, dx\, dy$
45. $\int_0^1 \int_{y^2}^1 4ye^{x^2}\, dx\, dy$
46. $\int_0^4 \int_{\sqrt{x}}^2 \sqrt{3x + y^2}\, dy\, dx$

In Problems 47–52, use a graphing calculator to graph the region R bounded by the graphs of the indicated equations. Use approximation techniques to find intersection points correct to two decimal places. Describe R in set notation with double inequalities, and evaluate the indicated integral correct to two decimal places.

47. $y = 1 + \sqrt{x}, \quad y = x^2, \quad x = 0; \quad \iint_R x\, dA$

48. $y = 1 + \sqrt[3]{x}, y = x, x = 0; \quad \iint_R x\, dA$

49. $y = \sqrt[3]{x}, y = 1 - x, y = 0; \quad \iint_R 24xy\, dA$

50. $y = x^3, y = 1 - x, y = 0; \quad \iint_R 48xy\, dA$

51. $y = e^{-x}, \quad y = 3 - x; \quad \iint_R 4y\, dA$

52. $y = e^x, \quad y = 2 + x; \quad \iint_R 8y\, dA$

Applications

53. **Stadium construction.** The floor of a glass-enclosed atrium at a football stadium is the region bounded by $y = 0$ and $y = 100 - 0.01x^2$. The ceiling lies on the graph of $f(x,y) = 90 - 0.5x$. (Each unit on the x, y, and z axes represents one foot.) Find the volume of the atrium (in cubic feet).

54. **Museum design.** The floor of an art museum gallery is the region bounded by $x = 0, x = 40, y = 0$, and $y = 50 - 0.3x$. The ceiling lies on the graph of $f(x,y) = 25 - 0.125x$. (Each unit on the x, y, and z axes represents one foot.) Find the volume of the atrium (in cubic feet).

55. **Convention center expansion.** A new exhibit hall at a convention center has a floor bounded by $x = 0$, $x = 200, y = -100 + 0.01x$, and $y = 100 - 0.01x$. The ceiling lies on the graph of $f(x,y) = 50 - 0.12x$. (Each unit on the x, y, and z axes represents one foot.) Find the volume of the exhibit hall (in cubic feet).

56. **Concert hall architecture.** The floor of a concert hall is the region bounded by $x = 0$ and $x = 100 - 0.04y^2$. The ceiling lies on the graph of $f(x,y) = 50 - 0.0025x^2$. (Each unit on the x, y, and z axes represents one foot.) Find the volume of the concert hall (in cubic feet).

The average value of a function $f(x, y)$ over a regular region R is defined to be

$$\frac{\iint_R f(x,y)\,dA}{\iint_R dA}$$

Use this definition of average value in Problems 57 and 58.

57. **Air quality.** An industrial plant is located on the lakefront of a city. Let (0, 0) be the coordinates of the plant. The city's residents live in the region R bounded by $y = 0$ and $y = 10 - 0.1x^2$. (Each unit on the x and y axes represents 1 mile.) Suppose that the concentration of fine particulate matter (in micrograms per cubic meter) at a point d miles from the plant is given by

$$C = 60 - 0.5d^2$$

Find the average concentration of fine particulate matter (to one decimal place) over the region R.

58. **Air quality.** Repeat Problem 57 for the region bounded by $y = 0$ and $y = 5 - 0.2x^2$.

Answers to Matched Problems

1. $R = \{(x,y)\,|\,y^2 \le x \le 6 - y,\ 0 \le y \le 2\}$
2. R is both a regular x region and a regular y region:
$R = \{(x,y)\,|\,\frac{1}{2}x + 2 \le y \le \sqrt{x+4},\ \ -4 \le x \le 0\}$
$R = \{(x,y)\,|\,y^2 - 4 \le x \le 2y - 4,\ 0 \le y \le 2\}$
3. $\frac{13}{40}$ **4.** $-\frac{77}{20}$ **5.** $\frac{64}{15}$
6. $\int_0^2 [\int_2^{4-y} f(x,y)\,dx]\,dy$
7. $\frac{2}{3}$

Chapter 9 Summary and Review

Important Terms, Symbols, and Concepts

9.1 Functions of Several Variables

EXAMPLES

- An equation of the form $z = f(x, y)$ describes a **function of two independent variables** if, for each permissible ordered pair (x, y), there is one and only one value of z determined by $f(x, y)$. The variables x and y are **independent variables**, and z is a **dependent variable**. The set of all ordered pairs of permissible values of x and y is the **domain** of the function, and the set of all corresponding values $f(x, y)$ is the **range**. Functions of more than two independent variables are defined similarly. Ex. 1, p. 524 Ex. 2, p. 525 Ex. 3, p. 525 Ex. 4, p. 526
- The graph of $z = f(x, y)$ consists of all ordered triples (x, y, z) in a **three-dimensional coordinate system** that satisfy the equation. The graphs of the functions $z = f(x,y) = x^2 + y^2$ and $z = g(x,y) = x^2 - y^2$, for example, are **surfaces**; the first has a local minimum, and the second has a **saddle point**, at (0, 0). Ex. 5, p. 527 Ex. 6, p. 527 Ex. 7, p. 529

9.2 Partial Derivatives

- If $z = f(x, y)$, then the **partial derivative of f with respect to x**, denoted as $\partial z/\partial x$, f_x, or $f_x(x, y)$, is
$$\frac{\partial z}{\partial x} = \lim_{h\to 0}\frac{f(x+h,y) - f(x,y)}{h}$$
Similarly, the **partial derivative of f with respect to y**, denoted as $\partial z/\partial y, f_y$, or $f_y(x, y)$, is
$$\frac{\partial z}{\partial y} = \lim_{k\to 0}\frac{f(x,y+k) - f(x,y)}{k}$$
The partial derivatives $\partial z/\partial x$ and $\partial z/\partial y$ are said to be **first-order partial derivatives**. Ex. 1, p. 534 Ex. 2, p. 535 Ex. 3, p. 535 Ex. 4, p. 535
- There are four **second-order partial derivatives** of $z = f(x, y)$: Ex. 5, p. 537

$$f_{xx} = f_{xx}(x,y) = \frac{\partial^2 z}{\partial x^2} = \frac{\partial}{\partial x}\left(\frac{\partial z}{\partial x}\right)$$

$$f_{xy} = f_{xy}(x,y) = \frac{\partial^2 z}{\partial y\,\partial x} = \frac{\partial}{\partial y}\left(\frac{\partial z}{\partial x}\right)$$

$$f_{yx} = f_{yx}(x,y) = \frac{\partial^2 z}{\partial x\,\partial y} = \frac{\partial}{\partial x}\left(\frac{\partial z}{\partial y}\right)$$

$$f_{yy} = f_{yy}(x,y) = \frac{\partial^2 z}{\partial y^2} = \frac{\partial}{\partial y}\left(\frac{\partial z}{\partial y}\right)$$

9.3 Maxima and Minima

- If $f(a, b) \geq f(x, y)$ for all (x, y) in a circular region in the domain of f with (a, b) as center, then $f(a, b)$ is a **local maximum**. If $f(a, b) \leq f(x, y)$ for all (x, y) in such a region, then $f(a, b)$ is a **local minimum**.
- If a function $f(x, y)$ has a local maximum or minimum at the point (a, b), and f_x and f_y exist at (a, b), then both first-order partial derivatives equal 0 at (a, b) [Theorem 1, p. 543]. Ex. 1, p. 544 Ex. 2, p. 544
- The second-derivative test for local extrema (Theorem 2, p. 543) gives conditions on the first- and second-order partial derivatives of $f(x, y)$, which guarantee that $f(a, b)$ is a local maximum, local minimum, or saddle point. Ex. 3, p. 546 Ex. 4, p. 547

9.4 Maxima and Minima Using Lagrange Multipliers

- The **method of Lagrange multipliers** can be used to find local extrema of a function $z = f(x, y)$ subject to the constraint $g(x, y) = 0$. A procedure that lists the key steps in the method is given on page 552. Ex. 1, p. 552 Ex. 2, p. 553
- The method of Lagrange multipliers can be extended to functions with arbitrarily many independent variables with one or more constraints (see Theorem 1, p. 551, and Theorem 2, p. 555, for the method when there are two and three independent variables, respectively). Ex. 3, p. 555

9.5 Method of Least Squares

- **Linear regression** is the process of fitting a line $y = ax + b$ to a set of data points $(x_1, y_1), (x_2, y_2), \ldots, (x_n, y_n)$ by using the **method of least squares**.
- We minimize $F(a, b) = \sum_{k=1}^{n} (y_k - ax_k - b)^2$, the **sum of the squares of the residuals**, by computing the first-order partial derivatives of F and setting them equal to 0. Solving for a and b gives the formulas Ex. 1, p. 564

$$a = \frac{n\left(\sum_{k=1}^{n} x_k y_k\right) - \left(\sum_{k=1}^{n} x_k\right)\left(\sum_{k=1}^{n} y_k\right)}{n\left(\sum_{k=1}^{n} x_k^2\right) - \left(\sum_{k=1}^{n} x_k\right)^2}$$

$$b = \frac{\sum_{k=1}^{n} y_k - a\left(\sum_{k=1}^{n} x_k\right)}{n}$$

- Graphing calculators have built-in routines to calculate linear—as well as quadratic, cubic, quartic, logarithmic, exponential, power, and trigonometric—regression equations. Ex. 2, p. 566

9.6 Double Integrals over Rectangular Regions

- The **double integral** of a function $f(x, y)$ over a rectangle Ex. 1, p. 570 Ex. 2, p. 571 Ex. 3, p. 572 Ex. 4, p. 573 Ex. 5, p. 574

$$R = \{(x, y) \mid a \leq x \leq b, \quad c \leq y \leq d\}$$

is

$$\iint_R f(x, y)\, dA = \int_a^b \left[\int_c^d f(x, y)\, dy\right] dx$$

$$= \int_c^d \left[\int_a^b f(x, y)\, dx\right] dy$$

- In the double integral $\iint_R f(x, y)\, dA$, $f(x, y)$ is called the **integrand** and R is called the **region of integration.** The expression dA indicates that this is an integral over a two-dimensional region. The integrals

$$\int_a^b \left[\int_c^d f(x, y)\, dy\right] dx \quad \text{and} \quad \int_c^d \left[\int_a^b f(x, y)\, dx\right] dy$$

are referred to as **iterated integrals** (the brackets are often omitted), and the order in which dx and dy are written indicates the order of integration.

- The **average value** of the function $f(x, y)$ over the rectangle

$$R = \{(x, y) \mid a \le x \le b, \quad c \le y \le d\}$$

is

$$\frac{1}{(b-a)(d-c)} \iint_R f(x, y)\, dA$$

Ex. 6, p. 574

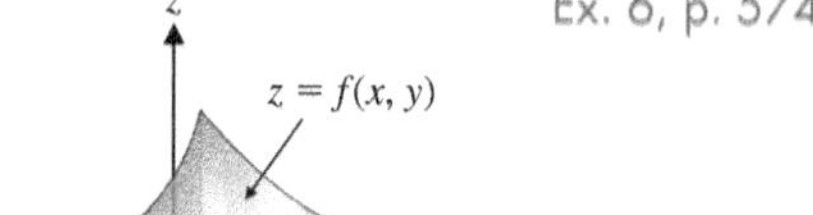

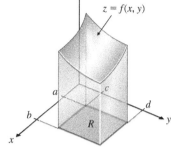

- If $f(x, y) \ge 0$ over a rectangle $R = \{(x, y) \mid a \le x \le b, c \le y \le d\}$, then the volume of the solid formed by graphing f over the rectangle R is given by

$$V = \iint_R f(x, y)\, dA$$

Ex. 7, p. 575

9.7 Double Integrals over More General Regions

- A region R in the xy plane is a **regular x region** if there exist functions $f(x)$ and $g(x)$ and numbers a and b such that Ex. 1, p. 580

$$R = \{(x, y) \mid g(x) \le y \le f(x), \quad a \le x \le b\}$$

- A region R in the xy plane is a **regular y region** if there exist functions $h(y)$ and $k(y)$ and numbers c and d such that Ex. 2, p. 581

$$R = \{(x, y) \mid h(y) \le x \le k(y), \quad c \le y \le d\}$$

- The double integral of a function $F(x, y)$ over a regular x region $R = \{(x, y) \mid g(x) \le y \le f(x), a \le x \le b\}$ is

$$\iint_R F(x, y)\, dA = \int_a^b \left[\int_{g(x)}^{f(x)} F(x, y)\, dy\right] dx$$

- The double integral of a function $F(x, y)$ over a regular y region $R = \{(x, y) \mid h(y) \le x \le k(y), c \le y \le d\}$ is

$$\iint_R F(x, y)\, dA = \int_c^d \left[\int_{h(y)}^{k(y)} F(x, y)\, dx\right] dy$$

Ex. 3, p. 583
Ex. 4, p. 583
Ex. 5, p. 584
Ex. 6, p. 585
Ex. 7, p. 585

Review Exercises

Work through all the problems in this chapter review and check your answers in the back of the book. Answers to all review problems are there, along with section numbers in italics to indicate where each type of problem is discussed. Where weaknesses show up, review appropriate sections of the text.

1. For $f(x, y) = 2{,}000 + 40x + 70y$, find $f(5, 10), f_x(x, y)$, and $f_y(x, y)$.
2. For $z = x^3y^2$, find $\partial^2 z/\partial x^2$ and $\partial^2 z/\partial x\, \partial y$.
3. Evaluate $\int (6xy^2 + 4y)\, dy$.
4. Evaluate $\int (6xy^2 + 4y)\, dx$.
5. Evaluate $\int_0^1 \int_0^1 4xy\, dy\, dx$.
6. For $f(x, y) = 6 + 5x - 2y + 3x^2 + x^3$, find $f_x(x, y)$, and $f_y(x, y)$, and explain why $f(x, y)$ has no local extrema.
7. For $f(x, y) = 3x^2 - 2xy + y^2 - 2x + 3y - 7$, find $f(2, 3) f_y(x, y)$, and $f_y(2, 3)$.
8. For $f(x, y) = -4x^2 + 4xy - 3y^2 + 4x + 10y + 81$, find $[f_{xx}(2, 3)][f_{yy}(2, 3)] - [f_{xy}(2, 3)]^2$.
9. If $f(x, y) = x + 3y$ and $g(x, y) = x^2 + y^2 - 10$, find the critical points of $F(x, y, \lambda) = f(x, y) + \lambda g(x, y)$.
10. Use the least squares line for the data in the following table to estimate y when $x = 10$.

x	y
2	12
4	10
6	7
8	3

11. For $R = \{(x, y) \mid -1 \le x \le 1, \quad 1 \le y \le 2\}$, evaluate the following in two ways:

$$\iint_R (4x + 6y)\, dA$$

12. For $R = \{(x, y) \mid \sqrt{y} \le x \le 1, \quad 0 \le y \le 1\}$, evaluate

$$\iint_R (6x + y)\, dA$$

13. For $f(x, y) = e^{x^2+2y}$, find f_x, f_y, and f_{xy}.

14. For $f(x, y) = (x^2 + y^2)^5$, find f_x and f_{xy}.

15. Find all critical points and test for extrema for

$$f(x, y) = x^3 - 12x + y^2 - 6y$$

16. Use Lagrange multipliers to maximize $f(x, y) = xy$ subject to $2x + 3y = 24$.

17. Use Lagrange multipliers to minimize $f(x, y, z) = x^2 + y^2 + z^2$ subject to $2x + y + 2z = 9$.

18. Find the least squares line for the data in the following table.

x	y	x	y
10	50	60	80
20	45	70	85
30	50	80	90
40	55	90	90
50	65	100	110

19. Find the average value of $f(x, y) = x^{2/3}y^{1/3}$ over the rectangle

$$R = \{(x, y) \mid -8 \le x \le 8, \quad 0 \le y \le 27\}$$

20. Find the volume of the solid under the graph of $z = 3x^2 + 3y^2$ over the rectangle

$$R = \{(x, y) \mid 0 \le x \le 1, \quad -1 \le y \le 1\}$$

21. Without doing any computation, predict the average value of $f(x, y) = x + y$ over the rectangle $R = \{(x, y) \mid -10 \le x \le 10, \quad -10 \le y \le 10\}$. Then check the correctness of your prediction by evaluating a double integral.

22. (A) Find the dimensions of the square S centered at the origin such that the average value of

$$f(x, y) = \frac{e^x}{y + 10}$$

over S is equal to 5.

(B) Is there a square centered at the origin over which

$$f(x, y) = \frac{e^x}{y + 10}$$

has average value 0.05? Explain.

23. Explain why the function $f(x, y) = 4x^3 - 5y^3$, subject to the constraint $3x + 2y = 7$, has no maxima or minima.

24. Find the volume of the solid under the graph of $F(x, y) = 60x^2y$ over the region R bounded by the graph of $x + y = 1$ and the coordinate axes.

Applications

25. **Maximizing profit.** A company produces x units of product A and y units of product B (both in hundreds per month). The monthly profit equation (in thousands of dollars) is given by

$$P(x, y) = -4x^2 + 4xy - 3y^2 + 4x + 10y + 81$$

(A) Find $P_x(1, 3)$ and interpret the results.

(B) How many of each product should be produced each month to maximize profit? What is the maximum profit?

26. **Minimizing material.** A rectangular box with no top and six compartments (see the figure) is to have a volume of 96 cubic inches. Find the dimensions that will require the least amount of material.

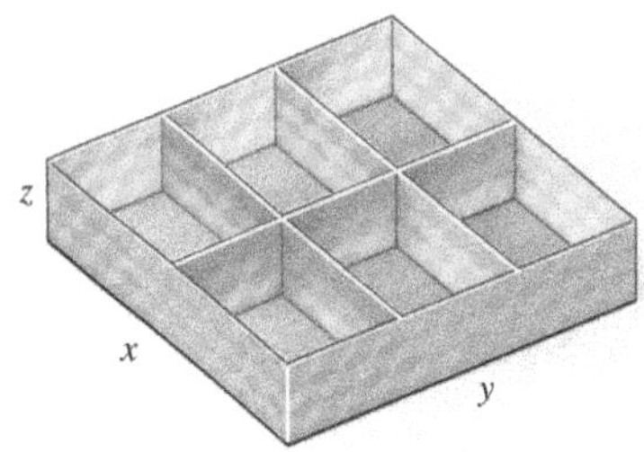

27. **Profit.** A company's annual profits (in millions of dollars) over a 5-year period are given in the following table. Use the least squares line to estimate the profit for the sixth year.

Year	Profit
1	2
2	2.5
3	3.1
4	4.2
5	4.3

28. **Productivity.** The Cobb–Douglas production function for a product is

$$N(x, y) = 10x^{0.8}y^{0.2}$$

where x is the number of units of labor and y is the number of units of capital required to produce N units of the product.

(A) Find the marginal productivity of labor and the marginal productivity of capital at $x = 40$ and $y = 50$. For the greatest increase in productivity, should management encourage increased use of labor or increased use of capital?

(B) If each unit of labor costs \$100, each unit of capital costs \$50, and \$10,000 is budgeted for production of this product, use the method of Lagrange multipliers to determine the allocations of labor and capital that will maximize the number of units produced and find the maximum production. Find the marginal productivity of money and approximate the increase in production that would result from an increase of \$2,000 in the amount budgeted for production.

(C) If $50 \le x \le 100$ and $20 \le y \le 40$, find the average number of units produced. Set up a double integral, and evaluate it.

29. **Marine biology.** When diving using scuba gear, the function used for timing the duration of the dive is

$$T(V, x) = \frac{33V}{x + 33}$$

where T is the time of the dive in minutes, V is the volume of air (in cubic feet, at sea-level pressure) compressed into tanks, and x is the depth of the dive in feet. Find $T_x(70, 17)$ and interpret the results.

30. Air quality. A heavy industrial plant located in the center of a small town emits particulate matter into the atmosphere. Suppose that the concentration of fine particulate matter (in parts per million) at a point d miles from the plant is given by

$$C = 65 - 6d^2$$

If the boundaries of the town form a square 4 miles long and 4 miles wide, what is the average concentration of fine particulate matter throughout the town? Express C as a function of x and y, and set up a double integral and evaluate it.

31. Sociology. A sociologist found that the number n of long-distance telephone calls between two cities during a given period varied (approximately) jointly as the populations P_1 and P_2 of the two cities and varied inversely as the distance d between the cities. An equation for a period of 1 week is

$$n(P_1, P_2, d) = 0.001\frac{P_1P_2}{d}$$

Find $n(100{,}000, 50{,}000, 100)$.

32. Education. At the beginning of the semester, students in a foreign language course take a proficiency exam. The same exam is given at the end of the semester. The results for 5 students are shown in the following table. Use the least squares line to estimate the second exam score of a student who scored 40 on the first exam.

First Exam	Second Exam
30	60
50	75
60	80
70	85
90	90

33. Population density. The following table gives the U.S. population per square mile for the years 1960–2010:

U.S. Population Density

Year	Population (per square mile)
1960	50.6
1970	57.5
1980	64.1
1990	70.4
2000	79.7
2010	87.4

(A) Find the least squares line for the data, using $x = 0$ for 1960.

(B) Use the least squares line to estimate the population density in the United States in the year 2025.

(C) Now use quadratic regression and exponential regression to obtain the estimate of part (B).

34. Life expectancy. The following table gives life expectancies for males and females in a sample of Central and South American countries:

Life Expectancies for Central and South American Countries

Males	Females	Males	Females
62.30	67.50	70.15	74.10
68.05	75.05	62.93	66.58
72.40	77.04	68.43	74.88
63.39	67.59	66.68	72.80
55.11	59.43		

(A) Find the least squares line for the data.

(B) Use the least squares line to estimate the life expectancy of a female in a Central or South American country in which the life expectancy for males is 60 years.

(C) Now use quadratic regression and logarithmic regression to obtain the estimate of part (B).

Appendices

Basic Algebra Review

Appendix B reviews some important basic algebra concepts usually studied in earlier courses. The material may be studied systematically before beginning the rest of the book or reviewed as needed.

A.1 Real Numbers

- Set of Real Numbers
- Real Number Line
- Basic Real Number Properties
- Further Properties
- Fraction Properties

The rules for manipulating and reasoning with symbols in algebra depend, in large measure, on properties of the real numbers. In this section we look at some of the important properties of this number system. To make our discussions here and elsewhere in the book clearer and more precise, we occasionally make use of simple *set* concepts and notation.

Set of Real Numbers

Informally, a **real number** is any number that has a decimal representation. The decimal representation may be terminating or repeating or neither. The decimal representation 4.713 516 94 is terminating (the space after every third decimal place is used to help keep track of the number of decimal places). The decimal representation $5.254\,7\overline{47}$ is repeating (the overbar indicates that the block "47" repeats indefinitely). The decimal representation 3.141 592 653 . . . of the number π, the ratio of the circumference to the diameter of a circle, is neither terminating nor repeating. Table 1 describes the set of real numbers and some of its important subsets. Figure 1 illustrates how these sets of numbers are related.

Table 1 **Set of Real Numbers**

Symbol	Name	Description	Examples
N	Natural numbers	Counting numbers (also called positive integers)	$1, 2, 3, \ldots$
Z	Integers	Natural numbers, their negatives, and 0	$\ldots, -2, -1, 0, 1, 2, \ldots$
Q	Rational numbers	Numbers that can be represented as a/b, where a and b are integers and $b \neq 0$; decimal representations are repeating or terminating	$-4, 0, 1, 25, \frac{-3}{5}, \frac{2}{3}, 3.67, -0.33\overline{3}, 5.272\,7\overline{27}$
I	Irrational numbers	Numbers that can be represented as nonrepeating and nonterminating decimal numbers	$\sqrt{2}, \pi, \sqrt[3]{7}, 1.414\,213\ldots, 2.718\,281\,82\ldots$
R	Real numbers	Rational and irrational numbers	

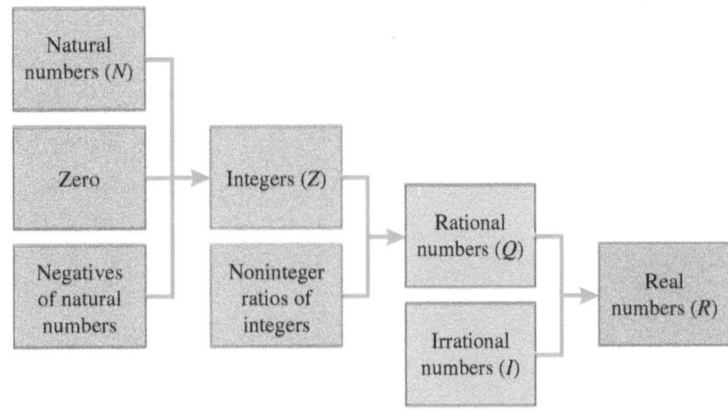

Figure 1 Real numbers and important subsets

The set of integers contains all the natural numbers and something else—their negatives and 0. The set of rational numbers contains all the integers and something else—noninteger ratios of integers. And the set of real numbers contains all the rational numbers and something else—irrational numbers.

Real Number Line

A one-to-one correspondence exists between the set of real numbers and the set of points on a line. That is, each real number corresponds to exactly one point, and each point corresponds to exactly one real number. A line with a real number associated with each point, and vice versa, as shown in Figure 2, is called a **real number line**, or simply a **real line**. Each number associated with a point is called the coordinate of the point.

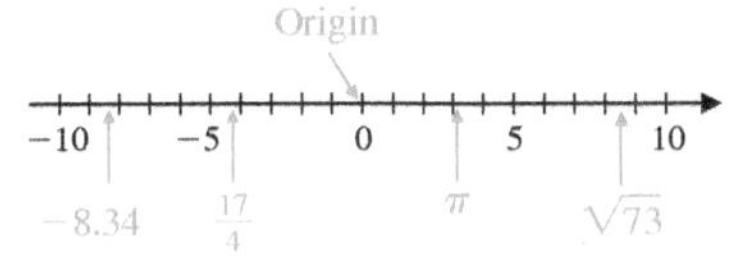

Figure 2 Real number line

The point with coordinate 0 is called the **origin**. The arrow on the right end of the line indicates a positive direction. The coordinates of all points to the right of the origin are called **positive real numbers**, and those to the left of the origin are called **negative real numbers**. The real number 0 is neither positive nor negative.

Basic Real Number Properties

We now take a look at some of the basic properties of the real number system that enable us to convert algebraic expressions into *equivalent forms*.

SUMMARY Basic Properties of the Set of Real Numbers

Let a, b, and c be arbitrary elements in the set of real numbers R.

Addition Properties

Associative: $(a + b) + c = a + (b + c)$

Commutative: $a + b = b + a$

Identity: 0 is the additive identity; that is, $0 + a = a + 0 = a$ for all a in R, and 0 is the only element in R with this property.

Inverse: For each a in R, $-a$, is its unique additive inverse; that is, $a + (-a) = (-a) + a = 0$ and $-a$ is the only element in R relative to a with this property.

Multiplication Properties

Associative: $(ab)c = a(bc)$

Commutative: $ab = ba$

Identity: 1 is the multiplicative identity; that is, $(1)a = a(1) = a$ for all a in R, and 1 is the only element in R with this property.

Inverse: For each a in R, $a \neq 0$, $1/a$ is its unique multiplicative inverse; that is, $a(1/a) = (1/a)a = 1$, and $1/a$ is the only element in R relative to a with this property.

Distributive Properties

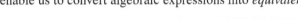

$a(b + c) = ab + ac \quad (a + b)c = ac + bc$

You are already familiar with the **commutative properties** for addition and multiplication. They indicate that the order in which the addition or multiplication of two numbers is performed does not matter. For example,

$$7 + 2 = 2 + 7 \quad \text{and} \quad 3 \cdot 5 = 5 \cdot 3$$

Is there a commutative property relative to subtraction or division? That is, does $a - b = b - a$ or does $a \div b = b \div a$ for all real numbers a and b (division by 0 excluded)? The answer is no, since, for example,

$$8 - 6 \neq 6 - 8 \quad \text{and} \quad 10 \div 5 \neq 5 \div 10$$

When computing

$$3 + 2 + 6 \quad \text{or} \quad 3 \cdot 2 \cdot 6$$

why don't we need parentheses to indicate which two numbers are to be added or multiplied first? The answer is to be found in the **associative properties**. These properties allow us to write

$$(3 + 2) + 6 = 3 + (2 + 6) \quad \text{and} \quad (3 \cdot 2) \cdot 6 = 3 \cdot (2 \cdot 6)$$

so it does not matter how we group numbers relative to either operation. Is there an associative property for subtraction or division? The answer is no, since, for example,

$$(12 - 6) - 2 \neq 12 - (6 - 2) \quad \text{and} \quad (12 \div 6) \div 2 \neq 12 \div (6 \div 2)$$

Evaluate each side of each equation to see why.

What number added to a given number will give that number back again? What number times a given number will give that number back again? The answers are 0 and 1, respectively. Because of this, 0 and 1 are called the **identity elements** for the real numbers. Hence, for any real numbers a and b,

$$0 + 5 = 5 \quad \text{and} \quad (a + b) + 0 = a + b$$

$$1 \cdot 4 = 4 \quad \text{and} \quad (a + b) \cdot 1 = a + b$$

We now consider **inverses**. For each real number a, there is a unique real number $-a$ such that $a + (-a) = 0$. The number $-a$ is called the **additive inverse** of a, or the **negative** of a. For example, the additive inverse (or negative) of 7 is -7, since $7 + (-7) = 0$. The additive inverse (or negative) of -7 is $-(-7) = 7$, since $-7 + [-(-7)] = 0$.

CONCEPTUAL INSIGHT

Do not confuse negation with the sign of a number. If a is a real number, $-a$ is the negative of a and may be positive or negative. Specifically, if a is negative, then $-a$ is positive and if a is positive, then $-a$ is negative.

For each nonzero real number a, there is a unique real number $1/a$ such that $a(1/a) = 1$. The number $1/a$ is called the **multiplicative inverse** of a, or the **reciprocal** of a. For example, the multiplicative inverse (or reciprocal) of 4 is $\frac{1}{4}$, since $4\left(\frac{1}{4}\right) = 1$. (Also note that 4 is the multiplicative inverse of $\frac{1}{4}$.) The number 0 has no multiplicative inverse.

We now turn to the **distributive properties**, which involve both multiplication and addition. Consider the following two computations:

$$5(3 + 4) = 5 \cdot 7 = 35 \qquad 5 \cdot 3 + 5 \cdot 4 = 15 + 20 = 35$$

Thus,

$$5(3 + 4) = 5 \cdot 3 + 5 \cdot 4$$

and we say that multiplication by 5 *distributes* over the sum $(3 + 4)$. In general, **multiplication distributes over addition** in the real number system. Two more illustrations are

$$9(m + n) = 9m + 9n \qquad (7 + 2)u = 7u + 2u$$

EXAMPLE 1 **Real Number Properties** State the real number property that justifies the indicated statement.

Statement	Property Illustrated
(A) $x(y + z) = (y + z)x$	Commutative $(\cdot)$
(B) $5(2y) = (5 \cdot 2)y$	Associative $(\cdot)$
(C) $2 + (y + 7) = 2 + (7 + y)$	Commutative $(+)$
(D) $4z + 6z = (4 + 6)z$	Distributive
(E) If $m + n = 0$, then $n = -m$.	Inverse $(+)$

MATCHED PROBLEM 1 State the real number property that justifies the indicated statement.

(A) $8 + (3 + y) = (8 + 3) + y$

(B) $(x + y) + z = z + (x + y)$

(C) $(a + b)(x + y) = a(x + y) + b(x + y)$

(D) $5xy + 0 = 5xy$

(E) If $xy = 1, x \neq 0$, then $y = 1/x$.

Further Properties

Subtraction and *division* can be defined in terms of addition and multiplication, respectively:

DEFINITION Subtraction and Division

For all real numbers a and b,

Subtraction: $a - b = a + (-b)$ $\quad 7 - (-5) = 7 + [-(-5)] = 7 + 5 = 12$

Division: $a \div b = a\left(\frac{1}{b}\right), b \neq 0$ $\quad 9 \div 4 = 9\left(\frac{1}{4}\right) = \frac{9}{4}$

To subtract b from a, add the negative (the additive inverse) of b to a. To divide a by b, multiply a by the reciprocal (the multiplicative inverse) of b. Note that division by 0 is not defined, since 0 does not have a reciprocal. **0 can never be used as a divisor!**

The following properties of negatives can be proved using the preceding assumed properties and definitions.

THEOREM 1 Negative Properties

For all real numbers a and b,

1. $-(-a) = a$
2. $(-a)b = -(ab) = a(-b) = -ab$
3. $(-a)(-b) = ab$
4. $(-1)a = -a$
5. $\frac{-a}{b} = -\frac{a}{b} = \frac{a}{-b}, b \neq 0$
6. $\frac{-a}{-b} = -\frac{-a}{b} = -\frac{a}{-b} = \frac{a}{b}, b \neq 0$

We now state two important properties involving 0.

THEOREM 2 Zero Properties

For all real numbers a and b,

1. $a \cdot 0 = 0$ $\quad 0 \cdot 0 = 0 \quad (-35)(0) = 0$
2. $ab = 0$ if and only if $a = 0$ or $b = 0$

   If $(3x + 2)(x - 7) = 0$, then either $3x + 2 = 0$ or $x - 7 = 0$.

Fraction Properties

Recall that the quotient $a \div b(b \neq 0)$ written in the form a/b is called a **fraction**. The quantity a is called the **numerator**, and the quantity b is called the **denominator**.

THEOREM 3 Fraction Properties

For all real numbers a, b, c, d, and k (division by 0 excluded):

1. $\frac{a}{b} = \frac{c}{d}$ if and only if $ad = bc$ $\quad \frac{4}{6} = \frac{6}{9}$ since $4 \cdot 9 = 6 \cdot 6$

2. $\frac{ka}{kb} = \frac{a}{b}$ $\quad \frac{7 \cdot 3}{7 \cdot 5} = \frac{3}{5}$

3. $\frac{a}{b} \cdot \frac{c}{d} = \frac{ac}{bd}$ $\quad \frac{3}{5} \cdot \frac{7}{8} = \frac{3 \cdot 7}{5 \cdot 8}$

4. $\frac{a}{b} \div \frac{c}{d} = \frac{a}{b} \cdot \frac{d}{c}$ $\quad \frac{2}{3} \div \frac{5}{7} = \frac{2}{3} \cdot \frac{7}{5}$

5. $\frac{a}{b} + \frac{c}{b} = \frac{a + c}{b}$ $\quad \frac{3}{6} + \frac{5}{6} = \frac{3 + 5}{6}$

6. $\frac{a}{b} - \frac{c}{b} = \frac{a - c}{b}$ $\quad \frac{7}{8} - \frac{3}{8} = \frac{7 - 3}{8}$

7. $\frac{a}{b} + \frac{c}{d} = \frac{ad + bc}{bd}$ $\quad \frac{2}{3} + \frac{3}{5} = \frac{2 \cdot 5 + 3 \cdot 3}{3 \cdot 5}$

A fraction is a quotient, not just a pair of numbers. So if a and b are real numbers with $b \neq 0$, then $\frac{a}{b}$ corresponds to a point on the real number line. For example, $\frac{17}{2}$ corresponds to the point halfway between $\frac{16}{2} = 8$ and $\frac{18}{2} = 9$. Similarly, $-\frac{21}{5}$ corresponds to the point that is $\frac{1}{5}$ unit to the left of -4.

EXAMPLE 2 **Estimation** Round $\frac{22}{7} + \frac{18}{19}$ to the nearest integer.

SOLUTION Note that a calculator is not required: $\frac{22}{7}$ is a little greater than 3, and $\frac{18}{19}$ is a little less than 1. Therefore the sum, rounded to the nearest integer, is 4.

MATCHED PROBLEM 2 Round $\frac{6}{93}$ to the nearest integer.

Fractions with denominator 100 are called **percentages**. They are used so often that they have their own notation:

$$\frac{3}{100} = 3\% \qquad \frac{7.5}{100} = 7.5\% \qquad \frac{110}{100} = 110\%$$

So 3% is equivalent to 0.03, 7.5% is equivalent to 0.075, and so on.

EXAMPLE 3 **State Sales Tax** Find the sales tax that is owed on a purchase of \$947.69 if the tax rate is 6.5%.

SOLUTION $6.5\%(\$947.69) = 0.065(947.69) = \$61.60$

MATCHED PROBLEM 3 You intend to give a 20% tip, rounded to the nearest dollar, on a restaurant bill of \$78.47. How much is the tip?

Exercises A.1

All variables represent real numbers.

A *In Problems 1–6, replace each question mark with an appropriate expression that will illustrate the use of the indicated real number property.*

1. Commutative property $(\cdot)$: $uv = ?$
2. Commutative property $(+)$: $x + 7 = ?$
3. Associative property $(+)$: $3 + (7 + y) = ?$
4. Associative property $(\cdot)$: $x(yz) = ?$
5. Identity property $(\cdot)$: $1(u + v) = ?$
6. Identity property $(+)$: $0 + 9m = ?$

In Problems 7–26, indicate true (T) or false (F).

7. $5(8m) = (5 \cdot 8)m$

8. $a + cb = a + bc$

9. $5x + 7x = (5 + 7)x$

10. $uv(w + x) = uvw + uvx$

11. $-2(-a)(2x - y) = 2a(-4x + y)$

12. $8 \div (-5) = 8\left(\frac{1}{-5}\right)$

13. $(x + 3) + 2x = 2x + (x + 3)$

14. $\frac{x}{3y} \div \frac{5y}{x} = \frac{15y^2}{x^2}$

15. $\frac{2x}{-(x + 3)} = -\frac{2x}{x + 3}$

16. $-\frac{2x}{-(x - 3)} = \frac{2x}{x - 3}$

17. $(-3)\left(\frac{1}{-3}\right) = 1$

18. $(-0.5) + (0.5) = 0$

19. $-x^2y^2 = (-1)x^2y^2$

20. $[-(x + 2)](-x) = (x + 2)x$

21. $\frac{a}{b} + \frac{c}{d} = \frac{a + c}{b + d}$

22. $\frac{k}{k + b} = \frac{1}{1 + b}$

23. $(x + 8)(x + 6) = (x + 8)x + (x + 8)6$

24. $u(u - 2v) + v(u - 2v) = (u + v)(u - 2v)$

25. If $(x - 2)(2x + 3) = 0$, then either $x - 2 = 0$ or $2x + 3 = 0$.

26. If either $x - 2 = 0$ or $2x + 3 = 0$, then $(x - 2)(2x + 3) = 0$.

B 27. If $uv = 1$, does either u or v have to be 1? Explain.

28. If $uv = 0$, does either u or v have to be 0? Explain.

29. Indicate whether the following are true (T) or false (F):

(A) All integers are natural numbers.

(B) All rational numbers are real numbers.

(C) All natural numbers are rational numbers.

30. Indicate whether the following are true (T) or false (F):

(A) All natural numbers are integers.

(B) All real numbers are irrational.

(C) All rational numbers are real numbers.

31. Give an example of a real number that is not a rational number.

32. Give an example of a rational number that is not an integer.

33. Given the sets of numbers N (natural numbers), Z (integers), Q (rational numbers), and R (real numbers), indicate to which set(s) each of the following numbers belongs:

(A) 8 (B) $\sqrt{2}$ (C) -1.414 (D) $\frac{-5}{2}$

34. Given the sets of numbers N, Z, Q, and R (see Problem 33), indicate to which set(s) each of the following numbers belongs:

(A) -3 (B) 3.14 (C) π (D) $\frac{2}{3}$

35. Indicate true (T) or false (F), and for each false statement find real number replacements for a, b, and c that will provide a counterexample. For all real numbers a, b, and c,

(A) $a(b - c) = ab - c$

(B) $(a - b) - c = a - (b - c)$

(C) $a(bc) = (ab)c$

(D) $(a \div b) \div c = a \div (b \div c)$

36. Indicate true (T) or false (F), and for each false statement find real number replacements for a and b that will provide a counterexample. For all real numbers a and b,

(A) $a + b = b + a$

(B) $a - b = b - a$

(C) $ab = ba$

(D) $a \div b = b \div a$

C 37. If $c = 0.151515\ldots$, then $100c = 15.1515\ldots$ and

$$100c - c = 15.1515\ldots - 0.151515\ldots$$
$$99c = 15$$
$$c = \frac{15}{99} = \frac{5}{33}$$

Proceeding similarly, convert the repeating decimal $0.090909\ldots$ into a fraction. (All repeating decimals are rational numbers, and all rational numbers have repeating decimal representations.)

38. Repeat Problem 37 for $0.181818\ldots$.

Use a calculator to express each number in Problems 39 and 40 as a decimal to the capacity of your calculator. Observe the repeating decimal representation of the rational numbers and the nonrepeating decimal representation of the irrational numbers.

39. (A) $\frac{13}{6}$ (B) $\sqrt{21}$ (C) $\frac{7}{16}$ (D) $\frac{29}{111}$

40. (A) $\frac{8}{9}$ (B) $\frac{3}{11}$ (C) $\sqrt{5}$ (D) $\frac{11}{8}$

In Problems 41–44, without using a calculator, round to the nearest integer.

41. (A) $\frac{43}{13}$ (B) $\frac{37}{19}$

42. (A) $\frac{9}{17}$ (B) $-\frac{12}{25}$

43. (A) $\frac{7}{8} + \frac{11}{12}$ (B) $\frac{55}{9} - \frac{7}{55}$

44. (A) $\frac{5}{6} - \frac{18}{19}$ (B) $\frac{13}{5} + \frac{44}{21}$

Applications

45. **Sales tax.** Find the tax owed on a purchase of \$182.39 if the state sales tax rate is 9%. (Round to the nearest cent).

46. **Sales tax.** If you paid \$29.86 in tax on a purchase of \$533.19, what was the sales tax rate? (Write as a percentage, rounded to one decimal place).

47. **Gasoline prices.** If the price per gallon of gas jumped from \$4.25 to \$4.37, what was the percentage increase? (Round to one decimal place).

48. **Gasoline prices.** The price of gas increased 4% in one week. If the price last week was \$4.30 per gallon, what is the price now? (Round to the nearest cent).

Answers to Matched Problems

1. (A) Associative (+) (B) Commutative (+)
   (C) Distributive (D) Identity (+)
   (E) Inverse (•)
2. 0
3. \$16

A.2 Operations on Polynomials

- Natural Number Exponents
- Polynomials
- Combining Like Terms
- Addition and Subtraction
- Multiplication
- Combined Operations

This section covers basic operations on *polynomials*. Our discussion starts with a brief review of natural number exponents. Integer and rational exponents and their properties will be discussed in detail in subsequent sections. (Natural numbers, integers, and rational numbers are important parts of the real number system; see Table 1 and Figure 1 in Appendix A.1.)

Natural Number Exponents

We define a **natural number exponent** as follows:

DEFINITION Natural Number Exponent

For n a natural number and b any real number,

$$b^n = b \cdot b \cdot \cdots \cdot b \quad n \text{ factors of } b$$

$$3^5 = 3 \cdot 3 \cdot 3 \cdot 3 \cdot 3 \quad 5 \text{ factors of } 3$$

where n is called the exponent and b is called the **base**.

Along with this definition, we state the **first property of exponents**:

THEOREM 1 First Property of Exponents

For any natural numbers m and n, and any real number b:

$$b^m b^n = b^{m+n} \quad (2t^4)(5t^3) = 2 \cdot 5t^{4+3} = 10t^7$$

Polynomials

Algebraic expressions are formed by using constants and variables and the algebraic operations of addition, subtraction, multiplication, division, raising to powers, and taking roots. Special types of algebraic expressions are called *polynomials*. A **polynomial in one variable** x is constructed by adding or subtracting constants and terms of the form ax^n, where a is a real number and n is a natural number. A **polynomial in two variables** x and y is constructed by adding and subtracting constants and terms of the form ax^my^n, where a is a real number and m and n are natural numbers. Polynomials in three and more variables are defined in a similar manner.

Polynomials		Not Polynomials	
8	0	$\frac{1}{x}$	$\frac{x-y}{x^2+y^2}$
$3x^3 - 6x + 7$ $2x^2 - 7xy - 8y^2$ $2x - 3y + 2$	$6x + 3$ $9y^3 + 4y^2 - y + 4$ $u^5 - 3u^3v^2 + 2uv^4 - v^4$	$\sqrt{x^3 - 2x}$	$2x^{-2} - 3x^{-1}$

Polynomial forms are encountered frequently in mathematics. For the efficient study of polynomials, it is useful to classify them according to their *degree.* If a term in a polynomial has only one variable as a factor, then the **degree of the term** is the power of the variable. If two or more variables are present in a term as factors, then the **degree of the term** is the sum of the powers of the variables. The **degree of a polynomial** is the degree of the nonzero term with the highest degree in the polynomial. Any nonzero constant is defined to be a **polynomial of degree 0**. The number 0 is also a polynomial but is not assigned a degree.

EXAMPLE 1 Degree

(A) The degree of the first term in $5x^3 + \sqrt{3}x - \frac{1}{2}$ is 3, the degree of the second term is 1, the degree of the third term is 0, and the degree of the whole polynomial is 3 (the same as the degree of the term with the highest degree).

(B) The degree of the first term in $8u^3v^2 - \sqrt{7}uv^2$ is 5, the degree of the second term is 3, and the degree of the whole polynomial is 5.

Matched Problem 1

(A) Given the polynomial $6x^5 + 7x^3 - 2$, what is the degree of the first term? The second term? The third term? The whole polynomial?

(B) Given the polynomial $2u^4v^2 - 5uv^3$, what is the degree of the first term? The second term? The whole polynomial?

In addition to classifying polynomials by degree, we also call a single-term polynomial a **monomial**, a two-term polynomial a **binomial**, and a three-term polynomial a **trinomial**.

Combining Like Terms

The concept of *coefficient* plays a central role in the process of combining *like terms.* A constant in a term of a polynomial, including the sign that precedes it, is called the **numerical coefficient**, or simply, the **coefficient**, of the term. If a constant does not appear, or only a + sign appears, the coefficient is understood to be 1. If only a − sign appears, the coefficient is understood to be −1. Given the polynomial

$$5x^4 - x^3 - 3x^2 + x - 7 = 5x^4 + (-1)x^3 + (-3)x^2 + 1x + (-7)$$

the coefficient of the first term is 5, the coefficient of the second term is −1, the coefficient of the third term is −3, the coefficient of the fourth term is 1, and the coefficient of the fifth term is −7.

The following distributive properties are fundamental to the process of combining *like terms.*

THEOREM 2 Distributive Properties of Real Numbers

1. $a(b + c) = (b + c)a = ab + ac$
2. $a(b - c) = (b - c)a = ab - ac$
3. $a(b + c + \cdots + f) = ab + ac + \cdots + af$

Two terms in a polynomial are called **like terms** if they have exactly the same variable factors to the same powers. The numerical coefficients may or may not be the same. Since constant terms involve no variables, all constant terms are like terms. If a polynomial contains two or more like terms, these terms can be combined into a single term by making use of distributive properties. The following example illustrates the reasoning behind the process:

$$
\begin{aligned}
3x^2y - 5xy^2 + x^2y - 2x^2y &= 3x^2y + x^2y - 2x^2y - 5xy^2 \\
&= (3x^2y + 1x^2y - 2x^2y) - 5xy^2 \\
&= (3 + 1 - 2)x^2y - 5xy^2 \\
&= 2x^2y - 5xy^2
\end{aligned}
$$

Note the use of distributive properties.

Free use is made of the real number properties discussed in Appendix A.1.

How can we simplify expressions such as $4(x - 2y) - 3(2x - 7y)$? We clear the expression of parentheses using distributive properties, and combine like terms:

$$
\begin{aligned}
4(x - 2y) - 3(2x - 7y) &= 4x - 8y - 6x + 21y \\
&= -2x + 13y
\end{aligned}
$$

EXAMPLE 2 **Removing Parentheses** Remove parentheses and simplify:

(A) $2(3x^2 - 2x + 5) + (x^2 + 3x - 7) = 2(3x^2 - 2x + 5) + 1(x^2 + 3x - 7)$
$= 6x^2 - 4x + 10 + x^2 + 3x - 7$
$= 7x^2 - x + 3$

(B) $(x^3 - 2x - 6) - (2x^3 - x^2 + 2x - 3)$
$= 1(x^3 - 2x - 6) + (-1)(2x^3 - x^2 + 2x - 3)$ Be careful with the sign here
$= x^3 - 2x - 6 - 2x^3 + x^2 - 2x + 3$
$= -x^3 + x^2 - 4x - 3$

(C) $[3x^2 - (2x + 1)] - (x^2 - 1) = [3x^2 - 2x - 1] - (x^2 - 1)$
$= 3x^2 - 2x - 1 - x^2 + 1$
$= 2x^2 - 2x$

MATCHED PROBLEM 2 Remove parentheses and simplify:

(A) $3(u^2 - 2v^2) + (u^2 + 5v^2)$

(B) $(m^3 - 3m^2 + m - 1) - (2m^3 - m + 3)$

(C) $(x^3 - 2) - [2x^3 - (3x + 4)]$

Addition and Subtraction

Addition and subtraction of polynomials can be thought of in terms of removing parentheses and combining like terms, as illustrated in Example 2. Horizontal and vertical arrangements are illustrated in the next two examples. You should be able to work either way, letting the situation dictate your choice.

EXAMPLE 3 **Adding Polynomials** Add horizontally and vertically:

$$x^4 - 3x^3 + x^2, \quad -x^3 - 2x^2 + 3x, \quad \text{and} \quad 3x^2 - 4x - 5$$

SOLUTION Add horizontally:

$$
\begin{aligned}
&(x^4 - 3x^3 + x^2) + (-x^3 - 2x^2 + 3x) + (3x^2 - 4x - 5) \\
&= x^4 - 3x^3 + x^2 - x^3 - 2x^2 + 3x + 3x^2 - 4x - 5 \\
&= x^4 - 4x^3 + 2x^2 - x - 5
\end{aligned}
$$

Or vertically, by lining up like terms and adding their coefficients:

$$
\begin{array}{rrrrr}
x^4 & - 3x^3 & + x^2 & & \\
 & - x^3 & - 2x^2 & + 3x & \\
 & & 3x^2 & - 4x & - 5 \\
\hline
x^4 & - 4x^3 & + 2x^2 & - x & - 5
\end{array}
$$

MATCHED PROBLEM 3 Add horizontally and vertically:

$$3x^4 - 2x^3 - 4x^2, \quad x^3 - 2x^2 - 5x, \quad \text{and} \quad x^2 + 7x - 2$$

EXAMPLE 4 **Subtracting Polynomials** Subtract $4x^2 - 3x + 5$ from $x^2 - 8$, both horizontally and vertically.

SOLUTION $(x^2 - 8) - (4x^2 - 3x + 5)$ or

$$= x^2 - 8 - 4x^2 + 3x - 5$$
$$= -3x^2 + 3x - 13$$

$$\begin{array}{r} x^2 \qquad\quad - 8 \\ -4x^2 + 3x - 5 \\ \hline -3x^2 + 3x - 13 \end{array}$$

← Change signs and add.

MATCHED PROBLEM 4 Subtract $2x^2 - 5x + 4$ from $5x^2 - 6$, both horizontally and vertically.

Multiplication

Multiplication of algebraic expressions involves the extensive use of distributive properties for real numbers, as well as other real number properties.

EXAMPLE 5 **Multiplying Polynomials** Multiply: $(2x - 3)(3x^2 - 2x + 3)$

SOLUTION

$$\begin{aligned}(2x - 3)(3x^2 - 2x + 3) &= 2x(3x^2 - 2x + 3) - 3(3x^2 - 2x + 3) \\ &= 6x^3 - 4x^2 + 6x - 9x^2 + 6x - 9 \\ &= 6x^3 - 13x^2 + 12x - 9\end{aligned}$$

Or, using a vertical arrangement,

$$\begin{array}{rrrr} & 3x^2 & - 2x & + 3 \\ & 2x & - 3 & \\ \hline 6x^3 & - 4x^2 & + 6x & \\ & - 9x^2 & + 6x & - 9 \\ \hline 6x^3 & - 13x^2 & + 12x & - 9 \end{array}$$

MATCHED PROBLEM 5 Multiply: $(2x - 3)(2x^2 + 3x - 2)$

Thus, to multiply two polynomials, multiply each term of one by each term of the other, and combine like terms.

Products of binomial factors occur frequently, so it is useful to develop procedures that will enable us to write down their products by inspection. To find the product $(2x - 1)(3x + 2)$ we proceed as follows:

$$\begin{aligned}(2x - 1)(3x + 2) &= 6x^2 + 4x - 3x - 2 \\ &= 6x^2 + x - 2\end{aligned}$$

The inner and outer products are like terms, so combine into a single term.

To speed the process, we do the step in the dashed box mentally.

Products of certain binomial factors occur so frequently that it is useful to learn formulas for their products. The following formulas are easily verified by multiplying the factors on the left.

THEOREM 3 Special Products

1. $(a - b)(a + b) = a^2 - b^2$
2. $(a + b)^2 = a^2 + 2ab + b^2$
3. $(a - b)^2 = a^2 - 2ab + b^2$

EXAMPLE 6 **Special Products** Multiply mentally, where possible.

(A) $(2x - 3y)(5x + 2y)$ (B) $(3a - 2b)(3a + 2b)$

(C) $(5x - 3)^2$ (D) $(m + 2n)^3$

SOLUTION

(A) $(2x - 3y)(5x + 2y) = 10x^2 + 4xy - 15xy - 6y^2$
$= 10x^2 - 11xy - 6y^2$

(B) $(3a - 2b)(3a + 2b) = (3a)^2 - (2b)^2$
$= 9a^2 - 4b^2$

(C) $(5x - 3)^2 = (5x)^2 - 2(5x)(3) + 3^2$
$= 25x^2 - 30x + 9$

(D)
$$\begin{aligned}(m + 2n)^3 &= (m + 2n)^2(m + 2n)\\ &= (m^2 + 4mn + 4n^2)(m + 2n)\\ &= m^2(m + 2n) + 4mn(m + 2n) + 4n^2(m + 2n)\\ &= m^3 + 2m^2n + 4m^2n + 8mn^2 + 4mn^2 + 8n^3\\ &= m^3 + 6m^2n + 12mn^2 + 8n^3\end{aligned}$$

MATCHED PROBLEM 6 Multiply mentally, where possible.

(A) $(4u - 3v)(2u + v)$ (B) $(2xy + 3)(2xy - 3)$

(C) $(m + 4n)(m - 4n)$ (D) $(2u - 3v)^2$

(E) $(2x - y)^3$

Combined Operations

We complete this section by considering several examples that use all the operations just discussed. Note that in simplifying, we usually remove grouping symbols starting from the inside. That is, we remove parentheses ( ) first, then brackets [ ], and finally braces { }, if present. Also, we observe the following order of operations.

DEFINITION Order of Operations

Multiplication and division precede addition and subtraction, and taking powers precedes multiplication and division.

$$2 \cdot 3 + 4 = 6 + 4 = 10, \quad \text{not} \quad 2 \cdot 7 = 14$$

$$\frac{10^2}{2} = \frac{100}{2} = 50, \quad \text{not} \quad 5^2 = 25$$

EXAMPLE 7 **Combined Operations** Perform the indicated operations and simplify:

(A)
$$\begin{aligned}3x - \{5 - 3[x - x(3 - x)]\} &= 3x - \{5 - 3[x - 3x + x^2]\}\\ &= 3x - \{5 - 3x + 9x - 3x^2\}\\ &= 3x - 5 + 3x - 9x + 3x^2\\ &= 3x^2 - 3x - 5\end{aligned}$$

(B)
$$\begin{aligned}(x - 2y)(2x + 3y) - (2x + y)^2 &= 2x^2 - xy - 6y^2 - (4x^2 + 4xy + y^2)\\ &= 2x^2 - xy - 6y^2 - 4x^2 - 4xy - y^2\\ &= -2x^2 - 5xy - 7y^2\end{aligned}$$

MATCHED PROBLEM 7 Perform the indicated operations and simplify:

(A) $2t - \{7 - 2[t - t(4 + t)]\}$

(B) $(u - 3v)^2 - (2u - v)(2u + v)$

Exercises A.2

A *Problems 1–8 refer to the following polynomials:*

(A) $2x - 3$ (B) $2x^2 - x + 2$ (C) $x^3 + 2x^2 - x + 3$

1. What is the degree of (C)?

2. What is the degree of (A)?

3. Add (B) and (C).

4. Add (A) and (B).

5. Subtract (B) from (C).

6. Subtract (A) from (B).

7. Multiply (B) and (C).

8. Multiply (A) and (C).

In Problems 9–30, perform the indicated operations and simplify.

9. $2(u - 1) - (3u + 2) - 2(2u - 3)$

10. $2(x - 1) + 3(2x - 3) - (4x - 5)$

11. $4a - 2a[5 - 3(a + 2)]$

12. $2y - 3y[4 - 2(y - 1)]$

13. $(a + b)(a - b)$

14. $(m - n)(m + n)$

15. $(3x - 5)(2x + 1)$

16. $(4t - 3)(t - 2)$

17. $(2x - 3y)(x + 2y)$

18. $(3x + 2y)(x - 3y)$

19. $(3y + 2)(3y - 2)$

20. $(2m - 7)(2m + 7)$

21. $-(2x - 3)^2$

22. $-(5 - 3x)^2$

23. $(4m + 3n)(4m - 3n)$

24. $(3x - 2y)(3x + 2y)$

25. $(3u + 4v)^2$

26. $(4x - y)^2$

27. $(a - b)(a^2 + ab + b^2)$

28. $(a + b)(a^2 - ab + b^2)$

29. $[(x - y) + 3z][(x - y) - 3z]$

30. $[a - (2b - c)][a + (2b - c)]$

B *In Problems 31–44, perform the indicated operations and simplify.*

31. $m - \{m - [m - (m - 1)]\}$

32. $2x - 3\{x + 2[x - (x + 5)] + 1\}$

33. $(x^2 - 2xy + y^2)(x^2 + 2xy + y^2)$

34. $(3x - 2y)^2(2x + 5y)$

35. $(5a - 2b)^2 - (2b + 5a)^2$

36. $(2x - 1)^2 - (3x + 2)(3x - 2)$

37. $(m - 2)^2 - (m - 2)(m + 2)$

38. $(x - 3)(x + 3) - (x - 3)^2$

39. $(x - 2y)(2x + y) - (x + 2y)(2x - y)$

40. $(3m + n)(m - 3n) - (m + 3n)(3m - n)$

41. $(u + v)^3$

42. $(x - y)^3$

43. $(x - 2y)^3$

44. $(2m - n)^3$

45. Subtract the sum of the last two polynomials from the sum of the first two: $2x^2 - 4xy + y^2$, $3xy - y^2$, $x^2 - 2xy - y^2$, $-x^2 + 3xy - 2y^2$

46. Subtract the sum of the first two polynomials from the sum of the last two: $3m^2 - 2m + 5$, $4m^2 - m$, $3m^2 - 3m - 2$, $m^3 + m^2 + 2$

C *In Problems 47–50, perform the indicated operations and simplify.*

47. $[(2x - 1)^2 - x(3x + 1)]^2$

48. $[5x(3x + 1) - 5(2x - 1)^2]^2$

49. $2\{(x - 3)(x^2 - 2x + 1) - x[3 - x(x - 2)]\}$

50. $-3x\{x[x - x(2 - x)] - (x + 2)(x^2 - 3)\}$

51. If you are given two polynomials, one of degree m and the other of degree n, where m is greater than n, what is the degree of their product?

52. What is the degree of the sum of the two polynomials in Problem 51?

53. How does the answer to Problem 51 change if the two polynomials can have the same degree?

54. How does the answer to Problem 52 change if the two polynomials can have the same degree?

55. Show by example that, in general, $(a + b)^2 \neq a^2 + b^2$. Discuss possible conditions on a and b that would make this a valid equation.

56. Show by example that, in general, $(a - b)^2 \neq a^2 - b^2$. Discuss possible conditions on a and b that would make this a valid equation.

Applications

57. Investment. You have \$10,000 to invest, part at 9% and the rest at 12%. If x is the amount invested at 9%, write an algebraic expression that represents the total annual income from both investments. Simplify the expression.

58. Investment. A person has \$100,000 to invest. If \$$x$ are invested in a money market account yielding 7% and twice that amount in certificates of deposit yielding 9%, and if the rest is invested in high-grade bonds yielding 11%, write an algebraic expression that represents the total annual income from all three investments. Simplify the expression.

59. **Gross receipts.** Four thousand tickets are to be sold for a musical show. If x tickets are to be sold for \$20 each and three times that number for \$30 each, and if the rest are sold for \$50 each, write an algebraic expression that represents the gross receipts from ticket sales, assuming all tickets are sold. Simplify the expression.

60. **Gross receipts.** Six thousand tickets are to be sold for a concert, some for \$20 each and the rest for \$35 each. If x is the number of \$20 tickets sold, write an algebraic expression that represents the gross receipts from ticket sales, assuming all tickets are sold. Simplify the expression.

61. **Nutrition.** Food mix A contains 2% fat, and food mix B contains 6% fat. A 10-kilogram diet mix of foods A and B is formed. If x kilograms of food A are used, write an algebraic expression that represents the total number of kilograms of fat in the final food mix. Simplify the expression.

62. **Nutrition.** Each ounce of food M contains 8 units of calcium, and each ounce of food N contains 5 units of calcium. A 160-ounce diet mix is formed using foods M and N. If x is the number of ounces of food M used, write an algebraic expression that represents the total number of units of calcium in the diet mix. Simplify the expression.

Answers to Matched Problems

1. (A) 5, 3, 0, 5 (B) 6, 4, 6
2. (A) $4u^2 - v^2$ (B) $-m^3 - 3m^2 + 2m - 4$ (C) $-x^3 + 3x + 2$
3. $3x^4 - x^3 - 5x^2 + 2x - 2$
4. $3x^2 + 5x - 10$
5. $4x^3 - 13x + 6$
6. (A) $8u^2 - 2uv - 3v^2$ (B) $4x^2y^2 - 9$ (C) $m^2 - 16n^2$ (D) $4u^2 - 12uv + 9v^2$ (E) $8x^3 - 12x^2y + 6xy^2 - y^3$
7. (A) $-2t^2 - 4t - 7$ (B) $-3u^2 - 6uv + 10v^2$

A.3 Factoring Polynomials

- Common Factors
- Factoring by Grouping
- Factoring Second-Degree Polynomials
- Special Factoring Formulas
- Combined Factoring Techniques

A positive integer is **written in factored form** if it is written as the product of two or more positive integers; for example, $120 = 10 \cdot 12$. A positive integer is **factored completely** if each factor is prime; for example, $120 = 2 \cdot 2 \cdot 2 \cdot 3 \cdot 5$. (Recall that an integer $p > 1$ is **prime** if p cannot be factored as the product of two smaller positive integers. So the first ten primes are 2, 3, 5, 7, 11, 13, 17, 19, 23, and 29). A **tree diagram** is a helpful way to visualize a factorization (Fig 1).

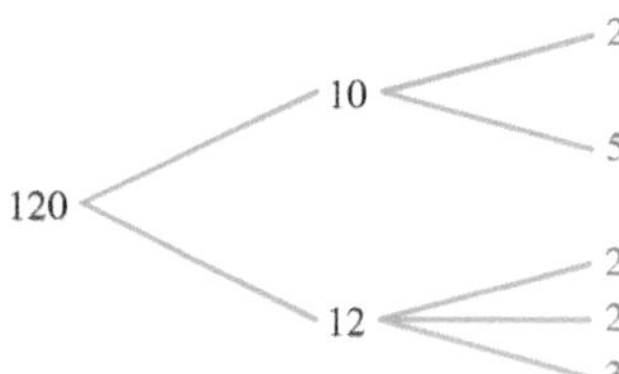

Figure 1

A polynomial is **written in factored form** if it is written as the product of two or more polynomials. The following polynomials are written in factored form:

$$4x^2y - 6xy^2 = 2xy(2x - 3y) \qquad 2x^3 - 8x = 2x(x - 2)(x + 2)$$
$$x^2 - x - 6 = (x - 3)(x + 2) \qquad 5m^2 + 20 = 5(m^2 + 4)$$

Unless stated to the contrary, we will limit our discussion of factoring polynomials to polynomials with integer coefficients.

A polynomial with integer coefficients is said to be **factored completely** if each factor cannot be expressed as the product of two or more polynomials with integer coefficients, other than itself or 1. All the polynomials above, as we will see by the conclusion of this section, are factored completely.

Writing polynomials in completely factored form is often a difficult task. But accomplishing it can lead to the simplification of certain algebraic expressions and to the solution of certain types of equations and inequalities. The distributive properties for real numbers are central to the factoring process.

Common Factors

Generally, a first step in any factoring procedure is to factor out all factors common to all terms.

EXAMPLE 1 **Common Factors** Factor out all factors common to all terms.

(A) $3x^3y - 6x^2y^2 - 3xy^3$

(B) $3y(2y + 5) + 2(2y + 5)$

SOLUTION

(A) $3x^3y - 6x^2y^2 - 3xy^3 = (3xy)x^2 - (3xy)2xy - (3xy)y^2$
$= 3xy(x^2 - 2xy - y^2)$

(B) $3y(2y + 5) + 2(2y + 5) = 3y(2y + 5) + 2(2y + 5)$
$= (3y + 2)(2y + 5)$

MATCHED PROBLEM 1 Factor out all factors common to all terms.

(A) $2x^3y - 8x^2y^2 - 6xy^3$ (B) $2x(3x - 2) - 7(3x - 2)$

Factoring by Grouping

Occasionally, polynomials can be factored by grouping terms in such a way that we obtain results that look like Example 1B. We can then complete the factoring following the steps used in that example. This process will prove useful in the next subsection, where an efficient method is developed for factoring a second-degree polynomial as the product of two first-degree polynomials, if such factors exist.

EXAMPLE 2 **Factoring by Grouping** Factor by grouping.

(A) $3x^2 - 3x - x + 1$

(B) $4x^2 - 2xy - 6xy + 3y^2$

(C) $y^2 + xz + xy + yz$

SOLUTION

(A) $3x^2 - 3x - x + 1$
$= (3x^2 - 3x) - (x - 1)$
$= 3x(x - 1) - (x - 1)$
$= (x - 1)(3x - 1)$

Group the first two and the last two terms. Factor out any common factors from each group. The common factor $(x - 1)$ can be taken out, and the factoring is complete.

(B) $4x^2 - 2xy - 6xy + 3y^2 = (4x^2 - 2xy) - (6xy - 3y^2)$
$= 2x(2x - y) - 3y(2x - y)$
$= (2x - y)(2x - 3y)$

(C) If, as in parts (A) and (B), we group the first two terms and the last two terms of $y^2 + xz + xy + yz$, no common factor can be taken out of each group to complete the factoring. However, if the two middle terms are reversed, we can proceed as before:

$$\begin{aligned} y^2 + xz + xy + yz &= y^2 + xy + xz + yz \\ &= (y^2 + xy) + (xz + yz) \\ &= y(y + x) + z(x + y) \\ &= y(x + y) + z(x + y) \\ &= (x + y)(y + z) \end{aligned}$$

MATCHED PROBLEM 2 Factor by grouping.

(A) $6x^2 + 2x + 9x + 3$

(B) $2u^2 + 6uv - 3uv - 9v^2$

(C) $ac + bd + bc + ad$

Factoring Second-Degree Polynomials

We now turn our attention to factoring second-degree polynomials of the form

$$2x^2 - 5x - 3 \quad \text{and} \quad 2x^2 + 3xy - 2y^2$$

into the product of two first-degree polynomials with integer coefficients. Since many second-degree polynomials with integer coefficients cannot be factored in this way, it would be useful to know ahead of time that the factors we are seeking actually exist. The factoring approach we use, involving the *ac test*, determines at the beginning whether first-degree factors with integer coefficients do exist. Then, if they exist, the test provides a simple method for finding them.

THEOREM 1 *ac* Test for Factorability

If in polynomials of the form

$$ax^2 + bx + c \quad \text{or} \quad ax^2 + bxy + cy^2 \qquad (1)$$

the product ac has two integer factors p and q whose sum is the coefficient b of the middle term; that is, if integers p and q exist so that

$$pq = ac \quad \text{and} \quad p + q = b \qquad (2)$$

then the polynomials have first-degree factors with integer coefficients. If no integers p and q exist that satisfy equations (2), then the polynomials in equations (1) will not have first-degree factors with integer coefficients.

If integers p and q exist that satisfy equations (2) in the ac test, the factoring always can be completed as follows: Using $b = p + q$, split the middle terms in equations (1) to obtain

$$ax^2 + bx + c = ax^2 + px + qx + c$$

$$ax^2 + bxy + cy^2 = ax^2 + pxy + qxy + cy^2$$

Complete the factoring by grouping the first two terms and the last two terms as in Example 2. This process always works, and it does not matter if the two middle terms on the right are interchanged.

Several examples should make the process clear. After a little practice, you will perform many of the steps mentally and will find the process fast and efficient.

EXAMPLE 3 **Factoring Second-Degree Polynomials** Factor, if possible, using integer coefficients.

(A) $4x^2 - 4x - 3$ (B) $2x^2 - 3x - 4$ (C) $6x^2 - 25xy + 4y^2$

SOLUTION

(A) $4x^2 - 4x - 3$

Step 1 Use the ac test to test for factorability. Comparing $4x^2 - 4x - 3$ with $ax^2 + bx + c$, we see that $a = 4$, $b = -4$, and $c = -3$. Multiply a and c to obtain

$$ac = (4)(-3) = -12$$

List all pairs of integers whose product is -12, as shown in the margin. These are called **factor pairs** of -12. Then try to find a factor pair that sums to $b = -4$, the coefficient of the middle term in $4x^2 - 4x - 3$. (In practice, this part of Step 1 is often done mentally and can be done rather quickly.) Notice that the factor pair 2 and -6 sums to -4. By the ac test, $4x^2 - 4x - 3$ has first-degree factors with integer coefficients.

pq
$(1)(-12)$
$(-1)(12)$
$(2)(-6)$
$(-2)(6)$
$(3)(-4)$
$(-3)(4)$

All factor pairs of $-12 = ac$

Step 2 Split the middle term, using $b = p + q$, and complete the factoring by grouping. Using $-4 = 2 + (-6)$, we split the middle term in $4x^2 - 4x - 3$ and complete the factoring by grouping:

$$\begin{aligned} 4x^2 - 4x - 3 &= 4x^2 + 2x - 6x - 3 \\ &= (4x^2 + 2x) - (6x + 3) \\ &= 2x(2x + 1) - 3(2x + 1) \\ &= (2x + 1)(2x - 3) \end{aligned}$$

The result can be checked by multiplying the two factors to obtain the original polynomial.

(B) $2x^2 - 3x - 4$

Step 1 Use the ac test to test for factorability:

$$ac = (2)(-4) = -8$$

pq
$(-1)(8)$
$(1)(-8)$
$(-2)(4)$
$(2)(-4)$

All factor pairs of $-8 = ac$

Does -8 have a factor pair whose sum is -3? None of the factor pairs listed in the margin sums to $-3 = b$, the coefficient of the middle term in $2x^2 - 3x - 4$. According to the ac test, we can conclude that $2x^2 - 3x - 4$ does not have first-degree factors with integer coefficients, and we say that the polynomial is **not factorable**.

(C) $6x^2 - 25xy + 4y^2$

Step 1 Use the ac test to test for factorability:

$$ac = (6)(4) = 24$$

Mentally checking through the factor pairs of 24, keeping in mind that their sum must be $-25 = b$, we see that if $p = -1$ and $q = -24$, then

$$pq = (-1)(-24) = 24 = ac$$

and

$$p + q = (-1) + (-24) = -25 = b$$

So the polynomial is factorable.

Step 2 Split the middle term, using $b = p + q$, and complete the factoring by grouping. Using $-25 = (-1) + (-24)$, we split the middle term in $6x^2 - 25xy + 4y^2$ and complete the factoring by grouping:

$$\begin{aligned} 6x^2 - 25xy + 4y^2 &= 6x^2 - xy - 24xy + 4y^2 \\ &= (6x^2 - xy) - (24xy - 4y^2) \\ &= x(6x - y) - 4y(6x - y) \\ &= (6x - y)(x - 4y) \end{aligned}$$

The check is left to the reader.

MATCHED PROBLEM 3 Factor, if possible, using integer coefficients.

(A) $2x^2 + 11x - 6$

(B) $4x^2 + 11x - 6$

(C) $6x^2 + 5xy - 4y^2$

Special Factoring Formulas

The factoring formulas listed in the following box will enable us to factor certain polynomial forms that occur frequently. These formulas can be established by multiplying the factors on the right.

THEOREM 2 Special Factoring Formulas

Perfect square:	1. $u^2 + 2uv + v^2 = (u + v)^2$
Perfect square:	2. $u^2 - 2uv + v^2 = (u - v)^2$
Difference of squares:	3. $u^2 - v^2 = (u - v)(u + v)$
Difference of cubes:	4. $u^3 - v^3 = (u - v)(u^2 + uv + v^2)$
Sum of cubes:	5. $u^3 + v^3 = (u + v)(u^2 - uv + v^2)$

CAUTION Notice that $u^2 + v^2$ is not included in the list of special factoring formulas. In fact,

$$u^2 + v^2 \neq (au + bv)(cu + dv)$$

for any choice of real number coefficients a, b, c, and d.

EXAMPLE 4 **Factoring** Factor completely.

(A) $4m^2 - 12mn + 9n^2$ (B) $x^2 - 16y^2$ (C) $z^3 - 1$
(D) $m^3 + n^3$ (E) $a^2 - 4(b + 2)^2$

SOLUTION

(A) $4m^2 - 12mn + 9n^2 = (2m - 3n)^2$

(B) $x^2 - 16y^2 = x^2 - (4y)^2 = (x - 4y)(x + 4y)$

(C) $z^3 - 1 = (z - 1)(z^2 + z + 1)$ Use the ac test to verify that $z^2 + z + 1$ cannot be factored.

(D) $m^3 + n^3 = (m + n)(m^2 - mn + n^2)$ Use the ac test to verify that $m^2 - mn + n^2$ cannot be factored.

(E) $a^2 - 4(b + 2)^2 = [a - 2(b + 2)][a + 2(b + 2)]$

MATCHED PROBLEM 4 Factor completely:

(A) $x^2 + 6xy + 9y^2$ (B) $9x^2 - 4y^2$ (C) $8m^3 - 1$
(D) $x^3 + y^3z^3$ (E) $9(m - 3)^2 - 4n^2$

Combined Factoring Techniques

We complete this section by considering several factoring problems that involve combinations of the preceding techniques.

PROCEDURE Factoring Polynomials

Step 1 Take out any factors common to all terms.
Step 2 Use any of the special formulas listed in Theorem 2 that are applicable.
Step 3 Apply the ac test to any remaining second-degree polynomial factors.

Note: It may be necessary to perform some of these steps more than once. Furthermore, the order of applying these steps can vary.

EXAMPLE 5 **Combined Factoring Techniques** Factor completely.

(A) $3x^3 - 48x$ (B) $3u^4 - 3u^3v - 9u^2v^2$
(C) $3m^2 - 24mn^3$ (D) $3x^4 - 5x^2 + 2$

SOLUTION

(A) $3x^3 - 48x = 3x(x^2 - 16) = 3x(x - 4)(x + 4)$

(B) $3u^4 - 3u^3v - 9u^2v^2 = 3u^2(u^2 - uv - 3v^2)$

(C) $3m^4 - 24mn^3 = 3m(m^3 - 8n^3) = 3m(m - 2n)(m^2 + 2mn + 4n^2)$
(D) $3x^4 - 5x^2 + 2 = (3x^2 - 2)(x^2 - 1) = (3x^2 - 2)(x - 1)(x + 1)$

MATCHED PROBLEM 5 Factor completely.

(A) $18x^3 - 8x$
(B) $4m^3n - 2m^2n^2 + 2mn^3$
(C) $2t^4 - 16t$
(D) $2y^4 - 5y^2 - 12$

Exercises A.3

A *In Problems 1–8, factor out all factors common to all terms.*

1. $6m^4 - 9m^3 - 3m^2$
2. $6x^4 - 8x^3 - 2x^2$
3. $8u^3v - 6u^2v^2 + 4uv^3$
4. $10x^3y + 20x^2y^2 - 15xy^3$
5. $7m(2m - 3) + 5(2m - 3)$
6. $5x(x + 1) - 3(x + 1)$
7. $4ab(2c + d) - (2c + d)$
8. $12a(b - 2c) - 15b(b - 2c)$

In Problems 9–18, factor by grouping.

9. $2x^2 - x + 4x - 2$
10. $x^2 - 3x + 2x - 6$
11. $3y^2 - 3y + 2y - 2$
12. $2x^2 - x + 6x - 3$
13. $2x^2 + 8x - x - 4$
14. $6x^2 + 9x - 2x - 3$
15. $wy - wz + xy - xz$
16. $ac + ad + bc + bd$
17. $am - 3bm + 2na - 6bn$
18. $ab + 6 + 2a + 3b$

B *In Problems 19–56, factor completely. If a polynomial cannot be factored, say so.*

19. $3y^2 - y - 2$
20. $2x^2 + 5x - 3$
21. $u^2 - 2uv - 15v^2$
22. $x^2 - 4xy - 12y^2$
23. $m^2 - 6m - 3$
24. $x^2 + x - 4$
25. $w^2x^2 - y^2$
26. $25m^2 - 16n^2$
27. $9m^2 - 6mn + n^2$
28. $x^2 + 10xy + 25y^2$
29. $y^2 + 16$
30. $u^2 + 81$
31. $4z^2 - 28z + 48$
32. $6x^2 + 48x + 72$
33. $2x^4 - 24x^3 + 40x^2$
34. $2y^3 - 22y^2 + 48y$
35. $4xy^2 - 12xy + 9x$
36. $16x^2y - 8xy + y$
37. $6m^2 - mn - 12n^2$
38. $6s^2 + 7st - 3t^2$
39. $4u^3v - uv^3$
40. $x^3y - 9xy^3$
41. $2x^3 - 2x^2 + 8x$
42. $3m^3 - 6m^2 + 15m$
43. $8x^3 - 27y^3$
44. $5x^3 + 40y^3$
45. $x^4y + 8xy$
46. $8a^3 - 1$

C

47. $(x + 2)^2 - 9y^2$
48. $(a - b)^2 - 4(c - d)^2$
49. $5u^2 + 4uv - 2v^2$
50. $3x^2 - 2xy - 4y^2$
51. $6(x - y)^2 + 23(x - y) - 4$
52. $4(A + B)^2 - 5(A + B) - 6$
53. $y^4 - 3y^2 - 4$
54. $m^4 - n^4$
55. $15y(x - y)^3 + 12x(x - y)^2$
56. $15x^2(3x - 1)^4 + 60x^3(3x - 1)^3$

In Problems 57–60, discuss the validity of each statement. If the statement is true, explain why. If not, give a counterexample.

57. If n is a positive integer greater than 1, then $u^n - v^n$ can be factored.

58. If m and n are positive integers and $m \neq n$, then $u^m - v^n$ is not factorable.

59. If n is a positive integer greater than 1, then $u^n + v^n$ can be factored.

60. If k is a positive integer, then $u^{2k+1} + v^{2k+1}$ can be factored.

Answers to Matched Problems

1. (A) $2xy(x^2 - 4xy - 3y^2)$ (B) $(2x - 7)(3x - 2)$
2. (A) $(3x + 1)(2x + 3)$ (B) $(u + 3v)(2u - 3v)$ (C) $(a + b)(c + d)$
3. (A) $(2x - 1)(x + 6)$ (B) Not factorable (C) $(3x + 4y)(2x - y)$
4. (A) $(x + 3y)^2$ (B) $(3x - 2y)(3x + 2y)$ (C) $(2m - 1)(4m^2 + 2m + 1)$ (D) $(x + yz)(x^2 - xyz + y^2z^2)$ (E) $[3(m - 3) - 2n][3(m - 3) + 2n]$
5. (A) $2x(3x - 2)(3x + 2)$ (B) $2mn(2m^2 - mn + n^2)$ (C) $2t(t - 2)(t^2 + 2t + 4)$ (D) $(2y^2 + 3)(y - 2)(y + 2)$

A.4 Operations on Rational Expressions

- Reducing to Lowest Terms
- Multiplication and Division
- Addition and Subtraction
- Compound Fractions

We now turn our attention to fractional forms. A quotient of two algebraic expressions (division by 0 excluded) is called a **fractional expression**. If both the numerator and the denominator are polynomials, the fractional expression is called a **rational expression**. Some examples of rational expressions are

$$\frac{1}{x^3 + 2x} \qquad \frac{5}{x} \qquad \frac{x + 7}{3x^2 - 5x + 1} \qquad \frac{x^2 - 2x + 4}{1}$$

In this section, we discuss basic operations on rational expressions. Since variables represent real numbers in the rational expressions we will consider, the properties of real number fractions summarized in Appendix A.1 will play a central role.

AGREEMENT Variable Restriction

Even though not always explicitly stated, we always assume that variables are restricted so that division by 0 is excluded.

For example, given the rational expression

$$\frac{2x + 5}{x(x + 2)(x - 3)}$$

the variable x is understood to be restricted from being 0, -2, or 3, since these values would cause the denominator to be 0.

Reducing to Lowest Terms

Central to the process of reducing rational expressions to *lowest terms* is the *fundamental property of fractions*, which we restate here for convenient reference:

THEOREM 1 Fundamental Property of Fractions

If a, b, and k are real numbers with $b, k \neq 0$, then

$$\frac{ka}{kb} = \frac{a}{b} \qquad \frac{5 \cdot 2}{5 \cdot 7} = \frac{2}{7} \qquad \frac{x(x + 4)}{2(x + 4)} = \frac{x}{2} \quad x \neq -4$$

Using this property from left to right to eliminate all common factors from the numerator and the denominator of a given fraction is referred to as **reducing a fraction to lowest terms**. We are actually dividing the numerator and denominator by the same nonzero common factor.

Using the property from right to left—that is, multiplying the numerator and denominator by the same nonzero factor—is referred to as **raising a fraction to higher terms**. We will use the property in both directions in the material that follows.

EXAMPLE 1 **Reducing to Lowest Terms** Reduce each fraction to lowest terms.

(A) $\dfrac{1 \cdot 2 \cdot 3 \cdot 4}{1 \cdot 2 \cdot 3 \cdot 4 \cdot 5 \cdot 6} = \dfrac{\cancel{1} \cdot \cancel{2} \cdot \cancel{3} \cdot \cancel{4}}{\cancel{1} \cdot \cancel{2} \cdot \cancel{3} \cdot \cancel{4} \cdot 5 \cdot 6} = \dfrac{1}{5 \cdot 6} = \dfrac{1}{30}$

(B) $\dfrac{2 \cdot 4 \cdot 6 \cdot 8}{1 \cdot 2 \cdot 3 \cdot 4} = \dfrac{\overset{2}{\cancel{2}} \cdot \overset{2}{\cancel{4}} \cdot \overset{2}{\cancel{6}} \cdot \overset{2}{8}}{\cancel{1} \cdot \cancel{2} \cdot \cancel{3} \cdot \cancel{4}} = 2 \cdot 2 \cdot 2 \cdot 2 = 16$

MATCHED PROBLEM 1 Reduce each fraction to lowest terms.

(A) $\dfrac{1 \cdot 2 \cdot 3 \cdot 4 \cdot 5}{1 \cdot 2 \cdot 1 \cdot 2 \cdot 3}$ (B) $\dfrac{1 \cdot 4 \cdot 9 \cdot 16}{1 \cdot 2 \cdot 3 \cdot 4}$

CONCEPTUAL INSIGHT

Using Theorem 1 to divide the numerator and denominator of a fraction by a common factor is often referred to as **canceling**. This operation can be denoted by drawing a slanted line through each common factor and writing any remaining factors above or below the common factor. Canceling is often incorrectly applied to individual terms in the numerator or denominator, instead of to common factors. For example,

$$\frac{14-5}{2} = \frac{9}{2}$$ Theorem 1 does not apply. There are no common factors in the numerator.

$$\frac{14-5}{2} \neq \frac{\overset{7}{\cancel{14}}-5}{\underset{1}{\cancel{2}}} = 2$$ Incorrect use of Theorem 1. To cancel 2 in the denominator, 2 must be a factor of each term in the numerator.

EXAMPLE 2 **Reducing to Lowest Terms** Reduce each rational expression to lowest terms.

(A) $$\frac{6x^2+x-1}{2x^2-x-1} = \frac{(2x+1)(3x-1)}{(2x+1)(x-1)}$$ Factor numerator and denominator completely.

$$= \frac{3x-1}{x-1}$$ Divide numerator and denominator by the common factor $(2x+1)$.

(B) $$\frac{x^4-8x}{3x^3-2x^2-8x} = \frac{x(x-2)(x^2+2x+4)}{x(x-2)(3x+4)}$$

$$= \frac{x^2+2x+4}{3x+4}$$

MATCHED PROBLEM 2 Reduce each rational expression to lowest terms.

(A) $\dfrac{x^2-6x+9}{x^2-9}$ (B) $\dfrac{x^3-1}{x^2-1}$

Multiplication and Division

Since we are restricting variable replacements to real numbers, multiplication and division of rational expressions follow the rules for multiplying and dividing real number fractions summarized in Appendix A.1.

THEOREM 2 Multiplication and Division

If a, b, c, and d are real numbers, then

1. $\dfrac{a}{b}\cdot\dfrac{c}{d} = \dfrac{ac}{bd}$, $b, d \neq 0$ $\qquad \dfrac{3}{5}\cdot\dfrac{x}{x+5} = \dfrac{3x}{5(x+5)}$
2. $\dfrac{a}{b}\div\dfrac{c}{d} = \dfrac{a}{b}\cdot\dfrac{d}{c}$, $b, c, d \neq 0$ $\qquad \dfrac{3}{5}\div\dfrac{x}{x+5} = \dfrac{3}{5}\cdot\dfrac{x+5}{x}$

EXAMPLE 3 **Multiplication and Division** Perform the indicated operations and reduce to lowest terms.

(A) $$\frac{10x^3y}{3xy+9y}\cdot\frac{x^2-9}{4x^2-12x}$$ Factor numerators and denominators. Then divide any numerator and any denominator with a like common factor.

$$= \frac{\overset{5x^2}{\cancel{10x^3y}}}{\underset{3\cdot 1}{\cancel{3y(x+3)}}}\cdot\frac{\overset{1\cdot 1}{\cancel{(x-3)(x+3)}}}{\underset{2\cdot 1}{\cancel{4x(x-3)}}}$$

$$= \frac{5x^2}{6}$$

(B) $\dfrac{4 - 2x}{4} \div (x - 2) = \dfrac{\overset{1}{\cancel{2}}(2 - x)}{\underset{2}{\cancel{4}}} \cdot \dfrac{1}{x - 2}$ $x - 2 = \dfrac{x - 2}{1}$

$= \dfrac{2 - x}{2(x - 2)} = \dfrac{\overset{-1}{\cancel{-(x - 2)}}}{2\underset{1}{\cancel{(x - 2)}}}$ $b - a = -(a - b)$, a useful change in some problems

$= -\dfrac{1}{2}$

MATCHED PROBLEM 3 Perform the indicated operations and reduce to lowest terms.

(A) $\dfrac{12x^2y^3}{2xy^2 + 6xy} \cdot \dfrac{y^2 + 6y + 9}{3y^3 + 9y^2}$ (B) $(4 - x) \div \dfrac{x^2 - 16}{5}$

Addition and Subtraction

Again, because we are restricting variable replacements to real numbers, addition and subtraction of rational expressions follow the rules for adding and subtracting real number fractions.

THEOREM 3 Addition and Subtraction

For *a*, *b*, and *c* real numbers,

1. $\dfrac{a}{b} + \dfrac{c}{b} = \dfrac{a + c}{b}, \quad b \neq 0$ $\dfrac{x}{x + 5} + \dfrac{8}{x + 5} = \dfrac{x + 8}{x + 5}$
2. $\dfrac{a}{b} - \dfrac{c}{b} = \dfrac{a - c}{b}, \quad b \neq 0$ $\dfrac{x}{3x^2y^2} - \dfrac{x + 7}{3x^2y^2} = \dfrac{x - (x + 7)}{3x^2y^2}$

We add rational expressions with the same denominators by adding or subtracting their numerators and placing the result over the common denominator. If the denominators are not the same, we raise the fractions to higher terms, using the fundamental property of fractions to obtain common denominators, and then proceed as described.

Even though any common denominator will do, our work will be simplified if the *least common denominator (LCD)* is used. Often, the LCD is obvious, but if it is not, the steps in the next box describe how to find it.

PROCEDURE Least Common Denominator

The least common denominator (LCD) of two or more rational expressions is found as follows:

1. Factor each denominator completely, including integer factors.
2. Identify each different factor from all the denominators.
3. Form a product using each different factor to the highest power that occurs in any one denominator. This product is the LCD.

EXAMPLE 4 **Addition and Subtraction** Combine into a single fraction and reduce to lowest terms.

(A) $\dfrac{3}{10} + \dfrac{5}{6} - \dfrac{11}{45}$ (B) $\dfrac{4}{9x} - \dfrac{5x}{6y^2} + 1$ (C) $\dfrac{1}{x - 1} - \dfrac{1}{x} - \dfrac{2}{x^2 - 1}$

SOLUTION

(A) To find the LCD, factor each denominator completely:

$$\left.\begin{aligned} 10 &= 2 \cdot 5 \\ 6 &= 2 \cdot 3 \\ 45 &= 3^2 \cdot 5 \end{aligned}\right\} \quad LCD = 2 \cdot 3^2 \cdot 5 = 90$$

Now use the fundamental property of fractions to make each denominator 90:

$$\frac{3}{10} + \frac{5}{6} - \frac{11}{45} = \frac{9 \cdot 3}{9 \cdot 10} + \frac{15 \cdot 5}{15 \cdot 6} - \frac{2 \cdot 11}{2 \cdot 45}$$

$$= \frac{27}{90} + \frac{75}{90} - \frac{22}{90}$$

$$= \frac{27 + 75 - 22}{90} = \frac{80}{90} = \frac{8}{9}$$

(B)

$$\left.\begin{aligned} 9x &= 3^2 x \\ 6y^2 &= 2 \cdot 3y^2 \end{aligned}\right\} \quad LCD = 2 \cdot 3^2 xy^2 = 18xy^2$$

$$\frac{4}{9x} - \frac{5x}{6y^2} + 1 = \frac{2y^2 \cdot 4}{2y^2 \cdot 9x} - \frac{3x \cdot 5x}{3x \cdot 6y^2} + \frac{18xy^2}{18xy^2}$$

$$= \frac{8y^2 - 15x^2 + 18xy^2}{18xy^2}$$

(C)

$$\frac{1}{x-1} - \frac{1}{x} - \frac{2}{x^2 - 1}$$

$$= \frac{1}{x-1} - \frac{1}{x} - \frac{2}{(x-1)(x+1)} \quad LCD = x(x-1)(x+1)$$

$$= \frac{x(x+1) - (x-1)(x+1) - 2x}{x(x-1)(x+1)}$$

$$= \frac{x^2 + x - x^2 + 1 - 2x}{x(x-1)(x+1)}$$

$$= \frac{1 - x}{x(x-1)(x+1)}$$

$$= \frac{-(x-1)}{x(x-1)(x+1)} = \frac{-1}{x(x+1)}$$

MATCHED PROBLEM 4 Combine into a single fraction and reduce to lowest terms.

(A) $\frac{5}{28} - \frac{1}{10} + \frac{6}{35}$

(B) $\frac{1}{4x^2} - \frac{2x + 1}{3x^3} + \frac{3}{12x}$

(C) $\frac{2}{x^2 - 4x + 4} + \frac{1}{x} - \frac{1}{x - 2}$

Compound Fractions

A fractional expression with fractions in its numerator, denominator, or both is called a **compound fraction**. It is often necessary to represent a compound fraction as a **simple fraction**—that is (in all cases we will consider), as the quotient of two polynomials. The process does not involve any new concepts. It is a matter of applying old concepts and processes in the correct sequence.

EXAMPLE 5 **Simplifying Compound Fractions** Express as a simple fraction reduced to lowest terms:

(A) $\dfrac{\dfrac{1}{5+h} - \dfrac{1}{5}}{h}$ (B) $\dfrac{\dfrac{y}{x^2} - \dfrac{x}{y^2}}{\dfrac{y}{x} - \dfrac{x}{y}}$

SOLUTION We will simplify the expressions in parts (A) and (B) using two different methods—each is suited to the particular type of problem.

(A) We simplify this expression by combining the numerator into a single fraction and using division of rational forms.

$$\frac{\dfrac{1}{5+h} - \dfrac{1}{5}}{h} = \left[\frac{1}{5+h} - \frac{1}{5}\right] \div \frac{h}{1}$$

$$= \frac{5 - 5 - h}{5(5+h)} \cdot \frac{1}{h}$$

$$= \frac{-h}{5(5+h)h} = \frac{-1}{5(5+h)}$$

(B) The method used here makes effective use of the fundamental property of fractions in the form

$$\frac{a}{b} = \frac{ka}{kb} \qquad b, k \neq 0$$

Multiply the numerator and denominator by the LCD of all fractions in the numerator and denominator—in this case, x^2y^2:

$$\frac{x^2y^2\left(\dfrac{y}{x^2} - \dfrac{x}{y^2}\right)}{x^2y^2\left(\dfrac{y}{x} - \dfrac{x}{y}\right)} = \frac{x^2y^2\dfrac{y}{x^2} - x^2y^2\dfrac{x}{y^2}}{x^2y^2\dfrac{y}{x} - x^2y^2\dfrac{x}{y}} = \frac{y^3 - x^3}{xy^3 - x^3y}$$

$$= \frac{\overset{1}{\cancel{(y - x)}}(y^2 + xy + x^2)}{xy\underset{1}{\cancel{(y - x)}}(y + x)}$$

$$= \frac{y^2 + xy + x^2}{xy(y + x)} \quad \text{or} \quad \frac{x^2 + xy + y^2}{xy(x + y)}$$

MATCHED PROBLEM 5 Express as a simple fraction reduced to lowest terms:

(A) $\dfrac{\dfrac{1}{2+h} - \dfrac{1}{2}}{h}$ (B) $\dfrac{\dfrac{a}{b} - \dfrac{b}{a}}{\dfrac{a}{b} + 2 + \dfrac{b}{a}}$

Exercises A.4

A *In Problems 1–22, perform the indicated operations and reduce answers to lowest terms.*

1. $\dfrac{5 \cdot 9 \cdot 13}{3 \cdot 5 \cdot 7}$

2. $\dfrac{10 \cdot 9 \cdot 8}{3 \cdot 2 \cdot 1}$

3. $\dfrac{12 \cdot 11 \cdot 10 \cdot 9}{4 \cdot 3 \cdot 2 \cdot 1}$

4. $\dfrac{15 \cdot 10 \cdot 5}{20 \cdot 15 \cdot 10}$

5. $\dfrac{d^5}{3a} \div \left(\dfrac{d^2}{6a^2} \cdot \dfrac{a}{4d^3}\right)$

6. $\left(\dfrac{d^5}{3a} \div \dfrac{d^2}{6a^2}\right) \cdot \dfrac{a}{4d^3}$

7. $\frac{x^2}{12} + \frac{x}{18} - \frac{1}{30}$

8. $\frac{2y}{18} - \frac{-1}{28} - \frac{y}{42}$

9. $\frac{4m - 3}{18m^3} + \frac{3}{4m} - \frac{2m - 1}{6m^2}$

10. $\frac{3x + 8}{4x^2} - \frac{2x - 1}{x^3} - \frac{5}{8x}$

11. $\frac{x^2 - 9}{x^2 - 3x} \div (x^2 - x - 12)$

12. $\frac{2x^2 + 7x + 3}{4x^2 - 1} \div (x + 3)$

13. $\frac{2}{x} - \frac{1}{x - 3}$

14. $\frac{5}{m - 2} - \frac{3}{2m + 1}$

15. $\frac{2}{(x + 1)^2} - \frac{5}{x^2 - x - 2}$

16. $\frac{3}{x^2 - 5x + 6} - \frac{5}{(x - 2)^2}$

17. $\frac{x + 1}{x - 1} - 1$

18. $m - 3 - \frac{m - 1}{m - 2}$

19. $\frac{3}{a - 1} - \frac{2}{1 - a}$

20. $\frac{5}{x - 3} - \frac{2}{3 - x}$

21. $\frac{2x}{x^2 - 16} - \frac{x - 4}{x^2 + 4x}$

22. $\frac{m + 2}{m^2 - 2m} - \frac{m}{m^2 - 4}$

B *In Problems 23–34, perform the indicated operations and reduce answers to lowest terms. Represent any compound fractions as simple fractions reduced to lowest terms.*

23. $\frac{x^2}{x^2 + 2x + 1} + \frac{x - 1}{3x + 3} - \frac{1}{6}$

24. $\frac{y}{y^2 - y - 2} - \frac{1}{y^2 + 5y - 14} - \frac{2}{y^2 + 8y + 7}$

25. $\frac{1 - \frac{x}{y}}{2 - \frac{y}{x}}$

26. $\frac{2}{5 - \frac{3}{4x + 1}}$

27. $\frac{c + 2}{5c - 5} - \frac{c - 2}{3c - 3} + \frac{c}{1 - c}$

28. $\frac{x + 7}{ax - bx} + \frac{y + 9}{by - ay}$

29. $\frac{1 + \frac{3}{x}}{x - \frac{9}{x}}$

30. $\frac{1 - \frac{y^2}{x^2}}{1 - \frac{y}{x}}$

31. $\frac{\frac{1}{2(x + h)} - \frac{1}{2x}}{h}$

32. $\frac{\frac{1}{x + h} - \frac{1}{x}}{h}$

33. $\frac{\frac{x}{y} - 2 + \frac{y}{x}}{\frac{x}{y} - \frac{y}{x}}$

34. $\frac{1 + \frac{2}{x} - \frac{15}{x^2}}{1 + \frac{4}{x} - \frac{5}{x^2}}$

In Problems 35–42, imagine that the indicated "solutions" were given to you by a student whom you were tutoring in this class.

(A) Is the solution correct? If the solution is incorrect, explain what is wrong and how it can be corrected.

(B) Show a correct solution for each incorrect solution.

35. $\frac{x^2 + 4x + 3}{x + 3} = \frac{x^2 + 4x}{x} = x + 4$

36. $\frac{x^2 - 3x - 4}{x - 4} = \frac{x^2 - 3x}{x} = x - 3$

37. $\frac{(x + h)^2 - x^2}{h} = (x + 1)^2 - x^2 = 2x + 1$

38. $\frac{(x + h)^3 - x^3}{h} = (x + 1)^3 - x^3 = 3x^2 + 3x + 1$

39. $\frac{x^2 - 3x}{x^2 - 2x - 3} + x - 3 = \frac{x^2 - 3x + x - 3}{x^2 - 2x - 3} = 1$

40. $\frac{2}{x - 1} - \frac{x + 3}{x^2 - 1} = \frac{2x + 2 - x - 3}{x^2 - 1} = \frac{1}{x + 1}$

41. $\frac{2x^2}{x^2 - 4} - \frac{x}{x - 2} = \frac{2x^2 - x^2 - 2x}{x^2 - 4} = \frac{x}{x + 2}$

42. $x + \frac{x - 2}{x^2 - 3x + 2} = \frac{x + x - 2}{x^2 - 3x + 2} = \frac{2}{x - 2}$

C *Represent the compound fractions in Problems 43–46 as simple fractions reduced to lowest terms.*

43. $\frac{\frac{1}{3(x + h)^2} - \frac{1}{3x^2}}{h}$

44. $\frac{\frac{1}{(x + h)^2} - \frac{1}{x^2}}{h}$

45. $x - \frac{2}{1 - \frac{1}{x}}$

46. $2 - \frac{1}{1 - \frac{2}{a + 2}}$

Answers to Matched Problems

1. (A) 10 (B) 24

2. (A) $\frac{x - 3}{x + 3}$ (B) $\frac{x^2 + x + 1}{x + 1}$

3. (A) $2x$ (B) $\frac{-5}{x + 4}$

4. (A) $\frac{1}{4}$ (B) $\frac{3x^2 - 5x - 4}{12x^3}$ (C) $\frac{4}{x(x - 2)^2}$

5. (A) $\frac{-1}{2(2 + h)}$ (B) $\frac{a - b}{a + b}$

A.5 Integer Exponents and Scientific Notation

- Integer Exponents
- Scientific Notation

We now review basic operations on integer exponents and scientific notation.

Integer Exponents

DEFINITION Integer Exponents

For n an integer and a a real number:

1. For n a positive integer,

$$a^n = a \cdot a \cdot \cdots \cdot a \quad n \text{ factors of } a \quad 5^4 = 5 \cdot 5 \cdot 5 \cdot 5$$

2. For $n = 0$,

$$a^0 = 1 \quad a \neq 0 \quad 12^0 = 1$$

0^0 is not defined.

3. For n a negative integer,

$$a^n = \frac{1}{a^{-n}} \quad a \neq 0 \quad a^{-3} = \frac{1}{a^{-(-3)}} = \frac{1}{a^3}$$

[If n is negative, then $(-n)$ is positive.]

Note: It can be shown that for *all* integers n,

$$a^{-n} = \frac{1}{a^n} \quad \text{and} \quad a^n = \frac{1}{a^{-n}} \quad a \neq 0 \quad a^5 = \frac{1}{a^{-5}} \quad a^{-5} = \frac{1}{a^5}$$

The following properties are very useful in working with integer exponents.

THEOREM 1 Exponent Properties

For n and m integers and a and b real numbers,

1. $a^m a^n = a^{m+n}$ $\qquad a^8 a^{-3} = a^{8+(-3)} = a^5$
2. $(a^n)^m = a^{mn}$ $\qquad (a^{-2})^3 = a^{3(-2)} = a^{-6}$
3. $(ab)^m = a^m b^m$ $\qquad (ab)^{-2} = a^{-2}b^{-2}$
4. $\left(\frac{a}{b}\right)^m = \frac{a^m}{b^m} \quad b \neq 0$ $\qquad \left(\frac{a}{b}\right)^5 = \frac{a^5}{b^5}$
5. $\frac{a^m}{a^n} = a^{m-n} = \frac{1}{a^{n-m}} \quad a \neq 0$ $\qquad \frac{a^{-3}}{a^7} = \frac{1}{a^{7-(-3)}} = \frac{1}{a^{10}}$

Exponents are frequently encountered in algebraic applications. You should sharpen your skills in using exponents by reviewing the preceding basic definitions and properties and the examples that follow.

EXAMPLE 1 **Simplifying Exponent Forms** Simplify, and express the answers using positive exponents only.

(A) $(2x^3)(3x^5) = 2 \cdot 3x^{3+5} = 6x^8$

(B) $x^5x^{-9} = x^{-4} = \frac{1}{x^4}$

(C) $\frac{x^5}{x^7} = x^{5-7} = x^{-2} = \frac{1}{x^2}$ or $\frac{x^5}{x^7} = \frac{1}{x^{7-5}} = \frac{1}{x^2}$

(D) $\dfrac{x^{-3}}{y^{-4}} = \dfrac{y^4}{x^3}$

(E) $(u^{-3}v^2)^{-2} = (u^{-3})^{-2}(v^2)^{-2} = u^6v^{-4} = \dfrac{u^6}{v^4}$

(F) $\left(\dfrac{y^{-5}}{y^{-2}}\right)^{-2} = \dfrac{(y^{-5})^{-2}}{(y^{-2})^{-2}} = \dfrac{y^{10}}{y^4} = y^6$

(G) $\dfrac{4m^{-3}n^{-5}}{6m^{-4}n^3} = \dfrac{2m^{-3-(-4)}}{3n^{3-(-5)}} = \dfrac{2m}{3n^8}$

MATCHED PROBLEM 1 Simplify, and express the answers using positive exponents only.

(A) $(3y^4)(2y^3)$ (B) m^2m^{-6} (C) $(u^3v^{-2})^{-2}$

(D) $\left(\dfrac{y^{-6}}{y^{-2}}\right)^{-1}$ (E) $\dfrac{8x^{-2}y^{-4}}{6x^{-5}y^2}$

EXAMPLE 2 **Converting to a Simple Fraction** Write $\dfrac{1-x}{x^{-1}-1}$ as a simple fraction with positive exponents.

SOLUTION First note that

$$\frac{1-x}{x^{-1}-1} \neq \frac{x(1-x)}{-1} \qquad \text{A common error}$$

The original expression is a compound fraction, and we proceed to simplify it as follows:

$$\frac{1-x}{x^{-1}-1} = \frac{1-x}{\frac{1}{x}-1} \qquad \text{Multiply numerator and denominator by } x \text{ to clear internal fractions.}$$

$$= \frac{x(1-x)}{x\left(\frac{1}{x}-1\right)}$$

$$= \frac{x(1-x)}{1-x} = x$$

MATCHED PROBLEM 2 Write $\dfrac{1+x^{-1}}{1-x^{-2}}$ as a simple fraction with positive exponents.

Scientific Notation

In the real world, one often encounters very large and very small numbers. For example,

- The public debt in the United States in 2016, to the nearest billion dollars, was

  $19,573,000,000,000

- The world population in the year 2025, to the nearest million, is projected to be

  7,947,000,000

- The sound intensity of a normal conversation is

  0.000 000 000 316 watt per square centimeter

It is generally troublesome to write and work with numbers of this type in standard decimal form. The first and last example cannot even be entered into many calculators as they are written. But with exponents defined for all integers, we can now express any finite decimal form as the product of a number between 1 and 10 and an integer power of 10, that is, in the form

$$a \times 10^n \qquad 1 \le a < 10, \quad a \text{ in decimal form}, \quad n \text{ an integer}$$

A number expressed in this form is said to be in **scientific notation.** The following are some examples of numbers in standard decimal notation and in scientific notation:

Decimal and Scientific Notation	
$7 = 7 \times 10^0$	$0.5 = 5 \times 10^{-1}$
$67 = 6.7 \times 10$	$0.45 = 4.5 \times 10^{-1}$
$580 = 5.8 \times 10^2$	$0.0032 = 3.2 \times 10^{-3}$
$43{,}000 = 4.3 \times 10^4$	$0.000\,045 = 4.5 \times 10^{-5}$
$73{,}400{,}000 = 7.34 \times 10^7$	$0.000\,000\,391 = 3.91 \times 10^{-7}$

Note that the power of 10 used corresponds to the number of places we move the decimal to form a number between 1 and 10. The power is positive if the decimal is moved to the left and negative if it is moved to the right. Positive exponents are associated with numbers greater than or equal to 10, negative exponents are associated with positive numbers less than 1, and a zero exponent is associated with a number that is 1 or greater but less than 10.

EXAMPLE 3 **Scientific Notation**

(A) Write each number in scientific notation:

$$7{,}320{,}000 \quad \text{and} \quad 0.000\,000\,54$$

(B) Write each number in standard decimal form:

$$4.32 \times 10^6 \quad \text{and} \quad 4.32 \times 10^{-5}$$

SOLUTION

(A) $7{,}320{,}000 = 7.320\,000. \times 10^6 = 7.32 \times 10^6$

6 places left
Positive exponent

$0.000\,000\,54 = 0.000\,000\,5.4 \times 10^{-7} = 5.4 \times 10^{-7}$

7 places right
Negative exponent

(B) $4.32 \times 10^6 = 4{,}320{,}000.$ 6 places right; Positive exponent 6

$4.32 \times 10^{-5} = \dfrac{4.32}{10^5} = 0.000\,043\,2$ 5 places left; Negative exponent −5

Matched Problem 3

(A) Write each number in scientific notation: 47,100; 2,443,000,000; 1.45

(B) Write each number in standard decimal form: 3.07×10^8; 5.98×10^{-6}

Exercises A.5

A *In Problems 1–14, simplify and express answers using positive exponents only. Variables are restricted to avoid division by 0.*

1. $2x^{-9}$ **2.** $3y^{-5}$ **3.** $\frac{3}{2w^{-7}}$

4. $\frac{5}{4x^{-9}}$ **5.** $2x^{-8}x^{5}$ **6.** $3c^{-9}c^{4}$

7. $\frac{w^{-8}}{w^{-3}}$ **8.** $\frac{m^{-11}}{m^{-5}}$ **9.** $(2a^{-3})^2$

10. $7d^{-4}d^{4}$ **11.** $(a^{-3})^2$ **12.** $(5b^{-2})^2$

13. $(2x^4)^{-3}$ **14.** $(a^{-3}b^4)^{-3}$

In Problems 15–20, write each number in scientific notation.

15. 82,300,000,000 **16.** 5,380,000

17. 0.783 **18.** 0.019

19. 0.000 034 **20.** 0.000 000 007 832

In Problems 21–28, write each number in standard decimal notation.

21. 4×10^4 **22.** 9×10^6

23. 7×10^{-3} **24.** 2×10^{-5}

25. 6.171×10^7 **26.** 3.044×10^3

27. 8.08×10^{-4} **28.** 1.13×10^{-2}

B *In Problems 29–38, simplify and express answers using positive exponents only. Assume that variables are nonzero.*

29. $(22 + 31)^0$ **30.** $(2x^3y^4)^0$

31. $\frac{10^{-3} \cdot 10^4}{10^{-11} \cdot 10^{-2}}$ **32.** $\frac{10^{-17} \cdot 10^{-5}}{10^{-3} \cdot 10^{-14}}$

33. $(5x^2y^{-3})^{-2}$ **34.** $(2m^{-3}n^2)^{-3}$

35. $\left(\frac{-5}{2x^3}\right)^{-2}$ **36.** $\left(\frac{2a}{3b^2}\right)^{-3}$

37. $\frac{8x^{-3}y^{-1}}{6x^2y^{-4}}$ **38.** $\frac{9m^{-4}n^3}{12m^{-1}n^{-1}}$

In Problems 39–42, write each expression in the form $ax^p + bx^q$ or $ax^p + bx^q + cx^r$, where a, b, and c are real numbers and p, q, and r are integers. For example,

$$\frac{2x^4 - 3x^2 + 1}{2x^3} = \frac{2x^4}{2x^3} - \frac{3x^2}{2x^3} + \frac{1}{2x^3} = x - \frac{3}{2}x^{-1} + \frac{1}{2}x^{-3}$$

39. $\frac{7x^5 - x^2}{4x^5}$ **40.** $\frac{5x^3 - 2}{3x^2}$

41. $\frac{5x^4 - 3x^2 + 8}{2x^2}$ **42.** $\frac{2x^3 - 3x^2 + x}{2x^2}$

Write each expression in Problems 43–46 with positive exponents only, and as a single fraction reduced to lowest terms.

43. $\frac{3x^2(x-1)^2 - 2x^3(x-1)}{(x-1)^4}$

44. $\frac{5x^4(x+3)^2 - 2x^5(x+3)}{(x+3)^4}$

45. $2x^{-2}(x-1) - 2x^{-3}(x-1)^2$

46. $2x(x+3)^{-1} - x^2(x+3)^{-2}$

In Problems 47–50, convert each number to scientific notation and simplify. Express the answer in both scientific notation and in standard decimal form.

47. $\frac{9{,}600{,}000{,}000}{(1{,}600{,}000)(0.000\,000\,25)}$

48. $\frac{(60{,}000)(0.000\,003)}{(0.0004)(1{,}500{,}000)}$

49. $\frac{(1{,}250{,}000)(0.000\,38)}{0.0152}$

50. $\frac{(0.000\,000\,82)(230{,}000)}{(625{,}000)(0.0082)}$

51. What is the result of entering 2^{3^2} on a calculator?

52. Refer to Problem 51. What is the difference between $2^{(3^2)}$ and $(2^3)^2$? Which agrees with the value of 2^{3^2} obtained with a calculator?

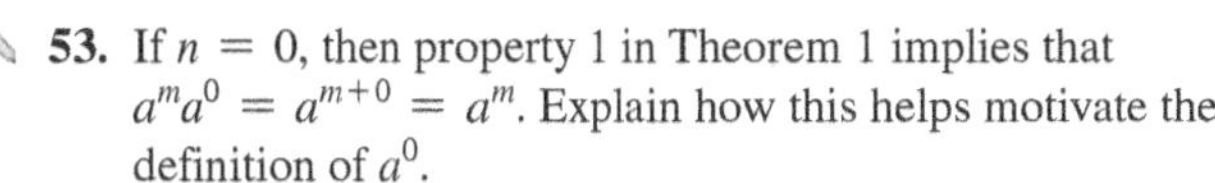

53. If $n = 0$, then property 1 in Theorem 1 implies that $a^m a^0 = a^{m+0} = a^m$. Explain how this helps motivate the definition of a^0.

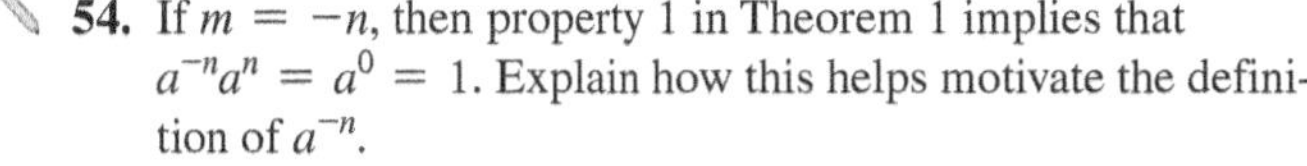

54. If $m = -n$, then property 1 in Theorem 1 implies that $a^{-n}a^n = a^0 = 1$. Explain how this helps motivate the definition of a^{-n}.

C *Write the fractions in Problems 55–58 as simple fractions reduced to lowest terms.*

55. $\frac{u + v}{u^{-1} + v^{-1}}$ **56.** $\frac{x^{-2} - y^{-2}}{x^{-1} + y^{-1}}$

57. $\frac{b^{-2} - c^{-2}}{b^{-3} - c^{-3}}$ **58.** $\frac{xy^{-2} - yx^{-2}}{y^{-1} - x^{-1}}$

Applications

Problems 59 and 60 refer to Table 1.

Table 1 **U.S. Public Debt, Interest on Debt, and Population**

Year	Public Debt ($)	Interest on Debt ($)	Population
2000	5,674,000,000,000	362,000,000,000	281,000,000
2016	19,573,000,000,000	433,000,000,000	323,000,000

59. Public debt. Carry out the following computations using scientific notation, and write final answers in standard decimal form.

(A) What was the per capita debt in 2016 (to the nearest dollar)?

(B) What was the per capita interest paid on the debt in 2016 (to the nearest dollar)?

(C) What was the percentage interest paid on the debt in 2016 (to two decimal places)?

60. Public debt. Carry out the following computations using scientific notation, and write final answers in standard decimal form.

(A) What was the per capita debt in 2000 (to the nearest dollar)?

(B) What was the per capita interest paid on the debt in 2000 (to the nearest dollar)?

(C) What was the percentage interest paid on the debt in 2000 (to two decimal places)?

Air pollution. *Air quality standards establish maximum amounts of pollutants considered acceptable in the air. The amounts are frequently given in parts per million (ppm). A standard of 30 ppm also can be expressed as follows:*

$$30 \text{ ppm} = \frac{30}{1{,}000{,}000} = \frac{3 \times 10}{10^6}$$

$$= 3 \times 10^{-5} = 0.000\,03 = 0.003\%$$

In Problems 61 and 62, express the given standard:

(A) In scientific notation

(B) In standard decimal notation

(C) As a percent

61. 9 ppm, the standard for carbon monoxide, when averaged over a period of 8 hours

62. 0.03 ppm, the standard for sulfur oxides, when averaged over a year

63. Crime. In 2015, the United States had a violent crime rate of 373 per 100,000 people and a population of 320 million people. How many violent crimes occurred that year? Compute the answer using scientific notation and convert the answer to standard decimal form (to the nearest thousand).

64. Population density. The United States had a 2016 population of 323 million people and a land area of 3,539,000 square miles. What was the population density? Compute the answer using scientific notation and convert the answer to standard decimal form (to one decimal place).

Answers to Matched Problems

1. (A) $6y^7$ (B) $\frac{1}{m^4}$ (C) $\frac{v^4}{u^6}$

(D) y^4 (E) $\frac{4x^3}{3y^6}$

2. $\frac{x}{x-1}$

3. (A) 4.7×10^4; 2.443×10^9; 1.45×10^0
(B) 307,000,000; 0.000 005 98

A.6 Rational Exponents and Radicals

- *n*th Roots of Real Numbers
- Rational Exponents and Radicals
- Properties of Radicals

Square roots may now be generalized to *nth roots*, and the meaning of exponent may be generalized to include all rational numbers.

*n*th Roots of Real Numbers

Consider a square of side r with area 36 square inches. We can write

$$r^2 = 36$$

and conclude that side r is a number whose square is 36. We say that r is a **square root** of b if $r^2 = b$. Similarly, we say that r is a **cube root** of b if $r^3 = b$. And, in general,

DEFINITION *n*th Root

For any natural number n,

$$r \text{ is an } \textbf{\textit{n}th root} \text{ of } b \text{ if } r^n = b$$

So 4 is a square root of 16, since $4^2 = 16$; -2 is a cube root of -8, since $(-2)^3 = -8$. Since $(-4)^2 = 16$, we see that -4 is also a square root of 16. It can be shown that any positive number has two real square roots; two real 4th roots; and, in general, two real nth roots if n is even. Negative numbers have no real square roots; no real 4th roots; and, in general, no real nth roots if n is even. The reason is that no real number raised to an even power can be negative. For odd roots, the situation is simpler. Every real number has exactly one real cube root; one real 5th root; and, in general, one real nth root if n is odd.

Additional roots can be considered in the *complex number system*. In this book, we restrict our interest to *real roots of real numbers*, and *root* will always be interpreted to mean "real root."

Rational Exponents and Radicals

We now turn to the question of what symbols to use to represent nth roots. For n a natural number greater than 1, we use

$$b^{1/n} \quad \text{or} \quad \sqrt[n]{b}$$

to represent a **real nth root of b**. The exponent form is motivated by the fact that $(b^{1/n})^n = b$ if exponent laws are to continue to hold for rational exponents. The other form is called an **nth root radical**. In the expression below, the symbol $\sqrt{\ }$ is called a **radical**, n is the **index** of the radical, and b is the **radicand**:

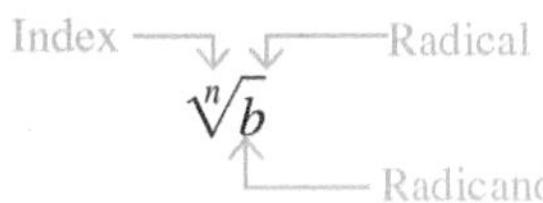

When the index is 2, it is usually omitted. That is, when dealing with square roots, we simply use $\sqrt{b}$ rather than $\sqrt[2]{b}$. If there are two real nth roots, both $b^{1/n}$ and $\sqrt[n]{b}$ denote the positive root, called the **principal nth root.**

EXAMPLE 1 **Finding nth Roots** Evaluate each of the following:

(A) $4^{1/2}$ and $\sqrt{4}$ (B) $-4^{1/2}$ and $-\sqrt{4}$ (C) $(-4)^{1/2}$ and $\sqrt{-4}$

(D) $8^{1/3}$ and $\sqrt[3]{8}$ (E) $(-8)^{1/3}$ and $\sqrt[3]{-8}$ (F) $-8^{1/3}$ and $-\sqrt[3]{8}$

SOLUTION

(A) $4^{1/2} = \sqrt{4} = 2 \quad (\sqrt{4} \neq \pm 2)$ (B) $-4^{1/2} = -\sqrt{4} = -2$

(C) $(-4)^{1/2}$ and $\sqrt{-4}$ are not real numbers

(D) $8^{1/3} = \sqrt[3]{8} = 2$ (E) $(-8)^{1/3} = \sqrt[3]{-8} = -2$

(F) $-8^{1/3} = -\sqrt[3]{8} = -2$

MATCHED PROBLEM 1 Evaluate each of the following:

(A) $16^{1/2}$ (B) $-\sqrt{16}$ (C) $\sqrt[3]{-27}$ (D) $(-9)^{1/2}$ (E) $(\sqrt[4]{81})^3$

CAUTION The symbol $\sqrt{4}$ represents the single number 2, not ± 2. Do not confuse $\sqrt{4}$ with the solutions of the equation $x^2 = 4$, which are usually written in the form $x = \pm\sqrt{4} = \pm 2$. ▲

We now define b^r for any rational number $r = m/n$.

DEFINITION Rational Exponents

If m and n are natural numbers without common prime factors, b is a real number, and b is nonnegative when n is even, then

$$b^{m/n} = \begin{cases} (b^{1/n})^m = (\sqrt[n]{b})^m & 8^{2/3} = (8^{1/3})^2 = (\sqrt[3]{8})^2 = 2^2 = 4 \\ (b^m)^{1/n} = \sqrt[n]{b^m} & 8^{2/3} = (8^2)^{1/3} = \sqrt[3]{8^2} = \sqrt[3]{64} = 4 \end{cases}$$

and

$$b^{-m/n} = \frac{1}{b^{m/n}} \quad b \neq 0 \qquad 8^{-2/3} = \frac{1}{8^{2/3}} = \frac{1}{4}$$

Note that the two definitions of $b^{m/n}$ are equivalent under the indicated restrictions on m, n, and b.

CONCEPTUAL INSIGHT

All the properties for integer exponents listed in Theorem 1 in Section A.5 also hold for rational exponents, provided that b is nonnegative when n is even. This restriction on b is necessary to avoid nonreal results. For example,

$$(-4)^{3/2} = \sqrt{(-4)^3} = \sqrt{-64} \quad \text{Not a real number}$$

To avoid nonreal results, all variables in the remainder of this discussion represent positive real numbers.

EXAMPLE 2 **From Rational Exponent Form to Radical Form and Vice Versa** Change rational exponent form to radical form.

(A) $x^{1/7} = \sqrt[7]{x}$

(B) $(3u^2v^3)^{3/5} = \sqrt[5]{(3u^2v^3)^3}$ or $(\sqrt[5]{3u^2v^3})^3$ The first is usually preferred.

(C) $y^{-2/3} = \dfrac{1}{y^{2/3}} = \dfrac{1}{\sqrt[3]{y^2}}$ or $\sqrt[3]{y^{-2}}$ or $\sqrt[3]{\dfrac{1}{y^2}}$

Change radical form to rational exponent form.

(D) $\sqrt[5]{6} = 6^{1/5}$

(E) $-\sqrt[3]{x^2} = -x^{2/3}$

(F) $\sqrt{x^2 + y^2} = (x^2 + y^2)^{1/2}$ Note that $(x^2 + y^2)^{1/2} \neq x + y$. Why?

MATCHED PROBLEM 2 Convert to radical form.

(A) $u^{1/5}$ (B) $(6x^2y^5)^{2/9}$ (C) $(3xy)^{-3/5}$

Convert to rational exponent form.

(D) $\sqrt[4]{9u}$ (E) $-\sqrt[7]{(2x)^4}$ (F) $\sqrt[3]{x^3 + y^3}$

EXAMPLE 3 **Working with Rational Exponents** Simplify each and express answers using positive exponents only. If rational exponents appear in final answers, convert to radical form.

(A) $(3x^{1/3})(2x^{1/2}) = 6x^{1/3+1/2} = 6x^{5/6} = 6\sqrt[6]{x^5}$

(B) $(-8)^{5/3} = [(-8)^{1/3}]^5 = (-2)^5 = -32$

(C) $(2x^{1/3}y^{-2/3})^3 = 8xy^{-2} = \dfrac{8x}{y^2}$

(D) $\left(\dfrac{4x^{1/3}}{x^{1/2}}\right)^{1/2} = \dfrac{4^{1/2}x^{1/6}}{x^{1/4}} = \dfrac{2}{x^{1/4-1/6}} = \dfrac{2}{x^{1/12}} = \dfrac{2}{\sqrt[12]{x}}$

MATCHED PROBLEM 3 Simplify each and express answers using positive exponents only. If rational exponents appear in final answers, convert to radical form.

(A) $9^{3/2}$ (B) $(-27)^{4/3}$ (C) $(5y^{1/4})(2y^{1/3})$

(D) $(2x^{-3/4}y^{1/4})^4$ (E) $\left(\dfrac{8x^{1/2}}{x^{2/3}}\right)^{1/3}$

EXAMPLE 4 **Working with Rational Exponents** Multiply, and express answers using positive exponents only.

(A) $3y^{2/3}(2y^{1/3} - y^2)$ (B) $(2u^{1/2} + v^{1/2})(u^{1/2} - 3v^{1/2})$

SOLUTION

(A) $3y^{2/3}(2y^{1/3} - y^2) = 6y^{2/3+1/3} - 3y^{2/3+2}$

$= 6y - 3y^{8/3}$

(B) $(2u^{1/2} + v^{1/2})(u^{1/2} - 3v^{1/2}) = 2u - 5u^{1/2}v^{1/2} - 3v$

MATCHED PROBLEM 4 Multiply, and express answers using positive exponents only.

(A) $2c^{1/4}(5c^3 - c^{3/4})$ (B) $(7x^{1/2} - y^{1/2})(2x^{1/2} + 3y^{1/2})$

EXAMPLE 5 **Working with Rational Exponents** Write the following expression in the form $ax^p + bx^q$, where a and b are real numbers and p and q are rational numbers:

$$\frac{2\sqrt{x} - 3\sqrt[3]{x^2}}{2\sqrt[3]{x}}$$

SOLUTION

$$\begin{aligned} \frac{2\sqrt{x} - 3\sqrt[3]{x^2}}{2\sqrt[3]{x}} &= \frac{2x^{1/2} - 3x^{2/3}}{2x^{1/3}} && \text{Change to rational exponent form.} \\ &= \frac{2x^{1/2}}{2x^{1/3}} - \frac{3x^{2/3}}{2x^{1/3}} && \text{Separate into two fractions.} \\ &= x^{1/6} - 1.5x^{1/3} \end{aligned}$$

MATCHED PROBLEM 5 Write the following expression in the form $ax^p + bx^q$, where a and b are real numbers and p and q are rational numbers:

$$\frac{5\sqrt[3]{x} - 4\sqrt{x}}{2\sqrt{x^3}}$$

Properties of Radicals

Changing or simplifying radical expressions is aided by several properties of radicals that follow directly from the properties of exponents considered earlier.

THEOREM 1 Properties of Radicals

If n is a natural number greater than or equal to 2, and if x and y are positive real numbers, then

1. $\sqrt[n]{x^n} = x$ $\quad \sqrt[3]{x^3} = x$
2. $\sqrt[n]{xy} = \sqrt[n]{x}\sqrt[n]{y}$ $\quad \sqrt[5]{xy} = \sqrt[5]{x}\sqrt[5]{y}$
3. $\sqrt[n]{\frac{x}{y}} = \frac{\sqrt[n]{x}}{\sqrt[n]{y}}$ $\quad \sqrt[4]{\frac{x}{y}} = \frac{\sqrt[4]{x}}{\sqrt[4]{y}}$

EXAMPLE 6 **Applying Properties of Radicals** Simplify using properties of radicals.

(A) $\sqrt[4]{(3x^4y^3)^4}$ (B) $\sqrt[4]{8}\sqrt[4]{2}$ (C) $\sqrt[3]{\frac{xy}{27}}$

SOLUTION

(A) $\sqrt[4]{(3x^4y^3)^4} = 3x^4y^3$ Property 1

(B) $\sqrt[4]{8}\sqrt[4]{2} = \sqrt[4]{16} = \sqrt[4]{2^4} = 2$ Properties 2 and 1

(C) $\sqrt[3]{\frac{xy}{27}} = \frac{\sqrt[3]{xy}}{\sqrt[3]{27}} = \frac{\sqrt[3]{xy}}{3}$ or $\frac{1}{3}\sqrt[3]{xy}$ Properties 3 and 1

MATCHED PROBLEM 6 Simplify using properties of radicals.

(A) $\sqrt[7]{(x^3 + y^3)^7}$ (B) $\sqrt[3]{8y^3}$ (C) $\frac{\sqrt[3]{16x^4y}}{\sqrt[3]{2xy}}$

What is the best form for a radical expression? There are many answers, depending on what use we wish to make of the expression. In deriving certain formulas, it is sometimes useful to clear either a denominator or a numerator of radicals. The process is referred to as **rationalizing** the denominator or numerator. Examples 7 and 8 illustrate the rationalizing process.

EXAMPLE 7 **Rationalizing Denominators** Rationalize each denominator.

(A) $\dfrac{6x}{\sqrt{2x}}$ (B) $\dfrac{6}{\sqrt{7}-\sqrt{5}}$ (C) $\dfrac{x-4}{\sqrt{x}+2}$

SOLUTION

(A) $\dfrac{6x}{\sqrt{2x}} = \dfrac{6x}{\sqrt{2x}}\cdot\dfrac{\sqrt{2x}}{\sqrt{2x}} = \dfrac{6x\sqrt{2x}}{2x} = 3\sqrt{2x}$

(B) $$\dfrac{6}{\sqrt{7}-\sqrt{5}} = \dfrac{6}{\sqrt{7}-\sqrt{5}}\cdot\dfrac{\sqrt{7}+\sqrt{5}}{\sqrt{7}+\sqrt{5}} = \dfrac{6(\sqrt{7}+\sqrt{5})}{2} = 3(\sqrt{7}+\sqrt{5})$$

(C) $$\dfrac{x-4}{\sqrt{x}+2} = \dfrac{x-4}{\sqrt{x}+2}\cdot\dfrac{\sqrt{x}-2}{\sqrt{x}-2} = \dfrac{(x-4)(\sqrt{x}-2)}{x-4} = \sqrt{x}-2$$

MATCHED PROBLEM 7 Rationalize each denominator.

(A) $\dfrac{12ab^2}{\sqrt{3ab}}$ (B) $\dfrac{9}{\sqrt{6}+\sqrt{3}}$ (C) $\dfrac{x^2-y^2}{\sqrt{x}-\sqrt{y}}$

EXAMPLE 8 **Rationalizing Numerators** Rationalize each numerator.

(A) $\dfrac{\sqrt{2}}{2\sqrt{3}}$ (B) $\dfrac{3+\sqrt{m}}{9-m}$ (C) $\dfrac{\sqrt{2+h}-\sqrt{2}}{h}$

SOLUTION

(A) $\dfrac{\sqrt{2}}{2\sqrt{3}} = \dfrac{\sqrt{2}}{2\sqrt{3}}\cdot\dfrac{\sqrt{2}}{\sqrt{2}} = \dfrac{2}{2\sqrt{6}} = \dfrac{1}{\sqrt{6}}$

(B) $\dfrac{3+\sqrt{m}}{9-m} = \dfrac{3+\sqrt{m}}{9-m}\cdot\dfrac{3-\sqrt{m}}{3-\sqrt{m}} = \dfrac{9-m}{(9-m)(3-\sqrt{m})} = \dfrac{1}{3-\sqrt{m}}$

(C) $$\dfrac{\sqrt{2+h}-\sqrt{2}}{h} = \dfrac{\sqrt{2+h}-\sqrt{2}}{h}\cdot\dfrac{\sqrt{2+h}+\sqrt{2}}{\sqrt{2+h}+\sqrt{2}} = \dfrac{h}{h(\sqrt{2+h}+\sqrt{2})} = \dfrac{1}{\sqrt{2+h}+\sqrt{2}}$$

MATCHED PROBLEM 8 Rationalize each numerator.

(A) $\dfrac{\sqrt{3}}{3\sqrt{2}}$ (B) $\dfrac{2-\sqrt{n}}{4-n}$ (C) $\dfrac{\sqrt{3+h}-\sqrt{3}}{h}$

Exercises A.6

A *Change each expression in Problems 1–6 to radical form. Do not simplify.*

1. $6x^{3/5}$
2. $7y^{2/5}$
3. $(32x^2y^3)^{3/5}$
4. $(7x^2y)^{5/7}$
5. $(x^2+y^2)^{1/2}$
6. $x^{1/2}+y^{1/2}$

Change each expression in Problems 7–12 to rational exponent form. Do not simplify.

7. $5\sqrt[4]{x^3}$
8. $7m\sqrt[5]{n^2}$
9. $\sqrt[5]{(2x^2y)^3}$
10. $\sqrt[7]{(8x^4y)^3}$
11. $\sqrt[3]{x}+\sqrt[3]{y}$
12. $\sqrt[3]{x^2+y^3}$

In Problems 13–24, find rational number representations for each, if they exist.

13. $25^{1/2}$ **14.** $64^{1/3}$ **15.** $16^{3/2}$

16. $16^{3/4}$ **17.** $-49^{1/2}$ **18.** $(-49)^{1/2}$

19. $-64^{2/3}$ **20.** $(-64)^{2/3}$ **21.** $\left(\frac{4}{25}\right)^{3/2}$

22. $\left(\frac{8}{27}\right)^{2/3}$ **23.** $9^{-3/2}$ **24.** $8^{-2/3}$

In Problems 25–34, simplify each expression and write answers using positive exponents only. All variables represent positive real numbers.

25. $x^{4/5}x^{-2/5}$ **26.** $y^{-3/7}y^{4/7}$ **27.** $\frac{m^{2/3}}{m^{-1/3}}$

28. $\frac{x^{1/4}}{x^{3/4}}$ **29.** $(8x^3y^{-6})^{1/3}$ **30.** $(4u^{-2}v^4)^{1/2}$

31. $\left(\frac{4x^{-2}}{y^4}\right)^{-1/2}$ **32.** $\left(\frac{w^4}{9x^{-2}}\right)^{-1/2}$

33. $\frac{(8x)^{-1/3}}{12x^{1/4}}$ **34.** $\frac{6a^{3/4}}{15a^{-1/3}}$

Simplify each expression in Problems 35–40 using properties of radicals. All variables represent positive real numbers.

35. $\sqrt[5]{(2x+3)^5}$ **36.** $\sqrt[3]{(7+2y)^3}$

37. $\sqrt{6x}\sqrt{15x^3}\sqrt{30x^7}$ **38.** $\sqrt[5]{16a^4}\sqrt[5]{4a^2}\sqrt[5]{8a^3}$

39. $\frac{\sqrt{6x}\sqrt{10}}{\sqrt{15x}}$ **40.** $\frac{\sqrt{8}\sqrt{12y}}{\sqrt{6y}}$

B *In Problems 41–48, multiply, and express answers using positive exponents only.*

41. $3x^{3/4}(4x^{1/4} - 2x^8)$

42. $2m^{1/3}(3m^{2/3} - m^6)$

43. $(3u^{1/2} - v^{1/2})(u^{1/2} - 4v^{1/2})$

44. $(a^{1/2} + 2b^{1/2})(a^{1/2} - 3b^{1/2})$

45. $(6m^{1/2} + n^{-1/2})(6m - n^{-1/2})$

46. $(2x - 3y^{1/3})(2x^{1/3} + 1)$

47. $(3x^{1/2} - y^{1/2})^2$

48. $(x^{1/2} + 2y^{1/2})^2$

Write each expression in Problems 49–54 in the form $ax^p + bx^q$, where a and b are real numbers and p and q are rational numbers.

49. $\frac{\sqrt[3]{x^2} + 2}{2\sqrt[3]{x}}$ **50.** $\frac{12\sqrt{x} - 3}{4\sqrt{x}}$ **51.** $\frac{2\sqrt[4]{x^3} + \sqrt[3]{x}}{3x}$

52. $\frac{3\sqrt[3]{x^2} + \sqrt{x}}{5x}$ **53.** $\frac{2\sqrt[3]{x} - \sqrt{x}}{4\sqrt{x}}$ **54.** $\frac{x^2 - 4\sqrt{x}}{2\sqrt[3]{x}}$

Rationalize the denominators in Problems 55–60.

55. $\frac{12mn^2}{\sqrt{3mn}}$ **56.** $\frac{14x^2}{\sqrt{7x}}$ **57.** $\frac{2(x+3)}{\sqrt{x-2}}$

58. $\frac{3(x+1)}{\sqrt{x+4}}$ **59.** $\frac{7(x-y)^2}{\sqrt{x} - \sqrt{y}}$ **60.** $\frac{3a - 3b}{\sqrt{a} + \sqrt{b}}$

Rationalize the numerators in Problems 61–66.

61. $\frac{\sqrt{5xy}}{5x^2y^2}$ **62.** $\frac{\sqrt{3mn}}{3mn}$

63. $\frac{\sqrt{x+h} - \sqrt{x}}{h}$ **64.** $\frac{\sqrt{2(a+h)} - \sqrt{2a}}{h}$

65. $\frac{\sqrt{t} - \sqrt{x}}{t^2 - x^2}$ **66.** $\frac{\sqrt{x} - \sqrt{y}}{\sqrt{x} + \sqrt{y}}$

Problems 67–70 illustrate common errors involving rational exponents. In each case, find numerical examples that show that the left side is not always equal to the right side.

67. $(x+y)^{1/2} \neq x^{1/2} + y^{1/2}$ **68.** $(x^3 + y^3)^{1/3} \neq x + y$

69. $(x+y)^{1/3} \neq \frac{1}{(x+y)^3}$ **70.** $(x+y)^{-1/2} \neq \frac{1}{(x+y)^2}$

C *In Problems 71–82, discuss the validity of each statement. If the statement is true, explain why. If not, give a counterexample.*

71. $\sqrt{x^2} = x$ for all real numbers x

72. $\sqrt{x^2} = |x|$ for all real numbers x

73. $\sqrt[3]{x^3} = |x|$ for all real numbers x

74. $\sqrt[3]{x^3} = x$ for all real numbers x

75. If $r < 0$, then r has no cube roots.

76. If $r < 0$, then r has no square roots.

77. If $r > 0$, then r has two square roots.

78. If $r > 0$, then r has three cube roots.

79. The fourth roots of 100 are $\sqrt{10}$ and $-\sqrt{10}$.

80. The square roots of $2\sqrt{6} - 5$ are $\sqrt{3} - \sqrt{2}$ and $\sqrt{2} - \sqrt{3}$.

81. $\sqrt{355 - 60\sqrt{35}} = 5\sqrt{7} - 6\sqrt{5}$

82. $\sqrt[3]{7 - 5\sqrt{2}} = 1 - \sqrt{2}$

In Problems 83–88, simplify by writing each expression as a simple or single fraction reduced to lowest terms and without negative exponents.

83. $-\frac{1}{2}(x-2)(x+3)^{-3/2} + (x+3)^{-1/2}$

84. $2(x-2)^{-1/2} - \frac{1}{2}(2x+3)(x-2)^{-3/2}$

85. $\frac{(x-1)^{1/2} - x(\frac{1}{2})(x-1)^{-1/2}}{x-1}$

86. $\frac{(2x-1)^{1/2} - (x+2)(\frac{1}{2})(2x-1)^{-1/2}(2)}{2x-1}$

87. $\frac{(x+2)^{2/3} - x(\frac{2}{3})(x+2)^{-1/3}}{(x+2)^{4/3}}$

88. $\frac{2(3x-1)^{1/3} - (2x+1)(\frac{1}{3})(3x-1)^{-2/3}(3)}{(3x-1)^{2/3}}$

In Problems 89–94, evaluate using a calculator. (Refer to the instruction book for your calculator to see how exponential forms are evaluated.)

89. $22^{3/2}$

90. $15^{5/4}$

91. $827^{-3/8}$

92. $103^{-3/4}$

93. $37.09^{7/3}$

94. $2.876^{8/5}$

In Problems 95 and 96, evaluate each expression on a calculator and determine which pairs have the same value. Verify these results algebraically.

95. (A) $\sqrt{3} + \sqrt{5}$ (B) $\sqrt{2 + \sqrt{3}} + \sqrt{2 - \sqrt{3}}$
(C) $1 + \sqrt{3}$ (D) $\sqrt[3]{10 + 6\sqrt{3}}$
(E) $\sqrt{8 + \sqrt{60}}$ (F) $\sqrt{6}$

96. (A) $2\sqrt[3]{2 + \sqrt{5}}$ (B) $\sqrt{8}$
(C) $\sqrt{3} + \sqrt{7}$ (D) $\sqrt{3 + \sqrt{8}} + \sqrt{3 - \sqrt{8}}$
(E) $\sqrt{10 + \sqrt{84}}$ (F) $1 + \sqrt{5}$

Answers to Matched Problems

1. (A) 4 (B) −4
(C) −3 (D) Not a real number
(E) 27

2. (A) $\sqrt[5]{u}$ (B) $\sqrt[9]{(6x^2y^5)^2}$ or $(\sqrt[9]{(6x^2y^5)})^2$
(C) $1/\sqrt[5]{(3xy)^3}$ (D) $(9u)^{1/4}$
(E) $-(2x)^{4/7}$ (F) $(x^3 + y^3)^{1/3}$ (not $x + y$)

3. (A) 27 (B) 81
(C) $10y^{7/12} = 10\sqrt[12]{y^7}$ (D) $16y/x^3$
(E) $2/x^{1/18} = 2/\sqrt[18]{x}$

4. (A) $10c^{13/4} - 2c$ (B) $14x + 19x^{1/2}y^{1/2} - 3y$

5. $2.5x^{-7/6} - 2x^{-1}$

6. (A) $x^3 + y^3$ (B) $2y$ (C) $2x$

7. (A) $4b\sqrt{3ab}$ (B) $3(\sqrt{6} - \sqrt{3})$
(C) $(x + y)(\sqrt{x} + \sqrt{y})$

8. (A) $\dfrac{1}{\sqrt{6}}$ (B) $\dfrac{1}{2 + \sqrt{n}}$ (C) $\dfrac{1}{\sqrt{3 + h} + \sqrt{3}}$

A.7 Quadratic Equations

- Solution by Square Root
- Solution by Factoring
- Quadratic Formula
- Quadratic Formula and Factoring
- Other Polynomial Equations
- Application: Supply and Demand

In this section we consider equations involving second-degree polynomials.

DEFINITION Quadratic Equation

A **quadratic equation** in one variable is any equation that can be written in the form

$$ax^2 + bx + c = 0 \qquad a \neq 0 \qquad \text{Standard form}$$

where x is a variable and a, b, and c are constants.

The equations

$$5x^2 - 3x + 7 = 0 \qquad \text{and} \qquad 18 = 32t^2 - 12t$$

are both quadratic equations, since they are either in the standard form or can be transformed into this form.

We restrict our review to finding real solutions to quadratic equations.

Solution by Square Root

The easiest type of quadratic equation to solve is the special form where the first-degree term is missing:

$$ax^2 + c = 0 \qquad a \neq 0$$

The method of solution of this special form makes direct use of the square-root property:

THEOREM 1 Square-Root Property

If $a^2 = b$, then $a = \pm\sqrt{b}$.

EXAMPLE 1 **Square-Root Method** Use the square-root property to solve each equation.

(A) $x^2 - 7 = 0$ (B) $2x^2 - 10 = 0$

(C) $3x^2 + 27 = 0$ (D) $(x - 8)^2 = 9$

SOLUTION

(A) $x^2 - 7 = 0$

$x^2 = 7$ What real number squared is 7?

$x = \pm\sqrt{7}$ Short for $\sqrt{7}$ or $-\sqrt{7}$

(B) $2x^2 - 10 = 0$

$2x^2 = 10$

$x^2 = 5$ What real number squared is 5?

$x = \pm\sqrt{5}$

(C) $3x^2 + 27 = 0$

$3x^2 = -27$

$x^2 = -9$ What real number squared is -9?

No real solution, since no real number squared is negative.

(D) $(x - 8)^2 = 9$

$$x - 8 = \pm\sqrt{9}$$
$$x - 8 = \pm 3$$
$$x = 8 \pm 3 = 5 \quad \text{or} \quad 11$$

MATCHED PROBLEM 1 Use the square-root property to solve each equation.

(A) $x^2 - 6 = 0$ (B) $3x^2 - 12 = 0$

(C) $x^2 + 4 = 0$ (D) $(x + 5)^2 = 1$

Solution by Factoring

If the left side of a quadratic equation when written in standard form can be factored, the equation can be solved very quickly. The method of solution by factoring rests on a basic property of real numbers, first mentioned in Section A.1.

CONCEPTUAL INSIGHT

Theorem 2 in Section A.1 states that if a and b are real numbers, then $ab = 0$ if and only if $a = 0$ or $b = 0$. To see that this property is useful for solving quadratic equations, consider the following:

$$x^2 - 4x + 3 = 0 \qquad (1)$$
$$(x - 1)(x - 3) = 0$$
$$x - 1 = 0 \quad \text{or} \quad x - 3 = 0$$
$$x = 1 \quad \text{or} \quad x = 3$$

You should check these solutions in equation (1).

If one side of the equation is not 0, then this method cannot be used. For example, consider

$$x^2 - 4x + 3 = 8 \qquad (2)$$
$$(x - 1)(x - 3) = 8$$
$$x - 1 \neq 8 \quad \text{or} \quad x - 3 \neq 8$$
$$x = 9 \quad \text{or} \quad x = 11$$

$ab = 8$ does not imply that $a = 8$ or $b = 8$.

Verify that neither $x = 9$ nor $x = 11$ is a solution for equation (2).

EXAMPLE 2 **Factoring Method** Solve by factoring using integer coefficients, if possible.

(A) $3x^2 - 6x - 24 = 0$ (B) $3y^2 = 2y$ (C) $x^2 - 2x - 1 = 0$

SOLUTION

(A)
$$3x^2 - 6x - 24 = 0$$ Divide both sides by 3, since 3 is a factor of each coefficient.
$$x^2 - 2x - 8 = 0$$ Factor the left side, if possible.
$$(x - 4)(x + 2) = 0$$
$$x - 4 = 0 \quad \text{or} \quad x + 2 = 0$$
$$x = 4 \quad \text{or} \quad x = -2$$

(B)
$$3y^2 = 2y$$
$$3y^2 - 2y = 0$$ We lose the solution $y = 0$ if both sides are divided by y ($3y^2 = 2y$ and $3y = 2$ are not equivalent).
$$y(3y - 2) = 0$$
$$y = 0 \quad \text{or} \quad 3y - 2 = 0$$
$$3y = 2$$
$$y = \frac{2}{3}$$

(C) $x^2 - 2x - 1 = 0$

This equation cannot be factored using integer coefficients. We will solve this type of equation by another method, considered below.

MATCHED PROBLEM 2 Solve by factoring using integer coefficients, if possible.

(A) $2x^2 + 4x - 30 = 0$ (B) $2x^2 = 3x$ (C) $2x^2 - 8x + 3 = 0$

Note that an equation such as $x^2 = 25$ can be solved by either the square-root or the factoring method, and the results are the same (as they should be). Solve this equation both ways and compare.

Also, note that the factoring method can be extended to higher-degree polynomial equations. Consider the following:

$$x^3 - x = 0$$
$$x(x^2 - 1) = 0$$
$$x(x - 1)(x + 1) = 0$$
$$x = 0 \quad \text{or} \quad x - 1 = 0 \quad \text{or} \quad x + 1 = 0$$
$$\text{Solution: } x = 0, 1, -1$$

Check these solutions in the original equation.

The factoring and square-root methods are fast and easy to use when they apply. However, there are quadratic equations that look simple but cannot be solved by either method. For example, as was noted in Example 2C, the polynomial in

$$x^2 - 2x - 1 = 0$$

cannot be factored using integer coefficients. This brings us to the well-known and widely used *quadratic formula*.

Quadratic Formula

There is a method called *completing the square* that will work for all quadratic equations. After briefly reviewing this method, we will use it to develop the quadratic formula, which can be used to solve any quadratic equation.

The method of **completing the square** is based on the process of transforming a quadratic equation in standard form,

$$ax^2 + bx + c = 0$$

into the form

$$(x + A)^2 = B$$

where A and B are constants. Then, this last equation can be solved easily (if it has a real solution) by the square-root method discussed above.

Consider the equation from Example 2C:

$$x^2 - 2x - 1 = 0 \tag{3}$$

Since the left side does not factor using integer coefficients, we add 1 to each side to remove the constant term from the left side:

$$x^2 - 2x = 1 \tag{4}$$

Now we try to find a number that we can add to each side to make the left side a square of a first-degree polynomial. Note the following square of a binomial:

$$(x + m)^2 = x^2 + 2mx + m^2$$

We see that the third term on the right is the square of one-half the coefficient of x in the second term on the right. To complete the square in equation (4), we add the square of one-half the coefficient of x, $(-\frac{2}{2})^2 = 1$, to each side. (This rule works only when the coefficient of x^2 is 1, that is, $a = 1$.) Thus,

$$x^2 - 2x + 1 = 1 + 1$$

The left side is the square of $x - 1$, and we write

$$(x - 1)^2 = 2$$

What number squared is 2?

$$x - 1 = \pm\sqrt{2}$$

$$x = 1 \pm \sqrt{2}$$

And equation (3) is solved!

Let us try the method on the general quadratic equation

$$ax^2 + bx + c = 0 \qquad a \neq 0 \tag{5}$$

and solve it once and for all for x in terms of the coefficients a, b, and c. We start by multiplying both sides of equation (5) by $1/a$ to obtain

$$x^2 + \frac{b}{a}x + \frac{c}{a} = 0$$

Add $-c/a$ to both sides:

$$x^2 + \frac{b}{a}x = -\frac{c}{a}$$

Now we complete the square on the left side by adding the square of one-half the coefficient of x, that is, $(b/2a)^2 = b^2/4a^2$ to each side:

$$x^2 + \frac{b}{a}x + \frac{b^2}{4a^2} = \frac{b^2}{4a^2} - \frac{c}{a}$$

Writing the left side as a square and combining the right side into a single fraction, we obtain

$$\left(x + \frac{b}{2a}\right)^2 = \frac{b^2 - 4ac}{4a^2}$$

Now we solve by the square-root method:

$$x + \frac{b}{2a} = \pm\sqrt{\frac{b^2 - 4ac}{4a^2}}$$

$$x = -\frac{b}{2a} \pm \frac{\sqrt{b^2 - 4ac}}{2a} \qquad \text{Since } \pm\sqrt{4a^2} = \pm 2a \text{ for any real number } a$$

When this is written as a single fraction, it becomes the **quadratic formula**:

Quadratic Formula

If $ax^2 + bx + c = 0$, $a \neq 0$, then

$$x = \frac{-b \pm \sqrt{b^2 - 4ac}}{2a}$$

This formula is generally used to solve quadratic equations when the square-root or factoring methods do not work. The quantity $b^2 - 4ac$ under the radical is called the **discriminant**, and it gives us the useful information about solutions listed in Table 1.

Table 1

$b^2 - 4ac$	$ax^2 + bx + c = 0$
Positive	Two real solutions
Zero	One real solution
Negative	No real solutions

EXAMPLE 3 **Quadratic Formula Method** Solve $x^2 - 2x - 1 = 0$ using the quadratic formula.

SOLUTION

$x^2 - 2x - 1 = 0$

$$x = \frac{-b \pm \sqrt{b^2 - 4ac}}{2a} \qquad a = 1, b = -2, c = -1$$

$$= \frac{-(-2) \pm \sqrt{(-2)^2 - 4(1)(-1)}}{2(1)}$$

$$= \frac{2 \pm \sqrt{8}}{2} = \frac{2 \pm 2\sqrt{2}}{2} = 1 \pm \sqrt{2} \approx -0.414 \quad \text{or} \quad 2.414$$

CHECK

$x^2 - 2x - 1 = 0$

When $x = 1 + \sqrt{2}$,

$$(1 + \sqrt{2})^2 - 2(1 + \sqrt{2}) - 1 = 1 + 2\sqrt{2} + 2 - 2 - 2\sqrt{2} - 1 = 0$$

When $x = 1 - \sqrt{2}$,

$$(1 - \sqrt{2})^2 - 2(1 - \sqrt{2}) - 1 = 1 - 2\sqrt{2} + 2 - 2 + 2\sqrt{2} - 1 = 0$$

MATCHED PROBLEM 3 Solve $2x^2 - 4x - 3 = 0$ using the quadratic formula.

If we try to solve $x^2 - 6x + 11 = 0$ using the quadratic formula, we obtain

$$x = \frac{6 \pm \sqrt{-8}}{2}$$

which is not a real number. (Why?)

Quadratic Formula and Factoring

As in Section A.3, we restrict our interest in factoring to polynomials with integer coefficients. If a polynomial cannot be factored as a product of lower-degree polynomials with integer coefficients, we say that the polynomial is **not factorable in the integers**.

How can you factor the quadratic polynomial $x^2 - 13x - 2{,}310$? We start by solving the corresponding quadratic equation using the quadratic formula:

$$x^2 - 13x - 2{,}310 = 0$$

$$x = \frac{-(-13) \pm \sqrt{(-13)^3 - 4(1)(-2{,}310)}}{2}$$

$$x = \frac{-(-13) \pm \sqrt{9{,}409}}{2}$$

$$= \frac{13 \pm 97}{2} = 55 \quad \text{or} \quad -42$$

Now we write

$$x^2 - 13x - 2{,}310 = [x - 55][x - (-42)] = (x - 55)(x + 42)$$

Multiplying the two factors on the right produces the second-degree polynomial on the left.

What is behind this procedure? The following two theorems justify and generalize the process:

THEOREM 2 Factorability Theorem

A second-degree polynomial, $ax^2 + bx + c$, with integer coefficients can be expressed as the product of two first-degree polynomials with integer coefficients if and only if $\sqrt{b^2 - 4ac}$ is an integer.

THEOREM 3 Factor Theorem

If r_1 and r_2 are solutions to the second-degree equation $ax^2 + bx + c = 0$, then

$$ax^2 + bx + c = a(x - r_1)(x - r_2)$$

EXAMPLE 4 **Factoring with the Aid of the Discriminant** Factor, if possible, using integer coefficients.

(A) $4x^2 - 65x + 264$ (B) $2x^2 - 33x - 306$

SOLUTION (A) $4x^2 - 65x + 264$

Step 1 Test for factorability:

$$\sqrt{b^2 - 4ac} = \sqrt{(-65)^2 - 4(4)(264)} = 1$$

Since the result is an integer, the polynomial has first-degree factors with integer coefficients.

Step 2 Factor, using the factor theorem. Find the solutions to the corresponding quadratic equation using the quadratic formula:

$$4x^2 - 65x + 264 = 0$$

From step 1

$$x = \frac{-(-65) \pm 1}{2 \cdot 4} = \frac{33}{4} \quad \text{or} \quad 8$$

Thus,

$$4x^2 - 65x + 264 = 4\left(x - \frac{33}{4}\right)(x - 8)$$
$$= (4x - 33)(x - 8)$$

(B) $2x^2 - 33x - 306$

Step 1 Test for factorability:

$$\sqrt{b^2 - 4ac} = \sqrt{(-33)^2 - 4(2)(-306)} = \sqrt{3{,}537}$$

Since $\sqrt{3{,}537}$ is not an integer, the polynomial is not factorable in the integers.

MATCHED PROBLEM 4 Factor, if possible, using integer coefficients.

(A) $3x^2 - 28x - 464$ (B) $9x^2 + 320x - 144$

Other Polynomial Equations

There are formulas that are analogous to the quadratic formula, but considerably more complicated, that can be used to solve any cubic (degree 3) or quartic (degree 4) polynomial equation. It can be shown that no such general formula exists for solving quintic (degree 5) or polynomial equations of degree greater than five. Certain polynomial equations, however, can be solved easily by taking roots.

EXAMPLE 5 **Solving a Quartic Equation** Find all real solutions to $6x^4 - 486 = 0$.

SOLUTION

$$6x^4 - 486 = 0 \quad \text{Add 486 to both sides}$$
$$6x^4 = 486 \quad \text{Divide both sides by 6}$$
$$x^4 = 81 \quad \text{Take the 4th root of both sides}$$
$$x = \pm 3$$

MATCHED PROBLEM 5 Find all real solutions to $6x^5 + 192 = 0$.

Application: Supply and Demand

Supply-and-demand analysis is a very important part of business and economics. In general, producers are willing to supply more of an item as the price of an item increases and less of an item as the price decreases. Similarly, buyers are willing to buy less of an item as the price increases, and more of an item as the price decreases. We have a dynamic situation where the price, supply, and demand fluctuate until a price is reached at which the supply is equal to the demand. In economic theory, this point is called the **equilibrium point**. If the price increases from this point, the supply will increase and the demand will decrease; if the price decreases from this point, the supply will decrease and the demand will increase.

EXAMPLE 6 **Supply and Demand** At a large summer beach resort, the weekly supply-and-demand equations for folding beach chairs are

$$p = \frac{x}{140} + \frac{3}{4} \quad \text{Supply equation}$$

$$p = \frac{5{,}670}{x} \quad \text{Demand equation}$$

The supply equation indicates that the supplier is willing to sell x units at a price of p dollars per unit. The demand equation indicates that consumers are willing to buy x units at a price of p dollars per unit. How many units are required for supply to equal demand? At what price will supply equal demand?

SOLUTION Set the right side of the supply equation equal to the right side of the demand equation and solve for x.

$$\frac{x}{140} + \frac{3}{4} = \frac{5,670}{x} \qquad \text{Multiply by } 140x \text{, the LCD.}$$

$$x^2 + 105x = 793,800 \qquad \text{Write in standard form.}$$

$$x^2 + 105x - 793,800 = 0 \qquad \text{Use the quadratic formula.}$$

$$x = \frac{-105 \pm \sqrt{105^2 - 4(1)(-793,800)}}{2}$$

$$x = 840 \text{ units}$$

The negative root is discarded since a negative number of units cannot be produced or sold. Substitute $x = 840$ back into either the supply equation or the demand equation to find the equilibrium price (we use the demand equation).

$$p = \frac{5,670}{x} = \frac{5,670}{840} = \$6.75$$

At a price of \$6.75 the supplier is willing to supply 840 chairs and consumers are willing to buy 840 chairs during a week.

MATCHED PROBLEM 6 Repeat Example 6 if near the end of summer, the supply-and-demand equations are

$$p = \frac{x}{80} - \frac{1}{20} \qquad \text{Supply equation}$$

$$p = \frac{1,264}{x} \qquad \text{Demand equation}$$

Exercises A.7

Find only real solutions in the problems below. If there are no real solutions, say so.

A *Solve Problems 1–4 by the square-root method.*

1. $2x^2 - 22 = 0$

2. $3m^2 - 21 = 0$

3. $(3x - 1)^2 = 25$

4. $(2x + 1)^2 = 16$

Solve Problems 5–8 by factoring.

5. $2u^2 - 8u - 24 = 0$

6. $3x^2 - 18x + 15 = 0$

7. $x^2 = 2x$

8. $n^2 = 3n$

Solve Problems 9–12 by using the quadratic formula.

9. $x^2 - 6x - 3 = 0$

10. $m^2 + 8m + 3 = 0$

11. $3u^2 + 12u + 6 = 0$

12. $2x^2 - 20x - 6 = 0$

B *Solve Problems 13–30 by using any method.*

13. $\frac{2x^2}{3} = 5x$

14. $x^2 = -\frac{3}{4}x$

15. $4u^2 - 9 = 0$

16. $9y^2 - 25 = 0$

17. $8x^2 + 20x = 12$

18. $9x^2 - 6 = 15x$

19. $x^2 = 1 - x$

20. $m^2 = 1 - 3m$

21. $2x^2 = 6x - 3$

22. $2x^2 = 4x - 1$

23. $y^2 - 4y = -8$

24. $x^2 - 2x = -3$

25. $(2x + 3)^2 = 11$

26. $(5x - 2)^2 = 7$

27. $\frac{3}{p} = p$

28. $x - \frac{7}{x} = 0$

29. $2 - \frac{2}{m^2} = \frac{3}{m}$

30. $2 + \frac{5}{u} = \frac{3}{u^2}$

In Problems 31–38, factor, if possible, as the product of two first-degree polynomials with integer coefficients. Use the quadratic formula and the factor theorem.

31. $x^2 + 40x - 84$

32. $x^2 - 28x - 128$

33. $x^2 - 32x + 144$

34. $x^2 + 52x + 208$

35. $2x^2 + 15x - 108$

36. $3x^2 - 32x - 140$

37. $4x^2 + 241x - 434$

38. $6x^2 - 427x - 360$

39. Solve $A = P(1 + r)^2$ for r in terms of A and P; that is, isolate r on the left side of the equation (with coefficient 1) and end up with an algebraic expression on the right side involving A and P but not r. Write the answer using positive square roots only.

40. Solve $x^2 + 3mx - 3n = 0$ for x in terms of m and n.

41. Consider the quadratic equation

$$x^2 + 4x + c = 0$$

where c is a real number. Discuss the relationship between the values of c and the three types of roots listed in Table 1 on page 562.

42. Consider the quadratic equation

$$x^2 - 2x + c = 0$$

where c is a real number. Discuss the relationship between the values of c and the three types of roots listed in Table 1 on page 562.

In Problems 43–48, find all real solutions.

43. $x^3 + 8 = 0$

44. $x^3 - 8 = 0$

45. $5x^4 - 500 = 0$

46. $2x^3 + 250 = 0$

47. $x^4 - 8x^2 + 15 = 0$

48. $x^4 - 12x^2 + 32 = 0$

Applications

49. **Supply and demand.** A company wholesales shampoo in a particular city. Their marketing research department established the following weekly supply-and-demand equations:

$$p = \frac{x}{450} + \frac{1}{2} \quad \text{Supply equation}$$

$$p = \frac{6{,}300}{x} \quad \text{Demand equation}$$

How many units are required for supply to equal demand? At what price per bottle will supply equal demand?

50. **Supply and demand.** An importer sells an automatic camera to outlets in a large city. During the summer, the weekly supply-and-demand equations are

$$p = \frac{x}{6} + 9 \quad \text{Supply equation}$$

$$p = \frac{24{,}840}{x} \quad \text{Demand equation}$$

How many units are required for supply to equal demand? At what price will supply equal demand?

51. **Interest rate.** If P dollars are invested at $100r$ percent compounded annually, at the end of 2 years it will grow to $A = P(1 + r)^2$. At what interest rate will \$484 grow to \$625 in 2 years? (*Note:* If $A = 625$ and $P = 484$, find r.)

52. **Interest rate.** Using the formula in Problem 51, determine the interest rate that will make \$1,000 grow to \$1,210 in 2 years.

53. **Ecology.** To measure the velocity v (in feet per second) of a stream, we position a hollow L-shaped tube with one end under the water pointing upstream and the other end pointing straight up a couple of feet out of the water. The water will then be pushed up the tube a certain distance h (in feet) above the surface of the stream. Physicists have shown that $v^2 = 64h$. Approximately how fast is a stream flowing if $h = 1$ foot? If $h = 0.5$ foot?

54. **Safety research.** It is of considerable importance to know the least number of feet d in which a car can be stopped, including reaction time of the driver, at various speeds v (in miles per hour). Safety research has produced the formula $d = 0.044v^2 + 1.1v$. If it took a car 550 feet to stop, estimate the car's speed at the moment the stopping process was started.

Answers to Matched Problems

1. (A) $\pm\sqrt{6}$ (B) ± 2 (C) No real solution (D) $-6, -4$
2. (A) $-5, 3$ (B) $0, \frac{3}{2}$ (C) Cannot be factored using integer coefficients
3. $(2 \pm \sqrt{10})/2$
4. (A) Cannot be factored using integer coefficients (B) $(9x - 4)(x + 36)$
5. -2
6. 320 chairs at \$3.95 each

B Special Topics

B.1 Sequences, Series, and Summation Notation

- Sequences
- Series and Summation Notation

If someone asked you to list all natural numbers that are perfect squares, you might begin by writing

$$1, 4, 9, 16, 25, 36$$

But you would soon realize that it is impossible to actually list all the perfect squares, since there are an infinite number of them. However, you could represent this collection of numbers in several different ways. One common method is to write

$$1, 4, 9, \ldots, n^2, \ldots \qquad n \in N$$

where N is the set of natural numbers. A list of numbers such as this is generally called a *sequence*.

Sequences

Consider the function f given by

$$f(n) = 2n + 1 \tag{1}$$

where the domain of f is the set of natural numbers N. Note that

$$f(1) = 3, \quad f(2) = 5, \quad f(3) = 7, \quad \ldots$$

The function f is an example of a sequence. In general, a **sequence** is a function with domain a set of successive integers. Instead of the standard function notation used in equation (1), sequences are usually defined in terms of a special notation.

The range value $f(n)$ is usually symbolized more compactly with a symbol such as a_n. Thus, in place of equation (1), we write

$$a_n = 2n + 1$$

and the domain is understood to be the set of natural numbers unless something is said to the contrary or the context indicates otherwise. The elements in the range are called **terms of the sequence**; a_1 is the first term, a_2 is the second term, and a_n is the ***n*th term**, or **general term**.

$$a_1 = 2(1) + 1 = 3 \quad \text{First term}$$
$$a_2 = 2(2) + 1 = 5 \quad \text{Second term}$$
$$a_3 = 2(3) + 1 = 7 \quad \text{Third term}$$
$$\vdots$$
$$a_n = 2n + 1 \quad \text{General term}$$

The ordered list of elements

$$3, 5, 7, \ldots, 2n + 1, \ldots$$

obtained by writing the terms of the sequence in their natural order with respect to the domain values is often informally referred to as a sequence. A sequence also may be represented in the abbreviated form $\{a_n\}$, where a symbol for the nth term is written within braces. For example, we could refer to the sequence $3, 5, 7, \ldots, 2n + 1, \ldots$ as the sequence $\{2n + 1\}$.

If the domain of a sequence is a finite set of successive integers, then the sequence is called a **finite sequence**. If the domain is an infinite set of successive integers, then the sequence is called an **infinite sequence.** The sequence $\{2n + 1\}$ discussed above is an infinite sequence.

EXAMPLE 1 **Writing the Terms of a Sequence** Write the first four terms of each sequence:

(A) $a_n = 3n - 2$ (B) $\left\{\frac{(-1)^n}{n}\right\}$

SOLUTION

(A) 1, 4, 7, 10 (B) $-1, \frac{1}{2}, \frac{-1}{3}, \frac{1}{4}$

MATCHED PROBLEM 1 Write the first four terms of each sequence:

(A) $a_n = -n + 3$ (B) $\left\{\frac{(-1)^n}{2^n}\right\}$

Now that we have seen how to use the general term to find the first few terms in a sequence, we consider the reverse problem. That is, can a sequence be defined just by listing the first three or four terms of the sequence? And can we then use these initial terms to find a formula for the nth term? In general, without other information, the answer to the first question is no. Many different sequences may start off with the same terms. Simply listing the first three terms (or any other finite number of terms) does not specify a particular sequence.

What about the second question? That is, given a few terms, can we find the general formula for at least one sequence whose first few terms agree with the given terms? The answer to this question is a qualified yes. If we can observe a simple pattern in the given terms, we usually can construct a general term that will produce that pattern. The next example illustrates this approach.

EXAMPLE 2 **Finding the General Term of a Sequence** Find the general term of a sequence whose first four terms are

(A) 3, 4, 5, 6, . . . (B) 5, −25, 125, −625, . . .

SOLUTION

(A) Since these terms are consecutive integers, one solution is $a_n = n, n \geq 3$. If we want the domain of the sequence to be all natural numbers, another solution is $b_n = n + 2$.

(B) Each of these terms can be written as the product of a power of 5 and a power of -1:

$$5 = (-1)^0 5^1 = a_1$$
$$-25 = (-1)^1 5^2 = a_2$$
$$125 = (-1)^2 5^3 = a_3$$
$$-625 = (-1)^3 5^4 = a_4$$

If we choose the domain to be all natural numbers, a solution is

$$a_n = (-1)^{n-1} 5^n$$

MATCHED PROBLEM 2 Find the general term of a sequence whose first four terms are

(A) 3, 6, 9, 12, . . . (B) 1, -2, 4, -8, . . .

In general, there is usually more than one way of representing the nth term of a given sequence (see the solution of Example 2A). However, unless something is stated to the contrary, we assume that the domain of the sequence is the set of natural numbers N.

Series and Summation Notation

If $a_1, a_2, a_3, \ldots, a_n, \ldots$ is a sequence, the expression

$$a_1 + a_2 + a_3 + \cdots + a_n + \cdots$$

is called a **series**. If the sequence is finite, the corresponding series is a **finite series**. If the sequence is infinite, the corresponding series is an **infinite series**. We consider only finite series in this section. For example,

$$1, 3, 5, 7, 9 \qquad \text{Finite sequence}$$

$$1 + 3 + 5 + 7 + 9 \qquad \text{Finite series}$$

Notice that we can easily evaluate this series by adding the five terms:

$$1 + 3 + 5 + 7 + 9 = 25$$

Series are often represented in a compact form called **summation notation**. Consider the following examples:

$$\sum_{k=3}^{6} k^2 = 3^2 + 4^2 + 5^2 + 6^2$$
$$= 9 + 16 + 25 + 36 = 86$$

$$\sum_{k=0}^{2} (4k + 1) = (4 \cdot 0 + 1) + (4 \cdot 1 + 1) + (4 \cdot 2 + 1)$$
$$= 1 + 5 + 9 = 15$$

In each case, the terms of the series on the right are obtained from the expression on the left by successively replacing the **summing index k** with integers, starting with the number indicated below the **summation sign Σ** and ending with the number that appears above Σ. The summing index may be represented by letters other than k and may start at any integer and end at any integer greater than or equal to the starting integer. If we are given the finite sequence

$$\frac{1}{2}, \frac{1}{4}, \frac{1}{8}, \ldots, \frac{1}{2^n}$$

the corresponding series is

$$\frac{1}{2} + \frac{1}{4} + \frac{1}{8} + \cdots + \frac{1}{2^n} = \sum_{j=1}^{n} \frac{1}{2^j}$$

where we have used j for the summing index.

EXAMPLE 3 **Summation Notation** Write

$$\sum_{k=1}^{5} \frac{k}{k^2 + 1}$$

without summation notation. Do not evaluate the sum.

SOLUTION

$$\sum_{k=1}^{5} \frac{k}{k^2 + 1} = \frac{1}{1^2 + 1} + \frac{2}{2^2 + 1} + \frac{3}{3^2 + 1} + \frac{4}{4^2 + 1} + \frac{5}{5^2 + 1}$$

$$= \frac{1}{2} + \frac{2}{5} + \frac{3}{10} + \frac{4}{17} + \frac{5}{26}$$

MATCHED PROBLEM 3 Write

$$\sum_{k=1}^{5} \frac{k + 1}{k}$$

without summation notation. Do not evaluate the sum.

If the terms of a series are alternately positive and negative, we call the series an **alternating series**. The next example deals with the representation of such a series.

EXAMPLE 4 **Summation Notation** Write the alternating series

$$\frac{1}{2} - \frac{1}{4} + \frac{1}{6} - \frac{1}{8} + \frac{1}{10} - \frac{1}{12}$$

using summation notation with

(A) The summing index k starting at 1

(B) The summing index j starting at 0

SOLUTION

(A) $(-1)^{k+1}$ provides the alternation of sign, and $1/(2k)$ provides the other part of each term. So, we can write

$$\frac{1}{2} - \frac{1}{4} + \frac{1}{6} - \frac{1}{8} + \frac{1}{10} - \frac{1}{12} = \sum_{k=1}^{6} \frac{(-1)^{k+1}}{2k}$$

(B) $(-1)^j$ provides the alternation of sign, and $1/[2(j + 1)]$ provides the other part of each term. So, we can write

$$\frac{1}{2} - \frac{1}{4} + \frac{1}{6} - \frac{1}{8} + \frac{1}{10} - \frac{1}{12} = \sum_{j=0}^{5} \frac{(-1)^j}{2(j + 1)}$$

MATCHED PROBLEM 4 Write the alternating series

$$1 - \frac{1}{3} + \frac{1}{9} - \frac{1}{27} + \frac{1}{81}$$

using summation notation with

(A) The summing index k starting at 1

(B) The summing index j starting at 0

Summation notation provides a compact notation for the sum of any list of numbers, even if the numbers are not generated by a formula. For example, suppose that the results of an examination taken by a class of 10 students are given in the following list:

87, 77, 95, 83, 86, 73, 95, 68, 75, 86

If we let $a_1, a_2, a_3, \ldots, a_{10}$ represent these 10 scores, then the average test score is given by

$$\frac{1}{10}\sum_{k=1}^{10} a_k = \frac{1}{10}(87 + 77 + 95 + 83 + 86 + 73 + 95 + 68 + 75 + 86)$$
$$= \frac{1}{10}(825) = 82.5$$

More generally, in statistics, the **arithmetic mean** $\bar{a}$ of a list of n numbers $a_1, a_2, \ldots, a_n$ is defined as

$$\bar{a} = \frac{1}{n}\sum_{k=1}^{n} a_k$$

EXAMPLE 5 **Arithmetic Mean** Find the arithmetic mean of 3, 5, 4, 7, 4, 2, 3, and 6.

SOLUTION

$$\bar{a} = \frac{1}{8}\sum_{k=1}^{8} a_k = \frac{1}{8}(3 + 5 + 4 + 7 + 4 + 2 + 3 + 6) = \frac{1}{8}(34) = 4.25$$

MATCHED PROBLEM 5 Find the arithmetic mean of 9, 3, 8, 4, 3, and 6.

Exercises B.1

A *Write the first four terms for each sequence in Problems 1–6.*

1. $a_n = 2n + 3$

2. $a_n = 4n - 3$

3. $a_n = \dfrac{n + 2}{n + 1}$

4. $a_n = \dfrac{2n + 1}{2n}$

5. $a_n = (-3)^{n+1}$

6. $a_n = (-\frac{1}{4})^{n-1}$

7. Write the 10th term of the sequence in Problem 1.

8. Write the 15th term of the sequence in Problem 2.

9. Write the 99th term of the sequence in Problem 3.

10. Write the 200th term of the sequence in Problem 4.

In Problems 11–16, write each series in expanded form without summation notation, and evaluate.

11. $\sum_{k=1}^{6} k$

12. $\sum_{k=1}^{5} k^2$

13. $\sum_{k=4}^{7} (2k - 3)$

14. $\sum_{k=0}^{4} (-2)^k$

15. $\sum_{k=0}^{3} \frac{1}{10^k}$

16. $\sum_{k=1}^{4} \frac{1}{2^k}$

Find the arithmetic mean of each list of numbers in Problems 17–20.

17. 5, 4, 2, 1, and 6

18. 7, 9, 9, 2, and 4

19. 96, 65, 82, 74, 91, 88, 87, 91, 77, and 74

20. 100, 62, 95, 91, 82, 87, 70, 75, 87, and 82

B *Write the first five terms of each sequence in Problems 21–26.*

21. $a_n = \dfrac{(-1)^{n+1}}{2^n}$

22. $a_n = (-1)^n(n - 1)^2$

23. $a_n = n[1 + (-1)^n]$

24. $a_n = \dfrac{1 - (-1)^n}{n}$

25. $a_n = \left(-\dfrac{3}{2}\right)^{n-1}$

26. $a_n = \left(-\dfrac{1}{2}\right)^{n+1}$

In Problems 27–42, find the general term of a sequence whose first four terms agree with the given terms.

27. $-2, -1, 0, 1, \ldots$

28. $4, 5, 6, 7, \ldots$

29. $4, 8, 12, 16, \ldots$

30. $-3, -6, -9, -12, \ldots$

31. $\frac{1}{2}, \frac{3}{4}, \frac{5}{6}, \frac{7}{8}, \ldots$

32. $\frac{1}{2}, \frac{2}{3}, \frac{3}{4}, \frac{4}{5}, \ldots$

33. $1, -2, 3, -4, \ldots$

34. $-2, 4, -8, 16, \ldots$

35. $1, -3, 5, -7, \ldots$

36. $3, -6, 9, -12, \ldots$

37. $1, \frac{2}{5}, \frac{4}{25}, \frac{8}{125}, \ldots$

38. $\frac{4}{3}, \frac{16}{9}, \frac{64}{27}, \frac{256}{81}, \ldots$

39. $x, x^2, x^3, x^4, \ldots$

40. $1, 2x, 3x^2, 4x^3, \ldots$

41. $x, -x^3, x^5, -x^7, \ldots$

42. $x, \frac{x^2}{2}, \frac{x^3}{3}, \frac{x^4}{4}, \ldots$

Write each series in Problems 43–50 in expanded form without summation notation. Do not evaluate.

43. $\sum_{k=1}^{5}(-1)^{k+1}(2k-1)^2$ **44.** $\sum_{k=1}^{4}\frac{(-2)^{k+1}}{2k+1}$

45. $\sum_{k=2}^{5}\frac{2^k}{2k+3}$ **46.** $\sum_{k=3}^{7}\frac{(-1)^k}{k^2-k}$

47. $\sum_{k=1}^{5}x^{k-1}$ **48.** $\sum_{k=1}^{3}\frac{1}{k}x^{k+1}$

49. $\sum_{k=0}^{4}\frac{(-1)^k x^{2k+1}}{2k+1}$ **50.** $\sum_{k=0}^{4}\frac{(-1)^k x^{2k}}{2k+2}$

Write each series in Problems 51–54 using summation notation with

(A) The summing index k starting at $k = 1$

(B) The summing index j starting at $j = 0$

51. $2 + 3 + 4 + 5 + 6$

52. $1^2 + 2^2 + 3^2 + 4^2$

53. $1 - \frac{1}{2} + \frac{1}{3} - \frac{1}{4}$

54. $1 - \frac{1}{3} + \frac{1}{5} - \frac{1}{7} + \frac{1}{9}$

Write each series in Problems 55–58 using summation notation with the summing index k starting at $k = 1$.

55. $2 + \frac{3}{2} + \frac{4}{3} + \cdots + \frac{n+1}{n}$

56. $1 + \frac{1}{2^2} + \frac{1}{3^2} + \cdots + \frac{1}{n^2}$

57. $\frac{1}{2} - \frac{1}{4} + \frac{1}{8} - \cdots + \frac{(-1)^{n+1}}{2^n}$

58. $1 - 4 + 9 - \cdots + (-1)^{n+1}n^2$

C *In Problems 59–62, discuss the validity of each statement. If the statement is true, explain why. If not, give a counterexample.*

59. For each positive integer n, the sum of the series $1 + \frac{1}{2} + \frac{1}{3} + \cdots + \frac{1}{n}$ is less than 4.

60. For each positive integer n, the sum of the series $\frac{1}{2} + \frac{1}{4} + \frac{1}{8} + \cdots + \frac{1}{2^n}$ is less than 1.

61. For each positive integer n, the sum of the series $\frac{1}{2} - \frac{1}{4} + \frac{1}{8} - \cdots + \frac{(-1)^{n+1}}{2^n}$ is greater than or equal to $\frac{1}{4}$.

62. For each positive integer n, the sum of the series $1 - \frac{1}{2} + \frac{1}{3} - \frac{1}{4} + \cdots + \frac{(-1)^{n+1}}{n}$ is greater than or equal to $\frac{1}{2}$.

Some sequences are defined by a **recursion formula**—*that is, a formula that defines each term of the sequence in terms of one or more of the preceding terms. For example, if $\{a_n\}$ is defined by*

$$a_1 = 1 \quad \text{and} \quad a_n = 2a_{n-1} + 1 \quad \text{for} \quad n \ge 2$$

then

$$a_2 = 2a_1 + 1 = 2 \cdot 1 + 1 = 3$$
$$a_3 = 2a_2 + 1 = 2 \cdot 3 + 1 = 7$$
$$a_4 = 2a_3 + 1 = 2 \cdot 7 + 1 = 15$$

and so on. In Problems 63–66, write the first five terms of each sequence.

63. $a_1 = 2$ and $a_n = 3a_{n-1} + 2$ for $n \ge 2$

64. $a_1 = 3$ and $a_n = 2a_{n-1} - 2$ for $n \ge 2$

65. $a_1 = 1$ and $a_n = 2a_{n-1}$ for $n \ge 2$

66. $a_1 = 1$ and $a_n = -\frac{1}{3}a_{n-1}$ for $n \ge 2$

If A is a positive real number, the terms of the sequence defined by

$$a_1 = \frac{A}{2} \quad \text{and} \quad a_n = \frac{1}{2}\left(a_{n-1} + \frac{A}{a_{n-1}}\right) \quad \text{for } n \ge 2$$

can be used to approximate $\sqrt{A}$ to any decimal place accuracy desired. In Problems 67 and 68, compute the first four terms of this sequence for the indicated value of A, and compare the fourth term with the value of $\sqrt{A}$ obtained from a calculator.

67. $A = 2$ **68.** $A = 6$

69. The sequence defined recursively by $a_1 = 1, a_2 = 1, a_n = a_{n-1} + a_{n-2}$ for $n \ge 3$ is called the *Fibonacci sequence*. Find the first ten terms of the Fibonacci sequence.

70. The sequence defined by $b_n = \frac{\sqrt{5}}{5}\left(\frac{1+\sqrt{5}}{2}\right)^n$ is related to the Fibonacci sequence. Find the first ten terms (to three decimal places) of the sequence $\{b_n\}$ and describe the relationship.

Answers to Matched Problems

1. (A) 2, 1, 0, −1 (B) $\frac{-1}{2}, \frac{1}{4}, \frac{-1}{8}, \frac{1}{16}$

2. (A) $a_n = 3n$ (B) $a_n = (-2)^{n-1}$

3. $2 + \frac{3}{2} + \frac{4}{3} + \frac{5}{4} + \frac{6}{5}$

4. (A) $\sum_{k=1}^{5}\frac{(-1)^{k-1}}{3^{k-1}}$ (B) $\sum_{j=0}^{4}\frac{(-1)^j}{3^j}$

5. 5.5

B.2 Arithmetic and Geometric Sequences

- Arithmetic and Geometric Sequences
- *n*th-Term Formulas
- Sum Formulas for Finite Arithmetic Series
- Sum Formulas for Finite Geometric Series
- Sum Formula for Infinite Geometric Series
- Applications

For most sequences, it is difficult to sum an arbitrary number of terms of the sequence without adding term by term. But particular types of sequences—*arithmetic sequences* and *geometric sequences*—have certain properties that lead to convenient and useful formulas for the sums of the corresponding *arithmetic series* and *geometric series*.

Arithmetic and Geometric Sequences

The sequence $5, 7, 9, 11, 13, \ldots, 5 + 2(n - 1), \ldots$, where each term after the first is obtained by adding 2 to the preceding term, is an example of an arithmetic sequence. The sequence $5, 10, 20, 40, 80, \ldots, 5(2)^{n-1}, \ldots$, where each term after the first is obtained by multiplying the preceding term by 2, is an example of a geometric sequence.

DEFINITION Arithmetic Sequence

A sequence of numbers

$$a_1, a_2, a_3, \ldots, a_n, \ldots$$

is called an **arithmetic sequence** if there is a constant d, called the **common difference**, such that

$$a_n - a_{n-1} = d$$

That is,

$$a_n = a_{n-1} + d \qquad \text{for every } n > 1$$

DEFINITION Geometric Sequence

A sequence of numbers

$$a_1, a_2, a_3, \ldots, a_n, \ldots$$

is called a **geometric sequence** if there exists a nonzero constant r, called a **common ratio**, such that

$$\frac{a_n}{a_{n-1}} = r$$

That is,

$$a_n = ra_{n-1} \quad \text{for every } n > 1$$

EXAMPLE 1 **Recognizing Arithmetic and Geometric Sequences** Which of the following can be the first four terms of an arithmetic sequence? Of a geometric sequence?

(A) $1, 2, 3, 5, \ldots$ (B) $-1, 3, -9, 27, \ldots$

(C) $3, 3, 3, 3, \ldots$ (D) $10, 8.5, 7, 5.5, \ldots$

SOLUTION

(A) Since $2 - 1 \neq 5 - 3$, there is no common difference, so the sequence is not an arithmetic sequence. Since $2/1 \neq 3/2$, there is no common ratio, so the sequence is not geometric either.

(B) The sequence is geometric with common ratio -3. It is not arithmetic.

(C) The sequence is arithmetic with common difference 0, and is also geometric with common ratio 1.

(D) The sequence is arithmetic with common difference -1.5. It is not geometric.

MATCHED PROBLEM 1 Which of the following can be the first four terms of an arithmetic sequence? Of a geometric sequence?

(A) 8, 2, 0.5, 0.125, . . . (B) −7, −2, 3, 8, . . . (C) 1, 5, 25, 100, . . .

*n*th-Term Formulas

If $\{a_n\}$ is an arithmetic sequence with common difference d, then

$$a_2 = a_1 + d$$
$$a_3 = a_2 + d = a_1 + 2d$$
$$a_4 = a_3 + d = a_1 + 3d$$

This suggests that

THEOREM 1 *n*th Term of an Arithmetic Sequence

$$a_n = a_1 + (n - 1)d \quad \text{for all } n > 1 \qquad (1)$$

Similarly, if $\{a_n\}$ is a geometric sequence with common ratio r, then

$$a_2 = a_1 r$$
$$a_3 = a_2 r = a_1 r^2$$
$$a_4 = a_3 r = a_1 r^3$$

This suggests that

THEOREM 2 *n*th Term of a Geometric Sequence

$$a_n = a_1 r^{n-1} \quad \text{for all } n > 1 \qquad (2)$$

EXAMPLE 2 **Finding Terms in Arithmetic and Geometric Sequences**

(A) If the 1st and 10th terms of an arithmetic sequence are 3 and 30, respectively, find the 40th term of the sequence.

(B) If the 1st and 10th terms of a geometric sequence are 3 and 30, find the 40th term to three decimal places.

SOLUTION

(A) First use formula (1) with $a_1 = 3$ and $a_{10} = 30$ to find d:

$$a_n = a_1 + (n - 1)d$$
$$a_{10} = a_1 + (10 - 1)d$$
$$30 = 3 + 9d$$
$$d = 3$$

Now find a_{40}:

$$a_{40} = 3 + 39 \cdot 3 = 120$$

(B) First use formula (2) with $a_1 = 3$ and $a_{10} = 30$ to find r:

$$a_n = a_1 r^{n-1}$$
$$a_{10} = a_1 r^{10-1}$$
$$30 = 3r^9$$
$$r^9 = 10$$
$$r = 10^{1/9}$$

Now find a_{40}:

$$a_{40} = 3(10^{1/9})^{39} = 3(10^{39/9}) = 64{,}633.041$$

MATCHED PROBLEM 2

(A) If the 1st and 15th terms of an arithmetic sequence are -5 and 23, respectively, find the 73rd term of the sequence.

(B) Find the 8th term of the geometric sequence

$$\frac{1}{64}, \frac{-1}{32}, \frac{1}{16}, \ldots$$

Sum Formulas for Finite Arithmetic Series

If $a_1, a_2, a_3, \ldots, a_n$ is a finite arithmetic sequence, then the corresponding series $a_1 + a_2 + a_3 + \cdots + a_n$ is called a *finite arithmetic series.* We will derive two simple and very useful formulas for the sum of a finite arithmetic series. Let d be the common difference of the arithmetic sequence $a_1, a_2, a_3, \ldots, a_n$ and let S_n denote the sum of the series $a_1 + a_2 + a_3 + \cdots + a_n$. Then

$$S_n = a_1 + (a_1 + d) + \cdots + [a_1 + (n-2)d] + [a_1 + (n-1)d]$$

Reversing the order of the sum, we obtain

$$S_n = [a_1 + (n-1)d] + [a_1 + (n-2)d] + \cdots + (a_1 + d) + a_1$$

Something interesting happens if we combine these last two equations by addition (adding corresponding terms on the right sides):

$$2S_n = [2a_1 + (n-1)d] + [2a_1 + (n-1)d] + \cdots + [2a_1 + (n-1)d] + [2a_1 + (n-1)d]$$

All the terms on the right side are the same, and there are n of them. Thus,

$$2S_n = n[2a_1 + (n-1)d]$$

and we have the following general formula:

THEOREM 3 Sum of a Finite Arithmetic Series: First Form

$$S_n = \frac{n}{2}[2a_1 + (n-1)d] \qquad (3)$$

Replacing

$$[a_1 + (n-1)d] \quad \text{in} \quad \frac{n}{2}[a_1 + a_1 + (n-1)d]$$

by a_n from equation (1), we obtain a second useful formula for the sum:

THEOREM 4 Sum of a Finite Arithmetic Series: Second Form

$$S_n = \frac{n}{2}(a_1 + a_n) \qquad (4)$$

EXAMPLE 3 **Finding a Sum** Find the sum of the first 30 terms in the arithmetic sequence:

$$3, 8, 13, 18, \ldots$$

SOLUTION Use formula (3) with $n = 30$, $a_1 = 3$, and $d = 5$:

$$S_{30} = \frac{30}{2}[2 \cdot 3 + (30 - 1)5] = 2{,}265$$

MATCHED PROBLEM 3 Find the sum of the first 40 terms in the arithmetic sequence:

$$15, 13, 11, 9, \ldots$$

EXAMPLE 4 **Finding a Sum** Find the sum of all the even numbers between 31 and 87.

SOLUTION First, find n using equation (1):

$$a_n = a_1 + (n - 1)d$$
$$86 = 32 + (n - 1)2$$
$$n = 28$$

Now find S_{28} using formula (4):

$$S_n = \frac{n}{2}(a_1 + a_n)$$
$$S_{28} = \frac{28}{2}(32 + 86) = 1{,}652$$

MATCHED PROBLEM 4 Find the sum of all the odd numbers between 24 and 208.

Sum Formulas for Finite Geometric Series

If $a_1, a_2, a_3, \ldots, a_n$ is a finite geometric sequence, then the corresponding series $a_1 + a_2 + a_3 + \cdots + a_n$ is called a *finite geometric series.* As with arithmetic series, we can derive two simple and very useful formulas for the sum of a finite geometric series. Let r be the common ratio of the geometric sequence $a_1, a_2, a_3, \ldots, a_n$ and let S_n denote the sum of the series $a_1 + a_2 + a_3 + \cdots + a_n$. Then

$$S_n = a_1 + a_1r + a_1r^2 + \cdots + a_1r^{n-2} + a_1r^{n-1}$$

If we multiply both sides by r, we obtain

$$rS_n = a_1r + a_1r^2 + a_1r^3 + \cdots + a_1r^{n-1} + a_1r^n$$

Now combine these last two equations by subtraction to obtain

$$rS_n - S_n = (a_1r + a_1r^2 + a_1r^3 + \cdots + a_1r^{n-1} + a_1r^n) - (a_1 + a_1r + a_1r^2 + \cdots + a_1r^{n-2} + a_1r^{n-1})$$
$$(r - 1)S_n = a_1r^n - a_1$$

Notice how many terms drop out on the right side. Solving for S_n, we have

THEOREM 5 Sum of a Finite Geometric Series: First Form

$$S_n = \frac{a_1(r^n - 1)}{r - 1} \qquad r \neq 1 \qquad (5)$$

Since $a_n = a_1r^{n-1}$, or $ra_n = a_1r^n$, formula (5) also can be written in the form

THEOREM 6 Sum of a Finite Geometric Series: Second Form

$$S_n = \frac{ra_n - a_1}{r - 1} \qquad r \neq 1 \qquad (6)$$

EXAMPLE 5 **Finding a Sum** Find the sum (to 2 decimal places) of the first ten terms of the geometric sequence:

$$1, 1.05, 1.05^2, \ldots$$

SOLUTION Use formula (5) with $a_1 = 1, r = 1.05$, and $n = 10$:

$$S_n = \frac{a_1(r^n - 1)}{r - 1}$$

$$S_{10} = \frac{1(1.05^{10} - 1)}{1.05 - 1}$$

$$\approx \frac{0.6289}{0.05} \approx 12.58$$

MATCHED PROBLEM 5 Find the sum of the first eight terms of the geometric sequence:

$$100, 100(1.08), 100(1.08)^2, \ldots$$

Sum Formula for Infinite Geometric Series

Given a geometric series, what happens to the sum S_n of the first n terms as n increases without stopping? To answer this question, let us write formula (5) in the form

$$S_n = \frac{a_1 r^n}{r - 1} - \frac{a_1}{r - 1}$$

It is possible to show that if $-1 < r < 1$, then r^n will approach 0 as n increases. The first term above will approach 0 and S_n can be made as close as we please to the second term, $-a_1/(r - 1)$ [which can be written as $a_1/(1 - r)$], by taking n sufficiently large. So, if the common ratio r is between -1 and 1, we conclude that the sum of an infinite geometric series is

THEOREM 7 Sum of an Infinite Geometric Series

$$S_\infty = \frac{a_1}{1 - r} \qquad -1 < r < 1 \qquad (7)$$

If $r \le -1$ or $r \ge 1$, then an infinite geometric series has no sum.

Applications

EXAMPLE 6 **Loan Repayment** A person borrows \$3,600 and agrees to repay the loan in monthly installments over 3 years. The agreement is to pay 1% of the unpaid balance each month for using the money and \$100 each month to reduce the loan. What is the total cost of the loan over the 3 years?

SOLUTION Let us look at the problem relative to a time line:

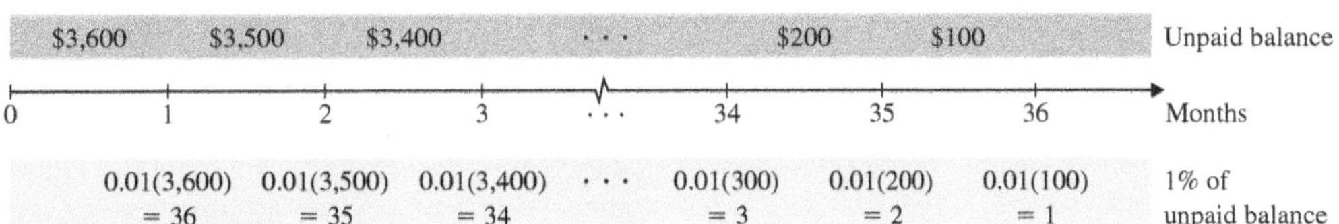

The total cost of the loan is

$$1 + 2 + \cdots + 34 + 35 + 36$$

The terms form a finite arithmetic series with $n = 36$, $a_1 = 1$, and $a_{36} = 36$, so we can use formula (4):

$$S_n = \frac{n}{2}(a_1 + a_n)$$

$$S_{36} = \frac{36}{2}(1 + 36) = \$666$$

We conclude that the total cost of the loan over 3 years is $666.

MATCHED PROBLEM 6 Repeat Example 6 with a loan of $6,000 over 5 years.

EXAMPLE 7 **Economy Stimulation** The government has decided on a tax rebate program to stimulate the economy. Suppose that you receive $1,200 and you spend 80% of this, and each of the people who receive what you spend also spend 80% of what they receive, and this process continues without end. According to the **multiplier principle** in economics, the effect of your $1,200 tax rebate on the economy is multiplied many times. What is the total amount spent if the process continues as indicated?

SOLUTION We need to find the sum of an infinite geometric series with the first amount spent being $a_1 = (0.8)(\$1{,}200) = \$960$ and $r = 0.8$. Using formula (7), we obtain

$$S_\infty = \frac{a_1}{1 - r}$$

$$= \frac{\$960}{1 - 0.8} = \$4{,}800$$

Assuming the process continues as indicated, we would expect the $1,200 tax rebate to result in about $4,800 of spending.

MATCHED PROBLEM 7 Repeat Example 7 with a tax rebate of $2,000.

Exercises B.2

A *In Problems 1 and 2, determine whether the indicated sequence can be the first three terms of an arithmetic or geometric sequence, and, if so, find the common difference or common ratio and the next two terms of the sequence.*

1. (A) $-11, -16, -21, \ldots$ (B) $2, -4, 8, \ldots$
(C) $1, 4, 9, \ldots$ (D) $\frac{1}{2}, \frac{1}{6}, \frac{1}{18}, \ldots$

2. (A) $5, 20, 100, \ldots$ (B) $-5, -5, -5, \ldots$
(C) $7, 6.5, 6, \ldots$ (D) $512, 256, 128, \ldots$

In Problems 3–8, determine whether the finite series is arithmetic, geometric, both, or neither. If the series is arithmetic or geometric, find its sum.

3. $\sum_{k=1}^{101} (-1)^{k+1}$

4. $\sum_{k=1}^{200} 3$

5. $1 + \frac{1}{2} + \frac{1}{3} + \cdots + \frac{1}{50}$

6. $3 - 9 + 27 - \cdots - 3^{20}$

7. $5 + 4.9 + 4.8 + \cdots + 0.1$

8. $1 - \frac{1}{4} + \frac{1}{9} - \cdots - \frac{1}{100^2}$

B *Let $a_1, a_2, a_3, \ldots, a_n, \ldots$ be an arithmetic sequence. In Problems 9–14, find the indicated quantities.*

9. $a_1 = 7; d = 4; a_2 = ?; a_3 = ?$

10. $a_1 = -2; d = -3; a_2 = ?; a_3 = ?$

11. $a_1 = 2; d = 4; a_{21} = ?; S_{31} = ?$

12. $a_1 = 8; d = -10; a_{15} = ?; S_{23} = ?$

13. $a_1 = 18; a_{20} = 75; S_{20} = ?$

14. $a_1 = 203; a_{30} = 261; S_{30} = ?$

Let $a_1, a_2, a_3, \ldots, a_n, \ldots$ be a geometric sequence. In Problems 15–24, find the indicated quantities.

15. $a_1 = 3; r = -2; a_2 = ?; a_3 = ?; a_4 = ?$

16. $a_1 = 32; r = -\frac{1}{2}; a_2 = ?; a_3 = ?; a_4 = ?$

17. $a_1 = 1; a_7 = 729; r = -3; S_7 = ?$

18. $a_1 = 3; a_7 = 2{,}187; r = 3; S_7 = ?$

19. $a_1 = 100; r = 1.08; a_{10} = ?$

20. $a_1 = 240; r = 1.06; a_{12} = ?$

21. $a_1 = 100; a_9 = 200; r = ?$

22. $a_1 = 100; a_{10} = 300; r = ?$

23. $a_1 = 500; r = 0.6; S_{10} = ?; S_\infty = ?$

24. $a_1 = 8{,}000; r = 0.4; S_{10} = ?; S_\infty = ?$

25. $S_{41} = \sum_{k=1}^{41}(3k + 3) = ?$ 26. $S_{50} = \sum_{k=1}^{50}(2k - 3) = ?$

27. $S_8 = \sum_{k=1}^{8}(-2)^{k-1} = ?$ 28. $S_8 = \sum_{k=1}^{8}2^k = ?$

29. Find the sum of all the odd integers between 12 and 68.

30. Find the sum of all the even integers between 23 and 97.

31. Find the sum of each infinite geometric sequence (if it exists).
(A) $2, 4, 8, \ldots$ (B) $2, -\frac{1}{2}, \frac{1}{8}, \ldots$

32. Repeat Problem 31 for:
(A) $16, 4, 1, \ldots$ (B) $1, -3, 9, \ldots$

C 33. Find $f(1) + f(2) + f(3) + \cdots + f(50)$ if $f(x) = 2x - 3$.

34. Find $g(1) + g(2) + g(3) + \cdots + g(100)$ if $g(t) = 18 - 3t$.

35. Find $f(1) + f(2) + \cdots + f(10)$ if $f(x) = (\frac{1}{2})^x$.

36. Find $g(1) + g(2) + \cdots + g(10)$ if $g(x) = 2^x$.

37. Show that the sum of the first n odd positive integers is n^2, using appropriate formulas from this section.

38. Show that the sum of the first n even positive integers is $n + n^2$, using formulas in this section.

39. If $r = 1$, neither the first form nor the second form for the sum of a finite geometric series is valid. Find a formula for the sum of a finite geometric series if $r = 1$.

40. If all of the terms of an infinite geometric series are less than 1, could the sum be greater than 1,000? Explain.

41. Does there exist a finite arithmetic series with $a_1 = 1$ and $a_n = 1.1$ that has sum equal to 100? Explain.

42. Does there exist a finite arithmetic series with $a_1 = 1$ and $a_n = 1.1$ that has sum equal to 105? Explain.

43. Does there exist an infinite geometric series with $a_1 = 10$ that has sum equal to 6? Explain.

44. Does there exist an infinite geometric series with $a_1 = 10$ that has sum equal to 5? Explain.

Applications

45. **Loan repayment.** If you borrow \$4,800 and repay the loan by paying \$200 per month to reduce the loan and 1% of the unpaid balance each month for the use of the money, what is the total cost of the loan over 24 months?

46. **Loan repayment.** If you borrow \$5,400 and repay the loan by paying \$300 per month to reduce the loan and 1.5% of the unpaid balance each month for the use of the money, what is the total cost of the loan over 18 months?

47. **Economy stimulation.** The government, through a subsidy program, distributes \$5,000,000. If we assume that each person or agency spends 70% of what is received, and 70% of this is spent, and so on, how much total increase in spending results from this government action? (Let $a_1 = \$3{,}500{,}000$.)

48. **Economy stimulation.** Due to reduced taxes, a person has an extra \$1,200 in spendable income. If we assume that the person spends 65% of this on consumer goods, and the producers of these goods in turn spend 65% on consumer goods, and that this process continues indefinitely, what is the total amount spent (to the nearest dollar) on consumer goods?

49. **Compound interest.** If \$1,000 is invested at 5% compounded annually, the amount A present after n years forms a geometric sequence with common ratio $1 + 0.05 = 1.05$. Use a geometric sequence formula to find the amount A in the account (to the nearest cent) after 10 years. After 20 years. (*Hint:* Use a time line.)

50. **Compound interest.** If \$$P$ is invested at $100r\%$ compounded annually, the amount A present after n years forms a geometric sequence with common ratio $1 + r$. Write a formula for the amount present after n years. (*Hint:* Use a time line.)

Answers to Matched Problems

1. (A) The sequence is geometric with $r = \frac{1}{4}$. It is not arithmetic.
(B) The sequence is arithmetic with $d = 5$. It is not geometric.
(C) The sequence is neither arithmetic nor geometric.
2. (A) 139 (B) -2
3. -960 4. 10,672 5. 1,063.66 6. \$1,830 7. \$8,000

B.3 Binomial Theorem

- Factorial
- Development of the Binomial Theorem

The binomial form

$$(a + b)^n$$

where n is a natural number, appears more frequently than you might expect. The coefficients in the expansion play an important role in probability studies. The *binomial formula,* which we will derive informally, enables us to expand $(a + b)^n$ directly for

n any natural number. Since the formula involves *factorials*, we digress for a moment here to introduce this important concept.

Factorial

For n a natural number, ***n* factorial**, denoted by $n!$, is the product of the first n natural numbers. **Zero factorial** is defined to be 1. That is,

DEFINITION *n* Factorial

$$n! = n \cdot (n-1) \cdot \cdots \cdot 2 \cdot 1$$
$$1! = 1$$
$$0! = 1$$

It is also useful to note that $n!$ can be defined recursively.

DEFINITION *n* Factorial—Recursive Definition

$$n! = n \cdot (n-1)! \quad n \geq 1$$

EXAMPLE 1 **Factorial Forms** Evaluate.

(A) $5! = 5 \cdot 4 \cdot 3 \cdot 2 \cdot 1 = 120$

(B) $\frac{8!}{7!} = \frac{8 \cdot \cancel{7!}}{\cancel{7!}} = 8$

(C) $\frac{10!}{7!} = \frac{10 \cdot 9 \cdot 8 \cdot \cancel{7!}}{\cancel{7!}} = 720$

MATCHED PROBLEM 1 Evaluate.

(A) $4!$ (B) $\frac{7!}{6!}$ (C) $\frac{8!}{5!}$

The following formula involving factorials has applications in many areas of mathematics and statistics. We will use this formula to provide a more concise form for the expressions encountered later in this discussion.

THEOREM 1 For *n* and *r* integers satisfying $0 \leq r \leq n$,

$$_nC_r = \frac{n!}{r!(n-r)!}$$

EXAMPLE 2 **Evaluating $_nC_r$**

(A) $_9C_2 = \frac{9!}{2!(9-2)!} = \frac{9!}{2!7!} = \frac{9 \cdot 8 \cdot \cancel{7!}}{2 \cdot \cancel{7!}} = 36$

(B) $_5C_5 = \frac{5!}{5!(5-5)!} = \frac{5!}{5!0!} = \frac{5!}{5!} = 1$

MATCHED PROBLEM 2 Find

(A) $_5C_2$ (B) $_6C_0$

Development of the Binomial Theorem

Let us expand $(a + b)^n$ for several values of n to see if we can observe a pattern that leads to a general formula for the expansion for any natural number n:

$$(a + b)^1 = a + b$$
$$(a + b)^2 = a^2 + 2ab + b^2$$
$$(a + b)^3 = a^3 + 3a^2b + 3ab^2 + b^3$$
$$(a + b)^4 = a^4 + 4a^3b + 6a^2b^2 + 4ab^3 + b^4$$
$$(a + b)^5 = a^5 + 5a^4b + 10a^3b^2 + 10a^2b^3 + 5ab^4 + b^5$$

CONCEPTUAL INSIGHT

1. The expansion of $(a + b)^n$ has $(n + 1)$ terms.
2. The power of a decreases by 1 for each term as we move from left to right.
3. The power of b increases by 1 for each term as we move from left to right.
4. In each term, the sum of the powers of a and b always equals n.
5. Starting with a given term, we can get the coefficient of the next term by multiplying the coefficient of the given term by the exponent of a and dividing by the number that represents the position of the term in the series of terms. For example, in the expansion of $(a + b)^4$ above, the coefficient of the third term is found from the second term by multiplying 4 and 3, and then dividing by 2 [that is, the coefficient of the third term $= (4 \cdot 3)/2 = 6$].

We now postulate these same properties for the general case:

$$(a + b)^n = a^n + \frac{n}{1}a^{n-1}b + \frac{n(n-1)}{1 \cdot 2}a^{n-2}b^2 + \frac{n(n-1)(n-2)}{1 \cdot 2 \cdot 3}a^{n-3}b^3 + \cdots + b^n$$
$$= \frac{n!}{0!(n-0)!}a^n + \frac{n!}{1!(n-1)!}a^{n-1}b + \frac{n!}{2!(n-2)!}a^{n-2}b^2 + \frac{n!}{3!(n-3)!}a^{n-3}b^3 + \cdots + \frac{n!}{n!(n-n)!}b^n$$
$$= {}_nC_0a^n + {}_nC_1a^{n-1}b + {}_nC_2a^{n-2}b^2 + {}_nC_3a^{n-3}b^3 + \cdots + {}_nC_nb^n$$

And we are led to the formula in the binomial theorem:

THEOREM 2 Binomial Theorem

For all natural numbers n,

$$(a + b)^n = {}_nC_0a^n + {}_nC_1a^{n-1}b + {}_nC_2a^{n-2}b^2 + {}_nC_3a^{n-3}b^3 + \cdots + {}_nC_nb^n$$

EXAMPLE 3 **Using the Binomial Theorem** Use the binomial theorem to expand $(u + v)^6$.

SOLUTION

$$(u + v)^6 = {}_6C_0u^6 + {}_6C_1u^5v + {}_6C_2u^4v^2 + {}_6C_3u^3v^3 + {}_6C_4u^2v^4 + {}_6C_5uv^5 + {}_6C_6v^6$$
$$= u^6 + 6u^5v + 15u^4v^2 + 20u^3v^3 + 15u^2v^4 + 6uv^5 + v^6$$

MATCHED PROBLEM 3 Use the binomial theorem to expand $(x + 2)^5$.

EXAMPLE 4 **Using the Binomial Theorem** Use the binomial theorem to find the sixth term in the expansion of $(x - 1)^{18}$.

SOLUTION Sixth term $= {}_{18}C_5x^{13}(-1)^5 = \dfrac{18!}{5!(18 - 5)!}x^{13}(-1)$

$= -8{,}568x^{13}$

MATCHED PROBLEM 4 Use the binomial theorem to find the fourth term in the expansion of $(x - 2)^{20}$.

Exercises B.3

A *In Problems 1–20, evaluate each expression.*

1. $6!$ **2.** $7!$ **3.** $\dfrac{10!}{9!}$

4. $\dfrac{20!}{19!}$ **5.** $\dfrac{12!}{9!}$ **6.** $\dfrac{10!}{6!}$

7. $\dfrac{5!}{2!3!}$ **8.** $\dfrac{7!}{3!4!}$ **9.** $\dfrac{6!}{5!(6-5)!}$

10. $\dfrac{7!}{4!(7-4)!}$ **11.** $\dfrac{20!}{3!17!}$ **12.** $\dfrac{52!}{50!2!}$

13. ${}_5C_3$ **14.** ${}_7C_3$ **15.** ${}_6C_5$ **16.** ${}_7C_4$

17. ${}_5C_0$ **18.** ${}_5C_5$ **19.** ${}_{18}C_{15}$ **20.** ${}_{18}C_3$

B *Expand each expression in Problems 21–26 using the binomial theorem.*

21. $(a + b)^4$ **22.** $(m + n)^5$

23. $(x - 1)^6$ **24.** $(u - 2)^5$

25. $(2a - b)^5$ **26.** $(x - 2y)^5$

Find the indicated term in each expansion in Problems 27–32.

27. $(x - 1)^{18}$; 5th term **28.** $(x - 3)^{20}$; 3rd term

29. $(p + q)^{15}$; 7th term **30.** $(p + q)^{15}$; 13th term

31. $(2x + y)^{12}$; 11th term **32.** $(2x + y)^{12}$; 3rd term

C **33.** Show that ${}_nC_0 = {}_nC_n$ for $n \geq 0$.

34. Show that ${}_nC_r = {}_nC_{n-r}$ for $n \geq r \geq 0$.

35. The triangle shown here is called **Pascal's triangle**. Can you guess what the next two rows at the bottom are? Compare these numbers with the coefficients of binomial expansions.

```
            1
          1   1
        1   2   1
      1   3   3   1
    1   4   6   4   1
```

36. Explain why the sum of the entries in each row of Pascal's triangle is a power of 2. (*Hint:* Let $a = b = 1$ in the binomial theorem.)

37. Explain why the alternating sum of the entries in each row of Pascal's triangle (e.g., $1 - 4 + 6 - 4 + 1$) is equal to 0.

38. Show that ${}_nC_r = \frac{n - r + 1}{r}{}_nC_{r-1}$ for $n \geq r \geq 1$.

39. Show that ${}_nC_{r-1} + {}_nC_r = {}_{n+1}C_r$ for $n \geq r \geq 1$.

Answers to Matched Problems

1. (A) 24 (B) 7 (C) 336
2. (A) 10 (B) 1
3. $x^5 + 10x^4 + 40x^3 + 80x^2 + 80x + 32$
4. $-9{,}120x^{17}$

B.4 Interpolating Polynomials and Divided Differences

- Introduction
- The Interpolating Polynomial
- Divided Difference Tables
- Application

Given two points in the plane with distinct x coordinates, we can use the point-slope form of the equation of a line to find a polynomial whose graph passes through these two points. If we are given a set of three, four, or more points with distinct x coordinates, is there a polynomial whose graph will pass through all the given points? In this section, we will see that the answer to this question is yes, and we will discuss several methods for finding this polynomial, called the *interpolating polynomial*. The principal use of interpolating polynomials is to approximate y coordinates for points not in the given set. For example, a retail sales firm may have obtained a table of prices at various demands by examining past sales records. Prices for demands not in the table can be approximated by an interpolating polynomial. Interpolating polynomials also have applications to computer graphics. If a computer user selects a set of points on a drawing, the interpolating polynomial can be used to produce a smooth curve that passes through the selected points.

Introduction

We usually write polynomials in standard form using either increasing or decreasing powers of x. Both of the following polynomials are written in standard form:

$$p(x) = 1 + x^2 - 2x^3 \quad q(x) = -3x^5 + 2x^4 - 5x$$

In this section, we will find it convenient to write polynomials in a different form. The following activity will give you some experience with this new form.

Explore and Discuss 1

Consider the points in Table 1.

(A) Let $p_1(x) = a_0 + a_1(x - 1)$. Determine a_0 and a_1 so that the graph of $y = p_1(x)$ passes through the first two points in Table 1.

(B) Let $p_2(x) = a_0 + a_1(x - 1) + a_2(x - 1)(x - 2)$. Determine a_0, a_1, and a_2 so that the graph of $y = p_2(x)$ passes through the first three points in Table 1.

(C) Let

$$p_3(x) = a_0 + a_1(x - 1) + a_2(x - 1)(x - 2) + a_3(x - 1)(x - 2)(x - 3).$$

Determine a_0, a_1, a_2, and a_3 so that the graph of $y = p_3(x)$ passes through all four points in Table 1.

Table 1

x	1	2	3	4
y	4	7	4	1

The following example will illustrate basic concepts.

EXAMPLE 1 **Approximating Revenue** A manufacturing company has defined the revenue function for one of its products by examining past records and listing the revenue (in thousands of dollars) for certain levels of production (in thousands of units). Use the revenue function defined by Table 2 to estimate the revenue if 3,000 units are produced and if 7,000 units are produced.

Table 2 **Revenue R Defined as a Function of Production x by a Table**

x	1	4	6	8
$R(x)$	65	80	40	16

SOLUTION

One way to approximate values of a function defined by a table is to use a **piecewise linear approximation**. To form the piecewise linear approximation for Table 2, we simply use the point-slope formula to find the equation of the line joining each successive pair of points in the table (see Fig. 1).

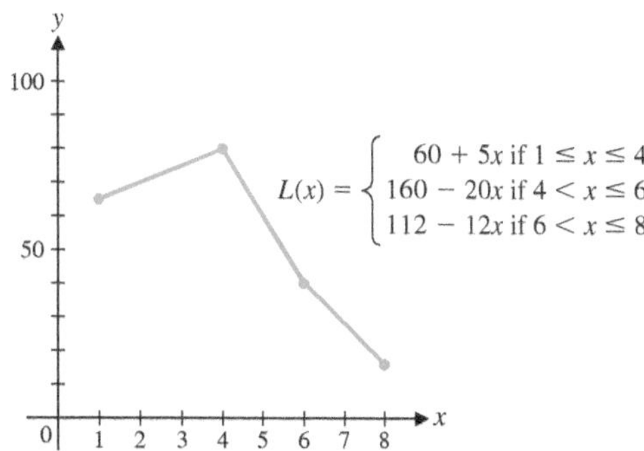

Figure 1 $L(x)$ is the piecewise linear approximation for $R(x)$.

This type of approximation is very useful in certain applications, but it has several disadvantages. First, the piecewise linear approximation usually has a sharp corner at each point in the table and thus is not differentiable at these points. Second, the piecewise linear approximation requires the use of a different formula between each successive pair of points in the table (see Fig. 1).

Instead of using the piecewise linear approximation, we will outline a method that will produce a polynomial whose values agree with $R(x)$ at each point in Table 2. This will provide us with a differentiable function given by a single formula that can be used to approximate $R(x)$ for any value of x between 1 and 8.

Suppose $p(x)$ is a polynomial whose values agree with the values of $R(x)$ at the four x values given in Table 2. Instead of expressing $p(x)$ in terms of powers of x, the standard method for writing polynomial forms, we use the first three x values in the table to write

$$p(x) = a_0 + a_1(x - 1) + a_2(x - 1)(x - 4) + a_3(x - 1)(x - 4)(x - 6)$$

As we will see, writing $p(x)$ in this special form will greatly simplify our work.

Since $p(x)$ is to agree with $R(x)$ at each x value in Table 2, we can write the following equations involving the coefficients a_0, a_1, a_2, and a_3:

$$65 = R(1) = p(1) = a_0 \qquad (1)$$
$$80 = R(4) = p(4) = a_0 + 3a_1 \qquad (2)$$
$$40 = R(6) = p(6) = a_0 + 5a_1 + 10a_2 \qquad (3)$$
$$16 = R(8) = p(8) = a_0 + 7a_1 + 28a_2 + 56a_3 \qquad (4)$$

From equation (1), we see that $a_0 = 65$. Solving equation (2) for a_1 and substituting for a_0, we have

$$a_1 = \frac{1}{3}(80 - a_0) = \frac{1}{3}(80 - 65) = 5$$

Proceeding the same way with equations (3) and (4), we have

$$a_2 = \frac{1}{10}(40 - a_0 - 5a_1) = \frac{1}{10}(40 - 65 - 25) = -5$$

$$a_3 = \frac{1}{56}(16 - a_0 - 7a_1 - 28a_2) = \frac{1}{56}(16 - 65 - 35 + 140) = 1$$

Therefore,

Table 2

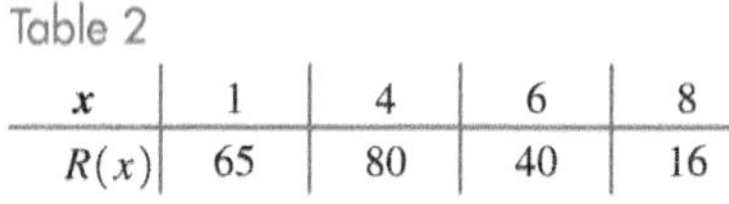

x	1	4	6	8
$R(x)$	65	80	40	16

$$p(x) = 65 + 5(x - 1) - 5(x - 1)(x - 4) + (x - 1)(x - 4)(x - 6)$$

The polynomial $p(x)$ agrees with $R(x)$ at each x value in Table 2 (verify this) and can be used to approximate $R(x)$ for values of x between 1 and 8 (see Fig. 2).

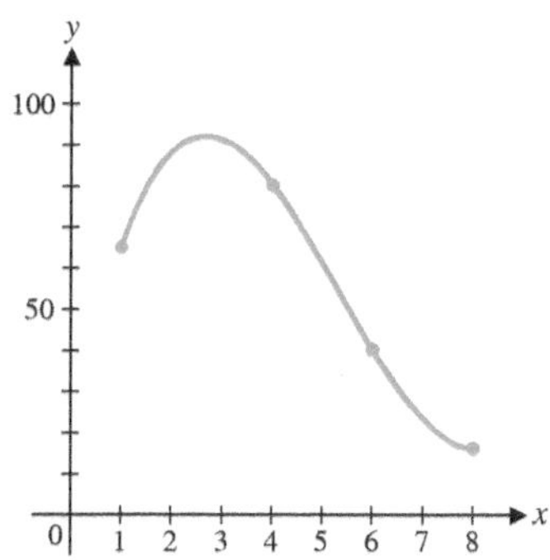

Figure 2 $p(x) = 65 + 5(x - 1) - 5(x - 1)(x - 4) + (x - 1)(x - 4)(x - 6)$

If 3,000 units are produced, then the revenue can be approximated by evaluating $p(3)$:

$$R(3) \approx p(3) = 65 + 5(2) - 5(2)(-1) + (2)(-1)(-3)$$
$$= 91 \text{ or } \$91{,}000$$

If 7,000 units are produced, then

$$R(7) \approx p(7) = 65 + 5(6) - 5(6)(3) + (6)(3)(1)$$
$$= 23 \text{ or } \$23{,}000$$

MATCHED PROBLEM 1 Refer to Example 1. Approximate the revenue if 2,000 units are produced and if 5,000 units are produced.

Since the revenue function in Example 1 was defined by a table, we have no information about this function for any value of x other than those listed in the table. So, we cannot say anything about the accuracy of the approximations obtained by using $p(x)$. As we mentioned earlier, the piecewise linear approximation might provide a better approximation in some cases. The primary advantage of using $p(x)$ is that we have a differentiable function that is defined by a single equation and agrees with the revenue function at every value of x in the table.

The Interpolating Polynomial

The procedure we used to find a polynomial approximation for the revenue function in Example 1 can be applied to any function that is defined by a table. The polynomial that is obtained in this way is referred to as the *interpolating polynomial.* The basic concepts are summarized in the next box.

DEFINITION The Interpolating Polynomial

If $f(x)$ is the function defined by the following table of $n + 1$ points,

x	x_0	x_1	$\cdots$	x_n
$f(x)$	y_0	y_1	$\cdots$	y_n

then the **interpolating polynomial** for $f(x)$ is the polynomial $p(x)$ of degree less than or equal to n that satisfies

$$\begin{aligned} p(x_0) &= y_0 = f(x_0) \\ p(x_1) &= y_1 = f(x_1) \\ &\vdots \quad\;\; \vdots \\ p(x_n) &= y_n = f(x_n) \end{aligned}$$

Newton's form for the interpolating polynomial is

$$\begin{aligned} p(x) = a_0 + a_1(x - x_0) + a_2(x - x_0)(x - x_1) + \cdots \\ + a_n(x - x_0)(x - x_1)\cdot\cdots\cdot(x - x_{n-1}) \end{aligned}$$

Notice that if we graph the points in the defining table and the interpolating polynomial $p(x)$ on the same set of axes, then the graph of $p(x)$ will pass through every point given in the table (see Fig. 2). Is it possible to find a polynomial that is different from $p(x)$ and also has a graph that passes through all the points in the table? In more advanced texts, it is shown that

The interpolating polynomial is the only polynomial of degree less than or equal to n whose graph will pass through every point in the table.

Any other polynomial whose graph goes through all these points must be of degree greater than n. The steps we used in finding the interpolating polynomial are summarized in the following box.

PROCEDURE Steps for Finding the Interpolating Polynomial

Step 1. Write Newton's form for $p(x)$.

Step 2. Use the conditions $p(x_i) = y_i, i = 0, 1, \ldots, n$ to write $n + 1$ linear equations for the coefficients. Do not change the order of these equations. This system of equations is called a **lower triangular system.**

Step 3. Starting with the first and proceeding down the list, solve each equation for the coefficient with the largest subscript and substitute all the previously determined coefficients. This method of solving for the coefficients is called **forward substitution.**

EXAMPLE 2 **Finding the Interpolating Polynomial** Find the interpolating polynomial for the function defined by the following table:

x	0	1	2	3
$f(x)$	5	4	−3	−4

SOLUTION

Step 1. Newton's form for $p(x)$ is

$$p(x) = a_0 + a_1x + a_2x(x-1) + a_3x(x-1)(x-2)$$

Step 2. The lower triangular system is

$$\begin{aligned} a_0 &= 5 \quad p(0) = f(0) = 5 \\ a_0 + a_1 &= 4 \quad p(1) = f(1) = 4 \\ a_0 + 2a_1 + 2a_2 &= -3 \quad p(2) = f(2) = -3 \\ a_0 + 3a_1 + 6a_2 + 6a_3 &= -4 \quad p(3) = f(3) = -4 \end{aligned}$$

Step 3. Solving this system by forward substitution, we have

$$a_0 = 5$$

$$a_1 = 4 - a_0 = 4 - 5 = -1$$

$$a_2 = \frac{1}{2}(-3 - a_0 - 2a_1) = \frac{1}{2}(-3 - 5 + 2) = -3$$

$$a_3 = \frac{1}{6}(-4 - a_0 - 3a_1 - 6a_2) = \frac{1}{6}(-4 - 5 + 3 + 18) = 2$$

Newton's form for the interpolating polynomial is

$$p(x) = 5 - x - 3x(x-1) + 2x(x-1)(x-2)$$

This form of $p(x)$ is suitable for evaluating the polynomial. For other operations, such as differentiation, integration, or graphing, it may be preferable to perform the indicated operations, collect like terms, and express $p(x)$ in the standard polynomial form

$$p(x) = 2x^3 - 9x^2 + 6x + 5$$

The graph of $p(x)$ is shown in Figure 3.

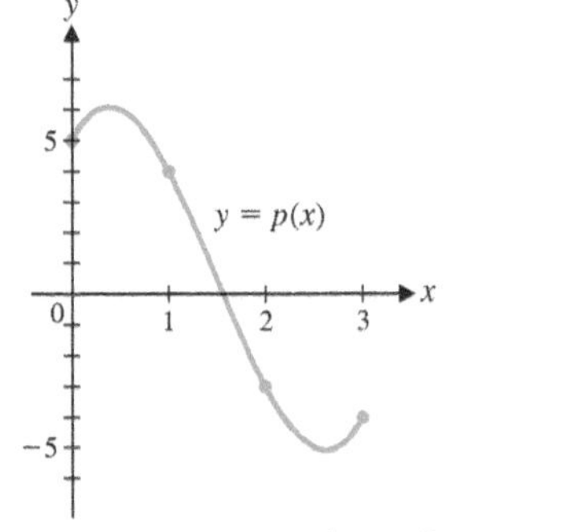

Figure 3 $p(x) = 2x^3 - 9x^2 + 6x + 5$

MATCHED PROBLEM 2 Find the interpolating polynomial for the function defined by the following table:

x	−1	0	1	2
$f(x)$	5	3	3	11

Explore and Discuss 2

Given the following polynomial and table,

$$p(x) = x^3 - 10x^2 + 29x - 17$$

x	1	3	6
y	3	7	13

(A) Show that the graph of $p(x)$ passes through each point in the table.

(B) Is $p(x)$ the interpolating polynomial for this table? If not, what is the interpolating polynomial for this table?

(C) Discuss the relationship between the number of points in a table and the degree of the interpolating polynomial for that table.

Divided Difference Tables

We now present a simple computational procedure for finding the coefficients $a_0, a_1, \ldots, a_n$ in Newton's form for an interpolating polynomial. To introduce this method, we return to Table 2 in Example 1, which we restate here.

Table 2

x	1	4	6	8
$f(x)$	65	80	40	16

The coefficients in Newton's form for the interpolating polynomial for this table were $a_0 = 65$, $a_1 = 5$, $a_2 = -5$, and $a_3 = 1$. We will now construct a table, called a *divided difference table*, which will produce these coefficients with a minimum of computation. To begin, we place the x and y values in the first two columns of a new table. Then we compute the ratio of the change in y to the change in x for each successive pair of points in the table, and place the result on the line between the two points (see Table 3). These ratios are called the **first divided differences.**

To form the next column in the table, we repeat this process, using the change in the first divided differences in the numerator and the change in *two* successive values of x in the denominator. These ratios are called the **second divided differences** and are placed on the line between the corresponding first divided differences (see Table 4).

Table 3 First Divided Differences

x_k	y_k	First Divided Difference
1	65	
		$\frac{80-65}{4-1} = \frac{15}{3} = 5$
4	80	
		$\frac{40-80}{6-4} = \frac{-40}{2} = -20$
6	40	
		$\frac{16-40}{8-6} = \frac{-24}{2} = -12$
8	16	

Table 4 Second Divided Differences

x_k	y_k	First Divided Difference	Second Divided Difference
1	65		
		5	
4	80		$\frac{-20-5}{6-1} = \frac{-25}{5} = -5$
		-20	
6	40		$\frac{-12-(-20)}{8-4} = \frac{8}{4} = 2$
		-12	
8	16		

To form the next column of the table, we form the ratio of the change in the second divided differences to the change in *three* successive values of x. These ratios are called the **third divided differences** and are placed on the line between the corresponding second divided differences (see Table 5). Since our table has only two second divided differences, there is only one third divided difference and this process is now complete.

Table 5 Third Divided Differences

x_k	y_k	First Divided Difference	Second Divided Difference	Third Divided Difference
1	65			
		5		
4	80		−5	
		−20		$\frac{2-(-5)}{8-1} = \frac{7}{7} = 1$
6	40		2	
		−12		
8	16			

We have presented each step in constructing the divided difference table here in a separate table to clearly illustrate this process. In applications of this technique, these steps are combined into a single table. With a little practice, you should be able to proceed quickly from the defining table for the function (Table 2) to the final form of the divided difference table (Table 6).

Table 6 Divided Difference Table—Final Form

x_k	y_k	First Divided Difference	Second Divided Difference	Third Divided Difference
1	65			
		$\frac{80-65}{4-1} = 5$		
4	80		$\frac{-20-5}{6-1} = -5$	
		$\frac{40-80}{6-4} = -20$		$\frac{2-(-5)}{8-1} = 1$
6	40		$\frac{-12-(-20)}{8-4} = 2$	
		$\frac{16-40}{8-6} = -12$		
8	16			

Now that we have computed the divided difference table, how do we use it? If we write the first number from each column of the divided difference table, beginning with the second column:

$$65 \quad 5 \quad -5 \quad 1$$

we see that these numbers are the coefficients of the interpolating polynomial for Table 2 (see Example 1). Thus, Table 6 contains all the information we need to write the interpolating polynomial:

$$p(x) = 65 + 5(x-1) - 5(x-1)(x-4) + (x-1)(x-4)(x-6)$$

The divided difference table provides an alternate method for finding interpolating polynomials that generally requires fewer computations and can be implemented easily on a computer. The ideas introduced in the preceding discussion are summarized in the following box.

PROCEDURE Divided Difference Tables and Interpolating Polynomials

Given the defining table for a function $f(x)$ with $n + 1$ points,

x	x_0	x_1	$\cdots$	x_n
$f(x)$	y_0	y_1	$\cdots$	y_n

where $x_0 < x_1 < \cdots < x_n$, then the **divided difference table** is computed as follows:

Column 1: x values from the defining table

Column 2: y values from the defining table

Column 3: First divided differences computed using columns 1 and 2

Column 4: Second divided differences computed using columns 1 and 3

⋮

Column n + 2: nth divided differences computed using columns 1 and $n + 1$

The coefficients in Newton's form for the interpolating polynomial,

$$p(x) = a_0 + a_1(x - x_0) + a_2(x - x_0)(x - x_1) + \cdots + a_n(x - x_0)(x - x_1) \cdot \cdots \cdot (x - x_{n-1})$$

are the first numbers in each column of the divided difference table, beginning with column 2.

CONCEPTUAL INSIGHT

1. The points in the defining table must be arranged with increasing x values before computing the divided difference table. If the x values are out of order, then the divided difference table will not contain the coefficients of Newton's form for the interpolating polynomial.
2. Since each column in the divided difference table uses all the values in the preceding column, it is necessary to compute all the numbers in every column, even though we are interested only in the first number in each column.
3. Other methods can be used to find interpolating polynomials. Referring to Table 1, we could write $p(x)$ in standard polynomial notation

$$p(x) = b_3x^3 + b_2x^2 + b_1x + b_0$$

and use the points in the table to write the following system of linear equations:

$$\begin{aligned} p(1) &= b_3 + b_2 + b_1 + b_0 = 65 \\ p(4) &= 64b_3 + 16b_2 + 4b_1 + b_0 = 80 \\ p(6) &= 216b_3 + 36b_2 + 6b_1 + b_0 = 40 \\ p(8) &= 512b_3 + 64b_2 + 8b_1 + b_0 = 16 \end{aligned}$$

The computations required to solve this system of equations are far more complicated than those involved in finding the divided difference table.

EXAMPLE 3 Using a Divided Difference Table

Table 7

x	0	1	2	3	4
$f(x)$	35	25	19	−7	−29

(A) Find the divided difference table for the points in Table 7.

(B) Use the divided difference table to find the interpolating polynomial.

SOLUTION

(A) The divided difference table is as follows.

x_k	y_k	First Divided Difference	Second Divided Difference	Third Divided Difference	Fourth Divided Difference
0	35				
		$\frac{25-35}{1-0} = -10$			
1	25		$\frac{-6-(-10)}{2-0} = 2$		
		$\frac{19-25}{2-1} = -6$		$\frac{-10-2}{3-0} = -4$	
2	19		$\frac{-26-(-6)}{3-1} = -10$		$\frac{4-(-4)}{4-0} = 2$
		$\frac{-7-19}{3-2} = -26$		$\frac{2-(-10)}{4-1} = 4$	
3	−7		$\frac{-22-(-26)}{4-2} = 2$		
		$\frac{-29-(-7)}{4-3} = -22$			
4	−29				

(B) Newton's form for the interpolating polynomial is

$$p(x) = a_0 + a_1x + a_2x(x-1) + a_3x(x-1)(x-2) + a_4x(x-1)(x-2)(x-3)$$

Substituting the values from the divided difference table for the coefficients in Newton's form, we have

$$\begin{aligned} p(x) &= 35 - 10x + 2x(x-1) - 4x(x-1)(x-2) + 2x(x-1)(x-2)(x-3) \\ &= 35 - 32x + 36x^2 - 16x^3 + 2x^4 \quad \text{Standard form} \end{aligned}$$

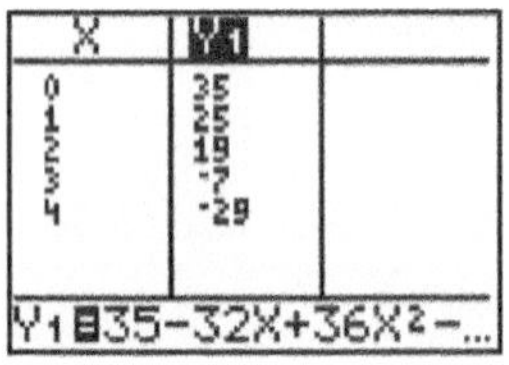

Multiplication details for the standard form are omitted. Figure 4 verifies that the values of the interpolating polynomial agree with the values in Table 7.

Figure 4

Table 8

x	0	1	2	3	4
$f(x)$	5	1	−1	−7	1

Matched Problem 3

(A) Find the divided difference table for the points in Table 8.

(B) Use the divided difference table to find the interpolating polynomial.

Explore and Discuss 3

A graphing calculator can be used to calculate a divided difference table. Figure 5A shows a program on a TI-84 Plus CE that calculates divided difference tables and Figure 5B shows the input and output generated when we use this program to solve Example 3.

(A) Program

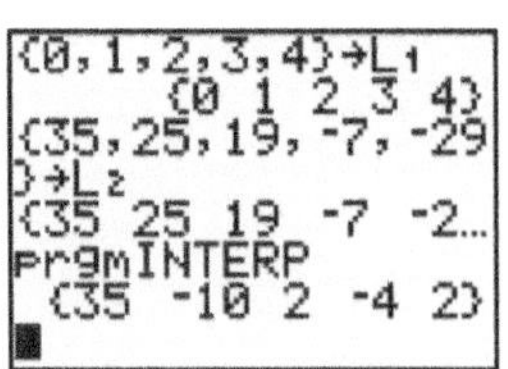

(B) Input and output

Figure 5

Enter this program into your graphing calculator and use it to solve Matched Problem 3.

Application

EXAMPLE 4 **Inventory** A store orders 8,000 units of a new product. The inventory I on hand t weeks after the order arrived is given in the following table:

Inventory

t	0	2	4	6	8
$I(t)$	8,000	5,952	3,744	1,568	0

Use the interpolating polynomial to approximate the inventory after 5 weeks and the average inventory during the first 5 weeks after the order arrived.

SOLUTION The divided difference table is as follows:

t_k	y_k	First Divided Difference	Second Divided Difference	Third Divided Difference	Fourth Divided Difference
0	8,000				
		−1,024			
2	5,952		−20		
		−1,104		4	
4	3,744		4		1
		−1,088		12	
6	1,568		76		
		−784			
8	0				

The interpolating polynomial is

$$p(t) = 8{,}000 - 1{,}024t - 20t(t-2) + 4t(t-2)(t-4) + t(t-2)(t-4)(t-6)$$

or, after simplifying,

$$p(t) = t^4 - 8t^3 - 1{,}000t + 8{,}000$$

The inventory after 5 weeks is given approximately by

$$p(5) = 5^4 - 8(5)^3 - 1{,}000(5) + 8{,}000 = 2{,}625 \text{ units}$$

The average inventory during the first 5 weeks is given approximately by

$$\frac{1}{5}\int_0^5 p(t)\,dt = \frac{1}{5}\int_0^5 (t^4 - 8t^3 - 1{,}000t + 8{,}000)\,dt$$
$$= \frac{1}{5}\left(\frac{1}{5}t^5 - 2t^4 - 500t^2 + 8{,}000t\right)\Big|_0^5$$
$$= \frac{1}{5}(625 - 1{,}250 - 12{,}500 + 40{,}000) - \frac{1}{5}(0)$$
$$= 5{,}375 \text{ units}$$

MATCHED PROBLEM 4 Refer to Example 4. Approximate the inventory after 7 weeks and the average inventory during the first 7 weeks.

Exercises B.4

A *In Problems 1–4,*

(A) Write Newton's form for the interpolating polynomial.

(B) Write the associated lower triangular system for the coefficients.

(C) Use forward substitution to find the interpolating polynomial.

1.

x	1	3	4
$f(x)$	2	6	11

2.

x	−1	1	2
$f(x)$	1	3	7

3.

x	−1	0	2	4
$f(x)$	6	5	15	−39

4.

x	−1	0	2	3
$f(x)$	5	1	5	1

In Problems 5–10, find the divided difference table and then find the interpolating polynomial.

5.

x	1	2	3
$f(x)$	4	8	14

6.

x	1	2	3
$f(x)$	1	3	7

7.

x	−1	0	1	2
$f(x)$	−3	1	3	9

8.

x	−1	0	1	2
$f(x)$	5	6	3	2

9.

x	−2	1	2	4
$f(x)$	25	10	17	13

10.

x	−1	0	3	5
$f(x)$	17	10	25	5

B **11.** Can a table with three points have a linear interpolating polynomial? A quadratic interpolating polynomial? A cubic interpolating polynomial? Explain.

12. Can a table with four points have a linear interpolating polynomial? A quadratic interpolating polynomial? A cubic interpolating polynomial? A quartic interpolating polynomial? Explain.

In Problems 13–20, use the interpolating polynomial to approximate the value of the function defined by the table at the indicated values of x.

13.

x	−4	0	4	8
$f(x)$	−64	32	0	224

(A) $f(2) \approx ?$ (B) $f(6) \approx ?$

14.

x	−5	0	5	10
$f(x)$	250	50	100	−350

(A) $f(-3) \approx ?$ (B) $f(8) \approx ?$

15.

x	−1	0	1	4
$f(x)$	0	0	0	15

(A) $f(2) \approx ?$ (B) $f(3) \approx ?$

16.

x	−2	0	2	6
$f(x)$	0	0	0	−96

(A) $f(1) \approx ?$ (B) $f(4) \approx ?$

17.

x	−4	−2	0	2	4
$f(x)$	24	2	0	−6	8

(A) $f(-3) \approx ?$ (B) $f(1) \approx ?$

18.

x	-6	-2	0	2	6
$f(x)$	19	3	10	3	19

(A) $f(1) \approx ?$ (B) $f(5) \approx ?$

19.

x	-3	-2	-1	1	2	3
$f(x)$	-24	-6	0	0	6	24

(A) $f(-0.5) \approx ?$ (B) $f(2.5) \approx ?$

20.

x	-3	-2	-1	0	1	2	3
$f(x)$	40	0	0	4	0	0	40

(A) $f(-2.5) \approx ?$ (B) $f(1.5) \approx ?$

In Problems 21–30, find the interpolating polynomial. Graph the interpolating polynomial and the points in the given table on the same set of axes.

21.

x	-2	0	2
$f(x)$	2	0	2

22.

x	-2	0	2
$f(x)$	2	0	-2

23.

x	0	1	2
$f(x)$	-4	-2	0

24.

x	0	1	2
$f(x)$	-4	-3	0

25.

x	-1	0	2	3
$f(x)$	0	2	0	-4

26.

x	-3	-1	0	1
$f(x)$	0	4	3	0

27.

x	-2	-1	0	1	2
$f(x)$	1	5	3	1	5

28.

x	-2	-1	0	1	2
$f(x)$	-8	0	2	4	12

29.

x	-2	-1	0	1	2
$f(x)$	-3	0	5	0	-3

30.

x	-1	0	1	2	3
$f(x)$	6	2	0	-6	2

In Problems 31–34, use the quartic regression routine on a graphing calculator to fit a fourth degree polynomial to the tables in the indicated problems. Compare this polynomial with the interpolating polynomial.

31. Problem 27 **32.** Problem 28

33. Problem 29 **34.** Problem 30

C **35.** The following table was obtained from the function $f(x) = \sqrt{x}$:

x	1	4	9
$f(x)$	1	2	3

Find the interpolating polynomial for this table. Compare the values of the interpolating polynomial $p(x)$ and the original function $f(x) = \sqrt{x}$ by completing the table below. Use a calculator to evaluate $\sqrt{x}$ and round each value to one decimal place.

x	1	2	3	4	5	6	7	8	9
$p(x)$	1			2					3
$\sqrt{x}$	1			2					3

36. The following table was obtained from the function $f(x) = 6/\sqrt{x}$:

x	1	4	9
$f(x)$	6	3	2

Find the interpolating polynomial for this table. Compare the values of the interpolating polynomial $p(x)$ and the original function $f(x) = 6/\sqrt{x}$ by completing the table below. Use a calculator to evaluate $6/\sqrt{x}$ and round each value to one decimal place.

x	1	2	3	4	5	6	7	8	9
$p(x)$	6			3					2
$6/\sqrt{x}$	6			3					2

37. The following table was obtained from the function $f(x) = 10x/(1 + x^2)$:

x	-2	-1	0	1	2
$f(x)$	-4	-5	0	5	4

Find the interpolating polynomial $p(x)$ for this table. Graph $p(x)$ and $f(x)$ on the same set of axes.

38. The following table was obtained from the function $f(x) = (9 - x^2)/(1 + x^2)$:

x	-2	-1	0	1	2
$f(x)$	1	4	9	4	1

Find the interpolating polynomial $p(x)$ for this table. Graph $p(x)$ and $f(x)$ on the same set of axes.

39. Find the equation of the parabola whose graph passes through the points $(-x_1, y_1)$, $(0, y_2)$, and (x_1, y_1), where $x_1 > 0$ and $y_1 \neq y_2$.

40. Find the equation of the parabola whose graph passes through the points $(0, 0)$, (x_1, y_1), and $(2x_1, 0)$, where $x_1 > 0$ and $y_1 \neq 0$.

Applications

41. **Cash reserves.** Suppose the cash reserves C (in thousands of dollars) for a small business are given by the following table, where t is the number of months after the first of the year.

t	0	4	8	12
$C(t)$	2	32	38	20

(A) Find the interpolating polynomial for this table.

(B) Use the interpolating polynomial to approximate (to the nearest thousand dollars) the cash reserves after 6 months.

(C) Use the interpolating polynomial to approximate (to the nearest hundred dollars) the average cash reserves for the first quarter.

42. **Inventory.** A hardware store orders 147 lawn mowers. The inventory I of lawn mowers on hand t months after the order arrived is given in the table.

t	0	1	2	3
$I(t)$	147	66	19	0

(A) Find the interpolating polynomial for this table.

(B) Use the interpolating polynomial to approximate (to the nearest integer) the average number of lawn mowers on hand for this three-month period.

43. **Income distribution.** The income distribution for the United States in 1999 is represented by the Lorenz curve $y = f(x)$, where $f(x)$ is given in the table.

x	0	0.2	0.8	1
$f(x)$	0	0.04	0.52	1

(A) Find the interpolating polynomial for this table.

(B) Use the interpolating polynomial to approximate (to four decimal places) the index of income concentration.

44. **Income distribution.** Refer to Problem 43. After making a series of adjustments for things like taxes, fringe benefits, and returns on home equity, the income distribution for the United States in 1999 is represented by the Lorenz curve $y = g(x)$, where $g(x)$ is given in the table.

x	0	0.2	0.8	1
$g(x)$	0	0.06	0.54	1

(A) Find the interpolating polynomial for this table.

(B) Use the interpolating polynomial to approximate (to four decimal places) the index of income concentration.

45. **Maximum revenue.** The revenue R (in thousands of dollars) from the sale of x thousand table lamps is given in the table.

x	2	4	6
$R(x)$	24.4	36	34.8

(A) Find the interpolating polynomial for this table.

(B) Use the interpolating polynomial to approximate (to the nearest thousand dollars) the revenue if 5,000 table lamps are produced.

(C) Use the interpolating polynomial to approximate (to the nearest integer) the production level that will maximize the revenue.

46. **Minimum average cost.** The cost C (in thousands of dollars) of producing x thousand microwave ovens is given in the table.

x	1	3	5
$C(x)$	215	535	1,055

(A) Find the interpolating polynomial for this table.

(B) Use the interpolating polynomial to approximate (to the nearest thousand dollars) the cost of producing 4,000 ovens.

(C) Use the interpolating polynomial to approximate (to the nearest integer) the production level that will minimize the average cost.

47. **Temperature.** The temperature C (in degrees celsius) in an artificial habitat after t hours is given in the table.

t	0	1	2	3	4
$C(t)$	14	13	16	17	10

(A) Find the interpolating polynomial for this table.

(B) Use the interpolating polynomial to approximate (to the nearest tenth of a degree) the average temperature over this 4-hour period.

48. **Drug concentration.** The concentration C (in milligrams per cubic centimeter) of a particular drug in a patient's bloodstream t hours after the drug is taken is given in the table.

t	0	1	2	3	4
$C(t)$	0	0.032	0.036	0.024	0.008

(A) Find the interpolating polynomial for this table.

(B) Use the interpolating polynomial to approximate (to two decimal places) the number of hours it will take for the drug concentration to reach its maximum level.

49. **Bacteria control.** A lake that is used for recreational swimming is treated periodically to control harmful bacteria growth. The concentration C (in bacteria per cubic centimeter) t days after a treatment is given in the table.

t	0	2	4	6
$C(t)$	450	190	90	150

(A) Find the interpolating polynomial for this table.

(B) Use the interpolating polynomial to approximate (to two decimal places) the number of days it will take for the bacteria concentration to reach its minimum level.

50. **Medicine respiration.** Physiologists use a machine called a pneumotachograph to produce a graph of the rate of flow R on air into the lungs (inspiration) and out (expiration). The figure gives the graph of the inspiration phase of the breathing cycle of an individual at rest.

(A) Use the values given by the graph at $t = 0,1,2,$ and 3 to find the interpolating polynomial for R.

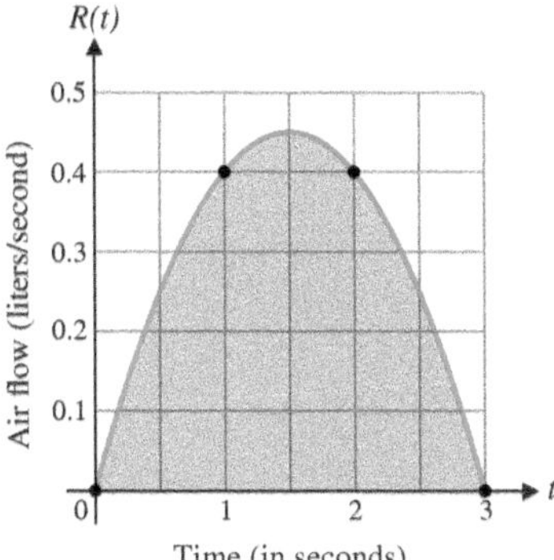

(B) Use the interpolating polynomial to approximate (to one decimal place) the total volume of air inhaled.

51. **Voter registration.** The number N of registered voters in a precinct over a 30-year period is given in the table.

t	0	10	20	30
$N(t)$	10,000	13,500	20,000	23,500

(A) Find the interpolating polynomial for this table.

(B) Use the interpolating polynomial to approximate (to the nearest thousand) the average number of voters over the first 20 years of this period.

52. **Voter registration.** The number N of registered voters in a precinct over a 10-year period is given in the table.

t	0	4	6	10
$N(t)$	15,000	18,800	22,200	26,000

(A) Find the interpolating polynomial for this table.

(B) Use the interpolating polynomial to approximate (to the nearest integer) the year t in which the rate of increase in the number of voters is most rapid.

Answers to Matched Problems

1. $p(2) = 88$ or \$88,000; $p(5) = 61$ or \$61,000
2. $p(x) = 5 - 2(x+1) + (x+1)x + (x+1)x(x-1)$
3. (A)

x_k	y_k	First Divided Difference	Second Divided Difference	Third Divided Difference	Fourth Divided Difference
0	5				
		−4			
1	1		1		
		−2		−1	
2	−1		−2		1
		−6		3	
3	−7		7		
		8			
4	1				

(B) $p(x) = 5 - 4x + x(x-1) - x(x-1)(x-2) + x(x-1)(x-2)(x-3)$
$= 5 - 13x + 15x^2 - 7x^3 + x^4$

4. 657 units; 4,294.2 units

Appendix

Integration Formulas

Table 1 Integration Formulas

Integrals Involving u^n

1. $\int u^n\,du = \dfrac{u^{n+1}}{n+1}, \quad n \neq -1$

2. $\int u^{-1}\,du = \int \dfrac{1}{u}\,du = \ln|u|$

Integrals Involving $a + bu$, $a \neq 0$ and $b \neq 0$

3. $\int \dfrac{1}{a+bu}\,du = \dfrac{1}{b}\ln|a+bu|$

4. $\int \dfrac{u}{a+bu}\,du = \dfrac{u}{b} - \dfrac{a}{b^2}\ln|a+bu|$

5. $\int \dfrac{u^2}{a+bu}\,du = \dfrac{(a+bu)^2}{2b^3} - \dfrac{2a(a+bu)}{b^3} + \dfrac{a^2}{b^3}\ln|a+bu|$

6. $\int \dfrac{u}{(a+bu)^2}\,du = \dfrac{1}{b^2}\left(\ln|a+bu| + \dfrac{a}{a+bu}\right)$

7. $\int \dfrac{u^2}{(a+bu)^2}\,du = \dfrac{(a+bu)}{b^3} - \dfrac{a^2}{b^3(a+bu)} - \dfrac{2a}{b^3}\ln|a+bu|$

8. $\int u(a+bu)^n\,du = \dfrac{(a+bu)^{n+2}}{(n+2)b^2} - \dfrac{a(a+bu)^{n+1}}{(n+1)b^2}, \quad n \neq -1, -2$

9. $\int \dfrac{1}{u(a+bu)}\,du = \dfrac{1}{a}\ln\left|\dfrac{u}{a+bu}\right|$

10. $\int \dfrac{1}{u^2(a+bu)}\,du = -\dfrac{1}{au} + \dfrac{b}{a^2}\ln\left|\dfrac{a+bu}{u}\right|$

11. $\int \dfrac{1}{u(a+bu)^2}\,du = \dfrac{1}{a(a+bu)} + \dfrac{1}{a^2}\ln\left|\dfrac{u}{a+bu}\right|$

12. $\int \dfrac{1}{u^2(a+bu)^2}\,du = -\dfrac{a+2bu}{a^2u(a+bu)} + \dfrac{2b}{a^3}\ln\left|\dfrac{a+bu}{u}\right|$

Integrals Involving $a^2 - u^2$, $a > 0$

13. $\int \dfrac{1}{u^2-a^2}\,du = \dfrac{1}{2a}\ln\left|\dfrac{u-a}{u+a}\right|$

14. $\int \dfrac{1}{a^2-u^2}\,du = \dfrac{1}{2a}\ln\left|\dfrac{u+a}{u-a}\right|$

Integrals Involving $(a + bu)$ and $(c + du)$, $b \neq 0$, $d \neq 0$, and $ad - bc \neq 0$

15. $\int \dfrac{1}{(a+bu)(c+du)}\,du = \dfrac{1}{ad-bc}\ln\left|\dfrac{c+du}{a+bu}\right|$

16. $\int \dfrac{u}{(a+bu)(c+du)}\,du = \dfrac{1}{ad-bc}\left(\dfrac{a}{b}\ln|a+bu| - \dfrac{c}{d}\ln|c+du|\right)$

17. $\int \dfrac{u^2}{(a+bu)(c+du)}\,du = \dfrac{1}{bd}u - \dfrac{1}{ad-bc}\left(\dfrac{a^2}{b^2}\ln|a+bu| - \dfrac{c^2}{d^2}\ln|c+du|\right)$

[*Note:* **The constant of integration is omitted for each integral, but must be included in any particular application of a formula.** The variable u is the variable of integration; all other symbols represent constants.]

Table 1 Integration Formulas Continued

18. $\int \frac{1}{(a+bu)^2(c+du)}\,du = \frac{1}{ad-bc}\frac{1}{a+bu} + \frac{d}{(ad-bc)^2}\ln\left|\frac{c+du}{a+bu}\right|$

19. $\int \frac{u}{(a+bu)^2(c+du)}\,du = -\frac{a}{b(ad-bc)}\frac{1}{a+bu} - \frac{c}{(ad-bc)^2}\ln\left|\frac{c+du}{a+bu}\right|$

20. $\int \frac{a+bu}{c+du}\,du = \frac{bu}{d} + \frac{ad-bc}{d^2}\ln|c+du|$

Integrals Involving $\sqrt{a+bu}$, $a \neq 0$ and $b \neq 0$

21. $\int \sqrt{a+bu}\,du = \frac{2\sqrt{(a+bu)^3}}{3b}$

22. $\int u\sqrt{a+bu}\,du = \frac{2(3bu-2a)}{15b^2}\sqrt{(a+bu)^3}$

23. $\int u^2\sqrt{a+bu}\,du = \frac{2(15b^2u^2-12abu+8a^2)}{105b^3}\sqrt{(a+bu)^3}$

24. $\int \frac{1}{\sqrt{a+bu}}\,du = \frac{2\sqrt{a+bu}}{b}$

25. $\int \frac{u}{\sqrt{a+bu}}\,du = \frac{2(bu-2a)}{3b^2}\sqrt{a+bu}$

26. $\int \frac{u^2}{\sqrt{a+bu}}\,du = \frac{2(3b^2u^2-4abu+8a^2)}{15b^3}\sqrt{a+bu}$

27. $\int \frac{1}{u\sqrt{a+bu}}\,du = \frac{1}{\sqrt{a}}\ln\left|\frac{\sqrt{a+bu}-\sqrt{a}}{\sqrt{a+bu}+\sqrt{a}}\right|, \quad a > 0$

28. $\int \frac{1}{u^2\sqrt{a+bu}}\,du = -\frac{\sqrt{a+bu}}{au} - \frac{b}{2a\sqrt{a}}\ln\left|\frac{\sqrt{a+bu}-\sqrt{a}}{\sqrt{a+bu}+\sqrt{a}}\right|, \quad a > 0$

Integrals Involving $\sqrt{a^2-u^2}$, $a > 0$

29. $\int \frac{1}{u\sqrt{a^2-u^2}}\,du = -\frac{1}{a}\ln\left|\frac{a+\sqrt{a^2-u^2}}{u}\right|$

30. $\int \frac{1}{u^2\sqrt{a^2-u^2}}\,du = -\frac{\sqrt{a^2-u^2}}{a^2u}$

31. $\int \frac{\sqrt{a^2-u^2}}{u}\,du = \sqrt{a^2-u^2} - a\ln\left|\frac{a+\sqrt{a^2-u^2}}{u}\right|$

Integrals Involving $\sqrt{u^2+a^2}$, $a > 0$

32. $\int \sqrt{u^2+a^2}\,du = \frac{1}{2}\left(u\sqrt{u^2+a^2} + a^2\ln|u+\sqrt{u^2+a^2}|\right)$

33. $\int u^2\sqrt{u^2+a^2}\,du = \frac{1}{8}\left[u(2u^2+a^2)\sqrt{u^2+a^2} - a^4\ln|u+\sqrt{u^2+a^2}|\right]$

34. $\int \frac{\sqrt{u^2+a^2}}{u}\,du = \sqrt{u^2+a^2} - a\ln\left|\frac{a+\sqrt{u^2+a^2}}{u}\right|$

35. $\int \frac{\sqrt{u^2+a^2}}{u^2}\,du = -\frac{\sqrt{u^2+a^2}}{u} + \ln|u+\sqrt{u^2+a^2}|$

36. $\int \frac{1}{\sqrt{u^2+a^2}}\,du = \ln|u+\sqrt{u^2+a^2}|$

37. $\int \frac{1}{u\sqrt{u^2+a^2}}\,du = \frac{1}{a}\ln\left|\frac{u}{a+\sqrt{u^2+a^2}}\right|$

38. $\int \frac{u^2}{\sqrt{u^2+a^2}}\,du = \frac{1}{2}\left(u\sqrt{u^2+a^2} - a^2\ln|u+\sqrt{u^2+a^2}|\right)$

39. $\int \frac{1}{u^2\sqrt{u^2+a^2}}\,du = -\frac{\sqrt{u^2+a^2}}{a^2u}$

[*Note:* **The constant of integration is omitted for each integral, but must be included in any particular application of a formula.** The variable u is the variable of integration; all other symbols represent constants.]

Integrals Involving $\sqrt{u^2 - a^2}, a > 0$

40. $\int \sqrt{u^2 - a^2}\, du = \frac{1}{2}(u\sqrt{u^2 - a^2} - a^2 \ln|u + \sqrt{u^2 - a^2}|)$

41. $\int u^2\sqrt{u^2 - a^2}\, du = \frac{1}{8}[u(2u^2 - a^2)\sqrt{u^2 - a^2} - a^4 \ln|u + \sqrt{u^2 - a^2}|]$

42. $\int \frac{\sqrt{u^2 - a^2}}{u^2}\, du = -\frac{\sqrt{u^2 - a^2}}{u} + \ln|u + \sqrt{u^2 - a^2}|$

43. $\int \frac{1}{\sqrt{u^2 - a^2}}\, du = \ln|u + \sqrt{u^2 - a^2}|$

44. $\int \frac{u^2}{\sqrt{u^2 - a^2}}\, du = \frac{1}{2}(u\sqrt{u^2 - a^2} + a^2 \ln|u + \sqrt{u^2 - a^2}|)$

45. $\int \frac{1}{u^2\sqrt{u^2 - a^2}}\, du = \frac{\sqrt{u^2 - a^2}}{a^2 u}$

Integrals Involving $e^{au}, a \neq 0$

46. $\int e^{au}\, du = \frac{e^{au}}{a}$

47. $\int u^n e^{au}\, du = \frac{u^n e^{au}}{a} - \frac{n}{a}\int u^{n-1}e^{au}\, du$

48. $\int \frac{1}{c + de^{au}}\, du = \frac{u}{c} - \frac{1}{ac}\ln|c + de^{au}|, \quad c \neq 0$

Integrals Involving $\ln u$

49. $\int \ln u\, du = u \ln u - u$

50. $\int \frac{\ln u}{u}\, du = \frac{1}{2}(\ln u)^2$

51. $\int u^n \ln u\, du = \frac{u^{n+1}}{n+1}\ln u - \frac{u^{n+1}}{(n+1)^2}, \quad n \neq -1$

52. $\int (\ln u)^n\, du = u(\ln u)^n - n\int (\ln u)^{n-1}\, du$

Integrals Involving Trigonometric Functions of $au, a \neq 0$

53. $\int \sin au\, du = -\frac{1}{a}\cos au$

54. $\int \cos au\, du = \frac{1}{a}\sin au$

55. $\int \tan au\, du = -\frac{1}{a}\ln|\cos au|$

56. $\int \cot au\, du = \frac{1}{a}\ln|\sin au|$

57. $\int \sec au\, du = \frac{1}{a}\ln|\sec au + \tan au|$

58. $\int \csc au\, du = \frac{1}{a}\ln|\csc au - \cot au|$

59. $\int (\sin au)^2\, du = \frac{u}{2} - \frac{1}{4a}\sin 2au$

60. $\int (\cos au)^2\, du = \frac{u}{2} + \frac{1}{4a}\sin 2au$

61. $\int (\sin au)^n\, du = -\frac{1}{an}(\sin au)^{n-1}\cos au + \frac{n-1}{n}\int (\sin au)^{n-2}\, du, \quad n \neq 0$

62. $\int (\cos au)^n\, du = \frac{1}{an}\sin au(\cos au)^{n-1} + \frac{n-1}{n}\int (\cos au)^{n-2}\, du, \quad n \neq 0$

[*Note:* **The constant of integration is omitted for each integral, but must be included in any particular application of a formula.** The variable u is the variable of integration; all other symbols represent constants.]

ANSWERS

Diagnostic Prerequisite Test

Section references are provided in parentheses following each answer to guide students to the specific content in the book where they can find help or remediation.

1. (A) $(y + z)x$ (B) $(2 + x) + y$ (C) $2x + 3x$ *(B.1)* **2.** $x^3 - 3x^2 + 4x + 8$ *(B.2)* **3.** $x^3 + 3x^2 - 2x + 12$ *(B.2)* **4.** $-3x^5 + 2x^3 - 24x^2 + 16$ *(B.2)* **5.** (A) 1 (B) 1 (C) 2 (D) 3 *(B.2)* **6.** (A) 3 (B) 1 (C) -3 (D) 1 *(B.2)* **7.** $14x^2 - 30x$ *(B.2)* **8.** $6x^2 - 5xy - 4y^2$ *(B.2)* **9.** $(x + 2)(x + 5)$ *(B.3)* **10.** $x(x + 3)(x - 5)$ *(B.3)* **11.** 7/20 *(B.1)* **12.** 0.875 *(B.1)* **13.** (A) 4.065×10^{12} (B) 7.3×10^{-3} *(B.5)* **14.** (A) 255,000,000 (B) 0.000 406 *(B.5)* **15.** (A) T (B) F *(B.1)* **16.** 0 and -3 are two examples of infinitely many. *(B.1)* **17.** $6x^5y^{15}$ *(B.5)* **18.** $3u^4/v^2$ *(B.5)* **19.** 6×10^2 *(B.5)* **20.** x^6/y^4 *(B.5)* **21.** $u^{7/3}$ *(B.6)* **22.** $3a^2/b$ *(B.6)* **23.** $\frac{5}{9}$ *(B.5)* **24.** $x + 2x^{1/2}y^{1/2} + y$ *(B.6)* **25.** $\dfrac{a^2 + b^2}{ab}$ *(B.4)* **26.** $\dfrac{a^2 - c^2}{abc}$ *(B.4)* **27.** $\dfrac{y^5}{x}$ *(B.4)* **28.** $\dfrac{1}{xy^2}$ *(B.4)* **29.** $\dfrac{-1}{7(7 + h)}$ *(B.4)* **30.** $\dfrac{xy}{y - x}$ *(B.6)* **31.** (A) Subtraction (B) Commutative (+) (C) Distributive (D) Associative (·) (E) Negatives (F) Identity (+) *(B.1)* **32.** (A) 6 (B) 0 *(B.1)* **33.** $4x = x - 4$; $x = -4/3$ *(A.1)* **34.** $-15/7$ *(A.2)* **35.** (4/7, 0) *(A.2)* **36.** $(0, -4)$ *(A.2)* **37.** $(x - 5y)(x + 2y)$ *(B.3)* **38.** $(3x - y)(2x - 5y)$ *(B.3)* **39.** $3x^{-1} + 4y^{1/2}$ *(B.6)* **40.** $8x^{-2} - 5y^{-4}$ *(B.5)* **41.** $\frac{2}{5}x^{-3/4} - \frac{7}{6}y^{-2/3}$ *(B.6)* **42.** $\frac{1}{3}x^{-1/2} + 9y^{-1/3}$ *(B.6)* **43.** $\frac{2}{7} + \frac{1}{14}\sqrt{2}$ *(B.6)* **44.** $\frac{14}{11} - \frac{5}{11}\sqrt{3}$ *(B.6)* **45.** $x = 0, 5$ *(B.7)* **46.** $x = \pm\sqrt{7}$ *(B.7)* **47.** $x = -4, 5$ *(B.7)* **48.** $x = 1, \frac{1}{6}$ *(B.7)* **49.** $x = -1 \pm \sqrt{2}$ *(B.7)* **50.** $x = \pm 1, \pm\sqrt{5}$ *(B.7)*

Chapter 1

Exercises 1.1

1. $x = 5$ **3.** $x = 2$ **5.** $x = -19$ **7.** $4 \le x < 13$ **9.** $-2 < x < 7$ **11.** $x \le 4$ **13.** $(-8, 2]$ **15.** $(-\infty, 9)$ **17.** $(-7, -5]$ **19.** $x = -\frac{3}{2}$ **21.** $y < -\frac{15}{2}$ **23.** $u = -\frac{3}{4}$ **25.** $x = 10$ **27.** $y \ge 3$ **29.** $x = 36$ **31.** $m < \frac{36}{7}$ **33.** $3 \le x < 7$ or $[3, 7)$ **35.** $-20 \le C \le 20$ or $[-20, 20]$ **37.** $y = \frac{3}{4}x - 3$ **39.** $y = -(A/B)x + (C/B) = (-Ax + C)/B$ **41.** $C = \frac{5}{9}(F - 32)$ **43.** $-2 < x \le 1$ or $(-2, 1]$ **45.** Negative **47.** 4,500 \$35 tickets and 5,000 \$55 tickets **49.** Fund A: \$180,000; Fund B: \$320,000 **51.** \$15,405 **53.** (A) \$420 (B) \$55 **55.** 34 rounds **57.** \$32,000 **59.** 5,851 books **61.** (B) 6,180 books (C) At least \$11.50 **63.** 5,000 **65.** 12.6 yr

Exercises 1.2

1. (D) **3.** (C) **5.** **7.**

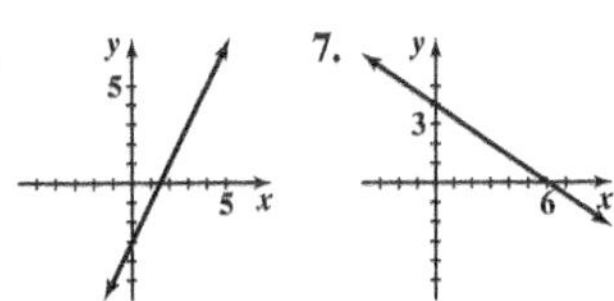

9. Slope = 5; y int. = -7 **11.** Slope = $-\frac{5}{2}$; y int. = -9 **13.** Slope = $\frac{1}{4}$; y int. = $\frac{2}{3}$ **15.** Slope = 2; x int. = -5 **17.** Slope = 8; x int. = 5 **19.** Slope = $\frac{6}{7}$; x int. = -7 **21.** $y = 2x + 1$ **23.** $y = -\frac{1}{3}x + 6$ **25.** x int.: $\frac{1}{2}$; y int.: 1; $y = -2x + 1$ **27.** x int.: -3; y int.: 1; $y = \frac{x}{3} + 1$ **29.**

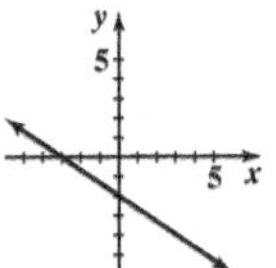

31. **33.** **35.** -4 **37.** $-\frac{3}{5}$ **39.** 2 **41.** **43.**

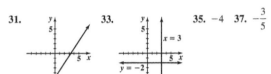

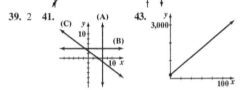

45. (A) (B) x int.: 3.5; y int.: -4.2

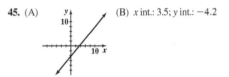

(C)

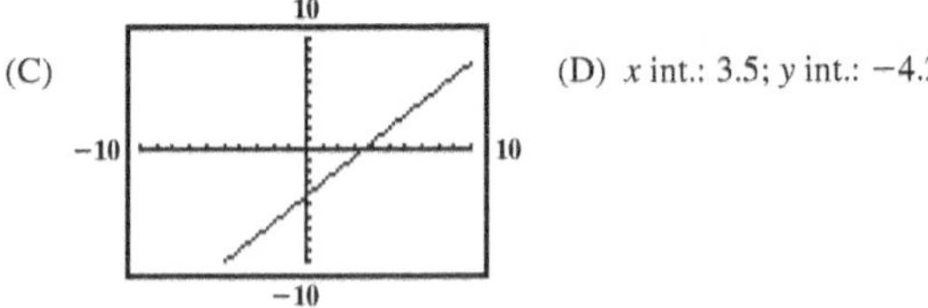

(D) x int.: 3.5; y int.: -4.2

47. $x = 4, y = -3$ **49.** $x = -1.5, y = -3.5$ **51.** $y = 5x - 15$ **53.** $y = -2x + 7$ **55.** $y = \frac{1}{3}x - \frac{20}{3}$ **57.** $y = -3.2x + 30.86$ **59.** (A) $m = \frac{2}{3}$ (B) $-2x + 3y = 11$ (C) $y = \frac{2}{3}x + \frac{11}{3}$ **61.** (A) $m = -\frac{5}{4}$ (B) $5x + 4y = -14$ (C) $y = -\frac{5}{4}x - \frac{7}{2}$ **63.** (A) Not defined (B) $x = 5$ (C) None **65.** (A) $m = 0$ (B) $y = 5$ (C) $y = 5$ **67.** The graphs have the same y int., (0, 2). **69.** $C = 124 + 0.12x$; 1,050 donuts **71.** (A) $C = 75x + 1{,}647$ (B) (C) The y int., \$1,647, is the fixed cost and the slope, \$75, is the cost per club. **73.** (A) $R = 1.4C - 7$ (B) \$137 **75.** (A) $V = -7{,}500t + 157{,}000$ (B) \$112,000 (C) During the 12th year (D)

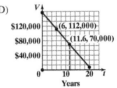

77. (A) $T = -1.84x + 212$ (B) 205.56°F (C) 6,522 ft

(D)

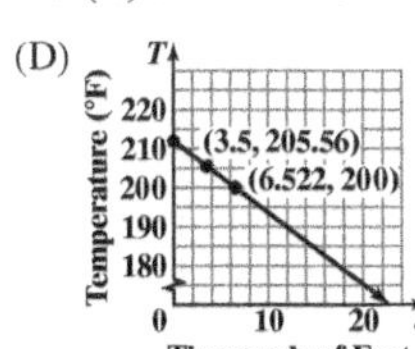

79. (A) $T = 70 - 3.6A$ (B) 10,000 ft

81. (A) $N = -0.0063t + 2.76$ (B) 2.45 persons **83.** (A) $f = -0.49t + 21$ (B) 2028 **85.** (A) $p = 0.001x + 5.4$ (B) $p = -0.001x + 13$

(C) (3,800, 9.2) (D)

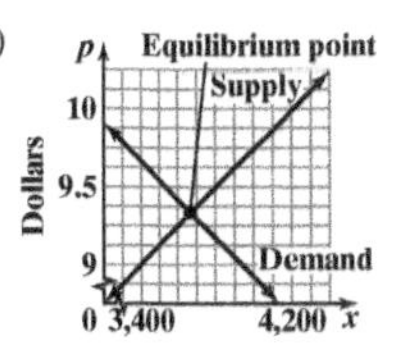

87. (A) $s = \frac{2}{5}w$ (B) 8 in. (C) 9 lb

Exercises 1.3

1. (A) $w = 49 + 1.7h$ (B) The rate of change of weight with respect to height is 1.7 kg/in. (C) 55.8 kg (D) 5′6.5″

3. (A) $P = 0.44\overline{5}d + 14.7$ (B) The rate of change of pressure with respect to depth is $0.44\overline{5}$ lb/in.^{2} per ft. (C) 37 lb/in.^{2} (D) 99 ft

5. (A) $a = 2{,}880 - 24t$ (B) −24 ft/sec (C) 24 ft/sec

7. $s = 0.6t + 331$; the rate of change of the speed of sound with respect to temperature is 0.6 m/s per °C. **9.** (A)

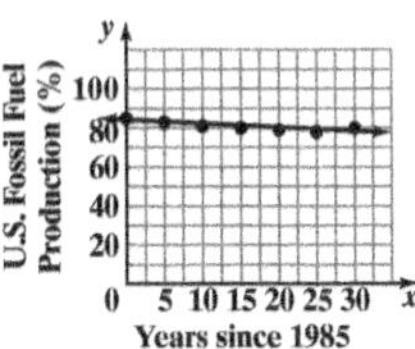

(B) The rate of change of fossil fuel production is −0.19% per year. (C) 76% of total production (D) 2058 **11.** (A)

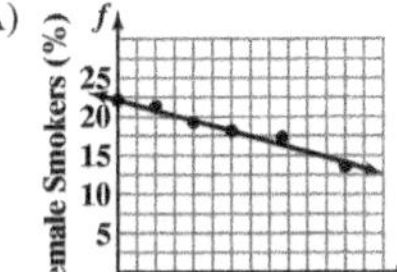

(B) 2025 **13.** (A)

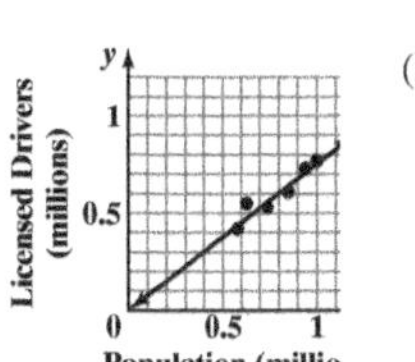

(B) 1,050,000 (C) 1,359,000

15. (A)

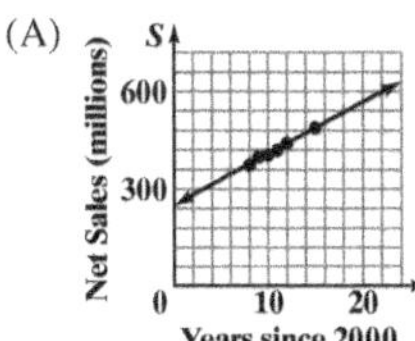

(B) \$662 billion

17. (A)

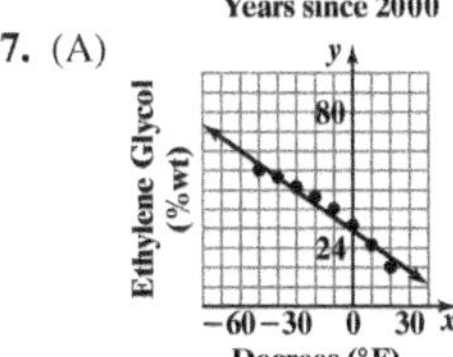

(B) 2°F (C) 22.75%

19. (A) The rate of change of height with respect to Dbh is 1.37 ft/in. (B) Height increases by approximately 1.37 ft. (C) 18 ft (D) 20 in.

21. (A) Undergraduate male enrollment is increasing at a rate of 87,000 students per year; undergraduate female enrollment is increasing at a rate of 140,000 students per year. (B) Male: 8.6 million; female: 11.5 million (C) 2026 **23.** $y = 0.061x + 50.703$; 54.67°F

25. Men: $y = -0.070x + 49.058$; women: $y = -0.085x + 54.858$; yes

27. Supply: $y = 0.2x + 0.87$; demand: $y = -0.15x + 3.5$; equilibrium price = \$2.37

Chapter 2

Exercises 2.1

1.

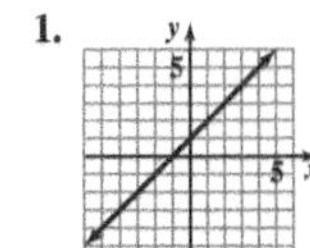

3.

5.

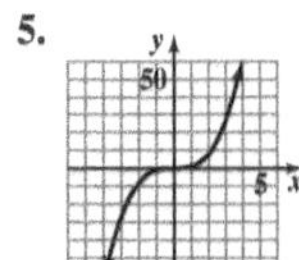

7.

9. A function **11.** Not a function **13.** A function **15.** A function **17.** Not a function **19.** A function **21.** Linear **23.** Linear **25.** Neither **27.** Constant

29.

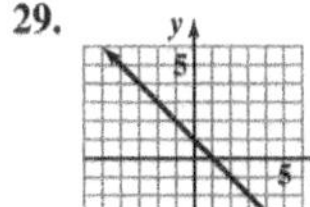

31.

33.

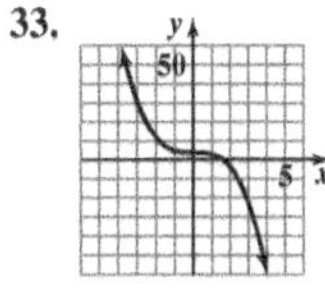

35.

37.

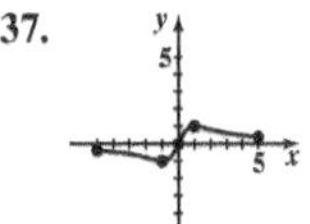

39. $y = 0$ **41.** $y = -2$

43. $x = -5$ **45.** $x = -6$ **47.** All real numbers **49.** All real numbers except −4 **51.** $x \le 7$ **53.** Yes; all real numbers **55.** No; for example, when $x = 0$, $y = \pm 2$ **57.** Yes; all real numbers except 0

59. No; when $x = 1$, $y = \pm 1$ **61.** $25x^2 - 4$ **63.** $x^2 + 6x + 5$

65. $x^4 - 4$ **67.** $x - 4$ **69.** $h^2 - 4$ **71.** $4h + h^2$ **73.** $4h + h^2$

75. (A) $4x + 4h - 3$ (B) $4h$ (C) 4

77. (A) $4x^2 + 8xh + 4h^2 - 7x - 7h + 6$ (B) $8xh + 4h^2 - 7h$ (C) $8x + 4h - 7$

79. (A) $20x + 20h - x^2 - 2xh - h^2$ (B) $20h - 2xh - h^2$ (C) $20 - 2x - h$

81. $P(w) = 2w + \frac{50}{w}, w > 0$ **83.** $A(l) = l(50 - l), 0 < l < 50$

85. (A) 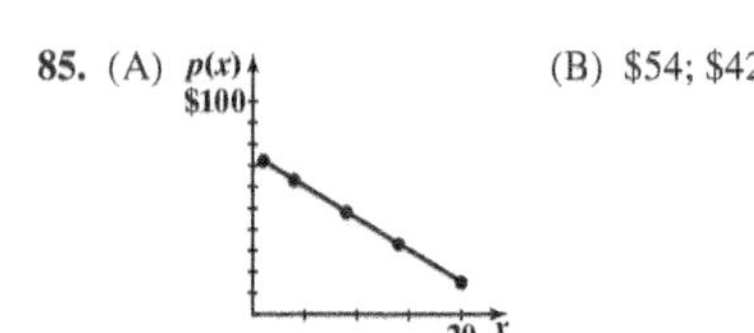

(B) \$54; \$42

87. (A) $R(x) = (75 - 3x)x, 1 \le x \le 20$ (B)

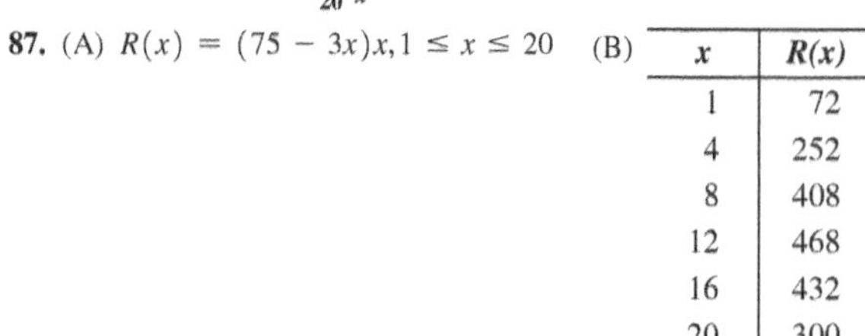

x	$R(x)$
1	72
4	252
8	408
12	468
16	432
20	300

(C) 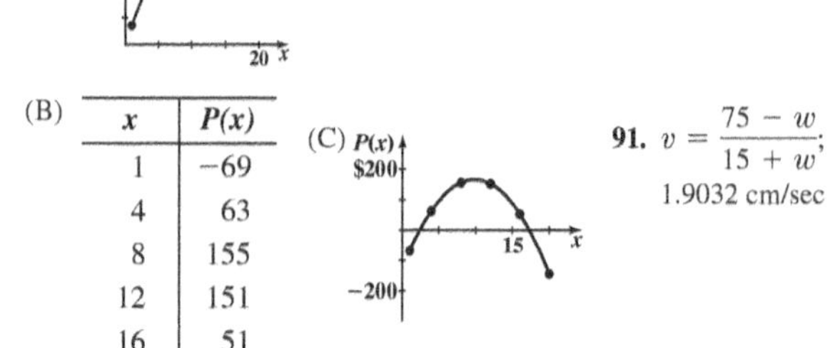

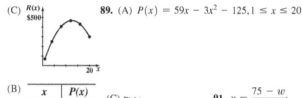

89. (A) $P(x) = 59x - 3x^2 - 125, 1 \le x \le 20$

(B)

x	$P(x)$
1	−69
4	63
8	155
12	151
16	51
20	−145

(C) P(x) \$200 −200 15 x

91. $v = \dfrac{75 - w}{15 + w}$; 1.9032 cm/sec

92. (A) $v = 0.625s + 0.125$; 44.4% (B) $s = 1.6v - 0.2$; 61.6%

Exercises 2.2

1. Domain: all real numbers; range: $[-4, \infty]$ 3. Domain:all real numbers; range: all real numbers 5. Domain: $[0, \infty)$; range: $(-\infty, 8]$ 7. Domain: all real numbers; range: all real numbers 9. Domain: all real numbers; range: $[9, \infty)$

11. 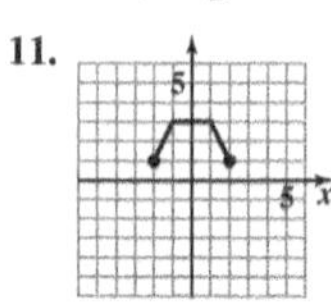

13. 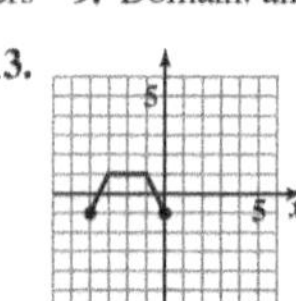

15. 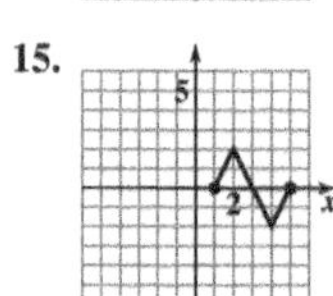

17. 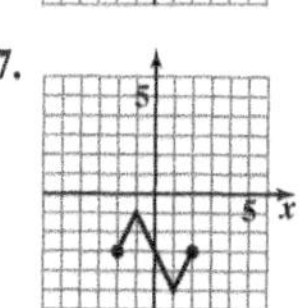

19. 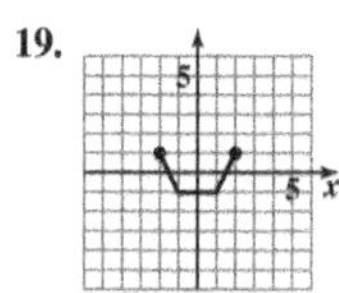

21. 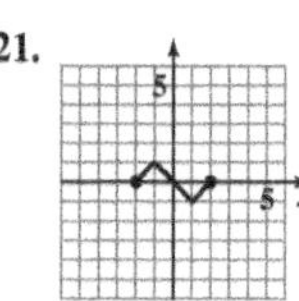

23. 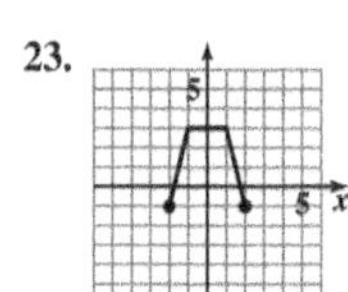

25. 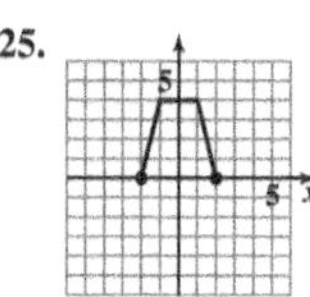

27. The graph of $g(x) = -|x + 3|$ is the graph of $y = |x|$ reflected in the x axis and shifted 3 units to the left.

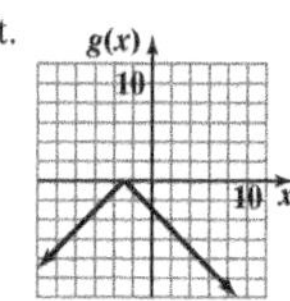

29. The graph of $f(x) = (x - 4)^2 - 3$ is the graph of $y = x^2$ shifted 4 units to the right and 3 units down.

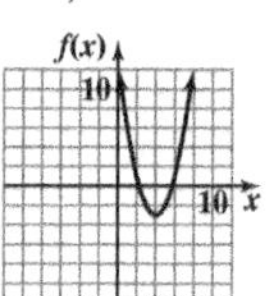

31. The graph of $f(x) = 7 - \sqrt{x}$ is the graph of $y = \sqrt{x}$ reflected in the x axis and shifted 7 units up.

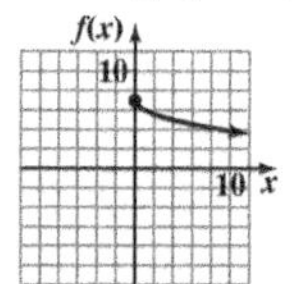

33. The graph of $h(x) = -3|x|$ is the graph of $y = |x|$ reflected in the x axis and vertically stretched by a factor of 3.

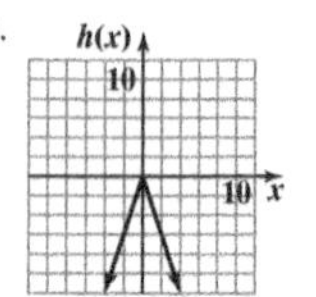

35. The graph of the basic function $y = x^2$ is shifted 2 units to the left and 3 units down. Equation: $y = (x + 2)^2 - 3$. 37. The graph of the basic function $y = x^2$ is reflected in the x axis and shifted 3 units to the right and 2 units up. Equation: $y = 2 - (x - 3)^2$. 39. The graph of the basic function $y = \sqrt{x}$ is reflected in the x axis and shifted 4 units up. Equation: $y = 4 - \sqrt{x}$. 41. The graph of the basic function $y = x^3$ is shifted 2 units to the left and 1 unit down. Equation: $y = (x + 2)^3 - 1$.

43. $g(x) = \sqrt{x + 3} + 2$

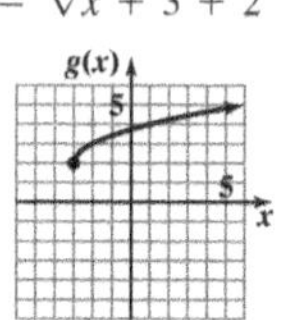

45. $g(x) = |x + 3|$

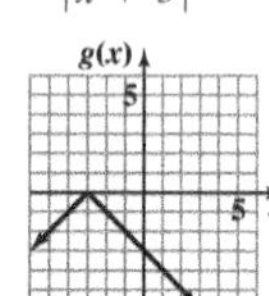

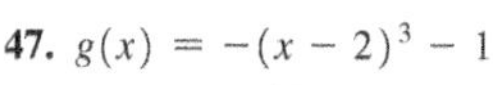

47. $g(x) = -(x - 2)^3 - 1$

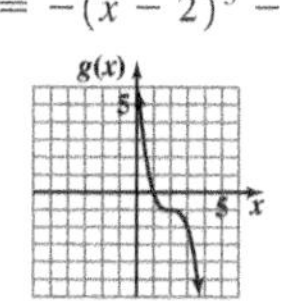

49. 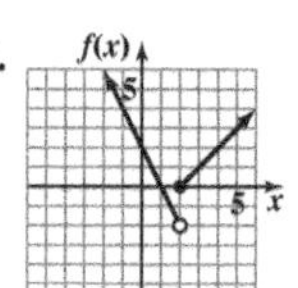

51. 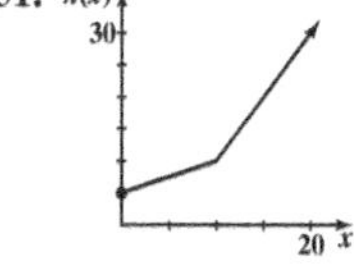

53. 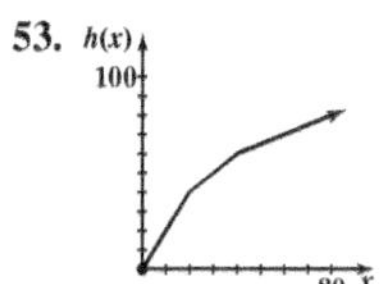

55. The graph of the basic function $y = |x|$ is reflected in the x axis and vertically shrunk by a factor of 0.5. Equation: $y = -0.5|x|$. **57.** The graph of the basic function $y = x^2$ is reflected in the x axis and vertically stretched by a factor of 2. Equation: $y = -2x^2$. **59.** The graph of the basic function $y = \sqrt[3]{x}$ is reflected in the x axis and vertically stretched by a factor of 3. Equation: $y = -3\sqrt[3]{x}$. **61.** Reversing the order does not change the result. **63.** Reversing the order can change the result. **65.** Reversing the order can change the result. **67.** (A) The graph of the basic function $y = \sqrt{x}$ is reflected in the x axis, vertically expanded by a factor of 4, and shifted up 115 units. (B)

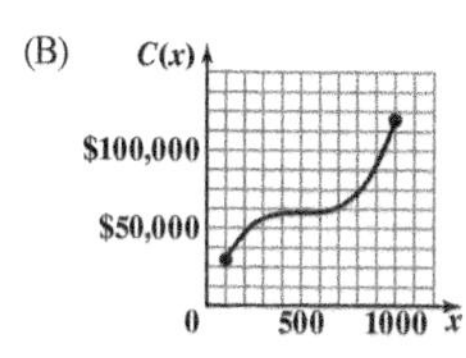

69. (A) The graph of the basic function $y = x^3$ is vertically contracted by a factor of 0.000 48 and shifted right 500 units and up 60,000 units.

(B)

71. (A) $V(x) = \begin{cases} 1.34 + 0.32x & \text{if } 0 \le x \le 11 \\ 1.01 + 0.35x & \text{if } x > 11 \end{cases}$

(B)

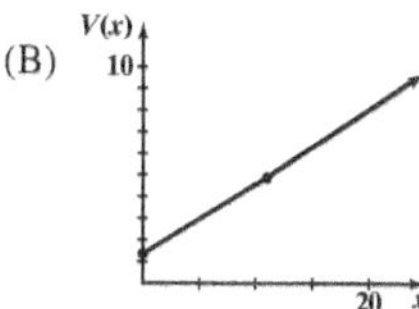

73. (A) $T(x) = \begin{cases} 0.002x & \text{if } 0 \le x \le 15 \\ 0.006x - 0.06 & \text{if } 15 \le x \le 60 \\ 0.010x - 0.30 & \text{if } x > 60 \end{cases}$

(B)

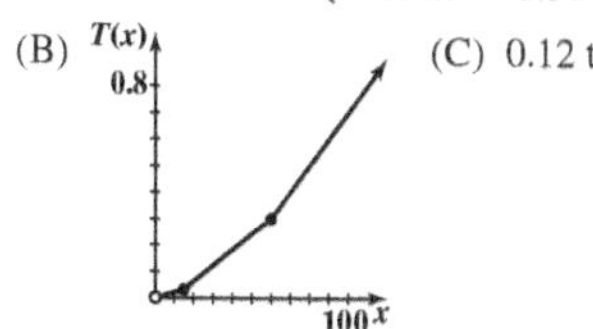

(C) 0.12 tax units; 0.60 tax units

75. (A) The graph of the basic function $y = x$ is vertically stretched by a factor of 5.5 and shifted down 220 units.

(B)

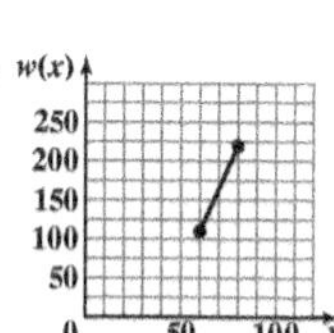

77. (A) The graph of the basic function $y = \sqrt{x}$ is vertically stretched by a factor of 7.08.

(B)

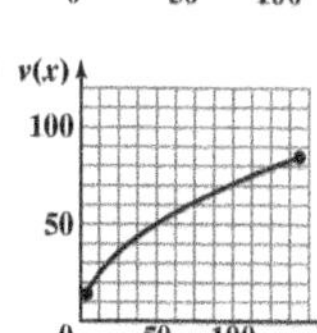

Exercises 2.3

1. $f(x) = (x - 5)^2 - 25$ **3.** $f(x) = (x + 10)^2 - 50$

5. $f(x) = -2(x - 1)^2 - 3$ **7.** $f(x) = 2\left(x + \frac{1}{2}\right)^2 + \frac{1}{2}$

9. The graph of $f(x)$ is the graph of $y = x^2$ shifted right 2 units and down 1 unit. **11.** The graph of $m(x)$ is the graph of $y = x^2$ reflected in the x axis, then shifted right 5 units and up 9 units. **13.** (A) m (B) g (C) f (D) n **15.** (A) x int.: 1, 3; y int.: -3 (B) Vertex: $(2, 1)$ (C) Max.: 1 (D) Range: $y \le 1$ or $(-\infty, 1]$ **17.** (A) x int.: $-3, -1$; y int.: 3 (B) Vertex: $(-2, -1)$ (C) Min.: -1 (D) Range: $y \ge -1$ or $[-1, \infty)$ **19.** (A) x int.: $3 \pm \sqrt{2}$; y int.: -7 (B) Vertex: $(3, 2)$ (C) Max.: 2 (D) Range: $y \le 2$ or $(-\infty, 2]$ **21.** (A) x int.: $-1 \pm \sqrt{2}$; y int.: -1 (B) Vertex: $(-1, -2)$ (C) Min.: -2 (D) Range: $y \ge -2$ or $[-2, \infty)$

23. $y = -[x - (-2)]^2 + 5$ or $y = -(x + 2)^2 + 5$ **25.** $y = (x - 1)^2 - 3$ **27.** Vertex form: $(x - 4)^2 - 4$ (A) x int.: 2, 6; y int.: 12 (B) Vertex: $(4, -4)$ (C) Min.: -4 (D) Range: $y \ge -4$ or $[-4, \infty)$ **29.** Vertex form: $-4(x - 2)^2 + 1$ (A) x int.: 1.5, 2.5; y int.: -15 (B) Vertex: $(2, 1)$ (C) Max.: 1 (D) Range: $y \le 1$ or $(-\infty, 1]$ **31.** Vertex form: $0.5(x - 2)^2 + 3$ (A) x int.: none; y int.: 5 (B) Vertex: $(2, 3)$ (C) Min.: 3 (D) Range: $y \ge 3$ or $[3, \infty)$ **33.** (A) $-4.87, 8.21$ (B) $-3.44, 6.78$ (C) No solution **35.** 651.0417 **37.** $g(x) = 0.25(x - 3)^2 - 9.25$ (A) x int.: $-3.08, 9.08$; y int.: -7 (B) Vertex: $(3, -9.25)$ (C) Min.: -9.25 (D) Range: $y \ge -9.25$ or $[-9.25, \infty)$ **39.** $f(x) = -0.12(x - 4)^2 + 3.12$ (A) x int.: $-1.1, 9.1$; y int.: 1.2 (B) Vertex: $(4, 3.12)$ (C) Max.: 3.12 (D) Range: $y \le 3.12$ or $(-\infty, 3.12]$ **41.** $(-\infty, -5) \cup (3, \infty)$ **43.** $[-3, 2]$ **45.** $x = -5.37, 0.37$ **47.** $-1.37 < x < 2.16$ **49.** $x \le -0.74$ or $x \ge 4.19$ **51.** Axis: $x = -4$; vertex: $(-4, -9)$; range: $y \le -9$ or $(-\infty, -9)$; no x intercept. **53.** (A)

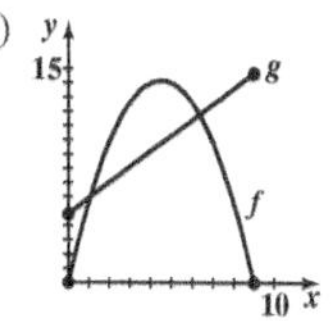

(B) 1.64, 7.61

(C) $1.64 < x < 7.61$ (D) $0 \le x < 1.64$ or $7.61 < x \le 10$

55. (A)

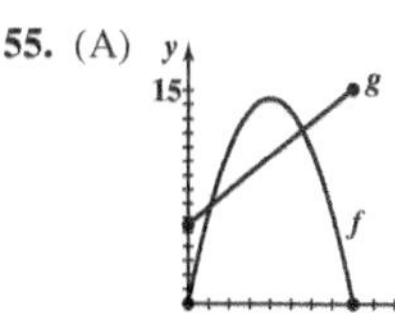

(B) 1.10, 5.57 (C) $1.10 < x < 5.57$ (D) $0 \le x < 1.10$ or $5.57 < x \le 8$

65. (A)

x	28	30	32	34	36
Mileage	45	52	55	51	47
$f(x)$	45.3	51.8	54.2	52.4	46.5

(B)

(C) $f(31) = 53.50$ thousand miles; (D) $f(35) = 49.95$ thousand miles;

69. (A)

(B) 12.5 (12,500,000 chips); $468,750,000 (C) $37.50

71. (A)

(B) 2,415,000 chips and 17,251,000 chips (C) Loss: $1 \le x < 2.415$ or $17.251 < x \le 20$; profit: $2.415 < x < 17.251$

73. (A) $P(x) = 59x - 3x^2 - 125$

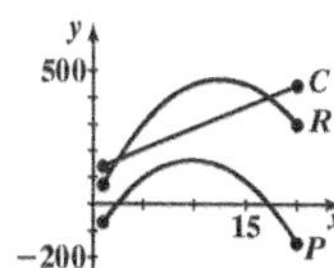

(C) Intercepts and break-even points: 2,415,000 chips and 17,251,000 chips (D) Maximum profit is $165,083,000 at a production level of 9,833,000 chips. This is much smaller than the maximum revenue of $468,750,000.

75. $x = 0.14$ cm **77.** 10.6 mph

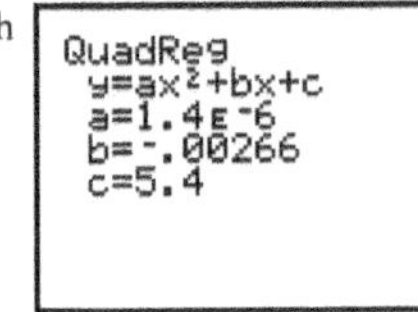

Exercises 2.4

1. (A) 1 (B) −3 (C) 21 **3.** (A) 2 (B) −5, −4 (C) 20 **5.** (A) 10 (B) None (C) 9 **7.** (A) 5 (B) 0, −6 (C) 0 **9.** (A) 11 (B) −5, −2, 5 (C) −12,800 **11.** (A) 4 (B) Negative **13.** (A) 5 (B) Negative **15.** (A) 1 (B) Negative **17.** (A) 6 (B) Positive **19.** 10 **21.** 1 **23.** (A) x int.: −2; y int.: −1 (B) Domain: all real numbers except 2 (C) Vertical asymptote: $x = 2$; horizontal asymptote: $y = 1$

(D)

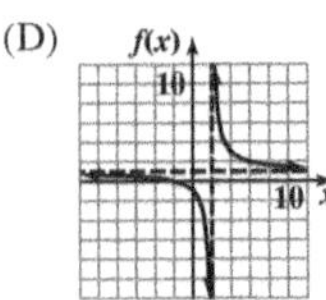

25. (A) x int.: 0; y int.: 0 (B) Domain: all real numbers except −2 (C) Vertical asymptote: $x = -2$; horizontal asymptote: $y = 3$ (D)

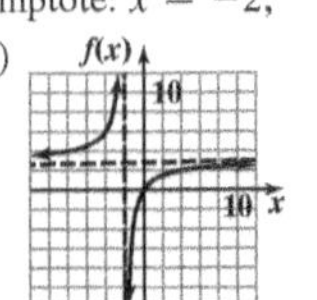

27. (A) x int.: 2; y int.: −1 (B) Domain: all real numbers except 4 (C) Vertical asymptote: $x = 4$; horizontal asymptote: $y = -2$ (D)

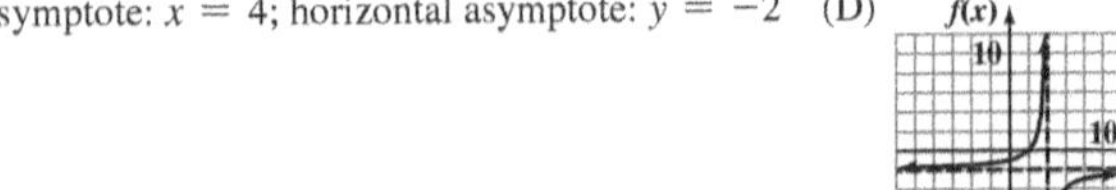

29. (A)

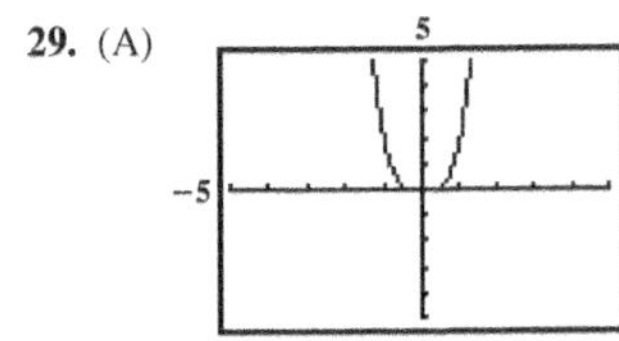

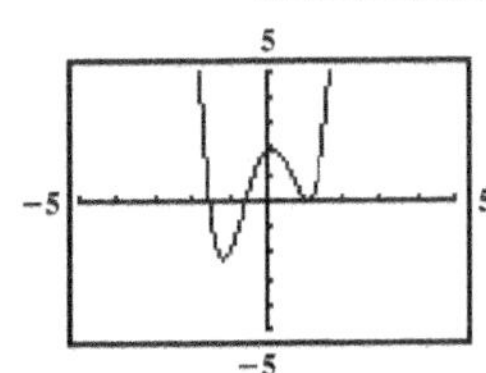

(B)

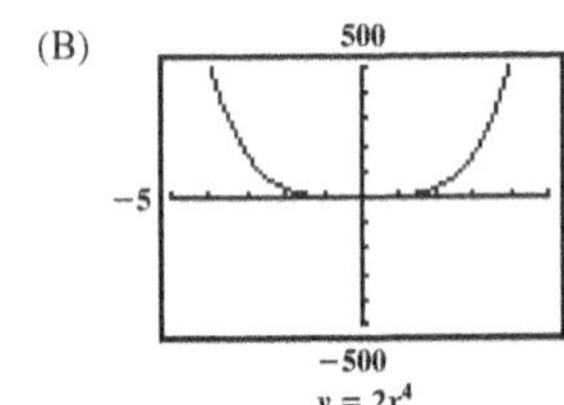
$y = 2x^4$

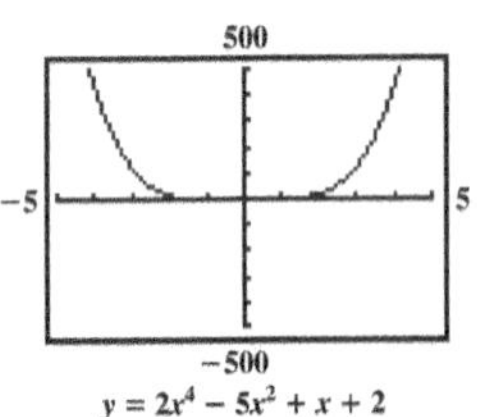
$y = 2x^4 - 5x^2 + x + 2$

31. (A)

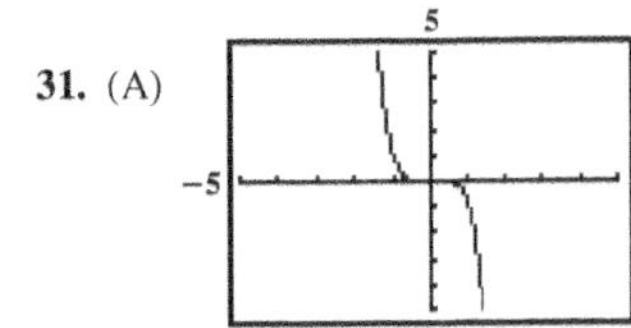

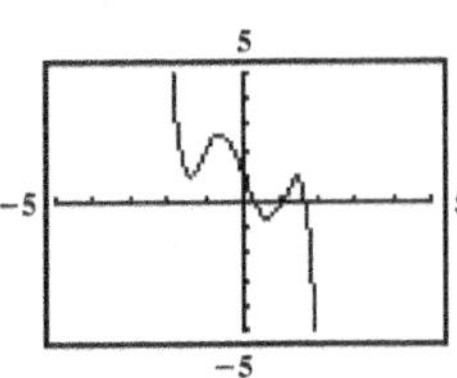

(B)

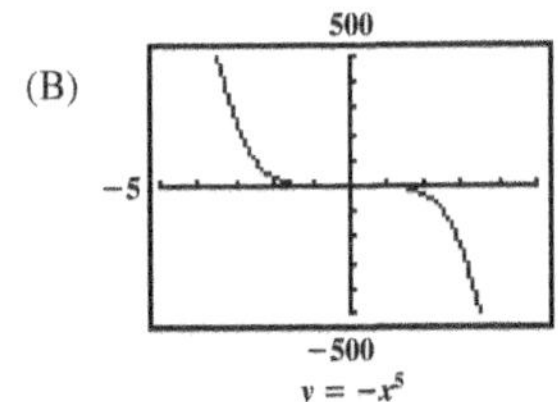
$y = -x^5$

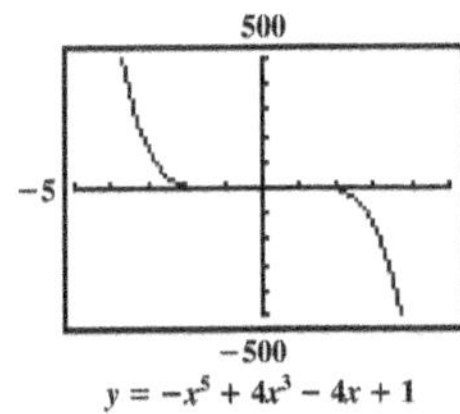
$y = -x^5 + 4x^3 - 4x + 1$

33. $y = \frac{4}{5}$ **35.** $y = \frac{1}{4}$ **37.** $y = 0$ **39.** None **41.** $x = -1, x = 1, x = -3, x = 3$ **43.** $x = 5$ **45.** $x = -7, x = 7$ **47.** (A) x int.: 0; y int.: 0 (B) Vertical asymptotes: $x = -2, x = 3$; horizontal asymptote: $y = 2$

(C)

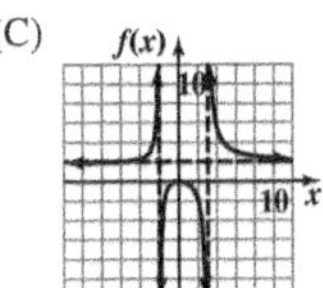

(D)

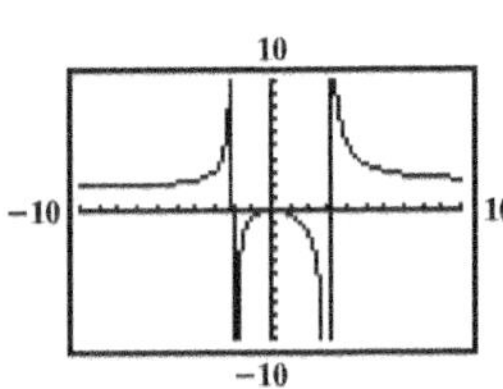

49. (A) x int.: $\pm\sqrt{3}$; y int.: $-\frac{2}{3}$ (B) Vertical asymptotes: $x = -3, x = 3$; horizontal asymptote: $y = -2$

(C)

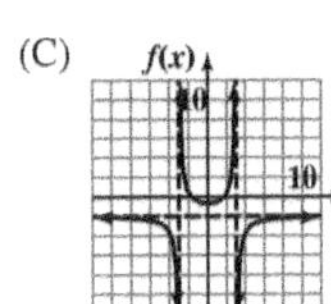

(D)

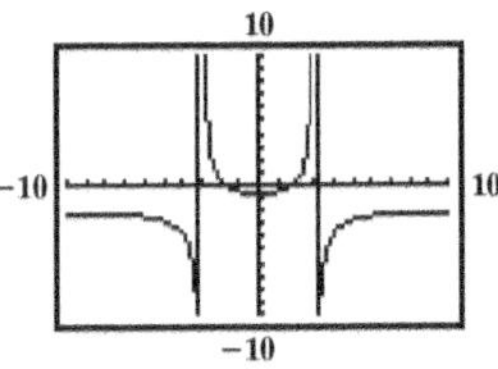

51. (A) x int.: 6; y int.: −4 (B) Vertical asymptotes: $x = -3, x = 2$; horizontal asymptote: $y = 0$

(C)

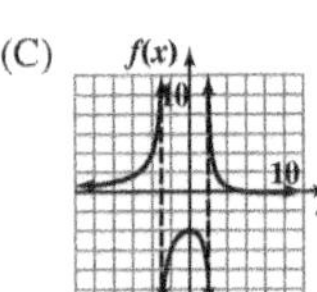

(D)

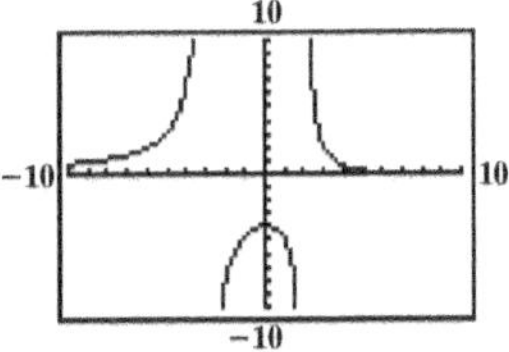

53. $f(x) = x^2 + 2x - 3$ **55.** $f(x) = x^3 + x^2 - 2x$

57. (A) $C(x) = 180x + 200$ (B) $\overline{C}(x) = \dfrac{180x + 200}{x}$

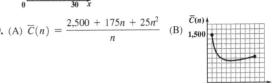

(C) $\overline{C}(x)$; 500; 0; 30 x (D) $180 per board

59. (A) $\overline{C}(n) = \dfrac{2{,}500 + 175n + 25n^2}{n}$ (B) $\overline{C}(n)$; 1,500; 0; 20 n

(C) 10 yr; $675.00 per year (D) 10 yr; $675.00 per year

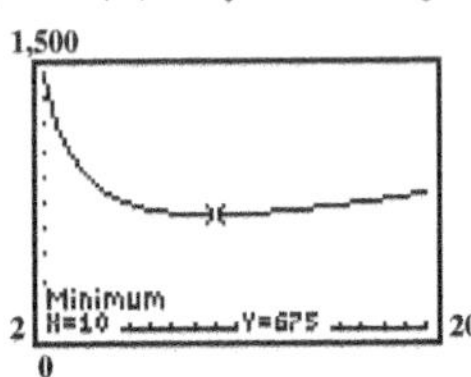

61. (A) $\overline{C}(x) = \dfrac{0.00048(x - 500)^3 + 60{,}000}{x}$

(B)

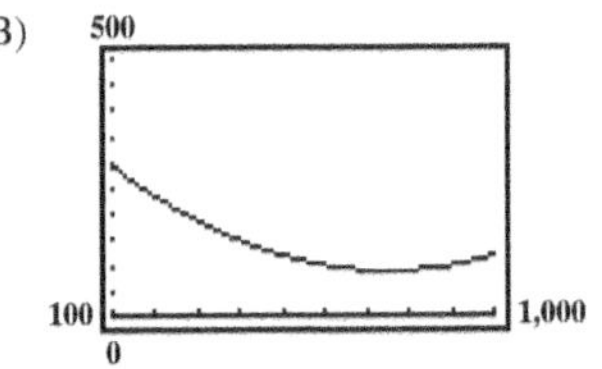

(C) 750 cases per month; $90 per case

63. (A) 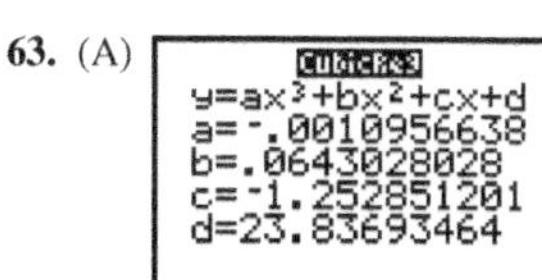

(B) 1.7 lb **65.** (A) 0.06 cm/sec

(B) 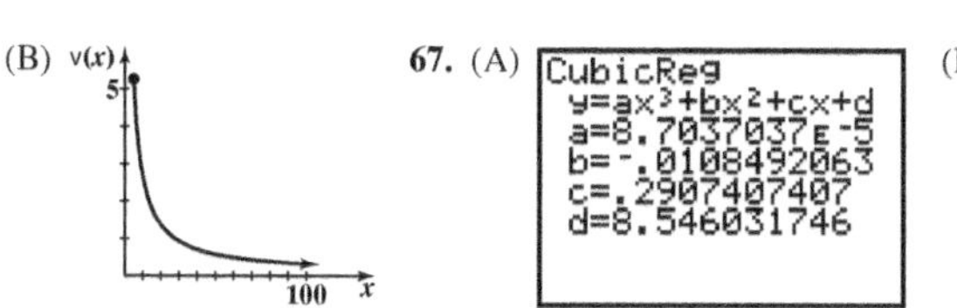

67. (A) (B) 5.5

Exercises 2.5

1. (A) k (B) g (C) h (D) f **3.**

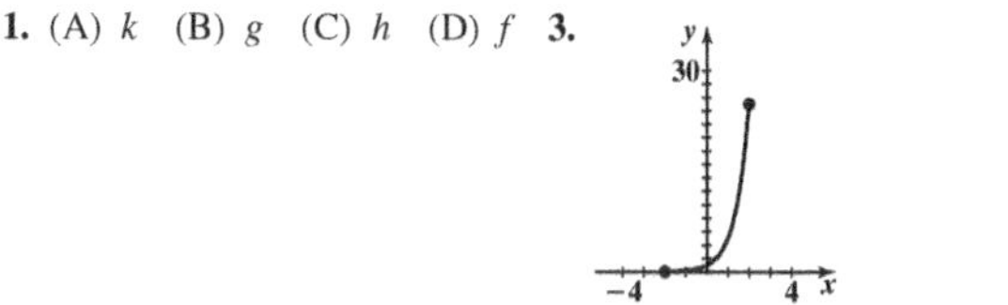

5. **7.** **9.**

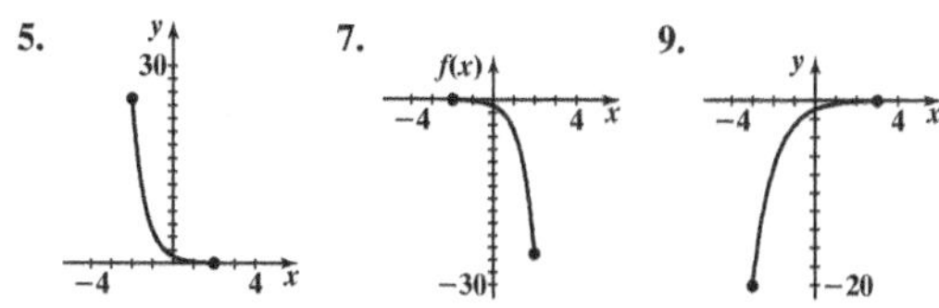

11. The graph of g is the graph of f reflected in the x axis. **13.** The graph of g is the graph of f shifted 1 unit to the left. **15.** The graph of g is the graph of f shifted 1 unit up. **17.** The graph of g is the graph of f vertically stretched by a factor of 2 and shifted to the left 2 units.

19. (A) (B) (C) (D) **21.** **23.**

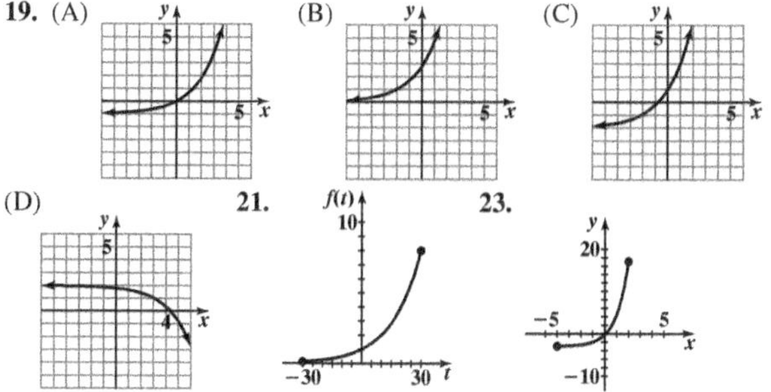

25.

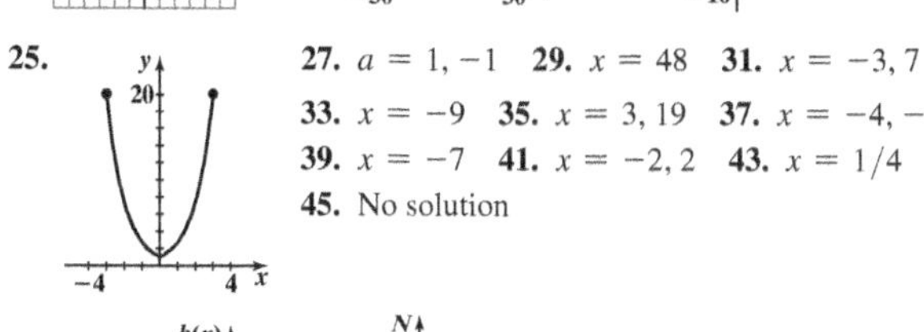

27. $a = 1, -1$ **29.** $x = 48$ **31.** $x = -3, 7$ **33.** $x = -9$ **35.** $x = 3, 19$ **37.** $x = -4, -3$ **39.** $x = -7$ **41.** $x = -2, 2$ **43.** $x = 1/4$ **45.** No solution

47. **49.**

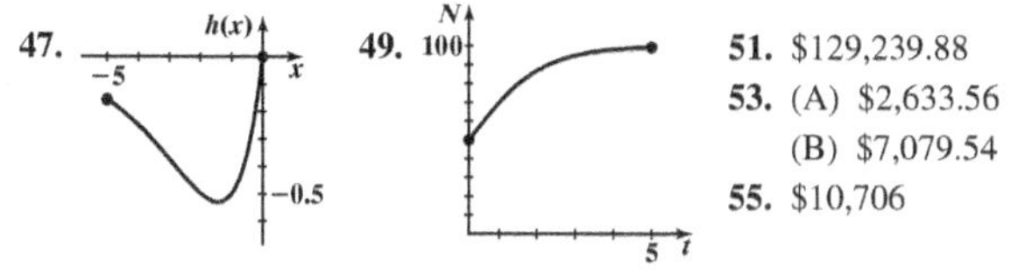

51. $129,239.88 **53.** (A) $2,633.56 (B) $7,079.54 **55.** $10,706

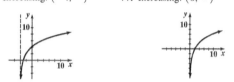

57. (A) $10,491.24 (B) $10,509.45 (C) $10,526.76 **59.** N approaches 2 as t increases without bound.

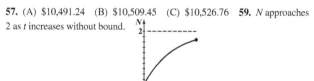

61. (A) 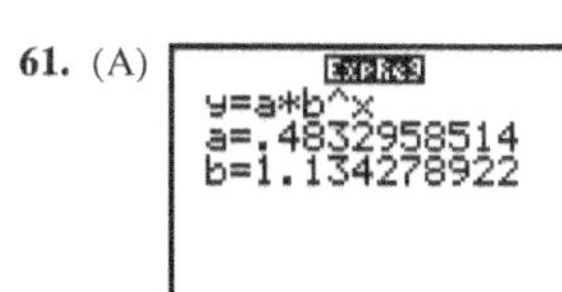

(B) 9.94 billion **63.** (A) 10% (B) 1% **65.** (A) $P = 12e^{0.0402x}$ (B) 17.9 million **67.** (A) $P = 127e^{-0.0016x}$ (B) 124 million

Exercises 2.6

1. $27 = 3^3$ **3.** $10^0 = 1$ **5.** $8 = 4^{3/2}$ **7.** $\log_7 49 = 2$ **9.** $\log_4 8 = \frac{3}{2}$ **11.** $\log_b A = u$ **13.** 6 **15.** -5 **17.** 7 **19.** -3 **21.** Not defined **23.** $\log_b P - \log_b Q$ **25.** $5 \log_b L$ **27.** q^p **29.** $x = 1/10$ **31.** $b = 4$ **33.** $y = -3$ **35.** $b = 1/3$ **37.** $x = 8$ **39.** False **41.** True **43.** True **45.** False **47.** $x = 2$ **49.** $x = 8$ **51.** $x = 7$ **53.** No solution

55.

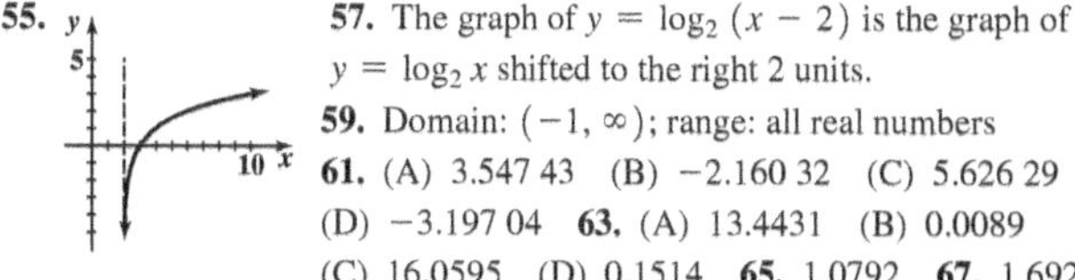

57. The graph of $y = \log_2 (x - 2)$ is the graph of $y = \log_2 x$ shifted to the right 2 units. **59.** Domain: $(-1, \infty)$; range: all real numbers **61.** (A) 3.547 43 (B) -2.160 32 (C) 5.626 29 (D) -3.197 04 **63.** (A) 13.4431 (B) 0.0089 (C) 16.0595 (D) 0.1514 **65.** 1.0792 **67.** 1.6923

69. 18.3559 **71.** Increasing: $(0, \infty)$

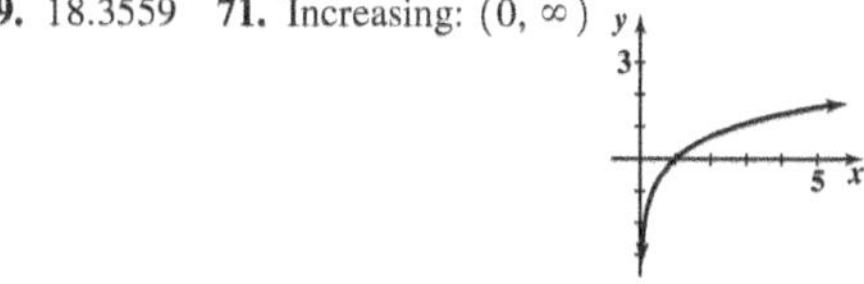

73. Decreasing: $(0, 1]$ Increasing: $[1, \infty)$

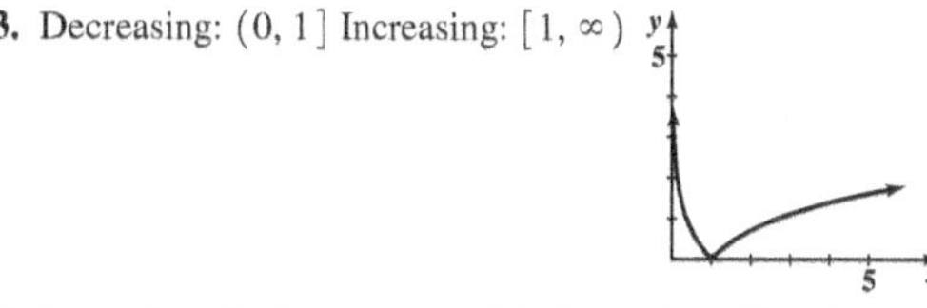

75. Increasing: $(-4, \infty)$ **77.** Increasing: $(0, \infty)$

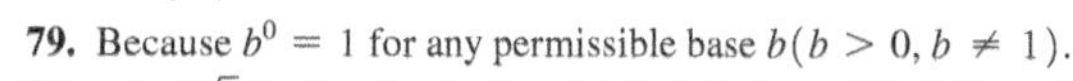

79. Because $b^0 = 1$ for any permissible base $b (b > 0, b \neq 1)$.
81. $x > \sqrt{x} > \ln x$ for $1 < x \leq 16$ **83.** 4 yr **85.** 9.87 yr; 9.80 yr
87. 7.51 yr **89.** (A) 5,373

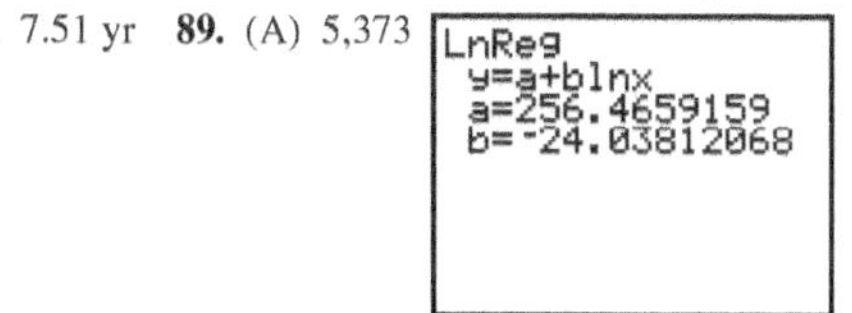

(B) 7,220

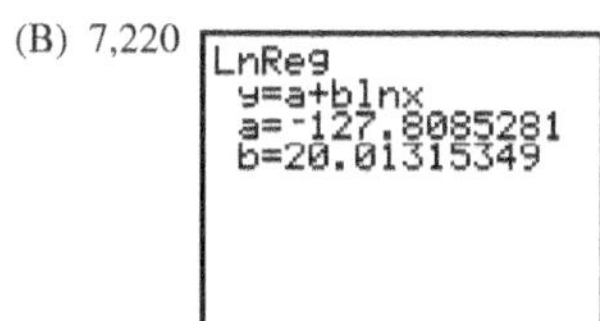

93. 168 bushels/acre

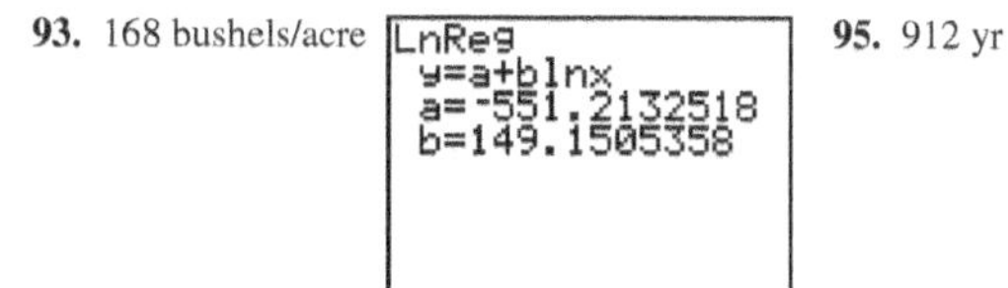

95. 912 yr

Chapter 2 Review Exercises

1. 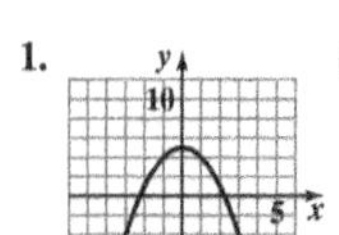

(2.1) **2.** (2.1) **3.** 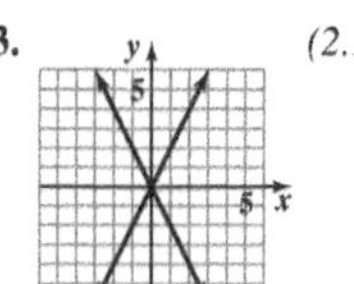

(2.1)

4. (A) Not a function (B) A function (C) A function (D) Not a function *(2.1)* **5.** (A) −1 (B) 0 (C) $-\frac{1}{3}$ (D) −3 *(2.1)*
6. $v = \ln u$ *(2.6)* **7.** $e^k = m$ *(2.6)* **8.** $x = \ln k$ *(2.6)* **9.** $z = \log m$ *(2.6)*
10. $x = 64$ *(2.6)* **11.** $z = 7$ *(2.6)* **12.** $x = 3$ *(2.6)* **13.** $x = 2.116$ *(2.6)*
14. $y = 5.298$ *(2.6)* **15.** $z = 141.254$ *(2.6)* **16.** $x = 0.318$ *(2.6)*
17. (A) $y = 4$ (B) $x = 0$ (C) $y = 1$ (D) $x = -1$ or 1 (E) $y = -2$ (F) $x = -5$ or 5 *(2.1)*

18. (A) 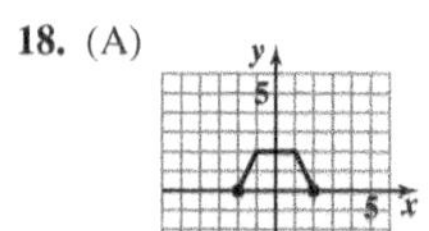

(B) 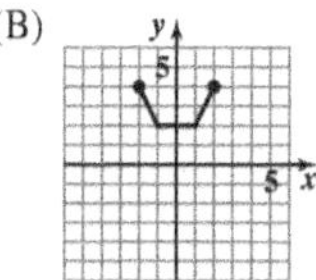

(C) 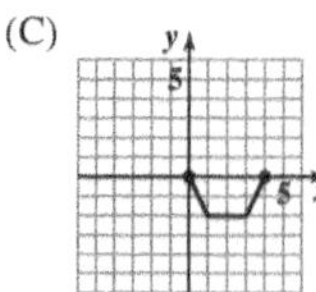

(D) 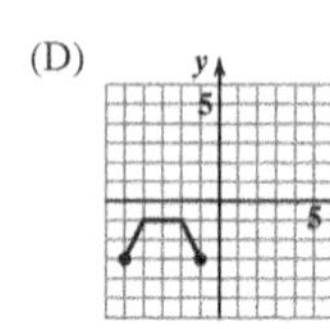

(2.2) **19.** $f(x) = -(x - 2)^2 + 4$. The graph of $f(x)$ is the graph of $y = x^2$ reflected in the x axis, then shifted right 2 units and up 4 units. *(2.2)* **20.** (A) g (B) m (C) n (D) f *(2.2, 2.3)*

21. (A) x intercepts: −4, 0; y intercept: 0 (B) Vertex: $(-2, -4)$ (C) Minimum: −4 (D) Range: $y \geq -4$ or $[-4, \infty)$ *(2.3)* **22.** Quadratic *(2.3)*
23. Linear *(2.1)* **24.** None *(2.1, 2.3)* **25.** Constant *(2.1)* **26.** $x = 8$ *(2.6)*
27. $x = 3$ *(2.6)* **28.** $x = 3$ *(2.5)* **29.** $x = -1, 3$ *(2.5)* **30.** $x = 0, \frac{1}{3}$ *(2.5)*
31. $x = -2$ *(2.6)* **32.** $x = \frac{1}{2}$ *(2.6)* **33.** $x = 27$ *(2.6)* **34.** $x = 13.3113$ *(2.6)*
35. $x = 158.7552$ *(2.6)* **36.** $x = 0.0097$ *(2.6)* **37.** $x = 1.4359$ *(2.6)*
38. $x = 1.4650$ *(2.6)* **39.** $x = 230.2609$ *(2.6)* **40.** $x = 9.0065$ *(2.6)*
41. $x = 2.1081$ *(2.6)* **42.** (A) All real numbers except $x = -2$ and 3 (B) $x < 5$ *(2.1)* **43.** Vertex form: $4\left(x + \frac{1}{2}\right)^2 - 4$; x intercepts: $-\frac{3}{2}$ and $\frac{1}{2}$; y intercept: −3; vertex: $(-\frac{1}{2}, -4)$; minimum: −4; range: $y \geq -4$ or $[-4, \infty)$ *(2.3)* **44.** (0.99, 0.69); (−0.79, −1.54) *(2.5, 2.6)*

45. 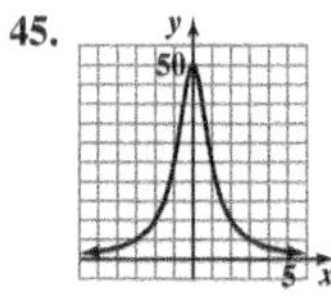

(2.1) **46.** 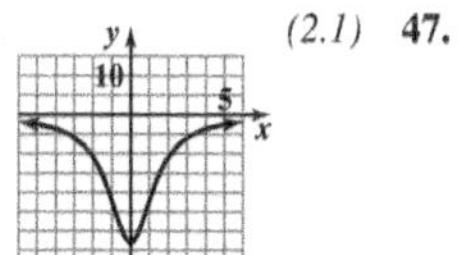

(2.1) **47.** 6 *(2.1)*

48. −19 *(2.1)* **49.** $10x - 4$ *(2.1)* **50.** $21 - 5x$ *(2.1)* **51.** (A) −1 (B) $-1 - 2h$ (C) $-2h$ (D) −2 *(2.1)* **52.** (A) −5 (B) $-5 - 3h$ (C) $-3h$ (D) −3 *(2.1)* **53.** The graph of function m is the graph of $y = |x|$ reflected in the x axis and shifted to the right 6 units. *(2.2)* **54.** The graph of function g is the graph of $y = x^3$ vertically shrunk by a factor of 0.6 and shifted up 5 units. *(2.2)* **55.** The graph of $y = x^2$ is vertically expanded by a factor of 2, reflected in the x axis, and shifted to the left 3 units. Equation: $y = -2(x + 3)^2$. *(2.2)* **56.** $f(x) = 2\sqrt{x + 3} - 1$ *(2.2)*

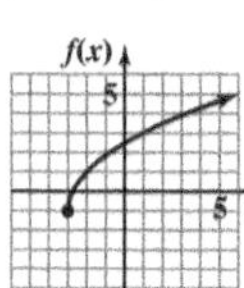

57. $y = 0$ *(2.4)* **58.** $y = \frac{3}{4}$ *(2.4)* **59.** None *(2.4)*
60. $x = -10, x = 10$ *(2.4)* **61.** $x = -2$ *(2.4)*
62. True *(2.3)* **63.** False *(2.3)* **64.** False *(2.3)*
65. True *(2.4)* **66.** True *(2.5)* **67.** True *(2.3)*

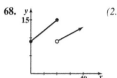

68. *(2.2)* **69.** *(2.2)*

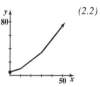

70. $y = -(x - 4)^2 + 3$ *(2.2, 2.3)* **71.** $f(x) = -0.4(x - 4)^2 + 7.6$
(A) x intercepts: −0.4, 8.4; y intercept: 1.2 (B) Vertex: (4.0, 7.6)
(C) Maximum: 7.6 (D) Range: $y \leq 7.6$ or $(-\infty, 7.6]$ *(2.3)*

72. 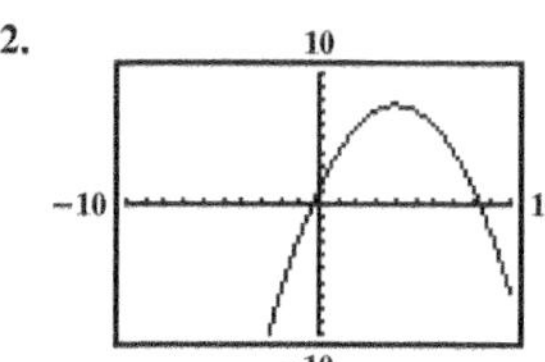

(A) x intercepts: −.4, 8.4; y intercept: 1.2 (B) Vertex: (4.0, 7.6) (C) Maximum: 7.6 (D) Range: $y \leq 7.6$ or $(-\infty, 7.6]$ *(2.3)*

73. $\log 10^\pi = \pi$ and $10^{\log\sqrt{2}} = \sqrt{2}$; $\ln e^\pi = \pi$ and $e^{\ln\sqrt{2}} = \sqrt{2}$ *(2.6)*
74. $x = 4$ *(2.6)* **75.** $x = 2$ *(2.6)* **76.** $x = \frac{6}{7}$ *(2.6)* **77.** $x = 300$ *(2.6)*
78. $y = be^{-7t}$ *(2.6)* **79.** If $\log_1 x = y$, then $1^y = x$; that is, $1 = x$ for all positive real numbers x, which is not possible. *(2.6)* **80.** The graph of $y = \sqrt[3]{x}$ is vertically expanded by a factor of 2, reflected in the x axis, and shifted 1 unit left and 1 unit down. Equation: $y = -2\sqrt[3]{x + 1} - 1$. *(2.2)*
81. $G(x) = 0.4(x + 2)^2 - 8.1$ (A) x int.: −6.527, 2.527; y int.: −6.5 (B) Vertex: $(-2, -8.1)$ (C) Min.: −8.1 (D) Range: $y \geq -8.1$ or $[-8.1, \infty)$ *(2.3)*

82. 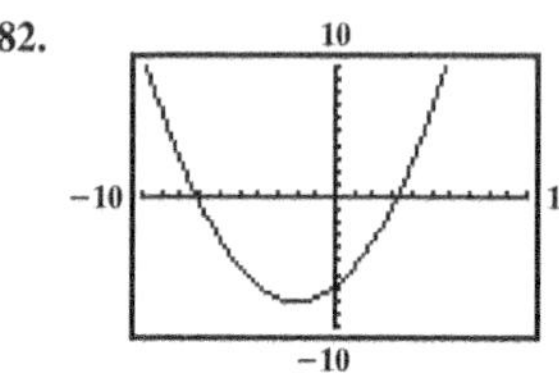

(A) x intercepts: −7.2. 3.2; y intercept: −6.9 (B) Vertex: $(-2, -8.1)$ (C) Minimum: −8.1 (D) Range: $y \geq -8.1$ or $[-8.1, \infty)$ *(2.3)*

83. (A) $S(x) = \begin{cases} 3 & \text{if } 0 \leq x \leq 20 \\ 0.057x + 1.86 & \text{if } 20 < x \leq 200 \\ 0.0346x + 6.34 & \text{if } 200 < x \leq 1{,}000 \\ 0.0217x + 19.24 & \text{if } x > 1{,}000 \end{cases}$

(B) 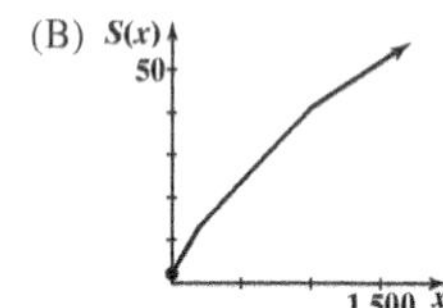

(2.2) **84.** \$5,321.95 *(2.5)*
85. \$5,269.51 *(2.5)*

86. 201 months (≈16.7 years) *(2.5)* **87.** 9.38 yr *(2.5)*

88. (A) 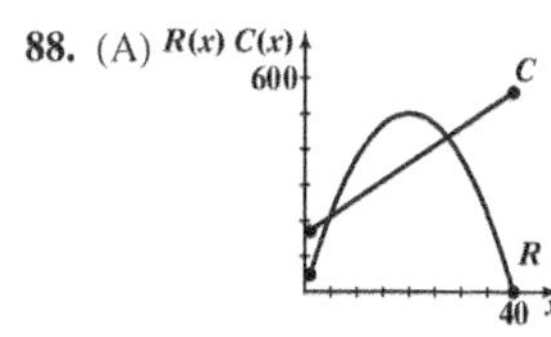

(B) $R = C$ for $x = 4.686$ thousand units (4,686 units) and for $x = 27.314$ thousand units (27,314 units); $R < C$ for $1 \leq x < 4.686$ or $27.314 < x \leq 40$; $R > C$ for $4.686 < x < 27.314$. (C) Maximum revenue is 500 thousand dollars (\$500,000). This occurs at an output of 20 thousand units (20,000 units). At this output, the wholesale price is $p(20) = \$25$. *(2.3)*

89. (A) $P(x) = R(x) - C(x) = x(50 - 1.25x) - (160 + 10x)$

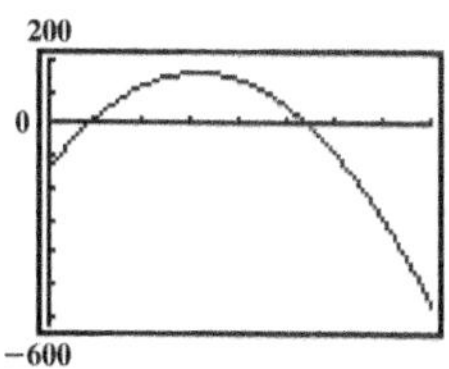

(B) $P = 0$ for $x = 4.686$ thousand units (4,686 units) and for $x = 27.314$ thousand units (27,314 units); $P < 0$ for $1 \le x < 4.686$ or $27.314 < x \le 40$; $p > 0$ for $4.686 < x < 27.314$. (C) Maximum profit is 160 thousand dollars ($160,000). This occurs at an output of 16 thousand units (16,000 units). At this output, the wholesale price is $p(16) = \$30$. *(2.3)*

90. (A) $A(x) = -\frac{3}{2}x^2 + 420x$ (B) Domain: $0 \le x \le 280$

(C)

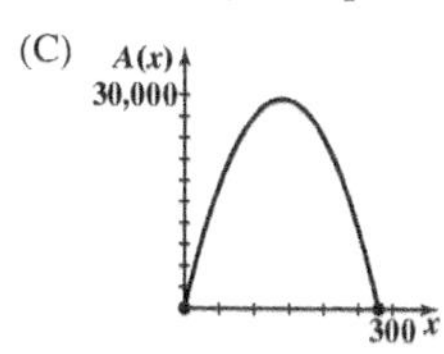

(D) There are two solutions to the equation $A(x) = 25{,}000$, one near 90 and another near 190. (E) 86 ft; 194 ft (F) Maximum combined area is 29,400 ft^2. This occurs for $x = 140$ ft and $y = 105$ ft. *(2.3)*

91. (A) 2,833 sets

QuadReg
y=ax²+bx+c
a=5.9477212E-6
b=-.1024018814
c=422.3467853

(B) 4,836

LinReg
y=ax+b
a=.0387421907
b=-7.364689544

(C) Equilibrium price: $131.59; equilibrium quantity: 3,587 cookware sets *(2.3)*

92. (A)

CubicReg
y=ax³+bx²+cx+d
a=.3039472614
b=-12.99286831
c=38.29231232
d=5604.782066

(B) 4976 *(2.4)*

93. (A) $N = 2^{2t}$ or $N = 4^t$ (B) 15 days *(2.5)* **94.** $k = 0.009\,42$; 489 ft *(2.6)*

95. (A) 6,134,000 *(2.6)*

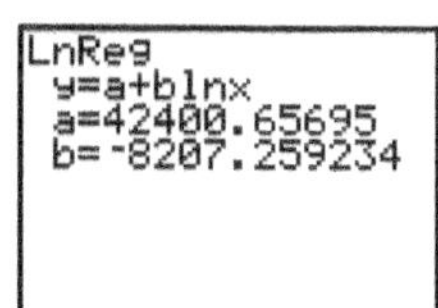

96. 23.1 yr *(2.5)* **97.** (A) $1,319 billion (B) 2031 *(2.5)*

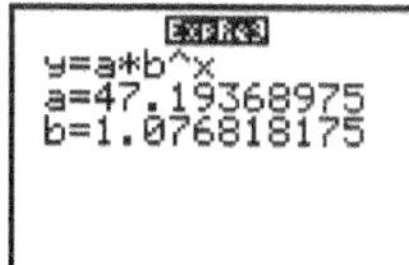

Chapter 3

Exercises 3.1

1. $25.42 **3.** 76% **5.** Slope = 120; y int. = 12,000 **7.** Slope = 50; y int. = 2,000 **9.** 0.015 **11.** 0.6% **13.** 0.004 **15.** 24.99% **17.** $\frac{1}{2}$ yr **19.** $\frac{1}{3}$ yr **21.** $\frac{5}{4}$ yr **23.** $\frac{6}{13}$ yr **25.** $42 **27.** $1,800 **29.** 0.12 or 12% **31.** $\frac{1}{2}$ yr **33.** $4,612.50 **35.** $875 **37.** 0.27 or 27% **39.** 1 yr **41.** $r = I/(Pt)$ **43.** $P = A/(1 + rt)$ **45.** $t = \frac{A - P}{Pr}$ **47.** The graphs are linear, all with y intercept $1,000; their slopes are 40, 80, and 120, respectively. **49.** $45 **51.** $30 **53.** $7,647.20 **55.** 8.1% **57.** 18% **59.** $1,604.40; 20.88% **61.** 4.298% **63.** $992.38 **65.** $24.31 **67.** $27 **69.** 5.396% **71.** 6.986% **73.** 12.085% **75.** 109.895% **77.** 87.158% **79.** $118.94 **81.** $1,445.89 **83.** $7.27 **85.** $824.85 **87.** 292% **89.** 60%

Exercises 3.2

1. $P = 950$ **3.** $x = 17$ **5.** $i = 0.5$ **7.** $n = 4$ **9.** $5,983.40 **11.** $4,245.07 **13.** $3,125.79 **15.** $1,733.04 **17.** 2.5 yr **19.** 6.79% **21.** 1.65% **23.** 0.85% **25.** 0.02% **27.** 2.43% **29.** 3.46% **31.** 6.36% **33.** 8.76% **35.** 2.19% **37.** (A) $126.25; $26.25 (B) $126.90; $26.90 (C) $127.05; $27.05 **39.** (A) $5,524.71 (B) $6,104.48 **41.** $12,175.69 **43.** All three graphs are increasing, curve upward, and have the same y intercept; the greater the interest rate, the greater the increase. The amounts at the end of 8 years are $1,376.40, $1,892.46, and $2,599.27, respectively.

45.

Period	Interest	Amount
0		$1,000.00
1	$97.50	$1,097.50
2	$107.01	$1,204.51
3	$117.44	$1,321.95
4	$128.89	$1,450.84
5	$141.46	$1,592.29
6	$155.25	$1,747.54

47. (A) $7,440.94 (B) $5,536.76 **49.** (A) $19,084.49 (B) $11,121.45 **51.** (A) 3.97% (B) 2.32% **53.** (A) 5.28% (B) 5.27% **55.** $11\frac{2}{3}$ yr **57.** 6 yr **59.** $n \approx 12$ **61.** (A) $7\frac{1}{4}$ yr (B) 6 yr **63.** (A) 23.1 yr (B) 11.6 yr **65.** $65,068.44 **67.** $282,222.44 **69.** $19.78 per ft^2 per mo **71.** (A) In 2026, 250 years after the signing, it would be worth $175,814.55. (B) If interest were compounded monthly, daily, or continuously, it would be worth $179,119.92, $180,748.53, or $180,804.24, respectively.

(C)

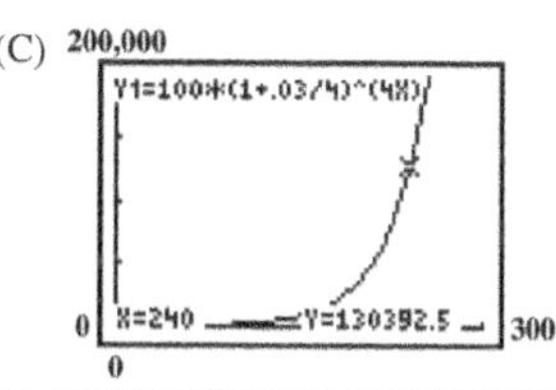

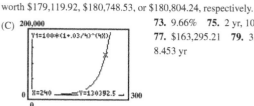

73. 9.66% **75.** 2 yr, 10 mo **77.** $163,295.21 **79.** 3,615 days; 8.453 yr

81.

Years	Exact Rate	Rule of 72
6	12.2	12.0
7	10.4	10.3
8	9.1	9.0
9	8.0	8.0
10	7.2	7.2
11	6.5	6.5
12	5.9	6.0

83. 14 quarters **85.** To maximize earnings, choose 10% simple interest for investments lasting fewer than 11 years and 7% compound interest otherwise. **87.** 3.33% **89.** 7.02% **91.** $15,843.80 **93.** 4.53% **95.** 13.44% **97.** 17.62%

Exercises 3.3

1. 1,023 **3.** 3,000 **5.** 71,744,530 **7.** $i = 0.02$; $n = 80$ **9.** $i = 0.0375$; $n = 24$ **11.** $i = 0.0065$; $n = 84$ **13.** $i = 0.0625$; $n = 15$ **15.** $FV = \$13{,}435.19$ **17.** $PMT = \$310.62$ **19.** $n = 17$ **21.** $i = 0.09$ **25.** $n = \dfrac{\ln\left(1 + i\dfrac{FV}{PMT}\right)}{\ln(1 + i)}$ **27.** Value: $84,895.40; interest: $24,895.40 **29.** $20,931.01 **31.** $176.25 **33.** $763.39

35.

Period	Amount	Interest	Balance
1	$1,000.00	$0.00	$1,000.00
2	$1,000.00	$83.20	$2,083.20
3	$1,000.00	$173.32	$3,256.52
4	$1,000.00	$270.94	$4,527.46
5	$1,000.00	$376.69	$5,904.15

37. First year: $33.56; second year: $109.64; third year: $190.41 **39.** $111,050.77 **41.** $1,308.75 **43.** (A) 1.650% (B) $528.89 **45.** 33 months **47.** 7.77% **49.** 0.75% **51.** After 11 quarterly

Exercises 3.4

1. 511/256 **3.** 33,333,333/1,000,000 **5.** 547/729 **7.** $i = 0.0045; n = 84$ **9.** $i = 0.02475; n = 40$ **11.** $i = 0.03375; n = 50$ **13.** $i = 0.0548; n = 9$ **15.** $PV = \$3,458.41$ **17.** $PMT = \$586.01$ **19.** $n = 29$ **21.** $i = 0.029$ **27.** $60,304.25 **29.** $11,241.81; $1,358.19 **31.** $69.58; $839.84 **33.** 31 months **35.** 71 months **37.** For 0% financing, the monthly payments should be $242.85, not $299. If a loan of $17,485 is amortized in 72 payments of $299, the rate is 7.11% compounded monthly. **39.** The monthly payments with 0% financing are $455. If you take the rebate, the monthly payments are $434.24. You should choose the rebate. **41.** $314.72; $17,319.68

43.

Payment Number	Payment	Interest	Unpaid Balance Reduction	Unpaid Balance
0				$5,000.00
1	$706.29	$140.00	$566.29	4,433.71
2	706.29	124.14	582.15	3,851.56
3	706.29	107.84	598.45	3,253.11
4	706.29	91.09	615.20	2,637.91
5	706.29	73.86	632.43	2,005.48
6	706.29	56.15	650.14	1,355.34
7	706.29	37.95	668.34	687.00
8	706.24	19.24	687.00	0.00
Totals	$5,650.27	$650.27	$5,000.00	

45. First year: $466.05; second year: $294.93; third year: $107.82 **47.** £15,668.64; £1,083.36 **49.** $143.85/mo; $904.80 **51.** Monthly payment: $908.99 (A) $125,862 (B) $81,507 (C) $46,905 **53.** (A) Monthly payment: $1,015.68; interest: $114,763 (B) 197 months; interest saved: $23,499 **55.** (A) 157 (B) 243 (C) The withdrawals continue forever. **57.** (A) Monthly withdrawals: $1,229.66; total interest: $185,338.80 (B) Monthly deposits: $162.65 **59.** $65,584 **61.** $34,692 **63.** All three graphs are decreasing, curve downward, and have the same x intercept; the unpaid balances are always in the ratio 2:3:4. The monthly payments are $402.31, $603.47, and $804.62, with total interest amounting to $94,831.60, $142,249.20, and $189,663.20, respectively. **65.** 14.45% **67.** 10.21%

Chapter 3 Review Exercises

1. $A = \$212$ *(3.1)* **2.** $P = \$869.57$ *(3.1)* **3.** $t = 3.543$ yr, or 43 mo *(3.1)* **4.** $r = 5\%$ *(3.1)* **5.** $A = \$1,578.12$ *(3.2)* **6.** $P = \$4,140.73$ *(3.2)* **7.** $A = \$6,064.18$ *(3.2)* **8.** $P = \$25,601.80$ *(3.2)* **9.** $PMT = \$117.95$ *(3.3)* **10.** $FV = \$99,897.40$ *(3.3)* **11.** $PV = \$39,536.26$ *(3.4)* **12.** $PMT = \$594.08$ *(3.4)* **13.** $n \approx 16$ *(3.2)* **14.** $n \approx 41$ *(3.3)* **15.** $4,570.00; $570.00 *(3.1)* **16.** $19,654 *(3.2)* **17.** $12,944.67 *(3.2)*

18. (A)

Period	Interest	Amount
0		$400.00
1	$21.60	$421.60
2	$22.77	$444.37
3	$24.00	$468.36
4	$25.29	$493.65

(3.2)

(B)

Period	Interest	Payment	Balance
1		$100.00	$100.00
2	$5.40	$100.00	$205.40
3	$11.09	$100.00	$316.49
4	$17.09	$100.00	$433.58

(3.3)

19. To maximize earnings, choose 13% simple interest for investments lasting less than 9 years and 9% compound interest for investments lasting 9 years or more. *(3.2)* **20.** $164,402 *(3.2)* **21.** 7.83% *(3.2)* **22.** 9% compounded quarterly, since its effective rate is 9.31%, while the effective rate of 9.25% compounded annually is 9.25% *(3.2)* **23.** $25,861.65; $6,661.65 *(3.3)* **24.** 288% *(3.1)* **25.** $1,725.56 *(3.1)* **26.** $29,354 *(3.2)* **27.** $18,021 *(3.2)* **28.** 15% *(3.1)* **29.** The monthly payments with 0% financing are $450. If you take the rebate, the monthly payments are $426.66. You should choose the rebate. *(3.4)* **30.** (A) 6.43% (B) 6.45% *(3.2)* **31.** 9 quarters or 2 yr, 3 mo *(3.2)* **32.** 139 mo; 93 mo *(3.2)* **33.** (A) $571,499 (B) $1,973,277 *(3.3)* **34.** 10.45% *(3.2)* **35.** (A) 174% (B) 65.71% *(3.1)* **36.** $725.89 *(3.3)* **37.** (A) $140,945.57 (B) $789.65 (C) $136,828 *(3.3, 3.4)* **38.** $102.99; $943.52 *(3.4)* **39.** $576.48 *(3.3)* **40.** 3,374 days; 10 yr *(3.2)* **41.** $175.28; $2,516.80 *(3.4)* **42.** $13,418.78 *(3.2)* **43.** 5 yr, 10 mo *(3.3)* **44.** 18 yr *(3.4)* **45.** 28.8% *(3.1)*

46.

Payment Number	Payment	Interest	Unpaid Balance Reduction	Unpaid Balance
0				$1,000.00
1	$265.82	$25.00	$240.82	759.18
2	265.82	18.98	246.84	512.34
3	265.82	12.81	253.01	259.33
4	265.81	6.48	259.33	0.00
Totals	$1,063.27	$63.27	$1,000.00	

47. 28 months *(3.3)* **48.** $55,347.48; $185,830.24 *(3.3)* **49.** 2.47% *(3.2)* **50.** 6.33% *(3.1)* **51.** 44 deposits *(3.3)* **52.** (A) $1,189.52 (B) $72,963.07 (C) $7,237.31 *(3.4)* **53.** The certificate would be worth $53,394.30 when the 360th payment is made. By reducing the principal, the loan would be paid off in 252 months. If the monthly payment were then invested at 7% compounded monthly, it would be worth $67,234.20 at the time of the 360th payment. *(3.2, 3.3, 3.4)* **54.** The lower rate would save $12,247.20 in interest payments. *(3.4)* **55.** $3,807.59 *(3.2)* **56.** 5.79% *(3.2)* **57.** $4,844.96 *(3.1)* **58.** $6,697.11 *(3.4)* **59.** 7.24% *(3.2)* **60.** (A) $398,807 (B) $374,204 *(3.3)* **61.** $15,577.64 *(3.2)* **62.** (A) 30 yr: $569.26; 15 yr: $749.82 (B) 30 yr: $69,707.99; 15 yr: $37,260.74 *(3.4)* **63.** $20,516 *(3.4)* **64.** 33.52% *(3.4)* **65.** (A) 10.74% (B) 15 yr: 40 yr *(3.3)*

Chapter 4

Exercises 4.1

1. $(0, 7)$ **3.** $(24, 0)$ **5.** $(5, -18)$ **7.** $y - 7 = -6(x - 2)$ **9.** (B); no solution **11.** (A); $x = -3, y = 1$ **13.** $x = 2, y = 4$ **15.** No solution (parallel lines) **17.** $x = 4, y = 5$ **19.** $x = 1, y = 4$ **21.** $u = 2, v = -3$ **23.** $m = 8, n = 6$ **25.** $x = 1, y = 1$ **27.** No solution (inconsistent) **29.** Infinitely many solutions (dependent) **31.** $m = \frac{1}{2}, n = \frac{11}{10}$ **33.** $x = -1, y = 2$ **35.** $x = 7, y = 3$ **37.** $x = \frac{7}{6}, y = -\frac{8}{9}$ **39.** $x = 0, y = 0$ **41.** $x = 14, y = 5$ **43.** Price tends to come down. **49.** $(1.125, 0.125)$ **51.** No solution (parallel lines) **53.** $(4.176, -1.235)$ **55.** $(-3.310, -2.241)$

57. **59.**

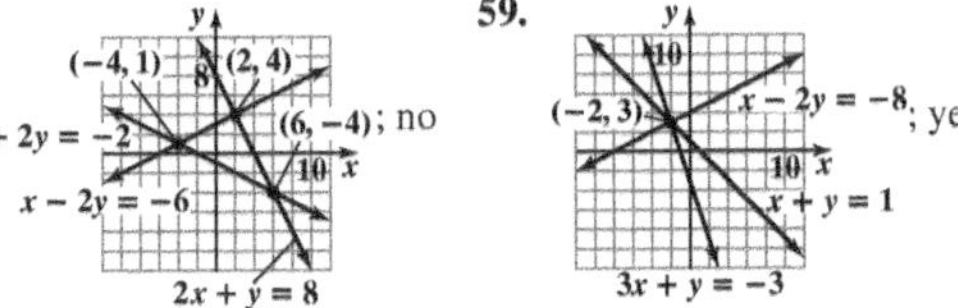

61.

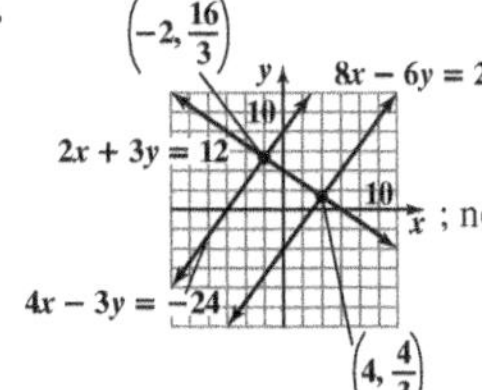

63. (A) $(20, -24)$ (B) $(-4, 6)$ (C) No solution **65.** (A) Supply: 143 T-shirts; demand: 647 T-shirts (B) Supply: 857 T-shirts; demand: 353 T-shirts (C) Equilibrium price $= \$6.50$; equilibrium quantity $= 500$ T-shirts

(D)

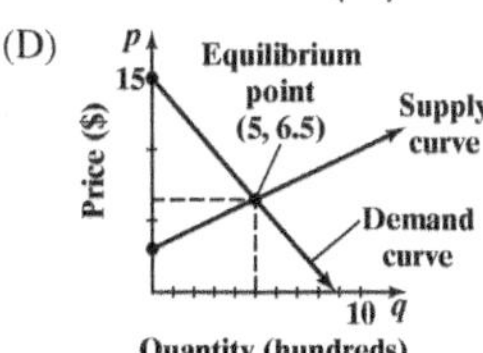

67. (A) $p = 1.5x + 1.95$ (B) $p = -1.5x + 7.8$ (C) Equilibrium price: \$4.875; equilibrium quantity: 1.95 billion bushels

(D)

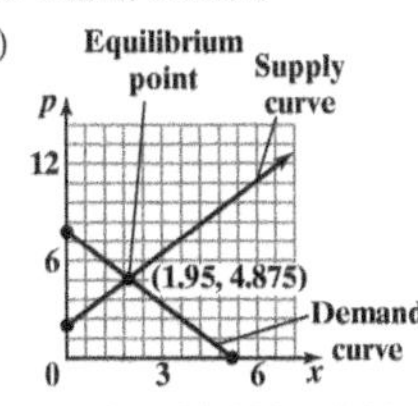

69. (A) 120 mowers

(B)

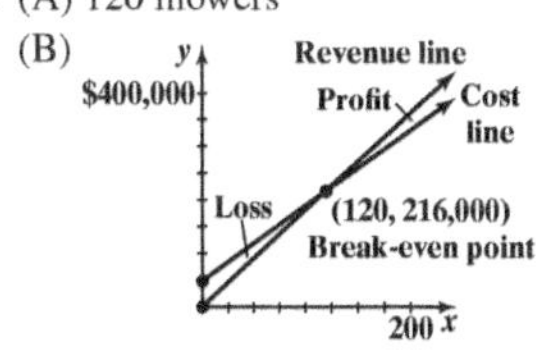

71. (A) $C = 24{,}000 + 7.45x$; $R = 19.95x$ (B) 1,920

(C)

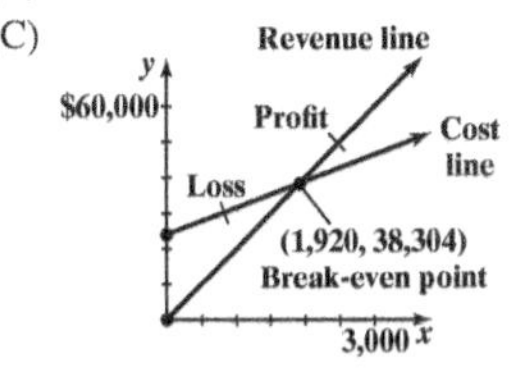

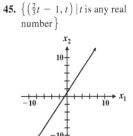

73. Base price $=$ €10.56; surcharge $=$ €1.56/kg **75.** 5,720 lb robust blend; 6,160 lb mild blend **77.** Mix *A*: 80 g; mix *B*: 60 g **79.** Operate the Mexico plant for 75 hours and the Taiwan plant for 50 hours. **81.** (A) $a = 196$, $b = -16$ (B) 196 ft (C) 3.5 sec **83.** 40 sec, 24 sec, 120 mi

85. (A)

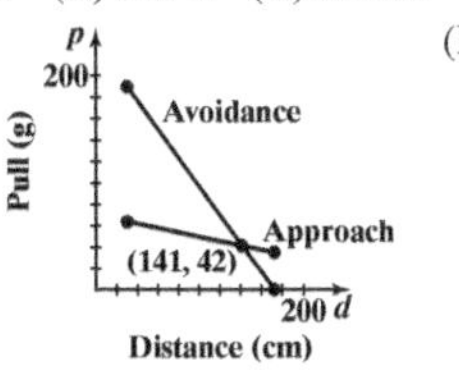

(B) $d = 141$ cm (approx.) (C) Vacillate

Exercises 4.2

1. 6; 3 **3.** 3×3; 2×1 **5.** *D* **7.** *B* **9.** 2, 1 **11.** $-4, 9, 0$ **13.** -1

15. $\begin{bmatrix} 3 & 5 \\ 2 & -4 \end{bmatrix}$; $\left[\begin{array}{cc|c} 3 & 5 & 8 \\ 2 & -4 & -7 \end{array}\right]$ **17.** $\begin{bmatrix} 1 & 4 \\ 6 & 0 \end{bmatrix}$; $\left[\begin{array}{cc|c} 1 & 4 & 15 \\ 6 & 0 & 18 \end{array}\right]$

19. $\begin{aligned} 2x_1 + 5x_2 &= 7 \\ x_1 + 4x_2 &= 9 \end{aligned}$ **21.** $\begin{aligned} 4x_1 &= -10 \\ 8x_2 &= 40 \end{aligned}$

23. $\left[\begin{array}{cc|c} 1 & -3 & 5 \\ 2 & -4 & 6 \end{array}\right]$ **25.** $\left[\begin{array}{cc|c} 2 & -4 & 6 \\ 2 & -6 & 10 \end{array}\right]$ **27.** $\left[\begin{array}{cc|c} 3 & -7 & 11 \\ 1 & -3 & 5 \end{array}\right]$

29. $\left[\begin{array}{cc|c} -1 & 2 & -3 \\ 1 & -3 & 5 \end{array}\right]$ **31.** $\left[\begin{array}{cc|c} 1 & -1 & 1 \\ 1 & -3 & 5 \end{array}\right]$ **33.** $\left[\begin{array}{cc|c} -1 & 5 & -9 \\ 1 & -3 & 5 \end{array}\right]$

35. $\frac{1}{3}R_2 \to R_2$ **37.** $6R_1 + R_2 \to R_2$ **39.** $\frac{1}{3}R_2 + R_1 \to R_1$ **41.** $R_1 \leftrightarrow R_2$

43. $\{(6, 6)\}$

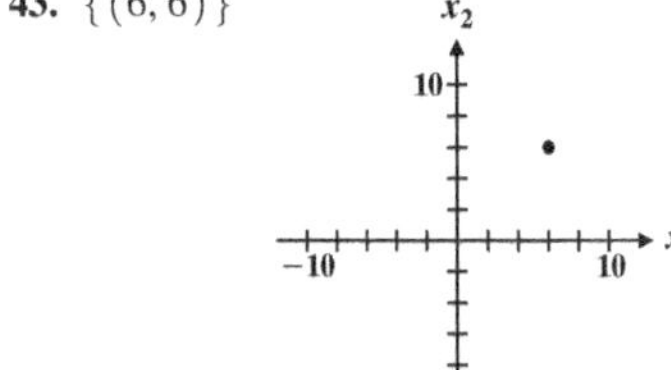

45. $\{(\frac{2}{3}t - 1, t) \mid t$ is any real number$\}$

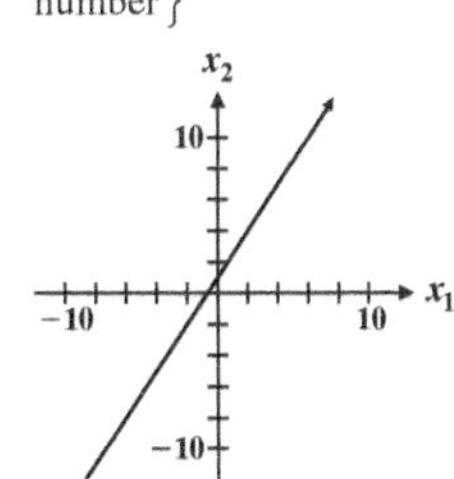

47. $x_1 = 3$, $x_2 = 2$; each pair of lines has the same intersection point.

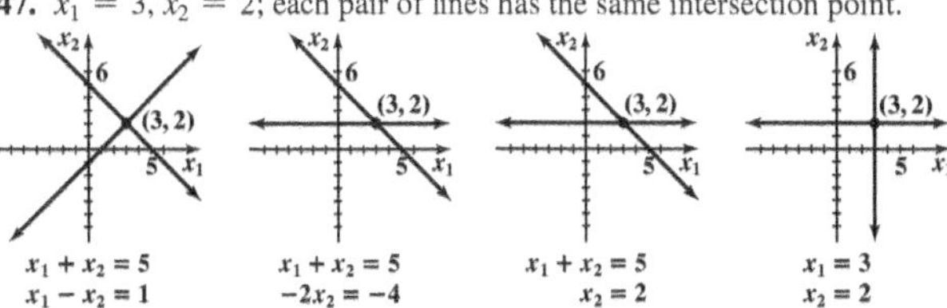

(3, 2)
$x_1 + x_2 = 5$
$x_1 - x_2 = 1$
(3, 2)
$x_1 + x_2 = 5$
$-2x_2 = -4$
(3, 2)
$x_1 + x_2 = 5$
$x_2 = 2$
(3, 2)
$x_1 = 3$
$x_2 = 2$

49. $x_1 = -4$, $x_2 = 6$ **51.** No solution **53.** $x_1 = 2t + 15$, $x_2 = t$ for any real number t **55.** $x_1 = 3$, $x_2 = 1$ **57.** $x_1 = 3$, $x_2 = -2$ **59.** $x_1 = 2$, $x_2 = 4$ **61.** No solution **63.** $x_1 = 1$, $x_2 = 4$ **65.** Infinitely many solutions: $x_2 = s$, $x_1 = 2s - 3$ for any real number s **67.** Infinitely many solutions; $x_2 = s$, $x_1 = \frac{1}{2}s + \frac{1}{2}$ for any real number s **69.** $x_1 = -1$, $x_2 = 3$ **71.** No solution **73.** Infinitely many solutions: $x_2 = t$, $x_1 = \frac{4}{3}t + 3$ for any real number t **75.** $x_1 = 2$, $x_2 = -1$ **77.** $x_1 = 2$, $x_2 = -1$ **79.** $x_1 = 1.1$, $x_2 = 0.3$ **81.** $x_1 = -23.125$, $x_2 = 7.8125$ **83.** $x_1 = 3.225$, $x_2 = -6.9375$

Exercises 4.3

1. $\left[\begin{array}{cc|c} 1 & 2 & 3 \;\; 12 \end{array}\right]$ → $\left[\begin{array}{ccc} 1 & 2 & 3 \\ 1 & 7 & -5 \end{array}\right.\left|\begin{array}{c} 12 \\ 15 \end{array}\right]$ **3.** $\left[\begin{array}{ccc|c} 1 & 0 & 6 & 2 \\ 0 & 1 & -1 & 5 \\ 1 & 3 & 0 & 7 \end{array}\right]$ **5.** $\begin{aligned} x_1 - 3x_2 &= 4 \\ 3x_1 + 2x_2 &= 5 \\ -x_1 + 6x_2 &= 3 \end{aligned}$

7. $5x_1 - 2x_2 + 8x_4 = 4$ **9.** Reduced form **11.** Not reduced form; $R_1 \leftrightarrow R_2$ **13.** Not reduced form; $\frac{1}{4}R_1 \to R_1$ **15.** Not reduced form; $-7R_2 + R_3 \to R_3$ **17.** Not reduced form; $-\frac{1}{2}R_2 \to R_2$ **19.** $x_1 = -2$, $x_2 = 3$, $x_3 = 0$ **21.** $x_1 = 2t + 3$, $x_2 = -t - 5$, $x_3 = t$ for any real number t **23.** No solution **25.** $x_1 = 3t + 5$, $x_2 = -2t - 7$, $x_3 = t$ for any real number t **27.** $x_1 = 2s + 3t - 5$, $x_2 = s$, $x_3 = -3t + 2$, $x_4 = t$ for any real numbers s and t **29.** 19 **31.** 21, 25, 27 **33.** False **35.** True **37.** False

39. $\left[\begin{array}{cc|c} 1 & 0 & -7 \\ 0 & 1 & 3 \end{array}\right]$ **41.** $\left[\begin{array}{ccc|c} 1 & 0 & -1 & 23 \\ 0 & 1 & 2 & -7 \end{array}\right]$ **43.** $\left[\begin{array}{ccc|c} 1 & 0 & 0 & -5 \\ 0 & 1 & 0 & 4 \\ 0 & 0 & 1 & -2 \end{array}\right]$

45. $\left[\begin{array}{ccc|c} 1 & 0 & 2 & 1 \\ 0 & 1 & -2 & -1 \\ 0 & 0 & 0 & 0 \end{array}\right]$ **47.** $x_1 = -2$, $x_2 = 3$, $x_3 = 1$ **49.** $x_1 = 0$, $x_2 = -2$, $x_3 = 2$ **51.** $x_1 = 2t + 3$, $x_2 = t - 2$, $x_3 = t$ for any real number t **53.** $x_1 = 1$, $x_2 = 2$

55. No solution **57.** $x_1 = t - 1$, $x_2 = 2t + 2$, $x_3 = t$ for any real number t **59.** $x_1 = -2s + t + 1$, $x_2 = s$, $x_3 = t$ for any real numbers s and t **61.** No solution **63.** (A) Dependent system with two parameters and an infinite number of solutions (B) Dependent system with one parameter and an infinite number of solutions (C) Independent system with a unique solution (D) Impossible **65.** $x_1 = 2s - 3t + 3$, $x_2 = s + 2t + 2$, $x_3 = s$, $x_4 = t$ for s and t any real numbers **67.** $x_1 = -0.5$, $x_2 = 0.2$, $x_3 = 0.3$, $x_4 = -0.4$ **69.** $x_1 = 2s - 1.5t + 1$, $x_2 = s$, $x_3 = -t + 1.5$, $x_4 = 0.5t - 0.5$, $x_5 = t$ for any real numbers s and t **71.** $a = 2$, $b = -4$, $c = -7$

73. (A) $x_1 =$ no. of one-person boats
$x_2 =$ no. of two-person boats
$x_3 =$ no. of four-person boats

$$\begin{aligned} 0.5x_1 + \quad x_2 + 1.5x_3 &= 380 \\ 0.6x_1 + 0.9x_2 + 1.2x_3 &= 330 \\ 0.2x_1 + 0.3x_2 + 0.5x_3 &= 120 \end{aligned}$$

20 one-person boats, 220 two-person boats, and 100 four-person boats

(B) $\begin{aligned} 0.5x_1 + \quad x_2 + 1.5x_3 &= 380 \\ 0.6x_1 + 0.9x_2 + 1.2x_3 &= 330 \end{aligned}$
$(t - 80)$ one-person boats, $(420 - 2t)$ two-person boats, and t four-person boats, where t is an integer satisfying $80 \le t \le 210$

(C) $\begin{aligned} 0.5x_1 + \quad x_2 &= 380 \\ 0.6x_1 + 0.9x_2 &= 330 \\ 0.2x_1 + 0.3x_2 &= 120 \end{aligned}$

There is no production schedule that will use all the labor-hours in all departments.

75. $x_1 =$ no. of 8,000-gal tank cars
$x_2 =$ no. of 16,000-gal tank cars
$x_3 =$ no. of 24,000-gal tank cars

$$\begin{aligned} x_1 + x_2 + x_3 &= 24 \\ 8{,}000x_1 + 16{,}000x_2 + 24{,}000x_3 &= 520{,}000 \end{aligned}$$

$(t - 17)$ 8,000-gal tank cars, $(41 - 2t)$ 16,000-gal tank cars, and t 24,000-gal tank cars, where $t = 17, 18, 19$, or 20

77. The minimum monthly cost is \$24,100 when 716,000-gallon and 17 24,000-gallon tank cars are leased.

79. x_1 = federal income tax
x_2 = state income tax
x_3 = local income tax

$$\begin{aligned} x_1 + 0.5x_2 + 0.5x_3 &= 3{,}825{,}000 \\ 0.2x_1 + x_2 + 0.2x_3 &= 1{,}530{,}000 \\ 0.1x_1 + 0.1x_2 + x_3 &= 765{,}000 \end{aligned}$$

Tax liability is 57.65%.

81. x_1 = taxable income of company *A*
x_2 = taxable income of company *B*
x_3 = taxable income of company *C*
x_4 = taxable income of company *D*

$$\begin{aligned} x_1 - 0.08x_2 - 0.03x_3 - 0.07x_4 &= 2.272 \\ -0.12x_1 + x_2 - 0.11x_3 - 0.13x_4 &= 2.106 \\ -0.11x_1 - 0.09x_2 + x_3 - 0.08x_4 &= 2.736 \\ -0.06x_1 - 0.02x_2 - 0.14x_3 + x_4 &= 3.168 \end{aligned}$$

Taxable incomes are $2,927,000 for company *A*, $3,372,000 for company *B*, $3,675,000 for company *C*, and $3,926,000 for company *D*.

83. (A) x_1 = no. of ounces of food *A*
x_2 = no. of ounces of food *B*
x_3 = no. of ounces of food *C*

$$\begin{aligned} 30x_1 + 10x_2 + 20x_3 &= 340 \\ 10x_1 + 10x_2 + 20x_3 &= 180 \\ 10x_1 + 30x_2 + 20x_3 &= 220 \end{aligned}$$

8 oz of food *A*, 2 oz of food *B*, and 4 oz of food *C*

(B) $30x_1 + 10x_2 = 340$
$10x_1 + 10x_2 = 180$
$10x_1 + 30x_2 = 220$
There is no combination that will meet all the requirements.

(C) $30x_1 + 10x_2 + 20x_3 = 340$
$10x_1 + 10x_2 + 20x_3 = 180$
8 oz of food *A*, $(10 - 2t)$ oz of food *B*, and t oz of food *C* where $0 \le t \le 5$

85. x_1 = no. of barrels of mix *A*
x_2 = no. of barrels of mix *B*
x_3 = no. of barrels of mix *C*
x_4 = no. of barrels of mix *D*

$$\begin{aligned} 30x_1 + 30x_2 + 30x_3 + 60x_4 &= 900 \\ 50x_1 + 75x_2 + 25x_3 + 25x_4 &= 750 \\ 30x_1 + 20x_2 + 20x_3 + 50x_4 &= 700 \end{aligned}$$

$(10 - t)$ barrels of mix *A*, $(t - 5)$ barrels of mix *B*, $(25 - 2t)$ barrels of mix *C*, and t barrels of mix *D*, where t is an integer satisfying $5 \le t \le 10$

87. 0 barrels of mix *A*, 5 barrels of mix *B*, 5 barrels of mix *C*, and 10 barrels of mix *D*

89. $y = 0.0025x^2 + 0.2x + 34{,}55$ million **91.** $y = 0.004x^2 + 0.06x + 77.6$; 1995–2000: 79.4 years; 2000–2005: 80.4 years

93.

90
0 25
70

95. x_1 = no. of hours for company *A*
x_2 = no. of hours for company *B*
$30x_1 + 20x_2 = 600$
$10x_1 + 20x_2 = 400$
Company *A*: 10 hr; company *B*: 15 hr

97. (A) Old Street and Baker Street: $x_1 + x_4 = 1{,}200$; Bridge Street and Baker Street: $x_1 + x_2 = 1{,}000$; Bridge Street and Market Street: $x_2 + x_3 = 900$; Old Street and Market Street: $x_3 + x_4 = 1{,}100$
(B) $x_1 = 1{,}200 - t$, $x_2 = t - 200$, $x_3 = 1{,}100 - t$, and $x_4 = t$, where $200 \le t \le 1{,}100$
(C) 1,100; 200 (D) Baker Street: 600; Bridge St.: 400; Market Street: 500

Exercises 4.4

1. $\begin{bmatrix} 4 & 15 \end{bmatrix}$ **3.** $\begin{bmatrix} 2 & 4 \\ -2 & 6 \end{bmatrix}$ **5.** Not defined **7.** $\begin{bmatrix} 21 & -35 & 63 & 28 \end{bmatrix}$

9. $\begin{bmatrix} 5 \\ -3 \end{bmatrix}$ **11.** $\begin{bmatrix} 2 & 4 \\ 1 & -5 \end{bmatrix}$ **13.** $\begin{bmatrix} 1 & -5 \\ -2 & -4 \end{bmatrix}$ **15.** $\begin{bmatrix} 5 & 10 \\ 15 & 20 \end{bmatrix}$ **17.** $\begin{bmatrix} 5 & 10 \\ 15 & 20 \end{bmatrix}$

19. $\begin{bmatrix} 7 & 9 \\ 0 & 0 \end{bmatrix}$ **21.** $\begin{bmatrix} 0 & 3 \\ 0 & 7 \end{bmatrix}$ **23.** $\begin{bmatrix} -23 \end{bmatrix}$ **25.** $\begin{bmatrix} -15 & 10 \\ 12 & -8 \end{bmatrix}$ **27.** $\begin{bmatrix} 1 \end{bmatrix}$

29. $\begin{bmatrix} -2 & 0 & 2 \\ -1 & 0 & 1 \\ -3 & 0 & 3 \end{bmatrix}$ **31.** $\begin{bmatrix} -12 & 12 & 18 \\ 20 & -18 & -6 \end{bmatrix}$ **33.** $\begin{bmatrix} -1 & 6 \\ 13 & -3 \\ -1 & 11 \end{bmatrix}$

35. $\begin{bmatrix} 11 & 2 \\ 4 & 27 \end{bmatrix}$ **37.** $\begin{bmatrix} 6 & 4 \\ 0 & -3 \end{bmatrix}$ **39.** $\begin{bmatrix} -1.3 & -0.7 \\ -0.2 & -0.5 \\ 0.1 & 1.1 \end{bmatrix}$ **41.** $\begin{bmatrix} -66 & 69 & 39 \\ 92 & -18 & -36 \end{bmatrix}$

43. Not defined **45.** $\begin{bmatrix} -18 & 48 \\ 54 & -34 \end{bmatrix}$ **47.** $\begin{bmatrix} -26 & -15 & -25 \\ -4 & -18 & 4 \\ 2 & 43 & -19 \end{bmatrix}$

49. $AB = \begin{bmatrix} 0 & 0 \\ 0 & 0 \end{bmatrix}$, $BA = \begin{bmatrix} a^2 + ab & a^2 + ab \\ -a^2 - ab & -a^2 - ab \end{bmatrix}$ **51.** $\begin{bmatrix} 0 & 0 \\ 0 & 0 \end{bmatrix}$

53. B^n approaches $\begin{bmatrix} 0.25 & 0.75 \\ 0.25 & 0.75 \end{bmatrix}$; AB^n approaches $\begin{bmatrix} 0.25 & 0.75 \end{bmatrix}$

55. $a = -1, b = 1, c = 3, d = -5$ **57.** $a = 3, b = 4, c = 1, d = 2$

59. False **61.** True **63.** (A) True (B) True (C) True

65.

Guitar	Banjo	
$51.50	$40.50	Materials
$87.00	$120.00	Labor

67.

	Basic car	Air	AM/FM radio	Cruise control
Model A	$2,937	$459	$200	$118
Model B	$2,864	$201	$88	$52
Model C	$2,171	$417	$177	$101

69. (A) €29.21 (B) €14.54 (C) *MN* gives the labor costs at each plant.
(D)

$MN =$	IT	PL	
	€18.68	€14.54	Small shelving unit
	€29.21	€22.76	Medium shelving unit
	€40.03	€31.24	Large shelving unit

71. (A) 70 g (B) 30 g (C) *MN* gives the amount (in grams) of protein, carbohydrate, and fat in 20 oz of each mix.
(D)

$MN =$	Mix X	Mix Y	Mix Z	
	70	60	50	Protein
	380	360	340	Carbohydrate
	50	40	30	Fat

73. (A) £10,830 (B) £14,080
(C)

$NM =$	Cost per borough	
	£10,830	Greenwich
	£14,080	Bromley

The entries are the total cost per borough.

Exercises 4.5

1. (A) -4; $1/4$ (B) 3; $-1/3$ (C) 0; not defined **3.** (A) $-2/3$; $3/2$ (B) $1/7$; -7 (C) -1.6; 0.625 **5.** No **7.** No **9.** (A) $\begin{bmatrix} 2 & -3 \\ 0 & 0 \end{bmatrix}$ (B) $\begin{bmatrix} 2 & 0 \\ 4 & 0 \end{bmatrix}$

11. (A) $\begin{bmatrix} 0 & 0 \\ 4 & 5 \end{bmatrix}$ (B) $\begin{bmatrix} 0 & -3 \\ 0 & 5 \end{bmatrix}$ **13.** (A) $\begin{bmatrix} 2 & -3 \\ 4 & 5 \end{bmatrix}$ (B) $\begin{bmatrix} 2 & -3 \\ 4 & 5 \end{bmatrix}$

15. $\begin{bmatrix} -2 & 1 & 3 \\ 2 & 4 & -2 \\ 5 & 1 & 0 \end{bmatrix}$ **17.** $\begin{bmatrix} -2 & 1 & 3 \\ 2 & 4 & -2 \\ 5 & 1 & 0 \end{bmatrix}$ **19.** Yes **21.** No **23.** Yes **25.** Yes **27.** No

39. $\begin{bmatrix} -1 & 0 \\ -3 & 1 \end{bmatrix}$ **41.** $\begin{bmatrix} 3 & -2 \\ -1 & 1 \end{bmatrix}$ **43.** $\begin{bmatrix} 9 & -2 \\ -4 & 1 \end{bmatrix}$

45. $\begin{bmatrix} -5 & -12 & 3 \\ -2 & -4 & 1 \\ 2 & 5 & -1 \end{bmatrix}$ **47.** $\begin{bmatrix} 6 & -2 & -1 \\ -5 & 2 & 1 \\ -3 & 1 & 1 \end{bmatrix}$ **49.** $\begin{bmatrix} -2 & -3 \\ 3 & 4 \end{bmatrix}$

51. Does not exist **53.** $\begin{bmatrix} 1.5 & -0.5 \\ -2 & 1 \end{bmatrix}$ **55.** $\begin{bmatrix} 0.35 & 0.01 \\ 0.05 & 0.03 \end{bmatrix}$

57. $\begin{bmatrix} \frac{1}{3} & 0 \\ 0 & \frac{1}{3} \end{bmatrix}$ **59.** $\begin{bmatrix} \frac{1}{2} & 0 \\ 0 & 2 \end{bmatrix}$ **61.** $\begin{bmatrix} 1 & 2 & 2 \\ -2 & -3 & -4 \\ -1 & -2 & -1 \end{bmatrix}$

63. Does not exist **65.** $\begin{bmatrix} -3 & -2 & 1.5 \\ 4 & 3 & -2 \\ 3 & 2 & -1.25 \end{bmatrix}$ **67.** $\begin{bmatrix} -1.75 & -0.375 & 0.5 \\ -5.5 & -1.25 & 1 \\ 0.5 & 0.25 & 0 \end{bmatrix}$

71. M^{-1} exists if and only if all the elements on the main diagonal are nonzero. **73.** $A^{-1} = A$; $A^2 = I$ **75.** $A^{-1} = A$; $A^2 = I$ **77.** 41 50 28 35 37 55 22 31 47 60 24 36 49 71 39 54 21 22
79. PRIDE AND PREJUDICE
81. 37 47 10 58 103 67 47 123 121 75 53 142 58 68 23 91 90 74 38 117 83 59 39 103 113 97 45 147 76 57 38 95 **83.** RAWHIDE TO WALTER REED **85.** 30 28 58 15 38 13 19 26 12 30 39 56 48 43 40 9 30 29 12 33
87. DOUBLE DOUBLE TOIL AND TROUBLE

Exercises 4.6

1. $-3/5$ **3.** $-7/4$ **5.** $9/8$ **7.** $1/10$ **9.** $3x_1 + x_2 = 5$ $2x_1 - x_2 = -4$
11. $\begin{aligned} -3x_1 + x_2 &= 3 \\ 2x_1 + x_3 &= -4 \\ -x_1 + 3x_2 - 2x_3 &= 2 \end{aligned}$

13. $\begin{bmatrix} 3 & -4 \\ 2 & 1 \end{bmatrix}\begin{bmatrix} x_1 \\ x_2 \end{bmatrix} = \begin{bmatrix} 1 \\ 5 \end{bmatrix}$

15. $\begin{bmatrix} 1 & -3 & 2 \\ -2 & 3 & 0 \\ 1 & 1 & 4 \end{bmatrix}\begin{bmatrix} x_1 \\ x_2 \\ x_3 \end{bmatrix} = \begin{bmatrix} -3 \\ 1 \\ -2 \end{bmatrix}$ **17.** $x_1 = -8, x_2 = 2$ **19.** $x_1 = -29, x_2 = 52$ **21.** $x_1 = 3, x_2 = -2$

23. $x_1 = 11, x_2 = 4$ **25.** $x_1 = 3, x_2 = 2$ **27.** No solution **29.** $x_1 = 2, x_2 = 5$ **31.** (A) $x_1 = -3, x_2 = 2$ (B) $x_1 = -1, x_2 = 2$ (C) $x_1 = -8, x_2 = 3$ **33.** (A) $x_1 = 5, x_2 = -2$ (B) $x_1 = -35, x_2 = 16$ (C) $x_1 = 20, x_2 = -9$ **35.** (A) $x_1 = 1, x_2 = 0, x_3 = 0$ (B) $x_1 = -7, x_2 = -2, x_3 = 3$ (C) $x_1 = 17, x_2 = 5, x_3 = -7$ **37.** (A) $x_1 = 8, x_2 = -6, x_3 = -2$ (B) $x_1 = -6, x_2 = 6, x_3 = 2$ (C) $x_1 = 20, x_2 = -16, x_3 = -10$ **39.** $X = A^{-1}B$ **41.** $X = BA^{-1}$ **43.** $X = A^{-1}BA$ **45.** No solution
47. No solution **49.** $x_1 = 13t + 3, x_2 = 8t + 1, x_3 = t$, for any real number t
51. $X = (A - B)^{-1}C$ **53.** $X = (A + I)^{-1}C$
55. $X = (A + B)^{-1}(C + D)$ **57.** $x_1 = 3, x_2 = 8$
59. $x_1 = 10.2, x_2 = 4.4, x_3 = 7.3$
61. $x_1 = 3.1, x_2 = 4.3, x_3 = -2.7, x_4 = 8$
63. $x_1 =$ no. of \$25 tickets
$x_2 =$ no. of \$35 tickets
$x_1 + x_2 = 10{,}000$ seats
$25x_1 + 35x_2 = k$ Return
(A) Concert 1: 7,500 \$25 tickets, 2,500 \$35 tickets
Concert 2: 5,000 \$25 tickets, 5,000 \$35 tickets
Concert 3: 2,500 \$25 tickets, 7,500 \$35 tickets
(B) No (C) $250{,}000 + 10t, 0 \le t \le 10{,}000$
65. $x_1 =$ no. of hours plant A operates
$x_2 =$ no. of hours plant B operates
$10x_1 + 8x_2 = k_1$ no. of car frames produced
$5x_1 + 8x_2 = k_2$ no. of truck frames produced
Order 1: 280 hr at plant A and 25 hr at plant B
Order 2: 160 hr at plant A and 150 hr at plant B
Order 3: 80 hr at plant A and 225 hr at plant B
67. $x_1 =$ president's bonus
$x_2 =$ executive vice-president's bonus
$x_3 =$ associate vice-president's bonus
$x_4 =$ assistant vice-president's bonus

$$\begin{aligned} x_1 + 0.03x_2 + 0.03x_3 + 0.03x_4 &= 60{,}000 \\ 0.025x_1 + x_2 + 0.025x_3 + 0.025x_4 &= 50{,}000 \\ 0.02x_1 + 0.02x_2 + x_3 + 0.02x_4 &= 40{,}000 \\ 0.015x_1 + 0.015x_2 + 0.015x_3 + x_4 &= 30{,}000 \end{aligned}$$

President: \$56,600; executive vice-president: \$47,000; associate vice-president: \$37,400; assistant vice-president: \$27,900
69. (A) $x_1 =$ no. of ounces of mix A
$x_2 =$ no. of ounces of mix B
$0.20x_1 + 0.14x_2 = k_1$ Protein
$0.04x_1 + 0.03x_2 = k_2$ Fat
Diet 1: 50 oz mix A and 500 oz mix B
Diet 2: 450 oz mix A and 0 oz mix B
Diet 3: 150 oz mix A and 500 oz mix B (B) No

Exercises 4.7

1. -3 **3.** 100 **5.** 4 **7.** 8 **9.** 40¢ from A; 20¢ from E
11. $\begin{bmatrix} 0.6 & -0.2 \\ -0.2 & 0.9 \end{bmatrix}; \begin{bmatrix} 1.8 & 0.4 \\ 0.4 & 1.2 \end{bmatrix}$ **13.** $X = \begin{bmatrix} x_1 \\ x_2 \end{bmatrix} = \begin{bmatrix} 16.4 \\ 9.2 \end{bmatrix}$

15. 30¢ from A; 20¢ from B; 30¢ from E **17.** $\begin{bmatrix} 0.8 & -0.3 & -0.2 \\ -0.1 & 0.8 & -0.1 \\ -0.1 & -0.3 & 0.9 \end{bmatrix}$
19. Agriculture: \$31.3 billion; building: \$27 billion; energy: \$34.7 billion
21. $I - M$ is singular; X does not exist **23.** $\begin{bmatrix} 1.75 & 1 \\ 1 & 2 \end{bmatrix}; \begin{bmatrix} 78.75 \\ 95 \end{bmatrix}$

25. $\begin{bmatrix} 1.58 & 0.24 & 0.58 \\ 0.4 & 1.2 & 0.4 \\ 0.22 & 0.16 & 1.22 \end{bmatrix}; \begin{bmatrix} 38.6 \\ 18 \\ 17.4 \end{bmatrix}$ **27.** (A) Agriculture: \$80 million; manufacturing: \$64 million. (B) The final demand for agriculture increases to \$54 million and the final demand for manufacturing decreases to \$38 million.
29. $\begin{bmatrix} 0.25 & 0.1 \\ 0.25 & 0.3 \end{bmatrix}$
31. The total output of the energy sector should be 75% of the total output of the mining sector.
33. Each element should be between 0 and 1, inclusive.
35. Coal: \$28 billion; steel: \$26 billion
37. Agriculture: \$165 million; tourism: \$164 million
39. Agriculture: \$40.1 billion; manufacturing: \$29.4 billion; energy: \$34.4 billion
41. Year 1: agriculture: \$65 billion; energy: \$83 billion; labor: \$71 billion; manufacturing: \$88 billion
Year 2: agriculture: \$81 billion; energy: \$97 billion; labor: \$83 billion; manufacturing: \$99 billion
Year 3: agriculture: \$117 billion; energy: \$124 billion; labor: \$106 billion; manufacturing: \$120 billion

Chapter 4 Review Exercises

1. $x = 4, y = 4$ *(4.1)* **2.** $x = 4, y = 4$ *(4.1)* **3.** (A) Not in reduced form; $R_1 \leftrightarrow R_2$ (B) Not in reduced form; $\frac{1}{3}R_2 \leftrightarrow R_2$ (C) Reduced form (D) Not in reduced form; $(-1)R_2 + R_1 \rightarrow R_1$ *(4.3)* **4.** (A) 2×5, 3×2 (B) $a_{24} = 3$, $a_{15} = 2$, $b_{31} = -1$, $b_{22} = 4$ (C) AB is not defined; BA is defined *(4.2, 4.4)* **5.** (A) $x_1 = 8, x_2 = 2$ (B) $x_1 = -15.5, x_2 = 23.5$ *(4.6)* **6.** $\begin{bmatrix} 8 & 7 \\ 8 & 5 \end{bmatrix}$ *(4.4)*
7. Not defined *(4.4)* **8.** $\begin{bmatrix} 7 & 8 \\ 10 & 4 \end{bmatrix}$ *(4.4)* **9.** $\begin{bmatrix} 22 \\ 8 \end{bmatrix}$ *(4.4)* **10.** Not defined *(4.4)*
11. $\begin{bmatrix} 5 \\ 5 \end{bmatrix}$ *(4.4)* **12.** $\begin{bmatrix} 2 & 3 \\ 4 & 6 \end{bmatrix}$ *(4.4)* **13.** $\begin{bmatrix} 22 & 16 \end{bmatrix}$ *(4.4)* **14.** Not defined *(4.4)*
15. $\begin{bmatrix} -2 & 3 \\ 3 & -4 \end{bmatrix}$ *(4.5)* **16.** $m_1 = -3, m_2 = 3$ *(4.1)* **17.** $x_1 = 9, x_2 = -11$ *(4.2)*
18. $x_1 = 9, x_2 = -11; x_1 = 16, x_2 = -19; x_1 = -2, x_2 = 4$ *(4.6)*
19. Not defined *(4.4)* **20.** $\begin{bmatrix} 10 & -8 \\ 4 & 6 \end{bmatrix}$ *(4.4)* **21.** $\begin{bmatrix} -2 & 8 \\ 8 & 6 \end{bmatrix}$ *(4.4)*
22. $\begin{bmatrix} -2 & -1 & -3 \\ 4 & 2 & 6 \\ 6 & 3 & 9 \end{bmatrix}$ *(4.4)* **23.** $\begin{bmatrix} 9 \end{bmatrix}$ *(4.4)* **24.** $\begin{bmatrix} 10 & -5 & 1 \\ -1 & -4 & -5 \\ 1 & -7 & -2 \end{bmatrix}$ *(4.4)*
25. $\begin{bmatrix} -\frac{5}{2} & 2 & -\frac{1}{2} \\ 1 & -1 & 1 \\ \frac{1}{2} & 0 & -\frac{1}{2} \end{bmatrix}$ *(4.5)* **26.** (A) $x_1 = 2, x_2 = 1, x_3 = -1$ (B) $x_1 = -5t - 12, x_2 = 3t + 7, x_3 = t$ for t any real number (C) $x_1 = -2t + 5$, $x_2 = t + 3, x_3 = t$ for t any real number *(4.3)*
27. $x_1 = 2, x_2 = 1, x_3 = -1; x_1 = 1, x_2 = -2, x_3 = 1; x_1 = -1, x_2 = 2, x_3 = -2$ *(4.6)* **28.** The system has an infinite no. of solutions for $k = 3$ and a unique solution for any other value of k. *(4.3)*
29. $(I - M)^{-1} = \begin{bmatrix} 1.4 & 0.3 \\ 0.8 & 1.6 \end{bmatrix}; X = \begin{bmatrix} 48 \\ 56 \end{bmatrix}$ *(4.7)* **30.** $\begin{bmatrix} 0.3 & 0.4 \\ 0.15 & 0.2 \end{bmatrix}$ *(4.7)*
31. $I - M$ is singular; X does not exist. *(4.5)* **32.** $x = 3.46, y = 1.69$ *(4.1)*

33. $\begin{bmatrix} -0.9 & -0.1 & 5 \\ 0.8 & 0.2 & -4 \\ 0.1 & -0.1 & 0 \end{bmatrix}$ *(4.5)* **34.** $x_1 = 1{,}400, x_2 = 3{,}200, x_3 = 2{,}400$ *(4.6)*

35. $x_1 = 1{,}400, x_2 = 3{,}200, x_3 = 2{,}400$ *(4.3)*

36. $(I\text{-}M)^{-1} = \begin{bmatrix} 1.3 & 0.4 & 0.7 \\ 0.2 & 1.6 & 0.3 \\ 0.1 & 0.8 & 1.4 \end{bmatrix}; X = \begin{bmatrix} 81 \\ 49 \\ 62 \end{bmatrix}$ *(4.7)*

37. (A) Unique solution (B) Either no solution or an infinite no. of solutions *(4.6)*
38. (A) Unique solution (B) No solution (C) Infinite no. of solutions *(4.3)*
39. (B) is the only correct solution. *(4.6)* **40.** (A) $C = 253{,}000 + 35.50x$; $R = 199.99x$ (B) $x = 1{,}538$ computers; $R = C = \$307{,}602.10$ (C) Profit occurs if $x > 1{,}538$; loss occurs if $x < 1{,}538$. *(4.1)*

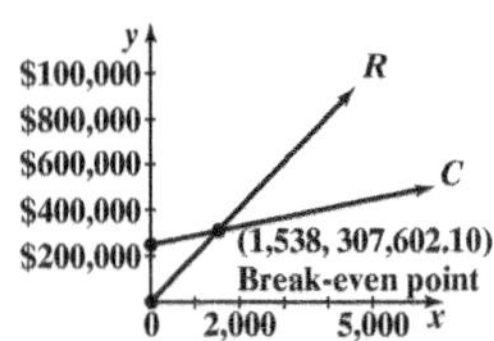

41. x_1 = no. of tons Port Hedland ore
x_2 = no. of tons of Jack Hills ore
$0.02x_1 + 0.03x_2 = 6$
$0.04x_1 + 0.02x_2 = 8$
x_1 = 150 tons of Port Hedland ore
x_2 = 100 tons of Jack Hills ore *(4.3)*

42. (A) $\begin{bmatrix} x_1 \\ x_2 \end{bmatrix} = \begin{bmatrix} -25 & 37.5 \\ 50 & -25 \end{bmatrix} \begin{bmatrix} 6 \\ 8 \end{bmatrix} = \begin{bmatrix} 150 \\ 100 \end{bmatrix}$
x_1 = 150 tons of Port Hedland ore
x_2 = 100 tons of Jack Hills ore
(B) $\begin{bmatrix} x_1 \\ x_2 \end{bmatrix} = \begin{bmatrix} -25 & 37.5 \\ 50 & -25 \end{bmatrix} \begin{bmatrix} 7.5 \\ 7 \end{bmatrix} = \begin{bmatrix} 75 \\ 200 \end{bmatrix}$
x_1 = 75 tons of Port Hedland ore
x_2 = 200 tons of Jack Hills ore *(4.6)*

43. (A) x_1 = no. of 3,000-ft^3 hoppers
x_2 = no. of 4,500-ft^3 hoppers
x_3 = no. of 6,000-ft^3 hoppers
$x_1 + x_2 + x_3 = 20$
$3{,}000x_1 + 4{,}500x_2 + 6{,}000x_3 = 108{,}000$
$x_1 = (t - 12)$ 3,000-ft^3 hoppers
$x_2 = (32 - 2t)$ 4,500-ft^3 hoppers
$x_3 = t$ 6,000-ft^3 hoppers
where t = 12, 13, 14, 15, or 16
(B) The minimum monthly cost is $5,700 when 8 4,500-ft^3 and 12 6,000-ft^3 hoppers are leased. *(4.3)*

44. (A) Elements in MN give the cost of materials for each alloy from each supplier.
(B)

$MN = \begin{bmatrix} \$7{,}620 & \$7{,}530 \\ \$13{,}880 & \$13{,}930 \end{bmatrix}$ (columns: Supplier A, Supplier B; rows: Alloy 1, Alloy 2)

(C) Supplier A Supplier B
$[1\ 1]MN = [\$21{,}500 \quad \$21{,}460]$
Total material costs *(4.4)*

45. (A) $6.35 (B) Elements in MN give the total labor costs for each calculator at each plant.
(C)

$MN = \begin{bmatrix} \$3.65 & \$3.00 \\ \$6.35 & \$5.20 \end{bmatrix}$ (columns: CA, TX; rows: Model A, Model B) *(4.4)*

46. x_1 = amount invested at 5% x_2 = amount invested at 10%
$x_1 + x_2 = 5{,}000$ $0.05x_1 + 0.1x_2 = 400$ $2,000 at 5%, $3,000 at 10% *(4.3)*

47. $2,000 at 5% and $3,000 at 10% *(4.6)* **48.** No to both. The annual yield must be between $250 and $500 inclusive. *(4.6)*

49. x_1 = no. of $8 tickets
x_2 = no. of $12 tickets
x_3 = no. of $20 tickets
$x_1 + x_2 + x_3 = 25{,}000$
$8x_1 + 12x_2 + 20x_3 = k_1$ Return required
$x_1 - x_3 = 0$
Concert 1: 5000 $8 tickets, 15,000 $12 tickets, and 5,000 $20 tickets
Concert 2: 7,500 $8 tickets, 10,000 $12 tickets, and 7,500 $20 tickets
Concert 3: 10,000 $8 tickets, 5,000 $12 tickets, and 10,000 $20 tickets *(4.6)*

50. $x_1 + x_2 + x_3 = 25{,}000$
$8x_1 + 12x_2 + 20x_3 = k_1$ Return required
Concert 1: $(2t - 5{,}000)$ $8 tickets, $(30{,}000 - 3t)$ $12 tickets, and t $20 tickets, where t is an integer satisfying $2{,}500 \le t \le 10{,}000$
Concert 2: $(2t - 7{,}500)$ $8 tickets, $(32{,}500 - 3t)$ $12 tickets, and t $20 tickets, where t is an integer satisfying $3{,}750 \le t \le 10{,}833$
Concert 3: $(2t - 10{,}000)$ $8 tickets, $(35{,}000 - 3t)$ $12 tickets, and t $20 tickets, where t is an integer satisfying $5{,}000 \le t \le 11{,}666$ *(4.3)*

51. (A) Wheat: 825 metric tons; Oil: 1425 metric tons
(B) Wheat: 1372 metric tons; Oil: 2850 metric tons *(4.7)*

52. BEWARE THE IDES OF MARCH *(4.5)*

53. (A) 1st and Elm: $x_1 + x_4 = 1{,}300$
2nd and Elm: $x_1 - x_2 = 400$
2nd and Oak: $x_2 + x_3 = 700$
1st and Oak: $x_3 - x_4 = -200$
(B) $x_1 = 1{,}300 - t$, $x_2 = 900 - t$, $x_3 = t - 200$, $x_4 = t$, where $200 \le t \le 900$
(C) 900; 200
(D) Elm St.: 800; 2nd St.: 400; Oak St.: 300 *(4.3)*

Chapter 5

Exercises 5.1

1. No **3.** Yes **5.** No **7.** No **9.** **11.**

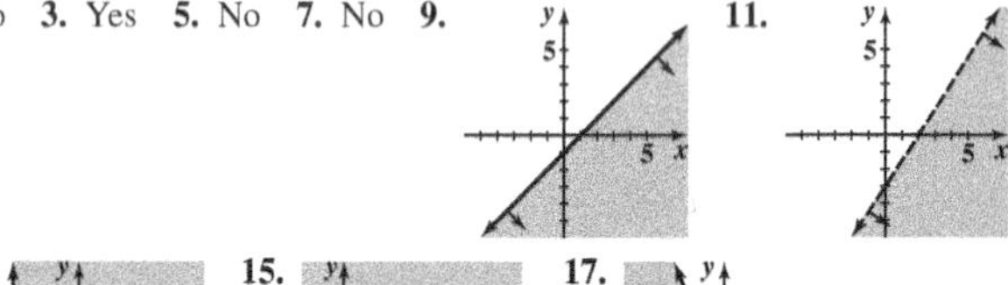

13. **15.** **17.**

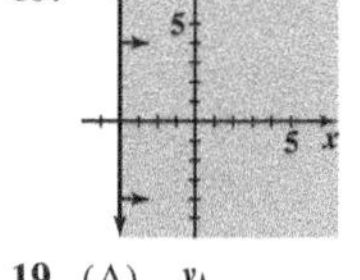

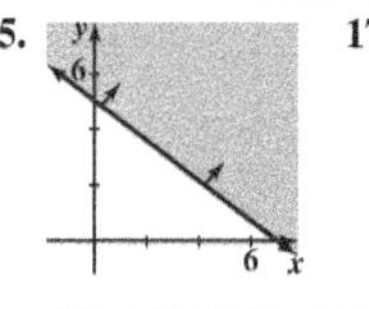

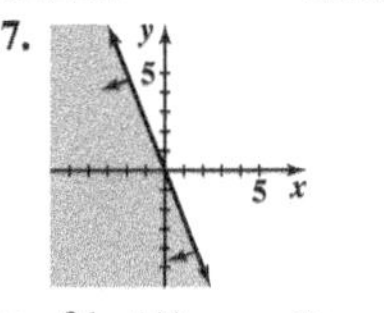

19. (A) (B) **21.** (A)

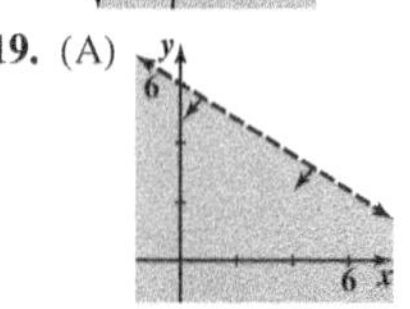

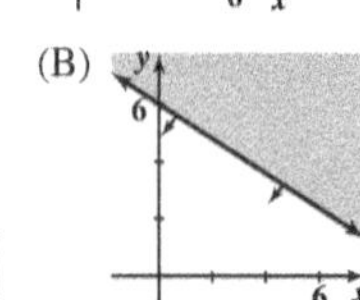

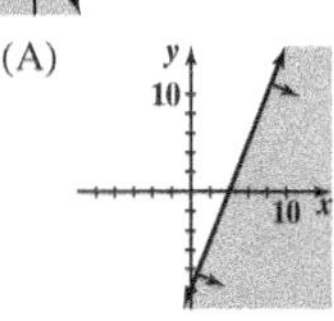

(B)

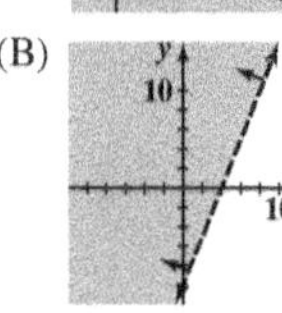

23. Let a = no. of applicants; $a < 10$
25. Let h = no. of hours of practice per day; $h \ge 2.5$ **27.** Let s = success rate; $s < 20\%$ **29.** Let f = annual fee; $f > \$45{,}000$
31. Let e = enrollment; $e \le 30$

33. $2x + 3y = -6$; $2x + 3y \ge -6$ **35.** $y = 3$; $y < 3$ **37.** $4x - 5y = 0$; $4x - 5y \ge 0$ **39.** Let x = enrollment in finite mathematics; let y = enrollment in calculus; $x + y < 300$ **41.** Let x = revenue; y = cost; $x \le y - 20{,}000$ **43.** Let x = no. of grams of protein in rice; let y = number of grams of proteins in potato; $x > 2y$

45. **47.** **49.**

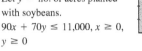

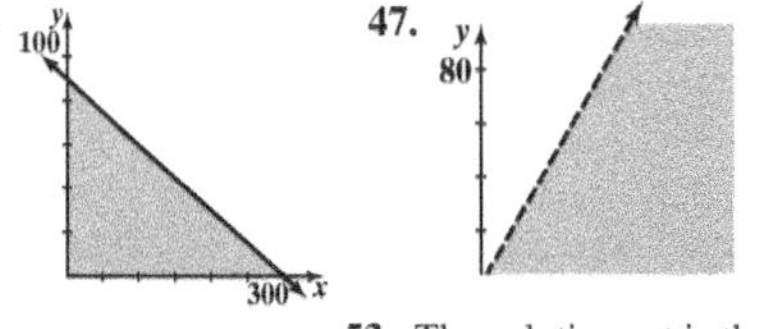

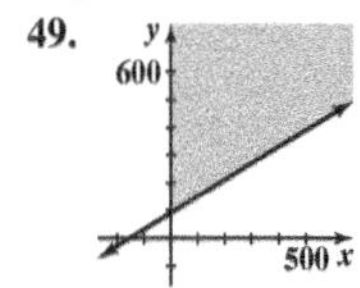

51.

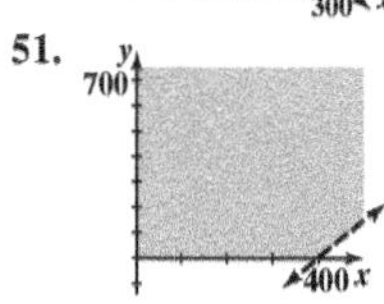

53. The solution set is the empty set and has no graph.
55. Let x = no. of acres planted with corn.
Let y = no. of acres planted with soybeans.
$90x + 70y \le 11{,}000$, $x \ge 0$, $y \ge 0$

57. Let x = no. of lbs of brand A.
Let y = no. of lbs of brand B.
(A) $0.26x + 0.16y \ge 120$, $x \ge 0, y \ge 0$ (B) $0.03x + 0.08y \le 28$, $x \ge 0, y \ge 0$

59. Let x = no. of kilograms of commercial bronze.
Let y = no. of kilograms of architechtural bronze.
$0.90x + 0.57y \ge 0.75(x + y), x \ge 0, y \ge 0$

61. Let x = no. of weeks Plant A is operated.
Let y = no. of weeks Plant B is operated.
$10x + 8y \ge 400, x \ge 0, y \ge 0$

63. Let x = no. of radio spots.
Let y = no. of television spots.
$200x + 800y \le 10{,}000, x \ge 0, y \ge 0$

65. Let x = no. of regular mattresses cut per day.
Let y = no. of king mattresses cut per day
$5x + 6y \le 3{,}000, x \ge 0, y \ge 0$

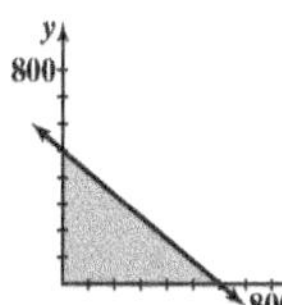

Exercises 5.2

1. Yes **3.** No **5.** No **7.** Yes **9.** IV **11.** I **13.**

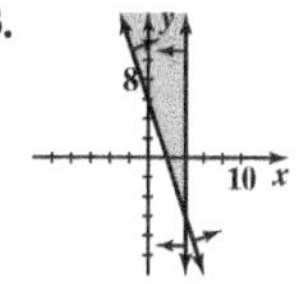

15. **17.** IV; $(8, 0)$, $(18, 0)$, $(6, 4)$ **19.** I; $(0, 16)$, $(6, 4)$, $(18, 0)$

21. Unbounded **23.** Unbounded **25.** Bounded **27.** Bounded

29. Bounded

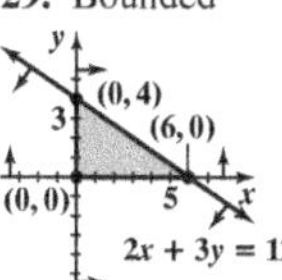

31. Unbounded

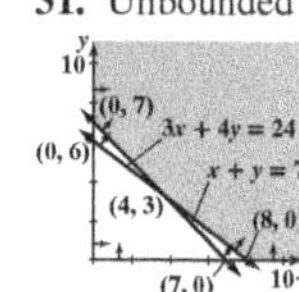

33. Bounded

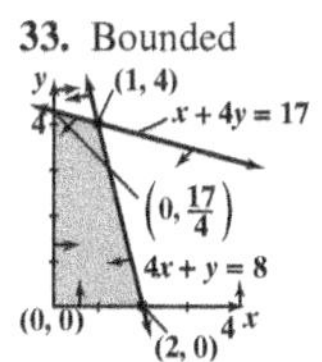

35. Unbounded

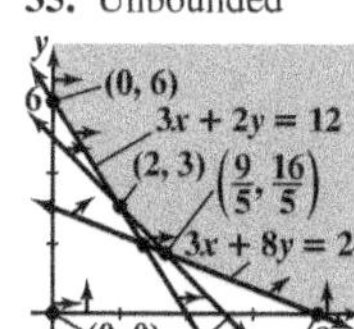

37. Bounded

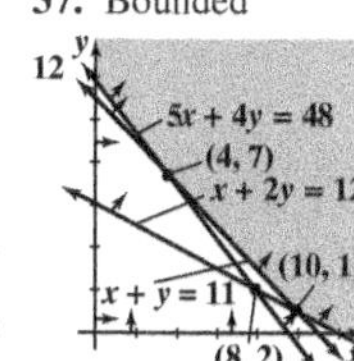

39. Empty

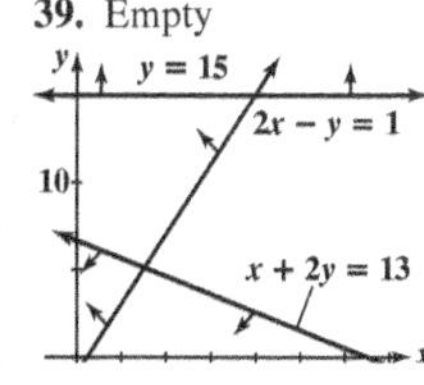

41. Bounded

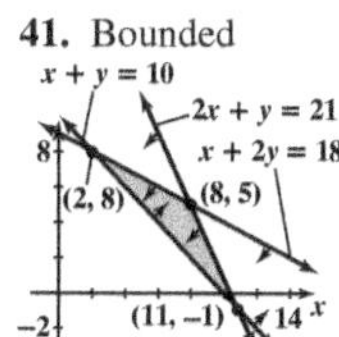

43. Unbounded

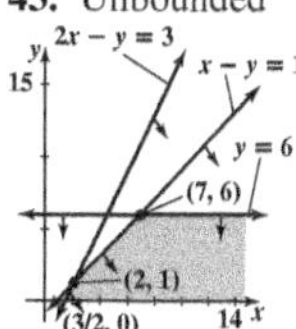

45. Bounded

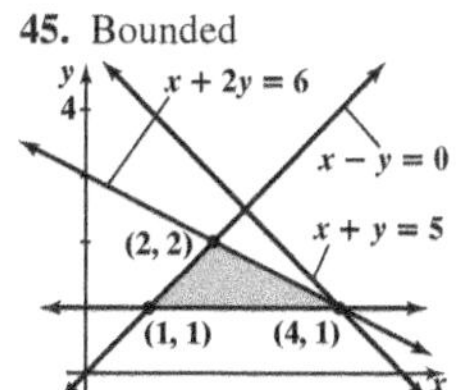

47. Bounded

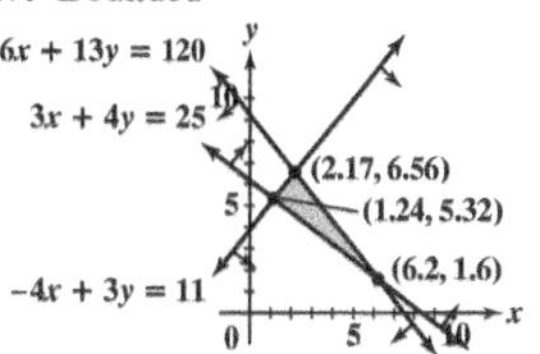

49. (A) $3x + 4y = 36$ and $3x + 2y = 30$ intersect at $(8, 3)$;
$3x + 4y = 36$ and $x = 0$ intersect at $(0, 9)$;
$3x + 4y = 36$ and $y = 0$ intersect at $(12, 0)$;
$3x + 2y = 30$ and $x = 0$ intersect at $(0, 15)$;
$3x + 2y = 30$ and $y = 0$ intersect at $(10, 0)$;
$x = 0$ and $y = 0$ intersect at $(0, 0)$
(B) $(8, 3)$, $(0, 9)$, $(10, 0)$, $(0, 0)$

51. $6x + 4y \le 108$
$x + y \le 24$
$x \ge 0$
$y \ge 0$

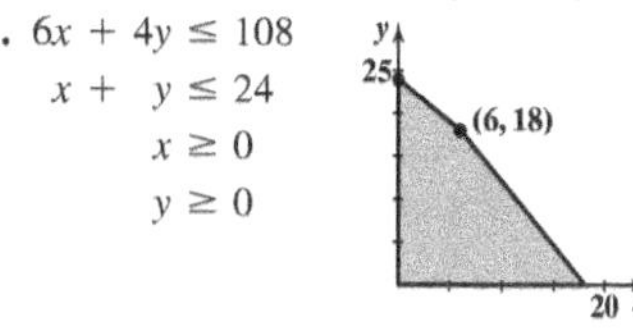

53. (A) All production schedules in the feasible region that are on the graph of $50x + 60y = 1{,}100$ will result in a profit of \$1,100. (B) There are many possible choices. For example, producing 5 trick skis and 15 slalom skis will produce a profit of \$1,150. All the production schedules in the feasible region that are on the graph of $50x + 60y = 1{,}150$ will result in a profit of \$1,150.

55. $20x + 10y \ge 460$
$30x + 30y \ge 960$
$5x + 10y \ge 220$
$x \ge 0$
$y \ge 0$

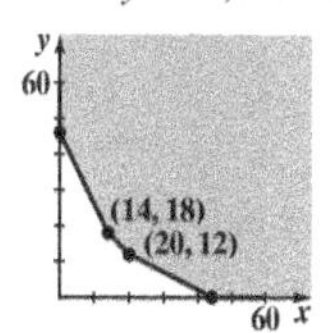

57. $10x + 20y \le 800$
$20x + 10y \le 640$
$x \ge 0$
$y \ge 0$

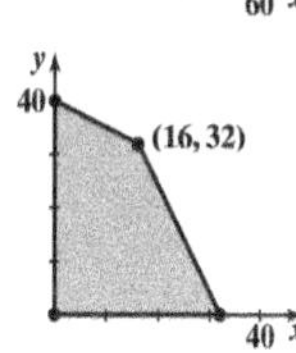

Exercises 5.3

1. Max $Q = 154$; Min $Q = 0$ **3.** Max $Q = 120$; Min $Q = -60$ **5.** Max $Q = 0$; Min $Q = -32$ **7.** Max $Q = 40$; Min $Q = -48$ **9.** Max $P = 16$ at $x = 7$ and $y = 9$ **11.** Max $P = 84$ at $x = 7$ and $y = 9$, at $x = 0$ and $y = 12$, and at every point on the line segment joining the preceding two points. **13.** Min $C = 32$ at $x = 0$ and $y = 8$ **15.** Min $C = 36$ at $x = 4$ and $y = 3$ **17.** Max $P = 78$ at $x = 0$ and $y = 6$ **19.** Min $C = 35$ at $x = 0$ and $y = 5$ **21.** Max $P = 200$ at $x = 4$ and $y = 12$ **23.** Min $z = 10$ at $x = 0$ and $y = 5$ **25.** Min $z = 218$ at $x = \frac{9}{5}$ and $y = \frac{16}{5}$ **27.** Max $P = 180$ at $x = 6$ and $y = 2$ **29.** Min $P = 20$ at $x = 0$ and $y = 2$; Max $P = 150$ at $x = 5$ and $y = 0$ **31.** Feasible region empty; no optimal solutions **33.** Min $P = 180$ at $x = 6$ and $y = 2$ **35.** Max $P = 20{,}000$ at $x = 0$ and $y = 1{,}000$ **37.** Max $P = 5{,}507$ at $x = 6.62$ and $y = 4.25$ **39.** Max $z = 2$ at $x = 4$ and $y = 2$; min z does not exist **41.** $5 < a < 30$ **43.** $a > 30$ **45.** $a = 30$ **47.** $a = 0$

49. (A) Let: x = no. of trick skis
y = no. of slalom skis
Maximize $P = 40x + 30y$
subject to $6x + 4y \le 108$
$x + y \le 24$
$x \ge 0, y \ge 0$
Max profit = \$780 when 6 trick skis and 18 slalom skis are produced.
(B) Max profit decreases to \$720 when 18 trick skis and no slalom skis are produced.
(C) Max profit increases to \$1,080 when no trick skis and 24 slalom skis are produced.

51. (A) Let x = no. of days to operate plant A
y = no. of days to operate plant B
Maximize $C = 1000x + 900y$
subject to $20x + 25y \geq 200$
$60x + 50y \geq 500$
$x \geq 0, y \geq 0$
Plant A: 5 days; Plant B: 4 days; min cost \$8,600
(B) Plant A: 10 days; Plant B: 0 days; min cost \$6,000
(C) Plant A: 0 days; Plant B: 10 days; min cost \$8,000

53. Let x = no. of buses
y = no. of vans
Maximize $C = 1{,}200x + 100y$
subject to $40x + 8y \geq 400$
$3x + y \leq 36$
$x \geq 0, y \geq 0$
7 buses, 15 vans; min cost \$9,900

55. Let x = amount invested in the CD
y = amount invested in the mutual fund
Maximize $P = 0.05x + 0.09y$
subject to $x + y \leq 60{,}000$
$y \geq 10{,}000$
$x \geq 2y$
$x, y \geq 0$
\$40,000 in the CD and \$20,000 in the mutual fund; max return is \$3,800

57. (A) Let x = no. of gallons produced by the old process
y = no. of gallons produced by the new process
Maximize $P = 60x + 20y$
subject to $20x + 5y \leq 16{,}000$
$40x + 20y \leq 30{,}000$
$x \geq 0, y \geq 0$
Max P = \$450 when 750 gal are produced using the old process exclusively.
(B) Max P = \$380 when 400 gal are produced using the old process and 700 gal are produced using the new process.
(C) Max P = \$288 when 1,440 gal are produced using the new process exclusively.

59. (A) Let x = no. of bags of brand A
y = no. of bags of brand B
Maximize $N = 8x + 3y$
subject to $4x + 4y \geq 1{,}000$
$2x + y \leq 400$
$x \geq 0, y \geq 0$
150 bags brand A, 100 bags brand B;
Max nitrogen = 1,500 lb
(B) 0 bags brand A, 250 bags brand B;
Min nitrogen = 750 lb

61. Let x = no. of cubic yards of mix A
y = no. of cubic yards of mix B
Minimize $C = 30x + 35y$
subject to $20x + 10y \geq 460$
$30x + 30y \geq 960$
$5x + 10y \geq 220$
$x \geq 0, y \geq 0$
20 yd³ A, 12 yd³ B; \$1,020

63. Let x = no. of mice used
y = no. of rats used
Maximize $P = x + y$
subject to $10x + 20y \leq 800$
$20x + 10y \leq 640$
$x \geq 0, y \geq 0$
48; 16 mice, 32 rats

Chapter 5 Review Exercises

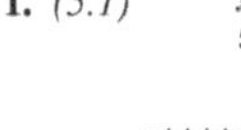

1. *(5.1)*

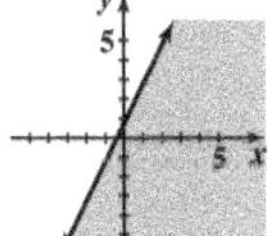

2. *(5.1)*

3. Bounded *(5.2)*

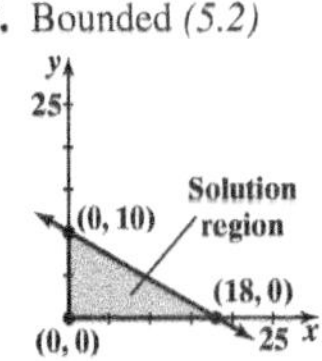

4. Unbounded *(5.2)*

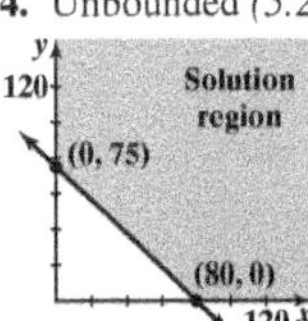

5. Bounded *(5.2)*

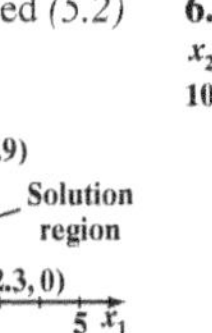

6. Unbounded *(5.2)*

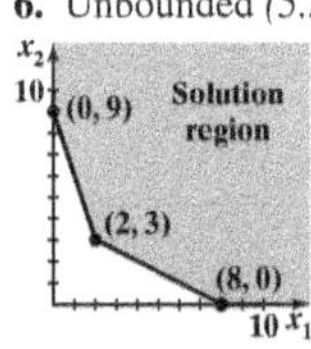

7. $2x + 3y = 2$, $2x + 3y \geq 2$ *(5.1)* **8.** $4x + y = 8$; $4x + y \geq 8$ *(5.1)*
9. Max $P = 18$ at $x = 6$ and $y = 0$ *(5.3)* **10.** Max $P = 18.08$ at $x = 17.54$ and $y = 0$ *(5.3)* **11.** Max $P = 26$ at $x = 2$ and $y = 5$ *(5.3)* **12.** Min $C = 51$ at $x = 3$ and $y = 9$ *(5.3)* **13.** Max $P = 84$ at $x = 12$ and $y = 12$ *(5.3)*

14. Let x = no. of calculator boards. *(5.1)*
y = no. of toaster boards
(A) $4x + 3y \leq 300, x \geq 0, y \geq 0$ (B) $2x + y \leq 120, x \geq 0, y \geq 0$

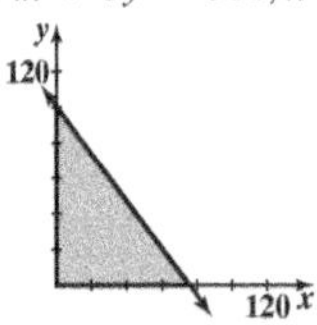

15. (A) Let x = no. of regular sails
y = no. of competition sails
Maximize $P = 100x + 200y$
subject to $2x + 3y \leq 150$
$4x + 10y \leq 380$
$x, y \geq 0$
Max P = \$8,500 when 45 regular and 20 competition sails are produced.
(B) Max profit increases to \$9,880 when 38 competition and no regular sails are produced.
(C) Max profit decreases to \$7,500 when no competition and 75 regular sails are produced. *(5.3)*

16. (A) Let x = no. of grams of mix A
y = no. of grams of mix B
Minimize $C = 0.04x + 0.09y$
subject to $2x + 5y \geq 850$
$2x + 4y \geq 800$
$4x + 5y \geq 1{,}150$
$x, y \geq 0$
Min C = \$16.50 when 300 g mix A and 50 g mix B are used
(B) The minimum cost decreases to \$13.00 when 100 g mix A and 150 g mix B are used
(C) The minimum cost increases to \$17.00 when 425 g mix A and no mix B are used *(5.3)*

Chapter 6

Exercises 6.1

1. $(x - 9)(x + 9)$ **3.** $(x - 7)(x + 3)$ **5.** $x(x - 3)(x - 4)$
7. $(2x - 1)(3x + 1)$ **9.** 2 **11.** 1.25 **13.** (A) 2 (B) 2 (C) 2 (D) 2
15. (A) 1 (B) 2 (C) Does not exist (D) 2 **17.** 2 **19.** 0.5
21. (A) 1 (B) 2 (C) Does not exist (D) Does not exist
23. (A) 1 (B) 1 (C) 1 (D) 3 **25.** (A) −2 (B) −2 (C) −2 (D) 1
27. (A) 2 (B) 2 (C) 2 (D) Does not exist **29.** 12 **31.** 1 **33.** −4
35. −1.5 **37.** 3 **39.** 15 **41.** −6 **43.** $\frac{7}{5}$ **45.** 3

47.

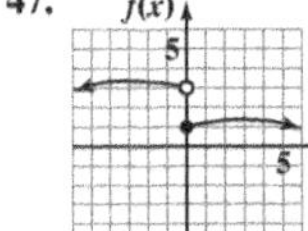

49.

51. (A) 1 (B) 1 (C) 1 (D) 1

53. (A) 2 (B) 1 (C) Does not exist (D) Does not exist **55.** (A) −6 (B) Does not exist (C) 6 **57.** (A) 1 (B) −1 (C) Does not exist (D) Does not exist **59.** (A) Does not exist (B) $\frac{1}{2}$ (C) $\frac{1}{4}$ **61.** (A) −5 (B) −3 (C) 0 **63.** (A) 0 (B) −1 (C) Does not exist **65.** (A) 1 (B) $\frac{1}{3}$ (C) $\frac{3}{4}$ **67.** False **69.** False **71.** True **73.** Yes; 2 **75.** No; Does not exist **77.** Yes; 7/5 **79.** No; 0 **81.** 3 **83.** 4 **85.** −7 **87.** 1

89. (A) 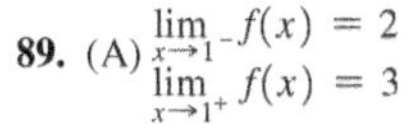
$\lim_{x\to 1^-} f(x) = 2$, $\lim_{x\to 1^+} f(x) = 3$
(B) 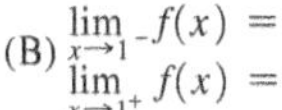
$\lim_{x\to 1^-} f(x) = 3$, $\lim_{x\to 1^+} f(x) = 2$
(C) 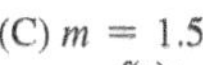
$m = 1.5$

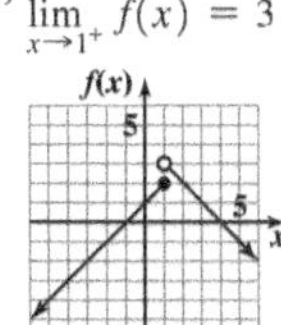
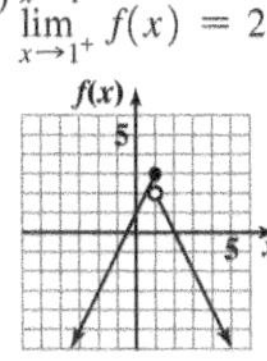
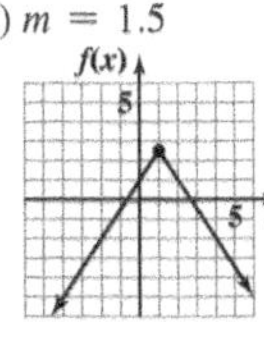

(D) The graph in (A) is broken when it jumps from (1, 2) up to (1, 3). The graph in (B) is also broken when it jumps down from (1, 3) to (1, 2). The graph in (C) is one continuous piece, with no breaks or jumps.

91. (A) $F(x) = \begin{cases} 50 & \text{if } 0 \le x \le 10 \\ 9x - 40 & \text{if } x > 10 \end{cases}$ (B)

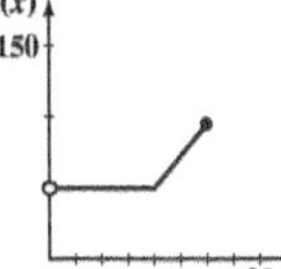

(C) All 3 limits are 50.

95. (A) $D(x) = \begin{cases} x & \text{if } 0 \le x < 300 \\ 0.97x & \text{if } 300 \le x < 1{,}000 \\ 0.95x & \text{if } 1{,}000 \le x < 3{,}000 \\ 0.93x & \text{if } 3{,}000 \le x < 5{,}000 \\ 0.9x & \text{if } x \ge 5{,}000 \end{cases}$

(B) $\lim_{x\to 1{,}000} D(x)$ does not exist because $\lim_{x\to 1{,}000^-} D(x) = 970$ and $\lim_{x\to 1{,}000^+} D(x) = 950$; $\lim_{x\to 3{,}000^-} D(x)$ does not exist because $\lim_{x\to 3{,}000^-} D(x) = 2{,}850$ and $\lim_{x\to 3{,}000^+} D(x) = 2{,}790$

97. $F(x) = \begin{cases} 20x & \text{if } 0 < x \le 4{,}000 \\ 80{,}000 & \text{if } x \ge 4{,}000 \end{cases}$
$\lim_{x\to 4{,}000} F(x) = 80{,}000$; $\lim_{x\to 8{,}000} F(x) = 80{,}000$

99. $\lim_{x\to 5} f(x)$ does not exist; $\lim_{x\to 10} f(x) = 0$; $\lim_{x\to 5} g(x) = 0$; $\lim_{x\to 10} g(x) = 1$

Exercises 6.2

1. $y = 4$ **3.** $x = -6$ **5.** $2x - y = -13$ **7.** $7x + 9y = 63$ **9.** −2 **11.** $-\infty$ **13.** Does not exist **15.** 0 **17.** (A) $-\infty$ (B) ∞ (C) Does not exist **19.** (A) $-\infty$ (B) $-\infty$ (C) $-\infty$ **21.** (A) 3 (B) 3 (C) 3 **23.** (A) $-\infty$ (B) ∞ (C) Does not exist **25.** (A) $-5x^3$ (B) $-\infty$ (C) ∞ **27.** (A) $-6x^4$ (B) $-\infty$ (C) $-\infty$ **29.** (A) x^2 (B) ∞ (C) ∞ **31.** (A) $2x^5$ (B) ∞ (C) $-\infty$ **33.** (A) $\frac{47}{41} \approx 1.146$ (B) $\frac{407}{491} \approx 0.829$ (C) $\frac{4}{5} = 0.8$ **35.** (A) $\frac{2{,}011}{138} \approx 14.572$ (B) $\frac{12{,}511}{348} \approx 35.951$ (C) ∞ **37.** (A) $-\frac{8{,}568}{46{,}653} \approx -0.184$ (B) $-\frac{143{,}136}{1{,}492{,}989} \approx -0.096$ (C) 0 **39.** (A) $-\frac{7{,}010}{996} \approx -7.038$ (B) $-\frac{56{,}010}{7{,}996} \approx -7.005$ (C) −7 **41.** $\lim_{x\to 2^-} f(x) = -\infty$; $\lim_{x\to 2^+} f(x) = \infty$; $x = 2$ is a vertical asymptote

43. $\lim_{x\to -1} f(x) = -0.5$; $\lim_{x\to 1^-} f(x) = -\infty$; $\lim_{x\to 1^+} f(x) = \infty$; $x = 1$ is a vertical asymptote
45. No zeros of denominator; no vertical asymptotes
47. $\lim_{x\to -2^-} f(x) = -\infty$; $\lim_{x\to -2^+} f(x) = \infty$; $\lim_{x\to 5^-} f(x) = \infty$; $\lim_{x\to 5^+} f(x) = -\infty$; $x = -2$ and $x = 5$ are vertical asymptotes
49. $\lim_{x\to -2} f(x) = -\frac{2}{3}$; $\lim_{x\to 0^-} f(x) = -\infty$; $\lim_{x\to 0^+} f(x) = \infty$; $\lim_{x\to 1^-} f(x) = \infty$; $\lim_{x\to 1^+} f(x) = -\infty$; $x = 0$ and $x = 1$ are vertical asymptotes
51. Horizontal asymptote: $y = 2$; vertical asymptote: $x = -2$
53. Horizontal asymptote: $y = 1$; vertical asymptotes: $x = -1$ and $x = 1$
55. No horizontal asymptotes; no vertical asymptotes
57. Horizontal asymptote: $y = 0$; no vertical asymptotes
59. No horizontal asymptotes; vertical asymptote: $x = 3$
61. Horizontal asymptote: $y = 2$; vertical asymptotes: $x = -1$ and $x = 2$
63. Horizontal asymptote: $y = 3$; vertical asymptote: $x = 4$
65. $\lim_{x\to\infty} f(x) = 0$ **67.** $\lim_{x\to\infty} f(x) = \infty$ **69.** $\lim_{x\to -\infty} f(x) = -\frac{1}{4}$
71. $\lim_{x\to -\infty} f(x) = \infty$ **73.** False **75.** False **77.** True
79. If $n \ge 1$ and $a_n > 0$, then the limit is ∞. If $n \ge 1$ and $a_n < 0$, then the limit is $-\infty$.
81. (A) $C(x) = 40x + 300$ (B) $\overline{C}(x) = \frac{40x + 300}{x}$
(C)

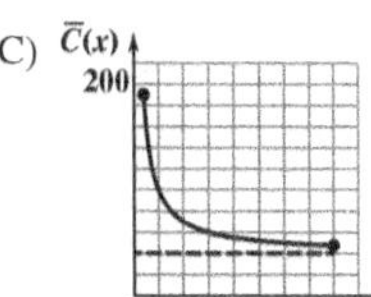

(D) $40 per chair

83. (A) 20%; 50%; 80% (B) $P(t) \to 100\%$
85. The long-term drug concentration is 5 mg/ml.
87. (A) $18 million (B) $38 million (C) $\lim_{x\to 1^-} P(x) = \infty$
89. 
(C) $V_{max} = 4$, $K_M = 20$
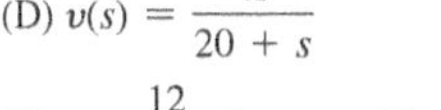
(D) $v(s) = \frac{4s}{20 + s}$

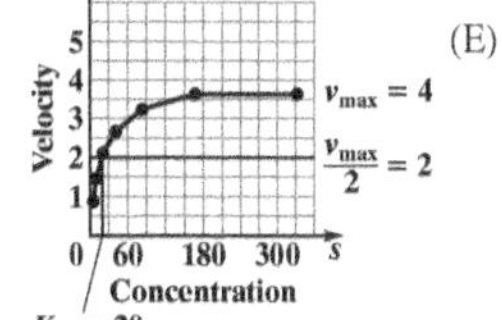

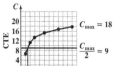

(E) $v = \frac{12}{7}$ when $s = 15$; $s = 60$ when $v = 3$

91. (A) $C_{max} = 18$, $M = 150$
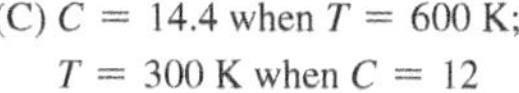
(B) $C(T) = \frac{18T}{150 + T}$
(C) $C = 14.4$ when $T = 600$ K; $T = 300$ K when $C = 12$

Exercises 6.3

1. $[-3, 5]$ **3.** $(-10, 100)$ **5.** $(-\infty, -5) \cup (5, \infty)$ **7.** $(-\infty, -3) \cup (4, \infty)$
9. f is continuous at $x = 1$, since $\lim_{x\to 1} f(x) = f(1)$.

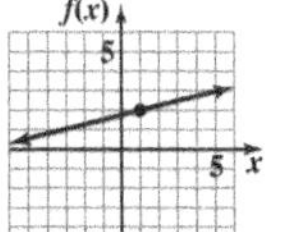

11. f is discontinuous at $x = 1$, since $\lim_{x\to 1} f(x) \ne f(1)$.

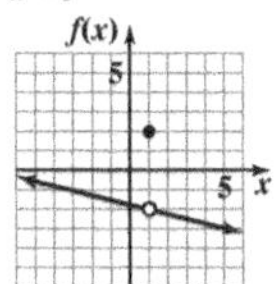

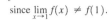

13. f is discontinuous at $x = 1$, since $\lim_{x\to 1} f(x)$ does not exist.

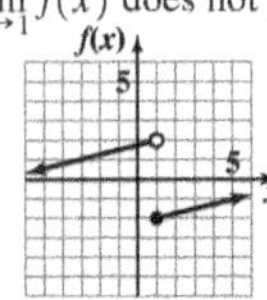

15. 1.9 **17.** 1.01 **19.** (A) 2 (B) 1 (C) Does not exist (D) 1 (E) No **21.** (A) 1 (B) 1 (C) 1 (D) 3 (E) No **23.** −0.1 **25.** 0.1 **27.** (A) −1 (B) −1 (C) −1 (D) −1 (E) Yes **29.** (A) $\frac{3}{2}$ (B) $\frac{3}{2}$ (C) $\frac{3}{2}$ (D) $\frac{3}{2}$ (E) Yes

31. All x **33.** All x, except $x = -2$ **35.** All x, except $x = -4$ and $x = 1$ **37.** All x **39.** All x, except $x = \pm\frac{3}{2}$ **41.** $-\frac{8}{3}, 4$ **43.** $-1, 1$ **45.** $-7, 0, 4, 8$ **47.** $-3 < x < 4$; $(-3, 4)$ **49.** $x < 3$ or $x > 7$; $(-\infty, 3) \cup (7, \infty)$ **51.** $x < -2$ or $0 < x < 2$; $(-\infty, -2) \cup (0, 2)$ **53.** $-5 < x < 0$ or $x > 3$; $(-5, 0) \cup (3, \infty)$ **55.** (A) $(-4, -2) \cup (0, 2) \cup (4, \infty)$ (B) $(-\infty, -4) \cup (-2, 0) \cup (2, 4)$ **57.** (A) $(-\infty, -2.5308) \cup (-0.7198, \infty)$ (B) $(-2.5308, -0.7198)$ **59.** (A) $(-\infty, -2.1451) \cup (-1, -0.5240) \cup (1, 2.6691)$ (B) $(-2.1451, -1) \cup (-0.5240, 1) \cup (2.6691, \infty)$ **61.** $[6, \infty)$ **63.** $(-\infty, \infty)$ **65.** $(-\infty, -3] \cup [3, \infty)$ **67.** $(-\infty, \infty)$

69. Since $\lim_{x\to 1^-} f(x) = 2$ and $\lim_{x\to 1^+} f(x) = 4$, $\lim_{x\to 1} f(x)$ does not exist and f is not continuous at $x = 1$.

71. This function is continuous for all x.

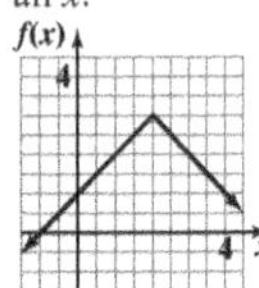

73. Since $\lim_{x\to 0} f(x) = 0$ and $f(0) = 1$, $\lim_{x\to 0} f(x) \neq f(0)$ and f is not continuous at $x = 0$.

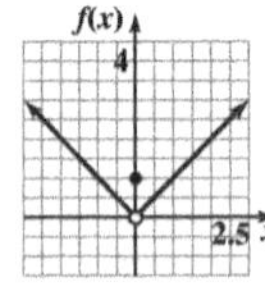

75. (A) Yes (B) No (C) Yes (D) No (E) Yes **77.** True **79.** False **81.** True

83. x int.: −5, 2

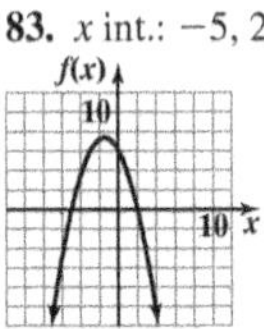

85. x int.: $x = -6, -1, 4$

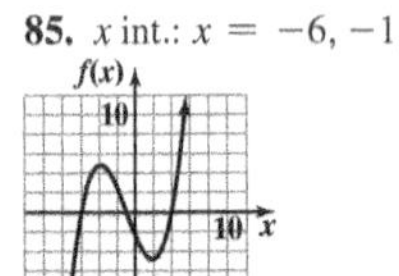

87. No, but this does not contradict Theorem 2, since f is discontinuous at $x = 1$.

89. (A) $P(x) = \begin{cases} 0.47 & \text{if } 0 < x \le 1 \\ 0.68 & \text{if } 1 < x \le 2 \\ 0.89 & \text{if } 2 < x \le 3 \\ 1.10 & \text{if } 3 < x \le 3.5 \end{cases}$

(B)

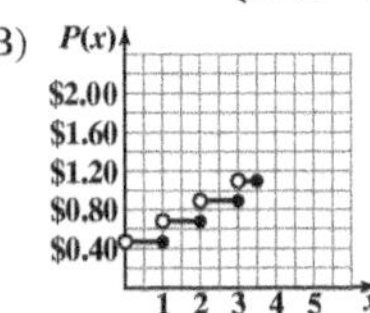

(C) Yes; no

93. (A) $S(x) = \begin{cases} 71 + 3.9x & \text{if } 0 \le x \le 50 \\ 171 + 1.9x & \text{if } x > 50 \end{cases}$

(B)

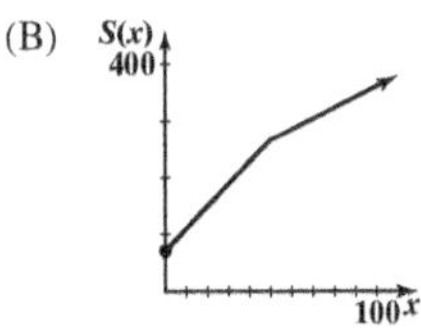

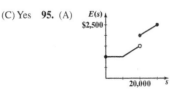

(C) Yes **95.** (A)

(B) $\lim_{x\to 10{,}000} E(s) = \$1{,}000$; $E(10{,}000) = \$1{,}000$
(C) $\lim_{x\to 20{,}000} E(s)$ does not exist; $E(20{,}000) = \$2{,}000$
(D) Yes; no

97. (A) t_2, t_3, t_4, t_6, t_7 (B) $\lim_{t\to t_5} N(t) = 7$; $N(t_5) = 7$ (C) $\lim_{t\to t_3} N(t)$ does not exist; $N(t_3) = 4$

Exercises 6.4

1. $\frac{9}{4} = 2.25$ **3.** $-\frac{27}{5} = -5.4$ **5.** $\frac{1}{3}\sqrt{3}$ **7.** $\frac{15}{2} - \frac{5}{2}\sqrt{7}$

9. (A) −3; slope of the secant line through $(1, f(1))$ and $(2, f(2))$ (B) $-2 - h$; slope of the secant line through $(1, f(1))$ and $(1 + h, f(1 + h))$ (C) −2; slope of the tangent line at $(1, f(1))$ **11.** (A) 15 (B) $6 + 3h$ (C) 6 **13.** (A) 40 km/hr (B) 40 (C) $y - 80 = 45(x - 2)$ or $y = 45x - 10$ **15.** $y - \frac{1}{2} = -\frac{1}{2}(x - 1)$ or $y = -\frac{x}{2} + 1$ **17.** $y - 16 = -32(x + 2)$ or $y = -32x - 48$ **19.** $f'(x) = 0$; $f'(1) = 0$, $f'(2) = 0$, $f'(3) = 0$ **21.** $f'(x) = 3$; $f'(1) = 3$, $f'(2) = 3$, $f'(3) = 3$ **23.** $f'(x) = -6x$; $f'(1) = -6$, $f'(2) = -12$, $f'(3) = -18$ **25.** $f'(x) = 2x - 2$; $f'(1) = 0$, $f'(2) = 2$, $f'(3) = 4$ **27.** $f'(x) = 8x + 3$; $f'(1) = 11$, $f'(2) = 19$, $f'(3) = 27$ **29.** $f'(x) = -2x + 5$; $f'(1) = 3$, $f'(2) = 1$, $f'(3) = -1$ **31.** $f'(x) = 20x - 9$; $f'(1) = 11$, $f'(2) = 31$, $f'(3) = 51$ **33.** $f'(x) = 6x^2$; $f'(1) = 6$, $f'(2) = 24$, $f'(3) = 54$ **35.** $f'(x) = -\frac{4}{x^2}$; $f'(1) = -4$, $f'(2) = -1$, $f'(3) = -\frac{4}{9}$ **37.** $f'(x) = \frac{3}{2\sqrt{x}}$; $f'(1) = \frac{3}{2}$, $f'(2) = \frac{3}{2\sqrt{2}}$ or $\frac{3\sqrt{2}}{4}$, $f'(3) = \frac{3}{2\sqrt{3}}$ or $\frac{\sqrt{3}}{2}$ **39.** $f'(x) = \frac{5}{\sqrt{x+5}}$; $f'(1) = \frac{5}{\sqrt{6}}$ or $\frac{5\sqrt{6}}{6}$, $f'(2) = \frac{5}{\sqrt{7}}$ or $\frac{5\sqrt{7}}{7}$, $f'(3) = \frac{5}{2\sqrt{2}}$ or $\frac{5\sqrt{2}}{4}$ **41.** $f'(x) = -\frac{1}{(x-4)^2}$; $f'(1) = -\frac{1}{9}$; $f'(2) = -\frac{1}{4}$; $f'(3) = -1$ **43.** $f'(x) = \frac{1}{(x+1)^2}$; $f'(1) = \frac{1}{4}$; $f'(2) = \frac{1}{9}$; $f'(3) = \frac{1}{16}$ **45.** (A) 5 (B) $3 + h$ (C) 3 (D) $y = 3x - 1$ **47.** (A) 5 m/s (B) $3 + h$ m/s (C) 3 m/s **49.** Yes **51.** No **53.** Yes **55.** Yes **57.** (A) $f'(x) = 2x - 4$ (B) −4, 0, 4 (C)

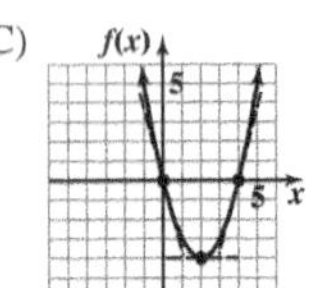

59. $v = f'(x) = 8x - 2$; 6 ft/s, 22 ft/s, 38 ft/s **61.** (A) The graphs of g and h are vertical translations of the graph of f. All three functions should have the same derivative. (B) $2x$ **63.** True **65.** False **67.** False

69. f is nondifferentiable at $x = 1$

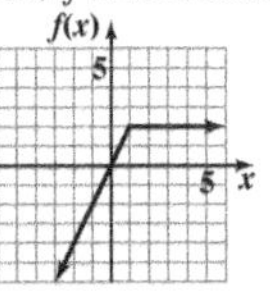

71. f is differentiable for all real numbers

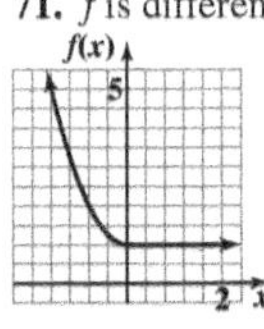

73. No **75.** No **77.** $f'(0) = 0$ **79.** 6 s; 192 ft/s **81.** (A) \$8.75 (B) $R'(x) = 60 - 0.05x$ (C) $R(1{,}000) = 35{,}000$; $R'(1{,}000) = 10$; At a production level of 1,000 car seats, the revenue is \$35,000 and is increasing at the rate of \$10 per seat. **83.** (A) $S'(t) = 1/(2\sqrt{t})$ (B) $S(4) = 6$; $S'(4) = 0.25$; After 4 months, the total sales are \$6 million and are increasing at the rate of \$0.25 million per month. (C) \$6.25 million; \$6.5 million **85.** (A) $p'(t) = 634t + 4{,}067$ (B) $p(10) = 104{,}970$, $p'(10) = 10{,}407$; In 2020, 104,970 tons of zinc are produced and this quantity is increasing at the rate of 10,407 tonnes per year.

87. (A)

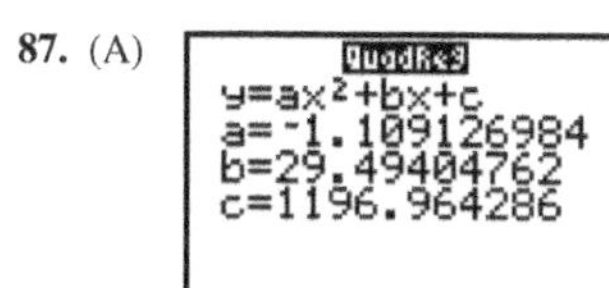

(B) $R(30) \approx 1083.6$ billion kilowatts, $R'(30) \approx -37.1$ billion kilowatts per year. In 2030, 1083.6 billion kilowatts will be sold and the amount sold is decreasing at the rate of 37.1 billion kilowatts per year.

89. (A) $P'(t) = 12 - 2t$ (B) $P(3) = 107$; $P'(3) = 6$. After 3 hours, the ozone level is 107 ppb and is increasing at the rate of 6 ppb per hour.

Exercises 6.5

1. $x^{1/2}$ **3.** x^{-5} **5.** x^{12} **7.** $x^{-1/4}$ **9.** 0 **11.** $7x^6$ **13.** $4x^3$ **15.** $-3x^{-4}$ **17.** $\frac{4}{3}x^{1/3}$ **19.** $-\frac{9}{x^{10}}$ **21.** $6x^2$ **23.** $1.8x^5$ **25.** $\frac{x^3}{3}$ **27.** 12 **29.** 2 **31.** 17 **33.** 2 **35.** $6t - 5$ **37.** $-10x^{-3} - 9x^{-2}$ **39.** $1.5u^{-0.7} - 8.8u^{1.2}$ **41.** $0.5 - 3.3t^2$ **43.** $-\frac{8}{5}x^{-5}$ **45.** $3x + \frac{14}{5}x^{-3}$ **47.** $-\frac{20}{9}\omega^{-5} + \frac{5}{3}\omega^{-2/3}$ **49.** $2u^{-1/3} - \frac{5}{3}u^{-2/3}$ **51.** $-\frac{9}{5}t^{-8/5} + 3t^{-3/2}$ **53.** $-\frac{1}{3}x^{-4/3}$ **55.** $-0.6x^{-3/2} + 6.4x^{-3} + 1$ **57.** (A) $f'(x) = 6 - 2x$ (B) $f'(2) = 2$; $f'(4) = -2$ (C) $y = 2x + 4$; $y = -2x + 16$ (D) $x = 3$ **59.** (A) $f'(x) = 12x^3 - 12x$ (B) $f'(2) = 72$; $f'(4) = 720$ (C) $y = 72x - 127$; $y = 720x - 2{,}215$ (D) $x = -1, 0, 1$ **61.** (A) $v = f'(x) = 176 - 32x$ (B) $f'(0) = 176$ ft/s; $f'(3) = 80$ ft/s (C) 5.5 s **63.** (A) $v = f'(x) = 3x^2 - 18x + 15$ (B) $f'(0) = 15$ ft/s; $f'(3) = -12$ ft/s (C) $x = 1$ s, $x = 5$ s **65.** $f'(x) = 2x - 3 - 2x^{-1/2} = 2x - 3 - \frac{2}{x^{1/2}}$; $x = 2.1777$ **67.** $f'(x) = 4\sqrt[3]{x} - 3x - 3$; $x = -2.9018$ **69.** $f'(x) = 0.2x^3 + 0.3x^2 - 3x - 1.6$; $x = -4.4607, -0.5159, 3.4765$ **71.** $f'(x) = 0.8x^3 - 9.36x^2 + 32.5x - 28.25$; $x = 1.3050$ **77.** $8x - 4$ **79.** $-20x^{-2}$ **81.** $-\frac{1}{5}x^{-2} + \frac{1}{2}x^{-3}$ **83.** False **85.** True **89.** (A) $S'(t) = 0.09t^2 + t + 2$ (B) $S(5) = 29.25$, $S'(5) = 9.25$. After 5 months, sales are \$29.25 million and are increasing at the rate of \$9.25 million per month. (C) $S(10) = 103$, $S'(10) = 21$. After 10 months, sales are \$103 million and are increasing at the rate of \$21 million per month. **91.** (A) $N'(x) = 3{,}780/x^2$ (B) $N'(10) = 37.8$. At the \$10,000 level of advertising, sales are increasing at the rate of 37.8 boats per \$1,000 spent on advertising. $N'(20) = 9.45$. At the \$20,000 level of advertising, sales are increasing at the rate of 9.45 boats per \$1,000 spent on advertising.

93. (A)

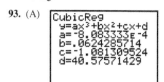

CubicReg
y=ax³+bx²+cx+d
a=-8.083333E-4
b=.0624285714
c=-1.081309524
d=40.57571429

(B) In 2025, 35.5% of male high school graduates enroll in college and the percentage is decreasing at the rate of 1.5% per year. **95.** (A) −1.37 beats/min (B) −0.58 beats/min **97.** (A) 25 items/hr (B) 8.33 items/hr

Exercises 6.6

1. 3; 3.01 **3.** 2.8; 2.799 **5.** 0; 0.01 **7.** 100; 102.01 **9.** $\Delta x = 3$; $\Delta y = 75$; $\Delta y/\Delta x = 25$ **11.** 20 **13.** 20 **15.** $dy = (24x - 3x^2)dx$ **17.** $dy = \left(2x - \frac{x^2}{3}\right)dx$ **19.** $dy = -\frac{295}{x^{3/2}}dx$ **21.** (A) $12 + 3\Delta x$ (B) 12 **23.** $dy = 6(3x - 1)dx$ **25.** $dy = \left(\frac{x^2 + 9}{x^2}\right)dx$ **27.** $dy = 1.4$; $\Delta y = 1.44$ **29.** $dy = -12$; $\Delta y = -12.77$ **31.** 120 in.^{3} **33.** (A) $\Delta y = \Delta x + (\Delta x)^2$; $dy = \Delta x$

(B) (C)

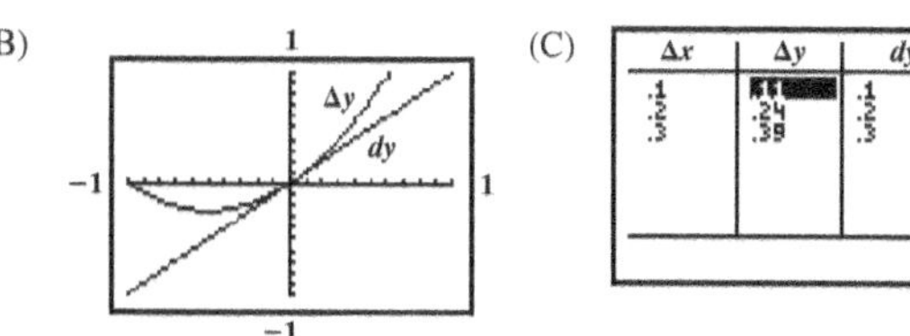

35. (A) $\Delta y = -\Delta x + (\Delta x)^2 + (\Delta x)^3$; $dy = -\Delta x$

(B) (C)

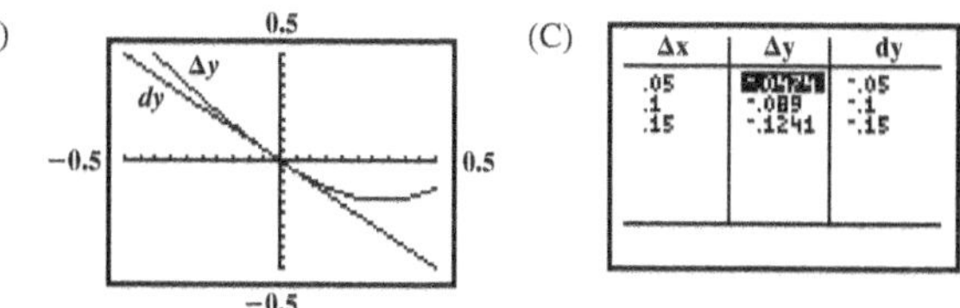

37. True **39.** False **41.** $dy = \left(\frac{2}{3}x^{-1/3} - \frac{10}{3}x^{2/3}\right)dx$ **43.** $dy = 3.9$; $\Delta y = 3.83$ **45.** 40-unit increase; 20-unit increase **47.** −\$2.50; \$1.25 **49.** −1.37 beats/min; −0.58 beats/min **51.** 1.26 mm^2 **53.** 3 wpm **55.** (A) 2,100 increase (B) 4,800 increase (C) 2,100 increase

Exercises 6.7

1. \$22,889.80 **3.** \$110.20 **5.** \$32,000.00 **7.** \$230.00 **9.** $C'(x) = 0.7$ **11.** $C'(x) = -0.2(0.1x - 23)$ **13.** $R'(x) = 4 - 0.02x$ **15.** $R'(x) = 12 - 0.08x$ **17.** $P'(x) = 3.3 - 0.02x$ **19.** $P'(x) = 7.4 - 0.06x$ **21.** $\overline{C}(x) = 1.5 + \frac{408}{x}$ **23.** $\overline{C}'(x) = -\frac{408}{x^2}$ **25.** $P(x) = 7.5x - 0.03x^2 - 408$ **27.** $\overline{P}(x) = 7.5 - 0.03x - \frac{408}{x}$ **29.** True **31.** False **33.** (A) \$29.50 (B) \$30 **35.** (A) \$420 (B) $\overline{C}'(500) = -0.24$. At a production level of 500 frames, average cost is decreasing at the rate of 24¢ per frame. (C) Approximately \$419.76 **37.** (A) \$14.70 (B) \$15 **39.** (A) $P'(450) = 0.5$. At a production level of 450 sweatshirts, profit is increasing at the rate of 50¢ per sweatshirt. (B) $P'(750) = -2.5$. At a production level of 750 sweatshirts, profit is decreasing at the rate of \$2.50 per sweatshirt. **41.** (A) \$13.50 (B) $\overline{P}'(50) = \$0.27$. At a production level of 50 mowers, the average profit per mower is increasing at the rate of \$0.27 per mower. (C) Approximately \$13.77 **43.** (A) $p = 100 - 0.025x$, domain: $0 \le x \le 4{,}000$ (B) $R(x) = 100x - 0.025x^2$, domain: $0 \le x \le 4{,}000$ (C) $R'(1{,}600) = 20$. At a production level of 1,600 pairs of running shoes, revenue is increasing at the rate of \$20 per pair. (D) $R'(2{,}500) = -25$. At a production level of 2,500 pairs of running shoes, revenue is decreasing at the rate of \$25 per pair.

45. (A) $p = 200 - \frac{1}{30}x$, domain: $0 \le x \le 6{,}000$ (B) $C'(x) = 60$ (C) $R(x) = 200x - (x^2/30)$, domain: $0 \le x \le 6{,}000$ (D) $R'(x) = 200 - (x/15)$ (E) $R'(1{,}500) = 100$. At a production level of 1,500 saws, revenue is increasing at the rate of \$100 per saw. $R'(4{,}500) = -100$. At a production level of 4,500 saws, revenue is decreasing at the rate of \$100 per saw. (F) Break-even points: (600, 108,000) and (3,600, 288,000)

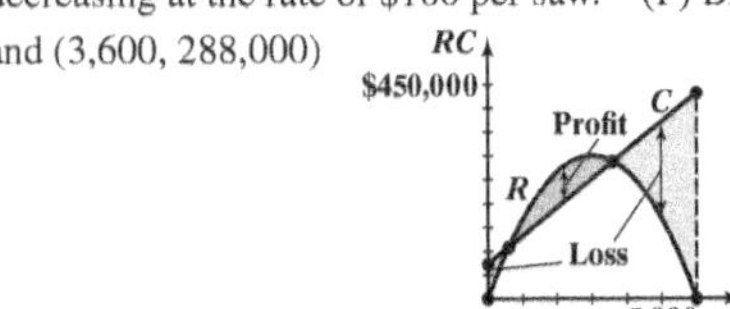

(G) $P(x) = -(x^2/30) + 140x - 72{,}000$

(H) $P'(x) = -(x/15) + 140$

(I) $P'(1{,}500) = 40$. At a production level of 1,500 saws, profit is increasing at the rate of \$40 per saw. $P'(3{,}000) = -60$. At a production level of 3,000 saws, profit is decreasing at the rate of \$60 per saw.

47. (A) $p = 50 - 0.025x$, domain: $0 \le x \le 2{,}000$

(B) $R(x) = 50x - 0.025x^2$, domain: $0 \le x \le 2{,}000$

(C) $C(x) = 10x + 7{,}000$

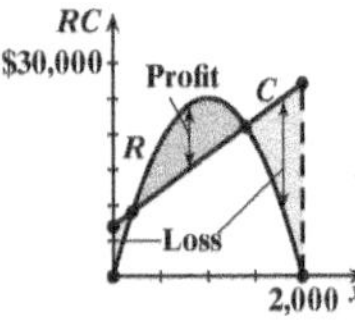

(D) Break-even points: (200, 9,000) and (1,400, 21,000)

(E) $P(x) = 40x - 0.025x^2 - 7{,}000$

(F) $P'(500) = 15$. At a production level of 500 mixers, profit is increasing at the rate of \$15 per mixer. $P'(900) = -5$. At a production level of 900 mixers, profit is decreasing at the rate of \$5 per mixer.

49. (A) $x = 500$ (B) $P(x) = 176x - 0.2x^2 - 21{,}900$ (C) $x = 440$

(D) Break-even points: (150, 25, 500) and (730, 39, 420); x intercepts for $P(x)$: $x = 150$ and $x = 730$

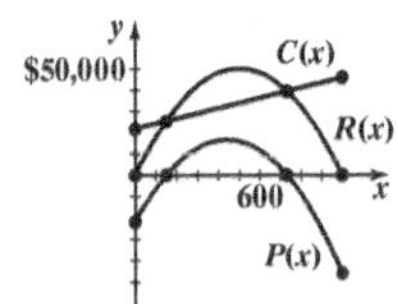

51. (A) $R(x) = 20x - x^{3/2}$

(B) Break-even points: (44, 588), (258, 1,016)

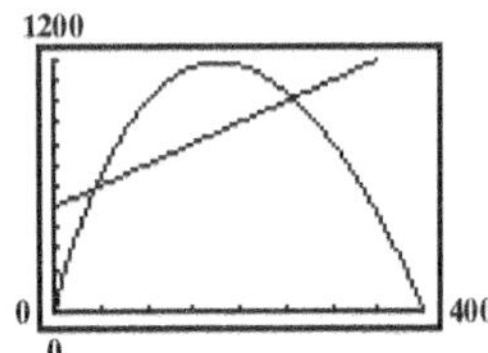

53. (A)

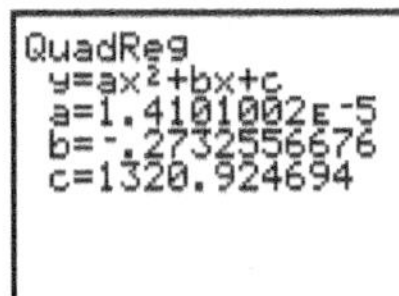

(B) Fixed costs ≈ \$721,680; variable costs ≈ \$121

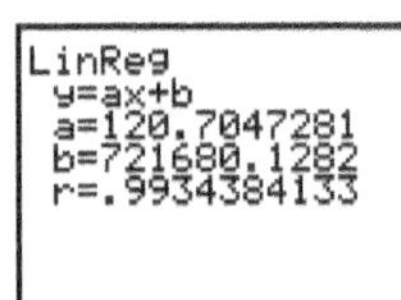

(C) (713, 807,703), (5,423, 1,376,227) (D) $\$254 \le p \le \$1{,}133$

Chapter 6 Review Exercises

1. (A) 40 (B) 20 (C) 20 (D) 14 (E) 14 (F) 14 *(6.2)* **2.** $f'(x) = 4$ *(6.2)* **3.** (A) 65 (B) 44 (C) $\frac{4}{11}$ (D) 96 *(6.1)* **4.** 1.5 *(6.1)* **5.** 3.5 *(6.1)* **6.** 3.75 *(6.1)* **7.** 3.75 *(6.1)* **8.** (A) 1 (B) 1 (C) 1 (D) 1 *(6.1)* **9.** (A) 2 (B) 3 (C) Does not exist (D) 3 *(6.1)* **10.** (A) 4 (B) 4 (C) 4 (D) Does not exist *(6.1)* **11.** (A) Does not exist (B) 3 (C) No *(6.3)* **12.** (A) 2 (B) Not defined (C) No *(6.3)* **13.** (A) 1 (B) 1 (C) Yes *(6.3)* **14.** 10 *(6.2)* **15.** 5 *(6.2)* **16.** ∞ *(6.2)* **17.** $-\infty$ *(6.2)* **18.** ∞ *(6.2)* **19.** ∞ *(6.2)* **20.** ∞ *(6.2)* **21.** $x = 2$; $x = 6$ *(6.2)* **22.** $y = 5$; $y = 10$ *(6.2)* **23.** $x = 2$; $x = 6$ *(6.3)* **24.** $f'(x) = 12x^2$ *(6.4)* **25.** (A) 6 (B) −4 (C) −9 (D) 1 (E) −12 **26.** $x + 2$ *(6.5)*

27. $x^{-2/3} + 4$ *(6.5)* **28.** 0 *(6.5)*

29. $-\frac{3}{2}x^{-2} + \frac{15}{4}x^2 = \frac{-3}{2x^2} + \frac{15x^2}{4}$ *(6.5)*

30. $-2x^{-5} + x^3 = \frac{-2}{x^5} + x^3$ *(6.5)*

31. $f'(x) = 12x^3 + 9x^2 - 2$ *(6.5)* **32.** $\Delta x = 3, \Delta y = 57, \Delta y/\Delta x = 19$ *(6.6)* **33.** 19 *(6.6)* **34.** 39 *(6.6)* **35.** $\Delta y = 1.32$; $dy = 1.3$ *(6.6)* **36.** (A) 4 (B) 6 (C) Does not exist (D) 6 (E) No *(6.3)* **37.** (A) 3 (B) 3 (C) 3 (D) 3 (E) Yes *(6.3)* **38.** (A) $(8, \infty)$ (B) $[0, 8]$ *(6.3)* **39.** $(-3, 4)$ *(6.3)* **40.** $(-3, 0) \cup (5, \infty)$ *(6.3)* **41.** $(-2.3429, -0.4707) \cup (1.8136, \infty)$ *(6.3)* **42.** (A) 3 (B) $2 + 0.5h$ (C) 2 *(6.4)* **43.** $-x^{-5} + 4x^{-3}$ *(6.4)*

44. $\frac{3}{4}x^{-1/2} - \frac{5}{6}x^{-3/2} = \frac{3}{4\sqrt{x}} - \frac{5}{6\sqrt{x^3}}$ *(6.5)*

45. $0.6x^{-2/3} - 0.3x^{-4/3} = \frac{0.6}{x^{2/3}} - \frac{0.3}{x^{4/3}}$ *(6.4)*

46. $-\frac{20}{7}(-3)x = \frac{9}{5x^4}$ *(6.5)* **47.** (A) $m = f'(4) = 2$ (B) $y = 2x - 2$ *(6.4, 6.5)* **48.** $x = 0$ *(6.4)* **49.** $x = -5, x = -1$ *(6.5)* **50.** $x = -1.3401, 0.5771, 2.2630$ *(6.4)* **51.** ± 2.4824 *(6.5)* **52.** (A) $v = f'(y) = 30 + 16t$ (B) 62 ft/sec *(6.5)* **53.** (A) $v = f'(x) = -6x + 50$ (B) $v(2) = 38$ ft/s *(6.5)*

54. (A) The graph of g is the graph of f shifted 4 units to the right, and the graph of h is the graph of f shifted 4 units down:

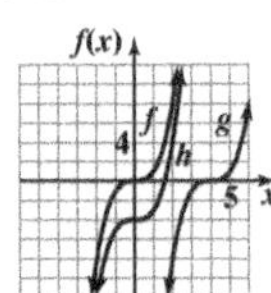

(B) The graph of g' is the graph of f' shifted 4 units to the right, and the graph of h' is the graph of f':

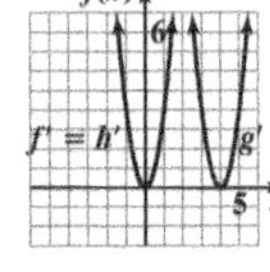

55. $(-\infty, \infty)$ *(6.3)* **56.** $(-\infty, 2) \cup (2, \infty)$ *(6.3)* **57.** $(-\infty, -4) \cup (-4, 1) \cup (1, \infty)$ *(6.3)* **58.** $(-\infty, \infty)$ *(6.3)*

59. $[-2, 2]$ *(6.3)* **60.** (A) $-\frac{3}{5}$ (B) Does not exist (C) $-\frac{3}{7}$ *(6.1)*

61. (A) $\frac{1}{2}$ (B) 0 (C) Does not exist *(6.1)* **62.** (A) −1 (B) 1 (C) Does not exist *(6.1)*

63. (A) $-\frac{1}{6}$ (B) Does not exist (C) $-\frac{1}{3}$ *(6.1)* **64.** (A) 0 (B) −1 (C) Does not exist *(6.1)* **65.** (A) $\frac{2}{3}$ (B) $\frac{2}{3}$ (C) Does not exist *(6.3)*

66. (A) ∞ (B) $-\infty$ (C) ∞ *(6.3)* **67.** (A) 0 (B) 0 (C) Does not exist *(6.2)* **68.** 2 *(6.1)* **69.** $\frac{-6}{x^3}$ *(6.1)*

70. $2x - 1$ *(6.4)* **71.** $1/(2\sqrt{x})$ *(6.4)* **72.** Yes *(6.4)* **73.** No *(6.4)*

74. No *(6.4)* **75.** No *(6.4)* **76.** Yes *(6.4)* **77.** Yes *(6.4)*
78. Horizontal asymptote: $y = 11$; vertical asymptote: $x = 5$ *(6.2)*
79. Horizontal asymptote: $y = 0$; vertical asymptote: $x = 4$ *(6.2)*
80. No horizontal asymptote; vertical asymptote: $x = 3$ *(6.2)*
81. Horizontal asymptote: $y = 1$; vertical asymptotes: $x = -2, x = 1$ *(6.2)*
82. Horizontal asymptote: $y = 1$; vertical asymptotes: $x = -1, x = 1$ *(6.2)*
83. The domain of $f'(x)$ is all real numbers except $x = 0$. At $x = 0$, the graph of $y = f(x)$ is smooth, but it has a vertical tangent. *(6.4)*
84. (A) $\lim_{x \to 1^-} f(x) = 1$; $\lim_{x \to 1^+} f(x) = -1$

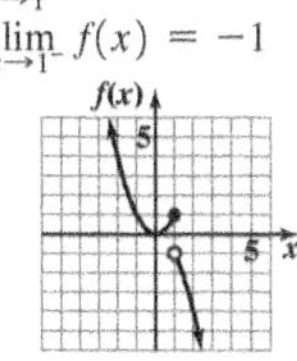

(B) $\lim_{x \to 1^-} f(x) = -1$; $\lim_{x \to 1^+} f(x) = 1$

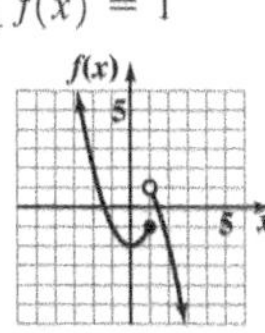

(C) $m = 1$

(D) The graphs in (A) and (B) have discontinuities at $x = 1$; the graph in (C) does not. *(6.2)*
85. (A) 1 (B) -1 (C) Does not exist (D) No *(6.4)*

86. (A) $S(x) = \begin{cases} 7.47 + 0.4x & \text{if } 0 \le x \le 90 \\ 24.786 + 0.2076x & \text{if } 90 < x \end{cases}$

(B)

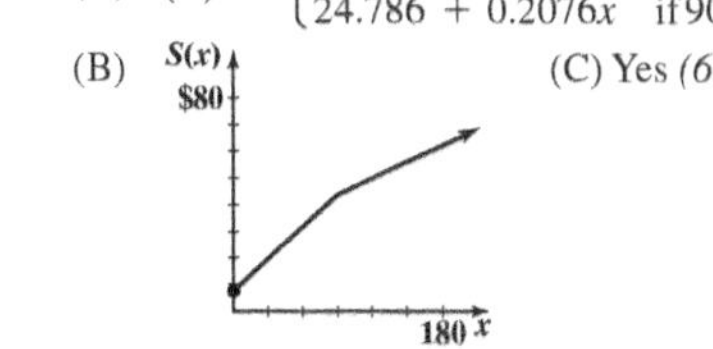

(C) Yes *(6.2)*

87. (A) \$121.00 (B) \$120.00 *(6.7)* **88.** (A) $C(200) = 111{,}200$; $C'(200) = 512$. At a production level of 200 motorcycles, the total cost is \$111,200, and cost is increasing at the rate of \$512 per motorcycle.
(B) $\overline{C}(200) = 556$; $\overline{C}'(200) = -0.22$. At a production level of 200 motorcycles, the average cost is \$556, and average cost is decreasing at a rate of \$0.22 per bicycle. *(6.7)*
89. The approximate cost of producing the 201st printer is greater than that of the 601st printer. Since these marginal costs are decreasing, the manufacturing process is becoming more efficient. *(6.7)*
90. (A) $C'(x) = 2$; $\overline{C}(x) = 2 + \frac{9{,}000}{x}$; $\overline{C}'(x) = \frac{-9{,}000}{x^2}$
(B) $R(x) = xp = 25x - 0.01x^2$; $R'(x) = 25 - 0.02x$; $\overline{R}(x) = 25 - 0.01x$; $\overline{R}'(x) = -0.01$ (C) $P(x) = R(x) - C(x) = 23x - 0.01x^2 - 9{,}000$; $P'(x) = 23 - 0.02x$; $\overline{P}(x) = 23 - 0.01x - \frac{9{,}000}{x}$;
$\overline{P}'(x) = -0.01 + \frac{9{,}000}{x^2}$
(D) (500, 10,000) and (1,800, 12,600)
(E) $P'(1{,}000) = 3$. Profit is increasing at the rate of \$3 per umbrella.
$P'(1{,}150) = 0$. Profit is flat.
$P'(1{,}400) = -5$. Profit is decreasing at the rate of \$5 per umbrella.
(F)

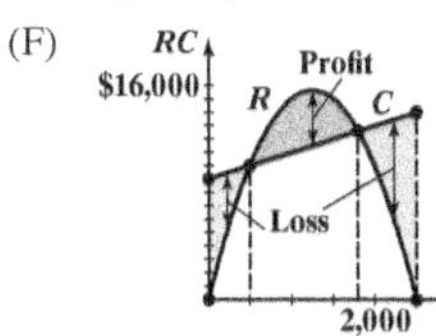

91. (A) 8 (B) 20 *(6.5)*
92. $N(9) = 27$; $N'(9) = 3.5$; After 9 months, 27,000 pools have been sold and the total sales are increasing at the rate of 3,500 pools per month. *(6.5)*

93. (A)

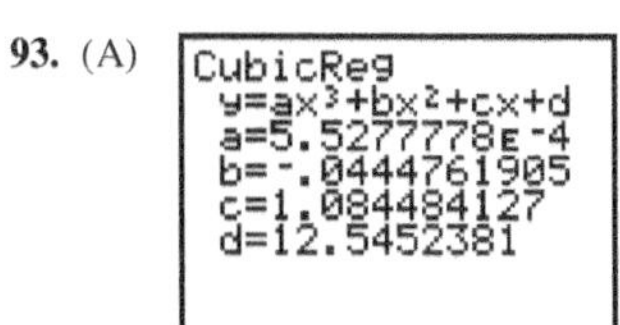

(B) $N(60) = 36.9$; $N'(60) = 1.7$. In 2020, natural-gas consumption is 36.9 trillion cubic feet and is increasing at the rate of 1.7 trillion cubic feet per year *(6.4)*

94. (A)

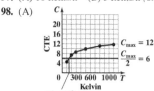

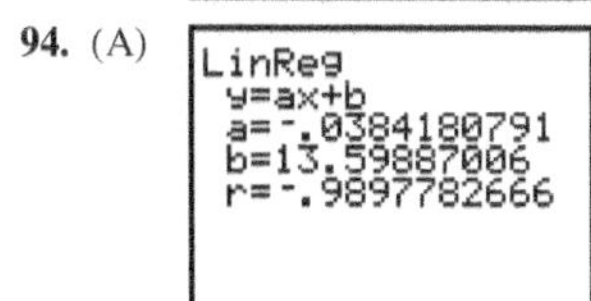

(B) Fixed costs: \$484.21; variable costs per kringle: \$2.11

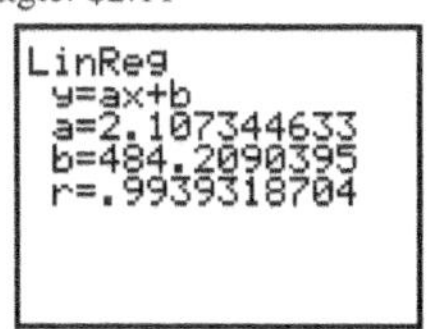

(C) (51, 591.15), (248, 1,007.62) (D) $\$4.07 < p < \$11.64$ *(6.7)*
95. $C'(10) = -1$; $C'(100) = -0.001(2.5)$ *(6.5)*
96. $F(4) = 98.16$; $F'(4) = -0.32$; After 4 hours the patient's temperature is 98.16°F and is decreasing at the rate of 0.32°F per hour. *(6.5)*
97. (A) 10 items/h (B) 5 items/h *(6.5)*
98. (A) (B) $C(T) = \frac{12T}{150 + T}$
(C) $C = 9.6$ at $T = 600$K; $T = 750$K when $C = 10$ *(6.3)*

Chapter 7

Exercises 7.1

1. $A = 1{,}465.68$ **3.** $P = 9{,}117.21$ **5.** $t = 5.61$ **7.** $r = 0.04$
9. \$11,051.71; \$12,214.03; \$13,498.59
11.

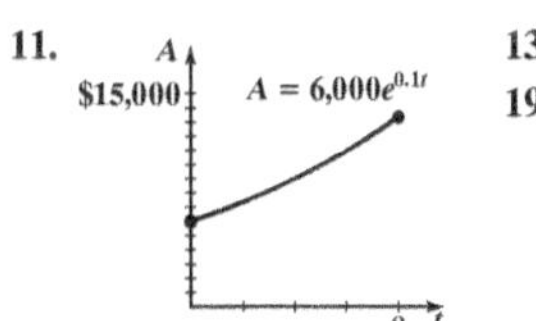

13. $t = 9.90$ **15.** $r = 0.08$ **17.** $t = 36.62$
19. $r = 0.11$

21.

n	$[1 + (1/n)]^n$
10	2.593 74
100	2.704 81
1,000	2.716 92
10,000	2.718 15
100,000	2.718 27
1,000,000	2.718 28
10,000,000	2.718 28
↓	↓
∞	$e = 2.718281828459\ldots$

23. $\lim_{n \to \infty} (1 + n)^{1/n} = 1$

25.

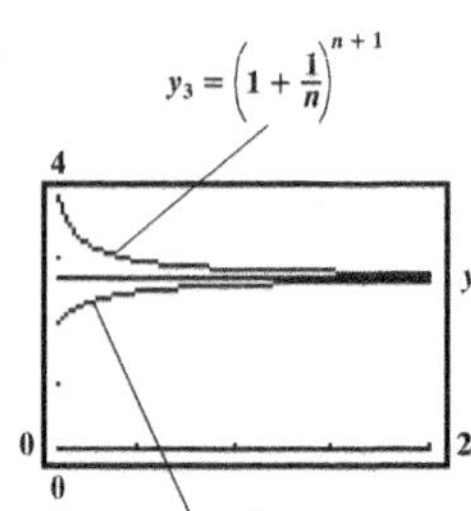
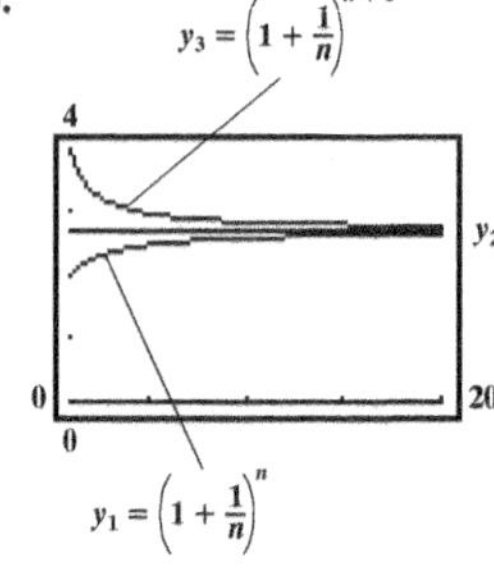

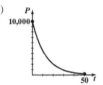

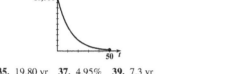

27. (A) \$12,398.62 (B) 27.34 yr
29. \$15,782.10 **31.** 8.11%

33. (A)

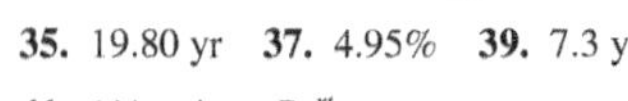

(B) $\lim_{t\to\infty} 10{,}000e^{-0.08t} = 0$

35. 19.80 yr **37.** 4.95% **39.** 7.3 yr

41. (A) $A = Pe^{rt}$
$2P = Pe^{rt}$
$2 = e^{rt}$
$rt = \ln 2$
$t = \dfrac{\ln 2}{r}$

(B)

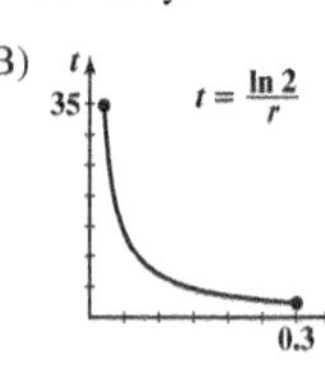

Although r could be any positive number, the restrictions on r are reasonable in the sense that most investments would be expected to earn a return of between 2% and 30%.

(C) The doubling times (in years) are 13.86, 6.93, 4.62, 3.47, 2.77, and 2.31, respectively.
43. $t = -(\ln 0.5)/0.000\,433\,2 \approx 1{,}600$ yr
45. $r = (\ln 0.5)/30 \approx -0.0231$ **47.** 61.3 yr **49.** 1.39%

Exercises 7.2

1. $y = 4$ **3.** $x = 1/5$ **5.** $y = 1/3$ **7.** $\ln x - \ln y$ **9.** $5 \ln x$
11. $\ln u + 2\ln v - \ln w$ **13.** $5e^x + 3$ **15.** $-\dfrac{2}{x} + 2x$ **17.** $3x^2 - 6e^x$
19. $e^x + 1 - \dfrac{1}{x}$ **21.** $\dfrac{3}{x}$ **23.** $5 - \dfrac{5}{x}$ **25.** $\dfrac{2}{x} + 4e^x$ **27.** $f'(x) = e^x + ex^{e-1}$
29. $f'(x) = (e+1)x^e$ **31.** $f'(x) = \dfrac{1}{x}$; $y = x + 2$
33. $f'(x) = 3e^x$; $y = 3x + 3$ **35.** $f'(x) = \dfrac{3}{x}$; $y = \dfrac{3x}{e}$
37. $f'(x) = 3e^x$; $y = 3e^x + 4$ **39.** Yes; yes **41.** No; no
43. $f(x) = 10x + \ln 10 + \ln x$; $f'(x) = 10 + \dfrac{1}{x}$
45. $f(x) = \ln 4 - 3\ln x$; $f'(x) = -\dfrac{3}{x}$ **47.** $\dfrac{1}{x \ln 2}$ **49.** $3^x \ln 3$
51. $2 - \dfrac{1}{x \ln 10}$ **53.** $1 + 10^x \ln 10$ **55.** $\dfrac{3}{x} + \dfrac{2}{x \ln 3}$ **57.** $2^x \ln 2$
59. $(-0.82, 0.44)$, $(1.43, 4.18)$, $(8.61, 5503.66)$ **61.** $(0.49, 0.49)$
63. (3.65, 1.30), (332,105.11, 12.71) **67.** \$28,447/yr; \$18,664/yr; \$11,021/yr
69. $A'(t) = 5{,}000(\ln 4)4^t$; $A'(1) = 27{,}726$ bacteria/hr (rate of change at the end of the first hour); $A'(5) = 7{,}097{,}827$ bacteria/hr (rate of change at the end of the fifth hour) **71.** At the 40-lb weight level, blood pressure would increase at the rate of 0.44 mm of mercury per pound of weight gain. At the 90-lb weight level, blood pressure would increase at the rate of 0.19 mm of mercury per pound of weight gain. **73.** $dR/dS = k/S$
75. (A) \$808.41 per year (B) \$937.50 per year

Exercises 7.3

1. (A) $5x^4$ (B) $4x^3$ **3.** (A) $15x^{14}$ (B) $50x^{13}$ **5.** (A) $3x^2$ (B) $2x^3$
7. (A) $-5x^{-6}$ (B) $\dfrac{2}{7}x^{-5}$ **9.** $2x^3(2x) + (x^2 - 2)(6x^2) = 10x^4 - 12x^2$
11. $(x-3)(2) + (2x-1)(1) = 4x - 7$
13. $\dfrac{(x-3)(1) - x(1)}{(x-3)^2} = \dfrac{-3}{(x-3)^2}$
15. $\dfrac{(x-2)(2) - (2x+3)(1)}{(x-2)^2} = \dfrac{-7}{(x-2)^2}$
17. $3xe^x + 3e^x = 3(x+1)e^x$ **19.** $x^3\left(\dfrac{1}{x}\right) + 3x^2 \ln x = x^2(1 + 3\ln x)$
21. $(x^2+1)(2) + (2x-3)(2x) = 6x^2 - 6x + 2$
23. $(0.4x+2)(0.5) + (0.5x-5)(0.4) = 0.4x - 1$
25. $\dfrac{(2x-3)(2x) - (x^2+1)(2)}{(2x-3)^2} = \dfrac{2x^2 - 6x - 2}{(2x-3)^2}$
27. $(x^2+3)2x + (x^2-5)2x = 4x^3 - 4x$
29. $\dfrac{(x^2-5)2x - (x^2+3)2x}{(x^2-5)^2} = \dfrac{-16x}{(x^2-5)^2}$
31. $\dfrac{(x^2+1)e^x - e^x(2x)}{(x^2+1)^2} = \dfrac{(x-1)^2 e^x}{(x^2+1)^2}$
33. $\dfrac{(1+x)\left(\frac{1}{x}\right) - \ln x}{(1+x)^2} = \dfrac{1 + x - x\ln x}{x(1+x)^2}$
35. $xf'(x) + f(x)$ **37.** $x^4 f'(x) + 4x^3 f(x)$ **39.** $\dfrac{x^2 f'(x) - 2xf(x)}{x^4}$
41. $\dfrac{f(x) - xf'(x)}{[f(x)]^2}$ **43.** $e^x f'(x) + f(x)e^x = e^x[f'(x) + f(x)]$
45. $\dfrac{f(x)\left(\frac{1}{x}\right) - (\ln x)f'(x)}{f(x)^2} = \dfrac{f(x) - (x\ln x)f'(x)}{xf(x)^2}$
47. $(2x+1)(2x-3) + (x^2-3x)(2) = 6x^2 - 10x - 3$
49. $(1.5t - t^2)(6) + (6t - 5.4)(1.5 - 2t) = -18t^2 + 28.8t - 8.1$
51. $\dfrac{(x^2+2x)(5) - (5x-3)(2x+2)}{(x^2+2x)^2} = \dfrac{-5x^2 + 6x + 6}{(x^2+2x)^2}$
53. $\dfrac{(w^2-1)(2w-3) - (w^2-3w+1)(2w)}{(w^2-1)^2} = \dfrac{3w^2 - 4w + 3}{(w^2-1)^2}$
55. $(3 - 2x + x^2)e^x + e^x(-2 + 2x) = (1 + x^2)e^x$
57. (A) $f'(x) = \dfrac{x \cdot 0 - 1 \cdot 1}{x^2} = -\dfrac{1}{x^2}$ (B) Note that $f(x) = x^{-1}$ and use the power rule: $f'(x) = -x^{-2} = -\dfrac{1}{x^2}$
59. (A) $f'(x) = \dfrac{x^4 \cdot 0 - (-3) \cdot 4x^3}{x^8} = \dfrac{12}{x^5}$ (B) Note that $f(x) = -3x^{-4}$ and use the power rule: $f'(x) = 12x^{-5} = \dfrac{12}{x^5}$
61. $f'(x) = (1+3x)(-2) + (5-2x)(3)$; $y = -11x + 29$
63. $f'(x) = \dfrac{(3x-4)(1) - (x-8)(3)}{(3x-4)^2}$; $y = 5x - 13$
65. $f'(x) = \dfrac{2^x - x(2^x \ln 2)}{2^{2x}}$; $y = \left(\dfrac{1 - 2\ln 2}{4}\right)x + \ln 2$

67. $f'(x) = (2x - 15)(2x) + (x^2 + 18)(2) = 6(x - 2)(x - 3); x = 2, x = 3$ **69.** $f'(x) = \frac{(x^2 + 1)(1) - x(2x)}{(x^2 + 1)^2} = \frac{1 - x^2}{(x^2 + 1)^2}; x = -1, x = 1$

71. $7x^6 - 3x^2$ **73.** $-27x^{-4} = -\frac{27}{x^4}$ **75.** $(w - 4)3^w \ln 3 + 3^w = [(w - 4)\ln 3 + 1]3^w$ **77.** $9x^{1/3}(3x^2) + (x^3 + 5)(3x^{-2/3}) = \frac{30x^3 + 15}{x^{2/3}}$

79. $\frac{(1 + x^2)\frac{1}{x \ln 2} - 2x \log_2 x}{(1 + x^2)^2} = \frac{1 + x^2 - 2x^2 \ln x}{x(1 + x^2)^2 \ln 2}$

81. $\frac{(x^2 - 3)(2x^{-2/3}) - 6x^{1/3}(2x)}{(x^2 - 3)^2} = \frac{-10x^2 - 6}{(x^2 - 3)^2 x^{2/3}}$

83. $g'(t) = \frac{(3t^2 - 1)(0.2) - (0.2t)(6t)}{(3t^2 - 1)^2} = \frac{-0.6t^2 - 0.2}{(3t^2 - 1)^2}$

85. $(20x)\frac{1}{x \ln 10} + 20 \log x = \frac{20(1 + \ln x)}{\ln 10}$

87. $(x + 3)(2x - 3) + (x^2 - 3x + 5)(1) = 3x^2 - 4$

89. $(x^2 + x + 1)(2x - 1) + (x^2 - x + 1)(2x + 1) = 4x^3 + 2x$

91. $\frac{e^t(1 + \ln t) - (t \ln t)e^t}{e^{2t}} = \frac{1 + \ln t - t \ln t}{e^t}$

93. (A) $S'(t) = \frac{(t^2 + 50)(180t) - 90t^2(2t)}{(t^2 + 50)^2} = \frac{9{,}000t}{(t^2 + 50)^2}$

(B) $S(10) = 60$; $S'(10) = 4$. After 10 months, the total sales are 60,000 video games, and sales are increasing at the rate of 4,000 video games per month. (C) Approximately 64,000 video games

95. (A) $\frac{dx}{dp} = \frac{(0.1p + 1)(0) - 4{,}000(0.1)}{(0.1p + 1)^2} = \frac{-400}{(0.1p + 1)^2}$

(B) $x = 800$; $dx/dp = -16$. At a price level of \$40, the demand is 800 DVD players per week, and demand is decreasing at the rate of 16 players per dollar. (C) Approximately 784 DVD players

97. (A) $C'(t) = \frac{(t^2 + 1)(0.14) - 0.14t(2t)}{(t^2 + 1)^2} = \frac{0.14 - 0.14t^2}{(t^2 + 1)^2}$

(B) $C'(0.5) = 0.0672$. After 0.5 hr, concentration is increasing at the rate of 0.0672 mg/cm^3 per hour. $C'(3) = -0.0112$. After 3 hr, concentration is decreasing at the rate of 0.0112 mg/cm^3 per hour.

Exercises 7.4

1. $f'(x) = 9x^8 + 10$ **3.** $f'(x) = \frac{7}{2}x^{-1/2} - 6x^{-3}$ **5.** $f'(x) = 8e^x$

7. $f'(x) = \frac{4}{x} + 8x$ **9.** 3 **11.** $-30x^5$ **13.** $2x$ **15.** $4x^3$

17. $-8(5 - 2x)^3$ **19.** $5(4 + 0.2x)^4(0.2) = (4 + 0.2x)^4$

21. $30x(3x^2 + 5)^4$ **23.** $5e^{5x}$ **25.** $-18e^{-6x}$ **27.** $(2x - 5)^{-1/2} = \frac{1}{(2x - 5)^{1/2}}$

29. $-8x^3(x^4 + 1)^{-3} = \frac{-8x^3}{(x^4 + 1)^3}$ **31.** $\frac{6x}{1 + x^2}$ **33.** $\frac{3(1 + \ln x)^2}{x}$

35. $f'(x) = 6(2x - 1)^2; y = 6x - 5; x = \frac{1}{2}$

37. $f'(x) = 2(4x - 3)^{-1/2} = \frac{2}{(4x - 3)^{1/2}}; y = \frac{2}{3}x + 1$; none

39. $f'(x) = 10(x - 2)e^{x^2 - 4x + 1}; y = -20ex + 5e; x = 2$

41. $12(x^2 - 2)^3(2x) = 24x(x^2 - 2)^3$

43. $-6(t^2 + 3t)^{-4}(2t + 3) = \frac{-6(2t + 3)}{(t^2 + 3t)^4}$

45. $\frac{1}{2}(w^2 + 8)^{-1/2}(2w) = \frac{w}{\sqrt{w^2 + 8}}$

47. $6e^{-7x} - 42xe^{-7x} = 6(1 - 7x)e^{-7x}$

49. $\frac{3x\left(\frac{1}{1 + x^2}\right)2x - 3\ln(1 + x^2)}{9x^2} = \frac{2x^2 - (1 + x^2)\ln(1 + x^2)}{3x^2(1 + x^2)}$

51. $6te^{3(t^2+1)}$ **53.** $\frac{3x}{x^2 + 3}$ **55.** $-5(w^3 + 4)^{-6}(3w^2) = \frac{-15w^2}{(w^3 + 4)^6}$

57. $f'(x) = (4 - x)^3 - 3x(4 - x)^2 = 4(4 - x)^2(1 - x); y = -16x + 48$

59. $f'(x) = \frac{(4x - 7)^5 - 20x(4x - 7)^4}{(4x - 7)^{10}} = \frac{-16x - 7}{(4x - 7)^6}; y = -39x + 80$

61. $f'(x) = \frac{1}{2x\sqrt{\ln x}}; y = \frac{x}{2e} + \frac{1}{2}$

63. $f'(x) = 2x(x - 5)^3 + 3x^2(x - 5)^2 = 5x(x - 5)^2(x - 2); x = 0, 2, 5$

65. $f'(x) = \frac{(4x + 6)^3 - 12x(4x + 6)^2}{(4x + 6)^6} = \frac{6 - 8x}{(4x + 6)^4}; x = \frac{3}{4}$

67. $f'(x) = (x^2 - 8x + 20)^{-1/2}(x - 4) = \frac{x - 4}{(x^2 - 8x + 20)^{1/2}}; x = 4$

69. No; yes **71.** Domain of f: $(0, \infty)$; domain of g: $[0, \infty)$; domain of m: $(0, \infty)$ **73.** Domain of f: $[0, \infty)$; domain of g: $(0, \infty)$; domain of m: $[1, \infty)$ **75.** Domain of f: $(0, \infty)$; domain of g: $(-\infty, \infty)$; domain of m: $(-2, 2)$ **77.** Domain of f: all real numbers except ± 1; domain of g: $(0, \infty)$; domain of m: all positive real numbers except e and $\frac{1}{e}$

79. $18x^2(x^2 + 1)^2 + 3(x^2 + 1)^3 = 3(x^2 + 1)^2(7x^2 + 1)$

81. $\frac{24x^5(x^3 - 7)^3 - (x^3 - 7)^4 6x^2}{4x^6} = \frac{3(x^3 - 7)^3(3x^3 + 7)}{2x^4}$

83. $\frac{1}{\ln 2}\left(\frac{20x^3}{5x^4 + 3}\right)$ **85.** $(2x + 1)(10^{x^2+x})(\ln 10)$ **87.** $\frac{12x^2 + 5}{(4x^3 + 5x + 7)\ln 3}$

89. $2^{x^3 - x^2 + 4x + 1}(3x^2 - 2x + 4)\ln 2$

91. (A) $C'(x) = (2x + 16)^{-1/2} = \frac{1}{(2x + 16)^{1/2}}$ (B) $C'(24) = \frac{1}{8}$, or \$12.50. At a production level of 24 cell phones, total cost is increasing at the rate of \$12.50 per cell phone and the cost of producing the 25th cell phone is approximately \$12.50. $C'(42) = \frac{1}{10}$, or \$10.00. At a production level of 42 cell phones, total cost is increasing at the rate of \$10.00 per cell phone and the cost of producing the 43rd cell phone is approximately \$10.00.

93. (A) $\frac{dx}{dp} = 40(p + 25)^{-1/2} = \frac{40}{(p + 25)^{1/2}}$ (B) $x = 400$ and $dx/dp = 4$. At a price of \$75, the supply is 400 bicycle helmets per week, and supply is increasing at the rate of 4 bicycle helmets per dollar.

95. (A) After 1 hr, the concentration is decreasing at the rate of 1.60 mg/mL per hour; after 4 hr, the concentration is decreasing at the rate of 0.08 mg/mL per hour.

(B)

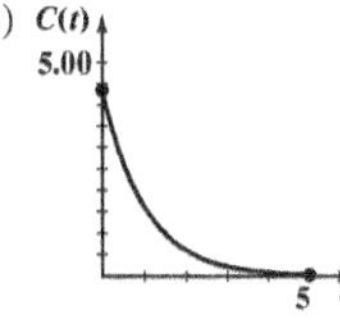

97. 2.27 mm of mercury/yr; 0.81 mm of mercury/yr; 0.41 mm of mercury/yr

Exercises 7.5

1. $y = -\frac{3}{2}x + 10$ **3.** $y = \pm\frac{5}{6}\sqrt{36 - x^2}$ **5.** $y = \frac{-x \pm \sqrt{4 - 3x^2}}{2}$

7. Impossible **9.** $y' = 4/3$ **11.** $y' = -\frac{4x}{y^2}$ **13.** $y' = -\frac{3}{e^y}$

15. $y' = 2xy$ **17.** $y' = 10x$; 10 **19.** $y' = \frac{2x}{3y^2}; \frac{4}{3}$ **21.** $y' = -\frac{6}{2y - 5}; 6$

23. $y' = -\frac{y}{x}; -\frac{3}{2}$ **25.** $y' = -\frac{2y}{2x + 1}; 4$ **27.** $y' = \frac{6 - 2y}{x}; -1$

29. $y' = \frac{2x}{e^y - 2y}; 2$ **31.** $y' = \frac{3x^2y}{y + 1}; \frac{3}{2}$ **33.** $y' = \frac{12x^3y - y \ln y}{x + 3y}; -6$

35. $x' = \dfrac{2tx - 3t^2}{2x - t^2}$; 8 **37.** $y'\big|_{(1.6, 1.8)} = -\dfrac{3}{4}$; $y'\big|_{(1.6, 0.2)} = \dfrac{3}{4}$

39. $y = -x - 4$ **41.** $y = \frac{2}{5}x - \frac{12}{5}$; $y = \frac{3}{5}x + \frac{12}{5}$ **43.** $y' = -\dfrac{1}{x}$

45. $y' = \dfrac{1}{3(1 + y)^2 + 1}$; $\dfrac{1}{13}$ **47.** $y' = \dfrac{(x - 3y)^2}{3(x - 3y)^2 + 4y^2}$; $\dfrac{1}{7}$

49. $y' = \dfrac{3x^2(7 + y^2)^{1/2}}{y}$; 16 **51.** $y' = \dfrac{y}{2xy^2 - x}$; 1 **53.** $y = 0.63x + 1.04$

55. $\dfrac{dp}{dx} = \dfrac{1}{p - 3}$ **57.** $\dfrac{dp}{dx} = -\dfrac{\sqrt{p + 25}}{15}$ **59.** $\dfrac{dL}{dV} = \dfrac{-(L + m)}{V + n}$

61. $\dfrac{dT}{dv} = \dfrac{2}{k}\sqrt{T}$ **63.** $\dfrac{dv}{dT} = \dfrac{k}{2\sqrt{T}}$

Exercises 7.6

1. 19.5 ft **3.** 52 m **5.** 34.5 ft **7.** 32 ft **9.** 30 **11.** $-\dfrac{16}{3}$ **13.** $-\dfrac{16}{7}$

15. Decreasing at 3 units/sec **17.** Approx. 3.03 ft/sec **19.** Approx. 126 ft²/sec

21. 47,124 cm³/min **23.** 6 lb/in.²/hr **25.** $\dfrac{9}{4}$ ft/sec **27.** $\dfrac{20}{3}$ ft/sec

29. 0.0214 ft/sec; 0.0135 ft/sec; yes, at $t = 0.000\,19$ sec

31. 3.835 units/sec **33.** (A) $\dfrac{dC}{dt} = \$15{,}000/\text{wk}$ (B) $\dfrac{dR}{dt} = -\$50{,}000/\text{wk}$

(C) $\dfrac{dP}{dt} = -\$65{,}000/\text{wk}$ **35.** $\dfrac{ds}{dt} = \$2{,}207/\text{wk}$

37. $\dfrac{dx}{dt} = 165\,\text{headphones/wk}$ **39.** $R(p) = p(6{,}000 - 0.15p^2)$;

$\dfrac{dR}{dt} = -\$2{,}775/\text{wk}$ **41.** $\dfrac{dx}{dt} = 160\,\text{lbs/wk}$ **43.** $\dfrac{dx}{dt} = \$2\,\text{million/wk}$

45. (A) $\dfrac{dx}{dt} = -12.73\,\text{units/month}$ (B) $\dfrac{dp}{dt} = \$1.53/\text{month}$

47. Approx. 100 ft³/min

Exercises 7.7

1. $x = f(p) = 105 - 2.5p, 0 \le p \le 42$

3. $x = f(p) = \sqrt{100 - 2p}, 0 \le p \le 50$

5. $x = f(p) = 20(\ln 25 - \ln p), 25/e \approx 9.2 \le p \le 25$

7. $x = f(p) = e^{8 - 0.1p}, 80 - 10\ln 30 \approx 46.0 \le p \le 80$

9. $\dfrac{35 - 0.8x}{35x - 0.4x^2}$ **11.** $-\dfrac{8e^{-x}}{9 + 8e^{-x}}$ **13.** $\dfrac{5}{x(12 + 5\ln x)}$ **15.** 0 **17.** -0.017

19. -0.034 **21.** 1.013 **23.** 0.405 **25.** 11.8% **27.** 5.4% **29.** -14.7%

31. -431.6% **33.** $E(p) = \dfrac{450p}{25{,}000 - 450p}$ **35.** $E(p) = \dfrac{8p^2}{4{,}800 - 4p^2}$

37. $E(p) = \dfrac{0.6pe^p}{98 - 0.6e^p}$ **39.** 0.07 **41.** 0.15 **43.** $\dfrac{x + 1}{x}$ **45.** $\dfrac{1}{x\ln x}$

47. (A) Inelastic (B) Unit elasticity (C) Elastic **49.** (A) Inelastic (B) Unit elasticity (C) Elastic **51.** $E(12) = 0.6$; 2.4% decrease **53.** $E(22) = 2.2$; 11% increase **55.** Elastic on $(16, 32)$ **57.** Increase **59.** Elastic on $(3.5, 7)$; inelastic on $(0, 3.5)$ **61.** Elastic on $(25/\sqrt{3}, 25)$; inelastic on $(0, 25/\sqrt{3})$ **63.** Elastic on $(48, 72)$; inelastic on $(0, 48)$ **65.** Elastic on $(25, 25\sqrt{2})$; inelastic on $(0, 25)$

67. $R(p) = 20p(10 - p)$

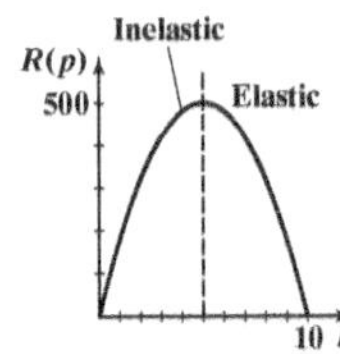

69. $R(p) = 40p(p - 15)^2$

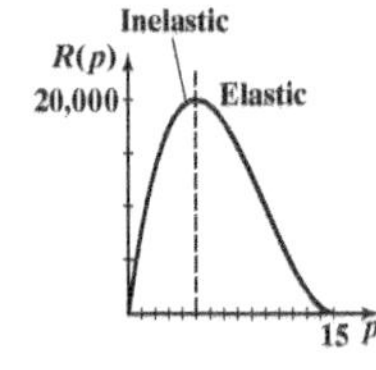

71. $R(p) = 30p - 10p\sqrt{p}$

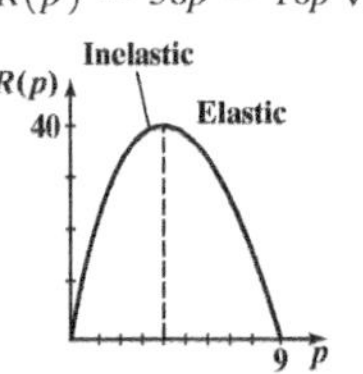

73. $\dfrac{3}{2}$ **75.** $\dfrac{1}{2}$ **77.** Elastic on $(0, 300)$; inelastic on $(300, 600)$ **79.** Elastic on $(0, 10\sqrt{3})$; inelastic on $(10\sqrt{3}, 30)$ **81.** k **83.** \$75 per day **85.** Increase **87.** Decrease **89.** \$3.75

91. $p(t) = \dfrac{23}{0.23t + 10.3}$

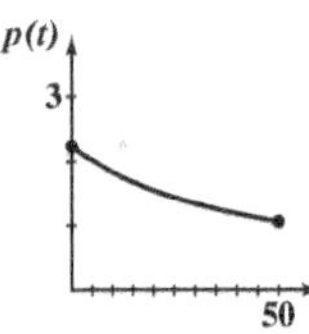

93. -0.035

Chapter 7 Review Exercises

1. \$3,136.62; \$4,919.21; \$12,099.29 *(7.1)* **2.** $\dfrac{3}{x} - 2e^{-x}$ *(7.2)* **3.** $2e^{2x-3}$ *(7.4)*

4. $\dfrac{3}{3x + 4}$ *(7.4)* **5.** $\dfrac{2e^{2x} + e^x}{e^{2x} + e^x + 4}$ *(7.4)* **6.** $y' = \dfrac{1 - 2x}{4xy^3}$; $-\dfrac{1}{4}$ *(7.5)*

7. $dy/dt = 576$ *(7.6)* **8.** $x = 5{,}000 - 200p$ *(7.7)* **9.** $E(p) = \dfrac{p}{25 - p}$ *(7.7)* **10.** $E(15) = 1.5$; 7.5% decrease *(7.7)* **11.** Elastic on (12.5, 25) *(7.7)* **12.** Increase *(7.7)*

13. 5 *(7.2)* **14.** $\lim\limits_{n \to \infty}\left(1 + \dfrac{2}{n}\right)^n = e^2 \approx 7.389\,06$ *(7.1)*

15. $\dfrac{7[(\ln z)^6 + 1]}{z}$ *(7.4)* **16.** $x^5(1 + 6\ln x)$ *(7.3)* **17.** $\dfrac{e^x(x - 6)}{x^7}$ *(7.3)*

18. $\dfrac{12x^5 + e^x}{2x^6 + e^x}$ *(7.4)* **19.** $(3x^2 - 2x)e^{x^3 - x^2}$ *(7.4)* **20.** $\dfrac{1 - 2x\ln 5x}{xe^{2x}}$ *(7.4)*

21. $y = -x + 2$; $y = -ex + 1$ *(7.4)* **22.** $y' = \dfrac{3y - 2x}{8y - 3x}$; $\dfrac{8}{19}$ *(7.5)*

23. $x' = \dfrac{6t^2x}{1 - 4t^3}$; $\dfrac{6}{5}$ *(7.5)* **24.** $y' = \dfrac{1}{e^y + 2y}$; 1 *(7.5)*

25. $y' = \dfrac{2xy}{1 + 2y^2}$; $\dfrac{2}{3}$ *(7.5)* **26.** 0.049 *(7.7)* **27.** $-\dfrac{3}{100 - 3p}$ *(7.7)*

28. $\dfrac{2x + e^x}{4 + x^2 + e^x}$ *(7.7)* **29.** $dx/dt = -\dfrac{3}{20}$ units/sec *(7.6)* **30.** 0.27 ft/sec *(7.6)*

31. $dC/dt \approx 3$ in.²/min *(7.6)* **32.** Elastic for $5 < p < 15$; inelastic for $0 < p < 5$ *(7.7)* **33.**

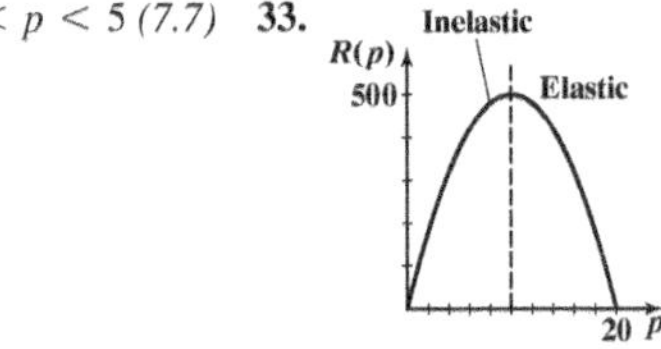

34. (A) $y = x^4$ (B) $\dfrac{dy}{dx} = 4x^3$ *(7.4)*

35. $4x(7^{2x^2+4})(\ln 7)$ *(7.4)* **36.** $\left(\dfrac{1}{\ln 5}\right)\dfrac{2x - 1}{x^2 - x}$ *(7.4)*

37. $\dfrac{e^{2x} + 4x}{(e^{2x} + 4x^2 + 3)\sqrt{\ln(e^{2x} + 4x^2 + 3)}}$ *(7.4)* **38.** $y' = \dfrac{2x - e^{xy}y}{xe^{xy} - 1}$; 0 *(7.5)*

39. The rate of increase of area is proportional to the radius R, so the rate is smallest when $R = 0$, and has no largest value. *(7.6)* **40.** Yes, for $x > 4$ *(7.6)*

41. (A) 14.2 yr (B) 13.9 yr *(7.1)*

42. $A'(t) = 10e^{0.1t}$; $A'(1) = \$11.05/\text{yr}$; $A'(10) = \$27.18/\text{yr}$ *(7.1)*

43. \$987.50/yr *(7.2)* **44.** $R'(x) = 3{,}000(0.998)^x(1 + x\ln 0.998)$ *(7.4)*

45. $\dfrac{-\sqrt{3{,}000 - 4p^5}}{10p^4}$ *(7.5)* **46.** $dR/dt = \$2{,}242/\text{day}$ *(7.6)*

47. Decrease price *(7.7)* **48.** 0.02125 *(7.7)* **49.** -1.111 mg/mL per hour; -0.335 mg/mL per hour *(7.4)* **50.** $dR/dt = -3/(2\pi)$; approx. 0.477 mm/day *(7.6)* **51.** (A) Increasing at the rate of 2.68 units/day at the end of 1 day of training; increasing at the rate of 0.54 unit/day after 5 days of training (B) 7 days *(7.4)* **52.** $dT/dt = -1/27 \approx -0.037$ min/hr *(7.6)*

Chapter 8

Exercises 8.1

1. Decreasing **3.** Increasing **5.** Increasing **7.** Decreasing **9.** (a, b); (d, f); (g, h) **11.** (b, c); (c, d); (f, g) **13.** c, d, f **15.** b, f **17.** Local maximum at $x = a$; local minimum at $x = c$; no local extrema at $x = b$ and $x = d$ **19.** $f(3) = 5$ is a local maximum; e **21.** No local extremum; d **23.** $f(3) = 5$ is a local maximum; f **25.** No local extremum; c **27.** (A) $f'(x) = 3x^2 - 3$ (B) $-1, 1$ (C) $-1, 1$ **29.** (A) $f'(x) = -\dfrac{-4}{(x+3)^2}$ (B) -3 (C) none **31.** (A) $f'(x) = \dfrac{1}{4}x^{-3/4}$ (B) 0 (C) 0 **33.** Decreasing on $(-\infty, 2)$; increasing on $(2, \infty)$; $f(2) = -10$ is a local minimum **35.** Increasing on $(-\infty, -4)$; decreasing on $(-4, \infty)$; $f(-4) = 7$ is a local maximum **37.** Increasing for all x; no local extrema **39.** Increasing on $(-\infty, -1)$ and $(1, \infty)$; decreasing on $(-1, 1)$; $f(-1) = 7$ is a local maximum, $f(1) = 3$ is a local minimum **41.** Decreasing on $(-\infty, -4)$ and $(2, \infty)$; increasing on $(-4, 2)$; $f(-4) = -220$ is a local minimum and $f(2) = 104$ is a local maximum **43.** Decreasing on $(-\infty, -3)$; increasing on $(-3, \infty)$; $f(-3) = 3$ is a local minimum **45.** Decreasing on $(-\infty, -4)$; increasing on $(-4, \infty)$; $f(-4) = -e^{-4} \approx -0.0183$ is a local minimum **47.** Decreasing on $(-\infty, -2)$ and $(0, 2)$; increasing on $(-2, 0)$ and $(2, \infty)$; $f(-2) = 0$ and $f(2) = 0$ are local minima; $f(0) = \sqrt[3]{8} \approx 2.5198$ is a local maximum

49. Increasing on $(-\infty, 4)$
Decreasing on $(4, \infty)$
Horizontal tangent at $x = 4$

51. Increasing on $(-\infty, -1)$, $(1, \infty)$
Decreasing on $(-1, 1)$
Horizontal tangents at $x = -1, 1$

53. Decreasing for all x
Horizontal tangent at $x = 2$

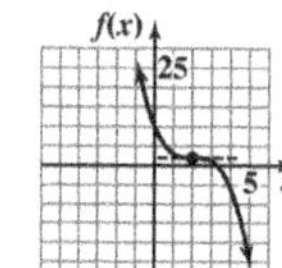

55. Decreasing on $(-\infty, -3)$ and $(0, 3)$; increasing on $(-3, 0)$ and $(3, \infty)$ Horizontal tangents at $x = -3, 0, 3$

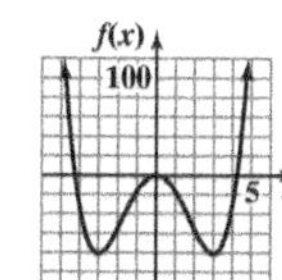

57. Critical numbers: $x = -0.77, 1.08, 2.69$; decreasing on $(-\infty, -0.77)$ and $(1.08, 2.69)$; increasing on $(-0.77, 1.08)$ and $(2.69, \infty)$; $f(-0.77) = -4.75$ and $f(2.69) = -1.29$ are local minima; $f(1.08) = 6.04$ is a local maximum **59.** Critical numbers: $x = -2.83, -0.20$; decreasing on $(-\infty, -2.83)$ and $(-0.20, \infty)$; increasing on $(-2.83, -0.20)$; $f(-2.83) = -7.08$ is a local minimum; $f(-0.20) = 1.10$ is a local maximum

61. **63.** **65.**

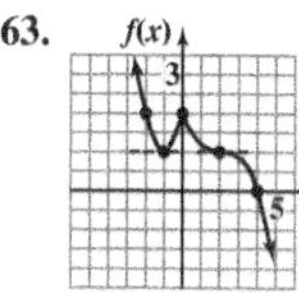

67. **69.** g_4 **71.** g_6 **73.** g_2 **75.** Increasing on $(-1, 2)$; decreasing on $(-\infty, -1)$ and $(2, \infty)$; local minimum at $x = -1$; local maximum at $x = 2$

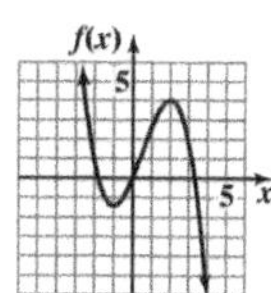

77. Increasing on $(-1, 2)$ and $(2, \infty)$; decreasing on $(-\infty, -1)$; local minimum at $x = -1$

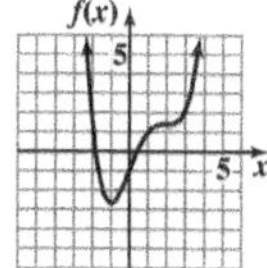

79. Increasing on $(-2, 0)$ and $(3, \infty)$; decreasing on $(-\infty, -2)$ and $(0, 3)$; local minima at $x = -2$ and $x = 3$; local maximum at $x = 0$

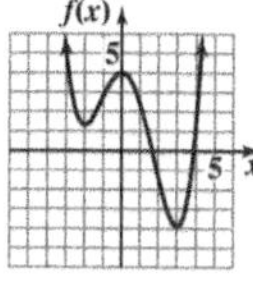

81. $f'(x) > 0$ on $(-\infty, -1)$ and $(3, \infty)$; $f'(x) < 0$ on $(-1, 3)$; $f'(x) = 0$ at $x = -1$ and $x = 3$

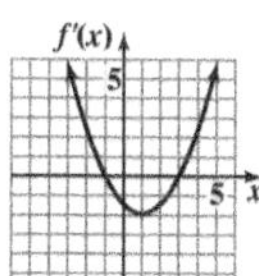

83. $f'(x) > 0$ on $(-2, 1)$ and $(3, \infty)$; $f'(x) < 0$ on $(-\infty, -2)$ and $(1, 3)$; $f'(x) = 0$ at $x = -2, x = 1$, and $x = 3$

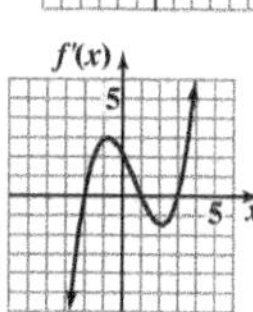

85. Critical numbers: $x = -2, x = 2$; increasing on $(-\infty, -2)$ and $(2, \infty)$; decreasing on $(-2, 0)$ and $(0, 2)$; $f(-2) = -4$ is a local maximum; $f(2) = 4$ is a local minimum

87. Critical numbers: $x = 0$; increasing on $(0, \infty)$; decreasing on $(-\infty, 0)$; $f(0) = 0$ is a local minimum **89.** Critical numbers: $x = 0, x = 4$; increasing on $(-\infty, 0)$ and $(4, \infty)$; decreasing on $(0, 2)$ and $(2, 4)$; $f(0) = 0$ is a local maximum; $f(4) = 8$ is a local minimum

91. (A) The marginal profit is positive on $(0, 600)$, 0 at $x = 600$, and negative on $(600, 1{,}000)$. (B)

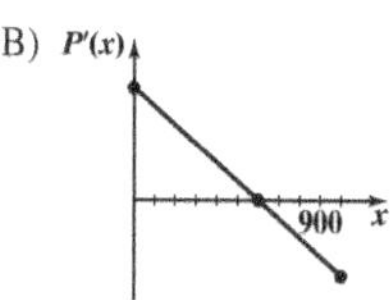

93. (A) The price decreases for the first 12 months to a local minimum, increases for the next 36 months to a local maximum, and then decreases for the remaining 12 months. (B)

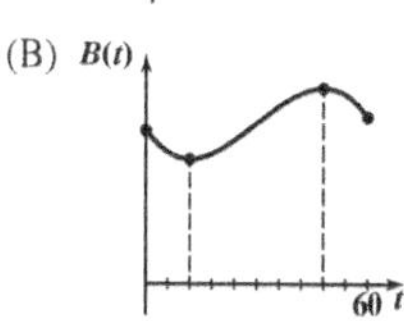

95. (A) $\overline{C}(x) = 0.05x + 20 + \dfrac{320}{x}$ (B) Critical number: $x = 80$; decreasing for $0 < x < 80$; increasing for $80 < x < 150$; $\overline{C}(80) = 28$ is a local minimum **97.** Critical number: $t = 2$; increasing on $(0, 2)$; decreasing on $(2, 24)$; $C(2) = 0.07$ is a local maximum.

Exercises 8.2

1. Concave up **3.** Concave down **5.** Concave down **7.** Neither **9.** (A) (a, c), (c, d), (e, g) (B) (d, e), (g, h) (C) (d, e), (g, h) (D) (a, c), (c, d), (e, g) (E) (a, c), (c, d), (e, g) (F) (d, e), (g, h) **11.** (A) $f(-2) = 3$ is a local maximum of f; $f(2) = -1$ is a local minimum of f. (B) $(0, 1)$ (C) 0

13. (C) **15.** (D) **17.** $12x - 8$ **19.** $4x^{-3} - 18x^{-4}$ **21.** $2 + \dfrac{9}{2}x^{-3/2}$

23. $48x^2(x^2+9)^2 + 8(x^2+9)^3 = 8(x^2+9)^2(7x^2+9)$
25. $(-10, 2{,}000)$ **27.** $(0, 2)$ **29.** None **31.** Concave upward on $(-\infty, -2)$ and $(2, \infty)$; concave downward on $(-2, 2)$; inflection points at $(-2, -80)$ and $(2, -80)$

33. Concave downward on $(-\infty, 1)$; concave upward on $(1, \infty)$; inflection point at $(1, 7)$ **35.** Concave upward on $(0, 6)$; concave downward on $(-\infty, 0)$ and $(6, \infty)$; inflection points at $(0, 10)$ and $(6, 1{,}264)$ **37.** Concave upward on $(-3, -1)$; concave downward on $(-\infty, -3)$ and $(-1, \infty)$; inflection points at $(-3, 0.6931)$ and $(-1, 0.6931)$ **39.** Concave upward on $(0, \infty)$; concave downward on $(-\infty, 0)$; inflection point at $(0, -5)$

41.
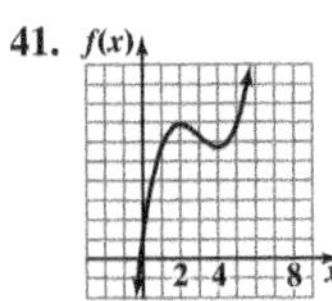

43.
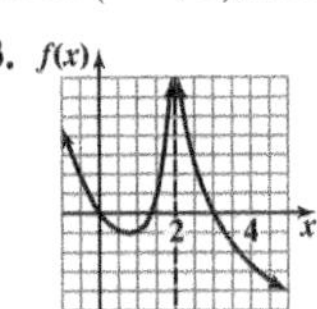

45.
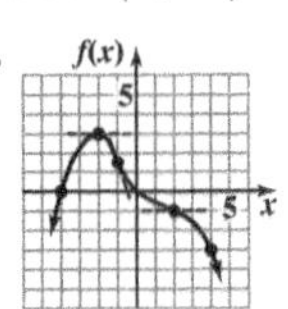

47.
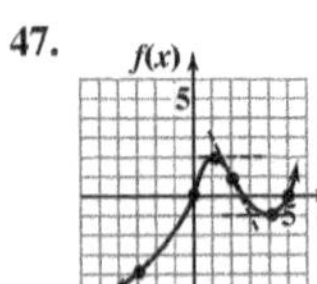

49.
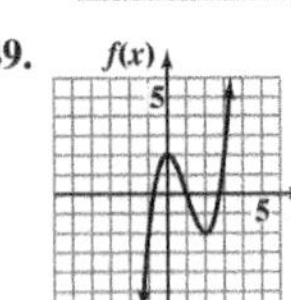

51.
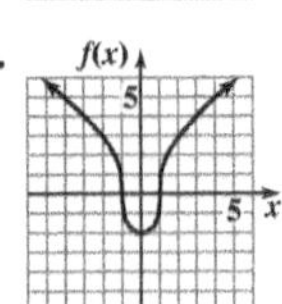

53. Domain: All real numbers
y int.: 16; x int.: $2 - 2\sqrt{3}, 2, 2 + 2\sqrt{3}$
Increasing on $(-\infty, 0)$ and $(4, \infty)$
Decreasing on $(0, 4)$
Local maximum: $f(0) = 16$; local minimum: $f(4) = -16$
Concave downward on $(-\infty, 2)$
Concave upward on $(2, \infty)$
Inflection point: $(2, 0)$

55. Domain: All real numbers
y int.: 2; x int.: -1
Increasing on $(-\infty, \infty)$
Concave downward on $(-\infty, 0)$
Concave upward on $(0, \infty)$
Inflection point: $(0, 2)$

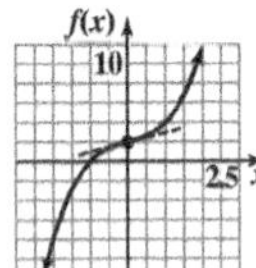

57. Domain: All real numbers
y int.: 0; x int.: 0, 4
Increasing on $(-\infty, 3)$
Decreasing on $(3, \infty)$
Local maximum: $f(3) = 6.75$
Concave upward on $(0, 2)$
Concave downward on $(-\infty, 0)$ and $(2, \infty)$
Inflection points: $(0, 0)$, $(2, 4)$

59. Domain: All real numbers;
y int.: 0; x int.: 0, 1
Increasing on $(0.25, \infty)$
Decreasing on $(-\infty, 0.25)$
Local minimum: $f(0.25) = -1.6875$
Concave upward on $(-\infty, 0.5)$ and $(1, \infty)$
Concave downward on $(0.5, 1)$
Inflection points: $(0.5, -1)$, $(1, 0)$

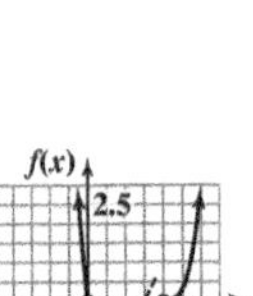

61. Domain: All real numbers
y int.: 27; x int.: $-3, 3$
Increasing on $(-\infty, -\sqrt{3})$ and $(0, \sqrt{3})$
Decreasing on $(-\sqrt{3}, 0)$ and $(\sqrt{3}, \infty)$
Local maxima: $f(-\sqrt{3}) = 36, f(\sqrt{3}) = 36$
Local minimum: $f(0) = 27$
Concave upward on $(-1, 1)$
Concave downward on $(-\infty, -1)$ and $(1, \infty)$
Inflection points: $(-1, 32)$, $(1, 32)$

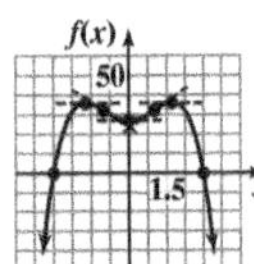

63. Domain: All real numbers
y int.: 16; x int.: $-2, 2$
Decreasing on $(-\infty, -2)$ and $(0, 2)$
Increasing on $(-2, 0)$ and $(2, \infty)$
Local minima: $f(-2) = 0, f(2) = 0$
Local maximum: $f(0) = 16$
Concave upward on $(-\infty, -2\sqrt{3}/3)$ and $(2\sqrt{3}/3, \infty)$
Concave downward on $(-2\sqrt{3}/3, 2\sqrt{3}/3)$
Inflection points: $(-1.15, 7.11)$, $(1.15, 7.11)$

65. Domain: All real numbers
y int.: 0; x int.: 0, 1.5
Decreasing on $(-\infty, 0)$ and $(0, 1.25)$
Increasing on $(1.25, \infty)$
Local minimum: $f(1.25) = -1.53$
Concave upward on $(-\infty, 0)$ and $(1, \infty)$
Concave downward on $(0, 1)$
Inflection points: $(0, 0)$, $(1, -1)$

67. Domain: All real numbers
y int.: 0; x int.: 0
Increasing on $(-\infty, \infty)$
Concave downward on $(-\infty, \infty)$

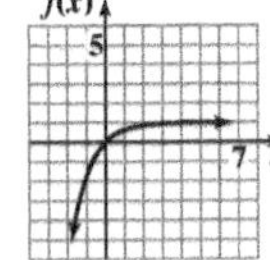

69. Domain: All real numbers
y int.: 5
Decreasing on $(-\infty, \ln 4)$
Increasing on $(\ln 4, \infty)$
Local minimum: $f(\ln 4) = 4$
Concave upward on $(-\infty, \infty)$

71. Domain: $(0, \infty)$
x int.: e^2
Increasing on $(-\infty, \infty)$
Concave downward on $(-\infty, \infty)$

73. Domain: $(-4, \infty)$
y int.: $-2 + \ln 4$; x int.: $e^2 - 4$
Increasing on $(-4, \infty)$
Concave downward on $(-4, \infty)$

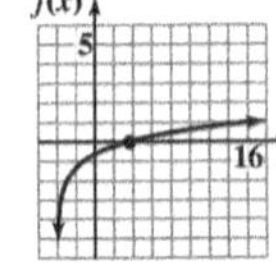

75.

x	$f'(x)$	$f(x)$
$-\infty < x < -1$	Positive and decreasing	Increasing and concave downward
$x = -1$	x intercept	Local maximum
$-1 < x < 0$	Negative and decreasing	Decreasing and concave downward
$x = 0$	Local minimum	Inflection point
$0 < x < 2$	Negative and increasing	Decreasing and concave upward
$x = 2$	Local max., x intercept	Inflection point, horiz. tangent
$2 < x < \infty$	Negative and decreasing	Decreasing and concave downward

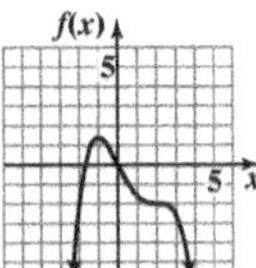

77.

x	$f'(x)$	$f(x)$
$-\infty < x < -2$	Negative and increasing	Decreasing and concave upward
$x = -2$	Local max., x intercept	Inflection point, horiz. tangent
$-2 < x < 0$	Negative and decreasing	Decreasing and concave downward
$x = 0$	Local minimum	Inflection point
$0 < x < 2$	Negative and increasing	Decreasing and concave upward
$x = 2$	Local max., x intercept	Inflection point, horiz. tangent
$2 < x < \infty$	Negative and decreasing	Decreasing and concave downward

79. Domain: All real numbers x int.: $-1.18, 0.61, 1.87, 3.71$; y int.: -5; Decreasing on $(-\infty, -0.53)$ and $(1.24, 3.04)$; Increasing on $(-0.53, 1.24)$ and $(3.04, \infty)$; Local minima: $f(-0.53) = -7.57, f(3.04) = -8.02$; Local maximum: $f(1.24) = 2.36$; Concave upward on $(-\infty, 0.22)$ and $(2.28, \infty)$; Concave downward on $(0.22, 2.28)$; Inflection points: $(0.22, -3.15)$, $(2.28, -3.41)$ **81.** Domain: All real numbers; x int.: $-2.40, 1.16$; y int.: 3 Increasing on $(-\infty, -1.58)$; Decreasing on $(-1.58, \infty)$; Local maximum: $f(-1.58) = 8.87$; Concave downward on $(-\infty, -0.88)$ and $(0.38, \infty)$; Concave upward on $(-0.88, 0.38)$; Inflection points: $(-0.88, 6.39)$, $(0.38, 2.45)$ **83.** The graph of the CPI is concave upward. **85.** The graph of $y = C'(x)$ is positive and decreasing. Since marginal costs are decreasing, the production process is becoming more efficient as production increases. **87.** (A) Local maximum at $x = 60$ (B) Concave downward on the whole interval $(0, 80)$ **89.** (A) Local maximum at $x = 1$ (B) Concave downward on $(-\infty, 2)$; concave upward on $(2, \infty)$

91. Increasing on $(0, 10)$; decreasing on $(10, 15)$; point of diminishing returns is $x = 10$; max $T'(x) = T'(10) = 500$

93. Increasing on (24, 36); decreasing on $(36, 45)$; point of diminishing returns is $x = 36$; max $N'(x) = N'(36) = 7{,}776$

95. (A)

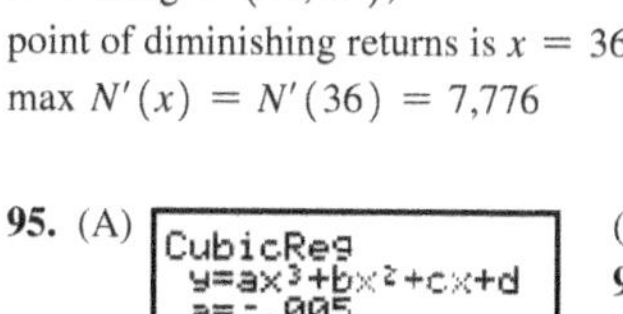
```
CubicReg
y=ax³+bx²+cx+d
a=-.005
b=.485
c=-1.85
d=300
```

(B) 32 ads to sell 574 cars per month **97.** (A) Increasing on $(0, 10)$; decreasing on $(10, 20)$ (B) Inflection point: $(10, 3000)$

(C)

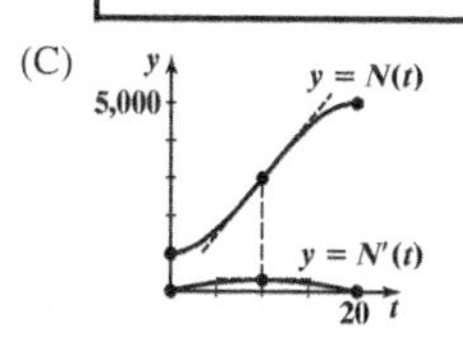

(D) $N'(10) = 300$ **99.** (A) Increasing on $(5, \infty)$; decreasing on $(0, 5)$ (B) Inflection point: $(5, 10)$

(C)

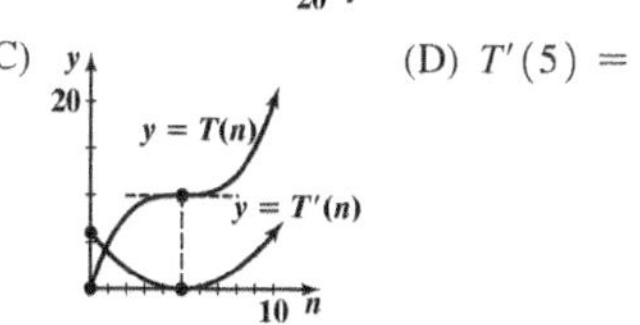

(D) $T'(5) = 0$

Exercises 8.3

1. 500 **3.** 0 **5.** 50 **7.** 0 **9.** 6 **11.** $-\frac{1}{10}$ **13.** 7 **15.** $-\frac{1}{2}$ **17.** $\frac{2}{5}$ **19.** 0 **21.** $-\infty$ **23.** $\frac{3}{4}$ **25.** $\frac{1}{4}$ **27.** $\frac{1}{5}$ **29.** ∞ **31.** ∞ **33.** 2 **35.** ∞ **37.** 8 **39.** 0 **41.** ∞ **43.** ∞ **45.** $\frac{1}{3}$ **47.** -2 **49.** $-\infty$ **51.** 0 **53.** 0 **55.** 0 **57.** $\frac{1}{4}$ **59.** $\frac{1}{3}$ **61.** 0 **63.** 0 **65.** ∞ **67.** $y = -10$ **69.** $y = -1$ and $y = \frac{3}{5}$

Exercises 8.4

1. Domain: All real numbers; x int.: -12; y int.: 36 **3.** Domain: $(-\infty, 25]$; x int.: 25; y int.: 5 **5.** Domain: All real numbers except 2; x int.: -1; y int.: $-\frac{1}{2}$ **7.** Domain: All real numbers except -1 and 1; no x intercept; y int.: -3 **9.** (A) $(-\infty, b), (0, e), (e, g)$ (B) $(b, d), (d, 0), (g, \infty)$ (C) $(b, d), (d, 0), (g, \infty)$ (D) $(-\infty, b), (0, e), (e, g)$ (E) $x = 0$ (F) $x = b, x = g$ (G) $(-\infty, a), (d, e), (h, \infty)$ (H) $(a, d), (e, h)$ (I) $(a, d), (e, h)$ (J) $(-\infty, a), (d, e), (h, \infty)$ (K) $x = a, x = h$ (L) $y = L$ (M) $x = d, x = e$

11. 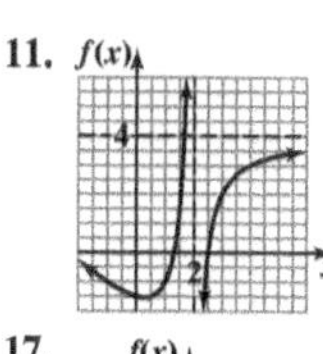 **13.** **15.** 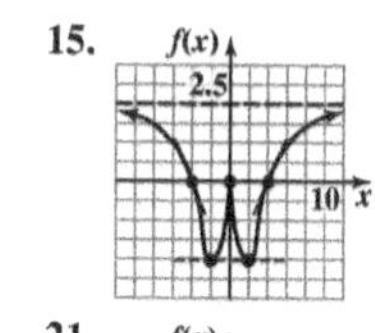

17. **19.** 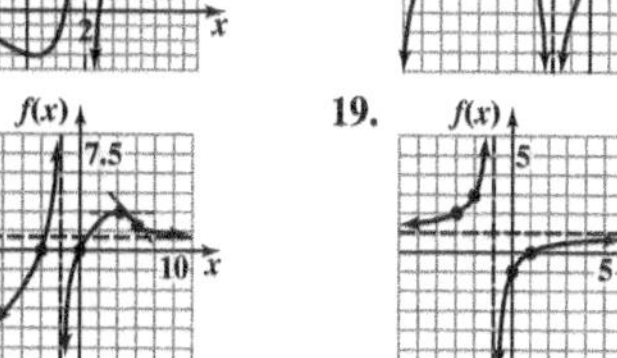 **21.** 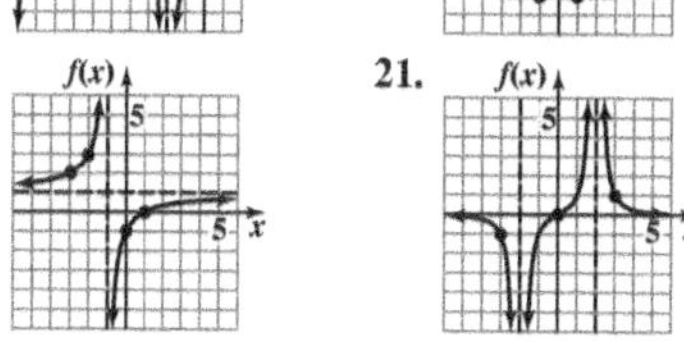

23. Domain: All real numbers, except 3
y int.: -1; x int.: -3
Horizontal asymptote: $y = 1$
Vertical asymptote: $x = 3$
Decreasing on $(-\infty, 3)$ and $(3, \infty)$
Concave upward on $(3, \infty)$
Concave downward on $(-\infty, 3)$

25. Domain: All real numbers, except 2; y int.: 0; x int.: 0
Horizontal asymptote: $y = 1$
Vertical asymptote: $x = 2$
Decreasing on $(-\infty, 2)$ and $(2, \infty)$
Concave downward on $(-\infty, 2)$
Concave upward on $(2, \infty)$

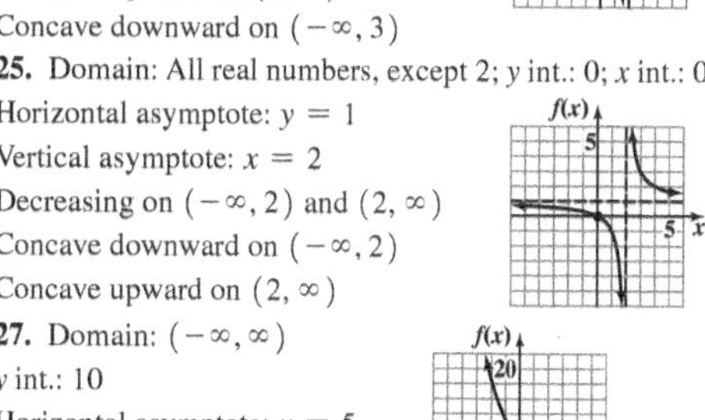

27. Domain: $(-\infty, \infty)$
y int.: 10
Horizontal asymptote: $y = 5$
Decreasing on $(-\infty, \infty)$
Concave upward on $(-\infty, \infty)$

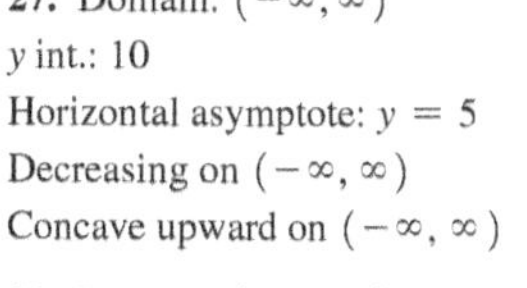
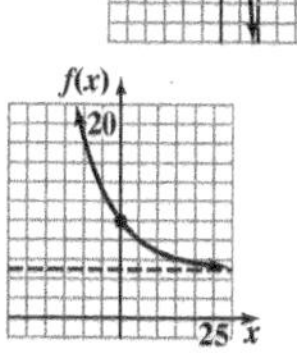

29. Domain: $(-\infty, \infty)$; y int.: 0; x int.: 0; Horizontal asymptote: $y = 0$
Increasing on $(-\infty, 5)$; Decreasing on $(5, \infty)$
Local maximum: $f(5) = 9.20$
Concave upward on $(10, \infty)$
Concave downward on $(-\infty, 10)$
Inflection point: $(10, 6.77)$

31. Domain: $(-\infty, 1)$
y int.: 0; x int.: 0
Vertical asymptote: $x = 1$
Decreasing on $(-\infty, 1)$
Concave downward on $(-\infty, 1)$

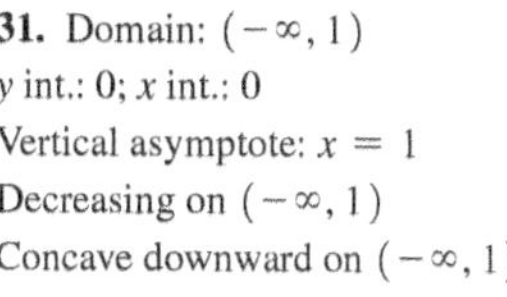
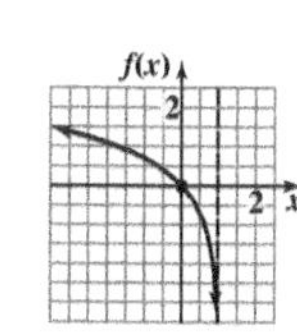

33. Domain: $(0, \infty)$
Vertical asymptote: $x = 0$
Increasing on $(1, \infty)$
Decreasing on $(0, 1)$
Local minimum: $f(1) = 1$
Concave upward on $(0, \infty)$

35. Domain: All real numbers, except ± 2; y int.: 0; x int.: 0; Horizontal asymptote: $y = 0$; Vertical asymptotes: $x = -2, x = 2$
Decreasing on $(-\infty, -2)$, $(-2, 2)$, and $(2, \infty)$
Concave upward on $(-2, 0)$ and $(2, \infty)$
Concave downward on $(-\infty, -2)$ and $(0, 2)$
Inflection point: $(0, 0)$

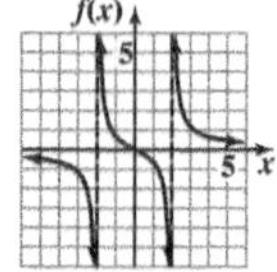

37. Domain: All real numbers; y int.: 1; Horizontal asymptote: $y = 0$
Increasing on $(-\infty, 0)$; Decreasing on $(0, \infty)$
Local maximum: $f(0) = 1$
Concave upward on $(-\infty, -\sqrt{3}/3)$ and $(\sqrt{3}/3, \infty)$
Concave downward on $(-\sqrt{3}/3, \sqrt{3}/3)$
Inflection points: $(-\sqrt{3}/3, 0.75)$, $(\sqrt{3}/3, 0.75)$

39. Domain: All real numbers except -1 and 1
y int.: 0; x int.: 0
Horizontal asymptote: $y = 0$
Vertical asymptote: $x = -1$ and $x = 1$
Increasing on $(-\infty, -1)$, $(-1, 1)$, and $(1, \infty)$
Concave upward on $(-\infty, -1)$ and $(0, 1)$
Concave downward on $(-1, 0)$ and $(1, \infty)$
Inflection point: $(0, 0)$

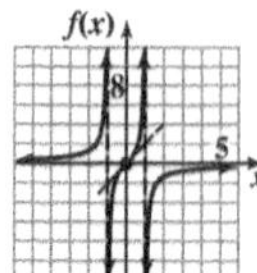

41. Domain: All real numbers except 1
y int.: 0; x int.: 0
Horizontal asymptote: $y = 0$
Vertical asymptote: $x = 1$
Increasing on $(-\infty, -1)$ and $(1, \infty)$
Decreasing on $(-1, 1)$
Local maximum: $f(-1) = 1.25$
Concave upward on $(-\infty, -2)$
Concave downward on $(-2, 1)$ and $(1, \infty)$
Inflection point: $(-2, 1.11)$

43. Domain: All real numbers except 0
Horizontal asymptote: $y = 1$
Vertical asymptote: $x = 0$
Increasing on $(0, 4)$
Decreasing on $(-\infty, 0)$ and $(4, \infty)$
Local maximum: $f(4) = 1.125$
Concave upward on $(6, \infty)$
Concave downward on $(-\infty, 0)$ and $(0, 6)$
Inflection point: $(6, 1.11)$

45. Domain: All real numbers except 1
y int.: 0; x int.: 0
Vertical asymptote: $x = 1$
Oblique asymptote: $y = x + 1$
Increasing on $(-\infty, 0)$ and $(2, \infty)$
Decreasing on $(0, 1)$ and $(1, 2)$
Local maximum: $f(0) = 0$
Local minimum: $f(2) = 4$
Concave upward on $(1, \infty)$
Concave downward on $(-\infty, 1)$

47. Domain: All real numbers except -3, 3
y int.: $-\frac{2}{9}$
Horizontal asymptote: $y = 3$
Vertical asymptotes: $x = -3, x = 3$
Increasing on $(-\infty, -3)$ and $(-3, 0)$
Decreasing on $(0, 3)$ and $(3, \infty)$
Local maximum: $f(0) = -0.22$
Concave upward on $(-\infty, -3)$ and $(3, \infty)$
Concave downward on $(-3, 3)$

49. Domain: All real numbers except 2
y int.: 0; x int.: 0
Vertical asymptote: $x = 2$
Increasing on $(3, \infty)$
Decreasing on $(-\infty, 2)$ and $(2, 3)$
Local minimum: $f(3) = 27$
Concave upward on $(-\infty, 0)$ and $(2, \infty)$
Concave downward on $(0, 2)$
Inflection point: $(0, 0)$

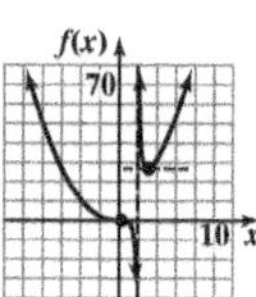

51. Domain: All real numbers
y int.: 3; x int.: 3
Horizontal asymptote: $y = 0$
Increasing on $(-\infty, 2)$
Decreasing on $(2, \infty)$
Local maximum: $f(2) = 7.39$
Concave upward on $(-\infty, 1)$
Concave downward on $(1, \infty)$
Inflection point: $(1, 5.44)$

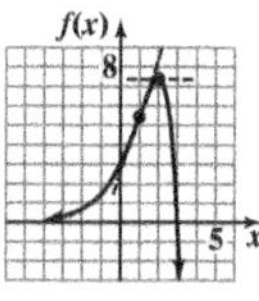

53. Domain: $(-\infty, \infty)$
y int.: 1
Horizontal asymptote: $y = 0$
Increasing on $(-\infty, 0)$
Decreasing on $(0, \infty)$
Local maximum: $f(0) = 1$
Concave upward on $(-\infty, -1)$ and $(1, \infty)$
Concave downward on $(-1, 1)$
Inflection points: $(-1, 0.61)$, $(1, 0.61)$

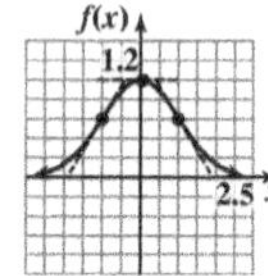

55. Domain: $(0, \infty)$
x int.: 1
Increasing on $(e^{-1/2}, \infty)$
Decreasing on $(0, e^{-1/2})$
Local minimum: $f(e^{-1/2}) = -0.18$
Concave upward on $(e^{-3/2}, \infty)$
Concave downward on $(0, e^{-3/2})$
Inflection point: $(e^{-3/2}, -0.07)$

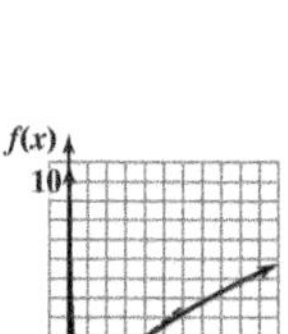

57. Domain: $(0, \infty)$
x int.: 1
Vertical asymptote: $x = 0$
Increasing on $(1, \infty)$
Decreasing on $(0, 1)$
Local minimum: $f(1) = 0$
Concave upward on $(0, e)$
Concave downward on (e, ∞)
Inflection point: $(e, 1)$

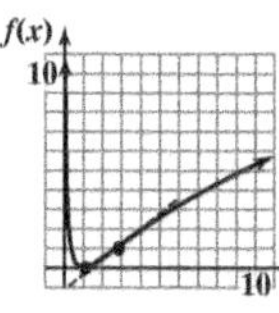

59. Domain: All real numbers except -4, 2
y int.: $-\frac{1}{8}$
Horizontal asymptote: $y = 0$
Vertical asymptote: $x = -4, x = 2$
Increasing on $(-\infty, -4)$ and $(-4, -1)$
Decreasing on $(-1, 2)$ and $(2, \infty)$
Local maximum: $f(-1) = -0.11$
Concave upward on $(-\infty, -4)$ and $(2, \infty)$
Concave downward on $(-4, 2)$

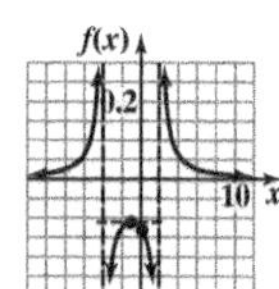

61. Domain: All real numbers except $-\sqrt{3}, \sqrt{3}$
y int.: 0; x int.: 0
Vertical asymptote: $x = -\sqrt{3}, x = \sqrt{3}$
Oblique asymptote: $y = -x$
Increasing on $(-3, -\sqrt{3})$, $(-\sqrt{3}, \sqrt{3})$, and $(\sqrt{3}, 3)$
Decreasing on $(-\infty, -3)$ and $(3, \infty)$
Local maximum: $f(3) = -4.5$
Local minimum: $f(-3) = 4.5$
Concave upward on $(-\infty, -\sqrt{3})$ and $(0, \sqrt{3})$
Concave downward on $(-\sqrt{3}, 0)$ and $(\sqrt{3}, \infty)$
Inflection point: $(0, 0)$

63. Domain: All real numbers except 0
Vertical asymptote: $x = 0$
Oblique asymptote: $y = x$
Increasing on $(-\infty, -2)$ and $(2, \infty)$
Decreasing on $(-2, 0)$ and $(0, 2)$
Local maximum: $f(-2) = -4$
Local minimum: $f(2) = 4$
Concave upward on $(0, \infty)$
Concave downward on $(-\infty, 0)$

65. Domain: All real numbers except 0; x int.: $\sqrt[3]{4}$
Vertical asymptote: $x = 0$; Oblique asymptote: $y = x$
Increasing on $(-\infty, -2)$ and $(0, \infty)$
Local maximum: $f(-2) = -3$
Decreasing on $(-2, 0)$
Concave downward on $(-\infty, 0)$ and $(0, \infty)$

67. $y = 90 + 0.02x$ **69.** $y = 210 + 0.1x$ **71.** Domain: All real numbers except $-1, 2$ y; int.: 1/2; x int.: 1; Vertical asymptote: $x = 2$
Horizontal asymptote: $y = 1$
Decreasing on $(-\infty, -1)$, $(-1, 2)$, and $(2, \infty)$
Concave upward on $(2, \infty)$
Concave downward on $(-\infty, -1)$ and $(-1, 2)$

73. Domain: All real numbers except -1
y int.: 2; x int.: -2
Vertical asymptote: $x = -1$
Horizontal asymptote: $y = 1$
Decreasing on $(-\infty, -1)$, and $(-1, \infty)$
Concave upward on $(-1, \infty)$
Concave downward on $(-\infty, -1)$

75. Domain: All real numbers except $-4, 3$
y int.: 1; x int.: $\frac{3}{2}$
Vertical asymptote: $x = 3$
Horizontal asymptote: $y = 2$
Decreasing on $(-\infty, -4)$, $(-4, 3)$, and $(3, \infty)$
Concave upward on $(3, \infty)$
Concave downward on $(-\infty, -4)$ and $(-4, 3)$

77. Domain: All real numbers except $-1, 3$
y int.: 0; x int.: $0, -7$
Vertical asymptote: $x = -1$
Oblique asymptote: $y = x + 6$
Increasing on $(-\infty, -1)$, $(-1, 3)$, and $(3, \infty)$
Concave upward on $(-\infty, -1)$
Concave downward on $(-1, 3)$ and $(3, \infty)$

79.

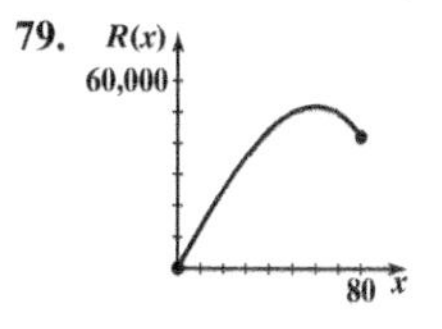

81. (A) Increasing on (0, 1) (B) Concave upward on (0, 1) (C) $x = 1$ is a vertical asymptote (D) The origin is both an x and a y intercept (E)

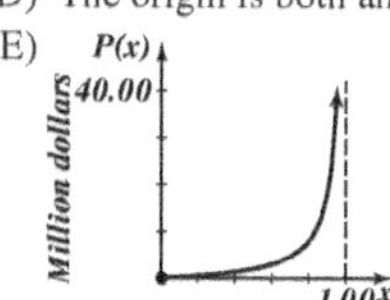

83. (A) $\overline{C}(n) = \dfrac{3{,}200}{n} + 250 + 50n$ (B)

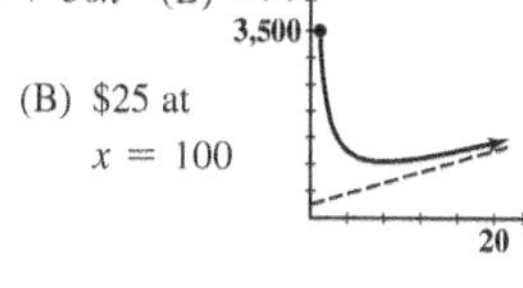

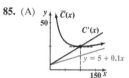

(C) 8 yr

85. (A)

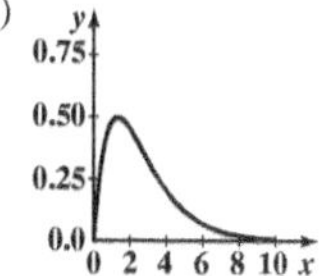

(B) \$25 at $x = 100$

87. (A) (B) $C(8) = \dfrac{8}{e^6} \approx 0.01983$ ppm
(C) $C(4/3) \approx 0.4905$

91.

Exercises 8.5

1. Max $f(x) = f(3) = 3$; Min $f(x) = f(-2) = -2$
3. Max $h(x) = h(-5) = 25$; Min $h(x) = h(0) = 0$
5. Max $n(x) = n(4) = 2$; Min $n(x) = n(3) = \sqrt{3}$
7. Max $q(x) = q(27) = -3$; Min $q(x) = q(64) = -4$
9. Min $f(x) = f(0) = 0$; Max $f(x) = f(10) = 14$
11. Min $f(x) = f(0) = 0$; Max $f(x) = f(3) = 9$
13. Min $f(x) = f(1) = f(7) = 5$; Max $f(x) = f(10) = 14$
15. Min $f(x) = f(1) = f(7) = 5$; Max $f(x) = f(3) = f(9) = 9$
17. Min $f(x) = f(5) = 7$; Max $f(x) = f(3) = 9$
19. (A) Max $f(x) = f(4) = 3$; Min $f(x) = f(0) = -5$
(B) Max $f(x) = f(10) = 15$; Min $f(x) = f(0) = -5$
(C) Max $f(x) = f(10) = 15$; Min $f(x) = f(-5) = -15$
21. (A) Max $f(x) = f(-1) = f(1) = 1$; Min $f(x) = f(0) = 0$
(B) Max $f(x) = f(5) = 25$; Min $f(x) = f(1) = 1$
(C) Max $f(x) = f(-5) = f(5) = 25$; Min $f(x) = f(0) = 0$
23. Max $f(x) = f(-1) = e \approx 2.718$; Min $f(x) = e^{-1} \approx 0.368$
25. Max $f(x) = f(0) = 9$; Min $f(x) = f(\pm 4) = -7$
27. Min $f(x) = f(2) = 0$ **29.** Max $f(x) = f(-2) = 10$ **31.** None
33. None **35.** None **37.** Min $f(x) = f(0) = -1.5$ **39.** None
41. Max $f(x) = f(0) = 0$ **43.** Min $f(x) = f(2) = -2$
45. Max $f(x) = f(2) = 4$ **47.** Min $f(x) = f(2) = 0$ **49.** No maximum
51. Max $f(x) = f(2) = 8$ **53.** Min $f(x) = f(4) = 22$
55. Min $f(x) = f(\sqrt{10}) = 14/\sqrt{10}$ **57.** Min $f(x) = f(2) = \dfrac{e^2}{4} \approx 1.847$
59. Max $f(x) = f(3) = \dfrac{27}{e^3} \approx 1.344$
61. Max $f(x) = f(e^{1.5}) = 2e^{1.5} \approx 8.963$
63. Max $f(x) = f(e^{2.5}) = \dfrac{e^5}{2} \approx 74.207$ **65.** Max $f(x) = f(1) = -1$
67. (A) Max $f(x) = f(1) = 28$; Min $f(x) = f(5) = -4$
(B) Max $f(x) = f(1) = 28$; Min $f(x) = f(-2) = -53$
(C) Max $f(x) = f(7) = 28$; Min $f(x) = f(5) = -4$
69. (A) Max $f(x) = f(0) = 126$; Min $f(x) = f(2) = -26$
(B) Max $f(x) = f(7) = 49$; Min $f(x) = f(2) = -26$
(C) Max $f(x) = f(6) = 6$; Min $f(x) = f(3) = -15$
71. (A) Max $f(x) = f(1) = 8$; Min $f(x) = f(-1) = 0$
(B) Max $f(x) = f(1) = 8$; Min $f(x) = f(-3) = -24$
(C) Max $f(x) = f(-4) = 3$; Min $f(x) = f(-3) = -24$
73. Local maximum **75.** Unable to determine **77.** Neither
79. Local minimum

Exercises 8.6

1. $f(x) = x(28 - x)$ **3.** $f(x) = \pi x^2/4$ **5.** $f(x) = \pi x^3$
7. $f(x) = x(60 - x)$ **9.** 6.5 and 6.5 **11.** 6.5 and −6.5
13. $\sqrt{13}$ and $\sqrt{13}$ **15.** $10\sqrt{2}$ ft by $10\sqrt{2}$ ft **17.** 37 ft by 37 ft
19. (A) Maximum revenue is $156,250 when 625 phones are produced and sold for $250 each. (B) Maximum profit is $124,000 when 600 phones are produced and sold for $260 each. **21.** (A) Max $R(x) = R(3{,}000) = +300{,}000$ (B) Maximum profit is $75,000 when 2,100 sets are manufactured and sold for $130 each. (C) Maximum profit is $64,687.50 when 2,025 sets are manufactured and sold for $132.50 each.
23. (A)

```
QuadReg
 y=ax²+bx+c
 a=-1.853976E-5
 b=-.1172685971
 c=401.66077739
```

(B)

```
LinReg
 y=ax+b
 a=91.90751445
 b=35317.91908
```

(C) The maximum profit is $139,179 when the price per backpack is $257.
25. (A) $4.80 (B) $8 **27.** $35; $6,125 **29.** 40 trees; 1,600 lb
31. $(10 - 2\sqrt{7})/3 = 1.57$ in. squares **33.** 20 ft by 40 ft (with the expensive side being one of the short sides) **35.** (A) 70 ft by 100 ft (B) 125 ft by 125 ft **37.** 8 production runs per year **39.** 10,000 books in 5 printings **41.** 34.64 mph **43.** (A) $x = 5.1$ mi (B) $x = 10$ mi
45. 4 days; 20 bacteria/cm^3 **47.** 1 month; 2 ft **49.** 4 yr from now

Chapter 8 Review Exercises

1. $(a, c_1), (c_3, c_6)$ *(8.1, 8.2)* **2.** $(c_1, c_3), (c_6, b)$ *(8.1, 8.2)* **3.** $(a, c_2), (c_4, c_5), (c_7, b)$ *(8.1, 8.2)* **4.** c_3 *(8.1)* **5.** c_1, c_6 *(8.1)* **6.** c_1, c_3, c_5 *(8.1)*
7. c_4, c_6 *(8.1)* **8.** c_2, c_4, c_5, c_7 *(8.2)*
9. *(8.2)*

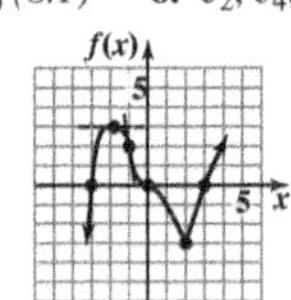

10. *(8.2)*

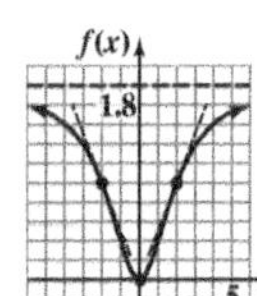

11. $f''(x) = 6 - \frac{1}{x^2}$ *(8.2)* **12.** $y'' = 8/x^3$ *(8.2)* **13.** Domain: All real numbers, except 1 and −1 y int.: 2; x int.: −2 *(8.2)* **14.** Domain: $(-2, \infty)$; y int.: ln 2; x int.: −1 *(8.2)* **15.** Horizontal asymptote: $y = 0$; Vertical asymptotes: $x = -4, x = 4$ *(8.4)* **16.** Horizontal asymptote: $y = \frac{2}{3}$; vertical asymptote: $x = -\frac{10}{3}$ *(8.4)* **17.** $(-\sqrt{2}, -20), (\sqrt{2}, -20)$ *(8.2)*
18. $(0, 10), (8, -4086)$ *(8.2)*
19. (A) $f'(x) = \left(\frac{2}{3}\right)x^{-2/3} - \left(\frac{2}{3}\right)x^{-1/3}$ (B) 0, 1 (C) 0, 1 *(8.1)*
20. (A) $f'(x) = -\frac{1}{5}x^{-6/5}$ (B) 0 (C) None *(8.1)* **21.** Domain: All real numbers; y int.: 0; x int.: 0, 9; Increasing on $(-\infty, 3)$ and $(9, \infty)$
Decreasing on $(3, 9)$
Local maximum: $f(3) = 108$
Local minimum: $f(9) = 0$
Concave upward on $(6, \infty)$
Concave downward on $(-\infty, 6)$
Inflection point: $(6, 54)$ *(8.4)*
22. Domain: All real numbers
y int.: 16; x int.: −4, 2
Increasing on $(-\infty, -2)$ and $(2, \infty)$
Decreasing on $(-2, 2)$
Local maximum: $f(-2) = 32$
Local minimum: $f(2) = 0$
Concave upward on $(0, \infty)$
Concave downward on $(-\infty, 0)$
Inflection point: $(0, 16)$ *(8.4)*

23. Domain: All real numbers
y int.: 0; x int.: 0, 4
Increasing on $(-\infty, 3)$
Decreasing on $(3, \infty)$
Local maximum: $f(3) = 54$
Concave upward on $(0, 2)$
Concave downward on $(-\infty, 0)$ and $(2, \infty)$
Inflection points: $(0, 0), (2, 32)$ *(8.4)*

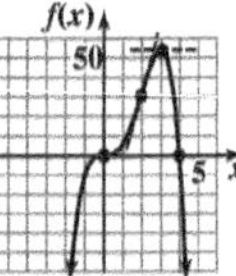

24. Domain: all real numbers
y int.: −3; x int.: −3, 1
No vertical or horizontal asymptotes
Increasing on $(-2, \infty)$
Decreasing on $(-\infty, -2)$
Local minimum: $f(-2) = -27$
Concave upward on $(-\infty, -1)$ and $(1, \infty)$
Concave downward on $(-1, 1)$
Inflection points: $(-1, -16), (1, 0)$ *(8.4)*

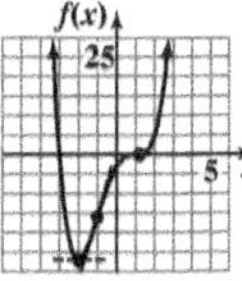

25. Domain: All real numbers, except −2
y int.: 0; x int.: 0
Horizontal asymptote: $y = 3$
Vertical asymptote: $x = -2$
Increasing on $(-\infty, -2)$ and $(-2, \infty)$
Concave upward on $(-\infty, -2)$
Concave downward on $(-2, \infty)$ *(8.4)*

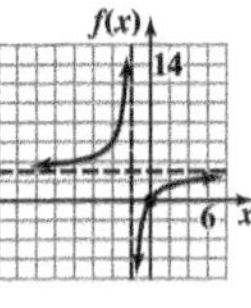

26. Domain: All real numbers; y int.: 0; x int.: 0; Horizontal asymptote: $y = 1$
Increasing on $(0, \infty)$; Decreasing on $(-\infty, 0)$
Local minimum: $f(0) = 0$
Concave upward on $(-3, 3)$
Concave downward on $(-\infty, -3)$ and $(3, \infty)$
Inflection points: $(-3, 0.25), (3, 0.25)$ *(8.4)*

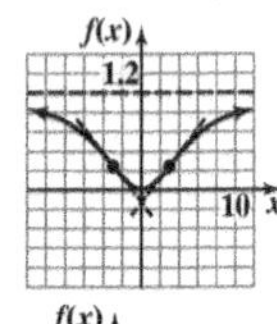

27. Domain: All real numbers except $x = -2$
y int.: 0; x int.: 0
Horizontal asymptote: $y = 0$
Vertical asymptote: $x = -2$
Increasing on $(-2, 2)$
Decreasing on $(-\infty, -2)$ and $(2, \infty)$
Local maximum: $f(2) = 0.125$
Concave upward on $(4, \infty)$
Concave downward on $(-\infty, -2)$ and $(-2, 4)$
Inflection point: $(4, 0.111)$ *(8.4)*

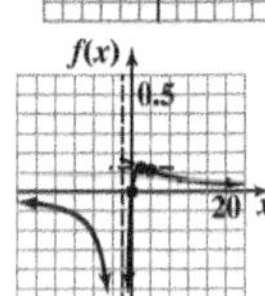

28. Domain: All real numbers
y int.: 0; x int.: 0
Oblique asymptote: $y = x$
Increasing on $(-\infty, \infty)$
Concave upward on $(-\infty, -3)$ and $(0, 3)$
Concave downward on $(-3, 0)$ and $(3, \infty)$
Inflection points: $(-3, -2.25), (0, 0), (3, 2.25)$ *(8.4)*

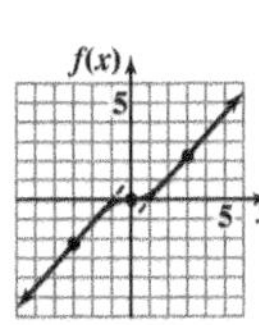

29. Domain: All real numbers
y int.: 0; x int.: 0
Horizontal asymptote: $y = 5$
Increasing on $(-\infty, \infty)$
Concave downward on $(-\infty, \infty)$ *(8.4)*

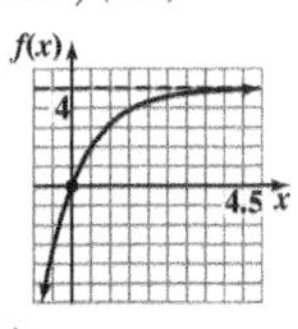

30. Domain: $(0, \infty)$
x int.: 1
Increasing on $(e^{-1/3}, \infty)$
Decreasing on $(0, e^{-1/3})$
Local minimum: $f(e^{-1/3}) = -0.123$
Concave upward on $(e^{-5/6}, \infty)$
Concave downward on $(0, e^{-5/6})$
Inflection point: $(e^{-5/6}, -0.068)$ *(8.4)*

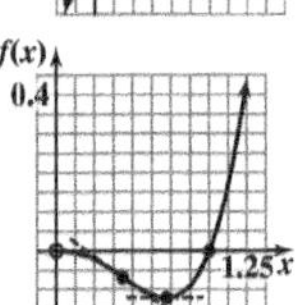

31. $\frac{-1}{2}$ *(8.3)* **32.** $\frac{5}{3}$ *(8.3)* **33.** 0 *(8.3)* **34.** 0 *(8.3)* **35.** 0 *(8.3)*
36. 0 *(8.3)* **37.** ∞ *(8.3)* **38.** ∞ *(8.3)* **39.** 0 *(8.3)* **40.** $\frac{1}{2}$ *(8.3)*

41.

x	$f'(x)$	$f(x)$
$-\infty < x < -2$	Negative and increasing	Decreasing and concave upward
$x = -2$	x intercept	Local minimum
$-2 < x < -1$	Positive and increasing	Increasing and concave upward
$x = -1$	Local maximum	Inflection point
$-1 < x < 1$	Positive and decreasing	Increasing and concave downward
$x = 1$	Local min., x intercept	Inflection point, horiz. tangent
$1 < x < \infty$	Positive and increasing	Increasing and concave upward

(8.2)
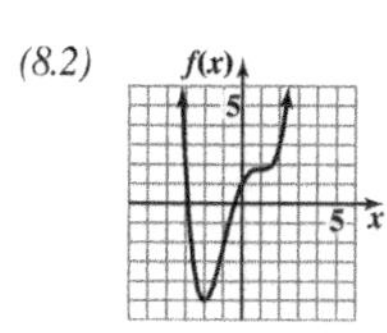

42. (C) *(8.2)* **43.** Local maximum $f(-2) = \frac{476}{3}$; local minimum $f(8) = 50.67$ *(8.5)*
44. Max $f(x) = f(5) = 77$; Min $f(x) = f(2) = -4$ *(8.5)*
45. Min $f(x) = f(1) = \frac{3}{4}$ *(8.5)*
46. Max $f(x) = f(e^{4.5}) = 2e^{4.5} \approx 180.03$ *(9.5)*
47. Max $f(x) = f(0.5) = 5e^{-1} \approx 1.84$ *(9.5)*
48. Yes. Since f is continuous on $[a, b]$, f has an absolute maximum on $[a, b]$. But neither $f(a)$ nor $f(b)$ is an absolute maximum, so the absolute maximum must occur between a and b. *(8.5)* **49.** No, increasing/decreasing properties apply to intervals in the domain of f. It is correct to say that $f(x)$ is decreasing on $(-\infty, 0)$ and $(0, \infty)$. *(8.1)*
number for $f'(x)$ that is also in the domain of f. For example, if $f(x) = x^{-1}$, then 0 is a partition number for $f'(x) = -x^{-2}$, but 0 is not a critical number of $f(x)$ since 0 is not in the domain of f. *(8.1)*
51. Max $f'(x) = f'(2) = 12$ *(8.2, 8.5)*

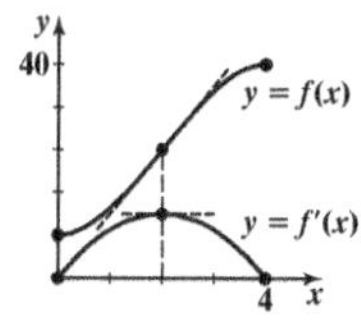

52. Each number is 20; minimum sum is 40 *(8.6)*
53. Domain: All real numbers; x int.: 0.79, 1.64; y int.: 4; Increasing on $(-1.68, -0.35)$ and $(1.28, \infty)$; Decreasing on $(-\infty, -1.68)$ and $(-0.35, 1.28)$; Local minima: $f(-1.68) = 0.97$, $f(1.28) = -1.61$
Local maximum: $f(-0.35) = 4.53$; Concave downward on $(-1.10, 0.60)$
Concave upward on $(-\infty, -1.10)$ and $(0.60, \infty)$; Inflection points: $(-1.10, 2.58)$, $(0.60, 1.08)$ *(8.4)* **54.** Domain: All real numbers
x int.: 0, 10.10; y int.: 0; Increasing on (1.87, 4.19) and $(8.94, \infty)$
Decreasing on $(-\infty, 1.87)$ and $(4.19, 8.94)$; Local maximum: $f(4.19) = -39.81$
Local minima: $f(1.87) = -52.14$, $f(8.94) = -123.81$
Concave upward on $(-\infty, 2.92)$ and $(7.08, \infty)$
Concave downward on (2.92, 7.08)
Inflection points: $(2.92, -46.41)$, $(7.08, -88.04)$ *(8.4)*
55. Max $f(x) = f(1.373) = 2.487$ *(8.5)*
56. Max $f(x) = f(1.763) = 0.097$ *(8.5)*
57. (A) For the first 15 months, the graph of the price is increasing and concave downward, with a local maximum at $t = 15$. For the next 15 months, the graph of the price is decreasing and concave downward, with an inflection point at $t = 30$. For the next 15 months, the graph of the price is decreasing and concave upward, with a local minimum at $t = 45$. For the remaining 15 months, the graph of the price is increasing and concave upward.

(B)
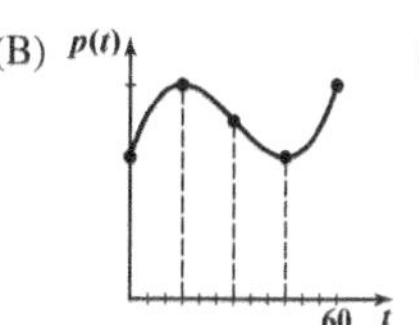

(8.2)

58. (A) Max $R(x) = R(12{,}000) = \$1{,}800{,}000$ (B) Maximum profit is \$100,000 when 4,000 phones are manufactured and sold for \$250 each. (C) Maximum profit is \$142,000 when 4,400 phones are manufactured and sold for \$245 each. *(8.6)*

59. (A) The expensive side is 50 ft; the other side is 100 ft. (B) The expensive side is 75 ft; the other side is 150 ft. *(8.6)* **60.** \$660; \$51,200 *(8.6)*
61. 12 orders/yr *(8.6)*
62. Min $\overline{C}(x) = \overline{C}(200) = \$50$ *(8.4)* **63.** Min $\overline{C}(x) = \overline{C}(e^5) \approx \$49.66$ *(8.4)*

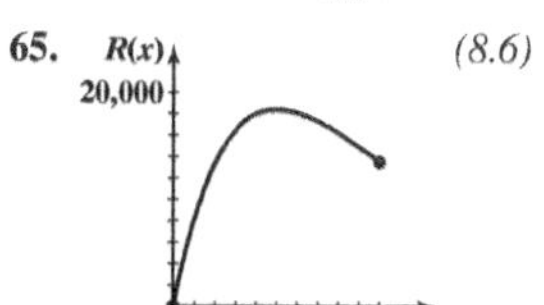

64. A maximum revenue of \$18,394 is realized at a production level of 50 units at \$367.88 each. *(8.6)*

65.
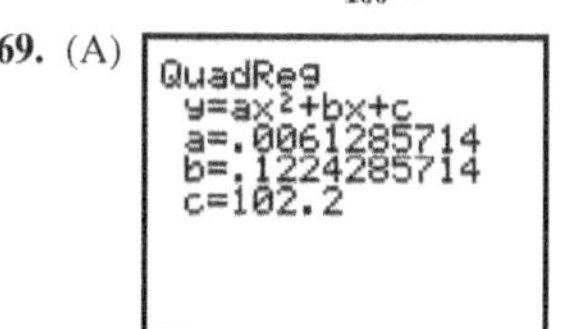

(8.6)

66. \$549.15; \$9,864 *(8.6)*
67. \$1.52 *(8.6)*
68. 20.39 ft *(8.6)*

69. (A)

```
QuadReg
 y=ax²+bx+c
 a=.0061285714
 b=.1224285714
 c=102.2
```

(B) Min $\overline{C}(x) = \overline{C}(129) = \$1.71$ *(8.4)*

70. Increasing on (0, 18); decreasing on (18, 24); point of diminishing returns is $x = 18$; max $N'(x) = N'(18) = 972$ *(8.2)*

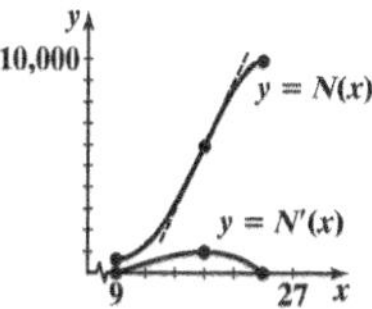

71. (A)
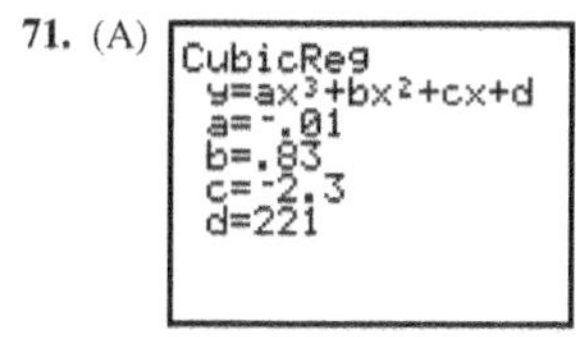

(B) 28 ads to sell 588 refrigerators per month *(8.2)* **72.** 8 days *(8.1)*
73. 2 yr from now *(8.1)*

Chapter 9

Exercises 9.1

1. 19.5 ft^2 **3.** 240 in.^{3} **5.** $32\pi \approx 100.5$ m^3 **7.** $1{,}440\pi \approx 4{,}523.9$ cm^2
9. -4 **11.** 11 **13.** 4 **15.** Not defined **17.** -1 **19.** -64 **21.** 154,440
23. $192\pi \approx 603.2$ **25.** $3\pi\sqrt{109} \approx 98.4$ **27.** 118 **29.** 6.2
31. $f(x) = x^2 - 7$ **33.** $f(y) = 38y + 20$ **35.** $f(y) = -2y^3 + 5$
37. $D(x, y) = x^2 + y^2$ **39.** $C(n, w) = 35nw$ **41.** $S(x, y, z) = \frac{x + y + z}{3}$
43. $L(d, h) = \frac{\pi}{12}d^2h$ **45.** $J(C, h) = \frac{C^2h}{4\pi}$ **47.** $y = 2$ **49.** $x = -\frac{1}{2}, 1$
51. $-1.926, 0.599$ **53.** $2x + h$ **55.** $2y^2$ **57.** $E(0, 0, 3)$; $F(2, 0, 3)$
59. (A) In the plane $y = c$, c any constant, $z = x^2$. (B) The y axis; the line parallel to the y axis and passing through the point $(1, 0, 1)$; the line parallel to the y axis and passing through the point $(2, 0, 4)$ (C) A parabolic "trough" lying on top of the y axis **61.** (A) Upper semicircles whose centers lie on the

y axis (B) Upper semicircles whose centers lie on the x axis (C) The upper hemisphere of radius 6 with center at the origin **63.** (A) $a^2 + b^2$ and $c^2 + d^2$ both equal the square of the radius of the circle. (B) Bell-shaped curves with maximum values of 1 at the origin (C) A bell, with maximum value 1 at the origin, extending infinitely far in all directions. **65.** \$13,200; \$18,000; \$21,300 **67.** $R(p, q) = -5p^2 + 6pq - 4q^2 + 200p + 300q$; $R(2, 3) = \$1{,}280$; $R(3, 2) = \$1{,}175$ **69.** 30,065 units **71.** (A) \$237,877.08 (B) 4.4% **73.** $T(70, 47) \approx 29$ min; $T(60, 27) = 33$ min **75.** $C(6, 8) = 75$; $C(8.1, 9) = 90$ **77.** $Q(12, 10) = 120$; $Q(10, 12) \approx 83$

Exercises 9.2

1. $f'(x) = 6$ **3.** $f'(x) = -5e + 14x$ **5.** $f'(x) = 3x^2 - 8\pi^2$ **7.** $f'(x) = 70x(e^2 + 5x^2)^6$ **9.** $\frac{dz}{dx} = e^x - 3e + ex^{e-1}$ **11.** $\frac{dz}{dx} = \frac{2x}{x^2 + \pi^2}$ **13.** $\frac{dz}{dx} = \frac{x + e}{x} + \ln x$ **15.** $\frac{dz}{dx} = \frac{(x^2 + \pi^2)5 - 10x^2}{(x^2 + \pi^2)^2} = \frac{5(\pi^2 - x^2)}{(x^2 + \pi^2)^2}$ **17.** $f_x(x, y) = 4$ **19.** $f_y(x, y) = -3x + 4y$ **21.** $\frac{\partial z}{\partial x} = 3x^2 + 8xy$ **23.** $\frac{\partial z}{\partial y} = 20(5x + 2y)^9$ **25.** 9 **27.** 3 **29.** -4 **31.** 0 **33.** 45.6 mpg; mileage is 45.6 mpg at a tire pressure of 32 psi and a speed of 40 mph **35.** 37.6 mpg; mileage is 37.6 mpg at a tire pressure of 32 psi and a speed of 50 mph **37.** 0.3 mpg per psi; mileage increases at a rate of 0.3 mpg per psi of tire pressure **39.** $f_{xx}(x, y) = 0$ **41.** $f_{xy}(x, y) = 0$ **43.** $f_{xy}(x, y) = y^2e^{xy^2}(2xy) + e^{xy^2}(2y) = 2y(1 + xy^2)e^{xy^2}$ **45.** $f_{yy}(x, y) = \frac{2 \ln x}{y^3}$ **47.** $f_{xx}(x, y) = 80(2x + y)^3$ **49.** $f_{xy}(x, y) = 720xy^3(x^2 + y^4)^8$ **51.** $C_x(x, y) = 6x + 10y + 4$ **53.** 2 **55.** $C_{xx}(x, y) = 6$ **57.** $C_{xy}(x, y) = 10$ **59.** 6 **61.** \$3,000; daily sales are \$3,000 when the temperature is 60° and the rainfall is 2 in. **63.** $-2{,}500$ \$/in.; daily sales decrease at a rate of \$2,500 per inch of rain when the temperature is 90° and rainfall is 1 in. **65.** -50 \$/in. per °F; S_r decreases at a rate of 50 \$/in. per degree of temperature **69.** $f_{xx}(x, y) = 2y^2 + 6x$; $f_{xy}(x, y) = 4xy = f_{yx}(x, y)$; $f_{yy}(x, y) = 2x^2$ **71.** $f_{xx}(x, y) = -2y/x^3$; $f_{xy}(x, y) = (-1/y^2) + (1/x^2) = f_{yx}(x, y)$; $f_{yy}(x, y) = 2x/y^3$ **73.** $f_{xx}(x, y) = (2y + xy^2)e^{xy}$; $f_{xy}(x, y) = (2x + x^2y)e^{xy} = f_{yx}(x, y)$; $f_{yy}(x, y) = x^3e^{xy}$ **75.** $x = 2$ and $y = 4$ **77.** $x = 1.200$ and $y = -0.695$ **79.** (A) $-\frac{13}{3}$ (B) The function $f(0, y)$, for example, has values less than $-\frac{13}{3}$. **81.** (A) $c = 1.145$ (B) $f_x(c, 2) = 0$; $f_y(c, 2) = 92.021$ **83.** (A) $2x$ (B) $4y$ **85.** $P_x(1{,}200, 1{,}800) = 24$; profit will increase approx. \$24 per unit increase in production of type A calculators at the $(1{,}200, 1{,}800)$ output level; $P_y(1{,}200, 1{,}800) = -48$; profit will decrease approx. \$48 per unit increase in production of type B calculators at the $(1{,}200, 1{,}800)$ output level **87.** $\partial x/\partial p = -5$: a \$1 increase in the price of brand A will decrease the demand for brand A by 5 lb at any price level (p, q); $\partial y/\partial p = 2$: a \$1 increase in the price of brand A will increase the demand for brand B by 2 lb at any price level (p, q) **89.** (A) $f_x(x, y) = 7.5x^{-0.25}y^{0.25}$; $f_y(x, y) = 2.5x^{0.75}y^{-0.75}$ (B) Marginal productivity of labor $= f_x(600, 100) \approx 4.79$; marginal productivity of capital $= f_y(600, 100) \approx 9.58$ (C) Capital **91.** Competitive **93.** Complementary **95.** (A) $f_w(w, h) = 6.65w^{-0.575}h^{0.725}$; $f_h(w, h) = 11.34w^{0.425}h^{-0.275}$ (B) $f_w(65, 57) = 11.31$: for a 65-lb child 57 in. tall, the rate of change in surface area is 11.31 in.^{2} for each pound gained in weight (height is held fixed); $f_h(65, 57) = 21.99$: for a child 57 in. tall, the rate of change in surface area is 21.99 in.^{2} for each inch gained in height (weight is held fixed) **97.** $C_W(6, 8) = 12.5$: index increases approx. 12.5 units for a 1-in. increase in width of head (length held fixed) when $W = 6$ and $L = 8$; $C_L(6, 8) = -9.38$: index decreases approx. 9.38 units for a 1-in. increase in length (width held fixed) when $W = 6$ and $L = 8$.

Exercises 9.3

1. $f'(0) = 0$; $f''(0) = -18$; local maximum **3.** $f'(0) = 0$; $f''(0) = 2$; local minimum **5.** $f'(0) = 0$; $f''(0) = -2$; local maximum **7.** $f'(0) = 1$; $f''(0) = -2$; neither **9.** $f_x(x, y) = 4$; $f_y(x, y) = 5$; the functions $f_x(x, y)$ and $f_y(x, y)$ never have the value 0. **11.** $f_x(x, y) = -1.2 + 4x^3$; $f_y(x, y) = 6.8 + 0.6y^2$; the function $f_y(x, y)$ never has the value 0. **13.** $f_x(x, y) = -2x + 2y - 4$; $f_y(x, y) = 2x - 2y + 5$; the system of equations $\begin{cases} -2x + 2y - 4 = 0 \\ 2x - 2y + 5 = 0 \end{cases}$ has no solution **15.** $f_x(x, y) = ye^x - 3$; $f_y(x, y) = e^x + 4$; the function $f_y(x, y)$ never has the value 0 **17.** $f(-4, 0) = 9$ is a local minimum. **19.** $f(6, -1) = 45$ is a local maximum. **21.** f has a saddle point at $(0, 0)$. **23.** $f(0, 0) = 100$ is a local maximum. **25.** $f(6, -5) = -22$ is a local minimum. **27.** f has a saddle point at $(0, 0)$. **29.** f has a saddle point at $(0, 0)$; $f(1, 1) = -1$ is a local minimum. **31.** f has a saddle point at $(0, 0)$; $f(3, 18) = -162$ and $f(-3, -18) = -162$ are local minima. **33.** The test fails at $(0, 0)$; f has saddle points at $(2, 2)$ and $(2, -2)$. **35.** f has a saddle point at $(0, -0.567)$. **37.** $f(x, y)$ is nonnegative and equals 0 when $x = 0$, so f has the local minimum 0 at each point of the y axis. **39.** (B) Local minimum **41.** 2,000 type A and 4,000 type B; max $P = P(2, 4) = \$15$ million **43.** (A) When $p = \$100$ and $q = \$120$, $x = 80$ and $y = 40$; when $p = \$110$ and $q = \$110$, $x = 40$ and $y = 70$ (B) A maximum weekly profit of \$4,800 is realized for $p = \$100$ and $q = \$120$. **45.** $P(x, y) = P(4, 2)$ **47.** 8 in. by 4 in. by 2 in. **49.** 20 in. by 20 in. by 40 in.

Exercises 9.4

1. Min $f(x, y) = f(-2, 4) = 12$ **3.** Min $f(x, y) = f(1, -1) = -4$ **5.** Max $f(x, y) = f(1, 0) = 2$ **7.** Max $f(x, y) = f(3, 3) = 18$ **9.** Min $f(x, y) = f(3, 4) = 25$ **11.** $F_x = -3 + 2\lambda = 0$ and $F_y = 4 + 5\lambda = 0$ have no simultaneous solution. **13.** Max $f(x, y) = f(3, 3) = f(-3, -3) = 18$; min $f(x, y) = f(3, -3) = f(-3, 3) = -18$ **15.** Maximum product is 25 when each number is 5. **17.** Min $f(x, y, z) = f(5, 5, 15) = 275$ **19.** Max $f(x, y, z) = f(4, 20, 10) = 220$ **21.** Max $f(x, y, z) = f(1, 10, 2) = 105$; Min $f(x, y, z) = f(-1, -10, -2) = -105$ **23.** Max $f(x, y, z) = f(2, -4, 2) = 12$; Min $f(x, y, z) = f(-2, 4, -2) = -12$ **25.** $F_x = e^x + \lambda = 0$ and $F_y = 3e^y - 2\lambda = 0$ have no simultaneous solution. **27.** Maximize $f(x, 5)$, a function of just one independent variable. **29.** (A) Max $f(x, y) = f(0.707, 0.5) = f(-0.707, 0.5) = 0.47$ **31.** 60 of model A and 30 of model B will yield a minimum cost of \$32,400 per week. **33.** (A) 8,000 units of labor and 1,000 units of capital; max $N(x, y) = N(8{,}000, 1{,}000) \approx 263{,}902$ units (B) Marginal productivity of money ≈ 0.6598; increase in production $\approx 32{,}990$ units **35.** 8 in. by 8 in. by $\frac{8}{3}$ in. **37.** $x = 50$ ft and $y = 200$ ft; maximum area is 10,000 ft^2

Exercises 9.5

1. 10 **3.** 98 **5.** 380
7. $y = 0.7x + 1$ **9.** $y = -2.5x + 10.5$ **11.** $y = x + 2$

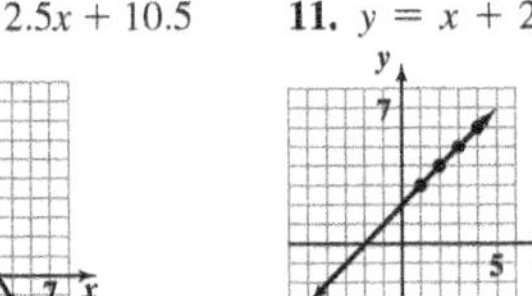

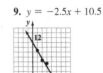

13. $y = -1.5x + 4.5$; $y = 0.75$ when $x = 2.5$ **15.** $y = 2.12x + 10.8$; $y = 63.8$ when $x = 25$ **17.** $y = -1.2x + 12.6$; $y = 10.2$ when $x = 2$ **19.** $y = -1.53x + 26.67$; $y = 14.4$ when $x = 8$ **21.** $y = 0.75x^2 - 3.45x + 4.75$ **27.** (A) $y = 1.52x - 0.16$; $y = 0.73x^2 - 1.39x + 1.30$ (B) The quadratic function

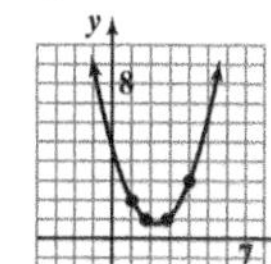

29. The normal equations form a system of 4 linear equations in the 4 variables a, b, c, and d, which can be solved by Gauss–Jordan elimination.

31. (A) $y = -85.089x + 3821.1$ (B) 1,694 crimes per 100,000 population **33.** (A) $y = -0.48x + 4.38$ (B) \$6.56 per bottle **35.** (A) $y = 0.0228x + 18.93$ (B) 19.93 ft **37.** (A) $y = 0.01814x - 0.365$ (B) 1.09°C

Exercises 9.6

1. $\pi x + \frac{x^2}{2} + C$ **3.** $x + \pi \ln|x| + C$ **5.** $\frac{e^{\pi x}}{\pi} + C$ **7.** (A) $3x^2y^4 + C(x)$ (B) $3x^2$ **9.** (A) $2x^2 + 6xy + 5x + E(y)$ (B) $35 + 30y$ **11.** (A) $\sqrt{y + x^2} + E(y)$ (B) $\sqrt{y+4} - \sqrt{y}$ **13.** (A) $\frac{\ln x \ln y}{x} + C(x)$ (B) $\frac{2 \ln x}{x}$ **15.** (A) $3y^2e^{x+y^3} + E(y)$ (B) $3y^2e^{1+y^3} - 3y^2e^{y^3}$ **17.** 9 **19.** 330 **21.** $(56 - 20\sqrt{5})/3$ **23.** 1 **25.** $e^9 - e^8 - e + 1 \approx 5{,}120.41$ **27.** 16 **29.** 49 **31.** $\frac{1}{8}\int_1^5\int_{-1}^1 (x+y)^2 dy\, dx = \frac{32}{3}$ **33.** $\frac{1}{15}\int_1^4\int_2^7 (x/y)\, dy\, dx = \frac{1}{2}\ln\frac{7}{2} \approx 0.6264$ **35.** $\frac{4}{3}$ cubic units **37.** $\frac{32}{3}$ cubic units **39.** $\int_0^1\int_1^2 xe^{xy}\, dy\, dx = \frac{1}{2} + \frac{1}{2}e^2 - e$ **41.** $\int_0^1\int_{-1}^1 \frac{2y + 3xy^2}{1 + x^2} dy\, dx = \ln 2$ **45.** (A) $\frac{1}{3} + \frac{1}{4}e^{-2} - \frac{1}{4}e^2$

(B)

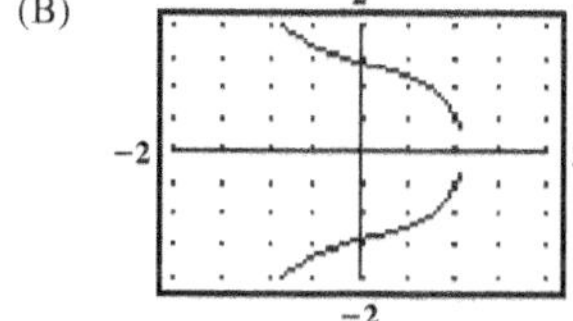

(C) Points to the right of the graph in part (B) are greater than 0; points to the left of the graph are less than 0.

47. $\frac{1}{0.4}\int_{0.6}^{0.8}\int_5^7 \frac{y}{1 - x} dy\, dx = 30 \ln 2 \approx$ \$20.8 billion **49.** $\frac{1}{10}\int_{10}^{20}\int_1^2 x^{0.75}y^{0.25} dy\, dx = \frac{8}{175}(2^{1.25} - 1)(20^{1.75} - 10^{1.75}) \approx 8.375$ or 8,375 units **51.** $\frac{1}{192}\int_{-8}^8\int_{-6}^6 [10 - \frac{1}{10}(x^2 + y^2)] dy\, dx = \frac{20}{3}$ insects/ft^2 **53.** $\frac{1}{8}\int_{-2}^2\int_{-1}^1 [50 - 9(x^2 + y^2)] dy\, dx = 35\ \mu\text{g/m}^3$ **55.** $\frac{1}{10{,}000}\int_{2{,}000}^{3{,}000}\int_{50}^{60} 0.000\,013\,3xy^2 dy\, dx \approx 100.86$ ft **57.** $\frac{1}{16}\int_8^{16}\int_{10}^{12} 100\frac{x}{y}\, dy\, dx = 600 \ln 1.2 \approx 109.4$

Exercises 9.7

1. 24 **3.** 0 **5.** 1 **7.** $R = \{(x, y) \mid 0 \le y \le 4 - x^2, 0 \le x \le 2\}$
$R = \{(x, y) \mid 0 \le x \le \sqrt{4 - y}, 0 \le y \le 4\}$

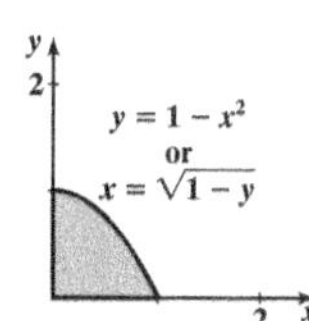

9. R is a regular x region:
$R = \{(x, y) \mid x^3 \le y \le 12 - 2x, 0 \le x \le 2\}$

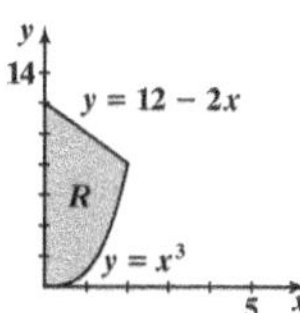

11. R is a regular y region:
$R = \{(x, y) \mid \frac{1}{2}y^2 \le x \le y + 4, -2 \le y \le 4\}$

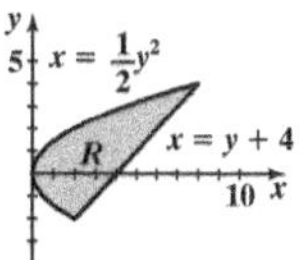

13. $\frac{1}{2}$ **15.** $\frac{39}{70}$ **17.** R consists of the points on or inside the rectangle with corners $(\pm 2, \pm 3)$; both **19.** R is the arch-shaped region consisting of the points on or inside the rectangle with corners $(\pm 2, 0)$ and $(\pm 2, 2)$ that are not inside the circle of radius 1 centered at the origin; regular x region **21.** $\frac{56}{3}$ **23.** $-\frac{3}{4}$ **25.** $\frac{1}{2}e^4 - \frac{5}{2}$ **27.** $R = \{(x, y) \mid 0 \le y \le x + 1, 0 \le x \le 1\}$
$\int_0^1\int_0^{x+1} \sqrt{1 + x + y}\, dy\, dx = (68 - 24\sqrt{2})/15$

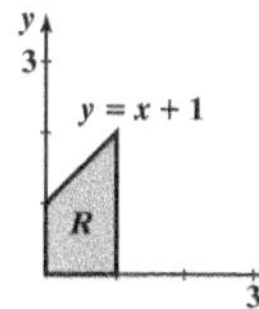

29. $R = \{(x, y) \mid 0 \le y \le 4x - x^2, 0 \le x \le 4\}$
$\int_0^4\int_0^{4x - x^2} \sqrt{y + x^2}\, dy\, dx = \frac{128}{5}$

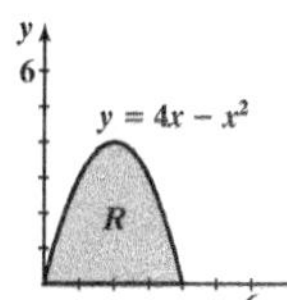

31. $R = \{(x, y) \mid 1 - \sqrt{x} \le y \le 1 + \sqrt{x}, 0 \le x \le 4\}$
$\int_0^4\int_{1-\sqrt{x}}^{1+\sqrt{x}} x(y - 1)^2 dy\, dx = \frac{512}{21}$

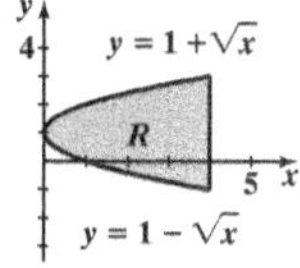

33. $\int_0^3\int_0^{3-y} (x + 2y)\, dx\, dy = \frac{27}{2}$

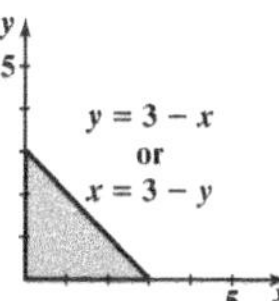

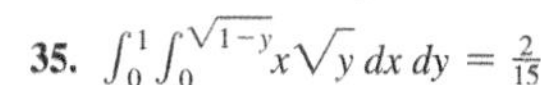

35. $\int_0^1\int_0^{\sqrt{1-y}} x\sqrt{y}\, dx\, dy = \frac{2}{15}$

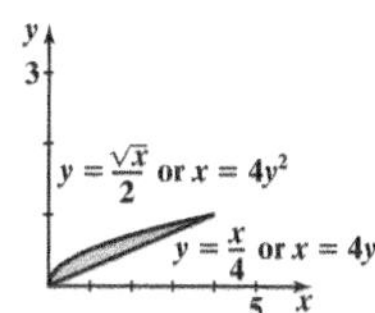

37. $\int_0^1 \int_{4y^2}^{4y} x\,dx\,dy = \frac{16}{15}$ **39.** $\int_0^4 \int_0^{4-x} (4 - x - y)\,dy\,dx = \frac{32}{3}$

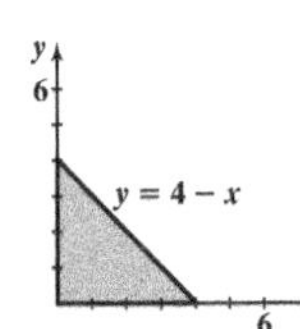

41. $\int_0^1 \int_0^{1-x^2} 4\,dy\,dx = \frac{8}{3}$

43. $\displaystyle\int_0^4 \int_0^{\sqrt{y}} \frac{4x}{1 + y^2}\,dx\,dy = \ln 17$

45. $\int_0^1 \int_0^{\sqrt{x}} 4ye^{x^2}\,dy\,dx = e - 1$

47. $R = \{(x, y) \mid x^2 \le y \le 1 + \sqrt{x}, 0 \le x \le 1.49\}$

$\int_0^{1.49} \int_{x^2}^{1+\sqrt{x}} x\,dy\,dx \approx 0.96$

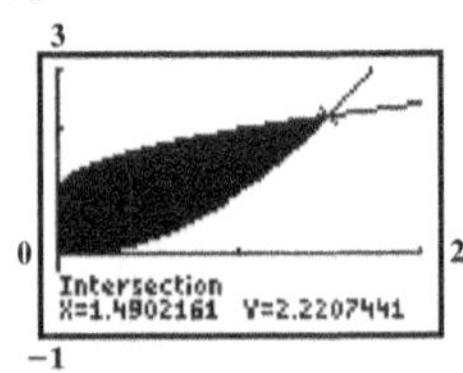

49. $R = \{(x, y) \mid y^3 \le x \le 1 - y, 0 \le y \le 0.68\}$

$\int_0^{0.68} \int_{y^3}^{1-y} 24xy\,dx\,dy \approx 0.83$

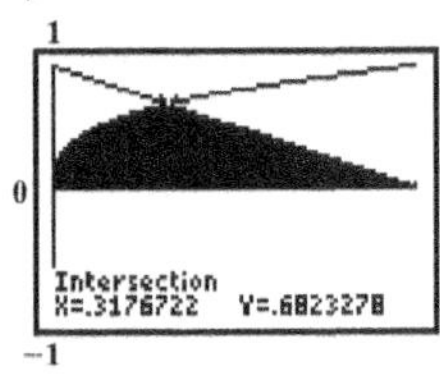

51. $R = \{(x, y) \mid e^{-x} \le y \le 3 - x, -1.51 \le x \le 2.95\}$; Regular x region
$R = \{(x, y) \mid -\ln y \le x \le 3 - y, 0.05 \le y \le 4.51\}$; Regular y region
$\int_{-1.51}^{2.95} \int_{e^{-x}}^{3-x} 4y\,dy\,dx = \int_{0.05}^{4.51} \int_{-\ln y}^{3-y} 4y\,dx\,dy \approx 40.67$

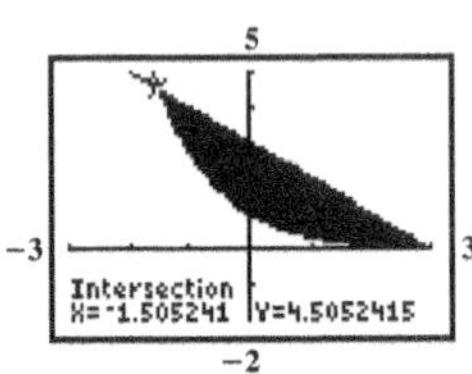

53. 1,200,000 ft^3 **55.** 1,506,400 ft^3 **57.** 38.6 μg/m^3

Chapter 9 Review Exercises

1. $f(5, 10) = 2{,}900$; $f_x(x, y) = 40$; $f_y(x, y) = 70$ *(9.1, 9.2)*
2. $\partial^2 z/\partial x^2 = 6xy^2$; $\partial^2 z/\partial x\,\partial y = 6x^2y$ *(9.2)* **3.** $2xy^3 + 2y^2 + C(x)$ *(9.6)*
4. $3x^2y^2 + 4xy + E(y)$ *(9.6)* **5.** 1 *(9.6)*
6. $f_x(x, y) = 5 + 6x + 3x^2$; $f_y(x, y) = -2$; the function $f_y(x, y)$ never has the value 0. *(9.3)*
7. $f(2, 3) = 7$; $f_y(x, y) = -2x + 2y + 3$; $f_y(2, 3) = 5$ *(9.1, 9.2)*
8. $(-8)(-6) - (4)^2 = 32$ *(9.2)* **9.** $(1, 3, -\frac{1}{2}), (-1, -3, \frac{1}{2})$ *(9.4)*
10. $y = -1.5x + 15.5$; $y = 0.5$ when $x = 10$ *(9.5)* **11.** 18 *(9.6)* **12.** $\frac{8}{5}$ *(9.7)*
13. $f_x(x, y) = 2xe^{x^2+2y}$; $f_y(x, y) = 2e^{x^2+2y}$; $f_{xy}(x, y) = 4xe^{x^2+2y}$ *(9.2)*
14. $f_x(x, y) = 10x(x^2 + y^2)^4$; $f_{xy}(x, y) = 80xy(x^2 + y^2)^3$ *(9.2)*
15. $f(2, 3) = -25$ is a local minimum; f has a saddle point at $(-2, 3)$. *(9.3)*
16. Max $f(x, y) = f(6, 4) = 24$ *(9.4)* **17.** Min $f(x, y, z) = f(2, 1, 2) = 9$ *(9.4)* **18.** $y = \frac{116}{165}x + \frac{100}{3}$ *(9.5)* **19.** $\frac{27}{5}$ *(9.6)* **20.** 4 cubic units *(9.6)*
21. 0 *(14.6)* **22.** (A) 12.56 (B) No *(9.6)* **23.** $F_x = 12x^2 + 3\lambda = 0$, $F_y = -15y^2 + 2\lambda = 0$, and $F_\lambda = 3x + 2y - 7 = 0$ have no simultaneous solution. *(9.4)* **24.** 1 *(9.7)* **25.** (A) $P_x(1, 3) = 8$; profit will increase \$8,000 for a 100-unit increase in product A if the production of product B is held fixed at an output level of $(1, 3)$. (B) For 200 units of A and 300 units of B, $P(2, 3) = \$100$ thousand is a local maximum. *(9.2, 9.3)*
26. $x = 6$ in., $y = 8$ in., $z = 2$ in. *(9.3)* **27.** $y = 0.63x + 1.33$; profit in sixth year is \$5.11 million *(9.4)* **28.** (A) Marginal productivity of labor ≈ 8.37; marginal productivity of capital ≈ 1.67; management should encourage increased use of labor. (B) 80 units of labor and 40 units of capital; max $N(x, y) = N(80, 40) \approx 696$ units; marginal productivity of money ≈ 0.0696; increase in production ≈ 139 units
(C) $\displaystyle\frac{1}{1{,}000}\int_{50}^{100}\int_{20}^{40} 10x^{0.8}y^{0.2}\,dy\,dx = \frac{(40^{1.2} - 20^{1.2})(100^{1.8} - 50^{1.8})}{216}$
$= 621$ items *(9.4)* **29.** $T_x(70, 17) = -0.924$ min/ft increase in depth when $V = 70$ ft^3 and $x = 17$ ft *(9.2)*
30. $\frac{1}{16}\int_{-2}^{2}\int_{-2}^{2}[65 - 6(x^2 + y^2)]dy\,dx = 49\ \mu g/m^3$ *(9.6)* **31.** 50,000 *(9.1)*
32. $y = \frac{1}{2}x + 48$; $y = 68$ when $x = 40$ *(9.5)* **33.** (A) $y = 0.734x + 49.93$ (B) 97.64 people/mi^2 (C) 101.10 people/mi^2; 103.70 people/mi^2 *(9.5)*
34. (A) $y = 1.069x + 0.522$ (B) 64.68 yr (C) 64.78 yr; 64.80 yr *(9.5)*

Appendix A

Exercises A.1

1. vu **3.** $(3 + 7) + y$ **5.** $u + v$ **7.** T **9.** T **11.** F **13.** T **15.** T **17.** T **19.** T **21.** F **23.** T **25.** T **27.** No **29.** (A) F (B) T (C) T **31.** $\sqrt{2}$ and π are two examples of infinitely many. **33.** (A) N, Z, Q, R (B) R (C) Q, R (D) Q, R **35.** (A) F, since, for example, $2(3 - 1) \ne 2 \cdot 3 - 1$ (B) F, since, for example, $(8 - 4) - 2 \ne 8 - (4 - 2)$ (C) T (D) F, since, for example, $(8 \div 4) \div 2 \ne 8 \div (4 \div 2)$. **37.** $\frac{1}{11}$
39. (A) 2.166 666 666 . . . (B) 4.582 575 69 . . . (C) 0.437 500 000 . . . (D) 0.261 261 261 . . . **41.** (A) 3 (B) 2 **43.** (A) 2 (B) 6 **45.** \$16.42 **47.** 2.8%

Exercises A.2

1. 3 **3.** $x^3 + 4x^2 - 2x + 5$ **5.** $x^3 + 1$
7. $2x^5 + 3x^4 - 2x^3 + 11x^2 - 5x + 6$ **9.** $-5u + 2$ **11.** $6a^2 + 6a$
13. $a^2 - b^2$ **15.** $6x^2 - 7x - 5$ **17.** $2x^2 + xy - 6y^2$ **19.** $9y^2 - 4$
21. $-4x^2 + 12x - 9$ **23.** $16m^2 - 9n^2$ **25.** $9u^2 + 24uv + 16v^2$
27. $a^3 - b^3$ **29.** $x^2 - 2xy + y^2 - 9z^2$ **31.** 1 **33.** $x^4 - 2x^2y^2 + y^4$
35. $-40ab$ **37.** $-4m + 8$ **39.** $-6xy$ **41.** $u^3 + 3u^2v + 3uv^2 + v^3$
43. $x^3 - 6x^2y + 12xy^2 - 8y^3$ **45.** $2x^2 - 2xy + 3y^2$
47. $x^4 - 10x^3 + 27x^2 - 10x + 1$ **49.** $4x^3 - 14x^2 + 8x - 6$ **51.** $m + n$
53. No change **55.** $(1 + 1)^2 \ne 1^2 + 1^2$; either a or b must be 0
57. $0.09x + 0.12(10{,}000 - x) = 1{,}200 - 0.03x$
59. $20x + 30(3x) + 50(4{,}000 - x - 3x) = 200{,}000 - 90x$
61. $0.02x + 0.06(10 - x) = 0.6 - 0.04x$

Exercises A.3

1. $3m^2(2m^2 - 3m - 1)$ **3.** $2uv(4u^2 - 3uv + 2v^2)$
5. $(7m + 5)(2m - 3)$ **7.** $(4ab - 1)(2c + d)$ **9.** $(2x - 1)(x + 2)$
11. $(y - 1)(3y + 2)$ **13.** $(x + 4)(2x - 1)$ **15.** $(w + x)(y - z)$
17. $(a - 3b)(m + 2n)$ **19.** $(3y + 2)(y - 1)$ **21.** $(u - 5v)(u + 3v)$
23. Not factorable **25.** $(wx - y)(wx + y)$ **27.** $(3m - n)^2$
29. Not factorable **31.** $4(z - 3)(z - 4)$ **33.** $2x^2(x - 2)(x - 10)$
35. $x(2y - 3)^2$ **37.** $(2m - 3n)(3m + 4n)$ **39.** $uv(2u - v)(2u + v)$
41. $2x(x^2 - x + 4)$ **43.** $(2x - 3y)(4x^2 + 6xy + 9y^2)$
45. $xy(x + 2)(x^2 - 2x + 4)$ **47.** $[(x + 2) - 3y][(x + 2) + 3y]$

49. Not factorable **51.** $(6x - 6y - 1)(x - y + 4)$
53. $(y - 2)(y + 2)(y^2 + 1)$ **55.** $3(x - y)^2(5xy - 5y^2 + 4x)$
57. True **59.** False

Exercises A.4

1. 39/7 **3.** 495 **5.** $8d^6$ **7.** $\frac{15x^2 + 10x - 6}{180}$ **9.** $\frac{15m^2 + 14m - 6}{36m^3}$

11. $\frac{1}{x(x - 4)}$ **13.** $\frac{x - 6}{x(x - 3)}$ **15.** $\frac{-3x - 9}{(x - 2)(x + 1)^2}$ **17.** $\frac{2}{x - 1}$

19. $\frac{5}{a - 1}$ **21.** $\frac{x^2 + 8x - 16}{x(x - 4)(x + 4)}$ **23.** $\frac{7x^2 - 2x - 3}{6(x + 1)^2}$ **25.** $\frac{x(y - x)}{y(2x - y)}$

27. $\frac{-17c + 16}{15(c - 1)}$ **29.** $\frac{1}{x - 3}$ **31.** $\frac{-1}{2x(x + h)}$ **33.** $\frac{x - y}{x + y}$

35. (A) Incorrect (B) $x + 1$ **37.** (A) Incorrect (B) $2x + h$

39. (A) Incorrect (B) $\frac{x^2 - x - 3}{x + 1}$ **41.** (A) Correct **43.** $\frac{-2x - h}{3(x + h)^2x^2}$

45. $\frac{x(x - 3)}{x - 1}$

Exercises A.5

1. $2/x^9$ **3.** $3w^7/2$ **5.** $2/x^3$ **7.** $1/w^5$ **9.** $4/a^6$ **11.** $1/a^6$ **13.** $1/8x^{12}$
15. 8.23×10^{10} **17.** 7.83×10^{-1} **19.** 3.4×10^{-5} **21.** 40,000

23. 0.007 **25.** 61,710,000 **27.** 0.000 808 **29.** 1 **31.** 10^{14} **33.** $y^6/25x^4$

35. $4x^6/25$ **37.** $4y^3/3x^5$ **39.** $\frac{7}{4} - \frac{1}{4}x^{-3}$ **41.** $\frac{5}{2}x^2 - \frac{3}{2} + 4x^{-2}$

43. $\frac{x^2(x - 3)}{(x - 1)^3}$ **45.** $\frac{2(x - 1)}{x^3}$ **47.** 2.4×10^{10}; 24,000,000,000

49. 3.125×10^4; 31,250 **51.** 64 **55.** uv **57.** $\frac{bc(c + b)}{c^2 + bc + b^2}$

59. (A) \$60,598 (B) \$1,341 (C) 2.21% **61.** (A) 9×10^{-6} (B) 0.000 009 (C) 0.0009% **63.** 1,194,000

Exercises A.6

1. $6\sqrt[5]{x^3}$ **3.** $\sqrt[5]{(32x^2y^3)^3}$ **5.** $\sqrt{x^2 + y^2}$ (not $x + y$) **7.** $5x^{3/4}$
9. $(2x^2y)^{3/5}$ **11.** $x^{1/3} + y^{1/3}$ **13.** 5 **15.** 64 **17.** −7 **19.** −16

21. $\frac{8}{125}$ **23.** $\frac{1}{27}$ **25.** $x^{2/5}$ **27.** m **29.** $2x/y^2$ **31.** $xy^2/2$

33. $1/(24x^{7/12})$ **35.** $2x + 3$ **37.** $30x^5\sqrt{3x}$ **39.** 2 **41.** $12x - 6x^{35/4}$

43. $3u - 13u^{1/2}v^{1/2} + 4v$ **45.** $36m^{3/2} - \frac{6m^{1/2}}{n^{1/2}} + \frac{6m}{n^{1/2}} - \frac{1}{n}$

47. $9x - 6x^{1/2}y^{1/2} + y$ **49.** $\frac{1}{2}x^{1/3} + x^{-1/3}$ **51.** $\frac{2}{3}x^{-1/4} + \frac{1}{3}x^{-2/3}$

53. $\frac{1}{2}x^{-1/6} - \frac{1}{4}$ **55.** $4n\sqrt{3mn}$ **57.** $\frac{2(x + 3)\sqrt{x - 2}}{x - 2}$

59. $7(x - y)(\sqrt{x} + \sqrt{y})$ **61.** $\frac{1}{xy\sqrt{5xy}}$ **63.** $\frac{1}{\sqrt{x + h} + \sqrt{x}}$

65. $\frac{1}{(t + x)(\sqrt{t} + \sqrt{x})}$ **67.** $x = y = 1$ is one of many choices.

69. $x = y = 1$ is one of many choices. **71.** False **73.** False **75.** False

77. True **79.** True **81.** False **83.** $\frac{x + 8}{2(x + 3)^{3/2}}$ **85.** $\frac{x - 2}{2(x - 1)^{3/2}}$

87. $\frac{x + 6}{3(x + 2)^{5/3}}$ **89.** 103.2 **91.** 0.0805 **93.** 4,588

95. (A) and (E); (B) and (F); (C) and (D)

Exercises A.7

1. $\pm\sqrt{11}$ **3.** $-\frac{4}{3}, 2$ **5.** −2, 6 **7.** 0, 2 **9.** $3 \pm 2\sqrt{3}$ **11.** $-2 \pm \sqrt{2}$

13. $0, \frac{15}{2}$ **15.** $\pm\frac{3}{2}$ **17.** $\frac{1}{2}, -3$ **19.** $(-1 \pm \sqrt{5})/2$ **21.** $(3 \pm \sqrt{3})/2$

23. No real solution **25.** $(-3 \pm \sqrt{11})/2$ **27.** $\pm\sqrt{3}$ **29.** $-\frac{1}{2}, 2$
31. $(x - 2)(x + 42)$ **33.** Not factorable in the integers
35. $(2x - 9)(x + 12)$ **37.** $(4x - 7)(x + 62)$ **39.** $r = \sqrt{A/P} - 1$
41. If $c < 4$, there are two distinct real roots; if $c = 4$, there is one real double root; and if $c > 4$, there are no real roots. **43.** −2 **45.** $\pm\sqrt{10}$
47. $\pm\sqrt{3}, \pm\sqrt{5}$ **49.** 1,575 bottles at \$4 each **51.** 13.64% **53.** 8 ft/sec; $4\sqrt{2}$ or 5.66 ft/sec